Lecture Notes in Computer Science 11187

Commenced Publication in 1973
Founding and Former Series Editors:
Gerhard Goos, Juris Hartmanis, and Jan van Leeuwen

More information about this series at http://www.springer.com/series/7407

Bernd Fischer · Tarmo Uustalu (Eds.)

Theoretical Aspects of Computing – ICTAC 2018

15th International Colloquium
Stellenbosch, South Africa, October 16–19, 2018
Proceedings

 Springer

Editors
Bernd Fischer 🆔
Stellenbosch University
Stellenbosch, South Africa

Tarmo Uustalu 🆔
Reykjavík University
Reykjavik, Iceland

and

Tallinn University of Technology
Tallinn, Estonia

ISSN 0302-9743   ISSN 1611-3349 (electronic)
Lecture Notes in Computer Science
ISBN 978-3-030-02507-6   ISBN 978-3-030-02508-3 (eBook)
https://doi.org/10.1007/978-3-030-02508-3

Library of Congress Control Number: 2018957486

LNCS Sublibrary: SL1 – Theoretical Computer Science and General Issues

This Springer imprint is published by the registered company Springer Nature Switzerland AG
The registered company address is: Gewerbestrasse 11, 6330 Cham, Switzerland

Preface

This volume is the proceedings of the 15th International Colloquium on Theoretical Aspects of Computing, ICTAC 2018, which was held in Stellenbosch, South Africa, during October 16–19, 2018, in colocation with the 14th African Conference on Research in Computer Science and Applied Mathematics, CARI 2018, October 14–16, and a jointly organized CARI/ICTAC spring school, October 12–15.

Established in 2004 by the International Institute for Software Technology of the United Nations University (UNU-IIST), the ICTAC conference series aims at bringing together researchers and practitioners from academia, industry, and government to present research and exchange ideas and experience addressing challenges in both theoretical aspects of computing and the exploitation of theory through methods and tools for system development. ICTAC also specifically aims to promote research cooperation between developing and industrial countries.

The topics of the conference include, but are not limited to, languages and automata; semantics of programming languages; logic in computer science; lambda calculus, type theory and category theory; domain-specific languages; theories of concurrency and mobility; theories of distributed, grid and cloud computing; models of objects and components; coordination models; models of software architectures; timed, hybrid, embedded, and cyber-physical systems; static analysis; software verification; software testing; program generation and transformation; model checking and automated theorem proving; interactive theorem proving; certified software, formalized programming theory.

Previous editions of ICTAC were held in Guiyang, China (2004), Hanoi, Vietnam (2005 and 2017), Tunis, Tunisia (2006), Macau (2007), Istanbul, Turkey (2008), Kuala Lumpur, Malaysia (2009), Natal, Brazil (2010), Johannesburg, South Africa (2011), Bangalore, India (2012), Shanghai, China (2013), Bucharest, Romania (2014), Cali, Colombia (2015), Taipei, Taiwan (2016). The proceedings of all these events were published in the LNCS series.

The program of ICTAC 2018 consisted of four invited talks and 25 contributed papers. We were proud to have as invited speakers Yves Bertot (Inria, France), Thomas Meyer (University of Cape Town, South Africa), Gennaro Parlato (University of Southampton, UK), and Peter Thiemann (Universität Freiburg, Germany). The talks of Meyer and Parlato are represented in this volume by abstracts, those by Bertot and Thiemann by an extended abstract and a paper.

The contributed papers were selected from among the 59 full submissions that we received in response to our call. Each of those was reviewed by at least three, and on average 3.4, Program Committee members or external reviewers. The Program Committee consisted of 28 researchers from academia and industry and from every continent.

The CARI/ICTAC spring school program consisted of seven half-day tutorials, taught by Yves Bertot, Vincent Cheval (Inria, France), Martin Leucker (Universität zu Lübeck, Germany), Thomas Meyer, Ina Schaefer (Technische Universität Braunschweig, Germany) with Loek Cleophas (Technische Universiteit Eindhoven, The Netherlands), Peter Thiemann, and Willem Visser (Stellenbosch University, South Africa).

We are grateful to all our invited speakers, submission authors, Program Committee members, and external reviewers for their contributions to the program, to the Steering Committee and especially its chair, Ana Cavalcanti, for advice, to Easychair for the platform for Program Committee work, and to the LNCS editorial team for producing this volume and for donating the best paper award money. We are thankful to the Stellenbosch Institute for Advanced Study (STIAS) for lending the premises, and to Hayley Du Plessis and Andrew Collett for administrative and technical support. Stellenbosch University, IFIP TC6 and DEC, Inria, and their partnering French agencies provided financial support toward the costs of the invited speakers and tutorialists.

August 2018   Bernd Fischer
                                                                Tarmo Uustalu

Organization

Steering Committee

Ana Cavalcanti	University of York, UK
Martin Leucker	Universität zu Lübeck, Germany
Zhiming Liu	Southwest University, China
Tobias Nipkow	Technische Universität München, Germany
Augusto Sampaio	Universidade Federal de Pernambuco, Brazil
Natarajan Shankar	SRI International, USA

General Chair

Bernd Fischer	Stellenbosch University, South Africa

Program Chairs

Bernd Fischer	Stellenbosch University, South Africa
Tarmo Uustalu	Reykjavík University, Iceland, and Tallinn University of Technology, Estonia

Program Committee

June Andronick	Data61, Australia
Éric Badouel	IRISA, France
Eduardo Bonelli	Universidad Nacional de Quilmes, Argentina
Ana Cavalcanti	University of York, UK
Dang Van Hung	VNU University of Engineering and Technology, Vietnam
Uli Fahrenberg	LIX, France
Anna Lisa Ferrara	University of Southampton, UK
Adrian Francalanza	University of Malta, Malta
Edward Hermann Haeusler	Pontifícia Universidade Católica do Rio de Janeiro, Brazil
Ross Horne	Nanyang Technological University, Singapore
Atsushi Igarashi	Kyoto University, Japan
Jan Křetínský	Technische Universität München, Germany
Martin Leucker	Universität zu Lübeck, Germany
Zhiming Liu	Southwest University, China
Radu Mardare	Aalborg University, Denmark
Tobias Nipkow	Technische Universität München, Germany
Maciej Piróg	University of Wrocław, Poland
Sanjiva Prasad	IIT Delhi, India

Murali Krishna Ramanathan	Uber Technologies, USA
Camilo Rueda	Pontificia Universidad Javeriana Cali, Colombia
Augusto Sampaio	Universidade Federal de Pernambuco, Brazil
Ina Schaefer	Technische Universität Braunschweig, Germany
Natarajan Shankar	SRI International, USA
Georg Struth	University of Sheffield, UK
Cong Tian	Xidian University, China
Lynette van Zijl	Stellenbosch University, South Africa

Additional Reviewers

Abdulrazaq Abba
Antonis Achilleos
Leonardo Aniello
Jaime Arias
S. Arun-Kumar
Pranav Ashok
Duncan Attard
Mauricio Ayala-Rincón
Giorgio Bacci
Giovanni Bacci
Joffroy Beauquier
Giovanni Bernardi
Silvio Capobianco
Ian Cassar
Sheng Chen
Lukas Convent
Alejandro Díaz-Caro
Eric Fabre
Nathanaël Fijalkow
Robert Furber
Ning Ge
Jeremy Gibbons
Stéphane Graham-Lengrand
Reiko Heckel
Willem Heijltjes
Wu Hengyang
Bengt-Ove Holländer
Juliano Iyoda
Mauro Jaskelioff
Yu Jiang
Christian Johansen
Dejan Jovanovic

Karam Kharraz
Hélène Kirchner
Alexander Knüppel
Jérémy Ledent
Karoliina Lehtinen
Benjamin Martin
Tobias Meggendorfer
Carroll Morgan
Madhavan Mukund
Kedar Namjoshi
Michael Nieke
Sidney C. Nogueira
Carlos Olarte
Marcel Vinicius Medeiros Oliveira
Hugo Paquet
Mathias Ruggaard
André Pedro
Gustavo Petri
Mathias Preiner
Adrian Puerto Aubel
Karin Quaas
Andrew Reynolds
Pedro Ribeiro
James Riely
Camilo Rocha
Nelson Rosa
Martin Sachenbacher
Gerardo M. Sarria M.
Torben Scheffel
Alexander Schlie
Malte Schmitz
Sven Schuster

Thomas Sewell
René Thiemann
Daniel Thoma
Thomas Thüm
Ashish Tiwari
Hazem Torfah
Szymon Toruńczyk

Dmitriy Traytel
Christian Urban
Frank Valencia
Maximilian Weininger
Pengfei Yang
Hengjun Zhao

Organizing Committee

Bernd Fischer	Stellenbosch University, South Africa
Katarina Britz	Stellenbosch University, South Africa
Hayley Du Plessis	Stellenbosch University, South Africa

Host Institution

Stellenbosch University Computer Science Division

Sponsors

Stellenbosch University
Springer
IFIP Technical Committee 6 and Digital Equity Committee
Inria
Agence universitaire de la Francophonie (AUF)
Centre de coopération internationale en recherche agronomique pour le développement (CIRAD)
Institut de recherche pour le développement (IRD)

Invited Talks (Abstracts)

What Is Knowledge Representation and Reasoning?

Thomas Meyer[ID]

Department of Computer Science and Centre for Artificial Intelligence Research,
University of Cape Town, Private Bag X3, Rondebosch 7701, South Africa
tmeyer@cs.uct.ac.za

Artificial Intelligence (AI) is receiving lots of attention at the moment, with all kinds of wild speculation in the media about its potential benefits. The excitement is mostly about recent successes in the subarea of AI known as Machine Learning. The current hype is reminiscent of the scenario about 20 years ago when logic-based AI, and more specifically, the subarea known as Knowledge Representation, had everyone in a state of euphoria about the future of AI.

My focus in this talk is on Knowledge Representation. I first provide an overview of the field as a whole, followed up by a more detailed presentation about some of the successful Knowledge Representation techniques and tools. The presentation is augmented with a discussion on the strengths and limitations of the Knowledge Representation approach to AI. Finally, I offer some thoughts on the recently revitalised suggestion that a combination of Knowledge Representation and Machine Learning techniques can lead to further advances in AI.

Finding Rare Concurrent Programming Bugs: An Automatic, Symbolic, Randomized, and Parallelizable Approach

Gennaro Parlato (ID)

School of Electronics and Computer Science,
University of Southampton, Highfield, Southampton SO17 1BJ, UK
gennaro@ecs.soton.ac.uk

Developing correct, scalable and efficient concurrent programs is a complex and difficult task, due to the large number of possible concurrent executions that need to be taken into account. Modern multi-core processors with weak memory models and lock-free algorithms make this task even more difficult, as they introduce additional executions that confound the developers' reasoning. Because of these complex interactions, concurrent programs often contain bugs that are difficult to find, reproduce, and fix. Stress testing is known to be very ineffective in detecting rare concurrency bugs as all possible executions of the programs have to be explored explicitly. Consequently, testing by itself is often inadequate for concurrent programs and needs to be complemented by automated analysis tools that enable detection of bugs in a systematic and symbolic way.

In the first part of the talk, I provide an overview of Lazy-CSeq, a symbolic method based on Bounded Model Checking (BMC) and Sequentialization. Lazy-CSeq first translates a multi-threaded C program into a nondeterministic sequential C program that preserves reachability for all round-robin schedules with a given bound on the number of rounds. It then reuses existing high-performance BMC tools as backends for the sequential verification problem. This translation is carefully designed to introduce very small memory overheads and very few sources of nondeterminism, so that it produces tight SAT/SMT formulae, and is thus very effective in practice.

In the second part of the talk, I present Swarm-CSeq, which extends Lazy-CSeq with a swarm-based bug-finding method. The key idea is to generate a set of simpler program instances, each capturing a reduced set of the original programs interleavings. These instances can then be verified independently in parallel. Our approach is parametrizable and allows us to fine-tune the nondeterminism and randomness used for the analysis. In our experiments, by using parallel analysis, we show that this approach is able, even with a small number of cores, to find bugs in the hardest known concurrency benchmarks in a matter of minutes, whereas other dynamic and static tools fail to do so in hours.

Contents

Invited Talks (Papers)

Formal Verification of a Geometry Algorithm: A Quest for Abstract Views
and Symmetry in Coq Proofs 3
  Yves Bertot

LTL Semantic Tableaux and Alternating ω-automata via Linear Factors 11
  Martin Sulzmann and Peter Thiemann

Contributed Talks

Proof Nets and the Linear Substitution Calculus 37
  Beniamino Accattoli

Modular Design of Domain-Specific Languages Using
Splittings of Catamorphisms 62
  Éric Badouel and Rodrigue Aimé Djeumen Djatcha

An Automata-Based View on Configurability and Uncertainty 80
  Martin Berglund and Ina Schaefer

Formalising Boost POSIX Regular Expression Matching 99
  Martin Berglund, Willem Bester, and Brink van der Merwe

Monoidal Multiplexing 116
  Apiwat Chantawibul and Paweł Sobociński

Input/Output Stochastic Automata with Urgency: Confluence
and Weak Determinism 132
  Pedro R. D'Argenio and Raúl E. Monti

Layer by Layer – Combining Monads 153
  Fredrik Dahlqvist, Louis Parlant, and Alexandra Silva

Layer Systems for Confluence—Formalized 173
  Bertram Felgenhauer and Franziska Rapp

A Metalanguage for Guarded Iteration 191
  Sergey Goncharov, Christoph Rauch, and Lutz Schröder

Generating Armstrong ABoxes for $\mathcal{ALC}$ TBoxes 211
  Henriette Harmse, Katarina Britz, and Aurona Gerber

Spatio-Temporal Domains: An Overview   231
  David Janin

Checking Modal Contracts for Virtually Timed Ambients   252
  Einar Broch Johnsen, Martin Steffen, Johanna Beate Stumpf,
  and Lars Tveito

Abstraction of Bit-Vector Operations for BDD-Based SMT Solvers.   273
  Martin Jonáš and Jan Strejček

Weak Bisimulation Metrics in Models with Nondeterminism
and Continuous State Spaces   292
  Ruggero Lanotte and Simone Tini

Symbolic Computation via Program Transformation   313
  Henrich Lauko, Petr Ročkai, and Jiří Barnat

Double Applicative Functors   333
  Härmel Nestra

Checking Sequence Generation for Symbolic Input/Output FSMs
by Constraint Solving   354
  Omer Nguena Timo, Alexandre Petrenko, and S. Ramesh

Explicit Auditing.   376
  Wilmer Ricciotti and James Cheney

Complexity and Expressivity of Branching- and Alternating-Time
Temporal Logics with Finitely Many Variables.   396
  Mikhail Rybakov and Dmitry Shkatov

Complexity Results on Register Context-Free Grammars and Register
Tree Automata   415
  Ryoma Senda, Yoshiaki Takata, and Hiroyuki Seki

Information Flow Certificates   435
  Manuel Töws and Heike Wehrheim

The Smallest FSSP Partial Solutions for One-Dimensional Ring Cellular
Automata: Symmetric and Asymmetric Synchronizers   455
  Hiroshi Umeo, Naoki Kamikawa, and Gen Fujita

Convex Language Semantics for Nondeterministic Probabilistic Automata . . .   472
  Gerco van Heerdt, Justin Hsu, Joël Ouaknine, and Alexandra Silva

Fast Computations on Ordered Nominal Sets   493
  David Venhoek, Joshua Moerman, and Jurriaan Rot

Non-preemptive Semantics for Data-Race-Free Programs   513
 Siyang Xiao, Hanru Jiang, Hongjin Liang, and Xinyu Feng

Author Index   533

Invited Talks (Papers)

Formal Verification of a Geometry Algorithm: A Quest for Abstract Views and Symmetry in Coq Proofs

Yves Bertot[(⊠)] [ID]

Inria Sophia Antipolis – Méditerranée and Université Côte d'Azur,
2004 route des Lucioles, 06902 Sophia Antipolis Cedex, France
yves.bertot@inria.fr

Abstract. This extended abstract is about an effort to build a formal description of a triangulation algorithm starting with a naive description of the algorithm where triangles, edges, and triangulations are simply given as sets and the most complex notions are those of boundary and separating edges. When performing proofs about this algorithm, questions of symmetry appear and this exposition attempts to give an account of how these symmetries can be handled. All this work relies on formal developments made with Coq and the mathematical components library.

1   Introduction

Over the years, proof assistants in higher-order logic have been advocated as tools to improve the quality of software, with a wide range of spectacular results, ranging from compilers, operating systems, distributed systems, and security and cryptography primitives. There are now good reasons to believe that any kind of software could benefit from a formal verification using a proof assistant.

Embedded software in robots or autonomous vehicles has to maintain a view of the geometry of the world around the device. We expect this software to rely on computational geometry. The work described in this extended abstract concentrates on an effort to provide a correctness proof for algorithms that construct triangulations.

2   An Abstract Description of Triangulation

Given a set of points, a triangulating algorithm returns a collection of triangles that must cover the space between these points (the convex hull), have no overlap, and such that all the points of the input set are vertices of at least one triangle. When the input points represent obstacles, the triangulation can help construct safe routes between these obstacles, thanks to Delaunay triangulations and Voronoï diagrams.

The formal verification work starts by providing a naive and abstract view of the algorithm that is later refined into a more efficient version. Mathematical properties are proved for the naive version and then modified for successive

© Springer Nature Switzerland AG 2018
B. Fischer and T. Uustalu (Eds.): ICTAC 2018, LNCS 11187, pp. 3–10, 2018.
https://doi.org/10.1007/978-3-030-02508-3_1

refinements. When the proof is about geometry and connected points, it is natural to expect symmetry properties to play a central role in the proofs. In this experiment, we start with a view of triangles simply as 3-point sets. We expect to refine this setting later into a more precise graph structure, where each triangle is also equipped with a link to its neighbors and costly operations over the whole set of triangles are replaced by low constant time operations that exploit information that is cached in memory.

From the point of view of formal verification, the properties that need to be verified for the naive version are the following ones: all triangles have the right number of elements, all points inside the convex hull are in a triangle, the union of all the triangles is exactly the input, and there is no overlap between two triangles.

The naive algorithm relies on the notion of separating edges of a triangle with respect to a point: for a triangle $\{a, b, c\}$ and a fourth point d, the point c is *separated* from d if c and d appear on different sides of the edge $\{a, b\}$. At this point, it appears that life is much easier if we take the simplifying assumption that three points of the input are never aligned. This assumption is often taken in the early literature on computational geometry and we will also take it.

The point d is inside the triangle $\{a, b, c\}$ exactly when no element of the triangle is separated from the point d. When the point d is outside the triangle, for instance when c is separated from d, the edge $\{a, b\}$ will be called *red*. An edge that is not red will be called *blue*.

Another important notion is the notion of boundary edge. An *edge* of the triangulation is a 2-point subset of one of the triangles in the triangulation, a *boundary edge* is an edge that belong to exactly one triangle. Boundary edges are triangle edges, and as such they can be blue or red with respect to a new point.

The algorithm then boils in the following few lines:

Take three points from the input: they constitute the first triangle, then take the points one by one.

- If the new point is inside an existing triangle, then remove this triangle from the triangulation and then add the three triangles produced by combining the new point and all edges of the removed triangle.
- If the new point is outside, then add all triangles obtained by combining the new point with all red boundary edges.

This algorithm terminates when all points from the input have been consumed.

3 Specifying the Correctness of the Algorithm

This algorithm is so simple that it seems proving it correct should be extremely simple. However, geometry properties play a significant role, as is already visible in the specification.

That the triangulation only contains 3-set seems obvious, as soon as the input set does contain three points. When there are more than 3 points, say n

points, we can assume by induction that the triangulation of the first n-1 points contains only-3 sets. Then, whether the new point is inside an existing triangle or outside, the new elements of the triangulation are obtained by adding the new point to edges of the previous triangulation. These operation always yield 3-point sets.

To verify that the union of all triangles is the input set, we need to show that at least one triangle is created when including a new point. This is surprising difficult, because it relies on geometry properties. If the new point is inside an existing triangle, the algorithm obviously includes in the triangulation three triangles that contain the new point. However, when the point is not inside a triangle, there is no simple logical reason for which there should exist a boundary edge that is also red. This requires an extra proof with geometrical content. Such a proof was already formally verified by Pichardie and Bertot [17].

With respect to boundary edges, when the triangulation is well-formed, all boundary edges should form the convex hull of the input set. In other words, for every point inside the convex hull, all boundary edges should be blue.

4 Formal Proof

When performing the proofs, it is interesting to exploit all the symmetry that can be found. In paper proofs, it is often enough to explicit one configuration and state rapidly that many other configurations can be proved similarly by symmetry.

4.1 Combinatorial Symmetries of Triangles

One example is the natural symmetry of triangles. When considering triangles, Knuth [13] proposed that they should be viewed as ordered triplets abc, such that one turns left when following the edges from a, b and then to c. Of course, if one views triangles simply as sets, it does not make sense to distinguish between oriented and non-oriented triangles. Thus, we need to add structure to the set, which we do by giving names to the elements. Now, when giving these names, we can do it in a way that ensures the obtained triangle to be oriented. When doing our formalization work, it becomes natural to name t_1, t_2, t_3 the three points of t.

In practice, we don't use integers for indexing the elements, because this means we would have to give a meaning to t_{18}. Instead, we use the type of integers smaller than 3 and we use the fact that this set can be given the structure of a group. The mathematical component library already provides such a structure, noted $'I\_3$. We profit from it and call 0, 1, and -1 the three elements. A characteristic property in our development will be that t_i, t_{i+1}, t_{i-1} form an oriented triangle, of course with the convention that $i+3 = i$ and $0-1 = 2$ when dealing with elements of $'I\_3$. This is a first way in which we attempt to deal with symmetry. This is supported by the finite group concepts in the library.

We define a function `three_points` that maps any set of type {set P} (this is the mathematical components' notation for sets of elements of P) to a function from 'I_3 to P. This function is defined in such a way that it is injective and its image is included in its first argument as soon as this set has at least three points and the images of 0, 1, and −1 form an oriented triplet.

4.2   Geometric Symmetries of Triangles

Other symmetries come up when considering oriented triangles in the plane. In his study of convex hull algorithms [13], Knuth expresses that the following 5 properties are to be expected from the orientation predicate, when the 5 points a, b, c, d, and e are taken to be pairwise distinct, and noting simply abc to express that one turns left when following the path from a to b and then c.

1. $abc \Rightarrow bca$
2. $abc \Rightarrow \neg bac$
3. $abc \lor bac$
4. $abd \land bcd \land cad \Rightarrow abc$
5. $abc \land abd \land abe \land acd \land ade \Rightarrow ace$.

Knuth calls these properties axioms of the orientation predicate and we will follow his steps, even though from the logical point of view, these properties are not really axioms because we can prove them for a suitable definition of the orientation predicate (using the points' coordinates and determinants).

The first axiom essentially says that from the geometrical point of view, triangles exhibit a ternary symmetry. The second one makes it slightly more precise by expressing that not any order sequence of three points forms an oriented triangle. The third one states that we are working under the assumption that no three points in the data set are aligned. The fourth axiom expresses that the combination of three adjacent oriented triangles lead to fourth one. It also has a natural ternary geometric symmetry, which is perhaps easier to see in the following drawing:

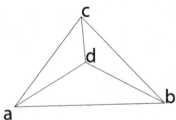

Axiom 5 describes relations of four points relative to a pivot, in this case a. It can be summarized by the following figure, where the topmost arrow (in blue) is a consequence of all others.

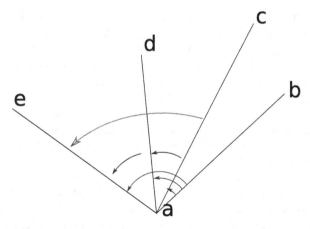

To have a symmetric collection of axioms, we would actually need a similar statement, but with all points pivoting around b. Knuth also recognizes this need and actually shows that the symmetric picture (an axial symmetry) is a logical consequence of all other axioms.

Using these axioms, we should be able to prove a statement like the following *if all vertices of a triangle $\{c, d, e\}$ lay on the left of a segment $[a, b]$, then any point f inside the triangle also lays on the left of the segment. This should also be true when one or both of a and b is element of $\{c, d, e\}$.*

A human readable form of this proof works by first studying the case the where sets $\{a, b\}$ and $\{c, d, e\}$ are disjoint, noting that there should be at least one edge of the triangle that is red with respect to both a and by supposing, without loss of generality that this edge is $[c, d]$. This proof already relies on 9 uses of Knuth's fifth axiom or its symmetric.

For a human reader, the exercise of renaming points is easily done, but for a computer, the three points c, d, and e are not interchangeable and performing the "without loss of generality" step requires a technical discussion with three cases to consider, where Knuth's fifth axiom is used once again. In total, if no step was taken to exploit the symmetry, this means that the proof would require 28 uses of Knuth's fifth axiom and since this proof has 5 premises, this corresponds to a proof complexity that it really cumbersome for the human mind.

More uses of symmetry have to be summoned to treat the cases when a and b may appear among the vertices c, d, and e, depending on whether it is a, b, or both that belongs to the triangle when c, d, or e are all on the left of the $[a, b]$ segment.

4.3   Symmetries with Respect to the Convex Hull

In two dimensions, the boundary edges of the convex hull form a loop where no edge plays a more significant role than the other. It is natural to think that the ternary symmetry of triangles should generalize to such a loop, but with the added ingredient that the size of the loop is an arbitrary number n, larger than 3. To cope with this source of symmetry, we did not choose to exhibit a mapping from 'I_n to the type of points, but rather to indicate that there exists a function f, such that $[x; f(x)]$ is always a boundary edge when x is taken from the union of the boundary edges, of the triangulation and all the other points of the triangulation are always on the left side of the segment $[x; f(x)]$.

To handle this point of view, the mathematical components library provides a notion of orbit of a point for a function.

When one considers the operation of adding a new point outside the convex hull, it is not true anymore that all boundary edges are equivalent. Some edges are red, some edges are blue. In fact, it is possible to show that all red boundary edges are connected together, so that there are exactly two points, which we can call the *purple* points that belong to two edges of different color. The role of these two points is symmetric, but they can be distinguished: for one of them, which we call p_1, the edge $[p_1, f(p_1)]$ is a red boundary edge and $[f^{n-1}(p_1), p_1]$ is a blue boundary edge, for the other, which we call p_2, the edge $[p_2, f(p_2)]$ is blue and $[f^{n-1}(p_2), p_2]$ is red. In fact, there exists a number n_r such that $f^{n_r}(p_1) = p_2$, all segments $[f^k(p_1), f^{k+1}(p_1)]$ are red boundary edges when $0 \le k < n_r$ and all segments $[f^k(p_1), f^{k+1}(p_1)$ are blue when $0 \le n_r < n$.

In principle, all statements made about p_1 are valid for p_2, mutatis mutandi. In practice, performing the proofs of the symmetric statement formally often relies on copying and pasting the proofs obtained for the first case, and guessing the right way to exploit the known symmetries, for example by replacing uses of Knuth's fifth axiom by its symmetric. The alternative is to make the proof only once and make the symmetry explicit, but the last step is often as difficult as the first one.

The existence of a cycle for the function f, so that $f^{k+n} = f^k$ also plays a role in the proof. Reasoning modulo n appears at several places during the proof, but for now we have not found a satisfactory way to exploit this fact.

5   Related Work

The formal verification of computational geometry algorithms is quite rare. A first attempt with convex hulls was provided by Pichardie and Bertot [17] where the only data structure used was that of lists but the question of non general positions (where points may be aligned) was also studied. Notable work is provided by Dufourd and his colleagues [1,3,5,6]. In particular, Dufourd advocated the use of hypermaps to represent many of the data-structures of computational geometry. In this work, we prefer to start with a much more naive data structure, closer to the mathematical perspective, which consists only of viewing the triangulation as a set of sets. Of course, when considering optimisations of the algorithm, where some data is pre-computed and cached in memory, it becomes useful to have more complex data-structure, but we believe that the correspondence between the naive algorithm and the clever algorithm can be described as a form of refinement which provides good structuring principles for the whole study and for the formal proof. In the end, the refinement will probably converge towards the data-structure advocated by Dufourd and his colleagues. It should be noted that the hypermap data-structure was also used by Gonthier in his study of the four-color theorem [7], but with a different formal representation. While Dufourd uses a list of darts and links between these darts, Gonthier has a more generic way to represent finite sets.

The computation of convex hulls was also studied Meikle and Fleuriot, with the focus on using Hoare logic to support the reasoning framework [16] and by Immler in the case of zonotopes, with applications to the automatic proof of formulas [12].

The algorithm we describe here is essentially the first phase of the one described in Sects. 3 and 4 of Lawson's report [14].

In the current state of our development, we benefit from the description of finite sets and finite groups provided by the mathematical components library [9,15]. This library was initially used for the four colour theorem [7] and further developed for the proof of the Feit-Thompson theorem [8].

Because it deals with the relative positions of points on a sphere, it is probable that the Flyspeck formal development also contains many of the ingredients necessary to formalize triangulations [10]. For instance, Hales published a proof of the Jordan Curve theorem [11] that has many similarities with the study of convex hulls and subdivisions of the plane.

6   Conclusion

The formal proofs described in this abstract have been developed with the Coq system [2] and the mathematical components library [15] and are available from

https://gitlab.inria.fr/bertot/triangles

This is a preliminary study of the problem of building triangulations for a variety of purposes. The naive algorithm is unsatisfactory as it does not provide a good way to find the triangle inside of which a new point may occur. This can be improved by using Delaunay triangulations, as already studied formally in [6] and a well-known algorithm of "visibility" walk in the triangulation [4], which can be proved to have guarantees to terminate only when the triangulation satisfies the Delaunay criterion. This is the planned future work.

Delaunay triangulations, and their dual Voronoï diagrams can be useful for practical problems concerning the motion of a device on a plane. It will be useful to extend this work to three dimensions and of course there already exists triangulation algorithms in three dimensions. At first sight, the naive algorithm described here can be used directly for arbitrary dimensions, as long the notion of separating facet is given a suitable definition. However, it seems that the proof done for the 2-dimensional case does not carry directly to a higher dimension d: the boundary facets do not form a loop but a closed hyper-surface (of dimension $d-1$), there is not just a pair of purple points but a collection of purple facets of dimension $d-2$. Still some properties are preserved: the red facets are contiguous, and there are probably equivalents to Knuth's axioms for the higher dimensions.

References

1. Brun, C., Dufourd, J.-F., Magaud, N.: Designing and proving correct a convex hull algorithm with hypermaps in Coq. Comput. Geom. **45**(8), 436–457 (2012). https://doi.org/10.1016/j.comgeo.2010.06.006
2. Coq Development Team: The Coq Proof Assistant Reference Manual, Version 8.8 (2018)
3. Dehlinger, C., Dufourd, J.-F.: Formalizing generalized maps in Coq. Theor. Comput. Sci. **323**(1–3), 351–397 (2004). https://doi.org/10.1016/j.tcs.2004.05.003
4. Devillers, O., Pion, S., Teillaud, M.: Walking in a triangulation. Int. J. Found. Comput. Sci. **13**(2), 181–199 (2002). https://doi.org/10.1142/s0129054102001047
5. Dufourd, J.-F.: An intuitionistic proof of a discrete form of the Jordan Curve theorem formalized in Coq with combinatorial hypermaps. J. Autom. Reason. **43**(1), 19–51 (2009). https://doi.org/10.1007/s10817-009-9117-x
6. Dufourd, J.-F., Bertot, Y.: Formal study of plane delaunay triangulation. In: Kaufmann, M., Paulson, L.C. (eds.) ITP 2010. LNCS, vol. 6172, pp. 211–226. Springer, Heidelberg (2010). https://doi.org/10.1007/978-3-642-14052-5_16
7. Gonthier, G.: The four colour theorem: engineering of a formal proof. In: Kapur, D. (ed.) ASCM 2007. LNCS (LNAI), vol. 5081, pp. 333–333. Springer, Heidelberg (2008). https://doi.org/10.1007/978-3-540-87827-8_28
8. Gonthier, G., et al.: A machine-checked proof of the odd order theorem. In: Blazy, S., Paulin-Mohring, C., Pichardie, D. (eds.) ITP 2013. LNCS, vol. 7998, pp. 163–179. Springer, Heidelberg (2013). https://doi.org/10.1007/978-3-642-39634-2_14
9. Gonthier, G., Mahboubi, A.: An introduction to small scale reflection in Coq. J. Form. Reason. **3**(2), 95–152 (2010). https://doi.org/10.6092/issn.1972-5787/1979
10. Hales, T., et al.: A formal proof of the Kepler conjecture. Forum Math. Pi **5**, 1–29 (2017). https://doi.org/10.1017/fmp.2017.1
11. Hales, T.C.: The Jordan Curve theorem, formally and informally. Am. Math. Mon. **114**(10), 882–894 (2007). http://www.jstor.org/stable/27642361
12. Immler, F.: A verified algorithm for geometric zonotope/hyperplane intersection. In: Proceedings of 2015 Conference on Certified Programs and Proofs, CPP 2015 (Mumbai, January 2015), pp. 129–136. ACM Press, New York (2015). https://doi.org/10.1145/2676724.2693164
13. Knuth, D.E. (ed.): Axioms and Hulls. LNCS, vol. 606. Springer, Heidelberg (1992). https://doi.org/10.1007/3-540-55611-7
14. Lawson, C.L.: Software for c^1 surface interpolation. JPL Publication 77–30, NASA Jet Propulsion Laboratory (1977). https://ntrs.nasa.gov/archive/nasa/casi.ntrs.nasa.gov/19770025881.pdf
15. Mahboubi, A., Tassi, E.: Mathematical components (2018). https://math-comp.github.io/mcb
16. Meikle, L.I., Fleuriot, J.D.: Mechanical theorem proving in computational geometry. In: Hong, H., Wang, D. (eds.) ADG 2004. LNCS (LNAI), vol. 3763, pp. 1–18. Springer, Heidelberg (2006). https://doi.org/10.1007/11615798_1
17. Pichardie, D., Bertot, Y.: Formalizing convex hull algorithms. In: Boulton, R.J., Jackson, P.B. (eds.) TPHOLs 2001. LNCS, vol. 2152, pp. 346–361. Springer, Heidelberg (2001). https://doi.org/10.1007/3-540-44755-5_24

LTL Semantic Tableaux and Alternating ω-automata via Linear Factors

Martin Sulzmann[1] and Peter Thiemann[2]

[1] Faculty of Computer Science and Business Information Systems,
Karlsruhe University of Applied Sciences,
Moltkestrasse 30, 76133 Karlsruhe, Germany
martin.sulzmann@hs-karlsruhe.de

[2] Faculty of Engineering, University of Freiburg,
Georges-Köhler-Allee 079, 79110 Freiburg, Germany
thiemann@acm.org

Abstract. Linear Temporal Logic (LTL) is a widely used specification framework for linear time properties of systems. The standard approach for verifying such properties is by transforming LTL formulae to suitable ω-automata and then applying model checking. We revisit Vardi's transformation of an LTL formula to an alternating ω-automaton and Wolper's LTL tableau method for satisfiability checking. We observe that both constructions effectively rely on a decomposition of formulae into *linear factors*. Linear factors have been introduced previously by Antimirov in the context of regular expressions. We establish the notion of linear factors for LTL and verify essential properties such as expansion and finiteness. Our results shed new insights on the connection between the construction of alternating ω-automata and semantic tableaux.

1 Introduction

Linear Temporal Logic (LTL) is a widely used specification framework for linear time properties of systems. An LTL formula describes a property of an infinite trace of a system. Besides the usual logical connectives, LTL supports the temporal operators $\bigcirc \varphi$ (φ holds in the next step of the trace) and $\varphi \, \mathbf{U} \, \psi$ (φ holds for all steps in the trace until ψ becomes true). LTL can describe many relevant safety and liveness properties.

The standard approach to verify a system against an LTL formula is model checking. To this end, the verifier translates a formula into a suitable ω-automaton, for example, a Büchi automaton or an alternating automaton, and applies the model checking algorithm to the system and the automaton. This kind of translation is widely studied because it is the enabling technology for model checking [19,20,23]. Significant effort is spent on developing translations that generate (mostly) deterministic automata or that minimize the number of states in the generated automata [2,7]. Any improvement in these dimensions is valuable as it speeds up the model checking algorithm.

© Springer Nature Switzerland AG 2018
B. Fischer and T. Uustalu (Eds.): ICTAC 2018, LNCS 11187, pp. 11–34, 2018.
https://doi.org/10.1007/978-3-030-02508-3_2

Our paper presents a new approach to understanding and proving the correctness of Vardi's construction of alternating automata (AA) from LTL formulae [18]. Our approach is based on a novel adaptation to LTL of *linear factors*, a concept arising in Antimirov's construction of partial derivatives of regular expressions [1]. Interestingly, a similar construction yields a new explanation for Wolper's construction of semantic tableaux [22] for checking satisfiability of LTL formulae. Thus, we uncover a deep connection between these constructions.

The paper contains the following contributions.

- Definition of linear factors and partial derivatives for LTL formulae (Sect. 3). We establish their properties and prove correctness.
- Transformation from LTL to AA based on linear factors. The resulting transformation is essentially the standard LTL to AA transformation [18]; it is correct by construction of the linear factors (Sect. 4).
- Construction of semantic tableaux to determine satisfiability of LTL formulae using linear factors (Sect. 5). Our method corresponds closely to Wolper's construction and comes with a free correctness proof.

Proofs are collected in the appendix of this paper and in a preprint[1].

1.1   Preliminaries

We write $\omega = \{0, 1, 2, \dots\}$ for the set of natural numbers with $n \in \omega$ and Σ^ω for the set of infinite words over alphabet Σ with symbols ranged over by $x, y \in \Sigma$. We regard a word $\sigma \in \Sigma^\omega$ as a map and write σ_n for the n-th symbol. We write $\sigma[n \dots]$ for the suffix of σ starting at n, that is, the function $i \mapsto \sigma_{n+i}$, for $i \in \omega$. We write $x\sigma$ for prepending symbol x to σ, that is, $(x\sigma)_0 = x$ and $(x\sigma)_{i+1} = \sigma_i$, for all $i \in \omega$. The notation $\mathbb{P}(X)$ denotes the power set of X.

2   Linear Temporal Logic

Linear temporal logic (LTL) [13] enhances propositional logic with the temporal operators $\bigcirc \varphi$ (φ will be true in the next step) and $\varphi \mathbf{U} \psi$ (φ holds until ψ becomes true). LTL formulae φ, ψ are defined accordingly where we draw atomic propositions p, q from a finite set **AP**.

Definition 1 (Syntax of LTL)

$$\varphi, \psi ::= p \mid \mathbf{tt} \mid \neg\varphi \mid \varphi \wedge \psi \mid \bigcirc \varphi \mid \varphi \mathbf{U} \psi$$

We apply standard precedence rules to parse a formula ($\neg$, $\bigcirc \varphi$, and other prefix operators bind strongest; then $\varphi \mathbf{U} \psi$ and the upcoming $\varphi \mathbf{R} \psi$ operator; then conjunction and finally disjunction with the weakest binding strength; as the latter are associative, we do not group their operands explicitly). We use parentheses to group subformulae explicitly.

---

[1] https://arxiv.org/abs/1710.06678.

A model of an LTL formula is an infinite word $\sigma \in \Sigma^\omega$ where $\Sigma = \mathbb{P}(\mathbf{AP})$, that is, from now on we identify a symbol with the set of true atomic propositions.

Definition 2 (Semantics of LTL). *The formula φ holds on word $\sigma \in \Sigma^\omega$ if the judgment $\sigma \models \varphi$ is provable.*

$$\sigma \models p \Leftrightarrow p \in \sigma_0$$
$$\sigma \models \mathbf{tt}$$
$$\sigma \models \neg\varphi \Leftrightarrow \sigma \not\models \varphi$$
$$\sigma \models \varphi \wedge \psi \Leftrightarrow \sigma \models \varphi \text{ and } \sigma \models \psi$$
$$\sigma \models \bigcirc\varphi \Leftrightarrow \sigma[1\ldots] \models \varphi$$
$$\sigma \models \varphi \mathbf{U} \psi \Leftrightarrow \exists n \in \omega, (\forall j \in \omega, j < n \Rightarrow \sigma[j\ldots] \models \varphi) \text{ and } \sigma[n\ldots] \models \psi$$

We say φ is satisfiable *if there exists $\sigma \in \Sigma^\omega$ such that $\sigma \models \varphi$.*

Definition 3 (Standard Derived LTL Operators)

$$\mathbf{ff} = \neg\mathbf{tt}$$
$$\varphi \vee \psi = \neg(\neg\varphi \wedge \neg\psi) \qquad\qquad\qquad disjunction$$
$$\varphi \mathbf{R} \psi = \neg(\neg\varphi \mathbf{U} \neg\psi) \qquad\qquad\qquad release$$
$$\Diamond\psi = \mathbf{tt} \mathbf{U} \psi \qquad\qquad eventually/finally$$
$$\Box\psi = \mathbf{ff} \mathbf{R} \psi \qquad\qquad always/globally$$

For many purposes, it is advantageous to restrict LTL formulae to positive normal form (PNF). In PNF, negation only occurs adjacent to atomic propositions. Using the derived operators, all negations can be pushed inside by using the de Morgan laws. Thanks to the release operator, this transformation runs in linear time and space. The resulting grammar of formulae in PNF is as follows.

Definition 4 (Positive Normal Form)

$$\varphi, \psi ::= p \mid \neg p \mid \mathbf{tt} \mid \mathbf{ff} \mid \varphi \wedge \psi \mid \varphi \vee \psi \mid \bigcirc\varphi \mid \varphi \mathbf{U} \psi \mid \varphi \mathbf{R} \psi$$

From now on, we assume that all LTL formulae are in PNF.

We make use of several standard equivalences in LTL.

Theorem 1 (Standard results about LTL)

1. $\bigcirc(\varphi \wedge \psi) \Leftrightarrow (\bigcirc\varphi) \wedge (\bigcirc\psi)$
2. $\bigcirc(\varphi \vee \psi) \Leftrightarrow (\bigcirc\varphi) \vee (\bigcirc\psi)$
3. $\varphi \mathbf{U} \psi \Leftrightarrow \psi \vee (\varphi \wedge \bigcirc(\varphi \mathbf{U} \psi))$
4. $\varphi \mathbf{R} \psi \Leftrightarrow \psi \wedge (\varphi \vee \bigcirc(\varphi \mathbf{R} \psi))$.

We also make use of the direct definition of a model for the release operation.

Lemma 1. $\sigma \models \varphi \mathbf{R} \psi$ *is equivalent to one of the following:*
$\forall n \in \omega, \sigma[n\ldots] \models \psi$ *or* $\exists j \in \omega, ((j < n) \wedge \sigma[j\ldots] \models \varphi)$
$\forall n \in \omega, \sigma[n\ldots] \models \psi$ *or* $\exists j \in \omega, \sigma[j\ldots] \models \varphi$ *and* $\forall i \in \omega, i \leq j \Rightarrow \sigma[i\ldots] \models \psi$.

3   Linear Factors and Partial Derivatives

Antimirov [1] defines a linear factor of a regular expression as a pair of an input symbol and a next regular expression to match the rest of the input. The analogue for LTL is a pair $\langle \mu, \varphi \rangle$ where μ is a propositional formula in monomial form (no modalities, see Definition 5) that models the set of first symbols whereas φ is a formal conjunction of temporal LTL formulae for the rest of the input. Informally, $\langle \mu, \varphi \rangle$ corresponds to $\mu \wedge \bigcirc \varphi$. A formula always gives rise to a set of linear factors, which is interpreted as their disjunction.

Definition 5 (Temporal Formulae, Literals and Monomials). *A temporal formula does not start with a conjunction or a disjunction.*

*A literal ℓ of **AP** is an element of $\mathbf{AP} \cup \neg\mathbf{AP}$. Negation of negative literals is defined by $\neg(\neg p) = p$.*

*A monomial μ, ν is either **ff** or a set of literals of **AP** such that $\ell \in \mu$ implies $\neg\ell \notin \mu$. The formula associated with a monomial μ is given by*

$$\Theta(\mu) = \begin{cases} \mathbf{ff} & \mu = \mathbf{ff} \\ \bigwedge \mu & \mu \text{ is a set of literals.} \end{cases}$$

In particular, if $\mu = \emptyset$, then $\Theta(\mu) = \mathbf{tt}$. Hence, we may write $\mathbf{tt}$ for the empty-set monomial. As a monomial is represented either by $\mathbf{ff}$ or by a set of non-contradictory literals, its representation is unique.

We define a smart conjunction operator on monomials that retains the monomial structure.

Definition 6. *Smart conjunction on monomials is defined as their union unless their conjunction $\Theta(\mu) \wedge \Theta(\nu)$ is equivalent to $\mathbf{ff}$.*

$$\mu \odot \nu = \begin{cases} \mathbf{ff} & \mu = \mathbf{ff} \vee \nu = \mathbf{ff} \\ \mathbf{ff} & \exists \ell \in \mu \cup \nu.\ \neg\ell \in \mu \cup \nu \\ \mu \cup \nu & \text{otherwise.} \end{cases}$$

Smart conjunction of monomials is correct in the sense that it produces results equivalent to the conjunction of the associated formulae.

Lemma 2. $\Theta(\mu) \wedge \Theta(\nu) \Leftrightarrow \Theta(\mu \odot \nu)$.

We define an operator $\mathcal{T}$ that transforms propositional formulae consisting of literals and temporal subformulae into sets of conjunctions. We assume that conjunction $\wedge$ simplifies formulae to normal form using associativity, commutativity, and idempotence. The normal form relies on a total ordering of formulae derived from an (arbitrary, fixed) total ordering on atomic propositions.

Definition 7 (Set-Based Conjunctive Normal Form)

$$\mathcal{T}(\varphi \wedge \psi) = \{\varphi' \wedge \psi' \mid \varphi' \in \mathcal{T}(\varphi), \psi' \in \mathcal{T}(\psi)\}$$
$$\mathcal{T}(\varphi \vee \psi) = \mathcal{T}(\varphi) \cup \mathcal{T}(\psi)$$
$$\mathcal{T}(\varphi) = \{\varphi\} \qquad\qquad \textit{if } \varphi \textit{ is a temporal formula}$$

Lemma 3. $\bigvee \mathcal{T}(\varphi) \Leftrightarrow \varphi$.

Definition 8 (Linear Factors). *The set of* linear factors $\mathrm{LF}(\varphi)$ *of an LTL formula* in PNF *is defined as a set of pairs of a monomial and a PNF formula in conjunctive normal form.*

$$
\begin{aligned}
\mathrm{LF}(\ell) &= \{\langle\{\ell\}, \mathbf{tt}\rangle\} \\
\mathrm{LF}(\mathbf{tt}) &= \{\langle\mathbf{tt}, \mathbf{tt}\rangle\} \\
\mathrm{LF}(\mathbf{ff}) &= \{\} \\
\mathrm{LF}(\varphi \vee \psi) &= \mathrm{LF}(\varphi) \cup \mathrm{LF}(\psi) \\
\mathrm{LF}(\varphi \wedge \psi) &= \{\langle\mu', \varphi' \wedge \psi'\rangle \mid \langle\mu, \varphi'\rangle \in \mathrm{LF}(\varphi), \langle\nu, \psi'\rangle \in \mathrm{LF}(\psi), \mu' = \mu \odot \nu \neq \mathbf{ff}\} \\
\mathrm{LF}(\bigcirc\varphi) &= \{\langle\mathbf{tt}, \varphi'\rangle \mid \varphi' \in \mathcal{T}(\varphi)\} \\
\mathrm{LF}(\varphi \, \mathbf{U} \, \psi) &= \mathrm{LF}(\psi) \cup \{\langle\mu, \varphi' \wedge \varphi \, \mathbf{U} \, \psi\rangle \mid \langle\mu, \varphi'\rangle \in \mathrm{LF}(\varphi)\} \\
\mathrm{LF}(\varphi \, \mathbf{R} \, \psi) &= \{\langle\mu', \varphi' \wedge \psi'\rangle \mid \langle\mu, \varphi'\rangle \in \mathrm{LF}(\varphi), \langle\nu, \psi'\rangle \in \mathrm{LF}(\psi), \mu' = \mu \odot \nu \neq \mathbf{ff}\} \\
&\quad \cup \{\langle\nu, \psi' \wedge \varphi \, \mathbf{R} \, \psi\rangle \mid \langle\nu, \psi'\rangle \in \mathrm{LF}(\psi)\}
\end{aligned}
$$

By construction, the first component of a linear factor is never $\mathbf{ff}$. Such pairs are eliminated from the beginning by the tests for $\mu \odot \nu \neq \mathbf{ff}$.

We can obtain shortcuts for the derived operators "eventually" and "always".

Lemma 4.
$$
\mathrm{LF}(\Diamond \psi) = \mathrm{LF}(\psi) \cup \{\langle\mathbf{tt}, \Diamond \psi\rangle\}
$$
$$
\mathrm{LF}(\Box \psi) = \{\langle\nu, \psi' \wedge \Box \psi\rangle \mid \langle\nu, \psi'\rangle \in \mathrm{LF}(\psi)\}
$$

Example 1. Consider the formula $\Box \Diamond p$.

$$
\begin{aligned}
\mathrm{LF}(\Diamond p) &= \mathrm{LF}(p) \cup \{\langle\mathbf{tt}, \Diamond p\rangle\} \\
&= \{\langle p, \mathbf{tt}\rangle, \langle\mathbf{tt}, \Diamond p\rangle\} \\
\mathrm{LF}(\Box \Diamond p) &= \{\langle\mu, \varphi' \wedge \Box \Diamond p\rangle \mid \langle\mu, \varphi'\rangle \in \mathrm{LF}(\Diamond p)\} \\
&= \{\langle\mu, \varphi' \wedge \Box \Diamond p\rangle \mid \langle\mu, \varphi'\rangle \in \{\langle p, \mathbf{tt}\rangle, \langle\mathbf{tt}, \Diamond p\rangle\}\} \\
&= \{\langle p, \Box \Diamond p\rangle, \langle\mathbf{tt}, \Diamond p \wedge \Box \Diamond p\rangle\}
\end{aligned}
$$

Definition 9 (Linear Forms). *A formula* $\varphi = \bigvee_{i \in I} b_i \wedge \bigcirc \varphi_i$ *is in* linear form *if each b_i is a conjunction of literals and each φ_i is a temporal formula.*

The formula associated to a set of linear factors is in linear form as given by the following mapping.

$$
\Theta(\{\langle\mu_i, \varphi_i\rangle \mid i \in I\}) = \bigvee_{i \in I} (\Theta(\mu_i) \wedge \bigcirc \varphi_i)
$$

Each PNF formula can be represented in linear form by applying the transformation to linear factors. The expansion theorem states the correctness of this transformation.

Theorem 2 (Expansion). *For all φ, $\Theta(\mathrm{LF}(\varphi)) \Leftrightarrow \varphi$.*

The partial derivative of a formula φ with respect to a symbol $x \in \Sigma$ is a set of formulae Ψ such that $x\sigma \models \varphi$ if and only if $\sigma \models \bigvee \Psi$. Partial derivatives only need to be defined for formal conjunctions of temporal formulae as we can apply the $\mathcal{T}$ operator first.

Definition 10 (Partial Derivatives). *The partial derivative of a formal conjunction of temporal formulae with respect to a symbol $x \in \Sigma$ is defined by*

$$\partial_x(\varphi) = \{\varphi' \mid \langle \mu, \varphi' \rangle \in \mathrm{LF}(\varphi), x \models \mu\} \qquad \text{if } \varphi \text{ is a temporal formula}$$

$$\partial_x(\mathbf{tt}) = \{\mathbf{tt}\}$$

$$\partial_x(\varphi \wedge \psi) = \{\varphi' \wedge \psi' \mid \varphi' \in \partial_x(\varphi), \psi' \in \partial_x(\psi)\}.$$

Example 2. Continuing the example of $\Box \Diamond p$, we find for $x \in \Sigma$:

$$\partial_x(\Box \Diamond p) = \{\varphi' \mid \langle \mu, \varphi' \rangle \in \mathrm{LF}(\Box \Diamond p), x \models \mu\}$$

$$= \{\varphi' \mid \langle \mu, \varphi' \rangle \in \{\langle p, \Box \Diamond p \rangle, \langle \mathbf{tt}, \Diamond p \wedge \Box \Diamond p \rangle\}, x \models \mu\}$$

$$= \begin{cases} \{\Box \Diamond p, \Diamond p \wedge \Box \Diamond p\} & p \in x \\ \{\Diamond p \wedge \Box \Diamond p\} & p \notin x \end{cases}$$

As it is sufficient to define the derivative for temporal formulae, it only remains to explore the definition of $\partial_x(\Diamond p)$.

$$\partial_x(\Diamond p) = \{\varphi' \mid \langle \mu, \varphi' \rangle \in \mathrm{LF}(\Diamond p), x \models \mu\}$$

$$= \{\varphi' \mid \langle \mu, \varphi' \rangle \in \{\langle p, \mathbf{tt} \rangle, \langle \mathbf{tt}, \Diamond p \rangle\}, x \models \mu\}$$

$$= \begin{cases} \{\mathbf{tt}, \Diamond p\} & p \in x \\ \{\Diamond p\} & p \notin x \end{cases}$$

A descendant of a formula is either the formula itself or an element of the partial derivative of a descendant by some symbol. As in the regular expression case, the set of descendants of a fixed LTL formula is finite. We refer to the online version for details.

4   Alternating ω-Automata

We revisit Vardi's construction [17] of alternating ω-automata from LTL formulas. The interesting observation is that the definition of the transition function for formulae in PNF corresponds to partial derivatives.

The transition function of an alternating automaton yields a set of sets of states, which we understand as a disjunction of conjunctions of states. The disjunction models the nondeterministic alternatives that the automaton can take in a step, whereas the conjunction models states that need to succeed together. Many presentations use positive Boolean formulae at this point, our presentation equivalently uses the set of minimal models of such formulae.

Definition 11. *A tuple $\mathcal{A} = (Q, \Sigma, \delta, \alpha_0, F)$ is an alternating ω-automaton (AA) [10] if Q is a finite set of states, Σ an alphabet, $\alpha_0 \subseteq \mathbb{P}(Q)$ a set of sets of states, $\delta : Q \times \Sigma \to \mathbb{P}(\mathbb{P}(Q))$ a transition function, and $F \subseteq Q$ a set of accepting states.*

A run of $\mathcal{A}$ on a word σ is a digraph $G = (V, E)$ with nodes $V \subseteq Q \times \omega$ and edges $E \subseteq \bigcup_{i \in \omega} V_i \times V_{i+1}$ where $V_i = Q \times \{i\}$, for all i.

- $\{q \in Q \mid (q, 0) \in V\} \in \alpha_0.$
- *For all $i \in \omega$:*
  - *If $(q', i+1) \in V_{i+1}$, then $((q, i), (q', i+1)) \in E$, for some $q \in Q$.*
  - *If $(q, i) \in V_i$, then $\{q' \in Q \mid ((q, i), (q', i+1)) \in E\} \in \delta(q, \sigma_i).$*

A run G on σ is accepting if every infinite path in G visits a state in F infinitely often (Büchi acceptance). Define the language of $\mathcal{A}$ as

$$\mathcal{L}(\mathcal{A}) = \{\sigma \mid \text{ there exists an accepting run of } \mathcal{A} \text{ on } \sigma\}.$$

Definition 12 ([11,17]). *The alternating ω-automaton $\mathcal{A}(\varphi) = (Q, \Sigma, \delta, \alpha_0, F)$ resulting from φ is defined by: the set of states $Q = \partial^+(\varphi)$, the set of initial states $\alpha_0 = \mathcal{T}(\varphi)$, the set of accepting states $F = \{\mathbf{tt}\} \cup \{\varphi \mathbf{R} \psi \mid \varphi \mathbf{R} \psi \in Q\}$, and the transition function δ by induction on the formula argument:*

- $\delta(\mathbf{tt}, x) = \{\{\mathbf{tt}\}\}$
- $\delta(\mathbf{ff}, x) = \{\}$
- $\delta(\ell, x) = \{\{\mathbf{tt}\}\}$, *if $x \models \ell$*
- $\delta(\ell, x) = \{\}$, *if $x \not\models \ell$*
- $\delta(\varphi \vee \psi, x) = \delta(\varphi, x) \cup \delta(\psi, x)$
- $\delta(\varphi \wedge \psi, x) = \{q_1 \cup q_2 \mid q_1 \in \delta(\varphi, x), q_2 \in \delta(\psi, x)\}$
- $\delta(\bigcirc \varphi, x) = \mathcal{T}(\varphi)$
- $\delta(\varphi \mathbf{U} \psi, x) = \delta(\psi, x) \cup \{q \cup \{\varphi \mathbf{U} \psi\} \mid q \in \delta(\varphi, x)\}$
- $\delta(\varphi \mathbf{R} \psi, x) = \{q_1 \cup q_2 \mid q_1 \in \delta(\varphi, x), q_2 \in \delta(\psi, x)\} \cup \{q \cup \{\varphi \mathbf{R} \psi\} \mid q \in \delta(\psi, x)\}$

We deviate slightly from Vardi's original definition by representing disjunction as a set of states. For example, in his definition $\delta(\mathbf{ff}, x) = \mathbf{ff}$, which is equivalent to the empty disjunction. Another difference is that we only consider formulae in PNF whereas Vardi covers LTL in general. Hence, Vardi's formulation treats negation by extending the set of states with negated subformulae. For example, we find $\delta(\neg\varphi, x) = \overline{\delta(\varphi, x)}$ where $\overline{\Phi}$ calculates the dual of a set Φ of formulae obtained by application of the de Morgan laws. The case for negation can be dropped because we assume that formulae are in PNF. In exchange, we need to state the cases for $\varphi \vee \psi$ and for $\varphi \mathbf{R} \psi$ which can be derived easily from Vardi's formulation by exploiting standard LTL equivalences.

The accepting states in Vardi's construction are all subformulae of the form $\neg(\varphi \mathbf{U} \psi)$, but $\neg(\varphi \mathbf{U} \psi) = (\neg\varphi) \mathbf{R} (\neg\psi)$, which matches our definition and others in the literature [6].

Furthermore, our construction adds $\mathbf{tt}$ to the set of accepting states, which is not present in Vardi's paper. It turns out that $\mathbf{tt}$ can be eliminated from the accepting states if we set $\delta(\mathbf{tt}, x) = \{\}$. This change transforms an infinite path with infinitely many $\mathbf{tt}$ states into a finite path that terminates when truth is established. Thus, it does not affect acceptance of the AA.

The same definition is given by Pelánek and Strejček [12] who note that the resulting automaton is in fact a 1-weak alternating automaton. For this class of automata there is a translation back to LTL.

We observe that the definition of the transition function in Definition 12 corresponds to the direct definition of partial derivatives in Definition 18.

Lemma 5. *Let $\mathcal{A}(\varphi)$ be the alternating ω-automaton for a formula φ according to Definition 12. For each $\psi \in Q$ and $x \in \Sigma$, we have that $\delta(\psi, x) = pd_x(\psi)$.*

Finally, we provide an independent correctness result for the translation from LTL to AA that relies on the correctness of our construction of linear factors.

Theorem 3. *Let φ be an LTL formula. Consider the alternating automaton $\mathcal{A}(\varphi)$ given by*

- $Q = \partial^+(\varphi)$,
- $\delta(\psi, x) = \partial_x(\psi)$, *for all* $\psi \in Q$ *and* $x \in \Sigma$,
- $\alpha_0 = \mathcal{T}(\varphi)$,
- $F = \{\mathbf{tt}\} \cup \{\varphi \mathbf{R} \psi \mid \varphi \mathbf{R} \psi \in Q\}$.

Then, $\mathcal{L}(\varphi) = \mathcal{L}(\mathcal{A}(\varphi))$ using the Büchi acceptance condition.

5   Semantic Tableaux

We revisit Wolper's [22] method of semantic tableaux to check satisfiability of an LTL formula. A tableau is represented as a directed graph built where nodes denote sets of formulae. A tableau for φ starts with the initial node $\{\varphi\}$. New nodes are generated by decomposition of formulae in existing nodes. A post-processing phase eliminates unsatisfiable nodes. The formula φ is satisfiable if there is a satisfiable path in the tableau. Our contribution is an explanation of decomposition in terms of linear factors, which obtains some of the elimination (post-processing) steps for free.

We largely follow Wolper's notation starting with PNF formulae. In the construction of a tableau, a formula φ may be *marked*, written as $\varphi*$. A formula is *elementary* if it is a literal or its outermost connective is $\bigcirc$. A node is called a *state* if the node consists solely of elementary or marked formulae. A node is called a *pre-state* if it is the initial node or the immediate child of a state. We let S and S_i range over sets of formulae.

Definition 13 (Wolper's Tableau Decision Method [22]). *Tableau construction for φ starts with node $S = \{\varphi\}$. New nodes are created as follows.*

- *Decomposition rules: For each non-elementary unmarked $\varphi \in S$ with decomposition rule $\varphi \to \{S_1, \ldots, S_k\}$ as defined below, create k child nodes where the ith child is of the form $(S - \{\varphi\}) \cup S_i \cup \{\varphi*\}$.*

$$\begin{aligned}
&(D1) \ \varphi \vee \psi \to \{\{\varphi\}, \{\psi\}\} \\
&(D2) \ \varphi \wedge \psi \to \{\{\varphi, \psi\}\} \\
&(D3) \quad \Diamond\varphi \to \{\{\varphi\}, \{\bigcirc \Diamond \varphi\}\} \\
&(D4) \quad \Box\varphi \to \{\{\varphi, \bigcirc\Box\varphi\}\} \\
&(D5) \ \varphi\,\mathbf{U}\,\psi \to \{\{\psi\}, \{\varphi, \bigcirc(\varphi\,\mathbf{U}\,\psi)\}\} \\
&(D6) \ \varphi\,\mathbf{R}\,\psi \to \{\{\psi, \varphi \vee \bigcirc(\varphi\,\mathbf{R}\,\psi)\}\}
\end{aligned}$$

- *Step rule: For each node S with only elementary or marked formulae, create a child node $\{\varphi \mid \bigcirc\varphi \in S\}$. Just create an edge if the node already exists.*

Elimination of (unsatisfiable) nodes proceeds as follows. A node S is elimi- nated if one of the conditions (E1)–(E3) applies.

(E1) The node contains p and its negation.
(E2) All successors of S have been eliminated.
(E3) The node S is a pre-state and contains an (unsatisfiable) formula of the form $\Diamond \psi$ or $\varphi \, \mathbf{U} \, \psi$ such that there is no path in the tableau leading from pre-state S to a node containing the formula ψ.

Theorem 4 (Wolper [22]). *An LTL formula φ is satisfiable iff the initial node generated by the tableau decision procedure is not eliminated.*

We argue that marked formulae and intermediate nodes are not essential in Wolper's tableau construction. Marked formulae can simply be dropped and intermediate nodes can be removed by exhaustive application of decomposition. This optimization reduces the size of the tableau and establishes a direct con- nection between states/pre-states and linear factors/partial derivatives.

Definition 14 (Decomposition and Elimination via Rewriting). *We define a rewrite relation among sets of sets of nodes ranged over by N.*

$$(Dec) \; \frac{\text{``}\varphi \to \{S_1, \dots, S_n\}\text{''} \in \{D1, \dots, D6\}}{\{S \cup \{\varphi\}\} \cup N \rightarrowtail \{S \cup S_1\} \cup \cdots \cup \{S \cup S_n\} \cup N}$$

$$(Elim) \; \frac{N' = \{S \mid S \in N \wedge (\forall \ell \in S) \; \neg \ell \notin S\}}{N \rightarrowtail N'}$$

The premise of the (Dec) rule corresponds to one of the decomposition rules (D1)–(D6). The (Elim) rule corresponds to the elimination rule (E1) applied globally. We write $N_1 \rightarrowtail^* N_k$ for $N_1 \rightarrowtail \cdots \rightarrowtail N_k$ where no further rewritings are possible on N_k. We write $\varphi \rightarrowtail^* N$ as a shorthand for $\{\{\varphi\}\} \rightarrowtail^* N$.

As the construction does not mark formulae, we call S a state node if S only consists of elementary formulae. By construction, for any set of formulae S we find that $\{S\} \rightarrowtail^* N$ for some N which only consists of state nodes. In our optimized Wolper-style tableau construction, each $S' \in N$ is a 'direct' child of S where intermediate nodes are skipped. Rule (Elim) integrates the elimination rule (E1) into the construction of new nodes.

The step rule is analogous to Wolper's, except that we represent a pre-state node with a single formula. That is, from state node S we generate the child pre-state node $\{\bigwedge_{\bigcirc \psi \in S} \psi\}$ whereas Wolper generates $\{\psi \mid \bigcirc \psi \in S\}$.

Definition 15 (Optimized Tableau Construction Method). *We consider tableau construction for φ. Let Q denote the set of pre-state formulae generated so far and $Q_j \subseteq Q$ the set of nodes considered in the j-th construction step. Initially, $Q = Q_0 = \{\varphi\}$. Then we perform the following steps for $j = 1, \dots$*

Decomposition: *For a pre-state node $\{\psi\} \in Q_j$, compute $\psi \rightarrowtail^* \{S_1, \dots, S_n\}$. Make each state node S_i a child of node $\{\psi\}$.*

Step: *For each state node S_i, we build $\varphi_i = \bigwedge_{\bigcirc \varphi \in S_i} \varphi$ where pre-state node $\{\varphi_i\}$ is a child of S_i. We set $Q_{j+1} = \{\varphi_1, \ldots, \varphi_n\} - Q$ and then update the set of pre-state formulae generated so far by setting $Q = Q \cup \{\varphi_1, \ldots, \varphi_n\}$.*

Construction continues until no new children are created.

Theorem 5 (Correctness of Optimized Tableau Construction). *For all φ, φ is satisfiable iff the initial node generated by the optimized Wolper-style tableau decision procedure is not eliminated by conditions (E2) and (E3).*

It turns out that states in the optimized variant of Wolper's tableau method correspond to linear factors and pre-states correspond to partial derivatives.

Let $S = \{\ell_1, \ldots, \ell_n, \bigcirc \varphi_1, \ldots, \bigcirc \varphi_m\}$ be a (state) node. We define $[\![S]\!] = \langle \ell_1 \odot \ldots \odot \ell_n, \varphi_1 \wedge \ldots \wedge \varphi_m \rangle$ using **tt** for empty conjunctions. Let $N = \{S_1, \ldots, S_n\}$ where each S_i is a state. We define $[\![N]\!] = \{[\![S_1]\!], \ldots, [\![S_n]\!]\}$.

Lemma 6. *For each $\varphi \neq \mathbf{ff}$, if $\varphi \rightarrowtail^* N$, then $\mathrm{LF}(\varphi) = [\![N]\!]$.*

Case **ff** is excluded because $LF(\mathbf{ff}) = \{\}$.

Hence, any state node generated during the optimized Wolper tableau construction corresponds to a linear factor. An immediate consequence is that each pre-state corresponds to a partial derivative. Hence, we can reformulate the optimized Wolper tableau construction as follows.

Theorem 6 (Tableau Construction via Linear Factors). *The optimized variant of Wolper's tableau construction for φ can be obtained as follows.*

1. *Each formula $\psi \neq \mathbf{tt}$ in the set of all partial derivative descendants $pd_{\Sigma^*}(\varphi)$ corresponds to a pre-state.*
2. *For each $\psi \in pd_{\Sigma^*}(\varphi)$ where $\psi \neq \mathbf{tt}$, each $\langle \nu, \psi' \rangle \in \mathrm{LF}(\psi)$ is state where $\langle \nu, \psi' \rangle$ is a child of ψ, and if $\psi' \neq \mathbf{tt}$, ψ' is a child of $\langle \nu, \psi' \rangle$.*

We exclude **tt** because Wolper's tableau construction stops once we reach **tt**.

The reformulation of Wolper's tableau construction in terms of linear factors and partial derivatives establishes a close connection to Vardi's construction of an alternating ω-automaton. Each path in the tableau labeled by LF and PD corresponds to a transition step in the automaton. The same applies to transitions with one exception. In Wolper's tableau, the state $\langle \ell, \mathbf{tt} \rangle$ is considered final whereas in Vardi's automaton has transitions $\delta(\ell, \mathbf{tt}) = \{\mathbf{tt}\}$. From Theorems 3 and 6 we obtain the following result.

Corollary 1. *Vardi's alternating ω-automaton derived from an LTL formula is isomorphic to Wolper's optimized LTL tableau construction assuming we ignore transitions $\delta(\ell, \mathbf{tt}) = \{\mathbf{tt}\}$.*

6   Related Work and Conclusion

Numerous works study the translation of LTL to ω-automata [4,9,11,17,18] and semantic tableaux [14,15,22]. The fact that there is a deep connection between both constructions appears to be folklore knowledge. For example [9]: "The central part of the automaton construction algorithm is a tableau-like procedure." Couvreur [4] mentions explicitly that "[his automaton construction] is also based on tableau procedures [21,22]." To the best of our knowledge, we are the first to establish a concise connection between the two constructions by means of linear factors and partial derivatives, as shown in Corollary 1. Both concepts have been studied previously in the standard regular expression setting [1] and also in the context of ω-regular languages [16]. We show that both concepts are applicable in the LTL setting and establish their essential properties.

Like some earlier works [4,9], our algorithm can operate on the fly and thus avoid the construction of the full automaton if the algorithm can provide an answer earlier. Further efficiency gains (in checking satisfiability) can be achieved by using Tarjan's algorithm [8] and this improvement is also compatible with our algorithm.

Some current work is dedicated to the direct construction of deterministic ω-automata from LTL formulae (e.g., [5]). Interestingly, that work relies on an "after function" *af* which is analogous to partial derivatives. Hence, it may be promising to further pursue our approach towards constructing deterministic automata.

A   Properties of Partial Derivatives

Our finiteness proof follows the method suggested by Broda et al. [3]. We look at the set of iterated partial derivatives of a formula φ, which turns out to be just the set of temporal subformulae of φ. This set is finite and closed under the partial derivative operation. Thus, finiteness follows.

Definition 16 (Iterated Partial Derivatives)

$$
\begin{aligned}
\partial^+(\ell) &= \{\ell\} \\
\partial^+(\mathbf{tt}) &= \{\mathbf{tt}\} \\
\partial^+(\mathbf{ff}) &= \{\mathbf{ff}\} \\
\partial^+(\varphi \vee \psi) &= \partial^+(\varphi) \cup \partial^+(\psi) \\
\partial^+(\varphi \wedge \psi) &= \partial^+(\varphi) \cup \partial^+(\psi) \\
\partial^+(\bigcirc \varphi) &= \{\bigcirc \varphi\} \cup \partial^+(\varphi) \\
\partial^+(\Diamond \varphi) &= \{\Diamond \varphi\} \cup \partial^+(\varphi) \\
\partial^+(\Box \varphi) &= \{\Box \varphi\} \cup \partial^+(\varphi) \\
\partial^+(\varphi \mathbf{U} \psi) &= \{\varphi \mathbf{U} \psi\} \cup \partial^+(\psi) \cup \partial^+(\varphi) \\
\partial^+(\varphi \mathbf{R} \psi) &= \{\varphi \mathbf{R} \psi\} \cup \partial^+(\psi) \cup \partial^+(\varphi)
\end{aligned}
$$

It is trivial to see that the set $\partial^+(\varphi)$ is finite because it is a subset of the set of subformulae of φ.

Lemma 7 (Finiteness). *For all φ, $\partial^+(\varphi)$ is finite.*

The iterated partial derivative only consider subformulae whereas the partial derivative elides disjunctions but returns a set of formal conjunctions. To connect both the following definition is required.

Definition 17 (Subsets of Formal Conjunctions). *For an ordered set $X = \{x_1, x_2, \dots\}$, we define the set of all formal conjunctions of X as follows.*

$$\mathcal{S}(X) = \{x_{i_1} \wedge \dots \wedge x_{i_n} \mid n \geq 0, i_1 < i_2 < \cdots < i_n\}$$

We regard a subset of $\mathcal{S}(X)$ as a positive Boolean formula over X in conjunctive normal form. We write **tt** *for the empty conjunction.*

Clearly, if a set of formulae Φ is finite, then so is $\mathcal{S}(\Phi)$, where we assume an arbitrary, but fixed total ordering on formulae.

The set of temporal subformulae of a given formula φ is also a formal conjunction of subformulae.

Lemma 8. *For all φ, $\mathcal{T}(\varphi) \subseteq \mathcal{S}(\partial^+(\varphi))$.*

Lemma 9 (Closedness under derivation)

1. *For all $x \in \Sigma$, $\partial_x(\varphi) \subseteq \mathcal{S}(\partial^+(\varphi))$.*
2. *For all $\varphi' \in \partial^+(\varphi)$ and $x \in \Sigma$, $\partial_x(\varphi') \subseteq \mathcal{S}(\partial^+(\varphi))$.*

From Lemmas 8 and 9 it follows that the set of descendants of a fixed LTL formula φ is finite. In fact, we can show that the cardinality of this set is exponential in the size of φ. We will state this result for a more "direct" definition of partial derivatives which does not require having to compute linear factors first.

Definition 18 (Direct Partial Derivatives). *Let $x \in \Sigma$. Then, $pd_x(\cdot)$ maps LTL formulae to sets of LTL formulae and is defined as follows.*

$$
\begin{aligned}
pd_x(\mathbf{tt}) &= \{\mathbf{tt}\} \\
pd_x(\mathbf{ff}) &= \{\} \\
pd_x(\ell) &= \begin{cases} \{\mathbf{tt}\} & x \models \ell \\ \{\} & \text{otherwise} \end{cases} \\
pd_x(\varphi \vee \psi) &= pd_x(\varphi) \cup pd_x(\psi) \\
pd_x(\varphi \wedge \psi) &= \{\varphi' \wedge \psi' \mid \varphi' \in pd_x(\varphi), \psi' \in pd_x(\psi)\} \\
pd_x(\bigcirc\varphi) &= \mathcal{T}(\varphi) \\
pd_x(\varphi \,\mathbf{U}\, \psi) &= pd_x(\psi) \cup \{\varphi' \wedge \varphi \,\mathbf{U}\, \psi \mid \varphi' \in pd_x(\varphi)\} \\
pd_x(\varphi \,\mathbf{R}\, \psi) &= \{\varphi' \wedge \psi' \mid \varphi' \in pd_x(\varphi), \psi' \in pd_x(\psi)\} \\
&\quad \cup \{\psi' \wedge \varphi \,\mathbf{R}\, \psi \mid \psi' \in pd_x(\psi)\} \\
pd_x(\Diamond\varphi) &= pd_x(\varphi) \cup \{\Diamond\varphi\} \\
pd_x(\square\varphi) &= \{\varphi' \wedge \square\varphi \mid \varphi' \in pd_x(\varphi)\}
\end{aligned}
$$

where conjunctions of temporal formulae are normalized as usual.

For $w \in \Sigma^*$, we define $pd_\varepsilon(\varphi) = \{\varphi\}$ and $pd_{xw}(\varphi) = \bigcup_{\varphi' \in pd_x(\varphi)} pd_w(\varphi')$. For $L \subseteq \Sigma^*$, we define $pd_L(\varphi) = \bigcup_{w \in L} pd_w(\varphi)$. We refer to the special case $pd_{\Sigma^*}(\varphi)$ as the set of partial derivative descendants *of φ.*

Example 3. Consider the formula $\Box \Diamond p$. We calculate

$$pd_p(\Diamond p) \quad = \{\mathbf{tt}, \Diamond p\}$$
$$pd_p(\Box \Diamond p) = \{\mathbf{tt} \wedge \Box \Diamond p, \Diamond p \wedge \Box \Diamond p\}$$
$$\text{(normalize)}$$
$$= \{\Box \Diamond p, \Diamond p \wedge \Box \Diamond p\}$$
$$pd_p(\Diamond p \wedge \Box \Diamond p)$$
$$= \{\mathbf{tt} \wedge \mathbf{tt} \wedge \Box \Diamond p, \Diamond p \wedge \Box \Diamond p, \mathbf{tt} \wedge \Diamond p \wedge \Box \Diamond p, \Diamond p \wedge \Diamond p \wedge \Box \Diamond p\}$$
$$\text{(normalize)}$$
$$= \{\Box \Diamond p, \Diamond p \wedge \Box \Diamond p\}$$

Lemma 10. *For all φ and $x \in \Sigma$, $\partial_x(\varphi) = pd_x(\varphi)$.*

The next result follows from Theorem 2 and Lemma 10.

Lemma 11. *For all φ, $\varphi \Leftrightarrow \bigvee_{x \in \Sigma, \varphi' \in pd_x(\varphi)} x \wedge \bigcirc \varphi'$.*

Definition 19. *The size of a temporal formula φ is the sum of the number of literals, temporal and Boolean operators in φ.*

If φ has size n, the number of subformulae in φ is bounded by $O(n)$.

Lemma 12. *For all φ, the cardinality of $pd_{\Sigma^*}(\varphi)$ is bounded by $O(2^n)$ where n is the size of φ.*

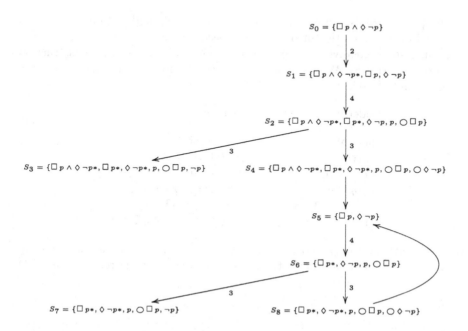

Fig. 1. Tableau before elimination: $\Box p \wedge \Diamond \neg p$

B   Tableau Examples

Example 4. Consider $\Box p \wedge \Diamond \neg p$. Figure 1 shows the tableau generated before elimination. In case of decomposition, edges are annotated with the number of the respective decomposition rule. For example, from the initial node S_0 we reach node S_1 by decomposition via (D2). Node S_4 consists of only elementary and marked nodes and therefore we apply the step rule to reach node S_5. The same applies to node S_3. For brevity, we ignore its child node because this node is obviously unsatisfiable (E1). The same applies to node S_7.

    We consider elimination of nodes. Nodes S_3, S_4, S_7 and S_8 are states. Therefore, S_0 and S_5 are pre-states. Nodes S_3 and S_7 can be immediately eliminated due to E1. Node S_5 contains $\Diamond \neg p$. This formula is not satisfiable because there is not path from S_5 along which we reach a node which contains $\neg p$. Hence, we eliminate S_5 due to E3. All other nodes are eliminated due to E3. Hence, we conclude that the formula $\Box p \wedge \Diamond \neg p$ is unsatisfiable.

Example 5. Consider $\Box p \wedge \Diamond \neg p$. Our variant of Wolper's tableau construction method yields the following.

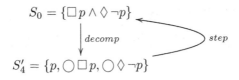

Node S_4' corresponds to node S_4 in Fig. 1. Nodes S_1, S_2, and S_3 from the original construction do not arise in our variant because we skip intermediate nodes and eliminate aggressively during construction whereas Wolper's construction method gives rise S_5. We avoid such intermediate nodes and immediately link S_4' to the initial node S_0.

Example 6. Consider $\neg p \wedge \bigcirc \neg p \wedge q \, \mathbf{U} \, p$ where

$$
\begin{aligned}
\text{LF}(\neg p) &= \{\langle \neg p, \mathbf{tt} \rangle\} \\
\text{LF}(\mathbf{tt}) &= \{\langle \mathbf{tt}, \mathbf{tt} \rangle\} \\
\text{LF}(\bigcirc \neg p) &= \{\langle \mathbf{tt}, \neg p \rangle\} \\
\text{LF}(q \, \mathbf{U} \, p) &= \{\langle p, \mathbf{tt} \rangle, \langle q, q \, \mathbf{U} \, p \rangle\} \\
\text{LF}(\neg p \wedge q \, \mathbf{U} \, p) &= \{\langle \neg p \wedge q, q \, \mathbf{U} \, p \rangle\} \\
\text{LF}(\neg p \wedge \bigcirc \neg p \wedge q \, \mathbf{U} \, p) &= \{\langle \neg p \wedge q, \neg p \wedge q \, \mathbf{U} \, p \rangle\}
\end{aligned}
$$

We carry out the tableau construction using linear factors notation where we use LF to label pre-state (derivatives) to state (linear factor) relations and PD to label state to pre-state relations.

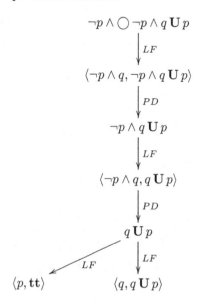

C   Proofs

C.1   Proof of Theorem 2

Proof. Show by induction on φ: for all $\sigma \in \Sigma^\omega$, $\sigma \models \varphi$ iff $\sigma \models \Theta(\mathrm{LF}(\varphi))$.

Case p.

$$\Theta(\mathrm{LF}(p)) = \Theta(\{\langle p, \mathbf{tt}\rangle\}) = p \wedge \bigcirc \mathbf{tt} \Leftrightarrow p$$

Case $\neg p$. Analogous.

Case $\mathbf{tt}$.

$$\Theta(\mathrm{LF}(\mathbf{tt})) = \Theta(\{\langle \mathbf{tt}, \mathbf{tt}\rangle\}) = \mathbf{tt} \wedge \bigcirc \mathbf{tt} \Leftrightarrow \mathbf{tt}$$

Case $\mathbf{ff}$.

$$\Theta(\mathrm{LF}(\mathbf{ff})) = \Theta(\{\}) = \mathbf{ff}$$

Case $\varphi \vee \psi$.

$$\Theta(\mathrm{LF}(\varphi \vee \psi)) = \Theta(\mathrm{LF}(\varphi) \cup \mathrm{LF}(\psi)) = \Theta(\mathrm{LF}(\varphi)) \vee \Theta(\mathrm{LF}(\psi))$$

Now

$$\sigma \models \varphi \vee \psi \Leftrightarrow (\sigma \models \varphi) \vee (\sigma \models \psi)$$
$$\text{by IH}$$
$$\Leftrightarrow (\sigma \models \Theta(\mathrm{LF}(\varphi))) \vee (\sigma \models \Theta(\mathrm{LF}(\psi)))$$
$$\Leftrightarrow (\sigma \models \Theta(\mathrm{LF}(\varphi)) \vee \Theta(\mathrm{LF}(\psi)))$$

Case $\varphi \wedge \psi$.

$$\Theta(\text{LF}(\varphi \wedge \psi)) = \Theta(\{\langle \mu \odot \nu, \varphi' \wedge \psi' \rangle \mid \langle \mu, \varphi' \rangle \in \text{LF}(\varphi), \langle \nu, \psi' \rangle \in \text{LF}(\psi)\})$$
$$= \bigvee \{(\mu \odot \nu) \wedge \bigcirc (\varphi' \wedge \psi') \mid \langle \mu, \varphi' \rangle \in \text{LF}(\varphi), \langle \nu, \psi' \rangle \in \text{LF}(\psi)\}$$

Now

$\sigma \models \varphi \wedge \psi$

$\Leftrightarrow (\sigma \models \varphi) \wedge (\sigma \models \psi)$

by IH

$\Leftrightarrow (\sigma \models \Theta(\text{LF}(\varphi))) \wedge (\sigma \models \Theta(\text{LF}(\psi)))$

$\Leftrightarrow (\sigma \models \bigvee \{\mu \wedge \bigcirc \varphi' \mid \langle \mu, \varphi' \rangle \in \text{LF}(\varphi)\})$

$\quad \wedge (\sigma \models \bigvee \{\nu \wedge \bigcirc \psi' \mid \langle \nu, \psi' \rangle \in \text{LF}(\psi)\})$

$\Leftrightarrow \sigma \models (\bigvee \{\mu \wedge \bigcirc \varphi' \mid \langle \mu, \varphi' \rangle \in \text{LF}(\varphi)\}) \wedge (\bigvee \{\nu \wedge \bigcirc \psi' \mid \langle \nu, \psi' \rangle \in \text{LF}(\psi)\})$

$\Leftrightarrow \sigma \models (\bigvee \{\mu \wedge \bigcirc \varphi' \wedge \nu \wedge \bigcirc \psi' \mid \langle \mu, \varphi' \rangle \in \text{LF}(\varphi), \langle \nu, \psi' \rangle \in \text{LF}(\psi)\})$

by Lemma 2 $\mu \wedge \nu \Leftrightarrow \Theta(\mu \odot \nu)$

$\Leftrightarrow \sigma \models (\bigvee \{(\mu \odot \nu) \wedge \bigcirc \varphi' \wedge \bigcirc \psi' \mid \langle \mu, \varphi' \rangle \in \text{LF}(\varphi), \langle \nu, \psi' \rangle \in \text{LF}(\psi)\})$

$\Leftrightarrow \sigma \models (\bigvee \{(\mu \odot \nu) \wedge \bigcirc (\varphi' \wedge \psi') \mid \langle \mu, \varphi' \rangle \in \text{LF}(\varphi), \langle \nu, \psi' \rangle \in \text{LF}(\psi)\})$

Case $\bigcirc \varphi$. (using Lemma 3)

$$\Theta(\text{LF}(\bigcirc \varphi)) = \Theta(\{\langle \mathbf{tt}, \varphi' \rangle \mid \varphi' \in \mathcal{T}(\varphi)\})$$
$$= \bigvee \{\mathbf{tt} \wedge \bigcirc \varphi' \mid \varphi' \in \mathcal{T}(\varphi)\}$$
$$= \bigcirc (\bigvee \mathcal{T}(\varphi))$$
$$\Leftrightarrow \bigcirc \varphi$$

Case $\varphi \mathbf{U} \psi$.

$$\Theta(\varphi \mathbf{U} \psi) = \Theta(\text{LF}(\psi) \cup \{\langle \mu, \varphi' \wedge \varphi \mathbf{U} \psi \rangle \mid \langle \mu, \varphi' \rangle \in \text{LF}(\varphi)\})$$
$$= \Theta(\text{LF}(\psi)) \vee \bigvee \{\mu \wedge \bigcirc (\varphi' \wedge \varphi \mathbf{U} \psi) \mid \langle \mu, \varphi' \rangle \in \text{LF}(\varphi)\}$$
$$\Leftrightarrow \Theta(\text{LF}(\psi)) \vee \bigvee \{\mu \wedge \bigcirc \varphi' \mid \langle \mu, \varphi' \rangle \in \text{LF}(\varphi)\} \wedge \bigcirc (\varphi \mathbf{U} \psi)$$
$$\Leftrightarrow \Theta(\text{LF}(\psi)) \vee (\Theta(\text{LF}(\varphi)) \wedge \bigcirc (\varphi \mathbf{U} \psi))$$

by IH

$$\Leftrightarrow \psi \vee (\varphi \wedge \bigcirc (\varphi \mathbf{U} \psi))$$
$$\Leftrightarrow \varphi \mathbf{U} \psi$$

Case $\varphi \mathbf{R} \psi$.

$$\Theta(\mathrm{LF}(\varphi \mathbf{R} \psi)) = \Theta\left(\begin{array}{l} \{\langle \mu \odot \nu, \varphi' \wedge \psi' \rangle \mid \langle \mu, \varphi' \rangle \in \mathrm{LF}(\varphi), \langle \nu, \psi' \rangle \in \mathrm{LF}(\psi)\} \\ \cup \{\langle \nu, \psi' \wedge \varphi \mathbf{R} \psi \rangle \mid \langle \nu, \psi' \rangle \in \mathrm{LF}(\psi)\} \end{array} \right)$$

$$= \bigvee\nolimits_{\langle \mu, \varphi' \rangle \in \mathrm{LF}(\varphi), \langle \nu, \psi' \rangle \in \mathrm{LF}(\psi)} (\Theta(\mu \odot \nu) \wedge \bigcirc (\varphi' \wedge \psi'))$$
$$\vee \bigvee\nolimits_{\langle \nu, \psi' \rangle \in \mathrm{LF}(\psi)} (\Theta(\nu) \wedge \bigcirc (\psi' \wedge \varphi \mathbf{R} \psi))$$

by Lemma 2 and the fact that $\bigcirc (\varphi \wedge \psi) \Leftrightarrow \bigcirc \varphi \wedge \bigcirc \psi$

$$\Leftrightarrow \bigvee\nolimits_{\langle \mu, \varphi' \rangle \in \mathrm{LF}(\varphi), \langle \nu, \psi' \rangle \in \mathrm{LF}(\psi)} (\Theta(\mu) \wedge \Theta(\nu) \wedge \bigcirc \varphi' \wedge \bigcirc \psi')$$
$$\vee \bigvee\nolimits_{\langle \nu, \psi' \rangle \in \mathrm{LF}(\psi)} (\Theta(\nu) \wedge \bigcirc \psi' \wedge \bigcirc (\varphi \mathbf{R} \psi))$$

by repeated application of the following distributivity laws

$$(\varphi_1 \wedge \varphi_2) \vee (\varphi_1 \wedge \varphi_3) \Leftrightarrow \varphi_1 \wedge (\varphi_2 \vee \varphi_3)$$
$$(\varphi_1 \wedge \varphi_2) \vee (\varphi_3 \wedge \varphi_2) \Leftrightarrow (\varphi_1 \vee \varphi_3) \wedge \varphi_2$$

$$\Leftrightarrow \bigvee\nolimits_{\langle \nu, \psi' \rangle \in \mathrm{LF}(\psi)} (\Theta(\nu) \wedge \bigcirc \psi')$$
$$\wedge (((\bigvee\nolimits_{\langle \mu, \varphi' \rangle \in \mathrm{LF}(\varphi)} (\Theta(\mu) \wedge \bigcirc \varphi'))) \vee \bigcirc (\varphi \mathbf{R} \psi))$$

$$= \Theta(\mathrm{LF}(\psi)) \wedge (\Theta(\mathrm{LF}(\varphi)) \vee \bigcirc (\varphi \mathbf{R} \psi))$$

by IH

$$\Leftrightarrow \psi \wedge (\varphi \vee \bigcirc (\varphi \mathbf{R} \psi))$$

by Theorem 1

$$\Leftrightarrow \varphi \mathbf{R} \psi$$

$\square$

C.2 Proof of Lemma 7

Proof. By straightforward induction on the linear temporal formula. $\square$

C.3 Proof of Lemma 8

Proof. By straightforward induction on the linear temporal formula. $\square$

C.4 Proof of Lemma 10

Proof. By induction on φ.

Case $\varphi \mathbf{R} \psi$. By definition,

$$\partial_x(\varphi \mathbf{R} \psi) = \{\varphi' \wedge \psi' \mid \langle \mu, \varphi' \rangle \in \mathrm{LF}(\varphi), \langle \nu, \psi' \rangle \in \mathrm{LF}(\psi), x \models \mu \odot \nu\} \quad (1)$$
$$\cup \{\psi' \wedge \varphi \mathbf{R} \psi \mid \langle \nu, \psi' \rangle \in \mathrm{LF}(\psi), x \models \nu\} \quad (2)$$

Consider (1). For $\mu \odot \nu = \mathbf{ff}$, the second components of the respective linear forms can be ignored. Hence, by IH we find that $\{\varphi' \wedge \psi' \mid \langle \mu, \varphi' \rangle \in \mathrm{LF}(\varphi), \langle \nu, \psi' \rangle \in \mathrm{LF}(\psi), x \models \mu \odot \nu\} \subseteq \{\varphi' \wedge \psi' \mid \varphi' \in pd_x(\varphi), \psi' \in pd_x(\psi)\}$. The other direction follows as well as $x \models \mu$ and $x \models \nu$ implies that $\mu \odot \nu \neq \mathbf{ff}$. Consider (2). By IH we have that $\{\psi' \wedge \varphi \mathbf{R} \psi \mid \langle \nu, \psi' \rangle \in \mathrm{LF}(\psi), x \models \nu\} = \{\psi' \wedge \varphi \mathbf{R} \psi \mid \psi' \in pd_x(\psi)\}$. Hence, $\partial_x(\varphi \mathbf{R} \psi) = pd_x(\varphi \mathbf{R} \psi)$.

The other cases can be proven similarly.

C.5   Proof of Lemma 12

Proof. The cardinality of $\partial^+(\varphi)$ is bounded by $O(n)$. By Lemma 9 (second part) elements in the set of descendants are in the set $\mathcal{S}(\partial^+(\varphi))$. The mapping $\mathcal{S}$ builds all possible (conjunctive) combinations of the underlying set. Hence, the cardinality of $\mathcal{S}(\partial^+(\varphi))$ is bounded by $O(2^n)$ and we are done.

C.6   Proof of Lemma 9

Proof. **First part.** By induction on φ we show that $\{\varphi' \mid \langle \mu, \varphi' \rangle \in \text{LF}(\varphi)\} \subseteq \mathcal{S}(\partial^+(\varphi))$.

Case tt. $\text{LF}(\mathbf{tt}) = \{\langle \mathbf{tt}, \mathbf{tt} \rangle\}$ and $\mathbf{tt} \in \mathcal{S}(\partial^+(\mathbf{tt}))$.

Case ℓ. Analogous.

Case ff. Holds vacuously.

Case $\varphi \vee \psi$. Immediate by induction.

Case $\varphi \wedge \psi$. Immediate by induction.

Case $\bigcirc \varphi$. $\text{LF}(\bigcirc \varphi) = \{\langle \mathbf{tt}, \varphi' \rangle \mid \varphi' \in \mathcal{T}(\varphi)\}$ and by Lemma 8, $\mathcal{T}(\varphi) \subseteq \mathcal{S}(\partial^+(\varphi))$.

Case $\varphi \mathbf{U} \psi$. $\text{LF}(\varphi \mathbf{U} \psi) = \text{LF}(\psi) \cup \{\langle \mu, \varphi' \wedge \varphi \mathbf{U} \psi \rangle \mid \langle \mu, \varphi' \rangle \in \text{LF}(\varphi)\}$. By induction, the second components of $\text{LF}(\psi)$ are in $\mathcal{S}(\partial^+(\psi)) \subseteq \mathcal{S}(\partial^+(\varphi \mathbf{U} \psi))$. By induction, the second components φ' of $\text{LF}(\varphi)$ are in $\mathcal{S}(\partial^+(\varphi))$, so that $\varphi' \wedge \varphi \mathbf{U} \psi \in \mathcal{S}(\partial^+(\varphi) \cup \{\varphi \mathbf{U} \psi\}) \subseteq \mathcal{S}(\partial^+(\varphi \mathbf{U} \psi))$.

Case $\varphi \mathbf{R} \psi$. $\text{LF}(\varphi \mathbf{R} \psi) = \{\langle \mu \odot \nu, \varphi' \wedge \psi' \rangle \mid \langle \mu, \varphi' \rangle \in \text{LF}(\varphi), \langle \nu, \psi' \rangle \in \text{LF}(\psi)\} \cup \{\langle \nu, \psi' \wedge \varphi \mathbf{R} \psi \rangle \mid \langle \nu, \psi' \rangle \in \text{LF}(\psi)\}$. By induction $\varphi' \in \mathcal{S}(\partial^+(\varphi))$ and $\psi' \in \mathcal{S}(\partial^+(\psi))$ so that $\varphi' \wedge \psi' \in \mathcal{S}(\partial^+(\varphi) \cup \partial^+(\psi)) \subseteq \mathcal{S}(\partial^+(\varphi \mathbf{R} \psi))$. Furthermore, $\psi' \wedge \varphi \mathbf{R} \psi \in \mathcal{S}(\partial^+(\psi) \cup \{\varphi \mathbf{R} \psi\}) \subseteq \mathcal{S}(\partial^+(\varphi \mathbf{R} \psi))$.

Second part. By induction on φ.

Case ℓ. If $\varphi' = \ell$ or $\varphi' = \mathbf{tt}$, then $\mathbf{tt} \in \mathcal{S}(\partial^+(\ell))$.

Case tt. Analogous.

Case ff. Vacuously true.

Case $\varphi \vee \psi$. Immediate by induction.

Case $\varphi \wedge \psi$. Immediate by induction.

Case $\varphi \mathbf{U} \psi$. By induction and the first part.

Case $\varphi \mathbf{R} \psi$. By induction and the first part.

C.7   Proof of Theorem 3

Proof. Suppose that $\sigma \models \varphi$. Show by induction on φ that $\sigma \in \mathcal{L}(\mathcal{A}(\varphi))$.

Case tt. Accepted by run $\mathbf{tt}, \mathbf{tt}, \ldots$ which visits $\mathbf{tt} \in F$ infinitely often.

Case ff. No run.

Case p. As $p \in \sigma_0$, σ is accepted by run $p, \mathbf{tt}, \mathbf{tt}, \ldots$.

Case $\neg p$. Accepted by run $\neg p, \mathbf{tt}, \mathbf{tt}, \ldots$.

Case $\varphi \wedge \psi$. By definition $\sigma \models \varphi$ and $\sigma \models \psi$. By induction, there are accepting runs $\alpha_0, \alpha_1, \ldots$ on σ in $\mathcal{A}(\varphi)$ and $\beta_0, \beta_1, \ldots$ on σ in $\mathcal{A}(\psi)$. But then $\alpha_0 \wedge \beta_0, \alpha_1 \wedge \beta_1, \ldots$ is an accepting run on σ in $\mathcal{A}(\varphi \wedge \psi)$ **because the state sets of the automata are disjoint.**

Case $\varphi \vee \psi$. By definition $\sigma \models \varphi$ or $\sigma \models \psi$. If we assume that $\sigma \models \varphi$, then induction yields an accepting run $\alpha_0, \alpha_1, \ldots$ on σ in $\mathcal{A}(\varphi)$. As the initial state of $\mathcal{A}(\varphi \vee \psi)$ is chosen from $\{\alpha_0, \beta_0\}$, for some β_0, we have that $\alpha_0, \alpha_1, \ldots$ is an accepting run on σ in $\mathcal{A}(\varphi \vee \psi)$.

Case $\bigcirc \varphi$. By definition $\sigma[1 \ldots] \models \varphi$. By induction, there is an accepting run $\alpha_0, \alpha_1, \ldots$ on $\sigma[1 \ldots]$ in $\mathcal{A}(\varphi)$ with $\alpha_0 = \mathcal{T}(\varphi)$. Thus, there is an accepting run $\bigcirc \varphi, \alpha_0, \alpha_1, \ldots$ on σ in $\mathcal{A}(\bigcirc \varphi)$.

Case $\varphi \mathbf{U} \psi$. By definition $\exists n \in \omega, \forall j \in \omega, j < n \Rightarrow \sigma[j \ldots] \models \varphi$ and $\sigma[n \ldots] \models \psi$. By induction, there is an accepting run on $\sigma[n \ldots]$ in $\mathcal{A}(\psi)$ and, for all $0 \leq j < n$, there are accepting runs on $\sigma[j \ldots]$ in $\mathcal{A}(\varphi)$.

We proceed by induction on n.

Subcase $n = 0$. In this case, there is an accepting run $\beta_0, \beta_1, \ldots$ on $\sigma[0 \ldots] = \sigma$ in $\mathcal{A}(\psi)$ so that $\beta_0 = \mathcal{T}(\psi)$. We want to show that $\varphi \mathbf{U} \psi, \beta_1, \ldots$ is an accepting run on σ in $\mathcal{A}(\varphi \mathbf{U} \psi)$. To see this, observe that $\beta_1 \in \partial_{\sigma_0}(\beta_0)$ and that $\partial_{\sigma_0}(\varphi \mathbf{U} \psi) = \partial_{\sigma_0}(\beta_0) \cup \partial_{\sigma_0}(\alpha_0) \wedge \varphi \mathbf{U} \psi$, where $\alpha_0 = \mathcal{T}(\varphi)$, which proves the claim.

Subcase $n > 0$. There must be an accepting run $\alpha_0, \alpha_1, \ldots$ on $\sigma[0 \ldots] = \sigma$ in $\mathcal{A}(\varphi)$ so that $\alpha_0 = \mathcal{T}(\varphi)$. By induction (on n) there must be an accepting run $\beta_0, \beta_1, \ldots$ on $\sigma[1 \ldots]$ in $\mathcal{A}(\varphi \mathbf{U} \psi)$ where $\beta_0 = \varphi \mathbf{U} \psi$. We need to show that $\varphi \mathbf{U} \psi, \alpha_1 \wedge \beta_0, \alpha_2 \wedge \beta_1, \ldots$ is an accepting run on σ in $\mathcal{A}(\varphi \mathbf{U} \psi)$. By the analysis in the base case, the automaton can step from $\varphi \mathbf{U} \psi$ to $\partial_{\sigma_0}(\alpha_0) \wedge \varphi \mathbf{U} \psi$.

Case $\varphi \mathbf{R} \psi$.

By definition, $\forall n \in \omega, (\sigma[n \ldots] \models \psi$ or $\exists j \in \omega, ((j < n) \wedge \sigma[j \ldots] \models \varphi))$. By induction, there is either an accepting run on $\sigma[n \ldots]$ in $\mathcal{A}(\psi)$, for each $n \in \omega$, or there exists some $j \in \omega$ such that there is an accepting run on $\sigma[j \ldots]$ in $\mathcal{A}(\varphi)$ and for all $0 \leq i \leq j$, there is an accepting run on $\sigma[i \ldots]$ in $\mathcal{A}(\psi)$.

If there is an accepting run $\pi_0^n, E_0^n, \pi_1^n, E_1^n, \ldots$ in $\mathcal{A}(\psi)$ on $\sigma[n \ldots]$ for each $n \in \omega$ where $\pi_0^n \in \mathcal{T}(\psi)$ and $\pi_{i+1}^n \in \partial_{\sigma_{i+n}}(\pi_i^n)$, then there is an accepting run in $\mathcal{A}(\varphi \mathbf{R} \psi)$:

$$\partial_{\sigma_0}(\varphi \mathbf{R} \psi) = \partial_{\sigma_0}(\varphi \wedge \psi) \cup \partial_{\sigma_0}(\psi) \wedge \varphi \mathbf{R} \psi.$$

Suppose that there is either an accepting run on $\sigma[n \ldots]$ in $\mathcal{A}(\psi)$, for each $n \in \omega$. In this case, there is an accepting run in $\mathcal{A}(\varphi \mathbf{R} \psi)$: there is infinite path of accepting states $\varphi \mathbf{R} \psi, \ldots$ and, as ψ holds at every n, every infinite path that starts in a state in $\partial_{\sigma_n}(\psi)$ visits infinitely many accepting states.

Otherwise, the run visits only finitely many states of the form $\varphi \mathbf{R} \psi$ and then continues according to the accepting runs on φ and ψ starting with $\partial_{\sigma_j}(\varphi \wedge \psi)$. Furthermore, any infinite path starting at some $\partial_{\sigma_i}(\psi) \wedge \varphi \mathbf{R} \psi$ that goes through $\partial_{\sigma_i}(\psi)$ visits infinitely many accepting states (for $0 \leq i < j$).

Suppose now that $\sigma \not\models \varphi$ and show that $\sigma \notin \mathcal{L}(\mathcal{A}(\varphi))$.

$\sigma \not\models \varphi$ is equivalent to $\sigma \models \neg \varphi$. We prove by induction on φ that $\sigma \notin \mathcal{L}(\mathcal{A}(\varphi))$.

Case tt. The statement $\sigma \not\models$ tt is contradictory.

Case ff. The statement $\sigma \not\models$ ff holds for all σ and the automaton $\mathcal{A}($ff$)$ has no transitions, so $\sigma \notin \mathcal{L}(\mathcal{A}(ff))$.

Case p. The statement $\sigma \not\models p$ is equivalent to $\sigma \models \neg p$. That is, $p \notin \sigma_0$. As $\mathrm{LF}(p) = \{\langle p, \mathbf{tt}\rangle\}$, we find that $\partial_{\sigma_0}(p) = \emptyset$ so that $\mathcal{A}(p)$ has no run on p.

Case $\neg p$. Similar.

Case $\varphi \wedge \psi$. If $\sigma \not\models \varphi \wedge \psi$, then $\sigma \not\models \varphi$ or $\sigma \not\models \psi$. If we assume that $\sigma \not\models \varphi$ and appeal to induction, then either there is no run of $\mathcal{A}(\varphi)$ on σ: in this case, there is no run of $\mathcal{A}(\varphi \wedge \psi)$ on σ, either. Alternatively, every run of $\mathcal{A}(\varphi)$ on σ has a path with only finitely many accepting states. This property is inherited by $\mathcal{A}(\varphi \wedge \psi)$.

Case $\varphi \vee \psi$. If $\sigma \not\models \varphi \vee \psi$, then $\sigma \not\models \varphi$ and $\sigma \not\models \psi$. By appeal to induction, every run of $\mathcal{A}(\varphi)$ on σ as well as every run of $\mathcal{A}(\psi)$ on σ has a path with only finitely many accepting states. Thus, every run of $\mathcal{A}(\varphi \vee \psi)$ on σ will have an infinite path with only finitely many accepting states.

Case $\bigcirc \varphi$. If $\sigma \not\models \bigcirc \varphi$, then $\sigma \models \neg \bigcirc \varphi$ which is equivalent to $\sigma \models \bigcirc \neg \varphi$ and thus $\sigma[1 \dots] \not\models \varphi$. By induction every run of $\mathcal{A}(\varphi)$ on $\sigma[1 \dots]$ has an infinite path with only finitely many accepting states, so has every run of $\mathcal{A}(\bigcirc \varphi)$ on σ.

Case $\varphi \mathbf{U} \psi$. If $\sigma \not\models \varphi \mathbf{U} \psi$, then it must be that $\sigma \models (\neg\varphi) \mathbf{R} (\neg\psi)$.

By definition, the release formula holds if

$$\forall n \in \omega, (\sigma[n \dots] \not\models \psi \text{ or } \exists j \in \omega, (j < n \wedge \sigma[j \dots] \not\models \varphi))$$

We obtain, by induction, for all $n \in \omega$ that either

1. every run of $\mathcal{A}(\psi)$ on $\sigma[n \dots]$ has an infinite path with only finitely many accepting states or
2. $\exists j \in \omega$ with $j < n$ and every run of $\mathcal{A}(\varphi)$ on $\sigma[j \dots]$ has an infinite path with only finitely many accepting states.

Now we consider a run of $\mathcal{A}(\varphi \mathbf{U} \psi)$ on σ.

$$\begin{aligned}
\partial_{\sigma_0}(\varphi \mathbf{U} \psi) &= \{\varphi' \mid \langle \mu, \varphi'\rangle \in \mathrm{LF}(\varphi \mathbf{U} \psi), \sigma_0 \models \mu\} \\
&= \{\psi' \mid \langle \nu, \psi'\rangle \in \mathrm{LF}(\psi), \sigma_0 \models \nu\} \\
&\quad \cup \{\varphi' \wedge \varphi \mathbf{U} \psi \mid \langle \mu, \varphi'\rangle \in \mathrm{LF}(\varphi), \sigma_0 \models \mu\}
\end{aligned}$$

To be accepting, the run cannot always choose the alternative that contains $\varphi \mathbf{U} \psi$ because that would give rise to an infinite path $(\varphi \mathbf{U} \psi)^\omega$ which contains no accepting state.

Thus, any accepting run must choose the alternative containing ψ' a derivative of ψ. Suppose this choice happens at σ_i. If the release formula is accepted because case 1 holds always, then a run of $\mathcal{A}(\psi)$ starting at σ_i has an infinite path with only finitely many accepting states. So this run cannot be accepting.

If the release formula is accepted because eventually case 2 holds, then $i < j$ is not possible for the same reason as just discussed. However, starting from σ_j, we have a state component from $\mathcal{A}(\varphi)$ which has an infinite path with only finitely many accepting states. So this run cannot be accepting, either.

Case $\varphi \mathbf{R} \psi$. If $\sigma \not\models \varphi \mathbf{R} \psi$, then $\sigma \models \neg(\varphi \mathbf{R} \psi)$ which is equivalent to $\sigma \models (\neg\varphi) \mathbf{U} (\neg\psi)$.

By definition, the until formula holds if

$$\exists n \in \omega, (\forall j \in \omega, j < n \Rightarrow \sigma[j\ldots] \not\models \varphi) \text{ and } \sigma[n\ldots] \not\models \psi$$

We obtain, by induction, that there is some $n \in \omega$ such that

1. for all $j \in \omega$ with $j < n$ every run of $\mathcal{A}(\varphi)$ on $\sigma[j\ldots]$ has an infinite path with only finitely many accepting states and
2. every run of $\mathcal{A}(\psi)$ on $\sigma[n\ldots]$ has an infinite path with only finitely many accepting states.

Now we assume that there is an accepting run of $\mathcal{A}(\varphi \mathbf{R} \psi)$ on σ. Consider

$$\partial_{\sigma_0}(\varphi \mathbf{R} \psi) = \partial_{\sigma_0}(\varphi \wedge \psi) \cup \partial_{\sigma_0}(\psi) \wedge \varphi \mathbf{R} \psi$$

Suppose that the run always chooses the alternative containing the formula $\varphi \mathbf{R} \psi$. However, at σ_n, this formula is paired with a run of $\mathcal{A}(\psi)$ on $\sigma[n\ldots]$ which has an infinite path with only finitely many accepting states. A contradiction.

Hence, there must be some $i \in \omega$ such that $\mathcal{A}(\varphi \mathbf{R} \psi)$ chooses its next states from $\partial_{\sigma_i}(\varphi \wedge \psi)$. If this index $i < n$, then this run cannot be accepting because it contains a run of $\mathcal{A}(\varphi)$ on $\sigma[i\ldots]$, which has an infinite path with only finitely many accepting states. Contradiction.

On the other hand, $i \geq n$ is not possible either because it would contradict case 2.

Hence, there cannot be an accepting run. $\qquad\qquad\qquad\qquad\qquad\qquad\qquad\square$

C.8   Proof of Theorem 5

We observe that exhaustive decomposition yields to the same set of states, regardless of the order decomposition rules are applied.

Example 7. Consider $\Box p \wedge \Diamond \neg p$. Starting with $\{\{\Box p \wedge \Diamond \neg p\}\}$ the following rewrite steps can be applied. Individual rewrite steps are annotated with the decomposition rule (number) that has been applied.

$$\Box p \wedge \Diamond \neg p \xrightarrow{2} \{\{\Box p, \Diamond \neg p\}\}$$
$$\xrightarrow{4} \{\{p, \bigcirc \Box p, \Diamond \neg p\}\}$$
$$\xrightarrow{3} \{\{p, \bigcirc \Box p, \neg p\}, \{p, \bigcirc \Box p, \bigcirc \Diamond \neg p\}\}$$

In the final set of nodes we effectively find nodes S_3 and S_4 from Wolper's tableau construction. Intermediate nodes S_1 and S_2 arise in some intermediate rewrite steps. See Fig. 1. The only difference is that marked formulae are dropped.

An interesting observation is that there is an alternative rewriting, which reaches the same set of children.

$$\Box p \wedge \Diamond \neg p \xrightarrow{2} \{\{\Box p, \Diamond \neg p\}\}$$
$$\xrightarrow{3} \{\{\Box p, \neg p\}, \{\Box p, \bigcirc \Diamond \neg p\}\}$$
$$\xrightarrow{4} \{\{p, \bigcirc \Box p, \neg p\}, \{\Box p, \bigcirc \Diamond \neg p\}\}$$
$$\xrightarrow{4} \{\{p, \bigcirc \Box p, \neg p\}, \{p, \bigcirc \Box p, \bigcirc \Diamond \neg p\}\}$$

We formalize the observations made in the above example. Decomposition yields the same set of nodes regardless of the choice of intermediate steps.

Lemma 13. *The rewrite relation $\rightarrowtail$ is terminating and confluent.*

Proof. By inspection of the decomposition rules D1–6.

Hence, our reformulation of Wolper's tableau construction method yields the same nodes (ignoring marked formulae and intermediate nodes).

Lemma 14. *Let S be a pre-state node in Wolper's tableau construction and S' be a node derived from S via some (possibly repeated) decomposition steps where S' is a state. Then, $\{S\} \rightarrowtail^* N$ for some N where $S'' \in N$ such that S'' and S' are equivalent modulo marked formulae.*

Proof. No further decomposition rules can be applied to a state. The only difference between our rewriting-based formulation of Wolper's tableau construction is that we drop marked formulae. Hence, the result follows immediately.

Wolper's proof does not require marked formulae nor does it make use of intermediate nodes in any essential way. Hence, correctness of the optimized Wolper-style tableau construction method follows from Wolper's proof.

C.9   Proof of Lemma 6

We first state some auxiliary result.

Lemma 15. *Let $\{S \cup \{\varphi\}\} \cup N \rightarrowtail \{S \cup S_1\} \cup \cdots \cup \{S \cup S_n\} \cup N \rightarrowtail^* N'$ where $\varphi \rightarrow \{S_1, \ldots, S_n\}$ and $\{\{\varphi\}\} \rightarrowtail^* \{S_1', \ldots, S_m'\}$. Then, $\{S \cup \{\varphi\}\} \cup N \rightarrowtail \{S \cup S_1'\} \cup \cdots \cup \{S \cup S_m'\} \cup N \rightarrowtail^* N'$.*

Proof. By induction over the length of the derivation $\{\{\varphi\}\} \rightarrowtail^* \{S_1', \ldots, S_m'\}$ and the fact that the rewriting relation is terminating and confluent (Lemma 13).

Lemma 15 says that we obtain the same result if we exhaustively decompose a single formula or apply decomposition steps that alternate among multiple formulae. This observation simplifies the up-coming inductive proof of Lemma 13.

By induction on φ we show that if $\varphi \rightarrowtail^* N$ then $\text{LF}(\varphi) = \llbracket N \rrbracket$.

Proof. **Case $\varphi \wedge \psi$.** By assumption $\varphi \wedge \psi \rightarrowtail \{\{\varphi, \psi\}\} \rightarrowtail^* N$. By induction we find that (1) $\text{LF}(\varphi) = \llbracket N_1 \rrbracket$ and (2) $\text{LF}(\psi) = \llbracket N_2 \rrbracket$ where $\varphi \rightarrowtail^* \{S_1, \ldots, S_n\}$, $\psi \rightarrowtail^* \{T_1, \ldots, T_m\}$, $N_1 = \{S_1, \ldots, S_n\}$ and $N_2 = \{T_1, \ldots, T_m\}$. By Lemma 15, we can conclude that $\varphi \wedge \psi \rightarrowtail \{\{\psi\} \cup S_1, \ldots, \{\psi\} \cup S_n\} \rightarrowtail \{S \cup T \mid S \in \{S_1, \ldots, S_n\}, T \in \{T_1, \ldots, T_m\}\}$ where $N = \{S \cup T \mid S \in \{S_1, \ldots, S_n\}, T \in \{T_1, \ldots, T_m\}\}$. From this and via (1) and (2), we can derive that $\text{LF}(\varphi \wedge \psi) = \llbracket N \rrbracket$. Elimination via (E1) is integrated as part of rewriting (see Definition 14).

Case $\varphi \, \mathbf{R} \, \psi$. By assumption

$$\varphi \, \mathbf{R} \, \psi \rightarrowtail \{\{\psi, \varphi \vee \bigcirc (\varphi \, \mathbf{R} \, \psi)\}\} \rightarrowtail \{\{\psi, \varphi\}, \{\psi, \bigcirc (\varphi \, \mathbf{R} \, \psi)\}\} \rightarrowtail^* N.$$

By reasoning analogously as in case of conjunction, we find that $\text{LF}(\varphi \, \mathbf{R} \, \psi) = \llbracket N \rrbracket$
The remaining cases follow the same pattern.

References

1. Antimirov, V.M.: Partial derivatives of regular expressions and finite automaton constructions. Theor. Comput. Sci. **155**(2), 291–319 (1996). https://doi.org/10.1016/0304-3975(95)00182-4
2. Babiak, T., Křetínský, M., Řehák, V., Strejček, J.: LTL to Büchi automata translation: fast and more deterministic. In: Flanagan, C., König, B. (eds.) TACAS 2012. LNCS, vol. 7214, pp. 95–109. Springer, Heidelberg (2012). https://doi.org/10.1007/978-3-642-28756-5_8
3. Broda, S., Machiavelo, A., Moreira, N., Reis, R.: Partial derivative automaton for regular expressions with shuffle. In: Shallit, J., Okhotin, A. (eds.) DCFS 2015. LNCS, vol. 9118, pp. 21–32. Springer, Cham (2015). https://doi.org/10.1007/978-3-319-19225-3_2
4. Couvreur, J.-M.: On-the-fly verification of linear temporal logic. In: Wing, J.M., Woodcock, J., Davies, J. (eds.) FM 1999. LNCS, vol. 1708, pp. 253–271. Springer, Heidelberg (1999). https://doi.org/10.1007/3-540-48119-2_16
5. Esparza, J., Křetínský, J., Sickert, S.: From LTL to deterministic automata: a safraless compositional approach. Form. Methods Syst. Des. **49**(3), 219–271 (2016). https://doi.org/10.1007/s10703-016-0259-2
6. Finkbeiner, B., Sipma, H.: Checking finite traces using alternating automata. Form. Methods Syst. Des. **24**(2), 101–127 (2004). https://doi.org/10.1023/b:form.0000017718.28096.48
7. Gastin, P., Oddoux, D.: Fast LTL to Büchi automata translation. In: Berry, G., Comon, H., Finkel, A. (eds.) CAV 2001. LNCS, vol. 2102, pp. 53–65. Springer, Heidelberg (2001). https://doi.org/10.1007/3-540-44585-4_6
8. Geldenhuys, J., Valmari, A.: More efficient on-the-fly LTL verification with Tarjan's algorithm. Theor. Comput. Sci. **345**(1), 60–82 (2005). https://doi.org/10.1016/j.tcs.2005.07.004
9. Gerth, R., Peled, D., Vardi, M.Y., Wolper, P.: Simple on-the-fly automatic verification of linear temporal logic. In: Dembinski, P., Sredniawa, M. (eds.) PSTV 1995. IFIPAICT, pp. 3–18. Springer, Boston (1996). https://doi.org/10.1007/978-0-387-34892-6_1
10. Loding, C., Thomas, W.: Alternating automata and logics over infinite words. In: van Leeuwen, J., Watanabe, O., Hagiya, M., Mosses, P.D., Ito, T. (eds.) TCS 2000. LNCS, vol. 1872, pp. 521–535. Springer, Heidelberg (2000). https://doi.org/10.1007/3-540-44929-9_36
11. Muller, D.E., Saoudi, A., Schupp, P.E.: Weak alternating automata give a simple explanation of why most temporal and dynamic logics are decidable in exponential time. In: Proceedings of 3rd Annual Symposium on Logic in Computer Science, LICS 1999, Edinburgh, July 1988, pp. 422–427. IEEE CS Press (1988). https://doi.org/10.1109/lics.1988.5139
12. Pelánek, R., Strejček, J.: Deeper connections between LTL and alternating automata. In: Farré, J., Litovsky, I., Schmitz, S. (eds.) CIAA 2005. LNCS, vol. 3845, pp. 238–249. Springer, Heidelberg (2006). https://doi.org/10.1007/11605157_20
13. Pnueli, A.: The temporal logic of programs. In: Proceedings of 18th Annual Symposium on Foundations of Computer Science, FOCS 1977, Providence, RI, October–November 1977, pp. 46–57. IEEE CS Press (1977). https://doi.org/10.1109/sfcs.1977.32

14. Reynolds, M.: A new rule for LTL tableaux. In: Cantone, D., Delzanno, G. (eds.) Proceedings of 7th International Symposium on Games, Automata, Logics and Formal Verification, GandALF 2016 (Catania, September 2016). Electronic Proceedings in Theoretical Computer Science, vol. 226, pp. 287–301. Open Public Association, Sydney (2016). https://doi.org/10.4204/eptcs.226.20

15. Schwendimann, S.: A new one-pass tableau calculus for **PLTL**. In: de Swart, H. (ed.) TABLEAUX 1998. LNCS (LNAI), vol. 1397, pp. 277–291. Springer, Heidelberg (1998). https://doi.org/10.1007/3-540-69778-0_28

16. Thiemann, P., Sulzmann, M.: From ω-regular expressions to Büchi automata via partial derivatives. In: Dediu, A.-H., Formenti, E., Martín-Vide, C., Truthe, B. (eds.) LATA 2015. LNCS, vol. 8977, pp. 287–298. Springer, Cham (2015). https://doi.org/10.1007/978-3-319-15579-1_22

17. Vardi, M.Y.: Nontraditional applications of automata theory. In: Hagiya, M., Mitchell, J.C. (eds.) TACS 1994. LNCS, vol. 789, pp. 575–597. Springer, Heidelberg (1994). https://doi.org/10.1007/3-540-57887-0_116

18. Vardi, M.Y.: Alternating automata: unifying truth and validity checking for temporal logics. In: McCune, W. (ed.) CADE 1997. LNCS, vol. 1249, pp. 191–206. Springer, Heidelberg (1997). https://doi.org/10.1007/3-540-63104-6_19

19. Vardi, M.Y., Wolper, P.: An automata-theoretic approach to automatic program verification (preliminary report). In: Proceedings of 1st Symposium on Logic in Computer Science, LICS 1986, Cambridge, MA, June 1986, pp. 332–344. IEEE CS Press (1986)

20. Vardi, M.Y., Wolper, P.: Reasoning about infinite computations. Inf. Comput. **115**(1), 1–37 (1994). https://doi.org/10.1006/inco.1994.1092

21. Wolper, P.: Temporal logic can be more expressive. Inf. Control **56**(1/2), 72–99 (1983). https://doi.org/10.1016/s0019-9958(83)80051-5

22. Wolper, P.: The tableau method for temporal logic: an overview. Log. Anal. **28**(110–111), 119–136 (1985). https://www.jstor.org/stable/44084125

23. Wolper, P., Vardi, M.Y., Sistla, A.P.: Reasoning about infinite computation paths (extended abstract). In: Proceedings of 24th Annual Symposium on Foundations of Computer Science, FOCS 1983, Tucson, AZ, November 1983, pp. 185–194. IEEE CS Press (1983). https://doi.org/10.1109/sfcs.1983.51

Contributed Talks

Proof Nets and the Linear Substitution Calculus

Beniamino Accattoli[✉]

Inria Saclay and LIX, École Polytechnique,
1 rue Honoré d'Estienne d'Orves, 91120 Palaiseau, France
beniamino.accattoli@inria.fr

Abstract. Since the very beginning of the theory of linear logic it is known how to represent the λ-calculus as linear logic proof nets. The two systems however have different granularities, in particular proof nets have an explicit notion of sharing—the exponentials—and a micro-step operational semantics, while the λ-calculus has no sharing and a small-step operational semantics. Here we show that the *linear substitution calculus*, a simple refinement of the λ-calculus with sharing, is isomorphic to proof nets at the operational level.

Nonetheless, two different terms with sharing can still have the same proof nets representation—a further result is the characterisation of the equality induced by proof nets over terms with sharing. Finally, such a detailed analysis of the relationship between terms and proof nets, suggests a new, abstract notion of proof net, based on rewriting considerations and not necessarily of a graphical nature.

1 Introduction

Girard's seminal paper on linear logic [23] showed how to represent intuitionistic logic—and so the λ-calculus—inside linear logic. During the nineties, Danos and Regnier provided a detailed study of such a representation via proof nets [15–17,41], which is nowadays a cornerstone of the field. Roughly, linear logic gives first-class status to *sharing*, accounted for by the *exponential* layer of the logic, and not directly visible in the λ-calculus. In turn, cut-elimination in linear logic provides a micro-step refinement of the small-step operational semantics of the λ-calculus, that is, β-reduction.

The Mismatch. Some of the insights provided by proof nets cannot be directly expressed in the λ-calculus, because of the mismatch of granularities. Typically, there is a *mismatch of states*: simulation of β on proofs passes through intermediate states/proofs that cannot be expressed as λ-terms. The mismatch does not allow, for instance, expressing fine strategies such as linear head evaluation [18,35] in the λ-calculus, nor to see in which sense proof nets quotient terms, as such a quotient concerns only the intermediate proofs. And when one starts to have a closer look, there are other mismatches, of which the lack of sharing in the λ-calculus is only the most macroscopic one.

B. Fischer and T. Uustalu (Eds.): ICTAC 2018, LNCS 11187, pp. 37–61, 2018.
https://doi.org/10.1007/978-3-030-02508-3_3

Some minor issues are due to a *mismatch of styles*: the fact that terms and proofs, despite their similarities, have different representations of variables and notions of redexes. Typically, two occurrences of a same variable in a term are smoothly identified by simply using the same name, while for proofs there is an explicit rule, contraction, to identify them. Name identification is obviously associative, commutative, and commutes with all constructors, while contractions do not have these properties for free[1]. For redexes, the linear logic representation of terms has many cuts with axioms that have no counterpart on terms. These points have been addressed in the literature, using for instance generalised contractions or interaction nets, but they are not devoid of further technical complications. Establishing a precise relationship between terms and proofs and their evaluations is, in fact, a very technical affair.

A serious issue is the *mismatch of operational semantics*. The two systems compute the same results, but with different rewriting rules, and linear logic is far from having the nice rewriting properties of the λ-calculus. Typically, the λ-calculus has a *residual system* [43][2], which is a strong form of confluence that allows building its famous advanced rewriting theory, given by standardisation, neededness, and Lévy's optimality [33]. In the ordinary presentations of linear logic cut-elimination is confluent but it does not admit residual systems[3], and so the advanced rewriting properties of the λ-calculus are lost. Put differently, linear logic is a structural refinement of the λ-calculus but it is far from refining it at the rewriting level.

A final point is the *mismatch of representations*: proofs in linear logic are usually manipulated in their graphical form, that is, as proof nets, and, while this is a handy formalism for intuitions, it is not amenable to formal reasoning— it is not by chance that there is not a single result about proof nets formalised in a proof assistant. And as already pointed out, the parallelism provided by proof nets, in the case of the λ-calculus, shows up only in the nets obtained as intermediate steps of the simulation of β, and so it cannot easily be seen on the λ-calculus. There is a way of expressing it, known as σ-equivalence, due to Regnier [42], but it is far from being natural.

The Linear Substitution Calculus. The linear substitution calculus (LSC) [2,8] is a refinement of the λ-calculus with sharing, introduced by Accattoli and Kesner as a minor variation over a calculus by Milner [39], and meant to correct all these problems at once.

---

[1] α-equivalence is subtle on terms, but this is an orthogonal issue, and a formal approach to proof net should also deal with α-equivalence for nodes, even if this is never done.

[2] For the unacquainted reader: having a residual system means to be a well-behaved rewriting system—related concepts are orthogonal systems, or the parallel moves or cube properties.

[3] Some presentations of proof nets (*e.g.* Regnier's in [41]) solve the operational semantics mismatch adapting proof nets to the λ-calculus, and do have residuals, but then they are unable to express typical micro-step proof nets concepts such as linear head reduction.

The LSC has been introduced in 2012 and then used in different settings—a selection of relevant studies concerning cost models, standardisation, abstract machines, intersection types, call-by-need, the π-calculus, and Lévy's optimality is [3,7–9,14,26,30]. The two design features of the LSC are its tight relationship with proof nets and the fact of having a residual system. The matching with proof nets, despite being one of the two reasons to be of the LSC, for some reason was never developed in detail, nor published. This paper corrects the situation, strengthening a growing body of research.

Contributions. The main result of the paper is the perfect correspondence between the LSC and the fragment of linear logic representing the λ-calculus. To this goal, the presentation of proof nets has to be adjusted, because the fault for the mismatch is not always on the calculus side. To overcome the mismatch of styles, we adopt a presentation of proof nets—already at work by the author [5]—that intuitively corresponds to interaction nets (to work modulo cut with axioms) with *hyper-wires*, that is, wires connecting more than two ports (to have smooth contractions). Our presentation of proof nets also refines the one in [5] with a micro-step operational semantics. Our exponential rewriting rules are slightly different than the others in the literature, and look more as the replication rule of the π-calculus—this is the key change for having a residual system.

Essentially, the LSC and our proof nets presentation are isomorphic. More precisely, our contribution is to establish the following tight correspondence:

1. *Transferable syntaxes*: every term translates to a proof net, and every proof net reads back to at least one term, removing the mismatch of states. We rely on a correctness criterion—Laurent's one for polarised proof nets [31,32]— to characterise proof nets and read them back. There can be many terms mapping to the same proof net, so at this level the systems are not isomorphic.
2. *Quotient*: we characterise the simple equivalence $\equiv$ on terms that is induced by the translation to proof nets. The quotient of terms by $\equiv$ is then isomorphic to proof nets, refining the previous point. The characterisation of the quotient is not usually studied in the literature on proof nets.
3. *Isomorphic micro-step operational semantics*: a term t and its associated proof net P have redexes in bijection, and such a bijection is a strong bisimulation: one step on one side is simulated by exactly one step on the other side, and vice-versa, and in both cases the reducts are still related by translation and read back. Therefore, the mismatch of operational semantics also vanishes.

The fact that the LSC has a residual system is proved in [8], and it is not treated here. But our results allow to smoothly transfer the residual system from the LSC to our presentation of proof nets.

These features allow to consider the LSC modulo $\equiv$ as an algebraic—that is, not graphical—reformulation of proof nets for the λ-calculus, providing the strongest possible solution to the mismatch of representations. At the end of the paper, we also suggest a new perspective on proof nets from a rewriting point of view, building on our approach.

The Value of this Paper. This work is a bit more than the filling of a gap in the literature. The development is detailed, and so necessarily technical, and yet clean. The study of correctness and sequentialisation is stronger than in other works in the literature, because beyond sequentialising we also characterise the quotient—the proof of the characterisation is nonetheless pleasantly simple. Another unusual point is the use of *context nets* corresponding to the contexts of the calculus, that are needed to deal with the rules of the LSC. Less technically, but maybe more importantly, the paper ends with the sketch of a new and high-level rewriting perspective on proof nets.

Proofs. For lack of space, all proofs are omitted. They can be found in the technical report [6].

1.1 Historical Perspective

The fine match between the LSC and proof nets does not come out of the blue: it rather is the final product of a decades-long quest for a canonical decomposition of the λ-calculus.

At the time of the introduction of linear logic, decompositions of the λ-calculus arose also from other contexts. Abadi, Cardelli, Curien, and Lévy introduced calculi with *explicit substitutions* [1], that are refinements of the λ-calculus where meta-level substitution is delayed, by introducing explicit annotations, and then computed in a micro-step fashion. A decomposition of a different nature appeared in concurrency, with the translations of the λ-calculus to the π-calculus [37], due to Milner.

These settings introduce an explicit treatment of *sharing*—called *exponentials* in linear logic, or explicit substitutions, or *replication* in the π-calculus. The first calculus of explicit substitutions suffered of a design issue, as showed by Melliès in [36]. A turning point was the link between explicit substitutions and linear logic proof nets by Di Cosmo and Kesner in [19]. Kesner and co-authors then explored the connection in various directions [20,28,29]. In none of these cases, however, do terms and proof nets behave exactly the same.

The graphical representation of λ-calculus based on linear logic in [10] induced a further calculus with explicit substitutions, the *structural λ-calculus* [11], isomorphic to their presentation of proof nets. The structural λ-calculus corrects most mentioned mismatches, but it lacks a residual system.

Independently, Milner developed a graphical framework for concurrency, *bigraphs* [38], able to represent the π-calculus and, consequently, the λ-calculus. He extracted from it a calculus with explicit substitutions [27,39], similar in spirit to the structural λ-calculus. Accattoli and Kesner later realised that Milner's calculus has a residual system. In 2011-12, they started to work on the LSC, obtained as a merge of Milner's calculus and the structural λ-calculus.

At first, the LSC was seen as a minor variation over existing systems. With time, however, a number of properties arose, and the LSC started to be used as a sharp tool for a number of investigations. Two of them are relevant for our story. First, the LSC also allows refining the relationship between the λ-calculus and the π-calculus, as shown by the author in [3]. The LSC can then be taken as the harmonious convergence and distillation of three different approaches— linear logic, explicit substitutions, and the π-calculus—at decomposing the λ-calculus. Second, Lévy's optimality adapts to the LSC as shown by Barenbaum and Bonelli in [14], confirming that the advanced rewriting theory of the λ-calculus can indeed be lifted to the micro-step granularity via the LSC.

1.2   Related Work on Proof Nets

The relationship between λ-calculi and proof nets has been studied repeatedly, beyond the already cited work (Danos & Regnier, Kesner & co-authors, Accattoli & Guerrini). A nice and detailed introduction to the relationship between λ-terms and proof nets is [24].

Laurent extends the translation to represent the $\lambda\mu$-calculus in [31, 32]. In this paper we use an adaptation of his correctness criterion. The translation of differential/resource calculi has also been studied at length: Ehrhard and Regnier [21] study the case without the promotion rule, while Vaux [46] and Tranquilli [44, 45] include promotion. Vaux also extends the relationship to the classical case (thus encompassing a differential $\lambda\mu$-calculus), while Tranquilli refines the differential calculus into a *resource calculus* that better matches proof nets. Vaux and Tranquilli use interaction nets to circumvent the minor issue of cuts with axioms.

Strategies rather than calculi are encoded in interaction nets in [34].

None of these works uses explicit substitutions, so they all suffer of the *mismatch of states*. Explicit substitutions are encoded in proof nets in [22], but the operational semantics are not isomorphic, nor correctness is studied. An abstract machine akin to the LSC is mapped to proof nets in [40], but the focus is on cost analyses, rather than on matching syntaxes.

Other works that connect λ-calculi and graphical formalisms with some logical background are [13, 25].

An ancestor of this paper is [5], that adopts essentially the same syntax for proof nets. In that work, however, the operational semantics is small-step rather than micro-step, there is no study of the quotient, and no use of contexts, nor it deals with the LSC.

2   The Linear Substitution Calculus

Expressions and Terms. One of the features of the LSC is the use of contexts to define the rewriting rules. Contexts are terms with a single occurrence of a special constructor called *hole*, and often noted $\langle\cdot\rangle$, that is a placeholder for a removed subterm. To study the relationship with proof nets, it is necessary to represent both terms and contexts, and, to reduce the number of cases in definitions and proofs, we consider a syntactic category generalizing both. *Expressions* may have 0, 1, or more holes. Proof nets also require holes to carry the set Δ of variables that can appear free in any subterm replacing the hole—*e.g.* $\Delta = \{x, y, z\}$. Expressions are then defined as follows:

EXPRESSIONS $\qquad e, f, g, h ::= x \mid \langle \cdot \rangle_\Delta \mid \lambda x.e \mid ef \mid e[x\leftarrow f]$

Terms are expressions without holes, noted t, s, u, and so on, and *contexts* are expressions with exactly one hole, noted C, D, E, etc.

The construct $t[x\leftarrow s]$ is an *explicit substitution*, shortened *ES*, of s for x in t—essentially, it is a more compact notation for let $x = s$ in t. Both $\lambda x.t$ and $t[x\leftarrow s]$ bind x in t. Meta-level, capture-avoiding substitution is rather noted $t\{x/s\}$. On terms, we silently work modulo α-equivalence, so that for instance $(\lambda x.((xyz)[y\leftarrow x])\{z/xy\} = \lambda x'.((x'y'(xy))[y'\leftarrow x'])$. Applications associate to the left. Free variables of holes are defined by $\mathtt{fv}(\langle \cdot \rangle_\Delta) := \Delta$, and for the other constructors as expected. The *multiplicity* of a variable x in a *term* t, noted $|t|_x$, is the number of free occurrences of x in t.

Contexts. The LSC uses contexts extensively, in particular *substitution contexts*:

SUBSTITUTION CONTEXTS $\quad L, L', L'' ::= \langle \cdot \rangle_\Delta \mid L[x\leftarrow t]$

Sometimes we write C_Δ for a context C whose hole $\langle \cdot \rangle_\Delta$ is annotated with Δ, and we call Δ the *interface* of C. Note that the free variables of C_Δ do not necessarily include those in its interface Δ, because the variables in Δ can be captured by the binders in C_Δ.

The basic operation over contexts is *plugging* of an expression e in the hole of the context C, that produces the expression $C\langle e \rangle$. The operation is defined only when the free variables $\mathtt{fv}(e)$ of e are included in the interface of the context.

PLUGGING OF e IN C_Δ (ASSUMING $\mathtt{fv}(e) \subseteq \Delta$)

$$\langle e \rangle_\Delta := e \qquad\qquad (\lambda x.C)\langle e \rangle := \lambda x.C\langle e \rangle$$
$$(Cs)\langle e \rangle := C\langle e \rangle s \qquad\qquad (sC)\langle e \rangle := sC\langle e \rangle$$
$$(C[x\leftarrow s])\langle e \rangle := C\langle e \rangle[x\leftarrow s] \qquad (s[x\leftarrow C])\langle e \rangle := s[x\leftarrow C\langle e \rangle]$$

An example of context is $C_{\{x,y\}} := \lambda x.(y\langle \cdot \rangle_{\{x,y\}}[z\leftarrow x])$, and one of plugging is $C_{\{x,y\}}\langle xx \rangle = \lambda x.(y(xx)[z\leftarrow x])$. Note the absence of side conditions in the cases for $\lambda x.C$ and $C[x\leftarrow s]$—it means that plugging in a context can capture variables, as in the given example. Clearly, $C\langle e \rangle$ is a term/context if and only if e is a term/context. Note also that if t is a term and s is a subterm of t then $t = C\langle s \rangle$ for some context C. Such a context C is unique up to the annotation Δ of the hole of C, which only has to satisfy $\mathtt{fv}(s) \subseteq \Delta$, and that can always be satisfied by some Δ.

We also define *the set* $\mathtt{cv}(C_\Delta)$ *of variables captured by a context* C_Δ:

VARIABLES CAPTURED BY A CONTEXT

$$\mathtt{cv}(\langle \cdot \rangle_\Delta) := \emptyset$$
$$\mathtt{cv}(\lambda x.C_\Delta) = \mathtt{cv}(C_\Delta[x\leftarrow t]) := \mathtt{cv}(C_\Delta) \cup \{x\}$$
$$\mathtt{cv}(tC_\Delta) = \mathtt{cv}(C_\Delta t) = \mathtt{cv}(t[x\leftarrow C_\Delta]) := \mathtt{cv}(C_\Delta)$$

Rewriting Rules for Terms. The rewriting rules of the LSC concern terms only. They are unusual as they use contexts in two ways: to allow their application anywhere in the term—and this is standard—and to define the rules at top level—this is less common (note the substitution context L and the context C in rules $\rightarrow_{\mathtt{m}}$ and $\rightarrow_{\mathtt{e}}$ below). We write $C\langle\!\langle t \rangle\!\rangle$ if C does not capture any free variable of t, that is, if $\mathtt{cv}(C) \cap \mathtt{fv}(t) = \emptyset$.

REWRITING RULES

MULTIPLICATIVE	$L\langle \lambda x.t \rangle s \;\rightarrow_{\mathtt{m}}\; L\langle t[x \leftarrow s] \rangle$
MILNER EXPONENTIAL	$C\langle\!\langle x \rangle\!\rangle [x \leftarrow s] \;\rightarrow_{\mathtt{e}}\; C\langle\!\langle s \rangle\!\rangle [x \leftarrow s]$
GARBAGE COLLECTION	$t[x \leftarrow s] \;\rightarrow_{\mathtt{gc}}\; t$ if $x \notin \mathtt{fv}(t)$

$$\text{CONTEXTUAL CLOSURES} \qquad \frac{t \rightarrow_a t'}{C\langle t \rangle \rightarrow_a C\langle t' \rangle} \quad \text{for } a \in \{\mathtt{m}, \mathtt{e}, \mathtt{gc}\}$$

$$\text{NOTATION} \qquad \rightarrow_{LSC} \;:=\; \rightarrow_{\mathtt{m}} \cup \rightarrow_{\mathtt{e}} \cup \rightarrow_{\mathtt{gc}}$$

Note that in $\rightarrow_{\mathtt{m}}$ (resp. $\rightarrow_{\mathtt{e}}$) we assume that L (resp. C) does not capture variables in $\mathtt{fv}(s)$—this is always possible by a (on-the-fly) α-renaming of $L\langle \lambda x.t \rangle$ (resp. $C\langle\!\langle x \rangle\!\rangle$), as we work modulo α. Similarly the interface of C can always be assumed to contain $\mathtt{fv}(s)$.

Structural Equivalence. The LSC is sometimes enriched with the following notion of structural equivalence $\equiv$ [8].

Definition 1 (Structural equivalence). *Structural equivalence $\equiv$ is defined as the symmetric, reflexive, transitive, and contextual closure of the following axioms:*

$$
\begin{aligned}
(\lambda y.t)[x \leftarrow s] &\equiv_\lambda \lambda y.t[x \leftarrow s] & &\text{if } y \notin \mathtt{fv}(s) \\
(t\,u)[x \leftarrow s] &\equiv_{@l} t[x \leftarrow s]\,u & &\text{if } x \notin \mathtt{fv}(u) \\
t[x \leftarrow s][y \leftarrow u] &\equiv_{com} t[y \leftarrow u][x \leftarrow s] & &\text{if } y \notin \mathtt{fv}(s) \text{ and } x \notin \mathtt{fv}(u)
\end{aligned}
$$

Its key property is that it commutes with evaluation in the following strong sense.

Proposition 2 ($\equiv$ is a strong bisimulation wrt $\rightarrow_{LSC}$ [8]). *Let $a \in \{\mathtt{m}, \mathtt{e}, \mathtt{gc}\}$. If $t \equiv s \rightarrow_a u$ then exists r such that $t \rightarrow_a r \equiv u$.*

Essentially, $\equiv$ never creates redexes, it can be postponed, and vanishes on normal forms (that have no ES). We are going to prove that $\equiv$ is exactly the quotient induced by translation to proof nets (Theorem 17, page 15). The absence of the axiom $(t\,u)[x \leftarrow s] \equiv_{@r} t\,u[x \leftarrow s]$ if $x \notin \mathtt{fv}(t)$ is correct: the two terms do not have the same proof net representation (defined in the next section), moreover adding this axiom to $\equiv$ breaks Proposition 2. The extension with $\equiv_{@r}$ has nonetheless been studied in [12].

3   Proof Nets

Introduction. Our presentation of proof nets, similar to the one in [5], is nonstandard in at least four points—we suggest to have a quick look to Fig. 3, page 12:

1. *Hyper-graphs*: we use directed hyper-graphs (for which formulas are nodes and links—*i.e.* logical rules—are hyper-edges) rather than the usual graphs with pending edges (for which formulas are edges and links are nodes). We prefer hyper-graphs—that despite the scaring name are nothing but bipartite graphs—because they give
    (a) *Contraction algebra for free*: contraction is represented modulo commutativity, associativity, and permutation with box borders *for free*, by admitting that exponential nodes can have more than one incoming link,
    (b) *Cut-axiom quotient for free*: cut and axiom links are represented implicitly, collapsing them on nodes. This is analogous to what happens in interaction nets. Intuitively, our multiplicative nodes are *wires*, with exponential nodes being *hyper*-wires, *i.e.* wires involving an arbitrary number of ports;
    (c) *Subnets as subsets*: subnets can be elegantly defined as subsets of links, which would not be possible when adopting other approaches such as generalized ?-links or a standard interaction nets formalism without hyper-wires.

    The choice of hyper-graphs, however, has various (minor) technical consequences, and the formulation of some usual notions (*e.g.* the nesting condition for boxes) shall be slightly different with respect to the literature.
2. *Directed links and polarity*: our links are directed and we apply a correctness criterion based on directed paths. Be careful, however, that we do not follow the usual premises-to-conclusions orientation for links, nor the input-output orientation sometimes at work for λ-calculi or intuitionistic settings. We follow, instead, the orientation induced by logical polarity according to Laurent's correctness criterion for polarised proof nets [31,32]. Let us point out that Laurent defines proof nets using the premises-to-conclusions orientation and then he switches to the polarised orientation for the correctness criterion. We prefer to adopt only one orientation, the polarised one, which we also employ to define proof nets.
3. *Syntax tree*: since we use proof nets to represent terms, we arrange them on the plane according to the syntax tree of the corresponding terms, and not according to the corresponding sequent calculus proof, analogously to the graph rewriting literature on the λ-calculus (*e.g.* [47]) but in contrast to the linear logic literature.
4. *Contexts*: to mimic the use of contexts in the LSC rewriting rules, we need to have a notion of context net. Therefore, we have a special link for context holes.

Nets. We first overview some choices and terminology.

- *Hyper-graphs*: nets are directed and labelled hyper-graphs $G = (\texttt{nodes}(G), \texttt{links}(G))$, *i.e.*, graphs where $\texttt{nodes}(G)$ is a set of labelled *nodes*

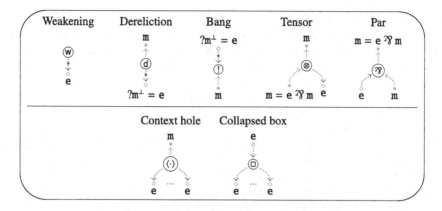

Fig. 1. Links. (Color figure online)

and links(G) is a set of labelled and *directed hyper-edges*, called *links*, which are edges with 0, 1, or more sources and 0, 1, or more targets[4].

- *Nodes*: nodes are labelled with a type in $\{e, m\}$, where e stands for *exponential* and m for *multiplicative*. If a node u has type e (resp. m) we say that it is a e-node (resp. m-node). The label of a node is usually left implicit, as e and m nodes are distinguished graphically, using both colours and different shapes: e-nodes are cyan and white-filled, while m-nodes are brown and dot-like. We come back to types below.

- *Links*: we consider hyper-graphs whose links are labelled from $\{!, d, w, ⅋, \otimes, \langle \cdot \rangle, \Box\}$, corresponding to the promotion, dereliction, weakening, par, and tensor rules of linear logic, plus a link $\langle \cdot \rangle$ for context holes and a link $\Box$ used for defining the correction graph—contraction is hard-coded on nodes, as already explained. The label of a link l forces the number and the type of the source and target nodes of l, as shown in Fig. 1 (types shall be discussed next). Similarly to nodes, we use colours and shapes for the type of the source/target connection of a link to a node: e-connections are blue and dotted, while m-connections are red and solid. Our choice of shapes allows reading the paper also if printed in black and white.

- *Principal conclusions*: note that every link except $\langle \cdot \rangle$ and $\Box$ has exactly one connection with a little circle: it denotes the *principal* node, *i.e.* the node on which the link can interact. Notice the principal node for tensor and !, which is not misplaced.

- *Typing*: nets are typed using a recursive type, usually noted $o = !o \multimap o$, but that we rename $m = !m \multimap m = ?m^\perp ⅋ m$ because m is a mnemonic for *multiplicative*. Let $e := ?m^\perp$, where e stands for *exponential*. Note that $m = e^\perp \multimap m = e ⅋ m$. Links are typed using m and e, but the types are omitted by all figures except Fig. 1 because they are represented using colours and with

---

[4] A hyper-graph G can be understood as a bipartite graph B_G, where $V_1(B_G)$ is nodes(G) and $V_2(B_G)$ is links(G), and the edges are determined by the relations *being a source* and *being a target* of a hyper-edge.

different shapes (m-nodes are brown and dot-like, e-nodes are white-filled cyan circles). Let us explain the types in Fig. 1. They may be counter-intuitive at first: note in particular the ! and $\otimes$ links, that have an unexpected type on their logical conclusion—it simply has to be negated, because the expected orientation would be the opposite one.

– *More on nodes*: a node is *initial* if it is not the target of any link; *terminal* if it is not the source of any link; *isolated* if it is initial and terminal; *internal* if it is not initial nor terminal.
– *Boxes*: every !-link has an associated *box*, *i.e.*, a sub-hyper-graph of P (have a look at Fig. 3), meant to be a sub-net.
– *Context holes and collapsed boxes*: it is natural to wonder if $\langle \cdot \rangle$ and $\square$ links can be merged into a single kind of link. They indeed play very similar roles, except that they have different polarised typings, which is why we distinguish them.

We first introduce *pre-nets*, and then add boxes on top of them, obtaining *nets*:

Definition 3 (Pre-nets). *A pre-net P is a triple $(|P|, \mathtt{fv}(P), r_P)$, where $|P|$ is a hyper-graph $(\mathtt{nodes}(P), \mathtt{links}(P))$ whose nodes are labelled with either $\mathtt{e}$ or $\mathtt{m}$ and whose hyper-edges are $\{!, \mathtt{d}, \mathtt{w}, \mathit{⅋}, \otimes, \langle \cdot \rangle, \square\}$-links, and such that:*

– Root: $r_P \in \mathtt{nodes}(P)$ *is a terminal $\mathtt{m}$-node of P, called the* root *of P.*
– Free variables: $\mathtt{fv}(P)$ *is the set of terminal $\mathtt{e}$-nodes of P, also called* free variables *of P, which are targets of $\{\mathtt{d}, \mathtt{w}, \langle \cdot \rangle, \square\}$-links (i.e. they are not allowed to be targets of $\otimes$-links, nor to be isolated).*
– Nodes: *every node has* at least *one incoming link and* at most *one outgoing link. Moreover,*
  • Multiplicative: $\mathtt{m}$-*nodes have* exactly one *incoming link;*
  • Exponential: *if an $\mathtt{e}$-node has more than one incoming link then they are* $\mathtt{d}$-*links.*

Definition 4 (Nets). *A net P is a pre-net together with a function $\mathtt{ibox}_P$ (or simply $\mathtt{ibox}$) associating to every !-link l a subset $\mathtt{ibox}(l)$ of $\mathtt{links}(P) \setminus \{l\}$ (i.e. the links of P except l itself), called the* interior of the box *of l, such that $\mathtt{ibox}(l)$ is a pre-net verifying (explanations follow):*

– Border: *the root $r_{\mathtt{ibox}(l)}$ is the source $\mathtt{m}$-nodes of l, and any free variable of $\mathtt{ibox}(l)$ is not the target of a weakening.*
– Nesting: *for any !-box $\mathtt{ibox}(h)$ if $\mathtt{ibox}(l)$ and $\mathtt{ibox}(h)$ have non-empty intersection—that is, if $\emptyset \neq I := |\mathtt{ibox}(l)| \cap |\mathtt{ibox}(h)|$—and one is not entirely contained in the other—that is, if $|\mathtt{ibox}(l)| \not\subseteq |\mathtt{ibox}(h)|$, and $|\mathtt{ibox}(h)| \not\subseteq |\mathtt{ibox}(l)|$—then all the nodes in I are free variables of both $\mathtt{ibox}(l)$ and $\mathtt{ibox}(h)$.*
– Internal closure:
  • Contractions: *if a contraction node is internal to $\mathtt{ibox}(l)$ then all its premises are in $\mathtt{ibox}(l)$—formally, $h \in \mathtt{ibox}(l)$ for any link h of P having as target an internal $\mathtt{e}$-node of $\mathtt{ibox}(l)$.*
  • Boxes: $\mathtt{ibox}(h) \subseteq \mathtt{ibox}(l)$ *for any !-link $h \in \mathtt{ibox}(l)$.*

A net is

- a term net *if it has no $\{\langle \cdot \rangle, \Box\}$-links;*
- a context net *if it has exactly one $\langle \cdot \rangle$-link;*
- a correction net *if it has no !-links.*

As for the calculus, the interface *of a $\langle \cdot \rangle$-link is the set of its free variables, and the interface of a context net is the interface of its $\langle \cdot \rangle$-link.*

Remark 5. Comments on the definition of net:

1. *Weakenings and box borders*: in the border condition for nets the fact that the free variables are not the target of a weakening means that weakenings are assumed to be pushed out of boxes as much as possible—of course the rewriting rules shall have to preserve this invariant.

2. *Weakenings are not represented as nullary contractions*: given the representation of contractions, it would be tempting to define weakenings as nullary contractions. However, such a choice would be problematic with respect to correctness (to be defined soon), as it would introduce many initial e-nodes in a correct net and thus blur the distinction between the root of the net, supposed to represent the output and to be unique (in a correct net), and substitutions on a variable with no occurrences (*i.e.* weakened subterms), that need not to be unique.

3. *Internal closure wrt contractions*: it is a by-product of collapsing contractions on nodes, which is also the reason for the unusual formulation of the nesting condition. In fact, two boxes that are intuitively disjoint can in our syntax share free variables, because of an implicit contraction merging two of them, as in the example in Fig. 3.

4. *Boxes as nets*: note that a box $\mathtt{ibox}(l)$ in a net P is only a *pre*-net, by definition. Every box in a net P, however, inherits a net structure from P. Indeed, one can restrict the box function $\mathtt{ibox}_P$ of P to the !-links of $\mathtt{ibox}(l)$, and see $\mathtt{ibox}(l)$ as a *net*, because all the required conditions are automatically satisfied by the internal boxes closure and by the fact that such boxes are boxes in P. Therefore, we freely consider boxes as *nets*.

5. *Tensors and !-boxes*: the requirements that the e-target of a $\otimes$-link cannot be the free variable of a net, nor the target of more than one link force these nodes to be sources of !-links. Therefore, every $\otimes$-link is paired to a !-link, and thus a box.

6. *Acyclic nesting*: the fact that a !-link does not belong to its box, plus the internal closure condition, imply that the nesting relation between boxes cannot be cyclic, as we now show. Let l and h be !-links. If $l \in \mathtt{ibox}(h)$ then by internal closure $\mathtt{ibox}(l) \subseteq \mathtt{ibox}(h)$. It cannot then be that $h \in \mathtt{ibox}(l)$, otherwise l would belong to its own box, because $l \in \mathtt{ibox}(h) \subseteq \mathtt{ibox}(l)$ by internal closure.

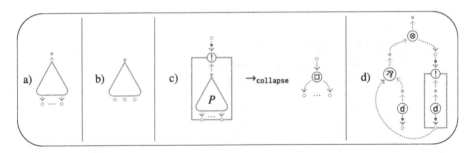

Fig. 2. Various images.

Terminology About Nets. Some further terminology and conventions:

- The *level* of a node/link/box is the maximum number of nested boxes in which it is contained[5] (a !-link is not contained in its own box). Note that the level is well defined by the acyclicity of nesting just pointed out. In particular, if a net has !-links then it has at least one !-link at level 0.
- A *variable* x is a e-node that is the target of a $\{\mathsf{d}, \mathsf{w}\}$-link—equivalently, that is not the target of a $\otimes$-link.
- Two links are *contracted* if they share an e-target. Note that the exponential condition states that only derelictions (*i.e.* d-links) can be contracted. In particular, no link can be contracted with a weakening.
- A *free weakening* in a net P is a weakening whose node is a free variable of P.
- The *multiplicity* of a variable x in P, noted $|P|_x$, is 0 if x is the target of a weakening, and $n \geq 1$ if it is the target of n derelictions.
- Sometimes (*e.g.* the bottom half of Fig. 3), the figures show a link in a box having as target a contracted e-node x which is outside the box: in those cases x is part of the box, it is outside of the box only in order to simplify the representation.

Translation. Nets representing terms have the general form in Fig. 2a, also represented as in Fig. 2b. The translation $\underline{\cdot}$ from expression to nets is in Fig. 3.

A net which is the translation of an expression is a *proof net*. Note the example in Fig. 3: two different terms translate to the same proof net, showing that proof nets quotient LSC terms.

The translation $\underline{\cdot}$ is refined to a translation $\underline{\cdot}_\Delta$, where Δ is a set of variables, in order to properly handle weakenings during cut-elimination. The reason is that an erasing step on terms simply erases a subterm, while on nets it also introduces some weakenings: without the refinement the translation would not be stable by reduction.

---

[5] Here the words *maximum* and *nested* are due to the fact that the free variables of !-boxes may belong to two not nested boxes, as in the example in Fig. 3, because of the way we represent contraction.

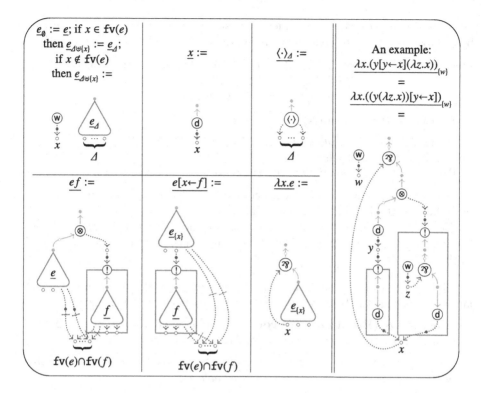

Fig. 3. Translation of expressions to nets, plus an example of translation.

Note that in some cases there are various edges entering an e-node, that is the way we represent contraction. In some cases the e-nodes have an incoming connection with a perpendicular little bar: it represents an arbitrary number (>0) of incoming connections. Structurally equivalent terms are translated to the same proof net, see Fig. 4 at page 16.

α-Equivalence. To circumvent an explicit and formal treatment of α-equivalence we assume that the set of e-nodes and the set of variable names for terms coincide. This convention removes the need to label the free variables of $\underline{t}_\Delta$ with the name of the corresponding free variables in t or Δ. Actually, before translating a term t it is necessary to pick a *well-named* α-equivalent term t', *i.e.* a term such that any two different variables (bound or free) have different names.

Paths. A *path* τ of length $k \in \mathbb{N}$ from u to w, noted $\tau : u \to^k w$, is an alternated sequence of nodes and links $u = u_1, l_1, \ldots, l_k, u_{k+1} = w$ such that link l_i has source u_i and target u_{i+1} for $i \in \{1, \ldots, k\}$. A *cycle* is a path $u \to^k u$ with $k > 0$.

Correctness. The correctness criterion is an adaptation of Laurent's criterion for polarized nets, and it is the simplest known criterion for proof nets. It is based on the notion of correction net, which—as usual for nets with boxes—is obtained by collapsing boxes into generalized axiom links, *i.e.* our □-links (see Fig. 1).

Definition 6 (Correction net). *Let P be a net. The* correction net P^0 *of P is the net obtained from P by collapsing each !-box at level 0 in P into a □-link with the same interface, by applying the rule in Fig. 2c.*

Definition 7 (Correctness). *A net P is* correct *if:*

- Root*: the root of P induces the only terminal m-node of P^0.*
- Acyclicity*: P^0 is acyclic.*
- Recursive correctness*: the box of every !-link at level 0 is correct.*

An example of net that is not correct is in Fig. 2d: the correction net obtained by collapsing the box indeed has a cycle.

Note that acyclicity provides an induction principle on correct nets, because it implies that there is a maximal length for paths in the correction net associated to the net.

Proof Nets are Correct. As usual, an easy and omitted induction on the translation shows that the translation of an expression is correct, *i.e.* that:

Proposition 8 (Proof nets are correct). *Let e be an expression and Δ a set of variables. Then $\underline{e}_\Delta$ is a correct net of free variables $\mathtt{fv}(e) \cup \Delta$. Moreover,*

1. *if e is a term then $\underline{e}_\Delta$ is a term net and their variables have the same multiplicity, that is, $|e|_x = |\underline{e}_\Delta|_x$ for every variable x.*
2. *if e is a context then $\underline{e}_\Delta$ is a context net.*

Linear Skeleton. We have the following strong structural property.

Lemma 9 (Linear skeleton). *Let P be a correct net. The* linear skeleton *of P^0, given by m-nodes and the red (or linear) paths between them, is a linear order.*

4   Sequentialisation and Quotient

In this section we prove the sequentialisation theorem and the fact that the quotient induced by the translation on terms is exactly the structural equivalence $\equiv$ of the LSC.

Subnets. The first concept that we need is the one of *subnet Q* of a correct net P, that is a subset of the links of P plus some closure conditions. These conditions avoid that Q prunes the interior of a box in P, or takes part of the interior without taking the whole box, or takes only some of the premises of an internal contraction.

For the sake of simplicity, in the following we specify sub-hyper-graphs of a net by simply specifying their set of links. This is an innocent abuse, because—by definition of (pre-)net—there cannot be isolated nodes, and so the set of nodes is retrievable from the set of links. Similarly, the boxes of !-links are inherited from the net.

Definition 10 (Subnet). *Let P be a correct net. A subnet Q of P is a subset of its links such that it is a correct net (with respect to the* ibox *function inherited from P) and satisfies the following closure conditions:*

- Contractions: *l ∈ Q for any link l of P having as target an internal* e*-node of Q.*
- Box interiors: ibox(*h*) ⊆ Q *for any* !*-link h ∈ Q.*
- Box free variables: ibox(*l*) ⊆ Q *if a free variable of* ibox(*l*) *is internal to Q.*

Decomposing Correct Nets. Sequentialisation shall read back an expression by progressively decomposing a correct net. We first need some terminology about boxes.

Definition 11 (Kinds of boxes). *Let P be a correct net. A* !*-link l of P is:*

- free *if it is at level 0 in P and its free variables are free variables of P.*
- *an* argument *if its* e*-node is the target of a ⊗-link;*
- *a* substitution *if its* e*-node is the target of a* {w, d, ⟨·⟩}*-link (or, equivalently, if it is not the target of a ⊗-link).*

The following lemma states that, in correct nets whose root structure is similar to the translation of an expression, it is always possible to decompose the net in correct subnets. The lemma does not state the correctness of the interior of boxes because they are correct by definition of correctness.

Lemma 12 (Decomposition). *Let P be a correct net.*

1. Free weakening: *if P has a free weakening l then* links(P) \ *l is a subnet of P.*
2. Root abstraction: *if the root link l of P is a ⅋-link then* links(P) \ *l is a subnet of P.*
3. Free substitution: *if P has a free substitution l then* links(P)\({*l*}∪ibox(*l*)) *is a subnet of P.*
4. Root application with free argument: *if the root link l of P is a ⊗-link whose argument is a free* !*-link h then* links(P) \ ({*l, h*} ∪ ibox(*h*)) *is a subnet of P.*

Definition 13 (Decomposable net). *A correct net P is decomposable if it is in one of the hypothesis of the decomposition lemma (Lemma 12), that is, if it has a free weakening, a root abstraction, a free substitution, or a root application with free argument.*

The last bit is to prove that every correct net is decomposable, and so, essentially corresponds to the translation of an expression.

Lemma 14 (Correct nets are decomposable). *Let P be a correct net with more than one link. Then P is decomposable.*

We now introduce the read back of correct net as expressions, which is the key notion for the sequentialisation theorem. Its definition relies, in turn, on the various ways in which a correct net can be decomposed, when it has more than one link.

Definition 15 (Read back). *Let P be a correct net and e be an expression. The relation e is a read back of P, noted $P \triangleright e$, is defined by induction on the number of links in P:*

- *One link term net: P is a d-link of e-node x. Then $P \triangleright x$;*
- *One link context net: P is a $\langle \cdot \rangle$-link of e-nodes Δ. Then $P \triangleright \langle \cdot \rangle_\Delta$;*
- *Free weakening: P has a free weakening l and $P \setminus l \triangleright e$. Then $P \triangleright e$;*
- *Root abstraction: the root link l of P is a $\mathcal{R}$-link of e-node x and $P \setminus l \triangleright e$. Then $P \triangleright \lambda x.e$;*
- *Free substitution: P has a free substitution l of e-node x, $P \setminus (\{l\} \cup \mathrm{ibox}(l)) \triangleright e$, and $\mathrm{ibox}(l) \triangleright f$. Then $P \triangleright e[x \leftarrow f]$.*
- *Root application with free argument: the root link l of P is a $\otimes$-link whose argument is a free !-link h, $P \setminus (\{l, h\} \cup \mathrm{ibox}(h)) \triangleright e$, and $\mathrm{ibox}(h) \triangleright f$. Then $P \triangleright ef$.*

We conclude the section with the sequentialisation theorem, that relates terms and proof nets at the static level. Its formulation is slightly stronger than similar theorems in the literature, that usually do not provide completeness.

Theorem 16 (Sequentialisation). *Let P be a correct net and Δ be the set of e-nodes of its free weakenings.*

1. *Read backs exist: there exists e such that $P \triangleright e$ with $\mathrm{fv}(e) = \mathrm{fv}(P)$.*
2. *The read back relation is correct: for all expressions e, $P \triangleright e$ implies $\underline{e}_\Delta = P$ and $\mathrm{fv}(P) = \mathrm{fv}(e) \cup \Delta$.*
3. *The read back relation is complete: if $\underline{e}_\Gamma = P$ then $P \triangleright e$ and $\Gamma \subseteq \mathrm{fv}(P) \cup \Delta$.*

Quotient. Next we prove that structural equivalence on the LSC is exactly the quotient induced by proof nets. We invite the reader to look at the proof of the following quotient theorem. The $\Leftarrow$ direction essentially follows from figure Fig. 4, where for simplicity we have omitted the contractions of common variables for the subnets. The $\Rightarrow$ direction is the tricky point. Note that $\equiv$-classes do not admit canonical representantives, because the $\equiv_{com}$ axiom is not orientable, and so it is not possible to rely on some canonical read back. The argument at work in the proof is however pleasantly simple.

Theorem 17 (Quotient). *Let P be correct term net. Then, $\underline{t} = P$ and $\underline{s} = P$ if and only if $t \equiv s$.*

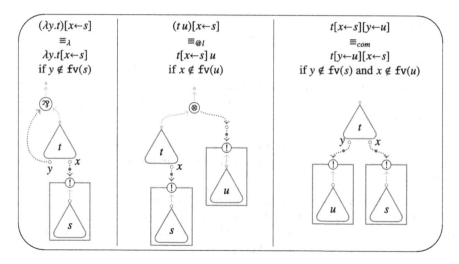

Fig. 4. Structural equivalent terms translate to the same proof nets (contractions of common variables are omitted).

5   Contexts

This short section develops a few notions about relating contexts in the two frameworks. We only deal with what is strictly needed to relate rewriting steps on terms and on term nets—a more general treatment is possible, but not explored here, for the sake of simplicity.

The plugging operation can also be done on context nets.

Definition 18 (Plugging on context nets). *Let P be a context net and let Δ be the free variables of its $\langle\cdot\rangle$-link l. The* plugging *of a net Q with free variables $\Gamma \subseteq \Delta$ in P is the net $P\langle Q\rangle$ obtained by*

- *if l is at level 0:*
  - Replacement: *replacing l with Q;*
  - Weakening unused variables in the interface: *adding a weakening h on every variable $x \in (\Delta \setminus \Gamma)$ not shared in P (or whose only incoming link in P is l).*
- *if l is in* ibox(h) *for a !-link h at level 0 then:*
  - Recursive plugging: *replacing the links of* ibox(h) *with those in* ibox$(h)\langle Q\rangle$*, inheriting the boxes;*
  - Pushing weakenings out of the box: *redefining* ibox(h) *as* ibox$(h)\langle Q\rangle$ *less its free weakenings, if any.*

The next lemma relies plugging in context nets with the corresponding read backs.

Lemma 19 (Properties of context nets plugging). *Let P be a context net of interface Δ, Q a correct net with free variables $\Gamma \subseteq \Delta$. Then*

1. Correctness: $P\langle Q\rangle$ is correct;
2. Read back: if $P \triangleright C_\Delta$ and $Q \triangleright e$ then $P\langle Q\rangle \triangleright C_\Delta\langle e\rangle$.

From the read back property, a dual property follows for the translation.

Lemma 20 (Context-free translation). Let C_Δ a context, e an expression such that $\mathrm{fv}(e) \subseteq \Delta$, and Γ a set of variables. Then $\underline{C_\Delta\langle e\rangle}_\Pi = \underline{C_{\Delta\Gamma}\langle e\rangle}$ where $\Pi = \Gamma \cup (\Delta \setminus \mathrm{cv}(C_\Delta))$.

The following lemma shall be used to relate the exponential steps in the two systems. The proof is a straightforward but tedious induction on $P \triangleright C_\Delta$, which is omitted.

Lemma 21 (Read back and free variable occurrences). Let $P \triangleright t$ be a term net with a fixed read back, l be a d-link of P whose e-node x is a free variable of P. Then for every set of variable names Δ there are a context C and a context net Q, both of interface $\Delta \cup \{x\}$, such that

1. Net factorisation: $Q\langle l\rangle = P$;
2. Term factorisation: $C\langle\!\langle x\rangle\!\rangle = t$; and
3. Read back: $Q \triangleright C$.

6   Micro-step Operational Semantics

Here we define the rewriting rules on proof nets and prove the isomorphism of rewriting systems with respect to the LSC. Since the rules of the LSC and those of proof nets match perfectly, we use the same names and the same notations for them.

The Rules. The rewriting rules are in Fig. 5. Let us explain them. First of all, note that the notion of cut in our syntax is implicit, because cut-links are not represented explicitly. A cut is given by a node whose incoming and outgoing connections are principal (*i.e.* with a little dot on the line).

The multiplicative rule $\to_{\mathrm{m}}$ is nothing but the usual elimination of a multiplicative cut, adapted to our syntax. The matching with the rule on terms is shown in Fig. 5.

The garbage collection rule $\to_{\mathrm{gc}}$ corresponds to a cut with a weakening. It is mostly as the usual rule, the only difference is with respect to the reduct. The box of the !-link is erased and replaced by a set of weakenings, one for every free variable of Q—this is standard. Each one of these new weakenings is also pushed out of all the m_i boxes closing on its e-node. This is done to preserve the invariant that weakenings are always pushed out of boxes as much as possible. Such an invariant is also used in the rule: note that the weakening is at the same level of Q. Last, if the weakenings created by the rule are contracted with any other link then they are removed on the fly, because by definition weakenings cannot be contracted.

The Milner exponential rule $\to_{\mathrm{e}}$ is the most unusual rule, and—to our knowledge—it has never been considered before on proof nets. There are two

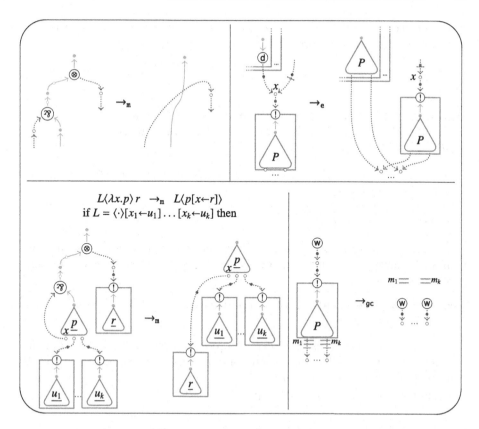

Fig. 5. Proof nets cut-elimination rules, plus—in the bottom-left corner—the matching of the multiplicative rule on terms and on term nets (forgetting, for simplicity, about the contraction of common variables for the boxes, and the fact that x_j can occur in u_i for $i < j$).

unusual points about it. The first one is that the redex crosses box borders, as the d-link is potentially inside many boxes, while the !-link is out of those boxes. In the literature, this kind of rules is usually paired with a small-step operational semantics (*e.g.* in [41]), that is, all the copies of the box are done in a single shot. Here instead we employ a micro-step semantics, as also done in [4]—that paper contains a discussion about this *box-crossing principle* and its impact on the rewriting theory of proof nets.

The second unusual point is the way the cut is eliminated. Roughly, it corresponds to a duplication of the box (so a contraction cut-elimination) immediately followed by commutation with all the boxes and opening of the box (so a dereliction cut-elimination). We say *roughly*, because there is a difference: the duplication happens also if the d-link is not contracted. Exactly as in the LSC, indeed, the $\rightarrow_e$ rule duplicates the ES even if there are no other occurrences of the replaced variable. In case the d-link is not contracted, the rule puts a weakening on the e-node source of the !-link.

The Isomorphism. Finally, we relate the evaluation of proof nets and of the LSC.

Theorem 22 (Dynamic isomorphism). *Let $P \triangleright t$ be a correct net with a fixed read back, and $a \in \{\mathtt{m}, \mathtt{e}, \mathtt{gc}\}$. There is a bijection ϕ between a-redexes of t and P such that:*

1. *Terms to proof nets: given a redex $R : t \to_a s$ then there exists Q such that $\phi(R) : P \to_a Q$ and $Q \triangleright s$.*
2. *Proof nets to terms: given a redex $R : P \to_a Q$ then there exists s such that $\phi^{-1}(R) : t \to_a s$ and $Q \triangleright s$.*

From Theorem 22 it immediately follows that cut-elimination preserves correctness, because the reduct of a correct net is the translation of a term, and therefore it is correct.

Corollary 23 (Preservation of correctness). *Let P be a term net and $P \to Q$. Then Q is correct.*

The perfect matching also transfers to proof nets the residual system of the LSC defined in [8]. Finally, the dynamic isomorphism (Theorem 22) combined with the quotient theorem (Theorem 17) also provides a new proof of the strong bisimulation property of structural equivalence (Proposition 2).

7   Abstracting Proof Nets from a Rewriting Point of View

In this section we provide a new, rewriting-based perspective on proof nets.

Cut Commutes with cut. One of the motivations for proof nets is the fact that cut-elimination in the sequent calculus has to face commutative cut-elimination cases. They are always a burden, but most of them are harmless. There is however at least one very delicate case, the commutation of cut with itself, given by:

$$
\cfrac{\begin{matrix}\gamma\\ \vdots\\ \vdash \Gamma, B\end{matrix} \quad \cfrac{\begin{matrix}\pi\\ \vdots\\ \vdash \Gamma, A\end{matrix} \quad \cfrac{\begin{matrix}\theta\\ \vdots\\ \vdash \Gamma, A, B\end{matrix}}{\vdash \Gamma, B}\;cut}{\vdash \Gamma}\;cut
\quad\to\quad
\cfrac{\begin{matrix}\pi\\ \vdots\\ \vdash \Gamma, A\end{matrix} \quad \cfrac{\begin{matrix}\gamma\\ \vdots\\ \vdash \Gamma, B\end{matrix} \quad \cfrac{\begin{matrix}\theta\\ \vdots\\ \vdash \Gamma, A, B\end{matrix}}{\vdash \Gamma, A}\;cut}{\vdash \Gamma}\;cut
$$

Such a commutation is delicate because it can be iterated, creating silly loops. If one studies weak normalisation (*i.e.* the *existence* of a normalising path) then it is enough to design a cut-elimination strategy that never commutes cut with itself—this is what is done in the vast majority of cut-elimination theorems. But if one is interested in strong normalisation (*i.e.*, *all* paths eventually normalise), then this is a serious issue. Morally, this is the conceptual problem behind proof nets and also behind the design of good explicit substitution calculi—it could be said that it is *the* rewriting issue of the Curry-Howard correspondence at the micro-step granularity.

One way to address this problem is to introduce an equivalence relation $\sim$ on proofs including the commutation of cut with itself, and then to switch to eliminate cuts modulo $\sim$. Rewriting modulo is a studied but technical and subtle topic, see [43] Chapter 14.3. The problem is that cut-elimination $\rightarrow$ and $\sim$ in general do not interact nicely, in particular $\sim$ cannot be postponed, because it *creates* $\rightarrow$-redexes.

Proof nets are a different, more radical solution: a change of syntax in which $\sim$-classes collapse on a single object, the proof net, so that the problem of the interaction between $\rightarrow$ and $\sim$ disappears. Proof nets seem, at first, elegant objects, and certainly a brilliant solution to the problem, providing many new intuitions about proofs. They are however heavy to manipulate formally, and it would be often preferable to have an alternative, more traditional syntax with similar properties.

Structural Rewriting Systems. The LSC is the prototype of a finer solution to the problem of commuting cut with itself. In general, we said, $\rightarrow$ and $\sim$ do not interact nicely. However, it is sometimes possible to *redefine* $\rightarrow$ so as to interact nicely with $\sim$. Typically, the contextual rules of the LSC interact nicely with $\equiv$ ($\equiv$ is the equivalence $\sim$ of the LSC, note in particular that axiom $\equiv_{com}$ is exactly commutation of cut with itself)—this is the motivation behind contextual rules, sometimes also called *at a distance*. This suggests the following notion, which is a special case of rewriting modulo an equivalence relation.

Definition 24 (Structural rewriting system). *Let T be a set of objects, $\rightarrow$ a rewriting relation and $\sim$ an equivalence relation over T. The triple $(T, \rightarrow, \sim)$ is a structural rewriting system (modulo) if $\sim$ is a strong bisimulation with respect to $\rightarrow$.*

Note that the definition does not mention graphs. We can then see proof nets and the LSC as instances of a single concept.

Proposition 25. *Let $\rightarrow_{PN}$ be the union of rules $\rightarrow_m$, $\rightarrow_e$, and $\rightarrow_{gc}$ on proof nets.*

1. *Proof nets with $\rightarrow_{PN}$ are a structural rewriting sytem, by taking $\sim$ to be the identity.*
2. *The LSC with $\rightarrow_{LSC}$ and $\equiv$ is a structural rewriting sytem.*

Structural rewriting sytems can be exported to different settings, with no need to bother about correctness criteria or graphical presentations, or the existence of a logical interpretation. For instance, in [3] there is a structural presentation of a fragment of the π-calculus based on contextual rules, independently of any logical interpretation.

8 Conclusions

This paper provides a perfect matching between the LSC and a certain presentation of the fragment of linear logic representing the λ-calculus. In particular, we prove that proof nets can be identified with the LSC up to structural equivalence $\equiv$, enabling one to reason about proof nets by means of a non-graphical language.

We also discuss our approach with respect to the basic proof theoretical problem of the cut rule commuting with itself. We try to suggest that the idea behind our result goes beyond proof nets and the LSC, as it also applies to other settings where rewriting has to interact with a notion of structural equivalence such as the π-calculus.

Acknowledgments. To the reviewers, for useful comments. This work has been partially funded by the ANR JCJC grant COCA HOLA (ANR-16-CE40-004-01).

References

1. Abadi, M., Cardelli, L., Curien, P.-L., Lévy, J.-J.: Explicit substitutions. J. Funct. Program. **1**(4), 375–416 (1991). https://doi.org/10.1017/S0956796800000186
2. Accattoli, B.: An abstract factorization theorem for explicit substitutions. In: Tiwari, A. (ed.) Proceedings of 28th International Conference on Rewriting Techniques and Applications, RTA 2012, May–June 2012, Nagoya, Leibniz International Proceedings in Informatics, vol. 15, pp. 6–21. Dagstuhl Publishing, Saarbrücken, Wadern (2012). https://doi.org/10.4230/lipics.rta.2012.6
3. Accattoli, B.: Evaluating functions as processes. In: Echahed, R., Plump, D. (eds.) Proceedings of 7th International Workshop on Computing with Terms and Graphs, TERMGRAPH 2013, March 2013, Rome, Electronic Proceedings in Theoretical Computer Science, vol. 110, pp. 41–55. Open Publishing Association, Sydney (2013). https://doi.org/10.4204/eptcs.110.6
4. Accattoli, B.: Linear logic and strong normalization. In: van Raamsdonk, F. (ed.) Proceedings of 29th International Conference on Rewriting Techniques and Applications, RTA 2013, June 2013, Eindhoven, Leibniz International Proceedings in Informatics, vol. 21, pp. 39–54. Dagstuhl Publishing, Saarbrücken, Wadern (2013). https://doi.org/10.4230/lipics.rta.2013.39
5. Accattoli, B.: Proof nets and the call-by-value λ-calculus. Theor. Comput. Sci. **606**, 2–24 (2015). https://doi.org/10.1016/j.tcs.2015.08.006
6. Accattoli, B.: Proof nets and the linear substitution calculus. arXiv preprint 1808.03395 (2018). https://arxiv.org/abs/1808.03395
7. Accattoli, B., Barenbaum, P., Mazza, D.: Distilling abstract machines. In: Proceedings of 19th ACM SIGPLAN International Conference on Functional Programming, ICFP 2014, Gothenburg, September 2014, pp. 363–376. ACM Press, New York (2014). https://doi.org/10.1145/2628136.2628154
8. Accattoli, B., Bonelli, E., Kesner, D., Lombardi, C.: A nonstandard standardization theorem. In: Proceedings of 41st ACM SIGPLAG-SIGACT Symposium on Principles of Programming Languages, POPL 2014, San Diego, CA, January 2014, pp. 659–670. ACM Press, New York (2014). https://doi.org/10.1145/2535838.2535886

9. Accattoli, B., Dal Lago, U.: (Leftmost-outermost) beta-reduction is invariant, indeed. Log. Methods Comput. Sci. **12**(1), Article 4 (2016). https://doi.org/10.2168/lmcs-12(1:4)2016

10. Accattoli, B., Guerrini, S.: Jumping boxes. In: Grädel, E., Kahle, R. (eds.) CSL 2009. LNCS, vol. 5771, pp. 55–70. Springer, Heidelberg (2009). https://doi.org/10.1007/978-3-642-04027-6_7

11. Accattoli, B., Kesner, D.: The structural λ-calculus. In: Dawar, A., Veith, H. (eds.) CSL 2010. LNCS, vol. 6247, pp. 381–395. Springer, Heidelberg (2010). https://doi.org/10.1007/978-3-642-15205-4_30

12. Accattoli, B., Kesner, D.: Preservation of strong normalisation modulo permutations for the structural λ-calculus. Log. Methods Comput. Sci. **8**(1), Article 28 (2012). https://doi.org/10.2168/lmcs-8(1:28)2012

13. Asperti, A., Laneve, C.: Comparing λ-calculus translations in sharing graphs. In: Dezani-Ciancaglini, M., Plotkin, G. (eds.) TLCA 1995. LNCS, vol. 902, pp. 1–15. Springer, Heidelberg (1995). https://doi.org/10.1007/BFb0014041

14. Barenbaum, P., Bonelli, E.: Optimality and the linear substitution calculus. In: Miller, D. (ed.) Proceedings of of 2nd International Conference on Formal Structures for Computation and Deduction, FSCD 2017, Oxford, September 2017. Leibniz International Proceedings in Informatics, vol. 84, Article 9. Dagstuhl Publishing, Saarbrücken/Wadern (2017). https://doi.org/10.4230/lipics.fscd.2017.9

15. Danos, V., Regnier, L.: Proof-nets and the Hilbert space. In: Girard, J.-Y., Lafont, Y., Regnier, L. (eds.) Advances in Linear Logic. London Mathematical Society Lecture Note Series, vol. 222, pp. 307–328. Cambridge University Press (1995). https://doi.org/10.1017/cbo9780511629150.016

16. Danos, V.: La Logique Linéaire appliqué à l'étude de divers processus de normalisation (principalement du λ-calcul). Ph.D. thesis, Université Paris 7 (1990)

17. Danos, V., Regnier, L.: Reversible, irreversible and optimal λ-machines. Theor. Comput. Sci. **227**(1–2), 79–97 (1999). https://doi.org/10.1016/s0304-3975(99)00049-3

18. Danos, V., Regnier, L.: Head linear reduction. Technical report (2004)

19. Di Cosmo, R., Kesner, D.: Strong normalization of explicit substitutions via cut elimination in proof nets (extended abstract). In: Proceedings of 12th Annual IEEE Symposium on Logic in Computer Science, LICS 1997, Warsaw, June–July 1997, pp. 35–46. IEEE CS Press, Washington, D.C. (1997). https://doi.org/10.1109/lics.1997.614927

20. Di Cosmo, R., Kesner, D., Polonowski, E.: Proof nets and explicit substitutions. Math. Struct. Comput. Sci. **13**(3), 409–450 (2003). https://doi.org/10.1017/s0960129502003791

21. Ehrhard, T., Regnier, L.: Differential interaction nets. Electron. Notes Theor. Comput. Sci. **123**, 35–74 (2005). https://doi.org/10.1016/j.entcs.2004.06.060

22. Fernández, M., Siafakas, N.: Labelled calculi of resources. J. Log. Comput. **24**(3), 591–613 (2014). https://doi.org/10.1093/logcom/exs021

23. Girard, J.-Y.: Linear logic. Theor. Comput. Sci. **50**, 1–102 (1987). https://doi.org/10.1016/0304-3975(87)90045-4

24. Guerrini, S.: Proof nets and the λ-calculus. In: Ehrhard, T., Girard, J.-Y., Ruet, P., Scott, P. (eds.) Linear Logic in Computer Science. London Mathematical Society Lecture Note Series, vol. 316, pp. 65–118. Cambridge University Press (2004). https://doi.org/10.1017/cbo9780511550850.003

25. Gundersen, T., Heijltjes, W., Parigot, M.: Atomic λ calculus: a typed λ-calculus with explicit sharing. In: Proceedings of 28th Annual ACM/IEEE Symposium on Logic in Computer Science, LICS 2013, New Orleans, LA, June 2015, pp. 311–320. IEEE CS Press, Washington, D.C. (2013). https://doi.org/10.1109/lics.2013.37

26. Kesner, D.: Reasoning about call-by-need by means of types. In: Jacobs, B., Löding, C. (eds.) FoSSaCS 2016. LNCS, vol. 9634, pp. 424–441. Springer, Heidelberg (2016). https://doi.org/10.1007/978-3-662-49630-5_25

27. Kesner, D., Conchúirl, S.Ó.: Milner's λ calculus with partial substitutions. Technical report, Université Paris 7 (2008). https://www.irif.fr/~kesner/papers/shortpartial.pdf

28. Kesner, D., Lengrand, S.: Extending the explicit substitution paradigm. In: Giesl, J. (ed.) RTA 2005. LNCS, vol. 3467, pp. 407–422. Springer, Heidelberg (2005). https://doi.org/10.1007/978-3-540-32033-3_30

29. Kesner, D., Renaud, F.: The prismoid of resources. In: Královič, R., Niwiński, D. (eds.) MFCS 2009. LNCS, vol. 5734, pp. 464–476. Springer, Heidelberg (2009). https://doi.org/10.1007/978-3-642-03816-7_40

30. Kesner, D., Ventura, D.: Quantitative types for the linear substitution calculus. In: Diaz, J., Lanese, I., Sangiorgi, D. (eds.) TCS 2014. LNCS, vol. 8705, pp. 296–310. Springer, Heidelberg (2014). https://doi.org/10.1007/978-3-662-44602-7_23

31. Laurent, O.: Étude de la polarisation en logique. Ph.D. thesis, University Aix-Marseille II (2002)

32. Laurent, O.: Polarized proof-nets and $\lambda\mu$-calculus. Theor. Comput. Sci. **290**(1), 161–188 (2003). https://doi.org/10.1016/s0304-3975(01)00297-3

33. Lévy, J.-J.: Réductions correctes et optimales dans le λ-calcul. Ph.D. thesis, University Paris VII (1978)

34. Mackie, I.: Encoding strategies in the Λ calculus with interaction nets. In: Butterfield, A., Grelck, C., Huch, F. (eds.) IFL 2005. LNCS, vol. 4015, pp. 19–36. Springer, Heidelberg (2006). https://doi.org/10.1007/11964681_2

35. Mascari, G., Pedicini, M.: Head linear reduction and pure proof net extraction. Theor. Comput. Sci. **135**(1), 111–137 (1994). https://doi.org/10.1016/0304-3975(94)90263-1

36. Mellies, P.-A.: Typed λ-calculi with explicit substitutions may not terminate. In: Dezani-Ciancaglini, M., Plotkin, G. (eds.) TLCA 1995. LNCS, vol. 902, pp. 328–334. Springer, Heidelberg (1995). https://doi.org/10.1007/BFb0014062

37. Milner, R.: Functions as processes. Math. Struct. Comput. Sci. **2**(2), 119–141 (1992). https://doi.org/10.1017/s0960129500001407

38. Milner, R.: Bigraphical reactive systems. In: Larsen, K.G., Nielsen, M. (eds.) CONCUR 2001. LNCS, vol. 2154, pp. 16–35. Springer, Heidelberg (2001). https://doi.org/10.1007/3-540-44685-0_2

39. Milner, R.: Local bigraphs and confluence: two conjectures (extended abstract). Electron. Notes Theor. Comput. Sci. **175**(3), 65–73 (2007). https://doi.org/10.1016/j.entcs.2006.07.035

40. Muroya, K., Ghica, D.R.: The dynamic geometry of interaction machine: a call-by-need graph rewriter. In: Goranko, V., Dam, M. (eds.) Proceeding of 26th EACSL Annual Conference, CSL 2017, Stockholm, August 2017. Leibniz International Proceedings in Informatics, vol. 82, Article 32. Dagstuhl Publishing, Saarbrücken/Wadern (2017). https://doi.org/10.4230/lipics.csl.2017.32

41. Regnier, L.: λ-calcul et réseaux. Ph.D. thesis, University Paris VII (1992)

42. Regnier, L.: Une équivalence sur les λ-termes. Theor. Comput. Sci. **126**(2), 281–292 (1994). https://doi.org/10.1016/0304-3975(94)90012-4

43. Terese: Term Rewriting Systems. Cambridge Tracts in Theoretical Computer Science, vol. 55. Cambridge University Press, Cambridge (2003)
44. Tranquilli, P.: Nets between determinism and nondeterminism. Ph.D. thesis, Universitá degli Studi Roma Tre/University Paris Diderot (2009)
45. Tranquilli, P.: Intuitionistic differential nets and λ-calculus. Theor. Comput. Sci. **412**(20), 1979–1997 (2011). https://doi.org/10.1016/j.tcs.2010.12.022
46. Vaux, L.: λ-calcul différentiel et logique classique: interactions calculatoires. Ph.D. thesis, University Aix-Marseille II (2007)
47. Wadsworth, C.P.: Semantics and pragmatics of the λ-calculus. Ph.D. thesis, University of Oxford (1971)

Modular Design of Domain-Specific Languages Using Splittings of Catamorphisms

Éric Badouel[1]([✉])[ID] and Rodrigue Aimé Djeumen Djatcha[2][ID]

[1] Inria Rennes – Bretagne Atlantique, IRISA, Campus universitaire de Beaulieu, 35042 Rennes Cedex, France
eric.badouel@inria.fr
[2] Faculty of Sciences, University of Douala, Douala, Cameroon
djeumenr@yahoo.fr

Abstract. Language oriented programming is an approach to software composition based on domain specific languages (DSL) dedicated to specific aspects of an application domain. In order to combine such languages we embed them into a host language (namely Haskell, a strongly typed higher-order lazy functional language). A DSL is then given by an algebraic type, whose operators are the constructors of abstract syntax trees. Such a multi-sorted signature is associated to a polynomial functor. An algebra for this functor tells us how to interpret the programs. Using Bekić's Theorem we define a modular decomposition of algebras that leads to a class of parametric multi-sorted signatures, associated with regular functors, allowing for the modular design of DSLs.

Keywords: Abstract syntax trees · Catamorphisms
Bekić's Theorem · Component-based design
Domain specific languages

1 Introduction

Component-based design is acknowledged as an important approach to improving the productivity in the design of complex software systems, as it allows pre-designed components to be reused in larger systems [14]. Instead of constructing standalone applications the focus is on the use of libraries viewed as toolboxes for the development of software product lines dedicated to some specific application domain. Using such "components on the shelf" improves productivity in developing software as well as the adaptability of the produced software with respect to changes. Thus intellectual investment is better preserved. In order to avoid redundancies a well designed domain specific library should have generic constituents (using parametrization, inheritance or polymorphism) and then it

---

This work was partially supported by ANR Headwork.

B. Fischer and T. Uustalu (Eds.): ICTAC 2018, LNCS 11187, pp. 62–79, 2018.
https://doi.org/10.1007/978-3-030-02508-3_4

can be seen as a small programming language in itself. Language oriented programming [5, 22] is an approach to software composition based on domain specific languages (DSL) dedicated to specific aspects of an application domain. A DSL captures the semantics of a specific application domain by packaging reusable domain knowledge into language features. It can be used by an expert of that domain who is provided with familiar notations and concepts rather that confronted with a general purpose programming language.

Many DSLs have been designed and used in the past decades, however their systematic study is a more recent concern. The design and implementation of a programming language, even a simple one, is a difficult task. One has to develop all the tools necessary to support programming and debugging in that language: a compiler for source text analysis, type checking, generation and optimisation of code, handling of errors... and also related tools for the generation of documentation, the integration of graphic and text editing facilities, the synchronization of multiple partial views, etc. Language adaptivity is another concern: it is very hard to make a change to the design of a programming language. However some domains of expertise may evolve in time, calling for frequent redesigns of the associated DSL: will we have to go through the process all over again every time? Finally, it might be difficult, if not impossible, to make different DSLs collaborate within some application even though most applications do involve different domains of expertise.

To alleviate these difficulties Hudak [10] suggested embedding the DSL into a chosen general-purpose host language; and coined the expression *Domain-Specific Embedded Languages* (or DSEL) to qualify them. Each DSEL inherits from the host language all parts that are not specific to the domain. It also inherits the compiler and the various tools used as a support to programming. Finally each DSEL is integrated into a general-purpose language, namely its host language; and several DSELs can communicate through their common host language. A higher-order strongly-typed lazy functional language like Haskell is an ideal host language since it can be viewed as a DSL for denotational semantics: a language that can be used to describe the semantics of various programming languages and thus also to combine them.

Recent language workbenches [7] like *Intentional Programming* [16, 21] or the *Meta Programming System* [5] from JetBrains envisage a system where one could systematically scope and design DSLs with the ability to compose a language for a particular problem by loading DSLs as various plug-ins. Each such plug-in would incorporate meta-programming tools allowing one to program in the corresponding DSL (browsing, navigating and editing syntax, extracting multiple views or executable code). The core of such intensional representations are abstract syntax trees associated to a multi-sorted signature whose operators are the basic contructions of the language. These operators are usually interpreted as closed higher-order functions (i.e., combinators). Following the higher-order interpretation of attribute grammars [2, 6, 11] we shall assume that these combinators derive from the semantic rules of an attribute grammar built on the multi-sorted signature.

Combining such DSLs requires considering a global grammar such that each DSL is associated with some subgrammar. The global grammar need not be constructed explicitly but we should be able to evaluate its abstract syntax trees by combining the catamorphisms of the corresponding subgrammars.

In this paper we address this problem by introducing the so-called modular grammars. The initial algebra of the polynomial functor associated with the operators of the language coincides with its least fixed-point. This fixed-point can be computed by a method of substitution using Bekić's Theorem [4]. By doing so the system of polynomial functors is transformed into a related system of regular functors. We introduce a splitting operation on algebras producing an algebra for the resulting system of regular functors from an algebra of the original system of polynomial functors. This transformation preserves the interpretation function (catamorphism).

2   Modular Domain Specific Languages

The syntax of a DSL is given by a multi-sorted signature $\Sigma = (S, \Omega)$ consisting of a set of sorts S and a set of operators $\omega \in \Omega$ where each operator has an *arity* in S^* and a *sort* in S. We let $\Omega(s_1 \cdots s_n, s)$ denote the set of operators $\omega \in \Omega$ with arity $s_1 \cdots s_n \in S^*$ and sort $s \in S$. Let us first assume that each sort appears as the sort of some operator. Then the signature can be associated with the endofunctor $F : |\mathbf{Set}|^S \to |\mathbf{Set}|^S$ such that

$$F(X)_s = \coprod_{\omega \in \Omega(s_1 \cdots s_n, s)} X_{s_1} \times \ldots \times X_{s_n}$$

which we may write

$$F(X)_s = \{\omega(x_1, \ldots, x_n) \mid \omega \in \Omega(s_1 \cdots s_n, s), \ (\forall 1 \leq i \leq n) \ x_i \in X_{s_i}\}$$

where $\omega(x_1, \ldots, x_n)$ is used to denote the element $(x_1, \ldots, x_n) \in X_{s_1} \times \ldots \times X_{s_n}$ that lies in the component indexed by ω. It is a polynomial functor (a sum of products) and it has a least fixed-point $F^\dagger$ made of the sorted Σ-trees. We readily show by induction that it is also the initial algebra. Hence there exists a unique morphism of F-algebra $(\!|\varphi|\!)_F : F^\dagger \to A$, called a *catamorphism* associated with each F-algebra $\varphi : F(A) \to A$. Note that such an F-algebra is nothing more than a Σ-algebra, namely a carrier set A_s associated with each sort $s \in S$ together with an interpretation function $\omega^\varphi : A_{s_1} \times A_{s_n} \to A_s$ for each $\omega \in \Omega(s_1 \cdots s_n, s)$. And the catamorphism amounts to interpreting the tree in the algebra by replacing each symbol ω by its interpretation ω^φ and evaluating the resulting expression.

Sorts that are used (they appear in arities of some operator) but not defined (they do not coincide with the sort of any operator) are called the *parameters* of the signature. When parameters exists the corresponding functor is no longer an endofunctor but has the form $F : |\mathbf{Set}|^{p+n} \to |\mathbf{Set}|^n$ where we have assumed an enumeration of the sorts with parameters coming first. Since $|\mathbf{Set}|^{p+n} \cong |\mathbf{Set}|^p \times$

$|\mathbf{Set}|^n$, functor F can be viewed as a parametric endofunctor $F : |\mathbf{Set}|^p \to (|\mathbf{Set}|^n \to |\mathbf{Set}|^n)$, and we can apply the results of the above discussion to each of the endofunctors $F\zeta$ for $\zeta \in |\mathbf{Set}|^p$. We readily verify that the fixed-point construction gives rise to a functor (the so-called *type functor* such that $F^\dagger\zeta = (F\zeta)^\dagger$) and the isomorphism $F\zeta\left(F^\dagger\zeta\right) \cong F^\dagger\zeta$ is natural in ζ. We let $in_{F,\zeta} : F\zeta\left(F^\dagger\zeta\right) \to F^\dagger\zeta$ and $out_{F,\zeta} : F^\dagger\zeta \to F\zeta\left(F^\dagger\zeta\right)$ stand for the inverse bijections associated with this isomorphism. Again a Σ-algebra is nothing more than a map $\varphi : F\zeta\xi \to \xi$ where $\zeta \in |\mathbf{Set}|^p$ and $\xi \in |\mathbf{Set}|^n$. The catamorphism $(\![\varphi]\!)_{F,\zeta} : F^\dagger\zeta \to \xi$ associated with φ and ζ is characterized by the identity:

$$(\![\varphi]\!)_{F,\zeta} \circ in_{F,\zeta} \;=\; \varphi \circ F\zeta\,(\![\varphi]\!)_{F,\zeta}$$

Haskell functions are however interpreted in the category $\mathcal{H} = \mathrm{DCPO}_\perp$ of pointed dcpos and continuous functions. Thus we should replace the category of sets and functions in the above discussion by $\mathcal{H}$. However (see [1, 15]) the category of pointed dcpos and continuous functions does not have coproducts and thus the above functorial interpretation of a signature does not seem to be possible. The trick used by Haskell to represent its data types is to resort to the subcategory $\mathcal{C} = \mathrm{DCPO}_{\perp!}$ of pointed dcpos and **strict** continuous functions. Finite products in $\mathcal{C}$ are given by the cartesian products and the finite coproduct of two dcpos is their *coalesced sum* $A \oplus B$ obtained from their disjoint union by identifying their respective least elements: $\perp_{A\oplus B} = \perp_A = \perp_B$. The lifting operator $(-)_\perp$ consists in adding a new least element to a given dcpo: $A_\perp = A \uplus \{\perp\}$. Finally, we let the sum of pointed dcpos be given by $\sum_{1\le i\le n} A_i \;=\; (A_1)_\perp \oplus \cdots \oplus (A_n)_\perp$ or equivalently by $\sum_{1\le i\le n} A_i \;=\; (A_1 \uplus \cdots \uplus A_n)_\perp$. When this sum has only two operands it will be written with an infix notation: $A + B \;=\; (A \uplus B)_\perp$. However, we should pay attention to the fact that this binary operation is not associative and that the corresponding n-ary operation cannot be presented as an iterated application of the binary one: we rather have a family of operators indexed by non-negative integers. The unary sum coincides with the lifting operator and the nullary sum gives $1 \;=\; ()_\perp \;=\; \{\perp, ()\}$. With these notations the following data type definition in Haskell

```
data Tree a = Node a (Forest a)
data Forest a  = Leaf | Cons  (Tree a) (Forest a)
```

is associated with the (parametric) polynomial functor $F : \mathcal{C}^3 \to \mathcal{C}^2$ such that $F(A, T, F) = ((A \times F)_\perp, 1 + (T \times F))$. Now, by observing that $\mathcal{C}(A_\perp, B) \cong \mathcal{H}(A, B)$ we deduce that an F-algebra $\varphi : F\zeta\alpha \to \alpha$ boils down to a continuous Σ-algebra in the sense that all the carrier sets are pointed dcpos and the interpretation functions are continuous functions. Hence the constituents of an algebra can be expressed by Haskell functions as intended.

All mentioned results holds more generally for *locally continuous* functors and in particular for the class of *regular functors* which is the least family of functors from $\mathcal{C}^n$ to $\mathcal{C}^m$ that contains the projections and is closed by sum, product, composition and the formation of type functors.

In the remaining parts of this section we introduce an example that will help us to explain our approach to modularity of domain specific languages embedded in Haskell.

2.1 DSL Associated with an Algebra

Let us consider a toy language for assembling elementary boxes. The following is an Haskell definition of a data structure for such boxes.

```
data Box = Elembox | Comp {pos :: Pos, first, second :: Box}
data Pos = Vert VPos | Hor  HPos
data VPos = Left_ | Right_
data HPos = Top | Bottom
```

Thus a box is either an elementary box (which we suppose has a unit size: its depth and height is 1) or is obtained by composing two sub-boxes. Two boxes can be composed either vertically with a left or right alignment or horizontally with a top or bottom alignment. The corresponding signature has a unique sort (Box), a constant standing for an elementary box and four binary operators associated with the various ways of assembling two sub-boxes in order to obtained a new box. The related notions of algebra and evaluation morphism can be expressed in Haskell as follows.

```
data AlgBox a = AlgBox {elembox :: a,  comp :: Pos -> a -> a -> a}
eval :: AlgBox a  -> Box -> a
eval (AlgBox elembox comp) = f where
  f Elembox = elembox
  f (Comp pos box1 box2) = comp (f box1) (f box2)
```

Now we need to make explicit the semantic aspects attached to a box: these are methods to extract useful information from a box. For instance we might be interested in representing a box by the list of origins of its elementary boxes, which of course depends on its own origin. Another property is the size of the box given by its height and depth. Thus a semantical domain for boxes would be an element of the following class:

```
data Size = Size {depth_, height_ :: Double} deriving Show
data Point = Point {xcoord, ycoord :: Double} deriving Show
class SemBox a where
  list :: a -> Point -> [Point]
  size :: a -> Size
```

An implementation of the language of boxes is given by an algebra whose domain of interpretation for boxes is an element of the class *SemBox*. One needs to specify the computations of the attributes *size* and *list* of a given box. For that purpose we use an attribute grammar that provides the required algebra following the higher-order functional approach to attribute grammars introduced in [2,6,11].

```
data SBox = SBox{list_ :: Point -> [Point]
                ,size_ :: Size}
instance SemBox SBox where
  list = list_
  size = size_
lang :: AlgBox SBox lang = AlgBox elembox comp where
 elembox = SBox (\ pt -> [pt])(Size 1 1)
 -- comp :: Pos -> SBox -> SBox -> SBox
 comp pos box1 box2 = SBox list' size' where
   list' pt = (list box1 (pi1 pt))++(list box2 (pi2 pt))
   size' = case pos of
   Vert _ -> Size (max d1 d2)(h1 + h2)
   Hor _  -> Size (d1 + d2)(max h1 h2)
   pi1 (Point x y) = case pos of
       Vert Left_  -> Point x y
       Vert Right_ -> Point (x + (max (d2-d1) 0)) y
       Hor Top     -> Point x y
       Hor Bottom  -> Point x (y + (max (h2-h1) 0))
   pi2 (Point x y) = case pos of
       Vert Left_  -> Point x (y+h1)
       Vert Right_ -> Point (x + (max (d1-d2) 0)) (y+h1)
       Hor Top     -> Point (x+d1) y
       Hor Bottom  -> Point x (y + (max (h1-h2) 0))
   Size d1 h1 = size box1
   Size d2 h2 = size box2
```

Using the algebra *lang* we can define derived operators

```
ebox :: SBox
ebox = elembox lang
hb, ht, vl, vr :: SBox -> SBox -> SBox
hb = cmp (Hor Bottom)
ht = cmp (Hor Top)
vl = cmp (Vert Left_)
vr = cmp (Vert Right_)
cmp = comp lang
```

We can also define their extensions on non-empty lists of boxes

```
hb*, ht*, vl*, vr* :: [SBox] -> SBox
hb* = foldl hb
ht* = foldl ht
vl* = foldl vl
vr* = foldl vr
```

For instance the following expression

```
box :: SBox
box = hb (vl (hb ebox ebox) ebox)
         (vr ebox (vl ebox (ht ebox ebox)))
```

is a description of the compound box displayed in Fig. 1. The shape of this expression follows exactly the shape of the corresponding data structure of type *Box* but it is an Haskell function of type *SBox*; thus the expression *size box* returns the size of that box.

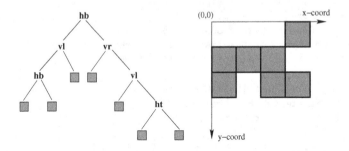

Fig. 1. A language of boxes

```
size box = Size{depth_=4, height_=3}
```

and the expression *list box* (*Point* 0 0) returns the corresponding list of located elementary boxes when the box is positioned at the origin.

```
list box (Point 0 0)= [Point{xcoord=0,ycoord=1},
Point{xcoord=1,ycoord=1}, Point{xcoord=0,ycoord=2},
Point{xcoord=3,ycoord=0}, Point{xcoord=2,ycoord=1},
Point{xcoord=2,ycoord=2}, Point{xcoord=3,ycoord=2}]
```

Therefore we have interpreted some static data structure as an active object on which one may operate using the corresponding methods

$$ebox :: SBox$$
$$cmp :: Pos \rightarrow SBox \rightarrow SBox \rightarrow SBox$$
$$size :: SBox \rightarrow Size$$
$$list \ :: SBox \rightarrow Point \rightarrow [Point]$$

(together with the derived operators: *hb*, *ht*, *vl*, and *vr* and their inductive extensions). That set of functions constitutes the interface of this embedded tiny language with its host language (Haskell).

Note that this language contains both the interpretation functions of the algebra (*ebox* and *cmp*) and the methods of the considered semantic domain (*size* and *list*). The description of the datatype *SBox* is not exported by the module dedicated to the language of boxes but only the functions that allows to build such boxes (*ebox* and *cmp*) or to use them (*size* and *list*).

2.2   Extension of a Domain Specific Language

Now, imagine that we seek to extend this language to allow an elementary box
to contain an image

```
data Image = Image {image :: a -> Point -> Maybe Color,
                    bb:: a -> Size}
```

represented as a function that returns the color of the point whose coordinates
relative to the upper left corner of the image are given as arguments. This function returns the undefined value *Nothing* (interpreted as "transparency") if the
coordinates exceed the bounding box of the image. However, the image itself may
contain some transparent parts. In addition we may wish to allow sub-boxes to
be centered when composed (horizontally and vertically, see Fig. 2).

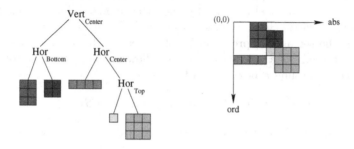

Fig. 2. A richer language of boxes (Color figure online)

The definition of the language can be adapted as follows:

```
data Box = Elembox  {image _ :: Image}
         | Comp {pos :: Pos, first, second :: Box}
data Pos = Vert VPos | Hor  HPos
data VPos = Left_ | Center_ | Right_
data HPos = Top | Center | Bottom
class SemBox a where
  list :: a -> Point -> [(Point,Image)]
  size :: a -> Size
```

The interface of a DSL is given by its algebra. An algebra consists of the
choice of a carrier set for each sort (the semantic domains of interpretation) and
a function of interpretation for each operator. Note that the precise definitions
of the carrier sets are not made visible. They are represented as abstract data
types (given by the two functions *list* and *size* for the basic version of our
example). If we want to reuse this DSL without modifying the existing code we
should kept the carrier sets unchanged. We may associate new methods with the
carrier sets of the algebra. But we are limited in this if the carrier sets cannot
simultaneously be extended. As far as the type *SBox* is concerned, it is clear

that any such function should be definable directly in terms of *list* and *size*; so these are just derived methods. Still, we may envisage adding new operators. For instance we may add the two operators $vc = Vert$ *(Vpos Center_)* and $hc =$ *Hor (Hpos Center)* to allow for extra ways of combining boxes. Then we should be able to extend the interpretation functions (*elembox* and *comp*) for handling these new operators while preserving the existing code. This problem has been referred to as the "expression problem" by Philip Walder:

> *The goal is to define a data type by cases, where one can add new cases to the data type and new functions over the datatype, without recompiling existing code, and while retaining static type safety.*

An elegant solution to this problem has been proposed by Wouter Swierstra in [18] using a method akin to an implementation of the visitor pattern. Nonetheless this method is no longer applicable if we are forced to reshape the carrier sets of the algebra, which is indeed the case for the extension considered here. We may even face more drastic changes imposed by the introduction of new operators. For instance the semantic representation of a box as a list of elementary boxes (containing an image of a given size) will not allow us to add a frame (of a given width and color) around a box using a function:

$$frame :: SBox \rightarrow Double \rightarrow Color \rightarrow SBox$$

The only reasonable choice to interpret the corresponding boxes seems to be the following:

```
class SemBox a where
    at   :: a -> Point -> Image
    size :: a -> Size
```

where *box 'at' pt* provides the image formed by anchoring the box at the given point. As in the preceding case, we have no other choice than to completely overwrite the interpretation functions *elembox* and *comp*.

3   Decomposition of Catamorphisms

3.1   Modular Grammar

The above example and discussion make it clear that a modular approach to DSLs requires that a basic module is dedicated to a specific set of sorts. Its interface is given by an algebra presented both by a set of interpretation functions for the operators and by methods that allow using objects of the carrier sets of the algebra. To be more precise let $\mathcal{L}$ be a language with signature $\Sigma = (S, \Omega)$ and $F : \mathcal{C}^{p+n} \rightarrow \mathcal{C}^n$ be its associated polynomial functor. Suppose that $n = n_1 + n_2$ and that the sorts S_2 corresponding to indices in n_2 are those defined by a particular module $\mathcal{L}_2$ of $\mathcal{L}$. Note that $S = S_0 \uplus S_1 \uplus S_2$ where S_0, such that $|S_0| = p$ are the parameters of the grammar and S_1, such that $|S_1| = n_1$, are the sorts defined by $\mathcal{L}$ outside the considered module. The signature of $\mathcal{L}_2$ is $\Sigma_2 = (S, \Omega_2)$ where Ω_2 is the set of operators in Ω whose sorts belong to S_2. Its associated polynomial functor is the composition of F with the second projection $\pi_2^{(n_1,n_2)} : \mathcal{C}^n \to \mathcal{C}^{n_2}$, namely $F_2 = \pi_2^{(n_1,n_2)} \circ F : \mathcal{C}^{p+n} \to \mathcal{C}^{n_2}$. Note that the parameters of Σ_2 are the elements of $S_0 \cup S_1$. Thus the sorts defined outside the module are extra parameters for this module. Of course a module would normally be given on a smaller set of sorts $S'' \subseteq S$ because it is usually defined prior to the language that uses it and we cannot anticipate all the potential usages of a module. Nonetheless, and for ease of presentation we assume as above that $S'' = S$. Indeed any signature can be viewed as a signature over a larger set of sorts where the additional sorts play the role of extra parameters, even though the interpretation functions will not use these arguments.

In order to implement language $\mathcal{L}$, assuming that its submodule $\mathcal{L}_2$ already exists, we have to define the interpretation functions for the operators in $\Omega \setminus \Omega_2$, namely to provide an algebra for the functor $F_1 = \pi_1^{(n_1,n_2)} \circ F : \mathcal{C}^{p+n} \to \mathcal{C}^{n_1}$. The parameters of this polynomial functor are the elements of $S_0 \cup S_2$. However we should distinguish between the parameters of the overall language $\mathcal{L}$ whose carrier sets $\zeta \in |\mathcal{C}|^p$ can be arbitrarily chosen (parametric polymorphism) from the sorts of S_2 whose value should lie in $F_2^\dagger \zeta \alpha_1$ if $\alpha_1 \in |\mathcal{C}|^{n_1}$ corresponds to the carrier sets for sorts in S_1. Hence the data that is needed to reconstruct the overall language from its submodule is an algebra for the residual functor F/F_2 defined in the following categorical version of Bekić's Theorem [4].

Theorem 1. *Let a locally continuous functor $F : \mathcal{C}^{p+n} \to \mathcal{C}^n$ with $n = n_1 + n_2$ be decomposed on the form $F = \langle F_1, F_2 \rangle$ where $F_1 = \pi_1^{(n_1,n_2)} \circ F : \mathcal{C}^{p+n} \to \mathcal{C}^{n_1}$ and $F_2 = \pi_2^{(n_1,n_2)} \circ F : \mathcal{C}^{p+n} \to \mathcal{C}^{n_2}$ where functors $\pi_1^{(n_1,n_2)} : \mathcal{C}^n \to \mathcal{C}^{n_1}$ and $\pi_2^{(n_1,n_2)} : \mathcal{C}^n \to \mathcal{C}^{n_2}$ are the two canonical projections. Then*

$$F^\dagger \zeta = H \zeta \times K \zeta$$

where

$$
\begin{aligned}
F/F_2 &= F_1 \circ \left\langle id_{p+n_1}, F_2^\dagger \right\rangle && : \mathcal{C}^{p+n_1} \to \mathcal{C}^{n_1} \\
H &= (F/F_2)^\dagger && : \mathcal{C}^p \to \mathcal{C}^{n_1} \\
F_2' &= F_2 \circ (\langle id_p, H \rangle \times id_{n_2}) && : \mathcal{C}^{p+n_2} \to \mathcal{C}^{n_2} \\
K &= F_2'^\dagger && : \mathcal{C}^p \to \mathcal{C}^{n_2}
\end{aligned}
$$

and $id_\ell : \mathcal{C}^\ell \to \mathcal{C}^\ell$ stands for the identity functor of $\mathcal{C}^\ell$.

Bekić's Theorem corresponds to the classical method of resolution by substitution. Indeed let $\mathbf{y}$, $\mathbf{x_1}$ and $\mathbf{x_2}$ be variables ranging respectively over $|\mathcal{C}|^p$, $|\mathcal{C}|^{n_1}$ and $|\mathcal{C}|^{n_2}$. Variable $\mathbf{x_1}$ of system F becomes a parameter for its subsystem F_2. By solving the latter we obtain a parametric solution $F_2^\dagger : \mathcal{C}^{p+n_1} \to \mathcal{C}^{n_2}$. We substitute this solution for variable $\mathbf{x_2}$ in the system F_1 thus leading to a new system $F/F_2 = F_1 \circ \langle id_{p+n_1}, F_2^\dagger \rangle : \mathcal{C}^{p+n_1} \to \mathcal{C}^{n_1}$ in which variable $\mathbf{x_2}$ no longer appears. Solving this new system provides us with the $\mathbf{x_1}$ component of the solution of the original system thus given by $H = (F/F_2)^\dagger : C^p \to C^{n_1}$. We can substitute that value into F_2 in order to derive the system $F_2' = F_2 \circ (\langle id_p, H \rangle \times id_{n_2}) : C^{p+n_2} \to C^{n_2}$ whose resolution gives the $\mathbf{x_2}$ component of the solution of the original system. The following lemma says that the $\mathbf{x_2}$ component of the solution of the original system can alternatively be obtained by substituting the $\mathbf{x_1}$ component of the solution of the original system (given by H) in the parametric solution $F_2^\dagger : C^{p+n_1} \to C^{n_2}$. The condition expressed by this lemma appears in several axiomatizations of parametric fixed-point operators [17], and in particular in the theory of traced monoidal categories [12].

Lemma 1. $K\zeta \simeq F_2^\dagger \zeta \, (H\,\zeta)$

Proof. First notice that $F_2'\zeta\,(K\zeta) = F_2\zeta\,(H\zeta)\,(K\zeta)$. The initial F_2', ζ-algebra

$$in_{F_2',\zeta} : F_2\zeta\,(H\zeta)\,(K\zeta) \to K\zeta$$

is thus an F_2-algebra with parameters $\zeta \times H\zeta$. We let

$$\iota_1 = \left(\!\left[in_{F_2',\zeta} \right]\!\right)_{F_2,\zeta \times H\zeta} : F_2^\dagger\zeta\,(H\,\zeta) \to K\zeta$$

be the corresponding catamorphism which, by definition, satisfies

$$\iota_1 \circ in_{F_2,\zeta \times H\zeta} = in_{F_2',\zeta} \circ F_2\zeta\,(H\zeta)\,\iota_1$$

Symmetrically, since $F_2\zeta(H\zeta)\left(F_2^\dagger\zeta\,(H\zeta)\right) = F_2'\zeta\left(F_2^\dagger\zeta\,(H\zeta)\right)$, we deduce that the initial $F_2, \zeta \times H\zeta$-algebra $in_{F_2,\zeta \times H\zeta} : F_2\zeta(H\zeta)\left(F_2^\dagger\zeta\,(H\zeta)\right) \to F_2^\dagger\zeta\,(H\zeta)$ is an F_2', ζ-algebra. Let $\iota_2 = \left(\!\left[in_{F_2,\zeta \times H\zeta} \right]\!\right)_{F_2',\zeta} : K\zeta \to F_2^\dagger\zeta\,(H\zeta)$ denote the corresponding catamorphism which, by definition, satisfies $\iota_2 \circ in_{F_2',\zeta} = in_{F_2,\zeta \times H\zeta} \circ F_2\zeta(H\zeta)\iota_2$. On the one hand it follows

$$\begin{aligned}
\iota_1 \circ \iota_2 \circ in_{F_2',\zeta} &= \iota_1 \circ in_{F_2,\zeta \times H\zeta} \circ F_2\zeta(H\zeta)\iota_2 \\
&= in_{F_2',\zeta} \circ F_2\zeta\,(H\zeta)\,\iota_1 \circ F_2\zeta(H\zeta)\iota_2 \\
&= in_{F_2',\zeta} \circ F_2\zeta\,(H\zeta)\,(\iota_1 \circ \iota_2) \\
&= in_{F_2',\zeta} \circ F_2'\zeta\,(\iota_1 \circ \iota_2)
\end{aligned}$$

and thus $\iota_1 \circ \iota_2 = \left(\!\left[in_{F_2',\zeta} \right]\!\right)_{F_2',\zeta} = id_{K\zeta}$. On the other hand

$$\begin{aligned}
\iota_2 \circ \iota_1 \circ in_{F_2,\zeta \times H\zeta} &= \iota_2 \circ in_{F_2',\zeta} \circ F_2\zeta\,(H\zeta)\,\iota_1 \\
&= in_{F_2,\zeta \times H\zeta} \circ F_2\zeta(H\zeta)\iota_2 \circ F_2\zeta\,(H\zeta)\,\iota_1 \\
&= n_{F_2,\zeta \times H\zeta} \circ F_2\zeta(H\zeta)\,(\iota_2 \circ \iota_1)
\end{aligned}$$

and thus $\iota_2 \circ \iota_1 = \left(\!\left[in_{F_2,\zeta \times H\zeta} \right]\!\right)_{F_2,\zeta \times H\zeta} = id_{F^\dagger\zeta(H\zeta)}$. The pair of morphisms $\iota_1 : F_2^\dagger\zeta\,(H\,\zeta) \to K\zeta$ and $\iota_2 : K\zeta \to F_2^\dagger\zeta\,(H\zeta)$ thus constitutes the required isomorphism $K\,\zeta \simeq F_2^\dagger\,\zeta\,(H\,\zeta)$. $\qquad\square$

Corollary 1. $F^\dagger = (F/F_2)^\dagger \bowtie F_2^\dagger$

where operation $\rtimes$ is given by

Definition 1. *The semidirect product (or cascaded composition) of functors $H : C^p \to C^n$ and $T : C^{p+n} \to C^m$ is given by*

$$H \rtimes T = \langle H, T \circ \langle id_p, H \rangle \rangle \; : \; C^p \to C^{n+m}$$

A module should be able to import other modules. This means that we should be able to apply a hierarchical decomposition of a signature. However, because of the presence of the type functor $F_2^\dagger$, we shall no longer stay within the frame of polynomial functors. Nonetheless, if we start from polynomial functors all constructions involved in Beckić's Theorem remain in the family of regular functors. We thus model a *modular grammar* as a combination of a polynomial functor, that describes the operators whose sorts are locally defined, and a regular functor associated with the imported definitions.

Definition 2. *A modular grammar $\mathbb{G} = (F, D)$ is a pair that consists of a polynomial functor $F : C^{p+n+m} \to C^n$ and a regular functor $D : C^{p+n} \to C^m$. The signature $\Sigma = (S, \Omega)$ associated with F concretizes the sorts and operators of the grammar where $S = S_p \uplus S_d \uplus S_i$ with $|S_p| = p$, $|S_d| = n$, and $|S_i| = m$. Sorts in S_p are the parameters of $\mathbb{G}$. A sort is said to be defined (respectively imported) by $\mathbb{G}$ if it belongs to S_d (resp. S_i). The regular functor represents the imported definitions of the grammar. The functor associated with the modular grammar is the (regular) functor*

$$F_\mathbb{G} = F \circ \langle id_{p+n}, D \rangle \; : \; C^{p+n} \to C^n$$

We let $F(\mathbb{G}) = F$ and $D(\mathbb{G}) = D$ denote the respective components of modular grammar $\mathbb{G}$.

The following proposition states that the family of modular grammars is closed by the operation of decomposition of a system into a subsystem and the corresponding residual system as described in Bekić's Theorem.

Proposition 1. *Let $\mathbb{G} = (F, D)$ be a modular grammar with polynomial functor $F : C^{p+n+m} \to C^n$ and regular functor $D : C^{p+n} \to C^m$. If $n = n_1 + n_2$ then $\pi_2^{(n_1,n_2)} \circ F_\mathbb{G} = F_{\mathbb{G}_2}$ and $F_{\mathbb{G}/\mathbb{G}_2} = F_\mathbb{G}/F_{\mathbb{G}_2}$ where the second projection $\mathbb{G}_2 = \pi_2^{(n_1,n_2)}(\mathbb{G})$ of modular grammar $\mathbb{G}$ is given by*

$$\begin{aligned} F(\mathbb{G}_2) &= \pi_2^{(n_1,n_2)} \circ F(\mathbb{G}) : C^{(p+n_1)+n_2+m} \to C^{n_2} \\ D(\mathbb{G}_2) &= D(\mathbb{G}) \qquad\qquad : C^{(p+n_1)+n_2} \to C^m \end{aligned}$$

and the residual operation is defined as

$$\begin{aligned} F(\mathbb{G}/\mathbb{G}_2) &= \pi_1^{(n_1,n_2)} \circ F(\mathbb{G}) : C^{p+n_1+(n_2+m)} \to C^{n_1} \\ D(\mathbb{G}/\mathbb{G}_2) &= F_{\mathbb{G}_2}^\dagger \rtimes D(\mathbb{G}) \quad : C^{p+n_1} \to C^{n_2+m} \end{aligned}$$

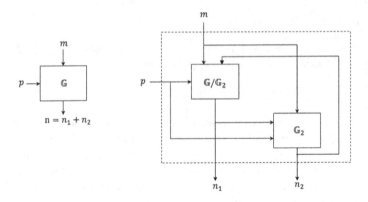

Fig. 3. Decomposition of modular grammars

The situation is depicted in Fig. 3 where we note that the sorts defined by the residual grammar $\mathbb{G}/\mathbb{G}_2$ (its outputs) are additional parameters for the sub-grammar $\mathbb{G}_2$, whereas the outputs of $\mathbb{G}_2$ are additional imported sorts for $\mathbb{G}/\mathbb{G}_2$.

Proof. The identity $\pi_2^{(n_1,n_2)} \circ F_{\mathbb{G}} = F_{\pi_2^{(n_1,n_2)}(\mathbb{G})}$ is immediate.

$$F_{\mathbb{G}}/F_{\mathbb{G}_2} = \pi_1^{(n_1,n_2)} \circ F_{\mathbb{G}} \circ \langle id_{p+n_1}, F_{\mathbb{G}_2}^\dagger \rangle$$
$$= \pi_1^{(n_1,n_2)} \circ F(\mathbb{G}) \circ \langle id_{p+n_1+n_2}, D(\mathbb{G}) \rangle \langle id_{p+n_1}, F_{\mathbb{G}_2}^\dagger \rangle$$

and

$$F_{\mathbb{G}/\mathbb{G}_2} = F(\mathbb{G}/\mathbb{G}_2) \circ \langle id_{p+n_1}, D(\mathbb{G}/\mathbb{G}_2) \rangle$$
$$= \pi_1^{(n_1,n_2)} \circ F(\mathbb{G}) \circ \langle id_{p+n_1}, F_{\mathbb{G}_2}^\dagger \rtimes D(\mathbb{G}) \rangle$$
$$= \pi_1^{(n_1,n_2)} \circ F(\mathbb{G}) \circ \langle id_{p+n_1}, \langle F_{\mathbb{G}_2}^\dagger, D(\mathbb{G}) \circ \langle id_{p+n_1}, F_{\mathbb{G}_2}^\dagger \rangle \rangle \rangle$$

In order to prove $F_{\mathbb{G}}/F_{\mathbb{G}_2} = F_{\mathbb{G}/\mathbb{G}_2}$ if suffices to show that

$$\langle id_{p+n_1+n_2}, D(\mathbb{G}) \rangle \langle id_{p+n_1}, F_{\mathbb{G}_2}^\dagger \rangle = \langle id_{p+n_1}, \langle F_{\mathbb{G}_2}^\dagger, D(\mathbb{G}) \circ \langle id_{p+n_1}, F_{\mathbb{G}_2}^\dagger \rangle \rangle \rangle$$

These two expressions are equal because they give rise to the same results when composed with the three projections from $\mathcal{C}^{(p+n_1)+n_2+m}$ to $\mathcal{C}^{p+n_1}$, $\mathcal{C}^{n_2}$, and $\mathcal{C}^m$ respectively:

$$\pi_1^{p+n_1,n_2,m} \circ E = id_{p+n_1}$$
$$\pi_2^{p+n_1,n_2,m} \circ E = F_{\mathbb{G}_2}^\dagger$$
$$\pi_3^{p+n_1,n_2,m} \circ E = D(\mathbb{G}) \circ \langle id_{p+n_1}, F_{\mathbb{G}_2}^\dagger \rangle$$

□

By Corollary 1 it follows that

Corollary 2. $F_{\mathbb{G}}^\dagger = \left(F_{\mathbb{G}/\mathbb{G}_2}^\dagger \right) \rtimes F_{\mathbb{G}_2}^\dagger$

3.2   Decomposition of Algebras

Using Bekić's Theorem we now define a decomposition of algebras.

Definition 3. *We let $F : C^{p+n} \to C^n$ be a locally continuous functor with $n = n_1 + n_2$. Let moreover $\Phi : F\zeta\alpha_1\alpha_2 \to \alpha_1 \times \alpha_2$ be an $F\zeta$-algebra ($\zeta \in |C|^p$) on the domain $\alpha = \alpha_1 \times \alpha_2$ ($\alpha_1 \in |C|^{n_1}$, and $\alpha_2 \in |C|^{n_2}$). Φ can be decomposed into*

$$\varphi_1 = \pi_1^{(n_1,n_2)}(\Phi) : F_1 \zeta \alpha_1 \alpha_2 \to \alpha_1$$
$$\varphi_2 = \pi_2^{(n_1,n_2)}(\Phi) : F_2 \zeta \alpha_1 \alpha_2 \to \alpha_2$$

The (n_1, n_2)-splitting of Φ is the pair consisting of the $(F/F_2) \zeta$-algebra of domain α_1

$$\pi_{F/F_2}\Phi \triangleq \varphi_1 \circ \left(F_1 \zeta \alpha_1 \, (\!|\varphi_2|\!)_{F_2,\zeta\times\alpha_1} \right) : F_1 \zeta \alpha_1 \left(F_2^\dagger \zeta \alpha_1 \right) \to \alpha_1$$

together with the $F_2 (\zeta \times \alpha_1)$-algebra of domain α_2

$$\pi_{F_2}\Phi \triangleq \varphi_2 : F_2 \zeta \alpha_1 \alpha_2 \to \alpha_2$$

The operation of decomposition of algebras is thus given as:

$$Split^{(n.m)} : Alg_{F,\zeta}(\alpha_1 \times \alpha_2) \to \left(Alg_{F/F_2,\zeta}(\alpha_1) \right) \times \left(Alg_{F_2,\zeta\times\alpha_1}(\alpha_2) \right)$$
$$Split^{(n_1,n_2)} \Phi = \left(\pi_{F/F_2}\Phi, \pi_{F_2}\Phi \right)$$

Thus an algebra $\Phi = \varphi_1 \times \varphi_2 : F\zeta\alpha_1\alpha_2 \to \alpha_1 \times \alpha_2$ is decomposed into an algebra $\pi_{F_2}\Phi = \varphi_2 : F_2 \zeta \alpha_1 \alpha_2 \to \alpha_2$ for the "subsystem" F_2 together with an algebra $\pi_{F/F_2}\Phi : F/F_2\zeta\alpha_1 \to \alpha_1$ for the "residual system" F/F_2. The following result shows that the catamorphism (evaluation function) associated with the algebra Φ for the overall system can be reconstructed from the catamorphisms associated respectively with $\pi_{F_2}\Phi$ and $\pi_{F/F_2}\Phi$ using a semidirect product operation which we first introduce.

In Definition 1 we defined the semidirect product of two functors $H : C^p \to C^n$ and $T : C^{p+n} \to C^m$ as

$$H \rtimes T = \langle H, T \circ \langle id_p, H \rangle \rangle : C^p \to C^{n+m}$$

By functoriality of the product and composition we deduce a related operation of semidirect product of natural transformations $\eta : H \to H'$ and $\tau : T \to T'$ where $H, H' : C^p \to C^n$ and $T, T' : C^{p+n} \to C^m$ given by

$$(\eta \rtimes \tau)_\zeta = \eta_\zeta \times (\tau_{\zeta,H'\zeta} \circ T\zeta\eta_\zeta) = \eta_\zeta \times (T'\zeta\eta_\zeta \circ \tau_{\zeta,H\zeta})$$

Considering the special case where the target functors H' and T' are constant functors leads us to the following definition

Definition 4. *The semidirect composition of two maps $f : H\zeta \to \alpha$ and $g : T\zeta\alpha \to \beta$ where $H : C^p \to C^n$ and $T : C^{p+n} \to C^m$ is the map $f \rtimes g : (H \rtimes T)\zeta \to \alpha \times \beta$ given by $(f \rtimes g) = f \times (g \circ T\zeta f)$.*

Using this operation we can now state

Theorem 2. *Up to the isomorphisms* $F^\dagger\zeta = H\zeta \times K\zeta$ *and* $K\zeta = F_2^\dagger\zeta\,(H\zeta)$ *one has*

$$(\!(\varPhi)\!)_{F,\zeta} = (\!([\pi_{F/F_2}\varPhi]\!)_{F/F_2,\zeta} \times (\!([\pi_{F_2}\varPhi]\!)_{F_2,\zeta\times\alpha_1}$$

Lemma 2. *Up to the isomorphism* $F^\dagger\zeta = H\zeta \times K\zeta$ *the initial algebra* $in_{F,\zeta}$: $F\zeta\,(F^\dagger\zeta) \to F^\dagger\zeta$ *decomposes to the form* $in_{F,\zeta} = in_{H,\zeta} \times in_{K,\zeta}$ *where* $in_{H,\zeta}$: $F_1\zeta(H\zeta)(K\zeta) \to H\zeta$ *and* $in_{K,\zeta} : F_2\zeta(H\zeta)(K\zeta) \to K\zeta$ *are respectively given by* $in_{H,\zeta} = in_{F/F_2,\zeta} \circ (F_1\zeta(H\zeta)\iota_2)$ *and* $in_{K,\zeta} = in_{F_2',\zeta}$.

Proof. The initial algebra is an isomorphism and the converse also holds true (any algebra which is an isomorphism is initial) when we have uniqueness of fixed-point (up to isomorphism) which is indeed the case here.

$$in_{H,\zeta} = in_{F/F_2,\zeta} \circ (F_1\zeta(H\zeta)\iota_2) : F_1\zeta(H\zeta)(K\zeta) \to H\zeta$$

and $in_{K,\zeta} = in_{F_2',\zeta} : F_2\zeta(H\zeta)(K\zeta) \to K\zeta$ are isomorphisms and thus

$$in_{H,\zeta} \times in_{K,\zeta} : F\zeta(H\zeta)(K\zeta) \to H\zeta \times K\zeta$$

is the initial algebra of functor F. $\qquad\square$

Corollary 3. *Up to the isomorphism* $F^\dagger\zeta = H\zeta \times K\zeta$, *the two parts* $f : H\zeta \to \alpha_1$ *and* $g : K\zeta \to \alpha_2$ *of catamorphism* $(\!(\varPhi)\!)_{F,\zeta} = f \times g$ *are characterized by* $f \circ in_{H,\zeta} = \varphi_1 \circ F\zeta fg$ *and* $g \circ in_{K,\zeta} = \varphi_2 \circ F_2\zeta fg$.

Lemma 3. *For any morphism* $f : H\zeta \to \alpha_1$ *one has*

$$(\!(\varphi_2 \circ F_2\zeta f\alpha_2)\!)_{F_2',\zeta} = (\!(\varphi_2)\!)_{F_2,\zeta\times\alpha_1} \circ \left(F_2^\dagger\zeta f\right) \circ \iota_2 : K\zeta \to \alpha_2$$

and that morphism $g(f)$ *satisfies* $g(f) \circ in_{K,\zeta} = \varphi_2 \circ (F_2\,\zeta\,f\,g(f))$.

Proof. By definition $F_2^\dagger\zeta f = \left(\!\left[in_{F_2,\zeta\times\alpha_1} \circ \left(F_2\zeta f\left(F_2^\dagger\zeta\alpha_1\right)\right)\right]\!\right)_{F_2,\zeta\times H\zeta}$ and that morphism satisfies

$$F_2^\dagger\zeta f \circ in_{F_2,\zeta\times H\zeta} = in_{F_2,\zeta\times\alpha_1} \circ \left(F_2\,\zeta\,f\left(F_2^\dagger\zeta\alpha_1\right)\right) \circ F_2\zeta\,(H\zeta)\left(F_2^\dagger\zeta f\right)$$

It follows that

$$(\!(\varphi_2)\!)_{F_2,\zeta\times\alpha_1} \circ \left(F_2^\dagger\zeta f\right) \circ \iota_2 \circ in_{F_2',\zeta}$$
$$= (\!(\varphi_2)\!)_{F_2,\zeta\times\alpha_1} \circ \left(F_2^\dagger\zeta f\right) \circ in_{F_2,\zeta\times H\zeta} \circ F_2\zeta(H\zeta)\iota_2$$
$$= (\!(\varphi_2)\!)_{F_2,\zeta\times\alpha_1} \circ in_{F_2,\zeta\times\alpha_1} \circ \left(F_2\,\zeta\,f\left(F_2^\dagger\zeta\alpha_1\right)\right) \circ F_2\zeta\,(H\zeta)\left(F_2^\dagger\zeta f\right) \circ$$
$$\qquad F_2\zeta(H\zeta)\iota_2$$
$$= \varphi_2 \circ F_2\zeta\alpha_1\,(\!(\varphi_2)\!)_{F_2,\zeta\times\alpha_1} \circ \left(F_2\,\zeta\,f\left(F_2^\dagger\zeta\alpha_1\right)\right) \circ F_2\zeta\,(H\zeta)\left(F_2^\dagger\zeta f \circ \iota_2\right)$$
$$= \varphi_2 \circ F_2\zeta f\alpha_2 \circ F_2\zeta\,(H\zeta)\,(\!(\varphi_2)\!)_{F_2,\zeta\times\alpha_1} \circ F_2\zeta\,(H\zeta)\left(F_2^\dagger\zeta f \circ \iota_2\right)$$
$$= (\varphi_2 \circ F_2\zeta f\alpha_2) \circ F_2\zeta\,(H\zeta)\left((\!(\varphi_2)\!)_{F_2,\zeta\times\alpha_1} \circ F_2^\dagger\zeta f \circ \iota_2\right)$$

and thus $(\![\varphi_2 \circ F_2\zeta f\alpha_2]\!)_{F_2',\zeta} = (\![\varphi_2]\!)_{F_2,\zeta\times\alpha_1} \circ \left(F_2^\dagger\zeta f\right) \circ \iota_2$. If we let $g(f) \triangleq$
$(\![\varphi_2]\!)_{F_2,\zeta\times\alpha_1} \circ \left(F_2^\dagger\zeta f\right) \circ \iota_2$ denote this morphism, we deduce $g(f) \circ in_{K,\zeta} =$
$\varphi_2 \circ F_2\zeta f\alpha_2 \circ F_2\zeta\,(H\zeta)\,g(f) = \varphi_2 \circ F_2\,\zeta\,f\,g(f)$ because $in_{K,\zeta} = in_{F_2',\zeta}$. $\square$

Lemma 4. *If $f : H\zeta \rightarrow \alpha_1$ and $g : K\zeta \rightarrow \alpha_2$ are, up the isomorphism $F^\dagger\zeta = H\zeta \times K\zeta$, the two parts of catamorphism $(\![\Phi]\!)_{F,\zeta} = f \times g$ then $f = \left(\![\varphi_1 \circ F_1\zeta\alpha_1\,(\![\varphi_2]\!)_{F_2,\zeta\times\alpha_1}]\!\right)_{F/F_2,\zeta}$ and $g = (\![\varphi_2 \circ F_2\zeta f\alpha_2]\!)_{F_2',\zeta}$.*

Proof. By Corollary 3 the two parts $f : H\zeta \rightarrow \alpha_1$ and $g : K\zeta \rightarrow \alpha_2$ of the catamorphism $(\![\Phi]\!)_{F,\zeta} = f \times g$ are characterized by $f \circ in_{H,\zeta} = \varphi_1 \circ F\zeta fg$ and $g \circ in_{K,\zeta} = \varphi_2 \circ F_2\zeta fg$. Set $f' = \left(\![\varphi_1 \circ F_1\zeta\alpha_1\,(\![\varphi_2]\!)_{F_2,\zeta\times\alpha_1}]\!\right)_{F/F_2,\zeta}$ and $g' = g(f') = (\![\varphi_2 \circ F_2\zeta f'\alpha_2]\!)_{F_2',\zeta}$. By the preceding lemma $g' \circ in_{K,\zeta} = \varphi_2 \circ F_2\,\zeta\,f'\,g'$, moreover

$$
\begin{aligned}
&f' \circ in_{H,\zeta} \\
&= f' \circ in_{F/F_2,\zeta} \circ F_1\zeta(H\zeta)\iota_2 \\
&= \varphi_1 \circ F_1\zeta\alpha_1\,(\![\varphi_2]\!)_{F_2,\zeta\times\alpha_1} \circ F_1\zeta f'\left(F_2^\dagger\zeta f'\right) \circ F_1\zeta(H\zeta)\iota_2 \\
&= \varphi_1 \circ F_1\zeta\alpha_1\,(\![\varphi_2]\!)_{F_2,\zeta\times\alpha_1} \circ F_1\zeta\alpha_1\left(F_2^\dagger\zeta f'\right) \circ F_1\zeta f'\left(F_2^\dagger\zeta(H\zeta)\right) \circ \\
&\quad F_1\zeta(H\zeta)\iota_2 \\
&= \varphi_1 \circ F_1\zeta\alpha_1\,(\![\varphi_2]\!)_{F_2,\zeta\times\alpha_1} \circ F_1\zeta\alpha_1\left(F_2^\dagger\zeta f'\right) \circ F_1\zeta\alpha_1\iota_2 \circ F_1\zeta f'(K\zeta) \\
&= \varphi_1 \circ F_1\zeta\alpha_1\left((\![\varphi_2]\!)_{F_2,\zeta\times\alpha_1} \circ F_2^\dagger\zeta f' \circ \iota_2\right) \circ F_1\zeta f'(K\zeta) \\
&= \varphi_1 \circ F_1\zeta\alpha_1 g' \circ F_1\zeta f'(K\zeta) \\
&= \varphi_1 \circ F_1\zeta f'g'
\end{aligned}
$$

From which it follows that $f' = f$ and $g' = g$. $\square$
Theorem 2 follows from Lemmas 3 and 4.

4   Conclusion

In this paper we relied on a modular decomposition of a (multi-sorted) signature based on a hierarchical decomposition of its set of sorts in order to reconstruct a language, specified by an algebra, by composition of the algebras associated with its sublanguages. As mentioned in the introduction the global laguage would normally be left implicit. Our result represents it as a cascaded composition of its constituent sublanguages. This representation preserves catamorphisms. One can then adopt an incremental approach consisting of growing a DSL by an operation of composition of modular grammars derived from Bekić's Theorem. This approach differs from the solution of the "expression problem" proposed by Swierstra in [18] which allows adding new operators for a fixed sort (or a fixed set of sorts) and thus stays confined to a given module in our context.

We intend to apply the work presented in this paper to Guarded Attribute Grammars [3]. It is a declarative model that describes the different ways of performing a task by recursively decomposing it into more elementary subtasks.

This is formalized by the productions of an abstract context-free grammar (i.e. a multi-sorted signature). The actual way a task is decomposed depends on the choices made by the person to whom the task is assigned and on the data attached to the task (inherited attributes whose values are refined over time). Productions of the grammar are associated with guards that filter the rules applicable in a given configuration. The evaluation of these guards is done incrementally which means that a rule is allowed as soon as its guard is satisfied. This allows the workspaces of different users to operate concurrently and in reactive mode. The local grammar of a user specifies how he can behave in order to solve the pending tasks in his workspace. It defines a DSL that captures the user's domain of expertise (his role). The lazy composition of roles is compatible with the choice of Haskell as host language. Still, it remains to take side effects into account, in particular for modelling user interactions. We might use the approach proposed in [18] to represent the set of involved input-output actions as a datatype in order to isolate the input-output side effects from the hierarchical description of the system that would be specified, using the method presented in this paper, with ordinary Haskell functions (without side effects).

As we have seen above, the splitting of algebras is an approach to modular attribute grammars. This approach is orthogonal to, and thus can be combined with, alternative approaches of modularity in attribute grammars [13] such as the descriptional composition [8,9] or the composition by aspects [19,20].

Acknowledgement. We are very grateful to the reviewers for the relevance of their comments which greatly helped us to improve the presentation of this work.

References

1. Abramsky, S., Jung, A.: Domain theory. In: Abramsky, S., Gabbay, D.M., Maibaum, T.S.E. (eds.) Handbook of Logic in Computer Science, Semantic Structures, vol. 3, pp. 1–168. Clarendon Press, Oxford (1994)
2. Backhouse, K.: A functional semantics of attribute grammars. In: Katoen, J.-P., Stevens, P. (eds.) TACAS 2002. LNCS, vol. 2280, pp. 142–157. Springer, Heidelberg (2002). https://doi.org/10.1007/3-540-46002-0_11
3. Badouel, E., Hélouët, L., Morvan, C., Kouamou, G., Nsaibirni, R.F.J.: Active workspaces: distributed collaborative systems based on guarded attribute grammars. SIGAPP Appl. Comput. Rev. **15**(3), 6–34 (2015). https://doi.org/10.1145/2695664.2695698
4. Bekić, H.: Definable operations in general algebras, and the theory of automata and flowcharts. In: Jones, C.B. (ed.) Programming Languages and Their Definition. LNCS, vol. 177, pp. 30–55. Springer, Heidelberg (1984). https://doi.org/10.1007/BFb0048939
5. Dmitriev, S.: Language oriented programming: The next paradigm. http://www.onboard.jetbrains.com/articles/04/10/lop/
6. Fokkinga, M.M., Jeuring, J., Meertens, L., Meijer, E.: A translation from attribute grammars to catamorphisms. Squiggolist **2**(1), 20–26 (1991)
7. Fowler, M.: Language workbenches: the killer-app for domain specific languages. http://www.martinfowler.com/articles/languageWorkbench.html

8. Ganzinger, H., Giegerich, R.: Attribute coupled grammars. In: Proceedings of 1984 SIGPLAN Symposium on Compiler Construction, Montréal, June 1984, pp. 157–170. ACM Press, New York (1984). https://doi.org/10.1145/502874.502890

9. Giegerich, R.: Composition and evaluation of attribute coupled grammars. Acta Inf. **25**(4), 355–423 (1988). https://doi.org/10.1007/bf02737108

10. Hudak, P.: Building domain-specific embedded languages. ACM Comput. Surv. **28**(4) (1996). article 196. https://doi.org/10.1145/242224.242477

11. Johnsson, T.: Attribute grammars as a functional programming paradigm. In: Kahn, G. (ed.) FPCA 1987. LNCS, vol. 274, pp. 154–173. Springer, Heidelberg (1987). https://doi.org/10.1007/3-540-18317-5_10

12. Joyal, A., Street, R., Verity, D.: Traced monoidal categories. In: Mathematical Proceedings of the Cambridge Philosophical Society, vol. 119, no. 3, pp. 447–468 (1996). https://doi.org/10.1017/s0305004100074338

13. Kastens, U., Waite, W.M.: Modularity and reusability in attribute grammars. Acta Inf. **31**(7), 601–627 (1994). https://doi.org/10.1007/bf01177548

14. Krueger, C.W.: Software reuse. ACM Comput. Surv. **24**(2), 131–183 (1992). https://doi.org/10.1145/130844.130856

15. Plotkin, G.: Post-graduate lectures notes in advanced domain theory (incorporating the "Pisa Notes"). University of Edinburgh (1981)

16. Simonyi, C.: The death of computer languages, the birth of intentional programming. In: Randell, B. (ed.) The Future of Software: Proceedings of Joint International Computers Ltd. and University of Newcastle Seminar. University of Newcastle (1995). (Also as Technical report MSR-TR-95-52, Microsoft Research, Redmond, WA)

17. Simpson, A.K., Plotkin, G.D.: Complete axioms for categorical fixed-point operators. In: Proceedings of 15th Annual IEEE Symposium on Logic in Computer Science, LICS 2000, Santa Barbara, CA, June 2000, pp. 30–41. IEEE CS Press, Washington (2000). https://doi.org/10.1109/lics.2000.855753

18. Swierstra, W.: Data types à la carte. J. Funct. Program. **18**(4), 423–436 (2008). https://doi.org/10.1017/s0956796808006758

19. Van Wyk, E.: Aspects as modular language extensions. Electron. Notes Theor. Comput. Sci. **82**(3), 555–574 (2003). https://doi.org/10.1016/s1571-0661(05)82628-3

20. Van Wyk, E.: Implementing aspect-oriented programming constructs as modular language extensions. Sci. Comput. Program. **68**(1), 38–61 (2007). https://doi.org/10.1016/j.scico.2005.06.006

21. Van Wyk, E., de Moor, O., Sittampalam, G., Piretti, I.S., Backhouse, K., Kwiatkowski, P.: Intensional programming: a host of language features. Technical report PRG-RR-01-21, Oxford University Computing Laboratory (2001)

22. Ward, M.P.: Language-oriented programming. Softw. Concepts Tools **15**(4), 147–161 (1994)

An Automata-Based View
on Configurability and Uncertainty

Martin Berglund[1](✉) and Ina Schaefer[2]

[1] Department of Information Science and Center for AI Research,
Stellenbosch University, Private Bag X1 Matieland,
Stellenbosch 7602, South Africa
pmberglund@sun.ac.za
[2] Institute of Software Engineering and Automotive Informatics,
Technische Universität Braunschweig, Mühlenpfordtstr. 23,
38106 Braunschweig, Germany
i.schaefer@tu-braunschweig.de

Abstract. In this paper, we propose an automata-based method for modeling the problem of communicating with devices operating in configurations which are uncertain, but where certain information is given about the possible *space* of configurations, as well as probabilities for the various configuration choices. Drawing inspiration from feature models for describing configurability, an extensible automata model is described, and two decision problems modeling the question of deciding the most likely configuration (as a set of extensions) for a given communicating device are given. A series of hardness results (the entirely general problems both being NP-complete) and efficient algorithms for relevant restricted cases are then given.

1 Introduction

More and more small interconnected devices, building the internet of things (IoT) [9], collaborate to complete spatial and temporal functionality. Communication between those devices is essential. This is complicated as devices in a neighborhood are heterogeneous and also highly configurable, and it may not necessarily be known for certain what configuration another system is in. However, to function robustly devices should be designed to be able to communicate independent of configuration.

In this paper, we formally capture the problem of heterogeneous devices and uncertain configuration. This is one of the first approaches to combine configurability and uncertainty. We rely on the notions used in software product line engineering [7] and represent configurability with feature models [6], considering a simplified concept of feature models then enhanced by the addition of probabilities, denoting the likelihood with which a feature is included in a configuration. This gives us a probability distribution over the configurations of devices and also about the possible behaviors of device variants.

© Springer Nature Switzerland AG 2018
B. Fischer and T. Uustalu (Eds.): ICTAC 2018, LNCS 11187, pp. 80–98, 2018.
https://doi.org/10.1007/978-3-030-02508-3_5

In particular, we concern ourselves with firstly the question "given the observed behavior, what is the likeliest configuration of this device", additionally considering the symmetrical "what is the likeliest configuration capable of handling the inputs we wish to send". A sketch of the process a device may go through in such circumstances is shown in Fig. 1.

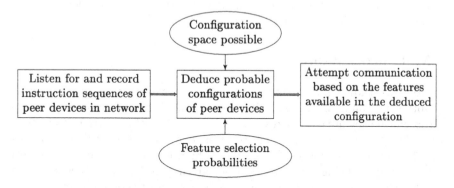

Fig. 1. Schematic view of a scenario where probabilistic deduction of the likely configuration of devices comes into play. The rectangles are the steps taken by the device concerned, first listening to the communications in the network, using that information to deduce the likeliest configurations of the peer devices (using the known information shown in ellipsis), and then using this deduced configuration to decide how to communicate with its peers.

That is, a device in the network may use the communications it observes happening, knowledge of the possible space of configurations (on either a device-by-device basis or globally), and the probabilities of configurations including certain features, to deduce the likeliest configuration of its peers. It may then use this deduced configuration to attempt communication. We model the device behaviors in terms of finite automata accepting languages. As a consequence, if communication fails the device can use the results to inform another attempt at deduction, in a process reminiscent of Angluin learning [1].

We split the problem of deduction into two cases: one where we are concerned with a *single sequence* of inputs or outputs, for example the execution of a sequence of instructions (here represented by a sequence of symbols), and one case where we have a whole family of inputs/outputs, here modeled as a, possibly infinite, language of such symbolic strings (specifically a regular language). In both cases we are primarily concerned with answering *what is, and how likely is, the most likely configuration* which a device can be in to understand/process these instructions. This is computed given a probabilistic model for how likely various features are. In this paper we give a mix of hardness results, showing that the natural way of phrasing these problems are NP-complete in general, and constructive algorithms which are demonstrated to be efficient in some circumstances of practical interest (while also being correct for the general case).

This paper starts in Sect. 2 with a more concrete example to set the scene for the model proposed, followed by basic definitions of languages and automata used in the later modeling in Sect. 3. In Sect. 4 the problem statements and initial hardness results for the general problems are given. The next two sections are primarily concerned with algorithms for restricted variants of the problems, Sect. 5 for the case where a single set of instructions is considered, and Sect. 6 for best-effort takes on the case where a family of instructions is considered. This is all followed by conclusions and future work in Sect. 7.

2   Motivating Example

The problems studied in this paper are well framed by a device in an IoT network attempting to communicate with its peers without certain knowledge of the features which they are equipped with (which may be either software features or hardware such as sensors and actuators). It is, however, assumed that the device knows for certain the space of possible configurations, and needs to analyze the probability of being understood either given observations of events in the network, or based on a family of instructions it wishes to communicate.

We capture the configurability of an IoT-device by a simplified and extended feature model [6]. A feature represents a configuration option, and a feature model defines the constraints between those features, i.e., which features are mandatory, optional and alternative and which features require or exclude each other (which we only model to a limited level here). A configuration of an IoT device is a subset of the features from the feature model satisfying the specified constraints. For each feature, a set of artifacts is specified capturing the semantics of the feature. By selecting the features for a configuration, the artifacts are assembled corresponding to the behavior of the configuration. We extend this view by attaching a probability to each feature in an IoT device's feature model, corresponding to the drop of probability[1] involved in assuming the existence of that feature in a deployed variant of the system (i.e., we model the likelihood that the system has *at least* a given set of features, independent of other constraints, so a system has a 100% chance of having at least the empty set of features). Below is given an informal example.

Example 1. As an example, consider the following simple feature model: we have a device which as base functionality can always accept the instruction "$read_X$" to query the value X. Beyond this it can be configured with the features:

F1. Monitoring drops probability by 10% but permits input sequences of the form "$monitor_X \cdot get_X \cdot get_X \cdots get_X \cdot unmonitor_X$" for any number of "$get_X$".

---

[1] The devices as eventually defined will state the "outright" probability of a feature, e.g. feature X has a 80% chance of being included, but as this probability does not account for how the feature may interact with other features (e.g. X cannot be combined with Y, which is very likely) it is often better for intuition to think about it as including feature X causing a 20% *drop* of probability.

F2. Logging drops probability by 50% but permits input sequences of the form "*log-read$_X$ · read$_X$*", it also cannot be combined with F1.

F3 Logging monitoring drops probability by 30% and requires F2, it permits sequences of both the form "*monitor$_X$ · get$_X$ · get$_X$ · · · · get$_X$ · unmonitor$_X$*" and "*log-mon$_X$ · monitor$_X$ · get$_X$ · get$_X$ · · · get$_X$ · unmonitor$_X$ · log-unmon$_X$*".

The most likely configuration which would be able to handle the instruction sequence "*log-mon· monitor$_X$ · get$_X$ · unmonitor$_X$ · log-unmon*" is a configuration including F2 with probability 50% times F3 with probability 70% (i.e. the drop of 30% from including F3) for a total probability of 35%. It is in this case also the *only* feature selection which will accept this sequence.

The product of the probabilities of all features in a configuration gives us the probability of the configuration in the set of all possible configurations that are compatible with the feature model. Considering the behaviors of the configurations, in this way we also obtain a probability distribution over the possible behaviors of the variants of an IoT device, or if we stick to the language-based characterization of the IoT device behavior, we have a probability distribution of the possible input languages.

The model can also equivalently be viewed as associating a *cost* to features (or even independent probabilities and costs melded into a single weight), making the results presented correspond to answering the question "how *cheaply* can a device variant with this behavior be constructed, given this feature model". These costs could be either monetary, or actually simply resource constraints (memory, storage, processing power, etc.)

Given such a framework many possible problems involving uncertainty and variability in IoT networks can be stated. For a given IoT device d with the output language L_d (which is known with certainty):

- Given that another IoT device b has been observed producing the output w (i.e. this sequence has been observed as output) what is the most likely configuration of b? Using this information, the device d can compute the input language L_b which the configuration gives b, letting it choose instructions only among $L_d \cap L_b$ when attempting to communicate.
- What is the most likely configuration which would let another IoT device b understand the device d, i.e., what is the likeliest configuration giving b an input language L_b such that the output language of d is fully included, having $L_d \subseteq L_b$?
- Looking forward into future work, given a set of IoT devices $\{d_1, \ldots, d_n\}$, how likely is it that a set of IoT devices of a given size understands the device d, i.e., $L_d \subseteq L_{d_i}$ for some i?

To keep matters manageable we do not consider the relation of inputs and outputs here, conflating all questions into configuring a single automaton to accept given strings or sublanguages. Replacing these devices with transducers, modeling a more full behavior, is left as future work.

3   Definitions

3.1   Basic Notation

For a set S we let 2^S denote the powerset of S. For a function f we let $\mathrm{dom}(f)$ denote its domain and $\mathrm{range}(f)$ its range. An alphabet is a finite set of symbols, usually denoted Σ, as usual we denote by Σ^* the set of all strings over Σ. The empty string is denoted ε.

3.2   Automata Definitions

The automata here considered will all be accept languages which are ultimately regular, though additional meaning and expressiveness will be achieved beyond simple finite automata. Let us, however start by recalling the definition of finite automata.

Definition 1. *A* finite automaton *(FA) A is a tuple $(Q, \Sigma, q_0, \delta, F)$ where (i) Q is the finite set of* states; *(ii) Σ is the* input alphabet; *(iii) $q_0 \in Q$ is the* initial state; *(iv) $\delta \subseteq Q \times \Sigma \times Q$ is the* transition relation; *and; (v) $F \subseteq Q$ is the set of* final states.

We distinguish the following properties: A is deterministic *(a DFA) if there exists at most one $(q, \alpha, q') \in \delta$ for each q and α. It is otherwise* non-deterministic *(an NFA). A is the (unique up to relabeling)* minimal DFA *if there exists no DFA B which accepts the same language but has fewer states.*

Definition 2. *For an FA $A = (Q, \Sigma, q_0, \delta, F)$ we write $q \xrightarrow{\alpha}_A q'$ if $q, q' \in Q$, $\alpha \in \Sigma$ and $(q, \alpha, q') \in \delta$. We may elide the A subscript if obvious from context, and if both $q \xrightarrow{\alpha} q'$ and $q' \xrightarrow{\beta} q''$ for $q'' \in Q$ and $\beta \in \Sigma$ we may write either $q \xrightarrow{\alpha} q' \xrightarrow{\beta} q''$, or, when the intervening state is not of interest, even $q \xrightarrow{\alpha\beta} q''$. When $q \xrightarrow{w} q'$ we say that q' is reachable from q on the string $w \in \Sigma^*$.*

The language accepted by *A, denoted $\mathcal{L}(A)$, is the set $\{w \in \Sigma^* \mid q_0 \xrightarrow{w}_A q_f$ for $q_f \in F\}$. The* size *of A is defined as $|\delta|$.*

With the usual finite automata out of the way we enter into the realm of extensible automata, which act as a template from which a (possibly exponentially large) family of automata can be constructed.

Definition 3. *An* extensible automaton *A is a tuple $A = (B, \Delta, wt)$ where*
(i) $B = (Q, \Sigma, q_0, \delta, F)$ is a DFA, the base automaton;
(ii) $\Delta \subseteq 2^{Q \times \Sigma \times Q}$ are the extension transition sets; *and; (iii) wt is the* weight *function, which as domain has 2^Δ and has an arbitrary totally ordered (by $\leq$) range. It is assumed that it can be evaluated in constant time (e.g., it is represented by a precomputed table).*

Here the common case is that the weight function will model the *probabilities* of the extensions, but it is left generic on the level of definitions. The extensible automata do not have language semantics in and of themselves, rather they in turn specify finite automata.

Definition 4. *For an extensible automaton $A = (B, \Delta, wt)$, taking the base automaton $B = (Q, \Sigma, q_0, \delta, F)$, define for each $\{\delta_1, \cdots, \delta_n\} \subseteq \Delta$ the finite automaton*

$$A_{+\{\delta_1,\ldots,\delta_n\}} = (Q, \Sigma, q_0, \delta \cup \delta_1 \cup \cdots \cup \delta_n, F).$$

Any such $A_{+\Delta'}$ is called a realization *of A. The weight of the realization $\Delta' \subseteq \Delta$ is $wt(\Delta')$. If $A_{+\Delta'}$ is deterministic the realization is called* proper.
   The size of A is defined as $|B| + \sum_{\delta \in \Delta} |\delta|$.

We call the additional sets of transitions *extensions*. An extension in our model captures the realization of a feature and, hence, its behavior. In this sense, an extension is similar to a feature module in feature-oriented programming (FOP) [2]. The separation of features and their associated extensions is a rather important distinction, as they, to make the algorithms straightforward and efficient, are necessarily a simplification of full feature models by requiring a one-to-one relationship between features and extensions.

Remark 1. There are three classes of weight functions which are of particular interest: constant, propositional formulas, and probabilistic.
   A *constant weight function,* where range(wt) = $\{c\}$ for some c. This in effect means that all realizations are equivalent, and thus the weight function plays no real part in decision procedures for this automaton.
   Propositional formulas is the case where range(wt) = $\{$true, false$\}$, and wt is represented by a propositional logic formula taking the set of extensions as variables (i.e. wt is in fact an arbitrary Boolean function over $\{$true, false$\}^\Delta$), permits capturing any set of constraints in a feature model on the compatibility of features and their associated extensions. Taking this view only the assignments which evaluate to *true* are permissible. However, this choice of cost function is in some cases inflexible (where there are quantitative costs) and dangerous (in that many questions are immediately made NP-hard due to the question of the satisfiability of the function). As such we in this paper mostly loosen the perspective a bit.
   Probabilistic weight functions are represented by a function $P : \Delta \to [0 \ldots 1]$, with $wt(\Delta') = \prod_{\delta \in \Delta'} P(\delta)$. That is, each extension (and thus its associated feature) is assigned a probability by P, and an overall realization is the compound probability of the extensions included. This, serving as a middle ground between the complexities of the propositional formulas and the freedom of no weights in the constant case, serves as the primary case for this paper.

Let us now show the simple feature model of Example 1 in the form of an extensible automaton (where each feature corresponds to one extension).

Example 2. We can construct an extensible automaton which corresponds to the feature model in Example 1 by taking $A = (B, \Delta, wt)$ where

- $B = (Q, \Sigma, q_0, \delta, F)$ where $Q = \{q_0, q_f, q_1, q_2, q_3, q_{3,1}, q_{3,2}, q_{3,3}\}$, $\Sigma = \{read_X, log\text{-}mon_X, monitor_X, get_X, unmonitor_X, log\text{-}unmon_X\}$, $F = \{q_f\}$, and, finally, $\delta = \{(q_0, read_X, q_f)\}$.

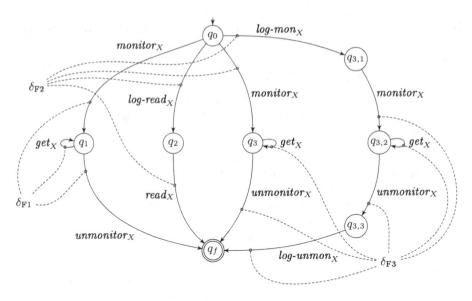

Fig. 2. The extensible automaton constructed in Example 2 to model the feature model given in Example 1. We elide the edge from q_0 to q_f which is in the base automaton, instead illustrating all the transitions which can be added by the extensions δ_{F1}, δ_{F2} and δ_{F3} (dashed edges indicated added transitions). Note in particular how δ_{F2} adds edges which enable sequences associated with the feature F3, making F3 "require" F2.

- $\Delta = \{\delta_{F1}, \delta_{F2}, \delta_{F3}\}$, where

$$\delta_{F1} = \{(q_0, monitor_X, q_1), (q_1, get_X, q_1), (q_1, unmonitor_X, q_f)\},$$
$$\delta_{F2} = \{(q_0, log\text{-}read_X, q_2), (q_2, read_X, q_f), (q_0, monitor_X, q_3),$$
$$(q_0, log\text{-}mon_X, q_{3,1})\}, \text{ and,}$$
$$\delta_{F3} = \{(q_3, get_X, q_3), (q_3, unmonitor_X, q_f), (q_{3,1}, monitor_X, q_{3,2}),$$
$$(q_{3,2}, get_X, q_{3,2}), (q_{3,3}, unmonitor_x, q_{3,3}, (q_{3,3}, log\text{-}mon_X, q_f)\}.$$

- $wt(S) = \prod_{\delta \in S} wt'(\delta)$, where $wt'(\delta_{F1}) = 0.9$, $wt'(\delta_{F2}) = 0.5$, and $wt'(\delta_{F3}) = 0.7$.

See Fig. 2 for an illustration of what this extensible automaton looks like. In particular, an extensible automaton has no special means of making a transition require another, but the feature model described in Example 1 has F3 require F2, the corresponding extensions instead has δ_{F2} add some of the transitions required by δ_{F3}, such that adding the latter without the former achieves nothing (meaning that the most probable realization, corresponding to the most probable configuration, will never include F3 if F2 is not included). That is, the requirement is modeled by making one extension pointless without including another. Also notice that δ_{F1} and δ_{F2} cannot both be added to a proper realization, as they both add a transition on $monitor_X$ from q_0.

Extensions "forbid" each other can be done in a more direct way as well (as will be used in, e.g., Lemma 2), but much like in this example, both forbidding and requiring can often be handled by straightforward modeling on the automaton.

To keep things general we consider one of the nice properties of probabilistic (and constant) weight functions specifically.

Definition 5. *A weight function wt, with domain 2^Δ, as in Definition 3 is monotonic, if and only if, for all $\Delta_1, \Delta_2 \subseteq \Delta$, we have $(\Delta_1 \subseteq \Delta_2) \Rightarrow (wt(\Delta_1) \geq wt(\Delta_2))$.*

Obviously this holds for both probabilistic and constant weight functions. Note that the reverse of the condition does not hold, as $\subseteq$ forms a partial order where $\leq$ is required to be total.

4 Problem Statements and Basic Hardness

As outlined in the introduction the primary purpose of the paper is to demonstrate the possibility of judging the probability that an agent (or device) of some form is configured such that it understands the (potentially infinite) set of instructions one wishes to issue to it. We phrase this as a decision problem.

Definition 6. *An instance of the cost-constrained superset realization (CCSR) problem is a tuple $(L, (A, \Delta, wt), c)$ where*

- *L is a language (assumed to be given as a DFA),*
- *(A, Δ, wt) is an extensible automaton,*
- *$c \in range(wt)$, such that*

there exists a proper realization $A_{+\Delta'}$ of A with $L \subseteq \mathcal{L}(A_{+\Delta'})$ and a weight greater than or equal to c.

This decision problem will be important for demonstrating hardness, when we get to algorithms solving some variants of it they will in fact be constructive. In many cases the language being checked will be very simple, for example when we have a single sequence of instructions we are wishing to send.

Definition 7. *The subproblem of CCSR where the language L is a singleton (i.e. consists of a single string) is called the cost-constrained membership realization (CCMR).*

Leaving these decision problems in their raw form does, however, make them problems quite hard, illustrating the need for additional restrictions and simplifications.

Lemma 1. *The CCRS and CCMR problems are NP-complete even for a constant wt.*

Fig. 3. The base automaton constructed in the reduction in the proof of Lemma 1, with a state for each variable and clause, plus an additional final state, but no transitions.

Proof. This can be established by a reduction from the, known to be NP-complete [5], problem of deciding whether a propositional logic formula on conjunctive normal form (cnf) is satisfiable.

Represent such a formula f over the variables $x_1, \ldots, x_n$ as a set of sets of literals. That is, letting $f = \{c_1, \ldots, c_n\}$, f represents the formula $\bigwedge_{i=1}^{n} \bigvee_{l \in c_i} l$. For example $(x \vee y \vee \neg z) \wedge (\neg x \vee z)$ is $\{\{x, y, \neg z\}, \{\neg x, z\}\}$. W.l.o.g. we assume that each variable occurs at least once and at most three times in f.

Then construct the extensible automaton $A = (B, \Delta, wt)$ as follows.

- Let $wt(\Delta') = 0$ for all $\Delta' \subseteq \Delta$.
- Let $B = (\{x_1, \ldots, x_n, c_1, \ldots, c_m, q_f\}, \{a\}, x_1, \emptyset, \{q_f\})$. That is, the base automaton has the form indicated in Fig. 3. Let $s(q)$ be the next state in the sequence $x_1, \ldots, x_n, c_1, \ldots, c_m, q_f$ (e.g. $s(c_m) = q_f$, $s(x_i) = x_{i+1}$ for $i < n$, but $s(x_n) = c_1$)
- Let Δ consist of precisely the following sets: for every literal l, letting x be the variable in l, and every $C \subseteq \{c \in \{c_1, \ldots, c_m\} \mid l \in c\}$ there is a set $\delta_{l,C}$ in Δ, defined by $\delta_{l,C} = \{(x, a, s(x))\} \cup \{(c, a, s(c)) \mid c \in C\}$.
  For example, if the literal $\neg x_2$ occurs in c_1 and the literal x_n occurs in c_3, then $B_{+\{\delta_{\neg x_2,\{c_1\}}, \delta_{x_n,\{c_3\}}\}}$ would exist and be of the form shown in Fig. 4. Note that for every extension there exist an extension with any subset of the edges outgoing from c_i-labeled states, e.g. the extension $\delta_{\neg x_2, \emptyset}$ also exists in the above example.

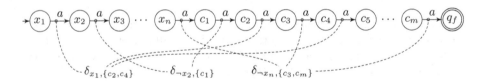

Fig. 4. Taking the extensible automaton constructed in the reduction in the proof of Lemma 1 when applied to a formula where the literal x_1 exists in clause 2 and 4, the literal $\neg x_2$ exists in clause 1, and the literal $\neg x_n$ exists in clause three and n, this sketches the realization $B_{+\{\delta_{x_1,\{c_2,c_4\}}, \delta_{\neg x_2,\{c_1\}}, \delta_{\neg x_n,\{c_3,c_m\}}\}}$. The dashed edges clarify which transitions are added by which extension.

The reduction is polynomial as there are $n + m + 1$ states and at most $16n$ extensions (each variable and its negation, and the eight options for including an occurrence of that literal or not).

We now argue that $(a^{n+m}, (B, \Delta, wt), 0)$ is an instance of CCMR (and thus CCSR) if and only if f is satisfiable. Intuitively, a realization which can accept a^{n+m} will in effect set each variable either true or false by choices of extensions needed in reading the a^n prefix, and the following a^m can only be matched if the truth assignment satisfies every clause. That $B_{+\Delta'}$ will match a^{n+m} if and only if one can select $\Delta_{l_1,C_1}, \ldots, \Delta_{l_n,C_n}$ such that each l_i is a literal on the variable x_i, and $C_1, \ldots, C_n$ are disjoint sets with the union equaling $\{c_1, \ldots, c_m\}$. No variable can repeat in the selection as it would add multiple a-labeled outgoing edges from the corresponding state in B, making the assignment improper.

The problem is *in* NP as a realization can be non-deterministically chosen and then verified in polynomial time.   □

In the next section we consider a restriction which will, in a reasonably natural way, avoid the issue highlighted by this hardness result.

5   Solving Restricted CCMR for Monotonic Weights

The nature of the reduction which is exploited to demonstrate hardness in Lemma 1 is of a somewhat artificial flavor as it involves an unbounded number of extension combinations being able to accept a certain common prefix of a string. That is, the first n symbols are possible to read in 2^n different ways, corresponding to setting the values of variables. In reality extensions would tend to either involve different strings, or they would be optional for most strings. As such we define this measure, and consider what happens to the CCSR and CCMR problems when it is bounded.

First a small supporting definition, which will be used when dealing with minimal realizations which can accept a given string.

Definition 8. *For a set of finite sets S let $\downarrow S \subseteq S$ denote the set of minimal incomparable sets of S, that is $s \in \downarrow S$ if and only if $s \in S$ but no strict subset of s exists in S.*

Note that, obviously and quite importantly, this makes all sets in $\downarrow S$ incomparable (i.e. for $s, t \in \downarrow S$ either $s = t$ or $s \not\subseteq t$ and $t \not\subseteq s$). We start with some trivial lemmas which clarify the algorithm for CCMR which follows.

Lemma 2. $\downarrow \{S \cup X \mid S \in \downarrow T\} = \downarrow \{S \cup X \mid S \in T\}$, *for all T and X.*

Proof. Trivially true as the subset relation is unchanged by adding elements on both sides, e.g. $(S \subseteq S') \Leftrightarrow ((S \cup X) \subseteq (S' \cup X))$ for all S, S' and X.   □

The reason for introducing this idea of the set of minimal incomparable sets is that it compresses the realizations we need to consider in a natural way.

Lemma 3. *Let L be any language and $A = (B, \Delta, wt)$ any extensible automaton with wt monotonic. Then for all $\Delta_1, \ldots, \Delta_n \subseteq \Delta$ such that*

- $L \subseteq \mathcal{L}(B_{+\Delta_i})$ *for all i, and,*
- *there exists at least one $\Delta' \in \{\Delta_1, \ldots, \Delta_n\}$ such that $B_{+\Delta'}$ is proper,*

there exists at least one $\Delta'' \in \downarrow \{\Delta_1, \ldots, \Delta_n\}$ such that; (i) $L \subseteq \mathcal{L}(B_{+\Delta''})$; (ii) $wt(\Delta'') \geq wt(\Delta')$; (iii) $B_{+\Delta''}$ is proper.

Proof. Condition (i) holds as $\downarrow S$ is a subset of S. Further, since either Δ' itself or a subset of it must exist in $\downarrow\{\Delta_1, \ldots, \Delta_n\}$ we have (ii) since wt is monotonic, and (iii) since any subset of a set of extensions giving a proper realization will give a proper realization. $\qquad\square$

Remark 2. Obviously $\downarrow S$ of a set S can be constructed in time $\mathcal{O}(n^2)$, where $n = \sum_{s \in S} |s|$ by simply comparing all sets.

With these definitions and lemmas in hand we are ready to define the restriction which will make clear the impact the number of incomparable realizations has on the difficulty of deciding the CCMR problem.

Definition 9. *The extension confusion depth of an extensible automaton $A = ((Q, \Sigma, q_0, \delta, F), \Delta, wt)$ is the smallest $k \in \mathbb{N}$ such that for all $\alpha_1, \ldots, \alpha_n \in \Sigma$ (for $n \in \mathbb{N}$) and $q \in Q$, we have $|\downarrow\{\Delta' \subseteq \Delta \mid q_0 \xrightarrow{\alpha_1}_{A+\Delta'} \cdots \xrightarrow{\alpha_n}_{A+\Delta'} q\}| \leq k$.*

Remark 3. Sperner's theorem [8] dictates that the extension confusion depth of extensible automata is bounded by $\binom{|\Delta|}{\lfloor|\Delta|/2\rfloor}$ (and this bound is tight). The assumption this section operates under, however, is that the confusion depth will in fact be bounded by some polynomial in $|\Delta|$.

Example 3. The automaton in Example 2 has extension confusion depth 2, as reaching q_f on the string $monitor_X \cdot get_X \cdot unmonitor_X$ can be done with either the realization $\{\delta_{F1}, \delta_{F2}\}$ or the realization $\{\delta_{F3}\}$, but no subset of either.

Further note that the construction in the proof of Lemma 1 will produce an extensible automaton with confusion depth at least 2^n (where n is the number of variables, as in the construction), as long as each variable occurs both negated and non-negated in the formula. To see this, pick the state c_1 and the string a^n, this string reaches the state c_1 by picking any realization consisting of n extensions setting each of the variables, for 2^n incomparable options.

With these definitions in hand Algorithm 1 solves CCMR for monotonic weight functions, and does so efficiently if the confusion depth is bounded.

Next to demonstrate the algorithm correct.

Theorem 1. *Algorithm 1 decides CCMR, for monotonic weight functions, in time $\mathcal{O}(nmk^2)$, where m and k is the size and extension confusion depth of the extensible automaton, and n the length of the input string.*

Proof. First we demonstrate, by induction on the iteration over the input string happening in step 3, the following invariant: Whenever step 3.1 is reached with $\alpha_1 \cdots \alpha_k$ already processed (for $0 \leq k \leq n$) we have $q_0 \xrightarrow{\alpha_1 \cdots \alpha_k}_{A+\Delta'} q$ if and only if $q \in \operatorname{dom}(T)$ and Δ' is a (not necessarily strict) superset of some set in $T(q)$. That is, $T(q)$ is complete list of minimal incomparable realizations which reaches q on the prefix so far processed.

This is obviously true in the base case, $T(q_0) = \emptyset$, as q_0 is reachable on the empty string with no extensions, the next T is then built by in step 3.1A simply

---

Algorithm 1. Solve-Monotonic-CCMR

Input: (i) a string $\alpha_1 \cdots \alpha_n$; (ii) an extensible automaton $A = (B, \Delta, wt)$ with extension confusion depth k and a monotonic weight function wt, letting $B = (Q, \Sigma, q_0, \delta, F)$; and; (iii) a minimum weight c.

Perform steps:

1. Initialize tables $T, T' : Q \to 2^{2^{\Delta}}$ to be undefined everywhere.
2. Set $T(q_0) := \emptyset$.
3. For each symbol α in $\alpha_1, \ldots, \alpha_n$, in order:
   3.1 For each $q \in \text{dom}(T)$:
      3.1A If $q \xrightarrow{\alpha}_B q'$ set $T'(q') := T(q)$.
      3.1B Otherwise, iteratively, for each $\delta' \in \Delta$ with $q \xrightarrow{\alpha}_{A+\{\delta'\}} q'$ for some $q' \in Q$, set

$$T'(q') := \begin{cases} \downarrow(T'(q') \cup \{\Delta' \cup \{\delta'\} \mid \Delta' \in T(q)) & \text{if } T'(q') \text{ is defined,} \\ \downarrow(\{\Delta' \cup \{\delta'\} \mid \Delta' \in T(q)) & \text{otherwise.} \end{cases}$$

   3.2 Set $T := T'$ and set T' to be undefined everywhere.
4. For each $q_f \in F$ and each $\Delta' \in T(q_f)$:
   4.1 check if $A_{+\Delta'}$ is a proper realization,
   4.2 if $wt(\Delta') \geq c$, answer "true".
5. Otherwise answer "false".

Algorithm 2. Construct-Monotonic-CCMR

Modifying Algorithm 1 to output the first matching (or, if desired, the greatest) realization in step 4(b) yields a constructive algorithm for proper high(est)-weight (e.g. most probable) realization, still running in $\mathcal{O}(nmk^2)$.

---

pushing the realizations that work forward to the next state if it can be reached in the base automaton, and (ignoring the use of $\downarrow$ at first) in step 3.1B adding the extensions needed to reach a next state to the set already gathered in the previous step (this may happen multiple times as different extensions may reach the state at the same iteration). Using $\downarrow$ each time in step 3(a)ii. does not make a difference from applying it once when retrieving the realizations by Lemma 2 (and is important to keep the size of the sets in T small).

By the induction all final states are reachable in some realization of A on $\alpha_1 \cdots \alpha_n$ in $F \cap \text{dom}(T)$ when step 4 is reached. We then need to check if any of those realizations are proper and have a weight greater than c, but by Lemma 3, it is then sufficient to check the minimal incomparable set of realizations which T, by induction, contains.

The complexity $\mathcal{O}(nmk^2)$ is incurred in step 3, for all q and at every step $|T(q)| \leq k$ (by definition, as it corresponds precisely to the confusion depth of A). That is, for each string symbol (n times), worst-case every transition in A (m times), we, worst-case, merge two table cells (each of size at most k) in T' and apply $\downarrow$ (which can be done in $\mathcal{O}(k^2)$ as noted in Remark 2). □

Algorithm 1 is a decision procedure, but can trivially be made constructive by the minor modification in Algorithm 2. Note that the above procedure does *not* work for weight functions which are not monotonic, as the $\downarrow$ applications may then be removing the highest-weight option. For example, for full propositional formulas (see Remark 1), one will often have to track every single possible realization, which may be exponential even with bounded confusion depth.

However, this restriction is not sufficient to make CCSR tractable, which can be demonstrated by a slightly different reduction.

Theorem 2. *CCSR is NP-complete even for extensible automata with extension confusion depth 1 and a constant wt.*

Proof. As in Lemma 1 we demonstrate this by a reduction from the satisfiability problem for a propositional logic formula on cnf. Without loss of generality we assume that each clause contains precisely three literals, and represent the formula by

$$f = (l_{1,1} \vee l_{1,2} \vee l_{1,3}) \wedge \cdots \wedge (l_{m,1} \vee l_{m,2} \vee l_{m,3})$$

where each $l_{i,j}$ is a literal over a variable from $\{x_1, \ldots, x_n\}$.

Then construct the extensible automaton $A = (B, \Delta, wt)$ as follows.

– Let $B = (Q, \{a, x_1, \ldots, x_n, c_1, \ldots, c_m\}, q_0, \emptyset, \{q_f\})$ where

$$Q = \{q_0, q_f, q_{1,1}, q_{1,2}, q_{1,3} \cdots, q_{m,1}, q_{m,2}, q_{m,3}\},$$

that is, the base automaton contains an initial and final state, and then one state for each literal of the formula.
– Let $\Delta = \{\delta_{x_1}, \delta_{\neg x_1}, \ldots, \delta_{x_n}, \delta_{\neg x_n}, \delta_{1,1}, \ldots, \delta_{m,3}\}$ where
   • $\delta_{x_i} = \{(q_0, x_i, q_f)\} \cup \{(q_{i,j}, a, q_{i,j}) \mid \text{literal } l_{i,j} \text{ equals } \neg x_i \text{ in } f\}$ for each variable x_i,
   • $\delta_{\neg x_i} = \{(q_0, x_i, q_f)\} \cup \{(q_{i,j}, a, q_{i,j}) \mid \text{literal } l_{i,j} \text{ equals } x_i \text{ in } f\}$ for each variable x_i, and
   • $\delta_{i,j} = \{(q_{i,j}, a, q_{i,j}), (q_0, c_i, q_f)\}$ for all $1 \leq i \leq m$ and $1 \leq j \leq 3$.
– Let $wt(\Delta') = 0$ for all $\Delta' \subseteq \Delta$.

Then $((\{x_1, x_2, \ldots, x_n, c_1, \ldots, c_m\}, A, wt), 0)$ is an instance of CCSR if and only if f is satisfiable. To see this, first note that the language L is the one accepted by the finite automaton shown in Fig. 5(a), while a realization of the extensible automaton A can be seen in Fig. 5(b). The example realization in the figure corresponds to a formula where $l_{1,2} = x_1$, $l_{4,2} = x_1$, and $l_{4,3} = \neg x_3$. The realization shown picks extensions $\delta_{\neg x_1}$, δ_{x_3}, $\delta_{1,3}$ and $\delta_{4,3}$. Referring to this picture it is fairly easy to see how the reduction works: for a realization to match all strings matched by the finite automaton in Fig. 5(a) either δ_{x_i} or $\delta_{\neg x_i}$ must be used for each x_i (to add the x_1 through x_n transitions), but choosing them adds an a-labeled self-loop to all states corresponding to literals which are made unsatisfiable by the indicated truth assignment. Further a transition must be added for each c_j by picking any one of $\delta_{j,1}$, $\delta_{j,2}$ or $\delta_{j,3}$, but this can only be done if all three are not rendered unsatisfiable by the choices of truth

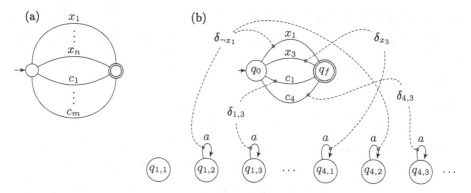

Fig. 5. (a). The deterministic finite automaton constructed as the L part of a CCSR instance constructed in the reduction in the proof of Theorem 2. **(b).** A realization of the extensible automaton A as constructed by the proof of Lemma 2. Specifically it shows the realization $A_{+\{\delta_{\neg x_1}, \delta_{x_3}, \delta_{1,3}, \delta_{4,3}\}}$ when the literal x_1 is the second literal of both the first and fourth clause, and $\neg x_3$ is the first literal of the fourth clause (the dashed lines indicate which extension adds which transitions). In the context of the reduction the realization corresponds to picking x_1 to be false, x_3 to be true, and satisfying clause c_1 and c_4 by literal $l_{1,3}$ and $l_{4,3}$, respectively.

assignments. In this way the extension choices perfectly mirror the satisfiability of the formula.

Finally, A has extension confusion depth 3 (the string c_j, for any $1 \le j \le m$, is matched by realizations containing one of $\delta_{j,1}$, $\delta_{j,2}$ and $\delta_{j,3}$). This can be reduced to 1 by constructing $\tilde{A}$ by splitting q_f into $2n + 3m$ final states, a distinct one used by each transition going to q_f in A.

The problem being *in* NP again follows from it being possible to simply non-deterministically choosing and verifying a realization.   □

In the next section we consider additional restrictions under which this problem is rendered tractable.

6 Solving Restricted CCSR for Monotonic Weights

The full superset problem appears to be very difficult, but we offer two straightforward restrictions where it is tractable. As a general scaffolding, first we consider Algorithm 3, which solves the problem in nondeterministic polynomial time. Obviously we can as before make this algorithm constructive by outputting Δ'.

Remark 4. Note that step 3.1B1 should, in practice, be performed in tandem with checking the various conditions placed on the extension chosen (i.e. find the transitions fulfilling the check in step 3.1B2 exist, and work from there). These details are to some extent a matter of selection of data structures etc., and we simply assume that the candidates can be enumerated in linear time.

Algorithm 3. Solve-Restricted-CCSR

Input: (i) a minimal DFA $D = (Q, \Sigma, q_0, \delta, F)$ (representing the language L); (ii) an extensible automaton $A = (B, \Delta, wt)$ with extension confusion depth k and a monotonic weight function wt, letting $B = (Q', \Sigma, q'_0, \delta', F')$; and; (iii) a minimum weight c.

Perform steps:
1. Initialize the sets $W := \{(q_0, q'_0)\}$ and $S := \emptyset$.
2. Initialize $\Delta' := \emptyset$.
3. For each $(q, q') \in W$:
   3.1 For each $\alpha \in \Sigma$ such that $(q, \alpha, p) \in \delta$ for some $p \in Q$:
       3.1A If $(q', \alpha, p') \in \delta' \cup \bigcup_{\delta'' \in \Delta'} \delta''$ for some p':
           3.1A1 If $p \in F$ but $p' \notin F'$ halt answering "no".
           3.1A2 Otherwise set $W := W \cup \{(p, p')\}$ and continue in step 3.1.
       3.1B Otherwise:
           3.1B1 Nondeterministically choose a $\delta'' \in \Delta \setminus \Delta'$ subject to the following checks (if no choice fulfilling all checks exists, halt answering "no").
           3.1B2 Check that $(q', \alpha, p') \in \delta''$ for some $p' \in Q'$.
           3.1B3 Check that if $p \in F$ then $p' \in F'$.
           3.1B4 Check that $A_{+\Delta' \cup \{\delta''\}}$ is a proper realization.
           3.1B5 Set $W := W \cup \{(p, p')\}$ and $\Delta' := \Delta' \cup \{\delta''\}$, and continue in step 3.1.
   3.2 Set $S := S \cup \{(q, q')\}$ and $W := W \setminus S$.
4 If $wt(\Delta') \geq c$ answer "yes", otherwise answer "no".

The way the algorithm works is very straightforward, with most of the work hidden in the nondeterministic choice of extension to add, but as an aid to understanding we elucidate the way it works in the following lemma.

Lemma 4. *Algorithm 3 decides the CCSR problem, in the cases where the weight function is monotonic, in nondeterministic polynomial time.*

Proof. (Sketch) The procedure operates by successively building up a realization, the set Δ', by relating the states of D to states in $A_{+\Delta}$. The realization is the smallest consistent with the state realization being attempted (which by monotonicity is to be preferred). The set W contains all pairs of states still to be shown to correspond between D and the current candidate realization, that is, being in W means the algorithm has established that they are reachable on some common string, but their outgoing transitions have not yet been checked (initially W equals $\{(q_0, q'_0)\}$, i.e. the initial states must correspond as they are reachable on the empty string). Step 3 picks one of these pairs from W and simulates one further step: for each alphabet symbol finding what state D reaches, and finding either what state the current candidate realization $A_{+\Delta'}$ goes to on the same symbol, or finds a new extension which makes it go to some state (or rejects if none can be found). As part of this it must also be checked that the realization is kept proper and that any final state in D corresponds to a final state in $A_{+\Delta'}$, or the latter would necessarily fail to accept some string in $\mathcal{L}(D)$. Note that it is not required that the reverse holds, as $A_{+\Delta'}$ is free to accept a *superset* of the strings in $\mathcal{L}(D)$ in a solution to CCSR. The pairs already checked are recorded in S, ensuring the loop runs only a polynomial number of steps.

The loop in step 3 only halts when W is empty, which will only happen if all states in D have been successfully assigned to state in the realized $A_{+\Delta'}$. If the realization has sufficient weight it is the solution and we accept.   □

The algorithm uses nondeterminism in the key step of picking an extension to add, making on the order of $|\Delta|$ such choices. The nondeterminism can be eliminated, as usual, by a deterministic search procedure, but in general this adds a factor $\mathcal{O}(2^{|\Delta|})$ to the running time (i.e. whenever a nondeterministic choice would be made all options are attempted, checking if some alternative answers "yes"). The exponential is base two as an extension gets considered for addition *at most once* on any computation path: *some* extension will be chosen, adding a transition which precludes all the other candidates in a proper realization.

This leads to the most straightforward restriction to place on a CCSR problem to make it tractable: limiting the number of instances of nondeterminism reachable in Algorithm 3. Let us recall some definitions to make this precise.

Definition 10. *For FA $A = (Q, \Sigma, q_0, \delta, F)$ and $B = (Q', \Sigma, q_0', \delta', F')$ the product automaton, denoted $A \times B$, equals $(Q \times Q', (q_0, q_0'), \{((q, q'), \alpha, (p, p')) \mid (q, \alpha, p) \in \delta, (q', \alpha, p') \in \delta'\}, \{(f, f') \mid f \in F, f' \in F'\})$.*

For a finite automaton A let f-prune(A) denote the automaton resulting when removing all states (and associated transitions) from A which cannot be reached from the initial state. Similarly, let b-prune(A) denote the automaton resulting when removing all states q from which no final state is reachable.

The degree of nondeterminism *of a finite automaton $A = (Q, \Sigma, q_0, \delta, F)$ is the sum $\sum_{q \in Q, \alpha \in \Sigma} \max(0, |\{q' \mid (q, \alpha, q') \in \delta\}| - 1)$. That is, informally, the total number of transitions making A nondeterministic.*

This is sufficient to phrase the complexity of applying Algorithm 3 using deterministic search in a more refined way.

Lemma 5. *For a CCSR instance $(L, A = (B, \Delta, wt), c)$, letting D be the minimal DFA accepting L, evaluating Algorithm 3 using deterministic search runs in time $\mathcal{O}(nml2^{\min(s,|\Delta|)})$ where n is the number of states in B, m the number of states in D, l the size of the input alphabet, and s is the degree of nondeterminism of f-prune($D \times A_{+\Delta}$).*

Proof. As a first observation, when e.g. $s = 0$, there is only ever a single choice in step 3.1B1 (as k choices imply a degree of nondeterminism of $k - 1$ in the indicated product automaton), and thus no searching happens. In this case the loop at step 3 will run at most nml times, and using appropriate data structures (e.g. bit vectors for W and S) the inner steps can be performed in constant time, giving an overall complexity of $\mathcal{O}(nml)$.

The $2^{\min(s,|\Delta|)}$ factor is the actual search procedure, in that both Δ and s bound the number of choices that can be made in step 3.1B1, and as each

---

Algorithm 4. Fast-Solve-Restricted-CCSR

Taking the same inputs as Algorithm 3, perform the following precomputation step:

0. Let $B = (Q \times Q') \setminus Q''$ where Q'' are the states of $b\text{-}prune(D \times A_{+\Delta})$.

That is, B consists of the states in the product automaton from which no final state is reachable. Then, add another check before updating W in step 3.1A2 and 3.1B5:

– Check that $(p, p') \notin B$ (if (p, p') is in B, halt answering "no").

I.e., when a state pair from B would be added to W in the algorithm (that is, the state pair are determined to be related by the current realization) realization, we now immediately reject (in the deterministic search case giving up on that path and realization, backtracking to try other options).

---

extension and (nondeterministic) transition is only considered for inclusion once along any search path (if they are not chosen when considered this means some other extension is chosen which precludes the original extensions inclusion in a proper realization). Note that $f\text{-}prune(D \times A_{+\Delta})$ contains precisely the states which will be explored as state pairs in W, as it will explore nothing that cannot be reached from (q_0, q_0') in the product. $\square$

Remark 5. Note that, in particular, if $A_{+\Delta}$ is deterministic the degree of nondeterminism in the product automaton is zero, making the decision procedure run in time $\mathcal{O}(nml)$.

The algorithm can be modified slightly, as shown in Algorithm 4, to improve the running times in typical cases, where relatively few of the state pairs possible are actually useful. Obviously these changes to Algorithm 3 can only lessen the amount of work done, in that the state pairs in B are never explored, and the rejection of the computation path may prevent further exploration of unrelated state pairs. It remains to argue that these shortcuts actually do not change the *outcome* of the algorithm.

Lemma 6. *Algorithm 3 and 4 are equivalent (answer the same on all inputs).*

Proof. Since D is a *minimal* DFA every state in D can reach some final state (i.e. $b\text{-}prune(D) = D$). As such, whenever Algorithm 3 adds a state pair (q, q') to W there exists some string w such that $q \xrightarrow{w}_D f$ for some final state f in D. However, if $(q, q') \in B$ we also know, by the construction of B in Algorithm 4, that there is no state (f, f'), where both f and f' are final, reachable from (q, q'). This means that as the algorithm exhaustively, from this point, explores the state pairs in W it will on every possible computation path either:

– Explore a state pair (f, p) reached when reading w from (q, q'), however, this means that f is final but p is not, so either step 3.1A1 or 3.1B3 (depending on whether the most recent step was taken by adding an extension or not) will then halt answering "no".

– Explore a transition in D for some prefix of w but then fail to find a corresponding transition in $A_{+\Delta}$, again having the computation halt answering "no" as there is no choice possible in step 3.1B1.

As all computation paths following from adding $(q, q') \in B$ to W in Algorithm 3 eventually answer "no" Algorithm 4 is equivalent, as the only change is having it answer "no" when such a state pair would be added.   □

This improvement can then be used to restate Lemma 5 with a bound which may improve many practical.

Theorem 3. *For a CCSR instance $(L, A = (B, \Delta, wt), c)$, letting D be the minimal DFA accepting L, evaluating Algorithm 4 using deterministic search runs in time $\mathcal{O}(nml2^{\min(s,|\Delta|)})$ where n is the number of states in B, m the number of states in D, l the size of the input alphabet, and s is the degree of nondeterminism of $b\text{-}prune(f\text{-}prune(D \times A_{+\Delta}))$.*

Proof. A trivial consequence of Lemma 5 with the additional observation that Algorithm 4 does not explore states removed by the application of *b-prune*, and thus any nondeterminism incurred in those states can be disregarded.   □

7   Conclusions and Future Work

Conclusions. This paper makes a first attempt to formalize the idea of uncertain configurations of software systems in an automata-theoretic framework. The main contributions are the extensible automata model itself, the various hardness results establishing the baseline for what may be efficiently computed, and the demonstration of Algorithms 2 and 4 being efficient in some interesting cases.

Related Work. From the automata perspective a key area of related work is weighted automata [4], which in a very general way model attaching weights to transitions. The key distinction is that for extensible automata an extension has a "one time" weight/probability/cost, adding some set of transitions which can then be used any number of times without any further interaction with the weights, whereas weighted automata compute weights as the product of a path which may include a transition weight any number of times. However, clearly an extensible automaton can be implemented by a weighted automaton by "stratifying" it: having transitions which correspond to adding an extension, going into an independent layer of the automaton, where the extension transitions are added. This may create an exponentially large weighted automaton, but should still be studied, as many results can no doubt be reused.

Future Work. For future work, the associated probabilistic feature model (sketched in Example 1) should itself be formalized to elucidate the gap with extensible automata. The automata themselves should be extended into extensible transducers, considering cases where related inputs and outputs (here origin information [3] should likely be assumed for tractability reasons) may be observed. Further, the *sum total* probability of a string or language being accepted should be considered, we have here considered only finding the most likely configuration, but when multiple configurations can handle a given input it may be more relevant to consider the aggregate probability of those configurations. The weighted automaton corresponding to an extensible automaton will likely be of great interest here.

Acknowledgements. This work is based on the research supported in part by the National Research Foundation of South Africa (Grant Number 115007).

References

1. Angluin, D.: Learning regular sets from queries and counterexamples. Inf. Comput. **75**(2), 87–106 (1987). https://doi.org/10.1016/0890-5401(87)90052-6
2. Apel, S., Batory, D.S., Kästner, C., Saake, G.: Feature-Oriented Software Product Lines: Concepts and Implementation. Springer, Heidelberg (2013). https://doi.org/10.1007/978-3-642-37521-7
3. Bojańczyk, M.: Transducers with origin information. In: Esparza, J., Fraigniaud, P., Husfeldt, T., Koutsoupias, E. (eds.) ICALP 2014. LNCS, vol. 8573, pp. 26–37. Springer, Heidelberg (2014). https://doi.org/10.1007/978-3-662-43951-7_3
4. Droste, M., Kuich, W., Vogler, H. (eds.): Handbook of Weighted Automata. Monographs in Theoretical Computer Science: An EATCS Series. Springer, Heidelberg (2009). https://doi.org/10.1007/978-3-642-01492-5
5. Garey, M.R., Johnson, D.S.: Computers and Intractability: A Guide to the Theory of NP-Completeness. W. H. Freeman & Co., New York (1979)
6. Meinicke, J., Thüm, T., Schröter, R., Benduhn, F., Leich, T., Saake, G.: Mastering Software Variability with FeatureIDE. Springer, Heidelberg (2017). https://doi.org/10.1007/978-3-319-61443-4
7. Pohl, K., Böckle, G., van der Linden, F.: Software Product Line Engineering: Foundations Principles and Techniques. Springer, Heidelberg (2005). https://doi.org/10.1007/3-540-28901-1
8. Sperner, E.: Ein Satz über Untermengen einer endlichen Menge. Math. Z. **27**(1), 544–548 (1928). https://eudml.org/doc/167993
9. Weiser, M.: The computer for the 21st century. In: Baecker, R.M., Grudin, J., Buxton, W.A.S., Greenberg, S. (eds.) Human-computer Interaction, pp. 933–940. Morgan Kaufmann Publishers (1995). (Reprinted in ACM SIGMOBILE Mobile Comput. Commun. Rev. **3**(3), 3–11 (1999). https://doi.org/10.1145/329124.329126)

Formalising Boost POSIX Regular Expression Matching

Martin Berglund[1] , Willem Bester[2](✉) , and Brink van der Merwe[2]

[1] Department of Information Science and Centre for AI Research,
University of Stellenbosch, Private Bag X1, Matieland,
7602 Stellenbosch, South Africa
pmberglund@sun.ac.za

[2] Division of Computer Science, University of Stellenbosch, Private Bag X1,
Matieland, 7602 Stellenbosch, South Africa
{whkbester,abvdm}@cs.sun.ac.za

Abstract. Whereas Perl-compatible regular expression matchers typically exhibit some variation of leftmost-greedy semantics, those conforming to the POSIX standard are prescribed leftmost-longest semantics. However, the POSIX standard leaves some room for interpretation, and Fowler and Kuklewicz have done experimental work to confirm differences between various POSIX matchers. The Boost library has an interesting take on the POSIX standard, where it maximises the leftmost match not with respect to subexpressions of the regular expression pattern, but rather, with respect to capturing groups. In our work, we provide the first formalisation of Boost semantics, and we analyse the complexity of regular expression matching when using Boost semantics.

Keywords: Regular expression matching · POSIX · Boost

1 Introduction

In his "casual stroll across the regex landscape", Friedl [9] identifies two regular expression flavours with which the typical user must become acquainted, namely, those that are Perl-compatible, called PCRE [1], and those that follow the POSIX standard [2]. PCRE matchers follow a leftmost-greedy disambiguation policy, but POSIX matchers favour the leftmost-longest match. These flavours differ not only in terms of their syntax, but also, more crucially, in terms of their matching semantics. The latter is particularly noteworthy where *ambiguity* enters the picture, which is to say, where an input string "can be matched in more than one way" [24].

Through the standardisation of languages such as Perl, with native support for regular expressions, and libraries such as those defined by POSIX, new features became available, but initially, without much attention to the theoretic investigation of issues such as ambiguity. If, after the publication of Thompson's famous construction [25] in 1968, regular expressions were viewed as the perfect

© Springer Nature Switzerland AG 2018
B. Fischer and T. Uustalu (Eds.): ICTAC 2018, LNCS 11187, pp. 99–115, 2018.
https://doi.org/10.1007/978-3-030-02508-3_6

marriage between theory and practice, then by the 1980s, the state of the art and the state of the theory had parted ways. Since the 1990s, when the growth of the World Wide Web led to an interest in parsing for markup languages [7], the academic community has responded with vigour, as various features and flavours of regular expressions were studied and formalised (for example, see Kearns [12]).

To this, we now add the following contributions: We extend regular expressions to *capturing regular expressions*, which define forest languages instead of the usual string languages, in an effort to place the notion of parsing, as found in implementations, on a secure theoretical footing. We go on to provide a series of varied instructive examples, highlighting the similarities and differences between standards, implementations, and our formalisation of matching semantics. Finally, we formalise the matching semantics and investigate the matching complexity of the Boost variant of POSIX regular expressions, which has not been attempted before.

1.1 Related Work

In the documentation to their system regular expression libraries, which claim POSIX-compatibility, BSD Unices like OpenBSD [4] point to the implementations of Henry Spencer [11] as foundation. Recent versions of macOS [3], also in the BSD family, cite in addition the TRE library [18] by Laurikari, who used the notion of tagged automata to formalise full matching with submatch addressing for POSIX [17,20]. Subsequently, Kuklewicz took issue with Laurikari's claims to efficiency and correctness [14,16], resulting in the Regex-TDFA library for Haskell [13], which passes an extensive test suite [15] based on Fowler's original version [8].

Okui and Suzuki [22] formalised leftmost-longest semantics in terms of a strict order based on the yield lengths of parse tree nodes, ordered lexicographically by position strings. In contrast, Sulzmann and Lu [23], inspired by Frisch and Cardelli's work on the formalisation of greedy matching semantics [10], used a different approach, that of viewing regular expressions as types, and then treating the parse trees as values of some regular expression type, in the process also establishing a strict order of various parse trees with respect to a particular regular expression.

1.2 Paper Outline

The paper outline is as follows. In the next section, we state some definitions and properties of regular expressions and formal languages. Then, in Sect. 3, we present detailed examples, which serve to illustrate some of the issues and complexities of POSIX and Boost matching. In Sect. 4, we give a formal statement of Boost matching semantics, and also discuss the complexity of doing regular expression macthing with Boost. We then present some experimental results, and we end with concluding remarks.

2   Preliminaries

Denote by $\mathbb{N}$ the set of positive integers, let $\mathbb{N}_0 = \mathbb{N} \cup \{0\}$, and as usual, let $\leq$ $(<)$ be the natural (strict) order on $\mathbb{N}_0$. We use $\bot$ and $\top$ to indicate undefined values, and assume that $\bot < n < \top$ for all $n \in \mathbb{N}_0$. Let Σ be a finite alphabet and ε the empty string. For any string w over Σ with $\Sigma' \subseteq \Sigma$, let $\pi_{\Sigma'}(w)$ be the maximal subsequence of w that contains only symbols from Σ', and let $|w|$ be the length of w, which is to say, the number of symbols (from Σ) in w. In particular, $|\varepsilon| = 0$.

We denote the empty set by $\varnothing$. For any set A, let $\mathcal{P}(A)$ be power set of A. If $g : A \rightarrow B$ is a function, we also use g to denote the function from $\mathcal{P}(A)$ to $\mathcal{P}(B)$ defined by mapping $A' \subseteq A$ to $\{g(a) \mid a \in A'\} \subseteq B$.

Next we define the notion of forests, that is, the concatenation of trees. This is used to formalise the concept of which substring of an input string is matched (or captured) by which subexpression of a given regular expression.

Definition 1. *The set of forests over Σ and the index set I, denoted by $\mathcal{F}(\Sigma, I)$, is defined inductively as follows. We assume $(\Sigma \cup \{\varepsilon\}) \subseteq \mathcal{F}(F, I)$, and for $f_1, f_2 \in \mathcal{F}(\Sigma, I)$ and $i \in I$, we have that $f_1 f_2$ (that is, the concatenation of f_1 and f_2) and $[_i f]_i$ are elements in $\mathcal{F}(\Sigma, I)$. A forest language L over Σ and I is a subset of $\mathcal{F}(\Sigma, I)$, whereas a* string language *over Σ is a subset of Σ^* (where Σ^* denotes the set of all strings over Σ).*

In the sequel, we shall assume $I \subseteq \mathbb{N}_0$. Note that $\mathcal{F}(\Sigma, I)$ properly contains all strings over Σ if I is non-empty, and is otherwise precisely equal to the set of strings over Σ. A forest can be considered either as being a string over $\Sigma \cup \{[_i,]_i \mid i \in I\}$ or as a concatenation of ordered unranked trees over $\{\varepsilon\} \cup \Sigma \cup I$, where $[_i f]_i$ is a tree with root node labelled by i, having the forest f of trees as descendants.

Since standard (theoretical) regular expressions do not formalise the parsing aspects related to regular expression matching, which is essential for our discussion on Boost and POSIX in general, we next extend the standard definition of regular expressions in a way suitable for our purpose.

Definition 2. *The set of* capturing regular expressions *over a finite alphabet Σ and an index set I, denoted by $\mathcal{R}(\Sigma, I)$, is defined inductively as follows:*

1. *the* empty language expression $\varnothing$;
2. *the* empty string expression ε;
3. *the* symbols $a \in \Sigma$;
4. *the* concatenation, *also known as the* product, $(r_0 \cdot r_1)$ *of $r_0, r_1 \in \mathcal{R}(\Sigma, I)$;*
5. *the* union, *also known as the* sum *or* alternation, $(r_0 + r_1)$ *of $r_0, r_1 \in \mathcal{R}(\Sigma, I)$;*
6. *the* (Kleene) closure (r^*) *of $r \in \mathcal{R}(\Sigma, I)$; and*
7. *the* capture group $(_i r)_i$ *for $r \in \mathcal{R}(\Sigma, I)$ and $i \in I$.*

Items 1 to 3 in Definition 2 are called the *atoms* of regular expressions. We assume the alphabet Σ is disjoint with the symbols used to define the operations in items 4 to 7. The parentheses around the expressions of items 4 to 6 are optional, and if some are left out, the operator precedence, from high to low, is (i) closure, (ii) concatenation, and (iii) union. In addition, we assume that any concatenation $r_0 \cdot r_1$ may be written by juxtaposition as r_0r_1.

Remark 1. For a Boost capturing regular expression r, it is assumed that all opening parentheses are indexed from 1 onward, from left to right, with the corresponding closing parentheses indexed correspondingly. A Boost matcher will also replace r by $(_0r)_0$, before starting the matching procedure. The Boost capturing regular expressions thus form a proper subset of $\mathcal{R}(\Sigma, I)$—if I contains enough elements to uniquely index each pair of opening and corresponding closing parentheses.

Next we define syntactic shortcuts used in practice and also in some of our examples.

Definition 3. *For $r \in \mathcal{R}(\Sigma, I)$, define the following additional iterative operators:*

1. *the* duplication $(r^{m,n})$ *abbreviates*

$$\Big(\underbrace{r \cdots r}_{m \ times} \ \underbrace{(r+\varepsilon) \cdots (r+\varepsilon)}_{n-m \ times} \Big)$$

   for $m, n \in \mathbb{N}_0$ with $m \leq n$ (with $r^{0,0}$ denoting ε);
2. *the* option $(r?)$ *abbreviates* $(r+\varepsilon)$;
3. *the* positive closure (r^+) *abbreviates* (rr^*).

The second parameter of duplication is optional, and here we distinguish between two cases, namely, r^m being equivalent to $r^{m,m}$, and $r^{m,}$ being equivalent to $r^m r^*$. Again, we assume the set of symbols used to define the shortcut iteration operators in Definition 3 is disjoint from the underlying alphabet Σ.

Definition 4. *We define the following operations on forest, and thus also on string languages:*

1. *the* concatenation $L_0 \cdot L_1 = L_0L_1 = \{w_0w_1 \mid w_0 \in L_0 \ and \ w_1 \in L_1\}$ *for two languages L_0 and L_1;*
2. *the* union $L_0 \cup L_1 = \{w \mid w \in L_0 \ or \ w \in L_1\}$ *for two languages L_0 and L_1;*
3. *the* nth power *of the language L, where $n \in \mathbb{N}_0$, is*

$$L^n = \begin{cases} \{\varepsilon\} & if \, n = 0, \\ L \cdot L^{n-1} & otherwise; \ and \end{cases}$$

4. *the* closure $L^* = \bigcup_{n \in \mathbb{N}_0} L^n$ *of the language L.*

Finally, we are ready to define the forest languages described by the expressions in $\mathcal{R}(\Sigma, I)$.

Definition 5. *The* forest language *described by* $r \in \mathcal{R}(\Sigma, I)$, *and denoted by* $\mathcal{L}(r)$, *is defined inductively as follows:* $\mathcal{L}(\varnothing) = \varnothing$, $\mathcal{L}(\varepsilon) = \{\varepsilon\}$, $\mathcal{L}(a) = \{\mathtt{a}\}$, $\mathcal{L}(r_0 \cdot r_1) = \mathcal{L}(r_0) \cdot \mathcal{L}(r_1)$, $\mathcal{L}(r_0 + r_1) = \mathcal{L}(r_0) \cup \mathcal{L}(r_1)$, $\mathcal{L}(r^*) = \mathcal{L}(r)^*$, *and* $\mathcal{L}((_i r)_i) = \{[_i\} \cdot \mathcal{L}(r) \cdot \{]_i\}$ *where* $r, r_0, r_1 \in \mathcal{R}(\Sigma, I)$ *and* $i \in I$.

Definition 6. *We define the* string language *described by* $r \in \mathcal{R}(\Sigma, I)$ *to be the set* $\pi_\Sigma(\mathcal{L}(r))$.

Remark 2. Note if r' is the regular expression obtained from $r \in \mathcal{R}(\Sigma, I)$ by replacing all capturing parentheses by normal parentheses, then $\mathcal{L}(r') = \pi_\Sigma(\mathcal{L}(r))$.

Definition 7. *A* forest disambiguation policy $D(\Sigma, I)$ *for* $\mathcal{R}(\Sigma, I)$ *is a set of functions* $\{d_r : \mathcal{L}(r) \rightarrow \mathcal{L}(r) \mid r \in \mathcal{R}(\Sigma, I)\}$, *such that for* $f, f' \in \mathcal{L}(r)$, *we have* $\pi_\Sigma(d_r(f)) = \pi_\Sigma(f)$ *and* $\pi_\Sigma(f) = \pi_\Sigma(f')$ *implies* $d_r(f) = d_r(f')$.

If for $f \in \mathcal{L}(r)$, we have $\pi_\Sigma(f) = w$, we refer to f as a *parse forest* for w. We can intuitively think of a regular expression matcher as not only deciding if a given string w is in $\pi_\Sigma(\mathcal{L}(r))$ or not, but also, if $w \in \pi_\Sigma(\mathcal{L}(r))$, to have a specification of which parse forest to associate with w, amongst the potentially many possible parse forests for w. However, for efficiency reasons, greedy, Boost, and other POSIX matchers do not have a forest disambiguation policy in general, but rather a disambiguation policy on matching information derived from parsing forests. In general, the corresponding forests can not uniquely be reconstructed from this derived information. In Sect. 4, we provide precise details on the structure of this derived information for Boost.

Example 1. Consider matching $w =$ "ab" with $E = /\mathtt{a?(ab)?b?}/$. The Okui–Suzuki disambiguation policy [22], modified here in terms of notation to align closer with our approach, first replaces E by an (almost) fully parenthesised expression $E' = /(_1\mathtt{a?})_1(_2(_3(\mathtt{ab})?)_3(_4\mathtt{b?})_4)_2/$, obtained by assuming concatenation is right-associative, and by numbering the opening parenthesis, in order, from left to right in E'. The following two forests are candidates for a full match:

$$t_0 = [_1\mathtt{a}]_1[_2[_3]_3[_4\mathtt{b}]_4]_2 \quad \text{and} \quad t_1 = [_1]_1[_2[_3\mathtt{ab}]_3[_4]_4]_2.$$

Using the natural order on $\mathbb{N}_0$ for the capture indices, this yields the two vectors $\langle 1, 1, 0, 1 \rangle$ and $\langle 0, 2, 2, 0 \rangle$ of lengths of captures for t_0 and t_1, respectively, by which t_0 is chosen when using a lexicographic order on these two vectors.

3 Examples

At this point, it is instructive to turn to some detailed examples. In particular, because POSIX [2] is a software engineering standard, its functional specification for regular expressions is written in English, without mathematical formalisms. As such, some parts of the specification might be open to multiple interpretations. Fowler [8] has argued that the specification is "surprisingly cavalier with terminology", and it is the implications of different readings of the standard that we now examine in detail.

Remark 3. An additional concern is that POSIX defines two different specifications for regular expressions, namely, *Basic Regular Expressions* (BREs) and *Extended Regular Expressions* (EREs), which although they share many similarities, especially in the specifications of atoms, are incompatible. For example, BREs supports backreferences, "operations which bind a substring to a variable, allowing it to be matched again verbatim", a feature that is non-regular and that makes matching NP-complete [6]. EREs do not support backreferences, removes the need for group and iteration bounds delimiters to be escaped, and supports the union of subexpressions, which BREs do not. Therefore—and it also bears mentioning that some implementers of POSIX regular expressions consider BREs obsolete [3,19]—we focus exclusively on EREs.

Remark 4. The specification language for regular expression patterns in POSIX differs from our Definitions 2 and 3. In particular, for the union $r + s$ of two expressions r and s, we would write r|s in POSIX, and the iterates r^*, r^m, $r^{m,}$, and $r^{m,n}$ are written as r*, r{m}, r{m,}, and r{m,n}, respectively. Until Sect. 5, we use the notation established in Sect. 2 exclusively.

Remark 5. In the POSIX standard for EREs [2, Sect. 9.4], each pair of parentheses, unless escaped or included in a *bracket expression*—where the escape sequences "\(" and "\)" match the literal opening and closing parenthesis characters, and whereas the bracket expression "[(ab)]" matches any one of the literal characters "(", "a", "b", or ")"—*always* automatically defines a *group*: They do not match literal occurrences of parentheses in the input string, but serve to override the default operator precedence, and also, allow the matcher to report which substring was *captured* (or matched) by which group. Consistent with Remark 1, groups are identified by positive integers, and internally, the matcher automatically numbers the pairs of parentheses from left to right, starting at 1; in addition, the entire regular expression is numbered as group 0. In our examples, we write group numbers explicitly, and depending on what is convenient, we either state group 0 explicitly, or do not indicate it at all.

Example 2. Consider matching the input string $w =$ "aba" with the regular expression $E_0 = /(_1 \mathsf{ab} + \mathsf{ba} + \mathsf{a})_1^*/$. Matching w with E_0 is ambiguous, because two different forests in $\mathcal{L}(E_0)$ that correspond to a full match, where the entire input string is matched by the regular expression, are possible, namely, $f_0 = [_1 \mathsf{ab}]_1 [_1 \mathsf{a}]_1$ and $f_1 = [_1 \mathsf{a}]_1 [_1 \mathsf{ba}]_1$. The forest f_0 means the matcher used the /ab/ subexpression of E_0 for the first iteration of the star, and the /a/ subexpression for the second, whereas the forest f_1 means the matcher used the /a/ subexpression of E_0 for the first iteration of the star, and the /ba/ subexpression for the second. The bracketed subforests in f_0 and f_1 indicate which substrings were matched by group 1 during consecutive iterations. For E_0, both leftmost-greedy and leftmost-longest matchers will use the forest f_0.

However, now consider matching $w =$ "aba" with $E_1 = /(_1 \mathsf{a} + \mathsf{ab} + \mathsf{ba})_1^*/$, and note that E_1 defines the same language as E_0, but that the order of the subexpressions inside the star has changed. Again, the two forests f_0 and f_1

correspond to a full match, but now, a leftmost-greedy matcher will use f_1, whereas a leftmost-longest matcher will still use f_0.   □

Remark 6. It should be noted that matchers typically do not report forests, but only substrings matched (or captured) by some subexpressions, and specifically, in the case of a subexpression s^*, most matchers only report the last capture by the subexpression s. Thus it is in fact only the simplicity of the previous example that makes it possible to reverse engineer the parse forests.

Intuitively, whenever more than one match is possible for a particular subexpression, a greedy matcher will return the first match with respect to the order in which this subexpression's subexpressions are written in the regular expression. This is to say, when a subexpression admits several choices for matching the same substring of the input string, the leftmost choice will prevail. In contrast, a leftmost-longest matcher must seemingly consider all possible matches for that subexpression, starting as early as possible in the input string, where "early" means "leftmost", unless this choice causes the entire match to fail; if the leftmost policy is not enough to distinguish between two submatches, we give preference to longer submatches.

Example 3. Again, consider the input string w and the regular expressions E_0 and E_1 from Example 2, but now let us examine what happens when these examples are run on Haskell's Regex-TDFA [13] and Boost [21], which both claim to be POSIX-compliant—but see Remark 7 below—and hence, where we expect both to return $[_1 \mathsf{ab}]_1 [_1 \mathsf{a}]_1$ for E_0 as well as E_1. However, whereas Regex-TDFA returns $[_1 \mathsf{ab}]_1 [_1 \mathsf{a}]_1$ with E_0 and E_1, and thus performs as expected, Boost returns $[_1 \mathsf{a}]_1 [_1 \mathsf{ba}]_1$, again for both E_0 and E_1. The disparity can be understood by realising that Regex-TDFA maximises all captures by a starred subexpression, from left to right, based on first considering the leftmost and secondly the length criteria, although it only reports the last match, while Boost does the maximisation only on the last submatch.   □

A case can be made that Boost is in fact POSIX-compliant, albeit with a different reading than, for example, Regex-TDFA of the salient points of the POSIX matching policy [2, Sect. 9.1]:

> The search for a matching sequence starts at the beginning of a string and stops when the first sequence matching the expression is found, where "first" is defined to mean "begins earliest in the string". If the pattern permits a variable number of matching characters and thus there is more than one such sequence starting at that point, the longest such sequence is matched. . . . Consistent with the whole match being the longest of the leftmost matches, each subpattern[1] from left to right shall match the longest possible string.

---

[1] Fowler [8] identifies the terms "subpattern" and "subexpression" as particular targets of abuse in the POSIX standard, especially since they are "central to the description of the matching algorithm". He goes on to note that, whereas "subpattern" is used but once, "subexpression" is used 70 times and always appears in the context of grouping.

POSIX therefore requires full matching with *submatch addressing*, where "the position and extent of the substrings matched by given subexpressions must be provided" [20]. Contrast this with the classic automata-theoretic approach, where a matcher simply determines whether the entire input string was matched by the regular expression or not.

Although Boost applies a leftmost-longest policy, it considers what its documentation calls "marked subexpressions" [21], instead of arbitrary subexpressions, such that we now render the last quoted sentence as: "Consistent with the whole match being the longest of the leftmost matches, each *marked* subpattern from left to right shall match the longest possible string." Thus Boost applies its leftmost-longest disambiguation policy not by maximising arbitrary subexpressions of a regular expression, but instead, by maximising marked subexpressions, in other words, those subexpressions surrounded by parentheses. Note when a regular expression is fully parenthesized, which is to say, when each subexpression is immediatedly surrounded by a pair of parentheses, then all subexpressions are marked. Since we distinguish between marked and other (that is, non-marked) subexpressions, the formalism of Sulzmann and Lu, and Frisch and Cardelli, of considering regular expressions as types and parse trees as values of types, is not directly applicable in our setting.

Remark 7. Boost also supports PCRE syntax and semantics, which is, in fact, its default mode of operation. (For detail, see the discussion after Remark 9 on page 11.) When we refer to Boost in this and following sections, we exclusively mean Boost in its POSIX mode of operation.

Example 4. Consider matching $w = $ "aa" with $E_2 = /(_0 a^*(_1 a^*)_1)_0/$ and $E_3 = /(_0(_1 a^*)_1(_2 a^*)_2)_0/$. Although both expressions define the same language, the first $/a^*/$ subexpression is a group in E_3, but not in E_2. For E_2, the forests $f_2 = [_0 aa[_1]_1]_0$, $f_3 = [_0 a[_1 a]_1]_0$, and $f_4 = [_0[_1 aa]_1]_0$ correspond to matching the entire input string w, and for E_3, we have the forests $f_5 = [_0[_1 aa]_1[_2]_2]_0$, $f_6 = [_0[_1 a]_1[_2 a]_2]_0$, and $f_7 = [_0[_1]_1[_2 aa]_2]_0$.

We consider matching with E_3 first: Boost and Regex-TDFA both prefer f_5, since all non-atomic subexpressions are parenthesised, and both matchers simply maximise the lengths of the substrings matched by the groups from left to right. However, for E_2, Regex-TDFA uses f_2, because this matcher maximises the lengths of *all* subexpressions from left to right, regardless of whether a subexpression is marked as a group. Boost, on the other hand, maximises groups—here, first with respect to group 0, and then with respect to group 1 (which is contained in group 0). Hence, Boost prefers f_4 to f_2.   □

Since unescaped and unbracketed parentheses always define groups, it does not matter that parentheses might have been necessitated by issues of operator precedence: Unlike the typical PCRE matcher or the Java regular expression matcher, which support non-capturing groups—for which parentheses has no other influence, save possibly changing how that abstract syntax tree of the regular expression is constructed—the user of POSIX-compliant matchers, including

Boost, has no choice in the matter of capturing groups. However, in our theoretical model of capturing regular expressions, we do in fact allow both capturing and non-capturing groups.

Example 5. Fowler gives the example $E_4 = /\texttt{a?}(_1\texttt{ab})_1\texttt{?b?}/$. Arguably, here the parentheses serve no other purpose except to delimit the subexpression to be matched by the second option operator. The two forests $f_8 = [_0\texttt{ab}]_0$ and $f_9 = [_0[_1\texttt{ab}]_1]_0$ correspond to a full match of the input string $w = $ "ab". Here, f_8 represents the matcher using the first $/\texttt{a}/$ and the last $/\texttt{b}/$ subexpressions, and f_9 the case where the second option, of the $/\texttt{ab}/$ subexpression, is used. As is to be expected for leftmost-longest semantics, Regex-TDFA returns f_8, but Boost, since it will maximise the only marked subexpression, returns f_9. Contrast this with matching the same input string w with $E_5 = /(_1\texttt{a?})_1(_2\texttt{ab})_2\texttt{?}(_3\texttt{b?})_3/$, where both Regex-TDFA and Boost will prefer the forest $f_{10} = [_0[_1\texttt{a}]_1[_3\texttt{b}]_3]_0$ to the forest $f_{11} = [_0[_1]_1[_2\texttt{ab}]_2[_3]_3]_0$. $\square$

Example 6. Consider the regular expression $E_6 = /(_1\texttt{a} + (_2\texttt{b}^*)_2)_1^*/$. Since all non-atomic subexpressions are parenthesised, for a given input string, matching with both Boost and Regex-TDFA succeed on the same forests. For the input strings $w_1 = $ "abb", $w_2 = $ "abba", and $w_3 = $ "abbab", the respective forests $f_{12} = [_0[_1\texttt{a}]_1[_1[_2\texttt{bb}]_2]_1]_0$, $f_{13} = [_0[_1\texttt{a}]_1[_1[_2\texttt{bb}]_2]_1[_1\texttt{a}]_1]_0$, and $f_{14} = [_0[_1\texttt{a}]_1[_1[_2\texttt{bb}]_2]_1[_1\texttt{a}]_1[_1[_2\texttt{b}]_2]_1]_0$ are preferred.

The way Boost reports the result, however, differs from Regex-TDFA. Using Fowler's format of reporting [8], we express the output (with grouping) of running a matcher as a sequence of pairs, one for each group, starting at 0 for the entire regular expression. The first element of a pair gives the start index of the substring of the input that was matched by the group subexpression, and the second element is the end index plus one of the substring. For f_{13}, Boost reports $(0,4)(3,4)(1,3)$, but Regex-TDFA reports $(0,4)(3,4)(?,?)$, where $(?,?)$ means the group subexpression did not participate in the match. $\square$

How the information is reported depends on the implementer's reading of the matching function's specification [2, "System interfaces—regcomp"], which we summarise as: (1) If a subexpression is not contained within another subexpression, then if the subexpression participated in a match multiple times, the last such match must be reported, or else, if it did not participate in a match, then it must be reported as non-participating; (2) if a subexpression is contained within another subexpression, and the outer subexpression participated in a match, then the match or non-match of the inner subexpression must be reported according to Rule (1), but with respect to the substring matched by the outer subexpression and not the entire input string. "Participation" is defined negatively: A subexpression *does not participate* in a match when one of the choices in a union is not taken, or when the empty string is matched with an iterative operator by matching zero times with the associated subexpression.

Essentially, Boost has elected to ignore Rule 2. Since group 2 is contained in group 1, and for the last match (by Rule 1) of group 1, group 2 did not participate in the match (by Rule 2), Regex-TDFA reported group 2 as $(?,?)$ by Rule 2.

This can be seen in the forest f_{13}, where the last subforest for group 1 does not contain a subforest for group 2. Boost, on the other hand, simply returns the last match information, regardless of whether one group is contained in another.

Incidentally, from the context in which the unqualified term "subexpression" is used in the POSIX specification for reporting submatches, it is clear that this term actually refers to parenthesised subexpressions, which is to say, groups. Elsewhere [2, Sect. 9.4], the same term can refer to arbitrary or parenthesised subexpressions, the latter of which is sometimes referred to by "grouping". These inconsistencies illustrate Fowler's critical stance on the standard.

Example 7. To see how reporting differs for an empty match as opposed to a non-participating subexpression, consider $E_7 = /(_0(_1a(_2(_3b)_3^*)_2)_1^*)_0/$ on input "aba". Both Boost and Regex-TDFA prefer the forest $f_{15} = [_0[_1a[_2[_3b]_3]_2]_1[_1a[_2]_2]_1]_0$, but Regex-TDFA reports the match as $(0,3)(2,3)(3,3)(?,?)$, whereas Boost reports $(0,3)(2,3)(3,3)(1,2)$. Note that both report an empty match for group 2 (by having the same index for the start and end). Since the iterative star operator is applied to group 3 inside group 2, and therefore, since the last match for group 2 is empty, group 3 did not participate in this match. Yet, although group 3 is inside group 2, Boost still reports the last match of group 3.   □

4   Boost Semantics and Matching Algorithm

We start this section by first providing three preliminary definitions, which is then used to formalise, in Definition 11, Boost semantics.

Definition 8. *The* capture history *for forests is the function* $C : \mathcal{F}(\Sigma, I) \times I \to \mathbb{N}_0 \times \mathbb{N}_0$, *defined as follows. Let* $f \in \mathcal{F}(\Sigma, I)$, $j \in I$, *and*

$$f(j) = \pi_{\Sigma \cup \{[_j,]_j\}}(f) = w_0[_j w_1]_j \cdots w_{2i}[_j w_{2i+1}]_j w_{2(i+1)} \cdots [_j w_{2k-1}]_j w_{2k}$$

where $w_i \in \Sigma^*$. *Then*

$$C(f, j) = \begin{cases} \{(|w_0 \cdots w_{2i}|, |w_{2i+1}|) \mid 0 \le i < k\} & \text{if } [_j \text{ appears in } f; \\ \varnothing & \text{otherwise.} \end{cases}$$

We assume that the tuples in $C(f, j)$ are always sorted by increasing first index. Also, $C_{\text{last}}(f, j)$ denotes the tuple in $C(f, j)$ with largest first index if $C(f, j)$ is non-empty, and $C_{\text{last}}(f, j) = (\top, \bot)$ otherwise.

Intuitively, Definition 5 allows us to express how substrings of an input string are captured by the capture groups of a regular expression, which is accomplished by decorating the input string with pairs of indexed brackets to delimit the substrings thus captured as matching proceeds. In turn, Definition 8 allows us to extract the capture history for a particular group, which yields a (possibly empty) set of pairs, where each pair gives the start index and the length of the captured substring. Note that we opted to record starting indices and length for captures in our formalisation in the previous definition, instead of starting and ending indices as is done typically by implementations.

Example 8. To illustrate the capture history, we revisit Example 5. For matching the input string $w =$ "ab" by $E_5 = /(_1a?)_1(_2ab)_2?(_3b?)_3/$, we consider the forests $f_{10} = [_0[_1a]_1[_3b]_3]_0$ and $f_{11} = [_0[_1]_1[_2ab]_2[_3]_3]_0$. They yield, first for f_{10}: $C(f_{10}, 0) = C([_0ab]_0) = \{(0, 2)\}$, $C(f_{10}, 1) = C([_1a]_1b, 1) = \{(0, 1)\}$, $C(f_{10}, 2) = C(ab, 2) = \{(\top, \bot)\}$, $C(f_{10}, 3) = C(a[_3b]_3, 3) = \{(1, 1)\}$; and then for f_{11}: $C(f_{11}, 0) = C([_0ab]_0) = \{(0, 2)\}$, $C(f_{11}, 1) = C([_1]_1ab, 1) = \{(0, 0)\}$, $C(f_{11}, 2) = C([_2ab]_2, 2) = \{(0, 2)\}$, and $C(f_{11}, 3) = C(ab[_3]_3, 3) = \{(2, 0)\}$. Note the difference between the empty captures such as $C(f_{11}, 1)$ and $C(f_{11}, 3)$, and a capture history in which a particular subexpression did not participate, such as $C(f_{10}, 2)$. □

Definition 9. *The* final capture history *for $f \in \mathcal{F}(\Sigma, I)$, denoted as $C_{fin}(f)$, is the set $\{(j, C_{last}(f, j)) \mid j \in I\}$.*

Remark 8. In the sequel, we abuse notation somewhat, and we write $C_{fin}(f)$ as a set of triplets instead of as a set of ordered pairs (of which each second element is also a pair).

Example 9. To illustrate the final capture history, we use the forest $f_{14} = [_0[_1a]_1[_1[_2bb]_2]_1[_1a]_1[_1[_2b]_2]_1]_0$ from Example 6. Recall, for this forest, we matched the input string $w_3 =$ "abbab" by the regular expression $E_6 = /(_1a + (_2b^*)_2)_1^*/$. From f_{14}, we extract the capture histories

$$C(f_{14}, 0) = C([_0abbab]_0, 0) = \{(0, 5)\},$$
$$C(f_{14}, 1) = C([_1a]_1[_1bb]_1[_1a]_1[_1b]_1, 1) = \{(0, 1), (1, 2), (3, 1), (4, 1)\}, \text{and}$$
$$C(f_{14}, 2) = C(a[_2bb]_2a[_2b]_2, 2) = \{(1, 2), (4, 1)\}.$$

Therefore, $C_{fin}(f_{14}) = \{(0, 0, 5), (1, 4, 1), (2, 4, 1)\}$. □

Definition 10. *We define the* Boost partial order, *denoted as $\prec_B$, on $\{C_{fin}(f) \mid f \in \mathcal{F}(\Sigma, I)\}$ as follows. Assume $\pi_\Sigma(f_1) = \pi_\Sigma(f_2)$, then $C_{fin}(f_1) \prec_B C_{fin}(f_2)$ if for the smallest element $j \in I$ such that $(j, s_1, \ell_1) \neq (j, s_2, \ell_2)$, where $(j, s_i, \ell_i) \in C_{fin}(f_i)$, we have $s_2 < s_1$, or $s_1 = s_2$ but $\ell_1 < \ell_2$.*

Definition 11. *For $r \in \mathcal{R}(\Sigma, I)$ and $w \in \pi_\Sigma(\mathcal{L}(r))$, the* Boost captures *of matching w with r, denoted as $B(r, w)$, is defined to be the largest element in $\{C_{fin}(f) \mid f \in \mathcal{L}(r), \pi_\Sigma(f) = w\}$ determined by $\prec_B$.*

Remark 9. It should be noted that $\prec_B$ is a total order on the finite set $\{C_{fin}(f) \mid f \in \mathcal{L}(r), \pi_\Sigma(f) = w\}$ used in the previous definition, and thus $B(r, w)$ is well-defined.

Example 10. To illustrate Boost partial order and captures, we continue Example 5. We match $w =$ "ab" with $E_4 = /a?(_1ab)_1?b?/$, and we consider the forests $f_8 = [_0ab]_0$ and $f_9 = [_0[_1ab]_1]_0$. By Definition 8, we have the capture histories $C(f_8, 0) = \{(0, 2)\}$, $C(f_8, 1) = \varnothing$, $C(f_9, 0) = \{(0, 2)\}$, and $C(f_9, 1) = \{(0, 2)\}$, whence by Definition 9, $C_{fin}(f_8) = \{(0, 0, 2), (1, \top, \bot)\}$ and $C_{fin}(f_9) = \{(0, 0, 2), (1, 0, 2)\}$. At $j = 1$, we find $s_8 = \top$ and $s_9 = 0$, so that

$s_9 < s_8$, and therefore, by Definition 10, $C_{\text{fin}}(f_8) \prec_B C_{\text{fin}}(f_9)$. Finally, by Definition 11, $B(E_4, \text{"ab"}) = \{(0,0,2),(1,0,2)\}$.

For matching w with $E_5 = /(_1\text{a}?)_1(_2\text{ab})_2?(_3\text{b}?)_3/$, and for the forests $f_{10} = [_0[_1\text{a}]_1[_3\text{b}]_3]_0$ and $f_{11} = [_0[_1]_1[_2\text{ab}]_2[_3]_3]_0$, we calculate, by way of Example 8,

$$C_{\text{fin}}(f_{10}) = \{(0,0,2),(1,0,1),(2,\top,\bot),(3,1,1)\} \text{ and}$$
$$C_{\text{fin}}(f_{11}) = \{(0,0,2),(1,0,0),(2,0,2),(3,2,0)\}.$$

At $j = 1$, we find $s_{10} = s_{11} = 0$, $\ell_{10} = 1$, and $\ell_{11} = 0$, so that $\ell_{11} < \ell_{10}$. Therefore, $C_{\text{fin}}(f_{11}) \prec_B C_{\text{fin}}(f_{10})$, and $B(E_5, w) = C_{\text{fin}}(f_{10})$.   □

The actual implementation of POSIX matching in Boost is implemented in a very straightforward way, in that it is a small modification of *another* matching engine. Boost contains a very complete implementation of PCRE/Java-style semantics, implemented by depth-first backtracking search on what is in effect an automaton constructed from the expression. See Berglund and Van der Merwe [5] for a complete discussion both of these semantics and the details of such search implementations, which applies fully to the PCRE-style mode in Boost, including the potential for very poor performance for some regular expressions [26] in instances where a significant amount of backtracking is necessary. The POSIX mode is derived from this engine as follows:

1. Apply the PCRE-style matching engine to the input, and record the resulting parse tree t. If the engine rejects the string then it is rejected (as the modes agree on simple membership though not on capturing semantics[2]).
2. Apply the PCRE-style matching engine to the input, and *each* time it *would* accept with a parse tree t':
   (a) if $C_{\text{fin}}(t) \prec_B C_{\text{fin}}(t')$, set $t \leftarrow t'$, with $\prec_B$ defined precisely as in Definition 10,
   (b) reject, as if the search had failed, causing the engine to backtrack.
3. Output the final t as the POSIX-style match result.

In effect the PCRE-style engine is simply made to explore every possible parse tree by triggering its backtracking. Unfortunately there are some edge cases where this does not quite work, as the PCRE-style engine fails to explore some trees which are from the PCRE perspective not useful candidates, but which are clearly more correct from a POSIX perspective—more on this follows in Sect. 5—but we view these instances as plain bugs rather than as intended semantics.

The larger issue with this implementation technique is that there may be exponentially many parse trees, and exploring them all may cause very poor performance. For example, with default settings, the Boost POSIX matcher will refuse to attempt to match the string "aaaaaaaaaaaaaa" with $/(\text{a}^*)^*/$, issuing a warning that the expression should be refactored to avoid "eternal" matching;

---

[2] The matching engine should also reject on syntax or operators not permitted, as not all PCRE-style features make sense in the POSIX context. The parsing and validation of the expression is not within the scope of this discussion however.

remove one "a", however, and the match will succeed. Again, see Weideman et al. [26] for a full treatment of this type of matching issues. Depending on the application, this may be a rather severe issue, but fortunately, the problem of computing the correct Boost match does not actually require exponential time, at least in theory (although this is not the case for current Boost implementations), as we will see next.

Theorem 1. *Boost captures $B(r, w)$, where $r \in \mathcal{R}(\Sigma, I)$ and $w \in \Sigma^*$, can be computed in time $\mathcal{O}(k|w||r| \log |w|)$, where k is the number of distinct capturing indices used in r.*

Proof. Without loss of generality, assume $I = \{1, \ldots, k\}$, and let $T(r)$ be a transducer, obtained via a modified Thompson construction, which on input w, outputs all matching forests of w; see Berglund and Van der Merwe [5] for a detailed description of such a construction. We associate with each $i \in I$ the sets of transitions O_i and C_i, from $T(r)$, that outputs $(_i$ and $)_i$, respectively. Next, we determine the capturing information for each $i \in I$ in order of priority, so starting with $i = 1$, we use binary search, in conjunction with a modified on-the-fly subset construction, on $T(r)$, to first find the leftmost position in w where we can use a transition, from O_i, for the last time, while matching w from left to right with $T(r)$. That is, the binary search proceeds by stating that "the last leftmost position is at or to the left of position p", then we simulate T on w by keeping track of all states reachable, verifying this assumption. If we succeed, we attempt a smaller p; if we fail, we attempt a larger one, until the precise leftmost last position possible is identified. To make this more precise, the condition is verified by up to position p simulating T, adding to each state reached a flag annotating whether it has been reached on a path which used some transition from O_1 at least once (if the same state is reached with and without using a transition from O_1, the flag is kept). When position p is reached, all states which have not used a transition from O_1 are discarded, and the simulation of T continues, but now *no* transition from O_1 may be used for the remainder of w.

Once we have this first position for capture $i = 1$ fixed—that is, every scan considered from here on should obey this condition on the paths they consider, but as this only *constrains* the possible paths in T, it has no negative impact on the matching performance—we again use the same search procedure to determine the rightmost position in w where we can use a transition from C_1, for the last time, while matching w from left to right with $T(r)$.

Combining this modified on-the-fly subset construction—which is to say, tracking of reachable states fulfilling the additional conditions placed by the capturing order—with binary search, allows us to determine the starting and ending positions of the capture on index 1 in time $\mathcal{O}(|w||r| \log |w|)$. This is the case as $|T| \in \mathcal{O}(r)$, and checking if T matches w can be done in time $\mathcal{O}(|T||w|)$, even with the added modifications, as the restrictions only *remove* paths which a full simulation would have to consider.

We now repeat this search for index $i = 2$, but while doing the search for starting and ending position of this capture, we use the additional restrictions that transitions from O_1 and C_1 has to be taken at the opening and closing positions of the capture on index 1. Repeating this procedure for each index gives us an $\mathcal{O}(k|E||w| \log |w|)$ algorithm to compute $B(w, r)$. $\square$

Remark 10. Theorem 1 does establish that matching consistent with the Boost semantics can be performed in polynomial time, which improves greatly on the exponential worst-case of Boost itself. However, this construction is primarily given for illustrative purposes, and it is clearly not the most efficient approach possible: The binary search proposed to optimize the moment when the state machine last uses the transitions corresponding to the captures can be replaced by a more complicated but more efficient linear scan which determines the correct placement outright. The details of such an algorithm are non-trivial, however, so we leave the construction and correctness proof details as future work.

5   Experimental Results

To test our formalism experimentally, we developed two applications in Python: (1) a small testing framework for existing matchers, and (2) a larger, extensible framework that allows us, given a regular expression $r \in \mathcal{R}(\Sigma, I)$ and an input string $w \in \Sigma^*$, to generate the forests $f \in \mathcal{L}(r)$, and then to apply the Boost or POSIX disambiguation policy, for the latter of which we used the Okui–Suzuki approach as proxy. For the sake of simplicity in the larger framework, we limited Σ to alphabetic characters, we did not implement the more involved POSIX regular expression atoms such as bracket expressions and collating elements, and beyond the barest minimum, we did not attempt to make forest generation and matching efficient in any way.

As sanity check for both frameworks, we generated 2 930 862 simple test cases, each containing a regular expression, an input string, and the expected output, taken from running the Boost matcher on the expression–input pair. The regular expressions were those consisting of the atoms a, b, and ., the operators *, +, ?, and |, as well as parentheses, and when counting all symbols in the expression, of all lengths up to and including 6; the input strings were all strings over the alphabet {a, b, c} of length up to and including 6. We used the small testing framework to run the test cases against output from the larger framework with our Boost semantics, and all of them passed.

Our principle source for in-depth testing was the 93 examples Fowler [8] designed specifically to tease out POSIX compliance: We retained the 49 ERE examples from `interpretation.dat`, removing a further three for containing bracket expressions. Of these, Boost was able to return matches, without resorting to partial matching, for 37 test cases; see Remark 11 for a discussion. We also wrote 19 additional test cases, designed to show the difference between Boost and POSIX disambiguation.

The implementation of our Boost formalism passed all of our own test cases with respect to what the Boost matcher returns. For the 37 test cases, our Boost formalism failed two, which we now discuss.

Example 11. Our formalism disagrees with the Boost matcher on Fowler's test case 10, matching "x" with the regular expression $(.?)\{2\}$, where the dot operator indicates a match with any character. Here, we get the forests $f_{16} = [_0[_1]_1[_1\mathtt{x}]_1]_0$ and $f_{17} = [_0[_1\mathtt{x}]_1[_1]_1]_0$. From Definitions 8 and 9, we get $C_{\mathrm{fin}}(f_{16}) = \{(0,0,1),(1,0,1)\}$ and $C_{\mathrm{fin}}(f_{17}) = \{(0,0,1),(1,1,0)\}$, and hence, by Definition 10, we have $C_{\mathrm{fin}}(f_{17}) \prec_B C_{\mathrm{fin}}(f_{16})$, so that our formalism selects f_{16}. However, the Boost matcher prefers f_{17}, which is to say, it returns $(0,1)(1,1)$ instead of the expected $(0,1)(0,1)$.

Running Regex-TDFA on the same example also returns $(0,1)(1,1)$. Therefore, we refer to the POSIX standard, which specifies that duplication "shall match what *repeated consecutive* occurrences" [emphasis added] would match [2, Sect. 9.4.6]. This would seem to suggest that $(.?)\{2\}$ is equivalent to the literal expansion $(.?)(.?)$. Both Boost and Regex-TDFA now return $(0,1)(0,1)(1,1)$ as expected, but note that we had no choice in the second pair of parentheses automatically defining a new group. We might now posit that (1) Boost has the internal forest representations $[_0[_1\mathtt{x}]_1[_2]_2]_0$ and $[_0[_1]_1[_2\mathtt{x}]_2]_0$, (2) it selects the former by our Boost formalism, but then (3) reports this choice as $[_0[_1\mathtt{x}]_1[_1]_1]_0$.

This postulation does not extend to Fowler's test case 17, matching "xxx" with $(.?.?)\{3\}$, where Boost returns $(0,3)(2,3)$, capturing the last "x" with group 1—unlike Regex-TDFA, which returns $(0,3)(3,3)$; when expanded to $(.?.?)(.?.?)(.?.?)$, both return $(0,3)(0,2)(2,3)(3,3)$. Our point is this: For sensible options of *internal* representation—non-capturing groups, group number reuse and reordering—we can cook up counterexamples, so that the same proposed representation does not work over all test cases. We believe this to be a bug in the Boost matcher: During code inspection, we found code that limits the forests to be explored, an optimisation that short-circuits a duplication when it first matches an empty string, which is fine for PCRE semantics—recall that Boost's POSIX matcher is a modified PCRE engine—but prevents all possibilities from being considered for POSIX semantics.   □

Remark 11. In our test setup, Boost only looks for full matches, that is, where the entire input string is matched by the regular expression. *Partial matching* allows a matcher to match a substring of the input string with a regular expression. Because Boost maximises groups (as opposed to subexpressions) from left to right, it is possible to simulate partial matching by prepending and appending .* to the regular expressions involved (and if necessary, surrounding the original expression with parentheses). For example, to allow Fowler's test case 28, matching "ababa" by $(\mathtt{aba}|\mathtt{a*b})$, to succeed, we rewrite the regular expression as .*$(\mathtt{aba}|\mathtt{a*b})$.*. Doing so allows Boost to return the partial match for the nine Fowler test cases that failed originally, and the results correspond to those returned by our own Boost ordering.

The same construction does not in general return correct results for a classic POSIX matcher set up to return full matches. It will match the first and last "a" in "aba" with the first and last .* of .*$(\mathtt{aba}|\mathtt{a*b})$.*, respectively, and "b" with group 1. A *lazy star*, which consumes as few symbols as possible, is necessary for the construction to work for POSIX matchers [5], but is not supported by the standard.

6   Future Work and Conclusion

Although we focused in this paper mostly on Boost semantics of regular expression matching, the overarching theme of this research is the more general notion of providing users of matching libraries the freedom to specify their own orders (or disambiguating policies) that can be used by more generic regular expression matching libraries. Thus, instead of being locked into the unclear semantics provided by current greedy and POSIX implementations, users can then specify their own policies, such as for example longest-leftmost, instead of the current leftmost-longest policy. Certainly, it might often be of more interest to find a longest submatch rather than a leftmost one. Given that comparators made generic sorting algorithms widely applicable, why not by analogy provide a generic way to specify classes of disambiguating policies to be used by a matcher, while still keeping the matching procedure efficient?

References

1. PCRE: Perl compatible regular expressions. https://www.pcre.org/. Accessed 26 May 2018
2. Portable Operating System Interface (POSIX) Base Specifications, Issue 7. IEEE Standard 1003.1-2017 (2017). (Revision of IEEE Standard 1003.1-2008) https://doi.org/10.1109/ieeestd.2008.4694976
3. Regex(3) BSD Library Functions Manual, September 2011. as available on macOS 10.11.6
4. Regular expression routines: OpenBSD library functions manual, May 2016. http://man.openbsd.org/regexec
5. Berglund, M., van der Merwe, B.: On the semantics of regular expression parsing in the wild. Theor. Comput. Sci. **679**, 69–82 (2017). https://doi.org/10.1016/j.tcs.2016.09.006
6. Berglund, M., van der Merwe, B.: Re-examining regular expressions with backreferences. In: Holub, J., Žd'árek, J. (eds.) Proceedings of Prague Stringology Conference, PSC 2017, Prague, August 2017, pp. 30–41. Czech Technical University Prague (2017). http://www.stringology.org/event/2017/p04.html
7. Brüggemann-Klein, A., Wood, D.: One-unambiguous regular languages. Inf. Comput. **140**(2), 229–253 (1998). https://doi.org/10.1006/inco.1997.2688
8. Fowler, G.: An interpretation of the POSIX regex standard. Technical report, AT&T Research, Florham Park, NJ (2003). http://gsf.cococlyde.org/download
9. Friedl, J.E.F.: Mastering Regular Expressions, 3rd edn. O'Reilly, Sebastopol (2006)
10. Frisch, A., Cardelli, L.: Greedy regular expression matching. In: Díaz, J., Karhumäki, J., Lepistö, A., Sannella, D. (eds.) ICALP 2004. LNCS, vol. 3142, pp. 618–629. Springer, Heidelberg (2004). https://doi.org/10.1007/978-3-540-27836-8_53

11. Houston, G.: Henry Spencer's regular expression libraries. Git repositories. https:// garyhouston.github.io/regex/. Accessed 26 May 2018
12. Kearns, S.M.: Extending regular expressions with context operators and parse extraction. Softw. Pract. Exp. **21**(8), 787–804 (1991). https://doi.org/10.1002/ spe.4380210803
13. Kuklewicz, C.: Regex-TDFA. https://hackage.haskell.org/package/regex-tdfa. Accessed 26 May 2018
14. Kuklewicz, C.: Summoned: Response to blog entry on lambda the ultimate: the programming languages weblog, February 2007. http://lambda-the-ultimate.org/ node/2064. Accessed 26 May 2018
15. Kuklewicz, C.: regex-posix-unittest (2009). https://hackage.haskell.org/package/ regex-posix-unittest. Accessed 26 May 2018
16. Kuklewicz, C.: Regex Posix. Haskell Wiki, March 2017. https://wiki.haskell.org/ Regex_Posix. Accessed 26 May 2018
17. Laurikari, V.: NFAs with tagged transitions, their conversion to deterministic automata and application to regular expressions. In: Proceedings of 7th International Symposium on String Processing and Information Retrieval, SPIRE 2000, A Coruña, September 2000, pp. 181–187. IEEE (2000). https://doi.org/10.1109/ spire.2000.878194
18. Laurikari, V.: TRE: The free and portable regex matching library. Git repository. https://github.com/laurikari/tre/. Accessed 26 May 2018
19. Laurikari, V.: TRE documentation. https://laurikari.net/tre/documentation/ regex-syntax/. Accessed 26 May 2018
20. Laurikari, V.: Efficient submatch addressing for regular expressions. Master's thesis, Helsinki University of Technology, November 2001
21. Maddock, J.: Boost.Regex (2013). https://www.boost.org/doc/libs/1_67_0/libs/ regex/doc/html/index.html. Accessed 26 May 2018
22. Okui, S., Suzuki, T.: Disambiguation in regular expression matching via position automata with augmented transitions. In: Domaratzki, M., Salomaa, K. (eds.) CIAA 2010. LNCS, vol. 6482, pp. 231–240. Springer, Heidelberg (2011). https:// doi.org/10.1007/978-3-642-18098-9_25
23. Sulzmann, M., Lu, K.Z.M.: POSIX regular expression parsing with derivatives. In: Codish, M., Sumii, E. (eds.) FLOPS 2014. LNCS, vol. 8475, pp. 203–220. Springer, Cham (2014). https://doi.org/10.1007/978-3-319-07151-0_13
24. Sulzmann, M., Lu, K.Z.M.: Derivative-based diagnosis of regular expression ambiguity. In: Han, Y.-S., Salomaa, K. (eds.) CIAA 2016. LNCS, vol. 9705, pp. 260–272. Springer, Cham (2016). https://doi.org/10.1007/978-3-319-40946-7_22
25. Thompson, K.: Programming techniques: regular expression search algorithm. Commun. ACM **11**(6), 419–422 (1968). https://doi.org/10.1145/363347.363387
26. Weideman, N., van der Merwe, B., Berglund, M., Watson, B.: Analyzing matching time behavior of backtracking regular expression matchers by using ambiguity of NFA. In: Han, Y.-S., Salomaa, K. (eds.) CIAA 2016. LNCS, vol. 9705, pp. 322–334. Springer, Cham (2016). https://doi.org/10.1007/978-3-319-40946-7_27

Monoidal Multiplexing

Apiwat Chantawibul[(✉)] and Paweł Sobociński

School of Electronics and Computer Science, University of Southampton,
Southampton SO17 1BJ, UK
billiska@gmail.com, ps@ecs.soton.ac.uk

Abstract. Given a classical algebraic structure—e.g. a monoid or
group—with carrier set X, and given a positive integer n, there is a
canonical way of obtaining the same structure on carrier set X^n by defining the required operations "pointwise". For resource-sensitive algebra
(i.e. based on mere symmetric monoidal, not cartesian structure), similar
"pointwise" operations are usually defined as a kind of syntactic sugar:
for example, given a comonoid structure on X, one obtains a comultiplication on $X \otimes X$ by tensoring two comultiplications and composing
with an appropriate permutation. This is a specific example of a general
construction that we identify and refer to as *multiplexing*. We obtain a
general theorem that guarantees that any equation that holds in the base
case will hold also for the multiplexed operations, thus generalising the
"pointwise" definitions of classical universal algebra.

Keywords: String diagrams · Resource sensitivity
Symmetric monoidal categories · Props

1 Introduction

In recent years there has been a significant amount of work that uses *string
diagrams* as a compositional syntax for various computational artefacts. A few
of the application domains are quantum foundations and quantum computing [1,
12,13], Petri nets [24,25], signal flow graphs in control theory [2,7,9,10,14],
electrical circuits [3,17,18], game theory [16] and functional programming [19,
23]. In applications, string diagrams are an intuitive, yet formal syntax and
often come equipped with an underlying algebraic theory with which one can
reason about the specific application domains using *diagrammatic reasoning*.
The deeper reason for this trend is that string diagrams are an appropriate
graphical representation for the arrows of symmetric monoidal categories, since
intuitive topological deformations capture the underlying algebraic laws. But
why symmetric monoidal categories?

In categorical universal algebra, following Lawvere [21], categories with finite
products are a canonical, categorical setting with which to capture the data
of any *classical* algebraic theory. Classical algebraic theories have an implicit
assumption that the underlying data is amenable to copying and discarding.

© Springer Nature Switzerland AG 2018
B. Fischer and T. Uustalu (Eds.): ICTAC 2018, LNCS 11187, pp. 116–131, 2018.
https://doi.org/10.1007/978-3-030-02508-3_7

Mathematically, this is reflected by the characterisation of cartesian categories as those symmetric monoidal categories where each object is equipped with a cocommutative comonoid structure and all arrows are comonoid homomorphisms [11,15]. In many applications (e.g. quantum), however, data is not classical. In others (e.g. concurrency, control), it is advisable to make copying and discarding explicit, whenever it is used. This boils down to passing from cartesian categories (Lawvere theories) to mere symmetric monoidal categories (props).

Classical universal algebra dates back to the 1930s, and is a mature subject. On the other hand, "resource-sensitive" universal algebra is still in a state of flux. The upshot of this state of affairs is that the same basic constructions are repeated in different articles, often without a clear picture of their generality. A consolidation effort is only just beginning, e.g. by extending Lawvere's functorial semantics to a suitable class of props [8] and by developing a general theory of rewriting modulo the structure of symmetric monoidal categories [4–6].

An example of a construction that appears in many of the aforementioned applications of string diagrams is "pointwise" definitions: e.g. given an operation such as multiplication $(2 \to 1)$, comultiplication $(1 \to 2)$, cup $(0 \to 2)$ or a cap $(2 \to 0)$, it is common to define its n-ary version, i.e. replacing the carrier 1 by n. For instance, two cups can be wired together appropriately to obtain a "2-cup":

In articles, the "obvious" recursive definitions are often given explicitly. Proving that "k-cups" behave as ordinary cups then reduces to a simple induction. This paper is devoted to continuing the consolidation effort through a close examination of such "pointwise" definitions, which we call *monoidal multiplexing*.

We start with an examination of *classical* "pointwise" definitions. A presentation of an algebraic theory is a pair (Σ, E) where Σ is a set of operations, each with an arity, and E is a set of equations between terms constructed from operations and variables. For a concrete example, consider the algebraic theory of a monoid. Its usual presentation is $\Sigma = \{m, e\}$, where m has arity 2 and e arity 0. The set of equations consists of associativity $(m(m(x_1, x_2), x_3) = m(x_1, m(x_2, x_3))$ and unitality $(m(x_1, e) = x_1, m(e, x_1) = x_1)$. To give a model (a concrete monoid) is to pick a carrier set X and interpretations: $m \colon X^2 \to X$, $e \colon X^0 \to X$, satisfying the required equations, given an implicit universal quantification over the variables that appear within them.

Given $k \in \mathbb{N}$, there is a canonical way to define this structure when the underlying carrier set is X^k: the operation $m{\cdot}k \colon (X^k)^2 \to X^k$ simply performs m "pointwise" on a pair of k-tuples. So, say letting $k = 3$, the multiplication takes (x_1, x_2, x_3), (y_1, y_2, y_3) to $(m(x_1, y_1), m(x_2, y_2), m(x_3, y_3))$ with unit (e, e, e). This idea is not specific to monoids and can be carried through similarly for any algebraic theory, as we shall see below.

Let us come back to Lawvere theories in more detail: the data of an algebraic theory with presentation (Σ, E) is captured by the Lawvere theory $\mathcal{L}_{\Sigma,E}$. This is a category with finite products where objects are natural numbers; moreover, the categorical product of m and n is $m + n$. A concrete description of an arrow $m \to n$ in $\mathcal{L}_{\Sigma,E}$ is as an n-tuple of terms constructed from operations of Σ and variables $x_1, x_2, \ldots x_m$, taken modulo the equations of E. Composition is substitution, in the obvious way. An outcome of this is *functorial semantics*: a classical model is a product-preserving functor $\mathcal{L}_{\Sigma,E} \to$ **Set**.

The "pointwise" construction can be explained concisely using Lawvere theories. Indeed, suppose that $\sigma \in \Sigma$ has arity n and consider some $k \in \mathbb{N}$. Write $n \cdot k$ for $\underbrace{k + k + \cdots + k}_{n \text{ times}}$ for the n-fold product of k in $\mathcal{L}_{\Sigma,E}$; recall that in a Lawvere theory $+$ is the categorical product on objects. The object k is itself a k-fold product of 1; for $1 \leq i \leq k$, denote the ith projection $\pi_i \colon k \to 1$. Note that as a term, π_i is simply the (1-tuple containing the) ith variable $\pi_i = (x_i)$.

Now let $\Pi_i \colon n \cdot k \to n = \underbrace{\pi_i + \pi_i + \cdots + \pi_i}_{n \text{ times}}$, which—concretely—is the n-tuple of variables $(x_i, x_{i+k}, \ldots, x_{i+(n-1)k})$. Together, $\{\Pi_1, \Pi_2, \ldots, \Pi_k\}$ is a complete set of projections of $n \cdot k$. Given this choice of projections, the pointwise definition of σ on k-tuples is the unique arrow $\sigma \cdot k : n \cdot k \to k$ induced by the universal property of products, where for each projection:

$$
\begin{array}{ccc}
k & \xrightarrow{\pi_i} & 1 \\
\scriptstyle{\sigma \cdot k} \Big\uparrow & & \Big\uparrow \scriptstyle{\sigma} \\
n \cdot k & \xrightarrow[\Pi_i]{} & n
\end{array}
$$

The above definition does not rely on the fact that σ is in Σ, and works for any arrow of $\mathcal{L}_{\Sigma,E}$. It is therefore easy to see that it defines a functor

$$(-) \cdot k : \mathcal{L}_{\Sigma,E} \to \mathcal{L}_{\Sigma,E}$$

with the heavy lifting taken care of by the fact that $\mathcal{L}_{\Sigma,E}$ has finite products. Now, given a model $M \colon \mathcal{L}_{\Sigma,E} \to$ **Set**, we obtain a canonical "pointwise" model on k-tuples: $M \circ [(-) \cdot k] \colon \mathcal{L}_{\Sigma,E} \to$ **Set**.

Although finite products seem to play an important role in the above development, they are in fact not necessary. To see why this is the case it is useful to note that any Lawvere theory is in fact a prop [11]. Then, returning the concrete example of the theory of monoids, $m \cdot 3$ is the string diagram

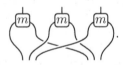

.

Our main result is that $(-) \cdot k$ defines a *strict* monoidal functor on any prop, where strict refers to preservation of $\otimes$ on the nose. An example of this for $k = 2$

and the arrow $A \otimes B$, where $A\colon 2 \to 2$ and $B\colon 2 \to 2$, is given below.

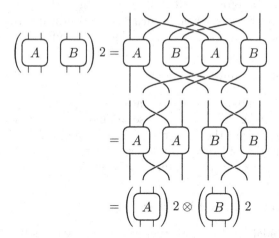

In order to define and reason about $(-)\cdot k$ *without* assuming that $\otimes$ is the categorical product, we need to carefully identify the required permutations, which feature in the diagrams above. We rely on the fact that the initial prop is the prop of permutations $\mathbb{P}$, which can be understood as the skeletal version of the category of finite sets and bijections. The latter category embeds faithfully in the category of finite sets and functions, which has both products and coproducts, and whose skeletal version can be presented as the symmetric monoidal theory of commutative monoids $\mathbb{CM}$ [20]. We use the structure of $\mathbb{CM}$ as a useful syntax with which to identify the required permutations.

Structure of the Paper. After recalling the necessary background definitions and graphical conventions in Sect. 2, we develop a toolbox of permutations in Sect. 3. We define the multiplexing operation in Sect. 4 where we prove our main result, and conclude in Sect. 5.

2   Preliminaries

2.1   Props

Props or **pro**duct and **p**ermutation categories are special cases of symmetric strict monoidal categories where the objects are generated from repeated monoidal product of a single generator object [22]. The strictness of monoidal categories means that the coherence morphisms (associator, left unitor, and right unitor) that mediate the different ways objects are combined with monoidal product are trivial: they are all identities.

The effect of strictness is that objects in props can be harmlessly identified with finite ordinals where the monoidal product on objects is addition and the monoidal unit is 0. Morphisms between props are symmetric strict monoidal functors, as described in Definition 2 that are, moreover, also identity-on-objects.

A common use of props is as a carrier of the data of an algebraic theory. Such "algebraic" props are often called *symmetric monoidal theories*. They strictly generalise Lawvere theories, which in turn can be identified with *cartesian* props where the monoidal product is also the categorical product.

2.2 Symmetric Monoidal Theory

By a symmetric monoidal theory we mean a prop that is generated from a *presentation*: a pair (Σ, E) of signature set Σ and a equation set E. As opposed to classical presentation, the elements of Σ are equipped with both arity and coarity. A presentation of particular relevance for us is the theory of commutative monoids, which appears at the beginning of Sect. 3.

2.3 Symmetric Monoidal Functors

Symmetric monoidal functors are structure-preserving maps between symmetric monoidal categories. They are typically defined with extra conditions ensuring their compatibility with the coherence conditions of monoidal categories. However, since the paper only concerns props which are symmetric strict monoidal categories, there are no further coherence conditions that the monoidal functors need to satisfy. The definition then reduces to:

Definition 1 (symmetric monoidal functor). *Let $\mathbb{C}$ and $\mathbb{D}$ be props. A symmetric monoidal functor $\mathcal{F}: \mathbb{C} \to \mathbb{D}$ consists of*

– *a functor*
$$F: \mathbb{C} \to \mathbb{D}$$

– *an isomorphism*
$$\varepsilon^{\mathcal{F}}: 0 \to F(0)$$

– *a natural isomorphism*
$$\mu^{\mathcal{F}}_{a,b}: F(a) \otimes F(b) \to F(a \otimes b)$$

for all objects $a, b \in \mathbb{C}$.

satisfying the preservation of symmetry condition:
$$\mu^{\mathcal{F}}_{b,a} \circ \sigma_{Fa,Fb} = F(\sigma_{a,b}) \circ \mu^{\mathcal{F}}_{a,b}$$

where σ denotes the symmetry natural transformation of the props.

The strictness of symmetric monoidal functors refers to the additional property that the preservation of symmetric monoidal structure is, in fact, on the nose.

Definition 2 (symmetric strict monoidal functor). *A symmetric monoidal functor* $\mathcal{F}\colon \mathbb{C} \to \mathbb{D}$ *is* strict *if* $\varepsilon^{\mathcal{F}}$ *is the identity morphism on* 0, *i.e.,*

$$0 = F(0)$$

and $\mu^{\mathcal{F}}$ *is the identity natural transformation, i.e.,*

$$F(a) \otimes F(b) = F(a \otimes b)$$

thus satisfying the strict preservation of symmetry condition:

$$\sigma_{Fa,Fb} = F(\sigma_{a,b})$$

2.4   Graphical Conventions

Props admit a particularly simple and topologically intuitive string diagrammatic notation. The objects (which, as we previously mentioned, can be considered as finite ordinals) are drawn as an ordered list of wires. We will draw a morphism $A\colon n \to m$ as an A-labelled box with n strings originating from the bottom and m strings coming out from the top. Sometimes, in specific cases such as $\mathbb{CM}$, a custom graphical notation is used instead to represent generators. The monoidal product of two morphisms is represented by juxtaposing two diagrams side-by-side and the composition of two morphisms is drawn by connecting the diagrams with matching number of strings vertically, as shown below.

3   Permutations Structured by $\mathbb{CM}$

The goal of this section is to assemble a toolbox of definitions and results about permutations, which are needed for a proper account of multiplexing. By permutations in an arbitrary prop $\mathbb{X}$, we refer to the morphisms of $\mathbb{X}$ contained within the image of the unique (but possibly non-faithful) morphism of props $\mathbb{P} \to \mathbb{X}$ where $\mathbb{P}$ is the initial prop which is equivalent to the category of finite ordinals and bijections. To manage the class of relevant permutations, we first note that $\mathbb{P}$ embeds in the prop of commutative monoids $\mathbb{CM}$ which is also equivalent to the category of finite ordinals and (all, i.e. possibly non-monotone) functions.

Remark 1. The embedding $\mathbb{P} \to \mathbb{CM}$ implies that we are able to use $\mathbb{CM}$ as a "sound and complete calculus" for permutations in $\mathbb{P}$—it is "sound" because equations involving the permutations in $\mathbb{CM}$ are reflected in $\mathbb{P}$ due to faithfulness of the embedding, and it is "complete" because equations involving permutations in $\mathbb{P}$ hold also in $\mathbb{CM}$ due to functoriality. Unlike $\mathbb{P}$, $\mathbb{CM}$ has finite (categorical) products and coproducts which, on objects, are the multiplication and addition of finite ordinals respectively; this is enough structure for description of the class of permutations of interest.

In Sect. 4, we will define the multiplexing operation on prop $\mathbb{X}$ by using the aforementioned class of permutations. Given the above embedding, we are able to do this without loss of generality.

In order to retain the "syntactic-flavour" of working with string diagrams, we use the well-known presentation [20] of $\mathbb{CM}$. The generators of $\mathbb{CM}$ are multiplication ⩓ and unit ⬦ while the commutative monoid equations are:

The permutations of interest follow from the universal properties of a *particular* choice of products and coproducts in $\mathbb{CM}$. Of course, the object part of products and coproducts is forced on us since $\mathbb{CM}$ is skeletal: the only choice is the projections and injections. In fact, these are determined by the following two conditions, which follow from usual conventions in diagrammatic reasoning:

1. the monoidal product of $\mathbb{CM}$ is diagrammatically represented by juxtaposing string diagrams side-by-side. Thus the left injection ought to "pick out" the left hand side of the composite diagram, the right the right hand side.
2. the product is *strictly right-distributive* over the coproduct, i.e., the canonical morphism:

$$n{\cdot}k + m{\cdot}k \longrightarrow (n+m){\cdot}k \qquad \text{(SRD)}$$

is required to be the identity. Informally, this translates to the identification of the following two ways of grouping of identity string diagrams:

The informal use of ellipses, as above, is part of what this work intends to eliminate.

Coproducts and Injections. From the above conditions, the inductive characterisations of projections and injections can be deduced. Fix the notation $\iota_{1,n,m}\colon n \to n+m$ and $\iota_{2,n,m}\colon m \to n+m$ for the left and right injections, respectively. Write $\sigma_{n,m}\colon n+m \to m+n$ for the isomorphism obtained from the universal property (of coproducts), which coincides with the symmetry of $\mathbb{CM}$:

$$(1)$$

The left injection can be given inductively as:

$$\iota_{1,0,0} = id_0,$$
$$\iota_{1,a,b+1} = \iota_{1,a,b} \otimes \blacklozenge,$$
$$\iota_{1,1+a,b} = id_1 \otimes \iota_{1,a,b}.$$

Products and Projections. We fix notation $\pi_{1,m,n}\colon m{\cdot}n \to m$ and $\pi_{2,m,n}\colon m{\cdot}n \to n$ for the left and right projections, respectively. Let $\rho_{n,m}\colon n{\cdot}m \to m{\cdot}n$ be defined by the universal property of products, as illustrated below:

$$
\begin{array}{ccc}
 & \xrightarrow{\quad\pi_{2,m,n}\quad} m{\cdot}n \xrightarrow{\quad\pi_{1,m,n}\quad} & \\
 & \rho_{n,m}\updownarrow\rho_{m,n} & \\
n \xleftarrow{\ \pi_{1,n,m}\ } n{\cdot}m \xrightarrow{\ \pi_{2,n,m}\ } m &
\end{array}
\tag{2}
$$

Note that $\rho_{n,m} = \rho_{m,n}^{-1}$. It is easy to check that $\rho_{m,n}$ is a natural transformation from $-_1{\cdot}-_2\colon \mathbb{CM} \times \mathbb{CM} \to \mathbb{CM}$ to $-_2{\cdot}-_1\colon \mathbb{CM} \times \mathbb{CM} \to \mathbb{CM}$. Similarly, the projections are natural transformations from $-_1{\cdot}-_2\colon \mathbb{CM} \times \mathbb{CM} \to \mathbb{CM}$ to the two projection functors. In subsequent mentions, the subscript of these natural transformations are omitted as they are implied by expressions of source and target objects.

Lemma 1. *The strict right-distributivity condition uniquely determines the inductive characterisation of the left projection π_1 as:*

$$\pi_{1,0,k} = id_0 \tag{3}$$
$$\pi_{1,1,1} = id_1 \tag{4}$$

$$\pi_{1,1,1+k} = \blacktriangle \circ (id_1 \otimes \pi_{1,1,k}) \tag{5}$$

$$\pi_{1,a+b,k} = \pi_{1,a,k} \otimes \pi_{1,b,k} \tag{6}$$

Proof. Projections given by (3), (4), and (5) are imposed by the universal properties of initial object 0 and terminal object 1. Lastly, (6) follows from fixing identity as the canonical right-distributor in the commutative diagram defining it as seen below:

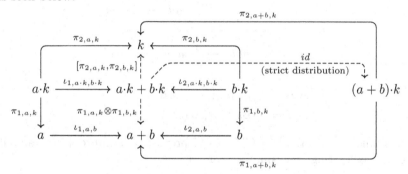

More explicitly, the derivation starts from noting that strict distribution condition equates the canonical right-distributor with identity:

$$id = (\pi_{1,a,k} \otimes \pi_{1,b,k}, [\pi_{2,a,k}, \pi_{2,b,k}])$$

Post-composing with the first projection of $(a+b)\cdot k$ on both sides results in

$$\pi_{1,a+b,k} = \pi_{1,a,k} \otimes \pi_{1,b,k}$$

□

3.1   Product Functor; Left and Right Multiplication

We take a closer look at the product functor that follows from our particular choice of projections and note the intuitive relationship it has with the desired multiplexing operation on arbitrary props. The induced product functor $-_1\cdot-_2\colon \mathbb{CM}\times\mathbb{CM} \to \mathbb{CM}$ maps $(A\colon a' \to a, B\colon b' \to b)$ to the morphism induced by the universal property of $a\cdot b$:

$$
\begin{array}{ccccc}
a & \xleftarrow{\ \pi_1\ } & a\cdot b & \xrightarrow{\ \pi_2\ } & b \\
{\scriptstyle A}\uparrow & & {\scriptstyle A\cdot B}\Big\uparrow & & \uparrow{\scriptstyle B} \\
a' & \xleftarrow{\ \pi_1\ } & a'\cdot b' & \xrightarrow{\ \pi_2\ } & b'
\end{array}
$$

Writing id_a as just a for brevity, $A\cdot B$ can be factorised using the universal property of products as:

$$
\begin{array}{ccc}
a\cdot b' & \xrightarrow{\ a\cdot B\ } & a\cdot b \\
{\scriptstyle A\cdot b'}\uparrow & {\scriptstyle A\cdot B}\ \nearrow & \uparrow{\scriptstyle A\cdot b} \\
a'\cdot b' & \xrightarrow{\ a'\cdot B\ } & a'\cdot b
\end{array}
\tag{7}
$$

We demonstrate in Lemma 2 that left multiplication $k\cdot(-)\colon \mathbb{CM} \to \mathbb{CM}$ is much easier to describe, namely as "k-fold monoidal product" and thus simple to define in arbitrary props. The right multiplication $(-)\cdot k\colon \mathbb{CM} \to \mathbb{CM}$, however, is used to define the multiplex operation in Sect. 4. To this end, we note the natural symmetry of product ρ can be used to express right multiplication in terms of left-multiplication instead as shown by the following commutative diagram:

$$
\begin{array}{ccccccc}
b'\cdot a & \xrightarrow{\ \rho\ } & a\cdot b' & \xrightarrow{\ a\cdot B\ } & a\cdot b & \xleftarrow{\ \rho\ } & b\cdot a \\
{\scriptstyle b'\cdot A}\uparrow & & {\scriptstyle A\cdot b'}\uparrow & {\scriptstyle A\cdot B}\nearrow\ {\scriptstyle A\cdot b}\uparrow & & & \uparrow{\scriptstyle b\cdot A} \\
b'\cdot a' & \xleftarrow{\ \rho\ } & a'\cdot b' & \xrightarrow{\ a'\cdot B\ } & a'\cdot b & \xrightarrow{\ \rho\ } & b\cdot a'
\end{array}
\tag{8}
$$

$$A\cdot B = \rho_{b,a} \circ (b\cdot A) \circ \rho_{a'\cdot b} \circ (a'\cdot B)$$
$$A\cdot B = (a\cdot B) \circ \rho_{b',a} \circ (b'\cdot A) \circ \rho_{a'\cdot b'}$$

The bifunctor $-_1\cdot-_2\colon \mathbb{CM}\times\mathbb{CM} \to \mathbb{CM}$ provides a useful tool for manipulation of $\mathbb{CM}$ as a string diagram, for example:

$$(\text{⚬}) \, 2 \circ (\text{⚬}) = (\text{⚬}) \cdot (\text{⚬}) = 2(\text{⚬}) \circ (\text{⚬}) \, 2$$

$= (\text{⚬}) \cdot (\text{⚬}) =$

(Note that the diagrams are only equal w.r.t. the equational theory of $\mathbb{CM}$.)
For any natural number k, the intuitive diagrammatic description of

- left multiplication $k \cdot (-)$ is k-fold monoidal product of the argument.
- right multiplication $(-) \cdot k$ is k copies of the argument 'placed in an overlapping cascade'.

Lemma 2. *Given any $A: a' \to a$ in $\mathbb{CM}$, the left multiplication $k \cdot (-) \colon \mathbb{CM} \to \mathbb{CM}$ satisfies:*

$$0 \cdot A = 0 \qquad\qquad k \cdot A = A \otimes (k-1) \cdot A$$

Proof. The first equation is forced by initiality of 0. The second equation follows from strict right-distributivity (SRD) inducing a natural identity:

$$(1 + (k-1)) \cdot (-) \Rightarrow 1 \cdot (-) \otimes (k-1) \cdot (-)$$

3.2 Natural Permutations Structured by $\mathbb{CM}$

We summarise the relationships between the natural family of permutations structured by $\mathbb{CM}$ here, ready to be transferred into arbitrary props on which multiplexing will be defined.

Let $\xi_{k,a,b} \colon (k \cdot a) + (k \cdot b) \to k \cdot (a + b)$ be the natural isomorphism defined by the canonical left-distribution of product over the coproduct (as opposed to the right-distribution which is required to be identity in (SRD)). Together with the symmetry of coproduct σ, the symmetry of product ρ, and the product functor defined previously, we obtain the following commutative diagram:

$$
\begin{array}{ccccccc}
 & & & k \cdot (\sigma) & & & \\
k \cdot (a+b) & \xrightarrow{\;\xi\;} & k \cdot a + k \cdot b & \xrightarrow{\;\sigma\;} & k \cdot b + k \cdot a & \xrightarrow{\;\xi\;} & k \cdot (b+a) \\
{\scriptstyle\rho}\downarrow & & {\scriptstyle\rho\otimes\rho}\downarrow & & {\scriptstyle\rho\otimes\rho}\downarrow & & {\scriptstyle\rho}\downarrow \\
(a+b) \cdot k & \xrightarrow{\;id\;} & a \cdot k + b \cdot k & \xrightarrow{\;\sigma\;} & b \cdot k + a \cdot k & \xrightarrow{\;id\;} & (b+a) \cdot k \\
 & & & (\sigma) \cdot k & & &
\end{array}
\qquad (9)
$$

which commutes because they are all canonical isomorphisms. In the diagram above, we omit the arrowheads and subscripts to emphasise that these are all isomorphisms.

Lemma 3. ξ *has an inductive characterisation with base case $\xi_{0,a,b} = id_0$ and inductive case as shown by the following commutative diagram:*

$$(1 + k)\cdot(a + b) \xleftarrow{\quad id \quad} a + b + k\cdot(a + b)$$

$$\xi_{(1+k),a,b} \uparrow \qquad\qquad\qquad \uparrow id_a \otimes id_b \otimes \xi_{k,a,b}$$

$$a + b + k\cdot a + k\cdot b$$

$$\uparrow id_a \otimes \sigma_{k\cdot a,b} \otimes id_{k\cdot b}$$

$$(1 + k)\cdot a + (1 + k)\cdot b \xrightarrow{\quad id \quad} a + k\cdot a + b + k\cdot b$$

Proof. The lemma is a special case where $n = 1$ of

$$(n + m)\cdot a + (n + m)\cdot b \xleftarrow{\quad \xi \quad} (n + m)\cdot(a + b) \xrightarrow{\quad id \quad} n\cdot(a + b) + m\cdot(a + b)$$

$$\left\downarrow id \qquad\qquad\qquad\qquad\qquad\qquad\qquad\qquad\qquad \right\downarrow \xi \otimes \xi$$

$$n\cdot a + m\cdot a + n\cdot b + m\cdot b \xrightarrow{\quad id_{n\cdot a} \otimes \sigma_{n\cdot b, m\cdot a} \otimes id_{m\cdot b} \quad} n\cdot a + n\cdot b + m\cdot a + m\cdot b$$

where the diagram commutes because they mediate canonical ways to distribute $(n + m)\cdot(a + b)$. □

Example 1. From the inductive definition of ξ, the string diagram of $\xi_{3,2,2}$ is:

4 Multiplexing

We have seen in the previous section that $(-)\cdot k \colon \mathbb{CM} \to \mathbb{CM}$ maps diagrams to our desired "pointwise" k-fold version. To define this as a functor on an arbitrary prop $\mathbb{X}$, we define it not through the product functor (which may not exists in $\mathbb{X}$) but through repeated tensor and permutations. With Remark 1 in mind, we abuse the notation and denote permutations in arbitrary props with the same symbols—ξ, ρ, σ—as the corresponding permutations defined in $\mathbb{CM}$.

Definition 3 (multiplexing map). *For an arbitrary prop $\mathbb{X}$, a morphism $A \colon a' \to a$ in $\mathbb{X}$, and any natural number k, define $k\cdot(-) \colon \mathbb{X}[a', a] \to \mathbb{X}[k\cdot a', k\cdot a]$ by recursion as:*

$$0\cdot A = id_0 \qquad\qquad\qquad k\cdot A = A \otimes (k - 1)\cdot A.$$

Next, we define $(-)\cdot k \colon \mathbb{X}[a', a] \to \mathbb{X}[a'\cdot k, a\cdot k]$ as:

$$A\cdot k = \rho_{k,a} \circ (k\cdot A) \circ \rho_{a',k}$$

where $\rho_{a,k} \colon a\cdot k \to k\cdot a$ denotes the permutation from (2). Call $k\cdot A$ the k-fold monoidal product of A and $A\cdot k$ the k-multiplex of A.

Example 2. Let $A\colon 2 \to 3$ be a morphism in $\mathbb{X}$, then

and

The above defines $k\cdot(-)$ and $(-)\cdot k$ as functions on homsets. On objects, we let $[k\cdot(-)](m) = k\cdot m = m\cdot k = [(-)\cdot k](m)$.

Lemma 4. *Both $k\cdot(-)$ and $(-)\cdot k$ strictly preserve the monoidal unit, i.e., on objects:*

$$0\cdot k = 0 = k\cdot 0$$

Lemma 5. *In the case $\mathbb{X} = \mathbb{CM}$, the definitions of $k\cdot(-)$ and $(-)\cdot k$ as defined inductively in Definition 3 agree with their definition as a one-argument product functor given in Sect. 3.1.*

Next, we verify that both $k\cdot(-)$ and $(-)\cdot k$ (strictly) preserve composition, i.e., are endofunctors on $\mathbb{X}$ as a plain category.

Lemma 6. *$k\cdot(-)$ strictly preserves composition.*

Proof. Using induction on k, the base case is derived by:

$$(0\cdot A) \circ (0\cdot B) = id_0 \circ id_0$$
$$= id_0$$
$$= 0\cdot(A \circ B)$$

and the inductive case is derived by:

$$
\begin{aligned}
(k\cdot A) \circ (k\cdot B) &= (A \otimes (k-1)\cdot A) \circ (B \otimes (k-1)\cdot B) &&; \text{distributivity}\\
&= (A \circ B) \otimes ((k-1)\cdot A) \circ ((k-1)\cdot B) &&; \text{interchange law}\\
&= (A \circ B) \otimes ((k-1)\cdot(A \circ B)) &&; \text{hypothesis}\\
&= k\cdot(A \circ B) &&; \text{distributivity}
\end{aligned}
$$

$\square$

Lemma 7. *$(-)\cdot k$ strictly preserves composition, i.e., the following diagram commutes in $\mathbb{X}$ for all $A\colon b \to a$ and $B\colon b' \to b$.*

$$
\begin{array}{ccc}
a{\cdot}k & \xrightarrow{\;id\;} & a{\cdot}k \\
\Big\uparrow{\scriptstyle A{\cdot}k} & & \Big\uparrow \\
b{\cdot}k & {\scriptstyle (A\circ B){\cdot}k} & \\
\Big\uparrow{\scriptstyle B{\cdot}k} & & \Big\uparrow \\
b'{\cdot}k & \xrightarrow{\;id\;} & b'{\cdot}k
\end{array}
$$

Proof. The following commutes by diagram pasting:

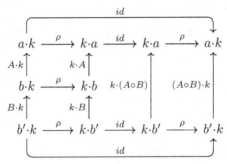

where the middle rectangle commutes by Lemma 6; the top and bottom rectangle commutes by (2); and other rectangles to the side commute as direct consequences of Definition 3.   □

The next two results demonstrate a significant difference between $k{\cdot}(-)$ and $(-){\cdot}k$: whereas the former preserves monoidal product only up to isomorphism, the latter preserves it on the nose.

Lemma 8. $k{\cdot}(-)$ *preserves tensor up to isomorphism via the naturality of* ξ.

Proof. The proof is by induction on k, relying on the inductive characterisation of ξ given in Lemma 3. The base case satisfies naturality condition because $(0{\cdot}A)\otimes(0{\cdot}B)=id_0\otimes id_0=id_0=0{\cdot}(A\otimes B)$ by Definition 3.

The inductive case is given by the commutativity of the outer perimeter of

$$
\begin{array}{ccc}
(1+k){\cdot}a+(1+k){\cdot}b & \xrightarrow{\;\xi_{(1+k),a,b}\;} & (1+k){\cdot}(a+b) \\
\Big\uparrow{\scriptstyle id} & & \Big\uparrow{\scriptstyle id} \\
a+k{\cdot}a+b+k{\cdot}b \xrightarrow{id_a\otimes\sigma_{k{\cdot}a,b}\otimes id_{k{\cdot}b}} a+b+k{\cdot}a+k{\cdot}b \xrightarrow{id_a\otimes id_b\otimes\xi_{k,a,b}} & & a+b+k{\cdot}(a+b) \\
\Big\uparrow{\scriptstyle (1+k){\cdot}A\otimes(k+1){\cdot}B}\quad \Big\uparrow{\scriptstyle A\otimes B\otimes k{\cdot}A\otimes k{\cdot}B} & & \Big\uparrow{\scriptstyle (1+k){\cdot}(A\otimes B)} \\
a'+k{\cdot}a'+b'+k{\cdot}b' \xrightarrow{id_{a'}\otimes\sigma_{k{\cdot}a',b'}\otimes id_{k{\cdot}b'}} a'+b'+k{\cdot}a'+k{\cdot}b' \xrightarrow{id_{a'}\otimes id_{b'}\otimes\xi_{k,a',b'}} & & a'+b'+k{\cdot}(a'+b') \\
\Big\uparrow{\scriptstyle id} & & \Big\uparrow{\scriptstyle id} \\
(1+k){\cdot}a'+(1+k){\cdot}b' & \xrightarrow{\;\xi_{(1+k),a',b'}\;} & (1+k){\cdot}(a'+b')
\end{array}
$$

which is obtained by pasting commutative diagrams where the top and bottom rectangles commute by Lemma 3; the middle-left rectangle commutes by naturality of symmetry σ; and the middle-right rectangle commutes by induction hypothesis.   □

Lemma 9. $(-) \cdot k$ *strictly preserves tensor.*

Proof. The lemma is represented by the front face of the following diagram

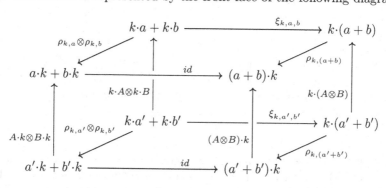

which commutes by diagram pasting with back face from Lemma 8, left and right faces from Definition 3, and top and bottom faces from the left rectangle in (9). □

Lemma 10. $(-) \cdot k$ *strictly preserves symmetry, i.e., the following commutes:*

$$
\begin{array}{ccc}
(b+a) \cdot k & \xrightarrow{\ id\ } & b \cdot k + a \cdot k \\
{\scriptstyle (\sigma_{a,b}) \cdot k} \uparrow & & \uparrow {\scriptstyle \sigma_{a \cdot k, b \cdot k}} \\
(a+b) \cdot k & \xrightarrow{\ id\ } & a \cdot k + b \cdot k
\end{array}
$$

Proof. Directly from the commutativity of the bottom rectangle in (9). □

Theorem 1. $(-) \cdot k$ *is a symmetric strict monoidal functor.*

Proof. Follows directly from Lemmas 4, 7, 9, and 10. □

The fact that $(-) \cdot k \colon \mathbb{X} \to \mathbb{X}$ is a strict monoidal functor is the main technical result of our work and it is worthwhile to examine its significance. First, its action on arrows gives us a concise definition of multiplexing: given an arrow $A \colon m \to n$ in $\mathbb{X}$, $A \cdot k$ is its k-multiplexed version. Moreover, functoriality means that any equation $A = B$ that holds for arrows in $\mathbb{X}$ will also hold for its k-multiplexed variation, i.e. $A \cdot k = B \cdot k$. Finally, given a notion of model as a symmetric monoidal functor $\mathbb{X} \to \mathbf{C}$, precomposition with $(-) \cdot k$ yields a model on which any algebraic structure of $\mathbb{X}$ is defined "pointwise", generalising the situation for classical models outlined in the Introduction.

5   Conclusions and Future Work

We showed that "pointwise" definitions of classical universal algebra generalise to resource-sensitive theories. Our main result shows that this operation defines a strict monoidal functor $(-) \cdot k$ on any prop $\mathbb{X}$. By identifying a suitable categorical setting in which to define and reason about the required permutations, we showed that although the similar operation on Lawvere theories seemingly requires the presence of categorical products, they are actually not necessary.

We note that this construction can be extended to braided monoidal categories: in fact, every string diagram for symmetry drawn in this article is already shown in compatible braiding scheme.

Our work fits into the recent trend of consolidating disparate strands of theory and applications of string diagrams in computer science and related fields, and through it, the crystallisation of a "resource-sensitive universal algebra".

References

1. Abramsky, S., Coecke, B.: A categorical semantics of quantum protocols. In: Proceedings of 19th Annual IEEE Symposium on Logic in Computer Science, LICS 2004, July 2004, Turku, pp. 415–425. IEEE CS Press, Washington, DC (2004). https://doi.org/10.1109/lics.2004.1319636
2. Baez, J.C., Erbele, J.: Categories in control. arXiv preprint 1405.6881 (2014). https://arxiv.org/abs/1405.6881
3. Baez, J.C., Fong, B.: A compositional framework for passive linear networks. arXiv preprint 1504.05625 (2015). https://arxiv.org/abs/1504.05625
4. Bonchi, F., Gadducci, F., Kissinger, A., Sobociński, P., Zanasi, F.: Rewriting modulo symmetric monoidal structure. In: Proceedings of 31st Annual ACM/IEEE Symposium on Logic and Computer Science, LICS 2016, pp. 710–719. ACM Press, New York (2016). https://doi.org/10.1145/2933575.2935316
5. Bonchi, F., Gadducci, F., Kissinger, A., Sobociński, P., Zanasi, F.: Confluence of graph rewriting with interfaces. In: Yang, H. (ed.) ESOP 2017. LNCS, vol. 10201, pp. 141–169. Springer, Heidelberg (2017). https://doi.org/10.1007/978-3-662-54434-1_6
6. Bonchi, F., Gadducci, F., Kissinger, A., Sobociński, P., Zanasi, F.: Rewriting with Frobenius. In: Proceedings of 33rd Annual ACM/IEEE Symposium on Logic and Computer Science, LICS 2018, July 2018, Oxford, pp. 165–174. ACM Press, New York (2018). https://doi.org/10.1145/3209108.3209137
7. Bonchi, F., Holland, J., Pavlovic, D., Sobociński, P.: Refinement for signal flow graphs. In: Meyer, R., Nestmann, U. (eds.) Proceedings of 28th International Conference on Concurrency Theory, CONCUR 2017, September 2017, Berlin, Leibniz International Proceedings in Informatics, vol. 85, p. 24. Dagstuhl Publishing, Saarbrücken, Wadern (2017). https://doi.org/10.4230/lipics.concur.2017.24
8. Bonchi, F., Pavlovic, D., Sobocinski, P.: Functorial semantics for relational theories. arXiv preprint 1711.08699 (2017). https://arxiv.org/abs/1711.08699
9. Bonchi, F., Sobociński, P., Zanasi, F.: Full abstraction for signal flow graphs. In: 42nd Annual ACM SIGPLAN-SIGACT Symposium on Principles of Programming Languages, POPL 2015, January 2015, Mumbai, pp. 515–526. ACM Press, New York (2015). https://doi.org/10.1145/2676726.2676993
10. Bonchi, F., Sobociński, P., Zanasi, F.: The calculus of signal flow diagrams I: linear relations on streams. Inf. Comput. **252**, 2–29 (2017). https://doi.org/10.1016/j.ic.2016.03.002
11. Bonchi, F., Sobociński, P., Zanasi, F.: Deconstructing Lawvere with distributive laws. J. Log. Algebr. Methods Program. **95**, 128–146 (2018). https://doi.org/10.1016/j.jlamp.2017.12.002

12. Coecke, B., Duncan, R.: Interacting quantum observables. In: Aceto, L., Damgård, I., Goldberg, L.A., Halldórsson, M.M., Ingólfsdóttir, A., Walukiewicz, I. (eds.) ICALP 2008. LNCS, vol. 5126, pp. 298–310. Springer, Heidelberg (2008). https://doi.org/10.1007/978-3-540-70583-3_25

13. Coecke, B., Kissinger, A.: Picturing Quantum Processes: A First Course in Quantum Theory and Diagrammatic Reasoning. Cambridge University Press, Cambridge (2017). https://doi.org/10.1017/9781316219317

14. Fong, B., Rapisarda, P., Sobociński, P.: A categorical approach to open and interconnected dynamical systems. In: Proceedings of 31st Annual ACM/IEEE Symposium on Logic and Computer Science, LICS 2016, July 2016, New York, NY, pp. 495–504. ACM Press, New York (2016). https://doi.org/10.1145/2933575.2934556

15. Fox, T.: Coalgebras and cartesian categories. Commun. Algebr. **4**(7), 665–667 (1976). https://doi.org/10.1080/00927877608822127

16. Ghani, N., Hedges, J., Winschel, V., Zahn, P.: Compositional game theory. In: Proceedings of 33rd Annual ACM/IEEE Symposium on Logic in Computer Science, LICS 2018, July 2018, Oxford, pp. 472–481. ACM Press, New York (2018). https://doi.org/10.1145/3209108.3209165

17. Ghica, D.R.: Diagrammatic reasoning for delay-insensitive asynchronous circuits. In: Coecke, B., Ong, L., Panangaden, P. (eds.) Computation, Logic, Games, and Quantum Foundations. The Many Facets of Samson Abramsky. LNCS, vol. 7860, pp. 52–68. Springer, Heidelberg (2013). https://doi.org/10.1007/978-3-642-38164-5_5

18. Ghica, D.R., Jung, A.: Categorical semantics of digital circuits. In: Proceedings of 2016 Conference on Formal Methods in Computer-Aided Design, FMCAD 2016, October 2016, Mountain View, CA, pp. 41–48. IEEE CS Press, Washington, DC (2016). https://doi.org/10.1109/fmcad.2016.7886659

19. Hinze, R.: Kan extensions for program optimisation *or*: art and dan explain an old trick. In: Gibbons, J., Nogueira, P. (eds.) MPC 2012. LNCS, vol. 7342, pp. 324–362. Springer, Heidelberg (2012). https://doi.org/10.1007/978-3-642-31113-0_16

20. Lack, S.: Composing PROPs. Theory Appl. Categ. **13**, 147–163 (2004). http://www.tac.mta.ca/tac/volumes/13/9/13-09abs.html

21. Lawvere, F.W.: Functorial semantics of algebraic theories. Proc. Natl. Acad. Sci. USA **50**(5), 869–872 (1963). https://doi.org/10.1073/pnas.50.5.869

22. Mac Lane, S.: Categorical algebra. Bull. Am. Math. Soc. **71**, 40–106 (1965). https://doi.org/10.1090/s0002-9904-1965-11234-4

23. Piróg, M., Wu, N.: String diagrams for free monads (functional pearl). In: Proceedings of 21st ACM SIGPLAN International Conference on Functional Programming, ICFP 2016, September 2016, Nara, pp. 490–501. ACM Press, New York (2016). https://doi.org/10.1145/2951913.2951947

24. Sobociński, P.: Representations of Petri net interactions. In: Gastin, P., Laroussinie, F. (eds.) CONCUR 2010. LNCS, vol. 6269, pp. 554–568. Springer, Heidelberg (2010). https://doi.org/10.1007/978-3-642-15375-4_38

25. Sobociński, P.: Nets, relations and linking diagrams. In: Heckel, R., Milius, S. (eds.) CALCO 2013. LNCS, vol. 8089, pp. 282–298. Springer, Heidelberg (2013). https://doi.org/10.1007/978-3-642-40206-7_21

Input/Output Stochastic Automata with Urgency: Confluence and Weak Determinism

Pedro R. D'Argenio[1,2,3]([⊠]) and Raúl E. Monti[1,2]

[1] Universidad Nacional de Córdoba, FAMAF, Córdoba, Argentina
{dargenio,rmonti}@famaf.unc.edu.ar
[2] CONICET, Córdoba, Argentina
[3] Saarland University, Department of Computer Science, Saarbrücken, Germany

Abstract. In a previous work, we introduced an input/output variant of stochastic automata (IOSA) that, once the model is closed (i.e., all synchronizations are resolved), the resulting automaton is fully stochastic, that is, it does not contain non-deterministic choices. However, such variant is not sufficiently versatile for compositional modelling. In this article, we extend IOSA with urgent actions. This extension greatly increases the modularization of the models, allowing to take better advantage on compositionality than its predecessor. However, this extension introduces non-determinism even in closed models. We first show that confluent models are weakly deterministic in the sense that, regardless the resolution of the non-determinism, the stochastic behaviour is the same. In addition, we provide sufficient conditions to ensure that a network of interacting IOSAs is confluent without the need to analyse the larger composed IOSA.

1 Introduction

The advantages of compositional modelling complex systems can hardly be overestimated. On the one hand, compositional modelling facilitates systematic design, allowing the designer to focus on the construction of small models for the components whose operational behavior is mostly well understood, and on the synchronization between the components, which are in general quite evident. On the other hand, it facilitates the interchange of components in a model, enables compositional analysis, and helps on attacking the state explosion problem.

In particular we focus on modelling of stochastic system for dependability and performance analysis, and aim to general models that require more than the usual negative exponential distribution. Indeed, phenomena such as timeouts in communication protocols, hard deadlines in real-time systems, human response times or the variability of the delay of sound and video frames (so-called jitter)

This work was supported by grants ANPCyT PICT-2017-3894 (RAFTSys), SeCyT-UNC 33620180100354CB (ARES), and the ERC Advanced Grant 695614 (POWVER).

© Springer Nature Switzerland AG 2018
B. Fischer and T. Uustalu (Eds.): ICTAC 2018, LNCS 11187, pp. 132–152, 2018.
https://doi.org/10.1007/978-3-030-02508-3_8

in modern multi-media communication systems are typically described by non-memoryless distributions such as uniform, log-normal, or Weibull distributions.

The analysis of this type of model quite often can only be performed through discrete event simulation [22]. However, simulation requires that the model under study is fully stochastic, that is, they should not contain non-deterministic choices. Unfortunately, compositional modelling languages such as stochastic process algebras with general distributions (see [5] and references therein) and Modest [4,18,19], were designed so that the non-determinism arises naturally as the result of composition.

Based on stochastic automata [10–12] and probabilistic I/O automata [26], we introduced input/output stochastic automata (IOSA) [13]. IOSAs were designed so that parallel composition works naturally and, moreover, the system becomes fully stochastic –not containing non-determinism– when closed, i.e., when all interactions are resolved and no input is left available in the model. IOSA splits the set of actions into inputs and outputs and let them behave in a reactive and generative manner respectively [17]. Thus, inputs are passive and their occurrence depends only on their interaction with outputs. Instead, occurrence of outputs are governed by the expiration of a timer which is set according to a given random variable. In addition, and not to block the occurrence of outputs, IOSAs are required to be input enabled.

We have used IOSA as input language of the rare event simulation tool FIG [6,7] and have experienced the limitations of the language, in particular when transcribing models originally given in terms of variants of dynamic fault trees (DFT) with repairs [24]. To illustrate the problem, suppose the simple digital system of Fig. 1.

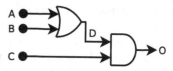

Fig. 1. A simple digital system.

We would like to measure the average time that the output O is 1 given that we know the distributions of the times in which the values on inputs A, B, and C change from 0 to 1 and vice-versa. The natural modelling of such system is to define 5 IOSA modules, three of them modelling the behaviour of the input signals and the other two modelling the OR and AND gates. Then we compose and synchronize the 5 modules properly. The main problem is that, while the dynamic behaviour of the input signal modules are governed by stochastically timed actions, the dynamic behavior of the gates are instantaneous and thus, for instance the output D of the OR gate, may change immediately after the arrival of signals A or B. Similar situations arise when modeling the behaviour of DFT under complex gates like priority AND, Spares or Repair boxes. As a consequence, we observe that the introduction of urgent actions will allow for a direct and simple compositional modelling of situations like the one recently described. Also, it is worth to notice that the need for instantaneous but causally dependent synchronization have been observed in many other timed modelling languages, notably, in Uppaal, with the introduction of committed locations, urgent locations and urgent synchronization [2,3].

Based on IMC [20] and, particularly, on I/O-IMC [9], in this article we extended IOSA with urgent actions (Sect. 2). Urgent actions are also partitioned in input and output actions and, though inputs behave reactively and passively as before, urgent outputs are executed instantaneously as soon as the enabling state is reached. We also give semantics to IOSA with urgent actions (from now on, we simply call it IOSA) in terms of NLMP [14,25] (Sect. 3), and define its parallel composition (Sect. 4).

The problem is that urgent actions on IOSA introduce non-determinism. Fortunately, non-determinism is limited to urgent actions and, in many occasions, it is introduced by confluent urgent output actions as a result of a parallel composition. Such non-determinism turns to be spurious in the sense that it does not change the stochastic behaviour of the model. In this paper, we characterize confluence on IOSAs (Sect. 5), define the concept of weak determinism, and show that a confluent closed IOSA is weakly deterministic (Sect. 6). Notably, a weakly deterministic IOSA is amenable to discrete event simulation. Milner [23] has provided a proof that confluence preserves weak determinism but it is confined to a discrete non-probabilistic setting. A similar proof has been used by Crouzen [9] on I/O-IMC but, though the model is stochastic, the proof is limited to discrete non-probabilistic transitions. Contrarily, our proof has to deal with continuous probabilities (since urgent action may sample on continuous random variables), hence making use of the solid measure theoretical approach. In particular, we address the complications of defining a particular form of weak transition on a setting that is normally elusive.

Based on the work of Crouzen [9] for I/O-IMC, in Sect. 7, we provide sufficient conditions to ensure that a closed IOSA is confluent and hence, weakly deterministic. If the IOSA is the result of composing several smaller IOSAs, the verification of the conditions is performed by inspecting the components rather than the resulting composed IOSA.

2   Input/Output Stochastic Automata with Urgency

Stochastic automata [10,11] use continuous random variables (called *clocks*) to observe the passage of time and control the occurrence of events. These variables are set to a value according to their associated probability distribution, and, as time evolves, they count down at the same rate. When a clock reaches zero, it may trigger some action. This allows the modelling of systems where events occur at random continuous time steps.

Following ideas from [26], IOSAs restrict Stochastic Automata by splitting actions into input and output actions which will act in a reactive and generative way respectively [17]. This splitting reflects the fact that input actions are considered to be controlled externally, while output actions are locally controlled.

Therefore, we consider the system to be input enabled. Moreover, output actions could be stochastically controlled or instantaneous. In the first case, output actions are controlled by the expiration of a single clock while in the second case the output actions take place as soon as the enabling state is reached.

We called these instantaneous actions *urgent*. A set of restrictions over IOSA will ensure that, almost surely, no two non-urgent outputs are enabled at the same time.

Definition 1. *An input/output stochastic automaton with urgency (IOSA) is a structure* $(\mathcal{S}, \mathcal{A}, \mathcal{C}, \rightarrow, C_0, s_0)$, *where* $\mathcal{S}$ *is a (denumerable) set of states,* $\mathcal{A}$ *is a (denumerable) set of labels partitioned into disjoint sets of* input labels $\mathcal{A}^i$ *and* output labels $\mathcal{A}^o$, *from which a subset* $\mathcal{A}^u \subseteq \mathcal{A}$ *is marked as* urgent. *We consider the distinguished* silent urgent action $\tau \in \mathcal{A}^u \cap \mathcal{A}^o$ *which is not amenable to synchronization.* $\mathcal{C}$ *is a (finite) set of clocks such that each* $x \in \mathcal{C}$ *has an associated continuous probability measure* μ_x *on* $\mathbb{R}$ *s.t.* $\mu_x(\mathbb{R}_{>0}) = 1$, $\rightarrow \subseteq \mathcal{S} \times \mathcal{C} \times \mathcal{A} \times \mathcal{C} \times \mathcal{S}$ *is a transition function,* C_0 *is the set of clocks that are initialized in the initial state, and* $s_0 \in \mathcal{S}$ *is the initial state.*

In addition, an IOSA with urgency should satisfy the following constraints:

(a) *If* $s \xrightarrow{C,a,C'} s'$ *and* $a \in \mathcal{A}^i \cup \mathcal{A}^u$, *then* $C = \varnothing$.

(b) *If* $s \xrightarrow{C,a,C'} s'$ *and* $a \in \mathcal{A}^o \setminus \mathcal{A}^u$, *then* C *is a singleton set.*

(c) *If* $s \xrightarrow{\{x\},a_1,C_1} s_1$ *and* $s \xrightarrow{\{x\},a_2,C_2} s_2$ *then* $a_1 = a_2$, $C_1 = C_2$ *and* $s_1 = s_2$.

(d) *For every* $a \in \mathcal{A}^i$ *and state* s, *there exists a transition* $s \xrightarrow{\varnothing,a,C} s'$.

(e) *For every* $a \in \mathcal{A}^i$, *if* $s \xrightarrow{\varnothing,a,C_1'} s_1$ *and* $s \xrightarrow{\varnothing,a,C_2'} s_2$, $C_1' = C_2'$ *and* $s_1 = s_2$.

(f) *There exists a function* active $: \mathcal{S} \to 2^{\mathcal{C}}$ *such that: (i)* active$(s_0) \subseteq C_0$, *(ii)* enabling$(s) \subseteq$ active(s), *(iii) if* s *is stable,* active$(s) =$ enabling(s), *and (iv) if* $t \xrightarrow{C,a,C'} s$ *then* active$(s) \subseteq ($active$(t) \setminus C) \cup C'$.

where enabling$(s) = \{y \mid s \xrightarrow{\{y\},\_,\_} \_\}$, *and* s *is stable, denoted* st(s), *if there is no* $a \in \mathcal{A}^u \cap \mathcal{A}^o$ *such that* $s \xrightarrow{\varnothing,a,\_} \_$. *(*$\_$ *indicates the existential quantification of a parameter.)*

The occurrence of an output transition is controlled by the expiration of clocks. If $a \in \mathcal{A}^o$, $s \xrightarrow{C,a,C'} s'$ indicates that there is a transition from state s to state s' that can be taken only when all clocks in C have expired and, when taken, it triggers action a and sets all clocks in C' to a value sampled from their associated probability distribution. Notice that if $C = \varnothing$ (which means $a \in \mathcal{A}^o \cap \mathcal{A}^u$) $s \xrightarrow{C,a,C'} s'$ is immediately triggered. Instead, if $a \in \mathcal{A}^i$, $s \xrightarrow{\varnothing,a,C'} s'$ is only intended to take place if an external output synchronizes with it, which means, in terms of an open system semantics, that it may take place at any possible time.

Restrictions (a) to (e) ensure that any *closed* IOSA without urgent actions is deterministic [13]. An IOSA is closed if all its synchronizations have been resolved, that is, the IOSA resulting from a composition does not have input actions ($\mathcal{A}^i = \varnothing$). Restriction (a) is two-folded: on the one hand, it specifies that output actions must occur as soon as the enabling state is reached, on the other hand, since input actions are reactive and their time occurrence can only depend on the interaction with an output, no clock can control their enabling.

Restriction (b) specifies that the occurrence of a non-urgent output is locally controlled by a single clock. Restriction (c) ensures that two different non-urgent output actions leaving the same state are always controlled by different clocks (otherwise it would introduce non-determinism). Restriction (d) ensures input enabling. Restriction (e) determines that IOSAs are input deterministic. Therefore, the same input action in the same state can not jump to different states, nor set different clocks. Finally, (f) guarantees that clocks enabling some output transition have not expired before, that is, they have not been used before by another output transition (without being reset in between) nor inadvertently reached zero. This is done by ensuring the existence of a function "active" that, at each state, collects clocks that are required to be active (i.e. that have been set but not yet expired). Notice that enabling clocks are required to be active (conditions (f)(ii) and (f)(iii)). Also note that every clock that is active in a state is allowed to remain active in a successor state as long as it has not been used, and clocks that have just been set may become active in the successor state (condition (f)(iv)).

Note that since clocks are set by sampling from a continuous random variable, the probability that the values of two different clocks are equal is 0. This fact along with restriction (c) and (f) guarantee that almost never two different non-urgent output transitions are enabled at the same time.

Example 1. Figure 2 depicts three simple examples of IOSAs. Although IOSAs are input enabled, we have omitted self loops of input enabling transitions for the sake of readability. In the figure, we represent output actions suffixed by '!' and by '!!' when they are urgent, and input actions suffixed by '?' and by '??' when they are urgent.

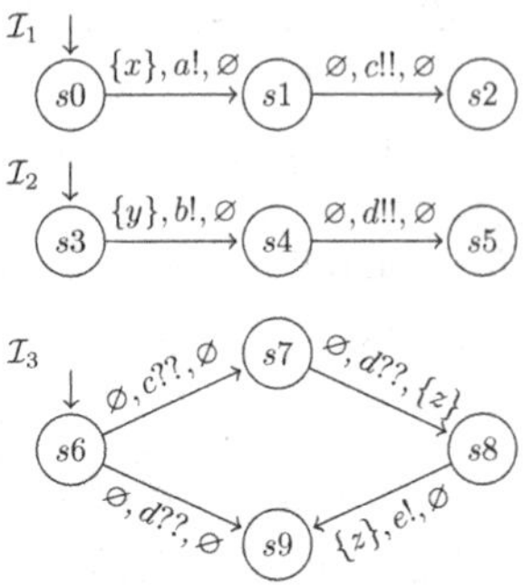

Fig. 2. Examples of IOSAs.

3   Semantics of IOSA

The semantics of IOSA is defined in terms of non-deterministic labeled Markov processes (NLMP) [14,25] which extends LMP [15] with *internal* non-determinism.

The foundations of NLMP is strongly rooted in measure theory, hence we recall first some basic definitions. Given a set S and a collection Σ of subsets of S, we call Σ a *σ-algebra* iff $S \in \Sigma$ and Σ is closed under complement and denumerable union. We call the pair (S, Σ) a *measurable space*. Let $\mathscr{B}(S)$ denote the Borel σ-algebra on the topology S. A function $\mu : \Sigma \to [0,1]$ is a *probability measure* if (i) $\mu(\bigcup_{i \in \mathbb{N}} Q_i) = \sum_{i \in \mathbb{N}} \mu(Q_i)$ for all countable family of pairwise disjoint measurable sets $\{Q_i\}_{i \in \mathbb{N}} \subseteq \Sigma$, and (ii) $\mu(S) = 1$. In particular, for $s \in S$, δ_s denotes the Dirac measure so that $\delta_s(\{s\}) = 1$. Let $\Delta(S)$ denote the set of all probability measures over (S, Σ). Let (S_1, Σ_1) and (S_2, Σ_2) be two measurable spaces. A function $f : S_1 \to S_2$ is said to be *measurable* if for all

$Q_2 \in \Sigma_2$, $f^{-1}(Q_2) \in \Sigma_1$. There is a standard construction to endow $\Delta(S)$ with a σ-algebra [16] as follows: $\Delta(\Sigma)$ is defined as the smallest σ-algebra containing the sets $\Delta^q(Q) \doteq \{\mu \mid \mu(Q) \geq q\}$, with $Q \in \Sigma$ and $q \in [0,1]$. Finally, we define the *hit σ-algebra* $H(\Delta(\Sigma))$ as the minimal σ-algebra containing all sets $H_\xi = \{\zeta \in \Delta(\Sigma) \mid \zeta \cap \xi \neq \varnothing\}$ with $\xi \in \Delta(\Sigma)$.

A *non-deterministic labeled Markov process* (NLMP for short) is a structure $(\mathbf{S}, \Sigma, \{T_a \mid a \in \mathcal{L}\})$ where Σ is a σ-algebra on the set of states $\mathbf{S}$, and for each label $a \in \mathcal{L}$ we have that $T_a : \mathbf{S} \to \Delta(\Sigma)$ is measurable from Σ to $H(\Delta(\Sigma))$.

The formal semantics of an IOSA is defined by a NLMP with two classes of transitions: one that encodes the discrete steps and contains all the probabilistic information introduced by the sampling of clocks, and another describing the time steps, that only records the passage of time synchronously decreasing the value of all clocks. For simplicity, we assume that the set of clocks has a total order and their current values follow the same order in a vector.

Definition 2. *Given an IOSA $\mathcal{I} = (\mathcal{S}, \mathcal{A}, \mathcal{C}, \to, C_0, s_0)$ with $\mathcal{C} = \{x_1, \ldots, x_N\}$, its semantics is defined by the NLMP $\mathcal{P}(\mathcal{I}) = (\mathbf{S}, \mathscr{B}(\mathbf{S}), \{T_a \mid a \in \mathcal{L}\})$ where*

- $S = (\mathcal{S} \cup \{init\}) \times \mathbb{R}^N$, $\mathcal{L} = \mathcal{A} \cup \mathbb{R}_{>0} \cup \{init\}$, *with* $init \notin \mathcal{S} \cup \mathcal{A} \cup \mathbb{R}_{>0}$
- $T_{init}(init, \vec{v}) = \{\delta_{s_0} \times \prod_{i=1}^N \mu_{x_i}\}$,
- $T_a(s, \vec{v}) = \{\mu_{C', s'}^{\vec{v}} \mid s \xrightarrow{C, a, C'} s', \bigwedge_{x_i \in C} \vec{v}(i) \leq 0\}$, *for all $a \in \mathcal{A}$, where* $\mu_{C', s'}^{\vec{v}} = \delta_{s'} \times \prod_{i=1}^N \overline{\mu}_{x_i}$ *with* $\overline{\mu}_{x_i} = \mu_{x_i}$ *if $x_i \in C'$ and* $\overline{\mu}_{x_i} = \delta_{\vec{v}(i)}$ *otherwise, and*
- $T_d(s, \vec{v}) = \{\delta_s \times \prod_{i=1}^N \delta_{\vec{v}(i)-d}\}$ *if there is no urgent $b \in \mathcal{A}^\circ \cap \mathcal{A}^u$ for which* $s \xrightarrow{\ -, b, -\ } \_$ *and $0 < d \leq \min\{\vec{v}(i) \mid \exists a \in \mathcal{A}^\circ, C' \subseteq \mathcal{C}, s' \in S : s \xrightarrow{\{x_i\}, a, C'} s'\}$, and* $T_d(s, \vec{v}) = \varnothing$ *otherwise, for all $d \in \mathbb{R}_{\geq 0}$.*

The state space is the product space of the states of the IOSA with all possible clock valuations. A distinguished initial state init is added to encode the random initialization of all clocks (it would be sufficient to initialize clocks in C_0 but we decided for this simplification). Such encoding is done by transition T_{init}. The state space is structured with the usual Borel σ-algebra. The discrete step is encoded by T_a, with $a \in \mathcal{A}$. Notice that, at state $(s, \vec{v})$, the transition $s \xrightarrow{C, a, C'} s'$ will only take place if $\bigwedge_{x_i \in C} \vec{v}(i) \leq 0$, that is, if the current values of all clocks in C are not positive. For the particular case of the input or urgent actions this will always be true. The next actual state would be determined randomly as follows: the symbolic state will be s' (this corresponds to $\delta_{s'}$ in $\mu_{C', s'}^{\vec{v}} = \delta_{s'} \times \prod_{i=1}^N \overline{\mu}_{x_i}$), any clock not in C' preserves the current value (hence $\overline{\mu}_{x_i} = \delta_{\vec{v}(i)}$ if $x_i \notin C'$), and any clock in C' is set randomly according to its respective associated distribution (hence $\overline{\mu}_{x_i} = \mu_{x_i}$ if $x_i \in C'$). The time step is encoded by $T_d(s, \vec{v})$ with $d \in \mathbb{R}_{\geq 0}$. It can only take place at d units of time if there is no output transition enabled at the current state within the next d time units (this is verified by condition $0 < d \leq \min\{\vec{v}(i) \mid \exists a \in \mathcal{A}^\circ, C' \subseteq \mathcal{C}, s' \in S : s \xrightarrow{\{x_i\}, a, C'} s'\}$). In this case, the system remains in the same symbolic state (this corresponds to δ_s in $\delta_{(s, \vec{v})}^{-d} = \delta_s \times \prod_{i=1}^N \delta_{\vec{v}(i)-d}$), and all clock values are

Table 1. Parallel composition on IOSA

$$\frac{s_1 \xrightarrow{C,a,C'}_1 s_1'}{s_1\|s_2 \xrightarrow{C,a,C'} s_1'\|s_2} \; a\in(\mathcal{A}_1\backslash\mathcal{A}_2)\cup\{\tau\} \;\; \text{(R1)} \qquad \frac{s_2 \xrightarrow{C,a,C'}_2 s_2'}{s_1\|s_2 \xrightarrow{C,a,C'} s_1\|s_2'} \; a\in(\mathcal{A}_2\backslash\mathcal{A}_1)\cup\{\tau\} \;\; \text{(R2)}$$

$$\frac{s_1 \xrightarrow{C_1,a,C_1'}_1 s_1' \quad s_2 \xrightarrow{C_2,a,C_2'}_2 s_2'}{s_1\|s_2 \xrightarrow{C_1\cup C_2,a,C_1'\cup C_2'} s_1'\|s_2'} \; a\in(\mathcal{A}_1\cap\mathcal{A}_2)\backslash\{\tau\} \;\; \text{(R3)}$$

decreased by d units of time (represented by $\delta_{\vec{v}(i)-d}$ in the same formula). Note the difference from the timed transitions semantics of pure IOSA [13]. This is due to the maximal progress assumption, which forces to take urgent transition as soon as they get enabled. We encode this by not allowing to make time transitions in presence of urgent actions, i.e. we check that there is no urgent $b \in \mathcal{A}^\circ \cap \mathcal{A}^u$ for which $s \xrightarrow{-,b,-} -$. (Notice that b may be τ.) Otherwise, $\mathcal{T}_d(s,\vec{v}) = \varnothing$. Instead, notice the *patient* nature of a state $(s,\vec{v})$ that has no output enabled. That is, $\mathcal{T}_d(s,\vec{v}) = \{\delta_s \times \prod_{i=1}^N \delta_{\vec{v}(i)-d}\}$ for all $d > 0$ whenever there is no output action $b \in \mathcal{A}^\circ$ such that $s \xrightarrow{-,b,-} -$.

In a similar way to [13], it is possible to show that $\mathcal{P}(\mathcal{I})$ is indeed a NLMP, i.e. that $\mathcal{T}_a$ maps into measurable sets in $\Delta(\mathscr{B}(\mathbf{S}))$, and that $\mathcal{T}_a$ is a measurable function for every $a \in \mathcal{L}$.

4   Parallel Composition

In this section, we define parallel composition of IOSAs. Since outputs are intended to be autonomous (or locally controlled), we do not allow synchronization between them. Besides, we need to avoid name clashes on the clocks, so that the intended behavior of each component is preserved and moreover, to ensure that the resulting composed automaton is indeed an IOSA. Furthermore, synchronizing IOSAs should agree on urgent actions in order to ensure their immediate occurrence. Thus we require to compose only *compatible* IOSAs.

Definition 3. *Two IOSAs $\mathcal{I}_1$ and $\mathcal{I}_2$ are compatible if they do not share synchronizable output actions nor clocks, i.e. $\mathcal{A}_1^\circ \cap \mathcal{A}_2^\circ \subseteq \{\tau\}$ and $\mathcal{C}_1 \cap \mathcal{C}_2 = \varnothing$ and, moreover, they agree on urgent actions, i.e. $\mathcal{A}_1 \cap \mathcal{A}_2^u = \mathcal{A}_2 \cap \mathcal{A}_1^u$.*

Definition 4. *Given two compatible IOSAs $\mathcal{I}_1$ and $\mathcal{I}_2$, the parallel composition $\mathcal{I}_1\|\mathcal{I}_2$ is a new IOSA $(\mathcal{S}_1 \times \mathcal{S}_2, \mathcal{A}, \mathcal{C}, \rightarrow, C_0, s_0^1\|s_0^2)$ where (i) $\mathcal{A}^\circ = \mathcal{A}_1^\circ \cup \mathcal{A}_2^\circ$ (ii) $\mathcal{A}^i = (\mathcal{A}_1^i \cup \mathcal{A}_2^i) \setminus \mathcal{A}^\circ$ (iii) $\mathcal{A}^u = \mathcal{A}_1^u \cup \mathcal{A}_2^u$ (iv) $\mathcal{C} = \mathcal{C}_1 \cup \mathcal{C}_2$ (v) $C_0 = C_0^1 \cup C_0^2$ and $\rightarrow$ is defined by rules in Table 1 where we write $s\|t$ instead of (s,t).*

Definition 4 does not ensure a priori that the resulting structure satisfies conditions (a)–(f) in Definition 1. This is only guaranteed by the following proposition.

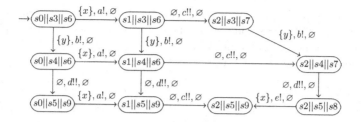

Fig. 3. IOSA resulting from the composition $\mathcal{I}_1||\mathcal{I}_2||\mathcal{I}_3$ of IOSAs in Fig. 2.

Proposition 1. *Let $\mathcal{I}_1$ and $\mathcal{I}_2$ be two compatible IOSAs. Then $\mathcal{I}_1||\mathcal{I}_2$ is indeed an IOSA.*

Example 2. The result of composing $\mathcal{I}_1||\mathcal{I}_2||\mathcal{I}_3$ from Example 1 is depicted in Fig. 3.

Larsen and Skou's probabilistic bisimulation [21] has been extended to NLMPs in [14]. It can be shown that the bisimulation equivalence is a congruence for parallel composition of IOSA. In fact, this has already been shown for IOSA without urgency in [13] and since the characteristics of urgency do not play any role in the proof over there, the result immediately extends to our setting. So we report the theorem and invite the reader to read the proof in [13].

Theorem 1. *Let $\sim$ denote the bisimulation equivalence relation on NLMPs [14] properly lifted to IOSA [13], and let $\mathcal{I}_1$, $\mathcal{I}_1'$, $\mathcal{I}_2$, $\mathcal{I}_2'$ be IOSAs such that $\mathcal{I}_1 \sim \mathcal{I}_1'$ $\mathcal{I}_2 \sim \mathcal{I}_2'$. Then, $\mathcal{I}_1||\mathcal{I}_2 \sim \mathcal{I}_1'||\mathcal{I}_2'$.*

5 Confluence

Confluence, as studied by Milner [23], is related to a form of weak determinism: two silent transitions taking place on an interleaving manner do not alter the behaviour of the process regardless of which happens first. In particular, we will eventually assume that urgent actions in a closed IOSA are silent as they do not delay the execution. Thus we focus on confluence of urgent actions only. The notion of confluence is depicted in Fig. 4 and formally defined as follows.

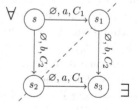

Fig. 4. Confluence in IOSA.

Definition 5. *An IOSA $\mathcal{I}$ is confluent with respect to actions $a, b \in \mathcal{A}^{\mathrm{u}}$ if, for every state $s \in S$ and transitions $s \xrightarrow{\varnothing, a, C_1} s_1$ and $s \xrightarrow{\varnothing, b, C_2} s_2$, there exists a state $s_3 \in S$ such that $s_1 \xrightarrow{\varnothing, b, C_2} s_3$ and $s_2 \xrightarrow{\varnothing, a, C_1} s_3$. $\mathcal{I}$ is confluent if it is confluent with respect to every pair of urgent actions.*

Note that we are asking that the two actions converge in a single state, which is stronger than Milner's strong confluence, where convergence takes place on bisimilar but potentially different states.

Confluence is preserved by parallel composition:

Proposition 2. *If both $\mathcal{I}_1$ and $\mathcal{I}_2$ are confluent w.r.t. actions $a, b \in \mathcal{A}^u$, then so is $\mathcal{I}_1 \| \mathcal{I}_2$. Therefore, if $\mathcal{I}_1$ and $\mathcal{I}_2$ are confluent, $\mathcal{I}_1 \| \mathcal{I}_2$ is also confluent.*

However, parallel composition may turn non-confluent components into a confluent composed system.

By looking at the IOSA in Fig. 5, one can notice that the non-determinism introduced by confluent urgent output actions is spurious in the sense that it does not change the stochastic behaviour of the model after the output urgent actions have been abstracted. Indeed, since time does not progress, it is the same to sample first clock x and then clock y passing through state s_1, or first y and then x passing through s_2, or even sampling both clocks simultaneously through a transition $s_1 \xrightarrow{\varnothing, \tau, \{x,y\}} s_3$. In any of the cases, the stochastic resolution of the execution of a or b in the stable state s_3 is the same. This could be generalized to any number of confluent transitions.

Thus, it will be convenient to use term rewriting techniques to collect all clocks that are active in the convergent stable state and have been activated through a path of urgent actions. Therefore, we recall some basic notions of rewriting systems. An *abstract reduction system* [1] is a pair $(E, \rightarrowtail)$, where the reduction $\rightarrowtail$ is a binary relation over the set E, i.e. $\rightarrowtail \subseteq E \times E$. We write $a \rightarrowtail b$ for $(a, b) \in \rightarrowtail$. We also write $a \overset{*}{\rightarrowtail} b$ to denote that there is a path $a_0 \rightarrowtail a_1 \ldots \rightarrowtail a_n$ with $n \geq 0$, $a_0 = a$ and $a_n = b$. An element $a \in E$ is in *normal form* if there is no b such that $a \rightarrowtail b$. We say that b is a normal form of a if $a \overset{*}{\rightarrowtail} b$ and b is in normal form. A reduction system $(E, \rightarrowtail)$ is *confluent* if for all $a, b, c \in E$ $a \overset{*}{\leftarrowtail} c \overset{*}{\rightarrowtail} b$ implies $a \overset{*}{\rightarrowtail} d \overset{*}{\leftarrowtail} b$ for some $d \in E$. This notion of confluence is implied by the following statement: for all $a, b, c \in E$, $a \leftarrowtail c \rightarrowtail b$ implies that either $a \rightarrowtail d \leftarrowtail b$ for some $d \in E$, or $a = b$. A reduction system is *normalizing* if every element has a normal form, and it is *terminating* if there is no infinite chain $a_0 \rightarrowtail a_1 \rightarrowtail \cdots$. A terminating reduction system is also normalizing. In a confluent reduction system every element has at most one normal form. If in addition it is also normalizing, then the normal form is unique.

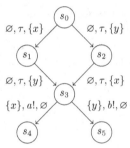

Fig. 5. Confluence is weakly deterministic

We now define the abstract reduction system introduced by the urgent transitions of an IOSA.

Definition 6. *Given an IOSA $\mathcal{I} = (\mathcal{S}, \mathcal{A}, \mathcal{C}, \rightarrow_{\mathcal{I}}, C_0, s_0)$, define the abstract reduction system $\mathcal{U}_I$ as $(\mathcal{S} \times \mathcal{P}(\mathcal{C}) \times \mathbb{N}_0, \rightarrowtail)$ where $(s, C, n) \rightarrowtail (s', C \cup C', n+1)$ if and only if there exists $a \in \mathcal{A}^u$ such that $s \xrightarrow{\varnothing, a, C'} s'$.*

An IOSA is *non-Zeno* if there is no loop of urgent actions. The following result can be straightforwardly proven.

Proposition 3. *Let the IOSA $\mathcal{I}$ be closed and confluent. Then $\mathcal{U}_{\mathcal{I}}$ is confluent, and hence every element has at most one normal form. Moreover, an element (s, C, n) is in normal form iff s is stable in $\mathcal{I}$. If in addition $\mathcal{I}$ is non-Zeno, $\mathcal{U}_{\mathcal{I}}$ is also terminating and hence every element has a unique normal form.*

6   Weak Determinism

As already shown in Fig. 5, the non-determinism introduced by confluence is spurious. In this section, we show that closed confluent IOSAs behave deterministically in the sense that the stochastic behaviour of the model is the same, regardless the way in which non-determinism is resolved. Thus, we say that a closed IOSA is *weakly deterministic* if (i) almost surely at most one discrete non-urgent transition is enabled at every time point, (ii) the election over enabled urgent transitions does not affect the non urgent-behavior of the model, and (iii) no non-urgent output and urgent output are enabled simultaneously. To avoid referring explicitly to time in (i), we say instead that a closed IOSA is weakly deterministic if it almost never reaches a state in which two different non-urgent discrete transitions are enabled. Moreover, to ensure (ii), we define the following weak transition.

For this definition and the rest of the section we will assume that the IOSA is closed and all its urgent actions have been abstracted, that is, all actions in $\mathcal{A}^u$ have been renamed to τ.

Definition 7. *For a non stable state s, and $v \in \mathbb{R}^N$, we define $(s, \vec{v}) \overset{C}{\Rightarrow}_n \mu$ inductively by the following rules:*

$$(T1) \quad \frac{s \xrightarrow{\varnothing, \tau, C} s' \quad \mathrm{st}(s')}{(s, \vec{v}) \overset{C}{\Rightarrow}_1 \mu_{C,s'}^{\vec{v}}} \qquad\qquad (T2) \quad \frac{s \xrightarrow{\varnothing, \tau, C'} s' \quad \forall \vec{v}' \in \mathbb{R}^N : \exists C'', \mu' : (s', \vec{v}') \overset{C''}{\Rightarrow}_n \mu'}{(s, \vec{v}) \overset{C' \cup C''}{\Longrightarrow}_{n+1} \hat{\mu}}$$

where $\mu_{C,s}^{\vec{v}}$ is defined as in Definition 2 and $\hat{\mu} = \int_{S \times \mathbb{R}^N} f_n^{C''} d\mu_{C',s'}^{\vec{v}}$, with $f_n^{C''}(t, \vec{w}) = \nu$, if $(t, \vec{w}) \overset{C''}{\Longrightarrow}_n \nu$, and $f_n^{C''}(t, \vec{w}) = 0$ otherwise. We define the weak transition $(s, \vec{v}) \Rightarrow \mu$ if $(s, \vec{v}) \overset{C}{\Rightarrow}_n \mu$ for some $n \geq 1$ and $C \subseteq \mathcal{C}$.

As given above, there is no guarantee that $\overset{C}{\Rightarrow}_n$ is well defined. In particular, there is no guarantee that $f_n^{C''}$ is a well defined measurable function. We postpone this to Lemma 1 below.

With this definition, we can introduce the concept of weak determinism:

Definition 8. *A closed IOSA $\mathcal{I}$ is weakly deterministic if $\Rightarrow$ is well defined in $\mathcal{I}$ and, in $P(\mathcal{I})$, any state $(s, v) \in \mathbf{S}$ that satisfies one of the following conditions is almost never reached from any $(\mathrm{init}, v_0) \in \mathbf{S}$: (a) s is stable and*

$\cup_{a \in \mathcal{A} \cup \{init\}} \mathcal{T}_a(s, v)$ *contains at least two different probability measures, (b)* s *is not stable,* $(s, v) \Rightarrow \mu$, $(s, v) \Rightarrow \mu'$ *and* $\mu \neq \mu'$, *or (c)* s *is not stable and* $(s, v) \xrightarrow{a} \mu$ *for some* $a \in \mathcal{A}^\circ \setminus \mathcal{A}^u$.

By "almost never" we mean that the measure of the set of all paths leading to any measurable set in $\mathscr{B}(\mathbf{S})$ containing only states satisfying (a), (b), or (c) is zero. Thus, Definition 8 states that, in a weakly deterministic IOSA, a situation in which a non urgent output action is enabled with another output action, being it urgent (case (c)) or non urgent (case (a)), or in which sequences of urgent transitions lead to different stable situations (case (b)), is almost never reached.

For the previous definition to make sense we need that $\mathcal{P}(\mathcal{I})$ satisfies *time additivity*, *time determinism*, and *maximal progress* [27]. This is stated in the following theorem whose proof follows as in [13, Theorem 16].

Theorem 2. *Let* $\mathcal{I}$ *be an IOSA* $\mathcal{I}$. *Its semantics* $\mathcal{P}(\mathcal{I})$ *satisfies, for all* $(s, \vec{v}) \in S$, $a \in \mathcal{A}^\circ$ *and* $d, d' \in \mathbb{R}_{>0}$, *(i)* $\mathcal{T}_a(s, \vec{v}) \neq \varnothing \Rightarrow \mathcal{T}_d(s, \vec{v}) = \varnothing$ *(maximal progress),* *(ii)* $\mu, \mu' \in \mathcal{T}_d(s, \vec{v}) \Rightarrow \mu = \mu'$ *(time determinism), and (iii)* $\delta_{(s,\vec{v})}^{-d} \in \mathcal{T}_d(s, \vec{v}) \wedge$ $\delta_{(s,\vec{v}-d)}^{-d'} \in \mathcal{T}_{d'}(s, \vec{v} - d) \iff \delta_{(s,\vec{v})}^{-(d+d')} \in \mathcal{T}_{d+d'}(s, \vec{v})$ *(time additivity).*

The next lemma states that, under the hypothesis that the IOSA is closed and confluent, $\xrightarrow{C}_n$ is well defined. Simultaneously, we prove that $\xrightarrow{C}_n$ is deterministic.

Lemma 1. *Let* $\mathcal{I}$ *be a closed and confluent IOSA. Then, for all* $n \geq 1$, *the following holds:*

1. *If* $(s, \vec{v}) \xrightarrow{C}_n \mu$ *then there is a stable state* s' *such that (i)* $\mu = \mu_{C,s'}^{\vec{v}}$, *(ii)* $(s, C', m) \xrightarrow{*} (s', C' \cup C, m+n)$ *for all* $C' \subseteq C$ *and* $m \geq 0$, *and (iii) if* $(s, \vec{v}') \xrightarrow{C'}_n \mu'$ *then* $C' = C$ *and moreover, if* $\vec{v}' = \vec{v}$, *also* $\mu' = \mu$; *and*
2. f_n^C *is a measurable function.*

The proof of the preceding lemma uses induction on n to prove item 1 and 2 simultaneously. It makes use of the previous results on rewriting systems in conjunction with measure theoretical tools such as Fubini's theorem to deal with Lebesgue integrals on product spaces. All these tools make the proof that confluence preserves weak determinism radically different from those of Milner [23] and Crouzen [9].

The following corollary follows by items 1.(ii) and 1.(iii) of Lemma 1.

Corollary 1. *Let* $\mathcal{I}$ *be a closed and confluent IOSA. Then, for all* $(s, \vec{v})$, *if* $(s, \vec{v}) \Rightarrow \mu_1$ *and* $(s, \vec{v}) \Rightarrow \mu_2$, $\mu_1 = \mu_2$.

This corollary already shows that closed and confluent IOSAs satisfy part (b) of Definition 8. In general, we can state:

Theorem 3. *Every closed confluent IOSA is weakly deterministic.*

The rest of the section is devoted to discuss the proof of this theorem. From now on, we work with the closed confluent IOSA $\mathcal{I} = (\mathcal{S}, \mathcal{C}, \mathcal{A}, \rightarrow, s_0, C_0)$, with $|\mathcal{C}| = N$, and its semantics $\mathcal{P}(\mathcal{I}) = (\mathbf{S}, \mathcal{B}(\mathbf{S}), \{T_a \mid a \in \mathcal{L}\})$.

The idea of the proof of Theorem 3 is to show that the property that all active clocks have non-negative values and they are different from each other is almost surely an invariant of $\mathcal{I}$, and that at most one non-urgent transition is enabled in every state satisfying such invariant. Furthermore, we want to show that, for unstable states, active clocks have strictly positive values, which implies that non-urgent transitions are never enabled in these states. Formally, the invariant is the set

$$
\begin{aligned}
\mathsf{Inv} = \ & \{(s, \vec{v}) \mid \mathsf{st}(s) \text{ and } \forall x_i, x_j \in \mathsf{active}(s) : i \neq j \Rightarrow \vec{v}(i) \neq \vec{v}(j) \wedge \vec{v}(i) \geq 0\} \\
& \cup \{(s, \vec{v}) \mid \neg\mathsf{st}(s) \text{ and } \forall x_i, x_j \in \mathsf{active}(s) : i \neq j \Rightarrow \vec{v}(i) \neq \vec{v}(j) \vec{v}(i) > 0\} \\
& \cup (\{\mathsf{init}\} \times \mathbb{R}^N)
\end{aligned}
\tag{1}
$$

with active as in Definition 1. Note that its complement is:

$$
\begin{aligned}
\mathsf{Inv}^c = \ & \{(s, \vec{v}) \mid \exists x_i, x_j \in \mathsf{active}(s) : i \neq j \wedge \vec{v}(i) = \vec{v}(j)\} \\
& \cup \{(s, \vec{v}) \mid \mathsf{st}(s) \text{ and } \exists x_i \in \mathsf{active}(s) : \vec{v}(i) < 0\} \\
& \cup \{(s, \vec{v}) \mid \neg\mathsf{st}(s) \text{ and } \exists x_i \in \mathsf{active}(s) : \vec{v}(i) \leq 0\}
\end{aligned}
\tag{2}
$$

It is not difficult to show that Inv^c is measurable and, in consequence, so is Inv. The following lemma states that Inv^c is almost never reached in one step from a state satisfying the invariant.

Lemma 2. *If $(s, \vec{v}) \in \mathsf{Inv}$, $a \in \mathcal{L}$, and $\mu \in T_a(s, \vec{v})$, then $\mu(\mathsf{Inv}^c) = 0$.*

From this lemma we have the following corollary.

Corollary 2. *The set Inv^c is almost never reachable in $\mathcal{P}(\mathcal{I})$.*

The proof of the corollary requires the definitions related to schedulers and measures on paths in NLMPs (see [25, Chap. 7] for a formal definition of scheduler and probability measures on paths in NLMPs.) We omit the proof of the corollary since it eventually boils down to an inductive application of Lemma 2.

The next lemma states that any stable state in the invariant Inv has at most one discrete transition enabled. Its proof is the same as that of [13, Lemma 20].

Lemma 3. *For all $(s, \vec{v}) \in \mathsf{Inv}$ with s stable or $s = \mathsf{init}$, the set $\bigcup_{a \in \mathcal{A} \cup \{\mathsf{init}\}} T_a(s, \vec{v})$ is either a singleton set or the empty set.*

The next lemma states that any unstable state in the invariant Inv can only produce urgent actions.

Lemma 4. *For every state $(s, \vec{v}) \in \mathsf{Inv}$, if $\neg\mathsf{st}(s)$ and $(s, \vec{v}) \xrightarrow{a} \mu$, then $a \in \mathcal{A}^u$.*

Proof. First recall that $\mathcal{I}$ is closed; hence $\mathcal{A}^{\mathsf{i}} = \varnothing$. If $(s, \vec{v}) \in \mathsf{Inv}$ and $\neg\mathsf{st}(s)$ then $\vec{v}_i > 0$ for all $x_i \in \mathsf{enabling}(s) \subseteq \mathsf{active}(s)$. Therefore, by Definition 2, $\mathcal{T}_a(s, \vec{v}) = \varnothing$ if $a \in \mathcal{A}^{\circ} \setminus \mathcal{A}^{\mathsf{u}}$. Furthermore, for any $d \in \mathbb{R}_{>0}$, $\mathcal{T}_d(s, \vec{v}) = \varnothing$ since s is not stable and hence $s \xrightarrow{-,b,-}$ _ for some $b \in \mathcal{A}^{\circ} \cap \mathcal{A}^{\mathsf{u}}$. $\square$

Finally, Theorem 3 is a consequence of Lemma 3, Lemma 4, Corollary 2, and Corollary 1.

7   Sufficient Conditions for Weak Determinism

Figure 3 shows an example in which the composed IOSA is weakly deterministic despite that some of its components are not confluent. The potential non-determinism introduced in state $s_1\|s_4\|s_6$ is never reached since urgent actions at states $s_0\|s_4\|s_6$ and $s_1\|s_3\|s_6$ prevent the execution of non urgent actions leading to such state. We say that state $s_1\|s_4\|s_6$ is not *potentially reachable*. The concept of potentially reachable can be defined as follows.

Definition 9. *Given an IOSA $\mathcal{I}$, a state s is* potentially reachable *if there is a path $s_0 \xrightarrow{-,a_0,-} s_1 \ldots, s_{n-1} \xrightarrow{-,a_{n-1},-} s_n = s$ from the initial state, with $n \geq 0$, such that for all $0 \leq i < n$, if $s_i \xrightarrow{-,b,-}$ _ for some $b \in \mathcal{A}^{\mathsf{u}} \cap \mathcal{A}^{\circ}$ then $a_i \in \mathcal{A}^{\mathsf{u}}$. In such case we call the path* plausible.

Notice that none of the paths leading to $s_1\|s_4\|s_6$ in Fig. 3 are plausible. Also, notice that an IOSA is bisimilar to the same IOSA when its set of states is restricted to only potentially reachable states.

Proposition 4. *Let $\mathcal{I}$ be a closed IOSA with set of states $\mathcal{S}$ and let $\overline{\mathcal{I}}$ be the same IOSA as $\mathcal{I}$ restricted to the set of states $\overline{\mathcal{S}} = \{s \in \mathcal{S} \mid$ is potentially reachable in $\mathcal{I}\}$. Then $\mathcal{I} \sim \overline{\mathcal{I}}$.*

Although we have not formally introduced bisimulation, it should be clear that both semantics are bisimilar through the identity relation since a transition $s \xrightarrow{\{x\},a,C} s'$ with s unstable does not introduce any concrete transition. (Recall the IOSA is closed so there is no input action on $\mathcal{I}$.)

For a state in a composed IOSA to be potentially reachable, necessarily each of the component states has to be potentially reachable in its respective component IOSA.

Lemma 5. *If a state $s_1\|\cdots\|s_n$ is potentially reachable in $\mathcal{I}_1\|\cdots\|\mathcal{I}_n$ then s_i is potentially reachable in $\mathcal{I}_i$ for all $i = 1, \ldots, N$.*

By Theorem 3, it suffices to check whether a closed IOSA is confluent to ensure that it is weakly deterministic. In this section, and following ideas introduced in [9], we build on a theory that allows us to ensure that a closed composed IOSA is confluent in a compositional manner, even when its components may not be confluent. Theorem 5 provides the sufficient conditions to guarantee that the composed IOSA is confluent. Because of Proposition 2, it suffices to check whether two urgent actions that are not confluent in a single component are potentially reached. Since potential reachability depends on the composition, the idea is to overapproximate by inspecting the components. The rest of the section builds on concepts that are essential to construct such overapproximation.

Let $\mathrm{uen}(s) = \{a \in \mathcal{A}^u \mid s \xrightarrow{-,a,-} \_\}$ be the set of urgent actions enabled in a state s. We say that a set B of output urgent actions is spontaneously enabled by a non-urgent action b if b is potentially reached and it transitions to a state enabling all actions in B.

Definition 10. *A set $B \subseteq \mathcal{A}^u \cap \mathcal{A}^\circ$ is spontaneously enabled by $a \in \mathcal{A} \setminus \mathcal{A}^u$ in $\mathcal{I}$, if either $B = \varnothing$ or there are potentially reachable states s and s' such that s is stable, $s \xrightarrow{-,a,-} s'$, and $B \subseteq \mathrm{uen}(s')$. B is maximal if for any B' spontaneously enabled by b in $\mathcal{I}$ such that $B \subseteq B'$, $B = B'$.*

A set that is spontaneously enabled in a composed IOSA, can be constructed as the union of spontaneously enabled sets in each of the components as stated by the following proposition. Therefore, spontaneously enabled sets in a composed IOSA can be overapproximated by unions of spontaneously enabled sets of its components.

Proposition 5. *Let B be spontaneously enabled by action a in $\mathcal{I}_1 \| \ldots \| \mathcal{I}_n$. Then, there are $B_1, \ldots, B_n$ such that each B_i is spontaneously enabled by a in $\mathcal{I}_i$, and $B = \bigcup_{i=1}^n B_i$. If in addition B is maximal, there are $B_1, \ldots, B_n$ such that each B_i is maximal spontaneously enabled by a in $\mathcal{I}_i$, and $B \subseteq \bigcup_{i=1}^n B_i$.*

Proof. We only prove it for $\mathcal{I}_1 \| \mathcal{I}_2$. The generalization to any n follows easily. Let $\bar{B}_i = B \cap \mathcal{A}_i$ for $i = 1, 2$ and note that $B = \bar{B}_1 \cup \bar{B}_2$. We show that $\bar{B}_1$ is spontaneously enabled by a in $\mathcal{I}_1$. The case of $\bar{B}_2$ follows similarly. Since B is spontaneously enabled by a in $\mathcal{I}_1 \| \mathcal{I}_2$, there exist potentially reachable states $s_1 \| s_2$ and $s_1' \| s_2'$, such that $s_1 \| s_2$ is stable, $s_1 \| s_2 \xrightarrow{-,a,-} s_1' \| s_2'$, and $B \subseteq \mathrm{uen}(s_1' \| s_2')$. First notice that $\bar{B}_1 \subseteq \mathrm{uen}(s_1)$. Also, suppose $\bar{B}_1 \neq \varnothing$, otherwise $\bar{B}_1$ is spontaneously enabled by a trivially. Consider first the case that $a \in \mathcal{A}_2 \setminus \mathcal{A}_1$. By (R2), $s_1 = s_1'$, but, since there is some $b \in \bar{B}_1$, $s_1 \xrightarrow{-,b,-} \_$ and hence $s_1 \| s_2 \xrightarrow{-,b,-} \_$ rendering $s_1 \| s_2$ unstable, which is a contradiction. So $a \in \mathcal{A}_1$ and $s_1 \xrightarrow{-,a,-} s_1'$. By Lemma 5, s_1 and s_1' are potentially reachable and, necessarily, s_1 is stable (otherwise $s_1 \| s_2$ has to be unstable as shown before). Therefore $\bar{B}_1$ is spontaneously enabled by a in $\mathcal{I}_1$. The second part of the proposition is immediate from the first part. $\square$

Spontaneously enabled sets refer to sets of urgent output actions that are enabled after some steps of execution. Urgent output actions can also be enabled at the initial state.

Definition 11. *A set $B \subseteq \mathcal{A}^u \cap \mathcal{A}^\circ$ is initial in an IOSA $\mathcal{I}$ if $B \subseteq \mathrm{uen}(s_0)$, with s_0 being the initial state of $\mathcal{I}$. B is maximal if $B = \mathrm{uen}(s_0) \cap \mathcal{A}^\circ$.*

An initial set of a composed IOSA can be constructed as the union of initial sets of its components. In particular the maximal initial set is the union of all the maximal sets of its components. The proof follows directly from the definition of parallel composition taking into consideration that IOSAs are input enabled.

Proposition 6. *Let B be initial in $\mathcal{I} = (\mathcal{I}_1|| \ldots ||\mathcal{I}_n)$. Then, there are $B_1, \ldots, B_2$, with B_i initial of $\mathcal{I}_i$, $1 \leq i \leq n$ and $B = \bigcup_{i=1}^{n} B_i$. Moreover, $\mathrm{uen}(s_0) \cap \mathcal{A}_{\mathcal{I}}^{\circ} = \bigcup_{i=1}^{n} \mathrm{uen}(s_i^0) \cap \mathcal{A}_i^{\circ}$.*

We say that an urgent action triggers an urgent output action if the first one enables the occurrence of the second one, which was not enabled before.

Definition 12. *Let $a \in \mathcal{A}^{\mathrm{u}}$ and $b \in \mathcal{A}^{\mathrm{u}} \cap \mathcal{A}^{\circ}$. a triggers b in an IOSA $\mathcal{I}$ if there are potentially reachable states s_1, s_2, and s_3 such that $s_1 \xrightarrow{-,a,-} s_2 \xrightarrow{-,b,-} s_3$ and, if $a \neq b$, $b \notin \mathrm{uen}(s_1)$.*

Notice that, for the particular case in which $a = b$, $b \notin \mathrm{uen}(s)$ is not required. The following proposition states that if one action triggers another one in a composed IOSA, then the same triggering occurs in a particular component.

Proposition 7. *Let $a \in \mathcal{A}^{\mathrm{u}}$ and $b \in \mathcal{A}^{\mathrm{u}} \cap \mathcal{A}^{\circ}$ such that a triggers b in $\mathcal{I}_1|| \ldots ||\mathcal{I}_n$. Then there is a component $\mathcal{I}_i$ such that $b \in \mathcal{A}_i^{\circ}$ and a triggers b in $\mathcal{I}_i$.*

Proof. We only prove it for $\mathcal{I}_1||\mathcal{I}_2$. The generalization to any n follows easily. Because $b \in \mathcal{A}^{\mathrm{u}} \cap \mathcal{A}^{\circ}$ necessarily $b \in \mathcal{A}_1^{\circ}$ or $b \in \mathcal{A}_2^{\circ}$. W.l.o.g. suppose $b \in \mathcal{A}_1^{\circ}$. Since a triggers b in $\mathcal{I}_1||\mathcal{I}_1$, $s_1||s_2 \xrightarrow{-,a,-} s_1'||s_2' \xrightarrow{-,b,-} s_1''||s_2''$ with $s_1||s_2$, $s_1'||s_2'$, and $s_1''||s_2''$ being potentially reachable.

Suppose first that $a \neq b$. Then $b \notin \mathrm{uen}(s_1||s_2)$. Recall that, by Lemma 5, s_1, s_1', and s_1'' are potentially reachable in $\mathcal{I}_1$. Since $b \in \mathcal{A}_1^{\circ}$, $s_1' \xrightarrow{-,b,-} s_1''$. Suppose $a \in \mathcal{A}_2 \backslash \mathcal{A}_1$. Then, necessarily, $s_1 = s_1'$ which gives $b \in \mathrm{uen}(s_1) \cap \mathcal{A}^{\circ} \subseteq \mathrm{uen}(s_1||s_2)$, yielding a contradiction. Thus, necessarily $a \in \mathcal{A}_1^{\mathrm{u}}$ and hence $s_1 \xrightarrow{-,a,-} s_1'$, by the definition of parallel composition. It remains to show that $b \notin \mathrm{uen}(s_1)$, but this is immediate since $\mathrm{uen}(s_1) \cap \mathcal{A}^{\circ} \subseteq \mathrm{uen}(s_1||s_2)$ and $b \notin \mathrm{uen}(s_1||s_2)$. Thus a triggers b in $\mathcal{I}_1$ in this case. If instead $a = b$, by the definition of parallel composition we immediately have that $s_1 \xrightarrow{-,b,-} s_1' \xrightarrow{-,b,-} s_1''$, proving thus the proposition. $\square$

Proposition 7 tells us that the triggering relation of a composed IOSA can be overapproximated by the union of the triggering relations of its components. Thus we define:

Definition 13. *The* approximate triggering relation *of $\mathcal{I}_1|| \ldots ||\mathcal{I}_n$ is defined by $\rightsquigarrow = \bigcup_{i=1}^{n} \{(a, b) \mid a \text{ triggers } b \text{ in } \mathcal{I}_i\}$. Its reflexive transitive closure $\rightsquigarrow^{*}$ is called* approximate indirect triggering relation.

The next definition characterizes all sets of urgent output actions that are simultaneously enabled in any potentially reachable state of a given IOSA.

Definition 14. *A set $B \subseteq \mathcal{A}^u \cap \mathcal{A}^\circ$ is an* enabled set *in an IOSA $\mathcal{I}$ if there is a potentially reachable state s such that $B \subseteq \text{uen}(s)$. If $a \in B$, we say that a is* enabled *in s. Let $\text{ES}_\mathcal{I}$ be the set of all enabled sets in $\mathcal{I}$.*

If an urgent output action is enabled in a potentially reachable state of a IOSA, then it is either initial, spontaneously enabled, or triggered by some action.

Theorem 4. *Let $b \in \mathcal{A}^u \cap \mathcal{A}^\circ$ be enabled in some potentially reachable state of the IOSA $\mathcal{I}$. Then there is a set B with $b \in B$ that is either initial or spontaneously enabled by some action $a \in \mathcal{A}^u$, or b is triggered by some action $a \in \mathcal{A}^\circ \setminus \mathcal{A}^u$.*

Proof. Let s be potentially reachable in $\mathcal{I}$ such that $b \in \text{uen}(s) \cap \mathcal{A}^\circ$. We prove the theorem for b by induction on the plausible path σ leading to s. If $|\sigma| = 0$, then $\sigma = s$ and s is the initial state. Then the set $\text{uen}(s) \cap \mathcal{A}^\circ$ is initial and we are done in this case. If $|\sigma| > 0$, then $\sigma = \sigma' \cdot (s' \xrightarrow{-,a,-} s)$ for some s', a, and plausible σ'. If $a \in \mathcal{A} \setminus \mathcal{A}^u$ then s' is stable (since σ is plausible) and thus $\text{uen}(s) \cap \mathcal{A}^\circ$ is spontaneously enabled by a. If instead $a \in \mathcal{A}^u$, two possibilities arise. If $b \notin \text{uen}(s')$, then b is triggered by a. If $b \in \text{uen}(s')$, the conditions are satisfied by induction since $|\sigma'| = |\sigma| - 1$. $\qquad\qquad\square$

The next definition is auxiliary to prove the main theorem of this section. It constructs a graph from a closed and composed IOSA whose vertices are sets of urgent output actions. It has the property that, if there is a path from one vertex to another, all actions in the second vertex are approximately indirectly triggered by actions in the first vertex (Lemma 7). This will allow to show that any set of simultaneously enabled urgent output actions is approximately indirectly triggered by initial actions or spontaneously enabled sets (Lemma 8).

Definition 15. *Let $\mathcal{I} = (\mathcal{I}_1 || \ldots || \mathcal{I}_n)$ be a closed IOSA. The* enabled graph *of $\mathcal{I}$ is defined by the labelled graph $\text{EG}_\mathcal{I} = (V, E)$, where $V \subseteq 2^{\mathcal{A}^\circ \cap \mathcal{A}^u}$ and $E \subseteq V \times (\mathcal{A}^u \cap \mathcal{A}^\circ) \times V$, with $V = \bigcup_{k \geq 0} V_k$ and $E = \bigcup_{k \geq 0} E_k$, and, for all $k \in \mathbb{N}$, V_k and E_k are inductively defined by*

$$V_0 = \bigcup_{a \in \mathcal{A}} \{ \bigcup_{i=1}^n B_i \mid \forall 1 \leq i \leq n :$$
$$B_i \text{ is spontaneously enabled by } a \text{ and maximal in } \mathcal{I}_i \}$$
$$\cup \{ \bigcup_{i=1}^n \text{uen}(s_i^0) \cap \mathcal{A}_i^\circ \mid \forall 1 \leq i \leq n : s_i^0 \text{ is the initial state in } \mathcal{I}_i \}$$
$$E_k = \{ (v, a, (v \setminus \{a\}) \cup \{b \mid a \rightsquigarrow b\}) \mid v \in V_k, a \in v \}$$
$$V_{k+1} = \{ v' \mid v \in V_i, (v, v') \in E_k, v' \notin \bigcup_{j=0}^k V_j \}$$

Notice that V_0 contains the maximal initial set of $\mathcal{I}$ and an overapproximation of all its maximal spontaneously enabled sets. Notice also that, by construction, there is a path from any vertex in V to some vertex in V_0.

The set closure of V in $\text{EG}_\mathcal{I}$, defined by $\overline{\text{ES}}_\mathcal{I} = \{ B \mid B \subseteq v, v \in V \}$, turns out to be an overapproximation of the actual set $\text{ES}_\mathcal{I}$ of all enabled sets in $\mathcal{I}$.

Lemma 6. *For any closed IOSA* $\mathcal{I} = (\mathcal{I}_1||\cdots||\mathcal{I}_n)$, $\mathsf{ES}_{\mathcal{I}} \subseteq \overline{\mathsf{ES}}_{\mathcal{I}}$.

Proof. Let $B \in \mathsf{ES}_{\mathcal{I}}$. We proceed by induction on the length of the plausible path σ that leads to the state s s.t. $B \subseteq \mathrm{uen}(s)$. If $|\sigma| = 0$ then s is the initial state and thus B is initial in $\mathcal{I}$. Thus, by Definition 11, Proposition 6, and Definition 15, $B \subseteq (\mathrm{uen}(s_0) \cap \mathcal{A}_{\mathcal{I}}^{\circ}) = (\bigcup_{i=1}^{n} \mathrm{uen}(s_i^0) \cap \mathcal{A}_i^{\circ}) \in V_0 \subseteq \overline{\mathsf{ES}}_{\mathcal{I}}$. As a consequence $B \in \overline{\mathsf{ES}}_{\mathcal{I}}$.

If $|\sigma| > 0$ then $\sigma = \sigma' \cdot (s' \xrightarrow{\,-,a,-\,} s)$, for some s', a, and plausible σ'. If $a \in \mathcal{A} \backslash \mathcal{A}^{\mathsf{u}}$ then s' is stable (since σ is plausible) and thus B is spontaneously enabled by a. By Proposition 5, there are $B_1, \ldots, B_n$ such that each B_i is spontaneously enabled by a and maximal in $\mathcal{I}_i$, and $B \subseteq \bigcup_{i=1}^{n} B_i$. Since $\bigcup_{i=1}^{n} B_i \in V_0 \subseteq \overline{\mathsf{ES}}_{\mathcal{I}}$, then $B \in \overline{\mathsf{ES}}_{\mathcal{I}}$. If instead $a \in \mathcal{A}^{\mathsf{u}}$, let $B' = \{a\} \cup (B \cap \mathrm{uen}(s'))$. Notice that $B' \subseteq \mathrm{uen}(s') \cap \mathcal{A}^{\circ}$. Since s' is the last state on σ' and $|\sigma'| = |\sigma| - 1$, $B' \in \overline{\mathsf{ES}}_{\mathcal{I}}$ by induction. Hence, there is a vertex $v' \in V$ in $\mathsf{EG}_{\mathcal{I}}$ such that $B' \subseteq v$ and, by Definition 15, $v' \in V_k$ for some $k \geq 0$. Let $v = (v' \backslash \{a\}) \cup \{b \mid a \leadsto b\}$, then $(v', a, v) \in E_k$ and hence $v \in V_{k+1}$. We show that $B \subseteq v$. Let $b \in B$. If $b = a$, then $a \in \mathrm{uen}(s) \cap \mathcal{A}^{\circ}$ and hence a triggers a in $\mathcal{I}$. By Proposition 7, $a \leadsto a$ which implies $a \in v$. Suppose, instead, that $b \neq a$. If $b \in \mathrm{uen}(s')$, then $b \in B' \backslash \{a\} \subseteq v' \backslash \{a\} \subseteq v$. If $b \notin \mathrm{uen}(s')$, then a triggers b in $\mathcal{I}$, and by Proposition 7, $a \leadsto b$ which implies $b \in v$. This proves $B \subseteq v \in \overline{\mathsf{ES}}_{\mathcal{I}}$ and hence $B \in \overline{\mathsf{ES}}_{\mathcal{I}}$. $\qquad\square$

The next lemma states that if there is a path from a vertex of $\mathsf{EG}_{\mathcal{I}}$ to another vertex, every action in the second vertex is approximately indirectly triggered by some action in the first vertex.

Lemma 7. *Let* $\mathcal{I}$ *be a closed IOSA, let* $v, v' \in V$ *be vertices of* $\mathsf{EG}_{\mathcal{I}}$ *and let* ρ *be a path following* E *from* v *to* v'. *Then for every* $b \in v'$ *there is an action* $a \in v$ *such that* $a \leadsto^* b$.

Proof. We proceed by induction in the length of ρ. If $|\rho| = 0$ then $v = v'$ and the lemma holds since $\leadsto^*$ is reflexive. If $|\rho| > 0$, there is a path ρ', $v'' \in V$, and $c \in \mathcal{A}^{\mathsf{u}} \cap \mathcal{A}^{\circ}$ such that $\rho = \rho' \cdot (v'', c, v')$. By induction, for every action $d \in v''$ there is some $a \in v$ such that $a \leadsto^* d$. Because of the definition of E in Definition 15, either $b \in v''$ or $c \leadsto b$ and $c \in v''$. The first case follows by induction. In the second case, also by induction, $a \leadsto^* c$ for some $a \in v$ and hence $a \leadsto^* b$. $\qquad\square$

The next lemma states that every enabled set B in a composed IOSA is either approximately triggered by a set of initial actions of the components of the IOSA or by a subset of the union of spontaneously enabled sets in each component where such sets are spontaneously enabled by the same event.

Lemma 8. *Let* $\mathcal{I} = (\mathcal{I}_1||\ldots||\mathcal{I}_n)$ *be a closed IOSA and let* $\{b_1, \ldots, b_m\} \subseteq \mathcal{A}^{\mathsf{u}} \cap \mathcal{A}^{\circ}$ *be enabled in* $\mathcal{I}$. *Then, there are (not necessarily different)* $a_1, \ldots, a_m$ *such that* $a_j \leadsto^* b_j$, *for all* $1 \leq j \leq m$, *and either (i)* $\{a_1, \ldots, a_m\} \subseteq \bigcup_{i=1}^{n} \mathrm{uen}(s_i^0) \cap \mathcal{A}_i^{\circ}$, *or (ii) there exists* $e \in \mathcal{A}$ *and (possibly empty) sets* $B_1, \ldots, B_n$ *spontaneously enabled by* e *in* $\mathcal{I}_1, \ldots, \mathcal{I}_n$ *respectively, such that* $\{a_1, \ldots, a_m\} \subseteq \bigcup_{i=1}^{n} B_i$.

Proof. Because of Lemma 6 there is a vertex v of $\mathsf{EG}_\mathcal{I}$ such that $\{b_1, \ldots, b_n\} \subseteq v$. Because of the inductive construction of E and V, there is a path from some $v' \in V_0$ to v in $\mathsf{EG}_\mathcal{I}$. From Lemma 7, for each $1 \leq j \leq m$, there is an $a_j \in v'$ such that $a_j \leadsto^* b_j$. Because $v' \in V_0$, then either $v' = \bigcup_{i=1}^n \mathrm{uen}(s_i^0) \cap \mathcal{A}_i^\circ$ or there is some $e \in \mathcal{A}$ such that $v' = \bigcup_{i=1}^n B_i$ with B_i spontaneously enabled by e in $\mathcal{I}_i$ $\square$

The following theorem is the main result of this section and provides sufficient conditions to guarantee that a closed composed IOSA is confluent or, as stated in the theorem, necessary conditions for the IOSA to be non-confluent.

Theorem 5. *Let* $\mathcal{I} = (\mathcal{I}_1 || \cdots || \mathcal{I}_n)$ *be a closed IOSA. If* $\mathcal{I}$ *potentially reaches a non-confluent state then there are actions* $a, b \in \mathcal{A}^{\mathrm{u}} \cap \mathcal{A}^\circ$ *such that some* $\mathcal{I}_i$ *is not confluent w.r.t.* a *and* b, *and there are* c *and* d *such that* $c \leadsto^* a$, $d \leadsto^* b$, *and, either (i)* c *and* d *are initial actions in any component, or (ii) there is some* $e \in \mathcal{A}$ *and (possibly empty) sets* $B_1, \ldots, B_n$ *spontaneously enabled by* e *in* $\mathcal{I}_1, \ldots, \mathcal{I}_n$ *respectively, such that* $c, d \in \bigcup_{i=1}^n B_i$.

Proof. Suppose $\mathcal{I}$ potentially reaches a non confluent state s. Then there are necessarily $a, b \in \mathrm{uen}(s)$ that show it and hence $\mathcal{I}$ is not confluent w.r.t. a and b. By Proposition 2, there is necessarily a component $\mathcal{I}_i$ that is not confluent w.r.t. a and b. Since $\{a, b\}$ is an enabled set in $\mathcal{I}$, the rest of the theorem follows by Lemma 8. $\square$

Because of Proposition 4 and Theorem 3, if all potentially reachable states in a closed IOSA $\mathcal{I}$ are confluent, then $\mathcal{I}$ is weakly deterministic. Thus, if no pair of actions satisfying conditions in Theorem 5 are found in $\mathcal{I}$, then $\mathcal{I}$ is weakly deterministic.

Notice that the IOSA $\mathcal{I} = \mathcal{I}_1 || \mathcal{I}_2 || \mathcal{I}_3$ of Example 2 (see also Figs. 2 and 3) is an example that does not meet the conditions of Theorem 5, and hence detected as confluent. c and d are the only potential non-confluent actions, which is noticed in state s_6 of $\mathcal{I}_3$. The approximate indirect triggering relation can be calculated to $\leadsto^* = \{(c, c), (d, d)\}$. Also, $\{c\}$ is spontaneously enabled by a in $\mathcal{I}_1$ and $\{d\}$ is spontaneously enabled by b in $\mathcal{I}_2$. Since both sets are spontaneously enabled by *different* actions and c and d are not initial, the set $\{c, d\}$ does not appear in V_0 of $\mathsf{EG}_\mathcal{I}$ which would be required to meet the conditions of the theorem.

Conditions in Theorem 5 are not sufficient and confluent IOSAs may satisfy them. Consider the IOSAs in Fig. 6. $\mathcal{I}_1 || \mathcal{I}_2 || \mathcal{I}_3$ is a closed IOSA with a single state and no outgoing transition. Hence, it is confluent. However, $\mathcal{I}_3$ is not confluent w.r.t. b and c, $\leadsto^* = \{(b, b), (c, c)\}$, $B_1 = \{b\}$ is spontaneously enabled by a in $\mathcal{I}_1$, and $B_2 = \{c\}$ is spontaneously enabled by a in $\mathcal{I}_2$. Hence $b, c \in \bigcup_{i=1}^n B_i$, thus meeting the conditions of Theorem 5.

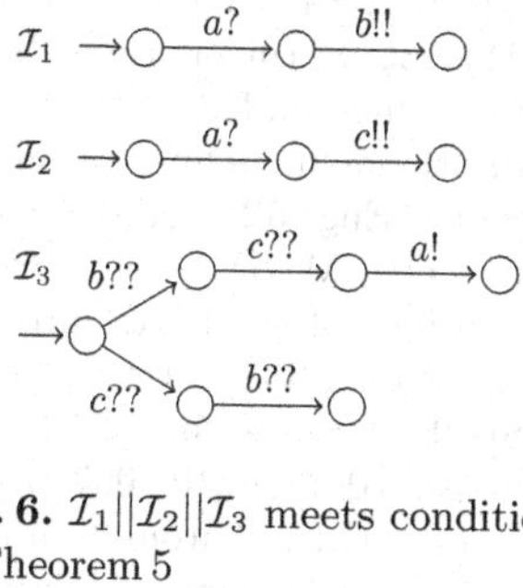

Fig. 6. $\mathcal{I}_1 || \mathcal{I}_2 || \mathcal{I}_3$ meets conditions in Theorem 5

8 Concluding Remarks

In this article, we have extended IOSA as introduced in [13] with urgent actions. Though such extension introduces non-determinism even if the IOSA is closed, it does so in a limited manner. We were able to characterize when a IOSA is weakly deterministic, which is an important concept since weakly deterministic IOSAs are amenable to discrete event simulation. In particular, we showed that closed and confluent IOSAs are weakly deterministic and provided conditions to check compositionally if a closed IOSA is confluent. Open IOSAs are naturally non-deterministic due to input enabledness: at any moment of time either two different inputs may be enabled or an input is enabled jointly with a possible passage of time. Thus, the property of non-determinism can only be possible in closed IOSAs. However, Theorem 5 relates open IOSAs to the concept of weak determinism by providing sufficient properties on open IOSAs whose composition leads to a closed weakly deterministic IOSA. In addition, we notice that languages like Modest [4,18,19], that have been designed for compositional modelling of complex timed and stochastic systems, embrace the concept of non-determinism as a fundamental property. Thus, ensuring weak determinism on Modest models using compositional tools like Theorem 5 will require significant limitations that may easily boil down to reduce it to IOSA. Notwithstanding this observation, we remark that some translation between IOSA and Modest is possible through Jani [8].

Finally, we remark that, though not discussed in this paper, the conditions provided by Theorem 5, can be verified in polynomial time respect to the size of the components and the number of actions.

References

1. Baader, F., Nipkow, T.: Term Rewriting and All That. Cambridge University Press, Cambridge (1998). https://doi.org/10.1017/cbo9781139172752
2. Behrmann, G., David, A., Larsen, K.G.: A tutorial on Uppaal. In: Bernardo, M., Corradini, F. (eds.) SFM-RT 2004. LNCS, vol. 3185, pp. 200–236. Springer, Heidelber (2004). https://doi.org/10.1007/978-3-540-30080-9_7
3. Bengtsson, J., et al.: Verification of an audio protocol with bus collision using UPPAAL. In: Alur, R., Henzinger, T.A. (eds.) CAV 1996. LNCS, vol. 1102, pp. 244–256. Springer, Heidelberg (1996). https://doi.org/10.1007/3-540-61474-5_73
4. Bohnenkamp, H.C., D'Argenio, P.R., Hermanns, H., Katoen, J.: MODEST: a compositional modeling formalism for hard and softly timed systems. IEEE Trans. Softw. Eng. **32**(10), 812–830 (2006). https://doi.org/10.1109/tse.2006.104
5. Bravetti, M., D'Argenio, P.R.: Tutte le algebre insieme: concepts, discussions and relations of stochastic process algebras with general distributions. In: Baier, C., Haverkort, B.R., Hermanns, H., Katoen, J.-P., Siegle, M. (eds.) Validation of Stochastic Systems. LNCS, vol. 2925, pp. 44–88. Springer, Heidelberg (2004). https://doi.org/10.1007/978-3-540-24611-4_2
6. Budde, C.E.: Automation of importance splitting techniques for rare event simulation. Ph.D. thesis, Universidad Nacional de Córdoba (2017)

7. Budde, C.E., D'Argenio, P.R., Monti, R.E.: Compositional construction of importance functions in fully automated importance splitting. In: Puliafito, A., Trivedi, K.S., Tuffin, B., Scarpa, M., Machida, F., Alonso, J. (eds.) Proceedings of 10th EAI International Conference on Performance Evaluation Methodologies and Tools, VALUETOOLS 2016, October 2016, Taormina. ICST (2017). https://doi.org/10.4108/eai.25-10-2016.2266501

8. Budde, C.E., Dehnert, C., Hahn, E.M., Hartmanns, A., Junges, S., Turrini, A.: JANI: quantitative model and tool interaction. In: Legay, A., Margaria, T. (eds.) TACAS 2017. LNCS, vol. 10206, pp. 151–168. Springer, Heidelberg (2017). https://doi.org/10.1007/978-3-662-54580-5_9

9. Crouzen, P.: Modularity and determinism in compositional markov models. Ph.D. thesis, Universität des Saarlandes, Saarbrücken (2014)

10. D'Argenio, P.R.: Algebras and automata for timed and stochastic systems. Ph.D. thesis, Universiteit Twente (1999)

11. D'Argenio, P.R., Katoen, J.P.: A theory of stochastic systems, part I: Stochastic automata. Inf. Comput. **203**(1), 1–38 (2005). https://doi.org/10.1016/j.ic.2005.07.001

12. D'Argenio, P.R., Katoen, J., Brinksma, E.: An algebraic approach to the specification of stochastic systems (extended abstract). In: Gries, D., de Roever, W.P. (eds.) PROCOMET 1998. IFIP Conference Proceedings, vol. 125, pp. 126–147. Chapman & Hall, Boca Raton (1998). https://doi.org/10.1007/978-0-387-35358-6_12

13. D'Argenio, P.R., Lee, M.D., Monti, R.E.: Input/Output stochastic automata. In: Fränzle, M., Markey, N. (eds.) FORMATS 2016. LNCS, vol. 9884, pp. 53–68. Springer, Cham (2016). https://doi.org/10.1007/978-3-319-44878-7_4

14. D'Argenio, P.R., Sánchez Terraf, P., Wolovick, N.: Bisimulations for nondeterministic labelled Markov processes. Math. Struct. Comput. Sci. **22**(1), 43–68 (2012). https://doi.org/10.1017/s0960129511000454

15. Desharnais, J., Edalat, A., Panangaden, P.: Bisimulation for labelled Markov processes. Inf. Comput. **179**(2), 163–193 (2002). https://doi.org/10.1006/inco.2001.2962

16. Giry, M.: A categorical approach to probability theory. In: Banaschewski, B. (ed.) Categorical Aspects of Topology and Analysis. LNM, vol. 915, pp. 68–85. Springer, Heidelberg (1982). https://doi.org/10.1007/BFb0092872

17. van Glabbeek, R.J., Smolka, S.A., Steffen, B.: Reactive, generative and stratified models of probabilistic processes. Inf. Comput. **121**(1), 59–80 (1995). https://doi.org/10.1006/inco.1995.1123

18. Hahn, E.M., Hartmanns, A., Hermanns, H., Katoen, J.: A compositional modelling and analysis framework for stochastic hybrid systems. Form. Methods Syst. Des. **43**(2), 191–232 (2013). https://doi.org/10.1007/s10703-012-0167-z

19. Hartmanns, A.: On the analysis of stochastic timed systems. Ph.D. thesis, Saarlandes University, Saarbrücken (2015). http://scidok.sulb.uni-saarland.de/volltexte/2015/6054/

20. Hermanns, H.: Interactive Markov Chains: And the Quest for Quantified Quality. LNCS, vol. 2428. Springer, Heidelberg (2002). https://doi.org/10.1007/3-540-45804-2

21. Larsen, K.G., Skou, A.: Bisimulation through probabilistic testing. Inf. Comput. **94**(1), 1–28 (1991). https://doi.org/10.1016/0890-5401(91)90030-6

22. Law, A.M., Kelton, W.D.: Simulation Modeling and Analysis, 3rd edn. McGraw-Hill Higher Education, New York City (1999)

23. Milner, R.: Communication and Concurrency. Prentice-Hall, Englewood Cliffs (1989)
24. Ruijters, E., Stoelinga, M.: Fault tree analysis: a survey of the state-of-the-art in modeling, analysis and tools. Comput. Sci. Rev. **15**, 29–62 (2015). https://doi.org/10.1016/j.cosrev.2015.03.001
25. Wolovick, N.: Continuous probability and nondeterminism in labeled transition systems. Ph.D. thesis, Universidad Nacional de Córdoba, Argentina (2012)
26. Wu, S., Smolka, S.A., Stark, E.W.: Composition and behaviors of probabilistic I/O automata. Theor. Comput. Sci. **176**(1–2), 1–38 (1997). https://doi.org/10.1016/S0304-3975(97)00056-X
27. Wang, Y.: Real-time behaviour of asynchronous agents. In: Baeten, J.C.M., Klop, J.W. (eds.) CONCUR 1990. LNCS, vol. 458, pp. 502–520. Springer, Heidelberg (1990). https://doi.org/10.1007/BFb0039080

Layer by Layer – Combining Monads

Fredrik Dahlqvist$^{(\boxtimes)}$, Louis Parlant, and Alexandra Silva

Department of Computer Science, University College London,
Gower Street, London WC1E 6BT, UK
{f.dahlqvist,l.parlant,a.silva}@cs.ucl.ac.uk

Abstract. We develop a modular method to build algebraic structures. Our approach is categorical: we describe the layers of our construct as monads, and combine them using distributive laws.

Finding such laws is known to be difficult and our method identifies precise sufficient conditions for two monads to distribute. We either (i) concretely build a distributive law which then provides a monad structure to the composition of layers, or (ii) pinpoint the algebraic obstacles to the existence of a distributive law and suggest a weakening of one layer that ensures distributivity.

This method can be applied to a step-by-step construction of a programming language. Our running example will involve three layers: a basic imperative language enriched first by adding non-determinism and then probabilistic choice. The first extension works seamlessly, but the second encounters an obstacle, resulting in an 'approximate' language very similar to the probabilistic network specification language Prob-NetKAT.

1 Introduction

The practical objective of this paper is to provide a systematic and modular understanding of the design of recent programming languages such as NetKAT [9] and ProbNetKAT [8,28] by re-interpreting their syntax as a layering of monads. However, in order to solve this problem, we develop a very general technique for building *distributive laws between monads* whose applicability goes far beyond understanding the design of languages in the NetKAT family. Indeed, the combination of monads has been an important area of research in theoretical computer science ever since Moggi developed a systematic understanding of computational effects as monads in [25]. In this paradigm – further developed by Plotkin, Power and others in e.g. [4,26] – the question of how to combine computational effects can be treated systematically by studying the possible ways of combining monads. This work can also be understood as a contribution to this area of research.

Combining effects is in general a non-trivial issue, but diverse methods have been studied in the literature. A *monad transformer*, as described in [4], is a

A. Silva—This work was partially supported by ERC grant ProfoundNet.

B. Fischer and T. Uustalu (Eds.): ICTAC 2018, LNCS 11187, pp. 153–172, 2018.
https://doi.org/10.1007/978-3-030-02508-3_9

way to enrich any theory with a specific effect. These transformers allow a step-by-step construction of computational structures, later exploited by Hudak et al. [20,21]. In [12], Hyland, Plotkin and Power systematized the study of effect combinations by introducing two canonical constructions for combining monads, which in some sense lie at the extreme ends of the collection of possible combination procedures. At one end of the spectrum they define the *sum* of monads which consists in the juxtaposition of both theories with no interaction whatsoever between computational effects. At the other end of the spectrum they define the *tensor* of two monads where both theories are maximally interacting in the sense that "each operator of one theory commutes with each operation of the other" [12]. In [11] they combine exceptions, side-effects, interactive input/output, non-determinism and continuations using these operations.

In some situations neither the sum nor the tensor of monads is the appropriate construction, and some intermediate level of interaction is required. From the perspective of understanding the design of recent programming languages which use layers of non-determinism and probabilities (e.g. ProbNetKAT), there are two reasons to consider combinations other than the sum or the tensor. First, there is the unavoidable mathematical obstacle which arises when combining sequential composition with non-deterministic choice (see the simple example below), two essential features of languages in the NetKAT family. When combining two monoid operations with the tensor construction, one enforces the equation $(p; q) + (r; s) = (p + r); (q + s)$ which means, by the Eckmann-Hilton argument, that the two operations collapse into a single commutative operation; clearly not the intended construction. Secondly, and much more importantly, the intended *semantics* of a language may force us to consider specific and limited interactions between its operations. This is the case for languages in the NetKAT family, where the intended trace semantics suggests *distributive laws* between operations, for instance that sequential composition distributes over non-deterministic choice (but not the converse). For this reason, the focus of this paper will be to explicitly construct *distributive laws* between monads.

It is worth noting that existence of distributive laws is a subtle question and having automatic tools to derive these is crucial in avoiding mistakes. As a simple example in which several mistakes have appeared in the literature, consider the composition of the powerset monad $\mathcal{P}$ with itself. Distributive laws of $\mathcal{P}$ over $\mathcal{P}$ were proposed in 1993 by King [15] and in 2007 [23], with a subsequent correction of the latter result by Manes and Mulry themselves in a follow-up paper. In 2015, Klin and Rot made a similar claim [16], but recently Klin and Salamanca have in fact showed that there is no distributive law of $\mathcal{P}$ over itself and explain carefully why all the mistakes in the previous results were so subtle and hard to spot [17]. This example shows that this question is very technical and sometimes counter-intuitive. Our general and modular approach provides a fine-grained method for determining (a) if a monad combination by distributive law is possible, (b) if it is not possible, exactly which features are broken by the extension and (c) suggests a way to fix the composition by modifying one of our monads. In other words, this enables informed design choices on which features we may accept to lose in order to achieve greater expressive power in a language through monad composition.

The original motivation for this work is very concrete and came from trying to understand the design of ProbNetKAT, a recently introduced programming language with non-determinism and probabilities [8,28]. The non-existence of a distributive law between the powerset monad and the distribution monad, first proved by Varacca [30] and discussed recently in [5], is a well known problem in semantics. As we will show, our method enables us to modularly build ProbNetKAT based on the composition of several monads capturing the desired algebraic features. The method derives automatically which equations have to be dropped when adding the probabilistic layer providing a principled justification to the work initially presented in [8,28].

A Simple Example. Let us consider a set P of atomic programs, and build a 'minimal' programming language as follows. Since sequential composition is essential to any imperative language we start by defining the syntax as:

$$p ::= \text{skip} \mid p\,;\,p \mid a \in P \tag{1}$$

and ask that the following programs be identified:

$$p\,;\,\text{skip} = p = \text{skip}\,;\,p \qquad \text{and} \qquad p\,;\,(q\,;\,r) = (p\,;\,q)\,;\,r \tag{2}$$

The language defined by the operations of (1) and the equations of (2) can equally be described as the application of the *free monoid monad* $(-)^*$ to the set of atomic programs P. If we assign a semantics to each basic program P, the semantics of the extended language can be defined as finite sequences (or traces) of the basic semantics. In a next step, we might want to enrich this basic language by adding a non-deterministic choice operation $+$ and the constant program abort, satisfying the equations:

$$\text{abort} + p = p = p + \text{abort} \quad p + p = p \quad p + q = q + p \quad p + (q + r) = (p + q) + r \tag{3}$$

The signature $(\text{abort}, +)$ and the axioms (3) define join-semilattices, and the monad building free semilattices is the *finitary powerset monad* $\mathcal{P}$. To build our language in a modular fashion we thus want to apply $\mathcal{P}$ on top of our previous construction and consider the programming language where the syntax and semantics arise from $\mathcal{P}(P^*)$. For this purpose we combine both monads to construct a new monad $\mathcal{P}(-^*)$ by building a distributive law $(-)^*\mathcal{P} \to \mathcal{P}(-)^*$. As explained above, this approach is semantically justified by the intended trace semantics of the language, and will ensure that operations from the inner layer distribute over the outer ones, i.e.

$$p\,;\,(q + r) = p\,;\,q + p\,;\,r \quad (q + r)\,;\,p = q\,;\,p + r\,;\,p \quad p\,;\,\text{abort} = \text{abort}\,;\,p = \text{abort} \tag{4}$$

Our method proves and relies on the following theorem: if $\mathcal{P}$ preserves the structure of $(-)^*$-algebra defined by (1)–(2), then the composition $\mathcal{P}(-^*)$ has a monad structure provided by the corresponding distributive law. Applying this theorem to our running example, the first step is to lift the signature (1), in other words to define new canonical interpretations in $\mathcal{P}(P^*)$ for ; and `skip`. Once this lifting is achieved, the equations in (2), arising from the inner layer, can be interpreted in $\mathcal{P}(-^*)$. We need to check if they still hold: is the new interpretation of ; still associative? To answer this question, our method makes use of categorical diagrams to obtain precise conditions on our monadic constructs. Furthermore, in the case where equations fail to hold, we provide a way to identify exactly what stands in the way of monad composition. We can then offer tailor-made adjustments to achieve the composition and obtain a 'best approximate' language, with slightly modified monads.

Structure of this Paper. Section 2 presents some basic facts about monads and distributive laws and fixes the notation. In Sect. 3 we recall the well-known fact [24,29] that there exists a distributive law of any polynomial functor over a monoidal **Set**-monad. In particular this shows that *operations* can be lifted by monoidal monads. In fact, the techniques presented in this paper can be extended beyond the monoidal case, but since we won't need such monads in our applications, we will focus on monoidal monads for which the lifting of operations is very straightforward. We then show in Sect. 4 when *equations* can also be lifted. We isolate two conditions on the lifting monad which guarantee that any equation can be lifted. These two conditions correspond to a monad being *affine* [18] and *relevant* [13]. We also characterise the general form of equations preserved by monads which only satisfy a subset of these conditions. Interestingly, together with the symmetry condition (SYM) which is always satisfied by monoidal **Set**-monads, we recover what are essentially the three structural laws of classical logic (see also [13]). In Sect. 5 we show how the $*$-free fragment of ProbNetKAT can be built in systematic way by construction distributive laws between the three layers of the language.

2   A Primer on Monads, Algebras and Distributive Laws

Monads and (Σ, E)-Algebras. For the purposes of this paper, we will always consider monads on **Set** [1,22,25]. The core language described in the introduction is defined by the signature $\Sigma = \{\ ;\ , \texttt{skip}\}$ and the set E of equations given by (2). More generally, we view programming languages as algebraic structures defined by a signature $(\Sigma, \mathrm{ar} : \Sigma \to \mathbb{N})$ and a set of equations E enforcing program equivalence. To formalize this we first define a Σ-algebra to be a set X together with an interpretation $[\![\sigma]\!] : X^{\mathrm{ar}(\sigma)} \to X$ of each operation $\sigma \in \Sigma$. A Σ-algebra can be conveniently represented as an algebra for the polynomial functor $\mathsf{H}_\Sigma = \coprod_{\sigma \in \Sigma} (-)^{\mathrm{ar}(\sigma)}$ defined by the signature, i.e. as a set X together with a map $\beta : \mathsf{H}_\Sigma X \to X$. A Σ-algebra morphism between $\beta : \mathsf{H}_\Sigma X \to X$ and $\gamma : \mathsf{H}_\Sigma Y \to Y$ is a map $f : X \to Y$ such that $\gamma \circ \mathsf{H}_\Sigma f = f \circ \beta$. The category of Σ-algebras and Σ-algebra morphisms is denoted $\mathbf{Alg}(\Sigma)$. In particular, the set $\mathsf{F}_\Sigma X$ of all Σ-terms is a Σ-algebra – the free Σ-algebra over X – and F_Σ is a functor $\mathbf{Set} \to \mathbf{Alg}(\Sigma)$ forming an adjunction

$$\mathsf{F}_\Sigma \dashv \mathsf{U}_\Sigma : \mathbf{Alg}(\Sigma) \to \mathbf{Set} \tag{5}$$

Since it will not lead to any ambiguity we will usually overload the symbol F_Σ to also denote the monad $U_\Sigma F_\Sigma : \mathbf{Set} \to \mathbf{Set}$ arising from this adjunction.

Given a Σ-algebra $\mathcal{A}$, a free Σ-term s built over variables in a set V, and a valuation map $v : V \to U_\Sigma \mathcal{A}$, we define the interpretation $[\![s]\!]_v$ of s in $\mathcal{A}$ recursively in the obvious manner. We say that an equation $s = t$ between free Σ-terms is valid in $\mathcal{A}$, denoted $\mathcal{A} \models s = t$, if for every valuation $v : V \to U_\Sigma \mathcal{A}$, $[\![s]\!]_v = [\![t]\!]_v$. Given a set E of equations we define a (Σ, E)-algebra as a Σ-algebra in which all the equations in E are valid. We denote by $\mathbf{Alg}(\Sigma, E)$ the subcategory of $\mathbf{Alg}(\Sigma)$ consisting of (Σ, E)-algebras. There exists a functor $F : \mathbf{Set} \to \mathbf{Alg}(\Sigma, E)$ building free (Σ, E)-algebras which is left adjoint to the obvious forgetful functor:

$$F \dashv U : \mathbf{Alg}(\Sigma, E) \to \mathbf{Set} \qquad (6)$$

In our running example all monads arise from a finitary syntax, and thus from an adjunction of the type (6).

Eilenberg-Moore Categories. An algebra for the monad T is a set X together with an map $\alpha : TX \to X$ such that the diagrams in (7) commute. A morphism $(X, \alpha) \xrightarrow{f} (Y, \beta)$ of T-algebras is a morphism $X \xrightarrow{f} Y$ in $\mathbf{Set}$ verifying $\beta \circ Tf = f \circ \alpha$.

$$
\begin{array}{ccc}
TTX \xrightarrow{\mu_X} TX & \qquad & X \xrightarrow{\eta_X} TX \\
\scriptstyle T\alpha \downarrow \qquad \downarrow \scriptstyle \alpha & & \scriptstyle 1 \searrow \quad \downarrow \scriptstyle \alpha \\
TX \xrightarrow{\ \alpha\ } X & & \qquad X
\end{array}
\qquad (7)
$$

The category of T-algebras and T-algebra morphisms is called the *Eilenberg-Moore* category of the monad T, and denoted $\mathcal{EM}(T)$. There is an obvious forgetful functor $U_E : \mathcal{EM}(T) \to \mathbf{Set}$ which sends an algebra to its carrier, it has a left adjoint $F_E : \mathbf{Set} \to \mathcal{EM}(T)$ which sends a set X to the free T-algebra $\mu_X : T^2 X \to TX$. Note that the adjunction $F_E \dashv U_E$ gives rise to the monad T. A *lifting* of a functor $F : \mathbf{Set} \to \mathbf{Set}$ to $\mathcal{EM}(T)$ is a functor $\hat{F}$ on $\mathcal{EM}(T)$ such that $U_E \circ \hat{F} = F \circ U_E$.

Lemma 1 *([22] VI.8. Theorem 1). For any adjunction of the form (6), $\mathcal{EM}(UF)$ and $\mathbf{Alg}(\Sigma, E)$ are equivalent categories.*

The functors connecting $\mathcal{EM}(UF)$ and $\mathbf{Alg}(\Sigma, E)$ are traditionally called *comparison functors*, and we will denote them by $M : \mathcal{EM}(UF) \to \mathbf{Alg}(\Sigma, E)$ and $K : \mathbf{Alg}(\Sigma, E) \to \mathcal{EM}(UF)$. Consider first the free monad F_Σ for a signature Σ (i.e. the monad generated by the adjunction (5)). The comparison functor $M : \mathbf{Alg}(\Sigma) \to \mathcal{EM}(F_\Sigma)$ maps the free F_Σ-algebra over X, that is $\mu_X^{F_\Sigma} : F_\Sigma^2 X \to F_\Sigma X$ to the free H_Σ-algebra over X which we shall denote by $\alpha_X : H_\Sigma F_\Sigma X \to F_\Sigma X$. It is well-known that α_X is an isomorphism. Moreover, the maps α_X define a natural transformation $H_\Sigma F_\Sigma \to F_\Sigma$. Similarly, in the presence of equations, if we consider the adjunction $F \dashv U$ of (6) and the associated monad $T = UF$, then the comparison functor $M' : \mathbf{Alg}(\Sigma, E) \to \mathcal{EM}(T)$

sends the free T-algebra $\mu_X^T : T^2X \to TX$ to an H_Σ-algebra which we shall denote $\rho_X : H_\Sigma TX \to TX$. Again, the maps ρ_X define a natural transformation $H_\Sigma T \to T$, but in general ρ_X is no longer an isomorphism: in the case of monoids and of a set $X = \{x, y, z\}$, we have $\rho_X(x; (y; z)) = \rho_X((x; y); z)$.

Distributive Laws. Let (S, η^S, μ^S) and (T, η^T, μ^T) be monads, a *distributive law of S over T* (see [3]) is a natural transformation $\lambda : ST \to TS$ satisfying:

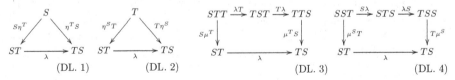

$$
\begin{array}{ccc}
& (DL.\ 1) & (DL.\ 2) \\
\end{array}
\qquad (DL.\ 3) \qquad\qquad (DL.\ 4)
$$

If λ only satisfies (DL. 2) and (DL. 4), we will say that λ is a distributive law of the the monad S over *functor* T, or in the terminology of [14], an $\mathcal{EM}$-law of S over T. Dually, if λ only satisfies (DL. 1) and (DL. 3), λ is known as a distributive law of the *functor* S over the monad T, or $\mathcal{Kl}$-law of S over T [14].

Theorem 1. [2,3,14] $\mathcal{EM}$-laws $\lambda : SF \to FS$ and liftings of F to $\mathcal{EM}(S)$ are in one-to-one correspondence.

If there exists a distributive law $\lambda : TS \to ST$ of the monad T over the monad S, then the composition of S and T also forms a monad (ST, u, m), whose unit u and multiplication m are given by:

$$
X \xrightarrow{\eta_X^T} TX \xrightarrow{\eta_{TX}^S} STX \qquad STSTX \xrightarrow{S\lambda_{TX}} SSTTX \xrightarrow{\mu_{TTX}^S} STTX \xrightarrow{S\mu_X^T} STX
$$
$$
\underbrace{\phantom{X \xrightarrow{\eta_X^T} TX \xrightarrow{\eta_{TX}^S}} }_{u_X} STX \qquad\qquad \underbrace{\phantom{STSTX \xrightarrow{S\lambda_{TX}} SSTTX \xrightarrow{\mu_{TTX}^S} STTX}}_{m_X}
$$

If $\mathcal{EM}(S) \simeq \mathbf{Alg}(\Sigma, E)$ and $\mathcal{EM}(T) \simeq \mathbf{Alg}(\Sigma', E')$, then a distributive law $ST \to TS$ implements the distributivity of the operations in Σ over those of Σ'.

3   Building Distributive Laws Between Monads

In this section we will show how to construct a distributive law $\lambda : ST \to TS$ between monads via a *monoidal structure* on T.

3.1   Monoidal Monads

Let us briefly recall some relatively well-known categorical notion. A *lax monoidal functor* on a monoidal category $(\mathbf{C}, \otimes, I)$, or simply a monoidal functor[1], is an endofunctor $F : \mathbf{C} \to \mathbf{C}$ together with natural transformations $\psi_{X,Y} : FX \otimes FY \to F(X \otimes Y)$ and $\psi^0 : I \to FI$ satisfying the diagrams:

---

[1] We will never consider the notion of *strong* monoidal functor, so this terminology should not lead to any confusion.

$$FX \otimes I \xrightarrow{\mathrm{id}_{FX}\otimes\psi^0} FX \otimes FI \qquad (FX \otimes FY) \otimes FZ \xrightarrow{\alpha_{FX,FY,FZ}} FX \otimes (FY \otimes FZ)$$

$$\begin{array}{ccc}
\downarrow{\rho_{FX}} & \quad \downarrow{\psi_{X,I}} & \qquad\qquad \downarrow{\psi_{X,Y}\otimes\mathrm{id}_{FZ}} \qquad\qquad\qquad\qquad \downarrow{\mathrm{id}_{FX}\otimes\psi_{Y,Z}}
\end{array}$$

$$FX \xleftarrow{\ F\rho_X\ } F(X \otimes I) \qquad F(X \otimes Y) \otimes FZ \qquad\qquad FX \otimes F(Y \otimes Z)$$

$$(\mathrm{MF.}\,1)$$

$$\downarrow{\psi_{X\otimes Y,Z}} \qquad\qquad\qquad \downarrow{\psi_{X,Y\otimes Z}}$$

$$F((X \otimes Y) \otimes Z) \xrightarrow{\ F\alpha_{X,Y,Z}\ } F(X \otimes (Y \otimes Z)))$$

$$I \otimes FX \xrightarrow{\psi^0\otimes\mathrm{id}_{FX}} FI \otimes FX \qquad\qquad\qquad (\mathrm{MF.}\,3)$$

$$\begin{array}{cc}
\downarrow{\rho'_{FX}} & \quad \downarrow{\psi_{I,X}}
\end{array}$$

$$FX \xleftarrow{\ F\rho'_X\ } F(I \otimes X)$$

$$(\mathrm{MF.}\,2)$$

where α is the associator of $(\mathbf{C}, \otimes, I)$ and ρ, ρ' the right and left unitors respectively. The diagrams (MF. 1), (MF. 2) and (MF. 3) play a key role in the lifting of operations and equations in this section and the next. In particular they ensure that any unital (resp. associative) operation lifts to a unital (resp. associative) operation. We will sometimes refer to ψ as the *Fubini transformation* of F.

A *monoidal monad* T on a monoidal category is a monad whose underlying functor is monoidal for a natural transformation $\psi_{X,Y} : TX \otimes TY \to T(X \otimes Y)$ and $\psi^0 = \eta_I$, the unit of the monad at I, and whose unit and multiplication are monoidal natural transformations, that is to say:

$$X \otimes Y \xrightarrow{\eta_X\otimes\eta_Y} TX \otimes TY \quad (\mathrm{MM.1}) \qquad T^2X \otimes T^2Y \xrightarrow{\psi_{TX,TY}} T(TX \otimes TY) \xrightarrow{T\psi_{X,Y}} TT(X \otimes Y) \quad (\mathrm{MM.2})$$

$$\begin{array}{cc}
\searrow{\eta_{X\otimes Y}} \quad \downarrow{\psi_{X,Y}} & \qquad \downarrow{\mu_X\otimes\mu_Y} \qquad\qquad\qquad\qquad\qquad \downarrow{\mu_X\otimes Y}
\end{array}$$

$$T(X \otimes Y) \qquad\qquad\qquad TX \otimes TY \xrightarrow{\qquad\qquad\psi_{X,Y}\qquad\qquad} T(X \otimes Y)$$

Moreover, a monoidal monad is called *symmetric monoidal* if

$$TX \otimes TY \xrightarrow{\psi_{X,Y}} T(X \otimes Y) \qquad\qquad (\mathrm{SYM})$$

$$\begin{array}{cc}
\downarrow{\mathsf{swap}_{TX,TY}} & \qquad \downarrow{T\mathsf{swap}_{X,Y}}
\end{array}$$

$$TY \otimes TX \xrightarrow{\psi_{Y,X}} T(Y \otimes X)$$

where $\mathsf{swap} : (-) \otimes (-) \to (-) \otimes (-)$ is the argument-swapping transformation (natural in both arguments).

We now present a result which shows that for monoidal categories which are sufficiently similar to $(\mathbf{Set}, \times, 1)$, being monoidal is equivalent to being symmetric monoidal. The criteria on $(\mathbf{C}, \otimes, I)$ in the following theorem are due to [27] and generalize the strength unicity result of [25, Proposition 3.4]. Our usage of the concept of strength in what follows is purely technical, it is the monoidal structure which is our main object of interest. We therefore refer the reader to e.g. [25] for the definitions of strength and commutative monad.

Theorem 2. *Let $T : \mathbf{C} \to \mathbf{C}$ be a monad over a monoidal category $(\mathbf{C}, \otimes, I)$ whose tensor unit I is a separator of $\mathbf{C}$ (i.e. $f, g : X \to Y$ and $f \neq g$ implies $\exists x : I \to X$ s.th. $f \circ x \neq g \circ x$) and such that for any morphism $z : I \to X \otimes Y$ there exist $x : I \to X, y \to Y$ such that $z = (x \otimes y) \circ \rho_I^{-1}$. Then t.f.a.e.*

(i) *There exists a unique natural transformation $\psi_{X,Y} : TX \otimes TY \to T(X \otimes Y)$ making T monoidal*

(ii) *There exists a unique strength $\mathsf{st}_{X,Y} : X \times TY \to T(X \otimes Y)$ making T commutative*

(iii) *There exists a unique natural transformation $\psi_{X,Y} : TX \otimes TY \to T(X \otimes Y)$ making T symmetric monoidal.*

In particular, monoidal monads on $(\mathbf{Set}, \times, 1)$ are necessarily symmetric (and thus commutative). As we will see in the next section (Theorem 7), this symmetry has deep consequences: it means that a large syntactically definable class of equations can always be lifted by monoidal monads.

3.2   Lifting Operations

First though, we show that being monoidal allows us to lift *operations*. The following Theorem is well-known and can be found in e.g. [24, 29].

Theorem 3. *Let $T : \mathbf{Set} \to \mathbf{Set}$ be a monoidal monad, then for any finitary signature Σ, there exists a distributive law $\lambda^\Sigma : \mathsf{H}_\Sigma T \to T\mathsf{H}_\Sigma$ of the polynomial functor associated with Σ over T.*

The distributive laws $\lambda^\Sigma : \mathsf{H}_\Sigma T \to T\mathsf{H}_\Sigma$ built from a monoidal structure ψ on T in Theorem 3 have the general shape

$$\mathsf{H}_\Sigma TX = \coprod_{s \in \Sigma} (TX)^{\mathrm{ar}(s)} \xrightarrow{\coprod_{s \in \Sigma} \psi_X^{(\mathrm{ar}(s))}} T\mathsf{H}_\Sigma X \tag{8}$$

where $\psi_X^{(0)} = \eta_1^T, \psi_X^{(1)} = \mathrm{id}_X, \psi_X^{(2)} = \psi_{X,X}$. For $k \geq 3$ if we wanted to be completely rigorous we should first give an evaluation order to the k-fold monoidal product $(TX)^k$ – for example evaluating the products from the left, e.g. $(TX)^3 := (TX \otimes TX) \otimes TX$ – and then define $\psi^{(k)} : (TX)^k \to T(X^k)$ accordingly by repeated application of the Fubini transformation ψ – for example defining

$$\psi_X^{(3)} = \psi_{X \otimes X, X} \circ (\psi_{X,X} \times \mathrm{id}) : (TX \otimes TX) \otimes TX \to T((X \otimes X) \otimes X)$$

However, we will in general be interested in a variety of evaluation orders for the tensors (depending on circumstances), and since in **Set** these different evaluation orders are related by a combination of associators $\alpha_{X,Y,Z}$ which simply re-bracket tuples, we will abuse notation slightly and write

$$\psi_X^{(k)} : (TX)^k \to T(X^k)$$

with the understanding that $\psi_X^{(k)}$ is only defined up to re-bracketing of tuples which is quietly taking place 'under the hood' as called for by the particular situation. The distributive laws defined by Theorem 3 can be extended to distributive laws for the free monad associated with the signature Σ.

Proposition 1. *Given a finitary signature Σ and a monad $T :$ **Set** $\to$ **Set**, there is a one-to-one correspondence between*

(i) *distributive laws $\lambda^\Sigma :$ $\mathsf{H}_\Sigma T \to T\mathsf{H}_\Sigma$ of the polynomial functor associated with Σ over T*
(ii) *distributive laws $\rho^\Sigma :$ $\mathsf{F}_\Sigma T \to T\mathsf{F}_\Sigma$ of the free monad associated with Σ over T.*

In particular, by Theorem 1, the distributive law (8) also corresponds to a lifting $\widehat{T}$ of T to $\mathcal{EM}(\mathsf{F}_\Sigma) \simeq \mathbf{Alg}(\Sigma)$. Explicitly, given an F_Σ-algebra $\beta : \mathsf{F}_\Sigma X \to X$, $\widehat{T}(X, \beta)$ is defined as the F_Σ-algebra

$$\mathsf{F}_\Sigma TX \xrightarrow{\rho_X^\Sigma} T\mathsf{F}_\Sigma X \xrightarrow{T\beta} TX \tag{9}$$

Thus whenever T is monoidal, we can 'lift' the operations of Σ, or, in programming language terms, we can define the operations of the outer layer (T) on the language defined by the operations of the inner layer (F_Σ).

3.3   Lifting Equations

We now show how to go from a lifting of T on $\mathcal{EM}(\mathsf{F}_\Sigma) \simeq \mathbf{Alg}(\Sigma)$ to a lifting of T on $\mathcal{EM}(S) \simeq \mathbf{Alg}(\Sigma, E)$. More precisely, we will now show how to 'quotient' the distributive law $\rho^\Sigma :$ $\mathsf{F}_\Sigma T \to T\mathsf{F}_\Sigma$ into a distributive law $\lambda : ST \to TS$. Of course this is not always possible, but in the next section we will give sufficient conditions under which the procedure described below does work. The first step is to define the natural transformation $q \colon \mathsf{F}_\Sigma \twoheadrightarrow S$ which quotients the free Σ-algebras by the equations of E to build the free (Σ, E)-algebra. At each set X, let EX denote the set of pairs $(s, t) \in \mathsf{F}_\Sigma X$ such that $SX \models s = t$ and let π_1, π_2 be the obvious projections. Then q can be constructed via the coequalizers:

$$EX \mathrel{\mathop{\rightrightarrows}^{\pi_1}_{\pi_2}} \mathsf{F}_\Sigma X \xrightarrow{q_X} SX \tag{10}$$

By construction q is a component-wise regular epi monad morphism ($q \circ \eta = \eta^S$ and $\mu^S \circ qq = q \circ \mu^T$), and it induces a functor $Q : \mathcal{EM}(S) \to \mathcal{EM}(\mathsf{F}_\Sigma)$ defined by

$$Q(\xi \colon SX \to X) = \xi \circ q_X : \mathsf{F}_\Sigma X \to X, \qquad Q(f) = f$$

which is well defined by naturality of q. This functor describes an embedding, in particular it is injective on objects: if $Q(\xi_1) = Q(\xi_2)$ then $\xi_1 \circ q_X = \xi_2 \circ q_X$, and therefore $\xi_1 = \xi_2$ since q_X is a (regular) epi.

Given two terms $u, v \in F_\Sigma V$, we will say that a lifting $\widehat{T} : \mathbf{Alg}(\Sigma) \to \mathbf{Alg}(\Sigma)$ preserves the equation $u = v$, or by a slight abuse of notation that the monad T preserves $u = v$, if $\widehat{T}\mathcal{A} \models u = v$ whenever $\mathcal{A} \models u = v$. Similarly, we will say that $\widehat{T}$ sends (Σ, E)-algebras to (Σ, E)-algebras if it preserves all the equations in E. Half of the following result can be found in [6] where a distributive law over a *functor* is built in a similar way.

Lemma 2. *If $q \colon F_\Sigma \twoheadrightarrow T$ is a component-wise epi monad morphism, ρ^Σ is a distributive law of the monad F_Σ over the monad T and if there exists a natural transformation $\lambda \colon ST \to TS$ such that the following diagram commutes*

$$
\begin{array}{ccc}
F_\Sigma T & \xrightarrow{\;qT\;} & ST \\
{\scriptstyle \rho^\Sigma}\downarrow & & \downarrow{\scriptstyle \lambda} \\
TF_\Sigma & \xrightarrow[\;Tq\;]{} & TS
\end{array}
\tag{11}
$$

then λ is a distributive law of the monad S over the monad T.

From this lemma we can give an abstract criterion which, when implemented concretely in the next section, will allow us to go from a lifting of T on $\mathcal{EM}(F_\Sigma) \simeq \mathbf{Alg}(\Sigma)$ to a lifting of T on $\mathcal{EM}(S) \simeq \mathbf{Alg}(\Sigma, E)$.

Theorem 4. *Suppose $T, S : \mathbf{Set} \to \mathbf{Set}$ are finitary monads, that T is monoidal and that $\mathcal{EM}(S) \simeq \mathbf{Alg}(\Sigma, E)$, and let $\widehat{T} : \mathbf{Alg}(\Sigma) \to \mathbf{Alg}(\Sigma)$ be the unique lifting of T defined via Theorems 1, 3 and Proposition 1. If $\widehat{T}$ sends (Σ, E)-algebras to (Σ, E)-algebras, then there exists a natural transformation $\lambda : ST \to TS$ satisfying (11), and therefore a distributive law of S over T.*

4   Checking Equation Preservation

In Sect. 3 we showed how to build a lifting of $T: \mathbf{Set} \to \mathbf{Set}$ to $\widehat{T} : \mathbf{Alg}(\Sigma) \to \mathbf{Alg}(\Sigma)$ using a Fubini transformation ψ via (8) and (9). In this section we provide a sound method to ascertain whether this lifting sends (Σ, E)-algebras to (Σ, E)-algebras, by giving sufficient conditions for the preservation of equations. We assume throughout this section that T is monoidal, in particular T lifts to $\mathbf{Alg}(\Sigma)$ for any finitary signature Σ. We will denote by $U_\Sigma : \mathbf{Alg}(\Sigma) \to \mathbf{Set}$ the obvious forgetful functor.

4.1   Residual Diagrams

We fix a finitary signature Σ and let u, v be Σ-terms over a set of variables V. Recall that the monad T preserves the equation $u = v$ if $\widehat{T}\mathcal{A} \models u = v$

whenever $\mathcal{A} \models u = v$. If t is a Σ-term, we will denote by $Var(t)$ the *set of variables* in t and by $Arg(t)$ the *list of arguments* used in t ordered as they appear in t. For example, the list of arguments of $t = f(x_1, g(x_3, x_2), x_1)$ is $Arg(t) = [x_1, x_3, x_2, x_1]$.

Let V be a set of variables and $\mathcal{A}$ be a Σ-algebra with carrier A, we define the morphism $\delta^V_{\mathcal{A}}(t) : A^{|V|} \to A^k$ where $k = |Arg(t)|$ as the following pairing of projections:

$$\text{if } Arg(t) = [x_{i_1}, x_{i_2}, x_{i_3}, \ldots x_{i_k}] \text{ then } \delta^V_{\mathcal{A}}(t) = \langle \pi_{i_1}, \pi_{i_2}, \pi_{i_3}, \ldots \pi_{i_k} \rangle$$

Intuitively, this pairing rearranges, copies and duplicates the variables used in t to match the arguments. Next, we define $\sigma^V_{\mathcal{A}}(t) : A^k \to A$ inductively by:

$$\sigma^V_{\mathcal{A}}(x) = \mathrm{id}_A$$

$$\sigma^V_{\mathcal{A}}(f(t_1, \ldots, t_i)) = A^k \xrightarrow{\sigma^V_{\mathcal{A}}(t_1) \times \ldots \times \sigma^V_{\mathcal{A}}(t_i)} A^i \xrightarrow{f_{\mathcal{A}}} A$$

With $f_{\mathcal{A}}$ the interpretation of $f \in \Sigma$ in $\mathcal{A}$. Finally we define $[\![t]\!]^V_{\mathcal{A}}$ as $\sigma^V_{\mathcal{A}}(t) \circ \delta^V_{\mathcal{A}}(t)$. The following lemma follows easily from the definitions.

Lemma 3. *For any* $t \in \mathsf{F}_\Sigma V$, $\delta^V_{\mathcal{A}}(t), \sigma^V_{\mathcal{A}}(t)$, *and thus* $[\![t]\!]^V_{\mathcal{A}}$, *are natural in* $\mathcal{A}$.

We can therefore re-interpret any term $t \in \mathsf{F}_\Sigma V$ as a natural transformation $[\![t]\!]^V : (-)^{(|V|)} \mathsf{U}_\Sigma \to \mathsf{U}_\Sigma$ which is itself the composition of two natural transformations. The first one, $\delta^V(t) : (-)^{|V|} \mathsf{U}_\Sigma \to (-)^k \mathsf{U}_\Sigma$, 'prepares' the variables by swapping, copying and deleting them as appropriate. The second one, $\sigma^V(t) : (-)^k \mathsf{U}_\Sigma \to \mathsf{U}_\Sigma$, performs the evaluation at each given algebra. Of course, the usual soundness and completeness property of term functions still holds.

Lemma 4. *For* $\mathcal{A}$ *a* Σ-*algebra and* $u, v \in \mathsf{F}_\Sigma V$, $[\![u]\!]^V_{\mathcal{A}} = [\![v]\!]^V_{\mathcal{A}}$ *iff* $\mathcal{A} \models u = v$.

Now consider the following diagram:

$$(12)$$

Since $\mathsf{U}_\Sigma \circ \widehat{T} = T \circ \mathsf{U}_\Sigma$ by definition of liftings it is clear that the vertical arrows $\psi^{(|V|)}_{\mathsf{U}_\Sigma}$ and $\psi^{(k)}_{\mathsf{U}_\Sigma}$ are well-typed. We define $Pres(T, t, V)$ as the outer square of Diagram (12) and we call the left-hand square $\textcircled{r}$ the *residual diagram* $\mathcal{R}(T, t, V)$. The following Lemma is at the heart of our method for building distributive laws.

Lemma 5. *If $\mathcal{R}(T,t,V)$ commutes, then $Pres(T,t,V)$ commutes.*

The following soundness theorem follows immediately from Lemma 5.

Theorem 5. *If $u,v \in \mathsf{F}_\Sigma V$ are such that $\mathcal{R}(T,u,V)$ and $\mathcal{R}(T,v,V)$ commute, then T preserves $u = v$.*

Proof. If $\mathcal{A} \models u = v$, then $[\![u]\!]_\mathcal{A}^V = [\![v]\!]_\mathcal{A}^V$ by Lemma 4 and thus $T[\![u]\!]_\mathcal{A}^V \circ \psi_\mathcal{A}^{(|V|)} = T[\![v]\!]_\mathcal{A}^V \circ \psi_\mathcal{A}^{(|V|)}$. Since $\mathcal{R}(T,u,V)$ and $\mathcal{R}(T,v,V)$ commute, so do $Pres(T,u,V)$ and $Pres(T,v,V)$ by Lemma 5, and therefore $[\![u]\!]_{\widehat{T}\mathcal{A}}^V = [\![v]\!]_{\widehat{T}\mathcal{A}}^V$, that is to say $\widehat{T}\mathcal{A} \models u = v$ by Lemma 4.

Therefore residual diagrams act as sufficient conditions for equation preservation. Note that these diagrams only involve ψ, projections and the monad T, sometimes inside pairings. In other words, the actual operations of Σ appearing in an equation have no impact on its preservation. What matters is the variable rearrangement transformations $\delta^V(u)$ and $\delta^V(v)$, and how they interact with the Fubini transformation ψ.

The converse of Theorem 5 does not hold. Consider the powerset monad $\mathcal{P}$ and a Σ-algebra $\mathcal{A}$ with Σ containing a binary operation $\bullet$. Clearly $\widehat{\mathcal{P}}\mathcal{A} \models x \bullet x = x \bullet x$ whenever $\mathcal{A} \models x \bullet x = x \bullet x$, because the equation trivially holds in any Σ-algebra. In other words, it is preserved by $\mathcal{P}$. However $\mathcal{R}(\mathcal{P}, x \bullet x, \{x\})$ does not commute: provided that X has more than one element, it is easy to see that $\mathcal{R}(\mathcal{P}, x \bullet x, \{x\})$ evaluated at X is

$$
\begin{array}{ccc}
\mathcal{P}\mathcal{A} & \xrightarrow{\Delta_{\mathcal{P}\mathcal{A}}} & (\mathcal{P}\mathcal{A})^2 \\
{\scriptstyle \mathrm{id}_{\mathcal{P}\mathcal{A}}} \downarrow & & \downarrow {\scriptstyle -\times-} \\
\mathcal{P}\mathcal{A} & \xrightarrow{\mathcal{P}(\Delta_\mathcal{A})} & \mathcal{P}(A^2)
\end{array}
$$

where Δ is the diagonal transformation and $-\times-$ is the monoidal structure for $\mathcal{P}$ which takes the Cartesian product. This diagram does not commute (in other words $\mathcal{P}$ is not 'relevant', see below).

4.2   Examples of Residual Diagrams

We need *a priori* two diagrams per equation to verify preservation. However, in many cases diagrams will be trivially commuting. For instance, associativity and unit produce trivial diagrams. For associativity we assume a binary operation $\bullet \in \Sigma$, let $V = \{x,y,z\}$ and compute that $\delta_\mathcal{A}^V(x \bullet (y \bullet z)) = \langle \pi_1, \pi_2, \pi_3 \rangle : A^3 \to A^3$ which is just id_{A^3}. It follows that $\mathcal{R}(T, x \bullet (y \bullet z), V)$ commutes since $\psi^3 \circ \mathrm{id}_{TA^3} = T\mathrm{id}_{A^3} \circ \psi^3$ which trivially holds. The argument for $(x \bullet y) \bullet z$ is identical, thus associativity is *always* lifted. The same argument shows that units are always lifted as well. This is not completely surprising since we have built-in units and associativity via Diagrams (MF. 1), (MF. 2) and (MF. 3).

Let us now consider commutativity: $x \bullet y = y \bullet x$. In this case, we put $V = \{x,y\}$ and hence $\delta_\mathcal{A}^V(x \bullet y) = \mathrm{id}_\mathcal{A}$ and $\mathcal{R}(T, x \bullet y, V)$ obviously commutes for the same reason as before. Similarly, it is not hard to check that $\mathcal{R}(T, y \bullet x, V)$ is just diagram (SYM), which we know holds by our assumption that T is monoidal and Theorem 2. It follows that:

Theorem 6. *Monoidal monads preserve associativity, unit and commutativity.*

Some equations are not always preserved by commutative monads, we present here two important examples.

Idempotency: $x \bullet x = x$
$\mathcal{R}(T, x \bullet x, \{x\})$ given by:

$$
\begin{array}{ccc}
TA & \xleftarrow{\ \ \text{id}\ \ } & TA \\
{\scriptstyle T\langle\pi_1,\pi_1\rangle}\downarrow & & \downarrow{\scriptstyle \langle\pi_1,\pi_1\rangle} \\
T(A^2) & \xleftarrow{\ \ \psi\ \ } & (TA)^2
\end{array}
$$

Absorption: $x \bullet 0 = 0$
$\mathcal{R}(T, x \bullet 0, \{x\})$ given by:

$$
\begin{array}{ccc}
TA & \xleftarrow{\ \ \text{id}\ \ } & TA \\
{\scriptstyle T!}\downarrow & & \downarrow{\scriptstyle !} \\
T1 & \xleftarrow{\ \ \eta_1\ \ } & 1
\end{array}
$$

$$(13)$$

These diagrams correspond to classes of monads studied in the literature. The residual diagram for idempotency can be expressed as the equation $\psi_{A,A} \circ \Delta_{TA} = T\Delta_A$, where Δ is the diagonal operator. A monad T verifying this condition is called *relevant* by Jacobs in [13]. Similarly, one easily shows that the commutativity of the absorption diagram is equivalent to the definition of *affine* monads in [13,18].

4.3   General Criteria for Equation Preservation

As shown in Lemma 5 and Theorem 5, the interaction between T and the variable rearrangements operated by δ^V can provide a sufficient condition for the preservation of equations. We will focus on three important types of interaction between a monad T and rearrangement operations. First, the residual diagram for commutativity, i.e. Diagram (SYM), which corresponds to saying that 'T preserves variable swapping', i.e. that T is commutative/symmetric monoidal, or in logical terms to the exchange rule. As we have seen, this condition *must* be satisfied in order to simply lift operations, so we must take it as a basic assumption. Second, the residual diagram for idempotency (leftmost diagram of (13)) which corresponds to 'T preserves variable duplications', i.e. that T is *relevant*, or in logical terms to the weakening rule. Finally, the residual diagram for absorption (rightmost diagram of (13)) which corresponds to 'T allows to drop variables', i.e. T is *affine*, or in logical terms to the contraction rule. To each of these residual diagrams corresponds a syntactically definable class of equations which are automatically preserved by a monad satisfying the residual diagram.

Theorem 7. *Let T be a commutative monad. If $Var(u) = Var(v)$ and if variables appear exactly once in u and in v, then T preserves $u = v$.*

Note that this theorem can be found in [23], where this type of equation is called *linear*. Moreover, $\mathcal{P}$ is within the scope of this result, which generalises one direction of Gautam's theorem [10]. Let us now present original results by first treating the case where variables may appear several times.

Theorem 8. *Let T be a commutative relevant monad. If $Var(u) = Var(v)$, then T preserves $u = v$.*

Commutative relevant monads seem to preserve many algebraic laws. However, in the case where both sides of the equation do not contain the same variables, for instance $x \bullet 0 = 0$, Theorem 8 does not apply. Intuitively, the missing piece is the ability to *drop* some of the variables in V.

Theorem 9. *Let T be a commutative affine monad. If variables appear at most once in u and in v, then T preserves $u = v$.*

Combining the results of Theorems 8 and 9, one gets a very economical – if very strong – criterion for the preservation of *all* equations.

Theorem 10. *Let T be a commutative, relevant and affine monad. For all u and v, T preserves $u = v$.*

Examining the existence of distributive laws between algebraic theories, as well as stating conditions on variable rearrangements, has been studied before in terms of Lawvere Theories (see for instance [7]). Note that for T commutative monad, being both relevant and affine (sometimes called *cartesian*) is equivalent to preserving products, as seen in [18]. This confirms that such a monad T preserves all equations of the underlying algebraic structure, in other words it always has a distributive law with any other monad. This is however a very strong condition. An example of this type of monad is $T(X) = X^Y$ for Y an object of **Set**.

4.4   Weakening the Inner Layer When Composition Fails

In the case where a residual diagram fails to commute, we cannot conclude that the equation lifts from $\mathcal{A}$ to $\widehat{T}\mathcal{A}$. The non-commutativity of the diagram often provides a counter-example which shows that the equation is in fact not valid in $\widehat{T}\mathcal{A}$ (this is the case of idempotency and distributivity in the next section).

However, if our aim is to build a structure combining all operations used to define T and S, then our method can provide an answer, since it allows us to identify precisely which equations fail to hold. Let E' be the subset of E containing the equations preserved by T. A new monad S' can be derived from signature Σ and equations E' using an adjunction of type (6). Since E' only contains equations preserved by T, by Theorem 4 the composition TS' creates a monad, and its algebraic structure contains all the constructs derived from the original signature Σ, as well as the new symbols arising from T.

This method for fixing a faulty monad composition follows the idea of loosening the constraints of the *inner* layer, meaning in this case modifying S to construct a monad resembling TS. The best approximate language we obtain has the desired signature, but has lost some of the laws described by S. We illustrate this method in the following section.

5 Application

As sketched in the introduction, our method aims to incrementally build an imperative language: starting with sequential composition, we add a layer providing non-deterministic choice, then a layer for probabilistic choice.

Adding the Non-deterministic Layer. We start with the simple programming language described in the introduction by the signature (1) and Eq. (2) – or, equivalently, by the monad $(-)^*$ – and let A be a set of atomic programs. Our minimal language is thus given by A^*. Note that the free monoid is not commutative and thus in our method it cannot be used as an outer layer, it has to constitute the core of the language we build. More generally, our method provides a simple heuristic for compositional language building: always start with the non-commutative monad.

We now add non-determinism via the finitary powerset monad $\mathcal{P}$, which is simply the free join semi-lattice monad. To build this extension, we want to combine both monads to create a new monad $\mathcal{P}((-)^*)$. As we have shown in Theorem 4, it suffices to build a lifting of monad $\mathcal{P}$ to **Mon**, the category of algebras for the signature (1) and Eq. (2). For this purpose we apply the method given in Sect. 4.

The first step is lifting $\mathcal{P}$ to the category of $\{\texttt{skip},;\}$-algebras, which means lifting the operations of A^* to $\mathcal{P}(A^*)$ using a Fubini map. It is well-known that the powerset monad is commutative, and it follows in particular that there exists a unique symmetric monoidal transformation $\psi \colon \mathcal{P} \times \mathcal{P} \to \mathcal{P}(- \times -)$ which is given by the Cartesian product: for $U \in \mathcal{P}(X), V \in \mathcal{P}(Y)$, we take $\psi_{X,Y}(U,V) = U \times V$. Using this Fubini transformation, we can now define the interpretation in $\mathcal{P}(A^*)$ of $\texttt{skip}$ and ; as:

$$\widehat{\texttt{skip}} = \mathcal{P}(\texttt{skip}) \circ \eta_1(*) = \{\varepsilon\}$$
$$\widehat{;} = \mathcal{P}(;) \circ \psi_{A^*,A^*} \colon (\mathcal{P}A^*)^2 \to \mathcal{P}A^*, \quad (U,V) \mapsto \{u \, ; \, v \mid u \in U, v \in V\}$$

To check that this lifting defines a lifting on **Mon**, we need to check that Eq. (2) hold in $\mathcal{P}(A^*)$. These equations describe associativity and unit: by Theorem 6, they are always preserved by a strong commutative monad like $\mathcal{P}$.

It follows from Theorems 4 and 5 that we obtain a distributive law $\lambda \colon (\mathcal{P}(-))^* \to \mathcal{P}((-)^*)$ between monads $(-)^*$ and $\mathcal{P}$, hence the composition $\mathcal{P}((-)^*)$ is also a monad, allowing us to apply our method again and potentially add another monadic layer. The language $\mathcal{P}(A^*)$ contains the lifted versions $\widehat{\texttt{skip}}$ and $\widehat{;}$ of our previous constructs as well as the new operations arising from $\mathcal{P}$, namely a non-deterministic choice operation $+$, which is associative, commutative and idempotent, and its unit **abort**. Note that since the monad structure on $\mathcal{P}((-)^*)$ is defined by a distributive law of $(-)^*$ over $\mathcal{P}$, the set of equations E

is made of the Eq. (2) arising from $(-)^*$, the Eq. (3) arising from $\mathcal{P}$, and finally the Eq. (4) expressing distributivity of operations of $(-)^*$ over those of $\mathcal{P}$. The language we have built so far has the structure of an *idempotent semiring*.

Adding the Probabilistic Layer. We will now enrich our language further by adding a probabilistic layer. Specifically, we will add the family of probabilistic choice operators $\oplus_\lambda$ for $\lambda \in [0,1]$ satisfying the axioms of convex algebras, i.e.

$$\mathsf{p} \oplus_\lambda \mathsf{p} = \mathsf{p} \quad \mathsf{p} \oplus_\lambda \mathsf{q} = \mathsf{q} \oplus_{1-\lambda} \mathsf{p} \quad \mathsf{p} \oplus_\lambda (\mathsf{q} \oplus_\tau \mathsf{r}) = (\mathsf{p} \oplus_{\frac{\lambda}{\lambda+(1-\lambda)\tau}} \mathsf{q}) \oplus_{\lambda+(1-\lambda)\tau} \mathsf{r} \tag{14}$$

From a monadic perspective, we want to examine the composition of monads $\mathcal{D}(\mathcal{P}((-)^*))$. It is known (see [30]) that $\mathcal{D}$ does not distribute over $\mathcal{P}$. We will see that our method confirms this result.

We start by lifting the constants and operations $\{\mathtt{skip}, \mathtt{abort}, ; , +\}$ of $\mathcal{P}((-)^*)$ by defining a Fubini map $\psi : \mathcal{D}(-) \times \mathcal{D}(-) \to \mathcal{D}(- \times -)$. It is well-known that $\mathcal{D}$ is a commutative monad and that the product of measures defines the Fubini transformation. In the case of finitely supported distributions the product of measures can be expressed simply as follows: given distributions $\mu \in \mathcal{D}X, \nu \in \mathcal{D}Y$, $\psi(\mu, \nu)$ is the distribution on $X \times Y$ defined on singletons $(x, y) \in X \times Y$ by $(\psi(\mu, \nu))(x, y) = \mu(x)\nu(y)$. Theorem 7 tells us that associativity, commutativity and unit are preserved by $\mathcal{D}$. It follows that the associativity of both ; and + is preserved by the lifting operation, and the liftings of $\mathtt{skip}$ and $\mathtt{abort}$ are their respective units. Furthermore, the lifting of + is commutative.

We know from Theorem 8 that the idempotency of + will be preserved if $\mathcal{D}$ is relevant. It is easy to see that $\mathcal{D}$ is badly non-relevant: consider the set $X = \{a, b\}, a \neq b$ and any measure μ on X which assigns non-zero probability to both a and b. We have:

$$\begin{aligned}
\psi(\Delta_{\mathcal{D}X}(\mu))(a, b) &= (\psi(\mu, \mu))(a, b) \\
&= \mu(a)\mu(b) \neq 0 \\
&= \mu(\emptyset) \\
&= \mu\{x \in X \mid \Delta_X(x) = (a, b)\} \\
&= \mathcal{D}(\Delta_X)(\mu)(a, b)
\end{aligned}$$

It follows that we *cannot* conclude that the lifting $\widehat{\mathcal{D}} : \mathbf{Alg}(\{\mathtt{skip}, \mathtt{abort}, ; , +\}) \to \mathbf{Alg}(\{\mathtt{skip}, \mathtt{abort}, ; , +\})$ defined by the product of measures following (8) sends idempotent semirings to idempotent semirings, and therefore we cannot conclude that $\mathcal{D}(\mathcal{P}(-)^*)$ is a monad (in fact we know it isn't). It is very telling that idempotency also had to be dropped in the design of the probabilistic network specification language ProbNetKAT (see [8, Lemma 1]) which is very similar to the language we are trying to incrementally build in this Section.

Requiring that + be idempotent is an algebraic obstacle, so let us now remove it and replace as our inner layer the monad building free idempotent semirings – that is to say $\mathcal{P}(-)^*$ – by the monad building free semirings – that is to say $\mathcal{M}(-)^*$, where $\mathcal{M}$ is the multiset monad ($\mathcal{M}$ can also be described as the free commutative monoid monad). Since we have already checked that the $\mathcal{D}$-liftings of binary operations preserve associativity, units and commutativity, it only remains to check that they preserve the distributivity of ; over $+$. The equation for distributivity belongs to the syntactic class covered by Theorem 8 since it has the same set of variables on each side (but one of them is duplicated, so we fall outside the scope of Theorems 7 and 9). Since we've just shown that $\mathcal{D}$ is not relevant, it follows that we cannot lift the distributivity axioms. So we must weaken our inner layer even further and consider a structure consisting of two monoids, one of which is commutative. Interestingly, the failure of distributivity was also observed in the development of ProbNetKAT ([8, Lemma 4]), and therefore should not come as a surprise.

Having removed the two distributivity axioms we are left with only the absorption laws to check. In this case the equation has no variable duplication, but has not got the same number of variables on each side of the equation, absorption therefore falls in the scope of Theorem 9, and we need to check if $\mathcal{D}$ is affine. Since $\mathcal{D}1 \simeq 1$, it is trivial to see that $\eta_1 \circ ! = \mathcal{D}!$ and hence $\mathcal{D}$ is affine. By Theorem 9, the absorption law is therefore preserved by the probabilistic extension. It follows that the probabilistic layer $\mathcal{D}$ can be composed with the inner layer consisting of the signature $\{\texttt{abort}, \texttt{skip}, ; , +\}$ and the axioms

(i) $\texttt{p} ; \texttt{skip} = \texttt{skip} ; \texttt{p} = \texttt{p}$ (iv) $\texttt{p} + \texttt{q} = \texttt{q} + \texttt{p}$

(ii) $(\texttt{p} ; \texttt{q}) ; \texttt{r} = \texttt{p} ; (\texttt{q} ; \texttt{r})$ (v) $(\texttt{p} + \texttt{q}) + \texttt{r} = \texttt{p} + (\texttt{q} + \texttt{r})$

(iii) $\texttt{p} + \texttt{abort} = \texttt{abort} + \texttt{p} = \texttt{p}$ (vi) $\texttt{p} ; \texttt{abort} = \texttt{abort} = \texttt{abort} ; \texttt{p}$

i.e. two monoids, one of them commutative, with the absorption law as the only interaction between the two operations. This structure, combined with the axioms of convex algebras (14) and the distributivity axioms

(Dst i) $\texttt{p} ; (\texttt{q} \oplus_\lambda \texttt{r}) = (\texttt{p} ; \texttt{q}) \oplus_\lambda (\texttt{p} ; \texttt{r})$ (Dst iii) $\texttt{p} + (\texttt{q} \oplus_\lambda \texttt{r}) = (\texttt{p} + \texttt{q}) \oplus_\lambda (\texttt{p} + \texttt{r})$

(Dst ii) $(\texttt{q} \oplus_\lambda \texttt{r}) ; \texttt{p} = (\texttt{q} ; \texttt{p}) \oplus_\lambda (\texttt{r} ; \texttt{p})$ (Dst iv) $(\texttt{q} \oplus_\lambda \texttt{r}) + \texttt{p} = (\texttt{q} + \texttt{p}) \oplus_\lambda (\texttt{r} + \texttt{p})$

forms the 'best approximate language' combining sequential composition, nondeterministic choice and probabilistic choice. Note that the distributive laws above makes good semantic sense, and indeed hold for the semantics of ProbNetKAT. What we have built modularly in this section is essentially the *-free and test-free fragment of ProbNetKAT.

6 Discussion and Future Work

We have provided a principled approach to building programming languages by incrementally layering features on the top one another. We believe that our approach is close in spirit to how programming languages are typically constructed, that is to say by an incremental enrichment of the list of features, and to the search for modularity initiated by foundational papers [20, 25].

Our method has assumed throughout that the monad for the outer layer had to be monoidal/commutative. Our method can in fact be straightforwardly extended to monads satisfying only (MM.1) and (MM.2). In practice however, the generality gained in this way is very limited: only a monoidal monad will lift an associative operation with a left and right unit, and given the importance of sequential composition with skip, the restriction we have placed on our method appears fairly natural and benign.

We must be careful about how layers are composed together: our approach yields distributive interactions between them, but one might want other sorts of interactions. Consider for example the minimal programming language P^* described in Sect. 1, and assume that we now want to add a concurrent composition operation $\parallel$ to this language with the natural axiom p $\parallel$ skip = p = p $\parallel$ skip. This addition is not as simple as layering described in Sect. 5, as the new construct has to interact with the core layer in a whole new way: skip must be the unit of $\parallel$ as well. In such cases our approach is not satisfactory, and two alternative strategies present themselves to us: we can consider 'larger' layers, for example the combined theory of sequential composition, skip and $\parallel$ described above as a single entity. However, the more complex an inner layer is, the less likely it is that an outer layer with lift it in its entirety. Alternatively, we may want to integrate our technique with Hyland and Power's methods [12] and combine some layers with sums and tensors, and others with distributive laws, depending on semantic and algebraic considerations.

A comment about our 'approximate language' strategy is also in order. As explained in Sect. 4, when an equation of the inner layer prevents the existence of a distributive law we choose to remove this equation, i.e. to loosen the inner layer. Another option is in principle possible: we could constrain the outer layer until it becomes compatible with the inner layer. We would obtain in this case a replacement candidate for one of our monads in order to achieve composition. In the case of $\mathcal{D}(\mathcal{P}(-)^*)$ this would be a particularly unproductive idea since the only elements of $\mathcal{D}(\mathcal{P}(-)^*)$ which satisfy the residual diagram for idempotency are Dirac deltas, i.e. we would get back the language $\mathcal{P}(-)^*$.

Another obvious avenue of research is to extend our method to programming languages specified by more than just equations. One example is the so-called 'exchange law' in concurrency theory given by $(p \parallel r) ; (q \parallel s) \sqsubseteq (p ; q) \parallel (r ; s)$ which involves a native pre-ordering on the collection of programs, i.e. moving from the category of sets to the category of posets. Another example are Kozen's quasi-equations [19] axiomatizing the Kleene star operations, for example $p ; x \leq x \Rightarrow p^* ; x \leq x$. This problem is much more difficult and involves moving away from monads and distributive laws altogether since quasi-varieties are in general not monadic categories.

References

1. Awodey, S.: Category Theory. Oxford Logic Guides, vol. 49, 2nd edn. Oxford University Press, Oxford (2010)
2. Balan, A., Kurz, A.: On coalgebras over algebras. Theor. Comput. Sci. **412**(38), 4989–5005 (2011). https://doi.org/10.1016/j.tcs.2011.03.021
3. Beck, J.: Distributive laws. In: Eckmann, B. (ed.) Seminar on Triples and Categorical Homology Theory: ETH 1966/67. LNM, vol. 80, pp. 119–140. Springer, Heidelberg (1969). https://doi.org/10.1007/BFb0083084
4. Benton, N., Hughes, J., Moggi, E.: Monads and effects. In: Barthe, G., Dybjer, P., Pinto, L., Saraiva, J. (eds.) APPSEM 2000. LNCS, vol. 2395, pp. 42–122. Springer, Heidelberg (2002). https://doi.org/10.1007/3-540-45699-6_2
5. Bonchi, F., Silva, A., Sokolova, A.: The power of convex algebras. arXiv preprint 1707.02344 (2017). https://arxiv.org/abs/1707.02344
6. Bonsangue, M.M., Hansen, H.H., Kurz, A., Rot, J.: Presenting distributive laws. Log. Methods. Comput. Sci. **11**(3), Article no. 2 (2015). https://doi.org/10.2168/lmcs-11(3:2)2015
7. Cheng, E.: Distributive laws for Lawvere theories. arXiv preprint 1112.3076 (2011). https://arxiv.org/abs/1112.3076
8. Foster, N., Kozen, D., Mamouras, K., Reitblatt, M., Silva, A.: Probabilistic NetKAT. In: Thiemann, P. (ed.) ESOP 2016. LNCS, vol. 9632, pp. 282–309. Springer, Heidelberg (2016). https://doi.org/10.1007/978-3-662-49498-1_12
9. Foster, N., Kozen, D., Milano, M., Silva, A., Thompson, L.: A coalgebraic decision procedure for NetKAT. In: Proceedings of 42nd Annual ACM SIGPLAN-SIGACT Symposium on Principles of Programming Languages, POPL 2015, Mumbai, January 2015, pp. 343–355. ACM Press, New York (2015). https://doi.org/10.1145/2676726.2677011
10. Gautam, N.: The validity of equations of complex algebras. Arch. Math. Log. Grundl. **3**(3–4), 117–124 (1957). https://doi.org/10.1007/bf01988052
11. Hyland, M., Levy, P., Plotkin, G., Power, J.: Combining algebraic effects with continuations. Theor. Comput. Sci. **375**(1–3), 20–40 (2007). https://doi.org/10.1016/j.tcs.2006.12.026
12. Hyland, M., Plotkin, G., Power, J.: Combining effects: sum and tensor. Theor. Comput. Sci. **357**(1–3), 70–99 (2006). https://doi.org/10.1016/j.tcs.2006.03.013
13. Jacobs, B.: Semantics of weakening and contraction. Ann. Pure Appl. Log. **69**(1), 73–106 (1994). https://doi.org/10.1016/0168-0072(94)90020-5
14. Jacobs, B., Silva, A., Sokolova, A.: Trace semantics via determinization. In: Pattinson, D., Schröder, L. (eds.) CMCS 2012. LNCS, vol. 7399, pp. 109–129. Springer, Heidelberg (2012). https://doi.org/10.1007/978-3-642-32784-1_7
15. King, D.J., Wadler, P.: Combining monads. In: Launchbury, J., Sansom, P.M. (eds.) Functional Programming, Glasgow 1992. Workshops in Computing, pp. 134–143. Springer, London (1993). https://doi.org/10.1007/978-1-4471-3215-8_12
16. Klin, B., Rot, J.: Coalgebraic trace semantics via forgetful logics. In: Pitts, A. (ed.) FoSSaCS 2015. LNCS, vol. 9034, pp. 151–166. Springer, Heidelberg (2015). https://doi.org/10.1007/978-3-662-46678-0_10
17. Klin, B., Salamanca, J.: Iterated covariant powerset is not a monad. Electron. Notes Theor. Comput. Sci. (to appear)
18. Kock, A.: Bilinearity and Cartesian closed monads. Math. Scand. **29**(2), 161–174 (1972). https://doi.org/10.7146/math.scand.a-11042

19. Kozen, D.: A completeness theorem for Kleene algebras and the algebra of regular events. In: Proceedings of the 6th Annual Symposium on Logic in Computer Science, LICS 1991, Amsterdam, July 1991, pp. 214–225. IEEE CS Press, Washington, DC (1991). https://doi.org/10.1109/lics.1991.151646
20. Liang, S., Hudak, P.: Modular denotational semantics for compiler construction. In: Nielson, H.R. (ed.) ESOP 1996. LNCS, vol. 1058, pp. 219–234. Springer, Heidelberg (1996). https://doi.org/10.1007/3-540-61055-3_39
21. Liang, S., Hudak, P., Jones, M.: Monad transformers and modular interpreters. In: Proceedings of 22nd ACM SIGPLAN-SIGACT Symposium on Principles of Programming Languages, POPL 1995, San Francisco, CA, USA, January 1995, pp. 333–343. ACM Press, New York (1995). https://doi.org/10.1145/199448.199528
22. Mac Lane, S.: Categories for the Working Mathematician. Graduate Texts in Mathematics, vol. 5, 2nd edn. Springer, Heidelberg (1978). https://doi.org/10.1007/978-1-4757-4721-8
23. Manes, E., Mulry, P.: Monad compositions I: general constructions and recursive distributive laws. Theor. Appl. Categ. **18**, 172–208 (2007). http://www.tac.mta.ca/tac/volumes/18/7/18-07abs.html
24. Milius, S., Palm, T., Schwencke, D.: Complete iterativity for algebras with effects. In: Kurz, A., Lenisa, M., Tarlecki, A. (eds.) CALCO 2009. LNCS, vol. 5728, pp. 34–48. Springer, Heidelberg (2009). https://doi.org/10.1007/978-3-642-03741-2_4
25. Moggi, E.: Notions of computation and monads. Inf. Comput. **93**(1), 55–92 (1991). https://doi.org/10.1016/0890-5401(91)90052-4
26. Plotkin, G., Power, J.: Notions of computation determine monads. In: Nielsen, M., Engberg, U. (eds.) FoSSaCS 2002. LNCS, vol. 2303, pp. 342–356. Springer, Heidelberg (2002). https://doi.org/10.1007/3-540-45931-6_24
27. Sato, T.: The Giry monad is not strong for the canonical symmetric monoidal closed structure on **Meas**. J. Pure Appl. Alg. **222**(10), 2888–2896 (2017). https://doi.org/10.1016/j.jpaa.2017.11.004
28. Smolka, S., Kumar, P., Foster, N., Kozen, D., Silva, A.: Cantor meets scott: semantic foundations for probabilistic networks. arXiv preprint 1607.05830 (2016). https://arxiv.org/1607.05830
29. Sokolova, A., Jacobs, B., Hasuo, I.: Generic trace semantics via coinduction. Log. Methods Comput. Sci. **3**(4), Article no. 11 (2007). https://doi.org/10.2168/lmcs-3(4:11)2007
30. Varacca, D.: Probability, nondeterminism and concurrency: two denotational models for probabilistic computation. BRICS Dissertation Series, vol. DS-03-14. Ph.D. thesis, Aarhus University (2003). http://www.brics.dk/DS/03/14/

Layer Systems
for Confluence—Formalized

Bertram Felgenhauer[1(✉)] and Franziska Rapp[2]

[1] Institut für Informatik, Universität Innsbruck,
Technikerstraße 21a, 6020 Innsbruck, Austria
bertram.felgenhauer@uibk.ac.at
[2] Allgemeines Rechenzentrum, Innsbruck, Austria

Abstract. Toyama's theorem states that the union of two confluent term rewrite systems with disjoint signatures is again confluent. This is a fundamental result in term rewriting, and several proofs appear in the literature. The underlying proof technique has been adapted to prove further results like persistence of confluence (if a many-sorted term rewrite system is confluent, then the underlying unsorted system is confluent) or the preservation of confluence by currying.

In this paper we present a formalization of modularity and related results in Isabelle/HOL. The formalization is based on layer systems, which cover modularity, persistence, currying (and more) in a single framework. The persistence result has been integrated into the certifier CeTA and the confluence tool CSI, allowing us to check confluence proofs based on persistent decomposition, of which modularity is a special case.

1 Introduction

Toyama's theorem [13,17,19] states that confluence is modular, i.e., that the union of two confluent term rewrite systems (TRSs) over disjoint signatures is confluent if and only if the two TRSs themselves are confluent. For example, Combinatory Logic extended with an equality test

$$@(@(\mathsf{K}, x), y) \to x \quad @(@(@(\mathsf{S}, x), y), z) \to @(@(x, z), @(y, z)) \quad \mathsf{e}(x, x) \to \top$$

is confluent because the first two rules are orthogonal, the last rule is terminating and has no critical pairs, and the signatures of these two sets of rules are disjoint. As the example shows, modularity opens up a decomposition approach to proving confluence, which is attractive, because different confluence criteria may apply to the constituent TRSs that do not apply to their union. By adapting the modularity proof, several other results have been proved in the literature.

- Confluence is persistent [1], i.e., a TRS is confluent if and only if it is confluent as a many-sorted TRS. This gives rise to a decomposition technique, and fully subsumes modularity.

This work is supported by FWF (Austrian Science Fund) project P27528.

B. Fischer and T. Uustalu (Eds.): ICTAC 2018, LNCS 11187, pp. 173–190, 2018.
https://doi.org/10.1007/978-3-030-02508-3_10

- Confluence is preserved by currying [11]. Currying is useful, for example, as a preprocessing step for deciding ground confluence.
- The notion of modularity has been generalized as well, by weakening the assumption that the signatures of the two TRSs are disjoint; for example, confluence is modular for layer-preserving composable TRSs [16], and for quasi-ground systems [12].

The list goes on. All of these proofs are based on decomposing terms into a maximal top and remaining aliens, but with different sets of admissible tops. In each case, confluence is established by induction on the number of nested tops in that decomposition (the *rank* of a term). Layer systems [7] were introduced as an abstraction from these proofs. A layer system $\mathfrak{L}$ is simply the set of admissible tops; for modularity, those are homogeneous multi-hole contexts, i.e., multi-hole contexts whose function symbols all belong to the signature of only one of the two given TRSs. At the heart of layer systems lies an adaptation of the modularity proof in [17]. When establishing confluence by layer systems, as remaining proof obligations, one has to check that a layer system satisfies so called layer conditions, which is easier than doing a full adaptation of the modularity proof.

Isabelle/HOL [15] is an interactive proof assistant based on higher-order logic with a Hindley-Milner type system, extended with type classes. It follows the LCF tradition [9] in having a trusted kernel, which ensures that theorems follow from the axioms by construction. Isabelle features a structured proof language [20]. Another useful feature are locales, which allow bundling of functions and assumptions that are shared by several definitions and theorems. (For example, locales are used to model groups in Isabelle/HOL). The locale mechanism in Isabelle is quite powerful; in particular, locales can be instantiated (so $\mathbb{Z}$ with addition, 0 as unit, and negation is a group) and extended (for example, the group locale is an extension of a semigroup locale, with additional operations (unit and inverse) and assumptions). Our main reason for using Isabelle/HOL is the existing **Isa**belle **Fo**rmalization of **R**ewriting, IsaFoR [18]. In addition to fundamental notions of term rewriting like terms, substitutions, contexts, multi-hole contexts, and so on, IsaFoR is also the foundation of CeTA (**C**ertified **T**ool **A**ssertions), which can certify termination and confluence proofs, among other things.

In this paper we describe a formalization of layer systems in Isabelle/HOL as part of IsaFoR. In fact, the prospect of formalization was one of the selling points of layer systems, with the idea of making large parts of the proof reusable. Note that whereas adapting existing proofs is convenient on paper, it becomes a burden when done in a formalization. The resulting duplication of code (that is, theorem statements and proofs) would decrease maintainability and is therefore best avoided. Our effort covers modularity of confluence, persistence of confluence, and preservation of confluence by currying for first order term rewrite systems. To the best of our knowledge, this is the first time that any of these results has been fully formalized in a proof assistant.

From a practical perspective, our interest in formalization is motivated by our work on an automated confluence prover, CSI [14]. As with all software, CSI potentially contains bugs. In order to increase the trust in CSI, proof output in a machine readable format is supported, which can be checked using CeTA [18]. As part of our formalization effort, we have extended CeTA with support for a decomposition technique based on persistence of confluence, allowing CSI and potentially other confluence tools to produce certifiable proofs using this technique. We have prepared a website with examples and information about the used software at http://cl-informatik.uibk.ac.at/software/lisa/ictac2018/.

For most theorems and many definitions, we provide the corresponding identifiers in the formalization; in the PDF version of this paper, they link to the HTML version of the formalization itself. Furthermore, links to selected defined symbols can be found on our website.

The remainder of this paper is structured as follows. We recall notations and basic definitions in Sect. 2. Then we present the layer conditions, which are central to our formalization, in Sect. 3. The next two sections are about persistence. Section 4 uses persistence as an example to illustrate how layer systems can be applied to obtain a confluence result, while Sect. 5 focuses on the persistent decomposition. In Sect. 6, we present details of the currying application. Finally, we conclude in Sect. 7.

2   Preliminaries

We use standard notation from term rewriting [3]. Let $\mathcal{F}$ be a signature and $\mathcal{V}$ be a set of variables. Then $\mathcal{T}(\mathcal{F}, \mathcal{V})$ is the set of terms over that signature. We denote by $\mathcal{P}os(t)$ the set of positions of t. The subterm of t at position p is $t|_p$, and $t[s]_p$ is the result of replacing the subterm at position p in t by s. We also write $\mathcal{P}os_X(r)$ for the set of positions p of t such that the root symbol of $t|_p$ is in X. If $X = \{x\}$ is a singleton set, we may omit the outer curly braces and write $\mathcal{P}os_x(t)$. The set of variables of t is $\mathcal{V}ar(t)$. The set of multi-hole contexts over $\mathcal{F}$ and $\mathcal{V}$ is denoted by $\mathcal{C}(\mathcal{F}, \mathcal{V})$. (Multi-hole contexts are terms that may contain occurrences of an extra constant $\square$, representing their holes.) If C is a multi-hole context with n holes, then $C[t_1, \ldots, t_n]$ denotes the term obtained by replacing the i-th hole in C by t_i for $1 \leqslant i \leqslant n$. On multi-hole contexts, we have a partial order $\sqsubseteq$ which is generated by $\square \sqsubseteq C$ and closure under contexts ($D \sqsubseteq D'$ implies $C[D] \sqsubseteq C[D']$). The corresponding partial supremum operation is denoted by $\sqcup$; intuitively it merges two multi-hole contexts.

A substitution $\sigma, \tau, \ldots$ is a map from variables to terms. The result of applying the substitution σ to the term t is denoted by $t\sigma$. A term rewrite system (TRS) $\mathcal{R}$ is a set of rules $\ell \to r$, where ℓ and r are terms, ℓ is not a variable, and $\mathcal{V}ar(r) \subseteq \mathcal{V}ar(\ell)$. There is a rewrite step from s to t ($s \to_{\mathcal{R}} t$) if $s = s[\ell\sigma]_p$ and $t = s[r\sigma]_p$ for a position $p \in \mathcal{P}os(s)$ and substitution σ.

Given a relation $\to$, we write $\leftarrow$ and $\to^*$ for its inverse and its reflexive transitive closure, respectively. A relation $\to$ is confluent if $t \, {}^*\!\leftarrow s \to^* u$ implies

$t \to^* \cdot {}^*\!\leftarrow u$. It is confluent on X if for all $s \in X$, $t \; {}^*\!\leftarrow s \to^* u$ implies $t \to^* \cdot {}^*\!\leftarrow u$.[3]

3   Layer Conditions

In the layer system approach to confluence, one sets up a layer system for a TRS $\mathcal{R}$ that satisfies the so-called layer conditions. These layer conditions constitute the interface between the reusable part of the formalization and the parts that are specific to a particular application of layer systems (e.g., modularity). Since they are central to the formalization, we recall the basic constructions and the layer conditions here. For full details please refer to [7].

Recall that modularity of confluence states that the union of two TRSs over disjoint signatures is confluent if each of the two TRSs is confluent (the converse is also true and fairly easy to prove). Modularity is proved by induction on the *rank* of a term; to obtain the rank, one decomposes the term into alternating layers of multi-hole contexts over the two signatures; the rank is the maximum nesting depth of the resulting layers.

Example 1. Let $\mathcal{F}_1 = \{\mathsf{A}, \mathsf{F}\}$ and $\mathcal{F}_2 = \{\mathsf{b}, \mathsf{g}\}$. Then $\mathrm{rank}(\mathsf{F}(\mathsf{F}(\mathsf{A}))) = 1$, while $\mathrm{rank}(\mathsf{g}(\mathsf{b}, \mathsf{F}(\mathsf{b}))) = 3$; the latter term is decomposed into $\mathsf{g}(\mathsf{b}, \square)$, $\mathsf{F}(\square)$ and b.

Layer systems abstract from this situation by considering all possible multi-hole contexts at the top of such a decomposition. So a layer system is a set of multi-hole contexts, and gives rise to tops and maximal tops as follows.

Definition 2 ([7, **Definition 3.1**]). *Let $\mathcal{F}$ be a signature and $\mathcal{V}$ be an infinite set of variables. Let $\mathfrak{L} \subseteq \mathcal{C}(\mathcal{F}, \mathcal{V})$ be a set of multi-hole contexts over $\mathcal{F}$. Then $L \in \mathfrak{L}$ is called a top of a context $C \in \mathcal{C}(\mathcal{F}, \mathcal{V})$ (according to $\mathfrak{L}$) if $L \sqsubseteq C$. A top is a* max-top *of C if it is maximal with respect to $\sqsubseteq$ among the tops of C.*

We want to prove that all terms are confluent, provided that terms of rank 1 are confluent. To this end we have to impose certain restrictions on the layer system.

- the rank must be well-defined, which is ensured if any term has a unique max-top that is not empty (i.e., not equal to $\square$);
- a rewrite step must span several layers (so it can be mimicked by a suitable rank 1 term); and
- the rank must not increase by rewriting.

Example 3. We illustrate a few obstructions to proving confluence in Fig. 1. (This example is an abridged version of [7, Example 3.4].)

---

[3] Another reasonable definition for "$\to$ is confluent on X" would be that $\to \cap (X \times X)$ is confluent; this is equivalent to the given definition whenever X is closed under rewriting by $\to$.

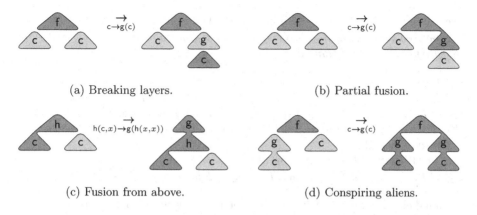

(a) Breaking layers.   (b) Partial fusion.

(c) Fusion from above.   (d) Conspiring aliens.

Fig. 1. Undesired behavior on layers.

(a) Here, we have the rewrite step $f(c, c) \rightarrow f(c, g(c))$, decomposed by some set of layers $\mathfrak{L}$. However, the c subterm becomes two layers after the rewrite step, increasing the rank. So rewriting a layer must again result in a layer.

(b) This is the same rewrite step as in (a). In this example, $g(c)$ may be a layer. However, the resulting term merges with the layer above (a phenomenon we call *fusion*). In the example, the fusion is *partial*; the fused context is broken apart. This is caused by there being a layer $f(\Box, g(\Box))$ but no layer $f(\Box, g(c))$.

(c) In this example, there is a root step $h(c, c) \rightarrow g(h(c, c))$. Note that both c constants in the result originate in the isolated c, but nevertheless, one of them has fused with the top in the result (so the rewrite step takes place above the point where fusion happens, hence *fusion from above*). In [7, Example 3.4] we show that the TRS

$$f(x, x) \rightarrow a \qquad f(x, g(x)) \rightarrow b \qquad h(c, x) \rightarrow g(h(x, x))$$

has a set of layers such that fusion from above is the sole reason for the system being non-confluent despite being confluent on terms of rank 1.

(d) Finally, it may happen that a rewrite step triggers fusion in a position that is parallel to the rewrite step. (*aliens* are what remains of a term after taking away its max-top; here a rewrite step in one alien causes another alien to fuse, hence *conspiring aliens*). As far as we know, this is not actually an obstruction to confluence, but nevertheless absence of conspiring aliens is required for our proof.

Definition 4 ([7, **Definition 3.3**]). *Let $\mathcal{F}$ be a signature. A set $\mathfrak{L} \subseteq \mathcal{C}(\mathcal{F}, \mathcal{V})$ of contexts is called a* layer system[4] *if it satisfies properties (L1), (L2), and (L3). The elements of $\mathfrak{L}$ are called* layers. *A TRS $\mathcal{R}$ over $\mathcal{F}$ is* weakly layered

---

[4] In [7] we use $\mathbb{L}$ for layer systems. We use $\mathfrak{L}$ here to be consistent with snippets like Fig. 2 that are generated from our Isabelle formalization, where $\mathbb{L}$ is not available.

(according to a layer system $\mathcal{L}$) if condition (W) is satisfied for each $\ell \to r \in \mathcal{R}$. It is layered (according to a layer system $\mathcal{L}$) if conditions (W), (C_1), and (C_2) are satisfied. The conditions are as follows.

(L_1) Each term in $\mathcal{T}(\mathcal{F}, \mathcal{V})$ has a non-empty top.
(L_2) If $x \in \mathcal{V}$ and $C \in \mathcal{C}(\mathcal{F}, \mathcal{V})$ then $C[x]_p \in \mathcal{L}$ if and only if $C[\square]_p \in \mathcal{L}$.
(L_3) If $L, N \in \mathcal{L}$, $p \in \mathcal{P}os_{\mathcal{F}}(L)$, and $L|_p \sqcup N$ is defined then $L[L|_p \sqcup N]_p \in \mathcal{L}$.
(W) If M is a max-top of s, $p \in \mathcal{P}os_{\mathcal{F}}(M)$, and $s \to_{p,\ell \to r} t$ then $M \to_{p,\ell \to r} L$
   for some $L \in \mathcal{L}$.
(C_1) In (W) either L is a max-top of t or $L = \square$.
(C_2) If $L, N \in \mathcal{L}$ and $L \sqsubseteq N$ then $L[N|_p]_p \in \mathcal{L}$ for any $p \in \mathcal{P}os_{\square}(L)$.

In a nutshell, (L_1) and (L_3) ensure that the rank is well-defined. Property (L_2) is a technical property that ensures that aliens can always be represented by suitable variables in the confluence proof. Condition (W) prevents breaking layers, and together with (L_3), fusion from above. The final two conditions, (C_1) and (C_2), prevent fusion from above and conspiring aliens, respectively. Now, let us formally define the rank and aliens of a term.

Definition 5 ([7, **Definition 3.6**]). *Let* $t = M[t_1, \dots, t_n]$ *with* M *the max-top of* t. *We define* $\text{rank}(t) = 1 + \max\{\text{rank}(t_i) \mid 1 \leqslant i \leqslant n\}$, *where* $\max(\varnothing) = 0$ *($t_1, \dots, t_n$ are the aliens of* t).

The main theorems of [7] are as follows (we omit [7, Theorem 4.3] because it has yet to be formalized).

Theorem 6 ([7, **Theorem 4.1**]). *Let* $\mathcal{R}$ *be a weakly layered TRS that is confluent on terms of rank one. If* $\mathcal{R}$ *is left-linear then* $\mathcal{R}$ *is confluent.*

Theorem 7 ([7, **Theorem 4.6**]). *Let* $\mathcal{R}$ *be a layered TRS that is confluent on terms of rank one. Then* $\mathcal{R}$ *is confluent.*

---

locale *layer_system_sig* = **fixes** $\mathcal{F} :: {}'f$ *sig* **and** $\mathcal{L} :: ({}'f, {}'v)$ *mctxt set*

locale *layer_system* = *layer_system_sig* $\mathcal{F}$ $\mathcal{L}$ **for** $\mathcal{F} :: {}'f$ *sig* **and**
   $\mathcal{L} :: ({}'f, {}'v :: infinite)$ *mctxt set* +
   assumes $\mathcal{L}\_sig$: $\mathcal{L} \subseteq \mathcal{C}$
   and L_1: $t \in \mathcal{T} \Longrightarrow \exists L \in \mathcal{L}.\ L \neq MHole \wedge L \leq mctxt\_of\_term\ t$
   and L_2: $p \in poss\_mctxt\ C \Longrightarrow$
      $mreplace\_at\ C\ p\ (MVar\ x) \in \mathcal{L} \longleftrightarrow mreplace\_at\ C\ p\ MHole \in \mathcal{L}$
   and L_3: $L \in \mathcal{L} \Longrightarrow N \in \mathcal{L} \Longrightarrow p \in funposs\_mctxt\ L \Longrightarrow$
      $(subm\_at\ L\ p,\ N) \in comp\_mctxt \Longrightarrow$
      $mreplace\_at\ L\ p\ (subm\_at\ L\ p \sqcup N) \in \mathcal{L}$

Fig. 2. Definitions of the *layer_system_sig* and *layer_system* locales in IsaFoR.

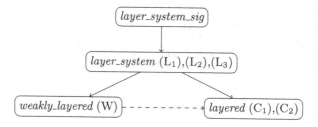

Fig. 3. Hierarchy of locales.

In Isabelle, we bundle these assumptions in locales [4]. Figure 2 shows how the first three layer conditions have been formalized in Isabelle. (A locale is declared using the **locale** keyword, followed by the locale name. It may declare constants using **fixes**, and make assumptions (often about those constants) using **assumes**. Furthermore, a locale may extend other locales; this is the case for *layer_system*, which extends *layer_system_sig*. In order to use a result from a locale, it has to be interpreted, meaning that one provides definitions for the types and constants that the locale depends on and prove that they satisfy the locale assumptions.) Inside the *layer_system_sig* locale, we define $\mathcal{T}$ and $\mathcal{C}$, the set of terms and multi-hole contexts over $\mathcal{F}$, and the concept of max-tops. In fact, max-tops are defined separately for terms and for multi-hole contexts, because while on paper, multi-hole contexts are just terms which may contain an extra constant $\Box$, in IsaFoR they have their own type. In total, four locales are defined, capturing the layer conditions, cf. Fig. 3. Note that condition (W) is not part of the *layered* locale; it would be redundant because (C_1) implies (W). In Isabelle we have encoded this fact by proving that *layered* is a sublocale of *weakly_layered*, as indicated by the dashed arrow. (Basically, a locale A is a sublocale of another locale B if the assumptions of B imply those of A.)

Within the formalization, Theorem 6 is established inside the *weakly_layered* locale as theorem *weakly_layered.CR_ll*, whereas Theorem 7 is holds in the *layered* locale as theorem *layered.CR*. (In fact these statements are declared as locale assumptions; they become theorems by proving suitable sublocale relationships. This is done in LS_Left_Linear.thy and LS_General.thy). The proofs of these main results correspond to Sect. 4 of [7]. The (lengthy) proof works by induction on the rank: assuming that terms of rank r are confluent, several auxiliary results are derived, and finally, confluence of terms of rank $r + 1$ follows. To this end, we use two more locales *weakly_layered_induct* and *weakly_layered_induct_dd* that capture the induction hypothesis, and an auxiliary assumption (namely that local peaks of so called *short steps* are joinable in a suitable way), respectively. For this use of locales it is crucial that they can be interpreted inside of a proof, since the induction hypothesis cannot be established for arbitrary r outside of an induction proof. This happens in the proof of the main lemma [7, Lemma 4.27] which we give in Fig. 4. Note that it does induction on the rank (called *rk* in the proof), and that it uses an **interpret** command to instantiate

lemma (in *weakly_layered*) *CR_main_lemma*:
  assumes *base*: *CR_on* (*rstep′ R*) {*t. mctxt_of_term t* ∈ $\mathfrak{L}$}
  and *step*: $\bigwedge$*rk. CR_on* (*rstep′ R*) {*t* ∈ $\mathcal{T}$. *rank t* ≤ *Suc rk*} $\Longrightarrow$
  weakly_layered_induct_dd $\mathcal{F}$ $\mathfrak{L}$ $\mathcal{R}$ *rk* (*R rk*)
  shows *CR_on* (*rstep′ R*) $\mathcal{T}$
proof −
  have *CR_on* (*rstep′ R*) {*t* ∈ $\mathcal{T}$. *rank t* ≤ *Suc rk*} **for** *rk*
  proof (*induct rk*)
    case *0*
    have *t* ∈ $\mathcal{T}$ ∧ *rank t* ≤ *Suc 0* $\longleftrightarrow$ *mctxt_of_term t* ∈ $\mathfrak{L}$ **for** *t*
      using *rank_1* [*of t*] *rank_gt_0* [*of t*] $\mathfrak{L}$_*sig* **by** (*fastforce simp: C_def T_def*)
    then show *?case* **using** *base* **by** *simp*
    next
    case (*Suc rk*)
    then interpret *weakly_layered_induct_dd* $\mathcal{F}$ $\mathfrak{L}$ $\mathcal{R}$ *rk R rk* **by** (*rule step*)
    show *?case* **using** *CR_Suc_rk* **by** (*simp only: native_terms_def*)
  qed
  then show *?thesis* **by** (*auto simp: CR_on_def*)
  (*metis less_Suc_eq less_Suc_eq_le less_Suc_eq_le*)
qed

Fig. 4. Proof of the "Main Lemma" for layer systems [7, Lemma 4.27]

the *weakly_layered_induct_dd* locale based on the induction hypothesis inside the proof.

One major benefit of using locales is separation of concerns; thanks to the abstraction of the layer conditions as locales, we could already work on the applications like modularity and currying before the proofs of the main results were complete, without having to worry about working with different assumptions. Basically, each application is an instantiation of these locales, which we could establish independently of the main results.

4 Persistence

To give an impression of what an application of layer systems entails, let us consider the case of persistence. This section overlaps with [7, Section 5.5], but here we focus on interesting aspects in the context of our formalization. In fact, given that the results presented here are both formalized and previously published, we focus on ideas rather than giving full proofs.

Definition 8 (*many_sorted_terms, persistent_cr_infinite_vars*)**.** *Let S be a set of sorts. A many-sorted signature $\mathcal{F}$ associates with each function symbol f of arity n a signature $f : \beta_1 \times \cdots \times \beta_n \to \alpha$, where $\beta_1, \ldots, \beta_n, \alpha \in S$. Furthermore we assume that there are pairwise disjoint, infinite sets of variables $\mathcal{V}_\alpha$ for $\alpha \in S$. The sets of of terms of sort α for $\alpha \in S$ are defined inductively by*

$$\mathcal{T}_\alpha ::= \mathcal{V}_\alpha \cup \{f(t_1, \ldots, t_n) \mid f : \beta_1 \times \cdots \times \beta_n \to \alpha, t_1 \in \mathcal{T}_{\beta_1}, \ldots, t_n \in \mathcal{T}_{\beta_n}\}$$

A many-sorted *TRS* $\mathcal{R}$ *is a TRS such that for every* $\ell \to r \in \mathcal{R}$, $\ell, r \in \mathcal{T}_\alpha$ *for some* $\alpha \in \mathcal{S}$.

We wish to establish the following theorem using layer systems.

Theorem 9 (many-sorted persistence, *CR_persist*). *Let* $\mathcal{R}$ *be a many-sorted TRS. We let* $\mathcal{V} = \bigcup_{\alpha \in \mathcal{S}} \mathcal{V}_\alpha$. *Then* $\mathcal{R}$ *is confluent on* $\mathcal{T}_\alpha$ *for all* $\alpha \in \mathcal{S}$ *if and only if* $\mathcal{R}$ *is confluent on* $\mathcal{T}(\mathcal{F}, \mathcal{V})$.

To this end we define a layer system $\mathfrak{L}$ as follows.

$$\mathfrak{L}_\alpha ::= \mathcal{V} \cup \{\Box\} \cup$$
$$\{f(C_1, \ldots, C_n) \mid f : \beta_1 \times \cdots \times \beta_n \to \alpha, C_1 \in \mathfrak{L}_{\beta_1}, \ldots, C_n \in \mathfrak{L}_{\beta_n}\}$$
$$\mathfrak{L} = \bigcup_{\alpha \in \mathcal{S}} \mathfrak{L}_\alpha$$

Showing that $\mathfrak{L}$ layers $\mathcal{R}$ is mostly straightforward. However, in order to show (W) (which is a prerequisite for showing (C_1)), one has to establish that if a rewrite step is applicable to a term at a position that is part of its max-top, then it is also applicable to the max-top itself. In order to obtain the substitution for the second rewrite step, it is helpful to define functions that compute the max-top:

$$\mathsf{mt}_\alpha(x) = x \qquad \text{for } x \in \mathcal{V}$$

$$\mathsf{mt}_\alpha(f(t_1, \ldots, t_n)) = \begin{cases} f(\mathsf{mt}_{\beta_1}(t_1), \ldots, \mathsf{mt}_{\beta_n}(t_n)) & \text{if } f : \beta_1 \times \cdots \times \beta_n \to \alpha \\ \Box & \text{if } f : \beta_1 \times \cdots \times \beta_n \to \alpha' \\ & \text{and } \alpha \neq \alpha' \end{cases}$$

The max-top of a term t equals $\mathsf{mt}_\alpha(t)$ for some $\alpha \in \mathcal{S}$ that can be obtained by looking at the root symbol of t.

Lemma 10 (*push_mt_subst, push_mt_ctxt*). *The following properties hold for* mt_α.

- *if* $s \in \mathcal{T}_\alpha$ *then* $\mathsf{mt}_\alpha(s\sigma) = s\sigma'$ *where* $\sigma'(x) = \mathsf{mt}_\alpha(\sigma(x))$ *for* $x \in \mathcal{V}_\alpha$; *and*
- *if* $p \in \mathcal{P}os(\mathsf{mt}_\alpha(t))$, *then for some* $\beta \in \mathcal{S}$, *all terms* s *satisfy* $\mathsf{mt}_\alpha(t[s]_p) = \mathsf{mt}_\alpha(t)[\mathsf{mt}_\beta(s)]$.

Now, given a rewrite step $s[\ell\sigma]_p \to s[r\sigma]_p$, with $p \in \mathcal{P}os_\mathcal{F}(\mathsf{mt}_\alpha(s))$ (as in (W)), the lemma entails

$$\mathsf{mt}_\alpha(s[\ell\sigma]_p) = \mathsf{mt}_\alpha(s)[\mathsf{mt}_\beta(\ell\sigma)]_p = \mathsf{mt}_\alpha(s)[\ell\sigma']_p$$
$$\to \mathsf{mt}_\alpha(s)[r\sigma']_p = \mathsf{mt}_\alpha(s)[\mathsf{mt}_\beta(r\sigma)]_p = \mathsf{mt}_\alpha(s[r\sigma]_p)$$

where $\ell, r \in \mathcal{T}_\beta$; this gives the desired rewrite step for (W). For (C_1) note that $s[r]_p$ can be a variable, in which case it is possible that $\mathsf{mt}_\alpha(s[r\sigma]_p) = \Box$, whereas the max-top is larger.

Remark 11. This idea of defining the max-top as a function is a recurring theme; it features in the formalizations of modularity and currying as well. The main benefit of (recursive) functions is that they come with an induction principle that is not available for the implicit notion of a "maximal top".

After showing that $\mathfrak{L}$ layers $\mathcal{R}$, Theorem 7 yields the following corollary.

Corollary 12 (*CR_on_union*). *If $\mathcal{R}$ is confluent on $\mathfrak{L} \cap T(\mathcal{F}, \mathcal{V})$,[5] then $\mathcal{R}$ is confluent on $T(\mathcal{F}, \mathcal{V})$.*

Let us now sketch a proof of Theorem 9. First note that if $\mathcal{R}$ is a many-sorted TRS, then the sets T_α are closed under rewriting by $\mathcal{R}$; hence confluence of $\mathcal{R}$ on $T(\mathcal{F}, \mathcal{V})$ implies confluence of $\mathcal{R}$ on T_α for any $\alpha \in \mathcal{S}$. For the converse, we want to use Corollary 12. We need to show that $\mathcal{R}$ is confluent on $\mathfrak{L} \cap T(\mathcal{F}, \mathcal{V})$. To this end, assume that $s \in \mathfrak{L} \cap T(\mathcal{F}, \mathcal{V})$, and we have a peak $t \ {}^*\!\leftarrow s \rightarrow^* t$. If s is a variable then $s = t = u$ and we're done. Otherwise, we can read off the sort α of s from its root symbol. Note that s is not necessarily an element of T_α, because $\mathfrak{L}$ disregards the sorts of variables. We modify s in two steps; first we annotate each variable with the type that is induced by its context (i.e., if x is the i-th argument of $f : \beta_1 \times \cdots \times \beta_n \rightarrow \gamma$, then we replace it by (x, β_i));[6] and secondly we rename the annotated variables in such a way that each (v, β) is replaced by an element of $\mathcal{V}_\beta$. In this fashion, we obtain a peak $t' \ {}^*\!\leftarrow s' \rightarrow^* u'$, where $s', t', u' \in T_\alpha$, and a substitution σ with $s = s'\sigma$, $t = t'\sigma$ and $u = u'\sigma$. By confluence of $\mathcal{R}$ on T_α, there is a valley $t' \rightarrow^* v' \ {}^*\!\leftarrow u'$, and hence a corresponding valley $t = t'\sigma \rightarrow^* v'\sigma \ {}^*\!\leftarrow u'\sigma = u$ in $\mathfrak{L} \cap T(\mathcal{F}, \mathcal{V})$.

5   Persistent Decomposition

Aoto and Toyama [1] pointed out that persistence gives rise to a decomposition technique for proving confluence. The basic idea is to attach sorts to a TRS. To obtain a decomposition, for each sort of the many-sorted TRS obtained in that way, the set of rules that are applicable to terms of that sort is computed. By persistence, if all of the resulting systems are confluent, the original TRS is confluent as well. In [2] a refined version of the persistent decomposition is presented, wherein only the maximal systems w.r.t. the subset relation are considered.

Example 13 ([1, Example 1]). Consider the TRS $\mathcal{R}$ consisting of the rules

$$f(x, y) \rightarrow f(g(x), g(y)) \qquad\qquad F(g(x), x) \rightarrow F(x, g(x))$$
$$g(x) \rightarrow h(x) \qquad\qquad F(h(x), x) \rightarrow F(x, h(x))$$

The following sort attachment makes the TRS $\mathcal{R}$ many-sorted:

$$f : 2 \times 2 \rightarrow 0 \quad g : 2 \rightarrow 2 \quad h : 2 \rightarrow 2 \quad F : 2 \times 2 \rightarrow 1$$

---

[5] Because multi-hole contexts are not terms, this is $\{t.\ mctxt\_of\_term\ t \in \mathfrak{L}\}$ in the formalization.

[6] This annotation procedure formalizes the following sentence in the proof of [7, Theorem 5.13]: "Note that for each p the sort of $s'|_p$ is uniquely determined by s.".

Looking at the sorts of possible subterms of terms of sort 0 (namely 0 and 2), 1 (1 and 2) and 2 (only 2), we obtain three induced TRSs, consisting of the first two rules, the last three rules, and only the second rule of $\mathcal{R}$, respectively. The last TRS is contained in the other two, and hence does not have to be considered. Confluence of $\mathcal{R}$ follows from confluence of the two systems

$$\mathsf{g}(x) \to \mathsf{h}(x) \qquad \mathsf{f}(x, y) \to \mathsf{f}(\mathsf{g}(x), \mathsf{g}(y))$$

(which is orthogonal) and

$$\mathsf{g}(x) \to \mathsf{h}(x) \qquad \mathsf{F}(\mathsf{g}(x), x) \to \mathsf{F}(x, \mathsf{g}(x)) \qquad \mathsf{F}(\mathsf{h}(x), x) \to \mathsf{F}(x, \mathsf{h}(x))$$

(which is terminating and has joinable critical pairs). Non-confluence of $\mathcal{R}$ would follow if any of the three TRSs induced by the sorts 0, 1, or 2 was non-confluent.

$$\frac{}{\alpha \unrhd \alpha} \text{ refl} \qquad \frac{\alpha \unrhd \beta \quad \beta \unrhd \gamma}{\alpha \unrhd \gamma} \text{ trans} \qquad \frac{f : \beta_1 \times \cdots \times \beta_n \to \alpha \quad 1 \leqslant i \leqslant n}{\alpha \unrhd \beta_i} \text{ arg}$$

Fig. 5. Syntactic order on sorts.

Definition 14. *Let $\mathcal{R}$ be a many-sorted TRS. Based on the signature, we define an order $\unrhd$ on sorts by the rules in Fig. 5. The TRS $\mathcal{R}_\alpha$ induced by $\alpha \in \mathcal{S}$ is given by*

$$\mathcal{R}_\alpha = \{\ell \to r \mid \ell \to r \in \mathcal{R}, \ell \in \mathcal{T}_\beta, \alpha \unrhd \beta\}$$

Remark 15. The notation $\unrhd$ is justified by the fact that $\mathcal{T}_\alpha \ni s \unrhd t \in \mathcal{T}_\beta$ implies $\alpha \unrhd \beta$. Note further that $\alpha \unrhd \beta$ implies $\mathcal{R}_\alpha \supseteq \mathcal{R}_\beta$, so the maximal induced TRSs $\mathcal{R}_\alpha$ w.r.t. subsets are induced by the maximal sorts α w.r.t. $\unrhd$.

Since only rules from $\mathcal{R}_\alpha$ are applicable to terms in $\mathcal{T}_\alpha$, we have the following lemma.

Lemma 16 (*CR_on_$\mathcal{T}_\alpha$_by_needed_rules*). *The system $\mathcal{R}$ is confluent on $\mathcal{T}_\alpha$ if and only if $\mathcal{R}_\alpha$ is confluent on $\mathcal{T}_\alpha$.*

We formalize the persistent decomposition result as follows.

Theorem 17 (*persistent_decomposition_nm*). *Let $\Sigma \subseteq \mathcal{S}$ be a set of sorts with the property that for each $\beta \in \mathcal{S}$, either $\mathcal{R}_\beta = \varnothing$, or $\alpha \in \Sigma$ for some $\alpha \unrhd \beta$. Then $\mathcal{R}$ is confluent on $\mathcal{T}(\mathcal{F}, \mathcal{V})$ if and only if $\mathcal{R}_\alpha$ is confluent on $\mathcal{T}(\mathcal{F}, \mathcal{V})$ for all $\alpha \in \Sigma$.*

Since no proof has been given in the literature[7] (as far as we know), we include one here.

---

[7] The proof is not difficult, but as a system description, [2] lacked space for a proof.

Proof. First assume that $\mathcal{R}_\alpha$ is confluent on $\mathcal{T}(\mathcal{F}, \mathcal{V})$ for all $\alpha \in \Sigma$. By Theorem 9, confluence of $\mathcal{R}$ on $\mathcal{T}(\mathcal{F}, \mathcal{V})$ follows if we can show that $\mathcal{R}$ is confluent on $\mathcal{T}_\beta$ for any $\beta \in \mathcal{S}$. By Lemma 16, this is equivalent to $\mathcal{R}_\beta$ being confluent on $\mathcal{T}_\beta$. If $\mathcal{R}_\beta = \varnothing$, we are done. Otherwise, by assumption, there is a sort $\alpha \unrhd \beta$ such that $\mathcal{R}_\alpha$ is confluent on $\mathcal{T}(\mathcal{F}, \mathcal{V})$. Because $\mathcal{T}_\beta$ is closed under rewriting by $\mathcal{R}_\alpha$, $\mathcal{R}_\alpha$ is confluent on $\mathcal{T}_\beta$, which implies that $(\mathcal{R}_\alpha)_\beta = \mathcal{R}_\beta$ is confluent on $\mathcal{T}_\beta$ by Lemma 16 and the fact that $\mathcal{R}_\alpha$ is a many-sorted TRS using the same signature as $\mathcal{R}$.

For the other direction, assume that $\mathcal{R}$ is confluent on $\mathcal{T}(\mathcal{F}, \mathcal{V})$. We show that $\mathcal{R}_\alpha$ is confluent on $\mathcal{T}(\mathcal{F}, \mathcal{V})$ for all $\alpha \in \mathcal{S}$ (and in particular those in Σ). Since $\mathcal{R}_\alpha$ is a many-sorted TRS, it is persistent (Theorem 9), so it suffices to show that $\mathcal{R}_\alpha$ is confluent on $\mathcal{T}_\beta$ for all $\beta \in \mathcal{S}$. So consider a peak $t \;_{\mathcal{R}_\alpha}^* \!\leftarrow s \rightarrow_{\mathcal{R}_\alpha}^* u$. We proceed by induction on $s \in \mathcal{T}_\beta$.

If $s \in \mathcal{V}$ then $s = t = u$ and we are done. Otherwise, $s = f(s_1, \ldots, s_n)$ for some $f : \beta_1 \times \cdots \times \beta_n \to \beta$, and $s_1 \in \mathcal{T}_{\beta_1}, \ldots, s_n \in \mathcal{T}_{\beta_n}$. There are two cases.

1. If $\alpha \unrhd \beta$, then since $\mathcal{R}$ is confluent on $\mathcal{T}_\beta$, $\mathcal{R}_\beta$ is confluent on $\mathcal{T}_\beta$. By Lemma 16 applied to $(\mathcal{R}_\alpha)_\beta = \mathcal{R}_\beta$, $\mathcal{R}_\alpha$ is confluent on $\mathcal{T}_\beta$ as well.
2. If $\alpha \ntrianglerighteq \beta$, then $\mathcal{R}_\alpha$ contains no rules whose root symbol has result sort β. Consequently there cannot be any root steps in $t \;_{\mathcal{R}_\alpha}^* \!\leftarrow s \;_{\mathcal{R}_\alpha}^* \!\leftarrow u$. Hence we obtain $t_1, \ldots, t_n$ and $u_1, \ldots, u_n$ with $t_i \;_{\mathcal{R}_\alpha}^* \!\leftarrow s_i \rightarrow_{\mathcal{R}_\alpha}^* u_i$ for $1 \leqslant i \leqslant n$, $t = f(t_1, \ldots, t_n)$, and $u = f(u_1, \ldots, u_n)$. We conclude by the induction hypothesis (s_i is confluent for $1 \leqslant i \leqslant n$). $\qquad \square$

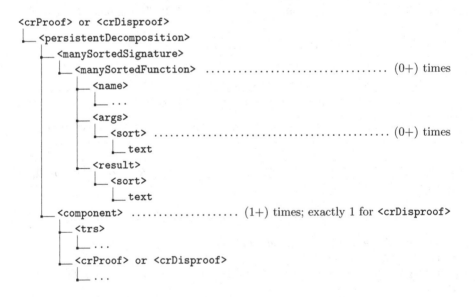

Fig. 6. CPF fragment for persistent decomposition proofs

We further integrated this result into CeTA. To this end, we implemented a function that computes the maximal sorts (with respect to $\unrhd$) for a given signature, a check function that checks the preconditions of Theorem 17, and extended CeTA's CPF parser with a certificate format for a persistent decomposition (CPF is an XML format. The fragment for persistent decomposition is given in Fig. 6, and may be of interest to tool authors who want to incorporate certifiable persistent decomposition into their confluence tools).

6   Currying

Currying is the most complicated application of layer systems that we have formalized so far. Currying is a transformation of term rewrite systems in which applications of n-ary functions are replaced by n applications of a single fresh binary function symbol to a constant, thereby applying arguments to the function one by one. More formally, we introduce a fresh function symbol $\bullet$ to denote application, whereas every other function symbol becomes a constant. We adopt the convention of writing f_n to denote a function symbol of arity n. Moreover, we denote the arity of a function symbol f with respect to the signature $\mathcal{F}$ by $a_\mathcal{F}(f)$. We identify $f_{a_\mathcal{F}(f)}$ with f.

Definition 18. *Given a TRS $\mathcal{R}$ over a signature $\mathcal{F}$, its* curried version $\mathsf{Cu}(\mathcal{R})$ *consists of rules* $\{\mathsf{Cu}(l) \to \mathsf{Cu}(r) \mid \ell \to r \in \mathcal{R}\}$, *where* $\mathsf{Cu}(t) = t$ *if t is a variable and* $\mathsf{Cu}(f(t_1,\ldots,t_n)) = f_0 \bullet \mathsf{Cu}(t_1) \bullet \cdots \bullet \mathsf{Cu}(t_n)$. *Here $\bullet$ is a fresh left-associative function symbol.*

Currying is useful for deciding properties such as confluence [5] or termination [10]. For analyzing confluence by currying, the following result is important.

Theorem 19 (*main_result_complete*)**.** *Let $\mathcal{R}$ be a TRS. If $\mathcal{R}$ is confluent, then $\mathsf{Cu}(\mathcal{R})$ is confluent.*

This result was proved by Kahrs [11]. Rather than working directly with $\mathsf{Cu}(\mathcal{R})$, Kahrs works with the *partial parametrization* of $\mathcal{R}$, which is given by $\mathsf{PP}(\mathcal{R}) = \mathcal{R} \cup \mathcal{U}_\mathcal{F}$, where $\mathcal{U}_\mathcal{F}$ is the set of uncurrying rules for $\mathcal{F}$ (see Definition 20). Confluence of $\mathsf{PP}(\mathcal{R})$ and $\mathsf{Cu}(\mathcal{R})$ are closely related, cf. Lemma 21.

Definition 20. *Given a signature $\mathcal{F}$, the* uncurrying *rules $\mathcal{U}_\mathcal{F}$ are rules*

$$f_i(x_1,\ldots,x_i) \bullet x_{i+1} \to f_{i+1}(x_1,\ldots,x_{i+1})$$

for every function symbol $f \in \mathcal{F}$ and $0 \leqslant i < a_\mathcal{F}(f)$.

Lemma 21 ([11, **Proposition 3.1**])**.** *Let $\mathcal{R}$ be a TRS. Then $\mathsf{Cu}(\mathcal{R})$ is confluent if $\mathsf{PP}(\mathcal{R})$ is.*

Hence in order to prove Theorem 19 it suffices to prove that $\mathsf{PP}(\mathcal{R})$ is confluent. To this end, we make use of Theorem 7. Hence we need to show that $\mathsf{PP}(\mathcal{R})$ is layered according to some set of layers $\mathfrak{L}$, and confluent on terms of rank one. First of all we have to define a suitable set of layers. We choose $\mathfrak{L} = \mathfrak{L}_1 \cup \mathfrak{L}_2$ letting $\mathcal{V}_\square = \mathcal{V} \cup \{\square\}$ and

$$\mathcal{L}_1 :: = \mathcal{V}_\Box \cup \{f_m(s_1, \ldots, s_m) \bullet s_{m+1} \bullet \cdots \bullet s_n \mid$$
$$f \in \mathcal{F}, 0 \leqslant m \leqslant n \leqslant \mathsf{a}_\mathcal{F}(f) \text{ and } s_1, \ldots, s_n \in \mathcal{L}_1\}$$
$$\mathcal{L}_2 = \{x \bullet t \mid x \in \mathcal{V}_\Box \text{ and } t \in \mathcal{L}_1\}$$

This definition realizes a separation between well-formed terms ($\mathcal{L}_1$), whose $\mathcal{U}_\mathcal{F}$-normal form contains no $\bullet$ symbol, and ill-formed terms ($\mathcal{L}_2$), whose $\mathcal{U}_\mathcal{F}$-normal form contains exactly one $\bullet$ symbol at the root. As required for condition (L_1), variables and holes are treated interchangeably.

Whereas for Lemma 21 we could follow the lines of the paper proof, the formalization of the fact that $\mathsf{PP}(\mathcal{R})$ is layered according to $\mathcal{L}$ turned out to be much more tedious. As with the modularity and persistence applications, we found it convenient to define functions that *compute* the max-top of a term, since the abstract definition of max-tops in the layer framework is not really suitable for proofs in Isabelle.

Definition 22. *The following function checks whether the number of arguments applied to the first non-$\bullet$ function symbol f is at most the arity $\mathsf{a}_\mathcal{F}(f)$ according to the original signature $\mathcal{F}$*

$$\mathsf{check}(t, m) = \begin{cases} \mathit{false} & \mathit{if}\ t \in \mathcal{V} \\ \mathsf{check}(t_1, m+1) & \mathit{if}\ t = t_1 \bullet t_2 \\ \mathsf{a}_\mathcal{F}(f) \geqslant m+n & \mathit{if}\ t = f_n(t_1, \ldots, t_n) \end{cases}$$

Let $\mathcal{F}^\bullet = \mathcal{F} \cup \{\bullet\}$. The max-top $\mathsf{mt_{Cu}}$ of a term $t \in \mathcal{T}(\mathcal{F}^\bullet, \mathcal{V})$ with respect to $\mathcal{L}$ is computed as

$$\mathsf{mt_{Cu}}(t) = \begin{cases} t & \mathit{if}\ t \in \mathcal{V} \\ f(\mathsf{mt_1}(t_1, 0), \ldots, \mathsf{mt_1}(t_n, 0)) & \mathit{if}\ t = f(t_1, \ldots, t_n) \\ & \mathit{and}\ (\mathsf{check}(t, 0)\ \mathit{or}\ t_1 \in \mathcal{V}) \\ \Box \bullet \mathsf{mt_1}(t_2, 0) & \mathit{otherwise}\ (\mathit{in\ which\ case}\ t = t_1 \bullet t_2) \end{cases}$$

Here $\mathsf{mt_1}(t, m)$ computes the max-top of t with respect to $\mathcal{L}_1$, where m is the number of already applied arguments:

$$\mathsf{mt_1}(t, m) = \begin{cases} t & \mathit{if}\ t \in \mathcal{V} \\ \mathsf{mt_1}(t_1, m+1) \bullet \mathsf{mt_1}(t_2, 0) & \mathit{if}\ t = t_1 \bullet t_2\ \mathit{and}\ \mathsf{check}(t, m) \\ f(\mathsf{mt_1}(t_1, 0), \ldots, \mathsf{mt_1}(t_n, 0)) & \mathit{if}\ t = f(t_1, \ldots, t_n), f \neq \bullet \\ & \mathit{and}\ \mathsf{check}(t, m) \\ \Box & \mathit{otherwise} \end{cases}$$

Note that there is some redundancy, since the check function does the same counting several times. It turns out, however, that this redundancy simplifies later proofs.

After proving the correctness of $\mathsf{mt_1}$ and $\mathsf{mt_{Cu}}$, the main difficulty was the proof of condition (C_1) for $\mathcal{L}$ and $\mathsf{PP}(\mathcal{R})$. Similar to Lemma 10, we proved facts about the interaction of $\mathsf{mt_1}$ (and hence $\mathsf{mt_{Cu}}$) with contexts and substitutions, in order to analyze a rewrite step $s = C[l\sigma]_p \to C[r\sigma]_p$ with p a function position of the max-top M of s.

Lemma 23 (*push_mt_in_ctxt*). *Let s be a term and p the hole position of context C such that $C[s]_p \in \mathcal{T}(\mathcal{F}^\bullet, \mathcal{V})$ and $p \in \mathcal{P}os_{\mathcal{F}^\bullet}(\mathsf{mt}_1(C[s], j))$. Then there exists a context D and a natural number k such that $\mathsf{mt}_1(C[s], j) = D[\mathsf{mt}_1(s, k)]$, and $\mathsf{mt}_1(C[t], j) = D[\mathsf{mt}_1(t, k)]$ for any term $t \in \mathcal{T}(\mathcal{F}^\bullet, \mathcal{V})$ having the same number of missing arguments as s.*

Lemma 24 (*push_mt_in_subst*). *Let $t \in \mathcal{T}(\mathcal{F}, \mathcal{V})$. Then $\mathsf{mt}_1(t \cdot \sigma, 0) = \mathsf{mt}_1(t, 0) \cdot \sigma'$ with $\sigma' = (\lambda x.\, \mathsf{mt}_1(x, 0)) \circ \sigma$.*

Using these two lemmas, we can obtain the desired rewrite step from M by the following computation, where for simplicity we only consider the case $M \in \mathfrak{L}_1$ and $l \to r \in \mathcal{R}$:

$$M = \mathsf{mt}(s) = \mathsf{mt}_1(C[l \cdot \sigma], 0) \overset{23}{=} D[\mathsf{mt}_1(l \cdot \sigma, k)] \overset{24}{=} D[\mathsf{mt}_1(l, 0) \cdot \sigma'] = D[l \cdot \sigma']$$

$$\to_{p, \ell \to r} D[r \cdot \sigma'] = D[\mathsf{mt}_1(r, 0) \cdot \sigma'] \overset{24}{=} D[\mathsf{mt}_1(r \cdot \sigma, k)] \overset{23}{=} \mathsf{mt}_1(C[r \cdot \sigma], 0)$$

The uses of the previous two lemmas are indicated above the equalities. Note that the number of missing arguments of r and l are equal (namely 0), so we can use Lemma 23 in both directions. For the same reason we must have $k = 0$, because otherwise $\mathsf{mt}_1(l \cdot \sigma, k) = \square$, contradicting the fact that the rewrite step would take place at a function position of M. Hence Lemma 24 is applicable. Furthermore, we use $\mathsf{mt}_1(l, 0) = l$ and $\mathsf{mt}_1(r, 0) = r$, using that l and r are well-formed. At this point we have established (W). For (C_1), we analyze the term $\mathsf{mt}_1(C[r \cdot \sigma], 0)$ some more: If $C = \square$, r is a variable and $\mathsf{check}(r \cdot \sigma)$ is false, $\mathsf{mt}_1(C[r \cdot \sigma], 0) = \square$. Otherwise, the max-top of $C[r \cdot \sigma]$ is equal to $\mathsf{mt}_1(C[r \cdot \sigma], 0)$.

Remark 25. As an anonymous reviewer suggested, it would most likely have been easier to use a different layer system, where each $\bullet$ symbol starts a new layer:

$$\mathfrak{L}'_1 = \mathcal{T}(\mathcal{F}, \mathcal{V}_\square)$$
$$\mathfrak{L}'_2 = \{f_m(s_1, \ldots, s_m) \bullet s_{m+1} \mid f \in \mathcal{F}, 0 \leqslant m < \mathsf{a}_{\mathcal{F}}(f) \text{ and } s_1, \ldots, s_{m+1} \in \mathfrak{L}'_1\}$$
$$\mathfrak{L}'_3 = \{x \bullet y \mid x, y \in \mathcal{V}_\square\} \cup$$
$$\{f_m(x_1, \ldots, x_m) \mid f \in \mathcal{F}, 0 \leqslant m < \mathsf{a}_{\mathcal{F}}(f) \text{ and } x_1, \ldots, x_m \in \mathcal{V}_\square\}$$

This would have avoided the complications of counting the number of "missing" arguments in the check function. Unfortunately we did not find this idea before starting our formalization. Adapting the existing formalization accordingly would be a substantial effort with no obvious gain—the final result would still be that currying preserves confluence.

7   Conclusion

We have presented a formalization of modularity, persistence, and currying, in the Isabelle proof assistant. The formalization spans about 12k lines of theory files and took approximately 9 person-months to develop. A breakdown of the effort is given in Fig. 7. (Note that modularity is subsumed by persistence. We formalized modularity first because it is the easiest application. Many proof ideas for modularity carried over to the other, more difficult applications.) The de Bruijn factor (which compares the size of the formalized proof to the paper version) varies wildly. We believe that the main reason for this is that the level of detail for proofs in [7] varies greatly; the core confluence proof (leading up to Theorem 7) is carried out in much more detail than the applications, where large parts of the proofs rely on the reader's intuition. A second contributing factor is that two people worked on different parts of the formalization.

As far as we know, this is the first formalization of modularity of confluence in any proof assistant. We would like to point out that even though the confluence proof for layer systems is based on a constructive proof of modularity of confluence [17], the formalized result is not constructive. This is because Isabelle/HOL is a classical logic. Producing a constructive proof in Isabelle/HOL would have to rely on discipline (including the avoidance of proof automation tools like Metis that are based on Skolemization). In fact, since the proof factors through decreasing diagrams (which were already part of the Archive of Formal Proofs [6]), we would first need a constructive proof for confluence by decreasing diagrams. In the end we would not reap any benefits from having a constructive proof (namely, an executable confluence result).

We integrated the persistence result into our theorem prover CSI (which already supported order-sorted persistence, so the main effort for extending CSI was adding the XML output.) We present experimental results in Fig. 8. The check mark ✓ indicates certified strategies; CSI✓ and +pd✓ are the certified strategies with and without persistent decomposition, respectively, while CSI refers to the uncertified, full strategy of CSI. As can be seen from the data, we have achieved a modest improvement in certified proofs over the Cops database of confluence problems.[8] It is worth noting that there is no progress in certified non-confluence proofs; in fact, there is no certification gap for non-confluence at all. For non-confluence, CSI employs tree automata [8], which (in theory,

topic	lines	dB factor
definitions, basic facts about layers	3.2k	20
Theorem 7	2.0k	13
modularity	0.8k	30
persistence	1.5k	55
currying	3.8k	40
executable persistence check	0.6k	—
total	12k	

Fig. 7. Formalization effort (dB = de Bruijn)

---

[8] Full results are available at http://cl-informatik.uibk.ac.at/software/lisa/ictac2018/.

	CSI✓	+pd✓	CSI
yes	148	154	244
no	162	162	162
maybe	127	121	31
total	437	437	437

Fig. 8. Impact of persistent decomposition on certifiable proofs by CSI.

and evidently also in practice) subsume the many-sorted decomposition result, because many-sorted terms are a regular tree language.

There are several parts of [7] that have not yet been formalized. For one, there are two more applications of layer systems, namely modularity of layer-preserving composable TRSs, and a modularity result for quasi-ground systems. The bigger missing part are *variable-restricted layer systems*, which are the foundation for a generalized persistence result with ordered sorts [7, Theorem 6.3]. Furthermore, while we have formalized preservation of confluence by currying, this is not integrated into CeTA. As far as we know, no confluence tool currently uses currying directly. However, currying is the basis of efficient decision procedures for ground TRSs, which are implemented in CSI, and are a target for future formalization efforts.

References

1. Aoto, T., Toyama, Y.: Extending persistency of confluence with ordered sorts. Technical report IS-RR-96-0025F, School of Information Science, JAIST (1996)
2. Aoto, T., Yoshida, J., Toyama, Y.: Proving confluence of term rewriting systems automatically. In: Treinen, R. (ed.) RTA 2009. LNCS, vol. 5595, pp. 93–102. Springer, Heidelberg (2009). https://doi.org/10.1007/978-3-642-02348-4_7
3. Baader, F., Nipkow, T.: Term Rewriting and All That. Cambridge University Press, Cambridge (1998). https://doi.org/10.1017/cbo9781139172752
4. Ballarin, C.: Locales: a module system for mathematical theories. J. Autom. Reason. **52**(2), 123–153 (2014). https://doi.org/10.1007/s10817-013-9284-7
5. Felgenhauer, B.: Deciding confluence of ground term rewrite systems in cubic time. In: Tiwari, A. (ed.) Proceedings of 23rd International Conference on Rewriting Techniques and Applications. RTA 2012, May–June 2012, Nagoya. Leibniz International Proceedings in Informatics, vol. 15, pp. 165–175. Dagstuhl Publishing, Saarbrücken, Wadern (2012). https://doi.org/10.4230/lipics.rta.2012.165
6. Felgenhauer, B.: Decreasing diagrams II. AFP, formal proof development (2015). https://www.isa-afp.org/entries/Decreasing-Diagrams-II.html
7. Felgenhauer, B., Middeldorp, A., Zankl, H., van Oostrom, V.: Layer systems for proving confluence. ACM Trans. Comput. Log. **16**(2), 14 (2015). https://doi.org/10.1145/2710017
8. Felgenhauer, B., Thiemann, R.: Reachability, confluence, and termination analysis with state-compatible automata. Inf. Comput. **253**(3), 467–483 (2017). https://doi.org/10.1016/j.ic.2016.06.011

9. Gordon, M.J., Milner, A.J., Wadsworth, C.P.: Edinburgh LCF. LNCS, vol. 78. Springer, Heidelberg (1979). https://doi.org/10.1007/3-540-09724-4
10. Hirokawa, N., Middeldorp, A., Zankl, H.: Uncurrying for termination. In: Cervesato, I., Veith, H., Voronkov, A. (eds.) LPAR 2008. LNCS (LNAI), vol. 5330, pp. 667–681. Springer, Heidelberg (2008). https://doi.org/10.1007/978-3-540-89439-1_46
11. Kahrs, S.: Confluence of curried term-rewriting systems. J. Symb. Comput. **19**(6), 601–623 (1995). https://doi.org/10.1006/jsco.1995.1035
12. Kitahara, A., Sakai, M., Toyama, Y.: On the modularity of confluent term rewriting systems with shared constructors. Tech. Rep. Inf. Process. Soc. Jpn. **95**(15), 11–20 (1995). (in Japanese)
13. Klop, J., Middeldorp, A., Toyama, Y., de Vrijer, R.: Modularity of confluence: a simplified proof. Inf. Process. Lett. **49**, 101–109 (1994). https://doi.org/10.1016/0020-0190(94)90034-5
14. Nagele, J., Felgenhauer, B., Middeldorp, A.: CSI: new evidence – a progress report. In: de Moura, L. (ed.) CADE 2017. LNCS (LNAI), vol. 10395, pp. 385–397. Springer, Cham (2017). https://doi.org/10.1007/978-3-319-63046-5_24
15. Nipkow, T., Wenzel, M., Paulson, L.C. (eds.): Isabelle/HOL. LNCS, vol. 2283. Springer, Heidelberg (2002). https://doi.org/10.1007/3-540-45949-9
16. Ohlebusch, E.: Modular properties of composable term rewriting systems. Ph.D. thesis, Universität Bielefeld (1994)
17. Oostrom, V.: Modularity of confluence. In: Armando, A., Baumgartner, P., Dowek, G. (eds.) IJCAR 2008. LNCS (LNAI), vol. 5195, pp. 348–363. Springer, Heidelberg (2008). https://doi.org/10.1007/978-3-540-71070-7_31
18. Thiemann, R., Sternagel, C.: Certification of termination proofs using CeTA. In: Berghofer, S., Nipkow, T., Urban, C., Wenzel, M. (eds.) TPHOLs 2009. LNCS, vol. 5674, pp. 452–468. Springer, Heidelberg (2009). https://doi.org/10.1007/978-3-642-03359-9_31
19. Toyama, Y.: On the Church-Rosser property for the direct sum of term rewriting systems. J. ACM **34**(1), 128–143 (1987). https://doi.org/10.1145/7531.7534
20. Wenzel, M.: Isar—a generic interpretative approach to readable formal proof documents. In: Bertot, Y., Dowek, G., Théry, L., Hirschowitz, A., Paulin, C. (eds.) TPHOLs 1999. LNCS, vol. 1690, pp. 167–183. Springer, Heidelberg (1999). https://doi.org/10.1007/3-540-48256-3_12

A Metalanguage for Guarded Iteration

Sergey Goncharov$^{(\boxtimes)}$, Christoph Rauch, and Lutz Schröder

Dept. Informatik, Friedrich-Alexander-Universität Erlangen-Nürnberg,
Martensstraße 3, 91058 Erlangen, Germany
{sergey.goncharov,christoph.rauch,lutz.schroeder}@fau.de

Abstract. Notions of guardedness serve to delineate admissible recursive definitions in various settings in a compositional manner. In recent work, we have introduced an axiomatic notion of guardedness in symmetric monoidal categories, which serves as a unifying framework for various examples from program semantics, process algebra, and beyond. In the present paper, we propose a generic *metalanguage for guarded iteration* based on combining this notion with the fine-grain call-by-value paradigm, which we intend as a unifying programming language for guarded and unguarded iteration in the presence of computational effects. We give a generic (categorical) semantics of this language over a suitable class of strong monads supporting guarded iteration, and show it to be in touch with the standard operational behaviour of iteration by giving a concrete big-step operational semantics for a certain specific instance of the metalanguage and establishing adequacy for this case.

1 Introduction

Guardedness is a recurring theme in programming and semantics, fundamentally distinguishing the view of computations as processes unfolding in time from the view that identifies computations with a final result they may eventually produce. Historically, the first perspective is inherent to process algebra (e.g. [27]), where the main attribute of a process is its *behaviour*, while the second is inherent to classical denotational semantics via domain theory [37], where the only information properly infinite computations may communicate to the outer world is the mere fact of their divergence. This gives rise to a distinction between *intensional* and *extensional* paradigms in semantics [1].

For example, in CCS [27] a process is guarded in a variable x if every occurrence of x in this process is preceded by an action. One effect of this constraint is that guarded recursive specifications can be solved uniquely, e.g. the equation $x = \bar{a}.x$, whose right-hand side is guarded in x, has the infinite stream $\bar{a}.\bar{a}....$ as its unique solution. If we view $\bar{a}$ as an action of producing an output, we can also view the process specified by $x = \bar{a}.x$ as *productive* and the respective solution $\bar{a}.\bar{a}...$ as a *trace* obtained by collecting its outputs. The view of guardedness as productivity is pervasive in programming and reasoning with coinductive types [11,14,15,20] as implemented in dependent type environments such as Coq and Agda. Semantic models accommodate this idea in various ways,

© Springer Nature Switzerland AG 2018
B. Fischer and T. Uustalu (Eds.): ICTAC 2018, LNCS 11187, pp. 191–210, 2018.
https://doi.org/10.1007/978-3-030-02508-3_11

handleit $e = \star$ in
   handle u in ($print$ ("think of a number") & raise$_u\star$) with
     (do $y \leftarrow random()$; $z \leftarrow read()$; if ($y = z$) then ret $\star$ else raise$_e\star$)

Fig. 1. Example of a guarded loop.

e.g. from a modal [2,29], (ultra-)metric [12,23], and a unifying topos-theoretic perspective [5,9].

In recent work, we have proposed a new *axiomatic* approach to unifying notions of guardedness [18,19], where the main idea is to provide an *abstract* notion of guardedness applicable to a wide range of (mutually incompatible) models, including, e.g., complete partial orders, complete metric spaces, and infinite-dimensional Hilbert spaces, instead of designing a concrete model carrying a specific notion of guardedness. A salient feature of axiomatic guardedness is that it varies in a large spectrum starting from *total guardedness* (everything is guarded) and ending at *vacuous guardedness* (very roughly, guardedness in a variable means non-occurrence of this variable in the defining expression) with proper examples as discussed above lying between these two extremes. The fact that axiomatic guardedness can be varied so broadly indicates that it can be used for bridging the gap between the intensional and extensional paradigms, which is indeed the perspective we are pursuing here by introducing a *metalanguage for guarded iteration*.

The developments in [18] are couched in terms of a special class of monoidal categories called *guarded traced symmetric monoidal categories*, equipped with a monoidal notion of guardedness and a monoidal notion of feedback allowing only such cyclic computations that are guarded in the corresponding sense. In the present work we explore a refinement of this notion by instantiating guarded traces to *Kleisli categories* of computational monads in sense of Moggi [28], with coproduct (inherited from the base category under fairly general assumptions) as the monoidal structure. The feedback operation is then equivalently given by *guarded effectful iteration*, i.e. a (partial) operator

$$\frac{f : X \to T(Y + X)}{f^\dagger : X \to TY} \tag{1}$$

to be thought of as iterating f over X until a result in Y is reached. As originally argued by Moggi, strong monads can be regarded as representing computational effects, such as nondeterminism, exceptions, or process algebra actions, and thus the corresponding internal language of strong monads, the *computational metalanguage* [28], can be regarded as a generic programming language over these effects. We extend this perspective by parametrizing such a language with a notion of guardedness and equipping it with guarded iteration. In doing so, we follow the approach of Geron and Levy [13] who already explored the case of unguarded iteration by suitably extending a fine-grain call-by-value language [24], a refined variant of Moggi's original computational λ-calculus.

A key insight we borrow from [13] is that effectful iteration can be efficiently organized via throwing and handling exceptions (also called *labels* in this context) in a loop, leading to a more convenient programming style in comparison to the one directly inspired by the typing of the iteration operator (1). We show that the exception handling metaphor seamlessly extends to the guarded case and is compatible with the axioms of guardedness. A quick illustration is presented in Fig. 1 where the handleit command implements a loop in which the raise command indexed with the corresponding label identifies the tail call. The *print* operation acts as a guard and makes the resulting program well-typed. Apart from this non-standard use of exceptions, they can be processed in a standard way with the handle command.

To interpret our metalanguage we derive and explore a notion of *strong guarded iteration* and give a generic (categorical) denotational semantics, for which the main subtlety are functional abstractions of guarded morphisms. We then define a big-step operational semantics for a concrete (simplistic) instance of our metalanguage and show an adequacy result w.r.t. a concrete choice of the underlying category and the strong monad.

Related Work. We have already mentioned work by Geron and Levy [13]. The instance of operational semantics we explore here is chosen so as to give the simplest proper example of guarded iteration, i.e. the one giving rise to infinite traces, making the resulting semantics close to one explored in a line of work by Nakata and Uustalu [30–33]. We regard our operational semantics as a showcase for the denotational semantics, and do not mean to address the notorious issue of undecidability of program termination, which is the main theme of Nakata and Uustalu's work. We do however regard our work as a stepping stone both for deriving more sophisticated styles of operational semantics and for developing concrete denotational models for addressing the operational behavior as discussed in op.cit. The *guarded* λ-calculus [9] is a recently introduced language for guarded recursion (as apposed to guarded iteration), on the one hand much more expressive than ours, but on the other hand capturing a very concrete model, the *topos of trees* [5].

Plan of the Paper. In Sect. 2 we give the necessary technical preliminaries, and discuss and complement the semantic foundations for guarded iteration [18,19]. In Sects. 3 and 4 we present our metalanguage for guarded iteration (without functional types) and its generic denotational semantics. In Sect. 5 we identify conditions for interpreting functional types and extend the denotational semantics to this case. In Sect. 6 we consider an instance of our metalanguage (for a specific choice of signature), give a big-step operation semantics and prove a corresponding adequacy result. Conclusions are drawn in Sect. 7.

2   Monads for Effectful Guarded Iteration

We use the standard language of category theory [25]. Some conventions regarding notation are in order. By $|\mathbf{C}|$ we denote the class of objects of a category $\mathbf{C}$, and by $\mathsf{Hom}_{\mathbf{C}}(A, B)$ (or $\mathsf{Hom}(A, B)$, if no confusion arises) the set of morphisms $f : A \to B$ from $A \in |\mathbf{C}|$ to $B \in |\mathbf{C}|$. We tend to omit object indices on natural transformations.

Coproduct Summands and Distributive Categories. We call a pair $\sigma = \langle \sigma_1 : Y_1 \to X, \sigma_2 : Y_2 \to X \rangle$ of morphisms a *summand* of X, denoted $\sigma : Y_1 \hookrightarrow X$, if it forms a coproduct cospan, i.e. X is a coproduct of Y_1 and Y_2 with σ_1 and σ_2 as coproduct injections. Each summand $\sigma = \langle \sigma_1, \sigma_2 \rangle$ thus determines a *complement summand* $\bar{\sigma} = \langle \sigma_2, \sigma_1 \rangle : Y_2 \hookrightarrow X$. We often identify a summand $\langle \sigma_1, \sigma_2 \rangle$ with its first component when there is a canonically predetermined σ_2. Summands of a given object X are naturally preordered by taking $\langle \sigma_1, \sigma_2 \rangle$ to be smaller than $\langle \theta_1, \theta_2 \rangle$ iff σ_1 factors through θ_1. In the presence of an initial object $\emptyset$, with unique morphisms $! : \emptyset \to X$, this preorder has a greatest element $\langle \mathsf{id}_X, ! \rangle$ and a least element $\langle !, \mathsf{id}_X \rangle$. By writing $X_1 + \ldots + X_n$ we designate the latter as a coproduct of the X_i and assign the canonical names $\mathsf{in}_i : X_i \hookrightarrow X_1 + \ldots + X_n$ to the corresponding summands. Dually, we write $\mathsf{pr}_i : X_1 \times \ldots \times X_n \to X_i$ for canonical *projections* (without introducing a special arrow notation). Note that in an *extensive category* [8], the second component of any coproduct summand $\langle \sigma_1, \sigma_2 \rangle$ is determined by the first up to isomorphism. However, we do not generally assume extensiveness, working instead with the weaker assumption of distributivity [10]: a category with finite products and coproducts (including a final and an initial object) is *distributive* if the natural transformation

$$X \times Y + X \times Z \xrightarrow{[\mathsf{id} \times \mathsf{inl}, \mathsf{id} \times \mathsf{inr}]} X \times (Y + Z)$$

is an isomorphism, whose inverse we denote by $\mathsf{dist}_{X,Y,Z}$.

Strong Monads. Following Moggi [28], we identify a *monad* $\mathbb{T}$ on a category $\mathbf{C}$ with the corresponding *Kleisli triple* $(T, \eta, (-)^\star)$ on $\mathbf{C}$ consisting of an endomap T on $|\mathbf{C}|$, a $|\mathbf{C}|$-indexed class of morphisms $\eta_X : X \to TX$, called the *unit* of $\mathbb{T}$, and the *Kleisli lifting* maps $(-)^\star : \mathsf{Hom}(X, TY) \to \mathsf{Hom}(TX, TY)$ such that

$$\eta^\star = \mathsf{id} \qquad f^\star \eta = f \qquad (f^\star g)^\star = f^\star g^\star.$$

These definitions imply that T is an endofunctor and η is a natural transformation. Provided that $\mathbf{C}$ has finite products, a monad $\mathbb{T}$ on $\mathbf{C}$ is *strong* if it is equipped with a *strength*, i.e. a natural transformation $\tau_{X,Y} : X \times TY \to T(X \times Y)$ satisfying a number of standard coherence conditions (e.g. [28]). Morphisms of the form $f : X \to TY$ form the *Kleisli category* of $\mathbb{T}$, which has the same objects as $\mathbf{C}$, units $\eta_X : X \to TX$ as identities, and composition $(f, g) \mapsto f^\star g$, also called *Kleisli composition*.

In programming language semantics, both the strength τ and the distributivity transformation dist essentially serve to propagate context variables. We often need to combine them into $(T \, \mathsf{dist}) \tau : X \times T(Y + Z) \to T(X \times Y + X \times Z)$. We denote the latter transformation by δ.

$$\textbf{(trv)} \quad \frac{f : X \to TY}{(T\,\mathsf{in}_1)f : X \to_{\mathsf{in}_2} T(Y+Z)} \qquad \textbf{(sum)} \quad \frac{f : X \to_\sigma TZ \qquad g : Y \to_\sigma TZ}{[f,g] : X+Y \to_\sigma TZ}$$

$$\textbf{(cmp)} \quad \frac{f : X \to_{\mathsf{in}_2} T(Y+Z) \qquad g : Y \to_\sigma TV \qquad h : Z \to TV}{[g,h]^\star f : X \to_\sigma TV}$$

$$\textbf{(str)} \quad \frac{f : X \to_\sigma TY}{\tau\,(\mathsf{id}_Z \times f) : Z \times X \to_{\mathsf{id} \times \sigma} T(Z \times Y)}$$

Fig. 2. Axioms of abstract guardedness.

Guarded Iteration. Let us fix a distributive category $\mathbf{C}$ and a strong monad $\mathbb{T}$ on $\mathbf{C}$. The monad $\mathbb{T}$ is *(abstractly) guarded* if it is equipped with a notion of guardedness, i.e. with a relation between Kleisli morphisms $f : X \to TY$ and summands $\sigma : Y' \hookrightarrow Y$ closed under the rules in Fig. 2, where $f : X \to_\sigma TY$ denotes the fact that f and σ are in the relation in question, in which case we also call f, σ-*guarded*. Let $\mathsf{Hom}_\sigma(X,Y)$ be the subset of $\mathsf{Hom}(X,TY)$ consisting of the morphisms $X \to_\sigma TY$. We also write $f : X \to_i TY$ for $f : X \to_{\mathsf{in}_i} TY$. More generally, we use the notation $f : X \to_{p,q,\dots} TY$ to indicate guardedness in the union of injections $\mathsf{in}_p, \mathsf{in}_q, \dots$ where $p, q, \dots$ are sequences over $\{1,2\}$ identifying the corresponding coproduct summand in Y. For example, we write $f : X \to_{12,2} T((Y+Z)+Z)$ to mean that f is $[\mathsf{in}_1\,\mathsf{in}_2, \mathsf{in}_2]$-guarded.

The axioms **(trv)**, **(sum)** and **(cmp)** come from [19]. Here, we also add the rule **(str)** stating compatibility of guardedness and strength. Note that since $\mathbf{C}$ is distributive, $\mathsf{id} \times \sigma$ is actually a summand.

Let us record some simple consequences of the axioms in Fig. 2.

Lemma 1. *The following rules are derivable:*

$$\textbf{(iso)} \quad \frac{f : X \to_\sigma TY \qquad \vartheta : Y \simeq Y'}{(T\vartheta)\,f : X \to_{\vartheta\sigma} TY'} \qquad\qquad \textbf{(wkn)} \quad \frac{f : X \to_\sigma TY}{f : X \to_{\sigma\vartheta} TY}$$

$$\textbf{(cmp}^\star\textbf{)} \quad \frac{f : X \to_{\sigma+\mathsf{id}} T(Y+Z) \qquad g : Y \to TV \qquad h : Z \to TV \qquad g\bar\sigma : Y' \to_\vartheta TV}{[g,h]^\star f : X \to_\vartheta TV}$$

Definition 2 (Guarded (pre-)iterative/Elgot monads). A strong monad $\mathbb{T}$ on a distributive category is *guarded pre-iterative* if it is equipped with a guarded iteration operator

$$\frac{f : X \to_2 T(Y+X)}{f^\dagger : X \to TY} \tag{2}$$

satisfying the

– *fixpoint law:* $f^\dagger = [\eta, f^\dagger]^\star f$.

We call a pre-iterative monad $\mathbb{T}$ *guarded Elgot* if it satisfies

– *naturality:* $g^\star f^\dagger = ([[(T\,\mathsf{inl})\,g, \eta\,\mathsf{inr}]^\star f)^\dagger$ for $f : X \to_2 T(Y+X)$, $g : Y \to TZ$;

- *codiagonal:* $(T[\mathsf{id}, \mathsf{inr}] \, f)^\dagger = f^{\dagger\dagger}$ for $f : X \to_{12,2} T((Y + X) + X)$;
- *uniformity:* $f \, h = T(\mathsf{id} + h) \, g$ implies $f^\dagger \, h = g^\dagger$ for $f : X \to_2 T(Y + X)$, $g : Z \to_2 T(Y + Z)$ and $h : Z \to X$;
- *strength:* $\tau \, \langle \mathsf{id}_X, f^\dagger \rangle = (T(\mathsf{id} + \mathsf{pr}_2) \, \delta \, \langle \mathsf{id}_X, f \rangle)^\dagger$ for any $f : X \to_2 T(Y + X)$;

and *guarded iterative* if $f^\dagger$ is a unique solution of the fixpoint law (the remaining axioms then are granted [19]).

The above axioms of iteration are standard (cf. [6]), except *strength* which we need here for the semantics of computations in multivariable contexts.

   The notion of (abstract) guardedness is a common generalization of various special cases occurring in practice. Every monad can be equipped with a least notion of guardedness, called *vacuous guardedness* and defined as follows: $f : X \to_2 T(Y + Z)$ iff f factors through $T \, \mathsf{inl} : Y \to T(Y + Z)$. On the other hand, the greatest notion of guardedness is *total guardedness*, defined by taking $f : X \to_2 T(Y + Z)$ for every $f : X \to T(Y + Z)$. This addresses *total iteration* operators on $\mathbb{T}$, whose existence depends on special properties of $\mathbb{T}$, such as being enriched over complete partial orders. Our motivating examples are mainly those that lie properly between these two extreme situations, e.g. *completely iterative monads* for which guardedness is defined via monad modules and the iteration operator is partial, but uniquely satisfies the fixpoint law [26]. For illustration, we consider several instances of guarded iteration.

Example 3. We fix the category of sets and functions **Set** as an ambient distributive category in the following examples.

1. *(Finitely branching processes)* Let $TX = \nu\gamma. \, \mathcal{P}_\omega(X + \mathsf{Act} \times \gamma)$, the final $\mathcal{P}_\omega(X + \mathsf{Act} \times -)$-coalgebra with $\mathcal{P}_\omega$ being the finite powerset functor. Thus, T is equivalently described as the set of finitely branching nondeterministic trees with edges labelled by elements of Act and with terminal nodes possibly labelled by elements of X (otherwise regarded as nullary nondeterminism, i.e. *deadlock*). Every $f : X \to T(Y + X)$ can be viewed as a family $(f(x) \in T(Y + X))_{x \in X}$ of trees whose terminal nodes are labelled in the disjoint union of X and Y. Each tree $f(x)$ thus can be seen as a recursive process definition for the process name x relative to the names in $X + Y$. The notion of guardedness borrowed from process algebra requires that every $x' \in X$ occurring in $f(x)$ must be preceded by a transition, and if this condition is satisfied, we can calculate a unique *solution* $f^\dagger : X \to TY$ of the system of definitions $(f(x) : T(Y + X))_{x \in X}$. In other words, $\mathbb{T}$ is guarded iterative with $f : X \to_2 T(Y + Z)$ iff

$$\mathsf{out} \, f : X \to \mathcal{P}_\omega((Y + Z) + \mathsf{Act} \times T(Y + Z))$$

   factors through $\mathcal{P}_\omega(\mathsf{inl} + \mathsf{id})$ where $\mathsf{out} : TX \cong \mathcal{P}_\omega(X + \mathsf{Act} \times TX)$ is the canonical final coalgebra isomorphism.

2. *(Countably branching processes)* A variation of the previous example is obtained by replacing finite with countable nondeterminism, i.e. by replacing $\mathcal{P}_\omega$ with the countable powerset functor $\mathcal{P}_{\omega_1}$. Note that in the previous

example we could not extend the iteration operator to a total one, because unguarded systems of recursive process equations may define infinitely branching processes [4]. The monad $TX = \nu\gamma.\,\mathcal{P}_{\omega_1}(X + \mathsf{Act} \times \gamma)$ does however support both partial guarded iteration in the sense of the previous example, and total iteration extending the former. Under total iteration, the fixpoints $f^\dagger$ are no longer unique. This setup is analysed more generally in detail in [17].

3. A very simple example of total guarded iteration is obtained from the (full) powerset monad $T = \mathcal{P}$. The corresponding Klesili category is enriched over complete partial orders and therefore admits total iteration calculated via least fixpoints.

4. *(Complete finite traces)* Let $TX = \mathcal{P}(\mathsf{Act}^\star \times X)$ be the monad obtained from $\mathcal{P}$ by an obvious modification ensuring that the first elements of the pairs from $\mathsf{Act}^\star \times X$, i.e. *finite traces*, are concatenated along Kleisli composition (c.f. [21, Theorem 12]). Like $\mathcal{P}$, this monad is *order-enriched* and thus supports a total iteration operator via least fixpoints (see e.g. [16]). From this, a guarded iteration operator is obtained by restricting to the guarded category with $f : X \to_2 \mathcal{P}(\mathsf{Act}^\star \times (Y + Z))$ iff f factors through the $\mathcal{P}(\mathsf{Act}^\star \times Y + \mathsf{Act}^+ \times Z) \to \mathcal{P}(\mathsf{Act}^\star \times Y + \mathsf{Act}^\star \times Z) \cong \mathcal{P}(\mathsf{Act}^\star \times (Y + Z))$ induced by the inclusion $\mathsf{Act}^+ \hookrightarrow \mathsf{Act}^\star$.

5. Finally, an example of partial guarded iteration can be obtained from Item 3 above by replacing $\mathcal{P}$ with the *non-empty powerset monad* $\mathcal{P}^+$. Total iteration as defined in Item 3 does not restrict to total iteration on $\mathcal{P}^+$, because empty sets can arise from solving systems not involving empty sets, e.g. $\eta \,\mathsf{inr} : 1 \to \mathcal{P}^+(1 + 1)$ would not have a solution in this sense. However, it is easy to see that total iteration does restrict to guarded iteration for $\mathcal{P}$ with the notion of guardedness defined as follows: $f : X \to_2 \mathcal{P}^+(Y + Z)$ iff for every x, $f(x)$ contains at least one element from Y.

For a pre-iterative monad $\mathbb{T}$, we derive a *strong iteration operator*:

$$\frac{f : W \times X \to_2 T(Y + X)}{f^\ddagger = (T(\mathsf{pr}_2 + \mathsf{id})\,\delta\langle \mathsf{pr}_1, f\rangle)^\dagger : W \times X \to TY} \tag{3}$$

which essentially generalizes the original operator $(-)^\dagger$ to morphisms extended with a context via $W \times -$. This will become essential in Sect. 3 for the semantics of our metalanguage.

To clarify the role of (3), we characterize it as iteration in a *simple slice category* $\mathbf{C}[W]$ arising for every fixed $W \in |\mathbf{C}|$ as the co-Kleisli category of the *product comonad* [7] $W \times -$, that is, $|\mathbf{C}[W]| = |\mathbf{C}|$, $\mathsf{Hom}_{\mathbf{C}[W]}(X, Y) = \mathsf{Hom}_{\mathbf{C}}(W \times X, Y)$, identities in $\mathbf{C}[W]$ are projections $\mathsf{pr}_2 : W \times X \to X$, and composition of $g : W \times X \to Y$ with $f : W \times Y \to Z$ is $f\,\langle \mathsf{pr}_1, g\rangle : W \times X \to Z$.

The monad $\mathbb{T}$ being strong means in particular that for every $W \in |\mathbf{C}|$, τ yields a distributive law of the monad $\mathbb{T}$ over the comonad $W \times -$, which extends $\mathbb{T}$ from $\mathbf{C}$ to $\mathbf{C}[W]$ [36]. Moreover, we obtain the following properties.

Theorem 4. *Let $\mathbb{T}$ be a strong monad on a distributive category $\mathbf{C}$, and let $W \in |\mathbf{C}|$. Then the following hold.*

1. $\mathbf{C}[W]$ *is distributive, and* $\mathbb{T}$ *extends to a strong monad over* $\mathbf{C}[W]$;
2. *if* $\mathbb{T}$ *is guarded pre-iterative on* $\mathbf{C}$ *then so is the extension of* $\mathbb{T}$ *to* $\mathbf{C}[W]$ *under the same definition of guardedness and iteration defined by* (3);
3. *if* $\mathbb{T}$ *is guarded Elgot on* $\mathbf{C}$ *then so is the extension of* $\mathbb{T}$ *to* $\mathbf{C}[W]$.

Proof (Sketch). The proof of Clause 1. runs along the following lines. Being a co-Kleisli category, $\mathbf{C}[W]$ inherits finite products from $\mathbf{C}$. Finite coproducts are inherited thanks to $\mathbf{C}$ being distributive; e.g.

$$\mathsf{Hom}_{\mathbf{C}[W]}(X+Y,Z) = \mathsf{Hom}_{\mathbf{C}}(W \times (X+Y),Z) \cong \mathsf{Hom}_{\mathbf{C}}(W \times X + W \times Y, Z)$$
$$\cong \mathsf{Hom}_{\mathbf{C}}(W \times X, Z) \times \mathsf{Hom}_{\mathbf{C}}(W \times Y, Z)$$
$$= \mathsf{Hom}_{\mathbf{C}[W]}(X,Z) \times \mathsf{Hom}_{\mathbf{C}[W]}(Y,Z).$$

Since both products and coproducts in $\mathbf{C}[W]$ are inherited from $\mathbf{C}$, so is distributivity. The unit of the extension of $\mathbb{T}$ to $\mathbf{C}[W]$ is $\eta\, \mathsf{pr}_2 : W \times X \to TX$ where η is the unit of $\mathbb{T}$ in $\mathbf{C}$; similarly, the strength is $\tau\, \mathsf{pr}_2 : W \times (X \times TY) \to T(X \times Y)$ where τ is the strength of $\mathbb{T}$ in $\mathbf{C}$. The Kleisli lifting of $f \in \mathsf{Hom}_{\mathbf{C}[W]}(X, TY)$ is $f^\star \tau$ where $f^\star : T(W \times X) \to TY$ is the Kleisli lifting of $f : W \times X \to TY$ in $\mathbf{C}$. The relevant laws and Clauses 2 and 3 are obtained by routine calculation.   □

3   A Metalanguage for Guarded Iteration

We proceed to define a variant of fine-grain call-by-value [24] following the ideas from [13] on *labelled iteration*. For our purposes we extend the standard setup by allowing a custom signature of operations Σ, but restrict the expressiveness of the language being defined slightly, mainly by excluding function spaces for the moment. The latter require some additional treatment, and we return to this point in Sect. 5.

We fix a supply Base of *base types* and define (composite) *types* A, B by the grammar

$$A, B, \ldots ::= C \mid 0 \mid 1 \mid A + B \mid A \times B \qquad (C \in \mathsf{Base}). \qquad (4)$$

The signature Σ consists of two disjoint parts: a *value signature* Σ_v containing signature symbols of the form $f : A \to B$, and an *effect signature* Σ_c containing signature symbols of the form $f : A \to B[C]$. While the former symbols represent pure functions, the latter capture morphisms of type $A \to_2 T(B+C)$, in particular they carry side-effects from T. The term language over these data is given in Fig. 3. We use a syntax inspired by Haskell's do-notation [22]. The metalanguage features two kinds of judgments:

$$\Gamma \vdash_\mathsf{v} v : A \qquad\qquad \text{and} \qquad\qquad \Delta \mid \Gamma \vdash_\mathsf{c} p : A \qquad (5)$$

for *values* and *computations* correspondingly. These involve two kinds of contexts: Γ denotes the usual context of typed *variables* $x : A$, and Δ denotes the context of typed *exceptions* $e : E^\alpha$ with E being a type from (4) and α being a tag from the two-element set $\{g, u\}$ to distinguish the exceptions raised in a guarded context (g) from those raised in an unguarded context (u) of the program code. Let us denote by $|\Delta|$ the list of pairs $e : E$ obtained from an exception context Δ by removing the g and u tags. Variable and exception names are drawn from the same infinite stock of symbols; they are required to occur non-repetitively in Γ and in Δ separately, but the same symbol may occur in Γ and in Δ at the same time.

Notation 5. As usual, we use the dash (-) to denote a fresh variable in binding expressions, e.g. $\mathsf{do}\text{-} \leftarrow p;\, q$, and use the standard conventions of shortening $\mathsf{do}\text{-} \leftarrow p;\, q$ to $\mathsf{do}\, p;\, q$ and $\mathsf{do}\, x \leftarrow p;\, (\mathsf{do}\, y \leftarrow q;\, r)$ to $\mathsf{do}\, x \leftarrow p;\, y \leftarrow q;\, r$. Moreover, we encode the if-then-else construct $\mathsf{if}\, b\, \mathsf{then}\, p\, \mathsf{else}\, q$ as $\mathsf{case}\, b\, \mathsf{of}\, \mathsf{inl}\text{-} \mapsto p;\, \mathsf{inr}\text{-} \mapsto q$, and also use the notation

$$f(v)\, \&\, \mathsf{raise}_e\, p \qquad \text{for} \qquad \mathsf{gcase}\, f(v)\, \mathsf{of}\, \mathsf{inl}\, x \mapsto \mathsf{init}\, x;\, \mathsf{inr}\text{-} \mapsto \mathsf{raise}_e\, p$$

whenever $f : X \to 0[1] \in \Sigma_c$.

The language constructs relating to products, coproducts, and the monad structure are standard (except maybe init, which forms unique morphisms from the null type 0 into any type A) and should be largely self-explanatory. The key features of our metalanguage, discussed next, concern algebraic operations on the one hand, and exception-based iteration on the other hand.

Algebraic Operations via Generic Effects. The signature symbols $f : A \to B[0]$ from Σ_c have Kleisli morphisms $A \to TB$ as their intended semantics, specifically, if $A = n$ and $B = m$, with n and m being identified with the corresponding n-fold and m-fold coproducts of 1, the respective morphisms $n \to Tm$ dually correspond to *algebraic operations*, i.e. certain natural transformations $T^m \to T^n$, as elaborated by Plotkin and Power [34]. In context of this duality the Kleisli morphisms of type $n \to Tm$ are also called *generic effects*. Hence we regard Σ_c as a stock of generic effects declared to be available to the language. The respective algebraic operations thus become automatically available – for a brief example consider the binary algebraic operation of nondeterministic choice $\oplus : T^2 \to T^1$, which is modeled by a generic effect $\mathsf{toss} : 1 \to T2$ as follows:

$$p \oplus q = \mathsf{do}\, c \leftarrow \mathsf{toss};\, \mathsf{case}\, c\, \mathsf{of}\, \mathsf{inl}\text{-} \mapsto p;\, \mathsf{inr}\text{-} \mapsto q.$$

Exception Raising. Following [13], we involve an exception raising/handling mechanism for organizing loops (we make the connection to exceptions more explicit, in particular, we use the term '*exceptions*' and not '*labels*', as the underlying semantics does indeed accurately match the standard exception semantics). A *guarded exception* $e : E^g$ is raised and recorded in the exception context Δ accordingly by the *guarded case* command

$$\mathsf{gcase}\, f(v)\, \mathsf{of}\, \mathsf{inl}\, x \mapsto p;\, \mathsf{inr}\, y \mapsto \mathsf{raise}_e\, q.$$

The $f(v)$ part acts as a *guard* partitioning the control flow into the left (unguarded) part in which a computation p is executed, and the right (guarded) part, in which the exception e is raised. Also, we allow raising of a standard *unguarded exception* $e : E^u$ with $\mathsf{raise}_e\, q$.

$$\frac{x : A \text{ in } \Gamma}{\Gamma \vdash_v x : A} \qquad \frac{f : A \to B \in \Sigma_v \quad \Gamma \vdash_v v : A}{\Gamma \vdash_v f(v) : B} \qquad \frac{}{\Gamma \vdash_v \star : 1}$$

$$\frac{\Gamma \vdash_v v : A \quad \Gamma \vdash_v w : B}{\Gamma \vdash_v \langle v, w \rangle : A \times B} \qquad \frac{\Gamma \vdash_v v : A}{\Gamma \vdash_v \text{inl}\, v : A + B} \qquad \frac{\Gamma \vdash_v w : B}{\Gamma \vdash_v \text{inr}\, w : A + B}$$

. . . .

$$\frac{e : E^g \text{ in } \Delta \quad f : A \to B[C] \in \Sigma_c \quad \Gamma \vdash_v v : A \quad \Delta \mid \Gamma, x : B \vdash_c p : D \quad \Gamma, y : C \vdash_v q : E}{\Delta \mid \Gamma \vdash_c \text{gcase}\, f(v) \text{ of inl}\, x \mapsto p;\ \text{inr}\, y \mapsto \text{raise}_e\, q : D}$$

$$\frac{f : A \to B[C] \in \Sigma_c \quad \Gamma \vdash_v v : A}{\Delta \mid \Gamma \vdash_c f(v) : B + C} \qquad \frac{\Gamma \vdash_v p : A \times B \quad \Delta \mid \Gamma, x : A, y : B \vdash_c q : C}{\Delta \mid \Gamma \vdash_c \text{case}\, p \text{ of } \langle x, y \rangle \mapsto q : C}$$

$$\frac{\Delta \mid \Gamma \vdash_c p : A \quad \Delta \mid \Gamma, x : A \vdash_c q : B}{\Delta \mid \Gamma \vdash_c \text{do}\, x \leftarrow p;\ q : B} \qquad \frac{\Gamma \vdash_v v : A}{\Delta \mid \Gamma \vdash_c \text{ret}\, v : A}$$

$$\frac{\Gamma \vdash_v t : 0}{\Gamma \vdash_c \text{init}\, t : A} \qquad \frac{\Gamma \vdash_v v : A + B \quad \Delta \mid \Gamma, x : A \vdash_c p : C \quad \Delta \mid \Gamma, y : B \vdash_c q : C}{\Delta \mid \Gamma \vdash_c \text{case}\, v \text{ of inl}\, x \mapsto p;\ \text{inr}\, y \mapsto q : C}$$

$$\frac{\Delta, e : E^g \mid \Gamma \vdash_c p : A \quad \Delta' \mid \Gamma, e : E \vdash_c q : A \quad |\Delta| = |\Delta'|}{\Delta \mid \Gamma \vdash_c \text{handle}\, e \text{ in } p \text{ with } q : A}$$

$$\frac{e : E^u \text{ in } \Delta \quad \Gamma \vdash_v q : E}{\Delta \mid \Gamma \vdash_c \text{raise}_e\, q : D} \qquad \frac{\Gamma \vdash_v p : E \quad \Delta, e : E^g \mid \Gamma, e : E \vdash_c q : A}{\Delta \mid \Gamma \vdash_c \text{handleit}\, e = p \text{ in } q : A}$$

Fig. 3. Term formation rules for values (top) and computations (bottom).

(Iterated) Exception Handling. The syntax for exception handing via handle e in p with q is meant to be understood as follows: p is a program possibly raising the exception e and q is a *handling term* for it. This can be compared to the richer exception handling syntax of Benton and Kennedy [3] whose construct try $x \Leftarrow p$ in q unless $\{e \mapsto r\}_{e \in E}$ we can encode as:

$$\text{do}\, z \leftarrow \text{handle}\, e \text{ in } (\text{do}\, x \leftarrow p;\ \text{ret inl}\, x) \text{ with } (\text{do}\, y \leftarrow r;\ \text{ret inr}\, y);$$
$$\text{case}\, z \text{ of inl}\, x \mapsto q;\ \text{inr}\, y \mapsto \text{ret}\, y$$

where p, q and r come from the judgments

$$\Delta, e : E^g \mid \Gamma \vdash_c p : A, \qquad \Delta \mid \Gamma, x : A \vdash_c q : B, \qquad \Delta \mid \Gamma, e : E \vdash_c r : B,$$

and the idea is to capture the following behavior: unless p raises exception $e : E^g$, the result is bound to x and passed to q (which may itself raise e), and otherwise the exception is handled by r. An analogous encoding is already discussed in [3] where the richer syntax is advocated and motivated by tasks in compiler optimization, but these considerations are not relevant to our present work and so we stick to the minimalist syntax.

```
do l ← length();
handleit m = l in
    case m − 1 of
    inl m' ↦ do (handleit j = 0 in
                    if m' <= j then ret ⋆
                    else do x ← get(j+1); y ← get(j);
                         (if x < y then swap(j, j+1));
                         print("swap at position ", j) & raise_j(j+1));
                print("proceed with ", m') & raise_m(m'));
    inr _ ↦ ret ⋆
```

Fig. 4. Example: bubble sort.

Note that we restrict to handling guarded exceptions only, although a construct for handling unguarded exceptions could be added without a trouble. The side condition $|\Delta| = |\Delta'|$ of the term construction rule for handle ensures that we can raise unguarded expressions in the handling term q and those become guarded in the resulting program. The reason for it is that the exception e being handled occurs in a guarded context thanks to p and so any exception in q becomes inherently guarded in this context.

The idea of the new construct handleit $e = p$ in q is to handle the exception in q recursively using q itself as the handling term, so that if q reraises e, handling continues repetitively. The value p is substituted into q to initialise the iteration.

Example 6. Let us illustrate the constructs introduced in Fig. 3 by the simple example of the familiar *bubble sort* algorithm in Fig. 4.

Here we assume that Base = $\{Nat, Str\}$ consists of natural numbers and character strings correspondingly, Σ_v consists of the obvious operations over natural numbers such as $+ : Nat \times Nat \to Nat$ (addition), $- : Nat \times Nat \to Nat + 1$ (subtraction) and $<= : Nat \times Nat \to 2$ (comparison) where $2 = 1 + 1$, and the effect signature Σ_c consists of $length : 1 \to Nat[0]$, $get : Nat \to Nat[0]$, $swap : Nat \times Nat \to 1[0]$ and $print : Str \times Nat \to 0[1]$. Intuitively, one should think of an underlying array for which $length()$ returns its length, get yields a value by index, and two cells of given indices can be interchanged with $swap$. The operation of printing acts as a loop guard, as follows from its type profile.

4   Generic Denotational Semantics

We proceed to give a denotational semantics of the guarded metalanguage assuming the following:

- a distributive category $\mathbf{C}$ (with initial objects);
- a strong guarded pre-iterative monad $\mathbb{T}$ on $\mathbf{C}$.

Supposing that every base type $A \in \mathsf{Base}$ is interpreted as an object $\underline{A}$ in $|\mathbf{C}|$, we define $\underline{A}$ for types A (see (4)) inductively by

$$\underline{0} = \emptyset, \qquad \underline{1} = 1, \qquad \underline{A+B} = \underline{A} + \underline{B}, \qquad \underline{A \times B} = \underline{A} \times \underline{B}.$$

To every $f : A \to B \in \Sigma_v$ we associate an interpretation $[\![f]\!] \in \mathsf{Hom}(\underline{A}, \underline{B})$ in $\mathbf{C}$ and to every $f : A \to B[C] \in \Sigma_c$ an interpretation $[\![f]\!] \in \mathsf{Hom_{inr}}(\underline{A}, T(\underline{B} + \underline{C}))$. Based on these we define the semantics of the term language from Fig. 3. The semantics of a value judgment $\Gamma \vdash_v p : A$ is a morphism $[\![\Gamma \vdash_v p : A]\!] \in \mathsf{Hom}(\underline{\Gamma}, \underline{A})$, and the semantics of a computation judgment $\Delta \mid \Gamma \vdash_c p : A$ is a morphism $[\![\Delta \mid \Gamma \vdash_c p : A]\!] \in \mathsf{Hom}_{!+\sigma_\Delta}(\underline{\Gamma}, T(\underline{A} + \underline{\Delta}))$ where

$$\underline{\Gamma} = \underline{A_1} \times \ldots \times \underline{A_n} \qquad \text{for } \Gamma = (x_1 : A_1, \ldots, x_n : A_n)$$
$$\underline{\Delta} = \underline{E_1} + \ldots + \underline{E_m} \qquad \text{for } \Delta = (e_1 : E_1^{\alpha_1}, \ldots, e_m : E_m^{\alpha_m})$$

and $\sigma_\Delta : \underline{\Delta'} \hookrightarrow \underline{\Delta}$ is the summand induced by removal of unguarded exceptions $e : E^u$ from Δ with Δ' denoting the result.

The semantic assignments for computation judgments are given in Fig. 5 (we skip the obvious standard rules for values) where $\mathsf{in}_e : \underline{E} \to \underline{\Delta}$ is the obvious coproduct injection of $\underline{E}$ to $\underline{\Delta}$ identified by e, assoc is the associativity isomorphism $X + (Y + Z) \cong (X + Y) + Z$, and $(-)^\ddagger$ is the strong iteration operator from (3).

The correctness of our semantic assignments is established by the following claim:

Proposition 7. *For every rule in Fig. 3, assuming the premises, the morphism in the conclusion is $(! + \sigma_\Delta)$-guarded.*

Proof. For **(fun)**, **(prod)**, **(ret)**, **(case)** and **(init)**, the verification is straightforward by the axioms of guardedness in $\mathbf{C}$. For **(gcase)** and **(do)**, we proceed analogously using the axioms of guardedness in $\mathbf{C}[\Gamma]$ and Theorem 4. Strong iteration as figuring in **(iter)** is, by Theorem 4, the standard guarded iteration in $\mathbf{C}[\Gamma]$, and the problem in question amounts to verifying that $f^\dagger : X \to_\sigma TY$ whenever $f : X \to_{\sigma + \mathsf{id}} T(Y + X)$. This is already shown in [19].

Consider the remaining rule **(handle)** in detail. By regarding g and h as morphisms in $\mathbf{C}[\Gamma]$, we reformulate the claim as follows: assuming $g : 1 \to_{! + (\sigma_\Delta + \mathsf{id})} T(\underline{A} + (\underline{\Delta} + \underline{E}))$ and $h : \underline{E} \to T(\underline{A} + \underline{\Delta})$, show that $[\eta, h]^\star (T \, \mathsf{assoc}) \, g : 1 \to_{! + \sigma_\Delta} T(\underline{A} + \underline{\Delta})$. Noting that $(T \, \mathsf{assoc}) \, g : 1 \to_{(! + \sigma_\Delta) + \mathsf{id}} T((\underline{A} + \underline{\Delta}) + \underline{E})$, we obtain the goal by using **(cmp*)** from Proposition 1. $\qquad\square$

5   Functional Types

In order to interpret functional types in fine-grain call-by-value, it normally suffices to assume existence of *Kleisli exponentials*, i.e. objects TB^A such that $\mathsf{Hom}(C, TB^A)$ and $\mathsf{Hom}(C \times A, TB)$ are naturaly isomorphic, or equivalently that all the *presheaves* $\mathsf{Hom}(- \times A, TB) : \mathbf{C}^{op} \to \mathbf{Set}$ are representable. In order

$$[\![\Gamma \vdash_v v : A]\!] = h : \underline{\Gamma} \to \underline{A}$$

(gcase)

$$[\![f : A \to B[C]]\!] = g : \underline{A} \to_2 T(\underline{B} + \underline{C})$$
$$[\![\Delta \mid \Gamma, x : B \vdash_c p : D]\!] = u : \underline{\Gamma} \times \underline{B} \to_{!+\sigma_\Delta} T(\underline{D} + \underline{\Delta})$$
$$[\![\Gamma, y : C \vdash_v q : E]\!] = w : \underline{\Gamma} \times \underline{C} \to \underline{E}$$

$$\overline{[\![\Delta \mid \Gamma \vdash_c \mathsf{gcase}\, f(v) \text{ of } \mathsf{inl}\, x \mapsto p;\ \mathsf{inr}\, y \mapsto \mathsf{raise}_e\, q : D]\!] =}$$
$$\underline{\Gamma} \xrightarrow{\delta\langle \mathsf{id},\, gh\rangle} T(\underline{\Gamma} \times \underline{B} + \underline{\Gamma} \times \underline{C}) \xrightarrow{[u,\eta\, \mathsf{in}_2\, \mathsf{in}_e\, w]^\star} T(\underline{D} + \underline{\Delta})$$

(fun)

$$\frac{[\![f : A \to B[C]]\!] = g : \underline{A} \to_2 T(\underline{B} + \underline{C}) \qquad [\![\Gamma \vdash_v t : A]\!] = h : \underline{\Gamma} \to \underline{A}}{[\![\Delta \mid \Gamma \vdash_c f(t) : B + C]\!] = (T\,\mathsf{in}_1)\, g\, h : \underline{\Gamma} \to T((\underline{B} + \underline{C}) + \underline{\Delta})}$$

(prod)

$$[\![\Gamma \vdash_v p : A \times B]\!] = g : \underline{\Gamma} \to \underline{A} \times \underline{B}$$
$$[\![\Delta \mid \Gamma, x : A, y : B \vdash_c q : C]\!] = h : \underline{\Gamma} \times \underline{A} \times \underline{B} \to_{!+\sigma_\Delta} T(\underline{C} + \underline{\Delta})$$

$$\overline{[\![\Delta \mid \Gamma \vdash_c \mathsf{case}\, p \text{ of } \langle x, y\rangle \mapsto q : C]\!] = h\langle \mathsf{id}_{\underline{\Gamma}}, g\rangle : \underline{\Gamma} \to T(\underline{C} + \underline{\Delta})}$$

(ret)

$$\frac{[\![\Gamma \vdash_v t : A]\!] = g : \underline{\Gamma} \to \underline{A}}{[\![\Delta \mid \Gamma \vdash_c \mathsf{ret}\, t : A]\!] = \eta\, \mathsf{in}_1\, g : \underline{\Gamma} \to T(\underline{A} + \underline{\Delta})}$$

(do)

$$[\![\Delta \mid \Gamma \vdash_c p : A]\!] = g : \underline{\Gamma} \to_{!+\sigma_\Delta} T(\underline{A} + \underline{\Delta})$$
$$[\![\Delta \mid \Gamma, x : A \vdash_c q : B]\!] = h : \underline{\Gamma} \times \underline{A} \to_{!+\sigma_\Delta} T(\underline{B} + \underline{\Delta})$$

$$\overline{[\![\Delta \mid \Gamma \vdash_c \mathsf{do}\, x \leftarrow p;\ q]\!] = [h, \eta\, \mathsf{in}_2\, \mathsf{pr}_2]^\star\, \delta\langle \mathsf{id}_{\underline{\Gamma}}, g\rangle : \underline{\Gamma} \to T(\underline{B} + \underline{\Delta})}$$

(init)

$$\frac{[\![\Gamma \vdash_v t : 0]\!] = g : \underline{\Gamma} \to \emptyset}{[\![\Delta \mid \Gamma \vdash_c \mathsf{init}\, t : A]\!] = !\, g : \underline{\Gamma} \to T(\underline{A} + \underline{\Delta})}$$

(case)

$$[\![\Gamma \vdash_v p : A + B]\!] = g : \underline{\Gamma} \to \underline{A} + \underline{B}$$
$$[\![\Delta \mid \Gamma, x : A \vdash_c q : C]\!] = h : \underline{\Gamma} \times \underline{A} \to_{!+\sigma_\Delta} T(\underline{C} + \underline{\Delta})$$
$$[\![\Delta \mid \Gamma, y : B \vdash_c r : C]\!] = u : \underline{\Gamma} \times \underline{B} \to_{!+\sigma_\Delta} T(\underline{C} + \underline{\Delta})$$

$$\overline{[\![\Delta \mid \Gamma \vdash_c \mathsf{case}\, p \text{ of } \mathsf{inl}\, x \mapsto q;\ \mathsf{inr}\, y \mapsto r : C]\!] =}$$
$$[h, u]\, \mathsf{dist}\langle \mathsf{id}_{\underline{\Gamma}}, g\rangle : \underline{\Gamma} \to T(\underline{C} + \underline{\Delta})$$

(raise)

$$\frac{[\![\Delta \mid \Gamma \vdash_v q : E]\!] = g : \underline{\Gamma} \to \underline{E}}{[\![\Delta \mid \Gamma \vdash_c \mathsf{raise}_e\, q : D]\!] = \eta\, \mathsf{in}_2\, \mathsf{in}_e\, g : \underline{\Gamma} \to T(\underline{D} + \underline{\Delta})}$$

(handle)

$$[\![\Delta, e : E^g \mid \Gamma \vdash_c p : A]\!] = g : \underline{\Gamma} \to_{!+(\sigma_\Delta + \mathsf{id})} T(\underline{A} + (\underline{\Delta} + \underline{E}))$$
$$[\![\Delta' \mid \Gamma, e : E \vdash_c q : A]\!] = h : \underline{\Gamma} \times \underline{E} \to T(\underline{A} + \underline{\Delta})$$

$$\overline{[\![\Delta \mid \Gamma \vdash_c \mathsf{handle}\, e \text{ in } p \text{ with } q : A]\!] =}$$
$$\underline{\Gamma} \xrightarrow{\delta\langle \mathsf{id}_{\underline{\Gamma}},\, (T\, \mathsf{assoc})\, g\rangle} T(\underline{\Gamma} \times (\underline{A} + \underline{\Delta}) + \underline{\Gamma} \times \underline{E}) \xrightarrow{[\eta\, \mathsf{pr}_2, h]^\star} T(\underline{A} + \underline{\Delta})$$

(iter)

$$[\![\Gamma \vdash_v p : E]\!] = g : \underline{\Gamma} \to \underline{E}$$
$$\frac{[\![\Delta, e : E^g \mid \Gamma, e : E \vdash_c q : A]\!] = h : \underline{\Gamma} \times \underline{E} \to_{!+(\sigma_\Delta + \mathsf{id})} T(\underline{A} + (\underline{\Delta} + \underline{E}))}{[\![\Delta \mid \Gamma \vdash_c \mathsf{handleit}\, e = p \text{ in } q : A]\!] = ((T\, \mathsf{assoc})\, h)^\ddagger \langle \mathsf{id}_{\underline{\Gamma}}, g\rangle : \underline{\Gamma} \to T(\underline{A} + \underline{\Delta})}$$

Fig. 5. Denotational semantics.

to add functional types to our metalanguage we additionally need to assume that all the presheaves $\mathsf{Hom}_\sigma(-, TA) : \mathbf{C}^{op} \to \mathbf{Set}$ are representable, i.e. for every A and $\sigma : A' \hookrightarrow A$ there is $A_\sigma \in |\mathbf{C}|$ such that

$$\xi : \mathsf{Hom}(X, A_\sigma) \cong \mathsf{Hom}_\sigma(X, TA) \tag{6}$$

naturally in X. By Yoneda lemma, this requirement is equivalent to the following.

Definition 8 (Greatest σ-algebra). Given $\sigma : A' \hookrightarrow A$, a pair (A_σ, ι_σ) consisting of an object $A_\sigma \in |\mathbf{C}|$ and a morphism $\iota_\sigma : A_\sigma \to_\sigma TA$ is called a *greatest σ-algebra* if for every $f : X \to_\sigma TA$ there is a unique $\hat{f} : X \to A_\sigma$ with the property that $f = \iota_\sigma \hat{f}$.

By the usual arguments, (A_σ, ι_σ) is defined uniquely up to isomorphism. The connection between ι_σ and ξ in (6) is as follows: $\iota_\sigma = \xi(\mathsf{id} : A_\sigma \to A_\sigma)$ and $\xi(f : X \to A_\sigma) = \iota_\sigma f$.

It immediately follows by definition that ι_σ is a monomorphism. The name 'σ-algebra' for (A, ι_σ) is justified as follows.

Proposition 9. *Suppose that (A, ι_σ) is a greatest σ-algebra. Then there is a unique $\alpha_\sigma : TA_\sigma \to A_\sigma$ such that $\iota_\sigma \alpha_\sigma = \iota_\sigma^\star$. The pair $(A_\sigma, \alpha_\sigma)$ is a $\mathbb{T}$-subalgebra of (TA, μ).*

Proof. Since $\iota_\sigma^\star : TA_\sigma \to TA$ is the Kleisli composite of $\iota_\sigma : A_\sigma \to_\sigma TA$ and $\mathsf{id} : TA_\sigma \to TA_\sigma$, $\iota_\sigma^\star$ is σ-guarded by **(cmp)**, so we obtain α_σ such that $\iota_\sigma \alpha_\sigma = \iota_\sigma^\star$ by the universal property of (A_σ, ι_σ). Since $\iota_\sigma^\star = \mu_A T \iota_\sigma$, it follows that $\iota_\sigma : (A_\sigma, \alpha_\sigma) \to (A, \mu_A)$ is a morphism of functor algebras. Since monad algebras are closed under taking functor subalgebras and ι_σ is monic as observed above, it follows that $(A_\sigma, \alpha_\sigma)$ is a $\mathbb{T}$-subalgebra of (A, μ_A). $\square$

Proposition 10. *1. Suppose that a greatest σ-algebra (A_σ, ι_σ) exists. Then*
(a) ι_σ is the greatest element in the class of all σ-guarded subobjects of TA;
(b) for every regular epic $e : X \to Y$ and every morphism $f : Y \to TA$, $fe : X \to_\sigma TA$ implies that $f : Y \to_\sigma TA$.
2. Assuming that every morphism in $\mathbf{C}$ admits a factorization into a regular epic and a monic, the converse of (1) is true: If (a) and (b) hold for (A_σ, ι_σ), then (A_σ, ι_σ) is a greatest σ-algebra.

Proof. 1.: Part 1a is immediate; we show 1b. Given a regular epic $e : X \to Y$ and a morphism $f : Y \to TA$ such that $fe : X \to_\sigma TA$, consider the diagram

$$Z \underset{g}{\overset{h}{\rightrightarrows}} X \xrightarrow{e} Y \xrightarrow{f} TA$$

where e is the coequalizer of h and g, and w exists uniquely by the universal property of ι_σ. Since $\iota_\sigma w h = f e h = f e g = \iota_\sigma w g$ and ι_σ is monic, $w h = w g$.

Hence, there is $u : Y \to A_\sigma$ such that $w = u\,e$. Therefore we have $\iota_\sigma\,u\,e = \iota_\sigma\,w = f\,e$. Since e is epi, this implies $f = \iota_\sigma\,u$. Since ι_σ is σ-guarded, so is f by **(cmp)**.

2.: Let $f : X \to_\sigma TA$, with factorization $f = m\,e$ into a mono m and a regular epi e. By 1b, m is σ-guarded; by 1a, it follows that m, and hence f, factor through ι_σ, necessarily uniquely since ι_σ is monic. □

Example 11. Let $\mathbb{T}$ be a strong monad on a distributive category $\mathbf{C}$ and let $\Sigma : \mathbf{C} \to \mathbf{C}$ be an endofunctor such that all the fixpoints $T_\Sigma X = \nu\gamma.\,T(X + \Sigma\gamma)$ exist. These extend to a strong monad $\mathbb{T}_\Sigma$, called the *generalized coalgebraic resumption monad transform* of $\mathbb{T}$ [19]. Moreover, $\mathbb{T}_\Sigma$ is guarded iterative with $f : X \to_\sigma T_\Sigma A$ iff $\mathrm{out}\,f : X \to T(A + \Sigma T_\Sigma A)$ factors as $T(\bar\sigma + \mathrm{id})\,g$ for some $g : X \to T(A' + \Sigma T_\Sigma A)$. Suppose that coproduct injections in $\mathbf{C}$ are monic and T preserves monics. Then for every $A \in |\mathbf{C}|$ and σ there is at most one g such that $\mathrm{out}\,f = T(\bar\sigma + \mathrm{id})\,g$. This entails an isomorphism

$$\mathsf{Hom}(X, T(A' + \Sigma T_\Sigma A)) \cong \mathsf{Hom}_\sigma(X, T_\Sigma A)$$

obviously natural in X, from which we obtain by comparison with (6) that $A_\sigma = T(A' + \Sigma T_\Sigma A)$.

Example 12. Let $\sigma : A'' \hookrightarrow A$, whose complement is $\bar\sigma : A' \hookrightarrow A$ and let us revisit Example 3.

1. $T = \nu\gamma.\,\mathcal{P}_\omega(- + \mathsf{Act} \times \gamma)$ is an instance of Example 11, and thus $A_\sigma = \mathcal{P}_\omega(A' + \mathsf{Act} \times TA)$.
2. For $T = \nu\gamma.\,\mathcal{P}_{\omega_1}(- + \mathsf{Act} \times \gamma)$ under total guardedness, $A_\sigma = TA$ independently of σ. For the other notion of guardedness on $\mathbb{T}$, A_σ is constructed in analogy to Item 1.
3. For $T = \mathcal{P}$ being totally guarded, again $A_\sigma = \mathcal{P}A$.
4. For $T = \mathcal{P}(\mathsf{Act}^\star \times -)$, it follows that $A_\sigma = \mathcal{P}(\mathsf{Act}^\star \times A' + \mathsf{Act}^+ \times A'')$.
5. Finally, for $T = \mathcal{P}^+$, it follows by definition that $A_\sigma = \mathcal{P}(A') \times \mathcal{P}^+(A'')$.

Assuming that greatest σ-algebras exist, we complement our metalanguage with functional types $A \to_\Delta B$ where the index Δ serves to store information about (guarded) exceptions of the curried function. Formally, these types are interpreted as $\underline{A \to_\Delta B} = \underline{A} \to (\underline{B} + \underline{\Delta})_{!+\sigma_\Delta}$. In the term language, this is reflected by the introduction of λ-abstraction and application, with syntax and semantics as shown in Fig. 6, where ξ is the isomorphism from (6).

6 Operational Semantics and Adequacy

We proceed to complement our denotational semantics from Sects. 4 and 5 with a big-step operational semantics. Following Geron and Levy [13], we choose the simplest concrete monad $\mathbb{T}$ sensibly illustrating all the main features and model it operationally. In [13] this is the *maybe monad* $TX = X + 1$ on **Set**, which suffices to give a sensible account of total iteration. The $+1$ part is necessary for modeling divergence. Since total iteration is still a guarded iteration, we could

$$\frac{\Delta \mid \Gamma, x : A \vdash_{\mathsf{c}} p : B}{\Gamma \vdash_{\mathsf{v}} \lambda x. p : A \to_\Delta B} \qquad \frac{\Gamma \vdash_{\mathsf{v}} w : A \qquad \Gamma \vdash_{\mathsf{v}} v : A \to_\Delta B}{\Delta \mid \Gamma \vdash_{\mathsf{c}} vw : B}$$

. . . .

$$\frac{[\![\Delta \mid \Gamma, x : A \vdash_{\mathsf{c}} p : B]\!] = g : \underline{\Gamma} \times \underline{A} \to_{!+\sigma_\Delta} T(\underline{B} + \underline{\Delta})}{[\![\Gamma \vdash_{\mathsf{v}} \lambda x. p : A \to_\Delta C]\!] = \mathsf{curry}(\xi^{-1}(g)) : \underline{\Gamma} \to \underline{A} \to (\underline{B} + \underline{\Delta})_{!+\sigma_\Delta}}$$

$$\frac{[\![\Gamma \vdash_{\mathsf{v}} w : A]\!] = g : \underline{\Gamma} \to \underline{A} \qquad [\![\Gamma \vdash_{\mathsf{v}} v : A \to_\Delta B]\!] = h : \underline{\Gamma} \to \underline{A} \to (\underline{B} + \underline{\Delta})_{!+\sigma_\Delta}}{[\![\Delta \mid \Gamma \vdash_{\mathsf{c}} vw : B]\!] = \xi(\mathsf{uncurry}(h)) \langle \mathsf{id}, g \rangle : \Gamma \to_{!+\sigma_\Delta} T(\underline{B} + \underline{\Delta})}$$

Fig. 6. Syntax (top) and semantics (bottom) of functional types.

formulate an adequate operational semantics over this monad too. To that end we would need to assume that the only operation $f : A \to B[C]$ in Σ_c with $C \neq 0$ is some distinguished element $tick : 1 \to 0[1]$ whose denotation is the unit of the monad (regarded as totally guarded). However, total iteration is only a degenerate instance of guarded iteration, and therefore, here we replace $X + 1$ with the guarded pre-iterative monad freely generated by an operation $put : \mathbf{N} \to 0[1]$ of outputting a natural number (say, to console), explicitly (on **Set**): $TX = (X \times \mathbf{N}^\star) \cup \mathbf{N}^\omega$. More abstractly, TX is the final $(X + \mathbf{N} \times -)$-coalgebra. The denotations in TX are of two types: pairs $(x, \tau) \in X \times \mathbf{N}^\star$ of a value x and a *finite trace* τ of outputs (for terminating iteration) and *infinite traces* $\pi \in \mathbf{N}^\omega$ of outputs (for non-terminating iteration).

We fix $TX = (X \times \mathbf{N}^\star) \cup \mathbf{N}^\omega$ for the rest of the section. Let us spell out the details of the structure of $\mathbb{T}$, which is in fact an instance of Example 11 under $T = \Sigma = \mathsf{Id}$. The unit of $\mathbb{T}$ sends x to $(x, \langle \rangle)$. Given $f : X \to TY$, we have

$$f^\star(x, \tau) = \begin{cases} (y, \tau + \!\!+ \tau') & \text{if } f(x) = (y, \tau'), \\ \tau + \!\!+ \pi & \text{if } f(x) = \pi, \end{cases} \qquad f^\star(\pi) = \pi.$$

for $x \in X$, $\tau \in \mathbf{N}^\star$, $\pi \in \mathbf{N}^\omega$ with $+\!\!+$ denoting concatenation of a finite trace with a possibly infinite one. Guardedness for $\mathbb{T}$ is defined as follows: $f : X \to_2 (Y + Z) \times \mathbf{N}^\star \cup \mathbf{N}^\omega$ if for every $x \in X$, either $f(x) \in \mathbf{N}^\omega$ or $f(x) = (\mathsf{in}_1 \, y, \tau)$ for some $y \in Y$, $\tau \in \mathbf{N}^\star$ or $f(x) = (\mathsf{in}_2 \, z, \tau)$ for some $z \in Z$, $\tau \in \mathbf{N}^+$. Finally, given $f : X \to_2 T(Y + X)$,

$$f^\dagger(x) = \begin{cases} (y, \tau_1 + \!\!+ \cdots + \!\!+ \tau_n) & \text{if } f(x) = (\mathsf{in}_2 \, x_1, \tau_1), \ldots, f(x_n) = (\mathsf{in}_1 \, y, \tau_n), \\ \tau_1 + \!\!+ \cdots + \!\!+ \tau_{n-1} + \!\!+ \pi & \text{if } f(x) = (\mathsf{in}_2 \, x_1, \tau_1), \ldots, f(x_n) = \pi, \\ \tau_1 + \!\!+ \cdots & \text{if } f(x) = (\mathsf{in}_2 \, x_1, \tau_1), \ldots \end{cases}$$

where the first clause addresses the situation when iteration finishes after finitely many steps, the second one addresses the situation when we hit divergence witnessed by some $x_n \in X$ reachable after finitely many iterations, and the third clause addresses the remaining situation of divergence via unfolding the loop at hand infinitely often. In the latter case, the guardedness assumption for f is

Values, Computations, Terminals:

$$v, w ::= x \mid \star \mid zero \mid succ\, v \mid \mathsf{inl}\, v \mid \mathsf{inr}\, v \mid \langle v, w \rangle \mid \lambda x.\, p$$

$$p, q ::= \mathsf{ret}\, v \mid pred(v) \mid put(v) \mid \mathsf{raise}_x\, v \mid \mathsf{gcase}\, put(v)\, \mathsf{of}\, \mathsf{inl} - \mapsto p;\, \mathsf{inr}\, x \mapsto \mathsf{raise}_y\, w$$
$$\mid \mathsf{case}\, v\, \mathsf{of}\, \langle x, y \rangle \mapsto p \mid init(v) \mid \mathsf{case}\, v\, \mathsf{of}\, \mathsf{inl}\, x \mapsto p;\, \mathsf{inr}\, y \mapsto q$$
$$\mid vw \mid \mathsf{do}\, x \leftarrow p;\, q \mid \mathsf{handle}\, x\, \mathsf{in}\, p\, \mathsf{with}\, q \mid \mathsf{handleit}\, y = v\, \mathsf{in}\, p$$

$$t ::= \mathsf{ret}\, v, \tau \mid \mathsf{raise}_x\, v, \tau \mid \pi \qquad (\tau \in \mathbf{N}^*, \pi \in \mathbf{N}^\omega)$$

Rules:

$$\overline{\mathsf{raise}_x\, v \Downarrow \mathsf{raise}_x\, v} \qquad \overline{\mathsf{gcase}\, put(v)\, \mathsf{of}\, \mathsf{inl} - \mapsto p;\, \mathsf{inr}\, x \mapsto \mathsf{raise}_y\, w \Downarrow \mathsf{raise}_y\, w[\star/x], \langle v \rangle}$$

$$\overline{put(v) \Downarrow \mathsf{ret}\, \star, \langle v \rangle} \qquad \overline{pred(zero) \Downarrow \mathsf{ret}\, \mathsf{in}_1\, \star, \langle \rangle} \qquad \overline{pred(succ(v)) \Downarrow \mathsf{ret}\, \mathsf{in}_2\, v, \langle \rangle}$$

$$\frac{p[v/x] \Downarrow t}{\mathsf{case}\, \mathsf{inl}\, v\, \mathsf{of}\, \mathsf{inl}\, x \mapsto p;\, \mathsf{inr}\, y \mapsto q \Downarrow t} \qquad \frac{q[w/y] \Downarrow t}{\mathsf{case}\, \mathsf{inr}\, w\, \mathsf{of}\, \mathsf{inl}\, x \mapsto p;\, \mathsf{inr}\, y \mapsto q \Downarrow t}$$

$$\frac{p \Downarrow \mathsf{ret}\, v, \tau \quad q[v/x] \Downarrow t, \tau'}{\mathsf{do}\, x \leftarrow p;\, q \Downarrow t, \tau + \!\!+ \, \tau'} \qquad \frac{p \Downarrow \mathsf{ret}\, v, \tau \quad q[v/x] \Downarrow \pi}{\mathsf{do}\, x \leftarrow p;\, q \Downarrow \tau + \!\!+ \, \pi} \qquad \frac{p \Downarrow \mathsf{raise}_x\, v, \tau}{\mathsf{do}\, x \leftarrow p;\, q \Downarrow \mathsf{raise}_x\, v, \tau}$$

$$\frac{p \Downarrow \pi}{\mathsf{do}\, x \leftarrow p;\, q \Downarrow \pi} \qquad \frac{p \Downarrow \mathsf{raise}_y\, v, \tau}{\mathsf{handle}\, x\, \mathsf{in}\, p\, \mathsf{with}\, q \Downarrow \mathsf{raise}_y\, v, \tau} \qquad \frac{p \Downarrow \mathsf{raise}_x\, v, \tau \quad q[v/x] \Downarrow t, \tau'}{\mathsf{handle}\, x\, \mathsf{in}\, p\, \mathsf{with}\, q \Downarrow t, \tau + \!\!+ \, \tau'}$$

$$\frac{p \Downarrow \pi}{\mathsf{handle}\, x\, \mathsf{in}\, p\, \mathsf{with}\, q \Downarrow \pi} \qquad \frac{p \Downarrow \mathsf{raise}_x\, v, \tau \quad q[v/x] \Downarrow \pi}{\mathsf{handle}\, x\, \mathsf{in}\, p\, \mathsf{with}\, q \Downarrow \tau + \!\!+ \, \pi} \qquad \frac{p \Downarrow \mathsf{ret}\, v, \tau}{\mathsf{handle}\, x\, \mathsf{in}\, p\, \mathsf{with}\, q \Downarrow \mathsf{ret}\, v, \tau}$$

$$\frac{}{\mathsf{ret}\, v \Downarrow \mathsf{ret}\, v, \langle \rangle} \qquad \frac{v_0 = v \quad q[v_0/x] \Downarrow \mathsf{raise}_x\, v_1, \tau_1 \quad \cdots \quad q[v_{n-1}/x] \Downarrow t, \tau_n}{\mathsf{handleit}\, x = v\, \mathsf{in}\, q \Downarrow t, \tau_1 + \!\!+ \cdots + \!\!+ \, \tau_n}$$

$$\frac{q[v/x, w/y] \Downarrow t}{\mathsf{case}\, \langle v, w \rangle\, \mathsf{of}\, \langle x, y \rangle \mapsto q \Downarrow t} \qquad \frac{v_0 = v \quad q[v_0/x] \Downarrow \mathsf{raise}_x\, v_1, \tau_1 \quad \cdots \quad q[v_{n-1}/x] \Downarrow \pi}{\mathsf{handleit}\, x = p\, \mathsf{in}\, q \Downarrow \tau_1 + \!\!+ \cdots + \!\!+ \, \tau_{n-1} + \!\!+ \, \pi}$$

$$\frac{p[v/x] \Downarrow t}{(\lambda x.\, p)v \Downarrow t} \qquad \frac{v_0 = v \quad q[v_0/x] \Downarrow \mathsf{raise}_x\, v_1, \tau_1 \quad q[v_1/x] \Downarrow \mathsf{raise}_x\, v_2, \tau_2 \quad \cdots}{\mathsf{handleit}\, x = p\, \mathsf{in}\, q \Downarrow \tau_1 + \!\!+ \, \tau_2 + \!\!+ \cdots}$$

Fig. 7. Operational semantics

crucial, as it ensures that each τ_i is nonempty, and therefore the resulting trace $\tau_1 + \!\!+ \, \tau_2 + \!\!+ \cdots$ is indeed infinite.

Operationally, guardedness in the above sense is modeled by cutting the control flow with the *put* command, which is the only one contributing to the traces. Concretely, let Base $= \{\mathbf{N}\}$, $\Sigma_v = \{zero : 1 \to \mathbf{N}, succ : \mathbf{N} \to \mathbf{N}\}$ and $\Sigma_c = \{pred : \mathbf{N} \to (1 + \mathbf{N})[0], put : \mathbf{N} \to 0[1]\}$. Operational semantics over these data is given in Fig. 7. Note that the bottom rule for handleit relies on the fact that each τ_i is nonempty, which can be easily established by induction.

Now we can state the main result of this section as follows.

Theorem 13 (Adequacy). *Let* $\Delta \mid - \vdash_c p : B$. *Then,*

1. *If* $p \Downarrow \text{ret}\, v, \tau$ *then* $[\![\Delta \mid - \vdash_c p : B]\!] = (\text{in}_1 v, \tau) \in (B + \Delta) \times \mathbf{N}^\star$.
2. *If* $p \Downarrow \text{raise}_x v, \tau$ *and* $x : E^g$ *is in* Δ *then* $[\![\Delta \mid - \vdash_c p : B]\!] = (\text{in}_2 \text{in}_x v, \tau) \in (B + \Delta) \times \mathbf{N}^+$.
3. *If* $p \Downarrow \text{raise}_x v, \tau$ *and* $x : E^u$ *is in* Δ *then* $[\![\Delta \mid - \vdash_c p : B]\!] = (\text{in}_2 \text{in}_x v, \tau) \in (B + \Delta) \times \mathbf{N}^\star$.
4. *If* $p \Downarrow \pi$, *then* $[\![\Delta \mid - \vdash_c p : B]\!] = \pi \in \mathbf{N}^\omega$.

Proof (Idea). The proof runs analogously to [13] by showing a stronger type-indexed property used as an induction invariant in the style of Tait [35]. $\quad\square$

7   Conclusions and Further Work

We have instantiated the notion of abstract guardedness [18,19] to a multi-variable setting in the form of a metalanguage for guarded iteration, keeping in touch with the seminal ideas of Moggi [28] and the fine-grain call-by-value perspective [24]. As a side product, this additionally resulted in a semantically justified unification of (guarded) iteration and exception handling, extending previous work by Geron and Levy [13].

In future work, we aim to investigate further applications of our unifying machinery, on the one hand for devising denotational (e.g. final coalgebra based) models for existing operational models, and on the other hand for developing operational accounts of phenomena whose denotational models can be taken as input. One prospective example is suggested by work of Nakata and Uustalu [33], who give a coinductive big-step trace semantics for a while-language. We conjecture that this work has an implicit guarded iterative monad $\mathbb{T}_\mathbb{R}$ under the hood, for which guardedness cannot be defined using the standard argument based on a final coalgebra structure of the monad because $\mathbb{T}_\mathbb{R}$ is not a final coalgebra. The relevant notion of guardedness is thus to be identified. Moreover, we will explore the relation of our work to call-by-push-value languages, using in particular a suitable notion of guardedness in Eilenberg-Moore algebras.

References

1. Abramsky, S.: Intensionality, definability and computation. In: Baltag, A., Smets, S. (eds.) Johan van Benthem on Logic and Information Dynamics, pp. 121–142. Springer, Cham (2014). https://doi.org/10.1007/978-3-319-06025-5_5
2. Appel, A.W., Melliès, P.A., Richards, C.D., Vouillon, J.: A very modal model of a modern, major, general type system. In: Proceedings of 34th Annual ACM SIGPLAN-SIGACT Symposium on Principles of Programming Languages. POPL 2007, January 2007, Nice, pp. 109–122. ACM Press, New York (2007). https://doi.org/10.1145/1190216.1190235
3. Benton, N., Kennedy, A.: Exceptional syntax. J. Funct. Program. **11**(4), 395–410 (2001). https://doi.org/10.1017/s0956796801004099
4. Bergstra, J., Ponse, A., Smolka, S. (eds.): Handbook of Process Algebra. Elsevier, New York City (2001). https://doi.org/10.1016/b978-0-444-82830-9.x5017-6

5. Birkedal, L., Møgelberg, R., Schwinghammer, J., Støvring, K.: First steps in synthetic guarded domain theory: step-indexing in the topos of trees. Log. Methods Comput. Sci. **8**(4), 1 (2012). https://doi.org/10.2168/lmcs-8(4:1)2012
6. Bloom, S., Ésik, Z.: Iteration Theories: The Equational Logic of Iterative Processes. EATCS Monographs on Theoretical Computer Science. Springer, Heidelberg (1993). https://doi.org/10.1007/978-3-642-78034-9
7. Brookes, S., Van Stone, K.: Monads and comonads in intensional semantics. Technical report CMU-CS-93-140, Department of Computer Science, Carnegie-Mellon University, Pittsburgh, PA (1993)
8. Carboni, A., Lack, S., Walters, R.: Introduction to extensive and distributive categories. J. Pure. Appl. Algebra **84**, 145–158 (1993). https://doi.org/10.1016/0022-4049(93)90035-r
9. Clouston, R., Bizjak, A., Grathwohl, H.B., Birkedal, L.: The guarded lambda-calculus: programming and reasoning with guarded recursion for coinductive types. Log. Methods Comput. Sci. **12**(3), 7 (2016). https://doi.org/10.2168/lmcs-12(3:7)2016
10. Cockett, J.R.B.: Introduction to distributive categories. Math. Struct. Comput. Sci. **3**(3), 277–307 (1993). https://doi.org/10.1017/s0960129500000232
11. Coquand, T.: Infinite objects in type theory. In: Barendregt, H., Nipkow, T. (eds.) TYPES 1993. LNCS, vol. 806, pp. 62–78. Springer, Heidelberg (1994). https://doi.org/10.1007/3-540-58085-9_72
12. Escardó, M.: A metric model of PCF. Paper Presented at Workshop on Realizability Semantics and Applications, June–July 1999, Trento (1999). http://www.cs.bham.ac.uk/~mhe/papers/metricpcf.pdf
13. Geron, B., Levy, P.B.: Iteration and labelled iteration. Electron. Notes Theor. Comput. Sci. **325**, 127–146 (2016). https://doi.org/10.1016/j.entcs.2016.09.035
14. Giménez, E.: Codifying guarded definitions with recursive schemes. In: Dybjer, P., Nordström, B., Smith, J. (eds.) TYPES 1994. LNCS, vol. 996, pp. 39–59. Springer, Heidelberg (1995). https://doi.org/10.1007/3-540-60579-7_3
15. Giménez, E.: Structural recursive definitions in type theory. In: Larsen, K.G., Skyum, S., Winskel, G. (eds.) ICALP 1998. LNCS, vol. 1443, pp. 397–408. Springer, Heidelberg (1998). https://doi.org/10.1007/BFb0055070
16. Goncharov, S., Milius, S., Rauch, C.: Complete Elgot monads and coalgebraic resumptions. Electron. Notes Theor. Comput. Sci. **325**, 147–168 (2016). https://doi.org/10.1016/j.entcs.2016.09.036
17. Goncharov, S., Rauch, C., Schröder, L.: Unguarded recursion on coinductive resumptions. Electron. Notes Theor. Comput. Sci. **319**, 183–198 (2015). https://doi.org/10.1016/j.entcs.2015.12.012
18. Goncharov, S., Schröder, L.: Guarded traced categories. In: Baier, C., Dal Lago, U. (eds.) FoSSaCS 2018. LNCS, vol. 10803, pp. 313–330. Springer, Cham (2018). https://doi.org/10.1007/978-3-319-89366-2_17
19. Goncharov, S., Schröder, L., Rauch, C., Piróg, M.: Unifying guarded and unguarded iteration. In: Esparza, J., Murawski, A.S. (eds.) FoSSaCS 2017. LNCS, vol. 10203, pp. 517–533. Springer, Heidelberg (2017). https://doi.org/10.1007/978-3-662-54458-7_30
20. Hancock, P., Setzer, A.: Guarded induction and weakly final coalgebras in dependent type theory. In: Crosilla, L., Schuster, P. (eds.) From Sets and Types to Topology and Analysis. Towards Practicable Foundations for Constructive Mathematics. Oxford Logic Guides, vol. 48, pp. 115–134. Clarendon Press, Oxford (2005)
21. Hyland, M., Plotkin, G., Power, J.: Combining effects: sum and tensor. Theor. Comput. Sci. **357**(1–3), 70–99 (2006). https://doi.org/10.1016/j.tcs.2006.03.013

22. Jones, S.P., et al.: Haskell 98: a non-strict, purely functional language (1999)
23. Krishnaswami, K., Benton, N.: Ultrametric semantics of reactive programs. In: Proceedings of 26th Annual IEEE Symposium on Logic in Computer Science. LICS 2011, June 2011, Toronto, ON, pp. 257–266. IEEE CS Press, Washington, DC (2011). https://doi.org/10.1109/lics.2011.38
24. Levy, P.B., Power, J., Thielecke, H.: Modelling environments in call-by-value programming languages. Inf. Comput. **185**(2), 182–210 (2003). https://doi.org/10.1016/s0890-5401(03)00088-9
25. Mac Lane, S.: Categories for the Working Mathematician. Graduate Texts in Mathematics, vol. 5. Springer, New York (1971). https://doi.org/10.1007/978-1-4612-9839-7
26. Milius, S.: Completely iterative algebras and completely iterative monads. Inf. Comput. **196**(1), 1–41 (2005). https://doi.org/10.1016/j.ic.2004.05.003
27. Milner, R.: Communication and Concurrency. Prentice-Hall, Upper Saddle River (1989)
28. Moggi, E.: A modular approach to denotational semantics. In: Pitt, D.H., Curien, P.-L., Abramsky, S., Pitts, A.M., Poigné, A., Rydeheard, D.E. (eds.) CTCS 1991. LNCS, vol. 530, pp. 138–139. Springer, Heidelberg (1991). https://doi.org/10.1007/BFb0013462
29. Nakano, H.: A modality for recursion. In: Proceedings of 15th Annual IEEE Symposium on Logic in Computer Science. LICS 2000, June 2000, Santa Barbara, CA, pp. 255–266. IEEE CS Press, Washington, DC (2000). https://doi.org/10.1109/lics.2000.855774
30. Nakata, K.: Resumption-based big-step and small-step interpreters for While with interactive I/O. In: Danvy, O., Shan, C. (eds.) Proceedings of IFIP Working Conference on Domain-Specific Languages. DSL 2011, Electronic Proceedings in Theoretical Computer Science, September 2011, Bordeaux, vol. 66, pp. 226–235. Open Publishing Association, Sydney (2011). https://doi.org/10.4204/eptcs.66.12
31. Nakata, K., Uustalu, T.: A Hoare logic for the coinductive trace-based big-step semantics of While. In: Gordon, A.D. (ed.) ESOP 2010. LNCS, vol. 6012, pp. 488–506. Springer, Heidelberg (2010). https://doi.org/10.1007/978-3-642-11957-6_26
32. Nakata, K., Uustalu, T.: Resumptions, weak bisimilarity and big-step semantics for While with interactive I/O: an exercise in mixed induction-coinduction. In: Aceto, L., Sobocinski, P. (eds.) Proceedings of 7th Workshop on Structural Operational Semantics. SOS 2010, Electronic Proceedings in Theoretical Computer Science, August 2010, Paris. vol. 32, pp. 57–75. Open Publishing Association, Sydney (2010). https://doi.org/10.4204/eptcs.32.5
33. Nakata, K., Uustalu, T.: A Hoare logic for the coinductive trace-based big-step semantics of While. Log. Methods Comput. Sci. **11**(1), 1 (2015). https://doi.org/10.2168/lmcs-11(1:1)2015
34. Plotkin, G., Power, J.: Adequacy for algebraic effects. In: Honsell, F., Miculan, M. (eds.) FoSSaCS 2001. LNCS, vol. 2030, pp. 1–24. Springer, Heidelberg (2001). https://doi.org/10.1007/3-540-45315-6_1
35. Tait, W.W.: Intensional interpretations of functionals of finite type I. J. Symb. Log. **32**(2), 198–212 (1967). https://doi.org/10.2307/2271658
36. Turi, D., Plotkin, G.: Towards a mathematical operational semantics. In: Proceedings of 12th Annual IEEE Symposium on Logic in Computer Science. LICS 1997, June–July 1997, Warsaw, pp. 280–291. IEEE CS Press, Washington, DC (1997). https://doi.org/10.1109/lics.1997.614955
37. Winskel, G.: The Formal Semantics of Programming Languages. MIT Press, Cambridge (1993)

Generating Armstrong ABoxes for $\mathcal{ALC}$ TBoxes

Henriette Harmse[1(✉)], Katarina Britz[2], and Aurona Gerber[1]

[1] Department of Informatics and Centre of AI Research, University of Pretoria,
Private Bag X20, Hatfield 0028, South Africa
henrietteharmse@gmail.com, aurona.gerber@up.ac.za
[2] Department of Information Science and Centre of AI Research,
Stellenbosch University, Private Bag X1, Matieland 7602, South Africa
abritz@sun.ac.za

Abstract. A challenge in ontology engineering is the mismatch in expertise between the ontology engineer and domain expert, which often leads to important constraints not being specified. Domain experts often only focus on specifying constraints that should hold and not on specifying constraints that could possibly be violated. In an attempt to bridge this gap we propose the use of "perfect test data". The generated test data is perfect in that it satisfies all the constraints of an application domain that are required, including ensuring that the test data violates constraints that can be violated. In the context of Description Logic ontologies we call this test data an "Armstrong ABox", a notion derived from Armstrong relations in relational database theory. In this paper we detail the theoretical development of Armstrong ABoxes for $\mathcal{ALC}$ TBoxes as well as an algorithm for generating such Armstrong ABoxes. The proposed algorithm is based, via the ontology completion algorithm of Baader et al. on attribute exploration in formal concept analysis.

1 Introduction

A challenge in ontology design is to know whether all the required constraints that correctly represent a domain of interest are specified. Any given set of constraints over a given domain can be classified into constraints that should hold and constraints that can possibly be violated. Ensuring that all constraints are classified explicitly avoids the situation where omission results in a constraint by default being classified as a constraint that can be violated.

The problem of incomplete specifications is well documented [5,6] and could be the result of domain experts that concentrate on specifying facts that should hold (such as "all prime numbers are integers") and not on facts that could possibly be violated (such as "all prime numbers are odd"). The problem of incomplete specifications is often exacerbated by a mismatch in expertise between an ontology engineer and domain expert. An ontology engineer usually has limited knowledge about the application domain and domain experts have limited knowledge regarding ontology engineering. However, domain experts are often

© Springer Nature Switzerland AG 2018
B. Fischer and T. Uustalu (Eds.): ICTAC 2018, LNCS 11187, pp. 211–230, 2018.
https://doi.org/10.1007/978-3-030-02508-3_12

well versed in the data of their application domain [13]. This motivates the idea of presenting the domain expert with "perfect test data" that satisfy the required constraints and refute constraints that could be violated. In relational database theory this idea of perfect test data is realized as Armstrong relations [8], which we extend here to description logics (DLs) as Armstrong ABoxes.

Description logics (DLs) are syntactic variants of fragments of first-order logic that are specifically designed for the conceptual representation of an application domain in terms of concepts and relationships between concepts. A key design goal for DLs is to ensure that the basic reasoning procedures like satisfiability and classification are decidable. A DL ontology consists of a TBox and an ABox. The TBox is used to define concepts and relationships between concepts and the ABox is used to assert knowledge regarding the domain of interest [1]. In this paper we concentrate on the DL $\mathcal{ALC}$, which we define in Sect. 2.1.

Armstrong ABoxes assume that an ontology engineer has created a TBox in collaboration with a domain expert, but it is unclear whether the TBox describes the application domain faithfully. By generating "perfect test data" for a given TBox, constraints that follow, as well as constraints that do not follow from the TBox, can be made explicit through example data. The Armstrong ABox (example data) can be reviewed to ensure the TBox is not over- or underspecified, after which the TBox can be amended as needed: if the TBox is overspecified constraints can be removed and if the TBox is underspecified constraints can be added. A new Armstrong ABox can then be generated for the amended TBox, which again can be reviewed until the TBox and Armstrong ABox accurately specify constraints that should hold and constraints that could be violated.

Armstrong ABoxes are formalized relative to particular classes of constraints, with each class of constraints resulting in a different Armstrong ABox formalization. Different Armstrong ABox formalizations may need to use different algorithms to generate an Armstrong ABox for the particular formalization. In previous research we have defined Armstrong ABoxes for the class of constraints consisting of n-ary relations with uniqueness- and null-free constraints [12], of which the practical applicability has been illustrated on RDF datasets [11]. However, this did not address the broader problem of the class of constraints that can be formulated using the full expressivity of a given DL. The current paper addresses this limitation by providing (1) a formalization for Armstrong ABoxes for the class of constraints that can be formulated in $\mathcal{ALC}$ and (2) the algorithms necessary for generating an Armstrong ABox for an $\mathcal{ALC}$ TBox.

This paper is structured as follows: In Sect. 2 we review key definitions and results that are of importance in the development of Armstrong ABoxes, in Sect. 3 we provide the core definitions and proofs related to Armstrong ABoxes and Sect. 4 concludes this paper.

2   Preliminaries

We define the syntax and semantics for $\mathcal{ALC}$ in Sect. 2.1. The algorithm for generating an Armstrong ABox for an $\mathcal{ALC}$ TBox is based on the ontology completion algorithm of Baader et al. [2] (Sect. 2.5), which is based on the attribute exploration algorithm of formal concept analysis (FCA) [9]. Core FCA definitions are reviewed in Sect. 2.3 and the attribute exploration algorithm is reviewed in Sect. 2.4. A key insight used in attribute exploration is to enumerate closed sets in lectic order, which we review in Sect. 2.2.

2.1 Description Logics (DLs)

The syntactic building blocks for an arbitrary DL are based on the disjoint sets N_C, N_R and N_I, where N_C is a set of concept names, N_R is a set of role names and N_I is a set of individual names. Concept names represent classes of entities (called concepts) that share common characteristics, roles names denote binary relations (called roles) that exist between individuals and individual names are used to refer to specific instances (called individuals) in a domain of interest [1].

$\mathcal{ALC}$ concept descriptions (referred to as concepts) are constructed using the following concept constructors

$$C := \top \mid A \mid \neg C \mid C_1 \sqcap C_2 \mid \exists r.C$$

where A is an atomic concept, C, C_1 and C_2 are (possibly complex) concepts and r is a role. The constructors $\sqcup$ and $\forall$, and the special concept $\bot$ are defined in terms of the others in the usual way [1].

The TBox consists of axioms $C_1 \sqsubseteq C_2$ called **general concept inclusions** (GCIs) stating that C_1 is subsumed by C_2. The ABox consists of **assertions** $C(x)$ and $r(x_1, x_2)$ stating respectively that individual x is an instance of C and that individuals x_1 and x_2 are associated via role r.

The semantics of concepts is given in terms of an interpretation $\mathcal{I} = (\Delta^{\mathcal{I}}, \cdot^{\mathcal{I}})$, where $\Delta^{\mathcal{I}}$ (the domain) is a non-empty set, and $\cdot^{\mathcal{I}}$ (the interpretation function) maps each concept name $A \in N_C$ to a set $A^{\mathcal{I}} \subseteq \Delta^{\mathcal{I}}$, each role name $r \in N_R$ to a binary relation $r^{\mathcal{I}} \subseteq \Delta^{\mathcal{I}} \times \Delta^{\mathcal{I}}$, and each individual name $a \in N_I$ to an element $a^{\mathcal{I}} \in \Delta^{\mathcal{I}}$.

Given an interpretation $\mathcal{I} = (\Delta^{\mathcal{I}}, \cdot^{\mathcal{I}})$, the function $\cdot^{\mathcal{I}}$ is extended to interpret complex concepts in the following way:

$$\top^{\mathcal{I}} = \Delta^{\mathcal{I}}, (\neg C)^{\mathcal{I}} = \Delta^{\mathcal{I}} \backslash C^{\mathcal{I}}, (C_1 \sqcap C_2)^{\mathcal{I}} = C_1^{\mathcal{I}} \cap C_2^{\mathcal{I}}$$
$$(\exists r.C)^{\mathcal{I}} = \{x \in \Delta^{\mathcal{I}} \mid A \; y \text{ exists such that } (x, y) \in r^{\mathcal{I}} \text{ and } y \in C^{\mathcal{I}}\}$$

When an interpretation $\mathcal{I}$ **satisfies** a GCI or assertion α it is denoted by $\mathcal{I} \Vdash \alpha$. Satisfaction of α is defined as follows: $\mathcal{I} \Vdash C_1 \sqsubseteq C_2$ iff $C_1^{\mathcal{I}} \subseteq C_2^{\mathcal{I}}$, $\mathcal{I} \Vdash C(x)$ iff $x^{\mathcal{I}} \in C^{\mathcal{I}}$, and $\mathcal{I} \Vdash r(x, y)$ iff $(x^{\mathcal{I}}, y^{\mathcal{I}}) \in r^{\mathcal{I}}$. $\mathcal{I}$ is a **model** of a TBox $\mathcal{T}$ or an ABox $\mathcal{A}$ if it satisfies all its GCIs or assertions. In case $\mathcal{I}$ is a model of both $\mathcal{T}$ and $\mathcal{A}$, it is also called a model of the ontology $(\mathcal{T}, \mathcal{A})$ and $(\mathcal{T}, \mathcal{A})$ is said to be **consistent** if such a model exists.

An axiom or assertion α is said to be **entailed** by an ontology $\mathcal{O}$, written as $\mathcal{O} \models \alpha$, if every model of $\mathcal{O}$ is also a model of α. For a set of axioms $\Sigma = \{\sigma_0, \ldots, \sigma_n\}$, we abbreviate $\mathcal{O} \models \sigma_0, \ldots, \mathcal{O} \models \sigma_n$ with $\mathcal{O} \models \Sigma$. If $\mathcal{O}$ is empty, we abbreviate $\mathcal{O} \models \alpha$ as $\models \alpha$.

2.2   Closed Sets in Lectic Order

A set M with n elements has 2^n subsets. The set of all subsets of M is denoted by 2^M and is called the **powerset of** M. For S a finite set and $\mathcal{C} \subseteq 2^S$, $\mathcal{C}$ is a set of subsets that is called a **closure system** on S if $S \in \mathcal{C}$, and $B_1, B_2 \in \mathcal{C}$ implies $B_1 \cap B_2 \in \mathcal{C}$ [7]. A mapping function $\varphi : 2^S \to 2^S$ is called a **closure operator** on S that assigns a **closure** $\varphi(B) \subseteq S$ to each subset $B \subseteq S$ if it is:

1. extensive: $B \subseteq \varphi(B)$ for all $B \subseteq S$,
2. monotone: $B_1 \subseteq B_2$ implies $\varphi(B_1) \subseteq \varphi(B_2)$, and
3. idempotent: $\varphi(\varphi(B)) = \varphi(B)$.

A subset $B \subseteq S$ is called a **closed set** w.r.t. φ if $\varphi(B) = B$ [7].

To generate all φ-closed sets for a set M, it is necessary to generate the closures for all $A \subseteq M$ w.r.t. φ. Assuming M consists of n elements, 2^n closures will be computed. Moreover, multiple sets $A \subseteq M$ may have the same closure. To only generate unique closures, lookups will have to be performed 2^n times. A more efficient means to generate closures for all subsets is to generate each closure only once. This can be achieved by generating closures in the lectic order [9].

Definition 1 [9]. *Assume that $M = \{m_1, \ldots, m_n\}$ and fix some linear order $m_1 < \ldots < m_n$ on M. This order imposes a linear order on 2^M, called the* **lectic order**, *which is denoted by $<$: For $m_i \in M$ and $A, B \subseteq M$ the* **order** $<_i$ *is defined as*

$$A <_i B \text{ iff } m_i \in B, m_i \notin A \text{ and } \forall j < i.(m_j \in A \Leftrightarrow m_j \in B).$$

The order $<$ is the union of the orders $<_i$, i.e.,

$$A < B \text{ iff } A <_i B \text{ for some } m_i \in M.$$

Definition 1 states that A is lectically smaller than B if the smallest i for which the element m_i differs between sets A and B, m_i belongs to B and not to A. Note that $<$ extends the strict subset order because if $A \subset B$ it follows that $A < B$ since all the elements in which sets A and B differ belong to B. Thus $\emptyset$ is the smallest and M the largest set w.r.t. $<$.

All φ-closed sets can be generated exactly once for a set M when the closed sets are generated in the lectic order. Given a set $A \subseteq M$ it is possible to determine the next closed set in the lectic order, which is shown in Proposition 1.

Proposition 1 [9]. *Given a closure operator φ on M and a φ-closed set $A \subset M$, the next φ-closed set following A in the lectic order is*

$$\varphi((A \cap \{m_1, \ldots, m_{i-1}\}) \cup \{m_i\})$$

where i is maximal such that $A <_i \varphi((A \cap \{m_1, \ldots, m_{i-1}\}) \cup \{m_i\})$.

The NextClosure algorithm (Algorithm 1) finds the next closed set in the lectic order for a given set $A \subseteq M$ and a closure operator φ. To find an m with maximal index i it traverses M in reverse linear order. Two cases need to be considered: either $m \in A$ or $m \notin A$. If $m \in A$ we can remove m from A since it will not result in a φ-closed set that is different from A. If $m \notin A$ we calculate $B := \varphi(A \cup \{m\})$ and if $B \setminus A$ has no element $< m$, we have found our next φ-closed set, otherwise we continue to the next m in reverse linear order. If no next φ-closed set can be found, the empty set is returned. All closed sets for M and φ can be generated by iterating through closed sets using NEXTCLOSURE starting with $A := \varphi(\emptyset)$ and terminating when $A = M$.

2.3   Formal Concept Analysis (FCA)

FCA [9] is a field of applied mathematics that is based on a lattice-theoretic formalization of the notions of concept and conceptual hierarchy.

Definition 2 [9]. *A **formal context** is a triple $\mathbb{K} = (G, M, I)$, where G is a set of objects, M is a set of attributes, and $I \subseteq G \times M$ is a relation that associates each object g with the attributes satisfied by g. In order to express that an object g is in relation I with an attribute m, we write gIm.*

A formal context can be visualised as a crosstable, where the rows represent the objects, and the columns represent the attributes. A cross in column m of row g means that object g has attribute m, absence of a cross means that object g does not have attribute m.

Let $\mathbb{K} = (G, M, I)$ be a formal context. For a set of objects $A \subseteq G$, the **intent** A' of A is the set of attributes that are satisfied by all objects in A, which is defined as $A' := \{p \in M | \forall a \in A : aIp\}$. For a set of attributes $B \subseteq M$, the **extent** B' of B is the set of objects that satisfy all attributes in B, which is defined as $B' := \{o \in G \mid \forall b \in B : oIb\}$. A **formal concept** of $\mathbb{K}$ is a pair (A, B) with $A \subseteq G$, $B \subseteq M$, $A' = B$ and $B' = A$. The sets A and B are called the **concept extent** and the **concept intent** of the formal concept (A, B), respectively [9].

For the operators $\cdot'$ and $\cdot''$ ($\cdot'$ applied twice) the following statements hold [9]:

1. $A_1 \subseteq A_2$ implies $A_2' \subseteq A_1'$ (resp. $B_1 \subseteq B_2$ implies $B_2' \subseteq B_1'$),
2. $A_1 \subseteq A_1''$ (resp. $B_1 \subseteq B_1''$), and
3. the $\cdot''$-operator is a closure operator on both G and M and the set of concept intents (resp. concept extents) is a closure system on M (resp. G).

A formal context can be analyzed by studying the implications between attributes in the context, which motivates the next definition.

Definition 3 [9].   *Let $\mathbb{K} = (G, M, I)$ be a formal context. An **implication** between the attributes in M is a pair of sets $L, R \subseteq M$, usually written as $L \rightarrow R$. An implication $L \rightarrow R$ **holds** in $\mathbb{K}$ if every object of $\mathbb{K}$ that has all the attributes in L also has all the attributes in R, i.e. if $L' \subseteq R'$. We denote the set of implications that hold in $\mathbb{K}$ by $Imp(\mathbb{K})$. A subset $X \subseteq M$ **respects an implication** $L \rightarrow R$ if $L \nsubseteq X$ or $R \subseteq X$. A subset $X \subseteq M$ **respects a set** $\mathcal{L}$ **of implications** if X respects every implication in $\mathcal{L}$. An implication $L \rightarrow R$ **follows** from a set of implications $\mathcal{L}$ if every subset $X \subseteq M$ that respects all implications in $\mathcal{L}$ also respects $L \rightarrow R$.*

Algorithm 1 NEXTCLOSURE(M, A, φ)

1: **for all** $m \in M$ in reverse order **do**
2:     **if** $m \in A$ **then**
3:         $A := A\backslash\{m\}$
4:     **else**
5:         $B := \varphi(A \cup \{m\})$
6:         **if** $B\backslash A$ contains no element $< m$ **then**
7:             **return** B
8:         **end if**
9:     **end if**
10: **end for**
11: **return** $\emptyset$

Algorithm 2 IMPLICATIONCLOSURE(X, $\mathcal{L}$)

1: **repeat**
2:     stable := true
3:     **for all** $L \to R \in \mathcal{L}$ **do**
4:         **if** $L \subseteq X$ **then**
5:             $X := X \cup R$
6:             stable := false
7:             $\mathcal{L} := \mathcal{L}\backslash\{L \to R\}$
8:         **end if**
9:     **end for**
10: **until** stable
11: **return** X

Algorithm 3 ATTRIBUTEEXPLORATION(M, $\mathbb{K}$)

1: $\mathcal{L} := \emptyset$; $L := \emptyset$
2: **while** $L \neq M$ **do**
3:     **if** $L \neq L''$ **then**
4:         Ask expert whether $L \to L''$ holds
5:         **if yes then**
6:             $\mathcal{L} := \mathcal{L} \cup \{L \to L''\}$
7:             $L :=$ NEXTCLOSURE(M, L, IMPLICATIONCLOSURE(L, $\mathcal{L}$))
8:         **else**
9:             Get an object o from the expert s.t. $L \subseteq o'$ and $L'' \not\subseteq o'$
10:            $\mathbb{K} := \mathbb{K} \cup \{o\}$
11:         **end if**
12:     **else**
13:         $L :=$ NEXTCLOSURE(M, L, IMPLICATIONCLOSURE(L, $\mathcal{L}$))
14:     **end if**
15: **end while**
16: **return** $\mathcal{L}$, $\mathbb{K}$

Proposition 2. *If $\mathcal{L}$ is a set of implications over M, then $Mod(\mathcal{L}) :=$ $\{X \subseteq M \mid X$ respects $\mathcal{L}\}$ is a closure system on M. If $\mathcal{L} = Imp(\mathbb{K})$ for some formal context $\mathbb{K}$, then $Mod(\mathcal{L})$ is the system of all concept intents.*

The **implication closure operator** for the closure system $Mod(\mathcal{L})$ is given by $\mathcal{L} : 2^M \to 2^M$, which can be defined iteratively as

$$X^{\mathcal{L}} := X \cup \bigcup\{R \mid L \to R \in \mathcal{L}, L \subseteq X\}$$
$$X^{\mathcal{LL}} := X^{\mathcal{L}} \cup \bigcup\{R \mid L \to R \in \mathcal{L}, L \subseteq X^{\mathcal{L}}\}$$

$$\vdots$$

From the sets $X^{\mathcal{L}}, X^{\mathcal{LL}}, X^{\mathcal{LLL}}, \ldots$ a set $\mathcal{L}(X) := X^{\mathcal{L} \cdots \mathcal{L}}$ is obtained with $\mathcal{L}(X)^{\mathcal{L}} = \mathcal{L}(X)$, which can be calculated by Algorithm 2. For a given set X of attributes and a given set $\mathcal{L}$ of implications, it repeatedly iterates through the implications in $\mathcal{L}$, expanding X with R and removing $L \to R$ from $\mathcal{L}$ whenever $L \subseteq X$. Once X can no longer be expanded, the algorithm terminates [9].

2.4   Attribute Exploration

Attribute exploration is used where $\mathbb{K}$ is not known but can become known by posing questions to a domain expert. It is assumed that the domain expert is able to answer whether an implication holds in $\mathbb{K}$ or, in case an implication does not hold, give a counterexample of the implication. In order to make efficient use of an expert's time, attribute exploration uses minimal implication bases. The set of implications $\mathcal{L}$ is an **implication base** of $\mathbb{K}$ if

1. $\mathcal{L}$ is sound for $\mathbb{K}$, i.e. every implication from $\mathcal{L}$ holds in $\mathbb{K}$,
2. $\mathcal{L}$ is complete for $\mathbb{K}$, i.e. every implication that holds in $\mathbb{K}$ follows from $\mathcal{L}$, and
3. $\mathcal{L}$ is non-redundant for $\mathbb{K}$, i.e. no implication in $\mathcal{L}$ follows from other implications in $\mathcal{L}$.

For a given formal context $\mathbb{K}$ multiple implication bases can exist, of which the simplest is the implication base consisting of all implications. But because such an implication base can be too large to be practical, there is an interest in implication bases with minimal cardinality. Duquenne and Guigues showed that a minimal implication base can be constructed for every formal context. This implication base relies on the notion of pseudo-intents, which is defined recursively as follows – A subset of attributes $L \subseteq M$ is called a **pseudo-intent** of the context $\mathbb{K} = (G, M, I)$ iff (1) $L \neq L''$ (L is not a concept intent), and (2) if $L_0 \subsetneq L$ is a pseudo-intent and a proper subset of L, then $L_0'' \subseteq L$ holds [9,10].

Theorem 1 [9,10]. *$\{L \to L'' \mid L$ is a pseudo-intent of $\mathbb{K}\}$ is a set of implications that is a minimal implication base of $\mathbb{K} = (G, M, I)$, called the **Duquenne-Guigues base** of $\mathbb{K}$.*

Algorithm 3 details the attribute exploration algorithm. It takes as input a set M of attributes and a context $\mathbb{K}$. The implication set $\mathcal{L}$ is initialized as the empty set. Based on Theorem 1 it iterates through the pseudo-intents of $\mathbb{K}$ (line 3), starting from the smallest $\mathcal{L}$-closed left-hand side (line 1), asking the expert implication questions of the form $L \to L''$ (line 4). If the expert answers "yes", the implication $L \to L''$ is added to the implication set $\mathcal{L}$ and the next closed set in the lectic order is determined (line 7). If the expert answers "no", the expert should provide a counterexample (line 9) with which the context $\mathbb{K}$ is expanded (line 10). For this reason L is kept constant while L'' is recalculated (line 3). When L is not a pseudo-intent, the next $\mathcal{L}$-closed set is considered (line 13). It is proven that Algorithm 3 terminates and on termination returns the completed context $\mathbb{K}$ and $\mathcal{L}$, where $\mathcal{L}$ is a Duquenne-Guigues base of $\mathbb{K}$ [9].

2.5   Ontology Completion

Classical attribute exploration assumes that an expert has complete information. I.e., the absence of a cross in a crosstable means that object g does not have attribute m. However, in practice experts often only have partial knowledge. This inspired the introduction of partial contexts [2,9,17,18]. The formalization of partial contexts we will use here is based on Baader et al. [2,18].

Definition 4 [18]. *A **partial object description (pod)** is a tuple (A, S) where $A, S \subseteq M$ are such that $A \cap S = \emptyset$. We call such a pod a **full object description (fod)** if $A \cup S = M$. A set of pods is called a **partial context** and a set of fods a **full context**.*

The pod (A, S) states that the object it describes is known to satisfy all attributes from A and to not satisfy any attribute from S. A full context coincides with a formal context: a set of fods $\overline{\mathcal{K}}$ corresponds to the formal context $\mathbb{K}_{\overline{\mathcal{K}}} := (\overline{\mathcal{K}}, M, I)$, where $(\overline{A}, \overline{S})Im$ if and only if $m \in \overline{A}$ for all $(\overline{A}, \overline{S}) \in \overline{\mathcal{K}}$. A partial context can be extended by adding new pods or extending existing pods.

Definition 5 [18]. *Let $\mathcal{L}$ be a set of implications and $\mathcal{K}$ a partial context. An implication is called **undecided** w.r.t. $\mathcal{K}$ and $\mathcal{L}$ if it neither follows from $\mathcal{L}$ nor is refuted by $\mathcal{K}$. It is **decided** w.r.t. $\mathcal{K}$ and $\mathcal{L}$ if it is not undecided w.r.t. $\mathcal{K}$ and $\mathcal{L}$.*

The attribute exploration of partial contexts tries to decide all undecided implications by either adding the implication to $\mathcal{L}$ or extending $\mathcal{K}$ such that it refutes the implication. If all implications are decided, then the goal is achieved.

Let $(\mathcal{T}, \mathcal{A})$ be a consistent DL ontology and M a finite set of concept descriptions. Any individual name a occurring in $\mathcal{A}$ gives rise to the partial object description $pod_{\mathcal{T},\mathcal{A}}(a, M) := (A, S)$ where $A := \{C \in M | \mathcal{T}, \mathcal{A} \models C(a)\}$ and $S := \{C \in M | \mathcal{T}, \mathcal{A} \models \neg C(a)\}$, and the whole ABox induces the partial context

$$\mathcal{K}_{\mathcal{T},\mathcal{A}}(M) := \{pod_{\mathcal{T},\mathcal{A}}(a, M) | a \text{ is an individual name occurring in } \mathcal{A}\}.$$

Any element $d \in \Delta^{\mathcal{I}}$ of an interpretation $\mathcal{I}$ gives rise to the full example

$$fod_{\mathcal{I}}(d, M) := (\overline{A}, \overline{S}) \text{ where } \overline{A} := \{C \in M \mid d \in C^{\mathcal{I}}\} \text{ and}$$
$$\overline{S} := \{C \in M \mid d \in (\neg C)^{\mathcal{I}}\},$$

and the whole interpretation induces the full context $\mathcal{K}_{\mathcal{I}}(M) := \{fod_{\mathcal{I}}(d, M) \mid d \in \Delta^{\mathcal{I}}\}$. Note that $fod_{\mathcal{I}}(d, M)$ is indeed a fod since every $d \in \Delta^{\mathcal{I}}$ satisfies either $d \in C^{\mathcal{I}}$ or $d \in \Delta^{\mathcal{I}} \backslash C^{\mathcal{I}} = (\neg C)^{\mathcal{I}}$.

Definition 6 [18]. *The implication $L \to R$ over the attributes M is **refuted** by the ontology $(\mathcal{T}, \mathcal{A})$ if it is refuted by $\mathcal{K}_{\mathcal{T},\mathcal{A}}(M)$, and it is **refuted** by the interpretation $\mathcal{I}$ if it is refuted by $\mathcal{K}_{\mathcal{I}}(M)$. If an implication is not refuted by $\mathcal{I}$, then we say that it **holds** in $\mathcal{I}$. The set of implications over M that hold in $\mathcal{I}$ is denoted by $Imp_M(\mathcal{I})$. In addition, we say that $L \to R$ **follows** from $\mathcal{T}$ if $\sqcap L \sqsubseteq_{\mathcal{T}} \sqcap R$, where $\sqcap L$ and $\sqcap R$ respectively stand for the conjunctions $\sqcap_{C \in L} C$ and $\sqcap_{D \in R} D$, and $\sqcap L \sqsubseteq_{\mathcal{T}} \sqcap R$ is a shorthand for $\mathcal{T} \vDash \sqcap L \sqsubseteq \sqcap R$.*

Similar to attribute exploration it is sufficient to only consider implications whose left-hand sides are $\mathcal{L}$-closed with the right-hand side the largest R such that $L \to R$ is not refuted by $\mathcal{K}_{\mathcal{T},\mathcal{A}}(M)$:

Proposition 3 [18]. *For a left-hand side L and a partial context $\mathcal{K}_{\mathcal{T},\mathcal{A}}(M)$, the largest right-hand side such that $L \to \mathcal{K}_{\mathcal{T},\mathcal{A}}(L)$ is not refuted by $\mathcal{K}_{\mathcal{T},\mathcal{A}}(M)$ is*

$$\mathcal{K}_{\mathcal{T},\mathcal{A}}(L) := M \backslash \bigcup \{D \in M \mid \exists a. \ L \subseteq \{C \mid \mathcal{T}, \mathcal{A} \vDash C(a)\} \wedge \mathcal{T}, \mathcal{A} \vDash \neg D(a)\}.$$

The aim is for the ontology to describe an intended model. For a fixed set M of concepts, the ontology is complete if it contains all the relevant knowledge about implications between these concepts: if an implication holds in the intended interpretation, then it should follow from the TBox, and if it does not hold in the intended interpretation, then the ABox should contain a counterexample.

Definition 7 [18]. *Let $(\mathcal{T}, \mathcal{A})$ be a DL ontology, M a finite set of concept descriptions, and $\mathcal{I}$ a model of $(\mathcal{T}, \mathcal{A})$. Then $(\mathcal{T}, \mathcal{A})$ is M-complete w.r.t. $\mathcal{I}$ if the following three statements are equivalent for all implications $L \to R$ over M:*

1. *$L \to R$ holds in $\mathcal{I}$.*
2. *$L \to R$ follows from $\mathcal{T}$.*
3. *$L \to R$ is not refuted by $(\mathcal{T}, \mathcal{A})$.*

Let $(\mathcal{T}_0, \mathcal{A}_0)$ be a DL ontology that also has $\mathcal{I}$ as a model. Then $(\mathcal{T}, \mathcal{A})$ is a completion of $(\mathcal{T}_0, \mathcal{A}_0)$ if it is complete and extends $(\mathcal{T}_0, \mathcal{A}_0)$, i.e., $\mathcal{T}_0 \subseteq \mathcal{T}$ and $\mathcal{A}_0 \subseteq \mathcal{A}$.

The attribute exploration algorithm for partial contexts can be adapted for ontology completion [2, 18] for which Proposition 4 and Theorem 2 state important results.

Proposition 4 [18]. *Let* $(\mathcal{T}, \mathcal{A}) := (\mathcal{T}_0, \mathcal{A}_0)$ *be an ontology, M a finite set of concept descriptions, and $\mathcal{I}$ a model of $(\mathcal{T}, \mathcal{A})$. Then the ontology completion algorithm terminates, and upon termination outputs an ontology $(\mathcal{T}, \mathcal{A}) := (\mathcal{T}_n, \mathcal{A}_n)$ and a set of implications $\mathcal{L}$ such that*

1. *$\mathcal{L}$ is sound and complete for $Imp_M(\mathcal{I})$, and*
2. *$(\mathcal{T}, \mathcal{A}) := (\mathcal{T}_n, \mathcal{A}_n)$ refutes every implication that is refuted by $\mathcal{I}$.*

Theorem 2 [18]. *Let $(\mathcal{T}, \mathcal{A}) := (\mathcal{T}_0, \mathcal{A}_0)$ be a ontology, M a finite set of concept descriptions, and $\mathcal{I}$ a model of $(\mathcal{T}, \mathcal{A}) := (\mathcal{T}_0, \mathcal{A}_0)$, and let $(\mathcal{T}, \mathcal{A}) := (\mathcal{T}_n, \mathcal{A}_n)$ be the knowledge base computed by the ontology completion algorithm. Then $(\mathcal{T}, \mathcal{A}) := (\mathcal{T}_n, \mathcal{A}_n)$ is a completion of $(\mathcal{T}, \mathcal{A}) := (\mathcal{T}_0, \mathcal{A}_0)$.*

3   Armstrong ABoxes

In this section we introduce Armstrong ABoxes for $\mathcal{ALC}$ TBoxes. The intent of Armstrong ABoxes is to create example data that satisfy all required constraints and violate all constraints that do not necessarily hold for a specific application domain. In this way Armstrong ABoxes are the DL equivalent of Armstrong relations of relational database theory.

3.1   Formal Definitions

For convenience the notation $\bigsqcap C_i$ and $\bigsqcap D_j$ will respectively be used as shorthand for $C_{i_0} \sqcap \ldots \sqcap C_{i_n}$ and $D_{j_0} \sqcap \ldots \sqcap D_{j_m}$.

To determine whether there are axioms that have been fortuitously missed, the ontology engineer wants to add assertions to the Armstrong ABox that serve as test data that violates these candidate axioms. This idea is motivated based on experimental results for Armstrong relations, where it was shown that experts more readily recognize meaningful constraints that have been missed when the missed constraints are violated by test data [14].

Definition 8. *Let $\mathcal{T}$ be a consistent $\mathcal{ALC}$ TBox and let*

$$\sigma' := \bigsqcap C_i \sqsubseteq \bigsqcap D_j$$

*for which $\mathcal{T} \nvDash \sigma'$ holds. An ABox $\mathcal{A}'$ is a **violating exemplar** of the entailment $\mathcal{T} \vDash \sigma'$ if*

$$\left\{ (\bigsqcap C_i)(x), (\neg \bigsqcap D_j)(x) \right\} \subseteq \mathcal{A}'$$

holds for some named individual x that does not appear in any other assertions of $\mathcal{A}'$. This is denoted by $\mathcal{A}' \nvDash \sigma'$.

Similar to Armstrong relations, Armstrong ABoxes include assertions that represent example data that satisfy the constraints of the TBox.

Definition 9. *Let $\mathcal{T}$ be a consistent $\mathcal{ALC}$ TBox, and let*

$$\sigma := \bigsqcap C_i \sqsubseteq \bigsqcap D_j$$

*for which $\mathcal{T} \vDash \sigma$ and $\nvDash \sigma$ holds. An ABox $\mathcal{A}$ is a **satisfying exemplar** of the entailment $\mathcal{T} \vDash \sigma$ if*

$$\left\{ (\bigsqcap C_i)(x), (\bigsqcap D_j)(x) \right\} \subseteq \mathcal{A}$$

holds for some named individual x that does not appear in any other assertions of $\mathcal{A}$. This is denoted by $\mathcal{A} \Vdash \sigma$.

In general, for a given TBox $\mathcal{T}$, the number of non-entailments and entailments can be infinite. For this reason, similar to ontology completion, Armstrong ABoxes consider for a TBox $\mathcal{T}$ a finite set M of interesting concept descriptions for which a partial context $\mathcal{K}_{\mathcal{T},\mathcal{A}}(M)$ can be constructed. The number of implications that can hold in such a context is finite. This is the reason why Definitions 8 and 9 are defined in terms of assertions contained in $\mathcal{A}$ and $\mathcal{A}'$ respectively, rather than assertions entailed by $(\mathcal{T},\mathcal{A})$ and $(\mathcal{T},\mathcal{A}')$ respectively.

In Sect. 3.3 a variation of ontology completion/attribute exploration will be used to generate Armstrong ABoxes. One of the aspects in which Armstrong ABoxes deviate from ontology completion is that for Armstrong ABoxes one of two possibilities must hold for each implication considered: either it follows from the TBox in which case a satisfying exemplar is added, or it does not follow from the TBox in which case a violating exemplar is added. To ensure that every implication not following from the TBox can indeed be refuted, we introduce the following definition.

Definition 10. *Let M be a set of concept descriptions. M is said to be **permissible** if it is finite and no concept in M is equivalent to $\top$. Furthermore, we define $M^{\rightarrow}$ to be the set of GCIs representing the finite set of all the implications $L \rightarrow R$ over M.*

Armstrong ABoxes assume that $\mathcal{T}$ is to the knowledge of the domain expert an accurate representation of the application domain. As such an interpretation $\mathcal{I}$ exists that is a model for $\mathcal{T}$ and is representative of the knowledge of the domain expert. Hence, in accordance with Definition 7, for all implications that hold over M it follows that $L \rightarrow R$ holds in $\mathcal{I}$ and $L \rightarrow R$ follows from $\mathcal{T}$.

Definition 11. *Let $\mathcal{T}$ be a consistent $\mathcal{ALC}$ TBox and let M be permissible. Let*

$$\Sigma' := \{ \sigma' \mid \mathcal{T} \nvDash \sigma' \text{ and } \sigma' \in M^{\rightarrow} \}.$$

*Σ' is called the **candidate axiom set** of $\mathcal{T}$ over M. Assume $\Sigma' = \{\sigma'_0, \ldots, \sigma'_n\}$. An ABox $\mathcal{A}'$ is a **violating exemplar** of $\mathcal{T} \vDash \Sigma'$ if $\mathcal{A}' \nVdash \sigma'_0, \ldots, \mathcal{A}' \nVdash \sigma'_n$ holds. An ABox $\mathcal{A}'$ is a **minimal violating exemplar** of $\mathcal{T} \vDash \Sigma'$ iff there is no ABox $\mathcal{A}'_0 \subset \mathcal{A}'$ that is violating exemplar of $\mathcal{T} \vDash \Sigma'$.*

Definition 12. *Let T be a consistent $\mathcal{ALC}$ TBox and let M be permissible. Let*

$$\Sigma := \{\sigma \mid T \vDash \sigma, \nvDash \sigma \text{ and } \sigma \in M^{\rightarrow}\}.$$

*Σ is called the **entailment set** of T over M. Assume $\Sigma = \{\sigma_0, \ldots, \sigma_n\}$. An ABox $\mathcal{A}$ is a **satisfying exemplar** of $T \vDash \Sigma$ if $\mathcal{A} \Vdash \sigma_0, \ldots, \mathcal{A} \Vdash \sigma_n$ holds, which is denoted by $\mathcal{A} \Vdash \Sigma$. An ABox $\mathcal{A}$ is a **minimal satisfying exemplar** of $T \vDash \Sigma$ iff there is no ABox $\mathcal{A}_0 \subset \mathcal{A}$ that is satisfying exemplar of $T \vDash \Sigma$.*

For the sake of brevity "over M" will sometimes be dropped with the tacit understanding that candidate axiom- and entailment sets are per definition constrained to some set M of concepts that is permissible.

The notion of an Armstrong ABox can now be defined. An Armstrong ABox is denoted by $\mathcal{A}_{\Box}$, which is pronounced as "A-shield".

Definition 13. *Let T be a consistent $\mathcal{ALC}$ TBox with Σ and Σ' respectively the entailment- and candidate axiom sets of T. $\mathcal{A}_{\Box}$ is said to be an **Armstrong ABox** for T if and only if:*

1. *for every $\sigma \in \Sigma$, $\mathcal{A}_{\Box} \Vdash \sigma$ holds,*
2. *for every $\sigma' \in \Sigma'$, $\mathcal{A}_{\Box} \nVdash \sigma'$ holds and*
3. *there is no proper subset of $\mathcal{A}_{\Box}$ such that properties (1) and (2) hold.*

*$\mathcal{O}_{\Box} = T \cup \mathcal{A}_{\Box}$ is called an **Armstrong ontology**.*

3.2   Key Attributes of Armstrong ABoxes

Before it can be proved that an Armstrong ontology is consistent, some intermediate results need to be proven first.

Lemma 1. *Let $(T, \mathcal{A})$ be a consistent $\mathcal{ALC}$ ontology. Let $\mathcal{A}_1$ be a set of assertions that is satisfiable w.r.t. T. Further assume that there is no individual x that appears in both $\mathcal{A}$ and $\mathcal{A}_1$. Then $(T, \mathcal{A} \cup \mathcal{A}_1)$ is consistent.*

Proof. Since $(T, \mathcal{A})$ is consistent and $(T, \mathcal{A}_1)$ is consistent, $\mathcal{A} \cup \mathcal{A}_1$ will only be inconsistent w.r.t. T if:

1. there is a clash in $\mathcal{A} \cup \mathcal{A}_1$, or
2. $\mathcal{A} \cup \mathcal{A}_1$ is unsatisfiable w.r.t. T.

For (1) to be the reason for the inconsistency there must be an individual x such that $\mathcal{A} \cup \mathcal{A}_1 \vDash C(x)$ and $\mathcal{A} \cup \mathcal{A}_1 \vDash \neg C(x)$, which is impossible because of the assumption that no individuals are shared between $\mathcal{A}$ and $\mathcal{A}_1$. For (2) to be the reason for the inconsistency, there must be some entailment $T \vDash C \sqsubseteq D$ for which there is an individual x such that $\mathcal{A} \cup \mathcal{A}_1 \vDash C(x)$ and $\mathcal{A} \cup \mathcal{A}_1 \vDash \neg D(x)$, which is impossible because no individuals are shared between $\mathcal{A}$ and $\mathcal{A}_1$. Since $\mathcal{A} \cup \mathcal{A}_1$ is consistent w.r.t. T the consistency of T is not affected by $\mathcal{A} \cup \mathcal{A}_1$ (see Proposition 3.6 of [16] or p. 142 of [3]). Hence, $(T, \mathcal{A} \cup \mathcal{A}_1)$ must be consistent.

Lemma 2. *Let T be a consistent $\mathcal{ALC}$ TBox with $\Sigma' = \{\sigma'_0, \ldots, \sigma'_n\}$ the candidate axiom set of T. Then $(T, \mathcal{A}'_0 \cup \ldots \cup \mathcal{A}'_n)$ is consistent where $\mathcal{A}'_0, \ldots, \mathcal{A}'_n$ are minimal violating exemplars corresponding to Σ'.*

Proof. Let $\mathcal{A}'_0 = \left\{ (\sqcap C_i)(x), (\neg \sqcap D_j)(x) \right\}$ be a violating exemplar. Then $\mathcal{A}'_0$ will only be unsatisfiable w.r.t. T if

1. $(\neg \sqcap D_j) \equiv \bot$, or
2. $\mathcal{A}'_0 \models C(y)$ and $\mathcal{A}'_0 \models \neg C(y)$ for a concept C and a named individual y.

(1) is in contradiction with M being permissible and (2) is in contradiction with $\mathcal{A}'_0$ being a minimal violating exemplar (Definition 11). Thus, $\mathcal{A}'_0$ is satisfiable w.r.t. T and from Lemma 1 it follows that $(T, \mathcal{A}'_0)$ is consistent. The result follows by induction over the n minimal violating exemplars using Lemma 1 and the fact that no individuals are shared between exemplars (Definition 8).

Lemma 3. *Let T be a consistent $\mathcal{ALC}$ TBox with $\Sigma = \{\sigma_0, \ldots, \sigma_n\}$ the entailment set of T. Then $(T, \mathcal{A}_0 \cup \ldots \cup \mathcal{A}_n)$ is consistent where $\mathcal{A}_0, \ldots, \mathcal{A}_n$ are minimal satisfying exemplars corresponding to Σ.*

Proof. Let $\mathcal{A}_0 = \left\{ (\sqcap C_i)(x), (\sqcap D_j)(x) \right\}$ be a satisfying exemplar. That $(T, \mathcal{A}_0)$ is consistent follows from Lemma 1, the fact that M is permissible and $\mathcal{A}_0$ being a minimal satisfying exemplar. The result follows by induction over the n minimal satisfying exemplars using Lemma 1 and the fact that no individuals are shared between exemplars (Definition 9).

From the preceding definitions it follows that an Armstrong ABox can be derived from TBox entailments and non-entailments. Conversely, TBox entailments and non-entailments can be derived from Armstrong ABoxes.

Theorem 3. *Let T be a consistent $\mathcal{ALC}$ TBox and let $\mathcal{O}_\sigma := T \cup \mathcal{A}_\sigma$. Then:*

1. *$\mathcal{O}_\sigma$ is consistent,*
2. *$\sigma' \in \Sigma'$ if and only if $\mathcal{A}_\sigma \nVdash \sigma'$ and*
3. *$\sigma \in \Sigma$ if and only if $\mathcal{A}_\sigma \Vdash \sigma$.*

Proof. (1) That $\mathcal{O}_\sigma$ is consistent is an immediate consequence of Lemmas 1, 2 and 3, the fact that an Armstrong ABox is minimal (it cannot be extended to contain assertions that clash) and $\Sigma \cap \Sigma' = \emptyset$.

(2) Let $\sigma' := \sqcap C_i \sqsubseteq \sqcap D_j$ where $\sigma' \in M^\rightarrow$. Then $\mathcal{A}_\sigma \nVdash \sigma'$ if and only if $\{(\sqcap C_i)(x), (\neg \sqcap D_j)(x)\} \subseteq \mathcal{A}_\sigma$ for some new individual x such that $T \nvDash \sigma'$ if and only if $\sigma' \in \Sigma'$.

(3) Let $\sigma := \sqcap C_i \sqsubseteq \sqcap D_j$ where $\sigma \in M^\rightarrow$. Then $\mathcal{A}_\sigma \Vdash \sigma$ if and only if $\{(\sqcap C_i)(x), (\sqcap D_j)(x)\} \subseteq \mathcal{A}_\sigma$ for some new individual x such that $T \vDash \sigma$ if and only if $\sigma \in \Sigma$.

Algorithm 4 NEWQUESTION$((\mathcal{T}, \mathcal{A}), L)$

1: $R := \mathcal{K}_{\mathcal{T},\mathcal{A}}(L)$ ▷ Proposition 3
2: undecided $:= L \neq R$
3: $C := \bigsqcap_{C \in L} C$
4: $D := \bigsqcap_{D \in \mathcal{K}_{\mathcal{T},\mathcal{A}}(L)} D$
5: **return** undecided, C, D

Algorithm 5 GENERATEARMSTRONGABOX$(\mathcal{T}, M)$

1: $\mathcal{L} := \emptyset; \mathcal{A}_0 := \emptyset; L := \emptyset; i := 0$
2: **while** $L \neq M$ **do**
3:      undecided := NEWQUESTION$((\mathcal{T}, \mathcal{A}_0), L)$
4:      **if** undecided = **true then**
5:          **if** $C \sqsubseteq_{\mathcal{T}} D$ **then**
6:              $\mathcal{L} := \mathcal{L} \cup \{L \to R\}$
7:              $L :=$ NEXTCLOSURE$(M, L,$ IMPLICATIONCLOSURE$(L, \mathcal{L}))$
8:              $\mathcal{A}_0 := \mathcal{A}_0 \cup \{C(x_i), D(x_i)\}; i := i + 1$
9:          **else**
10:             $\mathcal{A}_0 := \mathcal{A}_0 \cup \{C(x_i), \neg D(x_i)\}; i := i + 1$
11:          **end if**
12:      **else**
13:          $L :=$ NEXTCLOSURE$(M, L,$ IMPLICATIONCLOSURE$(L, \mathcal{L}))$
14:      **end if**
15: **end while**
16: **return** $\mathcal{L}, (\mathcal{T}, \mathcal{A}_0)$

3.3 Algorithm

The ontology completion algorithm can be adapted to generate Armstrong ABoxes. However, there are some differences between the assumptions for ontology completion versus for Armstrong ABoxes.

Armstrong ABoxes start with a non-empty consistent $\mathcal{ALC}$ TBox $\mathcal{T}$ which has been constructed in collaboration with a domain expert. Moreover, the assumption is that $\mathcal{T}$ is to the knowledge of the domain expert an accurate representation of the application domain. As such an interpretation $\mathcal{I}$ exists that is a model for $\mathcal{T}$ and is representative of the knowledge of the domain expert. In this regard Armstrong ABoxes differ from ontology completion since a model $\mathcal{I}$ of $\mathcal{T}$ matches the interpretation $\mathcal{I}$ known to the domain expert. Since the assumption is that $\mathcal{T}$ is representative of the application domain, $\mathcal{T}$ is not extended during the generation of an Armstrong ABox.

The main objective of Armstrong ABoxes is to generate an $\mathcal{A}_0$ corresponding to $\mathcal{T}$ in accordance with Definition 13. This can be achieved by checking whether $\sqcap L \sqsubseteq_{\mathcal{T}} \sqcap R$ follows from $\mathcal{T}$, in which case a satisfying exemplar (Definition 9) is added to $\mathcal{A}_0$ and the implication base $\mathcal{L}$ is extended with $L \to R$. If $\sqcap L \sqsubseteq \sqcap R$ does not follow from $\mathcal{T}$, a related violating exemplar (Definition 8) is added to $\mathcal{A}_0$. No questions are posed to an expert during Armstrong ABox generation.

To make the correspondence between Armstrong ABoxes and partial contexts induced by DL ontologies explicit, assume that $\mathcal{O} = (\mathcal{T}, \emptyset)$ represents the TBox for which an Armstrong ABox has to be generated. This will result in the ontology $\mathcal{O}_{\mho} = (\mathcal{T}, \mathcal{A}_{\mho})$ which has a model (Theorem 3). Assume that $\mathcal{I}_{\mho}$ is a model of $\mathcal{O}_{\mho}$. Then $\mathcal{O}_{\mho}$ induces the partial context

$$\mathcal{K}_{\mathcal{T}, \mathcal{A}_{\mho}} := \{ pod_{\mathcal{T}, \mathcal{A}_{\mho}}(a, M) \mid a \text{ is an individual name occurring in } \mathcal{A}_{\mho} \},$$

where M is a set of $\mathcal{ALC}$ concepts that is permissible, $pod_{\mathcal{T}, \mathcal{A}_{\mho}}$ is defined as before for $\mathcal{A}_{\mho}$ instead of $\mathcal{A}$ and $pod_{\mathcal{T}, \mathcal{A}_{\mho}}$ is a pod since $\mathcal{O}_{\mho}$ is consistent (Theorem 3).

Any element $d \in \triangle^{\mathcal{I}_{\mho}}$ of an interpretation $\mathcal{I}_{\mho}$ gives rise to the full example

$$fod_{\mathcal{I}_{\mho}}(d, M) := (\overline{A}, \overline{S}) \text{ where } \overline{A} := \{ C \in M \mid d \in C^{\mathcal{I}_{\mho}} \} \text{ and}$$
$$\overline{S} := \{ C \in M \mid d \in (\neg C)^{\mathcal{I}_{\mho}} \},$$

and the whole interpretation induces the full context

$$\mathcal{K}_{\mathcal{I}_{\mho}}(M) := \{ fod_{\mathcal{I}_{\mho}}(d, M) \mid d \in \triangle^{\mathcal{I}_{\mho}} \}.$$

Note that $fod_{\mathcal{I}_{\mho}}(d, M)$ is indeed a fod since every $d \in \triangle^{\mathcal{I}_{\mho}}$ satisfies either $d \in C^{\mathcal{I}_{\mho}}$ or $d \in \triangle^{\mathcal{I}_{\mho}} \backslash C^{\mathcal{I}_{\mho}} = (\neg C)^{\mathcal{I}_{\mho}}$.

For this reason many of the results of ontology completion applies directly to Armstrong ontologies with the assumption that $\mathcal{I} = \mathcal{I}_{\mho}$.

Algorithm 5 generates an Armstrong ABox $\mathcal{A}_{\mho}$, given a TBox $\mathcal{T}$ and M a set of concepts that is permissible. It initializes the implication set $\mathcal{L}$ and the Armstrong ABox $\mathcal{A}_{\mho}$ to be empty. L is initialized with the smallest set in the lectic order for $\mathcal{L}(\cdot)$ and a counter is initialized that is used in creating new individuals for which assertions are added to $\mathcal{A}_{\mho}$ (line 1).

Algorithm 4, which is called in line 3 of Algorithm 5, is introduced to simplify dealing with exemplars. It takes as input the TBox $\mathcal{T}$, the Armstrong ABox $\mathcal{A}_{\mho}$ calculated this far, and the left-hand side L of the current implication under consideration. In line 1 it calculates the largest R for L that is not refuted by the partial context $\mathcal{K}_{\mathcal{T}, \mathcal{A}}(M)$ (Proposition 3). Line 2 checks whether the implication is undecided in the context $\mathcal{K}_{\mathcal{T}, \mathcal{A}}$. Lines 3 and 4 are introduced to simplify the notation used in Algorithm 5.

Line 4 of Algorithm 5 ensures that only undecided implications are considered, otherwise it moves on to the next L in the lectic order under $\mathcal{L}(\cdot)$(line 13). An implication for which the related subsumption already follows from the TBox $\mathcal{T}$, the implication is added to $\mathcal{L}$ and a satisfying exemplar is added to $\mathcal{A}_{\mho}$ (lines 6-8), otherwise a violating exemplar is added to $\mathcal{A}_{\mho}$ (line 10). Since $\mathcal{L}$ changed in line 6, the next L in the lectic order under $\mathcal{L}(\cdot)$ is determined (line 7).

At termination Algorithm 5 returns an Armstrong ontology and a set of implications $\mathcal{L}$ that is sound and complete for $Imp_M(\mathcal{I}_{\mho})$ (Theorem 4).

Theorem 4. *Let $\mathcal{T}$ be a consistent $\mathcal{ALC}$ TBox and let M be permissible. Algorithm 5 terminates and upon termination it outputs the ontology $(\mathcal{T}, \mathcal{A}_{\mho})$ which is an Armstrong ontology and a set of implications $\mathcal{L}$ such that*

1. *$\mathcal{L}$ is sound and complete for $Imp_M(\mathcal{I}_{\mho})$, $\mathcal{I}_{\mho}$ a model of $(\mathcal{T}, \mathcal{A}_{\mho})$ and*
2. *$(\mathcal{T}, \mathcal{A}_{\mho})$ refutes every implication refuted by $\mathcal{I}_{\mho}$.*

Proof. That Algorithm 5 terminates and upon termination it outputs the set of implications $\mathcal{L}$ such that (1) and (2) holds, follows from Proposition 4.

That $(\mathcal{T}, \mathcal{A}_\sigma)$ is an Armstrong ontology follows from the following facts:

1. conditions (1) and (2) hold for the set of implications $\mathcal{L}$,
2. whenever $\sigma \in \Sigma$, a corresponding satisfying exemplar is added to $\mathcal{A}_\sigma$ (line 8),
3. for every $\sigma' \in \Sigma'$, a violating exemplar is added to $\mathcal{A}_\sigma$ (line 10),
4. no other other assertions are added to $\mathcal{A}_\sigma$, $\Sigma \cap \Sigma' = \emptyset$ and no variables are shared between exemplars (lines 8 and 10).

3.4 Example

Starting with $M = \{\text{Composite}, \text{Even}, \text{Odd}, \text{Prime}, \text{Square}\}$ and the TBox

$$\mathcal{T}_0 = \{\text{Composite} \sqsubseteq \top, \text{Even} \sqsubseteq \top, \text{Odd} \sqsubseteq \top, \text{Prime} \sqsubseteq \top, \text{Square} \sqsubseteq \top\},$$

Algorithm 5 generates no satisfying exemplars (because there are no implications that follow from $\mathcal{T}_0$ for $\mathcal{K}_{\mathcal{T}_0}(M)$) and the violating exemplars given in Table 1. Looking at the assertions for x_1, the expert realizes that some of these attributes will never occur together. Hence, the expert adds the axioms $\{\text{Even} \sqsubseteq \neg\text{Odd}, \text{Composite} \sqsubseteq \neg\text{Prime}, \text{Square} \sqsubseteq \neg\text{Prime}\}$. Regenerating the Armstrong ABox for $M = \{\text{Composite}, \text{Even}, \text{Square}\}$ and

$$\mathcal{T}_1 = \mathcal{T}_0 \cup \{\text{Even} \sqsubseteq \neg\text{Odd}, \text{Composite} \sqsubseteq \neg\text{Prime}, \text{Square} \sqsubseteq \neg\text{Prime}$$

results in no satisfying exemplars and the violating exemplars given in Table 2. Looking at the assertions for x_4 in Table 2 the expert realizes that every integer that is an Even and a Square, will necessarily be a Composite. Therefore the expert adds the GCI $\text{Even} \sqcap \text{Square} \sqsubseteq \text{Composite}$.

Generating an Armstrong ABox for $\mathcal{T}_2 = \mathcal{T}_1 \cup \{\text{Even} \sqcap \text{Square} \sqsubseteq \text{Composite}\}$ with $M = \{\text{Composite}, \text{Even}, \text{Square}\}$ will generate the same violating exemplars as in Table 2 except for x_4 that will be generated as a satisfying exemplar $\{(\text{Even} \sqcap \text{Square})(x_4), \text{Composite}(x_4)\}$.

Generating an Armstrong ABox for $\mathcal{T}_2$ with $M = \{\text{Composite}, \text{Odd}, \text{Square}\}$ will result in violating exemplars similar to Table 2, except that Even will be replaced with Odd. At this point the expert decides that $\mathcal{T}_2$ is sufficiently refined. Note that $\mathcal{T}_2$ defines constraints that should hold while the violating exemplars of the Armstrong ABoxes define constraints that can be violated.

3.5 Discussion

Our motivation for developing Armstrong ABoxes is to help identify ontologies of which the specification are incomplete, based on an idea that is inspired by Armstrong relations in relational database theory. Armstrong relations are used to assist domain experts to remedy incomplete specifications by identifying constraints that have been omitted, both with regard to constraints that should hold and constraints that do not necessarily hold [14]. By generating "perfect test

Table 1. Armstrong ABox for $\mathcal{T}_0$ and $M = \{$Composite, Even, odd, Prime, Square$\}$

Violating exemplars	
$\top(x_1)$	$\neg($Composite $\sqcap$ Even $\sqcap$ Odd $\sqcap$ Prime $\sqcap$ Square$)(x_1)$
Square(x_2)	$\neg($Composite $\sqcap$ Even $\sqcap$ Odd $\sqcap$ Prime$)(x_2)$
Prime(x_3)	$\neg($Composite $\sqcap$ Even $\sqcap$ Odd $\sqcap$ Square$)(x_3)$
(Prime $\sqcap$ Square)(x_4)	$\neg($Composite $\sqcap$ Even $\sqcap$ Odd$)(x_4)$
Odd(x_5)	$\neg($Composite $\sqcap$ Even $\sqcap$ Prime $\sqcap$ Square$)(x_5)$
(Odd $\sqcap$ Square)(x_6)	$\neg($Composite $\sqcap$ Even $\sqcap$ Prime$)(x_6)$
(Odd $\sqcap$ Prime)(x_7)	$\neg($Composite $\sqcap$ Even $\sqcap$ Square$)(x_7)$
(Odd $\sqcap$ Prime $\sqcap$ Square)(x_8)	$\neg($Composite $\sqcap$ Even$)(x_8)$
Even(x_9)	$\neg($Composite $\sqcap$ Odd $\sqcap$ Prime $\sqcap$ Square$)(x_9)$
(Even $\sqcap$ Square)(x_{10})	$\neg($Composite $\sqcap$ Odd $\sqcap$ Prime$)(x_{10})$
(Even $\sqcap$ Prime)(x_{11})	$\neg($Composite $\sqcap$ Odd $\sqcap$ Square$)(x_{11})$
(Even $\sqcap$ Prime $\sqcap$ Square)(x_{12})	$\neg($Composite $\sqcap$ Odd$)(x_{12})$
(Even $\sqcap$ Odd)(x_{13})	$\neg($Composite $\sqcap$ Prime $\sqcap$ Square$)(x_{13})$
(Even $\sqcap$ Odd $\sqcap$ Square)(x_{14})	$\neg($Composite $\sqcap$ Prime$)(x_{14})$
(Even $\sqcap$ Odd $\sqcap$ Prime)(x_{15})	$\neg($Composite $\sqcap$ Square$)(x_{15})$
(Even $\sqcap$ Odd $\sqcap$ Prime $\sqcap$ Square)(x_{16})	$\neg$Composite(x_{16})
Composite(x_{17})	$\neg($Even $\sqcap$ Odd $\sqcap$ Prime $\sqcap$ Square$)(x_{17})$
(Composite $\sqcap$ Square)(x_{18})	$\neg($Even $\sqcap$ Odd $\sqcap$ Prime$)(x_{18})$
(Composite $\sqcap$ Prime)(x_{19})	$\neg($Even $\sqcap$ Odd $\sqcap$ Square$)(x_{19})$
(Composite $\sqcap$ Prime $\sqcap$ Square)(x_{20})	$\neg($Even $\sqcap$ Odd$)(x_{20})$
(Composite $\sqcap$ Odd)(x_{21})	$\neg($Even $\sqcap$ Prime $\sqcap$ Square$)(x_{21})$
(Composite $\sqcap$ Odd $\sqcap$ Square)(x_{22})	$\neg($Even $\sqcap$ Prime$)(x_{22})$
(Composite $\sqcap$ Odd $\sqcap$ Prime)(x_{23})	$\neg($Even $\sqcap$ Square$)(x_{23})$
(Composite $\sqcap$ Odd $\sqcap$ Prime $\sqcap$ Square)(x_{24})	$\neg$Even(x_{24})
(Composite $\sqcap$ Even)(x_{25})	$\neg($Odd $\sqcap$ Prime $\sqcap$ Square$)(x_{25})$
(Composite $\sqcap$ Even $\sqcap$ Square)(x_{26})	$\neg($Odd $\sqcap$ Prime$)(x_{26})$
(Composite $\sqcap$ Even $\sqcap$ Prime)(x_{27})	$\neg($Odd $\sqcap$ Square$)(x_{27})$
(Composite $\sqcap$ Even $\sqcap$ Prime $\sqcap$ Square)(x_{28})	$\neg$Odd(x_{28})
(Composite $\sqcap$ Even $\sqcap$ Odd)(x_{29})	$\neg($Prime $\sqcap$ Square$)(x_{29})$
(Composite $\sqcap$ Even $\sqcap$ Odd $\sqcap$ Square)(x_{30})	$\neg$Prime(x_{30})
(Composite $\sqcap$ Even $\sqcap$ Odd $\sqcap$ Prime)(x_{31})	$\neg$Square(x_{31})

Table 2. Armstrong ABox for $\mathcal{T}_1$ and $M = \{$Composite, Even, Square$\}$

Violating exemplars	
$\top(x_1)$	$\neg($Composite $\sqcap$ Even $\sqcap$ Square$)(x_1)$
Square(x_2)	$\neg($Composite $\sqcap$ Even$)(x_2)$
Even(x_3)	$\neg($Composite $\sqcap$ Square$)(x_3)$
(Even $\sqcap$ Square)(x_4)	$\neg$Composite(x_4)
Composite(x_5)	$\neg($Even $\sqcap$ Square$)(x_5)$
(Composite $\sqcap$ Square)(x_6)	$\neg$Even(x_6)
(Composite $\sqcap$ Even)(x_7)	$\neg$Square(x_7)

data" in an Armstrong ABox we present the ontology engineer with exemplars that ensure that all the constraints of an application domain are specified. In particular the test data provides exemplars that violate constraints that do not necessarily hold.

Potential benefits of Armstrong ABoxes are that exemplars can make the meaning of entailments and non-entailments apparent, particularly for users that may not be well versed in DLs. Moreover, violating exemplars can alert a user to the fact that an entailment that should not follow from the TBox, does follow from the TBox. This can happen where $\mathcal{A}_\Box$ is generated for $\mathcal{T}_0$ after which $\mathcal{T}_0$ is amended resulting in $\mathcal{T}_1$, without regenerating $\mathcal{A}_\Box$. Assuming $\mathcal{T}_1$ is consistent and $(\mathcal{T}_1, \mathcal{A}_\Box)$ is inconsistent, the reason for the inconsistency will be due to a σ' such that $\mathcal{T}_0 \nvDash \sigma'$, $\mathcal{A}_\Box \nVdash \sigma'$ and $\mathcal{T}_1 \vDash \sigma'$. For $\mathcal{T}_0$ σ' represents a constraint that does not hold and for $\mathcal{T}_1$ a constraint that does hold. The question that the expert has to resolve is: Should σ' hold or is it an unintended side-effect of the changes to $\mathcal{T}_0$?

An advantage of Armstrong ABoxes over ontology completion is that there is no need to reclassify the ontology because no GCIs are added when an Armstrong ABox is generated. In the case of ontology completion the ontology has to be reclassified every time a new GCI is added [18] but for Armstrong ABoxes the ontology only needs to be reclassified after the expert reviewed the Armstrong ABox and decided to add GCIs.

Armstrong ABoxes give an expert the flexibility to focus only on exemplars of interest. Ontology completion (resp. attribute exploration) can be a time consuming process even though it is mathematically designed to minimize the number of questions posed to an expert. This problem is exacerbated when experts don't provide mathematically optimal counterexamples, which results in the number of questions that need to be answered to reduce at a much slower rate than what is possible through optimal counterexamples. Moreover, an expert may not be able to provide an answer without further investigation [9,18]. Onto-CompP, an implementation of ontology completion, deals with these challenges by trying to find a counterexample that may already be present in the ABox and it allows experts in certain situations to skip questions [4]. In contrast our Armstrong ABox algorithm will by definition always provide optimal counterexamples (Definition 8) and because such an Armstrong ABox is generated without expert interaction, it affords the expert the flexibility to choose which exemplars to focus on and which to ignore.

Limitations of our Armstrong ABox algorithm include its exponential complexity similar to attribute exploration/ontology completion. Less expressive DLs with favourable reasoning complexity like $\mathcal{FL}$, $\mathcal{AL}$ and $\mathcal{EL}$ are impractical given our current formalization of violating exemplars, which requires full negation. Moreover, ontology engineers and domain experts are likely to keep M small as to limit the cognitive load in reviewing an Armstrong ABox. This means the exponential complexity is likely to have a limited effect in practice, but this still needs to be evaluated in practice.

4   Conclusion

In order to assist with incomplete specifications when ontology engineers model a domain of interest, we propose the use of an Armstrong ABox, a notion derived from Armstrong relations in relational database theory. We formalized the notion of Armstrong ABoxes for TBoxes in the $\mathcal{ALC}$ DL, including an algorithm for generating such Armstrong ABoxes. The generated test data in the Armstrong ABox could be regarded as "perfect test data" that satisfies both the constraints of the domain that should hold, as well as constraints of the domain that do not hold. Our approach is novel in ontology engineering even though similar approaches have been used before in relational database specifications. Integrating our approach into ontology engineering tools will facilitate in detecting incomplete specifications.

References

1. Baader, F., Calvanese, D., McGuinness, D.L., Nardi, D., Patel-Schneider, P.F.: The Description Logic Handbook: Theory, Implementation and Applications. Cambridge University Press, Cambridge (2007). https://doi.org/10.1017/cbo9780511711787

2. Baader, F., Ganter, B., Sertkaya, B., Sattler, U.: Completing description logic knowledge bases using formal concept analysis. In: Veloso, M.M. (ed.) Proceedings of 20th International Joint Conference on Artificial Intelligence. IJCAI 2007, January 2007, Hyderabad, pp. 230–235. Morgan Kaufmann Publishers (2007). http://ijcai.org/Proceedings/07/Papers/035.pdf

3. Baader, F., Horrocks, I., Sattler, U.: Description logics. In: van Harmelen, F., Lifschitz, V., Porter, B. (eds.) Handbook of Knowledge Representation. Foundations of Articial Intelligence, vol. 3, pp. 135–179. Elsevier, Amsterdam (2008). https://doi.org/10.1016/s1574-6526(07)03003-9

4. Baader, F., Sertkaya, B.: Usability issues in description logic knowledge base completion. In: Ferré, S., Rudolph, S. (eds.) ICFCA 2009. LNCS (LNAI), vol. 5548, pp. 1–21. Springer, Heidelberg (2009). https://doi.org/10.1007/978-3-642-01815-2_1

5. Boehm, B., Basili, V.R.: Software defect reduction top 10 list. IEEE Comput. **34**(1), 135–137 (2001). https://doi.org/10.1109/2.962984

6. Brooks, F.P.: No silver bullet: essence and accidents of software engineering. IEEE Comput. **20**(4), 10–19 (1987). https://doi.org/10.1109/mc.1987.1663532

7. Davey, B.A., Priestley, H.A.: Introduction to Lattices and Order, 2nd edn. Cambridge University Press, Cambridge (2002). https://doi.org/10.1017/cbo9780511809088

8. Fagin, R., Vardi, M.Y.: Armstrong databases for functional and inclusion dependencies. Inf. Process Lett. **16**(1), 13–19 (1983). https://doi.org/10.1016/0020-0190(83)90005-4

9. Ganter, B., Obiedkov, S.: Conceptual Exploration. Springer, Heidelberg (2016). https://doi.org/10.1007/978-3-662-49291-8

10. Guigues, J.L., Duquenne, V.: Famille minimale d'implications informatives résultant d'un tableau de données binaires. Math. Sci. Hum. **24**(95), 5–18 (1986)

11. Harmse, H., Britz, K., Gerber, A.: Informative Armstrong RDF datasets for n-ary relations. In: Borgo, S., Hitzler, P. (eds.) Proceedings of 10th International Conference on Formal Ontology in Information Systems. Frontiers in Artificial Intelligence and Applications, pp. 187–199. IOS Press (2018). https://doi.org/10.3233/978-1-61499-910-2-187

12. Harmse, H., Britz, K., Gerber, A.: Armstrong relations for ontology design and evaluation. In: Lenzerini, M., Peñaloza, R. (eds.) Proceedings of 29th International Workshop on Description Logics. CEUR Workshop Proceedings, vol. 1577. CEUR-WS.org (2016). http://ceur-ws.org/Vol-1577/paper_4.pdf

13. Konev, B., Ozaki, A., Wolter, F.: A model for learning description logic ontologies based on exact learning. In: Schuurmans, D., Wellman, M.P. (eds.) Proceedings of 13th AAAI Conference on Artificial Intelligence, February 2016, Phoenix, AZ, pp. 1008–1015. AAAI Press (2016). https://www.aaai.org/ocs/index.php/AAAI/AAAI16/paper/view/11948/11696

14. Langeveldt, W., Link, S.: Empirical evidence for the usefulness of Armstrong relations in the acquisition of meaningful functional dependencies. Inf. Syst. **35**(3), 352–374 (2010). https://doi.org/10.1016/j.is.2009.11.002

15. Link, S.: Armstrong databases: validation, communication and consolidation of conceptual models with perfect test data. In: Ghose, A., Ferrarotti, F.A. (eds.) Proceedings of 8th Asia-Pacific Conference on Conceptual Modelling. APCCM 2012, CRPIT, January–February 2012, Melbourne, vol. 130, pp. 3–20. Australian Computer Society (2012). https://dl.acm.org/citation.cfm?id=2523784

16. Nebel, B.: Reasoning and Revision in Hybrid Representation Systems. LNCS, vol. 422. Springer, Heidelberg (1990). https://doi.org/10.1007/bfb0016445

17. Rudolph, S.: Relational Exploration: Combining Description Logics and Formal Concept Analysis for Knowledge Specification. Ph.D. thesis, Technische Universität Dresden (2006)

18. Sertkaya, B.: Formal Concept Analysis Methods for Description Logics. Ph.D. thesis, Technische Universität Dresden (2006)

Spatio-Temporal Domains: An Overview

David Janin[✉]

LaBRI, Bordeaux INP, Université de Bordeaux,
351 cours de la Libération, 33405 Talence Cedex, France
`janin@labri.fr`

Abstract. We consider the possibility of defining a general mathematical framework for the homogeneous modeling and analysis of heterogeneous spatio-temporal computations as they occur more and more in modern computerized systems of systems. It appears that certain fibrations of posets into posets, called here spatio-temporal domains, eventually provide a fully featured category that extends to space and time the category of cpos and continuous functions, aka Scott Domains, used in classical denotational semantics.

1   Introduction

Research Context. Program semantics is classically divided between two complementary approaches: *denotational semantics* and *operational semantics*. Denotational semantics generally refers to *what* the partial functions encoded by programs are: what is the relationship between (models of) their input values (or input memory state) and their output values (or output memory state). Operational semantics refers instead to *when* and *where* these values are read, transformed and eventually produced. To some extent, operational semantics defines effective models for implementing programs. It provides tools for analyzing the space and time behavior of programs therefore analyzing their complexity. On the other hand, denotational semantics provides instead methods for analyzing the (partial) correction of programs.

This suggests that semantic features can be distributed between typical operational features (time and space values) and denotational features (other data values). However, in many modern computerized systems such as, for instance, interactive music or animation systems [2,3,14,18], timing or spacing information plays a crucial rôle in the definition of system's inputs and outputs. There, many data values are implicitly parameterized by some space and/or time information: think of an augmented music system taking as input the melody played by a musician dancing on a stage. How the resulting spaced-and-timed signals can be read, combined and transformed in both an efficient and a sound way is one of the central questions of numerous domain specific language proposals such as, for instance, Fran [14] for animation or Euterpea [18] for music.

Work partially supported by Inria center Bordeaux-Sud-Ouest, from 09/2016 to 02/2017, long version at https://hal.archives-ouvertes.fr/hal-01634897.

B. Fischer and T. Uustalu (Eds.): ICTAC 2018, LNCS 11187, pp. 231–251, 2018.
https://doi.org/10.1007/978-3-030-02508-3_13

In all the underlying semantic models, compositionality is a key issue as it allows efficient, structure driven, development and analysis techniques. In fact, with compositionality, properties of complex systems/programs can be derived from certain combinations of the properties of their (simpler) components. As an immediate consequence, semantic models can also be studied and developed *per se*, adequate (domain specific) programming languages *deriving* a posteriori from the algebraic/combinatorial properties of these models.

Our Contribution. Following such a model-driven development of programming language, we consider the possibility of lifting space or time information into typical denotational models: Scott Domains. It happens that this can be done by restricting certain constructions known in topos and fibration theory to posets. We thus provide in this paper an elementary description of these constructions and illustrate their applicability by interpreting the induced algebras in terms of typical spaced or timed programming constructs.

Detailled Structure. Technically, we define spatio-temporal domain as certain discrete fibrations of posets into posets (Sect. 2). Simply said, elements of these domains are (partially ordered) computation histories indexed over spacetime scales. Relationships with other known semantic models are detailled in Sect. 3. Spatio-temporal morphisms are defined in Sect. 4 as monotone functions between spatio-temporal domains that *uniformly* act on the underlying spacetime scales. This eventually yields a fully featured category that extends to space and time the categories of posets/cpos/domains and monotone/continuous functions typically used in classical denotational semantics.

The proposed approach yields two layers of program constructs that have been long identified in Globally-Asynchronous Locally-Synchronous (GALS) system design [10,30]. More precisely, there appear:

(1) a *synchronous layer* of programming constructs available when components' inputs and outputs are located and timed on the same spacetime scale and received or produced in a synchronous way (Sect. 5),
(2) an *asynchronous layer* of programming constructs available when component's inputs and outputs are located and timed on possibly distinct spacetime scales (Sect. 6).

At the border of these two layers, when inputs and outputs are located on the same scale but without any synchronicity assumption, we show that feedback loop constructs are available for defining non trivial (least) fixpoints (Sect. 8), that is, infinite signals. Continuously spaced and timed posets are also studied in Sect. 7 where a tight relationship with various key concepts from Domain Theory is established.

It is known that fibration theory [29] is used in denotational semantics of higher-order dependently typed lambda calculus [20]. Restricting ourselves to discrete fibrations over posets yields a notion of types that weakly depends on spacetime scales (or clocks). These possibilities were already studied in language extension proposals [11,12] of the Synchronous Programming Language family [5,7]. Our approach provides a sound mathematical framework for the formal study of these possible extensions.

Concrete examples are detailed throughout, illustrating most concepts and their applicability to spacetime program's semantics.

2   Timed Posets

Throughout this text, an arbitrary poset T may be interpreted as a *spatio-temporal scale*. This means that for every element $u, v \in T$, we say that u lies *before* v, or v lays *after* u, when $u \leq v$, and that u lays *beside* v when u and v are incomparable. In other words, there is the *time dimension* that increases with the order, and, there is the *space dimension* where incomparable elements are also related.

Having said so, throughout the rest of this presentation, a spatio-temporal scale is simply referred to as a *time scale* and its elements are simply called *instants*.

Definition 2.1 (Timed poset). *Let T be a time scale. A poset* timed *over T is a poset P equipped with a* temporal projection $\pi : P \to T$ *such that:*

(IN1) *if $x \leq y$ then $\pi(x) \leq \pi(y)$, i.e. the temporal projection is monotone,*
(IN2) *for every $t \leq \pi(x)$ there is a unique element $x \downarrow t \in P$ such that $\pi(x \downarrow t) = t$ and $x \downarrow t \leq x$,*

for all $x, y \in P$. The element $x \downarrow t$ is called the temporal cut, *or simply the* cut *of x at instant t. This situation is depicted in (1). The cut function $(x, t) \mapsto x \downarrow t$ can be seen as sort of a (partial) action of the poset T over the poset P.*

$$
\begin{array}{ccc}
x \xrightarrow{\ \leq\ } y & \qquad & x \downarrow t \xrightarrow{\ \leq\ } x \\
\pi \downarrow \quad (\text{IN1}) \quad \downarrow \pi & & \exists!\pi \downarrow \quad (\text{IN2}) \quad \downarrow \pi \\
\pi(x) \xrightarrow[\leq]{} \pi(y) & & t \xrightarrow[\leq]{} \pi(x)
\end{array}
\tag{1}
$$

Example 2.1 (Self-timed poset). Every poset T is a timed poset over itself with identity *id* as temporal projection.

Example 2.2 (Sub-timed poset). Let P be a poset timed over T. Let $X \subseteq P$ be a downward closed subset of P. Let $inc_X : X \to P$ be the inclusion function. Then the set X ordered as in P with $\pi \circ inc_X$ as temporal projection is also a timed poset.

Example 2.3 (Timed impulses). Let T be a time scale and E a set of event values extended into $E_\perp = E \cup \{\perp\}$. The set $Imp(T, E) = T \times E_\perp$ is turned into a timed poset by equipping it with the temporal projection and partial order defined by $\pi(u, e) = u$ and $(t, e) \leq (t', e')$ when either $(t, e) = (t', e')$ or $t < t'$ and $e = \perp$.

An element $(t, e) \in Imp(T, E)$ with $e \neq \perp$ is a *timed impulse* with value e at instant t. Observe there are no elements strictly above (or after) such an impulse and all elements strictly below (or before) bear no value as they are of the form $(t', \perp)$ for some $t' < t$. Rephrased in terms of temporal cut, for every element $(t, e) \in Imp(T, E)$ and instant $t' \leq t$, two cases are possible: either $t' = t$ and we have $(t, e) \downarrow t' = (t, e)$, or $t' < t$ and we have $(t, e) \downarrow t' = (t', \perp)$.

Example 2.4 (Timed signals). With T and E as above, a *timed signal* is defined as a relation $S \subseteq T \times E$ that maps every instant $t \in T$ to the set $S(t) = \{e \in E : (t, e) \in S\}$ of event values received at instant t. Then a *partial timed signal* is a pair $(u, S) \in T \times \mathcal{P}(T \times E)$ such that for all $(t, e) \in S$ we have $t \leq u$.

The set $Sig(T, E)$ of partial timed signals is turned into a timed poset by equipping it with the temporal projection defined by $\pi(u, S) = u$ and the partial order relation defined by $(u, S) \leq (u', S')$ when $u \leq u'$ and $S(t) = S'(t)$ for all $t \leq u$, for all $(u, S), (u', S') \in Sig(T, E)$. Following [28], a pair $(u, S) \in Sig(T, E)$ represents the observation of a timed signal until the instant u. In some sense, it is the *temporal trace* of some computation until that instant.

Rephrased in terms of temporal cut, for every partial signal $(u, S) \in Sig(T, E)$ and instant $v \leq u = \pi(u, S)$ we have $(u, S) \downarrow v = (v, S \downarrow v)$ with $S \downarrow v = \{(t, e) \in S : t \leq v\}$. Such a temporal cut $(u, S) \downarrow v$ models the observation of the partial signal (u, S) until instant v that lies before instant u.

Definition 2.2 (Local cut). *Let P be a poset timed over T. For every $x \in P$, property (IN2) induces a (total) function $cut_x : \downarrow \pi(x) \to P$, called* local cut, *defined by $cut_x(u) = x \downarrow u$ for every $u \in T$ such that $u \leq \pi(x)$.*

Remark 2.1. In the definition above and later in the text, we use the notation $\downarrow X \subseteq P$ for the *downward closure* of a subset $X \subseteq P$ of a poset P defined by $\downarrow X = \{y \in P : \exists x \in X, y \leq x\}$ that extends to an element $x \in P$ by putting $\downarrow x = \{y \in P : y \leq x\}$. At first sight, this notation may clash with our chosen notation for cuts. However, for all $x \in P$ and all $u \leq \pi(x)$ we have $\downarrow(x \downarrow u) = (\downarrow x) \downarrow u$ as soon as we extent the (partially defined) cut point-wise. It follows that we can even write $\downarrow x \downarrow u$ without any parenthesis with no ambiguity.

Lemma 2.1 (Local cut properties). *Let $x, y \in P$ and $u, v \in T$ such that $u, v \leq \pi(x)$. Then:*

(1) $x \leq y$ if and only if $\pi(x) \leq \pi(y)$ and $x = y \downarrow \pi(x)$,
(2) $u \leq v$ if and only if $x \downarrow u \leq x \downarrow v$.

In particular, the (sub)posets $\downarrow x \subseteq P$ and $\downarrow \pi(x) \subseteq T$ are isomorphic posets as shown by the restriction of the cut to $\downarrow x$ and, as inverse, the temporal projection.

Corollary 2.1. *An element $x \in P$ is* minimal *(resp. minimum) in P if and only if its temporal projection $\pi(x) \in T$ is minimal (resp. minimum) in T. On the other hand, maximal elements in a timed poset can have arbitrary temporal projection as shown by timed impulse timed posets (see Example 2.3).*

3   Derived Notions

We review below several notions that derive from the notion of timed posets and that allow this notion to be related with other known concepts appearing in computer system modeling or programming language semantics.

Temporal Coherence. The following notion is inspired by Girard's notion of coherent space in linear logic [16]. A similar notion, even more closely related with timed domains, also appears in Winskel's notion of event structures [31].

Definition 3.1. *Let P be a poset timed over T. Let $x, y \in P$. We say that x and y are* coherent, *a property denoted by $x \frown y$, when, for every $x', y' \in P$ such that $x' \leq x$ and $y' \leq y$, if $\pi(x') = \pi(y')$ then $x' = y'$, or, equivalently, for all $u \leq \pi(x), \pi(y), x \downarrow u = y \downarrow u$. By extension, a subset $X \subseteq P$ is a* coherent subset *when $x \frown y$ for all $x, y \in X$.*

Lemma 3.1. *Let $x, y \in P$. Then $x \leq y$ if and only if $\pi(x) \leq \pi(y)$ and $x \frown y$.*

In other words, coherence offers an alternative to the definition of timed poset via an order relation.

Remark 3.1. In some sense, every coherent subset $X \subseteq P$ can be interpreted as the *trace* of a spatio-temporal computation that has been observed at the instants $\pi(X)$. The (sub)posets X and $\pi(X)$ are even isomorphic via the restriction of π to X and the downward closure $\downarrow X$ of a coherent subset is itself coherent.

Remark 3.2. The structure $(P, \leq, \not\frown)$ defined for every timed poset P is a special case of an event structure [31], though dropping the finite history requirement. The same computational interpretations are possible. Two elements x and y in P describe *concurrent* computations when they are coherent and incomparable: they can both appear in the same computation trace as suggested above.

On the other hand, two incoherent elements x and y in P describe *conflicting* computations: they cannot appear in the same computation trace. More precisely, by the definition of coherence, when $x \not\frown y$ there is $u \in T$ in the past of both $\pi(x)$ and $\pi(y)$ such that $x \downarrow u \neq y \downarrow u$. This means that two distinct computations occur at the same instant (and position) u, a case that is interpreted as impossible.

Remark 3.3. Relating timed posets with event structures, one can also observe that the equivalence induced by π, defined by $x \sim_\pi y$ when $\pi(x) = \pi(y)$ for every $x, y \in P$, essentially is a *symmetry*[1] as recently defined by Winskel in event structures [32].

This observation relates timed posets even more closely with the concepts introduced by Winskel in concurrency theory. However, the notion of timed poset is more restrictive than the notion of event structure. In a timed poset, coherence is *uniformly* defined via temporal projection. In an event structure, coherence is a given as part of the definition of that event structure.

Temporal Distance. Timed concurrent system semantics can also be modeled by means of generalized ultrametric distance, as already developed quite in the depth by Lee, Liu et Matsikoudis [25, 26, 28]. The following definition shows that timed posets also induce such distances over their elements.

Definition 3.2. *Let P be a poset timed over T. Let $\mathcal{P}^{\downarrow}(T)$ be the set of downward closed subsets of T ordered by reverse inclusion therefore with T itself as least element. The distance induced by π over P is the function*

$$d : P \times P \to \mathcal{P}^{\downarrow}(T) \quad \text{defined by} \quad d(x, y) = \{t \in T : t \leq \pi(x), \pi(y), x \downarrow t = y \downarrow t\}$$

when $x \neq y$ and by $d(x, y) = T$ when $x = y$.

One can easily check that $d(x, y) = \downarrow d(x, y)$ for all $x, y \in P$ hence the above definition is sound.

Lemma 3.2. *The function $d : P \times P \to \mathcal{P}^{\downarrow}(T)$ is a generalized ultrametric, that is, we have:*

(1) $d(x, y) = T$ if and only if $x = y$ (separation),
(2) $d(x, y) = d(y, x)$ (symmetry),
(3) $d(x, y) \supseteq d(x, z) \cap d(z, y)$ (ultra-metric inequality),

for all $x, y, z \in P$.

Temporal Presheaves. One last connection of timed posets with an existing notion, now complete, goes via the notion of categorical presheaves, a notion already used in concurrency theory especially by Catani, Stark and Winskel for modeling process calculi like CCS and the π-calculus [8, 9].

Let T be a poset. A *presheaf* on T is a functor $F : T^{op} \to Set$ from the category T^{op}, obtained from T by reversing the order relation, into the category Set of sets and functions. Then the following lemmas state that posets timed over T are isomorphic with what are known in category theory as the *categories of elements* of presheaves over T. This shows that timed posets and presheaves are essentially equivalent notions, an equivalence later stated as a categorical equivalence (see Theorem 4.1 below).

---

[1] Strictly speaking, for $\sim_\pi$ to be a symmetry, the timed poset P must be completed with sorts of "passing time" elements of the form (u, x) with $x \leq (u, x)$ and $\pi(u, x) = u$, defined for all $x \in P$ and $u \in T$ such that there is no y above x with $\pi(y) = u$.

Lemma 3.3. *Let* $F : T^{op} \rightarrow Set$ *be a presheaf over* T. *Then the set* $P_F = \Sigma_{t \in T} F(t) = \{(t, x) : t \in T, x \in F(t)\}$, *equipped with the temporal projection defined by* $\pi(u, x) = u$ *and the order relation defined by* $(u, x) \leq (v, y)$ *when* $u \leq v$ *and* $F(u \leq v)(y) = x$ *for all* $(u, x), (v, y) \in P_F$, *is a timed poset, also known as the category of elements of* F.

Lemma 3.4. *Let* P *be poset timed over* T. *Then the presheaf* $F_P : T^{op} \rightarrow Set$ *defined by* $F_P(t) = \{x \in P : \pi(x) = t\}$ *and* $F_P(u \leq v)(x) = x \downarrow u$ *for all* $t, u, v \in T$ *with* $u \leq v$ *and* $x \in F_P(v)$, *has an its category of elements isomorphic to* P.

4   Timed Morphisms

In this section, we define a class of timed morphisms between timed posets, called Δ-synchronous functions, as monotonic functions between timed posets that uniformly act on their underlying time scales. Somehow generalizing the approach of Colaço et al. [11,12], with timed posets interpreted as timed types, this uniformity requirement allows timed morphisms types to be defined not only as the domains and codomains of these morphisms, as in the simply-typed definition of function types, but also as the uniform transformation of time scales they induce.

Δ-synchronous Function. Throughout this section, let P and, resp. Q, be two posets timed over the time scales U and, resp. V.

Definition 4.1 (Δ-synchronous functions). *A function* $f : P \rightarrow Q$ *together with a monotone function* $\delta : U \rightarrow V$, *called the* temporal projection *of* f, *is Δ-synchronous when, as depicted in (2):*

(SD1) $\pi(f(x)) = \delta \circ \pi(x)$,
(SD2) *if* $x \leq y$ *then* $f(x) \leq f(y)$,
(SD3) $f(x \downarrow u) = f(x) \downarrow \delta(u)$,

for all $x, y \in P$ *and all* $u \in U$ *such that* $u \leq \pi(x)$.

$$
\begin{array}{ccc}
U \xleftarrow{\;\pi_P\;} P & \qquad & P \xrightarrow{\;\leq_P\;} P \\
\delta \downarrow \quad (\text{SD1}) \quad \downarrow f & & f \downarrow \quad (\text{SD2}) \quad \downarrow f \\
V \xleftarrow[\pi_Q]{} Q & & Q \xrightarrow[\leq_Q]{} Q
\end{array}
\qquad (2)
$$

Remark 4.1. As soon a $u \leq \pi(x)$ then, by monotonicity of δ we have $\delta(u) \leq \delta \circ \pi(x)$ hence, by (SD1), $\delta(u) \leq \pi(f(x))$ therefore property (SD3) is sound. Property (SD2) states that Δ-synchronous functions are poset functors. Property (SD1) formalizes the statement that they uniformly acts on the underlying time scales.

Example 4.1 (Self-synchronous). Every monotone increasing function $\delta : U \to V$ is a Δ-synchronous function between the self-timed posets U and V, with itself as temporal projection.

Lemma 4.1. *Under hypothesis (SD1), properties (SD2) and (SD3) are equivalent.*

On Coherence Preservation. It is easy to see that the Δ-synchronous image of a coherent subset bounded above is coherent. With a view towards application, this coherence preservation property is probably enough. Nevertheless, we show that without the boundedness condition this is no longer true and we provide sufficient additional conditions on time scale changes for coherence preservation.

Example 4.2. Let $U = \{\bot, a, b\}$, self-timed, with minimum element $\bot$ and a and b incomparable. Let $P = U$ ordered the same as U but timed over $V = \{0, 1\}$ by $\pi(\bot) = 0$, $\pi(a) = 1$ and $\pi(b) = 1$. The function $f : U \to P$ defined by $f(\bot) = \bot$, $f(a) = a$ and $f(b) = b$ is Δ-synchronous with temporal projection $\delta : U \to V$ defined by $\delta(\bot) = 0$, $\delta(a) = 1$ and $\delta(b) = 1$. Although $a \frown b$ in U we have $f(a) = a \not\frown b = f(b)$ in P. The function f does not preserve coherence.

Lemma 4.2. *Assume that both U and V are meet-semilattices. Let $\delta : U \to V$ be a meet-preserving function and let $f : P \to Q$ be a Δ-synchronous function with temporal projection δ. Then f is coherence preserving. Moreover, both P and Q are conditional meet-semilattice and the function f preserves conditional meet, i.e. it is stable in the sense of Berry [6].*

Corollary 4.1. *Let $Coh(P)$ and, resp. $Coh(Q)$ be the set of coherent subsets of P and, resp. of Q, ordered by inclusion. Then, equipped with the point-wise extension of their temporal projection, they both are posets timed over $\mathcal{P}(U)$ and $\mathcal{P}(V)$ respectively. Moreover, the function $f : Coh(P) \to Coh(Q)$ defined by extending f point-wise is Δ-synchronous, stable, and event linear in the sense of Girard [16], i.e. it is well-defined and we have $f(X \cap Y) = f(X) \cap f(Y)$ and $f(X \cup Y) = f(X) \cup f(X)$ for all $X, Y \in Coh(X)$.*

Remark 4.2. In Example 4.2, both U and V are meet semi-lattices, but the function $\delta : U \to V$ is indeed not meet-preserving since, $a \wedge b = \bot$ while $\delta(\bot) = 0 < 1 = \delta(x) \wedge \delta(b)$.

Synchronous Functions. We restrict our attention to a smaller class of timed morphisms we call *synchronous* in the sense that their outputs are timed the same way as their inputs.

Definition 4.2 (Synchronous function). *A function $f : P \to Q$, Δ-synchronous with temporal projection $\delta : U \to V$, is a synchronous function when $U = V$ and $\delta = id_U$. In other words, f is synchronous when:*

(SI1) $\pi(f(x)) = \pi(x)$,
(SI2) *if $x \leq y$ then $f(x) \leq f(y)$,*
(SI3) $f(x \downarrow u) = f(x) \downarrow u$,

for all $x \in P$ and $u \in U$ such that $u \leq \pi(x)$.

Theorem 4.1. *The category $TPoset(T)$ of posets timed over T and synchronous functions is equivalent to the category $Psh(T)$ of presheaves over T and natural transformations. The functor $\varphi : TPoset(T) \to Psh(T)$ defined, for every timed poset $P \in TPoset(T)$, by $\varphi(P) = F_P$ (see Lemma 3.4) and, for all synchronous function $f : P \to Q$ in $TPoset(T)$, by $\varphi(f) = \alpha$ with $\alpha_t(x) = f(x)$ for all $t \in T$ and $x \in F_P(t)$, is a categorical equivalence.*

This implies that the category $TPoset(T)$ is a Grothendieck topos. In the next section, we shall make explicit the constructions that prove it is, as a consequence, an elementary topos.

Δ-synchronous vs Synchronous Functions. We show that every time scale change δ induces a (simple) contravariant time scale change functor in such a way that every Δ-synchronous function f with temporal projection δ uniquely (and uniformly) factorizes into a synchronous function followed by a (simple) time scale change, this functor having a (less simple) left adjoint.

Theorem 4.2 (Left Kan extension). *Let $\delta : U \to V$ be a monotone function. Then there are two categorical functors $\delta^* : TPoset(V) \to TPoset(U)$ and $\delta_! : TPoset(U) \to TPoset(V)$ and, for every $P \in TPoset(U)$ and $Q \in TPoset(V)$, two Δ-synchronous functions $\omega_Q : \delta^*(Q) \to Q$ and $\alpha_P : P \to \delta_!(P)$ both with temporal projection δ, such that every Δ-synchronous $f : P \to Q$ with temporal projection δ we both have:*

(1) there is a unique synchronous function $f^* : P \to \delta^*(Q)$ such that $f = \omega_Q \circ f^*$,
(2) there is a unique synchronous function $f_! : \delta_!(P) \to Q$ such that $f = f_! \circ \alpha_P$,

i.e. f uniquely factorizes through α_P or ω_Q. In particular, there is the categorical adjunction $\delta_! \dashv \delta^*$. The functor $\delta_!$ is the left Kan extension operation along δ. This situation is depicted in (3).

$$
\begin{array}{ccccc}
V & & \delta_!(P) & \xrightarrow{\;\exists! f_!\;} & Q \\
{\scriptstyle\delta}\big\uparrow & & {\scriptstyle\alpha_P}\big\uparrow & \nearrow^{f} & \big\uparrow{\scriptstyle\omega_Q} \\
U & & P & \xrightarrow[\;\exists! f^*\;]{} & \delta^*(Q)
\end{array}
\qquad (3)
$$

Sketch of Proof (simplest case). The functor δ^* can be defined for every $Q \in TPoset(V)$ by $\delta^*(Q) = \{(u,y) \in U \times Q : \pi(y) = \delta(u)\}$ ordered pointwise with projection $\pi(u,y) = u$ for all $(u,y) \in \delta^*(Q)$ and for every synchronous function $h : Q \to Q'$ by $\delta^*(h) : \delta^*(Q) \to DS(Q')$ by $\delta^*(h)(u,y) = (y, h(y))$ for all $(u,y) \in \delta^*(Q)$. Then with $\omega_Q : \delta^*(Q) \to Q$ simply defined by $\omega_Q(u,y) = y$ for every $(u,y) \in \delta^*(Q)$, for every Δ-synchronous $f : P \to Q$ with projection δ we have $f^* : P \to \delta^*(Q)$ uniquely defined by $f^*(x) = (\pi(x), f(x))$. $\square$

Example 4.3 (Timed signals). Continuing examples on signals (see Example 2.4), with $P = Sig(U, A)$ and $Q = Sig(V, B)$, the "lower" part of the above theorem can defined within a slight extension of the notion signals as follows. We define $\delta^*(Q) = Sig^*(\delta, B)$ as the set of all pairs $(u, Y) \in U \times \mathcal{P}(V \times B)$ such that $v \leq \delta(u)$ for all $(v, b) \in Y$, with the cut defined by

$$(u, Y) \downarrow u' = (u', \{(v, b) \in Y : v \leq \delta(u')\})$$

for all $(u, Y) \in Sig^*(\delta, B)$ and $u' \leq u$. Then there is the Δ-synchronous function $\omega_Q : Sig^*(\delta, B) \to Sig(V, B)$ defined by $\omega_Q(u, Y) = (\delta(u), Y)$ for all $(u, Y) \in Sig^*(\delta, B)$ and, for every Δ-synchronous $f : Sig(U, A) \to Sig(V, B)$ with projection δ, the synchronous function $f^* : Sig(U, A) \to Sig^*(\delta, B)$ defined for all $(u, X) \in Sig(U, A)$ by $f^*(u, X) = (u, Y)$ when $f(u, X) = (\delta(u), Y)$ that uniquely factorizes f as above.

For the "upper" part, one can define over $Sig(U, A)$ the least equivalence $\simeq_\delta$ such that $(u, X) \simeq_\delta (u', X')$ whenever there is $u'' \in U$ such that $u, u' \leq u''$, $\delta(u) = \delta(u')$ and $X \downarrow u' = X' \downarrow u$. Then, one can check if $(u, X) \simeq_\delta (u', X')$ then $f(u, X) = f(u', X')$ for any Δ-synchronous function f with temporal projection δ. This means that $Sig(U, A)/\simeq_\delta$ can be used for defining $\delta_!(Q)$. However, in general, it does not seem that such a quotient is itself embeddable into (a sort of) a signal timed poset as done for the "lower" part above.

Remark 4.3. In some sense, in the above example, the function ω_Q acts as a *scheduler* that plans, within the time scale U, the events that will be emitted within the time scale V. Somehow dually, in the case both $\delta_!(Q)$ and α_P are definable over timed signals, for instance when δ is injective, then it can be observed that function α_P acts as a *buffer* that delays events timed on U until they are necessary for computation. More general conditions under which such an interpretation makes sense can be defined within timed signals, but we failed yet to find any general enough to be worth being detailed.

Remark 4.4. Every choice of a time scale provides a granularity at which a system behavior can be observed. The above result can thus be seen as a tool box that allows the behavior of a timed system to be analyzed at various granularity. There appear some potential links with abstraction/refinement techniques for system design [1] and abstract interpretation techniques for system analysis [13].

5   More on Synchronous Functions

Theorem 4.2 shows that Δ-synchronous functions are inherently linked with synchronous functions. Theorem 4.1 ensures that the category $TPoset(T)$ of posets timed over T and synchronous functions is a Grothendieck topos (see Theorem 5.1) therefore an elementary topos. We review below the concrete constructions over timed posets that derive from such a result and, with a view towards system modeling, describe their fairly intuitive interpretation.

Lemma 5.1 (Clock ticks). *Let P be a poset timed over T. Then the temporal projection $\pi : P \to T$ is the unique synchronous function from P into T. In other words, the self-timed poset T is terminal in $TPoset(T)$.*

Remark 5.1. In some sense, the time scale T, seen as a self-timed poset, can be understood as a clock. Indeed, every synchronous function $c : T \to P$ defines a timed constant which is produced, pieces after pieces, as time is passing. Observe however that the existence of such a function implies that $c(T)$ is a subset of P isomorphic to T. There are posets timed over T with no such a subset as shown by any strict downward closed subset of T (see Example 2.2). In other words, timed posets may also contain timed constants in which evolution in time may stop at some instant as if they were timed over a smaller (sub) time scale.

Definition 5.1 (Synchronous product). *Let P, Q be two posets timed over T. The* synchronous product *of P and Q is defined as the set $P \otimes Q = \{(x, y) \in P \times Q : \pi_P(x) = \pi_Q(y)\}$ ordered point-wise and equipped with the temporal projection defined by $\pi(x, y) = \pi(x) = \pi(y)$ for all $(x, y) \in P \otimes Q$.*

Example 5.1 (Timed signals). We have $Sig(T, A) \otimes Sig(T, B) \cong Sig(T, A \oplus B)$.

Lemma 5.2. *Then $P \otimes Q$ is a timed poset over T and, with projections $p_1 : P \otimes Q \to P$ and $p_2 : P \otimes Q \to Q$, it is the categorical product of P and Q in $TPoset(T)$.*

Remark 5.2. The interpretation of the above synchronous product shall be obvious. Thanks to the fact it is a categorical product, every pair of synchronous functions $f : R \to P$ and $g : R \to Q$ uniquely factorizes through some synchronous gluing $f \times g : R \to P \otimes Q$ of the functions f and g. Such a combinator over synchronous functions could be used is an arrow programming style [19].

Remark 5.3 (On coproduct). One can check that the coproduct[2] $P \oplus Q$ of two timed posets with canonical injection eventually leads to the definition of categorical coproduct of P and Q in $TPoset(T)$. Then the empty timed poset is the initial object in $TPoset(T)$. This shows that the category $TPoset(T)$ is bicartesian.

Such a coproduct can be used as a timed alternative. However, such an alternative is very likely to be solved at initialization time, before any instant in T. Indeed, as soon as T has a minimum, every coherent subset of $P \oplus Q$ is necessarily either the embeddings of a coherent subsets of P or the embedding of a coherent subset of Q. No mixed subset is coherent.

Definition 5.2 (Temporal cut of a synchronous function). *Let $f : P \to Q$ be a synchronous function on the time scale T. Let $u \in T$. The* temporal cut *of f at u is the function $f \downarrow u : P \downarrow u \to Q \downarrow u$ defined by $P \downarrow u = \{x \in P : \pi(x) \leq u\}$, $Q \downarrow u = \{y \in Q : \pi(y) \leq u\}$ and $(f \downarrow u)(x) = f(x)$ for all $x \in P \downarrow u$.*

---

[2] Possibly gluing minimal elements when considering the subcategory of timed posets with a minimum elements.

Observe that both $P \downarrow u$ and $Q \downarrow u$ are downward closed hence (see Example 2.2) they both are posets timed over T. Moroever, since f is synchronous, property (SI1) ensures that $f(x) \in Q \downarrow u$ for all $x \in P \downarrow u$ therefore $f \downarrow u$ is a well defined synchronous function from $P \downarrow u$ into $Q \downarrow u$.

Definition 5.3 (Synchronous exponent). *Let P and Q be two posets timed over T. The* synchronous exponent *of Q by P is defined to be the set $[P \to_T Q]$ of all pairs (u, h) with $u \in T$ and synchronous functions $h : P \downarrow u \to Q \downarrow u$, with temporal projection defined by $\pi(u, h) = u$ and partial order defined by $(u_1, h_1) \leq (u_2, h_2)$ when $u_1 \leq u_2$ and $h_1 = h_2 \downarrow u_1$ for all $(u, h), (u_1, h_2), (u_2, h_2) \in [P \to_T Q]$.*

Lemma 5.3. *Let P, Q, R be three posets timed over T. Then $[Q \to_T R]$ is a poset timed over T and the function eval $: Q^R \otimes Q \to R$ defined by $eval((u, h), y) = h(y)$ for all $((u, h), y) \in R^Q \otimes Q$ therefore with $\pi(y) = u$ is synchronous.*

The timed poset $[Q \to_T R]$ with function eval is the categorical exponent *of R by Q in $TPoset(T)$, i.e. for all synchronous function $g : P \otimes Q \to R$, the function $g^* : P \to R^Q$ defined, for all $x \in P$, by $g^*(x) = (\pi(x), \lambda y.g(x \downarrow \pi(y), y))$ is the unique synchronous function from P into R^Q such that $g(x, y) = eval(g^*(x), y)$ for all $(x, y) \in P \otimes Q$.*

Remark 5.4. This result states that every synchronous function $f : P \to Q$ can itself be represented by coherent subset $\{f \downarrow u\}_{u \in T}$ of exponent Q^P which can be transmitted and applied *on-the-fly* over the pieces $\{x \downarrow u\}_{u \leq \pi(x)}$ of an argument $x \in P$. Then, as soon as the instant $\pi(x)$ is reached, such an on-the-fly application stops since the remaining values $\{f \downarrow u\}_{u \not\leq \pi(x)}$ of the functions cannot be synchronized with any further argument. This property could perhaps be used designing a timed programming language where resources are indeed freed whenever a timed (sub)computation terminates.

The following lemma comes as a complement of the construction of timed posets from downward closed subsets of timed posets (see Example 2.2), by characterizing subobjects[3] of the category $TPoset(T)$ precisely as these downward closed subsets.

Lemma 5.4 (Timed subobjects). *Let $f : P \to Q$ be a synchronous function. Then $f(P) = \downarrow f(P)$, moreover, f is injective if and only if $P \simeq f(P)$ as posets.*

In the category *Set*, there is the powerset construction $\mathcal{P}(E)$ of subsets of a set E. In $TPoset(T)$ the analogous power object is defined below.

Definition 5.4 (Synchronous power). *Let P be a poset timed over T. The* synchronous power *of P is defined as the set $\Omega^P = \{(u, X) \in T \times \mathcal{P}(P) : X = \downarrow X, \pi(X) \leq u\}$ with temporal projection defined by $\pi(u, X) = u$ and partial order defined by $(u, X) \leq (v, Y)$ when $u \leq v$ and $X = Y \downarrow u$ for all $(u, X), (v, Y) \in \Omega^P$.*

---

[3] One can easily verify that the monomorphisms in $TPoset(T)$ are the injective synchronous functions. Then, as a consequence of the lemma, every injective synchronous function $f : Q \to P$ is equivalent (as sub-object) with the inclusion synchronous function $inc_{f(Q)} : f(Q) \to P$.

Lemma 5.5. *The synchronous power Ω^P of a timed poset P is a poset timed over T and the* power object *of P in $TPoset(P)$.*

Example 5.2 (Timed signals). Continuing Examples 2.3 and 2.4 one can show that we have $\Omega^{Imp(T,E)} \cong Sig(T,E)$. Indeed, every signal $(u, X) \in Sig(T, E)$ is a collection of (non trivial) timed impulses arrived before or at instant u.

Remark 5.5. The above example illustrates how power objects can be interpreted in terms of parallelism: a computation trace in Ω^P models arbitrarily many computation traces in P that are run synchronously. Moreover, just like subsets, two sub-traces identical at some instant are eventually merged into a single one. Alternatively, it also makes sense to interpret traces in the power object as pending nondeterministic choices much like in power domain constructions.

Remark 5.6. Following topos theory [4,27], the timed domain Ω^T defined by $\Omega^T = \{(u, V) \in T \times \mathcal{P}(T) : V = {\downarrow} V \leq u\}$, with function $true : T \rightarrow \Omega^T$, synchronous, defined by $true(t) = (t, {\downarrow} t)$ for all $t \in T$ is the *subobject classifier* in $TPoset(T)$. In other words, for every poset P timed over T, for every downward closed subset $X \subseteq P$, there is a unique synchronous function $\mathcal{X}_X : P \rightarrow \Omega$, the *characteristic synchronous function* of X, such that, given the synchronous inclusion $inc_X : X \rightarrow P$ we have $\mathcal{X}_f \circ inc_X = true \circ \pi$ and this is a pullback square, i.e. for all synchronous $f : Q \rightarrow P$ such that $\mathcal{X}_f \circ f = true \circ \pi$ we necessarily have $f(Q) = X$ therefore f uniquely factorizes through inc_X.

As an immediate consequence of Theorem 4.1, or gathering the results stated in this section[4], we have:

Theorem 5.1. *The category $TPoset(T)$ is an elementary topos, i.e. it is cartesian closed, finitely complete and has all powerobjects.*

6 More on Δ-synchronous Functions

Clearly, timed posets identities are synchronous functions and every composition of two Δ-synchronous functions is itself Δ-synchronous with temporal projection the composition of their temporal projections. It follows that every choice of a category $\mathbf{C} \subseteq Poset$ of time scales and time scale transformations yields the category $TPoset(\mathbf{C})$ of posets timed over time scales in $\mathbf{C}$ and Δ-synchronous functions with temporal projections that are morphisms in $\mathbf{C}$. In the most general case, one can choose for $\mathbf{C}$ the category $Poset$.

Throughout the rest of the section, we assume that the chosen time scale category $\mathbf{C} \subseteq Poset$ is cartesian closed with terminal poset $\{*\} \in \mathbf{C}$. We also assume some time scales U and $V \in \mathbf{C}$ and some posets P and, resp., $Q \in TPoset(\mathbf{C})$ timed over U and, resp., V.

---

[4] additionally proving that $TPoset(T)$ also has all equalizers, which is easy since they are essentially defined as in *Set*.

Lemma 6.1 (One instant clock). *Let* $\mathbf{1}$ *be the one element poset* $\{*\}$ *timed over itself. Then* $\mathbf{1}$ *is the terminal element in* $TPoset(\mathbf{C})$.

Definition 6.1 (Asynchronous product). *The* asynchronous product *of* P *and* Q *is defined as the cartesian product* $P \times Q$ *ordered pointwise with the temporal projection* $\pi : P \times Q \to U \times V$ *by* $\pi(x, y) = (\pi(x), \pi(y))$.

Lemma 6.2. *Then* $P \times Q$ *is a poset timed over* $U \times V \in \mathbf{C}$. *Both projections* $p_1 : P \times Q \to P$ *and* $p_2 : P \times Q \to Q$ *are* Δ-*synchronous with temporal projection* $\pi(p_1) = p_1 : U \times V \to U$ *in* $\mathbf{C}$ *and* $\pi(p_2) = p_2 : U \times V \to V$ *in* $\mathbf{C}$. *Together, they form the categorical product of* P *and* Q *in* $TPoset(\mathbf{C})$.

Definition 6.2 (Asynchronous exponent). *The* asynchronous exponent *of* Q *by* P *is defined as the set* Q^P *of* Δ-*synchronous function from* P *into* Q *with temporal projections in* $V^U \in \mathbf{C}$ *just as already defined in Definition 4.1.*

Lemma 6.3. *Then* Q^P *is a poset timed over* $V^U \in \mathbf{C}$. *The evaluation mapping* $eval : Q^P \times P \to Q$ *defined, for all* $f \in Q^P$ *and* $x \in P$, *by* $eval(f, x) = f(x)$ *is* Δ-*synchronous with, thanks to (SD1), temporal projection* $\pi(eval) = eval$ *in* $\mathbf{C}$. *Together, they form the exponent of* Q *by* P *in* $TPoset(\mathbf{C})$.

Theorem 6.1. *The category* $TPoset(\mathbf{C})$ *is cartesian closed whenever* $\mathbf{C}$ *is.*

Remark 6.1. The empty poset timed over the empty time scale is the initial object. The disjoint sum is the coproduct in $TPoset(\mathbf{C})$ therefore $TPoset(\mathbf{C})$ is even bi-cartesian closed whenever $\mathbf{C}$ is. The next theorem generalizes such a remark.

Definition 6.3 (Projection of diagram functor). *Let* $G = \langle V, E, s, t \rangle$ *be a graph with vertices* V, *edges* E, *source and target functions* $s, t : E \to V$. *Let* $F : G \to TPoset(\mathbf{C})$ *be a diagram functor[5]. The temporal projection of* F *is defined to be the diagram functor* $H : G \to \mathbf{C}$ *defined by, for all* $v \in V$, *the poset* $H(v)$ *is the time scale over which* $F(v)$ *is timed and, for all* $e \in E$, *the time scale transformation* $H(e)$ *is the temporal projection* $\pi \circ F(e)$ *of the* Δ-*synchronous function* $F(e)$.

Theorem 6.2 (Limit and colimit). *A diagram functor* $F : G \to TPoset(\mathbf{C})$ *has a limit (resp. a co-limit) in* $Poset(\mathbf{C})$ *whenever its temporal projection* $H : G \to \mathbf{C}$ *has a limit (resp. a colimit) in* $\mathbf{C}$.

As a particular case, a fixpoint equation of timed posets (or, as defined below, timed domains) has an inductive (resp. co-inductive) solution whenever the projection of this equation over time scales has an inductive (resp. co-inductive) solution.

---

[5] We call here a diagram functor a functor from the category freely generated by a graph G. As such a functor is fully determined by its value on graph vertices and edges it can simply be seen as a graph morphism from G into (the graph of) its codomain category.

7   Timed Domains

Timed domains ought to be cpos timed over cpos with continuous projections and cuts. Such a definition is formalized via the notion of pre-continuous timed posets so that timed domains can precisely be defined as pre-continuous timed posets timed over cpos.

Definition 7.1 (Pre-continous timed posets). *Let P be a poset timed over T. We say that P is a pre-continuous timed poset when*

(IN3) *if X is directed and $\bigvee \pi(X)$ is defined then so is $\bigvee X$, for all $X \subseteq P$.*

Remark 7.1. In general, neither $Imp(T, E)$ nor $Sig(T, E)$ (see Examples 2.3 and 2.4) are pre-continuous. Indeed, as soon as there is $t = \bigvee U$ with directed $U \subseteq T$ and $t \notin U$, then, in $Imp(T, E)$, we have $\{(t, e) \downarrow u\}_{u \in U} = \{(t, \bot) \downarrow u\}_{u \in U}$ therefore this set as no upper bound. A remedy to this fact is proposed below.

Example 7.1 (Observable timed signals). Let $\ll$ be the relation called here *way before*, defined for every instant $t, u \in T$ by $t \ll u$ when for every directed subset $U \subseteq X$ such that $\bigvee U = u$ there must exists $u' \in U$ such that $t \leq u'$. Let $Sig_C(T, E) \subseteq Sig(T, E)$ be the set of timed signals (u, X) such that $t \ll u$ for all $(t, e) \in X$, i.e. every event $(t, e) \in X$ is *observable* in the sense that it can be observed in any series of observations performed as any (directed) set of instants U such that $\bigvee U = u$. Then, with the cut $(u, X) \downarrow u' = (u', \{(t, e) \in X : t \ll u'\})$ defined for all $u' \leq u$, the resulting set of signals $Sig_C(T, E)$ is a pre-continuous timed poset though not, in general, a sub-timed poset of $Sig(T, E)$.

Lemma 7.1. *Let P be a pre-continous timed poset timed over T. Then, for every $x \in P$ the local cut $cut_x : \downarrow \pi(x) \to P$ (see Definition 2.2) is continuous.*

Remark 7.2. In general, the continuity of all local cuts in a timed poset *does not* imply the continuity of that timed poset as shown by the example $P_1 = \mathbb{N}$ timed as a timed subset of $T_1 = \overline{\mathbb{N}} = \mathbb{N} \cup \{\infty\}$ self-timed.

Also, the continuity of a timed poset *does not* imply the continuity of its temporal projection, as shown by the example $P_2 = \overline{\mathbb{N}}$ timed as a timed subset of $T_2 = \overline{\mathbb{N}} \cup \{\infty'\}$ self-timed, with ∞' another upper bound of $\mathbb{N}$, distinct and incomparable with ∞.

Lemma 7.2. *Let P be a pre-continuous timed poset, timed over T. Assume that T is complete. Then P is complete and its temporal projection is continuous.*

Definition 7.2 (Timed domain). *A timed domain is a pre-continuous timed poset timed over a complete time scale, hence, as proved above also a complete poset with continuous local cuts and temporal projection.*

Remark 7.3. As a consequence of Lemma 7.1, a timed domain P is continuous/algebraic in the sense of Scott if and only if T itself is continuous/algebraic. Indeed, it can be shown that for all $x, y \in P$, we have $x \ll y$ if and only if $\pi(x) \ll \pi(u)$.

Lemma 7.3 (Δ-synchronous vs continuous). *Let P and Q be two timed domains. Let $f : P \to Q$ be a Δ-synchronous function with temporal projection $\delta : U \to V$. Assume that δ is continuous. Then f is continuous.*

Remark 7.4. As a special case of the above lemma every synchronous function between timed domains is continuous.

Theorem 7.1. *Let T be a cpo. Then the category $TCpo(T)$ of timed domain over T and, when T has a least element, the category $TCpo_\perp(T)$ of timed domain over T with least element, with, in both cases, synchronous (and continuous) functions between them, are topoi.*

Proof (Sketch of). The proof goes by rephrasing the Scott topology in terms of a Grothendieck topology J over posets in such a way that (the categories of elements of the) sheaves in $Sh(T, J)$ are the pre-continuous timed posets timed over T. As a reminder, a subset X of a poset E is Scott closed when it is downward closed and for every directed $Y \subseteq X$, if $\bigvee Y$ is defined then $\bigvee Y \in X$. Then, for every $t \in T$, we define $J(t)$ to be the set of all downward closed subsets $U \subseteq T$ such that $U \leq t$, i.e. U is a sieve on t, and their Scott closure $\overline{U}$ equals $\downarrow t$.

One can easily check that J is a Grothendieck topology (see [27] p. 110). Moreover, one can also check that a timed poset $P \in TPoset(T)$ is pre-continuous if and only if its associated presheaf $F_P : T^{op} \to Set$ (see Lemma 3.4) is a sheaf for J (see [27] p. 121). This ensures that the categorical equivalence between $TPoset(T)$ and $Psh(T)$ (see Theorem 4.1) also defines a categorical equivalence between the subcategories $TCpo(T)$ and $Sh(T, J)$. It follows that $TCpo(T)$ is also a topos since $Sh(T, J)$ is.

For the category $TCpo_\perp(T)$ the argument is similar, though taking instead the topology J' defined from J, by letting $J'(t) = J(t)$ when $t > \perp$ and $J'(\perp) = \{\{\perp\}, \emptyset\}$. This forces every sheaf in $Sh(T, J')$ to be a singleton on $\perp$, and therefore its category of elements to have a least element. □

Remark 7.5. The terminal object, products and exponentials in both $TCpo(T)$ and $TCpo_\perp(T)$ are defined just in the same way as in $TPoset(T)$. The power object Ω^P differs from $TPoset(T)$ by the fact that it only contains pairs of the form $(u, X) \in T \times \mathcal{P}(P)$ where X is not only downward closed but also Scott closed. This follows from the fact that in both $TCpo(T)$ or $TCpo_\perp(T)$, subobjects correspond to Scott closed subsets of timed domains.

Theorem 7.2. *Both categories $TCpo(Cpo)$ of timed domains or $TCpo_\perp(Cpo_\perp)$ of timed domains with least elements, and, in both cases, Δ-synchronous functions with continuous temporal projections (therefore themselves continuous) are cartesian closed categories.*

Remark 7.6. Both categories above have an initial object when extended with the empty timed domain over the empty time scale. They also have coproducts: the disjoint sum in $TCpo(Cpo)$ and the coalescent sum in $TCpo_\perp(Cpo_\perp)$.

In other words, both (slightly extended) categories are bi-cartesian closed. More generally, it can be shown that Theorem 6.2 still holds when restricted to the category $TCpo_\perp(Cpo_\perp)$.

8   Timed Fixpoints and Causality

In the category $TCpo_\perp(Cpo_\perp)$ of timed domains with least elements, every Δ-synchronous function has a least fixpoint. Following the footsteps of Matsikoudis and Lee [28], we examine below the property of the induced least fixpoint operators.

Lemma 8.1. *Let $P \in TCpo_\perp(Cpo_\perp)$ be a timed domain with least element $\perp_P$ timed over a complete time scale T with least element $\perp_T$. Let $f : P \to P$ be a Δ-synchronous function with continuous temporal projection $\delta : T \to T$. Then both least fixpoints $\mu_P(f) \in P$ and $\mu_T(\delta) \in T$ are defined. Moreover, we have $\pi \circ \mu_P(f) = \mu_T(\delta)$.*

Example 8.1 (Timed signals). Let $T = \overline{\mathbb{R}^+}$ be the time scale of positive reals completed with a maximum element ∞. Let $f : Sig(T, E) \to Sig(T, E)$ defined for all $(u, X) \in Sig(T, E)$ by $f(u, X) = (u + 2, \{(0, e_0)\} \cup \{(t + 2, e) : (t, e) \in X\})$ for some fixed event value $e_0 \in E$. Then f is Δ-synchronous with temporal projection $t \mapsto t + 2$ with ∞ as least fixpoint. Then we have the least fixpoint $\mu(f) = (\infty, \{(2 * n, e_0) : n \in \mathbb{N}\})$.

Theorem 8.1. *Let P^P be the exponent in $TCpo_\perp(Cpo_\perp)$ of the timed domain P by itself and let T^T be the exponent of the object T by itself in $Cpo_\perp$. Then the least-fixpoint mapping $\mu_P : P^P \to P$ is a Δ-synchronous function with continuous temporal projection $\pi(\mu_P) = \mu_T : T^T \to T$.*

Remark 8.1. When computing the fixpoint of a function f the output of that function is sort of rewired on its input. In signal processing, there is a feedback loop. Since both inputs and outputs lie in the same timed domain, their temporal projections lie in the same time scale and can thus be compared. By default, every Δ-synchronous function is *locally causal* in the sense that, by monotonicity, for every $n \in \omega$, with $x_n = f^n(\perp_P)$, we have $x_n \leq f(x_n)$ and $\pi(x_n) \leq \pi(f(x_n))$. This suffices for Theorem 8.1 to hold. However, intuition suggests that we could require these functions to be globally causal as defined and studied below.

Definition 8.1 (Global causality). *Let P be a poset timed over T with least element $\perp_P \in P$ therefore also a least element $\perp_T \in T$. Let $f : P \to P$ be a Δ-synchronous function with temporal projection $\delta : T \to T$. We say that f is globally causal when $\pi(x) \leq \pi(f(x))$ for every $x \in P$. Equivalently, by (SD1), when $t \leq \delta(t)$ for all $t \in \pi(P)$.*

Though not needed in the general case, such a notion appears when restricting to $TCpo_\perp(SLattice_\perp)$ so that Δ-synchronous function preserves arbitrary coherence (Lemma 4.2). Indeed, in $SLattice_\perp$, the fixpoint function μ_T is not in general meet-preserving hence Theorem 8.1 fails.

Theorem 8.2. *In the category* $TCpo_\perp(CSLattice_\perp)$ *of domains timed over continuous meet-semilattices and* Δ-*synchronous functions with meet-preserving temporal projections, the fixpoint mapping* $\mu_P : P^P \to P$ *is* Δ-*synchronous provided we restrict ourselves to causal* Δ-*synchronous functions.*

Remark 8.2. Despite such a result, global causality remains quite an ad hoc restriction. We are still in need of some additional restrictions on the notion of Δ-synchronous functions in a category $TCpo_\perp(\mathbf{C}_\perp)$ that would guarantee their combinations to be globally causal whenever applicable. For such a purpose, adjunctions in posets could be a direction to investigate.

9   Conclusion

Along these pages, we have detailed a possible mathematical framework for the modeling of spatio-temporal system behaviors that extends to space and time the classical notion of cpos and continuous functions used in denotational semantics.

Bi-cartesian closed with internal fixpoint operators, and essentially all limits or co-limits that may exist in $Cpo_\perp$, the category $TCpo_\perp(Cpo_\perp)$ eventually turned out to be a fairly general and fully featured category for defining and analyzing the behaviors of timed programs with both synchronous and asynchronous versions of typical categorical constructs such as sum, products or exponents, as well as, in the synchronous case, power-objects.

Technically rooted in topos and fibration theory, via the category of elements of sheaves over certain Grothendieck topologies, the resulting definitions and constructions have (mostly) been stated in elementary mathematical terms. This means that, after some more polishing and more detailed application studies, such material could even be taught to standard students in computer science and software engineering.

With a view towards concrete applications, we have not yet developed at all the potential offered by the left Kan extension theorem (see Theorems 4.2 and 4.3). When time scales are built from concrete numerical scales such a $\mathbb{N}$, $\mathbb{Q}^+$ or $\mathbb{R}^+$, it allows us to define sound lifting of operators over these time scales such as delays, projections, stretches, etc., into timed program constructs. This would lead to pursuing the research program initiated by Paul Hudak for an algebraic and programming theory of Polymorphic Temporal Media [17] and the somehow related though earlier proposal of Functional Reactive Programming [14,15]. Links with the related ultrametric [24] or categorical models [21,22] could be investigated.

Examples over timed signals detailed throughout suggest that timed domains also may induce some notion of timed operational semantics, probably deeply linked with the existing state based timed system modeling frameworks such as IO-timed automata theory [23]. This surely necessitates focussing our attention on finite (or finitely representable) spaced and timed functions, a necessity that may benefit from our somewhat strong restriction to timed behaviors that uniformly act on the underlying time scales.

Acknowledgment. The author wishes to express his deep gratitude to Gordon Plotkin and Phil Scott for their early advice to look at the notion of presheaves, to Marek Zawadowski for his help in understanding Grothendieck topologies and sheaves, to referees for their numerous suggestions of improvement, and to Simon Archipoff, Michail Raskin and Bernard Serpette for many fruitful discussions on various aspects of this work.

References

1. Abrial, J.R.: Modeling in Event-B: System and Software Design. Cambridge University Press, Cambridge (2010). https://doi.org/10.1017/cbo9781139195881
2. Archipoff, S., Janin, D.: Structured reactive programming with polymorphic temporal tiles. In: Proceedings of 4th ACM SIGPLAN International Workshop on Functional Art, Music, Modeling and Design FARM 2016, pp. 29–40. ACM Press, New York (2016). https://doi.org/10.1145/2975980.2975984
3. Archipoff, S., Janin, D.: Unified media programming: an algebraic approach. In: Proceedings of 5th ACM SIGPLAN International Workshop on Functional Art, Music, Modeling and Design, FARM 2017, pp. 36–47. ACM Press, New York (2017). https://doi.org/10.1145/3122938.3122943
4. Barr, M., Wells, C.: Category Theory for Computing Science, 3rd edn. Centre de Recherche Mathématique (CRM), Montréal (1999)
5. Benveniste, A., Caspi, P., Edwards, S.A., Halbwachs, N., Le Guernic, P., De Simone, R.: The synchronous languages twelve years later. Proc. IEEE **91**(1), 64–83 (2003)
6. Berry, G.: Stable models of typed λ-calculi. In: Ausiello, G., Böhm, C. (eds.) ICALP 1978. LNCS, vol. 62, pp. 72–89. Springer, Heidelberg (1978). https://doi.org/10.1007/3-540-08860-1_7
7. Berry, G., Gonthier, G.: The Esterel synchronous programming language: design, semantics, implementation. Sci. Comput. Program. **19**(2), 87–152 (1992). https://doi.org/10.1016/0167-6423(92)90005-v
8. Cattani, G.L., Stark, I., Winskel, G.: Presheaf models for the π-calculus. In: Moggi, E., Rosolini, G. (eds.) CTCS 1997. LNCS, vol. 1290, pp. 106–126. Springer, Heidelberg (1997). https://doi.org/10.1007/BFb0026984
9. Cattani, G.L., Winskel, G.: Presheaf models for CCS-like languages. Theor. Comput. Sci. **300**(1–3), 47–89 (2003). https://doi.org/10.1016/s0304-3975(01)00209-2
10. Chapiro, D.M.: Globally-asynchronous locally-synchronous systems. Ph.D. thesis, Department of Computer Science, Stanford University (1985)
11. Colaço, J.L., Girault, A., Hamon, G., Pouzet, M.: Towards a higher-order synchronous data-flow language. In: Proceedings of 4th ACM International Conference on Embedded Software, EMSOFT 2004, Pisa, Septemebr 2004, pp. 230–239. ACM Press, New York (2004). https://doi.org/10.1145/1017753.1017792
12. Colaço, J.-L., Pouzet, M.: Clocks as first class abstract types. In: Alur, R., Lee, I. (eds.) EMSOFT 2003. LNCS, vol. 2855, pp. 134–155. Springer, Heidelberg (2003). https://doi.org/10.1007/978-3-540-45212-6_10
13. Cousot, P., Cousot, R., Mauborgne, L.: Logical abstract domains and interpretations. In: Nanz, S. (ed.) The Future of Software Engineering (Meyer Festschrift), pp. 48–71. Springer, Heidelberg (2010). https://doi.org/10.1007/BFb0026984

14. Elliott, C., Hudak, P.: Functional reactive animation. In: Proceedings of 2nd ACM International Conference on Functional Programming, ICFP 1997, Amsterdam, June 1997, pp. 263–273. ACM Press, New York (1997). https://doi.org/10.1145/258948.258973

15. Elliott, C.M.: Push-pull functional reactive programming. In: Proceedings of 2nd ACM SIGPLAN Symposium on Haskell, Haskell 2009, Edinburgh, September 2009, pp. 25–36. ACM Press, New York (2009) https://doi.org/10.1145/1596638.1596643

16. Girard, J.Y.: Linear logic. Theor. Comput. Sci. **50**, 1–102 (1987). https://doi.org/10.1016/0304-3975(87)90045-4

17. Hudak, P.: A sound and complete axiomatization of polymorphic temporal media. Technical report, RR-1259, Department of Computer Science, Yale University (2008)

18. Hudak, P.: The Haskell School of Music: From Signals to Symphonies. Department of Computer Science, Yale University (2013)

19. Hughes, J.: Programming with arrows. In: Vene, V., Uustalu, T. (eds.) AFP 2004. LNCS, vol. 3622, pp. 73–129. Springer, Heidelberg (2005). https://doi.org/10.1007/11546382_2

20. Jacobs, B.: Categorical Logic and Type Theory. Studies in Logic and the Foundations of Mathematics, vol. 141. North Holland, Amsterdam (1999). https://www.sciencedirect.com/bookseries/studies-in-logic-and-the-foundations-of-mathematics/vol/141/

21. Jeffrey, A.: Functional reactive types. In: Proceedings of EACSL Annual Conference and 29th Ann ACM/IEEE Symposium on Logic in Computer Science, CSL-LICS 2014, Vienna, July 2014, Article 54. ACM Press, New York (2014). https://doi.org/10.1145/2603088.2603106

22. Jeltsch, W.: An abstract categorical semantics for functional reactive programming with processes. In: Proceedings of 2014 ACM SIGPLAN Workshop on Programming Languages Meets Program Verification, PLPV 2014, San Diego, CA, January 2014, pp. 47–58. ACM Press, New York (2014). https://doi.org/10.1145/2541568.2541573

23. Kaynar, D.K., Lynch, N., Segala, R., Vaandrager, F.: The Theory of Timed I/O Automata. Synthesis Lectures on Computer Science. Morgan & Claypool Publishers (2006). https://doi.org/10.2200/s00006ed1v01y200508csl001

24. Krishnaswami, N.R.: Higher-order functional reactive programming without space-time leaks. In: Proceedings of 18th ACM SIGPLAN International Conference on Functional Programming, ICFP 2013, Boston, MA, September 2013, pp. 221–232. ACM Press, New York (2013). https://doi.org/10.1145/2500365.2500588

25. Krishnaswami, N.R., Benton, N.: Ultrametric semantics of reactive programs. In: Proceedings of 26th Annual IEEE Symposium on Logic in Computer Science, LICS 2011, Toronto, ON, June 2011, pp. 257–266. IEEE CS Press, Washington, DC (2011). https://doi.org/10.1109/lics.2011.38

26. Liu, X., Lee, E.A.: CPO semantics of timed interactive actor networks. Theor. Comput. Sci. **409**(1), 110–125 (2008). https://doi.org/10.1016/j.tcs.2008.08.044

27. Mac Lane, S., Moerdijk, I.: Sheaves in Geometry and Logic: A First Introduction to Topos Theory. Universitext. U. Springer, New York (1992). https://doi.org/10.1007/978-1-4612-0927-0

28. Matsikoudis, E., Lee, E.A.: The fixed-point theory of strictly causal functions. Theor. Comput. Sci. **574**, 39–77 (2015)

29. Streicher, T.: Fibred categories à la Jean Bénabou. Revised notes of a course on fibred categories given at a spring school in Munich 1999 (2014)

30. Teehan, P., Greenstreet, M.R., Lemieux, G.G.: A survey and taxonomy of GALS design styles. IEEE Des. Test. Comput. **24**(5), 418–428 (2007). https://doi.org/10.1109/mdt.2007.151

31. Winskel, G.: Event structures. In: Brauer, W., Reisig, W., Rozenberg, G. (eds.) ACPN 1986. LNCS, vol. 255, pp. 325–392. Springer, Heidelberg (1987). https://doi.org/10.1007/3-540-17906-2_31

32. Winskel, G.: Events, causality and symmetry. In: Proceedings of BCS International Academic Conference on Visions of Computer Science, London, September 2008, pp. 111–127. Electronic Workshops in Computing. British Computer Society (2008). https://ewic.bcs.org/content/ConWebDoc/22872

Checking Modal Contracts for Virtually Timed Ambients

Einar Broch Johnsen, Martin Steffen, Johanna Beate Stumpf$^{(\boxtimes)}$, and Lars Tveito

Inst. for informatikk, Universitetet i Oslo,
Postboks 1080, Blindern, 0316 Oslo, Norway
{einarj,msteffen,johanbst,larstvei}@ifi.uio.no

Abstract. The calculus of virtually timed ambients models timing aspects of resource management for virtual machines. With nested virtualization, virtual machines compete with other processes for the resources of their host environment. Resource provisioning in virtually timed ambients can be formalized by extending the capabilities of mobile ambients to model the dynamic creation, migration, and destruction of virtual machines. This paper introduces a logic to define modal contracts regarding resource management for virtually timed ambients. Service-level agreements are contracts between a service provider and a client, specifying properties that the service should fulfill with respect to quality of service (QoS). The proposed modal logic supports QoS statements about the resource consumption and nesting structure of a system during the timed reduction of its processes. Besides a formal definition of the logic, the paper provides a corresponding model checking algorithm and its prototype implementation in rewriting logic.

1 Introduction

In cloud-computing, a service-level agreement is an official commitment or contract between a cloud-service provider and a client. Service-level agreements are offered by service providers to specify the services that should be provided to the customer as well as properties the system has to satisfy with respect to quality of service, such as mean time between failures, responsibility for various data rates, resource consumption, etc. *Quality of service* (QoS) approaches in cloud computing have recently been surveyed [1], confirming that open challenges remain which require further research to provide trustworthy cloud computing services that deliver appropriate QoS. This paper provides a formalization to support QoS statements via modal contracts for virtually timed ambients.

The calculus of *virtually timed ambients* [22] is a calculus of explicit resource provisioning, based on mobile ambients [10]. It can be used to model nested virtualization in cloud systems. Virtualization technology enables the resources of an execution environment to be represented as a software layer, a so-called virtual machine. *Nested virtualization* [19] is a crucial technology to support the heterogeneous cloud [17], as it enables virtual machines to migrate between

B. Fischer and T. Uustalu (Eds.): ICTAC 2018, LNCS 11187, pp. 252–272, 2018.
https://doi.org/10.1007/978-3-030-02508-3_14

different cloud providers [38]. It is also necessary to host virtual machines with operating systems which themselves support virtualization [7], such as Microsoft Windows 7 and Linux KVM. The time model used to realize resource provisioning for virtually timed ambients is called *virtual time*. Virtual time is provided to a virtually timed ambient by its parental ambient, similar to the time slices that an operating system provisions to its processes. When considering multiple levels of nested virtualization, virtual time becomes a *local* notion of time which depends on a virtually timed ambient's position in the nesting structure. Virtually timed ambients are mobile, reflecting that virtual machines may migrate between host virtual machines. Observe that such migration affects the execution speed of processes in the migrating virtually timed ambient, as well as in the virtually timed ambient which is left, and in the virtually timed ambient which is entered.

This paper defines *modal contracts* which capture QoS statements for cloud systems modeled in virtually timed ambients. As virtually timed ambients can model nested virtualization in cloud systems, the modal contracts provide information on the resource consumption and nesting structure of a system of virtually timed ambients during the timed reduction of its processes. Modal contracts are formalized as properties in modal logic that a system has to satisfy. The modal logic we consider combines modal logic for mobile ambients with notions based on metric temporal logic to obtain a modal logic for virtually timed ambients. Modal logic for mobile ambients [9] enables us to make statements about the behavior of ambient systems during their reduction. Timing constraints on modalities are introduced in metric temporal logic [24,31,32], which is an extension of linear temporal logic.

To prove that a system satisfies a given modal contract, we define a simple *model checking algorithm*. We further contribute a *prototype-implementation* of the model checker in Maude [16], which is a formal specification and programming system based on rewriting logic [27].

Contributions. The main contributions of this paper are the following:

- we combine *modal logic* for mobile ambients with notions based on *metric temporal logic* in order to capture the special features of virtual time and resource provisioning in virtually timed ambients;
- we show that the resulting logic is a *conservative extension* of the modal logic for the ambient calculus, preserving satisfiability;
- we define a *model checking algorithm* for this modal logic, and develop a prototype implementation in the rewriting logic system *Maude*; and
- we illustrate all concepts by *examples*.

To the best of our knowledge, this is the first implementation of modal logic for mobile ambients in rewriting logic, and the first implementation of a model checker for mobile ambients considering time or resources.

Paper Overview. We introduce virtually timed ambients in Sect. 2. Section 3 considers modal logic for such ambients. Section 4 introduces a model checker algorithm. Section 5 presents the implementation of the model checker in rewriting logic. We discuss related work and conclude in Sects. 6 and 7.

Table 1. Syntax of virtually timed ambients, $x \in \mathbb{N}_0$.

n	name
tick	virtual time slice
Timed processes:	
$P, Q ::= \mathbf{0}$	inactive process
$\mid P \mid Q$	parallel composition
$\mid (\nu n)\, P$	restriction
$\mid\, !C.P$	replication
$\mid C.P$	prefixing
$\mid n[\text{SCHED} \mid \text{tick}^x \mid P]$	virtually timed ambient
Timed capabilities:	
$C ::= \mathbf{in}\ n$	enter n and adjust the local scheduler there
$\mid \mathbf{out}\ n$	exit n and adjust the local scheduler on the outside
$\mid \mathbf{open}\ n$	open n and adjust own local scheduler
$\mid \mathbf{c}$	consume a resource

2 Virtually Timed Ambients

Virtually timed ambients [22,23] is a calculus of explicit resource provisioning, based on mobile ambients. Mobile ambients [10] are processes with a concept of location, arranged in a dynamically evolving hierarchy. Interpreting these locations as places of deployment, virtually timed ambients extend mobile ambients with notions of virtual time and resource consumption. The timed behavior depends on the one hand on the *local* timed behavior, and on the other hand on the placement or deployment of the virtually timed ambient or process in the hierarchical ambient structure. Virtually timed ambients combine timed processes and timed capabilities with the features of mobile ambients.

Definition 1 (Virtually timed ambients). *The syntax of virtually timed ambients is given by the grammar in Table 1.*

Timed processes differ from mobile ambients in that each virtually timed ambient contains, besides possibly further (virtually timed) subambients, a *local scheduler*. In the sequel, we omit the qualification "timed" or "virtually timed", when speaking about processes, capabilities, or ambients when the context of virtually timed ambients is clear. In the calculus, the locations for processes, called *virtually timed ambients*, are represented by names, and time slices are written as tick. The inactive process **0** does nothing. The parallel composition $P \mid Q$ allows both processes P and Q to proceed concurrently, where the binary operator $|$ is commutative and associative. The restriction operator $(\nu n)P$ creates a new and unique name with process P as its scope. Replication of processes is given as $!C.P$. A process P located in an virtually timed ambient named n is written $n[\text{SCHED} \mid \text{tick}^x \mid P]$, where $\text{tick}^0 \equiv \mathbf{0}$. Ambients can be nested, and the nesting structure can change dynamically, this is specified by prefixing a process with a *capability C.P*. *Timed capabilities* extend the capabilities of mobile ambients by including a *resource consumption* capability **c** and by giving the *opening, exiting*, and *entering* capabilities of mobile ambients a *timed interpretation*. These capabilities restructure the hierarchy of an ambient system, so the behavior of local schedulers and resource consumption changes, as these depend on the placement of the timed ambient in the hierarchy.

The semantics of virtually timed ambients is given as a reduction system. The *reduction* relation $P \twoheadrightarrow Q$ for virtually timed ambients is captured by the rules in Tables 2 and 3. The rules for structural congruence $P \equiv Q$ are equivalent to those for mobile ambients (and thus omitted here). The rules in Table 2 make use of *observables,* also known as *barbs*. Barbs, originally introduced for the π-calculus [28], capture a notion of immediate observability. In the ambient calculus, these observations concern the presence of a top-level ambient whose name is not restricted. Let $\widetilde{m}$ describe a tuple of names, then the observability predicate $\downarrow_n$ or "barb" is defined as follows:

Definition 2 (Barbs, from [25]). *A process P strongly barbs on a name n, written $P\downarrow_n$, if $P \equiv (\nu\widetilde{m})(n[P_1] \mid P_2)$, where $n \notin \{\widetilde{m}\}$.*

A process that does not contain ν-binders is considered to be ν-*binder free*. By moving the ν-binders to the outside and only considering the inside of their scope, we can observe the bound ambients inside the scope of the ν-binders.

Definition 3 (Timed top-level ambients). *For a process P, let $P_\downarrow$ denote the set of all timed top-level ambients: $P_\downarrow = \{n \mid P \equiv (\nu\widetilde{m})P' \wedge P' is \nu\text{-}binderfree \wedge P'\downarrow_n \wedge speed_n > 0\}$.*

In a virtually timed ambient, the local scheduler is responsible for triggering timed behavior and local resource consumption. Each time slice emitted by a local scheduler triggers the scheduler of a subambient or is consumed by a process as a resource in a preemptive, yet *fair* way, which makes system behavior sensitive to co-located virtually timed ambients and resource consuming processes.

Definition 4 (Local and root schedulers). *Let the variables unserved and served denote sets containing names of virtually timed ambients as well as processes (represented directly, lacking names). A local scheduler is denoted by*

$$\text{SCHED}_{speed}\{in, out, rest, unserved, served\},$$

where $speed \in \mathbb{Q}$ relates externally received to internally emitted time slices; $in \in \mathbb{N}$ records the number of received time slices; $out \in \mathbb{N}$ records the number of time slices to be distributed for each incoming time slice, while $rest \in \mathbb{N}$ records *additional distributable time slices depending on the speed; and unserved contains local ambients with a positive speed and processes which are intended to receive one time slice in this round of the scheduling, while served contains processes scheduled for the next round.*

Root schedulers, *represented as* SCHED$^\dagger\{in, out, 0, unserved, served\}$, *are local schedulers which do not need an input to distribute time slices and therefore have no defined speed.*

The reduction rules for virtually timed ambients are given in Tables 2 and 3. The timed capabilities **in** n, **out** n, and **open** n enable virtually timed ambients to move in the hierarchical ambient structure. The local schedulers need to know about the current subambients, so their lists of subambients must be adjusted when virtually timed ambients move. Observe that without adjusting the schedulers, the moving subambient would not receive time slices from the scheduler in its new surrounding ambient. In TR-IN and TR-OUT, the schedulers of the old and new surrounding ambient of the moving ambient are updated by removing and adding, respectively, the name of the moving ambient, if it has a speed greater than zero. The scheduler of the moving subambient is also updated as it needs to contain the barbs of the process that was hidden behind the movement capability. In TR-OPEN, the scheduler of the opening ambient itself is updated by removing the name of the opened ambient and adding the barbs of the processes inside this ambient as well as the barbs of the process hidden behind the open capability. The scheduler of the opened ambient is deleted. In TR-RESOURCE, the time consuming process moves into the scheduler, where it awaits the distribution of a time slice as resource before it can continue. This reduction can only happen in virtually timed ambients with speed greater zero, meaning ambients which actually emit resources.

The rules in Table 3 distribute time slices via the local schedulers. We want to enable the schedulers to distribute time slices as soon as possible. The ratio of output time slices to input time slices is defined by the *speed* $\in \mathbb{Q}$ of the scheduler. For example, for a speed of $3/2$ the first incoming time slice (`tick`) should trigger one outgoing time slice and the second input should trigger two, emitting in total three time slices for two inputs. Thus, in order to implement a simple *eager scheduling strategy*, we make use of the so-called *Egyptian fraction decomposition* to determine the number of time slices to be distributed by the local scheduler for each incoming time slice `tick`. For every rational number $q \in \mathbb{Q}$ it holds that $q = x + \sum_{y=1}^{z} \frac{1}{b_y}$ for $x, b_y \in \mathbb{N}$, which is solvable in polynomial time. A greedy algorithm (e.g., [18]) additionally yields the desirable property that a time slice is distributed as soon as possible. From this decomposition, it follows that for each input time slice the local scheduler with speed q will distribute x time slices, plus one additional time slice for every b_y-th input.

In RR-TICK, the local scheduler receives a time slice, which it registers in the counter *in*. At the same time *out* and *rest* initiate the distribution of time slices depending on the Egyptian fraction decomposition of the speed of the scheduler. These steps of the time slice distribution are shown in the RR-TOCK rules, which allow transferring a new `tick` to a timed subambient or using the time slice as

Table 2. Reduction rules for timed capabilities. A blue backdrop marks the trigger of the reduction, red the changes in the schedulers, and green eventual constraints.

$\text{SDL}_k = \text{SCHED}_{speed_k}\{in_k, out_k, rest_k, U_k, S_k\}, \ n \in U_k \cup S_k$

$\text{SDL}_m = \text{SCHED}_{speed_m}\{in_m, out_m, rest_m, U_m, S_m\}$

$\text{SDL}_n = \text{SCHED}_{speed_n}\{in_n, out_n, rest_n, U_n, S_n\}$

$\text{SDL}'_k = \text{SCHED}_{speed_k}\{in_k, out_k, rest_k, \boxed{U_k \setminus \{n\}, S_k \setminus \{n\}}\}$

$\text{SDL}'_m = \text{SCHED}_{speed_m}\{in_m, out_m, rest_m, U_m, S_m \cup \boxed{\{n\}}\}, \ \text{if } speed_n > 0 \text{ else } \text{SDL}_m$

$\text{SDL}'_n = \text{SCHED}_{speed_n}\{in_n, out_n, rest_n, U_n, S_n \cup \boxed{P_\downarrow}\}$

$$k[\text{SDL}_k \mid n[\text{SDL}_n \mid \boxed{\mathbf{in}\ m.P} \mid Q] \mid m[\text{SDL}_m \mid R] \mid U] \qquad \text{(TR-In)}$$
$$\rightarrow k[\text{SDL}'_k \mid m[\text{SDL}'_m \mid R \mid n[\text{SDL}'_n \mid P \mid Q]] \mid U]$$

$\text{SDL}_k = \text{SCHED}_{speed_k}\{in_k, out_k, rest_k, U_k, S_k\}, \ n \in U_m \cup S_m$

$\text{SDL}_m = \text{SCHED}_{speed_m}\{in_m, out_m, rest_m, U_m, S_m\}$

$\text{SDL}_n = \text{SCHED}_{speed_n}\{in_n, out_n, rest_n, U_n, S_n\}$

$\text{SDL}'_k = \text{SCHED}_{speed_k}\{in_k, out_k, rest_k, U_k, S_k \cup \boxed{\{n\}}\}, \ \text{if } speed_n > 0 \text{ else } \text{SDL}_k$

$\text{SDL}'_m = \text{SCHED}_{speed_m}\{in_m, out_m, rest_m, \boxed{U_m \setminus \{n\}, S_m \setminus \{n\}}\}$

$\text{SDL}'_n = \text{SCHED}_{speed_n}\{in_n, out_n, rest_n, U_n, S_n \cup \boxed{P_\downarrow}\}$

$$k[\text{SDL}_k \mid m[\text{SDL}_m \mid n[\text{SDL}_n \mid \boxed{\mathbf{out}\ m.P} \mid Q] \mid R] \mid U] \qquad \text{(TR-Out)}$$
$$\rightarrow k[\text{SDL}'_k \mid n[\text{SDL}'_n \mid P \mid Q] \mid m[\text{SDL}'_m \mid R] \mid U]$$

$\text{SDL}_k = \text{SCHED}_{speed_k}\{in_k, out_k, rest_k, U_k, S_k\}, \ n \in U_k \cup S_k$

$\text{SDL}'_k = \text{SCHED}_{speed_k}\{in_k, out_k, rest_k, \boxed{U_k \setminus \{n\}, S_k \setminus \{n\} \cup P_\downarrow \cup R \downarrow}\}$

$$k[\text{SDL}_k \mid \boxed{\mathbf{open}\ n.P} \mid n[\text{SDL}_n \mid R] \mid Q] \rightarrow k[\text{SDL}'_k \mid P \mid R \mid Q] \qquad \text{(TR-Open)}$$

$\text{SDL}_m = \text{SCHED}_{speed_k}\{in_m, out_m, rest_m, U_m, S_m\}, \ \boxed{speed_m > 0}$

$\text{SDL}'_m = \text{SCHED}_{speed_m}\{in_m, out_m, rest_m, U_m, S_m \cup \boxed{\{\mathbf{c}.P\}}\}$

$$m[\text{SDL}_m \mid \boxed{\mathbf{c}.P} \mid R] \rightarrow m[\text{SDL}'_m \mid R] \qquad \text{(TR-Resource)}$$

a resource for a consume capability, which is waiting in the scheduler. The RR-Tock_1 rules concern the number x of time slices that are given out for every input time slice, while the RR-Tock_2 rules only allow to give out a time slice if the input step is a multiple of one of the fraction denominators b_y. This amounts to a concrete implementation of a fair scheduler where progress is uniform over the queue of timed subambients and time consuming processes. Once all waiting subambients and processes inside the set *unserved* have been served one time slice and are moved to the set *served*, either the rule RR-NewRound ensures

Table 3. Transition system for fair, preemptive distribution of virtual time slices, where $b_y \in \mathbb{N}$. A blue backdrop marks the reduction trigger and red the changes.

$$\text{SDL} = \text{SCHED}_{speed}\{in, 0, 0, \emptyset, \emptyset\}, \quad \text{SDL}' = \text{SCHED}_{speed}\{\,in+1\,, 0, 0, \emptyset, \emptyset\}, \; R \not\equiv \mathbf{c}\,.P \mid P'$$

$$\frac{}{a[\,\mathtt{tick}\, \mid \text{SDL} \mid R] \twoheadrightarrow a[\text{SDL}' \mid R]} \qquad \text{(RR-Empty)}$$

$$\text{SDL} = \text{SCHED}_{speed}\{in, 0, 0, U, S\}, \qquad U \cup S \neq \emptyset$$

$$\text{SDL}' = \text{SCHED}_{speed}\{\,in+1, x, z\,, U, S\}, \qquad speed = x + \textstyle\sum_{y=1}^{z} \frac{1}{b_y}, \; b_y > 1$$

$$\frac{}{a[\,\mathtt{tick}\, \mid \text{SDL} \mid R] \twoheadrightarrow a[\text{SDL}' \mid R]} \qquad \text{(RR-Tick)}$$

$$\text{SDL} = \text{SCHED}_{speed}\{in, out, rest, \,\emptyset, S\,\}, \qquad R \not\equiv \mathbf{c}\,.P \mid P'$$

$$\text{SDL}' = \text{SCHED}_{speed}\{in, out, rest, \,S, \emptyset\,\}$$

$$\frac{}{a[\text{SDL} \mid R] \twoheadrightarrow a[\text{SDL}' \mid R]} \qquad \text{(RR-NewRound)}$$

$$\boxed{out > 0}\,, \; a_i \in U, \; a_i \equiv \mathbf{c}\,.P, \qquad \text{SDL} = \text{SCHED}_{speed}\{in, out, rest, U, S\}$$

$$\text{SDL}' = \text{SCHED}_{speed}\{in, \,out-1\,, rest, U \setminus \,\{a_i\}\, \cup \,P_\downarrow\,, S\}$$

$$\frac{}{a[\text{SDL} \mid R] \twoheadrightarrow a[\text{SDL}' \mid R \mid P]} \qquad \text{(RR-Tock}_{1\text{-consume}})$$

$$\boxed{out > 0}\,, \; a_i \in U, \qquad R \equiv a_i[\text{SDL}_{a_i} \mid P'] \mid P, \qquad R' \equiv a_i[\text{SDL}_{a_i} \mid \,\mathtt{tick}\, \mid P'] \mid P$$

$$\text{SDL} = \text{SCHED}_{speed}\{in, out, rest, U, S\}$$

$$\text{SDL}' = \text{SCHED}_{speed}\{in, \,out-1\,, rest, U \setminus \,\{a_i\}\,, S \cup \,\{a_i\}\,\}$$

$$\frac{}{a[\text{SDL} \mid R] \twoheadrightarrow a[\text{SDL}' \mid R']} \qquad \text{(RR-Tock}_{1\text{-ambient}})$$

$$\boxed{rest > 0}\,, \; in \bmod b_{rest} = 0, \; a_i \in U, \; a_i \equiv \mathbf{c}\,.P, \; speed = x + \textstyle\sum_{y=1}^{z} \frac{1}{b_y}, \; b_y > 1$$

$$\text{SDL} = \text{SCHED}_{speed}\{in, out, rest, U, S\}$$

$$\text{SDL}' = \text{SCHED}_{speed}\{in, out, \,rest-1\,, U \setminus \,\{a_i\}\, \cup \,P_\downarrow\,, S\}$$

$$\frac{}{a[\text{SDL} \mid R] \twoheadrightarrow a[\text{SDL}' \mid R \mid P]} \qquad \text{(RR-Tock}_{2\text{-consume}})$$

$$\boxed{rest > 0}\,, \qquad a_i \in U, \quad R \equiv a_i[\text{SDL}_{a_i} \mid P'] \mid P, \quad R' \equiv a_i[\text{SDL}_{a_i} \mid \,\mathtt{tick}\, \mid P'] \mid P$$

$$\text{SDL} = \text{SCHED}_{speed}\{in, out, rest, U, S\}, \quad in \bmod b_{rest} = 0, \quad speed = x + \textstyle\sum_{y=1}^{z} \frac{1}{b_y}, \; b_y > 1$$

$$\text{SDL}' = \text{SCHED}_{speed}\{in, out, \,rest-1\,, U \setminus \,\{a_i\}\,, S \cup \,\{a_i\}\,\}$$

$$\frac{}{a[\text{SDL} \mid R] \twoheadrightarrow a[\text{SDL}' \mid R']} \qquad \text{(RR-Tock}_{2\text{-ambient}})$$

$$\boxed{rest > 0}\,, \; in \bmod b_{rest} \neq 0, \; speed = x + \textstyle\sum_{y=1}^{z} \frac{1}{b_y}, \; b_y > 1$$

$$\text{SDL} = \text{SCHED}_{speed}\{in, out, rest, U, S\}, \quad \text{SDL}' = \text{SCHED}_{speed}\{in, out, \,rest-1\,, U, S\}$$

$$\frac{}{a[\text{SDL} \mid R] \twoheadrightarrow a[\text{SDL}' \mid R]} \qquad \text{(RR-Tock}_{2\text{-no action}})$$

$$\text{SDL}^\dagger = \text{SCHED}^\dagger\{in, 0, 0, U, S\}, \; \text{SDL}_*^\dagger = \text{SCHED}^\dagger\{\,in+1, 1\,, 0, U, S\}$$

$$\frac{}{\text{SDL}^\dagger \twoheadrightarrow \,\text{SDL}_*^\dagger\,} \qquad \text{(RR-Root)}$$

---

that a new round of time slice distribution can begin, or, if the queue is empty, the rule RR-EMPTY is applied. This scheduling strategy ensures fairness in the competition for resources between processes, as the rounds ensure that no process can bypass another process more than once. The side condition $R \not\equiv \mathbf{c} . P \mid P'$ in the rules RR-NEWROUND and RR-EMPTY ensures that all resource-consuming processes, which are prefixed by a $\mathbf{c}$ capability, are included in the set to be scheduled for the next round. The root scheduler $\text{SCHED}^\dagger$ reduces without time slices from surrounding ambients in RR-ROOT.

In the sequel we will focus on a subset of the language of virtually timed ambients without replication and without restriction, denoted by VTA$^-$. Similarly, let MA$^-$ denote mobile ambients without replication and without restriction.

Example 1 (Virtually timed subambients, scheduling and resource consumption). The virtually timed ambient *cloud*, exemplifying a cloud server, emits one time slice for every time slice it receives, $\text{SDL}_{cloud} = \text{SCHED}_1\{0, 0, 0, \emptyset, \emptyset\}$. It contains two tick and is entered by a virtually timed subambient *vm*.

$$cloud\,[\text{SCHED}_1\{0, 0, 0, \emptyset, \emptyset\} \mid \text{tick} \mid \text{tick}]$$
$$\mid vm[\text{SCHED}_{3/4}\{0, 0, 0, \emptyset, \emptyset\} \mid \textbf{in } cloud.\ \mathbf{c}\ .P]$$

The ambient *vm* exemplifies a virtual machine containing a resource consuming task, where $\text{SDL}_{vm} = \text{SCHED}_{3/4}\{0, 0, 0, \emptyset, \emptyset\}$. The Egyptian fraction decomposition of the speed yields $3/4 = 0 + 1/2 + 1/4$ meaning that there is no time slice given out for every incoming time slice, but one time slice for every second incoming time slice, and one for every fourth. The process reduces as follows:

$$\rightarrow cloud\,[\text{SCHED}_1\{0, 0, 0, \emptyset, vm\} \mid \text{tick} \mid \text{tick}$$
$$\mid vm[\text{SCHED}_{3/4}\{0, 0, 0, \emptyset, \emptyset\} \mid \mathbf{c}\ .P]] \qquad\qquad \text{(TR-IN)}$$
$$\rightarrow cloud\,[\text{SCHED}_1\{0, 0, 0, vm, \emptyset\} \mid \text{tick} \mid \text{tick}$$
$$\mid vm[\text{SCHED}_{3/4}\{0, 0, 0, \emptyset, \emptyset\} \mid \mathbf{c}\ .P]] \qquad\qquad \text{(RR-NEWROUND)}$$
$$\rightarrow cloud\,[\text{SCHED}_1\{0, 0, 0, vm, \emptyset\} \mid \text{tick} \mid \text{tick}$$
$$\mid vm[\text{SCHED}_{3/4}\{0, 0, 0, \emptyset, \mathbf{c}\ .P\} \mid \mathbf{0}]] \qquad\qquad \text{(TR-RESOURCE)}$$
$$\rightarrow cloud\,[\text{SCHED}_1\{0, 0, 0, vm, \emptyset\} \mid \text{tick} \mid \text{tick}$$
$$\mid vm[\text{SCHED}_{3/4}\{0, 0, 0, \mathbf{c}\ .P, \emptyset\} \mid \mathbf{0}]] \qquad\qquad \text{(RR-NEWROUND)}.$$

Here, the ambient *vm* enters the ambient *cloud* and is registered in the scheduler. Furthermore, the resource consuming process in *vm* is registered. In the next steps the time slices move into the scheduler of the *cloud* ambient and are distributed further down in the hierarchy.

$$\rightarrow cloud\,[\textsc{Sched}_1\{1,1,0,vm,\emptyset\}\mid \texttt{tick}$$
$$\mid vm[\textsc{Sched}_{3/4}\{0,0,0,\mathbf{c}\,.P,\emptyset\}\mid \mathbf{0}]]\qquad\qquad\text{(RR-Tick)}$$
$$\rightarrow cloud\,[\textsc{Sched}_1\{1,0,0,\emptyset,vm\}\mid \texttt{tick}$$
$$\mid vm[\textsc{Sched}_{3/4}\{0,0,0,\mathbf{c}\,.P,\emptyset\}\mid \texttt{tick}]]\qquad\quad\text{(RR-Tock}_{\text{1-ambient}})$$
$$\rightarrow cloud\,[\textsc{Sched}_1\{2,0,0,vm,\emptyset\}$$
$$\mid vm[\textsc{Sched}_{3/4}\{0,0,0,\mathbf{c}\,.P,\emptyset\}\mid \texttt{tick}]]\qquad\quad\text{(RR-NewRound)}$$
$$\rightarrow cloud\,[\textsc{Sched}_1\{2,1,0,vm,\emptyset\}$$
$$\mid vm[\textsc{Sched}_{3/4}\{0,0,0,\mathbf{c}\,.P,\emptyset\}\mid \texttt{tick}]]\qquad\quad\text{(RR-Tick)}$$
$$\rightarrow cloud\,[\textsc{Sched}_1\{2,0,0,\emptyset,vm\}$$
$$\mid vm[\textsc{Sched}_{3/4}\{0,0,0,\mathbf{c}\,.P,\emptyset\}\mid \texttt{tick}\mid \texttt{tick}]]\qquad\text{(RR-Tock}_{\text{1-ambient}})$$
$$\rightarrow cloud\,[\textsc{Sched}_1\{2,0,0,vm,\emptyset\}$$
$$\mid vm[\textsc{Sched}_{3/4}\{0,0,0,\mathbf{c}\,.P,\emptyset\}\mid \texttt{tick}\mid \texttt{tick}]]\qquad\text{(RR-NewRound).}$$

Now the ambient vm can use the time signals to enable resource consumption.

$$\rightarrow cloud\,[\textsc{Sched}_1\{2,0,0,vm,\emptyset\}$$
$$\mid vm[\textsc{Sched}_{3/4}\{1,0,1,\mathbf{c}\,.P,\emptyset\}\mid \texttt{tick}]]\qquad\quad\text{(RR-Tick)}$$
$$\rightarrow cloud\,[\textsc{Sched}_1\{2,0,0,vm,\emptyset\}$$
$$\mid vm[\textsc{Sched}_{3/4}\{1,0,0,\mathbf{c}\,.P,\emptyset\}\mid \texttt{tick}]]\qquad\quad\text{(RR-Tock}_{\text{2-no action}})$$
$$\rightarrow cloud\,[\textsc{Sched}_1\{2,0,0,vm,\emptyset\}$$
$$\mid vm[\textsc{Sched}_{3/4}\{2,0,1,\mathbf{c}\,.P,\emptyset\}\mid \mathbf{0}]]\qquad\qquad\text{(RR-Tick)}$$
$$\rightarrow cloud\,[\textsc{Sched}_1\{2,0,0,vm,\emptyset\}$$
$$\mid vm[\textsc{Sched}_{3/4}\{2,0,0,P_\downarrow,\emptyset\}\mid P]]\qquad\qquad\text{(RR-Tock}_{\text{2-consume}})$$

Note that, as the calculus is non-deterministic, the reduction rules can be applied in arbitrary order, making several reduction paths possible.

3   Modal Logic for Virtually Timed Ambients

To capture the distinctive features of virtual time and resource provisioning in virtually timed ambients, the modal logic $\mathcal{ML}_{VTA}$ for VTA$^-$ combines the modal logic $\mathcal{ML}_{MA}$ for mobile ambients without the composition adjunct, with notions based on metric temporal logic [24, 31, 32].

The syntax of $\mathcal{ML}_{VTA}$ is shown in Table 4. The *sometime* operator (the name refers to *sometime in the reduction*) comes with a constraint giving the *maximal number of resources* $x \in \mathbb{N}_0 \cup \{\infty\}$ that a process may use inside an ambient named n before fulfilling formula $\mathcal{A}$. The *somewhere* operator refers to the formula being true in a sublocation of the process and specifies the *minimal speed* that the sublocation must possess relative to its surrounding ambients as well as the *maximal number of subambients* in this location. To define these operators, we adapt the sublocation relation from [9] to accommodate schedulers.

Table 4. Logical formulas, $n \in$ names, $x, s \in \mathbb{N}_0 \cup \{\infty\}$, $speed \in \mathbb{Q}$

$\mathcal{A}, \mathcal{B} ::=$ TRUE	True
$\neg \mathcal{A}$	Negation
$\mathcal{A} \vee \mathcal{B}$	Disjunction
$\mathbf{0}$	Void
$n[\mathcal{A}]$	Location
$\mathcal{A} \mid \mathcal{B}$	Composition
$\forall n.\mathcal{A}$	Universal quantification over names
$\mathcal{A}@n$	Local adjunct
$\mathfrak{c}$	Consumption
$\Diamond_{x@n}\mathcal{A}$	Sometime modality
$\Diamond_{(speed,s)}\mathcal{A}$	Somewhere modality

Definition 5 (Sublocation with schedulers). *A process P' is a sublocation of P, written $P \downarrow P'$, iff $P \equiv (n[\text{SDL} \mid P'] \mid P'')$ for some name n, scheduler SDL, and process P''. Let $P \downarrow^* P'$ denote the reflexive and transitive closure of $P \downarrow P'$; i.e., $P \downarrow^* P'$ iff $P \downarrow P'$ or $P \downarrow P''$ and $P'' \downarrow^* P'$ for some process P''.*

In order to capture the number of resources consumed in a given ambient, we define a *labeled reduction relation*. While $\rightarrow$ refers to all reduction steps in virtually timed ambients, we denote by $\xrightarrow{\text{tick}}$ the steps of the (RR-TICK) and (RR-EMPTY) rules; i.e., these labeled transitions capture the internal reductions in the schedulers enabling the timed reduction of processes. All other reduction steps are marked by $\xrightarrow{\tau}$.

Definition 6. *$P \xrightarrow{\text{tick}} P'$ iff $P \mid \text{tick} \rightarrow P'$. We write $\xrightarrow{\text{tick}^x}$ if x time signals tick are used; i.e., $P \xrightarrow{\text{tick}^x} P'$ iff $P \mid \text{tick} \mid \cdots \mid \text{tick} \rightarrow^* P'$, where the number of time signals tick is x. The weak version of this reduction is defined as $P \xRightarrow{\text{tick}^x} P'$ iff $P(\xrightarrow{\tau}^* \xrightarrow{\text{tick}} \xrightarrow{\tau}^*)^x P'$, where $\xrightarrow{\tau}^*$ describes the application of an arbitrary number of τ-steps.*

The relation $\xRightarrow{\text{tick}^x}_n$ captures the number of resources used inside an ambient n inside a process.

Definition 7. *$P \xRightarrow{\text{tick}^x}_n P'$ iff $P \rightarrow^* P'$ and there exists Q, Q' such that $P \downarrow^* n[Q]$, $P' \downarrow^* n[Q']$ and $Q \xRightarrow{\text{tick}^x} Q'$.*

We now define the notion of *accumulated speed*, based on the eager distribution strategy for time slices. The accumulated speed $accum\{m\}_P \in \mathbb{Q}$ in a subambient m which is part of a process P, is the relative speed of the ambient with respect to the scheduler of P and the siblings.

Table 5. Satisfaction of logical formulas, $n \in$ names, $x, s \in \mathbb{N}_0 \cup \{\infty\}$, $speed \in \mathbb{Q}$

$P \vDash \text{TRUE}$	
$P \vDash \neg\mathcal{A}$	iff $P \nvDash \mathcal{A}$
$P \vDash \mathcal{A} \vee \mathcal{B}$	iff $P \vDash \mathcal{A} \vee P \vDash \mathcal{B}$
$P \vDash \mathbf{0}$	iff $P \equiv \mathbf{0}$
$P \vDash n[\mathcal{A}]$	iff $\exists P'$ s.t. $P \equiv n[P'] \wedge P' \vDash \mathcal{A}$
$P \vDash \mathcal{A} \mid \mathcal{B}$	iff $\exists P', P''$ s.t. $P \equiv P' \mid P'' \wedge P' \vDash \mathcal{A} \wedge P'' \vDash \mathcal{B}$
$P \vDash \forall n.\mathcal{A}$	iff $\forall m : P \vDash \mathcal{A}\{n \leftarrow m\}$
$P \vDash \mathcal{A}@n$	iff $n[P] \vDash \mathcal{A}$
$P \vDash \mathfrak{c}$	iff $\exists P', P'', P'''$ s.t. $P \equiv P'. \mathfrak{c}. P'' \mid P''' \vee P \downarrow^*(P'. \mathfrak{c}. P'' \mid P''')$
$P \vDash \diamond_{x@n}\mathcal{A}$	iff $\exists P'$ s.t. $P \xrightarrow{\text{tick}^y}_n P' \wedge y \leq x \wedge P' \vDash \mathcal{A}$
$P \vDash \Diamond_{(speed,s)}\mathcal{A}$	iff $\exists P', P'', n$ s.t. $(P \equiv n[\text{SDL} \mid P'] \mid P'' \vee P \downarrow^* n[\text{SDL} \mid P'])$
	$\wedge P' \vDash \mathcal{A} \wedge accum\{n\}_P \geq speed \wedge \|U_{\text{SDL}} \cup S_{\text{SDL}}\| \leq s$

Definition 8 (Accumulated speed). *Let $speed_k \in \mathbb{Q}$ and $children(k)$ denote the speed and number of children of a virtually timed ambient* k. *Let* m *be a timed subambient of a process P, the name* parent *denoting the direct parental ambient of* m, *and* C *the path of all parental ambients of* m *up to the level of P. The* accumulated speed *for preemptive scheduling in a subambient* m *up to the level of the process P is given by*

$$accum\{m\}_P = speed_m \cdot {}^1/_{children(parent)} \cdot speed_{parent}$$

$$= speed_m \cdot \prod_{k \in C} {}^1/_{children(k)} \cdot \prod_{k \in C} speed_k$$

Schedulers distribute time slices preemptively, as child processes get one time slice at the time in iterative rounds. Consequently, an ambient's accumulated speed is influenced by both the speed and the number of children n of the parental ambient. Thus, scheduling is not only *path sensitive* but also *sibling sensitive*.

The satisfaction relation for logical formula, defined inductively in Table 5, can now be explained using these definitions. A process P satisfies the *negation* of a formula $\mathcal{A}$ iff P does not satisfy $\mathcal{A}$. The *disjunction* $\mathcal{A} \vee \mathcal{B}$ is satisfied by a process which satisfies either $\mathcal{A}$ or $\mathcal{B}$. A process satisfies the formula $\mathbf{0}$ (*void*) iff the process is equivalent to the inactive process $\mathbf{0}$. A process P satisfies a formula $\mathcal{A}$ *in location* n iff P is equivalent to $n[P']$ and P' satisfies $\mathcal{A}$. The *composition* $\mathcal{A} \mid \mathcal{B}$ is satisfied by a process iff the process can be split into two parallel processes, such that one satisfies $\mathcal{A}$ and the other $\mathcal{B}$. *Universal quantification* $\forall n.\mathcal{A}$ over names is satisfied iff $\mathcal{A}$ holds for all names n. A process satisfies the *local adjunct* iff it satisfies the formula $\mathcal{A}$ in location n. The *consumption* formula $\mathfrak{c}$ is satisfied by any process which contains a consumption capability. A process P satisfies the *sometime modality* iff it reduces to a process satisfying the formula, and uses less than x resources in ambient n in the reduction. The *somewhere modality* is satisfied iff there exists a sublocation of P satisfying the formula, the relative speed in the sublocation is greater or equal to the given *speed*, and the sublocation has less than or equal to s timed subambients.

We show that $\mathcal{ML}_{VTA}$ is conservative with respect to $\mathcal{ML}_{MA}$. It holds that every process in mobile ambients has an equivalent process in virtually timed ambients when timing aspects are ignored. We attach the names of the logics to the satisfaction relation to distinguish the relations in the presentation.

Lemma 1 (Correspondence to untimed processes). *Let $\mathcal{A} \in \mathcal{ML}_{MA}$ and $P \in MA^-$. If $P \vDash_{\mathcal{ML}_{MA}} \mathcal{A}$ then there exists $P' \in VTA^-$ such that $P' \vDash_{\mathcal{ML}_{VTA}} \mathcal{A}$.*

The satisfaction relation for the untimed definitions of the sometime and somewhere modalities in $\mathcal{ML}_{MA}$ is given as:

$$P \vDash_{\mathcal{ML}_{MA}} \Diamond\mathcal{A} \iff \exists P' \text{ s.t. } P \to^* P' \land P' \vDash_{\mathcal{ML}_{MA}} \mathcal{A}$$
$$P \vDash_{\mathcal{ML}_{MA}} \Diamond\!\!\!\!\Diamond\mathcal{A} \iff \exists P' \text{ s.t. } P \downarrow^* P' \land P' \vDash_{\mathcal{ML}_{MA}} \mathcal{A}.$$

These definitions correspond to timed modalities without restrictions on names and resources.

Lemma 2 (Correspondence to untimed modalities). *For all $P \in VTA^-$, $\mathcal{A} \in \mathcal{ML}_{MA}$ it holds that*

1. $P \vDash_{\mathcal{ML}_{MA}} \Diamond\mathcal{A} \iff P \vDash_{\mathcal{ML}_{VTA}} \neg\forall n\neg(\Diamond_{\infty@n}\mathcal{A})$
2. $P \vDash_{\mathcal{ML}_{MA}} \Diamond\!\!\!\!\Diamond\mathcal{A} \iff P \vDash_{\mathcal{ML}_{VTA}} \Diamond\!\!\!\!\Diamond_{(0,\infty)}\mathcal{A}.$

Proof. Follows from the definition of the satisfaction relation.

1. $P \vDash_{\mathcal{ML}_{VTA}} \neg\forall n\neg(\Diamond_{\infty@n}\mathcal{A})$

    $\iff P \nvDash_{\mathcal{ML}_{VTA}} \forall n\neg(\Diamond_{\infty@n}\mathcal{A})$

    $\iff \forall m : P \nvDash_{\mathcal{ML}_{VTA}} \neg(\Diamond_{\infty@n}\mathcal{A})\{n \leftarrow m\}$

    $\iff P \nvDash_{\mathcal{ML}_{VTA}} \neg(\Diamond_{\infty@m_1}\mathcal{A}) \land \cdots \land \neg(\Diamond_{\infty@m_k}\mathcal{A})$

    $\iff P \vDash_{\mathcal{ML}_{VTA}} \Diamond_{\infty@m_i}\mathcal{A}, \text{ for any } m_i$

    $\iff \exists P' \text{ s.t. } P \xoverset{\texttt{tick}^y}{\Longrightarrow}_{m_i} P' \land y \leq \infty \land P' \vDash_{\mathcal{ML}_{MA}} \mathcal{A}, \text{ for any } m_i$

    $\iff \exists P' \text{ s.t. } P \to^* P' \land P' \vDash_{\mathcal{ML}_{MA}} \mathcal{A}$

    $\iff P \vDash_{\mathcal{ML}_{MA}} \Diamond\mathcal{A}$

2. $P \vDash_{\mathcal{ML}_{VTA}} \Diamond\!\!\!\!\Diamond_{(0,\infty)}\mathcal{A}$

    $\iff \exists P', P'', n \text{ s.t. } (P \equiv n[\text{SDL} \mid P'] \mid P'' \lor P \downarrow^* n[\text{SDL} \mid P'])$
    $\qquad \land P' \vDash \mathcal{A} \land accum\{n\}_P \geq 0 \land |U_{\text{SDL}} \cup S_{\text{SDL}}| \leq \infty$

    $\iff \exists P' \text{ s.t. } P \downarrow^* P' \land P' \vDash_{\mathcal{ML}_{MA}} \mathcal{A}$

    $\iff P \vDash_{\mathcal{ML}_{MA}} \Diamond\!\!\!\!\Diamond\mathcal{A}$

For all other cases, the definition of the satisfaction relation in $\mathcal{ML}_{MA}$ is the same as in $\mathcal{ML}_{VTA}$. Thus, we can translate a $\mathcal{ML}_{MA}$-formula to $\mathcal{ML}_{VTA}$ by substituting untimed with timed modalities as given above. We now prove that $\mathcal{ML}_{VTA}$ is a conservative extension of $\mathcal{ML}_{MA}$.

Theorem 1 (Conservative extension). *Let $A \in \mathcal{ML}_{MA}$ and $P \in MA^-$. If $P \vDash_{\mathcal{ML}_{MA}} A$ then there exists $P' \in VTA^-$ such that $P' \vDash_{\mathcal{ML}_{VTA}} A^*$, where A^* is the translation of A to $\mathcal{ML}_{VTA}$.*

Proof. Follows from Lemmas 1 and 2 and the fact that for all other cases than the modalities, the satisfaction relation in $\mathcal{ML}_{MA}$ stays the same in $\mathcal{ML}_{VTA}$.

Example 2 (Modal contracts for virtually timed processes). Let process P consist of a cloud ambient containing a virtual machine vm, similar to Example 1, and a *task* to enter vm in order to consume a resource:

$$P \equiv cloud[\text{SDL}_{cloud} \mid \texttt{tick} \mid \texttt{tick} \mid vm[\text{SDL}_{vm} \mid \textbf{open } task] \mid task[\textbf{in } vm.\ \textbf{c}]].$$

This system satisfies the modal contract given by the formula $\diamond_{2@vm}(\neg\textbf{c})$, which expresses that after using two time slices the task can be executed. Example 1 illustrates how the time slices move from the *cloud* ambient into the virtual machine. Afterwards we can observe the following reduction process inside the *cloud* ambient:

$$vm[\text{SDL}_{vm} \mid \texttt{tick} \mid \texttt{tick} \mid \textbf{open } task] \mid task[\textbf{in } vm.\ \textbf{c}]$$
$$\rightarrow vm[\text{SDL}_{vm} \mid \texttt{tick} \mid \texttt{tick} \mid \textbf{open } task \mid task[\textbf{c}]]$$
$$\rightarrow vm[\text{SDL}_{vm} \mid \texttt{tick} \mid \texttt{tick} \mid \textbf{c}]$$
$$\rightarrow vm[\text{SDL}_{vm} \mid \textbf{0}]$$

This shows that $P \vDash \diamond_{2@vm}(\neg\textbf{c})$. With two time signals from the original active level the task can be executed. Therefore, we can say that P satisfies the modal contract stating that the system is able to execute with the use of two resources.

4   A Model Checker for Virtually Timed Ambients

To answer the question whether a process in VTA^- satisfies a given formula, we create a model checker algorithm for $\mathcal{ML}_{VTA}$. We extend the model checker algorithm for $\mathcal{ML}_{MA}$ [9] to cover the properties of virtually timed ambients. Technically, we add $\textbf{c}\ .P$ and $\texttt{tick}$ to the *prime processes* and use the same notion of *normal form*, where we add $Norm(n[\text{SDL} \mid P]) \triangleq [n[\text{SDL} \mid P]]$. Furthermore, the *Reachable* and *SubLocations* routines must account for our changes to the *sometime* and *somewhere* modalities and a *Consumption* routine is added to check if the formula $\textbf{c}$ holds for a process. These routines are now defined for $\mathcal{ML}_{VTA}$.

Definition 9. *Let $P \in VTA^-$, then*

- $Reachable_n^x(P) = [P_1, \ldots, P_k]$ iff $P \xRightarrow{\texttt{tick}^y}_n P_i$, for all $i \in 1, \ldots, k$, $y \leq x$ and for all Q, if $P \xRightarrow{\texttt{tick}^y}_n Q$ then $Q \equiv P_i$ for some $i \in 1, \ldots, k$ and $y \leq x$.
- $SubLocations_{(speed,s)}(P) = [P_1, \ldots, P_k]$ iff $P \equiv n[\text{SDL} \mid P_i] \mid P'$ or $P \downarrow^* n[\text{SDL} \mid P_i]$ for some n and $accum\{n\}_P \geq speed$ and $|S_{\text{SDL}_n} \cup T_{\text{SDL}_n}| \leq s$, for all $i \in 1, \ldots, k$. And for all Q, if $P \equiv n[\text{SDL} \mid Q \mid P'$ or $P \downarrow^* n[\text{SDL} \mid Q]$ some n and $accum\{n\}_P \geq speed$ and $|S_{\text{SDL}_n} \cup T_{\text{SDL}_n}| \leq s$, then $Q \equiv P_i$ for some $i \in 1, \ldots, k$.
- $Consumption(P) = \text{TRUE}$ iff $SubLocations_{(0,\infty)}(P) = [P_1, \ldots, P_k]$ and $\exists P'$, P'', P''', $P_i, i \in 1 \ldots k$ such that $P_i \equiv P'$. $\textbf{c}$.$P'' \mid P'''$.

The model checker algorithm for $\mathcal{ML}_{VTA}$ is defined inductively as follows:

Check$(P, \mathcal{A})$:   Checking whether process P satisfies formula $\mathcal{A}$

$Check(P, \text{TRUE}) \triangleq \text{TRUE}$

$Check(P, \neg\mathcal{A}) \triangleq \neg Check(P, \mathcal{A})$

$Check(P, \mathcal{A} \vee \mathcal{B}) \triangleq Check(P, \mathcal{A}) \vee Check(P, \mathcal{B})$

$Check(P, \mathbf{0}) \triangleq$ if $Norm(P) = []$ then TRUE else FALSE.

$Check(P, n[\mathcal{A}]) \triangleq$ if $Norm(P) = n[Q]$ for some Q then $Check(Q, \mathcal{A})$ else FALSE.

$Check(P, \mathcal{A} \mid \mathcal{B}) \triangleq$ Let $Norm(P) = [\pi_1, \ldots, \pi_k]$:
$\quad \exists I, J$ s.t. $I \cup J = \{1, \ldots, k\}$ and $I \cap J = \emptyset$:
$\quad \bigvee_{I,J} Check(\prod_{i \in I} \pi_i, \mathcal{A}) \wedge Check(\prod_{j \in J} \pi_j, \mathcal{B})$

$Check(P, \forall n.\mathcal{A}) \triangleq$ Let $\{m_1, \ldots, m_k\} = fn(P) \cup fn(\mathcal{A})$ and $m_0 \notin \{m_1, \ldots, m_k\}$:
$\quad \bigwedge_{i \in 0\ldots k} Check(P, \mathcal{A}\{n \leftarrow m_i\})$

$Check(P, \mathbf{c}) \triangleq Consumption(P)$

$Check(P, \diamond_{x@n}\mathcal{A}) \triangleq$ Let $Reachable_n^x(P) = [P_1, \ldots, P_k]$:
$\quad \bigvee_{i \in 1, \ldots, k} Check(P_i, \mathcal{A})$

$Check(P, \diamondsuit_{(speed,s)}\mathcal{A}) \triangleq$ Let $SubLocations_{(speed,s)}(P) = [P_1, \ldots, P_k]$:
$\quad \bigvee_{i \in 1, \ldots, k} Check(P_i, \mathcal{A})$

$Check(P, \mathcal{A}@n) \triangleq Check(n[P], \mathcal{A})$

As our extension only adds the simple predicate $\mathfrak{c}$ to the model checker and imposes discreet restrictions on the *Reachable* and *SubLocations* properties, it follows from results in [9] and [14] (regarding the equivalence of processes and their norms) that all recursive calls of the algorithm are on subformulas, therefore the algorithm always terminates.

Theorem 2. *For* $P \in VTA^-$, $\mathcal{A} \in \mathcal{ML}_{VTA}$ *it holds that:*

$$P \vDash \mathcal{A} \text{ iff } Check(P, \mathcal{A}) = \text{TRUE}.$$

Example 3 (Model checking). Reconsider Example 2, where the satisfaction of the sometime formula was demonstrated by considering the reduction. Let $P = vm[\text{SDL}_{vm} \mid \texttt{tick} \mid \texttt{tick} \mid \textbf{open } task] \mid task[\textbf{in } vm. \mathfrak{c}]$. We will now show that

$$Check(P, \diamond_{2@vm}(\neg\mathfrak{c})) = \text{TRUE}.$$

It holds that

$$Check(P, \diamond_{2@vm}(\neg\mathfrak{c})) \triangleq \text{Let } Reachable_{vm}^2(P) = [P_1, \ldots, P_k] :$$
$$\bigvee_{i \in 1, \ldots, k} Check(P_i, \neg\mathfrak{c})$$

$Reachable_{vm}^2(P)$ contains all states reachable from P with two timed steps and arbitrary many τ-steps. This includes $P_j = vm[\text{SDL}_{vm} \mid 0]$. For this process it holds that $Check(P_j, \neg\mathfrak{c}) \triangleq \neg Check(P_j, \mathfrak{c})$ and $Check(P_j, \mathfrak{c}) \triangleq Consumption(P_j)$ As $Consumption(P_j) = \text{FALSE}$ it follows that $Check(P, \diamond_{2@vm}(\neg\mathfrak{c})) = \text{TRUE}$.

5   Implementation in Maude

We implement a model checker for $\mathcal{ML}_{VTA}$ in the Maude [16, 30] rewriting logic system. Rewriting logic is a flexible, executable formal notation which can be used to represent a wide range of systems and logics with *low representational distance* [26]. Rewriting logic embeds *membership equational logic*, such that a specification or program may contain both equations and rewrite rules. When executing a Maude specification, rewrite steps are applied to normal forms in the equational logic. (The Maude system assumes that the equation set is terminating and confluent.) Thus, equations and rewrite rules constitute the *statics* and *dynamics* of a specification, respectively. Both equations and rewrite rules may be *conditional*, meaning that specified conditions must hold for the rule or equation to apply.

A translation of mobile ambients to Maude was proposed in [34], motivated by the application of the analysis tools that come with the Maude system. However, our primary goal is to build a model checker for virtually timed ambients. Hence, our implementation[1] consists of a translation for VTA$^-$ and $\mathcal{ML}_{VTA}$ to Maude, and will use the Maude engine as the model checker.

The syntax of VTA$^-$, given in Table 1, is represented by Maude terms, constructed from operators:

```
op zero : -> VTA [ctor] .
op _|_ : VTA VTA -> VTA [id: zero assoc comm] .
op _._ : Capability VTA -> VTA .
op _[_|_] : Name Scheduler VTA -> VTA .
```

The correlation between the formal definition and the Maude specification should be clear. The operator `zero` represents the inactive process, and parallel composition has the algebraic properties of being associative, commutative and having `zero` as identity element. Capability prefixing is represented with a dot. Virtually timed ambients are represented with a name followed by brackets,

---

[1] The full source code is available at https://github.com/larstvei/Check-VTA/tree/modal-contracts.

containing a scheduler and a process. Here all processes are defined with the data type VTA. The sort declarations for VTA, Capability, Name and Scheduler, as well as syntax for names and capabilities, are omitted.

The reduction rules for timed capabilities (Table 2) are represented as *rewrite rules*, which express that any term or subterm which matches the left hand side of the rewrite relation => may be rewritten into the right hand side; this corresponds to the reduction relation → in the calculus. Preconditions are expressed using conditional rewrite rules, where a condition is given after the keyword if. The TR-IN rule, for instance, may be expressed in Maude as follows:

```
crl [in] :
   K[sched SpdK {InK, OutK, RestK, UnSrvK, SrvK}
     | N[sched SpdN {InN, OutN, RestN, SrvN, UnSrvN} | in(M) . P | Q]
     | M[sched SpdM {InM, OutM, RestM, SrvM, UnSrvM} | R] | U]
   =>
   K[sched SpdK {InK, OutK, RestK, (UnSrvK \ N), (SrvK \ N)}
     | M[sched SpdM {InM, OutM, RestM, SrvM, union(UnSrvM, N)} | R
       | N[sched SpdN {InN, OutN, RestN, SrvN, union(UnSrvN, barb(P))}
         | P | Q]] | U]
   if N in union(UnSrvK, SrvK) .
```

The model checker algorithm *Check* (from Sect. 3) uses a normal form. Since rule matching in Maude is modulo associativity, commutativity and identity (so-called ACI-matching [16]), the satisfiability conditions of the modal logic can be represented directly, without this normal form. This results in a compact and flexible model checker which stays close to its mathematical formulation.

Terms representing logical formulas (defined in Table 4) are built from operator declarations in Maude and variable substitution on formulas is formalized using recursive equations. The semantics of formulas is interpreted with regards to the calculus of virtually timed ambients, and is formalized by defining the satisfaction relation as an operator:

```
op _|=_ : VTA Formula -> Bool [frozen] .
```

Here, the operator declaration's frozen attribute prevents the subterms of a satisfaction formula from being rewritten, giving the model checker control over the rewriting (i.e., the frozen attribute prohibits subterm matching). The semantics of the satisfaction relations from Table 5 is expressed as a set of equations and a single rewrite rule. For formulas which only depend on the current state of the process, the satisfaction predicate can be defined by an equation in Maude. For example, negation is defined as follows:

```
eq [Negation] : P |= ~ F = not (P |= F) .
```

Parallel composition relies on the matching of parallel processes, and there may be several possible solutions. Therefore, the satisfaction predicate for parallel processes must be defined as a rule. The rule uses reachability predicates as conditions, which allows the Maude implementation to closely reflect the satisfaction relation.

```
crl [Parallel] : P | Q |= F | G => true
        if P |= F => true /\ Q |= G => true
```

The *sometime modality* constructs formulas that depend on how a process evolves over time. The following conditional rewrite rule captures the semantics of a sometime formula:

```
crl [Sometime] : P |= <> A @ N F => true
    if contains(P, N) /\
        P => Q /\
        distance(P, Q, N) ≤ A /\
        contains(Q, N) /\
        Q |= F => true .
```

In this rule, the terms `contains` and `distance` define the existence of the name in the given process and the number of used resources, and are reduced by equations. Similar to the conditions of the `Parallel` rule, the condition `P => Q` expresses that the pattern `Q` is reachable from a pattern `P` (after substitution in the matching) by the rewrite relation `=>` in one or more steps. Maude will search for a `Q` such that the condition holds using a breadth-first strategy. This useful feature of Maude enables a straightforward implementation of the sometime modality. Note that `Q |= F => true` is used in favor of the simpler `Q |= F` to support nested modal formulas.

The execution of rewrite rules is represented in the syntax of the Maude model checker by providing the rewriting command `rewrite` with satisfaction relation containing a virtually timed ambient and a formula. The resulting Maude program can easily be used to check modal properties for virtually timed ambients and is demonstrated in the following example. The `rewrite` command applies the defined rewrite rules to the given satisfaction relation until termination, at which point the model checker returns a `result` in the form of a `Bool`.

Example 4 (Implementation of modal contracts for virtually timed processes). To illustrate the model checker we implement Example 2. A root ambient contains a virtual machine, which is entered by a request. We check if the system satisfies the quality of service contract stating that the request can be executed after the use of two time slices. The model checker confirms that after the use of two time signals in the root ambient there is no consume capability left, meaning that there exists a reduction path where at most two time signals are needed to execute the request in the virtual machine.

6   Related Work

Virtually timed ambients are based on mobile ambients [10]. The calculus is first described in [22]. Mobile ambients model both location mobility and nested locations, and capture processes executing at distributed locations in networks such as the Internet. Gordon proposed a simple formalism for virtualization loosely based on mobile ambients in [20]. The calculus of virtually timed ambients [22,23] stays closer to the syntax of the original mobile ambient calculus, while at the same time including notions of *time* and *explicit resource provisioning*.

Timed process algebras which originated from ACP and CSP can be found in, e.g., [5,6,29]. As virtually timed ambients build upon mobile ambients, we focus the discussion of related work on the π-calculus [35], which originated from CCS and is closely related to the ambient calculus. Timers have been studied for both the distributed π-calculus [8,33] and for mobile ambients [3,4,15]. In this line of work, timers, which are introduced to express the possibility of a timeout, are controlled by a global clock. In contrast, the root schedulers in our work recursively control local schedulers which define the execution power of the nested virtually timed ambients. Modeling timeouts is a straightforward extension of our work.

Modal logic for mobile ambients was introduced to describe properties of spatial configuration and mobile computation [9] for a fragment of mobile ambients without replication and restriction on names, and features a model checker algorithm for the given language fragment and modal logic using techniques from [12] to establish the *Reachable(P)* and *SubLocation(P)* properties. The complexity of model checking for mobile ambients is investigated in [13], and shown to be PSPACE-complete. After Cardelli and Gordon's work on logical properties for name restriction [11], the model checker algorithm was extended for private names [14] while preserving decidability and the complexity of the original fragment. Further it was shown that it is not possible to extend the algorithm for replication in the calculus or the local adjunct in the logic, as either of these extensions would lead to undecidability. For simplicity, we base our logic and model checker on the original fragment from [9]. The modal operators with restrictions on timing in this paper borrows ideas from metric temporal logic [24,31,32].

The Process Analysis Toolkit (PAT) [36] has been used to specify processes in the ambient calculus as well as properties in modal logic [37], to provide a basis for a possible model checker implementation. A model checker for ambient logic has been implemented by separating the analysis of temporal and spatial properties [2]: Mobile ambients are translated into Kripke structures and spatial modalities are replaced with atomic propositions in order to reduce ambient logic formulas to temporal logic formulas, while the analysis of temporal modalities are handled using the NuSMV model checker. In contrast to our work, none of the above model checkers consider notions of time or resources. We use Maude [16] to implement our model checker, exploiting the low representational distance which distinguishes this system [26]. The operational reduction rules for mobile ambients as well as a type system have been implemented in Maude in [34]. In contrast, our implementation focuses on capturing the timed reduction rules of virtually timed ambients as well as the modal formulas to define a model checker.

7   Concluding Remarks

Virtualization opens for new and interesting formal computational models. This paper introduces modal contracts to capture quality of service properties for virtually timed ambients, a formal model of hierarchical locations of execution. Resource provisioning for virtually timed ambients is based on virtual time, a local notion of time reminiscent of time slices for virtual machines in the context of nested virtualization. These time slices are locally distributed by means of fair, preemptive scheduling. Modal contracts are formalized as propositions in a modal logic for virtually timed ambients which features notions from metric temporal logic, enabling the timed behavior and resource consumption of a system to be expressed as modal logic properties of processes. We can now prove whether a system satisfies a certain quality of service agreement captured as a modal contract by means of a model checking algorithm which proves that a process satisfies a formula. We provide a proof of concept implementation of the model checking algorithm in the Maude rewriting logic system.

To model active resource management, future work will extend the model with constructs to support resource-aware scaling, as well as optimization strategies for scaling. We are also working on extending the implementation in that direction and intend to apply it to study corresponding examples involving resource management and load balancing. It is also interesting to investigate how the techniques developed here could be adapted to richer modelling languages for cloud-deployed software, such as ABS [21].

References

1. Abdelmaboud, A., Jawawi, D.N., Ghani, I., Elsafi, A., Kitchenham, B.: Quality of service approaches in cloud computing: a systematic mapping study. J. Syst. Softw. **101**, 159–179 (2015). https://doi.org/10.1016/j.jss.2014.12.015
2. Akar, O.: Model checking of ambient calculus specifications against ambient logic formulas. Bachelor's thesis, Istanbul Technical University (2009)
3. Aman, B., Ciobanu, G.: Mobile ambients with timers and types. In: Jones, C.B., Liu, Z., Woodcock, J. (eds.) ICTAC 2007. LNCS, vol. 4711, pp. 50–63. Springer, Heidelberg (2007). https://doi.org/10.1007/978-3-540-75292-9_4
4. Aman, B., Ciobanu, G.: Timers and proximities for mobile ambients. In: Diekert, V., Volkov, M.V., Voronkov, A. (eds.) CSR 2007. LNCS, vol. 4649, pp. 33–43. Springer, Heidelberg (2007). https://doi.org/10.1007/978-3-540-74510-5_7
5. Baeten, J.C.M., Bergstra, J.A.: Real time process algebra. Form. Aspects Comput. **3**(2), 142–188 (1991). https://doi.org/10.1007/bf01898401
6. Baeten, J.C.M., Middelburg, C.A.: Process Algebra with Timing. Monographs in Theoretical Computer Science: An EATCS Series. Springer, Heidelberg (2002). https://doi.org/10.1007/978-3-662-04995-2
7. Ben-Yehuda, M., et al.: The turtles project: design and implementation of nested virtualization. In: Proceedings of 9th USENIX Symposium on Operating Systems Design and Implementation, OSDI 2010, Vancouver, BC, October 2010, pp. 423–436. USENIX Association (2010). http://www.usenix.org/events/osdi10/tech/full_papers/Ben-Yehuda.pdf

8. Berger, M.: Towards abstractions for distributed systems. Ph.D. thesis, Imperial College, London (2004)
9. Cardelli, L., Gordon, A.D.: Anytime, anywhere: modal logics for mobile ambients. In: Proceedings of 27th ACM SIGPLAN-SIGACT Symposium on Principles of Programming Languages, POPL 2000, Boston, MA, January 2000, pp. 365–377. ACM Press, New York (2000). https://doi.org/10.1145/325694.325742
10. Cardelli, L., Gordon, A.D.: Mobile ambients. Theor. Comput. Sci. **240**(1), 177–213 (2000). https://doi.org/10.1016/s0304-3975(99)00231-5
11. Cardelli, L., Gordon, A.D.: Logical properites of name restriction. In: Abramsky, S. (ed.) TLCA 2001. LNCS, vol. 2044, pp. 46–60. Springer, Heidelberg (2001). https://doi.org/10.1007/3-540-45413-6_8
12. Cardelli, L., Gordon, A.D.: Equational properties of mobile ambients. Math. Struct. Comput. Sci. **13**(3), 371–408 (2003). https://doi.org/10.1017/s0960129502003742
13. Charatonik, W., Dal Zilio, S., Gordon, A.D., Mukhopadhyay, S., Talbot, J.-M.: The complexity of model checking mobile ambients. In: Honsell, F., Miculan, M. (eds.) FoSSaCS 2001. LNCS, vol. 2030, pp. 152–167. Springer, Heidelberg (2001). https://doi.org/10.1007/3-540-45315-6_10
14. Charatonik, W., Talbot, J.-M.: The decidability of model checking mobile ambients. In: Fribourg, L. (ed.) CSL 2001. LNCS, vol. 2142, pp. 339–354. Springer, Heidelberg (2001). https://doi.org/10.1007/3-540-44802-0_24
15. Ciobanu, G.: Interaction in time and space. Electron. Notes Theor. Comput. Sci. **203**(3), 5–18 (2008). https://doi.org/10.1016/j.entcs.2008.04.083
16. Clavel, M.: All About Maude - A High-Performance Logical Framework, How to Specify, Program, and Verify Systems in Rewriting Logic. Programming and Software Engineering, vol. 4350. Springer, Heidelberg (2007). https://doi.org/10.1007/978-3-540-71999-1
17. Crago, S., et al.: Heterogeneous cloud computing. In: Proceedings of 2011 IEEE International Conference on Cluster Computing, Austin, TX, September 2011, pp. 378–385. IEEE CS Press, Washington, DC (2011). https://doi.org/10.1109/cluster.2011.49
18. Fibonacci. Greedy algorithm for Egyptian fractions. https://en.wikipedia.org/wiki/Greedy_algorithm_for_Egyptian_fractions
19. Goldberg, R.P.: Survey of virtual machine research. IEEE Comput. **7**(6), 34–45 (1974). https://doi.org/10.1109/mc.1974.6323581
20. Gordon, A.D.: V for virtual. Electron. Notes Theor. Comput. Sci. **162**, 177–181 (2006). https://doi.org/10.1016/j.entcs.2006.01.030
21. Johnsen, E.B., Schlatte, R., Tapia Tarifa, S.L.: Integrating deployment architectures and resource consumption in timed object-oriented models. J. Log. Algebraic Methods Program. **84**(1), 67–91 (2015). https://doi.org/10.1016/j.jlamp.2014.07.001
22. Johnsen, E.B., Steffen, M., Stumpf, J.B.: A calculus of virtually timed ambients. In: James, P., Roggenbach, M. (eds.) WADT 2016. LNCS, vol. 10644, pp. 88–103. Springer, Cham (2017). https://doi.org/10.1007/978-3-319-72044-9_7
23. Johnsen, E.B., Steffen, M., Stumpf, J.B.: Virtually timed ambients: a calculus of nested virtualization. J. Log. Algebraic Methods Program. **94**, 109–127 (2018). https://doi.org/10.1016/j.jlamp.2017.10.001
24. Koymans, R.: Specifying real-time properties with metric temporal logic. Real-Time Syst. **2**(4), 255–299 (1990). https://doi.org/10.1007/bf01995674
25. Merro, M., Zappa Nardelli, F.: Behavioral theory for mobile ambients. J. ACM **52**(6), 961–1023 (2005). https://doi.org/10.1145/1101821.1101825

26. Meseguer, J.: Twenty years of rewriting logic. J. Log. Algebraic Program. **81**(7–8), 721–781 (2012). https://doi.org/10.1016/j.jlap.2012.06.003

27. Meseguer, J., Rosu, G.: The rewriting logic semantics project. Theor. Comput. Sci. **373**(3), 213–237 (2007). https://doi.org/10.1016/j.tcs.2006.12.018

28. Milner, R., Sangiorgi, D.: Barbed bisimulation. In: Kuich, W. (ed.) ICALP 1992. LNCS, vol. 623, pp. 685–695. Springer, Heidelberg (1992). https://doi.org/10.1007/3-540-55719-9_114

29. Nicollin, X., Sifakis, J.: The algebra of timed processes, ATP: theory and application. Inf. Comput. **114**(1), 131–178 (1994). https://doi.org/10.1006/inco.1994.1083

30. Ölveczky, P.C.: Designing Reliable Distributed Systems: A Formal Methods Approach Based on Executable Modeling in Maude. UTCS. Springer, London (2017). https://doi.org/10.1007/978-1-4471-6687-0

31. Ouaknine, J., Worrell, J.: On the decidability and complexity of metric temporal logic over finite words. Log. Methods Comput. Sci. **3**(1), Article 8 (2007). https://doi.org/10.2168/lmcs-3(1:8)2007

32. Ouaknine, J., Worrell, J.: Some recent results in metric temporal logic. In: Cassez, F., Jard, C. (eds.) FORMATS 2008. LNCS, vol. 5215, pp. 1–13. Springer, Heidelberg (2008). https://doi.org/10.1007/978-3-540-85778-5_1

33. Prisacariu, C., Ciobanu, G.: Timed distributed π-calculus. Technical report, FML-05-01, Inst. of Computer Science Iasi (2005) http://iit.iit.tuiasi.ro/TR/reports/fml1501.pdf

34. Rosa-Velardo, F., Segura, C., Verdejo, A.: Typed mobile ambients in maude. Electron. Notes Theor. Comput. Sci. **147**(1), 135–161 (2006). https://doi.org/10.1016/j.entcs.2005.06.041

35. Sangiorgi, D., Walker, D.: The Pi-Calculus: A Theory of Mobile Processes. Cambridge University Press, Cambridge (2001)

36. Sun, J., Liu, Y., Dong, J.S., Pang, J.: PAT: towards flexible verification under fairness. In: Bouajjani, A., Maler, O. (eds.) CAV 2009. LNCS, vol. 5643, pp. 709–714. Springer, Heidelberg (2009). https://doi.org/10.1007/978-3-642-02658-4_59

37. Sun, Y.: Toward a model checker for ambient logic using the process analysis toolkit. MSc thesis, Bishop's University, Sherbrooke, Quebec (2015)

38. Williams, D., Jamjoom, H., Weatherspoon, H.: The Xen-Blanket: virtualize once, run everywhere. In: Proceedings of 7th European Conference on Computer Systems, EuroSys 2012, Bern, April 2012, pp. 113–126. ACM Press, New York (2012). https://doi.org/10.1145/2168836.2168849

Abstraction of Bit-Vector Operations for BDD-Based SMT Solvers

Martin Jonáš[✉] and Jan Strejček

Faculty of Informatics, Masaryk University,
Botanicka 68á, 602 00 Brno, Czech Republic
{xjonas,strejcek}@fi.muni.cz

Abstract. BDD-based SMT solvers have recently shown to be competitive for solving satisfiability of quantified bit-vector formulas. However, these solvers reach their limits when the input formula contains complicated arithmetic. Hitherto, this problem has been alleviated by approximations reducing efficient bit-widths of bit-vector variables. In this paper, we propose an orthogonal abstraction technique working on the level of the individual instances of bit-vector operations. In particular, we compute only several bits of the operation result, which may be sufficient to decide the satisfiability of the formula. Experimental results show that our BDD-based SMT solver Q3B extended with these abstractions can solve more quantified bit-vector formulas from the SMT-LIB repository than state-of-the-art SMT solvers Boolector, CVC4, and Z3.

1 Introduction

In the modern world, as the computer software becomes still more ubiquitous and complex, there is an increasing need to test it and formally verify its correctness. Several approaches to software verification, such as symbolic execution or bounded model checking, rely on the ability to decide whether a given first-order formula in a suitable logical theory is satisfiable. To this end, many of the verifiers use Satisfiability Modulo Theories (SMT) solvers, which can solve precisely the task of checking satisfiability of a first-order formula in a given logical theory. For describing software, the natural choice of a logical theory is the theory of *fixed-size bit-vectors* in which the objects are vectors of bits and the operations on them precisely reflect operations performed by computers. Moreover, in applications such as synthesis of invariants, ranking functions, or loop summaries, the formulas in question also naturally contain quantifiers [6,7,10,12,17].

It is therefore not surprising that the development of SMT solvers for quantified formulas in the theory of fixed-size bit-vectors has seen several advances in the recent years. In particular, the support for arbitrarily quantified bit-vector formulas has been implemented to existing solvers Z3 [18], Boolector [15], and CVC4 [14]. Moreover, new tools that aim for precisely this theory, such as the solver Q3B [8], were developed. Approaches of these tools fall into two categories:

The research was supported by Czech Science Foundation, grant GA18-02177S.

B. Fischer and T. Uustalu (Eds.): ICTAC 2018, LNCS 11187, pp. 273–291, 2018.
https://doi.org/10.1007/978-3-030-02508-3_15

Z3, Boolector, and CVC4 use variants of quantifier instantiation that iteratively produces quantifier-free formulas that can be solved by a solver for quantifier-free bit-vector formulas. On the other hand, the solver Q3B uses Binary Decision Diagrams (BDDs) to represent quantified bit-vector formulas and to decide their satisfiability.

However, BDDs have inherent limitations. For example, if a formula contains multiplication of two variables, the BDD that represents it is guaranteed to be exponential in size regardless the chosen order of variables. Similarly, if the formula contains complicated arithmetic, the produced BDDs tend to grow in size very quickly. The solver Q3B tries to alleviate this problem by computing approximations [8] of the original formula to reduce sets of values that can be represented by the individual variables and, in turn, to reduce sizes of the resulting BDDs. In particular, if the set of possible values of all existentially quantified variables is reduced and the formula is still satisfiable, the original formula must have been satisfiable. Conversely, if the set of possible values of all universally quantified variables is reduced and the formula is still unsatisfiable, the original formula must have been unsatisfiable.

Although the approximations allowed Q3B to remain competitive with state-of-the-art SMT solvers, the approach has several drawbacks. Currently, Q3B cannot solve satisfiability of simple formulas such as

$$\exists x, y \; ((x < 2) \; \wedge \; (x > 4) \; \wedge \; (x \cdot y = 0)))\,,$$

$$\exists x, y \; ((x \ll 1) \cdot y = 1)\,,$$

$$\exists x, y \; (x > 0 \; \wedge \; x \leq 4 \; \wedge \; y > 0 \; \wedge \; y \leq 4 \; \wedge \; x \cdot y = 0)\,,$$

where all variables and constants have bit-width 32, and $\ll$ denotes bit-wise shift left. All these three formulas are unsatisfiable, but cannot be decided without approximations, because they contain non-linear multiplication. Moreover, they cannot be decided even with approximations, because they are unsatisfiable and contain no universally quantified variables that could be used to approximate the formula.

However, the three above-mentioned formulas have something in common: only a few of the bits of the multiplication results are sufficient to decide satisfiability of the formulas. The first formula can be decided unsatisfiable without computing any bits of $x \cdot y$ whatsoever. The second formula can be decided by computing only the least-significant bit of $(x \ll 1) \cdot y$ because it must always be zero. The third formula can be decided by computing 5 least-significant bits of $x \cdot y$, because they are enough to rule out all values of x and y between 1 and 4 as models.

With this in mind, we propose an improvement of BDD-based SMT solvers such as Q3B by allowing to compute only several bits of results of arithmetic operations. To achieve this, the paper defines abstract domains in which the operations can produce *do-not-know* values and shows that these abstract domains can be used to decide satisfiability of an input formula.

The paper is structured as follows. Section 2 provides necessary background and notations for SMT, bit-vector theory, and binary decision diagrams. Section 3 defines abstract domains for terms and formulas and shows how to use them to decide satisfiability of a formula. Section 4 introduces specific term and formula abstract domains that are used to compute only several bits from results of arithmetic bit-vector operations. Section 5 describes our implementation of these abstract domains in the SMT solver Q3B and the following Sect. 6 provides evaluation of this implementation both in comparison to the original Q3B and to other state-of-the-art SMT solvers.

2 Preliminaries

2.1 Bit-Vector Theory

This section briefly recalls the *theory of fixed sized bit-vectors* (*BV* or *bit-vector theory* for short). In the description, we assume familiarity with standard definitions of many-sorted logic, well-sorted terms, atomic formulas, and formulas. In the following, we denote the set of all well-sorted terms as T and the set of all well-sorted formulas as $\mathcal{F}$.

The bit-vector theory is a many-sorted first-order theory with infinitely many sorts corresponding to bit-vectors of various lengths. The BV theory uses only three predicates, namely *equality* ($=$), *unsigned inequality* of binary-encoded natural numbers ($\leq_u$), and *signed inequality* of integers in two's complement representation ($\leq_s$). The theory also contains various functions including *addition* ($+$), *multiplication* ($\cdot$), *unsigned division* ($\div$), *unsigned remainder* ($\%$), bit-wise *and* (bvand), bit-wise *or* (bvor), bit-wise *exclusive or* (bvxor), *left-shift* ($\ll$), *right-shift* ($\gg$), *concatenation* (concat), and *extraction* of n bits starting from position p (extract_p^n). The signature of BV theory also contains constants $c^{[n]}$ for each bit-width $n > 0$ and a number $0 \leq c \leq 2^n - 1$. If a bit-width of a constant or a variable is not specified, we suppose that it is equal to 32. We denote set of all bit-vectors as $\mathcal{BV}$ and the set of all variables as *vars*.

For a valuation μ that assigns to each variable from *vars* a value in its domain, $\llbracket \_ \rrbracket_\mu$ denotes the evaluation function, which assigns to each term t the bit-vector obtained by substituting variables in t by their values given by μ and evaluating all functions. Similarly, the function $\llbracket \_ \rrbracket_\mu$ assigns to each formula φ the value obtained by substituting free variables in φ by values given by μ and evaluating all functions, predicates, logic operators etc. A formula φ is *satisfiable* if $\llbracket \varphi \rrbracket_\mu = 1$ for some valuation μ; it is *unsatisfiable* otherwise.

The precise definition of many-sorted logic can be found for example in Barrett et al. [3]. The precise description of bit-vector theory and its operations can be found for example in the paper describing complexity of quantified bit-vector theory by Kovásznai et al. [9].

2.2 Binary Decision Diagrams

A binary decision diagram (BDD) is a data structure that can succinctly represent Boolean functions. Formally, it is a binary directed acyclic graph that has at most

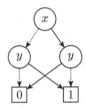

Fig. 1. BDD for $(x \text{ xor } y)$

two leaves, labelled by 0 and 1, and inner nodes labelled by formal arguments of the function. Each inner node has two children, called *high* and *low* children, that denote values 1 and 0, respectively, of the corresponding formal argument. Given a BDD that represents a Boolean function f, the value of f in a given assignment can be computed by traversing the BDD as follows: start in the root node; if the value of the argument corresponding to the current node is 1, continue to the high child, otherwise continue to the low child; continue with the traversal until reaching a leaf node and return its label. Given a BDD b and an assignment μ, we denote the result of the function represented by b as $[\![b]\!]_\mu$. For example, Fig. 1 shows a BDD that represents a binary function $f(x, y) = (x \text{ xor } y)$. According to the traditional notation, the high children are marked by solid edges, the low children are marked by dotted edges. The trivial BDDs $\boxed{0}$ and $\boxed{1}$ represent functions *false* (0) and *true* (1), respectively.

Alternatively, binary decision diagrams can be used to represent a set of satisfying assignments (also called *models*) of a Boolean formula φ. Such a BDD represents a function that has Boolean variables of the formula φ as formal arguments and that evaluates to 1 in a given assignment iff the assignment is a model of the formula φ. In this view, the BDD of Fig. 1 represents the set of assignments satisfying the formula $(x \wedge \neg y) \vee (\neg x \wedge y)$.

In this paper, we suppose that all binary decision diagrams are *reduced* and *ordered*. A BDD is *ordered* if for all pairs of paths in the BDD the order of common variables is the same. A BDD is *reduced* if it does not contain any inner node with the same high and low child. It has been shown that reduced and ordered BDDs (ROBDDs) are canonical – given a variable order, there is exactly one BDD for each given function [5].

Binary decision diagrams can be also used to represent an arbitrary *bit-vector function*, i.e., a function that assigns a bit-vector value to each assignment of bit variables. Such a function of a bit-width k (i.e., the produced bit-vectors have the bit-width k) can be represented by a vector of BDDs $\overline{b} = (b_i)_{0 \le i < k}$. Result of this function for an assignment μ is then the bit-vector $([\![b_i]\!]_\mu)_{0 \le i < k}$. For example, Fig. 2 shows a vector of BDDs representing addition $x_2 x_1 x_0 + y_2 y_1 y_0$ of two bit-vectors of size 3. In the following text, we denote the set of all BDDs as BDD and the set of all vectors of BDDs as BDDvec. We use the overlined symbols for both vectors of BDDs and bit-vectors.

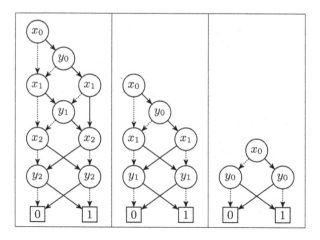

Fig. 2. Vector of BDDs representing the addition $x_2x_1x_0 + y_2y_1y_0$ of two bit-vectors of size 3. The least significant bit of the result is on the right.

2.3   Operations on Binary Decision Diagrams

It has been shown by Bryant [5] that given ROBDDs for Boolean functions f and g, one can compute a BDD for functions $f(\overline{x}) \wedge g(\overline{x})$ and $f(\overline{x}) \vee g(\overline{x})$ in polynomial time. A BDD for negation can be obtained by exchanging leaf nodes 0 and 1. Using these operations, a BDD for an arbitrary Boolean formula can be constructed by computing the corresponding BDDs for all subformulas from the smallest ones. Bryant has also described a function that modifies a given BDD by setting selected variables to given values. Using this function, it is possible to eliminate variable x from a given BDD representing $f(x, \overline{y})$ existentially or universally by computing the BDDs for $f(0, \overline{y}) \vee f(1, \overline{y})$ or $f(0, \overline{y}) \wedge f(1, \overline{y})$, respectively. We denote the functions for computing *conjunction, disjunction,* and *negation* of BDDs by the infix notations &, |, and !, respectively. Using these functions, we can define functions computing *equivalence* and *exclusive or* of two BDDs with the infix notations $\leftrightarrow$ and xor, respectively.

Further, given two vectors of BDDs that represent bit-vector functions f and g of the same bit-width, a vector of BDDs for the function $f(\overline{x}) + g(\overline{x})$, where $+$ is addition of two bit-vectors, can also be computed by using the basic logical operations on BDDs representing the individual bits. Listing 1.1 shows a pseudo-code of this computation, which is implemented for example in the BDD package BuDDy[1]. Other arithmetical operations such as *multiplication, division,* or *remainder* can also be computed in this way, although the algorithms are more involved in these cases.

Finally, given two vectors of BDDs that represent bit-vector functions f and g of the same bit-width, it is also possible to compute the BDD for their equality $f(\overline{x}) = g(\overline{x})$, the BDD for their unsigned inequality $f(\overline{x}) \leq_u g(\overline{x})$, and the BDD for

---

[1] http://sourceforge.net/projects/buddy.

Listing 1.1. Pseudo-codes computing operations *addition* (+) and *equality* (=) on vectors $\bar{a} = (a_i)_{0 \le i < k}$ and $\bar{b} = (b_i)_{0 \le i < k}$ of BDDs.

```
1   bvec_add(ā, b̄)
2   {
3       result ← (0̄,0̄,...,0̄) with the bit-width k;
4       carry ← 0̄;
5       for i from 0 to k - 1 {
6           result_i ← a_i xor b_i xor carry;
7           carry ← (a_i & b_i) | (carry & (a_i | b_i));
8       }
9       return result;
10  }
11
12  bvec_eq(ā, b̄)
13  {
14      result ← 1̄;
15      for i from 0 to k - 1 {
16          result ← result & (a_i ↔ b_i);
17      }
18      return result;
19  }
```

their signed inequality $f(\bar{x}) \le_s g(\bar{x})$. Listing 1.1 shows a pseudo-code computing the BDD for equality, which corresponds to the implementation in BuDDy.

Using these algorithms, it is possible to define a function t2BDDvec, which converts a bit-vector term to the vector of BDDs representing the function computed by the term. Consequently, it is possible to define a function f2BDD, which converts a bit-vector formula to the corresponding BDD.

3   Formula and Term Abstractions

Although it is often infeasible to compute functions t2BDDvec and f2BDD precisely, even an imprecise result can sometimes be enough to decide satisfiability of the input formula as illustrated in Introduction. In this section we describe notions of a *term abstract domain*, which captures an imprecise computation of t2BDDvec, and a *formula abstract domain*, which captures an imprecise computation of f2BDD. Generally, a term abstract domain defines a set of abstract objects A, a function α mapping terms to these abstract objects, and an evaluation function $[\![\_]\!]^A_\_$, which assigns to each abstract object a and a variable assignment μ the set $[\![a]\!]^A_\mu$ of bit-vectors represented by a.

Definition 1 (Term abstract domain). *A term abstract domain is a triple* $(A, \alpha, [\![\_]\!]^A_\_)$, *where A is a set of* abstract objects, $\alpha \colon \mathcal{T} \to A$ *is an* abstraction function, *and* $[\![\_]\!]^A_\_ \colon A \times \mathcal{BV}^{vars} \to 2^{\mathcal{BV}}$ *is an* abstract evaluation function.

As an example, consider the *precise* BDD *term abstract domain*, in which the corresponding vector of BDDs is assigned to each term. In particular, the precise BDD term abstract domain is the triple $(\text{BDDvec}, \text{t2BDDvec}, [\![\_]\!]\_^{\text{BDDvec}})$, where $[\![\overline{a}]\!]_\mu^{\text{BDDvec}}$ is the singleton set $\{bv\}$ such that bv is the result of evaluation of vector $\overline{a}$ of BDDs in the assignment μ, i.e., $bv = [\![\overline{a}]\!]_\mu$. This abstract domain enjoys two interesting properties: for each term and assignment, the corresponding abstract object contains the correct result and it does not contain any incorrect result. These properties are called *completeness* and *soundness*.

Definition 2. *A term abstract domain* $(A, \alpha, [\![\_]\!]\_^A)$ *is* complete *if each term* $t \in \mathcal{T}$ *and each assignment* μ *satisfy* $[\![t]\!]_\mu \in [\![\alpha(t)]\!]_\mu^A$. *Conversely, it is* sound *if each* t *and* μ *satisfy* $[\![\alpha(t)]\!]_\mu^A \subseteq \{[\![t]\!]_\mu\}$.

Similarly to the term abstract domain, the *formula abstract domain* defines a set of abstract objects A, a function α mapping formulas to these abstract objects, and an evaluation function $[\![\_]\!]^A$, which assigns to each abstract object a and a variable assignment μ the set $[\![a]\!]_\mu^A \subseteq \{0, 1\}$ of truth values associated to a.

Definition 3 (Formula abstract domain). *A formula abstract domain is a triple* $(A, \alpha, [\![\_]\!]\_^A)$, *where* A *is an arbitrary set of* abstract objects, $\alpha \colon \mathcal{F} \to A$ *is an* abstraction function, *and* $[\![\_]\!]\_^A \colon A \times \mathcal{BV}^{vars} \to 2^{\{1,0\}}$ *is an* abstract evaluation function.

Definition 4. *A formula abstract domain* $(A, \alpha, [\![\_]\!]\_^A)$ *is* complete *if each formula* $\varphi \in \mathcal{F}$ *and each assignment* μ *satisfy* $[\![\varphi]\!]_\mu \in [\![\alpha(\varphi)]\!]_\mu^A$. *Conversely, it is* sound *if each* φ *and* μ *satisfy* $[\![\alpha(\varphi)]\!]_\mu^A \subseteq \{[\![\varphi]\!]_\mu\}$.

As in the case of terms, the precise computation of the BDD corresponding to a formula yields a *precise* BDD *formula abstract domain*, which is complete and sound. The precise BDD formula abstract domain is a triple $(\text{BDD}, \text{f2BDD}, [\![\_]\!]\_^{\text{BDD}})$, where $[\![a]\!]_\mu^{\text{BDD}}$ is the singleton set $\{b\}$, where b is the result of evaluation of the BDD a in the assignment μ, i.e., $b = [\![a]\!]_\mu$.

In the following, we weaken the precise term and formula BDD abstract domains by dropping the requirement on the soundness, while still retaining the requirement of completeness. As the following theorem demonstrates, such an abstract domain can still be used for deciding satisfiability of the input formula.

Theorem 1. *Let* φ *be a formula and* $(A, \alpha, [\![\_]\!]\_^A)$ *be a complete formula abstract domain. If there exists an assignment* μ *such that* $[\![\alpha(\varphi)]\!]_\mu^A = \{1\}$, *the formula* φ *is satisfiable. On the other hand, if all assignments* μ *satisfy* $[\![\alpha(\varphi)]\!]_\mu^A = \{0\}$, *the formula is unsatisfiable.*

Note that for abstract domains in which abstract objects are BDDs with the standard evaluation function, the check for existence of the assignment μ from the previous theorem is easy to implement. Such an assignment exists precisely if the leaf node 1 is reachable from the root of the BDD. Furthermore, if the BDD is reduced and ordered, this happens precisely if the BDD is not $\boxed{0}$. Conversely, all assignments μ satisfy $[\![\alpha(\varphi)]\!]_\mu^A = \{0\}$ iff the reduced and ordered BDD $\alpha(\varphi)$ is $\boxed{0}$.

Fig. 3. Truncated result of addition of two three-bit bit-vectors.

4   Truncating Formula and Term Abstract Domains

This section describes a term abstract domain and a corresponding formula abstract domain that allow *truncating* results from bit-vector operations, i.e., computing only several bits from the result of arithmetic bit-vector operations.

In this whole section, we suppose that all formulas are in *negation normal form*, i.e., logical operations are conjunctions, disjunctions, and negations and negations are applied only on atomic subformulas. As traditional, we denote the literal $\neg(t_1 = t_2)$ as $t_1 \neq t_2$.

4.1   Truncating Term Abstract Domain

We introduce the *truncating term abstract domain* first. It is a complete but unsound term abstract domain, in which the terms are represented by vectors whose elements are BDDs, as in the precise term abstract domain, or *do-not-know values*. The do-not-know value, denoted as ?, represents an unknown value of the corresponding bit – it can be both 0 and 1.

For example, Fig. 3 shows the result of computing only the least-significant bit of an addition of two bit-vectors $x_2x_1x_0 + y_2y_1y_0$. The value of this abstract object under the assignment $\{x \mapsto 001, y \mapsto 100\}$ is the set $\{001, 011, 101, 111\}$, since only the value of the least-significant bit is computed precisely.

Formally, the truncating term abstract domain is a triple

$$(\texttt{tBDDvec}, \texttt{t2tBDDvec}, \llbracket\_\rrbracket_\_^{\texttt{tBDDvec}}),$$

where the set of abstract elements consists of vectors of BDDs and ? elements

$$\texttt{tBDDvec} = \{(b_i)_{0 \le i < k} \mid k \in \mathbb{N}, b_i \in \text{BDD} \cup \{?\} \text{ for all } 0 \le i < k\}$$

and the abstract evaluation function assigns to each $\bar{b} = (b_i)_{0 \le i < k} \in \texttt{tBDDvec}$ and an assignment μ the set of bit-vector values

$$\llbracket\bar{b}\rrbracket_\mu^{\texttt{tBDDvec}} = \{(v_i)_{0 \le i < k} \mid \text{if } b_i = ? \text{ then } v_i \in \{0, 1\} \text{ else } v_i = \llbracket b_i \rrbracket_\mu, 0 \le i < k\}.$$

There are many possible implementations of the `t2tBDDvec` function including the following two:

1. the number of computed bits is specified and other bits are set to ?,

2. the limit on BDD nodes in the result of the operation is specified and after reaching it, the remaining bits are set to ?.

In the following, we describe only the second option as our evaluation has shown that it outperforms the first one on the set of our benchmarks. Furthermore, it is easy to derive the implementation of the first option based on the description of the other option. In addition, we suppose that the limit on BDD nodes is fixed for the given domain. In the implementation, we use multiple abstract domains varying by the BDD node limit.

The function t2tBDDvec is computed recursively on the input term. The base case for the variables or constants is straightforward and it is the same as in the precise function t2BDDvec. On the other hand, the computation for bit-vector operations differs from t2BDDvec in two important aspects:

- The operations have to work correctly with ? elements. To achieve this, we modify the BDD operations &, |, and xor, which occurred in the computation of t2BDDvec. The handling of ? in the modified operations is similar to the definition of logical connectives in the three-valued logic and to the way bit-masks are computed in the SMT solver mcBV [19]. The modified BDD operations $\&_t$, $|_t$, and xor_t are computed as follows:

$$a \ \&_t \ b = \begin{cases} \boxed{0} & \text{if } a = \boxed{0} \text{ or } b = \boxed{0} \\ a \ \& \ b & \text{if } a, b \notin \{\boxed{0}, ?\} \\ ? & \text{otherwise} \end{cases}$$

$$a \ |_t \ b = \begin{cases} \boxed{1} & \text{if } a = \boxed{1} \text{ or } b = \boxed{1} \\ a \ | \ b & \text{if } a, b \notin \{\boxed{1}, ?\} \\ ? & \text{otherwise} \end{cases}$$

$$a \ \text{xor}_t \ b = \begin{cases} a \ \text{xor} \ b & \text{if } a \neq ? \text{ and } b \neq ? \\ ? & \text{otherwise} \end{cases}$$

Note that $? \ \text{xor}_t \ ?$ is not $\boxed{1}$ as each ? can represent a different value.
- Implementation of operations has to consider the given limit on the number of BDD nodes and set the bits that have not been computed precisely to ? after the limit has been reached. The example of modification of the original bvec_add that uses the node limit is shown in the Listing 1.2. The implementations of other operations are similar. However, they differ in the order in which the precise bits are produced: during computation of addition and multiplication, the first computed precise bits are the least significant ones; during computation of division, the first computed precise bits are the most-significant ones. Therefore if the computation of addition or multiplication reaches the BDD node limit, remaining most-significant bits are set to ?, while for division least-significant bits are set to ?.

Listing 1.2. Pseudo-code computing *truncated addition* of two tBDDvecs $\overline{a} = (a_i)_{0 \leq i < k}$ and $\overline{b} = (b_i)_{0 \leq i < k}$.

```
 1  bvec_add_nodeLimit (ā, b̄, limit)
 2  {
 3      result ← (⎡0⎤,⎡0⎤,...,⎡0⎤) with the bit-width k;
 4      carry  ← ⎡0⎤;
 5      for i from 0 to k - 1 {
 6          if (bddNodes (result) > limit) {
 7              resultᵢ ← ?;
 8          } else {
 9              resultᵢ ← aᵢ xorₜ bᵢ xorₜ carry;
10              carry   ← (aᵢ &ₜ bᵢ) |ₜ (carry &ₜ (aᵢ |ₜ bᵢ));
11          }
12      }
13      return result;
14  }
```

The set of values represented by the result of t2tBDDvec always contains the precise result of the given term because the t2tBDDvec can only make precise values imprecise by using ? elements. The truncating term abstract domain is therefore complete. However, it is not sound, as the abstract object can describe also incorrect results.

4.2   Truncating Formula Abstract Domain

We now define a formula abstract domain that uses results of truncated bit-vector operations. Intuitively, the abstract elements in this abstract domain are BDD pairs (b_{must}, b_{may}): the first one determines the assignments that satisfy the formula for all possible values of ? elements, and the second one determines the assignments that satisfy the formula for some values of ? elements.

Formally, the *truncating formula abstract domain* is a triple

$$(\texttt{BDDpair}, \texttt{f2BDDpair}, [\![\_]\!]^{\texttt{BDDpair}}_{\_}),$$

where $\texttt{BDDpair} = \texttt{BDD} \times \texttt{BDD}$ and the evaluation function assigns to each pair $(b_{must}, b_{may}) \in \texttt{BDDpair}$ the set of Boolean values

$$[\![(b_{must}, b_{may})]\!]^{\texttt{BDDpair}}_{\mu} = \{v \in \{0,1\} \mid [\![b_{must}]\!]_{\mu} \implies v \implies [\![b_{may}]\!]_{\mu}\}.$$

Observe that $[\![(b_{must}, b_{may})]\!]^{\texttt{BDDpair}}_{\mu}$ is $\{0\}$ when $[\![b_{must}]\!]_{\mu} = [\![b_{may}]\!]_{\mu} = 0$, it is $\{1\}$ when $[\![b_{must}]\!]_{\mu} = [\![b_{may}]\!]_{\mu} = 1$, and it is $\{0,1\}$ when $[\![b_{must}]\!]_{\mu} = 0$, $[\![b_{may}]\!]_{\mu} = 1$. While the result would be $\emptyset$ in the remaining case $[\![b_{must}]\!]_{\mu} = 1$, $[\![b_{may}]\!]_{\mu} = 0$, this situation never happens for the result of the defined function f2BDDpair.

The function $\texttt{f2BDDpair}(\varphi)$ is defined recursively as follows.

1. The formula φ is an atomic subformula or its negation, i.e., $\varphi \equiv t_1 \bowtie t_2$ for $\bowtie \in \{=, \neq, \leq_u, <_u, \leq_s, <_s\}$. The function f2BDDpair computes the pair (b_{must}, b_{may}) from t2tBDDvec(t_1) and t2tBDDvec(t_2) using modified algorithms for the corresponding operations on vectors of standard BDDs. For example, Listing 1.3 shows an algorithm for equality of t2tBDDvec(t_1) and t2tBDDvec(t_2) (compare with the algorithm for equality of vectors of standard BDDs presented in Listing 1.1). In this algorithm, the value b_{must} becomes 0 if there is ? in any of the input vectors, because then the arguments may differ for some value of the ?. On the other hand, the value b_{may} is the conjunction of equality of all pairs of corresponding bits that both have a known value. In particular, construction of b_{may} ignores the pairs of bits containing some ? as it could be the case that equality holds for these bits. Listing 1.3 also shows the algorithm for computing disequality of t2tBDDvec(t_1) and t2tBDDvec(t_2). The algorithms for other relational symbols are similar.

2. The formula φ has the form $\varphi_1 \wedge \varphi_2$ or $\varphi_1 \vee \varphi_2$. Let (b^1_{must}, b^1_{may}) be the result of f2BDDpair(φ_1) and (b^2_{must}, b^2_{may}) be the result of f2BDDpair(φ_2). Then we define

$$\texttt{f2BDDpair}(\varphi_1 \wedge \varphi_2) = ((b^1_{must} \ \& \ b^2_{must}), \ (b^1_{may} \ \& \ b^2_{may})),$$

$$\texttt{f2BDDpair}(\varphi_1 \vee \varphi_2) = ((b^1_{must} \ | \ b^2_{must}), \ (b^1_{may} \ | \ b^2_{may})).$$

3. The formula φ has the form $\forall x. \varphi_1$ or $\exists x. \varphi_1$. Let (b^1_{must}, b^1_{may}) be the result of f2BDDpair(φ_1). Then we define

$$\texttt{f2BDDpair}(\forall x. \varphi_1) = (bdd\_forall(x, b^1_{must}), \ bdd\_forall(x, b^1_{may})),$$

$$\texttt{f2BDDpair}(\exists x. \varphi_1) = (bdd\_exists(x, b^1_{must}), \ bdd\_exists(x, b^1_{may})),$$

where the function $bdd\_forall(x, \_)$ eliminates the variable x universally and $bdd\_exists(x, \_)$ eliminates it existentially as explained in Sect. 2.3.

Example 1. Let t, r, s, u be bit-vector terms, for which we have computed only the least-significant bit as computation of the other bits was infeasible. Formally,

$$\texttt{t2tBDDvec}(t) = (?, \ldots, ?, b_t), \qquad \texttt{t2tBDDvec}(r) = (?, \ldots, ?, b_r),$$

$$\texttt{t2tBDDvec}(s) = (?, \ldots, ?, b_s), \qquad \texttt{t2tBDDvec}(u) = (?, \ldots, ?, b_u),$$

where b_t, b_r, b_s, b_u are BDDs.

Consider the formula $t = r$. The function f2BDDpair applied on this formula returns the pair $(\boxed{0}, b_t \leftrightarrow b_r)$. This pair says that every assignment satisfying the formula must also satisfy the BDD $b_t \leftrightarrow b_r$. Therefore, if $t = r$ is put in conjunction with another formula implying that $b_t \leftrightarrow b_r$ is equal to $\boxed{0}$, the whole conjunction can be decided to be unsatisfiable.

Consider the formula $s \neq u$. The function f2BDDpair now produces the pair $(b_s \text{ xor } b_u, \boxed{1})$. Intuitively, if an assignment satisfies $b_s \text{ xor } b_u$, it also satisfies formula $s \neq u$, regardless the values of the remaining bits.

Finally, consider formulas $t = r \wedge s \neq u$ and $t = r \vee s \neq u$. The result of f2BDDpair($t = r \wedge s \neq u$) is $(\boxed{0}, b_t \leftrightarrow b_r)$, while the result of f2BDDpair($t = r \vee s \neq u$) is $(b_s \text{ xor } b_u, \boxed{1})$.

Listing 1.3. Pseudo-codes computing *truncated equality* and *truncated disequality* of two tBDDvecs $\overline{a} = (a_i)_{0 \le i < k}$ and $\overline{b} = (b_i)_{0 \le i < k}$.

```
1   bvec_eq_trunc(ā, b̄)
2   {
3       result_must  ← 1;
4       result_may   ← 1;
5       for i from 0 to k - 1 {
6           if (a_i == ? or b_i == ?) {
7               result_must  ← 0;
8           } else {
9               result_must  ← result_must & (a_i ↔ b_i);
10              result_may   ← result_may & (a_i ↔ b_i);
11          }
12      }
13      return (result_must, result_may);
14  }
15
16  bvec_neq_trunc(ā, b̄)
17  {
18      result_must  ← 0;
19      result_may   ← 0;
20      for i from 0 to k - 1 {
21          if (a_i == ? or b_i == ?) {
22              result_may   ← 1;
23          } else {
24              result_must  ← result_must | (a_i xor b_i);
25              result_may   ← result_may | (a_i xor b_i);
26          }
27      }
28      return (result_must, result_may);
29  }
```

Similarly to the truncating term abstract domain, the truncating formula abstract domain is also complete, as the following theorem shows.

Theorem 2. *The truncating formula abstract domain is complete.*

Proof. (*sketch*) It can be shown by induction on the structure of the formula that if $\texttt{f2BDDpair}(\varphi) = (b_{must}, b_{may})$, then the following must hold for each assignment μ:

$$[\![b_{must}]\!]_\mu \implies [\![\varphi]\!]_\mu \quad \text{and} \quad [\![\varphi]\!]_\mu \implies [\![b_{may}]\!]_\mu.$$

Therefore $[\![\varphi]\!]_\mu \in [\![\texttt{f2BDDpair}(\varphi)]\!]_\mu^{\texttt{BDDpair}}$ holds for each assignment μ, so the abstract domain is indeed complete. $\qquad\square$

Since the truncating formula abstract domain is complete, Theorem 1 can be used to check satisfiability of a given formula φ. Consider b_{must} and b_{may} such that

$$\texttt{f2BDDpair}(\varphi) = (b_{must}, b_{may}).$$

Then if b_{must} is not $\boxed{0}$, the formula φ is satisfiable. On the other hand, if b_{may} is $\boxed{0}$, the formula φ is not satisfiable.

This satisfiability check solves the formulas mentioned in Introduction as the motivation for the described approach. For all three of the formulas, the b_{may} after computing at least 5 bits from results of the multiplication is $\boxed{0}$ and the formulas can be decided as unsatisfiable.

5   Implementation

We have implemented the described truncated abstract formula domain into the SMT solver Q3B, which is written in C++. The solver Q3B uses the package CUDD [16] for BDD representation and operations, and the implementation of bit-vectors and bit-vector operations for CUDD by P. Navrátil [13]. We have modified this implementation to support ? elements and to support computing truncated results of bit-vector operations and computing (b_{must}, b_{may}) for all bit-vector relation operators and logical operators $\wedge$ and $\vee$. The operations that introduce ? elements, when the precise result would contain too many BDD nodes, are *addition, multiplication,* and *division*. We have selected these operations as the original version of Q3B often has difficulties to handle them. The implementation is available at GitHub[2].

In contrast to the description of computing formula abstraction from the previous section, the implementation does not convert the formula to the negation normal form. Instead, during the traversal of the formula, the solver maintains the *polarity* of the current subformula and uses it to perform the appropriate abstraction of atomic subformulas.

5.1   Further Optimizations

The described approach cannot solve simple formulas as $x \cdot y \leq_u 2 \wedge x \cdot y \geq_u 4$. Even if the subterms $x \cdot y$ are computed abstractly, the information that the ? elements in the two vectors representing the two occurrences of $x \cdot y$ have been the same is lost after computing BDD pairs for $x \cdot y \leq_u 2$ and $x \cdot y \geq_u 4$. Therefore, in the implementation, each multiplication and division is replaced by a fresh existentially quantified variable and the constraint specifying its relation to the multiplication or division, respectively, is added to the formula. For example, the previous formula is transformed to the equivalent formula

$$\exists m_{x,y}(\, m_{x,y} \leq_u 2 \wedge m_{x,y} \geq_u 4 \wedge m_{x,y} = x \cdot y).$$

---

[2] https://github.com/martinjonas/Q3B/releases/tag/ictac2018.

This formula is decided as unsatisfiable even if $x \cdot y$ is computed with arbitrarily low precision. Note that the transformed formula is still not solved by the original version of Q3B as the solver starts to build the precise BDDs for all three conjuncts. Although this particular case could be solved by computing precise BDDs for $m_{x,y} \leq_u 2 \wedge m_{x,y} \geq_u 4$ and not for the third conjunct as the conjunction is already unsatisfiable, the proposed formula modification is more general.

Similar problem arises for example in the unsatisfiable formula $x \cdot y \leq_u 2 \wedge \forall z\, (z \cdot y \geq_u 4)$. This formula cannot be solved even after performing the above-mentioned transformation. The transformation yields the formula

$$\exists m_{x,y}(m_{x,y} \leq_u 2 \wedge m_{x,y} = x \cdot y \wedge \forall z \exists m_{z,y}\,(m_{z,y} \geq_u 4 \wedge m_{z,y} = z \cdot y)),$$

which can not be decided unsatisfiable even by using the abstractions, because the solver can not infer the relationship between variables $m_{x,y}$ and $m_{z,y}$. To solve such formula, the implementation adds a congruence subformula stating that $x = z \rightarrow m_{x,y} = m_{z,y}$ to the formula. This results in the formula

$$\exists m_{x,y}\big(\, m_{x,y} \leq_u 2 \wedge m_{x,y} = x \cdot y \wedge$$
$$\wedge\, \forall z \exists m_{z,y}\,(m_{z,y} \geq_u 4 \wedge m_{z,y} = z \cdot y \wedge (x = z \rightarrow m_{x,y} = m_{z,y}))\big),$$

which can be decided unsatisfiable using the abstractions. Similarly to the previous transformation, the resulting formula is equivalent to the original one and its unsatisfiability can not be shown by the original solver without the abstractions, because it is infeasible to compute the precise BDD for the inner quantified subformula.

5.2   Combining Operation Abstractions and Formula Approximations

The solver Q3B employs formula approximations, which can in some cases help with solving input formulas with multiplication. This subsection elaborates on the interaction of these approximations with the newly implemented operation abstractions. Approximations of formulas are of two kinds: *underapproximation* and *overapproximation*. An underapproximation is a formula that logically entails the input formula; therefore if an underapproximation is satisfiable, the original formula is also satisfiable. On the other hand, an overapproximation is a formula that is logically entailed by the input formula; if an overapproximation is unsatisfiable, the original formula is also unsatisfiable.

The formula approximations are performed on formulas in negation normal form by reducing the *effective bit-width* of selected variables by fixing some of their bits to chosen values. The underapproximations are obtained by decreasing effective bit-widths of all existentially quantified variables and the overapproximations are obtained by decreasing effective bit-widths of all universally quantified variables. Q3B tries to solve the input formula by solving the original formula, underapproximations of the formula, and overapproximations of the formula in parallel. We have integrated the proposed operation abstractions

Listing 1.4. Algorithm combining operation abstractions with underapproximation.

```
1   solve_underapproximation (φ) {
2     effBW ← initialEffBW;
3     nodeLimit ← initialNodeLimit;
4     while (true) {
5       φ_u ← underApprox(φ, effBW);
6       (b_must, b_may) ← solveAbstract(φ_u, nodeLimit);
7       if (b_must != ⓪) return SAT;
8       if (b_must == ⓪ and φ == φ_u) return UNSAT;
9       if (b_must != b_may) {
10          nodeLimit ← increaseNodeLimit(nodeLimit);
11      }
12      else if (φ != underApprox(φ, effBW)) {
13          effBW ← increaseEffBW(effBW);
14      }
15    }
16  }
```

into the functions for solving underapproximations and overapproximations. The function solving the original formula can be adjusted to use operation abstractions as well, but the tool performs better if we keep this function unchanged.

Listing 1.4 shows the simplified implementation of solving underapproximations. The algorithm starts with the small initial values of the effective bit-width effBW for existential variables and the limit nodeLimit on the number of BDD nodes in the results of arithmetic operations. It repeatedly tries to solve the input formula and if the result is not determined, either the effective bit-width or the node limit is increased:

- if operation abstractions caused an imprecision, the node limit is increased;
- if the operation abstractions were precise, but the reduced effective bit-width could have caused imprecision, the effective bit-width is increased.

Currently, the initial effective bit-width is 1 and it is increased to $2, 4, 6, 8, \ldots$. The initial node limit is 1000 and the function increaseNodeLimit() multiplies it by 4 each time. The implementation for solving overapproximations is analogous.

6   Experimental Evaluation

We have compared Q3B with our implementation of operation abstractions (referenced as Q3B+OA) against the original Q3B [8] and state-of-the-art SMT solvers Z3 [11], Boolector [15], and CVC4 [1]. We used Z3 in the version 4.6.0, Boolector in the version that entered SMT-COMP 2017, and CVC4 in the version presented in the paper by Niemetz et al. [14]. We evaluated all 5 solvers on all 5151 quantified bit-vector formulas from the SMT-LIB repository [2] used in

Table 1. Numbers of benchmarks solved by the individual solvers divided by the satisfiability/unsatisfiability and the benchmark family.

	benchmark family	Boolector	CVC4	Z3	Q3B	Q3B+OA
UNSAT	heizmann	14	**107**	21	93	94
	preiner-keymaera	3919	3919	**3922**	3786	3906
	preiner-psyco	**62**	**62**	**62**	45	49
	preiner-scholl-smt08	**71**	37	68	52	69
	preiner-tptp	55	**56**	**56**	**56**	**56**
	preiner-ua	137	137	137	137	137
	wintersteiger-fixpoint	74	**75**	74	**75**	**75**
	wintersteiger-ranking	**20**	14	19	19	19
	Total UNSAT	4352	**4407**	4359	4263	4405
SAT	heizmann	17	18	13	19	**20**
	preiner-keymaera	**108**	78	**108**	104	104
	preinr-psyco	131	129	131	131	131
	preiner-scholl-smt08	248	215	203	239	**256**
	preiner-tptp	**17**	**17**	**17**	**17**	17
	preiner-ua	15	14	**16**	**16**	16
	wintersteiger-fixpoint	45	51	36	**54**	**54**
	wintersteiger-ranking	21	32	35	**40**	**40**
	Total SAT	602	554	559	620	**638**
	Total	4954	4961	4918	4883	**5043**

SMT-COMP 2017. The used benchmarks are divided into three benchmark sets: benchmarks from the tool Ultimate Automizer by M. Heizmann (marked as *heizmann*), benchmarks that were created by converting integer and real arithmetic benchmarks to bit-vectors by M. Preiner (marked as *preiner*), and benchmarks from software and hardware verification by C. M. Wintersteiger (marked as *wintersteiger*). The benchmark sets *preiner* and *wintersteiger* are further divided into smaller families of benchmarks.

All experiments were performed on a Debian machine with two six-core Intel Xeon E5-2620 2.00 GHz processors and 128 GB of RAM. Each benchmark run was limited to use 16 GB of RAM and 90 min of CPU time. All measured times are CPU times. For reliable benchmarking we employed BENCHEXEC [4], a tool that allocates resources for a program execution and measures their use precisely.

Table 1 shows numbers of solved benchmarks by the individual solvers. In total, Q3B+OA was able to solve 160 more benchmarks than the original version of Q3B. Moreover, Q3B+OA solved more benchmarks than other state-of-the art SMT solvers: 89 more than Boolector, 82 more than CVC4, and 125 more than Z3. We have also evaluated the effect of formula transformations described in Subsect. 5.1. The transformations helped only in two families of benchmarks:

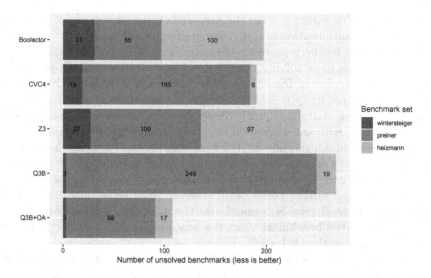

Fig. 4. The number of benchmarks unsolved by the individual solvers. The benchmarks are divided by the source of the benchmark.

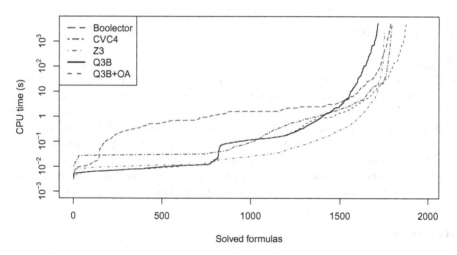

Fig. 5. Quantile plot of all solved non-trivial benchmarks from the SMT-LIB repository. Trivial benchmarks are those that all solvers solved within 0.1 s. The plot shows the number of non-trivial benchmarks (x-axis) that each solver was able to decide within a given CPU time limit (y-axis).

in the family *preiner-keymaera* the optimizations were necessary to solve 116 out of 120 newly decided benchmarks; in the family *wintersteiger-fixpoint* the solver Q3B+OA solved 1 benchmark less without the optimizations.

From the opposite point of view, Fig. 4 shows the number of benchmarks *unsolved* by the individual solvers. This graph shows that most of the benefit of abstractions is on formulas from the *preiner* benchmark set, where expensive operations like multiplication and division are frequently used.

Naturally, due to the repeated refinement of the abstractions, some benchmarks may require more solving time than without abstractions. In particular, there is one benchmark in the *heizmann* benchmark set that was solved by the original Q3B but not by Q3B+OA. Although this was the only such benchmark, the additional cost of abstractions is observable also on some benchmarks that were decided both with and without abstractions: computing abstractions slowed Q3B by more than 0.5 seconds on 115 benchmarks. On the other hand, there were 96 benchmarks decided by both versions of Q3B on which the version with abstraction was faster by more than 0.5 seconds.

To compare the solving times of all solvers, Fig. 5 shows quantile plots of solving times of *non-trivial benchmarks* for the individual solvers. We have filtered out 3168 trivial benchmarks, i.e., the benchmarks that were decided by all of the solvers in less than 0.1 s.

The detailed results of the evaluation, including the raw data files and further analyses, such as cross comparisons and scatter plots, are available at

$$\text{http://fi.muni.cz/~xstrejc/ictac2018/.}$$

7   Conclusions

We have presented operation abstractions that allow BDD-based SMT solvers to decide a formula by computing only some bits of results of arithmetic operations. The experimental evaluation shows that by using these abstractions, BDD-based SMT solver Q3B is able to solve more quantified bit-vector formulas from the SMT-LIB repository than state-of-the-art solvers Boolector, CVC4, and Z3.

In the implemented version, the solver computes overapproximations and underapproximations independently. It could be interesting to investigate whether sharing of the information obtained by an overapproximation with other parallel computations of the solver could improve the performance even more.

References

1. Barrett, C., et al.: CVC4. In: Gopalakrishnan, G., Qadeer, S. (eds.) CAV 2011. LNCS, vol. 6806, pp. 171–177. Springer, Heidelberg (2011). https://doi.org/10.1007/978-3-642-22110-1_14

2. Barrett, C., Fontaine, P., Tinelli, C.: The satisfiability modulo theories library (SMT-LIB) (2016). http://www.smt-lib.org/

3. Barrett, C.W., Sebastiani, R., Seshia, S.A., Tinelli, C.: Satisfiability modulo theories. In: Biere, A., Heule, M., van Maaren, H., Walsh, T. (eds.) Handbook of Satisfiability. Frontiers in Artificial Intelligence, vol. 185, pp. 825–885. IOS Press, Amsterdam (2009). https://doi.org/10.3233/978-1-58603-929-5-825

4. Beyer, D., Löwe, S., Wendler, P.: Benchmarking and resource measurement. In: Fischer, B., Geldenhuys, J. (eds.) SPIN 2015. LNCS, vol. 9232, pp. 160–178. Springer, Cham (2015). https://doi.org/10.1007/978-3-319-23404-5_12

5. Bryant, R.E.: Graph-based algorithms for Boolean function manipulation. IEEE Trans. Comput. **35**(8), 677–691 (1986). https://doi.org/10.1109/tc.1986.1676819
6. Cook, B., Kroening, D., Rümmer, P., Wintersteiger, C.M.: Ranking function synthesis for bit-vector relations. Form. Methods Syst. Des. **43**(1), 93–120 (2013). https://doi.org/10.1007/s10703-013-0186-4
7. Gulwani, S., Srivastava, S., Venkatesan, R.: Constraint-based invariant inference over predicate abstraction. In: Jones, N.D., Müller-Olm, M. (eds.) VMCAI 2009. LNCS, vol. 5403, pp. 120–135. Springer, Heidelberg (2008). https://doi.org/10.1007/978-3-540-93900-9_13
8. Jonáš, M., Strejček, J.: Solving quantified bit-vector formulas using binary decision diagrams. In: Creignou, N., Le Berre, D. (eds.) SAT 2016. LNCS, vol. 9710, pp. 267–283. Springer, Cham (2016). https://doi.org/10.1007/978-3-319-40970-2_17
9. Kovásznai, G., Fröhlich, A., Biere, A.: Complexity of fixed-size bit-vector logics. Theory Comput. Syst. **59**(2), 323–376 (2016). https://doi.org/10.1007/s00224-015-9653-1
10. Kroening, D., Lewis, M., Weissenbacher, G.: Under-approximating loops in C programs for fast counterexample detection. In: Sharygina, N., Veith, H. (eds.) CAV 2013. LNCS, vol. 8044, pp. 381–396. Springer, Heidelberg (2013). https://doi.org/10.1007/978-3-642-39799-8_26
11. de Moura, L., Bjørner, N.: Z3: an efficient SMT solver. In: Ramakrishnan, C.R., Rehof, J. (eds.) TACAS 2008. LNCS, vol. 4963, pp. 337–340. Springer, Heidelberg (2008). https://doi.org/10.1007/978-3-540-78800-3_24
12. Mrázek, J., Bauch, P., Lauko, H., Barnat, J.: SymDIVINE: tool for control-explicit data-symbolic state space exploration. In: Bošnački, D., Wijs, A. (eds.) SPIN 2016. LNCS, vol. 9641, pp. 208–213. Springer, Cham (2016). https://doi.org/10.1007/978-3-319-32582-8_14
13. Navrátil, P.: Adding support for bit-vectors to BDD libraries CUDD and sylvan. Bachelor's thesis, Faculty of Informatics, Masaryk University, Brno (2018). https://is.muni.cz/th/lij5a/
14. Niemetz, A., Preiner, M., Reynolds, A., Barrett, C., Tinelli, C.: On solving quantified bit-vectors using invertibility conditions. arXiv preprint 1804.05025 (2018). http://arxiv.org/abs/1804.05025
15. Preiner, M., Niemetz, A., Biere, A.: Counterexample-guided model synthesis. In: Legay, A., Margaria, T. (eds.) TACAS 2017. LNCS, vol. 10205, pp. 264–280. Springer, Heidelberg (2017). https://doi.org/10.1007/978-3-662-54577-5_15
16. Somenzi, F.: CUDD: CU decision diagram package release 3.0.0. University of Colorado at Boulder (2015). https://github.com/ivmai/cudd
17. Srivastava, S., Gulwani, S., Foster, J.S.: From program verification to program synthesis. In: Proceedings of 37th ACM SIGPLAN-SIGACT Symposium on Principles of Programming Languages, POPL 2010, Madrid, January 2010, pp. 313–326. ACM Press, New York (2010). https://doi.org/10.1145/1706299.1706337
18. Wintersteiger, C.M., Hamadi, Y., de Moura, L.M.: Efficiently solving quantified bit-vector formulas. Form. Methods Syst. Des. **42**(1), 3–23 (2013). https://doi.org/10.1007/s10703-012-0156-2
19. Zeljić, A., Wintersteiger, C.M., Rümmer, P.: Deciding bit-vector formulas with mcSAT. In: Creignou, N., Le Berre, D. (eds.) SAT 2016. LNCS, vol. 9710, pp. 249–266. Springer, Cham (2016). https://doi.org/10.1007/978-3-319-40970-2_16

Weak Bisimulation Metrics in Models with Nondeterminism and Continuous State Spaces

Ruggero Lanotte and Simone Tini[✉]

Dipartimento di Scienza e Alta Tecnologia, Università degli Studi dell'Insubria,
via Valleggio, 11, 22100 Como, Italy
{ruggero.lanotte,simone.tini}@uninsubria.it

Abstract. *Bisimulation metrics* are used to estimate the *behavioural distance* between *probabilistic systems*. They have been defined in discrete and continuous state space models. However, the *weak semantics approach*, where *non-observable* actions are abstracted away, has been adopted only in the discrete case. We fill this gap and provide a *weak bisimulation metric* for models with *continuous state spaces*. A difficulty is to provide a notion of *weak transition* leaving from a continuous distribution over states. Our weak bisimulation metric allows for *compositional* reasoning. Systems at distance zero are equated by a notion of *weak bisimulation*. We apply our theory in a case study where continuous distributions derive by the evolution of the physical environment.

Keywords: Weak bisimulation metric · Nondeterminism
Continuous state space

1 Introduction

Bisimulation metrics [8,11,31] are a successful instrument widely employed to estimate the *behavioural distance* between probabilistic systems. They can be viewed as the *quantitative* counterpart of the classic notion of *bisimulation* equivalence: Given two systems, bisimulation only allows us to say whether they behave exactly in the same way or not, whereas bisimulation metrics provide a notion of distance quantifying their disparity. The metrics approach is more robust than the equivalence approach, which can be clearly observed in the specification/implementation scenario: Any tiny variation of the probabilistic behaviour of a system implementation, which may be also due to a measurement error, will break the equality between such an implementation and its specification, without any further information on the *distance* of their behaviours. Actually, many implementations can only *approximate* the specification; thus, the verification task requires appropriate instruments to measure the *quality* of the approximation.

The bisimulation metrics in [8,11,31] have been defined for both *discrete* and *continuous* state space models. However, the *weak semantics approach*, where

B. Fischer and T. Uustalu (Eds.): ICTAC 2018, LNCS 11187, pp. 292–312, 2018.
https://doi.org/10.1007/978-3-030-02508-3_16

non-observable actions are abstracted away, has been adopted only in the discrete case [12]. One of the main technical difficulties to apply the weak semantic to the continuous case is in the definition of a suitable notion of *weak transition*, since this requires to lift transitions leaving from states to transitions leaving from continuous distributions over states.

Contribution. In this paper we fill the gap and we provide a *weak bisimulation metric* for models with nondeterminism and continuous state spaces. We will prove that: (i) as any reasonable notion of symmetric distance, our weak bisimulation metric is a *pseudometric*; (ii) our weak bisimulation metric allows for *compositional* reasoning, namely the distance between the parallel compositions $S_1 \parallel S_2$ and $T_1 \parallel T_2$ depends on distance between S_1 and T_1 and the distance between S_2 and T_2, the intuition being that if one fixes the maximal tolerable distance ϵ between the composed systems $S_1 \parallel S_2$ and $T_1 \parallel T_2$ then there are tolerances ϵ_i between the components S_i and T_i, with $i \in \{1, 2\}$, ensuring that the tolerance ϵ is respected; (iii) systems at *distance zero* are equated by a suitable notion of *weak bisimulation* equivalence.

We argue that our weak bisimulation metrics is suitable to reason on *cyber-physical systems*. In these systems, the description of the activity of the physical component requires to use *probability* as an *abstraction mechanism* that allows us to average over, thus abstracting away, the effect of inessential or unknown details of the evolution of physical quantities which may also be impossible to be observed in practice. These probabilities are inherently continuous. To show how our theory can be applied, we propose *Stochastic Hybrid Calculus* (SHC) as a process calculus extending Communicating Sequential Processes [19] with both primitives to deal with *discrete time*, inspired by those of Timed Process Algebra [18], and constructs to express *probabilistic behaviour*. In this calculus, we adopt a notion of *state*, which represents the *physical* component of the system, given by values of *physical quantities*, and a notion of *process*, which specifies the *cyber* component, or *logics* (controllers, IDS, supervisors) of the system. The logic interacts with both the physical component, by accessing the state, and with other cyber components by channel-based communication. Then, we provide a case study to illustrate how weak bisimulation metrics applied to our calculus can be used to reason on cyber physical systems.

Outline. In Sect. 2 we recall the notions on probability spaces used in the following. In Sect. 3 we introduce SHC. In Sect. 4 we introduce weak transitions. In Sect. 5 we define our weak bisimulation metric. In Sect. 6 we apply our theory to a case study. Section 7 contains conclusions and discussion of related work.

2   Background on Probability Spaces

A *σ-algebra* over a set Ω is a family $\mathcal{F}$ of subsets of Ω such that: (i) $\Omega \in \mathcal{F}$, (ii) $\mathcal{F}$ is closed under complementation, (iii) $\mathcal{F}$ is closed under countable union. The complement of any set $A \in \mathcal{F}$ is denoted $\mathcal{C}(A)$. Obviously, by (ii) and (iii) it follows that $\mathcal{F}$ is closed also under countable intersection.

It is well known that for a family Φ of subsets of Ω, the smallest σ-algebra over Ω containing Φ exists, and is unique. It is called the σ-algebra *generated* by Φ. In particular, for $n \in \mathbb{N}^+$, the *Borel σ-algebra* over $\mathbb{R}^n$, denoted $\mathcal{B}(\mathbb{R}^n)$, is the σ-algebra generated by the open sets in $\mathbb{R}^n$. A well-known result over Borel σ-algebras is given by the following proposition.

Proposition 1. *The σ-algebra generated by rectangles $A \times B$ with $A \in \mathcal{B}(\mathbb{R}^n)$ and $B \in \mathcal{B}(\mathbb{R}^m)$ is equal to $\mathcal{B}(\mathbb{R}^{n+m})$.*

A *measurable space* is a pair $(\Omega, \mathcal{F})$, with $\mathcal{F}$ a σ-algebra over Ω. The elements of $\mathcal{F}$ are called *measurable sets*. A *sub-probability measure* over $(\Omega, \mathcal{F})$ is a mapping $\mu \colon \mathcal{F} \to \mathbb{R}^{\geq 0}$ such that: (i) $\mu(\emptyset) = 0$; (ii) $\mu(\Omega) \leq 1$; (iii) for every countable family of pairwise disjoint measurable sets $\{A_i\}_{i \in I}$, we have $\mu(\bigcup_{i \in I} A_i) = \sum_{i \in I} \mu(A_i)$. We use $|\mu|$ to denote $\mu(\Omega)$.

We denote the set of sub-probability measures over $(\Omega, \mathcal{F})$ by $\mathcal{D}_{\mathrm{sub}}((\Omega, \mathcal{F}))$. For $\mu \in \mathcal{D}_{\mathrm{sub}}((\Omega, \mathcal{F}))$, the structure $(\Omega, \mathcal{F}, \mu)$ is called a *sub-probability space*. In particular, if $|\mu| = 1$, then μ is called a *probability measure* over $(\Omega, \mathcal{F})$ and $(\Omega, \mathcal{F}, \mu)$ is called a *probability space*. The set of probability measures over $(\Omega, \mathcal{F})$ is denoted by $\mathcal{D}((\Omega, \mathcal{F}))$. We introduce now some notions on sub-probability measures. Assume a measurable space $(\Omega, \mathcal{F})$. Then:

- For an element $\omega \in \Omega$, the *Dirac probability measure* is denoted by $\overline{\omega}$ and is defined by $\overline{\omega}(A) = 1$, if $\omega \in A$, and $\overline{\omega}(A) = 0$, otherwise, for all $A \in \mathcal{F}$.
- For a measurable set $A \in \mathcal{F}$ and a sub-probability measure $\mu \in \mathcal{D}_{\mathrm{sub}}((\Omega, \mathcal{F}))$, with $\mu \cap A$ we denote the sub-probability measure in $\mathcal{D}_{\mathrm{sub}}((\Omega, \mathcal{F}))$ defined by $(\mu \cap A)(B) = \mu(A \cap B)$, for all $B \in \mathcal{F}$.
- The *summation* of a set $\{\mu_i\}_{i \in I}$ of sub-probability measures in $\mathcal{D}_{\mathrm{sub}}((\Omega, \mathcal{F}))$ with $\sum_{i \in I} |\mu_i| \leq 1$ is the sub-probability measure $\sum_{i \in I} \mu_i$ in $\mathcal{D}_{\mathrm{sub}}((\Omega, \mathcal{F}))$ defined by $(\sum_{i \in I} \mu_i)(A) = \sum_{i \in I} \mu_i(A)$, for all $A \in \mathcal{F}$. The measures in the summation may be also weighted: $\sum_{i \in I} p_i \cdot \mu_i$ denotes the sub-probability measure defined by $(\sum_{i \in I} p_i \cdot \mu_i)(A) = \sum_{i \in I} p_i \mu_i(A)$, for all $A \in \mathcal{F}$, provided that $\sum_{i \in I} p_i |\mu_i| \leq 1$. Notice that this notation allows us to express mixed measures having both discrete and dense parts.
- A sub-probability measure $\mu \in \mathcal{D}_{\mathrm{sub}}((\Omega, \mathcal{F}))$ is called *discrete* if there exists a countable set of indexes I such that $\mu = \sum_{i \in I} p_i \cdot \overline{\omega_i}$, with $\omega_i \in \Omega$.

We need to recall also the notion of integral of a measurable function.

A function between two measurable spaces is called *measurable* if the preimage of any measurable set is a measurable set. In particular, if we consider any measurable space $(\Omega, \mathcal{F})$ and the Borel space $(\mathbb{R}, \mathcal{B}(\mathbb{R}))$, then $f \colon \Omega \to \mathbb{R}$ is measurable if $f^{-1}(A) \in \mathcal{F}$ for all $A \in \mathcal{B}(\mathbb{R})$.

For each measurable set $A \in \mathcal{F}$, the *indicator function* $\mathbf{1}_A \colon \Omega \to \mathbb{R}$ is defined by $\mathbf{1}_A(\omega) = 1$, if $\omega \in A$, and $\mathbf{1}_A(\omega) = 0$, otherwise. A *simple function* is of the form $\sum_{i=1}^{n} c_i \cdot \mathbf{1}_{A_i}$, with $A_1 \ldots, A_n$ measurable sets in $\mathcal{F}$ and $c_1, \ldots, c_n \in \mathbb{R}^+$. Notice that such a simple function is non negative and it can be rewritten such that $A_1, \ldots, A_n$ is a partition of Ω. Notice also that both indicator functions and simple functions are measurable. The following result is folklore (see, e.g. [28]).

Theorem 1. *Given a non negative measurable function $f \colon \Omega \to \mathbb{R}^{\geq 0}$, there is a non decreasing sequence of simple functions $\{f_i\}_{i \in \mathbb{N}}$ such that $f = \sup_{i \in \mathbb{N}} f_i$.*

For a probability space $(\Omega, \mathcal{F}, \mu)$ and a simple function $f = \sum_{i=1}^{n} c_i \cdot \mathbf{1}_{A_i}$, the integral of f wrt. the probability measure μ, denoted $\int f \, d\mu$, is defined as

$$\int \left(\sum_{i=1}^{n} c_i \cdot \mathbf{1}_{A_i} \right) d\mu = \sum_{i=1}^{n} c_i \cdot \mu(A_i)$$

We can extend this definition to any measurable non negative $f \colon \Omega \to \mathbb{R}^{\geq 0}$ by

$$\int f \, d\mu = \sup_{i \in \mathbb{N}} \int f_i \, d\mu, \text{ where } f = \sup_{i \in \mathbb{N}} f_i \text{ and } (f_i)_{i \in \mathbb{N}} \text{ are simple functions.}$$

Then, for an arbitrary measurable $f \colon \Omega \to \mathbb{R}$, we can consider the non-negative functions $f^{+} = \max\{f, 0\}$ and $f^{-} = -\min\{f, 0\}$, which gives $f = f^{+} - f^{-}$. If $\int f^{+} \, d\mu \neq \infty$ or $\int f^{-} \, d\mu \neq \infty$, then we say that f *is μ-integrable* and we define

$$\int f \, d\mu = \int f^{+} \, d\mu - \int f^{-} \, d\mu$$

We will use the following known properties for integrals.

Proposition 2. *The following facts hold:*
1. $\int f \, d(\overline{\omega}) = f(\omega)$
2. $\int \mathbf{1}_A \, d\mu = \mu(A)$
3. $\int c \cdot f \, d\mu = c \cdot \int f \, d\mu, \text{ for } c \in \mathbb{R}$
4. $\int f \, d(\mu_1 + \mu_2) = \int f \, d\mu_1 + \int f \, d\mu_2$
5. $\int f \, d\mu + \int g \, d\mu = \int (f + g) \, d\mu$
6. *If $f \leq g$, then $\int f \, d\mu \leq \int g \, d\mu$*

3   Stochastic Hybrid Calculus

In this section, we introduce *Stochastic Hybrid Calculus* (SHC) as a process calculus extending Communicating Sequential Processes (CSP) [19] with both primitives to deal with *discrete time*, inspired by those of Timed Process Algebra (TPL) [18], and constructs to express *probabilistic behaviour*. The calculus is tailored for specifying *cyber-physical systems*: we assume a notion of *state*, which represents the *physical* component of the system, given by values of physical quantities, sensors, actuators, etc., and a notion of *process*, which specifies the *cyber* component, or *logics* (controllers, IDS, supervisors) of the system. The logic interacts with both the physical component, by accessing the state, and with other cyber components by channel-based communication. Typically, physical quantities can be accessed by logic only through sensors and actuators. In order to simplify the calculus, we deliberately choose to abstract from this detail, assuming that the logic has the ability to directly access the physical quantities. This has no impact on the bisimulation metric theory developed in next section.

We stress that in the description of the activity of the physical component, we use *probability* as an *abstraction mechanism* that allows us to average over, thus abstracting away, the effect of inessential or unknown details of the evolution of physical quantities which may also be impossible to be observed in practice.

3.1 Syntax

The syntax of SHC is given as a three levels structure: we have *sequential processes*, ranged over by $P, Q, \ldots$, *networks of processes*, ranged over by $M, N, \ldots$, and *systems*, ranged over by $S, T, \ldots$. We refer to the set of all processes, networks and systems with $\mathbf{P}$, $\mathbf{N}$ and $\mathbf{S}$, respectively. A system $S \in \mathbf{S}$ is a pair of the form (N, s), where $N \in \mathbf{N}$ is a network of sequential processes in $\mathbf{P}$ running in parallel and s is a *state*, which is a tuple in $\mathbb{R}^n$ for some $n \in \mathbb{N}^+$.

Definition 1. *Systems, networks and processes are defined by:*

$$
\begin{aligned}
S, T &::= (M, s) \\
M, N &::= P \mid M \parallel_{\mathcal{A}} N \\
P, Q &::= \mathsf{nil}_n \mid \alpha. \bigoplus_{i \in I} p_i{:}P_i \mid \mathsf{if}\,(A)\,\{P\}\,\{Q\} \mid [i := c]P \mid \mathsf{tick}(\delta).P \mid X \mid \mathsf{rec}\,X.P
\end{aligned}
$$

In Definition 1 we assume a set of *actions* $\mathbf{A}$ containing: (i) a set of *synchronization actions*, ranged over by a, b, used to achieve a process multi-part synchronisation à la CSP [19]; (ii) the *silent action* τ, modelling internal computation steps that cannot be externally observed; (iii) the *timed action* tick, modelling the passage of one unit of time in a setting with a discrete notion of time [18]. Then, α, β range over *untimed actions* in $\mathbf{A} \setminus \{\mathsf{tick}\}$, λ ranges over the whole $\mathbf{A}$, and, finally, $\mathcal{A}, \mathcal{A}_1$ range over sets of synchronization actions, namely subsets of $\mathbf{A} \setminus \{\tau, \mathsf{tick}\}$.

A process $P \in \mathbf{P}$ interacts with a portion of the physical state, represented by a tuple in $\mathbb{R}^n$. In the following description we assume that this tuple is s. Since physical quantities accessed by P are fixed (only their values may change), the dimension of s cannot change at runtime. Process nil_n has terminated its task. We will formalise that nil_n requires that s has dimension n. Process $\alpha. \bigoplus_{i \in I} p_i{:}P_i$ performs the untimed action $\alpha \in \mathbf{A} \setminus \{\mathsf{tick}\}$ and, with probability p_i, it evolves to process P_i. If $\alpha \neq \tau$ then this computation step may serve to synchronise with other processes, otherwise, if $\alpha = \tau$ this is an internal computation step. Process $\mathsf{if}\,(A)\,\{P\}\,\{Q\}$, with $A \in \mathcal{B}(\mathbb{R}^n)$, is the standard conditional: If $s \in A$, then it behaves as P, otherwise as Q. Process $[i := c]P$ sets the ith coordinate of s to value $c \in \mathbb{R}$ and, then, it behaves as P. In process $\mathsf{tick}(\delta).P$, $\delta \colon \mathbb{R}^n \to \mathcal{D}((\mathbb{R}^n, \mathcal{B}(\mathbb{R}^n)))$ is a mapping from states to probability measures over states. Process $\mathsf{tick}(\delta).P$ sleeps for one unit of time, then at the next time step it will interact with states in $\{s' \colon s' \in A\}$ with probability $(\delta(s))(A)$, for any measurable set $A \in \mathcal{B}(\mathbb{R}^n)$. This models that in-between two time slots the value of state is updated by *the activity of the physical component* in a probabilistic way. In processes of the form $\mathsf{tick}(\delta).P$, the occurrence of P is said to be *time-guarded*. X is a *process variable*, $\mathsf{rec}\,X.P$ denotes *recursion*. We will consider only *time-guarded* recursion, where all occurrences of the process variable X may only occur time-guarded in P.

In network $M \parallel_{\mathcal{A}} N$, networks M and N must synchronize on actions in $\mathcal{A}$ (multi-part synchronisation à la CSP [19]) and also on action tick, namely they must agree on letting the time pass [18], whereas they are autonomous in performing the remaining actions (including the internal action τ).

The process variable X is *bound* in $\operatorname{rec} X.P$. This gives rise to the standard notions of *free/bound process variables*. We work only with *closed* processes/networks/systems containing no free process variable. The semantic rules will ensure that the absence of free variables is preserved at run-time. We write $S\{^P/_X\}$ for the substitution of process variable X with process P in system S.

The syntax is too permissive. We should restrict to networks running in states of the required dimension. To this purpose, we use a function $\#\colon \mathbf{N} \to \mathbb{N}^+ \cup \{\bot\}$, with $\#(N) = n$ if N can interact with states of dimension n, and $\#(N) = \bot$ if N is unable to interact with any state. We start with defining $\#\colon \mathbf{P} \to \mathbb{N}^+ \cup \{\bot\}$. We have $\#(P) \in \mathbb{N}^+$ if one of the following cases holds, otherwise $\#(P) = \bot$:

- $\#(\operatorname{nil}_n) = n$;
- $\#(\alpha.\bigoplus_{i \in I} p_i{:}P_i) = n$ if, for all $i \in I$, $\#(P_i) = n$;
- $\#(\operatorname{if}(A)\{P\}\{Q\}) = n$ if $A \in \mathcal{B}(\mathbb{R}^n)$ and $\#(P) = \#(Q) = n$;
- $\#([i := c]P) = \#(P)$ if $i \le \#(P)$ (namely the state has the i-th component);
- $\#(\operatorname{tick}(\delta).P) = n$ if $\delta\colon \mathbb{R}^n \to \mathcal{D}((\mathbb{R}^n, \mathcal{B}(\mathbb{R}^n)))$ and $\#(P) = n$;
- $\#(\operatorname{rec} X.P) = \#(P\{^{\operatorname{rec} X.P}/_X\})$ if $\#(P\{^{\operatorname{rec} X.P}/_X\}) \ne \bot$.

Then, $\#(M \parallel_{\mathcal{A}} N) = \#(M) + \#(N)$, with $\bot + n = n + \bot = \bot + \bot = \bot$.

Definition 2. *A process P is* well-formed *if $\#(P) \ne \bot$. Then, a network N is* well-formed *if $\#(N) \ne \bot$. Finally, a system $S = (N, s)$ is* well-formed *if for some $n \in \mathbb{N}^+$ we have $s \in \mathbb{R}^n$ and $\#(N) = n$.*

For well-formed systems $S_1 = (N_1, s_1)$ and $S_2 = (N_2, s_2)$, we write $S_1 \parallel_{\mathcal{A}} S_2$ for $(N_1 \parallel_{\mathcal{A}} N_2, s_1 \times s_2)$, where $s_1 \times s_2 = (c_1, \ldots, c_n, c_{n+1}, \ldots, c_{n+m})$ when $s_1 = (c_1, \ldots, c_n)$ and $s_2 = (c_{n+1}, \ldots, c_{n+m})$. Clearly, also $S_1 \parallel_{\mathcal{A}} S_2$ is well-formed.

3.2 Probabilistic Labelled Transition Semantics

In this section, we provide the dynamics of SHC in terms of a *probabilistic labelled transition system* (pLTS) [29]. Intuitively, a computation step takes a system in $\mathbf{S}$ to a probability measure over a suitable σ-algebra, whose measurable sets are sets of systems in $\mathbf{S}$. We start with introducing such a σ-algebra, denoted $\mathcal{F}_{\mathbf{S}}$. To this purpose, we rely on the notions of *dense-system*, which is a set of systems in $\mathbf{S}$ with the same network structure and with states giving a measurable set, and *meta-system*, which is an union of dense systems.

Definition 3. *The* dense-system *induced by a well-formed network $N \in \mathbf{N}$ and a measurable set $B \in \mathcal{B}(\mathbb{R}^{\#(N)})$ is the set of systems $(N, B) = \{(N, s)\colon s \in B\}$. Then, an at most countable union of dense systems is called a* meta-system.

Interestingly, a meta-system $\mathcal{S}$ can be always written in form $\mathcal{S} = \bigcup_{N \in \mathbf{N}}(N, B_N)$. Indeed, if for some network N, $\mathcal{S}$ contains no system (N, s), then the contribution of N to $\mathcal{S}$ can be represented by $(N, \emptyset)$, since $(N, \emptyset) = \emptyset$ and $(N, \emptyset)$ is a dense system, which follows by $\emptyset \in \mathcal{B}(\mathbb{R}^{\#(N)})$. Then, if for a countable set I, $\mathcal{S}$ contains all dense systems (N, B_i) with $i \in I$, then $\bigcup_{i \in I}(N, B_i) = (N, \bigcup_{i \in I} B_i)$, which is a dense system since $B_i \in \mathcal{B}(\mathbb{R}^{\#(N)})$ for all $i \in I$ implies $\bigcup_{i \in I} B_i \in \mathcal{B}(\mathbb{R}^{\#(N)})$.

We define $\mathcal{F}_{\mathbf{S}}$ as the family containing precisely all meta-systems.

Proposition 3. *The pair* $(\mathbf{S}, \mathcal{F}_\mathbf{S})$ *is a measurable space.*

We will use A, B to range over measurable sets in $\mathcal{B}(\mathbb{R}^n)$ and $\mathcal{S}, \mathcal{T}$ to range over measurable sets in $\mathcal{F}_\mathbf{S}$. Then, π ranges over (sub)-probability measures over $\mathcal{D}_{\mathrm{sub}}((\mathbb{R}^n, \mathcal{B}(\mathbb{R}^n)))$ and μ, ν over (sub)-probability measures over $\mathcal{D}_{\mathrm{sub}}((\mathbf{S}, \mathcal{F}_\mathbf{S}))$.

The notion of parallel composition can be lifted to measurable sets $\mathcal{S} = \bigcup_{M \in \mathbf{N}}(M, B_M)$ and $\mathcal{T} = \bigcup_{N \in \mathbf{N}}(N, C_N)$ in $\mathcal{F}_\mathbf{S}$ as follows:

$$\mathcal{S} \parallel_A \mathcal{T} = \bigcup_{M,N \in \mathbf{N}}(M \parallel_A N, B_M \times C_N)$$

By Proposition 1 we get that $\mathcal{F}_\mathbf{S}$ is closed wrt. this operation of parallel composition.

Proposition 4. *If* $\mathcal{S}, \mathcal{T} \in \mathcal{F}_\mathbf{S}$ *then* $\mathcal{S} \parallel_A \mathcal{T} \in \mathcal{F}_\mathbf{S}$.

We adapt now the notion of pLTS [29] to SHC.

Definition 4. *The pLTS for SHC is the triple* $(\mathbf{S}, \mathbf{A}, \rightarrow)$, *where* $\rightarrow \subseteq (\mathbf{S} \times \mathbf{A} \times \mathcal{D}_{\mathrm{sub}}((\mathbf{S}, \mathcal{F}_\mathbf{S})))$ *is the transition relation derived by the transition rules in Table 1.*

In the definition of the rules we use the following notations:

- For $s = (c_1, \ldots, c_n) \in \mathbb{R}^n$, $i \in \{1, \ldots, n\}$ and $c \in \mathbb{R}$, we let $s\{^c/_i\}$ denote the tuple $(c_1, \ldots, c_{i-1}, c, c_{i+1}, \ldots, c_n) \in \mathbb{R}^n$.
- For a process $P \in \mathbf{P}$ and a probability measure $\pi \in \mathcal{D}((\mathbb{R}^n, \mathcal{B}(\mathbb{R}^n)))$, with (P, π) we denote the probability measure over $(\mathbf{S}, \mathcal{F}_\mathbf{S})$ s.t. $(P, \pi)(\mathcal{S}) = \pi(B_P)$, if $B_P = \{s \colon (P, s) \in \mathcal{S}\}$.
- Given probability measures μ_1, μ_2 over $(\mathbf{S}, \mathcal{F}_\mathbf{S})$, we let $\mu_1 \parallel_A \mu_2$ denote the probability measure over $(\mathbf{S}, \mathcal{F}_\mathbf{S})$ s.t. $(\mu_1 \parallel_A \mu_2)(\mathcal{S}_1 \parallel_A \mathcal{S}_2) = \mu_1(\mathcal{S}_1) \cdot \mu_2(\mathcal{S}_2)$.

Let us comment on the rules of Table 1. For a process $P \in \mathbf{P}$, we get transitions from (P, s), where $s \in \mathbb{R}^{\#(P)}$ is the component of the global state used by P. Rule (Com) serves to model an untimed, possibly internal, computation step by a process. (We remind that $\alpha \in \mathbf{A} \setminus \{\text{tick}\}$.) Rules (True) and (False) serve to solve the conditional choice, which is an internal activity that cannot be externally observed. Rule (Res) models the update on the ith coordinate of s. Also this activity is internal. Rule (Del) models the passage of one unit of time. Rule (TimeNil) states that nil_n does not prevent passage of time. Rule (Rec) is the standard rule for recursion. Rule (Synch) serves to model CSP-like multi-part synchronisation on some action a. Rule (Asynch) serves to propagate to parallel components non-synchronising or internal actions. Its symmetric counterparts is obvious and thus omitted from the table. Rule (TPar) is standard and states that parallel components should agree on passage of time.

Example 1. In this example, for a bounded measurable set $A \in \mathcal{B}(\mathbb{R})$ and a probability mass $p \in (0, 1]$, with $\mathcal{U}(A, p)$ we denote the sub-probability measure in $\mathcal{D}_{\mathrm{sub}}((\mathbb{R}, \mathcal{B}(\mathbb{R})))$ which uniformly distributes the probability mass p on set A. Notice that $|\mathcal{U}(A, p)| = p$. Let $\delta \colon \mathbb{R} \to \mathcal{D}((\mathbb{R}, \mathcal{B}(\mathbb{R})))$ be the function mapping reals

Table 1. Probabilistic LTS for systems (Remind that $\overline{S}$ is the Dirac measure for S).

$$\text{(Com)}\ \frac{-}{(\alpha.\bigoplus_{i \in I} p_i{:}P_i, s) \xrightarrow{\alpha} \sum_{i \in I} p_i \cdot \overline{(P_i, s)}} \qquad \text{(Res)}\ \frac{-}{([i := c]P, s) \xrightarrow{\tau} \overline{(P, s\{^c/_i\})}}$$

$$\text{(True)}\ \frac{s \in A}{(\text{if}\,(A)\,\{P\}\,\{Q\}, s) \xrightarrow{\tau} \overline{(P, s)}} \qquad \text{(Del)}\ \frac{-}{(\text{tick}(\delta).P, s) \xrightarrow{\text{tick}} \overline{(P, \delta(s))}}$$

$$\text{(False)}\ \frac{s \notin A}{(\text{if}\,(A)\,\{P\}\,\{Q\}, s) \xrightarrow{\tau} \overline{(Q, s)}} \qquad \text{(TimeNil)}\ \frac{-}{(\text{nil}_n, s) \xrightarrow{\text{tick}} \overline{(\text{nil}_n, s)}}$$

$$\text{(TPar)}\ \frac{(N_1, s_1) \xrightarrow{\text{tick}} \mu_1 \quad (N_2, s_2) \xrightarrow{\text{tick}} \mu_2}{(N_1 \,\|_{\mathcal{A}}\, N_2, s_1 \times s_2) \xrightarrow{\text{tick}} \mu_1 \,\|_{\mathcal{A}}\, \mu_2} \qquad \text{(Rec)}\ \frac{(P\{^{\text{rec}\,X.P}/_X\}, s) \xrightarrow{\alpha} \mu}{(\text{rec}\,X.P, s) \xrightarrow{\alpha} \mu}$$

$$\text{(Synch)}\ \frac{(N_1, s_1) \xrightarrow{a} \mu_1 \quad (N_2, s_2) \xrightarrow{a} \mu_2 \quad a \in \mathcal{A}}{(N_1 \,\|_{\mathcal{A}}\, N_2, s_1 \times s_2) \xrightarrow{a} \mu_1 \,\|_{\mathcal{A}}\, \mu_2}$$

$$\text{(Asynch)}\ \frac{(N_1, s_1) \xrightarrow{\alpha} \mu_1 \quad \alpha \in (\mathbf{A} \setminus (\mathcal{A} \cup \{\text{tick}\}))}{(N_1 \,\|_{\mathcal{A}}\, N_2, s_1 \times s_2) \xrightarrow{a} \mu_1 \,\|_{\mathcal{A}}\, \overline{(N_2, s_2)}}$$

to uniform distributions over $\mathcal{D}((\mathbb{R}, \mathcal{B}(\mathbb{R})))$ defined by $\delta(s) = \mathcal{U}([s - 2, s + 2], 1)$ for all $s \in \mathbb{R}$. (Briefly, $\delta(s)$ is the continuous uniform distribution in $[s-2, s+2]$.)

Consider the process $P = \text{tick}(\delta).P'$, with $P' = \text{if}\,([-\infty, -1])\,\{a.\text{nil}_1\}\,\{[1 := 10]\,b.\text{nil}_1\}$, the state $0 \in \mathbb{R}$ and the system $S = (P, 0)$. Process P starts in state 0 and sleeps for one time unit (action tick). Then, it behaves as process P' running in a state expressed by the dense uniform distribution in $\mathcal{U}([-2, +2], 1)$. Formally, by rule (Del) we get $(P, 0) \xrightarrow{\text{tick}} (P', \mathcal{U}([-2, +2], 1))$. Now, if the state is in $[-2, -1]$ then by rule (True) the process P' becomes $a.\text{nil}_1$. Otherwise, by rule (False) P' becomes $[1 := 10]\,b.\text{nil}_1$ and will set the (first and unique component of the) state to 10 and becomes $b.\text{nil}_1$. This will be formalised in Example 2.

3.3 Properties of the pLTS

We conclude this section with some properties on our pLTS that will be useful in the following. First we show that whenever we have a transition $S \xrightarrow{\lambda} \mu$, then: (i) if $\lambda = \text{tick}$, then the underlying structure of processes in system S is maintained; (ii) if $\lambda \neq \text{tick}$, then μ is a discrete probability measure and, in this case, all the systems in the support of μ have the same number of parallel components of S (but may have a different process structure). Formally:

Proposition 5. *Assume a well-formed system $S = (M, s)$ with the network M of the form $M = P_1 \,\|_{\mathcal{A}_1} \cdots \|_{\mathcal{A}_{m-1}} P_m$ and $s \in \mathbb{R}^{\#(M)}$. If $S \xrightarrow{\lambda} \mu$, then:*

- *If $\lambda = \text{tick}$ then $\mu = (Q_1 \,\|_{\mathcal{A}_1} \cdots \|_{\mathcal{A}_{m-1}} Q_m, \pi)$ for suitable processes Q_i and probability measure $\pi \in \mathcal{D}((\mathbb{R}^{\#(M)}, \mathcal{B}(\mathbb{R}^{\#(M)})))$.*
- *If $\lambda \neq \text{tick}$ then $\mu = \sum_{i \in I} p_i \cdot \mu_i$ for a finite set I and, for any i, $\mu_i = (P_1^i \,\|_{\mathcal{A}_1} \cdots \|_{\mathcal{A}_{m-1}} P_m^i, \overline{s_i})$ for suitable processes $P_1^i, \ldots, P_m^i$ and $s_i \in \mathbb{R}^{\#(M)}$.*

Proposition 5 suggests a definition of normal form for measures in $\mathcal{D}_{\mathrm{sub}}((\mathbf{S}, \mathcal{F}_{\mathbf{S}}))$.

Definition 5. *A sub-probability measure* $\mu \in \mathcal{D}_{\mathrm{sub}}((\mathbf{S}, \mathcal{F}_{\mathbf{S}}))$ *is in* normal form *if* $\mu = \sum_{i \in I} p_i \cdot \mu_i$ *for a finite set* I, *and there exist naturals* $m, n \in \mathbb{N}^+$ *and sets of actions* $\mathcal{A}_1, \ldots, \mathcal{A}_{m-1}$ *s.t. for any* i, *we have* $\mu_i = (P_1^i \parallel_{\mathcal{A}_1} \cdots \parallel_{\mathcal{A}_{m-1}} P_m^i, \pi_i)$, *for suitable processes* P_j^i *and* $\pi_i \in \mathcal{D}_{\mathrm{sub}}((\mathbb{R}^n, \mathcal{B}(\mathbb{R}^n)))$.

Proposition 5 can be refined if we know that the action is τ.

Proposition 6. *Assume a well-formed system* $S = (M, s)$ *with the network* M *of the form* $M = P_1 \parallel_{\mathcal{A}_1} \cdots \parallel_{\mathcal{A}_{m-1}} P_m$ *and* $s = s_1 \times \cdots \times s_m$ *with* $s_i \in \mathbb{R}^{\#(P_i)}$. *If* $S \xrightarrow{\tau} \mu$, *then for some* $j \in 1 \ldots m$ *one of the following facts holds:*

- $P_j = \tau. \bigoplus_{i \in I} p_i : P_j^i$ *and* $\mu = \sum_{i \in I} p_i \cdot \overline{(P_1 \parallel_{\mathcal{A}_1} \cdots \parallel_{\mathcal{A}_{j-1}} P_j^i \parallel_{\mathcal{A}_j} \cdots \parallel_{\mathcal{A}_{m-1}} P_m, s)}$.
- $P_j = \text{if } (A) \{P_j^1\} \{P_j^2\}$ *and either* $\mu = \overline{(P_1 \parallel_{\mathcal{A}_1} \cdots \parallel_{\mathcal{A}_{j-1}} P_j^1 \parallel_{\mathcal{A}_j} \cdots \parallel_{\mathcal{A}_{m-1}} P_m, s)}$, *if* $s_j \in A$, *or* $\mu = \overline{(P_1 \parallel_{\mathcal{A}_1} \cdots \parallel_{\mathcal{A}_{j-1}} P_j^2 \parallel_{\mathcal{A}_j} \cdots \parallel_{\mathcal{A}_{m-1}} P_m, s)}$, *otherwise.*
- $P_j = [i := c] P_j'$ *and* $\mu = \overline{(P_1 \parallel_{\mathcal{A}_1} \cdots \parallel_{\mathcal{A}_{j-1}} P_j' \parallel_{\mathcal{A}_j} \cdots \parallel_{\mathcal{A}_{m-1}} P_m, s')}$ *with* $s' = s_1 \times \cdots \times s_j\{c/i\} \times \cdots \times s_m$.

4 Weak Transitions

In this section we define the notion of weak transition $S \xRightarrow{\hat{\lambda}} \mu$, which represents that the sub-probability measure μ is reached from system S by action λ, possibly preceded and followed by τ actions. Then, we will write $S \xRightarrow{\lambda!} \mu$ whenever $S \xRightarrow{\hat{\lambda}} \mu$ and no τ-transition from μ allows to reach a distribution different from μ. Intuitively, $\xRightarrow{\hat{\lambda}}$ introduce nondeterminism since it allows that only some processes able to perform a τ-transition perform it, whereas $\xRightarrow{\lambda!}$ solve such a nondeterminism by forcing all processes to perform their τ-transition.

In a probabilistic setting, the definition of weak transition is complicated by the fact that (strong) transitions take processes (in our case systems) to probability measures; consequently if we are to use weak transitions $\xRightarrow{\hat{\lambda}}$, which abstract away from non-observable actions, then we need to generalise transitions, so that they take (sub-)probability measures to (sub-)probability measures. An elegant solution to this problem was proposed in [10] for discrete measures. We provide here the necessary machinery to extend this approach to the dense case.

We proceed as follows. First, we lift transitions $S \xrightarrow{\lambda}$ performed by systems to transitions $\mu \xrightarrow{\hat{\lambda}}$ performed by (sub)-probability measures over systems. Then, for action τ we define the transition relation $\xRightarrow{\hat{\tau}}$ over (sub)-probability measures as the transitive and reflexive closure of $\xrightarrow{\hat{\tau}}$. Finally, we derive a transition $\overline{S} \xRightarrow{\hat{\lambda}} \mu$ from $\overline{S} \xRightarrow{\hat{\tau}} \mu'$, $\mu' \xrightarrow{\hat{\lambda}} \mu''$ and $\mu'' \xRightarrow{\hat{\tau}} \mu$. In the definition of these three transitions we assume that the left-hand-side is in normal form.

This is not restrictive, since $\overline{S}$ is a normal form and we will prove that transitions take normal forms to normal forms. Moreover, we will prove also that the target μ' of the first transition is discrete, which allows us to define $\mu' \xrightarrow{\lambda} \mu''$ for $\lambda \neq \tau$ assuming that μ' is discrete, besides a normal form.

We define the transition $\mu \xrightarrow{\lambda}$ for a normal form μ and an action $\lambda \in \mathbf{A}$ inductively wrt. the structure of μ. The base cases are $\mu = \overline{S}$ and $\mu = (M, \pi)$. The inductive step is $\mu = \sum_{i \in I} p_i \cdot \mu_i$.

BASE CASE $\mu = \overline{S}$. Distribution $\overline{S}$ inherits all transitions of system S. Moreover, we always have the transition $\overline{S} \xrightarrow{\hat{\tau}} \overline{S}$ since abstracting from τ-actions requires that we should not distinguish between performing τ or remaining inactive. Formally, if $\lambda = \tau$, then we write $\overline{S} \xrightarrow{\lambda} \nu$ whenever either $S \xrightarrow{\lambda} \nu$ or $\nu = \overline{S}$. Otherwise, if $\lambda \neq \tau$, then we write $\overline{S} \xrightarrow{\lambda} \nu$ whenever $S \xrightarrow{\lambda} \nu$. In case $\lambda \neq \tau$, we introduce a notation to represent if $\overline{S}$ does not make the λ-action: We write $\overline{S} \xrightarrow{\lambda}\!\!\!\!/\,$ if $S \xrightarrow{\lambda} \nu$ does not hold for any sub-probability measure ν.

BASE CASE $\mu = (M, \pi)$, **with** $M = P_1 \parallel_{A_1} \cdots \parallel_{A_{m-1}} P_m$. As anticipated above, we assume $\lambda = \tau$, since we need the transition $\mu \xrightarrow{\lambda}$ with $\lambda \neq \tau$ only if μ is discrete. A $\hat{\tau}$-transition from μ originates from τ-transitions from processes $P_1, \ldots, P_m$ (which are derived by rules (Com) with $\alpha = \tau$, (True), (False), (Res)) as follows. We take $H \subseteq \{1, \ldots, m\}$ as an arbitrary (possibly proper) subset of the indexes of the processes $P_1, \ldots, P_m$ that are able to perform a τ-transition. Then, for each $h \in H$ we take a meta-system $\mathcal{S}_h$ with $\mu(\mathcal{S}_h) > 0$ and we let systems in $\mathcal{S}_h$ inherit the τ-transition by P_h. Of course, for arbitrary $h, k \in H$ with $h \neq k$ we require that $\mathcal{S}_h \cap \mathcal{S}_k = \emptyset$. Then, also all systems in any measurable set $\mathcal{S} \subseteq \mathcal{C}(\bigcup_{h \in H} \mathcal{S}_h)$ with $\mu(\mathcal{S}) > 0$ can make the $\hat{\tau}$-transition, which is the analogous of the inactivity step $\overline{S} \xrightarrow{\hat{\tau}} \overline{S}$ already defined for Dirac measures. Formally, we define the transition $(M, \pi) \xrightarrow{\hat{\tau}} \nu + \sum_{h \in H} \nu_h$ if $H \subseteq \{1, \ldots, m\}$ and there are pairwise disjoint meta-systems $\mathcal{S}_h$ with $h \in H$ such that:

1. for each $h \in H$, $\mathcal{S}_h$ has the form $\mathcal{S}_h = (M, B_h)$, with $B_h \in \mathcal{B}(\mathbb{R}^{\#(M)})$ and $\pi(B_h) > 0$, and all systems in $\mathcal{S}_h$ inherit the τ-transition by P_h (with the effect described in Proposition 6). Precisely one of the following facts holds:

   (a) $P_h = \tau. \bigoplus_{i \in I} p_i : P_h^i$ and ν_h has the form

   $$\nu_h = \sum_{i \in I} p_i \cdot \left(P_1 \parallel_{A_1} \cdots \parallel_{A_{h-1}} P_h^i \parallel_{A_h} \cdots \parallel_{A_{m-1}} P_m, \pi \cap B_h \right)$$

   (b) $P_h = \text{if} (A) \{P'\} \{P''\}$, $\nu_h = \nu' + \nu''$ and for $n_1 = \sum_{l=1}^{h-1} \#(P_l)$ and $n_2 = \sum_{l=h+1}^{m} \#(P_l)$ the distributions ν' and ν'' have the form

   $$\nu' = \left(P_1 \parallel_{A_1} \cdots \parallel_{A_{h-1}} P' \parallel_{A_h} \cdots \parallel_{A_{m-1}} P_m, \pi \cap B_h \cap (\mathbb{R}^{n_1} \times A \times \mathbb{R}^{n_2}) \right)$$

   $$\nu'' = \left(P_1 \parallel_{A_1} \cdots \parallel_{A_{h-1}} P'' \parallel_{A_h} \cdots \parallel_{A_{m-1}} P_m, \pi \cap B_h \cap (\mathbb{R}^{n_1} \times \mathcal{C}(A) \times \mathbb{R}^{n_2}) \right)$$

(c) $P_h = [i := c]P_h'$ and the distribution ν_h has the form

$$\nu_h = (P_1 \parallel_{\mathcal{A}_1} \cdots \parallel_{\mathcal{A}_{h-1}} P_h' \parallel_{\mathcal{A}_h} \cdots \parallel_{\mathcal{A}_{m-1}} P_m, \pi')$$

where for $n_1 = (i-1) + \sum_{l=1}^{h-1} \#(P_l)$ and $n_2 = \#(P_h) - i + \sum_{l=h+1}^{m} \#(P_l)$, the distribution π' is defined so that for all $A \in \mathcal{B}(\mathbb{R}^{\#M})$ we have $\pi'(A) = (\pi \cap B_h)(\{s_1 \times \mathbb{R} \times s_2 \mid s_1 \times c \times s_2 \in A \wedge s_1 \in \mathbb{R}^{n_1} \wedge s_2 \in \mathbb{R}^{n_2}\})$.

2. $\nu = \mu \cap \mathcal{C}(\bigcup_{h \in H} \mathcal{S}_h)$.

Notice that: in case 1a, $\pi \cap B_h$ is in $\mathcal{D}_{\text{sub}}((\mathbb{R}^{\#(M)}, \mathcal{B}(\mathbb{R}^{\#(M)})))$; in case 1b, both $\pi \cap B_h \cap (\mathbb{R}^{n_1} \times A \times \mathbb{R}^{n_2})$ and $\pi \cap B_h \cap (\mathbb{R}^{n_1} \times \mathcal{C}(A) \times \mathbb{R}^{n_2})$ are in $\mathcal{D}_{\text{sub}}((\mathbb{R}^{\#(M)}, \mathcal{B}(\mathbb{R}^{\#(M)})))$; and, finally, in case 1c the set $\{s_1 \times \mathbb{R} \times s_2 \mid s_1 \times c \times s_2 \in A \wedge s_1 \in \mathbb{R}^{n_1} \wedge s_2 \in \mathbb{R}^{n_2}\})$ is Borel measurable and hence $\pi' \in \mathcal{D}_{\text{sub}}((\mathbb{R}^{\#(M)}, \mathcal{B}(\mathbb{R}^{\#(M)})))$. Summarising, we can conclude that $\nu + \sum_{h \in H} \nu_h$ is well-defined, which is formally stated by the following proposition.

Proposition 7. *If* $(M, \pi) \xrightarrow{\hat{\tau}} \nu + \sum_{h \in H} \nu_h$ *then* $\nu + \sum_{h \in H} \nu_h$ *is a (sub)-probability measure. Moreover,* $\nu + \sum_{h \in H} \nu_h$ *is in normal form.*

INDUCTIVE STEP $\mu = \sum_{i \in I} p_i \cdot \mu_i$. The $\hat{\lambda}$-transitions by μ are inherited from those by μ_i. Formally, we write $\mu \xrightarrow{\hat{\lambda}} \nu$ if there is a set of indexes $J \subseteq I$ s.t.: (i) $\mu_j \xrightarrow{\hat{\lambda}} \nu_j$, for all $j \in J$, (ii) $\mu_i \xrightarrow{\hat{\lambda}}\!\!\!\!/\,$, for all $i \in I \setminus J$, and (iii) $\nu = \sum_{j \in J} p_j \cdot \nu_j$. Note that for $\lambda \neq \tau$ it may happen that $|\nu| < |\mu|$. As regards the notation for the lack of $\hat{\lambda}$-action, we write $\mu \xrightarrow{\hat{\lambda}}\!\!\!\!/\,$ if $\mu_i \xrightarrow{\hat{\lambda}}\!\!\!\!/\,$ for all $i \in I$.

Proposition 8 below, relying on Propositions 5 and 7, ensures that all transitions $\overline{S} \xRightarrow{\hat{\lambda}} \mu$ are well defined. In detail, Proposition 8 ensures that all our weak transitions take normal forms to normal forms, thus implying that it was not too restrictive to define weak transitions only for normal form. Moreover, Proposition 8.3b ensures that it was not too restrictive to define $\xrightarrow{\hat{\lambda}}$ with $\lambda \neq \tau$ only for discrete distributions.

Proposition 8. *Assume a (sub)-probability measure* μ *in normal form. Then:*

1. *Given a transition* $\mu \xrightarrow{\widehat{\text{tick}}} \nu$, *if* μ *is discrete then* ν *is in normal form.*
2. *Given a transition* $\mu \xrightarrow{\hat{a}} \nu$ *with* $a \in \mathbf{A} \setminus \{\tau, \text{tick}\}$, *if* μ *is discrete then* ν *is a discrete (sub)-probability measure in normal form.*
3. *Given a transition* $\mu \xrightarrow{\hat{\tau}} \nu$ *or* $\mu \xRightarrow{\hat{\tau}} \nu$, *then:*
   (a) ν *is in normal form.*
   (b) *if* μ *is discrete then also* ν *is a discrete (sub-)probability measure.*

Example 2. Consider the systems in Example 1. We show how the transition $(P, 0) \xrightarrow{\text{tick}} (P', \mathcal{U}([-2, +2], 1))$ can be combined with two consecutive weak $\hat{\tau}$-transitions originating from the probability measure $(P', \mathcal{U}([-2, 2], 1)$ to obtain a $\widehat{\text{tick}}$-transition from $(P, 0)$. The first of such $\hat{\tau}$-transitions is derived assuming that all systems in meta system $\mathcal{S}_1 = (P', [-2, 2])$ perform the τ-transition inherited by process P', which, in turn, is derived from rule (True) or (False). More precisely, systems in $(P', [-2, 2] \cap [-\infty, -1])$ inherit the τ transition derived by rule (True) and those in $(P', (-2, 2] \cap (-1, \infty])$ inherit the τ-transition derived by rule (False). We get $(P', \mathcal{U}([-2, +2], 1)) \xrightarrow{\hat{\tau}} \nu + \nu_1$, with $\nu_1 = \nu' + \nu''$, where $\nu = \mathbf{0}$ is the sub-distribution assigning 0 to all measurable sets, $\nu' = (a.\mathrm{nil}_1, \mathcal{U}([-2, -1], 1/4))$ and $\nu'' = ([1 := 10] b.\mathrm{nil}_1, \mathcal{U}((-1, 2], 3/4))$. Notice that:

- the sub-probability measure ν represents the systems which do not evolve. It derives from the fact that $(P', \mathcal{U}([-2, +2], 1) \cap \mathcal{C}(\mathcal{S}_1) = \mathbf{0}$;
- the sub-probability measure ν' reached by exploiting rule (True) derives from the fact that $\mathcal{U}([-2, +2], 1) \cap [-\infty, -1]$ is equal to $\mathcal{U}([-2, -1], 1/4)$;
- the sub-probability measure ν'' reached by exploiting rule (False) derives from the fact that $\mathcal{U}([-2, +2], 1) \cap (-1, \infty]$ is equal to $\mathcal{U}((-1, 2], 3/4)$.

The second $\hat{\tau}$-transition is from ν'' and is derived assuming that all systems in meta system $\mathcal{S}_1' = ([1 := 10] b.\mathrm{nil}_1, (-1, 0] \cup [1, 2])$ make the τ-transition inherited by process $[1 := 10] b.\mathrm{nil}_1$ and derived by rule (Res), and those in $\mathcal{U}((-1, 2], 3/4) \cap \mathcal{C}(\mathcal{S}_1')$ make no move, which is represented by the inactivity step. We get $\nu'' \xrightarrow{\hat{\tau}} ([1 := 10] b.\mathrm{nil}_1, \mathcal{U}((0, 1), 1/4)) + 1/2 \cdot \overline{(b.\mathrm{nil}_1, 10)}$, where:

- the sub-probability measure $([1 := 10] b.\mathrm{nil}_1, \mathcal{U}((0, 1), 1/4))$ represents systems not evolving. It derives from $\mathcal{U}((-1, 2], 3/4) \cap \mathcal{C}(\mathcal{S}_1') = \mathcal{U}((0, 1), 1/4)$;
- the sub-probability measure $1/2 \cdot \overline{(b.\mathrm{nil}_1, 10)}$ is reached by systems inheriting the τ-step inferred from (Res) and derives from $\mathcal{U}((-1, 2], 3/4) \cap ((-1, 0] \cup [1, 2]) = \mathcal{U}((-1, 0] \cup [1, 2], 1/2)$ and $\mathcal{U}((-1, 0] \cup [1, 2], 1/2)(\mathbb{R}) = 1/2$.

It is immediate that we can derive also the transition $\nu' \xrightarrow{\hat{\tau}} \nu'$ and, then, $\nu' + \nu'' \xrightarrow{\hat{\tau}} \nu' + ([1 := 10] b.\mathrm{nil}_1, \mathcal{U}((0, 1), 1/4)) + 1/2 \cdot \overline{(b.\mathrm{nil}_1, 10)}$. By combining the transition $(P, 0) \xrightarrow{\mathrm{tick}} (P', \mathcal{U}([-2, +2], 1))$ derived in Example 1 and the two consecutive $\hat{\tau}$ transitions derived above we get $(P, 0) \xrightarrow{\widehat{\mathrm{tick}}} (a.\mathrm{nil}_1, \mathcal{U}([-2, -1], 1/4)) + ([1 := 10] b.\mathrm{nil}_1, \mathcal{U}((0, 1), 1/4)) + 1/2 \overline{(b.\mathrm{nil}_1, 10)}$. We notice that the probability measure reached is a normal form in $\mathcal{D}((\mathbf{S}, \mathcal{F}_\mathbf{S}))$ and is composed of a dense part and a discrete part.

We note that, as usual, weak transitions introduce nondeterminism. For instance, in base case $\mu = \overline{S}$, if $S \xrightarrow{\tau} \nu$, then we have both $\overline{S} \xLongrightarrow{\hat{\tau}} \overline{S}$ and $\overline{S} \xLongrightarrow{\hat{\tau}} \nu$. In base case $\mu = (M, \pi)$, the choice of the sets $\mathcal{S}_h$ is nondeterministic: The systems in $\mathcal{S}_h$ inherit the τ-transition from one of the processes running in parallel that is chosen nondeterministically. Clearly, in the inductive case, $\sum_{i \in I} p_i \cdot \mu_i$ inherit the nondeterminism from the μ_i. However, since we assume that recursion is time-guarded, we can easily define a notion of weak transition that limits such a nondeterminism by forcing all processes able to make a τ-transition to perform it. Simply, in base case $\mu = \overline{S}$, if $S \xrightarrow{\tau} \nu$ then we consider $\overline{S} \xLongrightarrow{\hat{\tau}} \nu$ and not $\overline{S} \xLongrightarrow{\hat{\tau}} \overline{S}$. In base case $\mu = (M, \pi)$, given the transition

$(M, \pi) \xrightarrow{\hat{\tau}} \nu + \sum_{h \in H} \nu_h$, from $\nu + \sum_{h \in H} \nu_h$ we can have another $\hat{\tau}$-transition where meta-systems in ν_h perform τ-transitions inherited by either some P_k, with $k \neq h$, or by the same P_h, if P_h had two consecutive non-observable steps derived by rules (Com), (True), (False), (Res), and, moreover, also meta-systems in ν may inherit transitions from the processes P_h that were nondeterministically rejected to perform an inactivity step. In words, each $\hat{\tau}$-step may leave pending some τ-transitions from processes P_h, which can always been performed in subsequent $\hat{\tau}$-steps.

Formally, we define $\mu \xRightarrow{\lambda!} \nu$ iff $\mu \xRightarrow{\hat{\lambda}} \nu$ and $\nu \xrightarrow{\hat{\tau}} \nu'$ implies $\nu = \nu'$. Notice that, since we assume only guarded recursion, these transitions $\nu \xrightarrow{\hat{\tau}} \nu'$ derive from inactivity steps and cannot be derived from τ-transitions by processes.

Example 3. In Example 2 we cannot label with tick! the transition $(P, 0) \xRightarrow{\widehat{\text{tick}}}$ $(a.\text{nil}_1, \mathcal{U}([-2, -1], 1/4)) + ([1 := 10] \, b.\text{nil}_1, \mathcal{U}((0, 1), 1/4)) + 1/2 \overline{(b.\text{nil}_1, 10)}$ since from the sub-probability measure $([1 := 10] \, b.\text{nil}_1, \mathcal{U}((0, 1), 1/4))$ we have the transition $([1 := 10] \, b.\text{nil}_1, \mathcal{U}((0, 1), 1/4)) \xrightarrow{\hat{\tau}} 1/4 \overline{(b.\text{nil}_1, 10)}$. By combining this transition with that above we get $(P, 0) \xRightarrow{\widehat{\text{tick}}} (a.\text{nil}_1, \mathcal{U}([-2, -1], 1/4)) + 3/4 \overline{(b.\text{nil}_1, 10)}$, which gives $(P, 0) \xRightarrow{\text{tick}!} (a.\text{nil}_1, \mathcal{U}([-2, -1], 1/4)) + 3/4 \overline{(b.\text{nil}_1, 10)}$.

We can state that $\xRightarrow{\lambda!}$ is finite branching.

Proposition 9. *There are finitely many distributions μ_i with $\overline{S} \xRightarrow{\lambda!} \mu_i$. Moreover, if $\lambda = \tau$, then there is only one μ_i with $\overline{S} \xRightarrow{\lambda!} \mu_i$.*

5   Weak Bisimulation Metrics

In this section we introduce the weak bisimilarity metric over SHC. This will be a function $\mathbf{d} \colon \mathbf{S} \times \mathbf{S} \to [0, 1]$ such that $\mathbf{d}(S, T)$ measures the behavioural disparity between S and T. Actually, $\mathbf{d}(S, T)$ will be the probability that S and T are unable to mimic each other's behaviour step by step, in the weak semantics approach. We will prove that: (i) as any reasonable notion of symmetric distance, $\mathbf{d}$ is a *pseudometric*; (ii) $\mathbf{d}$ allows for *compositional* reasoning; (iii) systems at *distance zero* are equated by a suitable notion of *weak bisimulation* equivalence.

To simplify our definitions, we enrich the syntax in Definition 1 by a special system Dead. Since Table 1 has no rule for Dead, we are sure that Dead is a deadlocked system unable to perform any transition.

We use $\mathcal{D}$ to denote the class of all functions $[0, 1]^{\mathbf{S} \times \mathbf{S}}$. The class $\mathcal{D}$ is equipped with the ordering $\sqsubseteq$ defined by $d_1 \sqsubseteq d_2$ iff $d_1(S, T) \leq d_2(S, T)$ for all $S, T \in \mathbf{S}$. The structure $(\mathcal{D}, \sqsubseteq)$ is a lattice, where for all $D \subseteq \mathcal{D}$ and $S, T \in \mathbf{S}$ we have $(\bigsqcup D)(S, T) = \sup_{d \in D} d(S, T)$ and $(\bigsqcap D)(S, T) = \inf_{d \in D} d(S, T)$. The constant function zero, which is the infimum of the lattice, will be denoted by $\mathbf{0}$.

Definition 6 (Pseudometric). *A function $d \in \mathcal{D}$ is a 1-bounded pseudometric over $\mathbf{S}$ if for all $S, T, U \in \mathbf{S}$ we have: (1) $d(S, S) = 0$, (2) $d(S, T) = d(T, S)$ (symmetry), and (3) $d(S, T) \leq d(S, U) + d(U, T)$ (triangle inequality).*

As anticipated above, we are interested in pseudometrics that assign to $S, T \in \mathbf{S}$ a numerical value in $[0,1]$ that corresponds to the difference in the probabilities of similar transitions. As a quantitative analogous of the bisimulation game, the intuition is that the distance between S and T is below a given value $\epsilon \in [0,1]$ if each transition $S \xrightarrow{\lambda} \mu$ is mimicked by a transition $T \xrightarrow{\lambda} \nu$ such that the distance between μ and ν is, in turn, below ϵ (and conversely). This notion of distance between μ and ν can be obtained by lifting the notion of pseudometric from $\mathbf{S}$ to probability measures over $\mathbf{S}$. To define this lifting, we rely on *1-Lipschitz functions* and *Kantorovich lifting*.

We recall that a function between two pseudometric spaces is called 1-Lipschitz if the distance between any two elements in the domain is not below the distance between their images. In the following definition we implicitly consider the metric over reals assigning to each pair $x, y \in \mathbb{R}$ the distance $| x - y |$.

Definition 7 (1-Lipschitz function). *Assume a function $d \colon \mathbf{S} \times \mathbf{S} \to \mathbb{R}$ and a measurable function $f \colon \mathbf{S} \to \mathbb{R}$ over the measurable spaces $(\mathbf{S}, \mathcal{F}_{\mathbf{S}})$ and $(\mathbb{R}, \mathcal{B}(\mathbb{R}))$. The function f is 1-Lipschitz over d iff $|f(S) - f(T)| \le d(S, T)$, for all $S, T \in \mathbf{S}$.*

We can define now the Kantorovich lifting. A really intuitive explanation of this notion requires to refer to a dual formulation based on the optimal transport problem. We refer the interested reader to [7,9,32].

Definition 8 (Kantorovich lifting). *Let $d \in \mathcal{D}$. The Kantorovich lifting of d is the function $\mathbf{K}(d) \colon \mathcal{D}(\mathbf{S}, \mathcal{F}_{\mathbf{S}}) \times \mathcal{D}(\mathbf{S}, \mathcal{F}_{\mathbf{S}}) \to [0,1]$ defined as:*

$$\mathbf{K}(d)(\mu, \nu) \stackrel{def}{=} \sup \left\{ \left| \int f \, d\mu - \int f \, d\nu \right| : f \colon \mathbf{S} \to \mathbb{R} \, is \, 1 - Lipschitz \, over \, d \right\}$$

Notice that the definition above is based on the property that all 1-Lipschitz functions f are μ- and ν-integrable, and $\int f \, d\mu \ne \infty \ne \int f \, d\nu$.

If d is a 1-bounded pseudometric over $\mathbf{S}$ then $\mathbf{K}(d)$ is a 1-bounded pseudometric over $\mathcal{D}(\mathbf{S}, \mathcal{F}_{\mathbf{S}})$ (see, e.g., [32]). It is not hard to see that function $\mathbf{K}$ is monotone, namely $d_1 \sqsubseteq d_2$ implies $\mathbf{K}(d_1) \sqsubseteq \mathbf{K}(d_2)$, and continuous, namely $\mathbf{K}(\bigsqcup D) = \bigsqcup \{\mathbf{K}(d) : d \in D\}$ for all $D \subseteq \mathcal{D}$.

Definition 9 (Weak bisimulation metric). *We say that a pseudometric $d \colon \mathbf{S} \times \mathbf{S} \to [0,1]$ is a weak bisimulation metric if for all systems $S, T \in \mathbf{S}$, with $d(S, T) < \epsilon$, whenever $S \xrightarrow{\lambda} \mu$ there is a transition $T \xrightarrow{\lambda} \nu$ such that $\mathbf{K}(d)(\mu + (1 - |\mu|)\overline{\mathsf{Dead}}, \nu + (1 - |\nu|)\overline{\mathsf{Dead}}) < \epsilon$.*

As in [23,25] we use Dead to ensure that $d(S, T)$ is at least the difference of the probability mass of μ and ν. An alternative formulation can be found in [13].

We can prove the existence of the minimal weak bisimulation metric. It will be the least fixed point of a functional $\mathbf{B}$ defined over the lattice $(\mathcal{D}, \sqsubseteq)$ such that $\mathbf{B}(d)(S, T)$ returns the minimum possible value for $d(S, T)$ in order to ensure that d is a weak bisimulation metric.

Definition 10 (Bisimulation metric functional). *Let* $\mathbf{B}\colon \mathcal{D} \to \mathcal{D}$ *be the functional such that for any* $d \in \mathcal{D}$ *and* $S, T \in \mathbf{S}$, $\mathbf{B}(d)(S,T) < \epsilon$ *if:*

- $\forall S \xrightarrow{\lambda!} \mu \exists T \xrightarrow{\lambda!} \nu$ *s.t.* $\mathbf{K}(d)(\mu + (1- |\mu|)\overline{\mathsf{Dead}}, \nu + (1- |\nu|)\overline{\mathsf{Dead}}) < \epsilon$.
- $\forall T \xrightarrow{\lambda!} \nu \exists S \xrightarrow{\lambda!} \mu$ *s.t.* $\mathbf{K}(d)(\mu + (1- |\mu|)\overline{\mathsf{Dead}}, \nu + (1- |\nu|)\overline{\mathsf{Dead}}) < \epsilon$.

Using $\xrightarrow{\lambda!}$ instead of $\xrightarrow{\lambda}$ in definition above may seem odd. We provide an alternative, and more classical, definition using $\xrightarrow{\lambda}$. We will prove that the two definitions can be used indifferently.

Definition 11 (Bisimulation metric functional - II). *Let* $\mathbf{B}'\colon \mathcal{D} \to \mathcal{D}$ *be the functional such that for any* $d \in \mathcal{D}$ *and* $S, T \in \mathbf{S}$, $\mathbf{B}'(d)(S,T) < \epsilon$ *if:*

- $\forall S \xrightarrow{\lambda} \mu \exists T \xrightarrow{\lambda} \nu$ *s.t.* $\mathbf{K}(d)(\mu + (1- |\mu|)\overline{\mathsf{Dead}}, \nu + (1- |\nu|)\overline{\mathsf{Dead}}) < \epsilon$.
- $\forall T \xrightarrow{\lambda} \nu \exists S \xrightarrow{\lambda} \mu$ *s.t.* $\mathbf{K}(d)(\mu + (1- |\mu|)\overline{\mathsf{Dead}}, \nu + (1- |\nu|)\overline{\mathsf{Dead}}) < \epsilon$.

Since $\mathbf{K}$ is monotone, it follows that $\mathbf{B}$ (resp. $\mathbf{B}'$) is monotone on lattice $(\mathcal{D}, \sqsubseteq)$. Furthermore, by Knaster-Tarski theorem it follows that $\mathbf{B}$ (resp. $\mathbf{B}'$) has a least prefixed point, which is also the least fixed point, which will be denoted by $\mathbf{d}$ (resp. $\mathbf{d}'$). Function $\mathbf{d}$ will be called the *weak bisimilarity metric*. We will prove that $\mathbf{d}$ and $\mathbf{d}'$ coincide. Since by the definition of $\mathbf{B}'$ it is clear that any 1-bounded pseudometric $d \in \mathcal{D}$ is a weak bisimulation metric if and only if d is a prefixed point of $\mathbf{B}'$, if we prove also that $\mathbf{d}$ is a 1-bounded pseudometric then we can conclude that $\mathbf{d}$ is the least weak bisimulation metric.

To prove that $\mathbf{d}$ is a 1-bounded pseudometric we first prove that $\mathbf{B}$ is Scott continuous. (We do not claim that also $\mathbf{B}'$ is.) By Kleene fixed point theorem, this allows us to infer that $\mathbf{d}$ is the limit of the ascending Kleene chain $\mathbf{0} \sqsubseteq \mathbf{B}(0) \sqsubseteq \mathbf{B}^2(0) \sqsubseteq \ldots$. Then, by a simple inductive argument one can prove that each element of this chain is a 1-bounded pseudometric. Finally, the 1-bounded pseudometric property for $\mathbf{d}$ can be easily derived. Notice that function $\mathbf{B}^n(0)$ is interesting in its own since, intuitively, quantifies the discrepancy in the behaviour of systems that accumulates in n steps. It will be denoted with $\mathbf{d}^n$ and called the *n-weak bisimilarity metric*. Having that $\mathbf{d} = \lim_{n \to \infty} \mathbf{d}^n$ not only allows us to relate the discrepancy between systems to the discrepancies that accumulate in n steps for all $n \in \mathbb{N}$, but, more in general, it allows one to prove interesting properties for $\mathbf{d}$ by using a simple inductive argument. Scott continuity of $\mathbf{B}$ derives from continuity of $\mathbf{K}$ and image finiteness (Proposition 9) ($\xrightarrow{\lambda}$ is not image finite, thus the following result does not apply to $\mathbf{B}'$).

Proposition 10. *The functional* $\mathbf{B}$ *is Scott continuous, i.e. for each non decreasing chain* $d_0 \sqsubseteq \ldots d_n \sqsubseteq \ldots$ *in* $\mathcal{D}$ *we have* $\mathbf{B}(\bigsqcup_{n \in \mathbb{N}} d_n) = \bigsqcup_{n \in \mathbb{N}} \mathbf{B}(d_n)$.

Proposition 11. *1. For all* $n \geq 0$, $\mathbf{d}^n$ *is a 1-bounded pseudometric.*
2. $\mathbf{d}$ *is a 1-bounded pseudometric.*

A crucial property of our pseudometrics is the possibility to reason on parallel systems in a *compositional* manner. Thus, for any notion of distance d between systems, the distance $d(S_1 \parallel_{\mathcal{A}} S_2, T_1 \parallel_{\mathcal{A}} T_2)$ should depend on distances $d(S_1, T_1)$ and $d(S_2, T_2)$, the intuition being that if one fixes the maximal tolerable distance ϵ between the composed systems $(S_1 \parallel_{\mathcal{A}} S_2)$ and $(T_1 \parallel_{\mathcal{A}} T_2)$, then there are tolerances ϵ_i between the components S_i and T_i, $i \in \{1, 2\}$, ensuring that the tolerance ϵ is respected. Following this intuition, several compositional criteria for bisimulation metrics can be found in the literature. Here, we show that our distances matches one of the most restrictive among those studied in [15,16], namely *non-expansiveness* [11,12], requiring that $\epsilon \leq \epsilon_1 + \epsilon_2$.

We start with a Lemma stating that Kantorovich pseudometric preserves non-expansiveness. This result is interesting in its own since it does not depend on the calculus we are using, but it is a general property of pLTSs. The same result was proved in [15], in the discrete case.

Lemma 1. *Given any function $d \in \mathcal{D}$, if for all systems $S_1, S_2, T_1, T_2 \in \mathbf{S}$ we have $d(S_1 \parallel_{\mathcal{A}} S_2, T_1 \parallel_{\mathcal{A}} T_2) \leq d(S_1, T_1) + d(S_2, T_2)$, then for all distributions $\mu_1, \mu_2, \nu_1, \nu_2$ we have $\mathbf{K}(d)(\mu_1 \parallel_{\mathcal{A}} \mu_2, \nu_1 \parallel_{\mathcal{A}} \nu_2) \leq \mathbf{K}(d)(\mu_1, \nu_1) + \mathbf{K}(d)(\mu_2, \nu_2)$.*

Theorem 2. *Assume arbitrary systems $S_1, S_2, T_1, T_2 \in \mathbf{S}$ and a set of actions $\mathcal{A} \subseteq \mathbf{A} \setminus \{\text{tick}, \tau\}$. We have:*

$$\mathbf{d}(S_1 \parallel_{\mathcal{A}} S_2, T_1 \parallel_{\mathcal{A}} T_2) \leq \mathbf{d}(S_1, T_1) + \mathbf{d}(S_2, T_2)$$

Now, we prove that $\mathbf{d}$ and $\mathbf{d}'$ coincide. This confirms that $\mathbf{d}$ is the least bisimulation metric. The proof exploits the non expansiveness of $\mathbf{d}$.

Theorem 3. $\mathbf{d}$ *is the least prefixed point of* $\mathbf{B}'$, *hence* $\mathbf{d} = \mathbf{d}'$.

To conclude this section, we discuss the kernel of our bisimulation metrics: We introduce the classical notion of weak-bisimulation equivalence for SHC and we prove that two systems are weakly bisimilar if and only if they are at distance zero according to $\mathbf{d}$.

For an equivalence relation $\mathcal{R} \subseteq \mathbf{S} \times \mathbf{S}$, we say that a measurable set $\mathcal{S} \in \mathcal{F}_{\mathbf{S}}$ is $\mathcal{R}$-*closed* if it is the union of equivalence classes of $\mathcal{R}$. Then, we say that two probability measures $\mu, \nu \in \mathcal{D}(\mathbf{S}, \mathcal{F}_{\mathbf{S}})$ are $\mathcal{R}$-*equivalent* if for all $\mathcal{R}$-closed sets $\mathcal{S} \in \mathcal{F}_{\mathbf{S}}$ we have $\mu(\mathcal{S}) = \nu(\mathcal{S})$.

Definition 12. *A symmetric relation* $\mathcal{R} \subseteq \mathbf{S} \times \mathbf{S}$ *is a* weak bisimulation *if, whenever* $S \mathcal{R} T$ *and* $S \overset{\hat{\lambda}}{\Longrightarrow} \mu$, *there is a transition* $T \overset{\hat{\lambda}}{\Longrightarrow} \nu$ *such that* $\mu \mathcal{R} \nu$.

Given any weak bisimulation metric $d \in \mathcal{D}$, we can prove that the pairs of systems at distance 0 give a weak bisimulation.

Proposition 12. *Given any weak bisimulation metric* $d \in \mathcal{D}$, *the relation* $\mathcal{R} \subseteq \mathbf{S} \times \mathbf{S}$ *defined as* $\mathcal{R} = \{(S, T) : d(S, T) = 0\}$ *is a weak bisimulation.*

This result combined with the properties expressed in the definition of weak bisimulation metrics imply that weak bisimulations are equivalences relations.

Moreover, the fact that $\mathbf{d}$ is the minimal weak bisimulation metric implies the existence of the greatest weak bisimulation. Following the tradition we call it *weak bisimilarity* and we denote it with $\sim$. Notice that $\sim = \{(S,T) : \mathbf{d}(S,T) = 0\}$. From compositionality of our pseudometrics (Theorem 2), we immediately derive the congruence property of weak bisimilarity.

Corollary 1. $S_1 \sim T_1$ and $S_2 \sim T_2$ imply $S_1 \parallel_A S_2 \sim T_1 \parallel_A T_2$.

6 Case Study

In this section, we provide a case study to illustrate how SHC can be used to specify and reason on cyber physical systems.

We model an engine whose temperature is maintained below a given threshold by means of a cooling system. This study was conducted in a non probabilistic setting in [21,22] and in the discrete probabilistic setting in [27]. The logic of the engine consists of a single process *Ctrl*, which models the controller activity and runs in a state s consisting in only one component, representing the temperature. Henceforth, $s \in \mathbb{R}$. Process *Ctrl* senses the temperature of the engine at each time interval. If the sensed temperature is above the threshold 10, the controller activates the coolant. The cooling activity is maintained for 5 time units. After that time, if the temperature does not drop below 10 then the system shuts down, which is represented by the action *s_down*; otherwise, if the sensed temperature is not above 10, the controller turns off the cooling and moves to the next time interval. In case of shutdown, there is a reset $[1 := 0]$ (we note that 1 refers to the first, and unique, component of the state). The evolution of the temperature is governed by dense uniform distributions over suitable intervals. When the cooling is off the temperature will increase probabilistically its value by an amount in $[0.6, 1.4]$, hence we consider the mapping $\delta^+ : \mathbb{R} \to \mathcal{D}((\mathbb{R}, \mathcal{B}(\mathbb{R})))$ with $\delta^+(s) = \mathcal{U}([s + 0.6, s + 1.4], 1)$, for all $s \in \mathbb{R}$. When the cooling is on, the temperature will decrease probabilistically its value by an amount in $[0.6, 1.4]$, hence we consider the mapping $\delta^- : \mathbb{R} \to \mathcal{D}((\mathbb{R}, \mathcal{B}(\mathbb{R})))$ with $\delta^-(s) = \mathcal{U}([s - 1.4, s - 0.6], 1)$, for all $s \in \mathbb{R}$. Formally:

$$Ctrl = \mathsf{rec}\, X. \text{ if } (10, +\infty) \, \{Cooling\} \, \{\mathsf{tick}(\delta^+).X\}$$
$$Cooling = (\mathsf{tick}(\delta^-))^5. \text{ if } (10, \infty) \, \{s\_down.[1 := 0]\mathsf{nil}_1\} \, \{\mathsf{tick}(\delta^+).X\}$$

We assume an initial temperature $s = 0$, hence the *whole engine* is defined as: $Eng = (Ctrl, 0)$. We consider also the process $NIL = (\mathsf{nil}_1, 0)$, which simply ticks at each time interval (see rule (TimeNil)).

We note that when the coolant is activated, the temperature cannot be above $10 + 1.4$. Then, in the worst case the cooling decreases the temperature to value $11.4 - 0.6 \cdot 5 = 8.4$. Hence the system never emits action *s_down*. This is formalised in the following proposition from which we infer that *Eng* never performs action *s_down*, which means that the cooling system works properly, since it is able to lead the temperature below the threshold in at most 5 time instants.

Proposition 13. $\mathbf{d}(Eng, NIL) = 0$.

An interesting question is if it is possible to improve the performance of the engine, for instance by reducing the power of the cooling system in order to save refrigerant. Assume that with such a reduced cooling power, when the coolant is on, the temperature decreases now probabilistically its value by an amount in $[0.26, 1.06]$. Formally, we consider the system $\widetilde{Eng} = (\widetilde{Ctrl}, 0)$, where in process $\widetilde{Ctrl}$ we use the mapping $\widetilde{\delta^-}$ instead of δ^-, with $\widetilde{\delta^-}(s) = \mathcal{U}([s - 1.06, s - 0.26, 1])$. Since when the coolant is activated the temperature is at most $10 + 1.4$, in the worst case the cooling decreases the temperature to the value $11.4 - 0.26 \cdot 5 = 10.1$. Hence we have a dense space $(10, 10.1]$ in which the system can emit the action s_down. This is formalized in the following proposition from which we infer that $\widetilde{Eng}$ may shutdown.

Proposition 14. For $S = ((\mathsf{tick}(id))^{15} .s\_down.\mathsf{nil}_1, 0)$, we have $\mathbf{d}(S, \widetilde{Eng}) < 1$.

Now it becomes crucial to have an estimation on the effective difference, in terms of behaviour, between the ideal system Eng and the system $\widetilde{Eng}$.

Proposition 15. For all $n \in \mathbb{N}$, we have $\mathbf{d}^n(Eng, \widetilde{Eng}) \leq 1 - (1 - (1/8)^5)^n$.

Note that after 5 tick-steps, the temperature is in $(10, 10.1]$ only if the coolant was activate with the temperature in $(11.3, 11.4]$ and after $k \leq 5$ tick the temperature is in $(11.3 - k \cdot 0.26, 11.4 - k \cdot 0.26]$, for all $k \leq 5$. The probability that the temperature drops from $(11.3 - k \cdot 0.26, 11.4 - k \cdot 0.26]$ to $(11.3 - (k+1) \cdot 0.26, 11.4 - (k+1) \cdot 0.26]$ is bounded by $1/8$, namely the ratio between the lengths of the intervals $(11.3 - (k+1) \cdot 0.26, 11.4 - (k+1) \cdot 0.26]$ and $[0.26, 1.06]$.

Thus, the probability that the two engines exhibit a different behaviour within n = 1000 computation steps is at most 0.03; a distance which may be considered still acceptable in specific contexts. Notice that in the (common) logics of the two engines, it is easy to see that two tick-actions are separated by at most 1 untimed actions. Thus, 1000 computation steps means around 500 time slots, i.e., about three hours for time slots lasting 20 s each.

7   Conclusions and Related Work

We have studied weak bisimulation metrics for models with nondeterminism and continuous probability, thus completing the theory of weak bisimulation metrics, which, up to now, was defined only in the discrete case. We have introduced a calculus for modelling stochastic hybrid systems for which we provide a suitable notion of weak transition. This is mathematically hard since it requires to lift transitions from states to transitions from continuous distributions over states. We have proved that our weak bisimulation metrics allows for compositional reasoning, we have proved that systems at distance zero are equated by a suitable notion of weak bisimulation and we have applied our theory in a case study where continuous distributions come from the evolution of physical environment.

We plan to adopt our weak bisimulation metric for estimating cyber-physical attacks, by extending the work [22], which deals with discrete probabilities. We intend to generalise n-weak bisimulation metrics to focus on timed actions only, along the line of [26].

Related Work. Several approaches have been proposed for modelling probabilistic behaviour of hybrid systems using formal methods (see, e.g., [1,4,14,17,20, 30,33]). Most of these papers introduce probability in transitions relation, or operators of probabilistic choice, or stochastic differential equations. Our calculus has several similarities with that in [33], where probabilistic choice replaces non-deterministic choice and stochastic differential equations replace differential equations. None of the mentioned papers introduce any notion of weak transition nor any notion to estimate the weak behavioural distance between systems.

A notion of weak behaviour for the continuous setting was introduced in [2,3]. The idea in [2] is that a weak transition is defined as a succession of non probabilistic τ-transitions followed by a probabilistic transition. In [6] measurability properties of stochastic transition systems with non-determinism and continuous state spaces are studied. To have a definition of measure on sets of paths, they identify the class of measurable schedulers. In this setting they define also a concept of weak transition based on measurable scheduler, but no notion to estimate the weak behavioural distance is given. In [5] the authors develop a notion of stochastic bisimulation for a category of general models for stochastic hybrid systems or, more generally, for the category of strong Markov processes defined on Borel spaces. Hence they consider neither weak behaviour nor behavioural distance.

Recent applications of weak bisimulation metrics in the discrete setting can be found in [23,24,26].

References

1. Abate, A., Prandini, M., Lygeros, J., Sastry, S.: Probabilistic reachability and safety for controlled discrete time stochastic hybrid systems. Automatica **44**(11), 2724–2734 (2008). https://doi.org/10.1016/j.automatica.2008.03.027
2. Bravetti, M.: Specification and analysis of stochastic real-time systems. Ph.D. thesis, Università di Bologna (2002)
3. Bravetti, M., Gorrieri, R.: The theory of interactive generalized semi-Markov processes. Theor. Comput. Sci. **282**(1), 5–32 (2002). https://doi.org/10.1016/s0304-3975(01)00043-3
4. Bujorianu, M.L.: Extended stochastic hybrid systems and their reachability problem. In: Alur, R., Pappas, G.J. (eds.) HSCC 2004. LNCS, vol. 2993, pp. 234–249. Springer, Heidelberg (2004). https://doi.org/10.1007/978-3-540-24743-2_16
5. Bujorianu, M.L., Lygeros, J., Bujorianu, M.C.: Bisimulation for general stochastic hybrid systems. In: Morari, M., Thiele, L. (eds.) HSCC 2005. LNCS, vol. 3414, pp. 198–214. Springer, Heidelberg (2005). https://doi.org/10.1007/978-3-540-31954-2_13

6. Cattani, S., Segala, R., Kwiatkowska, M., Norman, G.: Stochastic transition systems for continuous state spaces and non-determinism. In: Sassone, V. (ed.) FoSSaCS 2005. LNCS, vol. 3441, pp. 125–139. Springer, Heidelberg (2005). https://doi.org/10.1007/978-3-540-31982-5_8

7. Chatzikokolakis, K., Gebler, D., Palamidessi, C., Xu, L.: Generalized bisimulation metrics. In: Baldan, P., Gorla, D. (eds.) CONCUR 2014. LNCS, vol. 8704, pp. 32–46. Springer, Heidelberg (2014). https://doi.org/10.1007/978-3-662-44584-6_4

8. Deng, Y., Chothia, T., Palamidessi, C., Pang, J.: Metrics for action-labelled quantitative transition systems. Electron. Notes Theor. Comput. Sci. 153(2), 79–96 (2006). https://doi.org/10.1016/j.entcs.2005.10.033

9. Deng, Y., Du, W.: The Kantorovich metric in computer science: a brief survey. Electron. Notes Theor. Comput. Sci. 253(3), 73–82 (2009). https://doi.org/10.1016/j.entcs.2009.10.006

10. Deng, Y., van Glabbeek, R.J., Hennessy, M., Morgan, C.: Characterising testing preorders for finite probabilistic processes. Log. Methods Comput. Sci. 4(4), Article no. 4 (2008). https://doi.org/10.2168/lmcs-4(4:4)2008

11. Desharnais, J., Gupta, V., Jagadeesan, R., Panangaden, P.: Metrics for labelled Markov processes. Theor. Comput. Sci. 318(3), 323–354 (2004). https://doi.org/10.1016/j.tcs.2003.09.013

12. Desharnais, J., Jagadeesan, R., Gupta, V., Panangaden, P.: The metric analogue of weak bisimulation for probabilistic processes. In: Proceedings of 17th Annual IEEE Symposium on Logic in Computer Science, LICS 2002, Copenhagen, July 2002, pp. 413–422. IEEE CS Press, Washington, DC (2002). https://doi.org/10.1109/lics.2002.1029849

13. Du, W., Deng, Y., Gebler, D.: Behavioural pseudometrics for nondeterministic probabilistic systems. In: Fränzle, M., Kapur, D., Zhan, N. (eds.) SETTA 2016. LNCS, vol. 9984, pp. 67–84. Springer, Cham (2016). https://doi.org/10.1007/978-3-319-47677-3_5

14. Fränzle, M., Hahn, E.M., Hermanns, H., Wolovick, N., Zhang, L.: Measurability and safety verification for stochastic hybrid systems. In: Proceedings of 14th ACM International Conference on Hybrid Systems: Computation and Control, HSCC 2011, Chicago, IL, April 2011, pp. 43–52. ACM Press, New York (2011). https://doi.org/10.1145/1967701.1967710

15. Gebler, D., Larsen, K.G., Tini, S.: Compositional bisimulation metric reasoning with probabilistic process calculi. Log. Methods Comput. Sci. 12(4), Article no. 12 (2016). https://doi.org/10.2168/lmcs-12(4:12)2016

16. Gebler, D., Tini, S.: SOS specifications for uniformly continuous operators. J. Comput. Syst. Sci. 92, 113–151 (2018). https://doi.org/10.1016/j.jcss.2017.09.011

17. Hahn, E.M., Hartmanns, A., Hermanns, H., Katoen, J.-P.: A compositional modelling and analysis framework for stochastic hybrid systems. Form. Methods Syst. Des. 43(2), 191–232 (2013). https://doi.org/10.1007/s10703-012-0167-z

18. Hennessy, M., Regan, T.: A process algebra for timed systems. Inf. Comput. 117(2), 221–23 (1995). https://doi.org/10.1006/inco.1995.1041

19. Hoare, C.A.R.: Communicating Sequential Processes. Prentice Hall, Englewood Cliffs (1985)

20. Hu, J., Lygeros, J., Sastry, S.: Towards a theory of stochastic hybrid systems. In: Lynch, N., Krogh, B.H. (eds.) HSCC 2000. LNCS, vol. 1790, pp. 160–173. Springer, Heidelberg (2000). https://doi.org/10.1007/3-540-46430-1_16

21. Lanotte, R., Merro, M.: A calculus of cyber-physical systems. In: Drewes, F., Martín-Vide, C., Truthe, B. (eds.) LATA 2017. LNCS, vol. 10168, pp. 115–127. Springer, Cham (2017). https://doi.org/10.1007/978-3-319-53733-7_8

22. Lanotte, R., Merro, M., Muradore, R., Viganò, L.: A formal approach to cyber-physical attacks. In: Proceedings of 30th IEEE Computer Security Foundations Symposium, CSF 2017, Santa Barbara, CA, August 2017, pp. 436–450. IEEE CS Press, Washington, DC (2017). https://doi.org/10.1109/csf.2017.12

23. Lanotte, R., Merro, M., Tini, S.: Compositional weak metrics for group key update. In: Larsen, K.G., Bodlaender, H.L., Raskin, J.-F. (eds.) Proceedings of 42nd International Symposium on Mathematical Foundations of Computer Science, MFCS 2017. Leibniz International Proceedings in Informatics, Aalborg, August 2017, vol. 42, Article no. 72. Dagstuhl Publishing, Saarbrücken/Wadern (2017). https://doi.org/10.4230/lipics.mfcs.2017.72

24. Lanotte, R., Merro, M., Tini, S.: Equational reasonings in wireless network gossip protocols. arXiv preprint 1707.03215 (2017). https://arxiv.org/abs/1707.03215

25. Lanotte, R., Merro, M., Tini, S.: Weak simulation quasimetric in a gossip scenario. In: Bouajjani, A., Silva, A. (eds.) FORTE 2017. LNCS, vol. 10321, pp. 139–155. Springer, Cham (2017). https://doi.org/10.1007/978-3-319-60225-7_10

26. Lanotte, R., Merro, M., Tini, S.: Towards a formal notion of impact metric for cyber-physical attacks. In: Furia, C.A., Winter, K. (eds.) IFM 2018. LNCS, vol. 11023, pp. 296–315. Springer, Cham (2018). https://doi.org/10.1007/978-3-319-98938-9_17

27. Lanotte, R., Merro, M., Tini, S.: A probabilistic calculus of cyber-physical systems. Inf. Comput. (to appear)

28. Schiller, R.L.: Measures, Integrals and Martingales. Cambridge University Press, Cambridge (2005). https://doi.org/10.1017/cbo9780511810886

29. Segala, R.: Modeling and verification of randomized distributed real-time systems. Ph.D. thesis, MIT, Cambridge, MA (1995)

30. Sproston, J.: Decidable model checking of probabilistic hybrid automata. In: Joseph, M. (ed.) FTRTFT 2000. LNCS, vol. 1926, pp. 31–45. Springer, Heidelberg (2000). https://doi.org/10.1007/3-540-45352-0_5

31. van Breugel, F., Worrell, J.: A behavioural pseudometric for probabilistic transition systems. Theor. Comput. Sci. **331**(1), 115–142 (2005). https://doi.org/10.1016/j.tcs.2004.09.035

32. Villani, C.: Optimal Transport, Old and New. Grundlehren der mathematischen Wissenschaften, vol. 338. Springer, Heidelberg (2008). https://doi.org/10.1007/978-3-540-71050-9

33. Wang, S., Zhan, N., Zhang, L.: A compositional modelling and verification framework for stochastic hybrid systems. Form. Aspects Comput. **29**(4), 751–775 (2017). https://doi.org/10.1007/s00165-017-0421-7

Symbolic Computation via Program Transformation

Henrich Lauko[✉], Petr Ročkai, and Jiří Barnat

Faculty of Informatics, Masaryk University,
Botanická 68a, 602 00 Brno, Czech Republic
{xlauko1,xrockai,barnat}@fi.muni.cz

Abstract. Symbolic computation is an important approach in auto-mated program analysis. Most state-of-the-art tools perform symbolic computation as interpreters and directly maintain symbolic data. In this paper, we show that it is feasible, and in fact practical, to use a compiler-based strategy instead. Using compiler tooling, we propose and imple-ment a transformation which takes a standard program and outputs a program that performs a semantically equivalent, but partially sym-bolic, computation. The transformed program maintains symbolic values internally and operates directly on them; therefore, the program can be processed by a tool without support for symbolic manipulation.

The main motivation for the transformation is in symbolic verifica-tion, but there are many other possible use-cases, including test genera-tion and concolic testing. Moreover, using the transformation simplifies tools, since the symbolic computation is handled by the program directly. We have implemented the transformation at the level of LLVM bitcode. The paper includes an experimental evaluation, based on an explicit-state software model checker as a verification backend.

1 Introduction

It is common to use symbolic methods in program analysis and verification and related disciplines. Symbolic execution has found numerous use cases in test generation and concolic testing and is widely deployed in practice. Likewise, many modern software verification tools are based on bounded model checking, which combines symbolic execution with SMT solvers to successfully attack hard problems in their problem domain.

On one hand, multiple production-quality SMT solvers are readily available and even provide a common interface [3]. While a certain degree of integration is required to achieve optimal performance, solvers have attained nearly commodity status. This is in stark contrast to symbolic interpretation, which is usually implemented ad-hoc and is not re-usable across tools at all. The only exception may be KLEE [10], a symbolic interpreter for LLVM bitcode [20], which is used

---

This work has been partially supported by the Czech Science Foundation grant 18-02177S and by Red Hat, Inc.

© Springer Nature Switzerland AG 2018
B. Fischer and T. Uustalu (Eds.): ICTAC 2018, LNCS 11187, pp. 313–332, 2018.
https://doi.org/10.1007/978-3-030-02508-3_17

as a backend by a few analysis tools. Undoubtedly, the fact that it is based on the (ubiquitous) LLVM intermediate language has helped it foster wider adoption.

Arguably, interpreters (virtual machines) for controlled program execution, as required by dynamical analysis tools, are already complex enough, without involving symbolic computation. To faithfully interpret real-world programs, many features are required, including an efficient memory representation, support for threads, exceptions and a mechanism to deal with system calls. Complexity is, however, undesirable in any system and even more so in verification tools.

For these reasons, we propose to lift symbolic computation into a separate, self-contained module with minimal interfaces to the rest of the verification or analysis system (see Fig. 1). The best way to achieve this is to make it *compilation-based*, that is, provide a transformation that turns ordinary (explicit) programs into symbolic programs automatically. The transformed program only uses explicit operations, but it uses them to manipulate symbolic expressions and as a result can be executed using off-the-shelf components.

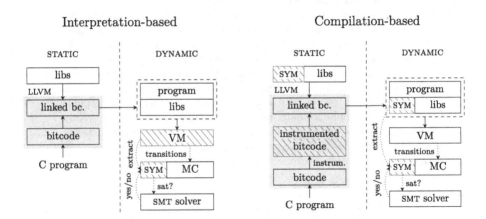

Fig. 1. Comparison of interpretation-based and compilation-based symbolic methods in the context of LLVM model checking. VM stands for 'virtual machine', while MC stands for 'model checker'. The hatched boxes represent components that work with symbolic data. In the compilation-based method, symbolic operations are instrumented into the bitcode, and their implementation is provided in the form of a library. The virtual machine does not need to know about symbolic values at all. The model checker, however, extracts symbolic data and a path condition from the executed program.

The expected result is that the proposed transformation can be combined with an existing solver and a standard explicit interpreter of LLVM bitcode. Depending on how one combines those ingredients, one will obtain different analysis tools. As an example, in Sect. 5.3, we use the transformation, an existing explicit-state model checker DIVINE and an SMT solver STP [15] to build a simple control-explicit, data-symbolic (CEDS) [4] model checker. Building a tool which implements symbolic execution would be even simpler.[1]

1.1 Goals

Our primary goal is to design a self-contained program transformation that can be used in conjunction with other components to piece together symbolic analysis and verification tools. We would like the transformation to exhibit the following properties:

1. allow mixing of explicit and symbolic computation in a single program,
2. expose a small interface to the rest of the system, and finally
3. impose minimal run-time overhead.

The first property is important because it often does not make sense to perform all computation within a program symbolically. For instance, a symbolic execution engine may wish to natively perform library calls requested by the program. Therefore, it ought to be possible to request, from the outset, that a particular value in the program is symbolic or explicit.

It is unfortunately not possible to execute the symbolised program in a context that is completely unaware of symbolic computation. However, the requirements imposed on the execution environment can be minimised and defined clearly (see Sect. 5.4). Finally, exploring all possible executions given a single input sequence is already expensive and when used in the context of model checking, we would like to incur as small a penalty as possible.

1.2 Contribution

The idea that various tasks can be shifted between compile time and run time is as old as higher-level programming languages. In the context of verification, there is a large variety of approaches that put different tasks at different points between these two extremes. Symbolic computation is traditionally found near the *interpretation* end of the spectrum.

Our contribution is to challenge this conventional wisdom and show that this technique can be shifted much farther towards the *compilation* end. Further, by treating symbolic computation as an *abstract domain*, we pave the way for other abstract domains to be approached in this manner. Finally, all relevant source code and benchmark data is freely available online.[2]

2 Related Work

Program verification techniques based on symbolic execution [18], symbolic program code analysis [24] and symbolic approach to model checking [21] have been the subject of extensive research.

---

[1] In fact, any control-explicit, data-symbolic model checker already contains a subroutine (in our case about 200 lines) which effectively implements a symbolic executor.
[2] https://divine.fi.muni.cz/2018/sym.

As for symbolic execution, the approach most closely related to ours is represented by the KLEE symbolic execution engine [10] that performs symbolic execution on top of LLVM IR [20]. Besides standalone usage as a symbolic executor, KLEE has become also a back-end tool for other types of analyses and for verification. For example, the tool Symbiotic [12] combines code instrumentation and slicing with KLEE to detect errors in C programs.

Besides symbolic execution, other forms of abstract interpretation, like predicate abstraction, is often used in code analysis. The most successful approaches are based either on counterexample-guided abstraction refinement (CEGAR) [13] or lazy abstraction with interpolants [2], which are implemented in tools such as BLAST [8] and CPAchecker [6]. There are numerous research results in this direction, summarised in e.g. [7,27,28].

A verification algorithm that goes beyond static program code analysis and combines predicate abstraction with concrete execution and dynamic analysis has been also introduced [14]. This approach can successfully verify programs that feature unbounded loops and recursion, unlike standard symbolic execution.

Using instrumentation (as opposed to interpretation) for symbolic verification was proposed a few times, but the only extant implementation that works with realistic programs is derived from the CUTE [26] family of concolic testing systems, i.e. the tools CREST [9] and jCUTE [25]. In particular, CREST uses the CIL toolkit[3] to insert additional calls into the program to perform the symbolic part of concolic execution. The approach as described in [26] is limited to symbolic computation, unlike the present paper, which works with arbitrary abstract domains.

A related process was proposed by Khurshid et al. [17]: in this case, hand-annotated code was processed by Java PathFinder [16], an explicit state model checker. Our approach, in contrast, is fully automatic and more general.

Finally, besides symbolic code analysis and symbolic execution, there are approaches that perform symbolic model checking as such. The key differentiating aspect of symbolic model checking is the ability to decide equality of symbolically represented states. This is important in particular for verification of parallel and reactive programs where the state space contains diamonds or loops, respectively. The tool SymDIVINE [22] is focused on bit-precise symbolic model checking of parallel C and C++ programs. It extends standard explicit state space exploration with SMT machinery to handle non-deterministic data values. As such, SymDIVINE is halfway between a symbolic executor and an explicit-state model checker. Unlike the solution presented in this paper, SymDIVINE does not separate the symbolic interpreter from the core of the model checker. In general, symbolic model checking is more often used with synchronous systems, for example [11].

---

[3] CIL is short for C Intermediate Language [23], and is a simplified subset of the C language. The toolkit can automatically translate standard C into the intermediate (CIL) form. The CIL form can be optionally brought into the form of three-address code and this feature is used in CREST.

3 Abstraction as a Transformation

While in the present work, our main goal is to transform a concrete program into one that performs symbolic computation, it is expedient to formulate the problem more generally. We will think in terms of an *abstraction*, in the sense of abstract interpretation, which has two main components: it affects how *program states* are represented and it affects the *computation of transitions* between those states. There are two levels on which the abstraction operates:

1. static, concerning syntactic constructs and the type system
2. dynamic, or semantic, which concerns actual execution and values

In the rest of this section, we will define *syntactic abstraction* (which covers the static aspects) as means of encoding abstract semantics into a concrete program. While it is convenient to think of the transformed program in terms of abstract values and abstract operations, it is also important to keep in mind that at a lower level, each abstract value is concretely represented (encoded). Likewise, abstract operations (instructions) are realised as sequences of concrete instructions which operate on the concrete representation of abstract values (see Fig. 4, left). Those considerations are at the core of the second, dynamic, aspect of abstraction. Reflecting this structure, the program transformation therefore proceeds in two steps:

1. the input program is (syntactically) abstracted
   – concrete values are replaced with abstract values
   – concrete instructions are replaced with abstract instructions
2. abstract instructions are replaced by their concrete realisation

The remainder of this section is organised as follows: in Sect. 3.1, we describe the expected concrete semantics of the input program. Section 3.2 then introduces syntactic abstraction, Sect. 3.3 deals with representation and typing of values in the abstracted program, Sect. 3.6 goes on to describe the treatment of instructions. Section 3.7 briefly discusses interactions of multiple domains within a program and finally Sect. 3.8 gives an overview of relational abstract domains that we use to perform a symbolic computation.

3.1 States and Transitions

We are interested in general programs, e.g. those written in the C programming language. Abstraction is often described in terms of *states* and *transitions*. In case of C programs, a state is described by the content of memory (including registers). Transitions describe how a state changes during computation performed by a given program. In this paper, we will use small-step semantics, partly because the prototype implementation is based on LLVM,[4] and in part because it is a natural choice for describing parallel programs.

---

[4] Programs in LLVM are in a partial SSA form, a special case of three-address code [1]. Three-address code is essentially small-step semantics in an executable form.

In this description, the transitions between program states are given by the effect of individual instructions on program state. Which instruction is executed and which part of the program state it affects is governed by the source state. Our discussion of *abstract transitions* will therefore focus on the effects of instructions: as an example, the **add** instruction obtains two values of a specified bit width from some locations in the program state, computes their sum and stores the result to a third location.

3.2 Syntactic Abstraction

The input program is given as a collection of functions, each consisting of a control flow graph where nodes are basic blocks – each a sequence of non-branching instructions. Memory access is always explicit: there are instructions for reading and writing memory, but memory is never directly copied, or directly used in computation. While this further restricts the semantics of the input program, it is not at the expense of generality: programs can be easily put in this form, often using commodity tools.

With these considerations in mind, the goal of what we will call *syntactic abstraction* is to replace some of the concrete instructions with their abstract counterparts. The general idea is illustrated in Fig. 2.

```
x : int ← input()              x : a_int ← lift(*)
y : int ← factorial(7)         y : int ← factorial(7)
z : int ← add(x, y)            z : a_int ← a_add(x, y)
b : bool ← leq(y, z)           b : a_bool ← a_leq(y, z)
assert(b)                      assert(b)
```

Fig. 2. An example of syntactic abstraction. In this example, a_int and a_bool represent abstract types (see also Sect. 3.3). We create the abstract value x with a lift(*) operation to represent an arbitrary value of type int (see Sect. 3.4). Also, notice that the concrete computation of factorial(7) remains intact.

Apart from a few special cases, an abstract instruction takes abstract values as its inputs and produces an abstract value as its result. The specific meaning of those abstract instructions and abstract values then defines the *semantic abstraction*. The result of *syntactic* abstraction being performed on the program is, therefore, that the modified program now performs abstract computation. In other words, the transformed program directly operates on abstract states and the effect of the program on abstract states defines the abstract transition system.

We posit that syntactic abstraction, as explained in following sections, will automatically lead to a good semantic abstraction – i.e. one that fits the standard definition: a set of concrete states can be mapped to an abstract state, an abstract state can be realised as a set of concrete states and those operations are compatible in the usual sense.

3.3   Abstract Values and Static Types

A distinguishing feature of the syntactic approach to abstraction is that it admits a static type system. In other words, the variables in the program can be assigned consistent types which respect the boundary between abstract and concrete values. While a type system is a useful consistency check, its main importance lies in facilitating a description of how syntactic abstraction operates.[5]

We start by assuming existence of a set of *concrete scalar types*, S, and of concrete pointer types. We define a map Γ that builds up all relevant types from the set of scalar types. The set of all types $\Gamma(T)$ derived from a set of scalars T is defined inductively as follows:

1. $T \subseteq (T)$, that is, each scalar type is included in $\Gamma(T)$
2. if $t_1, ..., t_n \in \Gamma(T)$ then also the product type $(t_1, ..., t_n) \in \Gamma(T)$, $n \in \mathbb{N}$
3. if $t_1, ..., t_n \in \Gamma(T)$ then also the disjoint union $t_1|t_2|...|t_n \in \Gamma(T)$, $n \in \mathbb{N}$
4. if $t \in \Gamma(T)$ then $t* \in \Gamma(T)$ ($t*$ denotes a pointer type)

In other words, the set $\Gamma(S)$ describes finite (non-recursive) algebraic types over the set of concrete scalars and pointers.

A fundamental building block of the syntactic abstraction is a bijective map α_i, defined for each abstract domain separately,[6] from the set of *concrete scalar types* S to the set of abstract scalar types $A_i = \alpha_i(S)$ (we let A be the union of all the A_i: $A = A_1 \cup A_2 \cup ...$). Each value which exists in the abstracted program then belongs to a type in $\Gamma(S \cup A)$ – in other words, values are built up from concrete and abstract scalars.

In particular, this means that the abstraction works with *mixed types* – products and unions with both concrete and abstract fields. Likewise, it is possible to form pointers to both abstract values and to mixed aggregates.

3.4   Semantic Abstraction

The maps α_i and α_i^{-1} let us move from concrete to abstract scalar *types* (and back) and are strictly a syntactic construct. The *semantic* (dynamic) counterpart of α_i are *lift_i* and *lower_i*: these are not maps, but rather abstract operations (instructions). Just as α_i and α_i^{-1} translate between concrete and abstract types, *lift_i* goes from concrete to abstract *values* and *lower_i* the other way around. While both the α_i and *lift_i* and *lower_i* are defined on scalar types S and scalar values respectively, they can be all naturally extended to the set of all types $\Gamma(S)$ (and their corresponding values).

---

[5] Additionally, since the SSA portion of the LLVM IR is already statically typed, we can take advantage of this existing type system in the implementation. Nonetheless, the treatment in this section does not depend on LLVM and would be applicable to any dataflow-oriented program representation.

[6] Since multiple abstract domains can co-exist in a single program, we use the lower index i to distinguish them.

3.5   Representation

Besides α_i, there is another type map, which we will call ρ_i, which maps each abstract scalar type in A_i to a concrete type in $\Gamma(S)$. This is the *representation map*, and describes how abstract values are *represented* at runtime. This is to emphasise that abstract values are, in the end, encoded using concrete values that belong to particular concrete types. Moreover, in general for $t \in \Gamma(S)$, $\rho_i(\alpha_i(t)) \neq t$: the representation is unrelated to the original concrete type. An abstract floating point number may be, for instance, represented by a concrete pointer to a concrete aggregate made of two 32-bit integers.

```
a : pointer ← malloc(4)        a : pointer ← malloc(4)
y : a_int ← lift(*)            y : term ← sym_lift(*)
store y → a                    freeze y → a
...                            ...
z : a_int ← load a             z : term ← thaw a
```

Fig. 3. Freezing and thawing of values transfers them between abstract representation and their concrete realisation. In this case, ρ sends a_int to term, which realises the term domain described in section Sect. 4. The *freeze* and *thaw* operations allow term to be bigger than the original 4-byte integer type.

While $lift_i$ and $lower_i$ are the value-level counterparts of the map α_i, we need another pair of operations to accompany the representation map ρ_i. We will call them $freeze_i$ and $thaw_i$, and they map between $t \in A_i$ and $\rho_i(t) \in \Gamma(S)$. The idea is that memory manipulation (and manipulation of any concrete aggregates) is done entirely in terms of the representation types (using frozen values), but abstraction operations on scalar values are defined in terms of the abstract type (i.e. thawed values). The use of freezing and thawing is illustrated in Fig. 3.

One challenge in the implementation of $freeze_i$ and $thaw_i$ is that the memory layout of a program should not change[7] as a side-effect of the transformation. This means that for many abstract domains, the *freeze* operation must be able to store additional data associated with a given address, and *thaw* must be able to obtain this data efficiently. While this is an implementation issue, it is an important part of the interface between the transformed program and the underlying execution or verification platform. However, since the program is

---

[7] The exact layout of data (structures, arrays, dynamic memory) is normally the responsibility of the program itself, more so in the case of intermediate or low-level languages. For this reason, it is often the case that the program will make various assumptions about relationships among addresses within the same memory object. It is impractical, if not impossible, to automatically adapt the program to a different data layout, e.g. in case the size of a scalar value would change due to abstraction.

transformed as a whole, there is no need to explicitly track this additional data at runtime.[8]

An additional role of the *freeze/thaw* pair is to maintain dynamic type information at runtime. While it is easy to assign static types to instruction operands and results, this is not true for memory locations: different parts of the program can load values of different static types from the same memory address. For this reason, the type system which governs memory use must be dynamic and allow dispatch on the runtime type of the value stored at a given memory location.

3.6   Abstract Instructions

As indicated at the start of this section, it is advantageous to formulate the transformation in two phases, using intermediate abstract instructions. Abstract instructions take abstract values as operands and give back abstract values as their results. It is, however, of crucial importance that each abstract instruction can be realised as a suitable sequence of concrete instructions. This is what makes it possible to eventually obtain an abstract program that does not actually contain any abstract instructions and execute it using standard (concrete, explicit) methods.

In the first (abstraction) phase, concrete instructions are replaced with their abstract versions: instruction `inst` with a type $(t_1, ..., t_n) \to t_r$ is replaced with `a_inst` of type $(\alpha(t_1), ..., \alpha(t_n)) \to (t_r)$. Additionally, *lift, lower, freeze* and *thaw* are inserted as required.[9] The implementation is free to decide which instructions to abstract and where to insert value lifting and lowering, as long as it obeys typing constraints. The specific approach we have taken is discussed in Sect. 3.7 and the implementation aspects are described in Sect. 5.2.

After the first phase is finished, the program may be further manipulated in its abstract form before continuing the second phase of the abstraction. This gives a practical, implementation-driven reason for performing the abstraction transformation in two steps, in addition to the conceptual clarity it provides.

In the second step, all abstract operations, including *lift* and *lower*, are realised using concrete subroutines. The realisation (implementation) of `a_inst` is of the type $(\rho(\alpha(t_1)), ..., \rho(\alpha(t_n))) \to \rho(\alpha(t_r)))$, clearly obviating the need for thawing and re-freezing the value.

3.7   Abstract Domains

Necessarily, in an abstracted program, the values it manipulates will come from at least two different domains: the concrete domain and the chosen abstract

---

[8] The only way a value can be copied from one memory address to another is via a `load` instruction followed by a `store`, both of which are instrumented and as such also transfer the supplementary data.

[9] For instance, concrete operands to abstract operations are lifted, arguments to necessarily concrete functions (e.g. real system calls) are lowered. Memory stores are replaced with *freeze* and loads with *thaw*.

domain, in line with the first requirement laid out in Sect. 1.1. This is because it is usually impractical to abstract *all* values that appear in the program. Additional abstract domains, therefore, do not pose any new conceptual problems.

For the sake of simplicity, we only consider instructions where all operands come from the same domain (this holds for both the concrete and for abstract domains). Moreover, the only instructions where the domain of the result does not agree with the domain of the operands are cross-domain conversion operations, which take care of transitioning values from one domain to another. The two most important instances of those operations are *lift* and *lower*[10] introduced in Sect. 3.3.

```
enum parity
   even, odd, undef

parity_add(a: parity, b: parity)
   if a is undef ∨ b is undef
      return undef
   if a is even: return b
   if b is even: return a
   return even # odd + odd
```

```
lifter_add(x: ?, y: ?)
   if x is int ∧ y is int
      return add(x, y)
   if x is int
      x : a_int ← lift(x)
   else # y is int
      y : a_int ← lift(y)
   return a_add(x, y)
```

Fig. 4. Left: Domain implementation can be provided in a high-level language (e.g. C++) and needs to provide a representation of abstract scalar values and operations on them. An abstract value (of type **parity**) can be **even**, **odd** or in a superposition of those (**undef** – unknown). The term domain described in Sect. 4 is constructed analogously. Right: A lifter ensures that both arguments to an operation are in the same domain.

Even though cross-domain conversions are necessary in the program, it is a major task of the proposed transformation to minimise their number. A natural approach that would minimise unwanted domain transitions is to propagate abstract domains along the data flow of the program. That is, if an abstract instruction a_inst is already in the program and its result a is also used as an operand elsewhere, we prefer to lift all the users of a into the abstract domain of a_inst (cf. Fig. 4, right), instead of lowering a into a set of concrete values. This simple technique, which we call *value propagation*, forms the core of our entire approach (see also Fig. 2). It is worth noting that this is particularly simple to do for programs in (partial) SSA form[11], although the variables which are not part of SSA are still somewhat challenging. Those are covered by the *freeze* and *thaw* operations, which are discussed in more detail in Sect. 5.1.

---

[10] The names *lift* and *lower* allude to the relationship of the abstract and the concrete domain. In applications with multiple abstract domains, it may be expedient to include additional instructions that convert directly from one abstract domain to another, although in theory it is always possible to go through the concrete domain.

[11] Again, this is true of LLVM bitcode – it is already in a partial SSA form. This simplifies our prototype implementation somewhat.

Given the above, a logical starting point is to pick an initial set of instructions that we wish to lift into an abstract domain. Those could be explicit *lift* instructions placed in the program by hand, they could be picked by static analysis, or could be the result of abstraction refinement. The abstract program can then be obtained by applying value propagation to this initial set of abstract instructions.

3.8   Constraints and Relational Domains

The last important aspect of abstraction is its effect on control flow of the program. It is often the case that the control flow depends on specific values of variables via conditional branching. The condition on the branch is typically a predicate on some value, or a relationship among multiple values that appear in the program. If the involved values are, in fact, abstract values, it is quite possible that *both* results of the predicate or comparison are admissible and that the conditional branch can therefore go both ways. The way we deal with this in the transformation is that the program makes a *nondeterministic choice* on the direction of the branch. How this nondeterministic choice is implemented is again deferred to the execution environment. In any case, the choice of direction provides additional information – constraints – on the possible values of variables (cf. Fig. 6).

We encode those constraints into *assume* instructions: given an abstract value and the constraint, *assume* computes the constrained value. Additionally, depending on the abstract domain, it may be desirable to constrain values other than those directly involved in the comparison. Alternatively, relational domains may be able to encode constraint information themselves: this is in particular the case in the *term domain* which realises symbolic computation. Therefore, for the purposes of the present paper, simply inserting a single *assume* instruction on each outgoing edge of the conditional is sufficient.

3.9   Summary

In the above, we have set up abstraction in such a way that it fits into a transformation-based approach. In particular, we have separated *syntactic* and *semantic* abstraction and shown how the former induces the latter. The proposed syntactic abstraction captures how the program is changed, while semantic abstraction captures the dynamic (execution) aspects of abstract interpretation.

4   Symbolic Computation

Now that we have described how to perform program abstraction as a transformation, the remaining task is to re-cast symbolic computation as an abstract domain. Fortunately, this is not very hard: the abstract values in the domain are *terms*, while the abstract instructions simply construct corresponding terms from their operands. In other words, symbolic computation is realised by a *free algebra* (that is, the *term algebra*). The *input values* of the program correspond to nullary symbols – in practice, a unique nullary symbol is created each time the program obtains a value from its input. All the remaining values are built up as terms of bit-vector operations and constants. We will refer to the abstract domain thus formed as the *term domain*.

It is not hard to see that a program transformed this way will simply perform part of its computation symbolically in the usual sense. Additionally, as the computation progresses, *assume* instructions impose a collection of *constraints* on the nullary symbols of the abstract algebra (i.e. the input values). Each constraint takes the form of a term with a relational symbol in the root position. These constraints become part of the abstract state, effectively ensuring that the term domain is fully relational.[12]

It is a requirement of abstract interpretation that it is possible to construct an abstract state from a set of concrete states. In the *term domain* this can be achieved by assigning, to each memory location that differs in some of the concrete states[13], a fresh nullary symbol. We then impose constraints that ensure that exactly the input set of concrete states is represented by the resulting abstract state. For instance, if the input set of concrete states differs by the value of a single variable a, and this variable takes values 1, 2, 3 and 4 in the 4 input states, a suitable constraint would be $a \geq 1 \wedge a \leq 4$.

In some cases, it is impossible to construct the requisite constraints using only conjunction and relational operators. To ensure that the term domain forms a lattice (in particular that a least upper bound always exists), it is necessary to allow the constraints to use logical disjunction.

While the above considerations regarding constraints are an important part of the theoretical underpinnings of the approach, it is almost always entirely impractical to shift back and forth between concrete and abstract states. In practice, therefore, the constraints described in this section simply arise through the *assume* mechanism described in Sect. 3.8. As such, the constraints that appear in a given state form a *path condition*. Finally, we note that the least upper bound of abstract states defined above corresponds to path conditions which arise from *path merging* in symbolic execution.

5   Implementation

We have implemented the proposed program transformation on top of LLVM, using its C++ API. Both the transformation and all additional code (model checker and solver integration) was done in C++. The transformation itself is the largest component, totalling 3200 lines of code.

---

[12] An abstract domain is called *relational* when it is capable of preserving information about relationships among various abstract values that appear in the program.

[13] In the present paper, we only deal with abstract (symbolic) *values*. The structure of the program state, that is, the arrangement of the program memory, is taken to be always represented explicitly, i.e., it belongs squarely to the concrete domain.

5.1   Freeze and Thaw

As mentioned in Sect. 3.7, our implementation is based on the simple idea of maximum propagation of abstract values along the data flow of the program. While the SSA part of the algorithm is essentially trivial, storing abstract values in program memory is slightly more challenging. The purpose of *freeze* and *thaw* is to overcome this issue.

While the dynamic type system that *freeze* and *thaw* provide to the transformed program and the ability to store additional data associated with a given memory address are largely orthogonal at the conceptual level, they are closely related at the level of implementation. This is because in principle, a dynamic type system only requires that additional information is attached to values manipulated by the program, and that this information is correctly propagated. Since apart from memory access, the program is statically typed, it is sufficient to perform dynamic type checks (and dispatch) when a value is *thawed*, while *freeze* simply stores the incoming static type.

Implementation-wise, our target platform is a virtual machine with provisions for associating user-defined metadata to arbitrary memory addresses. This makes the implementation of *freeze* and *thaw* simple and efficient. However, in case such a mechanism is not available, it is sufficient to implement an associative map, using addresses as keys, inside the program.

5.2   Domains

In real-world programs, there are often variables which do not benefit from abstraction or from symbolic treatment, and are best represented explicitly. For this reason, the toplevel abstract domain that we use is the disjoint union (i.e. the type-level sum) of the concrete domain and the term domain. If we denote the concrete domain with $\mathcal{C}$ and the symbolic (term) domain with $\mathcal{S}$, the type toplevel type is $\mathcal{C} \sqcup \mathcal{S}$.

Since the *freeze* and *thaw* operations maintain dynamic type information in the executing program, it is possible to quickly compute operations for which both operands are concrete (explicit). If both operands are symbolic, a symbolic operation is directly invoked, while in the remaining case – one symbolic and one concrete argument – the concrete argument is lifted into the symbolic (term) domain. The procedure is called a *lifter* and is automatically synthesized for each abstract operation that appears in the program. An example of a lifter is given in Fig. 4 (right).

It is also possible to use the domain $\mathcal{C} \sqcup (\mathcal{C} \times \mathcal{S})$, which corresponds to concolic execution (i.e. it maintains both a concrete and a symbolic value at the same time). This requires the additional provision that *assume* instructions obtain concrete values that satisfy the symbolic constraints on their abstract counterparts (an SMT solver will typically provide a model in case the assumptions were feasible, which can then be used to reconstruct the requisite concrete values).

```
a : pointer ← malloc(4)
w : a_int ← lift(*)
x : a_int ← lift(*)
y : a_int ← a_add(w, x)
z : a_int ← a_mul(y, 7)
freeze z → a
```

Fig. 5. Example of a formula tree as generated by the term domain. The boxes correspond to abstract variables, while the circles are the concrete representation of terms. Question marks denote unconstrained nullary symbols.

```
x : a_int ← lift(*)
if nondet()
    x': a_int ← assume(x < 10)
    y : a_int ← a_add(x', 1)
else
    x': a_int ← assume(x >= 10)
    y : a_int ← a_sub(x', 1)
```

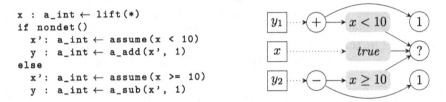

Fig. 6. The program on the left arises from instrumentation of conditional branching, in this case if x < 10. The formula tree on the right includes constraints arising from the *assume* instructions. Note that on any given path through the program, only one of the subtrees rooted in y_1 or y_2 can exist.

5.3   Execution and Model Checking

We represent the terms described in Sect. 4 by a simple tree data structure. The abstract instructions that correspond to operations on values construct a tree representation of the requisite term by joining their operands to a new root node, where only the operation in the root node depends on the specific abstract instruction. The approach is illustrated in Figs. 5, 6 and 7.

This arrangement makes it easy to extract the terms from program state and convert them to a form appropriate for further processing by the analysis tool. Recall that one of the motivating applications of the proposed approach was symbolic model checking. In this case, the state space is explored by an explicit-state model checker and the extracted terms are converted into SMT queries. To this end, the model checker must be slightly extended and coupled to an SMT solver, since:

1. transitions of the program must be checked for *feasibility*,
2. the state equality check must compare terms semantically, not syntactically.

Of course, the hitherto extracted terms must be left out of byte-wise comparison that is performed on the remaining (concrete) parts of program states. In our case, the required changes in the model checker were quite minor, amounting to about 1200 lines of code.

```
x : a_int ← lift(*)
for i : int ← 1 .. 2
    x : a_int ← a_add(x, 1)
```

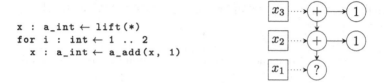

Fig. 7. An example of a formula tree arising from a `for` loop. Versions of the variable x which exist in different iterations of the loop are distinguished by an index in the picture.

5.4 Interfaces

One of the goals of the proposed approach was to minimise interfaces between the abstracted program and the verification or execution environment (recall goal 2 set in Sect. 1.1). In total, there are four interactions at play:

1. non-deterministic choice: under abstraction, conditionals in the program may be undetermined, and both branches may need to be explored; the abstraction uses a non-deterministic choice operator to capture this effect and defers an exploration strategy to the verifier
2. *freeze* and *thaw* must be provided as an interface for storing abstract values in program memory
3. enumeration of enabled (feasible) transitions must take the abstract values into account, if required by the domain(s) used in the program
4. state equality (if applicable in the verification approach) must be extended to take the employed abstract domains into account

The latter two points depend on the chosen abstract domains. For the term domains, both interfaces reduce to extracting abstract values (terms) from program state and executing an SMT query.

6 Evaluation

First of all, we have checked the performance of the transformation itself. On C programs from the SV-COMP suite, the transformation time was negligible. On more complex C++ programs, it took at most a few seconds, which is still fast compared to subsequent analysis.

As described in Sect. 5, we have built a simple tool which integrates the proposed transformation with an explicit-state model checker and an SMT solver. The experimental evaluation was done using this prototype integration (denoted 'DIVINE*' in summary tables).

6.1 Code Complexity

One of our criteria for the approach presented in this paper was reduced code complexity. While counting lines of code is not a very sophisticated metric, it is a reasonably good proxy for complexity and is easily obtained.[14] The results are summarised in Table 1.

Table 1. Summary of component sizes (thousands of lines of code) in a few symbolic verification and symbolic execution tools. Numbers in parentheses represent shared code (i.e. code not specific to the given approach to symbolic computation).

Component	DIVINE*	KLEE	SymDIVINE	CBMC
Transformation	3.2	0	0	(22)
Virtual machine	(10)	15	6	7.5
Exploration	(1.5)	1.2	1	2.3
Solver integration	1.2	8	0	14
SAT solver	(45)	(45)	(23)	(5.5)
SMT solver	(80)	(80)	(400)	16
Runtime support	1	0	0	0
Total unique	5.4	24.2	7	39.8
Total shared	136.5	125	423	27.5

6.2 Benchmarks

For benchmarking, we have used a subset of the SV-COMP [5] test cases, namely 7 categories, summarised in Table 2, along with statistics from our prototype tool. We have only taken examples with finite state spaces since the simple approach outlined in Sect. 5.3 cannot handle infinite recursion or infinite accumulation loops. In total, we have selected 1160 SV-COMP inputs. In many cases (especially in the `array` category), the benchmarks are parametric: we have included both the original SV-COMP instance and smaller instances to check that the approach works correctly, even if it takes a long time or exceeds the memory limit on the instances included in SV-COMP.

In all cases, the time limit, for each test case separately, was 10 minutes (wall time) and the memory limit was 10 GiB. The test machines were equipped with 4 Intel Xeon 5130 cores clocked at 2 GHz and 16 GiB of RAM.

In addition to the present approach, we have measured two additional tools: CBMC 5.8 and SymDIVINE, both of which are symbolic model checkers targeting C code. The overall results of the comparison, in terms of the number of cases solved, are presented in Table 3.

6.3 Comparison 1: CBMC

The results from CBMC 5.8 were obtained using the tool's default configuration. CBMC [19] is a mature bounded model checker for C programs with a good

---

[14] We have used the utility `sloccount` to get estimates of module size in terms of lines of code.

track record in SV-COMP and is built around a symbolic interpreter for 'goto programs', its own intermediate form, not entirely dissimilar to CIL or LLVM in its spirit. Besides KLEE, the CBMC toolkit is among the best established members of the interpretation-based school of symbolic computation.

Table 2. Summary of test cases from SV-COMP. The time limit was 10 min and memory limit was 10 GiB. The 'oot/oom' column is the number of test cases that did not finish within the limits, while 'solved' are those that gave the expected result; 'states' gives the number of states stored, 'search' gives the state space exploration time and 'ce' gives the counterexample generation time.

tag	solved	oot/oom	states	search	ce
array	96	94	170.3k	52:00	54:15
bitvector	17	15	3166	3:12	2:33
loops	72	106	14.0k	53:52	11:40
product-lines	336	239	20.2 M	4:36:44	43:11
pthread	9	36	609.4k	3:31	0:54
recursion	47	34	3955	16:16	7:41
systemc	14	45	25.0k	3:29	1:34
total	591	569			

Table 3. The number of benchmarks correctly solved by each of the evaluated tools. The best result in each category is rendered in boldface.

tag	total	DIVINE*	SymDIVINE	CBMC
array	190	**96**	68	93
bitvector	32	**17**	9	2
loops	178	**72**	67	9
product-lines	575	336	**411**	234
pthread	45	**9**	0	1
recursion	81	**47**	43	22
systemc	59	14	**27**	0
total	1160	591	**625**	361

Besides the total number of test cases solved (within the 10 min limit), we were interested in comparing the time required to do so. Time requirements are summarised in Table 4.

With regards to its state space exploration strategy, CBMC can be thought of as the middle ground between the approach taken by KLEE and that of our proposed tool. On one hand, KLEE, being a symbolic executor, does not attempt to identify already-visited program states. CBMC is a bounded model checker, which means it stores a single formula representing the entire set of reachable states. Our present approach, being based on an explicit-state model checker, stores sets of program states and compares them for equality using an SMT solver.

Table 4. Speed comparison: the columns 'models$_2$' and 'models$_1$' show the number of models which the respective pair of tools finished in common. In most cases, CBMC is substantially faster than the proposed approach, while SymDIVINE is significantly slower. The time shown is a sum across all the models in a given category.

tag	models$_1$	DIVINE*	CBMC	models$_2$	DIVINE*	SymDIVINE
array	73	34:16	13:58	58	3:18	42:54
bitvector	2	0:37	0:01	9	0:55	2:30
loops	4	0:03	0:02	62	22:25	19:04
product-lin.	182	4:08:24	7:25	183	0:30	28:33
pthread	0	0	0	0	0	0
recursion	22	0:01	0:13	43	4:02	13:58
systemc	0	0	0	14	3:29	6:43

6.4   Comparison 2: SymDIVINE

SymDIVINE [22] is a pre-existing, interpretation-based symbolic model checker which also works with LLVM bitcode. Similar to our approach, SymDIVINE relies on a state equality checker, in this case based on quantified bitvector formulae. In theory, this yields coarser state equivalence and consequently smaller state spaces, but we could not confirm this in our set of benchmarks: the total number of states stored across the benchmarks that finished using both tools was 802 thousand for SymDIVINE and 93 thousand with the approach described in this paper. Additionally, QBV satisfiability queries are typically much more expensive than those used by our prototype tool, which can help explain the speed difference between the tools.

7   Conclusion

We have presented an alternate approach to symbolic execution (and abstract interpretation in general), based on compilation-based techniques, instead of relying on the more traditional interpreter-based approach. We have shown that the proposed approach has important advantages and no serious drawbacks. Most importantly, our technique is modular to a degree not possible with symbolic or abstract interpreters. This makes implementation of software analysis and verification tools based on symbolic execution almost trivial. An important side benefit is that the approach allows for abstract domains other than the term domain, leading to a different class of verification algorithms with a comparatively small investment.

References

1. Aho, A.V.: Compilers: Principles, Techniques, and Tools. Addison-Wesley Series in Computer Science. Pearson/Addison Wesley, Boston (2007)
2. Albarghouthi, A., Gurfinkel, A., Chechik, M.: From under-approximations to over-approximations and back. In: Flanagan, C., König, B. (eds.) TACAS 2012. LNCS, vol. 7214, pp. 157–172. Springer, Heidelberg (2012). https://doi.org/10.1007/978-3-642-28756-5_12
3. Barrett, C., Fontaine, P., Tinelli, C.: SMT-LIB: the satisfiability modulo theories library. http://www.smt-lib.org/
4. Bauch, P., Havel, V., Barnat, J.: Control explicit-data symbolic model checking. ACM Trans. Softw. Eng. Methodol. **25**(2) (2016). Article no. 15. https://doi.org/10.1145/2888393
5. Beyer, D.: Reliable and reproducible competition results with BenchExec and witnesses (report on SV-COMP 2016). In: Chechik, M., Raskin, J.-F. (eds.) TACAS 2016. LNCS, vol. 9636, pp. 887–904. Springer, Heidelberg (2016). https://doi.org/10.1007/978-3-662-49674-9_55
6. Beyer, D., Keremoglu, M.E.: CPACHECKER: a tool for configurable software verification. In: Gopalakrishnan, G., Qadeer, S. (eds.) CAV 2011. LNCS, vol. 6806, pp. 184–190. Springer, Heidelberg (2011). https://doi.org/10.1007/978-3-642-22110-1_16
7. Beyer, D., Löwe, S.: Interpolation for value analysis. In: Aßmann, U., Demuth, B., Spitta, T., Püschel, G., Kaiser, R. (eds.) Software Engineering and Management. Lecture Notes in Informatics, vol. 239, pp. 73–74. Gesellschaft für Informatik, Bonn (2015). https://dl.gi.de/handle/20.500.12116/2495
8. Beyer, B., Henzinger, T.A., Jhala, R., Majumdar, R.: The software model checker BLAST. Int. J. Softw. Tools Technol. Transfer **9**(5), 505–525 (2007). https://doi.org/10.1007/s10009-007-0044-z
9. Burnim, J., Sen, K.: Heuristics for scalable dynamic test generation. In: Proceedings of 23rd IEEE/ACM International Conference on Automated Software Engineering, ASE 2008, L'Aquila, September 2008, pp. 443–446. IEEE CS Press, Washington, DC (2008). https://doi.org/10.1109/ase.2008.69
10. Cadar, C., Dunbar, D., Engler, D.R.: KLEE: unassisted and automatic generation of high-coverage tests for complex systems programs. In: Proceedings of 8th USENIX Symposium on Operating Systems Design and Implementation, San Diego, CA, December 2008, pp. 209–224. USENIX Association (2008). http://www.usenix.org/events/osdi08/tech/full_papers/cadar/cadar.pdf
11. Cavada, R., et al.: The NUXMV symbolic model checker. In: Biere, A., Bloem, R. (eds.) CAV 2014. LNCS, vol. 8559, pp. 334–342. Springer, Cham (2014). https://doi.org/10.1007/978-3-319-08867-9_22
12. Chalupa, M., Vitovská, M., Jonáš, M., Slaby, J., Strejček, J.: Symbiotic 4: beyond reachability. In: Legay, A., Margaria, T. (eds.) TACAS 2017. LNCS, vol. 10206, pp. 385–389. Springer, Heidelberg (2017). https://doi.org/10.1007/978-3-662-54580-5_28
13. Clarke, E., Grumberg, O., Jha, S., Lu, Y., Veith, H.: Counterexample-guided abstraction refinement. In: Emerson, E.A., Sistla, A.P. (eds.) CAV 2000. LNCS, vol. 1855, pp. 154–169. Springer, Heidelberg (2000). https://doi.org/10.1007/10722167_15
14. Daniel, J., Parízek, P.: PANDA: simultaneous predicate abstraction and concrete execution. In: Piterman, N. (ed.) HVC 2015. LNCS, vol. 9434, pp. 87–103. Springer, Cham (2015). https://doi.org/10.1007/978-3-319-26287-1_6

15. Ganesh, V., Dill, D.L.: A decision procedure for bit-vectors and arrays. In: Damm, W., Hermanns, H. (eds.) CAV 2007. LNCS, vol. 4590, pp. 519–531. Springer, Heidelberg (2007). https://doi.org/10.1007/978-3-540-73368-3_52

16. Havelund, K., Pressburger, T.: Model checking JAVA programs using JAVA PathFinder. Int. J. Softw. Tools Technol. Transfer 2(4), 366–381 (2000). https://doi.org/10.1007/s100090050043

17. Khurshid, S., Păsăreanu, C.S., Visser, W.: Generalized symbolic execution for model checking and testing. In: Garavel, H., Hatcliff, J. (eds.) TACAS 2003. LNCS, vol. 2619, pp. 553–568. Springer, Heidelberg (2003). https://doi.org/10.1007/3-540-36577-X_40

18. King, J.C.: Symbolic execution and program testing. Commun. ACM 19(7), 385–394 (1976). https://doi.org/10.1145/360248.360252

19. Kroening, D., Tautschnig, M.: CBMC – C bounded model checker. In: Ábrahám, E., Havelund, K. (eds.) TACAS 2014. LNCS, vol. 8413, pp. 389–391. Springer, Heidelberg (2014). https://doi.org/10.1007/978-3-642-54862-8_26

20. Lattner, C., Adve, V.: LLVM: a compilation framework for lifelong program analysis and transformation. In: Proceedings of 2nd IEEE/ACM International Symposium on Code Generation and Optimization, CGO 2004, Palo Alto, CA, March 2004, pp. 75–88. IEEE CS Press, Washington, DC (2004). https://doi.org/10.1109/cgo.2004.1281665

21. McMillan, K.L.: Symbolic Model Checking. Kluwer Academic Publishers, Boston (1993). https://doi.org/10.1007/978-1-4615-3190-6

22. Mrázek, J., Bauch, P., Lauko, H., Barnat, J.: SymDIVINE: tool for control-explicit data-symbolic state space exploration. In: Bošnački, D., Wijs, A. (eds.) SPIN 2016. LNCS, vol. 9641, pp. 208–213. Springer, Cham (2016). https://doi.org/10.1007/978-3-319-32582-8_14

23. Necula, G.C., McPeak, S., Rahul, S.P., Weimer, W.: CIL: intermediate language and tools for analysis and transformation of C programs. In: Horspool, R.N. (ed.) CC 2002. LNCS, vol. 2304, pp. 213–228. Springer, Heidelberg (2002). https://doi.org/10.1007/3-540-45937-5_16

24. Nielson, F., Nielson, H.R., Hankin, C.: Principles of Program Analysis. Springer, Heidelberg (1999). https://doi.org/10.1007/978-3-662-03811-6

25. Sen, K., Agha, G.: CUTE and jCUTE: concolic unit testing and explicit path model-checking tools. In: Ball, T., Jones, R.B. (eds.) CAV 2006. LNCS, vol. 4144, pp. 419–423. Springer, Heidelberg (2006). https://doi.org/10.1007/11817963_38

26. Sen, K., Marinov, D., Agha, G.: CUTE: a concolic unit testing engine for C. In: Proceedings of Joint 10th European Software Engineering Conference and 13th ACM SIGSOFT International Symposium on Foundations of Software Engineering, ESEC/FSE 2005, Lisbon, September 2005, pp. 263–272. ACM Press, New York (2005). https://doi.org/10.1145/1081706.1081750

27. Sousa, M., Rodríguez, C., D'Silva, V., Kroening, D.: Abstract interpretation with unfoldings. In: Majumdar, R., Kunčak, V. (eds.) CAV 2017. LNCS, vol. 10427, pp. 197–216. Springer, Cham (2017). https://doi.org/10.1007/978-3-319-63390-9_11

28. Weißenbacher, G.: Program analysis with interpolants. Ph.D. thesis, University of Oxford (2010)

Double Applicative Functors

Härmel Nestra[(⊠)][iD]

University of Tartu, Institute of Computer Science, J. Liivi 2, 50409 Tartu, Estonia
harmel.nestra@ut.ee

Abstract. Writing easily readable parser code is a classic application of monads in functional programming. For simpler cases, the Applicative and Alternative type classes in Haskell can be used for this purpose instead of the more powerful Monad and MonadPlus classes. Counterparts of all parsing expression grammar constructs except lookaheads are expressible via the Applicative and Alternative class methods. Yet their error handling capabilities are unsatisfactory even for simple applications. This paper proposes double applicative functors for increasing the flexibility of error handling without full monadic power, along with an extended set of operations, and studies relationships between mathematical laws that these operations are assumed to fulfill. Many properties of these operations are generalizations of semantic equivalences previously known for parsing expression grammars.

Keywords: Applicative functors · Monads · Parsing · Error handling

1 Introduction

In top-down parsing with backtracking, locating errors in the input is somewhat challenging. This is because ordinary parse errors work as indicators of being in a wrong branch and primarily cause taking a new one. Numerous backtrackings can have occurred at different locations before parsing ultimately fails and there are no trustworthy methods for telling afterwards where the input needs correction.

Parsing expression grammars (PEG) [7] specify formal languages using so-called *parsing expressions* which have the following syntax as minimum:

$$e \quad ::= \quad \epsilon \mid a \mid X \mid ee \mid e/e \mid !e \tag{1}$$

Here, ϵ means the empty string, a and X stand for terminal and non-terminal symbols, respectively, and juxtaposition refers to concatenation. The construct with slash (/) means left-biased choice between two expressions (if the first alternative succeeds then the second one is skipped) and the unary operator !, called *negation* or *negative lookahead*, inverts the success/failure status of its operand after trying it. Constructs like e? (option), e* (repetition), e+ (non-zero repetition) and &e (positive lookahead) are usually added as syntactic sugar.

Well-formed PEGs can be interpreted as top-down parsers for the languages they define, whereas negations and choices enable backtracking (recovery from

© Springer Nature Switzerland AG 2018
B. Fischer and T. Uustalu (Eds.): ICTAC 2018, LNCS 11187, pp. 333–353, 2018.
https://doi.org/10.1007/978-3-030-02508-3_18

failure). For overcoming the weakness described in the beginning, Maidl et al. [16] proposed a *labelled choice* construct of the form $e_1 /^E e_2$ where e_1, e_2 are parsing expressions and E is any finite set of errors. By the intended semantics, if e_1 fails with some error e such that $e \in E$ then e_2 is tried, otherwise e_2 is skipped.

The library module *Control.Applicative* [9] of the most popular implementation, GHC, of the functional programming language Haskell [8] provides an interface very close to the parsing expression language (1). The first paper advocating it as a distinct interface was by McBride and Paterson [17]. While there exist many more powerful parsing libraries, this interface is often the most natural choice for writing experimental parsers for simple languages because of its maximal simplicity. It defines two type classes, *Applicative* and *Alternative*:

> **class** *Functor f* $\Rightarrow$ *Applicative f* **where**
> $\quad pure :: a \rightarrow f\ a$
> $\quad (\circledast) :: f\ (a \rightarrow b) \rightarrow f\ a \rightarrow f\ b$
> **class** *Applicative f* $\Rightarrow$ *Alternative f* **where**
> $\quad (\diamondsuit) :: f\ a \qquad \rightarrow f\ a \rightarrow f\ a$

(The classes have more methods; only the most important ones are listed here.) The operators $\circledast$ and $\diamondsuit$ correspond to concatenation and choice, respectively. Types of the form $f\ a$ embed computations that, if successful, produce a return value of type a. Type constructors f to be included in the classes are assumed to be functors, whence they are called *applicative functors*. The method *pure*, corresponding to ϵ in (1), takes an operand and creates an empty computation that succeeds with returning the operand. Return values enable a PEG-like Haskell code to also specify parse results which are gradually composed from pieces. For instance, the type of $\circledast$ requires that its first argument computation, if successful, must return a function that can be applied to the potential result of the second one. The combined computation performs the application and returns the obtained result.

Similarly to PEGs, the Applicative-Alternative interface does not support different reactions to different errors. To handle errors smartly, the programmer must use operations outside this interface, like those of the exception monad transformer. Moreover, the interface lacks capabilities of the negation operator.

This paper studies an approach of *double applicative functors* to obtain higher expressivity for error handling within an applicative-style interface. Firstly, we introduce binary *lazy choice* operations to capture the power of the ternary labelled choice of [16]. We prefer binary infix operators to ternary functions to keep usage as familiar as possible. Distinction between errors being or not being handled at particular choice points is made by sum types (*Either e e'* in Haskell). Secondly, we introduce an operation that allows us to reinterpret normal values (i.e., results of successful computations) as errors and vice versa. A counterpart of negation is obtained as a special case. Thirdly, to increase flexibility of manipulating the numerous error types involved, we handle errors within an applicative-style interface similar to that used for normal values. That means, we use bifunctors applicative in both arguments, where different functor arguments stand for error and normal value types. Hence the term *double* (the word *biapplicative* is already used for another generalization of applicative functors [3,12]). A toy version of such interface is presented in Sect. 2.

Applicative functors are assumed to follow four laws [17]. In Sect. 3, we introduce laws for double applicative functors. In addition to carrying the classic laws over to both normal values and errors, we observe natural requirements that arise from coexistence of two applicative layers. We investigate the relationships between the laws imposed on different operators and select a small set of laws that imply all others. In Sect. 4, we prove that the laws are fulfilled by a hierarchy of bifunctors. Section 5 refers to related work and Sect. 6 concludes.

2   A Minimal Interface of Double Applicative Functors

We will use the *Bifunctor* type class provided by the GHC library along with its methods *first*, *second* and *bimap*. The latter method is analogous to the usual functor map function *fmap* but takes two functions as arguments, one for each functor argument. The methods *first* and *second* are special cases of *bimap* that take one argument function each (corresponding to the first resp. second functor argument), the other one is fixed to identity.

We assume the second argument type of the bifunctor to contain normal values and the first argument type to contain error values. This idea is designated by the type classes *Dipointed*, *Catenative* and *Triable*:

> **class** *Bifunctor f* $\Rightarrow$ *Dipointed f* **where**
> $\quad$ *raise* $\ :: e \to f\ e\ a$
> $\quad$ *invoke* :: $a \to f\ e\ a$
> **class** *Dipointed f* $\Rightarrow$ *Catenative f* **where**
> $\quad$ (∗∗∗) $\quad :: f\ e\ (a \to a') \to f\ e\ a \to f\ e\ a'$
> **class** *Dipointed f* $\Rightarrow$ *Triable f* $\qquad$ **where**
> $\quad$ (///) $\quad :: f\ (e \to e')\ a \to f\ e\ a \to f\ e'\ a$

The intended semantics of the operators ∗∗∗ and /// in parsing correspond to that of concatenation and choice in PEGs. The type of /// mimics that of ∗∗∗ with functor arguments interchanged. The method *invoke* of class *Dipointed*, by intention, creates an empty successful computation returning a specified normal value (we did not choose the name *return* as it is in use already). Similarly, *raise* creates an empty failing computation raising a specified error. Both methods of *Dipointed* play the role of the method *pure* of the classic *Applicative* interface; so the left section functors are applicative w.r.t. ∗∗∗ and *invoke*, whereas the right section functors are applicative w.r.t. /// and *raise*. Categorically, *invoke* and *raise* are units of the corresponding section functor each. Functors with units (in any category) are often called *pointed*—hence the name *Dipointed*.

One can implement the optional parse, the repetition and the non-zero repetition combinators in terms of these class methods. Assuming auxiliary infix operators ∗▷ and /▷ to be introduced as synonyms of the *second* and *first* methods of the *Bifunctor* type class, and ⊥ standing for the Haskell variable *undefined* that is used to denote values with no influence, the code looks as follows:

$$opt :: Triable\ f \qquad\qquad \Rightarrow f\ e\ a \to f\ e'\ (Maybe\ a)$$
$$opt\ \ p = raise\ \bot\ /\!/\!/\ Just \mathbin{*\!\!\!>} p\ /\!/\!/\ invoke\ Nothing$$
$$star :: (Catenative\ f, Triable\ f) \Rightarrow f\ e\ a \to f\ e\ [a]$$
$$star\ p = raise\ \bot\ /\!/\!/\ plus\ p\ /\!/\!/\ invoke\ [\,]$$
$$plus :: (Catenative\ f, Triable\ f) \Rightarrow f\ e\ a \to f\ e\ [a]$$
$$plus\ p = invoke\ (:) \mathbin{*\!\!*\!\!*} p \mathbin{*\!\!*\!\!*} star\ p$$

(Assume that product-like operators ($\mathbin{*\!\!*\!\!*}$, $\mathbin{*\!\!\!>}$, &&&) have higher priority than sum-like operators ($/\!/\!/$ and similar). The applicative-style methods ($\mathbin{*\!\!*\!\!*}$, $/\!/\!/$ etc.) associate left.) Unlike in usual definitions of these combinators, one must add *raise* ⊥ for type correctness, as $/\!/\!/$ expects functional return values in the l.h.s.

To embed selective error handling suggested in Sect. 1, we introduce the following class *LazyTriable* with two methods:

class *Triable f* $\Rightarrow$ *LazyTriable f* **where**
$$(\|\|\|) :: f\ (Either\ (e \to e')\ e'')\ a \to f\ (Either\ e\ e'')\ a \to f\ (Either\ e'\ e'')\ a$$
$$({}^{|||}_{|||}) :: f\ (Either\ (e \to e')\ e')\ a \to f\ e\ a \qquad\qquad \to f\ e'\ a$$

The operator $\|\|\|$ takes two computations, both of which can produce errors of two types. If an error of the second type (e'' in the signature) is raised by either argument computation then the whole computation fails and raises the same error. If it happens during the first argument computation then the second one is skipped. In the case of errors of the first type ($e \to e'$ and e in the signature), the operator $\|\|\|$ behaves like $/\!/\!/$. The operator ${}^{|||}_{|||}$ takes two argument computations, only the first of which can produce errors of two types. If an error of type $e \to e'$ is observed then ${}^{|||}_{|||}$ proceeds like $/\!/\!/$, but an error of type e' causes the second computation to be skipped. The semantics of the operators $/\!/\!/$, $\|\|\|$ and ${}^{|||}_{|||}$ differ only by the way they handle errors; if either argument computation being run is successful then they all stop normally and pass the result value.

The positive lookahead operator & of PEGs that runs the computation in its argument but consumes no input is usually desugared as double negation. Using lazy error handling, it can be defined without negation:

$$ignore :: (Catenative\ f, LazyTriable\ f) \Rightarrow f\ e\ a \to f\ e\ ()$$
$$ignore\ p = invoke\ \bot\ \mathbin{*\!\!*\!\!*} (Right\ /\!\!>\ p) \mathbin{*\!\!*\!\!*} raise\ (Left\ \bot)\ {}^{|||}_{|||}\ invoke\ ()$$

(A literal name was chosen to meet the naming rules of Haskell.) Let &&& be an infix operator that tries the first computation and, if successful, ignores it and runs the other one; if either computation fails then the whole computation fails:

$$(\&\&\&) :: (Catenative\ f, LazyTriable\ f) \Rightarrow f\ e\ a \to f\ e'\ b \to f\ (Either\ e\ e')\ b$$
$$p \mathbin{\&\&\&} q = invoke\ (flip\ const) \mathbin{*\!\!*\!\!*} (Left\ /\!\!>\ ignore\ p) \mathbin{*\!\!*\!\!*} (Right\ /\!\!>\ q)$$

The error type of the result remembers the origin of the error (either the left-hand or the right-hand argument). One can elegantly use $\&\&\&$ together with $|||$ to select a branch from among many, according to which parse test succeeds:

$$raise\ (Left\ \bot)\ |||\ test_1\ \&\&\&\ branch_1\ |||\ test_2\ \&\&\&\ branch_2\ |||\ \ldots$$

One can also define a binary branching function *branch* that chooses between its second and third argument computation according to the error raised by the first argument (*either id id* removes *Left* or *Right* tags from around error values):

$$branch :: (Catenative\ f, Lazy Triable\ f) \Rightarrow f\ e\ a \rightarrow (f\ e'\ b, f\ e'\ b) \rightarrow f\ e'\ b$$
$$branch\ p\ (q, r) = either\ id\ id\ /\!\!> (raise\ (Left\ \bot)\ |||\ p\ \&\&\&\ q\ |||\ (Right\ /\!\!> r))$$

More precisely, *branch* p (q, r) parses p and, if successful, also q. If p fails then r is tried as an alternative; if q fails then computation stops with raising the same error. This behaviour is analogous to the $A[B, C]$ construct of gTS/GTDPL [2, 4] (that can also be defined in PEG via negation [7]); the only essential difference is that *branch* cancels any input consumption performed during the test parse.

The following are "conditional" versions of optional parse, repetition and non-zero repetition operations, useful if one needs to distinguish syntax errors from failures arising because of wrong attempts:

$$condOpt :: (Catenative\ f, Lazy Triable\ f) \Rightarrow f\ e\ a \rightarrow f\ e'\ b \rightarrow f\ e'\ (Maybe\ b)$$
$$condOpt\ p\ q = branch\ p\ (Just\ *\!\!> q, invoke\ Nothing)$$
$$condStar :: (Catenative\ f, Lazy Triable\ f) \Rightarrow f\ e\ a \rightarrow f\ e'\ b \rightarrow f\ e'\ [b]$$
$$condStar\ p\ q = branch\ p\ (condPlus\ p\ q, invoke\ [\,])$$
$$condPlus :: (Catenative\ f, Lazy Triable\ f) \Rightarrow f\ e\ a \rightarrow f\ e'\ b \rightarrow f\ e'\ [b]$$
$$condPlus\ p\ q = invoke\ (:)\ *\!\!*\ q\ *\!\!*\ condStar\ p\ q$$

They differ from their unconditional counterparts by terminating conditions. The general idea is to deliver control over how many times the main computation (the second argument) is repeated to another computation (the first argument). An error raised by the first computation signals that the job of the whole computation is done and it must stop normally, while errors raised by the second argument computation mean unexpected events and have to be passed through.

For example, code like *condOpt* (*consumeIf isWhere*) *parseLocalDecl* (assuming that *consumeIf*, *isWhere* and *parseLocalDecl* have meanings suggested by the names) may parse a local declaration block of Haskell code after having confirmed that the next token is a **where** keyword. If no **where** keyword is recognized then parsing succeeds and consumes no input (a local declaration block is not expected) but if a **where** keyword exists and *parseLocalDecl* fails then the error raised passes through (a local declaration is expected but incorrect). Similarly, *condStar* (*consumeIf* (*not ∘ isCloseParen*)) *parseUnit* parses the list of tokens between two matching parentheses (if *parseUnit* parses either one token or a whole parenthesized block). Reaching a closing parenthesis causes parsing to stop normally while an error raised by *parseUnit* passes through.

The labelled choice operator of the extended PEG of Maidl et al. [16] can also be defined via lazy error handling as

$$lchoice :: (LazyTriable\ f) \Rightarrow (e \to Bool) \to f\ e\ a \to f\ e\ a \to f\ e\ a$$
$$lchoice\ p\ x\ y = bimap\ (\lambda e \to \textbf{if}\ p\ e\ \textbf{then}\ Left\ id\ \textbf{else}\ Right\ e)\ id\ x\ \substack{|||\\|||}\ y$$

The negation operator of PEG is expressible as follows:

$$negation :: (Catenative\ f, LazyTriable\ f) \Rightarrow f\ e\ a \to f\ ()\ ()$$
$$negation\ p = branch\ p\ (raise\ (), invoke\ ())$$

It tries the argument computation and inverts the success/failure status but forgets about result values and consumed input. Yet the result of the negated computation could be useful for producing informative error messages. The framework introduced so far has no means of remembering results of successful parsing within a failing one and vice versa. To fix this, define the following class *Mixable*:

$$\textbf{class}\ (Dipointed\ f) \Rightarrow Mixable\ f\ \textbf{where}$$
$$mixmap :: (Either\ e\ a \to Either\ e'\ a') \to f\ e\ a \to f\ e'\ a'$$

The expected semantics of the method *mixmap* is to apply a function (the first argument) to the result of a computation (the second argument). Thereby, errors and normal values are wrapped with the *Left* and *Right* tag, respectively. So a successful computation can be reinterpreted as a failure and vice versa; still whenever the final outcome is a failure, any consumption of input during the computation is cancelled. Using *mixmap*, one can define a pithier negation by

$$negation :: (Mixable\ f) \Rightarrow f\ e\ a \to f\ a\ e$$
$$negation = mixmap\ (either\ Right\ Left)$$

(The function *either Right Left* replaces *Left* tag with *Right* tag and vice versa.)

We will see in Subsect. 3.3 that each of the operations ||| and $\substack{|||\\|||}$ can be defined in terms of the other. Moreover, /// is expressible in terms of either of these two operations, and both these operations are expressible via /// and *mixmap*.

3   Laws

In the rest, we shall use the standard notation of category theory instead of Haskell function names. So, an application of a bifunctor F to functions h and f will be denoted by $F(h, f)$ rather than *bimap h f*. Thereby $+$ and $\times$ denote the binary sum and product functors, respectively. Injections *Left* and *Right* are denoted by inl and inr, respectively, and $h \triangledown f$ for arbitrary functions $h : E \to X$ and $f : A \to X$ means the same as *either h f* in Haskell, i.e., the unique strict function of type $E+A \to X$ that satisfies both $(h \triangledown f) \circ \text{inl} = h$ and $(h \triangledown f) \circ \text{inr} = f$. The composition operator $\circ$ is assigned a higher priority than other operators.

The only aims of using the notation of category theory are making formulae shorter and improving readability. Similarly, we denote the units of a pointed functor by η and mixmap by ϕ, as well as use the shorter $\circledast$, $/$, $|$ and $\wr$ for the operations ⁂, ///, ||| and ⦙⦙. As usual, we ignore partiality issues (a "moral" justification for this is given by Danielsson et al. [6]). In brief, we are working in the category **Set** in general, but will occasionally exclude the empty set.

3.1 Pointed Bifunctors

The library presented in Sect. 2 suggests that pointed bifunctors F have two units, raise : $E \to F(E, A)$ and invoke : $A \to F(E, A)$. In mathematics, it is often easier to work equivalently with a joint unit $\eta : E + A \to F(E, A)$; then raise = $\eta \circ \text{inl}$ and invoke = $\eta \circ \text{inr}$. The only law of pointed functors is naturality:

$$F(h, f) \circ \eta \;=\; \eta \circ (h + f) \qquad\qquad \text{(Unit-Nat)}$$

3.2 The *Mixable* Operations

We choose the letter ϕ to denote mixmap because of its functor-like nature. So $\phi : (E + A \to E' + A') \to (F(E, A) \to F(E', A'))$. Functoriality would mean preservation of identities and composition. To make mixmap applications a generalization of functor applications, we also require preservation of functor:

$$\phi(h + f) \;=\; F(h, f) \qquad\qquad \text{(Mixmap-Fun)}$$

This means that mixmap applications that keep errors as errors and normal values as normal values are equivalent to usual functor applications.

Alas, mixmaps of parsers do not always preserve composition. Indeed, consider $g : E + A \to E' + A'$ and $g' : E' + A' \to E'' + A''$ such that $g(\text{inr}\,a) = \text{inl}\,e$ and $g'(\text{inl}\,e) = \text{inr}\,a'$ for some a, a' and e. If g and g' are separately lifted to the parser level then the input consumption during a computation that returns a is forgotten by $\phi(g)$ since it creates an intermediate failing computation. If the composition $g' \circ g$ is lifted to the parser level as a whole then no failure occurs in the same circumstances, whence the input consumption remains in force.

We can trace all scenarios that sequential applications of ϕ might cause on the functor $E \ddagger A = (E + A) + A$. Normal values whose history contains at least one reinterpretation as failure should be kept separately in the extra A on the left, while other normal values should stay on the right. The idea is realized by defining sep : $(E + A \to E' + A') \to (E \ddagger A \to E' \ddagger A')$ by sep $g = \text{inl} \circ g \bigtriangledown (\text{inl} + \text{id}) \circ g \circ \text{inr}$. A desired law would now state that $\phi(g_m) \circ \ldots \circ \phi(g_1) = \phi(g'_n) \circ \ldots \circ \phi(g'_1)$ whenever sep $g_m \circ \ldots \circ$ sep $g_1 = $ sep $g'_n \circ \ldots \circ$ sep g'_1.

To find an equivalent law in equational form, note that all compositions of the form sep $g_l \circ \ldots \circ$ sep g_1 can be equivalently rewritten as sep $g'_2 \circ$ sep g'_1 where $g'_1 = (\text{inl} \bigtriangledown \text{id}) \circ (g_l \circ \ldots \circ g_1 \circ \text{inl} + \text{sep} g_l \circ \ldots \circ \text{sep} g_1 \circ \text{inr})$ and $g'_2 = \text{id} \bigtriangledown \text{inr}$. Thus sequential applications of ϕ should also be reducible to two applications. Along with naturality of the unit w.r.t. ϕ and preservation of the identity, we get the following axiom set (to

obtain MIXMAP-COMP from above, use MIXMAP-FUN and the rewrite
$\text{sep}\,g_1' = \text{sep}(\text{inl}\,\triangledown\,\text{id}) \circ \text{sep}(g_l \circ \ldots \circ g_1 \circ \text{inl} + \text{sep}g_l \circ \ldots \circ \text{sep}g_1 \circ \text{inr}))$:

$$\phi(g) \circ \eta \;=\; \eta \circ g \qquad\qquad\qquad\qquad (\text{MIXMAP-UNITNAT})$$

$$\phi(\text{id}) \;=\; \text{id} \qquad\qquad\qquad\qquad\qquad (\text{MIXMAP-ID})$$

$$\phi(g'') \circ \phi(g') \circ \phi(g) \;=\; \phi(\text{id}\,\triangledown\,\text{inr}) \circ \phi(\text{inl}\,\triangledown\,\text{id}) \circ F\,(h, f) \qquad (\text{MIXMAP-COMP})$$
$$\text{where } h = g'' \circ g' \circ g \circ \text{inl},\, f = \text{sep}\,g'' \circ \text{sep}\,g' \circ \text{sep}\,g \circ \text{inr}$$

Indeed these axioms imply all laws desired. Taking $g'' = g' = g = \text{id}$ in MIXMAP-COMP and applying MIXMAP-ID gives $\phi(\text{id}\,\triangledown\,\text{inr}) \circ \phi(\text{inl}\,\triangledown\,\text{id}) \circ F(\text{inl}, \text{inr}) = \text{id}$. Substituting $g'' = g' = \text{id}$ and $g = h + f$ to MIXMAP-COMP now gives MIXMAP -FUN. Furthermore, MIXMAP-COMP can be generalized from 3 to l operands by induction. The initially desired implication of $\phi(g_m) \circ \ldots \circ \phi(g_1) = \phi(g_n')$ $\circ \ldots \circ \phi(g_1')$ by $\text{sep}\,g_m \circ \ldots \circ \text{sep}\,g_1 = \text{sep}\,g_n' \circ \ldots \circ \text{sep}\,g_1'$ then follows directly. In addition, UNIT-NAT is implied by MIXMAP-FUN and MIXMAP-UNITNAT.

As a corollary of the axioms, it follows that $\phi(g') \circ \phi(g) = \phi(g' \circ g)$ whenever either $g = g'' \,\triangledown\, \text{inr} \circ f$ or $g' = \text{inl} \circ h \,\triangledown\, g''$, and in particular if either g or g' is of the form $h + f$. In formulae,

$$\phi(g') \circ \phi(g \,\triangledown\, \text{inr} \circ f) \;=\; \phi(g' \circ (g \,\triangledown\, \text{inr} \circ f)) \qquad (\text{MIXMAP-COMP-RPRES})$$

$$\phi(\text{inl} \circ h \,\triangledown\, g') \circ \phi(g) \;=\; \phi((\text{inl} \circ h \,\triangledown\, g') \circ g) \qquad (\text{MIXMAP-COMP-LPRES})$$

Another corollary is that $\phi(g') \circ \phi(g)$ is equivalent to $\phi(g' \circ g)$ if they are composed with the negation $\phi(\text{inr}\,\triangledown\,\text{inl})$ from either the right or the left. As negation loses all information about input consumption, the other applications of ϕ can cause no extra harm. In particular, triple negation is equivalent to single negation.

Denote negation like in PEGs by !; besides negation, four other cases of ϕ turn out to be particularly useful. So we have the following definitions, where swap = $\text{inr}\,\triangledown\,\text{inl}$, assocr = $(\text{id} + \text{inl})\,\triangledown\,\text{inr} \circ \text{inr}$ and assocl = $\text{inl} \circ \text{inl}\,\triangledown\,(\text{inr} + \text{id})$:

!	=	$\phi(\text{swap})$	: $F(E, A) \to F(A, E)$	(NEG-MIXMAP)
turnr	=	$\phi(\text{assocr})$	: $F(E + E', A) \to F(E, E' + A)$	(TURNR-MIXMAP)
turnl	=	$\phi(\text{assocl})$	: $F(E, E' + A) \to F(E + E', A)$	(TURNL-MIXMAP)
fuser	=	$\phi(\text{id}\,\triangledown\,\text{inr})$	: $F(E + A, A) \to F(E, A)$	(FUSER-MIXMAP)
fusel	=	$\phi(\text{inl}\,\triangledown\,\text{id})$	: $F(E, E + A) \to F(E, A)$	(FUSEL-MIXMAP)

Conversely, ϕ can be defined via fuser and fusel (an analogous definition via turnr and turnl is possible but not needed in this work):

$$\phi(g) \;=\; \text{fusel} \circ \text{fuser} \circ F\,(\text{inr} \circ g \circ \text{inl}, g \circ \text{inr}) \qquad (\text{MIXMAP-FUSELR})$$

Functions fuser and fusel defined via ϕ satisfy the following:

$$
\begin{array}{llll}
F(h, f) \circ \mathsf{fuser} & = & \mathsf{fuser} \circ F(h + f, f) & (\textsc{FuseR-Nat}) \\
F(h, f) \circ \mathsf{fusel} & = & \mathsf{fusel} \circ F(h, h + f) & (\textsc{FuseL-Nat}) \\
\mathsf{fusel} \circ \mathsf{fuser} \circ F(\mathsf{inr} \circ \mathsf{inl}, \mathsf{inr}) & = & \mathsf{id} & (\textsc{FuseLR-Id}) \\
\mathsf{fuser} \circ \mathsf{fuser} & = & \mathsf{fuser} \circ F(\mathsf{id} \triangledown \mathsf{inr}, \mathsf{id}) & (\textsc{FuseR-FuseR}) \\
\mathsf{fusel} \circ \mathsf{fusel} & = & \mathsf{fusel} \circ F(\mathsf{id}, \mathsf{inl} \triangledown \mathsf{id}) & (\textsc{FuseL-FuseL})
\end{array}
$$

One can show that these five laws imply $\mathsf{fusel} \circ \mathsf{fuser} \circ F(\mathsf{inr}, \mathsf{inr}) = \mathsf{fuser}$ and $\mathsf{fusel} \circ \mathsf{fuser} \circ F(\mathsf{inr} \circ \mathsf{inl}, \mathsf{id}) = \mathsf{fusel}$. By substituting $g = \mathsf{id} \triangledown \mathsf{inr}$ and $g = \mathsf{inl} \triangledown \mathsf{id}$ into Mixmap-FuseLR one thus regains the defining equations FuseR-Mixmap and FuseL-Mixmap, respectively. This means that if ϕ is given by Mixmap-FuseLR in terms of any operations fuser and fusel that meet the five laws then the operations fuser and fusel must have been the "correct" ones. Moreover, the equations FuseR-Mixmap, FuseL-Mixmap and Mixmap-FuseLR establish a one-to-one correspondence between pairs (fuser, fusel) satisfying FuseR-Nat, FuseL-Nat, FuseLR-Id, FuseR-FuseR, FuseL-FuseL and operations ϕ that satisfy Mixmap-Fun, Mixmap-Comp-RPres, Mixmap-Comp-LPres.

3.3 The *Catenative*, *Triable* and *LazyTriable* Class Operations

When McBride and Paterson introduced four axioms of applicative functors in their classical paper [17], the aim was to specify the necessary properties without referring to the functor or relying on functor laws. The functor (as it works on morphisms) was defined in terms of the applicative operation and unit. Instead, we assume a pointed bifunctor F being given and rely on it.

We consider seven laws about $\circledast : F(E, A \to A') \times F(E, A) \to F(E, A')$:

$$
\begin{array}{llll}
\eta(\mathsf{inr}\, f) \circledast u & = & F(\mathsf{id}, f)\, u & (\textsc{Cat-LUnit}) \\
t \circledast \eta(\mathsf{inr}\, a) & = & F(\mathsf{id}, \mathsf{T}\, a)\, t & (\textsc{Cat-RUnit}) \\
t \circledast (u \circledast v) & = & F(\mathsf{id}, \mathsf{B})\, t \circledast u \circledast v & (\textsc{Cat-Assoc}) \\
\eta(\mathsf{inl}\, e) \circledast u & = & \eta(\mathsf{inl}\, e) & (\textsc{Cat-LZero}) \\
t \circledast \eta(\mathsf{inl}\, e) & = & F(\mathsf{id} \triangledown \mathsf{K}\, e, \mathsf{id})\, (\phi(\mathsf{inl})\, t) & (\textsc{Cat-Raise}) \\
F(h, \mathsf{id})\, (t \circledast u) & = & F(h, \mathsf{id})\, t \circledast F(h, \mathsf{id})\, u & (\textsc{Cat-FunHom}) \\
!!(!t \circledast u) & = & !t \circledast !!u & (\textsc{Cat-DblNegHom})
\end{array}
$$

Here and below, T, B and K are the postfix application, function composition and constant function combinators, respectively, known from the lambda calculus, i.e., $\mathsf{T} = \lambda x f \,.\, f\, x$, $\mathsf{B} = \lambda g f x \,.\, g\, (f\, x)$ and $\mathsf{K} = \lambda x y \,.\, x$. Hence B and $\circ$ mean the same but their usages differ (prefix vs infix).

Given the pointed functor F and its laws, Cat-LUnit, Cat-RUnit and Cat-Assoc together are equivalent to the four classic axioms of [17] along with the additional assumption that the functor defined in terms of $\circledast$ and the unit coincides with F. The law Cat-LZero is analogous to the left zero law standardly assumed about monads with zero. The law CAT-RAISE tells that $t \circledast \eta(\text{inl } e)$ always raises an error after running t, whereby normal result values are replaced by e. The homomorphism law CAT-FUNHOM states that mapping of an error raised by $t \circledast u$ is equivalent to mapping the error at any stage it occurs. The law CAT-DBLNEGHOM generalizes a corresponding PEG semantic equivalence.

Using CAT-LUNIT, CAT-RUNIT and CAT-ASSOC, expressions built up from $\circledast$, η and functor mappings of normal values can be equivalently rewritten in a canonical form consisting of a sequence of operations $\circledast$ with parentheses from the left and a single functor mapping around the leftmost operand. An analogous fact is well known about classic applicative functors; Hinze [10] describes a linear time algorithm for this. The rewrite sequence can be straightened using two auxiliary laws $F(\text{id}, f)(t \circledast u) = F(\text{id}, \mathsf{B}\, f)\, t \circledast u$ and $t \circledast F(\text{id}, f)\, u = F(\text{id}, \mathsf{B}(\mathsf{T}\, f)\, \mathsf{B})\, t \circledast u$. We will call these and similar facts *straightening laws*. They are easily derivable from CAT-LUNIT, CAT-RUNIT and CAT-ASSOC.

The left zero law can be extended to $\phi(\text{inl})\, t \circledast u = \phi(\text{inl})\, t$. It can be proven using CAT-LZERO, CAT-RAISE and CAT-ASSOC under the assumption that types are non-empty (both sides are equal to $\phi(\text{inl})\, t \circledast (\eta(\text{inl } e) \circledast u)$).

We consider also seven laws about $/ : F(E \to E', A) \times F(E, A) \to F(E', A)$, among which all but the seventh are obtained from the corresponding laws of $\circledast$ by swapping the arguments of the bifunctor F:

$\eta(\text{inl } h) / u$	$=$	$F(h, \text{id})\, u$	(TRI-LUNIT)
$t / \eta(\text{inl } e)$	$=$	$F(\mathsf{T}\, e, \text{id})\, t$	(TRI-RUNIT)
$t / (u / v)$	$=$	$F(\mathsf{B}, \text{id})\, t / u / v$	(TRI-ASSOC)
$\eta(\text{inr } a) / u$	$=$	$\eta(\text{inr } a)$	(TRI-LZERO)
$t / \eta(\text{inr}a)$	$=$	$F(\text{id}, \mathsf{K}\, a \triangledown \text{id})\, (\phi(\text{inr})\, t)$	(TRI-INVOKE)
$F(\text{id}, f)(t / u)$	$=$	$F(\text{id}, f)\, t / F(\text{id}, f)\, u$	(TRI-FUNHOM)
$\text{turnr}(\text{turnl}(t / u))$	$=$	$\text{turnr}(\text{turnl}\, t) / \text{turnr}(\text{turnl}\, u)$	(TRI-TURNRLHOM)

The composition $\text{turnr} \circ \text{turnl}$ forgets consumed input if the computation succeeds with a result having tag inl but otherwise works as identity. Intuitively, TRI-TURNRLHOM holds since the partition of normal values into those causing cancellation of input consumption and the others is not affected by execution of the operation $/$ (the same is not true for $\circledast$). The situation is more general than in the case of double negation that always forgets consumed input. Indeed, $!!(t / u) = !!t / !!u$ can be deduced from TRI-FUNHOM and TRI-TURNRLHOM since $! \circ ! = F(\text{id}, \text{id} \triangledown \text{id}) \circ \text{turnr} \circ \text{turnl} \circ F(\text{id}, \text{inl})$ by mixmap laws.

The axioms imply straightening laws $F(h, \text{id})(t / u) = F(\mathsf{B}\, h, \text{id})\, t / u$ and $t / F(h, \text{id})\, u = F(\mathsf{B}(\mathsf{T}\, h)\, \mathsf{B}, \text{id})\, t / u$ and, for non-empty types, the left zero extension law $\phi(\text{inr})\, t / u = \phi(\text{inr})\, t$. The proofs are symmetric to the case of $\circledast$.

The operations $| : F((E \to E') + E'', A) \times F(E + E'', A) \to F(E' + E'', A)$ and $\wr : F((E \to E') + E', A) \times F(E, A) \to F(E', A)$ are discussed next. In the law names, we distinguish them by letters W and S (from *weak* and *strong*); this is suggested by the stronger associativity property of the second operation.

The ten laws for $|$ are presented in lines with those considered for $\circledast$ and $/$. Recall from Sect. 2 that the operation $|$ behaves with "errors of the second kind", i.e., those of type E'', differently from "ordinary errors", as errors of type E'' must remain uncaught by the operation $|$. The reader may notice that the behaviour on errors of type E'' mimics that on normal values:

$$\eta(\text{inl}(\text{inl}\,h)) \mid u \quad = \quad F\,(h + \text{id}, \text{id})\,u \qquad\qquad\qquad (\text{WTri-LUnit})$$

$$t \mid \eta(\text{inl}(\text{inl}\,e)) \quad = \quad F\,(\mathsf{T}\,e + \text{id}, \text{id})\,t \qquad\qquad\qquad (\text{WTri-RUnit})$$

$$t \mid (u \mid v) \quad = \quad F\,(\mathsf{B} + \text{id}, \text{id})\,t \mid u \mid v \qquad\qquad\quad (\text{WTri-Assoc})$$

$$\eta(\text{inr}\,a) \mid u \quad = \quad \eta(\text{inr}\,a) \qquad\qquad\qquad\qquad (\text{WTri-LZero-R})$$

$$\eta(\text{inl}(\text{inr}\,e)) \mid u \quad = \quad \eta(\text{inl}(\text{inr}\,e)) \qquad\qquad\qquad (\text{WTri-LZero-L})$$

$$t \mid \eta(\text{inr}\,a) \quad = \quad \phi((\mathsf{K}\,(\text{inr}\,a) \,\triangledown\, \mathsf{B}\,\text{inl}\,\text{inr}) \,\triangledown\, \text{inr})\,t \quad (\text{WTri-Invoke})$$

$$t \mid \eta(\text{inl}(\text{inr}\,e)) \quad = \quad F\,(\mathsf{B}\,\text{inr}\,(\mathsf{K}\,e \,\triangledown\, \text{id}), \text{id})\,t \qquad (\text{WTri-Raise})$$

$$F\,(\text{id}, f)\,(t \mid u) \quad = \quad F\,(\text{id}, f)\,t \mid F\,(\text{id}, f)\,u \qquad\quad (\text{WTri-FunHom-R})$$

$$F\,(\text{id} + f, \text{id})\,(t \mid u) \quad = \quad F\,(\text{id} + f, \text{id})\,t \mid F\,(\text{id} + f, \text{id})\,u \quad (\text{WTri-FunHom-L})$$

$$\mathsf{turnr}(\mathsf{turnl}(t \mid u)) \quad = \quad \mathsf{turnr}(\mathsf{turnl}\,t) \mid \mathsf{turnr}(\mathsf{turnl}\,u) \;(\text{WTri-TurnRLHom})$$

The axioms imply straightening laws $F\,(h + \text{id}, \text{id})\,(t \mid u) = F\,(\mathsf{B}\,h + \text{id}, \text{id})\,t \mid u$ and $t \mid F\,(h + \text{id}, \text{id})\,u = F\,(\mathsf{B}\,(\mathsf{T}\,h)\,\mathsf{B} + \text{id}, \text{id})\,t \mid u$, and also two extended left zero laws, $\phi(\text{inr})\,t \mid u = \phi(\text{inr})\,t$ and $F\,(\text{inr}, \text{id})\,t \mid u = F\,(\text{inr}, \text{id})\,t$, for non-empty types. Finally, we consider the following eight laws about $\wr$:

$$\eta(\text{inl}(\text{inl}\,h)) \wr u \quad = \quad F\,(h, \text{id})\,u \qquad\qquad\qquad (\text{STri-LUnit})$$

$$t \wr \eta(\text{inl}\,e) \quad = \quad F\,(\mathsf{T}\,e \,\triangledown\, \text{id}, \text{id})\,t \qquad\qquad (\text{STri-RUnit})$$

$$t \wr (u \wr v) \quad = \quad F\,((\lambda h\,.\,\mathsf{B}\,h + h) + \text{inr}, \text{id})\,t \wr u \wr v \quad (\text{STri-Assoc})$$

$$\eta(\text{inr}\,a) \wr u \quad = \quad \eta(\text{inr}\,a) \qquad\qquad\qquad\qquad (\text{STri-LZero-R})$$

$$\eta(\text{inl}(\text{inr}\,e)) \wr u \quad = \quad \eta(\text{inl}\,e) \qquad\qquad\qquad\quad (\text{STri-LZero-L})$$

$$t \wr \eta(\text{inr}a) \quad = \quad \phi((\mathsf{K}\,(\text{inr}\,a) \,\triangledown\, \text{inl}) \,\triangledown\, \text{inr})\,t \quad (\text{STri-Invoke})$$

$$F\,(\text{id}, f)\,(t \wr u) \quad = \quad F\,(\text{id}, f)\,t \wr F\,(\text{id}, f)\,u \qquad\quad (\text{STri-FunHom})$$

$$\mathsf{turnr}(\mathsf{turnl}(t \wr u)) \quad = \quad \mathsf{turnr}(\mathsf{turnl}\,t) \wr \mathsf{turnr}(\mathsf{turnl}\,u) \quad (\text{STri-TurnRLHom})$$

The associativity law looks complicated in comparison to the analogous laws imposed on the previous operations. The sophistication arises from the number of possible error types in the first operand being different from that in the second operand and in the result of the operation, whence rearranging of parentheses must conform to the changed number of error types.

Like for operations $\circledast$ and $/$, the laws STri-LUnit, STri-RUnit and STri-Assoc enable transforming expressions built up from $\wr$, η and functor mappings of errors to equivalent canonical forms with parentheses from the left and the only functor mapping applying to the first operand. Two straightening laws deducible are $F\,(h, \text{id})\,(t \wr u) = F\,(\mathsf{B}\,h + h, \text{id})\,t \wr u$ and $t \wr F\,(h, \text{id})\,u = F\,(\mathsf{B}\,(\mathsf{T}\,h)\,\mathsf{B} + \text{id}, \text{id})\,t \wr u$. Two extended left zero laws for $\wr$ are $\phi(\text{inr})\,t \wr u = \phi(\text{inr})\,t$ and $F\,(\text{inr}, \text{id})\,t \wr u = t$.

Each of the operations $/$, $|$ and $\wr$ is able to express the others:

$$t \mathbin{/} u \;=\; F\,(\mathrm{id}\;\triangledown\;\mathrm{id},\mathrm{id})\,(F\,(\mathrm{inl},\mathrm{id})\,t \mid F\,(\mathrm{inl},\mathrm{id})\,u) \qquad\qquad (\textsc{Tri-WTri})$$

$$t \mid u \;=\; \mathrm{turnl}(\mathrm{turnr}\,t \mathbin{/} \mathrm{turnr}\,u) \qquad\qquad (\textsc{WTri-Tri})$$

$$t \mid u \;=\; F\,((\lambda h\mathbin{.}h + \mathrm{id}) + \mathrm{inr},\mathrm{id})\,t \wr u \qquad\qquad (\textsc{WTri-STri})$$

$$t \wr u \;=\; F\,(\mathrm{id}\;\triangledown\;\mathrm{id},\mathrm{id})\,(t \mid F\,(\mathrm{inl},\mathrm{id})\,u) \qquad\qquad (\textsc{STri-WTri})$$

$$t \mathbin{/} u \;=\; F(\mathrm{inl},\mathrm{id})\,t \wr u \qquad\qquad (\textsc{Tri-STri})$$

$$t \wr u \;=\; \mathrm{fusel}\,(\mathrm{turnr}\,t \mathbin{/} F\,(\mathrm{id},\mathrm{inr})\,u) \qquad\qquad (\textsc{STri-Tri})$$

Thereby, STri-Tri follows directly from STri-WTri and WTri-Tri, while Tri-STri follows directly from Tri-WTri and STri-WTri. In addition, assume $\circledast$ and $/$ being related by two De Morgan laws:

$$!(t \mathbin{/} u) \;=\; !t \circledast !u \qquad\qquad (\textsc{Tri-Cat-DeM})$$

$$!(!t \circledast u) \;=\; !!t \mathbin{/} !u \qquad\qquad (\textsc{Cat-Tri-DeM})$$

Note that the double negation law Cat-DblNegHom can be obtained as an easy corollary of De Morgan laws. Two homomorphisms between structures with operations $/$ and $|$ related by WTri-Tri follow from Tri-FunHom and Tri-TurnRLHom, respectively:

$$F\,(\mathrm{inl},\mathrm{id})\,(t \mathbin{/} u) \;=\; F\,(\mathrm{inl},\mathrm{id})\,t \mid F\,(\mathrm{inl},\mathrm{id})\,u \qquad\qquad (\textsc{FunInL-Hom})$$

$$\mathrm{turnr}(t \mid u) \;=\; \mathrm{turnr}\,t \mathbin{/} \mathrm{turnr}\,u \qquad\qquad (\textsc{TurnR-Hom})$$

Furthermore, WTri-Tri together with FunInL-Hom implies Tri-WTri, while WTri-STri together with the straightening laws of $\wr$ implies STri-WTri. Thus if $|$ is given in terms of either $/$ or $\wr$ then the original operation must have been the one that the obtained operation $|$ determines. The converses (i.e., if one starts from $|$ and defines a new $|$ via either $/$ or $\wr$ then the original operation is obtained) must be postulated if necessary.

The seven laws of $/$ guarantee that $|$ defined via WTri-Tri meets its ten laws. The proofs are mostly straightforward. For establishing WTri-TurnRLHom, first prove $\mathrm{turnr}\circ\mathrm{turnl}\circ\mathrm{turnl} = \mathrm{turnl}\circ F\,(\mathrm{id},\mathrm{swap}')\circ\mathrm{turnr}\circ\mathrm{turnl}\circ F\,(\mathrm{id},\mathrm{swap}')$ and $\mathrm{turnr}\circ\mathrm{turnr}\circ\mathrm{turnl} = F\,(\mathrm{id},\mathrm{swap}')\circ\mathrm{turnr}\circ\mathrm{turnl}\circ F\,(\mathrm{id},\mathrm{swap}')\circ\mathrm{turnr}$ where $\mathrm{swap}' = \mathrm{assocr}\circ(\mathrm{swap}+\mathrm{id})\circ\mathrm{assocl}$ using mixmap laws. Similarly, the eight laws of $\wr$ guarantee that $|$ defined by WTri-STri satisfies its ten laws.

Conversely, if $/$ and $\wr$ are defined by Tri-WTri and STri-WTri via $|$ that meets the ten laws then one can establish all laws of $/$ and $\wr$ except associativities. However, the law Tri-Assoc can be proven if $|$ is given by WTri-STri via $\wr$ that satisfies at least the straightenings. We have not found any criteria succinctly expressible in terms of $|$ for establishing STri-Assoc.

The following theorem establishes a subset (presumably minimal) of laws considered in this subsection that imply all others. We included laws of the operation $/$ as far as they imply those of the other operations since they are probably easier to prove in practice. Associativity must be assumed for the operation $\wr$. The unit laws of $\wr$ are necessary for having straightenings that are liable for the correct correspondence between $\wr$ and $|$.

Theorem 1. *Let F be a pointed functor. Let ϕ satisfy* MIXMAP-UNITNAT, MIXMAP-ID *and* MIXMAP-COMP *and let* !, turnr, turnl *and* fusel *be given by* NEG-MIXMAP, TURNR-MIXMAP, TURNL-MIXMAP *and* FUSEL-MIXMAP. *Let the operations* ⊛, $/$, $|$ *and* $\wr$ *satisfy* CAT-LUNIT, CAT-RUNIT, CAT-ASSOC, CAT-LZERO, CAT-RAISE, CAT-FUNHOM, TRI-LZERO, TRI-INVOKE, TRI-FUNHOM, TRI-TURNRLHOM, TRI-CAT-DEM, CAT-TRI-DEM, STRI-LUNIT, STRI-RUNIT, STRI-ASSOC, WTRI-TRI *and* WTRI-STRI. *Then* ⊛, $/$, $|$ *and* $\wr$ *satisfy all laws mentioned above in this subsection.* □

3.4 Double Applicative Functors vs Monads

The Applicative class methods can be expressed via those of Monad [17]. Similar relationships between double applicative functors and bifunctors that are monads in both arguments are useful as in the bifunctor hierarchy in Sect. 4, defining ⊛ and proving its laws via the monad level is for some instances the easiest choice.

So let F be a pointed bifunctor along with bind and catch operations, denoted by $(\cdot)^{\vee}$ and $(\cdot)^{\wedge}$, of types $(\cdot)^{\vee} : (A \to F(E, A')) \to (F(E, A) \to F(E, A'))$ and $(\cdot)^{\wedge} : (E \to F(E', A)) \to (F(E, A) \to F(E', A))$ (characters $^{\vee}$ and $^{\wedge}$ were chosen because they resemble two opposite "half-stars"). Define ⊛ and $\wr$ by

$$t ⊛ u = (\lambda f \cdot F(\mathrm{id}, f)\, u)^{\vee}\, t \qquad\qquad \text{(CAT-BND)}$$

$$t \wr u = ((\lambda h \cdot F(h, \mathrm{id})\, u) \triangledown \eta \circ \mathrm{inl})^{\wedge}\, t \qquad\qquad \text{(STRI-CCH)}$$

Defining operations $/$ and $|$ similarly via $(\cdot)^{\wedge}$ is straightforward. What should be the laws of $^{\vee}$ and $^{\wedge}$ that would imply all laws of ⊛, $/$, $|$ and $\wr$ above? In the lines of Subsect. 3.3, we could choose the seven axioms below for $(\cdot)^{\vee}$:

$$k^{\vee} \circ \eta \circ \mathrm{inr} = k \qquad\qquad \text{(BND-LUNIT)}$$

$$(\eta \circ \mathrm{inr} \circ f)^{\vee} = F(\mathrm{id}, f) \qquad\qquad \text{(BND-RUNIT)}$$

$$l^{\vee} \circ k^{\vee} = (l^{\vee} \circ k)^{\vee} \qquad\qquad \text{(BND-ASSOC)}$$

$$k^{\vee} \circ \eta \circ \mathrm{inl} = \eta \circ \mathrm{inl} \qquad\qquad \text{(BND-LZERO)}$$

$$(\eta \circ \mathrm{inl} \circ f)^{\vee} = F(\mathrm{id} \triangledown f, \mathrm{id}) \circ \phi(\mathrm{inl}) \qquad\qquad \text{(BND-RAISE)}$$

$$F(h, \mathrm{id}) \circ k^{\vee} = (F(h, \mathrm{id}) \circ k)^{\vee} \circ F(h, \mathrm{id}) \qquad\qquad \text{(BND-FUNHOM)}$$

$$!\circ!\circ k^{\vee} \circ\, ! = (!\circ!\circ k)^{\vee} \circ\, ! \qquad\qquad \text{(BND-DBLNEGHOM)}$$

The first three of them state that $(\cdot)^{\vee}$ and $\eta \circ \mathsf{inr}$ together make functors of the form $F(E, \_)$ monads. Similarly for $(\cdot)^{\wedge}$ we would obtain:

$$h^{\wedge} \circ \eta \circ \mathsf{inl} \qquad = \quad h \qquad\qquad\qquad\qquad\qquad\qquad\qquad\qquad \text{(Cch-LUnit)}$$

$$(\eta \circ \mathsf{inl} \circ h)^{\wedge} \qquad = \quad F\,(h, \mathsf{id}) \qquad\qquad\qquad\qquad\qquad\qquad\qquad \text{(Cch-RUnit)}$$

$$g^{\wedge} \circ h^{\wedge} \qquad = \quad (g^{\wedge} \circ h)^{\wedge} \qquad\qquad\qquad\qquad\qquad\qquad\qquad \text{(Cch-Assoc)}$$

$$h^{\wedge} \circ \eta \circ \mathsf{inr} \qquad = \quad \eta \circ \mathsf{inr} \qquad\qquad\qquad\qquad\qquad\qquad\qquad \text{(Cch-LZero)}$$

$$(\eta \circ \mathsf{inr} \circ h)^{\wedge} \qquad = \quad F\,(\mathsf{id}, h \bigtriangledown \mathsf{id}) \circ \phi(\mathsf{inr}) \qquad\qquad\qquad\qquad \text{(Cch-Invoke)}$$

$$F\,(\mathsf{id}, f) \circ h^{\wedge} \qquad = \quad (F\,(\mathsf{id}, f) \circ h)^{\wedge} \circ F\,(\mathsf{id}, f) \qquad\qquad\qquad \text{(Cch-FunHom)}$$

$$\mathsf{turnr} \circ \mathsf{turnl} \circ h^{\wedge} \quad = \quad (\mathsf{turnr} \circ \mathsf{turnl} \circ h)^{\wedge} \circ \mathsf{turnr} \circ \mathsf{turnl} \, \text{(Cch-TurnRLHom)}$$

The first three axioms establish the monad laws for functors of the form $F(\_, A)$.

Similarly to the straightening laws of lower-level operations, one can deduce for $(\cdot)^{\vee}$ laws $F(\mathsf{id}, f) \circ k^{\vee} = (F(\mathsf{id}, f) \circ k)^{\vee}$ and $k^{\vee} \circ F(\mathsf{id}, f) = (k \circ f)^{\vee}$ and for $(\cdot)^{\wedge}$ laws $F(f, \mathsf{id}) \circ h^{\wedge} = (F(f, \mathsf{id}) \circ h)^{\wedge}$ and $h^{\wedge} \circ F(f, \mathsf{id}) = (h \circ f)^{\wedge}$. Extended left zero laws $k^{\vee} \circ \phi(\mathsf{inl}) = \phi(\mathsf{inl})$ and $h^{\wedge} \circ \phi(\mathsf{inr}) = \phi(\mathsf{inr})$ can also be deduced, whereby no assumption about non-emptyness is needed.

While bind of unit equals identity in the case of ordinary monads, it is reasonable to require the following for our bifunctor context:

$$\mathsf{fuser} \quad = \quad \eta^{\wedge} \qquad\qquad\qquad\qquad\qquad\qquad\qquad\qquad\qquad \text{(FuseR-Cch)}$$

$$\mathsf{fusel} \quad = \quad \eta^{\vee} \qquad\qquad\qquad\qquad\qquad\qquad\qquad\qquad\qquad \text{(FuseL-Bnd)}$$

Then also ϕ is expressible in terms of $(\cdot)^{\vee}$ and $(\cdot)^{\wedge}$. One can take FuseR-Cch and FuseL-Bnd as definitions of fuser and fusel; then the laws FuseR-Nat, FuseL-Nat, FuseR-FuseR and FuseL-FuseL are implied by the axioms of $(\cdot)^{\vee}$ and $(\cdot)^{\wedge}$ but FuseLR-Id must be required explicitly if needed. Together with the straightenings, FuseL-Bnd and FuseR-Cch imply $(\eta \circ g)^{\vee} = \mathsf{fusel} \circ F(\mathsf{id}, g)$ and $(\eta \circ g)^{\wedge} = \mathsf{fuser} \circ F(g, \mathsf{id})$; the former axioms Bnd-Raise and Cch-Invoke can be obtained as corollaries of these equations.

We finally introduce monad level De Morgan laws connecting $(\cdot)^{\vee}$ and $(\cdot)^{\wedge}$:

$$!\circ h^{\wedge} \quad = (!\circ h)^{\vee} \circ ! \qquad\qquad\qquad\qquad\qquad\qquad\qquad \text{(Cch-Bnd-DeM)}$$

$$!\circ k^{\vee} \circ ! = (!\circ k)^{\wedge} \circ !\circ ! \qquad\qquad\qquad\qquad\qquad\qquad \text{(Bnd-Cch-DeM)}$$

Together the De Morgan laws imply Bnd-DblNegHom.

Note that Bnd-FunHom and Cch-FunHom along with Unit-Nat, and Cch-TurnRLHom and Cch-Bnd-DeM along with mixmap laws, establish that $F(h, \mathsf{id})$, $F(\mathsf{id}, f)$, $\mathsf{turnr} \circ \mathsf{turnl}$ and $!$ are monad morphisms, i.e., natural transformations that preserve both monad unit and bind.

And indeed the laws of $\circledast$, $/$, $|$ and $\wr$ are also implied by the obtained set of monad-level axioms. Theorem 2 ties the pieces together:

Theorem 2. *Let F be a bifunctor equipped with operations η, $(\cdot)^{\vee}$ and $(\cdot)^{\wedge}$ and let* fuser, fusel, ϕ, !, turnr, turnl, $\circledast$, $\wr$, $\mid$ *and* $/$ *be defined by equations* FuseR-Cch, FuseL-Bnd, Mixmap-FuseLR, Neg-Mixmap, TurnR-Mixmap, TurnL-Mixmap, Cat-Bnd, STri-Cch, WTri-STri *and* Tri-WTri. *If* Bnd-LUnit, Bnd-RUnit, Bnd-Assoc, Bnd-LZero, Bnd-FunHom, Cch-LUnit, Cch-RUnit, Cch-Assoc, Cch-LZero, Cch-FunHom, Cch-TurnRLHom, Cch-Bnd-DeM, Bnd-Cch-DeM, FuseLR-Id *and* Mixmap-Comp *are satisfied then all laws considered so far in the paper are valid.*   □

We have considered parsing as the primary supposed application but chose the axioms rather conservatively in this context. We finish this section with treating some extra laws usable for a typical but not every reasonable instance.

Firstly, running a failing computation once or twice under similar conditions can often be treated as equivalent. This is useful, for instance, in the context of transforming parsing expressions to more efficient ones with the same result. Denoting by W the diagonal combinator $\lambda h x \, . \, h \, x \, x$, the corresponding law is:

$$F(h, \mathrm{id}) \, t \, / \, t \; = \; F(W \, h, \mathrm{id}) \, t \qquad\qquad (\text{Tri-Copy})$$

The standard applicative functor and monad axioms do not include equations like Tri-Copy because, in the presence of side effects, repeated computations always differ from singleton ones. Similarly, parsing can not have a law like Tri-Copy for the operation $\circledast$ as a successful parsing may consume input whence it can not be equivalently repeated. The copy law can be stated at the monad level as $(\lambda e \, . \, F(h \, e, \mathrm{id}) \, t)^{\wedge} \, t = F(W \, h, \mathrm{id}) \, t$. Monads satisfying a similar law are called *idempotent*[1] by King and Wadler [11] and *copy monads* by Cockett and Lack [5] and Uustalu and Veltri [23, 24] (but [5, 23, 24] in addition require commutativity of the monad).

A distributivity law between $\circledast$ and $/$ would generalize Tri-Copy and extend the similar distributivity law holding for PEGs:

$$F(h, \mathrm{id}) \, t \circledast u \, / \, t \circledast v \; = \; F(W \, h, \mathrm{id}) \, t \circledast (u \, / \, v) \qquad (\text{Cat-Tri-Distr})$$

To infer Tri-Copy from Cat-Tri-Distr, take $u = v = \eta(\mathrm{inr} \, \imath)$ where $\imath$ is the member of a one-element set. It may be reasonable to require distributivity at monad level between $(\cdot)^{\vee}$ and $/$, which is stronger than Cat-Tri-Distr:

$$k^{\vee}(F(h, \mathrm{id}) \, t) \, / \, l^{\vee} \, t \; = \; (\lambda a \, . \, k \, a \, / \, l \, a)^{\vee}(F(W \, h, \mathrm{id}) \, t) \qquad (\text{Bnd-Tri-Distr})$$

In order to provide ability to perform case study, one can use the law

$$
\begin{aligned}
& h_1{}^{\wedge} \circ f = g_1{}^{\wedge} \circ f \\
\& \quad & h_2{}^{\wedge} \circ f = g_2{}^{\wedge} \circ f \\
\Longrightarrow \quad & \mathrm{cond}(p, h_1, h_2)^{\wedge} \circ f = \mathrm{cond}(p, g_1, g_2)^{\wedge} \circ f
\end{aligned}
\qquad (\text{Cch-Cond})
$$

---

[1] Not to be confused with the standard notion of idempotent monads defined as those whose multiplication is an isomorphism.

Here $\text{cond}(p, k_1, k_2)$ denotes the function that works as k_1 on arguments satisfying p and as k_2 elsewhere. Intuitively, this law captures determinism: its counterpart for unary functors is valid for most well-known monads that operate with one value simultaneously (identity, error, reader, writer, state etc.) but not for lists. Expecting a parser monad to satisfy CCH-COND is therefore justified if single error values rather than assortments are thrown in the case of failures.

The law CCH-COND is enough to establish the following derivation schema for the operation $\wr$ with any number of operands:

$$
\begin{aligned}
& F(h_1, \text{id})\, t \wr u_1 \wr \ldots \wr u_l = F(g_1, \text{id})\, t \wr v_1 \wr \ldots \wr v_m \\
\&\quad & F(h_2, \text{id})\, t \wr u_1 \wr \ldots \wr u_l = F(g_2, \text{id})\, t \wr v_1 \wr \ldots \wr v_m \\
\implies\quad & F(\text{cond}(p, h_1, h_2), \text{id})\, t \wr u_1 \wr \ldots \wr u_l = F(\text{cond}(p, g_1, g_2), \text{id})\, t \wr v_1 \wr \ldots \wr v_m
\end{aligned}
$$
$$\text{(STRI-COND)}$$

For a concrete application, consider the labelled choice operation of Maidl et al. [16] that can be defined in our interface as shown in Sect. 2. The authors use finite sets of errors as labels and claim that this can be seen as syntactic sugar; $t /^{\{e_1, e_2, \ldots, e_l\}} u$ could be equivalently rewritten as $t /^{e_1} u /^{e_2} \ldots /^{e_n} u$. A direct translation of this equivalence into our framework can be proven using our laws if both TRI-COPY and STRI-COND are included.

The applicative functor language is known for its inability to express dynamic control flow, meaning that control flow cannot branch on a value obtained from a preceding computation [14,15]. Lazy error handling operations like $\wr$ enable binary (hence arbitrary finite) branching on earlier computation results. It is even possible to define an operation that mimics monadic bind: Suppose that $\mathbb{B} = 1 + 1$ where $1 = \{\imath\}$ and let $\text{bcatch} : (\mathbb{B} \to F(E, A)) \to (F(\mathbb{B}, A) \to F(E, A))$ be given by $\text{bcatch}\, h\, t = F(\text{K inr} + \text{K (inl id)}, \text{id})\, t \wr h(\text{inl}\,\imath) \wr h(\text{inr}\,\imath)$. The laws considered above (inclusive of the extended left zero laws) imply monad laws for bcatch (use STRI-COND for proving associativity). Moreover, if the operation $\wr$ is defined by STRI-CCH in terms of $(\cdot)^{\widehat{}}$ that satisfies the monad-level laws then bcatch works identically to $(\cdot)^{\widehat{}}$. Because of its restricted type, bcatch does not make functors of the form $F(\_, A)$ monads.

4   A Hierarchy of Instances

We build a hierarchy of bifunctors F with accompanying operations that satisfy the assumptions of Theorem 2, as well as BND-TRI-DISTR and CCH-COND. Thus all laws studied in this paper hold for all top-down parsers with error handling that are expressible in terms of these bifunctors. The hierarchy subsumes all monads that can be constructed by applying the classic reader, writer and state monad transformers [13,19,25] to an error monad. Here they are considered as bifunctors with the underlying error type as the supplementary (first) parameter.

We include also construction steps that by analogy with the classic monad transformers can be characterized as *update transformations* after *update monads* introduced by Ahman and Uustalu [1]. The update transformation coincides with the composition of the reader and writer transformations in the case of all operations except $\circledast$ and $(\cdot)^{\vee}$. The state transformation is a homomorphic image of the update transformation. These observations enable one to simplify proofs for the state transformation considerably.

The definitions of the functors and the operations are given in Fig. 1. The hierarchy starts from the sum functor. Let $\mathcal{R}$, $\mathcal{W}$, $\mathcal{U}$ and $\mathcal{S}$ denote the reader, writer, update and state transformers, respectively; note that here they apply to bifunctors. The definitions refer to arbitrary fixed sets R, S and monoid $(W, \cdot, 1)$. In the case of $\mathcal{U}$, we assume a right action $\bullet : S \times W \to S$ of $(W, \cdot, 1)$ on S, i.e., an operation satisfying $s \bullet 1 = s$ and $s \bullet (w \cdot w') = (s \bullet w) \bullet w'$. For brevity, we use the section syntax of Haskell in formulas: if $\oplus$ is a binary operator then $(a\oplus)$ and $(\oplus b)$ denote $\lambda b . a \oplus b$ and $\lambda a . a \oplus b$, respectively. This holds for pair-forming comma as well; so $(, 1)$ means $\lambda a . (a, 1)$ etc. Also references to functors are omitted from the formulae of η, $(\cdot)^{\vee}$ and $(\cdot)^{\wedge}$ for brevity. Just remember that operations on the left-hand sides belong to the new functor (i.e., $\mathcal{R} F$, $\mathcal{W} F$ etc.) while operations on the right-hand sides are those of the underlying functor (i.e., F).

Let the operations not defined in Fig. 1 be given by FuseR-Cch, FuseL-Bnd, Mixmap-FuseLR, Neg-Mixmap, TurnR-Mixmap, TurnL-Mixmap, Cat-Bnd, STri-Cch, WTri-STri and Tri-WTri uniformly for all functors. Note that the functor $\mathcal{U}$ equals the composition $\mathcal{R} \circ \mathcal{W}$ if $R = S$, but the operation $(\cdot)^{\vee}$ of $\mathcal{U}$ differs from that of $\mathcal{R} \circ \mathcal{W}$ as in the case of $\mathcal{U}$ the second computation is performed in a new state determined by the previous computation rather than in the original state. This difference is also inherited by $\circledast$ via Cat-Bnd. If the operand of $(\cdot)^{\vee}$ is negated, the difference disappears.

The sum functor:
$$\eta(x) = x$$
$$k^{\vee} t = (\text{inl} \triangledown k)\, t$$
$$h^{\wedge} t = (h \triangledown \text{inr})\, t$$

The reader transformation:
$$\mathcal{R} F(E, A) = R \to F(E, A)$$
$$\mathcal{R} F(h, f) = \lambda g . F(h, f) \circ g$$
$$\eta(x) = \lambda r . \eta(x)$$
$$k^{\vee} t = \lambda r . (\lambda a . k\, a\, r)^{\vee} (t\, r)$$
$$h^{\wedge} t = \lambda r . (\lambda e . h\, e\, r)^{\wedge} (t\, r)$$

The state transformation:
$$\mathcal{S} F(E, A) = S \to F(E, A \times S)$$
$$\mathcal{S} F(h, f) = \lambda g . F(h, f \times \text{id}) \circ g$$
$$\eta(x) = \lambda s . \eta((\text{id} + (, s))\, x)$$
$$k^{\vee} t = \lambda s . (\lambda(a, s') . k\, a\, s')^{\vee} (t\, s)$$
$$h^{\wedge} t = \lambda s . (\lambda e . h\, e\, s)^{\wedge} (t\, s)$$

The writer transformation:
$$\mathcal{W} F(E, A) = F(E, A \times W)$$
$$\mathcal{W} F(h, f) = F(h, f \times \text{id})$$
$$\eta(x) = \eta((\text{id} + (, 1))\, x)$$
$$k^{\vee} t = (\lambda(a, w) . F(\text{id}, \text{id} \times (w \cdot)) (k\, a))^{\vee} t$$
$$h^{\wedge} t = h^{\wedge} t$$

The update transformation:
$$\mathcal{U} F(E, A) = S \to F(E, A \times W)$$
$$\mathcal{U} F(h, f) = \lambda g . F(h, f \times \text{id}) \circ g$$
$$\eta(x) = \lambda s . \eta((\text{id} + (, 1))\, x)$$
$$k^{\vee} t = \lambda s . (\lambda(a, w) . F(\text{id}, \text{id} \times (w \cdot)) (k\, a\, (s \bullet w)))^{\vee} (t\, s)$$
$$h^{\wedge} t = \lambda s . (\lambda e . h\, e\, s)^{\wedge} (t\, s)$$

Fig. 1. Hierarchy of parser bifunctors along with monad-level operations

Theorem 3. *Let "the laws" refer to all axioms required by Theorem 2 along with* BND-TRI-DISTR *and* CCH-COND. *Then the sum functor* $F = +: \mathbf{Set} \times \mathbf{Set} \to \mathbf{Set}$ *fulfills the laws and, whenever a bifunctor* $F = M : \mathbf{Set} \times \mathbf{Set} \to \mathbf{Set}$ *fulfills the laws, functors* $F = \mathcal{R} M$, $F = \mathcal{W} M$, $F = \mathcal{U} M$ *and* $F = \mathcal{S} M$ *fulfill the laws.*   □

The proof of Theorem 3 is straightforward. To obtain the laws for $\mathcal{S}$ as easy corollaries from those of $\mathcal{U}$, use the following correspondence between $\mathcal{U}$ and $\mathcal{S}$: Define monoid $(W, \cdot, 1)$ by $W = 1 + S$ where $1 = \{\imath\}$, $w \cdot \mathsf{inr}\, s = \mathsf{inr}\, s$, $w \cdot \mathsf{inl}\, \imath = w$ and $1 = \mathsf{inl}\, \imath$ (so-called *overwrite monoid*). Let $\mathsf{retr} : \mathcal{U} M(E, A) \to \mathcal{S} M(E, A)$ and $\mathsf{sec} : \mathcal{S} M(E, A) \to \mathcal{U} M(E, A)$ be given by $\mathsf{retr}\, t = \lambda s \,.\, M(\mathsf{id}, \mathsf{id} \times (s \bullet))(t\, s)$ and $\mathsf{sec}\, t = \lambda s \,.\, M(\mathsf{id}, \mathsf{id} \times \mathsf{inr})(t\, s)$. Then $\mathsf{retr}(\mathcal{U} M(h, f) t) = \mathcal{S} M(h, f)(\mathsf{retr}\, t)$, $\mathsf{retr}(\eta(x)) = \eta(x)$, $\mathsf{retr}(k^{\vee} t) = (\mathsf{retr} \circ k)^{\vee}(\mathsf{retr}\, t)$ and $\mathsf{retr}(h^{\wedge} t) = (\mathsf{retr} \circ h)^{\wedge}(\mathsf{retr}\, t)$, whence retr is homomorphic w.r.t. all operations under consideration. Furthermore, we have $\mathsf{sec}(\mathcal{S} M(h, f) t) = \mathcal{U} M(h, f)(\mathsf{sec}\, t)$, $\mathsf{sec}(k^{\vee} t) = (\mathsf{sec} \circ k)^{\vee}(\mathsf{sec}\, t)$ and $\mathsf{sec}(h^{\wedge} t) = (\mathsf{sec} \circ h)^{\wedge}(\mathsf{sec}\, t)$. Moreover, $\mathsf{retr} \circ \mathsf{sec} = \mathsf{id}$. These equations are enough for reducing all necessary laws of $\mathcal{S}$ to those of $\mathcal{U}$.

Our transformations retr and sec are analogous to retr and sec between the update and state monad used by Ahman and Uustalu [1]. The homomorphism equations of retr for $^{\vee}$ and η imply that retr is a monad morphism in the second parameter of the functor; similarly, retr is a monad morphism in the first functor parameter due to the homomorphism equations for $^{\wedge}$ and η. Note however that $\mathsf{sec}(\eta(\mathsf{inr}\, a)) \neq \eta(\mathsf{inr}\, a)$ because the pair component added by η obtains the form $\mathsf{inr}\, s$ in the l.h.s. while it equals $\mathsf{inl}\, \imath$ in the r.h.s. Hence sec is not a monad morphism in the second functor parameter.[2] In general also $\mathsf{sec}(\phi(g)) \neq \phi(\mathsf{sec}\, g)$.

5   Related Work

Applicative functors (also known as *idioms*) were recognized by McBride and Paterson [17] as a useful generalization of monads with a number of application areas, but several authors had used such interfaces for writing parsers long before. For instance, parsing in the nhc compiler [20] was implemented in the Applicative-Alternative programming style, and a similar interface was proposed by Swierstra and Duponcheel [22] for creating error correcting parsers for LL(1) grammars. Error reporting in combinator parsing is discussed in a later paper by Swierstra [21] but only in the context of the longest valid prefix approach.

Kmett has created a Haskell library containing an implementation of *biapplicative bifunctors* [12] which differs from our double applicative functors (for instance, Kmett's bifunctor unit works on product type rather than sum type).

Ford [7] introduced PEGs and made intensive use of semantic equivalences of parsing expressions. Maidl et al. [16] discussed the incapacity of PEGs to distinguish severe errors from local failures and introduced the labelled choice operator as a remedy for the shortcoming. With a similar aim, Mizushima

---

[2] For similar reasons, sec of [1] is not a monad morphism though retr is (the paper incorrectly claims both to be monad morphisms).

et al. [18] used cut operators in parsing expressions to signal that backtracking is undesired.

Update monads were introduced and recognized as a useful link between reader, writer and state monads by Ahman and Uustalu [1]. The generalization to transformers in our paper is straightforward and follows the classic pattern [13, 19, 25]. To our knowledge, update monad transformers have not been used in research before, but implementations in Haskell exist on the web.

6 Conclusions

We introduced a new approach to error handling in applicative style parsers and studied the relationship between laws imposed on the parsing combinators.

Lindley et al. [15] showed that results of intermediate computations in the case of applicative functors can influence neither the choice of the next computations nor the parameter values passed to them; in other words, both control and data flow are static. Our approach involves operations that may skip lexically following computations depending on the error being raised; so it enables dynamic control flow while keeping data flow static. In Lindley's classification [14], this combination is called *strange* because of not having occurred in the literature; our work shows the strange combination also being reasonable.

In the case of parsing simple context-free languages, the need for dynamic control flow appears primarily in the context of error handling, whence we did not involve analogous operators for branching on normal values. Such operators would be reasonable to have; although one can reflect the branching operations defined for errors in the world of normal values via *mixmap*, the obtained operations would not enable accumulative input consumption.

We considered deterministic top-down parsing as the canonical application of double applicative functors. Other applications, which we are currently not aware of, might exist that would potentially break some of our laws. The latter seems likely in particular because of the pervasive asymmetry between the bifunctor arguments suggested by parsing needs but possibly undesired elsewhere.

Acknowledgement. The work was partially supported by the Estonian Research Council under R&D project No. IUT2-1.

The author thanks Tarmo Uustalu for fruitful discussions and also the anonymous reviewers for valuable feedback.

References

1. Ahman, D., Uustalu, T.: Update monads: cointerpreting directed containers. In: Matthes, R., Schubert, A. (eds.) 19th International Conference on Types for Proofs and Programs, TYPES 2013. Leibniz International Proceedings in Informatics, Toulouse, April 2013, vol. 26, pp. 1–23. Dagstuhl Publishing, Saarbrücken/Wadern (2014). https://doi.org/10.4230/lipics.types.2013.1
2. Aho, A.V., Ullman, J.D.: The Theory of Parsing, Translation, and Compiling. 1: Parsing. Prentice-Hall, Englewood Cliffs (1972)

3. Bifunctors and biapplicatives. https://github.com/purescript/purescript-bifunctors

4. Birman, A., Ullman, J.D.: Parsing algorithms with backtrack. Inf. Control **23**(1), 1–34 (1973). https://doi.org/10.1016/s0019-9958(73)90851-6

5. Cockett, J.R.B., Lack, S.: Restriction categories III: colimits, partial limits and extensivity. Math. Struct. Comput. Sci. **17**(4), 775–817 (2007). https://doi.org/10.1017/s0960129507006056

6. Danielsson, N.A., Hughes, J., Jansson, P., Gibbons, J.: Fast and loose reasoning is morally correct. In: Proceedings of 33rd ACM SIGPLAN-SIGACT Symposium on Principles of Programming Languages, POPL 2006, Charleston, SC, pp. 206–217. ACM Press, New York (2006). https://doi.org/10.1145/1111037.1111056

7. Ford, B.: Parsing expression grammars: a recognition-based syntactic foundation. In: Proceedings of 31st ACM SIGPLAN-SIGACT Symposium on Principles of Programming Languages, POPL 2004, Venice, January 2004, pp. 111–122. ACM Press, New York (2004). https://doi.org/10.1145/964001.964011

8. Haskell. https://www.haskell.org

9. Haskell hierarchical libraries. https://downloads.haskell.org/~ghc/latest/docs/html/libraries/index.html

10. Hinze, R.: Lifting operators and laws (2010). https://www.cs.ox.ac.uk/ralf.hinze/Lifting.pdf

11. King, D.J., Wadler, P.: Combining monads. In: Launchbury, J., Sansom, P.M. (eds.) Functional Programming, Glasgow 1992. Workshops in Computing, pp. 134–143. Springer, London (1993). https://doi.org/10.1007/978-1-4471-3215-8_12

12. Kmett, E.: Biapplicative bifunctors. https://hackage.haskell.org/package/bifunctors-3.2.0.1/docs/Data-Biapplicative.html

13. Liang, S., Hudak, P., Jones, M.P.: Monad transformers and modular interpreters. In: Conference Record of 22nd ACM SIGPLAN-SIGACT Symposium on Principles of Programming Languages, POPL 1995, San Francisco, CA, January 1995, pp. 333–343. ACM Press, New York (1995). https://doi.org/10.1145/199448.199528

14. Lindley, S.: Algebraic effects and effect handlers for idioms and arrows. In: Proceedings of 10th ACM SIGPLAN Workshop on Generic Programming, WGP 2014, Gothenburg, August 2014, pp. 47–58. ACM Press, New York (2014). https://doi.org/10.1145/2633628.2633636

15. Lindley, S., Wadler, P., Yallop, J.: Idioms are oblivious, arrows are meticulous, monads are promiscuous. Electron. Notes Theor. Comput. Sci. **229**(5), 97–117 (2011). https://doi.org/10.1016/j.entcs.2011.02.018

16. Maidl, A.M., Mascarenhas, F., Medeiros, S., Ierusalimschy, R.: Error reporting in parsing expression grammars. Sci. Comput. Program. **132**, 129–140 (2016). https://doi.org/10.1016/j.scico.2016.08.004

17. McBride, C., Paterson, R.: Applicative programming with effects. J. Funct. Program. **18**(1), 1–13 (2008). https://doi.org/10.1017/s0956796807006326

18. Mizushima, K., Maeda, A., Yamaguchi, Y.: Packrat parsers can handle practical grammars in mostly constant space. In: Proceedings of 9th ACM SIGPLAN-SIGSOFT Workshop on Program Analysis for Software Tools and Engineering, PASTE 2010, Toronto, ON, June 2010, pp. 29–36. ACM Press, New York (2010). https://doi.org/10.1145/1806672.1806679

19. Moggi, E.: An abstract view of programming languages. Technical report, ECS-LFCS-90-113, University of Edinburgh (1990)

20. Röjemo, N.: Highlights from nhc–a space-efficient Haskell compiler. In: Proceedings of 7th International Conference on Functional Programming Languages and Computer Architecture, FPCA 1995, La Jolla, CA, June 1995, pp. 282–292. ACM Press (1995). https://doi.org/10.1145/224164.224217

21. Swierstra, S.D.: Combinator parsing: a short tutorial. In: Bove, A., Barbosa, L.S., Pardo, A., Pinto, J.S. (eds.) LerNet 2008. LNCS, vol. 5520, pp. 252–300. Springer, Heidelberg (2009). https://doi.org/10.1007/978-3-642-03153-3_6

22. Swierstra, S.D., Duponcheel, L.: Deterministic, error-correcting combinator parsers. In: Launchbury, J., Meijer, E., Sheard, T. (eds.) AFP 1996. LNCS, vol. 1129, pp. 184–207. Springer, Heidelberg (1996). https://doi.org/10.1007/3-540-61628-4_7

23. Uustalu, T., Veltri, N.: The delay monad and restriction categories. In: Hung, D.V., Kapur, D. (eds.) ICTAC 2017. LNCS, vol. 10580, pp. 32–50. Springer, Cham (2017). https://doi.org/10.1007/978-3-319-67729-3_3

24. Uustalu, T., Veltri, N.: Partiality and container monads. In: Chang, B.-Y.E. (ed.) APLAS 2017. LNCS, vol. 10695, pp. 406–425. Springer, Cham (2017). https://doi.org/10.1007/978-3-319-71237-6_20

25. Wadler, P.: Comprehending monads. Math. Struct. Comput. Sci. **2**(4), 461–493 (1992). https://doi.org/10.1017/s0960129500001560

Checking Sequence Generation
for Symbolic Input/Output FSMs
by Constraint Solving

Omer Nguena Timo[1]([✉]), Alexandre Petrenko[1], and S. Ramesh[2]

[1] Computer Research Institute of Montreal, CRIM, Montreal, Canada
{omer.nguena-timo,petrenko}@crim.ca
[2] GM Global R&D, Warren, MI, USA
ramesh.s@gm.com

Abstract. The reset of reactive systems in testing can be impossible or
very costly, which could force testers to avoid it. In this context, testers
often want to generate a checking sequence, i.e., a unique sequence of
inputs satisfying a chosen test criterion. This paper proposes a method
for generating a checking sequence with complete fault coverage for a
given fault model of reactive systems. The systems are represented with
an extension of Finite State Machines (FSMs) with symbolic inputs and
outputs which are predicates on input and output variables having possibly infinite domains. In our setting, a checking sequence is made up
of symbolic inputs and the fault domain can represent complex faults.
The method consists in building and solving Boolean expressions to iteratively refine and extend a sequence of symbolic inputs. We evaluate the
efficiency of the approach with a prototype tool we have developed.

Keywords: Extended FSM · Symbolic input/output FSM
Checking sequence · Fault modeling · Fault detection
Constraint solving

1 Introduction

Model-based testing [26] has been developing for decades and is now getting
adopted in the industry. The industrial testers are concerned with the quality
of the tests and the cost of their application which also includes the cost of
resetting (re-initializing) the systems. In this paper, we consider the fault model
driven generation of tests for non-resettable systems modeled with symbolic
input/output finite state machines (SIOFSMs) and propose a method to generate
a checking sequence, i.e., a single symbolic input sequence detecting all faulty
implementations within a specified fault model.

SIOFSM [16] extends FSM with symbolic inputs and outputs; it is a restricted
type of extended FSM [18]. A symbolic input is a predicate over input variables.
A symbolic output is a predicate defining output variables with Boolean and

© Springer Nature Switzerland AG 2018
B. Fischer and T. Uustalu (Eds.): ICTAC 2018, LNCS 11187, pp. 354–375, 2018.
https://doi.org/10.1007/978-3-030-02508-3_19

arithmetic expressions over the input variables. SIOFSM is adequate for modeling both control and data specific behaviors, especially pre- and post-conditions of state transitions.

Fault model-driven testing [15,27] focuses on detecting specific faults and it can complement testing driven by code coverage [5,25,28]. In the theory of testing from FSM, mutation machine [10,24] was proposed for compact representation of fault domains, i.e., the set of possible implementations of a given specification FSM. The mutation machine contains the specification machine and extends it with mutated transitions modeling potential faults. Recently proposed methods for fault model-driven testing from FSM are based on constraint solving [20,21]. The methods are aimed to generate checking experiments [6,11,16] for an FSM, i.e., multiple input sequences for full coverage of a fault domain for an FSM specification. The methods in [20,21] have inspired the work in [13] on the generation of checking experiments for FSMs with symbolic inputs and concrete outputs (SIFSMs). The work in [13] considers complex faults on symbolic inputs including splitting and merging of symbolic inputs; such faults were not considered in [23]. Experimental results [13,21] have shown the efficiency of the methods based on constraint solving to generate checking experiments for FSM and SIFSM. The method in [16] generates checking experiments for SIOFSMs. It does not consider complex mutation operations on symbolic inputs and the experimental evaluation of the efficiency of the method was not performed. Checking experiments are applicable provided that systems under test can be reset prior to the application of each input sequence in a checking experiment, which is not always possible and motivates the generation of checking sequences.

The methods in [7,9,17,22] allow generating a checking sequence to detect all possible faulty implementations with the number of states not exceeding that of a specification FSM. The approach in [22] consists in searching a maximal acyclic path to a sink state of the distinguishing automaton of the specification and mutation FSMs. Searching a maximal acyclic path is a sufficient condition to find a checking sequence but it is not a necessary condition and the resulting checking sequence could be too long. No experimental evaluation of the efficiency of the method is provided in [22]. The approach in [17] generates a checking sequence during the inference of an FSM from input/output sequences; it is based on building and solving Boolean formulas. Extended FSMs, including SIOFSMs, have been increasingly used to represent embedded controllers and systems [1,19]. Generating checking sequences for SIOFSMs is an interesting challenge which, to the best of our knowledge, has not been addressed.

We propose a method for verifying whether an input sequence is a checking sequence for a specification SIOFSM; then we elaborate a method for generating checking sequence. Specification and implementation SIOFSMs in a fault model are assumed to be strongly-connected, i.e., every state is reachable from any other state. The fault model defined by a tester may represent complex faults on Boolean and arithmetic operations in the specification. To the best of our knowledge, this is the first work addressing the generation of checking sequences for SIOFSMs to detecting such complex faults. FSMs and SIFSMs have concrete outputs, while SIOFSM has symbolic ones, which significantly complicates determining the distinguishability achieved by a symbolic input sequence. This is needed to verify that an input sequence produces different output sequences in the specification SIOFSM and any faulty implementation SIOFSM. The proposed methods are based on constraint solving and avoid explicit enumeration of the implementations. The generation method iteratively refines and extends a symbolic input sequence (starting from the empty sequence) until it becomes a checking sequence. The paper also presents preliminary experimental results obtained with a prototype tool we have developed.

The remaining of the paper is organized as follows. Section 2 provides the main definitions related to SIOFSM. In Sect. 3, we elaborate Boolean formulas for specifying a fault domain, which we use in Sect. 4 to verify, refine and generate checking sequences. Section 5 presents experimental results obtained with a prototype tools we have developed. Section 6 summarizes our contributions and indicates future work.

2 Definitions

2.1 Preliminaries

Let G_V denote the universe of *inputs* that are predicates over *input variables* in a fixed set V for which a decision procedure exists, excluding the predicates that are always *false*. G_V^* denotes the universe of *input sequences* and ε denotes the empty sequence. Let I_V denote the set of all the *valuations* of the input variables in the set V, called *concrete inputs*. A set of concrete inputs is called a *symbolic input*; both, concrete and symbolic inputs are represented by predicates in G_V. Henceforth, we use set-theoretical operations on inputs. In particular, we say that concrete input $\mathbf{x}$ satisfies symbolic input g if $\mathbf{x} \in g$. We let $\overline{g}$ denote the negation of g, i.e., $\mathbf{x} \in g$ iff $\mathbf{x} \notin \overline{g}$. We also have that $I_V \subseteq G$. A set of inputs H is a *tautology* if each concrete input $x \in I_V$ satisfies at least one input in it, i.e., $\{x \in g \mid g \in H\} = I_V$.

We define some relations between input sequences in G_V^*. Given two input sequences $\alpha, \beta \in G^*$ of the same length k, $\alpha = g_1 g_2 \ldots g_k, \beta = g_1' g_2' \ldots g_k'$, we let $\alpha \cap \beta = g_1 \cap g_1' \ldots g_k \cap g_k'$ denote the sequence of intersections of inputs in sequences α and β. The sequences α and β are *compatible*, if for all $i = 1, \ldots, k$, $g_i \cap g_i' \neq \emptyset$. We say that α is a *reduction* of β, denoted $\alpha \subseteq \beta$, if $\alpha = \alpha \cap \beta$. If α is a sequence of concrete inputs as well as a reduction of β then it is called an *instance* of β.

We let $A(O, V)$ denote the universe of assignments that associate valuations of the *output variables* in a fixed set O with valuations of the input variables in V. Formally, an assignment in $A(O, V)$ is a function $a : I_V \to I_O$ and we write $\mathbf{y} = a(\mathbf{x})$ whenever assignment a associates the valuation $\mathbf{x} \in I_V$ to the valuation $\mathbf{y} \in I_O$, a *concrete* output. An assignment can be expressed with a mapping of every output variable to a meaningful (arithmetic, Boolean, etc.) expression defined over the input variables. We extend the definition of an assignment to symbolic inputs, namely $a(g) = \{\mathbf{y} \mid \mathbf{y} = a(\mathbf{x}), \mathbf{x} \in g\}$; $a(g)$ is a *symbolic output*.

Notice that an input variable of which the domain is a singleton is nothing else but a constant. Given two assignments a_1, a_2, we define the sets of valuations of the input variables on which the assignments are equal $eq(a_1, a_2) = \{\mathbf{x} \in I_V \mid a_1(\mathbf{x}) = a_2(\mathbf{x})\}$ and $neq(a_1, a_2) = \{\mathbf{x} \in I_V \mid a_1(\mathbf{x}) \neq a_2(\mathbf{x})\}$ the sets of valuations of the input variables on which the assignments are different. Both $eq(a_1, a_2)$ and $neq(a_1, a_2)$ can be represented with predicates on the inputs variables in V.

2.2 FSM with Symbolic Inputs and Outputs

We consider an extension of FSM called symbolic input/output finite state machine (SIOFSM) [16], which operates in discrete time as a synchronous machine reading values of input variables and setting up the values of output variables with arithmetic operations on the input variables. The sets of input and output valuations can be infinite.

Definition 1 (Symbolic input/output finite state machine). *A symbolic input/output finite state machine (SIOFSM or machine, for short) $\mathcal{S}$ is a 5-tuple (S, s_0, V, O, T), where S is a finite set of states with the initial state s_0, V is a finite set of input variables over which inputs are defined, O is a finite set of output variables, $V \cap O = \emptyset$, $T \subseteq S \times G_V \times A(O, V) \times S$ is a finite transition relation, $(s, g, a, s') \in T$ is a transition.*

Definition 2 (Suspicious transition). *Transitions from the same state with compatible inputs are said to be suspicious.*

The machine $\mathcal{S}$ is *deterministic* (DSIOFSM), if for every state s, $T(s)$ does not have suspicious transitions; otherwise $\mathcal{S}$ is a *nondeterministic* SIOFSM. The machine $\mathcal{S}$ is *complete*, if for each state s, $G(s)$ is a tautology. The machine $\mathcal{S}$ is *initially-connected*, if for any state $s \in S$, there exists an execution to s. The machine $\mathcal{S}$ is *strongly-connected*, if for any ordered pair of states $(s, s') \in S \times S$, there exists an execution from s to s'.

Definition 3 (Non deterministic and deterministic execution). *An execution of $\mathcal{S}$ from state s is a sequence $e = t_1 t_2 \ldots t_n$ of transitions $(t_i = (s_i, g_i, a_i, s_{i+1}))_{i=1..n}$ forming a path from s in the state transition diagram of $\mathcal{S}$. An execution with at least two suspicious transitions from an identical state is called* nondeterministic, *otherwise it is* deterministic.

Clearly, a DSIOFSM has only deterministic executions, while a nondeterministic SIOFSM can have both deterministic and nondeterministic executions. We use $inp(e)$, $src(e)$ and $tgt(e)$ to denote input sequence $g_1 g_2 \ldots g_n$, the starting state s_1 and the ending state s_{n+1} of an execution e as above defined, respectively. We let $Susp(e)$ denote the set of suspicious transitions in the execution e, $Susp(s)$ denote the set of all suspicious transitions in state s and $Susp(\mathcal{S})$ denote the set of all suspicious transitions of SIOFSM $\mathcal{S}$.

Given two executions e and e' such that $tgt(e) = src(e')$, ee' denotes the *concatenation* of e and e'; it is an execution of $\mathcal{S}$ from $src(e)$ to $tgt(e')$.

Definition 4 (Enabled and triggered executions). *Let e be an execution with input sequence $g_1 g_2 \ldots g_n$. An input sequence $\alpha = g'_1 g'_2 \ldots g'_n$ enables execution e if α and $inp(e)$ are compatible. The input sequence α triggers e if α is a reduction of the input sequence of e, i.e., $\alpha \subseteq inp(e)$.*

Note that an input sequence triggering an execution also enables the execution; however an input sequence enabling an execution does not necessarily trigger the execution.

The output of an execution e enabled by α is the sequence of symbolic outputs $out(e, \alpha) = a_1(g_1 \cap g'_1) a_2(g_2 \cap g'_2) \ldots a_n(g_n \cap g'_n)$. We let $out_8(s, \alpha) = \bigcup \{out(e, \alpha) \mid e$ is an execution of 8 in s triggered by $\alpha\}$ denote the set of the output sequences which can be produced by 8 in response to α at state s. Clearly, $out_8(s, \alpha)$ is the union of all symbolic output sequences which can be produced in response to α. We let $G(s)$ denote the set of predicates and $\Omega(s)$ denote the set of all symbolic input sequences defined in state s, i.e., $g_1 g_2 \ldots g_n \in \Omega(s)$ if there is an execution e from s such that $g_1 g_2 \ldots g_n = inp(e)$. The set of concrete output sequences which can be produced in response to the instances of α is the set of instances of $out(e, \alpha)$, i.e., $\bigcup_{x \in \alpha} out(e, x) = \{y \mid y \in out(e, \alpha)\}$.

We define distinguishability and equivalence relations between states of SIOFSM. Intuitively, states that produce different output sequences in response to some concrete input sequence are distinguishable.

Definition 5 (Distinguishable and equivalent states). *Let p and s be the states of two complete SIOFSMs over the same set of input and output variables V and O. Given an input sequence $\alpha \subseteq \alpha_1 \cap \alpha_2$, such that $\alpha_1 \in \Omega(p)$ and $\alpha_2 \in \Omega(s)$, p and s are distinguishable (with distinguishing input sequence α), denoted $p \not\simeq_\alpha s$, if the sets of concrete outputs in $out_8(p, \alpha)$ and $out_8(s, \alpha)$ differ, otherwise they are equivalent and we write $s \simeq p$, i.e., if the sets of concrete outputs coincide for all $\alpha \subseteq \alpha_1 \cap \alpha_2$, $\alpha_1 \in \Omega(p)$, and $\alpha_2 \in \Omega(s)$.*

Given SIOFSMs $\mathcal{M} = (S, s_0, V, O, T)$ and $\mathcal{P} = (P, p_0, V, O, N)$, $\mathcal{P}$ is a submachine of $\mathcal{M}$ if $p_0 = s_0$, $P \subseteq S$ and $N \subseteq T$.

2.3 Mutation Machine and Checking Sequence

Let $8 = (S, s_0, V, O, N)$ be a strongly- connected complete DSIOFSM.

Definition 6. *A SIOFSM $\mathcal{M} = (S, s_0, V, O, T)$ is a mutation machine of 8, if 8 is a submachine of $\mathcal{M}$. Then 8 is called the specification machine for $\mathcal{M}$.*

Let $\mathcal{P} = (P, p_0, V, O, D)$ be a submachine of mutation machine $\mathcal{M}$ of specification 8. We use the state equivalence relation $\simeq$ to define conforming submachines.

Definition 7 (Conforming submachine). *Submachine $\mathcal{P}$ is conforming to 8, if $p_0 \simeq s_0$, otherwise, it is nonconforming.*

We say that an input sequence α *detects* $\mathcal{P}$ if $p_0 \not\simeq_\alpha s_0$; otherwise $\mathcal{P}$ *survives* α. Submachine $\mathcal{P}$ is *involved* in an execution e of $\mathcal{M}$ if $Susp(e) \subseteq Susp(\mathcal{P})$. Nonconforming submachines are involved in minimal executions of $\mathcal{M}$ having unexpected output sequences and called revealing executions.

Definition 8 (Revealing execution). *Given an input sequence $\alpha \in G^*$, we say that an execution e_1 of a mutation machine $\mathcal{M}$ from s_0 is α-revealing (or simply revealing) if there exists an execution e_2 of the specification machine $\mathcal{S}$ from s_0 such that the sets of concrete outputs in $out(e_2, \alpha)$ and $out(e_1, \alpha)$ differ and α triggers both e_1 and e_2 while this does not hold for any prefix of α.*

We use mutation machines to compactly represent possible (faulty) implementations of a specification machine also called mutants.

Definition 9 (Mutant). *Given a mutation machine $\mathcal{M}$ for a specification machine $\mathcal{S}$, a mutant for $\mathcal{S}$ is a strongly-connected complete deterministic submachine of $\mathcal{M}$.*

Both the specification and mutation machines are defined over the same set of states. This means that we focus on mutants having no more states than the specification. We introduce several types of transitions in mutation machine depending on their use in mutants or the specification.

Definition 10 (Mutated and trusted transitions). *A transition of mutation machine $\mathcal{M}$ that is called* mutated *if it is not also a transition of the specification $\mathcal{S}$. A transition of $\mathcal{M}$ that is also a transition of the specification $\mathcal{S}$ is* trusted *if it is not suspicious; otherwise it is* untrusted.

Intuitively, mutated transitions are alternatives for untrusted transitions and they represent faults. There is no alternative for trusted which appear in all the mutants. We let $Untr(\mathcal{M})$ denote the set of untrusted transitions of the mutation machine $\mathcal{M}$.

The set of all mutants in mutation machine $\mathcal{M}$ is called a *fault domain* for $\mathcal{S}$, denoted $Mut(\mathcal{M})$. A subset of $Mut(\mathcal{M})$ is a fault sub-domain. If $\mathcal{M}$ is deterministic and complete then $\mathcal{S}$ is the only mutant in $Mut(\mathcal{M})$. A general *fault model* is the tuple $\langle \mathcal{S}, \simeq, Mut(\mathcal{M}) \rangle$ following [20, 21, 23]. The conformance relation partitions the set $Mut(\mathcal{M})$ into conforming mutants and nonconforming ones which we need to detect. The number of mutants in $Mut(\mathcal{M})$ is bounded by the number of deterministic complete submachines of $\mathcal{M}$. A state of the mutation machine may have suspicious transitions which must belong to different deterministic complete submachines, which motivates the following definition.

Definition 11 (Cluster of a state and suspicious state). *Given state s of $\mathcal{M}$, a subset of $T(s)$ is called a* cluster *of s if it is deterministic and the inputs of its transitions constitute a tautology. State s is said to be* suspicious *if it has more than one cluster.*

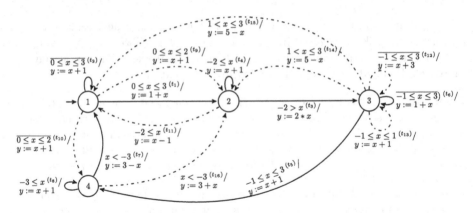

Fig. 1. A mutation SIOFSM $\mathcal{M}_1$ with 16 transitions from t_1 to t_{16}, state 1 is initial.

The number of deterministic complete submachines of mutation machine $\mathcal{M}$ is the product of the sizes of the clusters of the states; this is because each state of each complete deterministic submachine has one cluster. Let $Z(s)$ to denote the set of all clusters of s, we have that $|Mut(\mathcal{M})| \leq \Pi_{s \in S} |Z(s)|$. We use S_{susp} to denote the set of all suspicious states of $\mathcal{M}$.

Henceforth, we only consider mutation machines in which every mutated transition belongs to a cluster and thus to at least one mutant; such machines are called *well-formed* mutation machines [13].

Example 1. Figure 1 presents an example of a mutation SIOFSM $\mathcal{M}_1$ with 4 states and 16 transitions ranging from t_1 to t_{16}, an Integer input variable x and Integer output variable y. The solid lines represent the non-mutated transitions of the specification machine from t_1 to t_8. We let S_1 be the name of the specification machine. Machine $\mathcal{M}_1$ is nondeterministic and has 8 mutated transitions including transitions from t_9 to t_{16} represented with dashed lines. The mutated transitions represent faults which can be introduced in implementing the specification. The input $0 \leq x \leq 2$ of the mutated transition t_9 is a reduction of the input $0 \leq x \leq 3$ of transition t_1 of the specification; then both transitions are suspicious. All transitions but t_3 are suspicious as t_3 is the only trusted transition defined in every deterministic complete submachine of $\mathcal{M}_1$. States 1, 2, 3 and 4 define two, two, six and two clusters, respectively. The six clusters for states 3 are $Z_{3_1} = \{t_5, t_6\}$, $Z_{3_2} = \{t_6, t_{13}, t_{15}\}$, $Z_{3_3} = \{t_6, t_{13}, t_{14}\}$, $Z_{3_4} = \{t_{12}, t_{13}, t_{15}\}$, $Z_{3_5} = \{t_{12}, t_{13}, t_{14}\}$, $Z_{3_6} = \{t_5, t_{12}\}$. Mutation machine $\mathcal{M}_1$ is well-formed and includes $2 \times 2 \times 6 \times 2 = 48$ complete deterministic submachines; one of them is the specification, 12 others are not strongly-connected, e.g., the submachine specified with $\{t_1, t_2, t_3, t_4, t_5, t_6, t_8, t_{16}\}$ and the remaining 35 are the mutants we have to detect.

Definition 12 (Checking sequence). *A checking sequence for $\langle S, \simeq, Mut(\mathcal{M}) \rangle$ is an input sequence detecting every nonconforming mutant in $Mut(\mathcal{M})$.*

The goal of this paper is to elaborate a method to generate a checking sequence for a fault model. In our work, the mutated transitions in mutation machines can be introduced by various mutation operations including, but are not limited to, changing target states, merging/splitting inputs of transitions, replacing variables with default values, swapping occurrences of variables in inputs, substituting a variable for another, modifying arithmetic/logical operations in inputs and outputs. Mutations of arithmetic/logical operations defining the outputs which are not applicable to SIFSM [13] are considered in [2,3,8]. Note that merging and splitting of inputs are not considered in [16].

In the next section, we specify with a Boolean expression the deterministic complete submachines undetected by an input sequence all together avoiding their enumeration; an individual submachine could then be determined by resolving the expression and we could check if it is strongly-connected and non-conforming, i.e., a surviving mutant.

3   Specifying Mutants Surviving an Input Sequence

A submachine of a mutation machine survives an input sequence (a test) whenever it does not trigger a revealing execution of the mutation machine involving the submachine. Mutants are involved only in deterministic executions of the mutation machine and they are detected if these executions are revealing. First we elaborate a method for determining deterministic revealing executions of the mutation machine an input sequence triggers; then we use the executions to build a Boolean expression encoding mutants surviving the input sequence.

3.1   Determining Deterministic Revealing Executions

Both deterministic and nondeterministic revealing executions of a mutation machine can be determined using a distinguishing automaton obtained by composing the transitions of the specification and mutation machines as follows. The composition differs from that in [13] and was introduced in [16].

Definition 13. *Given a DSIOFSM* $S = (S, s_0, V, O, N)$ *and a mutation machine* $M = (S, s_0, V, O, T)$ *of* S*, a finite automaton* $D = (D \cup \{\nabla\}, d_0, G, \Theta, \nabla)$*, where* $D \subseteq S \times S$*,* ∇ *is an accepting (sink) state and* $\Theta \subseteq D \times G \times D$ *is the transition relation, is the* distinguishing automaton *for* S *and* M*, if it holds that* $d_0 = (s_0, s_0) \in D$ *is the initial state and for any* $(s_1, s_2) \in D$

- $((s_1, s_2), g_1 \cap g_2 \cap eq(a_1, a_2), (s_1', s_2')) \in \Theta$, *if there exist* $(s_1, g_1, a_1, s_1') \in N$, $(s_2, g_2, a_2, s_2') \in T$, *such that* $g_1 \cap g_2 \cap eq(a_1, a_2) \neq \emptyset$
- $((s_1, s_2), g_1 \cap g_2 \cap neq(a_1, a_2), \nabla) \in \Theta$, *if there exist* $(s_1, g_1, a_1, s_1') \in N$, $(s_2, g_2, a_2, s_2') \in T$, *such that* $g_1 \cap g_2 \cap neq(a_1, a_2) \neq \emptyset$

An execution of D from a state d_0 and ending at a sink state in ∇ is said to be *accepted*. The language of D, L_D is the set of input sequences labeling accepted executions of $\mathcal{D}$. By definition, every $\beta \in L_{\mathcal{D}}$ triggers a β-revealing execution of $\mathcal{M}$. Every execution of $\mathcal{D}$ is defined by an execution of the specification and an execution of $\mathcal{M}$.

Lemma 1. *An execution of $\mathcal{M}$ is revealing if and only if it defines an accepted execution of $\mathcal{D}$.*

The following lemma characterizes the inputs triggering revealing executions of $\mathcal{M}$.

Lemma 2. *An input sequence α triggers a revealing execution of $\mathcal{M}$ if and only if $\alpha \subseteq \beta$ for some $\beta \in L_{\mathcal{D}}$.*

Each non-revealing execution of $\mathcal{M}$ defines an unaccepted execution of $\mathcal{D}$ from d_0. However an unaccepted execution of $\mathcal{D}$ can be defined with a revealing execution of $\mathcal{M}$, in which case the input sequences of the two defined executions are incompatible. This situation may happen when the input of a specification's transition was split into two inputs of two mutated transitions.

Example 2. Consider the situation when transitions in $\mathcal{S}_1$ and $\mathcal{M}_1$ define a transition to a sink state and a transition to a non-sink state. E.g., $((4,3),(x = 2),(4,1))$ and $((4,3),(1 < x \leq 3 \land x \neq 2),\nabla)$ are two transitions of $\mathcal{D}_{\mathcal{M}_1}$ defined with t_8 and t_{15}.

Based on Lemma 1, we can use $\mathcal{D}$ to enumerate all the triggered revealing as well as non-revealing executions of $\mathcal{M}$. Verifying whether an input sequence is a checking sequence we will be interested in deterministic executions triggered or enabled by the sequence since mutants can only be involved in deterministic executions. Checking whether an execution of the distinguishing automaton is defined by a deterministic execution of the mutation machine can be done by verifying that it does not use two suspicious transitions of the mutation machine. This verification can be performed on-the-fly by enumerating all the executions of $\mathcal{D}$ for a given input sequence (test). Latter in refining an input sequence, we will be interested in executions it enables. They can be determined with a method similar to that for the triggered executions except that checking the intersection of inputs is used instead of checking the inclusion.

Let $\alpha \in G^*$ be an input sequence. We let E_α be the set of accepted deterministic executions of the $\mathcal{D}$ triggered by a prefix of α in $\mathcal{M}$ and F_α be the set of unaccepted deterministic executions triggered by α in $\mathcal{D}$. This set can be used for determining $E_{\alpha \downarrow \mathcal{M}}$ and $F_{\alpha \downarrow \mathcal{M}}$, the set of revealing and non-revealing executions for α. Clearly, an execution of $\mathcal{M}$ cannot define both an execution in E_α and an execution in F_α.

3.2   Encoding SIOFSMs Involved in Deterministic Revealing Executions

We use Boolean expressions over the variables representing the suspicious transitions of a mutation machine $\mathcal{M}$ for encoding SIOFSMs involved in revealing

Procedure Build_expression $(F_\alpha, \beta, \mathcal{D})$;

Let $c_{+\beta} :=$ *False*;

Determine $E_{+\beta}$ and $F_{\alpha\beta}$ from F_α and $\mathcal{D}$;

for *each* $d \in E_{+\beta\downarrow\mathcal{M}}$ **do**

$\quad | \quad c_d := \bigwedge_{t \in Susp(d)} t$;

$\quad | \quad c_{+\beta} := c_{+\beta} \vee c_d$;

end

return $(c_{+\beta}, F_{\alpha\beta})$

Algorithm 1. Building $c_{+\beta}$ s.t. $c_{\alpha\beta} = c_\alpha \vee c_{+\beta}$

executions, as we did in a previous work [13]. Each submachine of $\mathcal{M}$ has all the trusted transitions of $\mathcal{M}$ and a unique set of suspicious transitions. Hence each submachine can be identified by its set of suspicious transitions. We introduce a Boolean variable for each suspicious transition in $\mathcal{M}$ and we refer to both a variable and the corresponding transition with the same symbol t. A solution of such a Boolean expression is an assignment to True or False of every variable which makes the expression True; it can be obtained with solvers [4,12]. A solution *selects* (resp. *excludes*) transitions to which it assigns the value True (resp False); it *specifies* a (possibly nondeterministic and partially specified) submachine $\mathcal{P}$ of $\mathcal{M}$ if it selects a subset of $Susp(\mathcal{M})$ which together with the trusted transitions of $\mathcal{M}$ constitutes the submachine.

Given an execution e of a mutation machine, let $c_e \stackrel{\text{def}}{=} \bigwedge_{t \in Susp(e)} t$ be the conjunction of all the suspicious transitions in e. As usual, the disjunction over the empty set is *False* and the conjunction over the empty set is *True*. A solution of c_e selects not only all the transitions in $Susp(e)$ but also some arbitrary suspicious transitions not in e; this is because we assumed that every Boolean expression is defined over the set of the variables for all the suspicious transitions. Given an execution ee' obtained by concatenating e with e', it holds that $c_{ee'} = c_e \wedge c_{e'}$. Let us denote by $F_{\downarrow\mathcal{M}}$ the set of executions of the mutation machine $\mathcal{M}$ defining an execution in a set F of execution of $\mathcal{D}$. Given an input sequence $\alpha \in G^*$, we define $c_\alpha \stackrel{\text{def}}{=} \bigvee_{e \in E_{\alpha\downarrow\mathcal{M}}} c_e$. A submachine $\mathcal{P}$ of $\mathcal{M}$ is involved in an execution e of a mutation machine $\mathcal{M}$ if and only if c_e specifies $\mathcal{P}$.

Lemma 3. *The Boolean expression c_α specifies all the submachines involved in all revealing executions triggered by a prefix of α and detected by α.*

Let α and β be two input sequences. Assuming that we want to determine $F_{\alpha\beta}$ and $E_{\alpha\beta}$, given F_α, we will proceed as follows. We can determine $E_{+\beta} = \{ee' \mid e \in F_\alpha, ee'$ is an accepted deterministic execution, and $\beta' \subseteq inp(e')$ for some prefix β' of $\beta\}$ and $F_{\alpha\beta} = \{ee' \mid e \in F_\alpha, ee'$ is accepted and unaccepted deterministic execution, $\beta \subseteq inp(e')\}$. Then $E_{\alpha\beta} = E_\alpha \cup E_{+\beta}$. It holds that any solution of $c_{\alpha\beta}$ is a solution of $c_\alpha \vee \bigvee_{e \in E_{+\beta\downarrow\mathcal{M}}} c_e$ and vice versa.

Procedure *Build_expression* in Algorithm 1 is aimed at building the expression $c_{+\beta} = \bigvee_{e \in E_{+\beta\downarrow\mathcal{M}}} c_e$ to be added to c_α for obtaining $c_{\alpha\beta}$. The inputs and the outputs of the procedure are obvious and omitted. We observe that when the procedure is called with $F_\varepsilon = \{\varepsilon\}$, it returns exactly c_β.

Lemma 4. *Let α be a symbolic input sequence. A submachine is not involved in a deterministic α-revealing execution e if and only if it is specified with $\bar{c}_e$, where $\bar{c}_e$ denotes the negation of c_e.*

Thus the sets of suspicious transitions in all deterministic α-revealing executions represent all submachines detected by input sequence α and only them.

Lemma 5. *Input sequence $\alpha \in G^*$ does not detect any submachine specified with $\bar{c}_\alpha$.*

The Boolean expression $\bar{c}_\alpha$ specifies the submachines of a mutation machine not involved in deterministic revealing executions. These submachines exclude suspicious transitions in the revealing executions but they also include other transitions of the mutation machine, causing some of the specified submachines to be nondeterministic or partially specified. To determine the deterministic submachines (and so the mutants) undetected by an input sequence, we must exclude the nondeterministic and partially specified submachines from the submachines specified by $\bar{c}_\alpha$, by adding a constraint that only complete deterministic submachines should be considered.

3.3   Encoding (Un)detected Deterministic Complete Machines

The deterministic complete submachines of a mutation machine $\mathcal{M}$ can also be identified with the suspicious transitions as discussed in the previous subsection. So, we can specify them with Boolean expressions over the variables for the suspicious transitions.

Let s be a suspicious state, $Z(s) = \{Z_1, Z_2, \ldots, Z_n\}$ be the set of its clusters. Then the conjunction of variables of a cluster Z_i expresses the requirement that all these transitions must be present together to ensure that a submachine with the cluster Z_i is complete in state s. Moreover, only one cluster in $Z(s)$ can be chosen in a deterministic complete submachine, therefore, the transitions are restricted by the expressions determining clusters. Each cluster Z_i is uniquely specified by Boolean expression $z_i \stackrel{\text{def}}{=} (\bigwedge_{t \in Z_i} t) \wedge (\overline{\bigvee_{t \in Susp(s) \setminus Z_i} t})$ which permits the selection of exactly the suspicious transitions in Z_i. Given $Z_i, Z_j \in Z(s)$, every solution of z_i is not a solution of z_j. Then each state s in S_{susp} yields the expression $c_s \stackrel{\text{def}}{=} \bigvee_{i=1}^{n} z_i$ of which all the solutions determine all the clusters in $Z(s)$. The set of clusters specified by c_s is $Z(s)$.

The expression $\bigwedge_{s \in S_{susp}} c_s$ specifies the set of clusters of suspicious states either in the specification $\mathcal{S}$ or every mutant. Each such cluster in the specification has at least one untrusted transition in $Untr(\mathcal{S})$. Excluding the specification $\mathcal{S}$ can be expressed with the negation of the conjunction of the variables of all the untrusted transitions $\overline{\bigwedge_{t \in Untr(\mathcal{S})} t}$. Any of its solutions excludes at least one cluster in the specification and the negation cannot specify the $\mathcal{S}$. The Boolean expression $c_{clstr} \stackrel{\text{def}}{=} \bigwedge_{s \in S_{susp}} c_s \wedge \overline{\bigwedge_{t \in Untr(S)} t}$ excludes nondeterministic and partially specified submachines and the specification, meaning that c_{clstr} specifies only all deterministic submachines of $\mathcal{M}$ including the mutants in $Mut(\mathcal{M})$. To further exclude nondeterministic and partially specified submachines as well as the specification from the submachines specified by $\overline{c}_\alpha$, the Boolean expression c_{clstr} must be added to $\overline{c}_\alpha$. Combining the statements above with Lemma 5, we get Theorem 1.

Theorem 1. *Input sequence $\alpha \in G^*$ does not detect any deterministic submachine of mutation machine $\mathcal{M}$ specified with $\overline{c}_\alpha \wedge c_{clstr}$.*

The set of mutants $Mut(\mathcal{M})$ is included in the set of deterministic complete submachines of $\mathcal{M}$, which justifies the following corollary.

Corollary 1. *Input sequence $\alpha \in G^*$ does not detect any mutant in $Mut(\mathcal{M})$ specified with $\overline{c}_\alpha \wedge c_{clstr}$.*

Example 3. The Boolean expression specifying the clusters in state 3 of the mutation machine in Fig. 1 is $c_3 = \bigvee_{i=1..6} z_{3_i}$ where $z_{3_1} = t_5 t_6 \overline{t}_{12} \overline{t}_{13} \overline{t}_{14} \overline{t}_{15}$ for cluster $Z_{3_1} = \{t_5, t_6\}$ and the others z_{3_i} can be easily computed from the clusters in Example 1.

4 Verification and Generation of a Checking Sequence

In this section we address two problems. The first problem is verifying whether a given input sequence, which we call a (checking sequence) *conjecture*, is a checking sequence and the second is concerned with the generation of a checking sequence. Our approach to solving both problems consists in building and resolving Boolean expressions specifying mutants surviving input sequences.

4.1 Verifying a Checking Sequence Conjecture

Let φ be a Boolean expression specifying a set of complete deterministic submachines including a set of mutants to be detected. The set of submachines for φ can always be reduced with an expression specifying submachines a given input sequence detects.

Theorem 2. *An input sequence α is a checking sequence for a set of complete deterministic machines specified with an expression φ if and only if $\overline{c}_\alpha \wedge \varphi$ has no solution or each of the machines it specifies is conforming or not strongly-connected.*

The set of complete deterministic submachines of a mutation machine $\mathcal{M}$ is specified with c_{clstr}, which leads to Corollary 2.

Corollary 2. *Input sequence α is a checking sequence for $Mut(\mathcal{M})$ if and only if $\overline{c}_\alpha \wedge c_{clstr}$ has no solution or each of the machines it specifies is either conforming or not a mutant.*

Procedure Verify_checking_sequence $(\mathcal{D}, \alpha, \varphi_\alpha, F_\alpha, \beta)$;

Inputs : $\mathcal{D}$, the distinguishing automaton of $\mathcal{M}$ and $\mathcal{S}$; α, β a prefix and a suffix of the conjecture $\alpha\beta$; φ_α and F_α

Output: $isAChSeq$, a Boolean flag indicating whether $\alpha\beta$ is a checking sequence

Output: $\varphi_{\alpha\beta}$ a Boolean expression specifying the mutants undetected by $\alpha\beta$

Output: $\mathcal{D}_\mathcal{P}$ the distinguishing automaton of $\mathcal{S}$ and $\mathcal{P}$, a mutant undetected by $\alpha\beta$

Output: $F_{\alpha\beta}$ the set of unaccepted deterministic executions of $\mathcal{D}_\mathcal{P}$ triggered by $\alpha\beta$

$(c_{+\beta}, F_{\alpha\beta}) := Build\_expression(F_\alpha, \mathcal{D}, \beta)$;

Initialization: $c_\mathcal{P} := False$; $\varphi_{\alpha\beta} := \varphi_\alpha \wedge \overline{c}_{+\beta}$; $\mathcal{D}_\mathcal{P} := null$;

repeat

    $isAChSeq := true$;

    $\varphi_{\alpha\beta} := \varphi_{\alpha\beta} \wedge \overline{c}_\mathcal{P}$;

    Generate a deterministic complete machine $\mathcal{P}$ by resolving $\varphi_{\alpha\beta}$;

    if $\mathcal{P} \neq null$ **then**

        $isAChSeq := False$;

        Set $\mathcal{D}_\mathcal{P}$ to the distinguishing automaton of $\mathcal{S}$ and $\mathcal{P}$;

        if $\mathcal{P}$ *is not strongly-connected or* $\mathcal{D}_\mathcal{P}$ *has no sink state* **then**

            $c_\mathcal{P} := \bigwedge_{t \in Susp(\mathcal{P})} t$;

            Set $\mathcal{D}_\mathcal{P} := null$;

        end

    end

until $isAChSeq$ or $\mathcal{D}_\mathcal{P} \neq null$;

return $(isAChSeq, \mathcal{D}_\mathcal{P}, \varphi_{\alpha\beta}, F_{\alpha\beta})$;

Algorithm 2. Verifying a checking sequence conjecture

Based in Theorem 2 and Corollary 2, to verify whether a conjecture is a checking sequence for a given fault model we can iteratively exclude conforming mutants and non-strongly-connected submachines as solutions to a Boolean expression specifying the submachines the conjecture cannot detect, while no nonconforming mutant is found. This idea is implemented in Algorithm 2 with Procedure *Verify_checking_sequence*.

Procedure *Verify_checking_sequence* is aimed at verifying whether the conjecture $\alpha\beta$ constitutes a checking sequence, assuming that we have evidence that α is not. The evidence is expressed with a Boolean expression φ_α specifying a non-empty set of mutants having survived α and the set F_α of unaccepted deterministic executions of $\mathcal{D}$ triggered by α. The procedure takes also as inputs the distinguishing automaton for the specification and mutation machines and input sequence β. The procedure returns a Boolean flag $isAChSeq$ indicating whether $\alpha\beta$ is a checking sequence, evidence for whether $\alpha\beta$ is a checking sequence or not and the distinguishing automaton $\mathcal{D}_\mathcal{P}$ for the specification and a mutant $\mathcal{P}$ undetected by $\alpha\beta$. A call to the procedure with $\alpha = \varepsilon$, $F_\alpha = \{\varepsilon\}$ and $\varphi_\alpha = c_{clstr}$ allows verifying whether β is a checking sequence.

Verifying the conjecture $\alpha\beta$, the procedure makes a call to procedure *Build_expression* in Algorithm 1 to compute a Boolean expression specifying the submachines detected by $\alpha\beta$ but not by α. The negation of the latter expression is added to φ_α for obtaining $\varphi_{\alpha\beta}$ specifying the next surviving submachine. Iteratively, the procedure uses a solver to generate a next submachine undetected by $\alpha\beta$; the iteration stops when there is no surviving machine or a witness surviving submachine is neither strongly-connected nor conforming, i.e., it is a nonconforming mutant. The distinguishing automaton for the specification and a conforming mutant has no sink state. On the termination, $\alpha\beta$ is not a checking sequence if and only if a nonconforming mutant was generated, in which case the procedure returns the distinguishing automaton of the specification and the mutant. Later, the automaton will serve to refine $\alpha\beta$ and to determine a new input sequence to be appended to the refined sequence. Indeed, an input sequence which is not a checking sequence can always be extended to obtain a checking sequence since the mutants and the specification are strongly-connected.

In the next section we elaborate methods for determining extension sequences to be added to a conjecture to build a checking sequence.

4.2 Refining and Extending an Input Sequence to Detect Surviving Mutants

A given checking sequence conjecture leaves a nonconforming mutant undetected because it does not trigger any of the revealing executions involving the mutant, i.e., every prefix of the conjecture is not a reduction of the input sequence of the revealing executions involving the mutant. To obtain a checking sequence from a conjecture, we distinguish two situations on whether or not a prefix of conjecture is compatible with the input sequence of a revealing execution involving an undetected mutant. In case of compatibility, the conjecture can be reduced to an input sequence which triggers a revealing execution involving an undetected witness mutant. The reduced conjecture will all the mutants detected by the original conjecture as and other mutants including the witness undetected mutant. The refinement (by reduction) process will be repeated until there is no new undetected mutant or the length of the revealing executions involving a surviving mutant is greater than the length of the reduced conjecture, which corresponds to the second situation in which the reduced conjecture can be extended.

In the second situation, a nonconforming mutant is left undetected and all its executions enabled by the given conjecture are not revealing. Note that there always exists at least one such execution because mutants and the specification are complete and strongly-connected. Any of the execution enabled by the conjecture can be used to obtain a reduced conjecture and to determine an input sequence for extending the reduced conjecture. The concatenation of the reduced conjecture and the extension input sequence constitutes an extended conjecture. The extended conjecture triggers at least one new revealing execution; so it not only detects all the mutants detected by the given conjecture, but it also detects all the mutants involved in the revealing executions it triggers. The reduction

Procedure Refine_and_gen_extension $(\alpha, \mathcal{D}_{\mathcal{P}})$;

Input : α an input sequence

Input : $\mathcal{D}_{\mathcal{P}}$, the distinguishing automaton of $\mathcal{M}$ and a mutant $\mathcal{P}$ surviving α

Output: $\alpha_{ref} \subseteq \alpha$, a reduction of α for triggering the prefix of a revealing
execution in $\mathcal{P}$

Output: β, an input sequence such that $\alpha_{ref}\beta$ detects a $\mathcal{P}$; $\beta = \varepsilon$, if α_{ref} detects
$\mathcal{P}$

if $\mathcal{D}_{\mathcal{P}}$ *has an accepted execution enabled by a prefix of* α **then**

    | Let e be an accepted execution of $\mathcal{D}_{\mathcal{P}}$ enabled by a prefix of α;

    | $\alpha_{ref} := (\alpha[1...|e|] \cap inp(e))\alpha[|e| + 1...|\alpha|]$;

    | $\beta := \varepsilon$

else

    | Let e be an unaccepted execution of $\mathcal{D}_{\mathcal{P}}$ enabled by α;

    | $\alpha_{ref} := \alpha \cap inp(e)$;

    | Let s be the last state in e;

    | Let β be the input sequence of a path from s to a sink state;

end

return (α_{ref}, β);

      Algorithm 3. Refining a sequence and generating an extension

and extension processes can be repeated until every nonconforming mutants is detected. Theorem 3 formalizes the discussion above and specifies a way for reducing and extending a given input sequence to detect a mutant surviving the given conjecture. Given an input sequence α of length $|\alpha|$, we let $\alpha[i...j]$, with $1 \leq i, j \leq |\alpha|$, denote the subsequence obtained by extracting the elements in α from position i to j.

Theorem 3. *Let α be an input sequence detecting some mutants but not detecting a nonconforming mutant $\mathcal{P}$. Exactly one of the two following statements holds:*

- *A reduction γ of a prefix of α detects $\mathcal{P}$ and in which case $\gamma\alpha[|\gamma| + 1...|\alpha|]$ detects $\mathcal{P}$ and all the mutants involved in an execution in $E_{\gamma\alpha[|\gamma|+1...|\alpha|]}$ including those detected by α.*
- *$\mathcal{P}$ survives every reduction of every prefix of α; then there is a reduction γ of α and an input sequence β such that $\gamma\beta$ detects $\mathcal{P}$ and all the mutants involved in an execution in $E_{\gamma\beta}$ including the mutants detected by α.*

The mutant referenced in Theorem 3 identifies some revealing executions which α does not trigger. A revealing execution may allow reducing and extending α. The set of revealing executions involving the mutant can be determined with the distinguishing automaton of the specification machine and the mutant.

Procedure *Refine_and_gen_extension* in Algorithm 3 reduces and extends a given input sequence α to detect a nonconforming mutant $\mathcal{P}$ for which the distinguishing automaton $\mathcal{D}_{\mathcal{P}}$ is known. The procedure returns a reduction α_{ref} of α triggering an execution in the mutant and an input sequence β for extending the execution to a revealing execution in $\mathcal{P}$. The sequence β is empty in case a prefix of α_{ref} triggers a revealing execution. Computing α_{ref} and β, first an execution e from the initial to the sink state of $\mathcal{D}_{\mathcal{P}}$ enabled by a prefix of α is determined. The intersection of $inp(e)$ and a prefix of α is a reduction of the input of the revealing execution defining e, so it triggers a revealing execution and detects the mutant. Then α_{ref} is the concatenation of the intersection sequence with the suffix of α and β is set to empty. In case none of the prefixes of α can trigger a revealing execution in the mutant, the whole sequence α is reduced with the input sequence of an unaccepted execution it enables in $\mathcal{D}_{\mathcal{P}}$ and β becomes the input of an execution from the target state of the execution enabled by α but triggered by α_{ref}.

Example 4. Let $\alpha_{ex} = (0 \leq x \leq 3)(x < -3)(x < -1 \vee x > 3)$ be an input sequence of length $|\alpha_{ex}| = 3$. To verify whether α_{ex} is a checking sequence for $\mathcal{M}_1$, we can execute *Verify_checking_sequence*$(\mathcal{D}, \varepsilon, c_{clstr}, \{\varepsilon\}, \alpha_{ex})$ making a call to *Build_expression*$(\varepsilon, \mathcal{D}, \alpha_{ex})$ to determine the only accepted execution α_{ex} triggers in $\mathcal{D}$ defined by the execution of the specification $e_1 = t_1 t_3 t_6$ and the deterministic execution $e_2 = t_1 t_3 t_{12}$. All the transitions in e_1 are belong to the specification but t_{12} occurring in e_2 is mutated. The execution of $\mathcal{D}$ is accepted because the symbolic output sequences $out(e_1, \alpha_{ex}) = (1 \leq y \leq 4)(y < -4)(0 > y \vee y > 4)$ and $out(e_1, \alpha_{ex}) = (1 \leq y \leq 4)(y < -4)(2 > y \vee y > 6)$ do not have the same concrete outputs. Every mutant involved by e_2, e.g., the mutant composed of $t_1, t_2, t_3, t_4, t_{12}, t_5, t_7, t_8$ is nonconforming and detected by α_{ex}. Such a mutant is specified with $c_{e_2} = t_1 t_{12}$. However the mutant specified with Boolean expression $\mathcal{P}_1 = \{t_9, t_{10}, t_3, t_{11}, t_{12}, t_5, t_{16}, t_8\}$ specified with $\overline{c}_{e_2}$ survives α_{ex} because α_{ex} does not trigger an execution in it, so producing the empty output sequence different from $out(e_1, \alpha_{ex})$. α_{ex} does not trigger an execution in $\mathcal{P}_1$ because the first input in α_{ex} is not a reduction of the inputs of t_9 and t_{10}. At the end, *Verify_checking_sequence* returns that α_{ex} is not a checking sequence and it also returns $\mathcal{D}_{\mathcal{P}_1}$, $\varphi_{\alpha_{ex}} = \overline{c}_{e_2} \wedge c_{clstr}$ and $F_{\alpha_{ex}} = \{e_1\}$.

A call to *Refine_and_gen_extension*$(\alpha_{ex}, \mathcal{D}_{\mathcal{P}_1})$ refines the prefix of length two of α_{ex} to detect $\mathcal{P}_1$. Execution $e_3 = t_{10} t_{16}$ is a revealing execution involving $\mathcal{P}_1$; it is not triggered but enabled by $\alpha_{ex}[1..2]$ and it is used to determine the refined (reduced) sequence $\alpha_{ref} = (x = 3)(x < -3)(x < -1 \vee x > 3)$. The inputs in α_{ref} are obtained by intersecting the input in α_{ex} with those labeling the accepted execution of $\mathcal{D}_{\mathcal{P}_1}$ defined with e_3. At the end $\beta = \varepsilon$ since a prefix of α_{ex} detects $\mathcal{P}_1$.

4.3   Generating a Checking Sequence

We want to generate starting from a given input sequence a checking sequence for a given fault model. Our method iterates three actions: verifying whether a current input sequence is a checking sequence, refining and extending the current input sequence by detecting a witness nonconforming mutant surviving the current input sequence in case it is not a checking sequence. The iteration

Table 1. Checking sequence generation for $\mathcal{M}_1$ in Fig. 1.

Step	$\alpha \to \beta$	Suspicious transitions in revealing executions	Witness surviving mutant
1	$\varepsilon \to (0 \le x \le 3)(x < -3)(x < -1 \vee x > 3)$	$\{t_1, t_{12}\}$	$\{t_9, t_{10}, t_3, t_{11}, t_{12}, t_5, t_{16}, t_8\}$
2	$(x=3)(x<-3)(x<-1 \vee x>3) \to \varepsilon$	$\{t_{10}, t_{16}\}$	$\{t_9, t_{10}, t_3, t_{11}, t_{12}, t_5, t_7, t_8\}$
3	$(x=3)(x<-3)(x<-1 \vee x>3) \to \varepsilon$	$\{t_7, t_{10}\}$	$\{t_1, t_2, t_3, t_{11}, t_5, t_6, t_7, t_8\}$
4	$(x=3)(x<-3)(x<-1 \vee x>3) \to (-1 \le x \le 3)(x<-3)(0 \le x \le 3)(-2 \le x)$	$\{t_{16}, t_1, t_5, t_6\}$, $\{t_1, t_5, t_6, t_7, t_{11}\}$	$\{t_1, t_2, t_3, t_{11}, t_6, t_{13}, t_{14}\}$
5	$(x=3)(x<-3)(x<-1 \vee x>3)(1<x\le3 \wedge x \ne 2)(x<-3)(0 \le x \le 3)(-2 \le x) \to \varepsilon$	$\{t_1, t_6, t_{14}\}$	$\{t_1, t_2, t_3, t_{11}, t_6, t_{13}, t_{15}\}$
6	$(x=3)(x<-3)(x<-1 \vee x>3)(1<x\le3 \wedge x \ne 2)(x<-3)(0 \le x \le 3)(-2 \le x) \to \varepsilon$	$\{t_1, t_6, t_{15}\}$	No surviving mutant

process terminates when the current input sequence is a checking sequence. Procedure *Gen_check_seq* in Algorithm 4 takes as inputs an initial input sequence α_{init} and a fault model and generates a checking sequence α detecting all the nonconforming mutants in the fault model. Determining the checking sequence, the procedure performs an initialization phase followed by a computing phase. In the initialization phase, the procedure computes the expression specifying all the deterministic and complete submachines of the mutation machine. It also computes the distinguishing automaton $\mathcal{D}$ of the specification and mutation machines. Then it sets the prefix of the conjecture α to the empty sequence, F_α to the singleton $\{\varepsilon\}$, φ_α to c_{clstr} for specifying search space for the mutants and the suffix of the conjecture β to α_{init}.

In the computing phase, the procedure makes a call to *Verify_checking_sequence* to verify whether $\alpha\beta$ is a checking sequence knowing that α is not. *Verify_checking_sequence* returns a verdict in variable *isAChSeq* together with $\mathcal{D}_\mathcal{P}$ the distinguishing automaton of the specification and a mutant undetected by $\alpha\beta$, the Boolean expression $\varphi_{\alpha\beta}$ specifying the mutants undetected by $\alpha\beta$, and the set $F_{\alpha\beta}$. Then the current input sequence α becomes $\alpha\beta$, φ_α becomes $\varphi_{\alpha\beta}$. In case the current input sequence is not a checking sequence it is reduced and the non-null extension sequence β is generated via a call to *Refine_and_gen_extension*. β can be the empty input sequence in which case φ_α is updated to remove the detected mutants prior to the next iteration step. Another approach would have been to remove all the new mutants detected by α_{ref}, which requires determining all new accepted executions of $\mathcal{D}$ triggered by α_{ref}. In our work, we just remove the witness mutant and the others will be detected in the next iteration steps. When β is not empty, $\varphi_{\alpha\beta}$ is determined at the next iteration step. The computation phase terminates if the current input is a checking sequence, i.e., φ_α specifies no submachine. This termination happens after a finite number of iteration steps because each call to *Verify_checking_sequence* reduces the number of machines in the finite space of undetected mutants.

Procedure Gen_check_seq $(\alpha_{init}, \langle \mathcal{S}, \simeq, Mut(\mathcal{M}) \rangle)$;
Input : α_{init}, an initial input sequence and $\langle \mathcal{S}, \simeq, Mut(\mathcal{M}) \rangle$, a fault model
Output: α, a checking sequence for $\langle \mathcal{S}, \simeq, Mut(\mathcal{M}) \rangle$
Compute c_{clstr} and $\mathcal{D}$ the distinguishing automaton for $\mathcal{S}$ and $\mathcal{M}$;
Initialization : $\alpha := \varepsilon$ $\beta := \alpha_{init}$ $\varphi_\alpha := c_{clstr}$ $F_\alpha := \{\varepsilon\}$;
repeat

> $(isAChSeq, \mathcal{D}_\mathcal{P}, \varphi_{\alpha\beta}, F_{\alpha\beta}) := Verify\_checking\_sequence(\mathcal{D}, \alpha, \varphi_\alpha, F_\alpha, \beta)$;
> $\alpha := \alpha\beta$;
> $\varphi_\alpha := \varphi_{\alpha\beta}$;
> **if** *not (isAChSeq)* **then**
>> $(\alpha_{ref}, \beta) := Refine\_and\_gen\_extension(\alpha, \mathcal{D}_\mathcal{P})$;
>> $\alpha := \alpha_{ref}$;
>> **if** $\beta = \varepsilon$ **then**
>>> Let e be a revealing execution triggered by α in $\mathcal{P}$ obtained from $\mathcal{D}_\mathcal{P}$;
>>> $\varphi_\alpha := \varphi_\alpha \wedge \bar{c}_e$;
>>
>> **end**
>
> **end**

until *isAChSeq*;
return α is a checking sequence;
Algorithm 4. Generation of a checking sequence from an initial input sequence α_{init}

Example 5. Table 1 presents data produced in executing *Gen_check_seq* to compute a checking sequence for $\mathcal{M}_1$ from α_{ex}. The second column shows how β extends α. The witness mutant at step i is not involved in any current set of suspicious transitions. Each set specifies a revealing execution; such a mutant survives $\alpha\beta$ determined at the same step. The input sequence α extended with β at step $i + 1$ detects the witness mutant at step i; they are generated using procedure *Refine_and_gen_extension*. β is ε whenever the procedure has found a reduction of a previous input sequence detecting the witness mutant having survived the previous input sequence. After 6 iteration steps, *Gen_check_seq* produces the checking sequence $(x = 3)(x < -3)(x < -1 \vee x > 3)(1 < x \leq 3 \wedge x \neq 2)(x < -3)(0 \leq x \leq 3)(-2 \leq x)$ detecting all the 35 mutants in the fault domain.

5   Prototype Tool and Experimental Results

We performed an experimental evaluation of the scalability of the proposed method for generating checking sequences for DSIOFSM. We implemented in JAVA a prototype tool for verifying and generating a checking sequence. The tool is built on top of ANTLR [14] and a Z3 API [12]. In our experiments, we used a desktop computer equipped with 3.4 Ghz Intel Core i7-3770 CPU, 16.0 GB of RAM and Windows 7.

We used two industrial-like specification DSIOFSMs. Each DIOFSM represents an automotive HVAC system [19,21] with 13 states and 62 transitions.

Table 2. Experimental results with the second SIOFSM specification

Max. number of mutants	8191	$1.9E+5$	$2.6E+7$	$5E+15$
Length of check. seq.	50	42	52	133
Time (sec.)	297	266	695	3042

The first specification DIOFSM is in fact a deterministic SIFSM used in [13] to generate checking experiments, i.e., a set of input sequences detecting all nonconforming mutants. This experiment focuses on checking sequences which cannot be generated by the method in [13]. The DSIFSM uses symbolic input over 6 integer input variables and 5 Boolean input variables. All the outputs are concrete. We added mutated transitions to the deterministic SIFSM, obtaining a mutation SIFSM including 8191 deterministic submachines different from the specification; 8159 submachines are mutants of the fault domain and the other 32 are not mutants because they are not strongly-connected (this was computed by our tool). The tool has generated a checking sequence of length 49 detecting all the nonconforming SIFSM mutants.

The second specification DSIOFSM was obtained by replacing in the SIFSM concrete outputs with symbolic outputs using integer output variables and a Boolean output variable. The mutation machines were obtained by adding to the specification mutated transitions implementing different types of faults: transfer, output, changing of arithmetic and Boolean operators in inputs and assignments. Table 2 summarizes the results. The first row shows the numbers of complete deterministic machines in the fault domains; we have not determined the exact number of mutants in the fault domain. The second row shows the length of the generated checking sequences and the third row presents the computation time. For the SIOFSM mutation machine defining at most 8191 mutants, an execution of the tool lasted 297 s to generate a checking sequence of length 50.

The result of the experimental evaluation indicates that the more mutants in the fault domain, the longer are the checking sequence and the generation time. In some situation the generation time seems to be too long, which could prevent the application of the method. In practice, the generation of a checking sequence can be stopped at any time since it is incremental, which will permit obtaining a checking sequence for a fault subdomain. Then, one could generate checking experiments [13] to detect the remaining mutants not in the fault subdomain. Indeed, increasing the number of resets would reduce the time for detecting the remaining mutants.

6   Conclusion

In this paper, we generalized the checking sequence construction problem from a classical Mealy machine to a restricted type of extended FSM, SIOFSM, while modeling a fault domain by a mutation machine instead of limiting it just by a state number as in previous work. We elaborated a method for verifying whether an input sequence is a checking sequence for a given fault model. Then we used it to propose a method for generating a checking sequence by iterative extensions of a given (possibly empty) input sequence that avoids using the reset. The methods are based on solving Boolean expression. The novelty of the proposed method is that it generates a checking sequence for a user defined fault model of a finite state machine with infinite inputs and infinite outputs.

We have developed a prototype tool and used it to generate checking sequences for examples of industrial-like systems represented with SIOFSMs.

Our current work focuses on generating checking sequences of near-to-minimal lengths and checking sequences for timed extensions of SIOFSMs.

Acknowledgment. This work is supported in part by GM, NSERC of Canada and MESI (Ministère de l'Économie, Science et Innovation) of Gouvernement du Québec.

References

1. Androutsopoulos, K., Clark, D., Harman, M., Hierons, R.M., Li, Z., Tratt, L.: Amorphous slicing of extended finite state machines. IEEE Trans. Softw. Eng. **39**(7), 892–909 (2013). https://doi.org/10.1109/tse.2012.72
2. Bessayah, F., Cavalli, A., Maja, W., Martins, E., Valenti, A.W.: A fault injection tool for testing web services composition. In: Bottaci, L., Fraser, G. (eds.) TAIC PART 2010. LNCS, vol. 6303, pp. 137–146. Springer, Heidelberg (2010). https://doi.org/10.1007/978-3-642-15585-7_13
3. Delamaro, M.E., Maldonado, J.C., Pasquini, A., Mathur, A.P.: Interface mutation test adequacy criterion: an empirical evaluation. Empir. Softw. Eng. **6**(2), 111–142 (2001). https://doi.org/10.1023/a:1011429104252
4. Eén, N., Sörensson, N.: An extensible SAT-solver. In: Giunchiglia, E., Tacchella, A. (eds.) SAT 2003. LNCS, vol. 2919, pp. 502–518. Springer, Heidelberg (2004). https://doi.org/10.1007/978-3-540-24605-3_37
5. Godefroid, P., Klarlund, N., Sen, K.: DART: directed automated random testing. ACM SIGPLAN Not. **40**(6), 213–223 (2005). https://doi.org/10.1145/1064978.1065036
6. Hennie, F.C.: Fault detecting experiments for sequential circuits. In: Proceedings of 5th Annual Symposium on Switching Circuit Theory and Logical Design, SWCT 1964, November 1964, Princeton, NJ, pp. 95–110. IEEE CS Press, Washington, DC (1964). https://doi.org/10.1109/swct.1964.8
7. Hierons, R.M., Jourdan, G.V., Ural, H., Yenigun, H.: Checking sequence construction using adaptive and preset distinguishing sequences. In: Proceedings of 7th IEEE International Conference on Software Engineering and Formal Methods, SEFM 2009, November 2009, Hanoi, pp. 157–166. IEEE CS Press, Washington (2009). https://doi.org/10.1109/sefm.2009.12
8. Jia, Y., Harman, M.: An analysis and survey of the development of mutation testing. IEEE Trans. Softw. Eng. **37**(5), 649–678 (2011). https://doi.org/10.1109/tse.2010.62
9. Jourdan, G.V., Ural, H., Yenigün, H.: Reducing locating sequences for testing from finite state machines. In: Proceedings of 31st Annual ACM Symposium on Applied Computing, SAC 2016, April 2016, Pisa, pp. 1654–1659. ACM, New York (2016). https://doi.org/10.1145/2851613.2851831

10. Koufareva, I., Petrenko, A., Yevtushenko, N.: Test generation driven by user-defined fault models. In: Csopaki, G., Dibuz, S., Tarnay, K. (eds.) Testing of Communicating Systems. ITIFIP, vol. 21, pp. 215–233. Springer, Boston, MA (1999). https://doi.org/10.1007/978-0-387-35567-2_14

11. Moore, E.F.: Gedanken-experiments on sequential machines. In: Shannon, C., McCarthy, J. (eds.) Automata Studies, pp. 129–153. Princeton University Press, Princeton (1956)

12. de Moura, L., Bjørner, N.: Z3: an efficient SMT solver. In: Ramakrishnan, C.R., Rehof, J. (eds.) TACAS 2008. LNCS, vol. 4963, pp. 337–340. Springer, Heidelberg (2008). https://doi.org/10.1007/978-3-540-78800-3_24

13. Nguena Timo, O., Petrenko, A., Ramesh, S.: Multiple mutation testing from finite state machines with symbolic inputs. In: Yevtushenko, N., Cavalli, A.R., Yenigün, H. (eds.) ICTSS 2017. LNCS, vol. 10533, pp. 108–125. Springer, Cham (2017). https://doi.org/10.1007/978-3-319-67549-7_7

14. Parr, T.: The Definitive ANTLR 4 Reference, 2nd edn. Pragmatic Bookshelf, Dallas and Raleigh (2013)

15. Petrenko, A.: Fault model-driven test derivation from finite state models: annotated bibliography. In: Cassez, F., Jard, C., Rozoy, B., Ryan, M.D. (eds.) MOVEP 2000. LNCS, vol. 2067, pp. 196–205. Springer, Heidelberg (2001). https://doi.org/10.1007/3-540-45510-8_10

16. Petrenko, A.: Toward testing from finite state machines with symbolic inputs and outputs. Softw. Syst. Model. (2017, to appear). https://doi.org/10.1007/s10270-017-0613-x

17. Petrenko, A., Avellaneda, F., Groz, R., Oriat, C.: From passive to active FSM inference via checking sequence construction. In: Yevtushenko, N., Cavalli, A.R., Yenigün, H. (eds.) ICTSS 2017. LNCS, vol. 10533, pp. 126–141. Springer, Cham (2017). https://doi.org/10.1007/978-3-319-67549-7_8

18. Petrenko, A., Boroday, S., Groz, R.: Confirming configurations in EFSM testing. IEEE Trans. Softw. Eng. **30**(1), 29–42 (2004). https://doi.org/10.1109/tse.2004.1265734

19. Petrenko, A., Dury, A., Ramesh, S., Mohalik, S.: A method and tool for test optimization for automotive controllers. In: Workshops Proceedings of 6th IEEE International Conference on Software Testing, Verification and Validation, ICST 2013 Workshops, March 2013, Luxembourg, pp. 198–207. IEEE CS Press, Washington, DC (2013). https://doi.org/10.1109/icstw.2013.31

20. Petrenko, A., Nguena Timo, O., Ramesh, S.: Multiple mutation testing from FSM. In: Albert, E., Lanese, I. (eds.) FORTE 2016. LNCS, vol. 9688, pp. 222–238. Springer, Cham (2016). https://doi.org/10.1007/978-3-319-39570-8_15

21. Petrenko, A., Nguena Timo, O., Ramesh, S.: Test generation by constraint solving and FSM mutant killing. In: Wotawa, F., Nica, M., Kushik, N. (eds.) ICTSS 2016. LNCS, vol. 9976, pp. 36–51. Springer, Cham (2016). https://doi.org/10.1007/978-3-319-47443-4_3

22. Petrenko, A., Simao, A.: Generating checking sequences for user defined fault models. In: Yevtushenko, N., Cavalli, A.R., Yenigün, H. (eds.) ICTSS 2017. LNCS, vol. 10533, pp. 320–325. Springer, Cham (2017). https://doi.org/10.1007/978-3-319-67549-7_20

23. Petrenko, A., Simao, A.: Checking experiments for finite state machines with symbolic inputs. In: El-Fakih, K., Barlas, G., Yevtushenko, N. (eds.) ICTSS 2015. LNCS, vol. 9447, pp. 3–18. Springer, Cham (2015). https://doi.org/10.1007/978-3-319-25945-1_1

24. Petrenko, A., Yevtushenko, N.: Test suite generation from a FSM with a given type of implementation errors. In: Linn Jr., R.J., Uyar, M.Ü. (eds.) Proceedings of IFIP TC6/WG6.1 12th International Symposium on Protocol Specification, Testing and Verification, Lake Buena Vista, FL, June 1992. IFIP Transactions C: Communication Systems, vol. 8, pp. 229–243. North-Holland, Amsterdam (1992). https://doi.org/10.1016/b978-0-444-89874-6.50021-0

25. Thummalapenta, S., Xie, T., Tillmann, N., de Halleux, J., Su, Z.: Synthesizing method sequences for high-coverage testing. ACM SIGPLAN Not. **46**(10), 189–206 (2011). https://doi.org/10.1145/2076021.2048083

26. Utting, M., Pretschner, A., Legeard, B.: A taxonomy of model-based testing approaches. Softw. Test. Verif. Reliab. **22**(5), 297–312 (2012). https://doi.org/10.1002/stvr.456

27. Yannakakis, M., Lee, D.: Testing finite state machines: fault detection. J. Comput. Syst. Sci. **50**(2), 209–227 (1995). https://doi.org/10.1006/jcss.1995.1019

28. Zhu, H., Hall, P.A.V., May, J.H.R.: Software unit test coverage and adequacy. ACM Comput. Surv. **29**(4), 366–427 (1997). https://doi.org/10.1145/267580.267590

Explicit Auditing

Wilmer Ricciotti$^{(\boxtimes)}$ and James Cheney

LFCS, School of Informatics, University of Edinburgh,
10 Crichton Street, Edinburgh EH8 9AB, UK
research@wilmer-ricciotti.net, jcheney@inf.ed.ac.uk

Abstract. The Calculus of Audited Units (CAU) is a typed lambda calculus resulting from a computational interpretation of Artemov's Justification Logic under the Curry-Howard isomorphism; it extends the simply typed lambda calculus by providing *audited types*, inhabited by expressions carrying a *trail* of their past computation history. Unlike most other auditing techniques, CAU allows the inspection of trails at runtime as a first-class operation, with applications in security, debugging, and transparency of scientific computation.

An efficient implementation of CAU is challenging: not only do the sizes of trails grow rapidly, but they also need to be normalized after every beta reduction. In this paper, we study how to reduce terms more efficiently in an untyped variant of CAU by means of explicit substitutions and explicit auditing operations, finally deriving a call-by-value abstract machine.

Keywords: Lambda calculus · Justification Logic
Audited computation · Explicit substitutions · Abstract machines

1 Introduction

Transparency is an increasing concern in computer systems: for complex systems, whose desired behavior may be difficult to formally specify, auditing is an important complement to traditional techniques for verification and static analysis for security [2,6,12,16,19,27], program slicing [22,26], and provenance [21,24]. However, formal foundations of auditing as a programming language primitive are not yet well-established: most approaches view auditing as an extra-linguistic operation, rather than a first-class construct. Recently, however, Bavera and Bonelli [14] introduced a calculus in which recording and analyzing audit trails are first-class operations. They proposed a λ-calculus based on a Curry-Howard correspondence with Justification Logic [7–10] called *calculus of audited units*, or **CAU**. In recent work, we developed a simplified form of **CAU** and proved strong normalization [25].

The type system of **CAU** is based on modal logic, following Pfenning and Davies [23]: it provides a type $[\![s]\!]\, A$ of audited units, where s is "evidence", or

---

An extended version of this paper can be found at https://arxiv.org/abs/1808.00486.

B. Fischer and T. Uustalu (Eds.): ICTAC 2018, LNCS 11187, pp. 376–395, 2018.
https://doi.org/10.1007/978-3-030-02508-3_20

the expression that was evaluated to produce the result of type A. Expressions of this type $!_q M$ contain a value of type A along with a "trail" q explaining how M was obtained by evaluating s. Trails are essentially (skeletons of) proofs of reduction of terms, which can be *inspected* by structural recursion using a special language construct.

To date, most work on foundations of auditing has focused on design, semantics, and correctness properties, and relatively little attention has been paid to efficient execution, while most work on auditing systems has neglected these foundational aspects. Some work on tracing and slicing has investigated the use of "lazy" tracing [22]; however, to the best of our knowledge there is no prior work on how to efficiently evaluate a language such as **CAU** in which auditing is a built-in operation. This is the problem studied in this paper.

A naïve approach to implementing the semantics of **CAU** as given by Bavera and Bonelli runs immediately into the following problem: a **CAU** reduction first performs a *principal contraction* (e.g. beta reduction), which typically introduces a local trail annotation describing the reduction, that can block further beta-reductions. The local trail annotations are then moved up to the nearest enclosing audited unit constructor using one or more *permutation reductions*. For example:

$$!_q \mathcal{F}[(\lambda x.M)\ N] \xrightarrow{\ \beta\ } !_q \mathcal{F}[\beta \triangleright M\ \{N/x\}]$$
$$\xrightarrow{\ \tau\ } !_{\mathbf{t}(q,\mathcal{Q}[\beta])} \mathcal{F}[M\ \{N/x\}]$$

where $\mathcal{F}[]$ is a bang-free evaluation context and $\mathcal{Q}[\beta]$ is a subtrail that indicates where in context $\mathcal{F}$ the β-step was performed. As the size of the term being executed (and distance between an audited unit constructor and the redexes) grows, this evaluation strategy slows down quadratically in the worst case; eagerly materializing the traces likewise imposes additional storage cost.

While some computational overhead seems inevitable to accommodate auditing, both of these costs can in principle be mitigated. Trail permutations are computationally expensive and can often be delayed without any impact on the final outcome. Pushing trails to the closest outer bang does not serve any real purpose: it would be more efficient to keep the trail where it was created and perform normalization only if and when the trail must be inspected (and this operation does not even actually require an actual pushout of trails, because we can reuse term structure to compute the trail structure on-the-fly).

This situation has a well-studied analogue: in the λ-calculus, it is not necessarily efficient to eagerly perform all substitutions as soon as a β-reduction happens. Instead, calculi of *explicit substitutions* such as Abadi et al.'s $\lambda\sigma$ [1] have been developed in which substitutions are explicitly tracked and rewritten. Explicit substitution calculi have been studied extensively as a bridge between the declarative rewriting rules of λ-calculi and efficient implementations. Inspired by this work, we hypothesize that calculi with auditing can be implemented more efficiently by delaying the operations of trail extraction and erasure, using explicit symbolic representations for these operations instead of performing them eagerly.

Particular care must be placed in making sure that the trails we produce still correctly describe the order in which operations were actually performed (e.g. respecting call-by-name or call-by-value reduction): when we perform a principal contraction, pre-existing trail annotations must be recorded as history that happened *before* the contraction, and not after. In the original eager reduction style, this is trivial because we never contract terms containing trails; however, we will show that, thanks to the explicit trail operations, correctness can be achieved even when adopting a lazy normalization of trails.

Contributions. We study an extension of Abadi et al.'s calculus $\lambda\sigma$ [1] with explicit auditing operations. We consider a simplified, untyped variant **CAU⁻** of the Calculus of Audited Units (Sect. 2); this simplifies our presentation because type information is not needed during execution. We revisit $\lambda\sigma$ in Sect. 3, extend it to include auditing and trail inspection features, and discuss problems with this initial, naïve approach. We address these problems by developing a new calculus **CAU⁻$_\sigma$** with explicit versions of the "trail extraction" and "trail erasure" operations (Sect. 4), and we show that it correctly refines **CAU⁻** (subject to an obvious translation). In Sect. 5, we build on **CAU⁻$_\sigma$** to define an abstract machine for audited computation and prove its correctness. Some proofs have been omitted due to space constraints and are included in the extended version of this paper.

2   The Untyped Calculus of Audited Units

The language **CAU⁻** presented here is an untyped version of the calculi λ^h [14] and Ricciotti and Cheney's λ^{hc} [25] obtained by erasing all typing information and a few other related technicalities: this will allow us to address all the interesting issues related to the reduction of **CAU** terms, but with a much less pedantic syntax. To help us explain the details of the calculus, we adapt some examples from our previous paper [25]; other examples are described by Bavera and Bonelli [14].

Unlike the typed variant of the calculus, we only need one sort of variables, denoted by the letters $x, y, z \ldots$. The syntax of **CAU⁻** is as follows:

Terms $M, N ::= x \mid \lambda x.M \mid M\ N \mid \text{let}_!(x := M, N) \mid !_q M \mid q \triangleright M \mid \iota(\vartheta)$

Trails $q, q' ::= \mathbf{r} \mid \mathbf{t}(q, q') \mid \beta \mid \beta_! \mid \mathbf{ti} \mid \mathbf{lam}(q) \mid \mathbf{app}(q, q') \mid \mathbf{let}_!(q, q') \mid \mathbf{tb}(\zeta)$

CAU⁻ extends the pure lambda calculus with *audited units* $!_q M$ (colloquially, "bang M"), whose purpose is to decorate the term M with a log q of its computation history, called *trail* in our terminology: when M evolves as a result of computation, q will be updated by adding information about the reduction rules that have been applied. The form $!_q M$ is in general not intended for use in source programs: instead, we will write $!\ M$ for $!_\mathbf{r} M$, where $\mathbf{r}$ represents the empty execution history (*reflexivity* trail).

Audited units can then be employed in larger terms by means of the "let-bang" operator, which unpacks an audited unit and thus allows us to access its contents. The variable declared by a let$_!$ is bound in its second argument: in essence $\mathsf{let}_!(x := !_q M, N)$ will reduce to N, where free occurrences of x have been replaced by M; the trail q will not be discarded, but will be used to produce a new trail explaining this reduction.

The expression form $q \triangleright M$ is an auxiliary, intermediate annotation of M with partial history information which is produced during execution and will eventually stored in the closest surrounding bang.

Example 1. In **CAU**$^-$ we can express history-carrying terms explicitly: for instance, if we use $\bar{n}$ to denote the Church encoding of a natural number n, and *plus* or *fact* for lambda terms computing addition and factorial on said representation, we can write audited units like

$$!_q \bar{2} \qquad !_{q'} \bar{6}$$

where q is a trail representing the history of $\bar{2}$ i.e., for instance, a witness for the computation that produced $\bar{2}$ by reducing *plus* $\bar{1}$ $\bar{1}$; likewise, q' might describe how computing *fact* $\bar{3}$ produced $\bar{6}$. Supposing we wish to add these two numbers together, at the same time retaining their history, we will use the $\mathsf{let}_!$ construct to look inside them:

$$\mathsf{let}_!(x := !_q \bar{2}, \mathsf{let}_!(y := !_{q'} \bar{6}, plus\ x\ y)) \longrightarrow\!\!\!\rightarrow q'' \triangleright \bar{8}$$

where the final trail q'' is produced by composing q and q'; if this reduction happens inside an external bang, q'' will eventually be captured by it.

Trails, representing sequences of reduction steps, encode the (possibly partial) computation history of a given subterm. The main building blocks of trails are β (representing standard beta reduction), $\beta_!$ (contraction of a let-bang redex) and **ti** (denoting the execution of a trail inspection). For every class of terms we have a corresponding congruence trail (**lam, app, let**$_!$, **tb**, the last of which is associated with trail inspections), with the only exception of bangs, which do not need a congruence rule because they capture all the computation happening inside them. The syntax of trails is completed by reflexivity **r** (representing a null computation history, i.e. a term that has not reduced yet) and transitivity **t** (i.e. sequential composition of execution steps). As discussed by our earlier paper [25], we omit Bavera and Bonelli's symmetry trail form.

Example 2. We build a pair of natural numbers using Church's encoding:

$$! ((\lambda x, y, p.p\ x\ y)\ 2)\ 6 \rightarrow !_{\mathbf{t}(\mathbf{r},\mathbf{app}(\beta,\mathbf{r}))}\ (\lambda y, p.p\ 2\ y)\ 6$$
$$\rightarrow !_{\mathbf{t}(\mathbf{t}(\mathbf{r},\mathbf{app}(\beta,\mathbf{r})),\beta)}\ \lambda p.p\ 2\ 6$$

The trail for the first computation step is obtained by transitivity (trail constructor **t**) from the original trivial trail (**r**, i.e. reflexivity) composed with β, which describes the reduction of the applied lambda: this subtrail is wrapped in a congruence **app** because the reduction takes place deep inside the left-hand subterm of an application (the other argument of **app** is reflexivity, because no reduction takes place in the right-hand subterm).

The second beta-reduction happens at the top level and is thus not wrapped in a congruence. It is combined with the previous trail by means of transitivity.

The last term form $\iota(\vartheta)$, called *trail inspection*, will perform primitive recursion on the computation history of the current audited unit. The metavariables ϑ and ζ associated with trail inspections are *trail replacements*, i.e. maps associating to each possible trail constructor, respectively, a term or a trail:

$$\vartheta ::= \{M_1/\mathbf{r}, M_2/\mathbf{t}, M_3/\beta, M_4/\beta_!, M_5/\mathbf{ti}, M_6/\mathbf{lam}, M_7/\mathbf{app}, M_8/\mathbf{let}_!, M_9/\mathbf{tb}\}$$
$$\zeta ::= \{q_1/\mathbf{r}, q_2/\mathbf{t}, q_3/\beta, q_4/\beta_!, q_5/\mathbf{ti}, q_6/\mathbf{lam}, q_7/\mathbf{app}, q_8/\mathbf{let}_!, q_9/\mathbf{tb}\}$$

When the trail constructors are irrelevant for a certain ϑ or ζ, we will omit them, using the notations $\{\overrightarrow{M}\}$ or $\{\overrightarrow{q}\}$. These constructs represent (or describe) the nine cases of a structural recursion operator over trails, which we write as $q\vartheta$.

Definition 1. *The operation $q\vartheta$, which produces a term by structural recursion on q applying the inspection branches ϑ, is defined as follows:*

$$\mathbf{r}\vartheta \triangleq \vartheta(\mathbf{r}) \qquad \mathbf{t}(q,q')\vartheta \triangleq \vartheta(\mathbf{t}) \, (q\vartheta) \, (q'\vartheta) \qquad \beta\vartheta \triangleq \vartheta(\beta) \qquad \beta_!\vartheta \triangleq \vartheta(\beta_!)$$
$$\mathbf{ti}\vartheta \triangleq \vartheta(\mathbf{ti}) \qquad \mathbf{lam}(q)\vartheta \triangleq \vartheta(\mathbf{lam}) \, (q\vartheta) \qquad \mathbf{tb}(\{\overrightarrow{q}\})\vartheta \triangleq \vartheta(\mathbf{tb}) \, \overrightarrow{(q\vartheta)}$$
$$\mathbf{app}(q,q')\vartheta \triangleq \vartheta(\mathbf{app}) \, (q\vartheta) \, (q'\vartheta) \qquad \mathbf{let}_!(q,q')\vartheta \triangleq \vartheta(\mathbf{let}_!) \, (q\vartheta) \, (q'\vartheta)$$

where the sequence $\overrightarrow{(q\vartheta)}$ is obtained from $\overrightarrow{q}$ by pointwise recursion.

Example 3. Trail inspection can be used to count all of the contraction steps in the history of an audited unit, by means of the following trail replacement:

$$\vartheta_+ ::= \{\bar{0}/\mathbf{r}, plus/\mathbf{t}, \bar{1}/\beta, \bar{1}/\beta_!, \bar{1}/\mathbf{ti}, \lambda x.x/\mathbf{lam}, plus/\mathbf{app}, plus/\mathbf{let}_!, sum/\mathbf{tb}\}$$

where sum is a variant of $plus$ taking nine arguments, as required by the arity of $\mathbf{tb}$. For example, we can count the contractions in $q = \mathbf{t}(\mathbf{let}_!(\beta,\mathbf{r}),\beta_!)$ as:

$$q\vartheta_+ = plus \, (plus \, \bar{1} \, \bar{0}) \, \bar{1}$$

2.1 Reduction

Reduction in $\mathbf{CAU}^-$ includes rules to contract the usual beta redexes (applied lambda abstractions), "beta-bang" redexes, which unpack the bang term appearing as the definiens of a $\mathbf{let}_!$, and trail inspections. These rules, which we call *principal contractions*, are defined as follows:

$$(\lambda x.M) \, N \xrightarrow{\beta} \beta \triangleright M \, \{N/x\} \qquad \mathbf{let}_!(x := !_q M, N) \xrightarrow{\beta} \beta_! \triangleright N \, \{q \triangleright M/x\}$$
$$!_q \mathcal{F}[\iota(\vartheta)] \xrightarrow{\beta} !_q \mathcal{F}[\mathbf{ti} \triangleright q\vartheta]$$

Substitution $M \, \{N/x\}$ is defined in the traditional way, avoiding variable capture. The first contraction is familiar, except for the fact that the reduct $M \, \{N/x\}$ has been annotated with a β trail. The second one deals with unpacking a bang: from $!_q M$ we obtain $q \triangleright M$, which is then substituted for x in the target term N; the resulting term is annotated with a $\beta_!$ trail. The third contraction defines the result of a trail inspection $\iota(\vartheta)$. Trail inspection will be contracted by capturing the current history, as stored in the nearest enclosing bang, and performing structural recursion on it according to the branches defined by ϑ. The concept of "nearest enclosing bang" is made formal by contexts $\mathcal{F}$ in which the hole cannot appear inside a bang (or *bang-free* contexts, for short):

$$\mathcal{F} ::= \blacksquare \mid \lambda x.\mathcal{F} \mid \mathcal{F}\; M \mid M\; \mathcal{F} \mid \mathsf{let}_!(\mathcal{F}, M) \mid \mathsf{let}_!(M, \mathcal{F}) \mid q \rhd \mathcal{F} \mid \iota(\{\overrightarrow{M}, \mathcal{F}, \overrightarrow{N}\})$$

The definition of the principal contractions is completed, as usual, by a contextual closure rule stating that they can appear in any context $\mathcal{E}$:

$$\mathcal{E} ::= \blacksquare \mid \lambda x.\mathcal{E} \mid \mathcal{E}\; M \mid M\; \mathcal{E} \mid \mathsf{let}_!(\mathcal{E}, M) \mid \mathsf{let}_!(M, \mathcal{E}) \mid\; !_q\mathcal{E} \mid q \rhd \mathcal{E} \mid \iota(\{\overrightarrow{M}, \mathcal{E}, \overrightarrow{N}\})$$

$$\frac{M \xrightarrow{\;\beta\;} N}{\mathcal{E}[M] \xrightarrow{\;\beta\;} \mathcal{E}[N]}$$

The principal contractions introduce local trail subterms $q' \rhd M$, which can block other reductions. Furthermore, the rule for trail inspection assumes that the q annotating the enclosing bang really is a complete log of the history of the audited unit; but at the same time, it violates this invariant, because the **ti** trail created after the contraction is not merged with the original history q.

For these reasons, we only want to perform principal contractions on terms not containing local trails: after each principal contraction, we apply the following rewrite rules, called *permutation reductions*, to ensure that the local trail is moved to the nearest enclosing bang:

$$\mathbf{r} \rhd M \xrightarrow{\;\tau\;} M \qquad\qquad q \rhd (q' \rhd M) \xrightarrow{\;\tau\;} \mathbf{t}(q, q') \rhd M$$

$$!_q(q' \rhd M) \xrightarrow{\;\tau\;} !_{\mathbf{t}(q,q')}M \qquad\qquad \lambda x.(q \rhd M) \xrightarrow{\;\tau\;} \mathbf{lam}(q) \rhd \lambda x.M$$

$$(q \rhd M)\; N \xrightarrow{\;\tau\;} \mathbf{app}(q, \mathbf{r}) \rhd M\; N \qquad M\; (q \rhd N) \xrightarrow{\;\tau\;} \mathbf{app}(\mathbf{r}, q) \rhd M\; N$$

$$\mathsf{let}_!(x := q \rhd M, N) \xrightarrow{\;\tau\;} \mathsf{let}_!(q, \mathbf{r}) \rhd \mathsf{let}_!(x := M, N)$$

$$\mathsf{let}_!(x := M, q \rhd N) \xrightarrow{\;\tau\;} \mathsf{let}_!(\mathbf{r}, q) \rhd \mathsf{let}_!(x := M, N)$$

$$\iota(\{M_1, \ldots, q \rhd M_i, \ldots, M_9\}) \xrightarrow{\;\tau\;} \mathbf{tb}(\{\mathbf{r}, \ldots, q, \ldots, \mathbf{r}\}) \rhd \iota(\{M_1, \ldots, M_9\})$$

Moreover, the following rules are added to the $\xrightarrow{\;\tau\;}$ relation to ensure confluence:

$$\mathbf{t}(q, \mathbf{r}) \xrightarrow{\;\tau\;} q \qquad \mathbf{t}(\mathbf{r}, q) \xrightarrow{\;\tau\;} q \qquad \mathbf{tb}(\{\overrightarrow{\mathbf{r}}\}) \xrightarrow{\;\tau\;} \mathbf{r}$$

$$\mathbf{app}(\mathbf{r}, \mathbf{r}) \xrightarrow{\;\tau\;} \mathbf{r} \qquad \mathbf{lam}(\mathbf{r}) \xrightarrow{\;\tau\;} \mathbf{r} \qquad \mathsf{let}_!(\mathbf{r}, \mathbf{r}) \xrightarrow{\;\tau\;} \mathbf{r}$$

$$\mathbf{t}(\mathbf{t}(q_1, q_2), q_3) \xrightarrow{\;\tau\;} \mathbf{t}(q_1, \mathbf{t}(q_2, q_3))$$

$$\mathbf{t}(\mathbf{lam}(q), \mathbf{lam}(q')) \xrightarrow{\;\tau\;} \mathbf{lam}(\mathbf{t}(q, q'))$$

$$\mathbf{t}(\mathbf{lam}(q_1), \mathbf{t}(\mathbf{lam}(q_1'), q)) \xrightarrow{\;\tau\;} \mathbf{t}(\mathbf{lam}(\mathbf{t}(q_1, q_1')), q)$$

$$\mathbf{t}(\mathbf{app}(q_1, q_2), \mathbf{app}(q_1', q_2')) \xrightarrow{\;\tau\;} \mathbf{app}(\mathbf{t}(q_1, q_1'), \mathbf{t}(q_2, q_2'))$$

$$\mathbf{t}(\mathbf{app}(q_1, q_2), \mathbf{t}(\mathbf{app}(q_1', q_2'), q)) \xrightarrow{\;\tau\;} \mathbf{t}(\mathbf{app}(\mathbf{t}(q_1, q_1'), \mathbf{t}(q_2, q_2')), q)$$

$$\mathbf{t}(\mathsf{let}_!(q_1, q_2), \mathsf{let}_!(q_1', q_2')) \xrightarrow{\;\tau\;} \mathsf{let}_!(\mathbf{t}(q_1, q_1'), \mathbf{t}(q_2, q_2'))$$

$$\mathbf{t}(\mathsf{let}_!(q_1, q_2), \mathbf{t}(\mathsf{let}_!(q_1', q_2'), q)) \xrightarrow{\;\tau\;} \mathbf{t}(\mathsf{let}_!(\mathbf{t}(q_1, q_1'), \mathbf{t}(q_2, q_2')), q)$$

$$\mathbf{t}(\mathbf{tb}(\overrightarrow{q_1}), \mathbf{tb}(\overrightarrow{q_2})) \xrightarrow{\;\tau\;} \mathbf{tb}(\overrightarrow{\mathbf{t}(q_1, q_2)})$$

$$\mathbf{t}(\mathbf{tb}(\overrightarrow{q_1}), \mathbf{t}(\mathbf{tb}(\overrightarrow{q_2}), q)) \xrightarrow{\;\tau\;} \mathbf{t}(\mathbf{tb}(\overrightarrow{\mathbf{t}(q_1, q_2)}), q)$$

As usual, $\xrightarrow{\tau}$ is completed by a contextual closure rule. We prove

Lemma 1 ([14]). $\xrightarrow{\tau}$ *is terminating and confluent.*

When a binary relation $\xrightarrow{\mathcal{R}}$ on terms is terminating and confluent, we will write $\mathcal{R}(M)$ for the unique $\mathcal{R}$-normal form of M. Since principal contractions must be performed on τ-normal terms, it is convenient to merge contraction and τ-normalization in a single operation, which we will denote by $\xrightarrow{\mathbf{CAU}^-}$:

$$\frac{M \xrightarrow{\beta} N}{M \xrightarrow{\mathbf{CAU}^-} \tau(N)}$$

Example 4. We take again the term from Example 1 and reduce the outer $\mathsf{let}_!$ as follows:

$$\begin{aligned}
&!\ \mathsf{let}_!(x := !_q 2, \mathsf{let}_!(y := !_{q'} 6, plus\ x\ y)) \\
&\xrightarrow{\beta}\ !\ (\beta_! \rhd \mathsf{let}_!(y := !_{q'} 6, plus\ (q \rhd 2)\ y)) \\
&\xrightarrow{\tau}\ !_{\mathbf{t}(\beta_!, \mathsf{let}_!(\mathbf{r}, \mathbf{app}(\mathbf{app}(\mathbf{r},q),\mathbf{r})))}\ \mathsf{let}_!(y := !_{q'} 6, plus\ 2\ y)
\end{aligned}$$

This $\mathsf{let}_!$-reduction substitutes $q \rhd 2$ for x; a $\beta_!$ trail is produced immediately inside the bang, in the same position as the redex. Then, we τ-normalize the resulting term, which results in the two trails being combined and used to annotate the enclosing bang.

3   Naïve Explicit Substitutions

We seek to adapt the existing abstract machines for the efficient normalization of lambda terms to $\mathbf{CAU}^-$. Generally speaking, most abstract machines act on nameless terms, using de Bruijn's indices [15], thus avoiding the need to perform renaming to avoid variable capture when substituting a term into another.

Moreover, since a substitution $M\{N/x\}$ requires to scan the whole term M and is thus *not* a constant time operation, it is usually not executed immediately in an eager way. The abstract machine actually manipulates *closures*, or pairs of a term M and an environment s declaring lazy substitutions for each of the free variables in M: this allows s to be applied in an incremental way, while scanning the term M in search for a redex. In the $\lambda\sigma$-calculus of Abadi et al. [1], lazy substitutions and closures are manipulated explicitly, providing an elegant bridge between the classical λ-calculus and its concrete implementation in abstract machines. Their calculus expresses beta reduction as the rule

$$(\lambda.M)\ N \longrightarrow M[N]$$

where $\lambda.M$ is a nameless abstraction *à la de Bruijn*, and $[N]$ is a (suspended) *explicit substitution* mapping the variable corresponding to the first dangling index in M to N, and all the other variables to themselves. Terms in the form

$M[s]$, representing closures, are syntactically part of $\lambda\sigma$, as opposed to substitutions $M\{N/x\}$, which are meta-operations that *compute* a term. In this section we formulate a first attempt at adding explicit substitutions to $\mathbf{CAU}^-$. We will not prove any formal result for the moment, as our purpose is to elicit the difficulties of such a task. An immediate adaptation of $\lambda\sigma$-like explicit substitutions yields the following syntax:

Terms $\qquad M, N ::= 1 \mid \lambda.M \mid M\ N \mid \mathrm{let}_!(M, N) \mid {!_q}M \mid q \triangleright M \mid \iota(\vartheta) \mid M[s]$

Substitutions $s, t \quad ::= \langle\rangle \mid {\uparrow} \mid s \circ t \mid M \cdot s$

where 1 is the first de Bruijn index, the nameless λ binds the first free index of its argument, and similarly the nameless $\mathrm{let}_!$ binds the first free index of its second argument. Substitutions include the identity (or empty) substitution $\langle\rangle$, lift $\uparrow$ (which reinterprets all free indices n as their successor $n+1$), the composition $s \circ t$ (equivalent to the sequencing of s and t) and finally $M \cdot s$ (indicating a substitution that will replace the first free index with M, and other indices n with their predecessor $n-1$ under substitution s). Trails are unchanged.

We write $M[N_1 \cdots N_k]$ as syntactic sugar for $M[N_1 \cdots N_k \cdot \langle\rangle]$. Then, $\mathbf{CAU}^-$ reductions can be expressed as follows:

$$(\lambda.M)\ N \xrightarrow{\ \beta\ } \beta \triangleright M[N] \qquad \mathrm{let}_!({!_q}M, N) \xrightarrow{\ \beta\ } \beta_! \triangleright N[q \triangleright M]$$

$$!_q\mathcal{F}[\iota(\vartheta)] \xrightarrow{\ \beta\ } !_q\mathcal{F}[\mathbf{ti} \triangleright q\vartheta]$$

(trail inspection, which does not use substitutions, is unchanged). The idea is that explicit substitutions make reduction more efficient because their evaluation does not need to be performed all at once, but can be delayed, partially or completely; delayed explicit substitutions applied to the same term can be merged, so that the term does not need to be scanned twice. The evaluation of explicit substitution can be defined by the following σ-rules:

$$
\begin{array}{ll}
1[\langle\rangle] \xrightarrow{\ \sigma\ } 1 & \langle\rangle \circ s \xrightarrow{\ \sigma\ } s \\[4pt]
1[M \cdot s] \xrightarrow{\ \sigma\ } M & {\uparrow} \circ \langle\rangle \xrightarrow{\ \sigma\ } {\uparrow} \\[4pt]
(\lambda M)[s] \xrightarrow{\ \sigma\ } \lambda(M[1 \cdot (s \circ {\uparrow})]) & {\uparrow} \circ (M \cdot s) \xrightarrow{\ \sigma\ } s \\[4pt]
(M\ N)[s] \xrightarrow{\ \sigma\ } M[s]\ N[s] & (M \cdot s) \circ t \xrightarrow{\ \sigma\ } M[t] \cdot (s \circ t) \\[4pt]
({!_q}M)[s] \xrightarrow{\ \sigma\ } !_q(M[s]) & (s_1 \circ s_2) \circ s_3 \xrightarrow{\ \sigma\ } s_1 \circ (s_2 \circ s_3) \\[4pt]
\mathrm{let}_!(M, N)[s] \xrightarrow{\ \sigma\ } \mathrm{let}_!(M, N[1 \cdot (s \circ {\uparrow})]) & (q \triangleright M)[s] \xrightarrow{\ \sigma\ } q \triangleright (M[s]) \\[4pt]
\iota(\{\overrightarrow{M}\})[s] \xrightarrow{\ \sigma\ } \iota(\{\overrightarrow{M[s]}\}) & M[s][t] \xrightarrow{\ \sigma\ } M[s \circ t]
\end{array}
$$

These rules are a relatively minor adaptation from those of $\lambda\sigma$: as in that language, σ-normal forms do not contain explicit substitutions, save for the case of the index 1, which may be lifted multiple times, e.g.:

$$1[{\uparrow}^n] = 1[\underbrace{{\uparrow} \circ \cdots \circ {\uparrow}}_{n \text{ times}}]$$

If we take $1[{\uparrow}^n]$ to represent the de Bruijn index $n+1$, as in $\lambda\sigma$, σ-normal terms coincide with a nameless representation of $\mathbf{CAU}^-$.

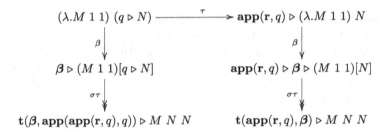

Fig. 1. Non-joinable reduction in **CAU⁻** with naïve explicit substitutions

The σ-rules are deferrable, in that we can perform β-reductions even if a term is not in σ-normal form. We would like to treat the τ-rules in the same way, perhaps performing τ-normalization only before trail inspection; however, we can see that changing the order of τ-rules destroys confluence even when β-redexes are triggered in the same order. Consider for example the reductions in Fig. 1: performing a τ-step before the beta-reduction, as in the right branch, yields the expected result. If instead we delay the τ-step, the trail q decorating N is duplicated by beta reduction; furthermore, the order of q and β gets mixed up: even though q records computation that happened (once) *before* β, the final trail asserts that q happened (twice) *after* β.[1] As expected, the two trails (and consequently the terms they decorate) are not joinable.

The example shows that β-reduction on terms whose trails have not been normalized is *anachronistic*. If we separated the trails stored in a term from the underlying, trail-less term, we might be able to define a *catachronistic*, or time-honoring version of β-reduction. For instance, if we write $\lfloor M \rfloor$ for trail-erasure and $\lceil M \rceil$ for the trail-extraction of a term M, catachronistic beta reduction could be written as follows:

$$(\lambda.M)\ N \xrightarrow{\beta} \mathbf{t}(\lceil (\lambda.M)\ N \rceil, \beta) \triangleright \lfloor M \rfloor \lfloor \lfloor N \rfloor \rfloor$$

$$\mathrm{let}_!(!_q M, N) \xrightarrow{\beta} \mathbf{t}(\lceil \mathrm{let}_!(!_q M, N) \rceil, \beta_!) \triangleright \lfloor N \rfloor [q \triangleright M]$$

$$!_q \mathcal{F}[\iota(\vartheta)] \xrightarrow{\beta} !_q \mathcal{F}[\mathbf{ti} \triangleright q'\vartheta] \quad (\text{where } q' = \tau(\mathbf{t}(q, \lceil \mathcal{F}[\iota(\vartheta)] \rceil)))$$

We could easily define trail erasure and extraction as operations on pure **CAU⁻** terms (without explicit substitutions), but the cost of eagerly computing their result would be proportional to the size of the input term; furthermore, the extension to explicit substitutions would not be straightforward. Instead, in the next section, we will describe an extended language to manipulate trail projections explicitly.

---

[1] Although the right branch describes an unfaithful account of history, it is still a coherent one: we will explain this in more detail in the conclusions.

4   The Calculus $\mathbf{CAU}_\sigma^-$

We define the untyped Calculus of Audited Units with explicit substitutions, or $\mathbf{CAU}_\sigma^-$, as the following extension of the syntax of $\mathbf{CAU}^-$ presented in Sect. 2:

$$M, N ::= 1 \mid \lambda.M \mid M\ N \mid \mathbf{let}_!(M, N) \mid !_q M \mid q \rhd M \mid \iota(\vartheta) \mid M[s] \mid \lfloor M \rfloor$$
$$q, q' ::= \mathbf{r} \mid \mathbf{t}(q, q') \mid \beta \mid \beta_! \mid \mathbf{ti} \mid \mathbf{lam}(q) \mid \mathbf{app}(q, q') \mid \mathbf{let}_!(q, q') \mid \mathbf{tb}(\zeta) \mid \lceil M \rceil$$
$$s, t ::= \langle\rangle \mid \uparrow \mid M \cdot s \mid s \circ t$$

$\mathbf{CAU}_\sigma^-$ builds on the observations about explicit substitutions we made in the previous section: in addition to closures $M[s]$, it provides syntactic trail erasures denoted by $\lfloor M \rfloor$; dually, the syntax of trails is extended with the explicit trail-extraction of a term, written $\lceil M \rceil$. In the naïve presentation, we gave a satisfactory set of σ-rules defining the semantics of explicit substitutions, which we keep as part of $\mathbf{CAU}_\sigma^-$. To express the semantics of explicit projections, we provide in Fig. 2 rules stating that $\lfloor \cdot \rfloor$ and $\lceil \cdot \rceil$ commute with most term constructors (but not with !) and are blocked by explicit substitutions. These rules are completed by congruence rules asserting that they can be used in any subterm or subtrail of a given term or trail.

$$
\begin{array}{ll}
\lfloor 1 \rfloor \xrightarrow{\sigma} 1 & \lceil 1 \rceil \xrightarrow{\sigma} \mathbf{r} \\
\lfloor 1[\uparrow^n] \rfloor \xrightarrow{\sigma} 1[\uparrow^n] & \lceil 1[\uparrow^n] \rceil \xrightarrow{\sigma} \mathbf{r} \\
\lfloor \lambda.M \rfloor \xrightarrow{\sigma} \lambda.\lfloor M \rfloor & \lceil \lambda.M \rceil \xrightarrow{\sigma} \mathbf{lam}(\lceil M \rceil) \\
\lfloor M\ N \rfloor \xrightarrow{\sigma} \lfloor M \rfloor\ \lfloor N \rfloor & \lceil M\ N \rceil \xrightarrow{\sigma} \mathbf{app}(\lceil M \rceil, \lceil N \rceil) \\
\lfloor !_q M \rfloor \xrightarrow{\sigma} !_q M & \lceil !_q M \rceil \xrightarrow{\sigma} \mathbf{r} \\
\lfloor \mathbf{let}_!(M, N) \rfloor \xrightarrow{\sigma} \mathbf{let}_!(\lfloor M \rfloor, \lfloor N \rfloor) & \lceil \mathbf{let}_!(M, N) \rceil \xrightarrow{\sigma} \mathbf{let}_!(\lceil M \rceil, \lceil N \rceil) \\
\lfloor q \rhd M \rfloor \xrightarrow{\sigma} \lfloor M \rfloor & \lceil q \rhd M \rceil \xrightarrow{\sigma} \mathbf{t}(q, \lceil M \rceil) \\
\left\lfloor \iota(\{\overrightarrow{M}\}) \right\rfloor \xrightarrow{\sigma} \iota(\{\lfloor \overrightarrow{M} \rfloor\}) & \left\lceil \iota(\{\overrightarrow{M}\}) \right\rceil \xrightarrow{\sigma} \mathbf{tb}(\{\lceil \overrightarrow{M} \rceil\})
\end{array}
$$

Fig. 2. σ-reduction for explicit trail projections

The τ rules from Sect. 2 are added to $\mathbf{CAU}_\sigma^-$ with the obvious adaptations. We prove that σ and τ, together, yield a terminating and confluent rewriting system.

Theorem 1. $(\xrightarrow{\sigma} \cup \xrightarrow{\tau})$ *is terminating and confluent.*

Proof. Tools like APROVE [17] are able to prove termination automatically. Local confluence can be proved easily by considering all possible pairs of rules: full confluence follows as a corollary of these two results.

4.1   Beta Reduction

We replace the definition of β-reduction by the following lazy rules that use trail-extraction and trail-erasure to ensure that the correct trails are eventually produced:

$$(\lambda.M)\; N \xrightarrow{\text{Beta}} \mathbf{t}(\mathbf{app}(\mathbf{lam}(\lceil M \rceil), \lceil N \rceil), \beta) \rhd \lfloor M \rfloor \, [\lfloor N \rfloor]$$

$$\mathbf{let}_!(!_q M, N) \xrightarrow{\text{Beta}} \mathbf{t}(\mathbf{let}_!(\mathbf{r}, \lceil N \rceil), \beta_!) \rhd \lfloor N \rfloor \, [q \rhd M]$$

$$!_q \mathcal{F}[\iota(\vartheta)] \xrightarrow{\text{Beta}} !_q \mathcal{F}[\mathbf{ti} \rhd q'\vartheta] \qquad (\text{where } q' = \sigma\tau(\mathbf{t}(q, \lceil \mathcal{F}[\iota(\vartheta)]\rceil)))$$

where $\mathcal{F}$ specifies that the reduction cannot take place within a bang, a substitution, or a trail erasure:

$$\mathcal{F} ::= \blacksquare \mid \lambda.\mathcal{F} \mid (\mathcal{F}\; N) \mid (M\; \mathcal{F}) \mid \mathbf{let}_!(\mathcal{F}, N) \mid \mathbf{let}_!(M, \mathcal{F}) \mid q \rhd \mathcal{F} \mid \iota(\overrightarrow{M}, \mathcal{F}, \overrightarrow{N}) \mid \mathcal{F}[s]$$

As usual, the relation is extended to inner subterms by means of congruence rules. However, we need to be careful: we cannot reduce within a trail-erasure, because if we did, the newly created trail would be erroneously erased:

$$
\begin{aligned}
\text{wrong: } & \lfloor (\lambda.M)\; N \rfloor \\
& \xrightarrow{\text{Beta}} \lfloor \mathbf{t}(\mathbf{app}(\mathbf{lam}(\lceil M \rceil), \lceil N \rceil), \beta) \rhd \lfloor M \rfloor \, [\lfloor N \rfloor] \rfloor \\
& \xrightarrow{\sigma} \lfloor \lfloor M \rfloor \, [\lfloor N \rfloor] \rfloor
\end{aligned}
$$

$$
\begin{aligned}
\text{correct: } & \lfloor (\lambda.M)\; N \rfloor \\
& \xrightarrow{\sigma} (\lambda.\lfloor M \rfloor)\; \lfloor N \rfloor \\
& \xrightarrow{\text{Beta}} \mathbf{t}(\mathbf{app}(\mathbf{lam}(\lceil \lfloor M \rfloor \rceil), \lceil \lfloor N \rfloor \rceil), \beta) \rhd \lfloor M \rfloor \, [\lfloor N \rfloor]
\end{aligned}
$$

This is why we express the congruence rule by means of contexts $\mathcal{E}_\sigma$ such that holes cannot appear within erasures (the definition also employs substitution contexts $\mathcal{S}_\sigma$ to allow reduction within substitutions):

$$\frac{M \xrightarrow{\text{Beta}} N}{\mathcal{E}_\sigma[M] \xrightarrow{\text{Beta}} \mathcal{E}_\sigma[N]}$$

Formally, evaluation contexts are defined as follows:

Definition 2 (evaluation context)

$$
\begin{aligned}
\mathcal{E}_\sigma ::=\ & \blacksquare \mid \lambda.\mathcal{E}_\sigma \mid (\mathcal{E}_\sigma\; N) \mid (M\; \mathcal{E}_\sigma) \mid \mathbf{let}_!(\mathcal{E}_\sigma, N) \mid \mathbf{let}_!(M, \mathcal{E}_\sigma) \mid !_q \mathcal{E}_\sigma \mid q \rhd \mathcal{E}_\sigma \\
& \mid \iota(\{\overrightarrow{M}, \mathcal{E}_\sigma, \overrightarrow{N}\}) \mid \mathcal{E}_\sigma[s] \mid M[\mathcal{S}_\sigma] \\
\mathcal{S}_\sigma ::=\ & \mathcal{S}_\sigma \circ t \mid s \circ \mathcal{S}_\sigma \mid \mathcal{E}_\sigma \cdot s \mid M \cdot \mathcal{S}_\sigma
\end{aligned}
$$

We denote $\sigma\tau$-equivalence (the reflexive, symmetric, and transitive closure of $\xrightarrow{\sigma\tau}$) by means of $\xleftrightarrow{\sigma\tau}$. As we will prove, $\sigma\tau$-equivalent $\mathbf{CAU}_\sigma^-$ terms can be interpreted as the same $\mathbf{CAU}^-$ term: for this reason, we define reduction in $\mathbf{CAU}_\sigma^-$ as the union of $\xrightarrow{\text{Beta}}$ and $\xleftrightarrow{\sigma\tau}$:

$$\xrightarrow{\mathbf{CAU}_\sigma^-} := \xrightarrow{\text{Beta}} \cup \xleftrightarrow{\sigma\tau} \tag{1}$$

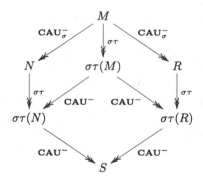

Fig. 3. Relativized confluence for $\mathbf{CAU}_\sigma^-$.

4.2   Properties of the Rewriting System

The main results we prove concern the relationship between $\mathbf{CAU}^-$ and $\mathbf{CAU}_\sigma^-$: firstly, every $\mathbf{CAU}^-$ reduction must still be a legal reduction within $\mathbf{CAU}_\sigma^-$; in addition, it should be possible to interpret every $\mathbf{CAU}_\sigma^-$ reduction as a $\mathbf{CAU}^-$ reduction over suitable $\sigma\tau$-normal terms.

Theorem 2. *If* $M \xrightarrow{\;CAU^-\;}\!\!\!\twoheadrightarrow N$, *then* $M \xrightarrow{\;CAU_\sigma^-\;}\!\!\!\twoheadrightarrow N$.

Theorem 3. *If* $M \xrightarrow{\;CAU_\sigma^-\;}\!\!\!\twoheadrightarrow N$, *then* $\sigma\tau(M) \xrightarrow{\;CAU^-\;}\!\!\!\twoheadrightarrow \sigma\tau(N)$.

Although $\mathbf{CAU}_\sigma^-$, just like $\mathbf{CAU}^-$, is *not* confluent (different reduction strategies produce different trails, and trail inspection can be used to compute on them, yielding different terms as well), the previous results allow us to use Hardin's interpretation technique [18] to prove a *relativized* confluence theorem:

Theorem 4. *If* $M \xrightarrow{\;CAU_\sigma^-\;}\!\!\!\twoheadrightarrow N$ *and* $M \xrightarrow{\;CAU_\sigma^-\;}\!\!\!\twoheadrightarrow R$, *and furthermore* $\sigma\tau(N)$ *and* $\sigma\tau(R)$ *are joinable in* $\mathbf{CAU}^-$, *then* N *and* R *are joinable in* $\mathbf{CAU}_\sigma^-$.

Proof. See Fig. 3.

While the proof of Theorem 2 is not overly different from the similar proof for the $\lambda\sigma$-calculus, Theorem 3 is more interesting. The main challenge is to prove that whenever $M \xrightarrow{\;\text{Beta}\;} N$, we have $\sigma\tau(M) \xrightarrow{\;CAU^-\;}\!\!\!\twoheadrightarrow \sigma\tau(N)$. However, when proceeding by induction on $M \xrightarrow{\;\text{Beta}\;} N$, the terms $\sigma\tau(M)$ and $\sigma\tau(N)$ are too normalized to provide us with a good enough induction hypothesis: in particular, we would want them to be in the form $q \rhd R$ even when q is reflexivity. We call terms in this quasi-normal form *focused*, and prove the theorem by reasoning on them. The details of the proof are discussed in the extended version.

5   A Call-by-Value Abstract Machine

In this section, we derive an abstract machine implementing a weak call-by-value strategy. More precisely, the machine will consider subterms shaped like $q \triangleright \lfloor \overline{M}[e] \rfloor$, where $\overline{M}$ is a pure $\mathbf{CAU}^-$ term with no explicit operators, and e is an *environment*, i.e. an explicit substitution containing only values. In the tradition of lazy abstract machines, values are *closures* (typically pairing a lambda and an environment binding its free variables); in our case, the most natural notion of closure also involves trail erasures and bangs:

Closures	C	$::= \lfloor (\lambda \overline{M})[e] \rfloor \mid !_q C$
Values	V, W	$::= q \triangleright C$
Environments e		$::= \langle \rangle \mid V \cdot e$

According to this definition, the most general case of closure is a telescope of bangs, each equipped with a complete history, terminated at the innermost level by a lambda abstraction applied to an environment and enclosed in an erasure.

$$!_{q_1} \cdots !_{q_n} \lfloor (\lambda \overline{M})[e] \rfloor$$

The environment e contains values with dangling trails, which may be captured by bangs contained in $\overline{M}$; however, the erasure makes sure that none of these trails may reach the external bangs; thus, along with giving meaning to free variables contained in lambdas, closures serve the additional purpose of making sure the history described by the $q_1, \ldots, q_n$ is complete for each bang.

The machine we describe is a variant of the SECD machine. To simplify the description, the code and environment are not separate elements of the machine state, but they are combined, together with a trail, as the top item of the stack. Another major difference is that a code κ can be not only a normal term without explicit operations, but also be a fragment of abstract syntax tree. The stack π is a list of tuples containing a trail, a code, and an environment, and represents the subterm currently being evaluated (the top of the stack) and the unevaluated context, i.e. subterms whose evaluation has been deferred (the remainder of the stack). As a pleasant side-effect of allowing fragments of the AST into the stack, we never need to set aside the current stack into the dump: D is just a list of values representing the evaluated context (i.e. the subterms whose evaluation has already been completed).

Codes	κ	$::= \overline{M} \mid @ \mid ! \mid \mathrm{let}_!(\overline{M}) \mid \iota$
Tuples	τ	$::= (q|\kappa|e)$
Stack	π	$::= \overrightarrow{\tau}$
Dumps	D	$::= \overrightarrow{V}$
Configurations ς		$::= (\pi, D)$

The AST fragments allowed in codes include application nodes $@$, bang nodes $!$, incomplete let bindings $\mathrm{let}_!(\overline{M})$, and inspection nodes ι. A tuple $(q|\overline{M}|e)$ in which the code happens to be a term can be easily interpreted as $q \triangleright \lfloor \overline{M}[e] \rfloor$; however, tuples whose code is an AST fragment only make sense within a certain machine state. The machine state is described by a configuration ς consisting of a stack and a dump.

$$(\epsilon, \epsilon) \ \mathbf{ctx}$$

$$\frac{(\pi, D) \ \mathbf{ctx}}{((q|\overline{M}|e) :: (q'|@|\langle\rangle) :: \pi, D) \ \mathbf{ctx}}$$

$$\frac{(\pi, D) \ \mathbf{ctx}}{((q|@|\langle\rangle) :: \pi, V :: D) \ \mathbf{ctx}}$$

$$\frac{(\pi, D) \ \mathbf{ctx}}{((q|\operatorname{let}_!(\overline{M})|e) :: \pi, D) \ \mathbf{ctx}}$$

$$\frac{(\pi, D) \ \mathbf{ctx}}{((q|!|\langle\rangle) :: \pi, D) \ \mathbf{ctx}}$$

$$\frac{(\pi, D) \ \mathbf{ctx}}{\left(\begin{array}{c}\overrightarrow{(q_i|\overline{M_i}|e_i)_{i=k+1,\ldots,9}} :: \\ (q'|\iota|\langle\rangle) :: \pi, \\ \overrightarrow{V_{\{j=1,\ldots,k-1\}}} :: D\end{array}\right) \ \mathbf{ctx}}$$

$$(\epsilon, V :: \epsilon) \ \mathbf{tm}$$

$$\frac{(\pi, D) \ \mathbf{ctx}}{((q|\overline{M}|e) :: \pi, D) \ \mathbf{tm}}$$

$$\frac{(\pi, D) \ \mathbf{ctx}}{((q|@|\langle\rangle) :: \pi, W :: V :: D) \ \mathbf{tm}}$$

$$\frac{(\pi, D) \ \mathbf{ctx}}{((q|\operatorname{let}_!(\overline{M})|e) :: \pi, V :: D) \ \mathbf{tm}}$$

$$\frac{(\pi, D) \ \mathbf{ctx}}{((q|!|\langle\rangle) :: \pi, V :: D) \ \mathbf{tm}}$$

$$\frac{(\pi, D) \ \mathbf{ctx}}{((q|\iota|\langle\rangle) :: \pi, \overrightarrow{V_9} :: D) \ \mathbf{ctx}}$$

Fig. 4. Term and context configurations

A meaningful state cannot contain just any stack and dump, but must have a certain internal coherence, which we express by means of the two judgments in Fig. 4: in particular, the machine state must be a *term configuration*; this notion is defined by the judgment $\varsigma \ \mathbf{tm}$, which employs a separate notion of *context configuration*, described by the judgment $\varsigma \ \mathbf{ctx}$.

We can define the denotation of configurations by recursion on their well-formedness judgment:

Definition 3

1. The denotation of a context configuration is defined as follows:

$$(\epsilon, \epsilon) \triangleq \blacksquare$$

$$((q|\overline{M}|e) :: (q'|@|\langle\rangle) :: \pi, D) \triangleq (\pi, D)[q' \rhd (\blacksquare \ (q \rhd \lfloor \overline{M}[e] \rfloor))]$$

$$((q|@|\langle\rangle) :: \pi, V :: D) \triangleq (\pi, D)[q \rhd (V \ \blacksquare)]$$

$$((q|\operatorname{let}_!(\overline{M})|e) :: \pi, D) \triangleq (\pi, D)[q \rhd \operatorname{let}_!(\blacksquare, \lfloor \overline{M}[1 \cdot (e \circ \uparrow)] \rfloor)]$$

$$((q|!|\langle\rangle) :: \pi, D) \triangleq (\pi, D)[q \rhd !\blacksquare]$$

$$\overrightarrow{((q_i|\overline{M_i}|e_i)} :: (q'|\iota|\langle\rangle) :: \pi, \overrightarrow{V_j} :: D) \triangleq (\pi, D)[q' \rhd \iota(\overrightarrow{V_j}, \blacksquare, \overrightarrow{(q_i \rhd \lfloor \overline{M_i}[e_i] \rfloor)})]$$

where in the last line $i + j + 1 = 9$.

	source		$\mapsto$	target	
1	$(q|\overline{M}\ \overline{N}|e) :: \pi$	D		$(\mathbf{r}|\overline{M}|e) :: (\mathbf{r}|\overline{N}|e) :: (q|@|\langle\rangle) :: \pi$	D
2	$(q|@|\langle\rangle) :: \pi$	$(q' \triangleright C) :: (q'' \triangleright \lfloor(\lambda\overline{M})[e]\rfloor) :: D$		$(q; \mathbf{app}(q'', q'); \beta|\overline{M}|(\mathbf{r} \triangleright C) \cdot e) :: \pi$	D
3	$(q|\lambda\overline{M}|e) :: \pi$	D		π	$(q \triangleright \lfloor(\lambda\overline{M})[e]\rfloor) :: D$
4	$(q|\operatorname{let}_!(\overline{M},\overline{N})|e) :: \pi$	D		$(\mathbf{r}|\overline{M}|e) :: (q|\operatorname{let}_!(\overline{N})|e) :: \pi$	D
5	$(q|\operatorname{let}_!(\overline{N})|e) :: \pi$	$(q' \triangleright !V) :: D$		$(q; \operatorname{let}_!(q',\mathbf{r}); \beta_!; q_{\overline{N},e,V}|\overline{N}|V \cdot e) :: \pi$	D
6	$(q|!_{q'}\overline{M}|e) :: \pi$	D		$(q'; \lceil \overline{M}[e]\rceil |\overline{M}|e) :: (q|!|\langle\rangle) :: \pi$	D
7	$(q|!|\langle\rangle) :: \pi$	$V :: D$		π	$(q \triangleright !V) :: D$
8	$(q|\iota(\overrightarrow{M_9})|e) :: \pi$	D		$\overrightarrow{(\mathbf{r}|M_i|e)_{i=1,\ldots,9}} :: (q|\iota|\langle\rangle) :: \pi$	D
9	$(q|\iota|\langle\rangle) :: \pi$	$\overrightarrow{(q_i \triangleright C_i)_{i=1,\ldots,9}} :: D$		$(q; \mathbf{tb}(\overrightarrow{q_i}); \operatorname{ti}|J_{q,\overrightarrow{q_i},\pi,D}|[(\mathbf{r} \triangleright C_i)]) :: \pi$	D
10	$(q|n|e) :: \pi$	D		π	$(q \triangleright e(n)) :: D$

$$q_{\overline{N},e,V} \triangleq \lceil \lfloor \overline{N}[1 \cdot (e \circ {\uparrow})]\rfloor [V]\rceil$$
$$J_{q,\overrightarrow{q_i},\pi,D} \triangleq \mathcal{I}((q; \mathbf{tb}(\overrightarrow{q_i})), \pi, D)$$
$$e(n) \triangleq \begin{cases} C & \text{if } e = (q \triangleright C) \cdot e' \text{ and } n = 1 \\ e'(m) & \text{if } e = V \cdot e' \text{ and } n = m + 1 \end{cases}$$

Fig. 5. Call-by-value abstract machine

2. *The denotation of a term configuration is defined as follows:*

$$\mathcal{T}(\epsilon, V :: \epsilon) \triangleq V$$
$$\mathcal{T}((q|\overline{M}|e) :: \pi, D) \triangleq \underline{(\pi, D)}[q \triangleright \lfloor \overline{M}[e]\rfloor]$$
$$\mathcal{T}((q|@|\langle\rangle) :: \pi, W :: V :: D) \triangleq \underline{(\pi, D)}[q \triangleright (V\ W)]$$
$$\mathcal{T}((q|\operatorname{let}_!(\overline{M})|e) :: \pi, V :: D) \triangleq \underline{(\pi, D)}[q \triangleright \operatorname{let}_!(V, \lfloor \overline{M}[1 \cdot (e \circ {\uparrow})]\rfloor)]$$
$$\mathcal{T}((q|!|\langle\rangle) :: \pi, V :: D) \triangleq \underline{(\pi, D)}[q \triangleright !V]$$
$$\mathcal{T}((q|\iota|\langle\rangle) :: \pi, \overrightarrow{V_9} :: D) \triangleq \underline{(\pi, D)}[q \triangleright \iota(\overrightarrow{V_9})]$$

We see immediately that the denotation of a term configuration is a $\mathbf{CAU}_\sigma^-$ term, while that of a context configuration is a $\mathbf{CAU}_\sigma^-$ context (Definition 2).

The call-by-value abstract machine for $\mathbf{CAU}^-$ is shown in Fig. 5: in this definition we use semi-colons as a compact notation for sequences of transitivity trails. The evaluation of a pure, closed term $\overline{M}$, starts with an empty dump and a stack made of a single tuple $(\mathbf{r}, \overline{M}, \langle\rangle)$: this is a term configuration denoting $\mathbf{r} \triangleright \lfloor \overline{M}[\langle\rangle]\rfloor$, which is $\sigma\tau$-equivalent to $\overline{M}$. Final states are in the form $\epsilon, V :: \epsilon$, which simply denotes the value V. When evaluating certain erroneous terms (e.g. $(!\ M)\ V$, where function application is used on a term that is not a function), the machine may get stuck in a non-final state; these terms are rejected by the

$$\mathcal{I}(q_\vartheta, (q'|!|\epsilon) :: \pi, D) = \sigma\tau(q_\vartheta)$$
$$\mathcal{I}(q_\vartheta, (q'|\overline{M}|e) :: (q''|@|\epsilon) :: \pi, D) = \mathcal{I}((q''; \mathbf{app}(q_\vartheta, q')), \pi, D)$$
$$\mathcal{I}(q_\vartheta, (q'|@|\langle\rangle) :: \pi, (q'' \triangleright C) :: D) = \mathcal{I}((q', \mathbf{app}(q'', q_\vartheta)), \pi, D)$$
$$\mathcal{I}(q_\vartheta, (q'|\operatorname{let}_!(\overline{M})|e) :: \pi, D) = \mathcal{I}((q'; \operatorname{let}_!(q_\vartheta, \mathbf{r})), \pi, D)$$
$$\mathcal{I}(q_\vartheta, \overrightarrow{(q_i|M_i|e_i)} :: (q'|\iota|\langle\rangle) :: \pi, \overrightarrow{(q_j \triangleright C_j)} :: D) = \mathcal{I}((q'; \mathbf{tb}(\overrightarrow{q_j}, q_\vartheta, \overrightarrow{q_i})), \pi, D)$$

Fig. 6. Materialization of trails for inspection

typed **CAU**. The advantage of our machine, compared to a naive evaluation strategy, is that in our case all the principal reductions can be performed in constant time, except for trail inspection which must examine a full trail, and thus will always require a time proportional to the size of the trail.

Let us now examine the transition rules briefly. Rules 1–3 and 10 closely match the "Split CEK" machine [3] (a simplified presentation of the SECD machine), save for the use of the @ code to represent application nodes, while in the Split CEK machine they are expressed implicitly by the stack structure.

Rule 1 evaluates an application by decomposing it, placing two new tuples on the stack for the subterms, along with a third tuple for the application node; the topmost trail remains at the application node level, and two reflexivity trails are created for the subterms; the environment is propagated to the subterm tuples.

The idea is that when the machine reaches a state in which the term at the top of the stack is a value (e.g. a lambda abstraction, as in rule 3), the value is moved to the dump, and evaluation continues on the rest of the stack. Thus when in rule 2 we evaluate an application node, the dump will contain two items resulting from the evaluation of the two subterms of the application; for the application to be meaningful, the left-hand subterm must have evaluated to a term of the form $\lambda \overline{M}$, whereas the form of the right-hand subterm is not important: the evaluation will then continue as usual on $\overline{M}$ under an extended environment; the new trail will be obtained by combining the three trails from the application node and its subexpressions, followed by a β trail representing beta reduction.

The evaluation of $\text{let}_!$ works similarly to that of applications; however, a term $\text{let}_!(\overline{M}, \overline{N})$ is split intro $\overline{M}$ and $\text{let}_!(\overline{N})$ (rule 4), so that $\overline{N}$ is never evaluated independently from the corresponding $\text{let}_!$ node. When in rule 5 we evaluate the $\text{let}_!(\overline{N})$ node, the dump will contain a value corresponding to the evaluation of $\overline{M}$ (which must have resulted in a value of the form $!V$): we then proceed to evaluate $\overline{N}$ in an environment extended with V; this step corresponds to a principal contraction, so we update the trail accordingly, by adding $\beta_!$; additionally, we need to take into account the trails from V after substitution into $\overline{N}$: we do this by extending the trail with $\lceil \lfloor \overline{N}[1 \cdot (e \circ \uparrow)] \rfloor [V] \rceil$.

Bangs are managed by rules 6 and 7. To evaluate $!_{q'}\overline{M}$, we split it into $\overline{M}$ and a $!$ node, placing the corresponding tuples on top of the stack; the original external trail q remains with the $!$ node, whereas the internal trail q' is placed in the tuple with $\overline{M}$; the environment e is propagated to the body of the bang but, since it may contain trails, we need to extend q' with the trails resulting from substitution into $\overline{M}$. When in rule 7 we evaluate the $!$ node, the top of the dump contains the value V resulting from the evaluation of its body: we update the dump by combining V with the bang and proceed to evaluate the rest of the stack.

The evaluation of trail inspections (rules 8 and 9) follows the same principle as that of applications, with the obvious differences due to the fact that inspections have nine subterms. The principal contraction happens in rule 9, which assumes that the inspection branches have been evaluated to $q_1 \rhd C_1, \ldots, q_9 \rhd C_9$ and put on the dump: at this point we have to reconstruct and normalize the inspection trail and apply the inspection branches. To reconstruct the inspection trail, we combine q and the $\overrightarrow{q_i}$ into the trail for the current subterm $(q; \mathbf{tb}(\overrightarrow{q_i}))$; then we must collect the trails in the context of the current bang, which are scattered in the stack and dump: this is performed by the auxiliary operator $\mathcal{I}$ of Fig. 6, defined by recursion on the well-formedness of the context configuration π, D; the definition is partial, as it lacks the case for ϵ, ϵ, corresponding to an inspection appearing outside all bangs: such terms are considered "inspection-locked" and cannot be reduced. Due to the operator $\mathcal{I}$, rule 9 is the only rule that cannot be performed in constant time.

$\mathcal{I}$ returns a $\sigma\tau$-normalized trail, which we need to apply to the branches $C_1, \ldots, C_9$; from the implementation point of view, this operation is analogous to a substitution replacing the trail nodes $(\mathbf{r}, \mathbf{t}, \beta, \mathbf{app}, \mathbf{lam}, \ldots)$ with the respective M_i. Suppose that trails are represented as nested applications of dangling de Bruijn indices from 1 to 9 (e.g. the trail $\mathbf{app}(\mathbf{r}, \beta)$ can be represented as $(1\ 2\ 3)$ for $\mathbf{app} = 1$, $\mathbf{r} = 2$ and $\beta = 3$); then trail inspection reduction amounts to the evaluation of a trail in an environment composed of the trail inspection branches. To sum it up, rule 9 produces a state in which the current tuple contains:

- a trail $(q; \mathbf{tb}(\overrightarrow{q_i}); \mathbf{ti})$ (combining the trail of the inspection node, the trails of the branches, and the trail $\mathbf{ti}$ denoting trail inspection
- the $\sigma\tau$-reduced inspection "trail" (operationally, an open term with nine dangling indices) which results from $\mathcal{I}((q; \mathbf{tb}(\overrightarrow{q_i})), \pi, D)$
- an environment $[\overrightarrow{(\mathbf{r} \triangleright C_i)}]$ which implements trail inspection by substituting the inspection branches for the dangling indices in the trail.

The machine is completed by rule 10, which evaluates de Bruijn indices by looking them up in the environment. Notice that the lookup operation $e(n)$, defined when the de Bruijn index n is closed by the environment e, simply returns the n-th closure in e, but *not* the associated trail; the invariants of our machine ensure that this trail is considered elsewhere (particularly in rules 5 and 6).

The following theorem states that the machine correctly implements reduction.

Theorem 5. *For all valid* ς, $\varsigma \mapsto \varsigma'$ *implies* $\mathcal{T}(\varsigma) \xrightarrow{\ \mathbf{CAU}_\sigma^- \ } \mathcal{T}(\varsigma')$.

6   Conclusions and Future Directions

The calculus $\mathbf{CAU}_\sigma^-$ which we introduced in this paper provides a finer-grained view over the reduction of history-carrying terms, and proved an effective tool in the study of the smarter evaluation techniques which we implemented in an abstract machine. $\mathbf{CAU}_\sigma^-$ is not limited to the call-by-value strategy used by our machine, and in future work we plan to further our investigation of efficient auditing to call-by-name and call-by-need. Another intriguing direction we are exploring is to combine our approach with recent advances in explicit substitutions, such as the linear substitution calculus of Accattoli and Kesner [5], and apply the *distillation* technique of Accattoli et al. [3]

In our discussion, we showed that the original definition of beta-reduction, when applied to terms that are not in trail-normal form, creates temporally unsound trails. We might wonder whether these anachronistic trails carry any meaning: let us take, as an example, the reduction on the left branch of Fig. 1:

$$(\lambda.M\ 1\ 1)\ (q \triangleright N) \longrightarrow \mathbf{t}(\beta, \mathbf{app}(\mathbf{app}(\mathbf{r}, q), q)) \triangleright M\ N\ N$$

We know that q is the trace left behind by the reduction that led to N from the original term, say R:

$$R \longrightarrow q \triangleright N$$

We can see that the anachronistic trail is actually consistent with the reduction of $(\lambda.M\ 1\ 1)\ R$ under a leftmost-outermost strategy:

$$(\lambda.M\ 1\ 1)\ R \longrightarrow \beta \triangleright M\ R\ R \longrightarrow \beta \triangleright M\ (q \triangleright N)\ (q \triangleright N)$$
$$\longrightarrow \mathbf{t}(\beta, \mathbf{app}(\mathbf{app}(\mathbf{r}, q), q)) \triangleright M\ N\ N$$

Under the anachronistic reduction, q acts as the witness of an original inner redex. Through substitution within M, we get evidence that the contraction of an inner redex can be swapped with a subsequent head reduction: this is a key result in the proof of standardization that is usually obtained using the notion of *residual* ([13], Lemma 11.4.5). Based on this remark, we conjecture that trails might be used to provide a more insightful proof: it would thus be interesting to see how trails relate to recent advancements in standardization [4,11,20,28].

Acknowledgments. Effort sponsored by the Air Force Office of Scientific Research, Air Force Material Command, USAF, under grant number FA8655-13-1-3006. The U.S. Government and University of Edinburgh are authorised to reproduce and distribute reprints for their purposes notwithstanding any copyright notation thereon. Cheney was also supported by ERC Consolidator Grant Skye (grant number 682315). We are grateful to James McKinna and the anonymous reviewers for comments.

References

1. Abadi, M., Cardelli, L., Curien, P.L., Lévy, J.J.: Explicit substitutions. J. Funct. Program. **1**(4), 375–416 (1991). https://doi.org/10.1017/s0956796800000186
2. Abadi, M., Fournet, C.: Access control based on execution history. In: Proceedings of Network and Distributed System Security Symposium, NDSS 2003, San Diego, CA. The Internet Society (2003) http://www.isoc.org/isoc/conferences/ndss/03/proceedings/papers/7.pdf
3. Accattoli, B., Barenbaum, P., Mazza, D.: Distilling abstract machines. In: Proceedings of 19th ACM SIGPLAN Conference on Functional Programming, ICFP 2014, Gothenburg, September 2014, pp. 363–376. ACM Press, New York (2014). https://doi.org/10.1145/2628136.2628154

4. Accattoli, B., Bonelli, E., Kesner, D., Lombardi, C.: A nonstandard standardization theorem. In: Proceedings of 41st Annual ACM SIGPLAN-SIGACT Symposium on Principles of Programming Languages, POPL 2014, San Diego, CA, January 2014, pp. 659–670. ACM Press, New York (2014). https://doi.org/10.1145/2535838.2535886

5. Accattoli, B., Kesner, D.: The structural λ-calculus. In: Dawar, A., Veith, H. (eds.) CSL 2010. LNCS, vol. 6247, pp. 381–395. Springer, Heidelberg (2010). https://doi.org/10.1007/978-3-642-15205-4_30

6. Amir-Mohammadian, S., Chong, S., Skalka, C.: Correct audit logging: theory and practice. In: Piessens, F., Viganò, L. (eds.) POST 2016. LNCS, vol. 9635, pp. 139–162. Springer, Heidelberg (2016). https://doi.org/10.1007/978-3-662-49635-0_8

7. Artemov, S.: Justification logic. In: Hölldobler, S., Lutz, C., Wansing, H. (eds.) JELIA 2008. LNCS (LNAI), vol. 5293, pp. 1–4. Springer, Heidelberg (2008). https://doi.org/10.1007/978-3-540-87803-2_1

8. Artemov, S.: The logic of justification. Rev. Symb. Log. 1(4), 477–513 (2008). https://doi.org/10.1017/s1755020308090060

9. Artemov, S.N.: Explicit provability and constructive semantics. Bull. Symb. Log. 7(1), 1–36 (2001). https://doi.org/10.2307/2687821

10. Artemov, S., Bonelli, E.: The intensional lambda calculus. In: Artemov, S.N., Nerode, A. (eds.) LFCS 2007. LNCS, vol. 4514, pp. 12–25. Springer, Heidelberg (2007). https://doi.org/10.1007/978-3-540-72734-7_2

11. Asperti, A., Levy, J.J.: The cost of usage in the λ-calculus. In: Proceedings of 28th Annual ACM/IEEE Symposium on Logic in Computer Science, LICS 2013, New Orleans, LA, June 2013, pp. 293–300. IEEE CS Press, Washington, DC (2013). https://doi.org/10.1109/lics.2013.35

12. Banerjee, A., Naumann, D.A.: History-based access control and secure information flow. In: Barthe, G., Burdy, L., Huisman, M., Lanet, J.-L., Muntean, T. (eds.) CASSIS 2004. LNCS, vol. 3362, pp. 27–48. Springer, Heidelberg (2005). https://doi.org/10.1007/978-3-540-30569-9_2

13. Barendregt, H.P.: The Lambda Calculus: Its Syntax and Semantics. Studies in Logic and the Foundations of Mathematic, vol. 103, 2nd edn. North-Holland, Amsterdam (1984). https://www.sciencedirect.com/science/bookseries/0049-237X/103

14. Bavera, F., Bonelli, E.: Justification logic and audited computation. J. Log. Comput. 28(5), 909–934 (2018). https://doi.org/10.1093/logcom/exv037

15. de Bruijn, N.: Lambda-calculus notation with nameless dummies: a tool for automatic formula manipulation with application to the Church-Rosser theorem. Indagationes Math. 34(5), 381–392 (1972). https://doi.org/10.1016/1385-7258(72)90034-0

16. Garg, D., Jia, L., Datta, A.: Policy auditing over incomplete logs: theory, implementation and applications. In: Proceedings of 18th ACM Conference on Computer and Communications Security, CCS 2011, Chicago, IL, October 2011, pp. 151–162. ACM Press, New York (2011). https://doi.org/10.1145/2046707.2046726

17. Giesl, J., et al.: Proving Termination of programs automatically with AProVE. In: Demri, S., Kapur, D., Weidenbach, C. (eds.) IJCAR 2014. LNCS (LNAI), vol. 8562, pp. 184–191. Springer, Cham (2014). https://doi.org/10.1007/978-3-319-08587-6_13

18. Hardin, T.: Confluence results for the pure strong categorical combinatory logic CCL: λ-calculi as subsystems of CCL. Theor. Comput. Sci. 65(3), 291–342 (1989). https://doi.org/10.1016/0304-3975(89)90105-9

19. Jia, L., et al.: AURA: a programming language for authorization and audit. In: Proceedings of 13th ACM SIGPLAN International Conference on Functional Programming, ICFP 2013, Victoria, BC, September 2008, pp. 27–38. ACM Press, New York (2008). https://doi.org/10.1145/1411204.1411212
20. Kashima, R.: A proof of the standardization theorem in lambda-calculus. Technical report, Research Reports on Mathematical and Computing Science, Tokyo Institute of Technology (2000)
21. Moreau, L.: The foundations for provenance on the web. Found. Trends Web Sci. **2**(2–3), 99–241 (2010). https://doi.org/10.1561/1800000010
22. Perera, R., Acar, U.A., Cheney, J., Levy, P.B.: Functional programs that explain their work. In: Proceedings of 17th ACM SIGPLAN International Conference on Functional Programming, ICFP 2012, Copenhagen, September 2002, pp. 365–376. ACM Press, New York (2012). https://doi.org/10.1145/2364527.2364579
23. Pfenning, F., Davies, R.: A judgmental reconstruction of modal logic. Math. Struct. Comput. Sci. **11**(4), 511–540 (2001). https://doi.org/10.1017/s0960129501003322
24. Ricciotti, W.: A core calculus for provenance inspection. In: Proceedings of 19th International Symposium on Principles and Practice of Declarative Programming, PPDP 2017, Namur, October 2017, pp. 187–198. ACM Press, New York (2017). https://doi.org/10.1145/3131851.3131871
25. Ricciotti, W., Cheney, J.: Strongly normalizing audited computation. In: Goranko, V., Dam, M. (eds.) Proceedings of 26th EACSL Annual Conference, CSL 2017, Stockholm, August 2017. Leibniz International Proceedings in Informatics, vol. 82, Article no. 36. Schloss Dagstuhl Publishing, Saarbrücken/Wadern (2017). https://doi.org/10.4230/lipics.csl.2017.36
26. Ricciotti, W., Stolarek, J., Perera, R., Cheney, J.: Imperative functional programs that explain their work. Proc. ACM Program. Lang. **1**(ICFP), Article no. 14 (2017). https://doi.org/10.1145/3110258
27. Vaughan, J.A., Jia, L., Mazurak, K., Zdancewic, S.: Evidence-based audit. In: Proceedings of 21st IEEE Computer Security Foundations Symposium, CSF 2008, Pittsburgh, PA, June 2008, pp. 177–191. IEEE CS Press, Washington, DC (2008). https://doi.org/10.1109/csf.2008.24
28. Xi, H.: Upper bounds for standardizations and an application. J. Symb. Log. **64**(1), 291–303 (1999). https://doi.org/10.2307/2586765

Complexity and Expressivity of Branching- and Alternating-Time Temporal Logics with Finitely Many Variables

Mikhail Rybakov[1,2] and Dmitry Shkatov[2(✉)]

[1] Tver State University, Tver, Russia
m_rybakov@mail.ru
[2] University of the Witwatersrand, Johannesburg, South Africa
shkatov@gmail.com

Abstract. We show that Branching-time temporal logics **CTL** and **CTL***, as well as Alternating-time temporal logics **ATL** and **ATL***, are as semantically expressive in the language with a single propositional variable as they are in the full language, i.e., with an unlimited supply of propositional variables. It follows that satisfiability for **CTL**, as well as for **ATL**, with a single variable is EXPTIME-complete, while satisfiability for **CTL***, as well as for **ATL***, with a single variable is 2EXPTIME-complete,—i.e., for these logics, the satisfiability for formulas with only one variable is as hard as satisfiability for arbitrary formulas.

Keywords: Branching-time temporal logics
Alternating-time temporal logics · Finite-variable fragments
Computational complexity · Semantic expressivity
Satisfiability problem

1 Introduction

The propositional Branching-time temporal logics **CTL** [4,7] and **CTL*** [7,11] have for a long time been used in formal specification and verification of (parallel) non-terminating computer programs [7,25], such as (components of) operating systems, as well as in formal specification and verification of hardware. More recently, Alternating-time temporal logics **ATL** and **ATL*** [1,7] have been used for formal specification and verification of multi-agent [35] and, more broadly, so-called open systems, i.e., systems whose correctness depends on the actions of external entities, such as the environment or other agents making up a multi-agent system.

This work has been supported by Russian Foundation for Basic Research, projects 16-07-01272 and 17-03-00818.

© Springer Nature Switzerland AG 2018
B. Fischer and T. Uustalu (Eds.): ICTAC 2018, LNCS 11187, pp. 396–414, 2018.
https://doi.org/10.1007/978-3-030-02508-3_21

Logics **CTL**, **CTL***, **ATL**, and **ATL*** have two main applications to computer system design, corresponding to two different stages in the system design process, traditionally conceived of as having specification, implementation, and verification phases. First, the task of verifying that an implemented system conforms to a specification can be carried out by checking that a formula expressing the specification is satisfied in the structure modelling the system,—for program verification, this structure usually models execution paths of the program; this task corresponds to the model checking problem [5] for the logic. Second, the task of verifying that a specification of a system is satisfiable—and, thus, can be implemented by some system—corresponds to the satisfiability problem for the logic. Being able to check that a specification is satisfiable has the obvious advantage of avoiding wasted effort in trying to implement unsatisfiable systems. Moreover, an algorithm that checks for satisfiability of a formula expressing a specification builds, explicitly or implicitly, a model for the formula, thus supplying a formal model of a system conforming to the specification; this model can subsequently be used in the implementation phase. There is hope that one day such models can be used as part of a "push-button" procedure producing an assuredly correct implementation from a specification model, avoiding the need for subsequent verification altogether. Tableaux-style satisfiability-checking algorithms developed for **CTL** in [10], for **CTL*** in [30], for **ATL** in [19], and for **ATL*** in [6] all implicitly build a model for the formula whose satisfiability is being checked.

In this paper, we are concerned with the satisfiability problem for **CTL**, **CTL***, **ATL**, and **ATL***; clearly, the complexity of satisfiability for these logics is of crucial importance to their applications to formal specification. It is well-known that, for formulas that might contain contain an arbitrary number of propositional variables, the complexity of satisfiability for all of these logics is quite high: it is EXPTIME-complete for **CTL** [10,13], 2EXPTIME-complete for **CTL*** [37], EXPTIME-complete for **ATL** [14,40], and 2EXPTIME-complete for **ATL*** [34].

It has, however, been observed (see, for example, [8]) that, in practice, formulas expressing formal specifications, despite being quite long and containing deeply nested temporal operators, usually contain only a very small number of propositional variables,—typically, two or three. The question thus arises whether limiting the number of propositional variables allowed to be used in the construction of formulas we take as inputs can bring down the complexity of the satisfiability problem for **CTL**, **CTL***, **ATL**, and **ATL***. Such an effect is not, after all, unknown in logic: examples are known of logics whose satisfiability problem goes down from "intractable" to "tractable" once we place a limit on the number of propositional variables allowed in the language: thus, satisfiability for the classical propositional logic as well as the extensions of the modal logic **K5** [27], which include such logics as **K45**, **KD45**, and **S5** (see also [21]), goes down from NP-complete to polynomial-time decidable once we limit the number of propositional variables in the language to an (arbitrary) finite number.[1] Similarly, as follows from [28], satisfiability for the intuitionistic propositional logic goes down from PSPACE-complete to polynomial-time decidable if we allow only a single propositional variable in the language.

The question of whether the complexity of satisfiability for **CTL**, **CTL***, **ATL**, and **ATL***can be reduced by restricting the number of propositional variables allowed to be used in the formulas has not, however, been investigated in the literature. The present paper is mostly meant to fill that gap.

A similar question has been answered in the negative for Linear-time temporal logic **LTL** in [8], where it was shown, using a proof technique peculiar to **LTL** (in particular, [8] relies on the fact that for **LTL** with a finite number of propositional variables satisfiability reduces to model-checking), that a single-variable fragment of **LTL** is PSPACE-complete, i.e., as computationally hard as the entire logic [36]. It should be noted that, in this respect, **LTL** behaves like most "natural" modal and temporal logics, for which the presence of even a single variable in the language is sufficient to generate a fragment whose satisfiability is as hard as satisfiability for the entire logic. The first results to this effect have been proven in [2] for logics for reasoning about linguistic structures and in [38] for provability logic. A general method of proving such results for PSPACE-complete logics has been proposed in [21]; even though [21] considers only a handful of logics, the method can be generalised to large classes of logics, often in the language without propositional variables [3,23] (it is not, however, applicable to **LTL**, as it relies on unrestricted branching in the models of the logic, which runs contrary to the semantics of **LTL**,—hence the need for a different approach, as in [8]). In this paper, we use a suitable modification of the technique from [21] (see [31,32]) to show that single-variable fragments of **CTL**, **CTL***, **ATL**, and **ATL*** are as computationally hard as the entire logics; thus, for these logics, the complexity of satisfiability cannot be reduced by restricting the number of variables in the language.

Before doing so, a few words might be in order to explain why the technique from [21] is not directly applicable to the logics we are considering in this paper. The approach of [21] is to model propositional variables by (the so-called pp-like) formulas of a single variable; to establish the PSPACE-harness results presented in [21], a substitution is made of such pp-like formulas for propositional variables into formulas encoding a PSPACE-hard problem. In the case of logics containing modalities corresponding to transitive relations, such as the modal logic **S4**, for such a substitution to work, the formulas into which the substitution is made need to satisfy the property referred to in [21] as "evidence in a structure,"—a formula is evident in a structure if it has a model satisfying the following heredity condition: if a propositional variable is true at a state, it has to be true at

---

[1] To avoid ambiguity, we emphasise that we use the standard complexity-theoretic convention of measuring the complexity of the input as its size; in our case, this is the length of the input formula. In other words, we do not measure the complexity of the input according to how many distinct variables it contains; limiting the number of variables simply provides a restriction on the languages we consider.

all the states accessible from that state. In the case of PSPACE-complete logics, formulas satisfying the evidence condition can always be found, as the intuitionistic logic, which is PSPACE-complete, has the heredity condition built into its semantics. The situation is drastically different for logics that are EXPTIME-hard, which is the case for all the logics considered in the present paper: to show that a logic is EXPTIME-hard, one uses formulas that require for their satisfiability chains of states of the length exponential in the size of the formula,—this cannot be achieved with formulas that are evident in a structure, as by varying the valuations of propositional variables that have to satisfy the heredity condition we can only describe chains whose length is linear in the size of the formula. Thus, the technique from [21] is not directly applicable to EXPTIME-hard logics with "transitive" modalities, as the formulas into which the substitution of pp-like formulas needs to be made do not satisfy the condition that has to be met for such a substitution to work. As all the logics considered in this paper do have a "transitive" modality—namely, the temporal connective "always in the future", which is interpreted by the reflexive, transitive closure of the relation corresponding to the temporal connective "at the next instance"—this limitation prevents the technique from [21] from being directly applied to them.

In the present paper, we modify the approach of [21] by coming up with substitutions of single-variable formulas for propositional variables that can be made into arbitrary formulas, rather than formulas satisfying a particular property, such as evidence in a structure. This allows us to break away from the class PSPACE and to deal with **CTL**, **CTL***, **ATL**, and **ATL***, all of which are at least EXPTIME-hard. A similar approach has recently been used in [31] and [32] for some other propositional modal logics.

A by-product of our approach, and another contribution of this paper, is that we establish that single-variable fragments of **CTL**, **CTL***, **ATL**, and **ATL*** are as semantically expressive as the entire logic, i.e., all properties that can be specified with any formula of the logic can be specified with a formula containing only one variable—indeed, our complexity results follow from this. In this light, the observation cited above—that in practice most properties of interest are expressible in these logics using only a very small number of variables—is not at all surprising from a purely mathematical point of view, either.

The paper is structured as follows. In Sect. 2, we introduce the syntax and semantics of **CTL** and **CTL***. Then, in Sect. 3, we show that **CTL** and **CTL*** can be polynomial-time embedded into their single-variable fragments. As a corollary, we obtain that satisfiability for the single variable fragment of **CTL** is EXPTIME-complete and satisfiability for the single variable of of **CTL*** is 2EXPTIME-complete. In Sect. 4, we introduce the syntax and semantics of **ATL** and **ATL***. Then, in Sect. 5, we prove results for **ATL** and **ATL*** that are analogous to those proven in Sect. 3 for **CTL** and **CTL***. We conclude in Sect. 6 by discussing other formalisms related to the logics considered in this paper to which our proof technique can be applied to obtain similar results.

2   Branching-Time Temporal Logics

We start by briefly recalling the syntax and semantics of **CTL** and **CTL***.

The language of **CTL*** contains a countable set $Var = \{p_1, p_2, \ldots\}$ of propositional variables, the propositional constant $\bot$ ("falsehood"), the Boolean connective $\to$ ("if ..., then ..."), the path quantifier $\forall$, and temporal connectives $\bigcirc$ ("next") and $\mathcal{U}$ ("until"). The language contains two kinds of formulas: state formulas and path formulas, so called because they are evaluated in the models at states and paths, respectively. State formulas φ and path formulas ϑ are simultaneously defined by the following BNF expressions:

$$\varphi ::= p \mid \bot \mid (\varphi \to \varphi) \mid \forall \vartheta,$$

$$\vartheta ::= \varphi \mid (\vartheta \to \vartheta) \mid (\vartheta \, \mathcal{U} \vartheta) \mid \bigcirc \vartheta,$$

where p ranges over Var. Other Boolean connectives are defined as follows: $\neg A := (A \to \bot)$, $(A \wedge B) := \neg(A \to \neg B)$, $(A \vee B) := (\neg A \to B)$, and $(A \leftrightarrow B) := (A \to B) \wedge (B \to A)$, where A and B can be either state or path formulas. We also define $\top := \bot \to \bot$, $\Diamond \vartheta := (\top \, \mathcal{U} \vartheta)$, $\Box \vartheta := \neg \Diamond \neg \vartheta$, and $\exists \vartheta := \neg \forall \neg \vartheta$.

Formulas are evaluated in Kripke models. A Kripke model is a tuple $\mathfrak{M} = (\mathcal{S}, \longmapsto, V)$, where $\mathcal{S}$ is a non-empty set (of states), $\longmapsto$ is a binary (transition) relation on $\mathcal{S}$ that is serial (i.e., for every $s \in \mathcal{S}$, there exists $s' \in \mathcal{S}$ such that $s \longmapsto s'$), and V is a (valuation) function $V : Var \to 2^{\mathcal{S}}$.

An infinite sequence $s_0, s_1, \ldots$ of states in $\mathfrak{M}$ such that $s_i \longmapsto s_{i+1}$, for every $i \geqslant 0$, is called a *path*. Given a path π and some $i \geqslant 0$, we denote by $\pi[i]$ the ith element of π and by $\pi[i, \infty]$ the suffix of π beginning at the ith element. If $s \in \mathcal{S}$, we denote by $\Pi(s)$ the set of all paths π such that $\pi[0] = s$.

The satisfaction relation between models $\mathfrak{M}$, states s, and state formulas φ, as well as between models $\mathfrak{M}$, paths π, and path formulas ϑ, is defined as follows:

- $\mathfrak{M}, s \models p_i \leftrightharpoons s \in V(p_i)$;
- $\mathfrak{M}, s \models \bot$ never holds;
- $\mathfrak{M}, s \models \varphi_1 \to \varphi_2 \leftrightharpoons \mathfrak{M}, s \models \varphi_1$ implies $\mathfrak{M}, s \models \varphi_2$;
- $\mathfrak{M}, s \models \forall \vartheta_1 \leftrightharpoons \mathfrak{M}, \pi \models \vartheta_1$ for every $\pi \in \Pi(s)$.
- $\mathfrak{M}, \pi \models \varphi_1 \leftrightharpoons \mathfrak{M}, \pi[0] \models \varphi_1$;
- $\mathfrak{M}, \pi \models \vartheta_1 \to \vartheta_2 \leftrightharpoons \mathfrak{M}, \pi \models \vartheta_1$ implies $\mathfrak{M}, \pi \models \vartheta_2$;
- $\mathfrak{M}, \pi \models \bigcirc \vartheta_1 \leftrightharpoons \mathfrak{M}, \pi[1, \infty] \models \vartheta_1$;
- $\mathfrak{M}, \pi \models \vartheta_1 \mathcal{U} \vartheta_2 \leftrightharpoons \mathfrak{M}, \pi[i, \infty] \models \vartheta_2$ for some $i \geqslant 0$ and $\mathfrak{M}, \pi[j, \infty] \models \vartheta_1$ for every j such that $0 \leqslant j < i$.

A **CTL***-formula is a state formula in this language. A **CTL***-formula is satisfiable if it is satisfied by some state of some model, and valid if it is satisfied by every state of every model. Formally, by **CTL*** we mean the set of valid **CTL***-formulas. Notice that this set is closed under uniform substitution.

Logic **CTL** can be thought of as a fragment of **CTL*** containing only formulas where a path quantifier is always paired up with a temporal connective.

This, in particular, disallows formulas whose main sign is a temporal connective and, thus, eliminates path-formulas. Such composite "modal" operators are $\forall \bigcirc$ (universal "next"), $\forall\, \mathcal{U}$ (universal "until"), and $\exists\, \mathcal{U}$ (existential "until"). Formulas are defined by the following BNF expression:

$$\varphi ::= p \mid \bot \mid (\varphi \to \varphi) \mid \forall \bigcirc \varphi \mid \forall (\varphi\, \mathcal{U}\varphi) \mid \exists (\varphi\, \mathcal{U}\varphi),$$

where p ranges over **Var**. We also define $\neg\varphi := (\varphi \to \bot)$, $(\varphi \wedge \psi) := \neg(\varphi \to \neg\psi)$, $(\varphi \vee \psi) := (\neg\varphi \to \psi)$, $\top = \bot \to \bot$, $\exists \bigcirc \varphi := \neg\forall\bigcirc\neg\varphi$, $\exists \Diamond \varphi := \exists(\top\, \mathcal{U}\varphi)$, and $\forall \Box \varphi := \neg\exists\Diamond\neg\varphi$.

The satisfaction relation between models $\mathfrak{M}$, states s, and formulas φ is inductively defined as follows (we only list the cases for the "new" modal operators):

- $\mathfrak{M}, s \models \forall\bigcirc\varphi_1 \leftrightharpoons \mathfrak{M}, s' \models \varphi_1$ whenever $s \longmapsto s'$;
- $\mathfrak{M}, s \models \forall(\varphi_1\, \mathcal{U}\varphi_2) \leftrightharpoons$ for every path $s_0 \longmapsto s_1 \longmapsto \ldots$ with $s_0 = s$, $\mathfrak{M}, s_i \models \varphi_2$, for some $i \geqslant 0$, and $\mathfrak{M}, s_j \models \varphi_1$, for every $0 \leqslant j < i$;
- $\mathfrak{M}, s \models \exists(\varphi_1\, \mathcal{U}\varphi_2) \leftrightharpoons$ there exists a path $s_0 \longmapsto s_1 \longmapsto \ldots$ with $s_0 = s$, such that $\mathfrak{M}, s_i \models \varphi_2$, for some $i \geqslant 0$, and $\mathfrak{M}, s_j \models \varphi_1$, for every $0 \leqslant j < i$.

Satisfiable and valid formulas are defined as for **CTL***. Formally, by **CTL** we mean the set of valid **CTL**-formulas; this set is closed under substitution.

For each of the logics described above, by a variable-free fragment we mean the subset of the logic containing only formulas without any propositional variables. Given formulas φ, ψ and a propositional variable p, we denote by $\varphi[p/\psi]$ the result of uniformly substituting ψ for p in φ.

3   Finite-Variable Fragments of CTL* and CTL

In this section, we consider the complexity of satisfiability for finite-variable fragments of **CTL** and **CTL***, as well as semantic expressivity of those fragments.

We start by noticing that for both **CTL** and **CTL*** satisfiability of the variable-free fragment is polynomial-time decidable. Indeed, it is easy to check that, for these logics, every variable-free formula is equivalent to either $\bot$ or $\top$. Thus, to check for satisfiability of a variable-free formula φ, all we need to do is to recursively replace each subformula of φ by either $\bot$ or $\top$, which gives us an algorithm that runs in time linear in the size of φ. Since both **CTL** and **CTL*** are at least EXPTIME-hard and P $\neq$ EXPTIME, variable-free fragments of these logics cannot be as expressive as the entire logic.

We next prove that the situation changes once we allow just one variable to be used in the construction of formulas. Then, we can express everything we can express in the full languages of **CTL** and **CTL***; as a consequence, the complexity of satisfiability becomes as hard as satisfiability for the full languages. In what follows, we first present the proof for **CTL***, and then point out how that work carries over to **CTL**.

Let φ be an arbitrary **CTL***-formula. Without a loss of generality we may assume that φ contains propositional variables $p_1, \ldots p_n$. Let p_{n+1} be a variable not occurring in φ. First, inductively define the translation $\cdot'$ as follows:

$$
\begin{aligned}
p_i' &= p_i, \quad \text{where } i \in \{1, \ldots, n\}; \\
\bot' &= \bot; \\
(\phi \to \psi)' &= \phi' \to \psi'; \\
(\forall \alpha)' &= \forall(\Box p_{n+1} \to \alpha'); \\
(\bigcirc \alpha)' &= \bigcirc \alpha'; \\
(\alpha \, \mathcal{U} \beta)' &= \alpha' \, \mathcal{U} \beta'.
\end{aligned}
$$

Next, let

$$
\Theta = p_{n+1} \wedge \forall \Box (\exists \bigcirc p_{n+1} \leftrightarrow p_{n+1}),
$$

and define

$$
\widehat{\varphi} = \Theta \wedge \varphi'.
$$

Intuitively, the translation $\cdot'$ restricts evaluation of formulas to the paths where every state makes the variable p_{n+1} true, while Θ acts as a guard making sure that all paths in a model satisfy this property. Notice that φ is equivalent to $\widehat{\varphi}[p_{n+1}/\top]$.

Lemma 1. *Formula φ is satisfiable if, and only if, formula $\widehat{\varphi}$ is satisfiable.*

Proof. Suppose that $\widehat{\varphi}$ is not satisfiable. Then, $\neg\widehat{\varphi} \in \mathbf{CTL}^*$ and, since $\mathbf{CTL}^*$ is closed under substitution, $\neg\widehat{\varphi}[p_{n+1}/\top] \in \mathbf{CTL}^*$. As $\widehat{\varphi}[p_{n+1}/\top] \leftrightarrow \varphi \in \mathbf{CTL}^*$, so $\neg\varphi \in \mathbf{CTL}^*$; thus, φ is not satisfiable.

Suppose that $\widehat{\varphi}$ is satisfiable. In particular, let $\mathfrak{M}, s_0 \models \widehat{\varphi}$ for some model $\mathfrak{M}$ and some s_0 in $\mathfrak{M}$. Define $\mathfrak{M}'$ to be the smallest submodel of $\mathfrak{M}$ such that

- s_0 is in $\mathfrak{M}'$;
- if x is in $\mathfrak{M}'$, $x \longmapsto y$, and $\mathfrak{M}, y \models p_{n+1}$, then y is also in $\mathfrak{M}'$.

Notice that, since $\mathfrak{M}, s_0 \models p_{n+1} \wedge \forall \Box(\exists \bigcirc p_{n+1} \leftrightarrow p_{n+1})$, the model $\mathfrak{M}'$ is serial, as required, and that p_{n+1} is true at every state of $\mathfrak{M}'$.

We now show that $\mathfrak{M}', s_0 \models \varphi$. Since $\mathfrak{M}, s_0 \models \varphi'$, it suffices to prove that, for every state x in $\mathfrak{M}'$ and every state subformula ψ of φ, we have $\mathfrak{M}, x \models \psi'$ if, and only if, $\mathfrak{M}', x \models \psi$; and that, for every path π in $\mathfrak{M}'$ and every path subformula α of φ, we have $\mathfrak{M}, \pi \models \alpha'$ if, and only if, $\mathfrak{M}', \pi \models \alpha$. This can be done by simultaneous induction on ψ and α.

The base case as well as Boolean cases are straightforward.

Let $\psi = \forall \alpha$, so $\psi' = \forall(\Box p_{n+1} \to \alpha')$. Assume that $\mathfrak{M}, x \not\models \forall(\Box p_{n+1} \to \alpha')$. Then, $\mathfrak{M}, \pi \not\models \alpha'$, for some $\pi \in \Pi(x)$ such that $\mathfrak{M}, \pi[i] \models p_{n+1}$, for every $i \geq 0$. By construction of $\mathfrak{M}'$, π is a path is $\mathfrak{M}'$; thus, we can apply the inductive hypothesis to conclude that $\mathfrak{M}', \pi \not\models \alpha$. Therefore, $\mathfrak{M}', x \not\models \forall \alpha$, as required. Conversely, assume that $\mathfrak{M}', x \not\models \forall \alpha$. Then, $\mathfrak{M}', \pi \not\models \alpha$, for some $\pi \in \Pi(x)$. Clearly, π is a path in $\mathfrak{M}$. Since p_{n+1} is true at every state in $\mathfrak{M}'$, and thus, at every state in π, using the inductive hypothesis, we conclude that $\mathfrak{M}, x \not\models \forall(\Box p_{n+1} \to \alpha')$.

The cases for the temporal connectives are straightforward.

Lemma 2. *If $\widehat{\varphi}$ is satisfiable, then it is satisfied in a model where p_{n+1} is true at every state.*

Proof. If $\widehat{\varphi}$ is satisfiable, then, as has been shown in the proof of Lemma 1, φ is satisfied in a model where p_{n+1} is true at every state; i.e., $\mathfrak{M}, s \models \varphi$ for some $\mathfrak{M} = (\mathcal{S}, \longmapsto, V)$ such that p_{n+1} is true at every state in $\mathcal{S}$ and some $s \in \mathcal{S}$. Since φ is equivalent to $\widehat{\varphi}[p_{n+1}/\top]$, clearly $\mathfrak{M}, s \models \widehat{\varphi}$.

Next, we model all the variables of $\widehat{\varphi}$ by single-variable formulas $A_1, \ldots, A_m$. This is done in the following way. Consider the class M of models that, for each $m \in \{1, \ldots, n+1\}$, contains a model $\mathfrak{M}_m = (\mathcal{S}_m, \longmapsto, V_m)$ defined as follows:

- $\mathcal{S}_m = \{r_m, b^m, a_1^m, a_2^m, \ldots, a_{2m}^m\}$;
- $\longmapsto = \{\langle r_m, b^m \rangle, \langle r_m, a_1^m \rangle\} \cup \{\langle a_i^m, a_{i+1}^m \rangle : 1 \leq m \leq 2m - 1\} \cup \{\langle s, s \rangle : s \in \mathcal{S}_m\}$;
- $s \in V_m(p)$ if, and only if, $s = r_m$ or $s = a_{2k}^m$, for some $k \in \{1, \ldots, m\}$.

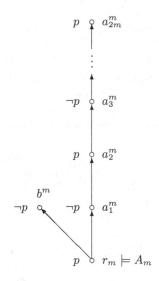

Fig. 1. Model $\mathfrak{M}_m$

The model $\mathfrak{M}_m$ is depicted in Fig. 1, where circles represent states with loops. With every such $\mathfrak{M}_m$, we associate a formula A_m, in the following way. First, inductively define the sequence of formulas

$$\chi_0 = \forall \Box p;$$
$$\chi_{k+1} = p \wedge \exists \bigcirc (\neg p \wedge \exists \bigcirc \chi_k).$$

Next, for every $m \in \{1, \ldots, n+1\}$, let

$$A_m = \chi_m \wedge \exists \bigcirc \forall \Box \neg p.$$

Lemma 3. *Let* $\mathfrak{M}_k \in \mathsf{M}$ *and let* x *be a state in* $\mathfrak{M}_k$. *Then,* $\mathfrak{M}_k, x \models A_m$ *if, and only if,* $k = m$ *and* $x = r_m$.

Proof. Straightforward.

Now, for every $m \in \{1, \ldots, n+1\}$, define

$$B_m = \exists \bigcirc A_m.$$

Finally, let σ be a (substitution) function that, for every $i \in \{1 \ldots n+1\}$, replaces p_i by B_i, and let

$$\varphi^* = \sigma(\widehat{\varphi}).$$

Notice that the formula φ^* contains only a single variable, p.

Lemma 4. *Formula φ is satisfiable if, and only if, formula φ^* is satisfiable.*

Proof. Suppose that φ is not satisfiable. Then, in view of Lemma 1, $\widehat{\varphi}$ is not satisfiable. Then, $\neg\widehat{\varphi} \in \mathbf{CTL}^*$ and, since $\mathbf{CTL}^*$ is closed under substitution, $\neg\varphi^* \in \mathbf{CTL}^*$. Thus, φ^* is not satisfiable.

Suppose that φ is satisfiable. Then, in view of Lemmas 1 and 2, $\widehat{\varphi}$ is satisfiable in a model $\mathfrak{M} = (\mathcal{S}, \longmapsto, V)$ where p_{n+1} is true at every state. We can assume without a loss of generality that every $x \in \mathcal{S}$ is connected by some path to s. Define model $\mathfrak{M}'$ as follows. Append to $\mathfrak{M}$ all the models from M (i.e., take their disjoint union), and for every $x \in \mathcal{S}$, make r_m, the root of $\mathfrak{M}_m$, accessible from x in $\mathfrak{M}'$ exactly when $\mathfrak{M}, x \models p_m$. The evaluation of p is defined as follows: for states from each $\mathfrak{M}_m \in \mathsf{M}$, the evaluation is the same as in $\mathfrak{M}_m$, and for every $x \in \mathcal{S}$, let $x \notin V'(p)$.

We now show that $\mathfrak{M}', s \models \varphi^*$. It is easy to check that $\mathfrak{M}', s \models \sigma(\Theta)$. It thus remains to show that $\mathfrak{M}', s \models \sigma(\varphi')$. Since $\mathfrak{M}, s \models \varphi'$, it suffices to prove that $\mathfrak{M}, x \models \psi'$ if, and only if, $\mathfrak{M}', x \models \sigma(\psi')$, for every state x in $\mathfrak{M}$ and every state subformula ψ of φ; and that $\mathfrak{M}, \pi \models \alpha'$ if, and only if, $\mathfrak{M}', \pi \models \sigma(\alpha')$, for every path π in $\mathfrak{M}$ and every path subformula α of φ. This can be done by simultaneous induction on ψ and α.

Let $\psi = p_i$, so $\psi' = p_i$ and $\sigma(\psi') = B_i$. Assume that $\mathfrak{M}, x \models p_i$. Then, by construction of $\mathfrak{M}'$, we have $\mathfrak{M}', x \models B_i$. Conversely, assume that $\mathfrak{M}', x \models B_i$. As $\mathfrak{M}', x \models B_i$ implies $\mathfrak{M}', x \models \exists \bigcirc p$ and since $\mathfrak{M}, y \not\models p$, for every $y \in \mathcal{S}$, this can only happen if $x \longmapsto^{\mathfrak{M}'} r_m$, for some $m \in \{1, \ldots, n+1\}$. Since, then, $r_m \models A_i$, in view of Lemma 3, $m = i$, and thus, by construction of $\mathfrak{M}'$, we have $\mathfrak{M}, x \models p_i$.

The Boolean cases are straightforward.

Let $\psi = \forall\alpha$, so $\psi' = \forall(\Box p_{n+1} \to \alpha')$ and $\sigma(\psi') = \forall(\Box B_{n+1} \to \sigma(\alpha'))$. Assume that $\mathfrak{M}, x \not\models \forall(\Box p_{n+1} \to \alpha')$. Then, for some $\pi \in \Pi(x)$ such that $\mathfrak{M}, \pi[i] \models p_{n+1}$ for every $i \geqslant 0$, we have $\mathfrak{M}, \pi \not\models \alpha'$. Clearly, π is a path in $\mathfrak{M}'$, and thus, by inductive hypothesis, $\mathfrak{M}', \pi[i] \models B_{n+1}$, for every $i \geqslant 0$, and $\mathfrak{M}', \pi \not\models \sigma(\alpha')$. Hence, $\mathfrak{M}', x \not\models \forall(\Box B_{n+1} \to \sigma(\alpha'))$, as required. Conversely, assume that $\mathfrak{M}', x \not\models \forall(\Box B_{n+1} \to \sigma(\alpha'))$. Then, for some $\pi \in \Pi(x)$ such that $\mathfrak{M}', \pi[i] \models B_{n+1}$ for every $i \geqslant 0$, we have $\mathfrak{M}', \pi \not\models \sigma(\alpha')$. Since by construction of $\mathfrak{M}'$, no state outside of $\mathcal{S}$ satisfies B_{n+1}, we know that π is a path in $\mathfrak{M}$. Thus, we can use the inductive hypothesis to conclude that $\mathfrak{M}, x \not\models \forall(\Box p_{n+1} \to \alpha')$.

The cases for the temporal connectives are straightforward.

Lemma 4, together with the observation that the formula φ^* is polynomial-time computable from φ, give us the following:

Theorem 1. *There exists a polynomial-time computable function e assigning to every $\mathbf{CTL}^*$-formula φ a single-variable formula $e(\varphi)$ such that $e(\varphi)$ is satisfiable if, and only if, φ is satisfiable.*

Theorem 2. *The satisfiability problem for the single-variable fragment of $\mathbf{CTL}^*$ is 2EXPTIME-complete.*

Proof. The lower bound immediately follows from Theorem 1 and 2EXPTIME-hardness of satisfiability for $\mathbf{CTL}^*$ [37]. The upper bound follows from the 2EXPTIME upper bound for satisfiability for $\mathbf{CTL}^*$ [37].

We now show how the argument presented above for $\mathbf{CTL}^*$ can be adapted to $\mathbf{CTL}$. First, we notice that if our sole purpose were to prove that satisfiability for the single-variable fragment of $\mathbf{CTL}$ is EXPTIME-complete, we would not need to work with the entire set of connectives present in the language of $\mathbf{CTL}$,— it would suffice to work with a relatively simple fragment of $\mathbf{CTL}$ containing the modal operators $\forall\bigcirc$ and $\forall\square$, whose satisfiability, as follows from [13], is EXPTIME-hard. We do, however, also want to establish that the single-variable fragment of $\mathbf{CTL}$ is as expressive the entire logic; therefore, we embed the entire $\mathbf{CTL}$ into its single-variable fragment. To that end, we can carry out an argument similar to the one presented above for $\mathbf{CTL}^*$.

First, we define the translation $\cdot'$ as follows:

$$
\begin{aligned}
p_i{}' &= p_i \quad \text{where } i \in \{1, \ldots, n\}; \\
(\bot)' &= \bot; \\
(\phi \rightarrow \psi)' &= \phi' \rightarrow \psi'; \\
(\forall\bigcirc\phi)' &= \forall\bigcirc(p_{n+1} \rightarrow \phi'); \\
(\forall\,(\phi\,\mathcal{U}\psi))' &= \forall\,(\phi'\,\mathcal{U}(p_{n+1} \wedge \psi')); \\
(\exists\,(\phi\,\mathcal{U}\psi))' &= \exists\,(\phi'\,\mathcal{U}(p_{n+1} \wedge \psi')).
\end{aligned}
$$

Next, let

$$
\Theta = p_{n+1} \wedge \forall\square(\exists\bigcirc p_{n+1} \leftrightarrow p_{n+1}).
$$

and define

$$
\widehat{\varphi} = \Theta \wedge \varphi'.
$$

Intuitively, the translation $\cdot'$ restricts the evaluation of formulas to the states where p_{n+1} is true. Formula Θ acts as a guard making sure that all states in a model satisfy this property. We can then prove the analogues of Lemmas 1 and 2.

Lemma 5. *Formula φ is satisfiable if, and only if, formula $\widehat{\varphi}$ is satisfiable.*

Proof. Analogous to the proof of Lemma 1. In the right-to-left direction, inductive steps for modal connectives rely on the fact that in a submodel we constructed every state makes the variable p_{n+1} true.

Lemma 6. *If $\widehat{\varphi}$ is satisfiable, then it is satisfied in a model where p_{n+1} is true at every state.*

Proof. Analogous to the proof of Lemma 2.

Next, we model propositional variables $p_1, \ldots, p_{n+1}$ in the formula $\widehat{\varphi}$ exactly as in the argument for **CTL***, i.e., we use formulas A_m and their associated models $\mathfrak{M}_m$, where $m \in \{1, \ldots, n+1\}$. This can be done since formulas A_m are, in fact, **CTL**-formulas. Lemma 3 can, thus, be reused for **CTL**, as well.

We then define a single-variable **CTL**-formula φ^* analogously to the way it had been done for **CTL***:

$$\varphi^* = \sigma(\widehat{\varphi}),$$

where σ is a (substitution) function that, for every $i \in \{1 \ldots n+1\}$, replaces p_i by $B_i = \exists \bigcirc A_i$. We can then prove the analogue of Lemma 4.

Lemma 7. *Formula φ is satisfiable if, and only if, formula φ^* is satisfiable.*

Proof. Analogous to the proof of Lemma 4. In the left-to-right direction, the inductive steps for the modal connectives rely on the fact that the formula B_{n+1} is true precisely at the states of the model that satisfies φ.

We, thus, obtain the following:

Theorem 3. *There exists a polynomial-time computable function e assigning to every **CTL**-formula φ a single-variable formula $e(\varphi)$ such that $e(\varphi)$ is satisfiable if, and only if, φ is satisfiable.*

Theorem 4. *The satisfiability problem for the single-variable fragment of **CTL** is EXPTIME-complete.*

Proof. The lower bound immediately follows from Theorem 3 and EXPTIME-hardness of satisfiability for **CTL** [13]. The upper bound follows from the EXPTIME upper bound for satisfiability for **CTL** [10].

4   Alternating-Time Temporal Logics

Alternating-time temporal logics **ATL*** and **ATL** can be conceived of as generalisations of **CTL*** and **CTL**, respectively. Their models incorporate transitions occasioned by simultaneous actions of the agents in the system rather than abstract transitions, as in **CTL*** and **CTL**, and we now reason about paths that can be forced by cooperative actions of coalitions of agents, rather than just about all ($\forall$) and some ($\exists$) paths. We do not lose the ability to reason about all and some paths in **ATL*** and **ATL**, however, so these logics are generalisations of **CTL*** and **CTL**, respectively.

The language of **ATL*** contains a non-empty, finite set $\mathbb{AG}$ of names of agents (subsets of $\mathbb{AG}$ are called coalitions); a countable set $\mathit{Var} = \{p_1, p_2, \ldots\}$ of propositional variables; the propositional constant $\bot$; the Boolean connective

$\rightarrow$; coalition quantifiers $\langle\!\langle C \rangle\!\rangle$, for every $C \subseteq \mathbb{AG}$; and temporal connectives $\bigcirc$ ("next"), $\mathcal{U}$ ("until"), and $\square$ ("always in the future"). The language contains two kinds of formulas: state formulas and path formulas. State formulas φ and path formulas α are simultaneously defined by the following BNF expressions:

$$\varphi ::= p \mid \bot \mid (\varphi \rightarrow \varphi) \mid \langle\!\langle C \rangle\!\rangle \vartheta,$$

$$\vartheta ::= \varphi \mid (\vartheta \rightarrow \vartheta) \mid (\vartheta \, \mathcal{U} \vartheta) \mid \bigcirc \vartheta \mid \square \vartheta,$$

where C ranges over subsets of $\mathbb{AG}$ and p ranges over **Var**. Other Boolean and temporal connectives are defined as for **CTL***.

Formulas are evaluated in concurrent game models. A concurrent game model is a tuple $\mathfrak{M} = (\mathbb{AG}, \mathcal{S}, Act, act, \delta, V)$, where

- $\mathbb{AG} = \{1, \ldots, k\}$ is a finite, non-empty set of agents;
- $\mathcal{S}$ is a non-empty set of states;
- Act is a non-empty set of actions;
- $act : \mathbb{AG} \times \mathcal{S} \mapsto 2^{Act}$ is an action manager function assigning a non-empty set of "available" actions to an agent at a state;
- δ is a transition function assigning to every state $s \in \mathcal{S}$ and every action profile $\alpha = (\alpha_1, \ldots, \alpha_k)$, where $\alpha_a \in act(a, s)$, for every $a \in \mathbb{AG}$, an outcome state $\delta(s, \alpha)$;
- V is a (valuation) function $V : \textbf{Var} \rightarrow 2^{\mathcal{S}}$.

A few auxiliary notions need to be introduced for the definition of the satisfaction relation.

A *path* is an infinite sequence $s_0, s_1, \ldots$ of states in $\mathfrak{M}$ such that, for every $i \geq 0$, the following holds: $s_{i+1} \in \delta(s_i, \alpha)$, for some action profile α. The set of all such sequences is denoted by $\mathcal{S}^\omega$. The notation $\pi[i]$ and $\pi[i, \infty]$ is used as for **CTL***. Initial segments $\pi[0, i]$ of paths are called *histories*; a typical history is denoted by h, and its last state, $\pi[i]$, is denoted by $last(h)$. Note that histories are non-empty sequences of states in $\mathcal{S}$; we denote the set of all such sequences by $\mathcal{S}^+$.

Given $s \in \mathcal{S}$ and $C \subseteq \mathbb{AG}$, a C-action at s is a tuple α_C such that $\alpha_C(a) \in act(a, s)$, for every $a \in C$, and $\alpha_C(a')$, for every $a' \notin C$, is an unspecified action of agent a' at s (technically, a C-action might be thought of as an equivalence class on action profiles determined by a vector of chosen actions for every $a \in C$); we denote by $act(C, s)$ the set of C-actions at s. An action profile α extends a C-action α_C, symbolically $\alpha_C \sqsubseteq \alpha$, if $\alpha(a) = \alpha_C(a)$, for every $a \in C$. The *outcome set* of the C-action α_C at s is the set of states $out(s, \alpha_C) = \{\delta(s, \alpha) \mid \alpha \in act(\mathbb{AG}, s) \text{ and } \alpha_C \sqsubseteq \alpha\}$.

A *strategy* for an agent a is a function $str_a(h) : \mathcal{S}^+ \mapsto act(a, last(h))$ assigning to every history an action available to a at the last state of the history. A C-strategy is a tuple of strategies for every $a \in C$. The function $out(s, \alpha_C)$ can be naturally extended to the functions $out(s, str_C)$ and $out(h, str_C)$ assigning to a given state s, or more generally a given history h, and a given C-strategy the set of states that can result from applying str_C at s or h, respectively. The set of all paths that can result when the agents in C follow the strategy str_C from a given state s is denoted by $\Pi(s, str_C)$ and defined as $\{\pi \in \mathcal{S}^\omega \mid \pi[0] = s$ and $\pi[j+1] \in out(\pi[0,j], str_C)$, for every $j \geqslant 0\}$.

The satisfaction relation between models $\mathfrak{M}$, states s, and state formulas φ, as well as between models $\mathfrak{M}$, paths π, and path formulas ϑ, is defined as follows:

- $\mathfrak{M}, s \models p_i \leftrightharpoons s \in V(p_i)$;
- $\mathfrak{M}, s \models \bot$ never holds;
- $\mathfrak{M}, s \models \varphi_1 \to \varphi_2 \leftrightharpoons \mathfrak{M}, s \models \varphi_1$ implies $\mathfrak{M}, s \models \varphi_2$;
- $\mathfrak{M}, s \models \langle\!\langle C \rangle\!\rangle \vartheta_1 \leftrightharpoons$ there exists a C-strategy str_C such that $\mathfrak{M}, \pi \models \vartheta_1$ holds for every $\pi \in \Pi(s, str_C)$;
- $\mathfrak{M}, \pi \models \varphi_1 \leftrightharpoons \mathfrak{M}, \pi[0] \models \varphi_1$;
- $\mathfrak{M}, \pi \models \vartheta_1 \to \vartheta_2 \leftrightharpoons \mathfrak{M}, \pi \models \vartheta_1$ implies $\mathfrak{M}, \pi \models \vartheta_2$;
- $\mathfrak{M}, \pi \models \bigcirc \vartheta_1 \leftrightharpoons \mathfrak{M}, \pi[1, \infty] \models \vartheta_1$;
- $\mathfrak{M}, \pi \models \Box \vartheta_1 \leftrightharpoons \mathfrak{M}, \pi[i, \infty] \models \vartheta_1$, for every $i \geqslant 0$;
- $\mathfrak{M}, \pi \models \vartheta_1 \mathcal{U} \vartheta_2 \leftrightharpoons \mathfrak{M}, \pi[i, \infty] \models \vartheta_2$ for some $i \geqslant 0$ and $\mathfrak{M}, \pi[j, \infty] \models \vartheta_1$ for every j such that $0 \leqslant j < i$.

An **ATL***-formula is a state formula in this language. An **ATL***-formula is satisfiable if it is satisfied by some state of some model, and valid if it is satisfied by every state of every model. Formally, by **ATL*** we mean the set of all valid **ATL***-formulas; notice that this set is closed under uniform substitution.

Logic **ATL** can be thought of as a fragment of **ATL*** containing only formulas where a coalition quantifier is always paired up with a temporal connective. This, as in the case of **CTL**, eliminates path-formulas. Such composite "modal" operators are $\langle\!\langle C \rangle\!\rangle \bigcirc$, $\langle\!\langle C \rangle\!\rangle \Box$, and $\langle\!\langle C \rangle\!\rangle \mathcal{U}$. Formulas are defined by the following BNF expression:

$$\varphi ::= p \mid \bot \mid (\varphi \to \varphi) \mid \langle\!\langle C \rangle\!\rangle \bigcirc \varphi \mid \langle\!\langle C \rangle\!\rangle \Box \varphi \mid \langle\!\langle C \rangle\!\rangle (\varphi \mathcal{U} \varphi),$$

where C ranges over subsets of $\mathbb{AG}$ and p ranges over Var. The other Boolean connectives and the constant $\top$ are defined as for **CTL**.

The satisfaction relation between concurrent game models $\mathfrak{M}$, states s, and formulas φ is inductively defined as follows (we only list the cases for the "new" modal operators):

- $\mathfrak{M}, s \models \langle\!\langle C \rangle\!\rangle \bigcirc \varphi_1 \leftrightharpoons$ there exists a C-action α_C such that $\mathfrak{M}, s' \models \varphi_1$ whenever $s' \in out(s, act_C)$;
- $\mathfrak{M}, s \models \langle\!\langle C \rangle\!\rangle \Box \varphi_1 \leftrightharpoons$ there exists a C-strategy str_C such that $\mathfrak{M}, \pi[i] \models \varphi_1$ holds for all $\pi \in out(s, str_C)$ and all $i \geqslant 0$;
- $\mathfrak{M}, s \models \langle\!\langle C \rangle\!\rangle (\varphi_1 \mathcal{U} \varphi_2) \leftrightharpoons$ there exists a C-strategy str_C such that, for all $\pi \in out(s, str_C)$, there exists $i \geqslant 0$ with $\mathfrak{M}, \pi[i] \models \varphi$ and $\mathfrak{M}, \pi[j] \models \varphi$ holds for every j such that $0 \leqslant j < i$.

Satisfiable and valid formulas are defined as for **ATL***. Formally, by **ATL** we mean the set of all valid **ATL***-formulas; this set is closed under substitution.

Remark 1. We have given definitions of satisfiability and validity for **ATL*** and **ATL** that assume that the set of all agents $\mathbb{AG}$ present in the language is "fixed in advance". At least two other notions of satisfiability (and, thus, validity) for these logics have been discussed in the literature (see, e.g., [40])—i.e., satisfiability of a formula in a model where the set of all agents coincides with the set of agents named in the formula and satisfiability of a formula in a model where the set of agents is any set including the agents named in the formula (in this case, it suffices to consider all the agents named in the formula plus one extra agent). In what follows, we explicitly consider only the notion of satisfiability for a fixed set of agents; other notions of satisfiability can be handled in a similar way.

5   Finite-Variable Fragments of ATL* and ATL

We start by noticing that satisfiability for variable-free fragments of both **ATL*** and **ATL** is polynomial-time decidable, using the algorithm similar to the one outlined for **CTL*** and **CTL**. It follows that variable-free fragments of **ATL*** and **ATL** cannot be as expressive as entire logics.

We also notice that, as is well-known, satisfiability for **CTL*** is polynomial-time reducible to satisfiability for **ATL*** and satisfiability for **CTL** is polynomial-time reducible to satisfiability for **ATL**, using the translation that replaces all occurrences of $\forall$ by $\langle\!\langle\varnothing\rangle\!\rangle$ and all occurrences of $\exists$ by $\langle\!\langle\mathbb{AG}\rangle\!\rangle$. Thus, Theorems 2 and 4, together with the known upper bounds [14,24,34], immediately give us the following:

Theorem 5. *The satisfiability problem for the single-variable fragment of* **ATL***
is 2EXPTIME-*complete.*

Theorem 6. *The satisfiability problem for the single-variable fragment of* **ATL**
is EXPTIME-*complete.*

In the rest of this section, we show that single-variable fragments of **ATL*** and **ATL** are as expressive as the entire logics by embedding both **ATL*** and **ATL** into their single-variable fragments. The arguments closely resemble the ones for **CTL*** and **CTL**, so we only provide enough detail for the reader to be able to easily fill in the rest.

First, consider **ATL***. The translation $\cdot'$ is defined as for **CTL***, except that the clause for $\forall$ is replaced by the following:

$$(\langle\!\langle C\rangle\!\rangle\alpha)' = \langle\!\langle C\rangle\!\rangle(\Box p_{n+1} \to \alpha').$$

Next, we define

$$\Theta = p_{n+1} \wedge \langle\!\langle\varnothing\rangle\!\rangle\Box(\langle\!\langle\mathbb{AG}\rangle\!\rangle\bigcirc p_{n+1} \leftrightarrow p_{n+1})$$

and

$$\widehat{\varphi} = \Theta \wedge \varphi'.$$

Then, we can prove the analogues of Lemmas 1 and 2.

We next model all the variables of $\widehat{\varphi}$ by single-variable formulas $A'_1, \ldots, A'_m$. To that end, we use the class of concurrent game models $\mathsf{M} = \{\mathfrak{M}'_1, \ldots, \mathfrak{M}'_m\}$ that closely resemble models $\mathfrak{M}_1, \ldots, \mathfrak{M}_m$ used in the argument for $\mathbf{CTL}^*$. For every $\mathfrak{M}'_i$, with $i \in \{1, \ldots, m\}$, the set of states and the valuation V are the same as for $\mathfrak{M}_i$; in addition, whenever $s \longmapsto s'$ holds in $\mathfrak{M}_i$, we set $\delta(s, \alpha) = s'$, for every action profile α. The actions available to an agent a at each state of $\mathfrak{M}_i$ are all the actions available to a at any of the states of the model $\mathfrak{M}$ to which we are going to attach models $\mathfrak{M}'_i$ when proving the analogue of Lemma 4, as well as an extra action d_a that we need to set up transitions from the states of $\mathfrak{M}$ to the roots of $\mathfrak{M}'_i$s.

With every $\mathfrak{M}'_i$ we associate the formula A'_i. First, inductively define the sequence of formulas

$$\chi'_0 = \langle\!\langle\varnothing\rangle\!\rangle \Box p;$$
$$\chi'_{k+1} = p \wedge \langle\!\langle\mathbb{AG}\rangle\!\rangle \bigcirc (\neg p \wedge \langle\!\langle\mathbb{AG}\rangle\!\rangle \bigcirc \chi_k).$$

Next, for every $m \in \{1, \ldots, n+1\}$, let

$$A'_m = \chi'_m \wedge \langle\!\langle\mathbb{AG}\rangle\!\rangle \bigcirc \langle\!\langle\varnothing\rangle\!\rangle \Box \neg p.$$

Lemma 8. *Let $\mathfrak{M}'_k \in \mathsf{M}$ and let x be a state in $\mathfrak{M}'_k$. Then, $\mathfrak{M}'_k, x \models A'_m$ if, and only if, $k = m$ and $x = r_m$.*

Proof. Straightforward.

Now, for every $m \in \{1, \ldots, n+1\}$, define

$$B'_m = \langle\!\langle\mathbb{AG}\rangle\!\rangle \bigcirc A'_m.$$

Finally, let σ be a (substitution) function that, for every $i \in \{1, \ldots, n+1\}$, replaces p_i by B'_i, and let

$$\varphi^* = \sigma(\widehat{\varphi}).$$

This allows us to prove the analogue of Lemma 4.

Lemma 9. *Formula φ is satisfiable if, and only if, formula φ^* is satisfiable.*

Proof. Analogous to the proof of Lemma 4. When constructing the model $\mathfrak{M}'$, whenever we need to connect a state s in $\mathfrak{M}$ to the root r_i of $\mathfrak{M}'_i$, we make an extra action, d_a, available to every agent a, and define $\delta(s, \langle d_a\rangle_{a \in \mathbb{AG}}) = r_i$.

Thus, we have the following:

Theorem 7. *There exists a polynomial-time computable function e assigning to every $\mathbf{ATL}^*$-formula φ a single-variable formula $e(\varphi)$ such that $e(\varphi)$ is satisfiable if, and only if, φ is satisfiable.*

We then can adapt the argument for $\mathbf{ATL}$ form the one just presented in the same way we adapted the argument for $\mathbf{CTL}$ from the one for $\mathbf{CTL}^*$, obtaining the following:

Theorem 8. *There exists a polynomial-time computable function e assigning to every $\mathbf{ATL}$-formula φ a single-variable formula $e(\varphi)$ such that $e(\varphi)$ is satisfiable if, and only if, φ is satisfiable.*

6   Discussion

We have shown that logics **CTL***, **CTL**, **ATL***, and **ATL** can be polynomial-time embedded into their single-variable fragments; i.e., their single-variable fragments are as expressive as the entire logics. Consequently, for these logics, satisfiability is as computationally hard when one considers only formulas of one variable as when one considers arbitrary formulas. Thus, the complexity of satisfiability for these logics cannot be reduced by restricting the number of variables allowed in the construction of formulas.

The technique presented in this paper can be applied to many other modal and temporal logics of computation considered in the literature. We will not here attempt a comprehensive list, but rather mention a few examples.

The proofs presented in this paper can be extended in a rather straightforward way to Branching- and Alternating-time temporal-epistemic logics [18, 22, 24, 39], i.e., logics that enrich the logics considered in this paper with the epistemic operators of individual, distributed, and common knowledge for the agents. Our approach can be used to show that single-variable fragments of those logics are as expressive as the entire logics and that, consequently, the complexity of satisfiability for them is as hard (EXPTIME-hard or 2EXPTIME-hard) as for the entire logics. Clearly, the same approach can be applied to epistemic logics [12, 16, 20], i.e., logics containing epistemic, but not temporal, operators—such logics are widely used for reasoning about distributed computation. Our argument also applies to logics with the so-called universal modality [15] to obtain EXPTIME-completeness of their variable-free fragments. The technique presented here has also been recently used [31] to show that propositional dynamic logics are as expressive in the language without propositional variables as in the language with an infinite supply of propositional variables. Since our method is modular in the way it tackles modalities present in the language, it naturally lends itself to modal languages combining various modalities—a trend that has been gaining prominence for some time now.

The technique presented in this paper can also be lifted to first-order languages to prove undecidability results about fragments of first-order modal and related logics,—see [33].

We conclude by noticing that, while we have been able to overcome the limitations of the technique from [21] described in the introduction, our modification thereof has limitations of its own. It is not applicable to logics whose semantics forbids branching, such as **LTL** or temporal-epistemic logics of linear time [17, 22]. Our technique cannot be used, either, to show that finite-variable fragments of logical systems that are not closed under uniform substitution—such as public announcement logic **PAL** [9, 29]—have the same expressive power as the entire system. This does not preclude it from being used in establishing complexity results for finite-variable fragments of such systems provided they contain fragments, as is the case with **PAL** [26], that are closed under substitution and have the same complexity as the entire system.

References

1. Alur, R., Henzinger, T.A., Kuperman, O.: Alternating-time temporal logic. J. ACM **49**(5), 672–713 (2002). https://doi.org/10.1145/585265.585270
2. Blackburn, P., Spaan, E.: A modal perspective on the computational complexity of attribute value grammar. J. Log. Lang. Inf. **2**, 129–169 (1993). https://doi.org/10.1007/bf01050635
3. Chagrov, A., Rybakov, M.: How many variables does one need to prove PSPACE-hardness of modal logics? In: Advances in Modal Logic, vol. 4, pp. 71–82. King's College Publications (2003)
4. Clarke, E.M., Emerson, E.A.: Design and synthesis of synchronization skeletons using branching time temporal logic. Logics of Programs. LNCS, vol. 131, pp. 52–71. Springer, Heidelberg (1981). https://doi.org/10.1007/bfb0025774
5. Clarke, E.M., Grumberg, O., Peled, D.A.: Model Checking. MIT Press, Cambridge (2000)
6. David, A.: Deciding ATL* satisfiability by tableaux. In: Felty, A.P., Middeldorp, A. (eds.) CADE 2015. LNCS (LNAI), vol. 9195, pp. 214–228. Springer, Cham (2015). https://doi.org/10.1007/978-3-319-21401-6_14
7. Demri, S., Goranko, V., Lange, M.: Temporal Logics in Computer Science. Cambridge Tracts in Theoretical Computer Science, vol. 58. Cambridge University Press, Cambridge (2016). https://doi.org/10.1017/cbo9781139236119
8. Demri, S., Schnoebelen, P.: The complexity of propositional linear temporal logics in simple cases. Inf. Comput. **174**(1), 84–103 (2002). https://doi.org/10.1006/inco.2001.3094
9. van Ditmarsch, H., van der Hoek, W., Kooi, B.: Dynamic Epistemic Logic. Studies In Epistemology, Logic, Methodology, and Philosophy of Science, vol. 337. Springer, Heidelberg (2008). https://doi.org/10.1007/978-1-4020-5839-4
10. Emerson, E.A., Halpern, J.: Decision procedures and expressiveness in temporal logic of branching time. J. Comput. Syst. Sci. **30**(1), 1–24 (1985). https://doi.org/10.1016/0022-0000(85)90001-7
11. Emerson, E.A., Halpern, J.Y.: "Sometimes and not never" revisited: on branching versus linear time temporal logic. J. ACM **33**(1), 151–178 (1986). https://doi.org/10.1145/4904.4999
12. Fagin, R., Halpern, J.Y., Moses, Y., Vardi, M.Y.: Reasoning About Knowledge. MIT Press, Cambridge (1995)
13. Fischer, M.J., Ladner, R.E.: Propositional dynamic logic of regular programs. J. Comput. Syst. Sci. **18**, 194–211 (1979). https://doi.org/10.1016/0022-0000(79)90046-1
14. Goranko, V., van Drimmelen, G.: Complete axiomatization and decidability of the alternating-time temporal logic. Theor. Comput. Sci. **353**(1–3), 93–117 (2006). https://doi.org/10.1016/j.tcs.2005.07.043
15. Goranko, V., Passy, S.: Using the universal modality: gains and questions. J. Log. Comput. **2**(1), 5–30 (1989). https://doi.org/10.1093/logcom/2.1.5
16. Goranko, V., Shkatov, D.: Tableau-based decision procedure for multi-agent epistemic logic with operators of common and distributed knowledge. In: Proceedings of 6th IEEE International Conference on Software Engineering and Formal Methods, SEFM 2008, Cape Town, November 2008, pp. 237–246. IEEE CS Press, Washington, DC (2008). https://doi.org/10.1109/sefm.2008.27

17. Goranko, V., Shkatov, D.: Tableau-based decision procedure for full coalitional multiagent temporal-epistemic logic of linear time. In: Sierra, C., Castelfranchi, C., Decker, K.S., Sichman, J.S. (eds.) Proceedings of 8th International Joint Conference on Autonomous Agents and Multiagent Systems, AAMAS 2009, Budapest, May 2009, vol. 2, pp. 969–976. International Federation AAMAS (2009). https://dl.acm.org/citation.cfm?id=1558147

18. Goranko, V., Shkatov, D.: Tableau-based decision procedure for the full coalitional multiagent temporal-epistemic logic of branching time. In: Baldoni, M., et al. (eds.) Proceedings of 2nd Multi-Agent Logics, Languages, and Organisations Federated Workshops, Turin, September 2009, CEUR Workshop Proceedings, vol. 494, CEUR-WS.org (2009). http://ceur-ws.org/Vol-494/famaspaper7.pdf

19. Goranko, V., Shkatov, D.: Tableau-based decision procedures for logics of strategic ability in multiagent systems. ACM Trans. Comput. Log. 11(1) (2009). https://doi.org/10.1145/1614431.1614434. Article 3

20. Goranko, V., Shkatov, D.: Tableau-based procedure for deciding satisfiability in the full coalitional multiagent epistemic logic. In: Artemov, S., Nerode, A. (eds.) LFCS 2009. LNCS, vol. 5407, pp. 197–213. Springer, Heidelberg (2008). https://doi.org/10.1007/978-3-540-92687-0_14

21. Halpern, J.Y.: The effect of bounding the number of primitive propositions and the depth of nesting on the complexity of modal logic. Artif. Intell. 75(2), 361–372 (1995). https://doi.org/10.1016/0004-3702(95)00018-a

22. Halpern, J.Y., Vardi, M.Y.: The complexity of reasoning about knowledge and time I: lower bounds. J. Comput. Syst. Sci. 38(1), 195–237 (1989). https://doi.org/10.1016/0022-0000(89)90039-1

23. Hemaspaandra, E.: The complexity of poor man's logic. J. Log. Comput. 11(4), 609–622 (2001). https://doi.org/10.1093/logcom/11.4.609

24. van der Hoek, W., Wooldridge, M.: Cooperation, knowledge, and time: alternating-time temporal epistemic logic and its applications. Studia Logica 75(1), 125–157 (2003). https://doi.org/10.1023/a:1026185103185

25. Huth, M., Ryan, M.: Logic in Computer Science: Modelling and Reasoning About Systems, 2nd edn. Cambridge University Press, Cambridge (2004). https://doi.org/10.1017/cbo9780511810275

26. Lutz, C.: Complexity and succinctness of public announcement logic. In: Nakashima, H., Wellman, M.P., Weiss, G., Stone, P. (eds.) Proceedings of 5th International Joint Conference on Autonomous Agents and Multiagent Systems, AAMAS 2006, Hakodate, May 2006, pp. 137–143. ACM Press (2006). https://doi.org/10.1145/1160633.1160657

27. Nagle, M.C., Thomason, S.K.: The extensions of the modal logic K5. J. Symb. Log. 50(1), 102–109 (1975). https://doi.org/10.2307/2273793

28. Nishimura, I.: On formulas of one variable in intuitionistic propositional calculus. J. Symb. Log. 25(4), 327–331 (1960). https://doi.org/10.2307/2963526

29. Plaza, J.A.: Logics of public communications. In: Emrich, M.L., Pfeifer, M.S., Hadzikadic, M., Ras, Z.W. (eds.) Proceedings of 4th International Symposium on Methodologies for Intelligent Systems: Poster Session Program, pp. 201–216, Oak Ridge National Laboratory (1989). (Reprinted as: Synthese 158(2), 165–179 (2007). https://doi.org/10.1007/s11229-007-9168-7)

30. Reynolds, M.: A tableau for CTL*. In: Cavalcanti, A., Dams, D.R. (eds.) FM 2009. LNCS, vol. 5850, pp. 403–418. Springer, Heidelberg (2009). https://doi.org/10.1007/978-3-642-05089-3_26

31. Rybakov, M., Shkatov, D.: Complexity and expressivity of propositional dynamic logics with finitely many variables. Log. J. IGPL **26**(5), 539–547 (2018). https://doi.org/10.1093/jigpal/jzy014

32. Rybakov, M., Shkatov, D.: Complexity of finite-variable fragments of propositional modal logics of symmetric frames. Log. J. IGPL (to appear). https://doi.org/10.1093/jigpal/jzy018

33. Rybakov, M., Shkatov, D.: Undecidability of first-order modal and intuitionistic logics with two variables and one monadic predicate letter. Studia Logica (to appear). https://doi.org/10.1007/s11225-018-9815-7

34. Schewe, S.: ATL* satisfiability Is 2EXPTIME-complete. In: Aceto, L., Damgård, I., Goldberg, L.A., Halldórsson, M.M., Ingólfsdóttir, A., Walukiewicz, I. (eds.) ICALP 2008. LNCS, vol. 5126, pp. 373–385. Springer, Heidelberg (2008). https://doi.org/10.1007/978-3-540-70583-3_31

35. Shoham, Y., Leyton-Brown, K.: Multiagent Systems: Algorithmic, Game-Theoretic, and Logical Foundations. Cambridge University Press, Cambridge (2008). https://doi.org/10.1017/cbo9780511811654

36. Sistla, A.P., Clarke, E.M.: The complexity of propositional linear temporal logics. J. ACM **32**(3), 733–749 (1985). https://doi.org/10.1145/3828.3837

37. Vardi, M.Y., Stockmeyer, L.: Improved upper and lower bounds for modal logics of programs (preliminary report). In: Proceedings of 17th Annual ACM Symposium on Theory of Computing, STOC 1985, Providence, RI, May 1985, pp. 240–251. ACM Press, New York (1985). https://doi.org/10.1145/22145.22173

38. Švejdar, V.: The decision problem of provability logic with only one atom. Arch. Math. Log. **42**(8), 763–768 (2003). https://doi.org/10.1007/s00153-003-0180-4

39. Walther, D.: ATEL with common and distributed knowledge is ExpTime-complete. In: Schlingloff, H. (ed.) Methods for Modalities 4. Informatik-Berichte, vol. 194, pp. 173–186. Humboldt-Universität zu Berlin (2005)

40. Walther, D., Lutz, C., Wolter, F., Wooldridge, M.: ATL satisfiability is indeed EXPTIME-complete. J. Log. Comput. **16**(6), 765–787 (2006). https://doi.org/10.1093/logcom/exl009

Complexity Results on Register Context-Free Grammars and Register Tree Automata

Ryoma Senda[1(✉)], Yoshiaki Takata[2], and Hiroyuki Seki[1]

[1] Graduate School of Information Science, Nagoya University,
Furo-cho, Chikusa, Nagoya 464-8601, Japan
`ryoma.private@sqlab.jp`, `seki@i.nagoya-u.ac.jp`
[2] Graduate School of Engineering, Kochi University of Technology,
Tosayamada, Kami City, Kochi 782-8502, Japan
`takata.yoshiaki@kochi-tech.ac.jp`

Abstract. Register context-free grammars (RCFG) and register tree automata (RTA) are an extension of context-free grammars and tree automata, respectively, to handle data values in a restricted way. RTA are paid attention as a model of query languages for structured documents such as XML with data values. This paper investigates the computational complexity of the basic decision problems for RCFG and RTA. We show that the membership and emptiness problems for RCFG are EXPTIME-complete and also show how the complexity reduces by introducing subclasses of RCFG. The complexity of these problems for RTA are also shown to be NP-complete and EXPTIME-complete.

1 Introduction

There have been studies on defining computational models having mild powers of processing data values by extending classical models. Some of them are shown to have the decidability on basic problems and the closure properties, including first-order and monadic second-order logics with data equality, linear temporal logic with freeze quantifier [7] and register automata [14]. Among them, register automata (abbreviated as RA) is a natural extension of finite automata defined by incorporating registers that can keep data values as well as the equality test between an input data value and the data value kept in a register. Regular expression was extended to regular expression with memory (REM), which have the same expressive power as RA [18].

Recently, attention has been paid to RA as a computational model of a query language for structured documents such as XML because a structured document can be modeled as a tree or a graph where data values are associated with nodes and a query on a document can be specified as the combination of a regular pattern and a condition on data values [17,19]. For query processing and optimization, the decidability (hopefully in polynomial time) of basic properties of queries is desirable. The membership problem that asks for a given query q

B. Fischer and T. Uustalu (Eds.): ICTAC 2018, LNCS 11187, pp. 415–434, 2018.
https://doi.org/10.1007/978-3-030-02508-3_22

and an element e in a document whether e is in the answer set of q is the most basic problem. The satisfiability or (non)emptiness problem asking whether the answer set of a given query is nonempty is also important because if the answer set is empty, the query can be considered to be redundant or meaningless when query optimization is performed. The membership and emptiness problems for RA were already shown to be decidable [14] and their computational complexities were also analyzed [7,22].

While RA have a power sufficient for expressing regular patterns on *paths* of a tree or a graph, it cannot represent tree patterns (or patterns over branching paths) that can be represented by some query languages such as XPath. Register context-free grammars (RCFG) were proposed in [6] as an extension of classical context-free grammars (CFG) in a similar way to extending FA to RA. In [6], properties of RCFG were shown including the decidability of the membership and emptiness problems, and the closure properties. However, the computational complexity of these problems has not been reported yet. In parallel with this, RA were extended to a model dealing with trees, called tree automata over an infinite alphabet [15,23]. For uniformity, we will call the latter register tree automata (abbreviated as RTA).

In this paper, we analyze the computational complexity of the membership and emptiness problems for general RCFG, some subclasses of them, and RTA. In the original definition of RCFG [6], an infinite alphabet is assumed and an RCFG is defined as a formal system that generates finite strings over the infinite alphabet as in the original definition of RA [14]. In a derivation, a symbol can be loaded to a register only when the value is different from any symbol stored in the other registers, by which the equality checking is indirectly incorporated. In recent studies on RA [18,19], more concrete notions suitable for modeling a query language are adopted, namely, a word is a finite string over the product of a finite alphabet and an infinite set of data values (called *data word*), and the equality check between an input data value and the data value kept in a register can be specified as the guard condition of a transition rule. Also, different registers can keep an identical value in general.

Following those modern notions, we first define an RCFG as a grammar that derives a data word. In a derivation of a k-RCFG, k data values are associated with each occurrence of a nonterminal symbol (called a *register assignment*) and a production rule can be applied only when the guard condition of the rule, which is a Boolean combination of the equality check between an input data value and the data value in a register, is satisfied. We introduce subclasses of RCFG, including ε-rule free RCFG, growing RCFG, and RCFG with bounded registers.

We then show that the membership problems for general RCFG, ε-rule free RCFG, growing RCFG, and RCFG with bounded registers are EXPTIME-complete, PSPACE-complete, NP-complete, and solvable in P, respectively. For example, to show the upper bound for general RCFG, we use the property that any RCFG can be translated into a classical CFG when the number of different data values used in the derivation is finite, which was shown in [6]. EXPTIME-hardness is proved by a polynomial time reduction from the membership

problem for polynomial space-bounded alternating Turing machines. We also
show that the emptiness problem for general RCFG is EXPTIME-complete and
the complexity does not decrease even if we restrict RCFG to be growing.

Finally, we analyze the computational complexity of these problems for RTA.
It is well-known that the class of tree languages accepted by tree automata
coincides with the class of derivation trees generated by CFG. The difference
of RCFG and RTA in the membership problem is that a derivation tree is not
specified as an input in the former case while a data tree is given as an input to
the problem in the latter case.

Main results of this paper is summarized in Table 1. Note that the complexity
of the membership problems is in terms of both the size of a grammar or an
automaton and that of an input word (*combined complexity*). The complexity of
the membership problem on the size of an input word only (*data complexity*) is
P for general RCFG and RTA. In application, the size of a query (a grammar or
an automaton) is usually much smaller than that of a data (an input word). It
is desirable that the data complexity is small while the combined complexity is
rather a criterion of the expressive succinctness of the query language.

Table 1. Complexity results on RCFG and RTA

	General RCFG	ε-rule free RCFG	Growing RCFG	RCFG w/ bounded regs	RTA
Membership	EXPTIMEc	PSPACEc	NPc	In P	NPc
Emptiness	EXPTIMEc	EXPTIMEc	EXPTIMEc	In P	EXPTIMEc

Related Work. Early studies on query optimization and static analysis for
structured documents used traditional models such as tree automata, two variable logic and LTL. While those studies were successful, most of them neglected
data values associated with documents. Later, researchers developed richer models that can be applied to structured documents with data values, including
extensions of automata (register automata, pebble automata, data automata)
and extensions of logics (two-variable logics with data equality, LTL with freeze
quantifier). We review each of them in the following.

Register Automata and Register Context-Free Grammars: As already mentioned,
register automata (RA) was first introduced in [14] as finite-memory automata
where they show that the membership and emptiness problems are decidable,
and RA are closed under union, concatenation and Kleene-star. Later, the computational complexity of the former two problems are analyzed in [7,22]. In [6],
register context-free grammars (RCFG) as well as pushdown automata over an
infinite alphabet were introduced and the equivalence of the two models as well
as the decidability results and closure properties similar to RA were shown.

Other Automata for Data Words: There are extensions of automata to deal with
data in a restricted way other than RA, namely, data automata [4] and pebble

automata (PA) [20]. It is desirable for a query language to have an efficient data complexity for the membership problem. Libkin and Vrgoč [19] argue that register automata (RA) is the only model that has this property among the above mentioned formalisms and adopt RA as the core computational model of their queries on graphs with data. Neven [21] considers variations of RA and PA, either they are one way or two ways, deterministic, nondeterministic or alternating shows inclusion and separation relationships among these automata, $FO(\sim, <)$ and $EMSO(\sim, <)$, and gives the answer to some open problems including the undecidability of the universality problem for RA.

LTL with Freeze Quantifier: Linear temporal logic (LTL) was extended to LTL↓ with freeze quantifier [7,8]. A data value is bound with a variable in a formula and is referred to later in the scope of a freeze quantifier of that variable. The relationship among subclasses of LTL↓ and RA as well as the decidability and complexity of the satisfiability (nonemptiness) problems are investigated [7]. Especially, they showed that the emptiness problem for (both nondeterministic and deterministic) RA are PSPACE-complete.

Two-Variable Logics with Data Equality: First-order logic (FO) and monadic second-order logic (MSO) are major logics for finite model theory. It is known that two-variable $FO^2(<, +1)$ where $<$ is the ancestor-descendant relation and $+1$ is the parent-child relation is decidable and corresponds to Core XPath. The logic was extended to those with data equality. It was shown in [3] that $FO^2(\sim, <, +1)$ with data equality $\sim$ is decidable on data words. Note that $FO^2(\sim, <, +1)$ is incomparable with LTL↓ of [7]. Also it was shown in [2] that $FO^2(\sim, +1)$ and existential $MSO^2(\sim, +1)$ are decidable on unranked data trees.

Tree Automata and Data XPath: In [15], tree automata over infinite alphabets are introduced as a natural extension of RA. We call them register tree automata (RTA) in this paper. They showed that the membership and emptiness problems for RTA are decidable and the universality and inclusion problems are undecidable, and also showed that a data language L is generated by an RCFG if and only if there is an RTA that accepts a data tree language whose yield is L. However, the complexity of those decidable problems was not shown. In connection with XPath, top-down tree automata for data trees called alternating tree register automata (ATRA) [12] which correspond to forward XPath were introduced, and the decidability of the emptiness problems for these classes was shown. While RTA work on ranked data trees, ATRA work on unranked data trees. Later, [9,10] extended ATRA so that (1) they can guess a data value to store it in a register, and also (2) they can universally quantify the data values encountered in a given run; the emptiness for the extended ATRA was shown to be decidable by identifying ATRA as well-structured transition systems. Also, bottom-up tree automata for unranked data trees, which correspond to vertical XPath were introduced and the decidability of the emptiness was shown in [11]. Since XML documents are usually modeled as unranked trees, ATRA may be a better model for XPath than RTA. However, the complexity of the emptiness for ATRA is not elementary and an appropriate subclass would be needed for broader applications.

2   Definitions

2.1   Preliminaries

A register context-free grammar was introduced in [6] as a grammar over an infinite alphabet. We define it as a grammar over the product of a finite alphabet and an infinite set of data values, following recent notions [18,19]. Note that these differences are not essential.

Let $\mathbb{N} = \{1, 2, \ldots\}$ and $\mathbb{N}_0 = \{0\} \cup \mathbb{N}$. We assume an infinite set D of data values as well as a finite alphabet Σ. For a given $k \in \mathbb{N}_0$ specifying the number of registers, a mapping $\nu : [k] \to D$ is called an assignment (of data values to k registers) where $[k] = \{1, 2, \ldots, k\}$. We assume that a data value $\perp \in D$ is designated as the initial value of a register. Let F_k denote the class of assignments to k registers. For $\nu, \nu' \in F_k$, we write $\nu' = \nu[i \leftarrow d]$ if $\nu'(i) = d$ and $\nu'(j) = \nu(j)$ $(j \neq i)$.

Let C_k denote the set of guard expressions over k registers defined by the following syntax rules:

$$\psi := \mathrm{tt} \mid \mathrm{ff} \mid x_i^= \mid x_i^{\neq} \mid \psi \wedge \psi \mid \psi \vee \psi \mid \neg \psi$$

where $x_i \in \{x_1, \ldots, x_k\}$. The description length of guard expression ψ is defined as

$$\|\psi\| = \begin{cases} 1 & \text{if } \psi = \mathrm{tt} \text{ or } \mathrm{ff}, \\ 1 + \log k & \text{if } \psi = x_i^= \text{ or } x_i^{\neq}, \\ 1 + \|\psi_1\| + \|\psi_2\| & \text{if } \psi = \psi_1 \wedge \psi_2 \text{ or } \psi_1 \vee \psi_2, \\ 1 + \|\psi_1\| & \text{if } \psi = \neg \psi_1. \end{cases}$$

For $d \in D$ and $\nu \in F_k$, the satisfaction of $\psi \in C_k$ by (d, ν) is recursively defined as follows. Intuitively, d is a current data value in the input, ν is a current register assignment, $d, \nu \models x_i^=$ means that the data value assigned to the i-th register by ν is equal to d and $d, \nu \models x_i^{\neq}$ means they are different.

- $d, \nu \models \mathrm{tt}$
- $d, \nu \not\models \mathrm{ff}$
- $d, \nu \models x_i^=$ iff $\nu(i) = d$
- $d, \nu \models x_i^{\neq}$ iff $\nu(i) \neq d$
- $d, \nu \models \psi_1 \wedge \psi_2$ iff $d, \nu \models \psi_1$ and $d, \nu \models \psi_2$
- $d, \nu \models \psi_1 \vee \psi_2$ iff $d, \nu \models \psi_1$ or $d, \nu \models \psi_2$
- $d, \nu \models \neg\psi$ iff $d, \nu \not\models \psi$

where $d, \nu \not\models \psi$ holds iff $d, \nu \models \psi$ does not hold.

For a finite alphabet Σ and a set D of data values disjoint from Σ, a *data word* over $\Sigma \times D$ is a finite sequence of elements of $\Sigma \times D$ and a subset of $(\Sigma \times D)^*$ is called a *data language* over $\Sigma \times D$. For a data word $w = (a_1, d_1)(a_2, d_2) \ldots (a_n, d_n)$, $a_1 a_2 \ldots a_n$ is the label of w and $d_1 d_2 \ldots d_n$ is the data part of w. $|\beta|$ denotes the cardinality of β if β is a set and the length of β if β is a finite sequence.

2.2 Register Context-Free Grammars

Let Σ be a finite alphabet, D be a set of data values such that $\Sigma \cap D = \emptyset$ and $k \in \mathbb{N}$. A k-register context-free grammar (k-RCFG) is a triple $G = (V, R, S)$ where

- V is a finite set of nonterminal symbols (abbreviated as nonterminals) where $V \cap (\Sigma \cup D) = \emptyset$,
- R is a finite set of production rules (abbreviated as rules) having either of the following forms:

$$(A, \psi, i) \to \alpha, \quad (A, \psi) \to \alpha$$

  where $A \in V$, $\psi \in C_k$, $i \in [k]$ and $\alpha \in (V \cup (\Sigma \times [k]))^*$; we call (A, ψ, i) (or (A, ψ)) the left-hand side and α the right-hand side of the rule, and,
- $S \in V$ is the start symbol.

A rule whose right-hand side is ε is an ε-*rule* and a rule whose right-hand side is a single nonterminal symbol is a *unit rule*. If R contains no ε-rule, G is called ε-*rule free*. If R contains neither ε-rule nor unit rule, G is called *growing*. The description length of a k-RCFG $G = (V, R, S)$ is defined as $\|G\| = |V| + |R| \max\{(|\alpha| + 1)(\log |V| + \log k) + \|\psi\| \mid (A, \psi, i) \to \alpha \in R \text{ or } (A, \psi) \to \alpha \in R\}$, where $\|\psi\|$ is the description length of ψ. In this definition, we assume that the description length of $\alpha \in (V \cup (\Sigma \times [k]))^*$ is $|\alpha|(\log |V| + \log k)$ because the description length of each element of α is $O(\log |V| + \log k)$ bits if we consider $|\Sigma|$ is a constant. Since the description length of the left-hand side of a rule $(A, \psi, i) \to \alpha$ is $\log |V| + \|\psi\| + \log k$, we let the description length of this rule be $(|\alpha| + 1)(\log |V| + \log k) + \|\psi\|$. We assume $k \leq \|G\|$ without loss of generality.

We define $\Rightarrow_G$ as the smallest relation containing the instantiations of rules in R and closed under the context as follows. For $A \in V$, $\nu \in F_k$ and $X \in ((V \times F_k) \cup (\Sigma \times D))^*$, we say (A, ν) directly derives X, written as $(A, \nu) \Rightarrow_G X$ if there exist $d \in D$ (regarded as an input data value) and $(A, \psi, i) \to c_1 \ldots c_n \in R$ (resp. $(A, \psi) \to c_1 \ldots c_n \in R$) such that

$$d, \nu \models \psi, \ X = c'_1 \ldots c'_n, \ \nu' = \nu[i \leftarrow d] \text{ (resp. } \nu' = \nu) \text{ where}$$
$$c'_j = \begin{cases} (B, \nu') & \text{if } c_j = B \in V, \\ (b, \nu'(l)) & \text{if } c_j = (b, l) \in \Sigma \times [k]. \end{cases}$$

For $X, Y \in ((V \times F_k) \cup (\Sigma \times D))^*$, we also write $X \Rightarrow_G Y$ if there are $X_1, X_2, X_3 \in ((V \times F_k) \cup (\Sigma \times D))^*$ such that $X = X_1 (A, \nu) X_2$, $Y = X_1 X_3 X_2$ and $(A, \nu) \Rightarrow_G X_3$.

Let $\overset{*}{\Rightarrow}_G$ and $\overset{+}{\Rightarrow}_G$ be the reflexive transitive closure and the transitive closure of $\Rightarrow_G$, respectively, meaning the derivation of zero or more steps (resp. the derivation of one or more steps). We abbreviate $\Rightarrow_G$, $\overset{*}{\Rightarrow}_G$ and $\overset{+}{\Rightarrow}_G$ as $\Rightarrow$, $\overset{*}{\Rightarrow}$ and $\overset{+}{\Rightarrow}$ if G is clear from the context.

We denote by $\bot$ the register assignment that assigns the initial value $\bot$ to every register. Figure 1 shows an example of a direct derivation from $(S, \bot)$

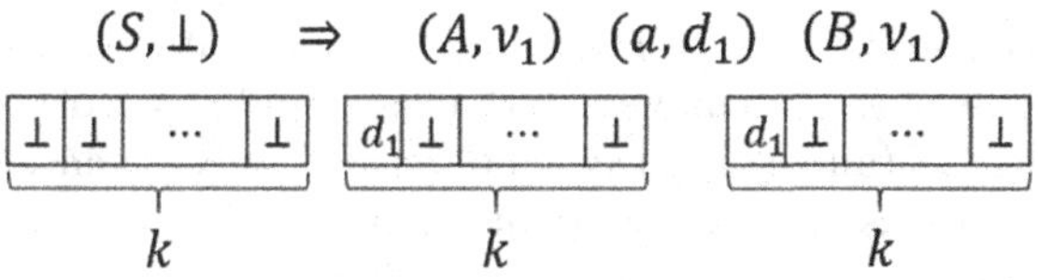

$$(S, \bot) \quad \Rightarrow \quad (A, \nu_1) \quad (a, d_1) \quad (B, \nu_1)$$

Fig. 1. An example of derivation from $(S, \bot)$ using $(S, \mathrm{tt}, 1) \rightarrow A(a, 1)B$

using $(S, \mathrm{tt}, 1) \rightarrow A(a, 1)B$. In the figure, d_1 is an arbitrary data value in D and $\nu_1 = \bot[1 \leftarrow d_1]$, because the guard of the rule is tt.

We let

$$L(G) = \{w \mid (S, \nu_0) \overset{*}{\Rightarrow} w \in (\Sigma \times D)^*\}.$$

$L(G)$ is called the data language generated by G. For example, if G is a 1-RCFG having two rules $(S, \mathrm{tt}, 1) \rightarrow (a, 1)S(a, 1)$ and $(S, \mathrm{tt}, 1) \rightarrow \varepsilon$, $L(G) = \{(a, d_1) \ldots (a, d_n)(a, d_n) \ldots (a, d_1) \mid n \geq 0\}$.

0-RCFG coincide with classical context-free grammars and we call a 0-RCFG a *context-free grammar (CFG)*.

Example 1. For a CFG G, it is well-known that if $L(G) \neq \emptyset$, then there exists a derivation tree of some word $w \in L(G)$ whose height is $O(\|G\|)$. However, this property does not hold for RCFG. Consider the following k-RCFG $G = (V, R, S)$, which satisfies $L(G) = \{(a, \bot)\}$. While $\|G\| = O(k \log k)$, the height of the derivation tree of $(a, \bot)$ is $\Omega(2^k)$.

$$V = \{A_{(i,b)} \mid 1 \leq i \leq k, \ b \in \{0, 1\}\}$$
$$\cup \{B_{(i,b)} \mid 1 \leq i < k, \ b \in \{0, 1\}\},$$
$$S = A_{(1,0)},$$

and R consists of the following rules:

$$(A_{(k,0)}, \mathrm{tt}) \rightarrow (a, k),$$

and for $1 \leq i < k$,

$$(A_{(i,0)}, x_k^= \wedge x_i^=) \rightarrow B_{(i,0)},$$
$$(A_{(i,1)}, x_k^= \wedge x_i^{\neq}) \rightarrow B_{(i,1)},$$
$$(B_{(i,0)}, x_k^{\neq}, i) \rightarrow A_{(1,0)} \mid A_{(1,1)},$$
$$(B_{(i,1)}, x_k^=, i) \rightarrow A_{(i+1,0)} \mid A_{(i+1,1)}.$$

The derivation of G from $(S, \bot)$ to $(a, \bot)$ simulates a $(k-1)$-bit binary counter. We consider that the ith bit of the binary counter is "0" (resp. "1") if the value of ith register is $\bot$ (resp. not $\bot$). The derivation keeps the value of the kth register being $\bot$. For $1 \leq i < k$ and $b \in \{0, 1\}$, derivation $(A_{(i,b)}, \nu) \Rightarrow_G (B_{(i,b)}, \nu)$ can exist if only if the ith bit of the binary counter represented by ν equals b. After this derivation, the ith bit is flipped by the derivation from $(B_{(i,b)}, \nu)$, and it derives $(A_{(j,0)}, \nu')$ and $(A_{(j,1)}, \nu')$ where ν' is the updated register assignment, and $j = i + 1$ if "the carry to the next bit" exists, and $j = 1$ otherwise. Because $(A_{(k,0)}, \nu)$ for some ν (and $(a, \perp)$) can be derived only when every bit of the binary counter becomes "1", the derivation from $(S, \perp)$ to $(a, \perp)$ must pass through the elements of $\{A_{(1,0)}, A_{(1,1)}\} \times F_k$ 2^{k-1} times.

3   Basic Properties of RCFG

The properties of RCFG in this section were first shown in [6]. We will give sketches of proofs to them to make this paper self-contained. We fix a finite alphabet Σ and a set D of data values.

Proposition 2. *Let G be an RCFG and $D' \subseteq D$ be a finite set. We can construct a CFG G' from G and D' that satisfies $L(G') = L(G) \cap (\Sigma \times D')^*$.*

Proof. Let $G = (V, R, S)$ be a k-RCFG and D' be a finite subset of D. We construct a CFG $G' = (V', R', S')$ from G and D' as follows. A nonterminal of G' is a nonterminal of G with k data values that represent a register assignment. The rules of G' are constructed accordingly. Note that whether a rule can be applied does not depend on data values themselves but depends on the equality among the data values given as an input or assigned to registers. By this fact, if $|D'| \geq k + 1$, then it suffices to consider data values in D' to simulate the derivations of G. Otherwise, i.e., $|D'| \leq k$, we need $k + 1$ different data values including those in D'.

- $V' = V \times D''^k$ where $D'' = D'$ if $|D'| \geq k+1$ and D'' is a set such that $D'' \supseteq D'$ and $|D''| = k + 1$ otherwise. Note that we can consider an assignment ν in F_k to be a k-tuple over D, i.e. an element of D^k, and thus $V' \subseteq V \times F_k$.
- $R' = \{(A, \nu) \to X \mid (A, \nu) \in V', X \in (V' \cup (\Sigma \times D'))^*, \text{ and } (A, \nu) \Rightarrow_G X\}$.
- $S' = (S, \perp)$.

We can show by induction on the length of derivations that for any $X \in (V' \cup (\Sigma \times D'))^*$, $S' \overset{*}{\Rightarrow}_{G'} X$ if and only if $(S, \perp) \overset{*}{\Rightarrow}_G X$. This establishes $L(G') = L(G) \cap (\Sigma \times D')^*$.

Proposition 3. *If a k-RCFG G generates a data word of length n, G generates a data word of length n that contains at most $k + 1$ different data values.*

Proof. Let $G = (V, R, S)$ be a k-RCFG and $w \in L(G)$ with $|w| = n$. Also, let $d_1, \ldots, d_{k+1} \in D$ be arbitrary data values that are mutually different and contain $\perp$. Consider a direct derivation of G:

$$(A, \nu) \Rightarrow_G X$$

where $A \in V$, $\nu \in F_k$, $X \in ((V \times F_k) \cup (\Sigma \times D))^*$ and $\nu(j) \in \{d_1, \ldots, d_{k+1}\}$ for every j $(1 \leq j \leq k)$. We alter the direct derivation as follows: Assume that an applied rule is $(A, \psi, i) \to \alpha$ and the content of i-th register of ν is updated as d, i.e., the register assignment appearing in X is $\nu' = \nu[i \leftarrow d]$. Let ν'' be the register assignment as follows:

- If there is j with $1 \leq j \leq k$ and $j \neq i$ such that $\nu(j) = d$, let $\nu'' = \nu'$.
- Otherwise, there is a data value $d' \in \{d_1, \ldots, d_{k+1}\}$ such that $\nu(j) \neq d'$ for every j $(1 \leq j \leq k)$. Let $\nu'' = \nu[i \leftarrow d']$.

Let X' be obtained from X by replacing every ν' in X with ν''. Then, $(A, \nu) \Rightarrow_G X'$ with X' containing at most $k+1$ different data values. For a given derivation $(S, \perp) \overset{*}{\Rightarrow}_G w$, by starting with $(S, \perp)$ and repeating the above transformation to each direct derivation in $(S, \perp) \overset{*}{\Rightarrow}_G w$, we obtain a desired derivation $(S, \perp) \overset{*}{\Rightarrow}_G w'$ with $|w'| = n$ and at most $k + 1$ different data values.

Proposition 4. *The membership problem for RCFG is decidable.*

Proof. Let G be an RCFG. It holds that $w = (a_1, d_1) \ldots (a_n, d_n) \in L(G)$ if and only if $w \in L(G) \cap (\Sigma \times \{d_1, \ldots, d_n\})^*$. By Proposition 2, we can construct a CFG G' from G and w that generates $L(G) \cap (\Sigma \times \{d_1, \ldots, d_n\})$. This implies the decidability of the membership problem of RCFG because the membership problem of CFG is decidable.

Proposition 5. *The emptiness problem for RCFG is decidable.*

Proof. For a given k-RCFG G, let $D_k = \{d_1, \ldots, d_{k+1}\} \subseteq D$ be an arbitrary subset of D consisting of $k + 1$ different data values. By Proposition 3, $L(G) = \emptyset$ if and only if $L(G) \cap (\Sigma \times D_k)^* = \emptyset$. By Proposition 2, we can construct a CFG G' from G and D_k such that $L(G') = L(G) \cap (\Sigma \times D_k)^*$. Hence, the emptiness for RCFG is decidable because the emptiness for CFG is decidable.

RCFG has the following closure properties [6].

Proposition 6. *The class of data languages generated by RCFG are closed under union, concatenation and Kleene-star.*

4   Upper Bounds

Lemma 7. *For the CFG G' constructed from a given k-RCFG G and a finite set $D' \subseteq D$ of data values by the construction of Proposition 2, we have $\|G'\| \in O(\|G\| \cdot |D''|^{k+1}k)$ where D'' is a subset of data values defined in the proof of Proposition 2.*

Proof. Let $G = (V, R, S)$ be a k-RCFG and $D' \subseteq D$ be a finite subset of data values. The following properties hold on the size of the CFG $G' = (V', R', S')$ constructed in the proof of Proposition 2.

$|V'| = |V \times D''^k| \in O(\|G\| \cdot |D''|^k)$.

$|R'| \leq |R| \cdot |D''|^k$.

$\|R'\| = |R| \max\{(|X| + 1)(\log |V| + k \log |D''| + \log |D'|) \mid (A, \nu) \rightarrow X \in R'\}$
$\qquad \in O(\|G\| \cdot |D''|^k \cdot k \log |D''|)$.

$\|S'\| \in O(1)$.

Hence, $\|G'\| \in O(\|G\| \cdot |D''|^{k+1}k)$ holds.

Lemma 8. *The membership problem for RCFG is decidable in EXPTIME.*

Proof. Assume we are given a k-RCFG G and a data word $w = (a_1, d_1) \ldots (a_n, d_n)$ as an input. Consider the CFG G' such that $L(G) \cap (\Sigma \times \{d_1, \ldots, d_n\})^*$, which is constructed in the proof of Proposition 4. By Lemma 7, $\|G'\| \in O(\|G\| c^{k+1} k)$ where $c = \max\{|w|, k+1\}$. Since the membership problem for CFG is decidable in deterministic polynomial time, the problem $w \in L(G)$ for k-RCFG G is decidable in deterministic time exponential to k.

Lemma 9. *The membership problem for ε-rule free RCFG is decidable in PSPACE.*

Proof. Let $G = (V, R, S)$ be an ε-rule free k-RCFG. Because G is ε-rule free, for any α such that $S \overset{*}{\Rightarrow}_G \alpha \overset{*}{\Rightarrow}_G w$, $|\alpha| \leq |w|$ holds. and the space needed for representing α is at most $\|G\| \cdot k(\log c) \cdot |w|$ where $c = \max\{|w|, k+1\}$. We can check whether $w \in L(G)$ by nondeterministically guessing a derivation from S to w and checking step by step whether $S \overset{*}{\Rightarrow}_G w$ in polynomial space in $\|G\|$, $|w|$, and k.

Lemma 10. *The membership problem for growing RCFG is decidable in NP.*

Proof. Let $G = (V, R, S)$ be a growing k-RCFG. Because G is a growing RCFG, for any α, α' such that $S \overset{*}{\Rightarrow}_G \alpha \Rightarrow_G \alpha'$, $|\alpha| < |\alpha'|$ holds. Therefore we can check whether $w \in L(G)$ by nondeterministically guessing a derivation from S to w, where the length of derivation is less than $|w|$, and checking step by step whether $S \overset{*}{\Rightarrow}_G w$ in nondeterministical polynomial time in $\|G\|$, $|w|$, and k.

Lemma 11. *The emptiness problem for RCFG is decidable in EXPTIME.*

Proof. Let G be a k-RCFG and $D_k = \{d_1, ..., d_{k+1}\} \subseteq D$. Assume that we construct the CFG G' from G and D_k such that $L(G) \cap (\Sigma \times D_k)^*$ according to the proof of Proposition 2. By Lemma 7, $\|G'\| \in O(\|G\| \cdot |D_k|^{k+1} k)$ holds. Because the emptiness problem for CFG is decidable in linear time, the problem of $L(G) = \emptyset$ for a k-RCFG is decidable in deterministic time exponential to k.

5   Lower Bounds

5.1   Alternating Turing Machine

An *alternating Turing machine* [5], [24, Sect. 10.3] (abbreviated as ATM) is a tuple $M = (Q, Q_e, Q_a, \Gamma, \Sigma, \delta, q_0, q_{acc}, q_{rej})$ where

- Q is a finite set of states, Q_e and Q_a are the set of *existential states* and the set of *universal states*, respectively, such that $Q_e \cup Q_a \cup \{q_{acc}, q_{rej}\} = Q$ and $Q_e, Q_a, \{q_{acc}, q_{rej}\}$ are mutually disjoint,

- Γ is a finite set of tape symbols containing a special symbol representing *blank*, $\sqcup \in \Gamma \backslash \Sigma$,
- $\Sigma \subseteq \Gamma$ a set of input symbols,
- $\delta : Q \times \Gamma \to \mathcal{P}(Q \times \Gamma \times \{L, R\})$ is a state transition function where $\mathcal{P}(A)$ denotes the powerset of a set A, and
- $q_0, q_{acc}, q_{rej} \in Q$ are the initial state, the accepting state and the rejecting state, respectively.

For a state $q \in Q$, a tape content $\alpha \in \Gamma^*$ and a head position j ($1 \le j \le |\alpha|$), (q, α, j) is called an *instantaneous description* (abbreviated as ID) of M. For two IDs $(q, \alpha, j), (q', \alpha', j')$, we say that (q, α, j) can transit to (q', α', j') or (q', α', j') is a successor of (q, α, j), written as $(q, \alpha, j) \to (q', \alpha', j')$ if $\exists a, b \in \Gamma$, $\exists \beta, \gamma \in \Gamma^*$, $|\beta| = j - 1$, $\alpha = \beta a \gamma$ such that

$$\alpha' = \begin{cases} \beta b \sqcup & \text{if } |\alpha| = j \text{ (i.e. } \gamma = \varepsilon) \text{ and } j' = j + 1, \\ \beta b \gamma & \text{otherwise,} \end{cases}$$

$$j' = \begin{cases} j - 1 & \delta(q, a) \ni (q', b, L), \text{ or} \\ j + 1 & \delta(q, a) \ni (q', b, R). \end{cases}$$

Let $\overset{*}{\to}$ be the reflexive transitive closure of $\to$.

We define the accepting condition $g : Q \times \Gamma^* \times N \to \{\text{tt}, \text{ff}\}$ of M as follows.

$$g(q, \alpha, j) = \begin{cases} \text{tt} & q = q_{acc} \\ \text{ff} & q = q_{rej} \\ \bigvee_{(q,\alpha,j) \to (q',\alpha',j')} g(q', \alpha', j') & q \in Q_e \\ \bigwedge_{(q,\alpha,j) \to (q',\alpha',j')} g(q', \alpha', j') & q \in Q_a \end{cases}$$

For an ATM $M = (Q, Q_e, Q_a, \Gamma, \Sigma, \delta, q_0, q_{acc}, q_{rej})$ and $u \in \Sigma^*$, if $g(q_0, u, 1) = \text{tt}$, then M accepts u, and if $g(q_0, u, 1) = \text{ff}$, then M rejects u. Let $L(M) = \{u \in \Sigma^* \mid g(q_0, u, 1) = \text{tt}\}$, which is the language recognized by M. Let $s : \mathbb{N}_0 \to \mathbb{N}_0$ be a function. If for any $u \in \Sigma^*$ and any (q, α, j) such that $(q_0, u, 1) \overset{*}{\to} (q, \alpha, j)$, $|\alpha| \le s(|u|)$ holds, then we say that M is an $s(n)$-space bounded ATM. If M is a $p(n)$-space bounded ATM for a polynomial $p(n)$, M is a polynomial space bounded ATM. It is well-known that APSPACE = EXPTIME where APSPACE is the class of languages accepted by polynomial space bounded ATM.

5.2 Membership for General RCFG

Theorem 12. *The membership problem for RCFG is EXPTIME-complete. This holds even for RCFG of which every guard expression refers to at most two registers.*

Proof. By Lemma 8, it is enough to show EXPTIME-hardness, which will be shown by a polynomial-time reduction from the membership problem for polynomial-space bounded ATM. In the reduction, we simulate tape contents of a given ATM M by a register assignment of the RCFG G constructed from M. For this purpose, we encode the state transition function of M by production rules of G.

Assume that we are given a $p(n)$-space bounded ATM $M = (Q, Q_e, Q_a, \Gamma, \Sigma, \delta, q_0, q_{acc}, q_{rej})$ where $p(n)$ is a polynomial and an input $u \in \Sigma^*$ to M. Then, we construct $(|\Gamma| + p(|u|))$-RCFG $G = (V, R, S)$ that satisfy $u \in L(M) \Leftrightarrow \varepsilon \in L(G)$, where

$$
\begin{aligned}
V = \ &\{T_{(i,j)} \mid 1 \le j < i \le |\Gamma|\} \cup \{T_{(1,0)}\} \\
&\cup \{W_i \mid 0 \le i \le |u|\} \\
&\cup \{A_q^{(i,j)} \mid q \in Q,\ 1 \le i \le |\Gamma|,\ 1 \le j \le p(|u|)\} \\
&\cup \{B_q^{(i,j)} \mid q \in Q,\ 1 \le i \le |\Gamma|,\ 1 \le j \le p(|u|)\} \\
&\cup \{C_q^{(i,j,k)} \mid q \in Q,\ 1 \le i \le |\Gamma|,\ 1 \le j \le p(|u|), \\
&\qquad 0 \le k \le \max_{q \in Q,\, a \in \Gamma} |\delta(q,a)|\},
\end{aligned}
$$

$$
S = T_{(1,0)},
$$

and R is constructed as follows. Without loss of generality, we assume that $\Gamma = \{1, 2, \ldots, |\Gamma|\} \subseteq \mathbb{N}$ and 1 is the blank symbol of M. In the following, we denote the ith element of a sequence α by α_i (i.e., $\alpha = \alpha_1 \alpha_2 \ldots \alpha_{|\alpha|}$).

- We construct production rules that load different data values in the first $|\Gamma|$ registers. Note that we keep the initial value $\perp$ in the first register. To the ith register $(i \ge 2)$, a data value different from $\perp$ is assigned by Rule (1), and that data value is guaranteed to be different from the value of every jth register $(2 \le j < i)$ by Rule (2).

$$
(T_{(i-1,i-2)}, x_1^{\neq}, i) \to T_{(i,1)} \quad \text{for } 2 \le i \le |\Gamma|, \tag{1}
$$

$$
(T_{(i,j-1)}, x_i^{=} \wedge x_j^{\neq}) \to T_{(i,j)} \quad \text{for } 2 \le j < i \le |\Gamma|. \tag{2}
$$

- To express the initial tape contents u, we construct the following production rules that load data values corresponding to the symbols in u from left to right into $(|\Gamma| + 1)$th to $(|\Gamma| + |u|)$th registers:

$$
(T_{(|\Gamma|, |\Gamma|-1)}, \text{tt}) \to W_0, \tag{3}
$$

$$
(W_{i-1}, x_{u_i}^{=}, |\Gamma| + i) \to W_i \quad \text{for } 1 \le i \le |u|. \tag{4}
$$

- Let $s(m) = -1$ if $m = L$ and $s(m) = 1$ if $m = R$. For encoding the state transition and accepting condition of M by G, we introduce a nonterminal symbol $A_q^{(i,j)}$ for $q \in Q$, $1 \le i \le |\Gamma|$, and $1 \le j \le p(n)$. $A_q^{(i,j)}$ represents a part of an ID (q, α, j) of M where $i = \alpha_j$, i.e. the tape symbol at the head position. The remaining information about α of (q, α, j) will be represented by a register assignment of G. More precisely, the content of $(|\Gamma| + j)$th register (i.e. $\nu(|\Gamma| + j)$) equals the data value $\nu(\alpha_j)$ representing the tape symbol α_j for $1 \le j \le |\alpha|$ and $\nu(|\Gamma| + j) = \perp$ for $|\alpha| < j \le p(|u|)$. Let ν_α denote such

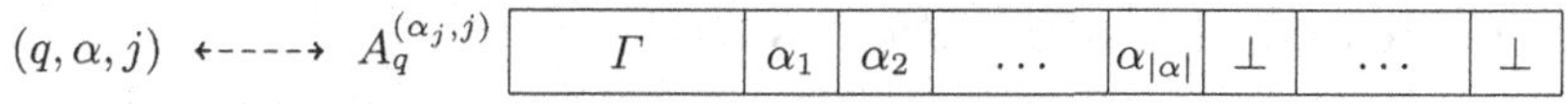

Fig. 2. The correspondence between M's ID and G's nonterminal symbol and registers.

a register assignment that represents the tape contents α. We illustrate the correspondence between an ID of M and a nonterminal symbol and a register assignment of G in Fig. 2.

- To derive the nonterminal symbol corresponding to the initial ID of M, we construct the following rule:

$$(W_{|u|}, \mathrm{tt}) \rightarrow A_{q_0}^{(u_1, 1)}. \tag{5}$$

- Consider $A_q^{(i,j)}$ and let $\{(q_1, b_1, m_1), \ldots, (q_t, b_t, m_t)\} = \delta(q, i)$. For each $a \in \Gamma$ and $1 \leq k \leq t$, we construct the following rules. If $q \in Q_e$, then:

$$(A_q^{(i,j)}, x_{b_k}^=, |\Gamma| + j) \rightarrow B_{q_k}^{(a, j+s(m_k))}. \tag{6}$$

If $q \in Q_a$, then:

$$(A_q^{(i,j)}, \mathrm{tt}) \rightarrow C_q^{(i,j,1)} \ldots C_q^{(i,j,t)}, \tag{7}$$

$$(C_q^{(i,j,k)}, x_{b_k}^=, |\Gamma| + j) \rightarrow B_{q_k}^{(a, j+s(m_k))}. \tag{8}$$

Note that if $t = 0$, then the right-hand side of Rule (7) is ε. We also construct the following rule for each $q' \in Q$, $a \in \Gamma$, and $1 \leq j' \leq p(n)$:

$$(B_{q'}^{(a,j')}, x_a^= \wedge x_{|\Gamma|+j'}^=) \rightarrow A_{q'}^{(a,j')}. \tag{9}$$

- Finally, we construct the following rules to express accepting IDs.

$$(A_{q_{acc}}^{(i,j)}, \mathrm{tt}) \rightarrow \varepsilon \tag{10}$$

We can show for each ID (q, α, j),

$$g(q, \alpha, j) = \mathrm{tt} \ \text{ iff } \ (A_q^{(\alpha_j, j)}, \nu_\alpha) \overset{*}{\Rightarrow}_G \varepsilon \tag{11}$$

by induction on the application number of the definition of accepting condition for only if part and by induction on the length of the derivation for if part.

We can easily prove that $(S, \bot) \overset{*}{\Rightarrow}_G (A_{q_0}^{(u_1, 1)}, \nu_u)$, and moreover, if $(S, \bot) \overset{*}{\Rightarrow}_G \varepsilon$, then this derivation must be $(S, \bot) \overset{*}{\Rightarrow}_G (A_{q_0}^{(u_1, 1)}, \nu_u) \overset{*}{\Rightarrow}_G \varepsilon$. By letting $(q, \alpha, k) = (q_0, u, 1)$ in property (11) and by the above-mentioned fact, we obtain $u \in L(M) \Leftrightarrow g(q_0, u, 1) = \mathrm{tt} \Leftrightarrow ((S, \bot) \overset{*}{\Rightarrow} \varepsilon) \Leftrightarrow \varepsilon \in L(G)$. By the definition of G, we can say that this EXPTIME-completeness holds even for RCFG of which every guard expression refers to at most two registers.

5.3 Membership for ε-rule Free RCFG

Theorem 13. *The membership problem for ε-rule free RCFG is PSPACE-complete. This holds even for ε-rule free RCFG with guards referring to at most two registers.*

Proof. By Lemma 9, it is enough to show PSPACE-hardness. We prove it by a polynomial-time reduction from the membership problem for polynomial-space bounded ordinary Turing machines (TM), in a similar way as the proof of Theorem 12. A TM can be regarded as an ATM that has no universal states, and hence we do not need to construct ε-rules for a universal state that has no successor (i.e. we do not need Rule (7), whose right-hand side is ε if $t = 0$). We modify Rule (10), the ε-rule for the accepting state, as $(A_{q_{acc}}^{(i,j)}, \text{tt}) \rightarrow (a, 1)$. The resultant RCFG G is ε-rule free, and we can show $u \in L(M) \Leftrightarrow (a, \bot) \in L(G)$ (because the data value in the first register is always $\bot$). ∎

5.4 Membership for Growing RCFG

Theorem 14. *The membership problem for growing RCFG is NP-complete. This holds even for growing RCFG in which every guard is either tt or $x_1^=$.*

Proof. By Lemma 10, it is enough to show NP-hardness. We prove it by a polynomial-time reduction from the satisfiability problem for 3-Conjunctive Normal Form (3CNF). Let $\phi = (a_1 \vee b_1 \vee c_1) \ldots (a_m \vee b_m \vee c_m)$ be a 3CNF over Boolean variables $y_1, \ldots, y_n$ where each a_i, b_i, c_i $(1 \leq i \leq m)$ is a literal y_j or $\overline{y_j}$ for some j $(1 \leq j \leq n)$. For i $(1 \leq i \leq m)$, we define register number r_{a_i} as $r_{a_i} = 2j$ if $a_i = y_j$ and $r_{a_i} = 2j + 1$ if $a_i = \overline{y_j}$. We also define the same notation r_{b_i} and r_{c_i} for b_i and c_i. We construct the growing $(2n+1)$-RCFG $G = (V, S, R)$ over $\Sigma = \{a\}$ where $V = \{S, A_{P_0}, \ldots, A_{P_n}, A_{C_0}, \ldots, A_{C_m}\}$ and

$$
\begin{aligned}
R = &\{(S, \text{tt}, 1) \rightarrow A_{P_0}(a, 1)\} \\
&\cup \{(A_{P_{i-1}}, x_1^=, 2i + j) \rightarrow A_{P_i}(a, 1) \mid 1 \leq i \leq n,\ j \in \{0, 1\}\} \\
&\cup \{(A_{P_n}, \text{tt}) \rightarrow A_{C_0}(a, 1)\} \\
&\cup \{(A_{C_{i-1}}, \text{tt}) \rightarrow A_{C_i}(a, r) \mid 1 \leq i \leq m,\ r \in \{r_{a_i}, r_{b_i}, r_{c_i}\}\} \\
&\cup \{(A_{C_m}, \text{tt}) \rightarrow (a, 1)\}.
\end{aligned}
$$

The first register of the constructed RCFG G is used for keeping a data value (possibly) different from $\bot$, and we use that value and $\bot$ for representing tt and ff, respectively. G nondeterministically loads the value representing tt to exactly one of the $(2i)$th and $(2i + 1)$th registers for each i, to encode a truth value assignment to $y_1, \overline{y_1}, y_2, \overline{y_2}, \ldots, y_n, \overline{y_n}$. Then G outputs the value of one of the literals a_i, b_i, c_i for each clause $a_i \vee b_i \vee c_i$ in ϕ. It is not difficult to show that ϕ is satisfiable if and only if $(a, d)^{n+m+3} \in L(G)$, where d is an arbitrary data value in $D \setminus \{\bot\}$. Since $(a, d_1)^{n+m+3} \in L(G)$ iff $(a, d_2)^{n+m+3} \in L(G)$ for any $d_1, d_2 \in D \setminus \{\bot\}$, we can choose any $d \in D \setminus \{\bot\}$ to make the input data word for the membership problem. Hence, we have shown the NP-hardness of the problem.

5.5   The Emptiness Problem

Theorem 15. *The emptiness problem for RCFG is EXPTIME-complete, even if RCFG are restricted to be growing and with guards referring to at most two registers.*

Proof. By Lemma 11, it is enough to show EXPTIME-hardness. In the proof of Theorem 12, we construct ε-rules when the state q under consideration is a universal state that has no successor (see Rule (7)) or q is the accepting state (see Rule (10)). We modify those production rules (7) and (10) as follows:

$$(A_q^{(i,j)}, \text{tt}) \rightarrow (a, 1) \quad \text{if } \delta(q, i) = \emptyset \text{ and } q \in Q_a,$$
$$(A_{q_{acc}}^{(i,j)}, \text{tt}) \rightarrow (a, 1).$$

Also, a unit rule, say $A \rightarrow B$ $(A, B \in V)$ can be replaced with $A \rightarrow (a, 1)B$ $(a \in \Sigma)$. With this modification, the constructed RCFG G has neither ε-rule nor unit rule, and $L(G)$ is nonempty iff the given ATM M accepts the input u. Therefore, we reduced the membership problem for polynomial-space bounded ATM to the emptiness problem for growing RCFG in polynomial time. Note that we cannot use this construction for proving Theorem 12 because the length of a (shortest) word in $L(G)$ is not guaranteed to be a polynomial of the sizes of M and u. □

As shown in Theorem 14, the membership problem for RCFG is NP-hard even if RCFG is restricted to have guards referring to at most one register. In contrast, the emptiness problem for RCFG with guards referring to at most one register is in P, as shown in the next theorem.

Theorem 16. *The emptiness problem for RCFG with guards referring to at most one register is decidable in linear time.*

Proof. If a guard expression ψ refers to at most one register, then for every register assignment ν, there must be a data value d that satisfies $d, \nu \models \psi$. That is, regardless of ν, rule $(A, \psi, i) \rightarrow \alpha$ or $(A, \psi) \rightarrow \alpha$ can be applied to expanding (A, ν).

Now, for a given RCFG G, let G' be the CFG obtained from G by removing the guard expression and register numbers in each production rule (e.g., replacing $(A, \psi, i) \rightarrow B(a, j)$ with $A \rightarrow Ba$). For a string $X \in ((V \times F_k) \cup (\Sigma \times D))^*$, let $r(X) \in (V \cup \Sigma)^*$ be the string obtained from X by removing the register assignments and the data values. By the discussion in the previous paragraph, if $X \Rightarrow_G Y$, then $r(X) \Rightarrow_{G'} r(Y)$, and if $r(X) \Rightarrow_{G'} Y'$ for some Y', then $X \Rightarrow_G Y$ for some Y such that $r(Y) = Y'$. Therefore $L(G) \neq \emptyset$ iff $L(G') \neq \emptyset$. Since $\|G'\| = O(\|G\|)$ and the emptiness problem for CFG is decidable in linear time, the emptiness problem for RCFG with guards referring to at most one register is also decidable in linear time.

5.6   RCFG with Bounded Registers

Theorem 17. *The membership problem and emptiness problem for RCFG with bounded registers are in P. The data complexity of the membership problem for general RCFG is in P.*

Proof. Let G be a k-RCFG over Σ and D and G' be the CFG constructed as in the proof of Proposition 2 from G and a finite set $D' \subseteq D$. Then $\|G'\| = O(\|G\| \cdot |D''|^{k+1}k)$ holds by Lemma 7. If k is a constant independent of the choice of G, then $\|G'\|$ is a polynomial of $\|G\|$ and $|D''|$. Hence, by Lemmas 8 and 11, both of the membership problem and the emptiness problem for RCFG with bounded registers are in P. By the same reason, the data complexity of the membership problem for general RCFG is in P.

6   Register Tree Automata

6.1   Definitions

A *ranked alphabet* Σ is a finite set of symbols, each of which is associated with a nonnegative integer called a rank. Let Σ_n be the set of symbols having rank n in Σ. Let T_Σ be the smallest set satisfying $f \in \Sigma_n$ and $t_j \in T_\Sigma (1 \le j \le n)$ imply $f(t_1, \ldots, t_n) \in T_\Sigma$. A member $t \in T_\Sigma$ is called a *tree* over Σ. The set of positions $Pos(t)$ of a tree $t = f(t_1, \ldots, f_n)$ $(f \in \Sigma_n)$ is defined by $Pos(t) = \{\varepsilon\} \cup \{jp \mid p \in Pos(t_j), 1 \le j \le n\}$. For $t = f(t_1, \ldots, t_n)$ $(f \in \Sigma_n)$ and $p \in Pos(t)$, the label $lab(t, p)$ and the subtree $t|_p$ of t at p is defined as $lab(t, \varepsilon) = f$, $t|_\varepsilon = t$, $lab(t, jp) = lab(t_j, p)$ and $t|_{jp} = t_j|_p$ $(1 \le j \le n)$. Let D be an infinite set of data values. A *data tree* over Σ and D is a pair $\tau = (t, \delta)$ where $t \in T_\Sigma$ and δ is a mapping $\delta : Pos(t) \to D$. We let $Pos(\tau) = Pos(t)$. The set of all data trees over Σ and D is denoted as $T_{\Sigma \times D}$.

Definition 18. *A k-register tree automaton (k-RTA) over a ranked alphabet Σ and a set D of data values is a tuple $A = (Q, q_0, T)$ where Q is a finite set of states, $q_0 \in Q$ is the initial state and T is a set of transition rules having one of the following forms:*

$$f(q, \psi, i) \to (q_1, \ldots, q_n) \ \ or \ \ f(q, \psi) \to (q_1, \ldots, q_n)$$

where $f \in \Sigma_n$, $q \in Q$, $\psi \in C_k$, $1 \le i \le k$ and q_j $(1 \le j \le n)$. When $n = 1$, we omit the parentheses in the right-hand side. When $n = 0$, we write only the left-hand side $f(q, \psi, i)$ or $f(q, \psi)$ to denote the rule. A run of A on a data tree $\tau = (t, \delta)$ is a mapping $\rho : Pos(t) \to Q \times F_k$ satisfying the following condition: For $p \in Pos(t)$, if $\rho(p) = (q, \nu)$, $lab(t, p) = f$, and $\rho(pj) = (q_j, \mu_j)$ for $1 \le j \le n$, then there is $f(q, \psi, i) \to (q_1, \ldots, q_n) \in T$ (resp. $f(q, \psi) \to (q_1, \ldots, q_n) \in T$) such that $\delta(p), \nu \models \psi$ and $\nu_j = \nu[i \leftarrow \delta(p)]$ (resp. $\nu_j = \nu$) $(1 \le j \le n)$. A run ρ is accepting if $\rho(\varepsilon) = (q_0, \perp)$. The data tree language recognized by A is $L(A) = \{\tau \in T_{\Sigma \times D} \mid there is an accepting run of A on $\tau\}$.

6.2 Computational Complexity

Theorem 19. *The membership problem for RTA is NP-complete. This holds even if Σ is monadic, i.e., $\Sigma = \Sigma_0 \cup \Sigma_1$.*

Proof. To prove an upper bound, assume we are given an RTA A and a data tree $\tau = (t, \delta) \in T_{\Sigma \times D}$ and simulate a run of A on τ. For one step transition, A reads the data value at a node of τ and moves down. Therefore, the number of transitions of A is exactly $|t|$ and A will not read the data value of any node more than once. Hence, we can decide whether $\tau \in L(A)$ by nondeterministically assign a state of A to each node of τ and verify that the guessed assignment of states constitutes an accepting run of A on τ in polynomial time.

The NP-hardness can be proved in a similar way to the proof of Theorem 14.

Theorem 20. *The emptiness problem for RTA is EXPTIME-complete.*

Proof. To prove the theorem, it suffices to prove the following two properties because the emptiness problem for ε-rule free RCFG is EXPTIME-complete (Theorem 15).

- For a given ε-rule free k-RCFG G, we can construct a k-RTA A_G such that $L(G) = \emptyset \Leftrightarrow L(A_G) = \emptyset$ in polynomial time.
- For a given k-RTA A, we can construct an ε-rule free k-RCFG G_A such that $L(A) = \emptyset \Leftrightarrow L(G_A) = \emptyset$ in polynomial time.

Let $G = (V, R, S)$ be a k-RCFG over Σ and D. We first translate G to a k-RCFG $G' = (V', R', S)$ such that $L(G') = L(G)$ and R consists of production rules having one of the following forms:

$$(A, \varphi, i) \to \alpha, \quad (A, \varphi) \to \alpha \quad (\alpha \in V^+)$$
$$(A, \mathrm{tt}) \to (a, j) \quad (a \in \Sigma, \; j \in [k])$$

by replacing $(a, j) \in \Sigma \times [k]$ in the right-hand side of a production rule in R with a new nonterminal, say X, and adding a rule $(X, \mathrm{tt}) \to (a, j)$. From G', we construct the following k-RTA $A_G = (Q, q_S, T)$ over Σ' and D where $\Sigma'_n = \{f_n \mid$ there is a production rule in R' such that the length of its right-hand side is $n\}$ and

- $Q = \{q_c \mid c \in V \cup \Sigma_0\}$, and
- $T = \{f_n(q_A, \varphi, i) \to (q_{B_1}, q_{B_2}, \ldots, q_{B_n}) \mid (A, \varphi, i) \to B_1 B_2 \ldots B_n \in R'\}$
  $\cup \{f_n(q_A, \varphi) \to (q_{B_1}, q_{B_2}, \ldots, q_{B_n}) \mid (A, \varphi) \to B_1 B_2 \ldots B_n \in R'\}$
  $\cup \{f_0(q_A, \mathrm{tt}) \mid (A, \mathrm{tt}) \to (a, j) \in R'\}$.

It is straightforward to check that this RTA A_G has the desired property.

Next, let $A = (Q, q_0, T)$ be a k-RTA over a ranked alphabet Σ and D and we construct k-register RCFG $G_A = (V, R, A_{q_0})$ where

- $V = \{A_c \mid c \in Q \cup \Sigma_0\}$ and

- $R = \{ (A_q, \varphi, i) \rightarrow A_{q_1} A_{q_2} \dots A_{q_n} \mid$

  $\quad f(q, \varphi, i) \rightarrow (q_1, q_2, \dots, q_n) \in T, \ f \in \Sigma_n \ (n \geq 1) \}$

  $\cup \{ (A_q, \varphi) \rightarrow A_{q_1} A_{q_2} \dots A_{q_n} \mid$

  $\quad f(q, \varphi) \rightarrow (q_1, q_2, \dots, q_n) \in T, \ f \in \Sigma_n \ (n \geq 1) \}$

  $\cup \{ (A_q, \varphi, i) \rightarrow c \mid c(q, \varphi, i) \in T \} \cup \{ (A_q, \varphi) \rightarrow c \mid c(q, \varphi) \in T \}.$

It is also straightforward to check that this RCFG G_A has the desired property and we are done.

7 Conclusion

We have discussed the computational complexity of the membership and emptiness problems for RCFG and RTA. The combined complexity of the membership problem for general RCFG is EXPTIME-complete and decreases when we consider subclasses of RCFG while the data complexity is in P for general RCFG. There is an interesting similarity of the computational hierarchies between RCFG and multiple context-free grammars (MCFG) [13] where an MCFG is another natural extension of CFG generating tuples of strings. The emptiness problem for RCFG remains EXPTIME-complete even if we restrict RCFG to be growing. We also analyze how the complexity reduces when we restrict the number of registers occurring in the guard of a production rule.

Introducing a logic such as FO($\sim$), EMSO($\sim$) and LTL$\downarrow$ on data trees that corresponds to or subsumes RCFG and RTA is a future study. Also, introducing recursive queries such as datalog in relational databases and fixed point logics as related logical foundations [1, Part D] [16, Chap. 10] would be an interesting topic to be pursued.

Acknowledgements. This work was supported by JSPS KAKENHI Grant Number JP15H02684.

References

1. Abiteboul, S., Hull, R., Vianu, V.: Foundations of Databases. Addison-Wesley, Reading (1995)
2. Bojańczyk, M., Muscholl, A., Schwentick, T., Segoufin, L.: Two-variable logic on data trees and XML reasoning. J. ACM **56**(3), Article no. 13 (2009). https://doi.org/10.1145/1516512.1516515.
3. Bojańczyk, M., David, C., Muscholl, A., Schwentick, T., Segoufin, L.: Two-variable logic on data words. ACM Trans. Comput. Log. **1**(4), Article no. 27 (2011). https://doi.org/10.1145/1970398.1970403
4. Bouyer, P.: A logical characterization of data languages. Inf. Process. Lett. **84**(2), 75–85 (2002). https://doi.org/10.1016/s0020-0190(02)00229-6
5. Chandra, A.K., Kozen, D., Stockmeyer, L.J.: Alternation. J. ACM **28**(1), 114–133 (1981). https://doi.org/10.1145/322234.322243

6. Cheng, E.Y.C., Kaminski, M.: Context-free languages over infinite alphabets. Acta Inf. **35**(3), 245–267 (1998). https://doi.org/10.1007/s002360050120

7. Demri, S., Lazić, R.: LTL with freeze quantifier and register automata. ACM Trans. Comput. Log. **10**(3), Article no. 16 (2009). https://doi.org/10.1145/1507244. 1507246

8. Demri, S., Lazić, R., Nowak, D.: On the freeze quantifier in constraint LTL: decidability and complexity. Inf. Comput. **205**(1), 2–24 (2007). https://doi.org/10.1016/j.ic.2006.08.003

9. Figueira, D.: Forward-XPath and extended register automata on data-trees. In: Proceedings of 13th International Conference on Database Theory, ICDT 2010, Lausanne, March 2010. ACM International Conference Proceedings Series, pp. 231–241. ACM Press, New York (2010). https://doi.org/10.1145/1804669.1804699

10. Figueira, D.: Alternating register automata on finite data words and trees. Log. Methods Comput. Sci. **8**(1), Article no. 22 (2012). https://doi.org/10.2168/lmcs-8(1:22)2012

11. Figueira, D., Segoufin, L.: Bottom-up automata on data trees and vertical XPath. In: Schwentick, T., Dürr, C. (eds.) Proceedings of 28th International Symposium on Theoretical Aspects of Computer Science, STACS 2011, Dortmund, March 2011. Leibniz International Proceedings in Information, vol. 9, pp. 93–104. Dagstuhl Publishing, Saarbrücken/Wadern (2011). https://doi.org/10.4230/lipics.stacs.2011.93

12. Jurdziński, M., Lazić, R.: Alternation-free modal mu-calculus for data trees. In: Proceedings of 22nd IEEE Symposium on Logic in Computer Science, LICS 2007, Wroclaw, July 2007, pp. 131–140. IEEE CS Press, Washington, DC (2007). https://doi.org/10.1109/lics.2007.11

13. Kaji, Y., Nakanishi, R., Seki, H., Kasami, T.: The computational complexity of the universal recognition problem for parallel multiple context-free grammars. Comput. Intell. **10**(4), 440–452 (1994). https://doi.org/10.1111/j.1467-8640.1994.tb00008.x

14. Kaminski, M., Franz, N.: Finite-memory automata. Theor. Comput. Sci. **134**(2), 322–363 (1994). https://doi.org/10.1016/0304-3975(94)90242-9

15. Kaminski, M., Tan, T.: Tree automata over infinite alphabets. In: Avron, A., Dershowitz, N., Rabinovich, A. (eds.) Pillars of Computer Science. LNCS, vol. 4800, pp. 386–423. Springer, Heidelberg (2008). https://doi.org/10.1007/978-3-540-78127-1_21

16. Libkin, L.: Elements of Finite Model Theory. TTCS. Springer, Heidelberg (2004). https://doi.org/10.1007/978-3-662-07003-1

17. Libkin, L., Martens, W., Vrgoč, D.: Querying graphs with data. J. ACM **63**(2), Article no. 14 (2016). https://doi.org/10.1145/2850413

18. Libkin, T., Tan, T., Vrgoč, D.: Regular expressions for data words. J. Comput. Syst. Sci. **81**(7), 1278–1297 (2015). https://doi.org/10.1016/j.jcss.2015.03.005

19. Libkin, L., Vrgoč, D.: Regular path queries on graphs with data. In: Proceedings of 15th International Conference on Database Theory, ICDT 2012, Berlin, March 2012, pp. 74–85. ACM Press, New York (2012). https://doi.org/10.1145/2274576. 2274585

20. Milo, T., Suciu, D., Vianu, V.: Type checking for XML transformers. In: Proceedings of 19th ACM SIGMOD-SIGACT-SIGART Symposium on Principles of Database Systems, PODS 2000, Dallas, TX, May 2000, pp. 11–22. ACM Press, New York (2000). https://doi.org/10.1145/335168.335171

21. Neven, F., Schwentick, T., Vianu, V.: Finite state machines for strings over infinite alphabets. ACM Trans. Comput. Log. **5**(3), 403–435 (2004). https://doi.org/10. 1145/1013560.1013562

22. Sakamoto, H., Ikeda, D.: Intractability of decision problems for finite-memory automata. Theor. Comput. Sci. **231**, 297–308 (2000). https://doi.org/10.1016/s0304-3975(99)00105-x

23. Segoufin, L.: Automata and logics for words and trees over an infinite alphabet. In: Ésik, Z. (ed.) CSL 2006. LNCS, vol. 4207, pp. 41–57. Springer, Heidelberg (2006). https://doi.org/10.1007/11874683_3

24. Sipser, M.: Introduction to the Theory of Computation, 3rd edn. Cengage Learning, Boston (2013)

Information Flow Certificates

Manuel Töws[(✉)] and Heike Wehrheim

Institut für Informatik, Universität Paderborn,
Warburger Straße 100, 33098 Paderborn, Germany
mtoews@mail.uni-paderborn.de, wehrheim@uni-paderborn.de

Abstract. Information flow analysis investigates the flow of data in applications, checking in particular for flows from private sources to public sinks. Flow- and path-sensitive analyses are, however, often too costly to be performed every time a security-critical application is run. In this paper, we propose a variant of *proof carrying code* for information flow security. To this end, we develop information flow (IF) *certificates* which get attached to programs as well as a method for IF certificate *validation*. We prove soundness of our technique, i.e., show it to be tamper-free. The technique is implemented within the program analysis tool CPACHECKER. Our experiments confirm that the use of certificates pays off for costly analysis runs.

1 Introduction

Information flow (IF) analysis [5,6,13,14,19,21,26,29,36] is concerned with the flow of data in software applications. It investigates how information flows along program statements and whether this flow adheres to given *security policies* [17,31]. In its simplest form, information flow analysis tries to detect the flow of information from sources classified as private to public sinks. Information flow analysis has recently been extensively studied in the context of smartphone apps [6,14].

A number of different approaches for IF analyses have been proposed in the past. They range from approaches based on type systems [21,36] over logic [5,13,26] to theorem proving [13]. Some approaches also employ a dependency analysis which operates either on the control flow [5] or the program dependence graph [19]. Information flow analyses differ in the precision in which they can detect policy violations. While all approaches based on testing [1,18,30,35] *under-approximate* the real flow in the program, all static analysis techniques [5,6,21,36] *over-approximate* flows. Static analysis techniques moreover vary with respect to the sensitivities they incorporate into their analysis (e.g., flow-, context- or path-sensitivities). Naturally, the more precise the analysis, the more costly in terms of runtime and memory consumption. However, in particular when downloading a new application from the Internet, it is

This work was partially supported by the German Research Foundation (DFG) within the Collaborative Research Centre "On-The-Fly Computing" (SFB 901).

© Springer Nature Switzerland AG 2018
B. Fischer and T. Uustalu (Eds.): ICTAC 2018, LNCS 11187, pp. 435–454, 2018.
https://doi.org/10.1007/978-3-030-02508-3_23

crucial to be able to ensure information flow security within a short amount of time.

In this paper, we therefore propose a *proof-carrying code* (PCC) variant for information flow. The basic idea is to have a provider of an application attach an information flow *certificate* to the code. This certificate might have been constructed via a time-consuming, precise analysis. The software consumer on the other hand just needs to check the validity of the certificate. Certificate validation has to be designed in such a way that it ensures *tamper-free* operation: validation should detect any manipulation of code or certificate which invalidates security.

So far, PCC techniques for information flow security have been based on reusing computed typing information [29] or logic-based information [11,12,25]. In [29] the certificate generation process operates on linear security policies and is build in a CEGAR-like fashion involving multiple information flow analysis runs. For the generation they run their information flow analysis with an initial typing as certificate. Whenever there is a violation, the violating entity will be lifted to a higher security class and the analysis will be restarted with the modified typing until no violation is left. This typing is the certificate for the checking process. Their certificate checking is then mainly a sole run of the same information flow analysis and a check whether no violation of the policy occurs. Their focus lies clearly on keeping the certificate small.

Since information flow analysis are costly, we did not want to put the burden of a complete information flow analysis run onto the consumer. Therefore, we aim at just executing the information flow analysis during the certificate generation process. For verifying the validity of a certificate, we use a more lightweight checking procedure.

Logic-based PCC techniques for information flow security rely on checking generated theorem proving results. These techniques consider constructing COQ-proofs [11,25] or *Isabelle/HOL*-proofs [12] containing both the information flow property as well as the source-code in it. The consumers task is then the validation of those constructed proofs. The *Mobius* [8] project aims at providing a proof-carrying code architecture with safety and security scenarios in mind. The techniques they use are both type-based and logic-based where the result are together with program transformed to COQ-proofs as certificates, which has to be verified by the consumer.

Here, we aim at automatic certificate generation as well as validation and base our certificates on the results of a static flow analysis taking data and control dependencies into account. Certificates basically record the over-approximated explicit and implicit dependencies between variables at every program location. For such certificates, we develop a certificate checking mechanism and prove it to be sound and relatively complete. Soundness in this context means that invalid certificates not showing security of a program will be rejected, and relative[1] completeness states that all certificates produced by our information flow analysis will be accepted by the certificate checker.

---

[1] Relative to the employed analysis.

We have implemented our certificate generation and checking algorithm within the configurable analysis tool CPACHECKER [10]. For the evaluation, we have taken example programs from the annual competition on software verification SV-COMP (see e.g. [9]) benchmark suite of C programs. The experiments show that certificate generation in particular pays off when a costly information flow analysis has to be carried out for a program.

The outline of the paper is as follows. In Sect. 2 we start with defining the program model we build on. There, we also outline the information flow analysis which we employ and have introduced in previous work [34]. In Sect. 3 we introduce the terminology for security certificates together with the soundness and completeness proofs and the checking algorithm. In Sect. 4 we evaluate our approach and Sect. 6 discusses related and future work and concludes.

2   Background

In this section, we formalize the basics we use later. We model a program S as a control-flow automaton (*CFA*) $CFA_S = (L, G, cd)$, where L is a set of program *locations*, $G \subseteq L \times Ops \times L$ (for the set of operations Ops see below) is a set of *control flow edges* and the mapping $cd : L \to 2^L$ is an extension of the control-flow graph that represents *control dependencies* (not standardly included in control flow graphs). A control dependency states that the execution of a statement in a program depends on another statement, typically a condition in an IF or WHILE-statement: $\ell' \in cd(\ell)$ if the execution of the statement in location ℓ depends on the evaluation of the statement in ℓ'. We require a pre-computation of control dependencies, e.g. like proposed in [20,27]. As operations on the edges in the CFA we allow for the following:

$$Ops ::= skip \mid assume(b) \mid x := expr$$

Therein, *skip* is an empty operation, *assume(b)* is an assumption corresponding to a boolean condition b (of an IF or WHILE-statement) and $x := expr$ is an assignment (*expr* being an element of the set of expressions *Expr*). We let V denote the set of variables. Locations without predecessors in the control flow relation are *initial* locations $init(CFA_S) \subseteq L$. For simplicity, we assume that $|init(CFA_S)| = 1$. Furthermore, we write $fv(expr) \subseteq V$ for the set of variables occurring in the expression *expr*.

The semantics of a control-flow automaton (L, G, cd) is given by a transition system $T = (C, \to)$. In this, the set of concrete states $C = L \times DS$ consists of two parts. Each concrete state $c = (pc, ds) \in C$ represents a program *position* given by a value $pc \in L$. The *concrete data state* $ds: V \to (\mathbb{Z} \cup \mathbb{B})$ assigns to each variable $v \in V$ a concrete integer or boolean value. For an expression $expr \in Expr$, a concrete data value $ds(expr)$ over $ds: Expr \to (\mathbb{Z} \cup \mathbb{B})$ can be also naturally derived from the concrete values of the variables of $fv(expr)$ by considering the semantics of arithmetic and boolean expressions. Furthermore, $\to \subseteq C \times G \times C$ denotes a transition between states. We let $c \xrightarrow{g} c'$ abbreviate $(c, g, c') \in \to$ and write $c \to c'$ if there exists a $g \in G$ s.t. $(c, g, c') \in \to$.

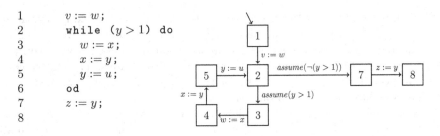

```
1        v := w ;
2        while (y > 1) do
3            w := x ;
4            x := y ;
5            y := u ;
6        od
7        z := y ;
8
```

Fig. 1. A small program snippet of a loop and its control flow automaton.

Following, we define the transitions for an edge (ℓ, op, ℓ') in a CFA: $((pc, ds), (\ell, op, \ell'), (pc', ds')) \in \, \to$ if $pc = \ell$ and $pc' = \ell'$ and the following holds:

$$\text{if } op \,\hat{=}\, skip, \text{ then } ds' = ds,$$

$$\text{if } op \,\hat{=}\, x := expr, \text{ then } ds'(y) = \begin{cases} ds(y) & \text{if } x \neq y \\ ds(expr) & \text{if } x = y \end{cases}$$

$$\text{if } op \,\hat{=}\, assume(b), \text{ then } ds(b) = true \text{ and } ds' = ds.$$

We call a sequence of transitions $c_0 \xrightarrow{g_1} c_1 \ldots \xrightarrow{g_n} c_n$ in a transition system $T = (C, \to)$ a *program path* of CFA_S if $c_0 = (\ell_0, \cdot)$ starts in the initial location, i.e., $\ell_0 \in init(CFA_S)$. We let $Paths_{CFA_S}$ denote the set of all program paths of S. The set of reachable concrete states from C' is defined as $Reach_S := \{c \in C \mid \exists c_0 \to \ldots \to c \in Paths_S\}$.

Program analyses typically operate on *abstractions* of concrete states. We denote the overall set of abstract states of an analysis by E. An abstract state $e \in E$ can represent several concrete states. The concretization function $[\![\cdot]\!] : E \to 2^C$ assigns to each abstract state its meaning – i.e. the set of concrete states it represents. In order to show specific properties, program analyses compute the set of reachable abstract states. To this end, they employ an abstract *transfer function* $\varphi : E \times G \to E$. In addition, we fix an initial abstract state $e_0 \in E$ abstracting the concrete states at the start location. We call (E, φ, e_0) an *abstract analysis*.

As a recurring example we use the following program snippet in Fig. 1. The associated CFA (L, G, cd) contains the set $L = \{1, 2, 3, 4, 5, 7, 8\}$ as locations and the control flow relation according to the graph. The control dependencies are $cd := \{1 \mapsto \emptyset, 2 \mapsto \{2\}, 3 \mapsto \{2\}, 4 \mapsto \{2\}, 5 \mapsto \{2\}, 7 \mapsto \emptyset, 8 \mapsto \emptyset\}$.

In the following, we give an abstract information flow analysis $(E_{\mathbb{IF}}, \varphi_{\mathbb{IF}}, e_0^{\mathbb{IF}})$ (sometimes omitting the subscript when clear from the context). Its purpose is the investigation of flows of information between program variables. We start with formalizing the notion of *non-interference*. The integration of control dependencies cd into the CFA_S specification has the purpose of enabling the computation of non-interferences and interferences between entities (i.e., program variables). More precisely, these are functions $NInf, Inf : (L \times V) \to 2^V$ mapping per location each variable to a set of variables that does not influence ($NInf$) respectively does influence (Inf) its value at that location.

$$NInf_\ell(v) := \{v' \in V \mid \forall p = \big(c_0 \to \ldots \overset{(\cdot,\cdot,\ell)}{\to} c_j\big), p' = \big(c_0' \to \ldots \overset{(\cdot,\cdot,\ell)}{\to} c_k'\big) \in Paths_S;$$
$$\forall v'' \in V \setminus \{v'\} : (pc_0 = pc_0' \wedge c_0(v'') = c_0'(v'')) \Rightarrow c_j(v) = c_k'(v)\},$$
$$Inf_\ell(v) := V \setminus NInf_\ell(v).$$

In our previous works [33,34] we integrated an information flow analysis into CPACHECKER. The analysis is configurable in its security configuration and can be used to over-approximate the non-interference property. On the basis of this, we also defined two extensions which for simplicity we will not consider in this paper: policy-dependent information flow analyses [34] and policy-driven CEGAR refinement [33].

We shortly recap our base analysis in this subsection. It is a data flow analysis computing analysis information of the form $E_{\mathbb{IF}} = L \to (Dp \times Cn)$ as abstract states. It describes a location and two sorts of information: a *dependency function* from $Dp = V \to 2^V$ which over-approximates the actual inferences per variable per location, and a *context function* $Cn = L \to 2^V$ which over-approximates the actual additional implicit inferences caused by branching at a location. For the initial abstract state $e_0^{\mathbb{IF}}$ each entity just depends on itself and has no implicit inferences. Hence, $e_0^{\mathbb{IF}} = (\{v \mapsto \{v\} \mid v \in V\}, \{\ell \mapsto \emptyset \mid \ell \in L\})$.

In the following, we define our analysis as a standard data flow analysis by giving the *transfer* (or flow) function, a join operation and an equation system. The transfer function $\varphi : E_{\mathbb{IF}} \times G \to E_{\mathbb{IF}}$ on this abstract domain states how program statements transform analysis information. More precisely, we have $\varphi((\ell, dp, cn), (\ell, op, \ell_1)) = (\ell', dp', cn')$ if $\ell' = \ell_1$ and the following holds:

if $op \,\hat{=}\, skip$, then $dp' = dp$ and $cn' = cn$,

if $op \,\hat{=}\, x := expr$, then $cn' = cn$ and

$$\forall v \in V : dp'(v) = \begin{cases} dp(fv(expr)) \cup \bigcup_{\ell'' \in cd(\ell)} cn(\ell'') & \text{if } v = x \\ dp(v) & \text{else,} \end{cases}$$

if $op \,\hat{=}\, assume(b)$; then $dp' = dp$ and

$$\forall \ell'' \in L : cn'(\ell'') = \begin{cases} cn(\ell'') \cup \bigcup_{v \in fv(b)} dp(v) & \text{if } \ell'' = \ell \\ cn(\ell'') & \text{else.} \end{cases}$$

If two information pairs (ℓ, dp, cn) and (ℓ', dp', cn') flow together at join points (i.e., where $\ell = \ell'$), we apply the following merge operator on the analysis information.

$$(\ell, dp, cn) \uplus (\ell, dp', cn') = (\ell, dp \cup dp', cn \cup cn') \text{ with}$$
$$\forall v \in V : (dp \cup dp')(v) = dp(v) \cup dp'(v)$$
$$\forall \ell \in L : (cn \cup cn')(\ell) = cn(\ell) \cup cn'(\ell)$$

The partial order for two information pairs (ℓ, dp, cn) and (ℓ', dp', cn') is given by

$$(\ell, dp, cn) \sqsubseteq (\ell', dp', cn') \text{ iff } (\ell = \ell') \wedge \forall v \in V : dp(v) \subseteq dp'(v)$$
$$\wedge \forall \ell'' \in L : cn(\ell'') \subseteq cn'(\ell'')$$

Table 1. Fixpoint computation result of $\mathbb{IF}$ for running example from Fig. 1. Simultaneously, it is the certificate.

$\mathbb{IF}_\ell = (dp, cn)$	dp						cn	
	u	v	w	x	y	z	2	$\{1,3,4,5,7,8\}$
$\mathbb{IF}_1$	$\{u\}$	$\{v\}$	$\{w\}$	$\{x\}$	$\{y\}$	$\{z\}$	$\emptyset$	$\emptyset$
$\mathbb{IF}_2$	$\{u\}$	$\{w\}$	$\{w,x,y,u\}$	$\{x,y,u\}$	$\{y,u\}$	$\{z\}$	$\{y,u\}$	$\emptyset$
$\mathbb{IF}_3$	$\{u\}$	$\{w\}$	$\{w,x,y,u\}$	$\{x,y,u\}$	$\{y,u\}$	$\{z\}$	$\{y,u\}$	$\emptyset$
$\mathbb{IF}_4$	$\{u\}$	$\{w\}$	$\{x,y,u\}$	$\{x,y,u\}$	$\{y,u\}$	$\{z\}$	$\{y,u\}$	$\emptyset$
$\mathbb{IF}_5$	$\{u\}$	$\{w\}$	$\{x,y,u\}$	$\{y,u\}$	$\{y,u\}$	$\{z\}$	$\{y,u\}$	$\emptyset$
$\mathbb{IF}_7$	$\{u\}$	$\{w\}$	$\{w,x,y,u\}$	$\{x,y,u\}$	$\{y,u\}$	$\{z\}$	$\{y,u\}$	$\emptyset$
$\mathbb{IF}_8$	$\{u\}$	$\{w\}$	$\{w,x,y,u\}$	$\{x,y,u\}$	$\{y,u\}$	$\{x,y,u\}$	$\{y,u\}$	$\emptyset$

The overall equation system $\mathbb{IF}_\ell$ per program location $\ell \in L$ solved by a standard fixpoint computation is then given by:

$$\mathbb{IF}_\ell = \begin{cases} e_0^{\mathbb{IF}} & \text{if } \ell \in init(CFA_S) \\ \biguplus\{\varphi(\mathbb{IF}_{\ell^*}, (\ell^*, op, \ell)) \mid (\ell^*, op, \ell) \in G\} & \text{otherwise.} \end{cases}$$

The solution to the equation system gives us one abstract state per program location. For the running example the computed fixpoint of the equation system is given in Table 1.

This information is now used to determine whether a program is *secure*. The specification of security violations, however, requires two additional inputs: a *security policy* P and a *security mapping* SC which together form a *security configuration* (P, SC). A *security mapping* $SC \colon V \to Sec$ connects program entities with *security classes* – denoted by the set Sec. A *security policy* $P \subseteq Sec \times 2^{Sec}$ provides the security classes with a semantics and thereby describes what flows in the program are allowed to exist between the security classes. Technically, a policy is a collection of pairs. The policy specifies the allowed flow of information for each individual security class. An element $(a, A) \in P$ is a *secure state*. It states that an element $a \in Sec$ is allowed to depend on information equal to the security classes $A \in 2^{Sec}$. On the contrary, an element (b, B) not being part of a policy – i.e. $(b, B) \in (Sec \times 2^{Sec}) \setminus P$ – is a *non-secure state*. To guarantee soundness in joining, removing some security classes from the right-hand side should not turn a secure state into a non-secure state. Hence, for all $a \in Sec, A \subseteq B \subseteq Sec : (a, B) \in P \Rightarrow (a, A) \in P$ must hold.

For the running example we consider a policy LHI consisting of three security classes $Sec_{LHI} = \{l, h, i\}$ which denotes *low*, *high* and *internal* entities. The policy allows for h and i to contain everything (i.e. for all $B \subseteq Sec_{LHI} : (h, B) \in LHI$ and $(i, B) \in LHI$). If l contains no high information it is a secure state (i.e. for all $B \subseteq Sec_{LHI} : (l, B \setminus \{h\}) \in LHI$), otherwise it is a non-secure state (i.e. for all $B \subseteq Sec_{LHI} : (l, B \cup \{h\}) \notin LHI$). Especially, h information should not be allowed to flow into l directly or transitively via i entities.

With this at hand, we can define violations of security configurations.

Definition 1. *Let* $T = (C, \rightarrow)$ *be a transition system. A concrete state* $c = (pc, \cdot) \in C$ *violates a security configuration* (P, SC) *iff there exists a* $v \in V$ *such that* $(SC(v), SC(Inf_{pc}(v))) \notin P$, *i.e. a non-secure state is occurring.*

In the absence of violations we say the concrete state is *secure*. A transition system is secure iff all of its reachable concrete states are. Analogously, a security configuration can be violated in an abstract state.

Definition 2. *Let* $(E_{\mathbb{IF}}, \cdot, \cdot)$ *be the abstract information flow analysis. An abstract state* $(\ell, dp, cn) \in E_{\mathbb{IF}}$ *violates a security configuration* (P, SC) *iff there exists a* $v \in V$ *such that* $(SC(v), SC(dp(v))) \notin P$.

Again, in the absence of violations we say that the abstract state is *secure*. A set of abstract states is secure iff all states in the set are. The solution to $\mathbb{IF}$ defines such a set of abstract states. We use this solution to derive information about the security of the program. Next, we simply restate the soundness result from [33]: Security of $\mathbb{IF}$ implies security of CFA_S.

Theorem 1. *Let* CFA_S *be a program model,* $\mathbb{IF}$ *the solution to the associated equation system and* (P, SC) *be the security configuration. If* $\mathbb{IF}$ *is secure w.r.t. to* (P, SC), *then* CFA_S *is secure w.r.t. to* (P, SC).

Considering the running example and the security configuration (LHI, SC^1) with $SC^1 = \{u \mapsto h; v \mapsto i; w \mapsto i; x \mapsto i; y \mapsto i; z \mapsto l\}$, the result in Table 1 is not secure since $\mathbb{IF}_8 : (SC(z), SC(dp(z))) = (l, \{i, h\}) \notin LHI$. When changing the security configuration to (LHI, SC^2) with $SC^2 = \{u \mapsto h; v \mapsto l; w \mapsto i; x \mapsto i; y \mapsto i; z \mapsto i\}$ the result is secure since no abstract state violates the policy. Hence the program is secure w.r.t. (LHI, SC^2).

3 Certification for Information Flow

Our objective now is the usage of this analysis information as a *certificate* in a proof-carrying code approach. The concept of proof-carrying code dates back to Necula [32]. The concept is generic and consists of two roles: A software producer and a software consumer. The producer aims at selling her software to the consumer and has to find a way of convincing the consumer of its quality, viz. the holding of a property. However, the consumer should not be bothered with costly correctness proofs. Therefore, the producer computes a proof (witness, certificate) certifying the holding of the property and ships this proof together with the software. The consumer's task is then simply certificate validation. A good PCC scheme guarantees that the majority of the workload is on the producer's side. Jakobs and Wehrheim developed a Configurable Program Certification approach (CPC) [23] for configurable program analysis frameworks and integrated it into the tool CPACHECKER. The basic idea is to reduce the consumer's cost of validation by omitting fixpoint computations. Our approach adapts CPC to information flow properties.

We start by defining our notion of a certificate.

Definition 3. *A certificate Z is a set of abstract states $Z \subseteq E_{\mathbb{IF}}$.*

The existence of a certificate alone is typically not enough for assuring that the program is secure: the certificate also has to be *valid*. For validity, a certificate on the one hand has to be secure w.r.t. to the given security configuration, and on the other hand has to faithfully represent the program in that each reachable concrete state is over-approximated by an abstract state.

Definition 4. *Let Z be a certificate and CFA_S the program model. We call a certificate Z valid for the program S and a security configuration (P, SC) iff*

1. *it contains one over-approximating abstract state for every reachable concrete state:* $\forall (\ell, ds) \in Reach_S \exists dp, cn$ *such that*
   - *$(\ell, dp, cn) \in Z$,*
   - *$\forall v \in V : Inf_{\ell}(v) \subseteq dp(v)$ and*
2. *the certificate is secure:*
   $\forall (\ell, dp, cn) \in Z; \forall v \in V : (SC(v), SC(dp(v))) \in P$.

In a PCC context, we need a way of *generating* valid certificates (for the producer) and of *checking* the validity of certificates (for the consumer). For certificate generation, the producer can just take the set of abstract states computed by the data flow analysis. A secure result will always be a valid certificate.

Lemma 1. *Let CFA_S be a program model, $\mathbb{IF}$ the information flow analysis result of S and (P, SC) a security configuration. If $\mathbb{IF}$ is secure w.r.t. (P, SC), then $\mathbb{IF}$ is a certificate which is valid w.r.t. S and (P, SC).*

Proof. The first property of validity holds. In [33] we have shown that $\mathbb{IF}$ computes abstract states that over-approximate the actual inferences in a forward analysis. The second property of validity is trivially fulfilled, since each $e \in \mathbb{IF}$ is secure w.r.t. the security configuration (P, SC). $\square$

Moreover, every valid certificate (not just the ones computed by the data flow analysis) certifies security of the program.

Lemma 2. *Let Z be a certificate, CFA_S the program model and (P, SC) a security configuration. If Z is valid w.r.t. S and (P, SC), then S is secure w.r.t. (P, SC).*

Proof. From property 1 of validity, it follows that for each $c_i = (\ell, ds) \in Reach_S$ there is an $e_i = (\ell, dp, cn) \in Z$ that over-approximates c_i. From property 2 it follows that for all $e_i = (\ell, dp, cn) \in Z$ and for all $v \in V$ $(SC(v), SC(dp(v)) \in P$ holds. Since $dp(v)$ over-approximates $Inf_{\ell}(v)$ and we are just considering policies for which $a \in Sec, A \subseteq B \subseteq Sec : (a, B) \in P \Rightarrow (a, A) \in P$ holds (subsets stays secure), this leads to $v \in V$ $(SC(v), SC(Inf_{\ell}(v)) \in P$. Hence, S is secure. $\square$

The consumer's task is now to check whether the received certificate is valid. Of course, such a validity check should be possible *without* considering concrete states of the program. To this end, we define a *coverage check* function which checks whether an abstract state is represented by the certificate.

Definition 5. *Let E be the set of all abstract states. A function cover : $E \times 2^E \to \mathbb{B}$ is a* coverage check *if for all $e \in E, R \subseteq E$*

$$cover(e, R) \Rightarrow e \sqsubseteq \biguplus_{e' \in R} e'$$

holds.

Here, we need to define a coverage check function $cover_{\mathbb{IF}} : E_{\mathbb{IF}} \times 2^{E_{\mathbb{IF}}} \to \mathbb{B}$ for our information flow analysis. We can do so by letting

$$cover_{\mathbb{IF}}(((\ell, dp, cn), R)) \hat{=} \exists(\ell', dp', cn') \in R : (\ell, dp, cn) \sqsubseteq (\ell', dp', cn').$$

Next, we show that $cover_{\mathbb{IF}}$ is a coverage-check according to Definition 5.

Lemma 3. *The function $cover_{\mathbb{IF}}$ is a coverage check function.*

Proof. By definition of $cover_{\mathbb{IF}}$. Let $(\ell, dp, cn) \in E_{\mathbb{IF}}, R \subseteq E_{\mathbb{IF}}$.

Let $cover_{\mathbb{IF}}((\ell, dp, cn), R) = \textbf{true}$
$\Rightarrow [\exists(\ell', dp', cn') \in R : (\ell, dp, cn) \sqsubseteq (\ell', dp', cn')]$

For $(\ell', dp', cn'), (\ell'', dp'', cn'')' \in R$ with $\ell' = \ell''$ it holds that $(\ell', dp', cn') \uplus (\ell'', dp'', cn'')'$ is computable[2]. Since, $\forall v \in V : dp'(v) \subseteq dp'(v) \cup dp''(v)$ and $\forall \ell \in L : cn'(\ell) \subseteq cn'(\ell) \cup cn''(\ell)$ it holds, that $(\ell', dp', cn') \sqsubseteq (\ell', dp', cn') \uplus (\ell'', dp'', cn'')$. Therefore, we conclude the following:

$\Rightarrow [\exists(\ell', dp', cn') \in R : (\ell, dp, cn) \sqsubseteq (\ell', dp', cn') \sqsubseteq \biguplus_{(\ell'', dp'', cn'') \in R}(\ell'', dp'', cn'')$.
$\square$

Our certificate checking approach furthermore demands the coverage check to be *well-behaving*, i.e., to be consistent with the partial order on abstract states and to be monotonic.

Definition 6. *Let cover : $E \times 2^E \to \mathbb{B}$ be a coverage check. Function cover is* well-behaving *if it is*

1. *consistent with $\sqsubseteq$:* $\forall e \in E, R \subseteq E : \exists e' \in R : e \sqsubseteq e' \Rightarrow cover(e, R)$, *and*
2. *monotonic:* $\forall e, e' \in E, R, R' \subseteq E :$
   $e \sqsubseteq e' \land R \sqsubseteq R' \land cover(e', R) \Rightarrow cover(e, R')$.

We next show that $cover_{\mathbb{IF}}$ is indeed well-behaving.

Lemma 4. *$cover_{\mathbb{IF}}$ is a well-behaving coverage-function.*

Proof

1. Consistent with partial order. $\forall(\ell, dp, cn) \in E_{\mathbb{IF}}, R \subseteq E_{\mathbb{IF}}, \exists(\ell', dp', cn') \in R:$

---

[2] The $\uplus$-operation is only defined if $\ell' = \ell''$. For the computation of the equation system $\mathbb{IF}$ the evaluation order of $\uplus$ is not specified. Hence, it is possible that the two listed abstract states weren't joined directly.

Algorithm 1. Validation algorithm for information flow certificates

---

Input: Program model $CFA_S = (L, G, cd)$ of S
Initial abstract state $e_0 \in E_{\mathbb{IF}}$, transfer function $\varphi_{\mathbb{IF}}$, cover function $cover_{\mathbb{IF}}$
certificate $Z \subseteq E_{\mathbb{IF}}$,
security configuration (P, SC).
Output: Boolean value indicating whether Z is valid.

1   **if** $(\neg cover_{\mathbb{IF}}(e_0, Z))$ **then**
2 | **return** *false*;

3   **for** each $(\ell, dp, cn) \in Z$ **do**
4 | **for** each $(\ell, op, \ell') \in G$ **do**
5 | | $(\ell', dp', cn') := \varphi_{\mathbb{IF}}((\ell, dp, cn), (\ell, op, \ell'))$;
6 | | **if** $(\neg cover_{\mathbb{IF}}((\ell', dp', cn'), Z))$ **then**
7 | | | **return** *false*;

8   **return** $[\forall(\ell, dp, cn) \in Z; \forall v \in V : (SC(v), SC(dp(v))) \in P]$;

Let $(\ell, dp, cn) \sqsubseteq (\ell', dp', cn') \wedge (\ell', dp', cn') \in R$
Since $(\ell', dp', cn') \in R$ it holds that
$\Rightarrow \exists(\ell'', dp'', cn'') \in R : (\ell, dp, cn) \sqsubseteq (\ell'', dp'', cn'')$
But this means according to the definition of $cover_{\mathbb{IF}}$ that
$\Rightarrow cover_{\mathbb{IF}}((\ell, dp, cn), R) = \textbf{true}$

2. Monotonic:
Let $(\ell, dp, cn) \sqsubseteq (\ell', dp', cn') \wedge R \sqsubseteq R' \wedge cover(e', R)$
$\Rightarrow \exists(\ell'', dp'', cn'') \in R : (\ell', dp', cn') \sqsubseteq (\ell'', dp'', cn'')$
Since $R \sqsubseteq R'$ it holds that
$\Rightarrow \exists(\ell'', dp'', cn'') \in R' : (\ell, dp, cn) \sqsubseteq (\ell', dp', cn') \sqsubseteq (\ell'', dp'', cn'')$
But this means according to the definition of $cover_{\mathbb{IF}}$ that
$\Rightarrow cover_{\mathbb{IF}}((\ell, dp, cn), R') = \textbf{true}$ $\square$

The coverage check operator is now used within our certificate validation algorithm (Algorithm 1). The algorithm is an adaption of the CCV-algorithm of Jakobs and Wehrheim [23], tailored to our setting. Basically, the algorithm checks validity of the certificate on the abstraction: First, it checks whether all initial concrete states are covered (lines 1 and 2). This is done by checking for covering of e_0 which itself covers all initial states and is – via the ordering $\sqsubseteq$ – the minimal such element. Second, the algorithm checks whether all abstract successors (using the transfer function) are covered by the certificate (lines 3 to 7). Finally, it examines security of the certificate (line 8).

It can be shown that Algorithm 1 accepts all secure solutions of the equations system $\mathbb{IF}$ as certificate. Hence the producer can safely use such a solution as certificate.

Lemma 5. *Let $\mathbb{IF} \subseteq E_{\mathbb{IF}}$ be a solution to the equation system for a program model CFA_S and (P, SC) a security configuration.*

If $\mathbb{IF}$ is secure w.r.t. (P, SC), then Algorithm 1 accepts $\mathbb{IF}$ as certificate (i.e., returns true).

Proof. We first show that Algorithm 1 will not terminate in line 2 – i.e. we show that when $\mathbb{IF}$ is secure w.r.t. (P, SC), then $cover_{\mathbb{IF}}(e_0, \mathbb{IF}) = \textbf{true}$ always in line 1.

1. In the process of computing $\mathbb{IF}$ the abstract state of the initial location $\mathbb{IF}_0$ is set and stays equal to the initial state $e_0^{\mathbb{IF}}$: $e_0^{\mathbb{IF}} = \mathbb{IF}_0$. Therefore, $e_0^{\mathbb{IF}} \sqsubseteq \mathbb{IF}_0$ holds. But this means $cover_{\mathbb{IF}}(e_0, Z) = \textbf{true}$.

We next show that Algorithm 1 will not terminate in line 7 – i.e. we show that when $\mathbb{IF}$ is secure w.r.t. (P, SC), then $cover_{\mathbb{IF}}((\ell', dp', cn'), \mathbb{IF}) = \textbf{true}$ always in line 6.

2. Let $(\ell, dp, cn) \in \mathbb{IF}$. This means $\mathbb{IF}_\ell = (\ell, dp, cn)$. For each $g = (\ell, op, \ell')$ there has to be an abstract state $\mathbb{IF}_{\ell'} = (\ell', dp', cn') \in \mathbb{IF}$. This is the case since the $\mathbb{IF}$ computes an over-approximating abstract state for all reachable locations.
   $\mathbb{IF}_{\ell'}$ is computed by a fixpoint computation $\biguplus \{\varphi(\mathbb{IF}_{\ell^*}, (\ell^*, op, \ell'))$ | $(\ell^*, op, \ell') \in G\}$. Especially, $\varphi(\mathbb{IF}_\ell, (\ell, op, \ell'))$ is contained in this join operation as operand.
   For $(\ell', dp', cn'), (\ell'', dp'', cn'')' \in E_{\mathbb{IF}}$ with $\ell' = \ell''$ it holds that $(\ell', dp', cn') \uplus (\ell'', dp'', cn'')'$ is computable (See footnote 2). Since, $\forall v \in V : dp'(v) \subseteq dp'(v) \cup dp''(v)$ and $\forall \ell \in L : cn'(\ell) \subseteq cn'(\ell) \cup cn''(\ell)$ it holds, that $(\ell', dp', cn') \sqsubseteq (\ell', dp', cn') \uplus (\ell'', dp'', cn'')$. But this means, we can conclude that $\varphi(\mathbb{IF}_\ell, (\ell, op, \ell')) \sqsubseteq \mathbb{IF}_{\ell'}$. Hence, $cover_{\mathbb{IF}}(\varphi(\mathbb{IF}_\ell, (\ell, op, \ell')), Z) = \textbf{true}$.

We next show that Algorithm 1 will terminate in line 8 with true – i.e. we show that if $\mathbb{IF}$ is secure, then $[\forall(\ell, dp, cn) \in \mathbb{IF}; \forall v \in V : (SC(v), SC(dp(v))) \in P] = \textbf{true}$ always in line 8.

3. This follows directly trivially from the definition that $\mathbb{IF}$ is secure.

All in all this means Algorithm 1 accepts secure solutions to the equations system $\mathbb{IF}$ as certificate $Z = \mathbb{IF}$.   □

Furthermore, whenever Algorithm 1 accepts a certificate, it is a valid certificate.

Lemma 6. *Let $Z \subseteq E_{\mathbb{IF}}$ be a certificate, CFA_S a program model and (P, SC) a security configuration.*
   If Algorithm 1 accepts Z, then Z is valid for S and (P, SC).

Proof. Suppose Algorithm 1 accepts Z. This means Algorithm 1 terminates in line 8 with **true** since the other return-possibilities in line 2 and 8 can only return **false**. But this means Z fulfills the second property (security) according to the valid certificate Definition 4.
   Let $p := \left(c_0 \to \ldots \overset{(\cdot, op_n, \ell_n)}{\to} c_n\right) \in Paths_{CFA_S}$ be arbitrary but fixed. $e_0 = (\ell_0, dp_0, cn_0) = (\ell_0, \{v \mapsto \{v\} \mid v \in V\}, \{\ell \mapsto \emptyset \mid \ell \in L\})$ is an over-approximation of c_0. Since the Algorithm 1 has not terminated in line 2 $cover_{\mathbb{IF}}(e_0, Z) = \textbf{true}$ holds in line 1. So there has to be an over-approximating abstract state $e = (\ell, dp, cn) \in Z$ s.t. $e_0 \sqsubseteq e$.

Table 2. Cover-checks in the validation algorithm for the running example from Fig. 1. If the cell is marked in gray, the set is a real subset ($\subset$), otherwise the sets are equal ($=$).

	dp						cn		
	u	v	w	x	y	z	2	$\{1,3,4,5,7,8\}$	
$e_1^{\mathbb{IF}}$	$\{u\}$	$\{v\}$	$\{w\}$	$\{x\}$	$\{y\}$	$\{z\}$	$\emptyset$	$\emptyset$	$\sqsubseteq \mathbb{IF}_1$
$\phi(\mathbb{IF}_1,(1,v:=w,2))$	$\{u\}$	$\{w\}$	$\{w\}$	$\{x\}$	$\{y\}$	$\{z\}$	$\emptyset$	$\emptyset$	$\sqsubseteq \mathbb{IF}_2$
$\phi(\mathbb{IF}_2,(2,(y>1),3))$	$\{u\}$	$\{w\}$	$\{w,x,y,u\}$	$\{x,y,u\}$	$\{y,u\}$	$\{z\}$	$\{y,u\}$	$\emptyset$	$\sqsubseteq \mathbb{IF}_3$
$\phi(\mathbb{IF}_3,(3,w:=x,4))$	$\{u\}$	$\{w\}$	$\{x,y,u\}$	$\{x,y,u\}$	$\{y,u\}$	$\{z\}$	$\{y,u\}$	$\emptyset$	$\sqsubseteq \mathbb{IF}_4$
$\phi(\mathbb{IF}_4,(4,x:=y,5))$	$\{u\}$	$\{w\}$	$\{x,y,u\}$	$\{y,u\}$	$\{y,u\}$	$\{z\}$	$\{y,u\}$	$\emptyset$	$\sqsubseteq \mathbb{IF}_5$
$\phi(\mathbb{IF}_5,(5,y:=u,2))$	$\{u\}$	$\{w\}$	$\{x,y,u\}$	$\{y,u\}$	$\{y,u\}$	$\{z\}$	$\{y,u\}$	$\emptyset$	$\sqsubseteq \mathbb{IF}_2$
$\phi(\mathbb{IF}_2,(2,\neg(y>1),7))$	$\{u\}$	$\{w\}$	$\{w,x,y,u\}$	$\{x,y,u\}$	$\{y,u\}$	$\{z\}$	$\{y,u\}$	$\emptyset$	$\sqsubseteq \mathbb{IF}_7$
$\phi(\mathbb{IF}_7,(7,z:=w,8))$	$\{u\}$	$\{w\}$	$\{w,x,y,u\}$	$\{x,y,u\}$	$\{y,u\}$	$\{x,y,u\}$	$\{y,u\}$	$\emptyset$	$\sqsubseteq \mathbb{IF}_8$

By now computing for each $\varphi((\ell, dp, cn),(\ell, op, \ell')) = (\ell', dp', cn')$ and $cover_{\mathbb{IF}}((\ell', dp', cn'), Z)) = \textbf{true}$ we have transitive (since $cover_{\mathbb{IF}}(e_0, Z) = \textbf{true}$) an over-approximating state per c_i that is covered by a more abstract state $(\ell'', dp'', cn'') \in Z$ in the certificate s.t. $(\ell', dp', cn') \sqsubseteq (\ell'', dp'', cn'')$. But this means Z fulfills the first property (over-approximation per reachable concrete state) according to the valid certificate Definition 4.

All in all this means Z is valid according to Definition 4.   □

We apply the validation algorithm to the certificate computed by the data-flow analysis of our running example from the previous section. Again we consider the first security configuration (LHI, SC^1). First, we check whether the initial abstract state is covered. Than per each abstract state of the certificate we check per outgoing edge whether the resulting abstract successor state is covered in the certificate. This is the case as stated in Table 2. For the validation we just compute a successor abstract state once per outgoing edge and check whether $cover_{\mathbb{IF}}$ holds. In contrary to the data flow analysis on the producer side – where we need at least 3 iterations for the fixpoint computation and that means 19 abstract states have to be computed and merged at least 12 times – we just compute 8 abstract states and check them for covering. For all 8 rows the cover relation holds. The second and sixth row $\mathbb{IF}_2$ are covered by abstract states in the certificate which are real over-approximations. The other six rows are computing the exactly same abstract states as the certificate they check for covering. However, this certificate is not secure, since $\mathbb{IF}_8$ is not secure and therefore it will be rejected in line 8 of Algorithm 1. If we would check for the other security configuration (LHI, SC^2), the validation would succeed as expected and return true in line 8.

However, Lemma 6 is only a one-sided implication; the other direction does not hold. Not all valid certificates are accepted. In [23], this phenomenon is called *relative completeness* of certificate validation. It occurs when a certificate over-approximates all concrete states, but is not closed under successor computation via the transfer function. Consider again the running example. If we replace the first row ($\mathbb{IF}_1$) of Table 1 by an abstract state $(Mod_1 = (\{v \mapsto V \mid v \in V\}, \{\ell \mapsto$

$\emptyset \mid \ell \in L\}))$, we get only a more over-approximating abstract state and we will still have a valid certificate. However, the certificate will be denied at line 7 of Algorithm 1 since the successor $Mod_2 = \phi(Mod_1, (1, v := w, 2)) = (\{v \mapsto V \mid v \in V\}, \{\ell \mapsto \emptyset \mid \ell \in L\})$ is not covered by $\mathbb{IF}_2$.

4   Experimental Results

We have integrated our approach into the configurable program analysis framework CPACHECKER [10] and carried out a number of experiments to see in particular whether the security certificate pays off. Our experiments were performed on a Intel(R) Core(TM)i7 4600U @ 2.10 GHz running Windows 7 with 8192 MB RAM. The installed Java version was JDK 1.8.0_77.

For the experiments we used the policy-independent analyses which we have explained in Sect. 2. We focused on the following two research questions:

RQ1 Is the checking of a certificate faster than running a complete analysis?
RQ2 How large can certificates become?

We run a number of experiments to answer these two research questions. As there is – to our knowledge – no established benchmark suite for non-interference properties, we took C programs from SV-COMP 2017[3] as examples. Such programs typically do not come with security configurations. For the experiments, we chose the *LHI* policy together with a mapping which assigns the security class i to all variables. As a consequence, all programs are secure and thus we could concentrate on the computation of interferences. Table 3 lists the results for those programs where the proof generation process exceeded 10 s, i.e. which are complex enough so that the use of certificates might potentially pay off.

Table 3 reads as follows: Each row represents a test-case with an identifier (program name) in the first column. The second column – denoted as *Loc* – gives an impression of the program size by listing the number of locations in the control flow automaton that is generated from the program code. The next four columns deliver statistics about the proof-generation process of the producer. The third column – denoted as *Analysis* – lists how much time in seconds the information flow analysis took. The fourth column *#Computed States* lists how many abstract states were computed in total during this analysis before the number was reduced by the join operation on abstract states to one per location. The fifth column *Writing* lists how much time in seconds the writing of the certificate took. The sixth column *Size* names the size of the generated certificate in bytes. The last two columns are reserved for the proof-checking on consumer side. The seventh column *Analysis* lists how much time in seconds the combined proof reading and proof checking of the certificate took. The eighth and last column *#Computed States* denotes how many abstract states were computed during the certificate checking and checked for covering.

---

[3] https://sv-comp.sosy-lab.org/2017/.

Table 3. Runtime and sizes of certificates for generation and checking.

Testcase	Loc	Proof-Generation				Proof-Checking	
		Analysis [s]	#Computed States	Writing [s]	Size [Bytes]	Analysis [s]	#Computed States
minepump_spec1_product21	603	13.379	22630	14.579	1372046	21.266	20385
minepump_spec1_product22	609	11.814	22671	16.393	1403330	19.058	20419
minepump_spec1_product41	601	13.839	22641	11.876	1332065	18.374	19623
minepump_spec1_product42	607	12.246	22682	15.068	1364208	19.501	19657
minepump_spec1_product43	611	21.099	28318	39.947	1701929	40.201	24589
minepump_spec2_product35	614	11.867	27660	15.710	1487781	21.726	23491
minepump_spec2_product36	620	14.383	27722	17.456	1505963	21.555	23536
minepump_spec3_product33	595	16.784	32642	22.521	1728841	24.586	26780
minepump_spec3_product34	601	15.681	32706	24.851	1750942	24.697	26820
minepump_spec4_product36	607	11.472	25090	10.508	1315027	17.009	21086
minepump_spec4_product41	601	16.481	29376	29.159	1666193	25.458	24564
minepump_spec5_product33	607	12.916	23430	11.177	1222606	16.839	19959
minepump_spec5_product34	613	11.695	23488	10.034	1244329	16.533	19995
minepump_spec5_product35	617	15.927	30703	24.748	1634312	24.134	26193
minepump_spec5_product36	623	15.854	30776	24.414	1657371	24.492	26241
psyco_abp_1_f-u-c_f-t_t-no-o	550	82.752	84799	56.373	4872606	45.558	21366
psyco_abp_1_t-u-c_f-t_t-no-o	547	69.922	84269	50.839	4764343	43.262	21362
s3_clnt_1_f-u-c_t-no-o.BV.c.cil	494	48.793	37535	8.001	1219858	5.719	4930
s3_clnt_1_f-u-c_t-t.cil	472	35.468	34526	7.688	1603181	7.833	4783
s3_clnt_1_t-u-c_t-no-o.BV.c.cil	495	42.318	39902	7.791	1445838	6.642	5168
s3_clnt_1_t-u-c_t-t.cil	472	32.837	34526	7.632	1598065	7.738	4783
s3_clnt_2_f-u-c_t-no-o.BV.c.cil	484	42.671	38296	8.061	1175382	6.370	5139
s3_clnt_2_f-u-c_t-t.cil	475	36.665	36340	8.730	1791864	8.862	5062
s3_clnt_2_t-u-c_t-no-o.BV.c.cil	485	39.352	40011	10.736	1270027	6.794	5390
s3_clnt_2_t-u-c_t-t.cil	475	37.031	36340	8.699	1929144	7.725	5062
s3_clnt_3.cil_t-u-c_t-t	456	21.809	35295	5.465	1112419	5.195	4790
s3_clnt_3_f-u-c_t-no-o.BV.c.cil	491	55.862	40946	13.328	1342443	6.621	5394
s3_clnt_3_f-u-c_t-t.cil	500	45.279	36234	11.538	2516347	9.016	4990
s3_clnt_3_t-u-c_t-no-o.BV.c.cil	492	40.344	40947	13.490	1301600	9.894	5395
s3_clnt_3_t-u-c_t-t.cil	493	45.051	36052	11.049	2378323	8.969	4983
s3_clnt_4_f-u-c_t-t.cil	478	36.807	36363	8.732	1841811	7.722	5072
s3_clnt_4_t-u-c_t-t.cil	475	36.728	36360	8.601	1749859	7.514	5069
s3_srvr_10_f-u-c_f-t.cil	534	86.684	62475	18.144	3291356	26.338	9045
s3_srvr_11_f-u-c_f-t.cil	542	106.699	72432	20.768	3682932	29.797	10221
s3_srvr_13_f-u-c_f-t.cil	550	80.682	59833	18.074	3155530	22.003	9014
s3_srvr_14_f-u-c_f-t.cil	548	88.365	63599	19.351	3429914	29.086	9573
s3_srvr_1_alt_t-u-c_t-no-o.BV.c.cil	544	79.062	50586	22.440	1850922	10.186	6582
s3_srvr_1_f-u-c_f-t.cil	520	62.655	51428	13.352	2545039	17.732	7270
s3_srvr_1_t-u-c_f-t.cil	524	59.544	49862	13.395	2507864	18.017	7914
s3_srvr_1_t-u-c_t-no-o.BV.c.cil	535	70.076	47575	11.692	1667117	9.076	6496
s3_srvr_2_alt_t-u-c_t-no-o-f-t.BV.c.cil	538	62.226	48204	15.125	1620684	10.617	6516
s3_srvr_2_f-u-c_f-t.cil	520	64.390	49179	12.305	2307516	16.448	7045
s3_srvr_2_t-u-c_f-t.cil	519	60.539	49178	12.428	2268504	16.541	7044
s3_srvr_2_t-u-c_t-no-o-f-t.BV.c.cil	538	84.643	48218	15.387	1621022	10.284	6516
s3_srvr_3_alt_t-u-c_t-no-o.BV.c.cil	536	72.667	47042	12.468	1556778	8.809	6404
s3_srvr_3_t-u-c_f-t.cil	518	61.948	50048	12.984	2390487	16.865	7220
s3_srvr_3_t-u-c_t-no-o.BV.c.cil	535	68.911	46835	12.425	1534821	8.840	6403
s3_srvr_4_t-u-c_f-t.cil	519	60.241	49587	12.680	2333254	16.653	7109
s3_srvr_6_f-u-c_f-t.cil	575	83.424	59646	19.155	3380035	28.363	9387
s3_srvr_6_t-u-c_f-t.cil	572	79.878	58710	18.207	3259491	29.190	9191
s3_srvr_7_t-u-c_f-t.cil	533	64.221	52172	14.101	2406142	20.308	7688
s3_srvr_8_t-u-c_f-t.cil	539	69.548	53888	15.072	2655016	19.877	8014

Let us first consider **RQ1**. We expected the certificate checking to be more efficient than applying a complete analysis despite the drawback that additionally to the checking time, the time for parsing a certificate – i.e. the proof reading – is added as an overhead. To better see the result, we marked those cells in Table 3 in gray which have a smaller runtime, either the complete information flow analysis or the certificate checking. We observe that checking is more efficient only when the overall number of computed abstract states in the checking process is significantly smaller than in the generation process. This is the case when the analysis performs many iterations during fixpoint computation due to loops in the program. Since fixpoints are already computed by the certificate generation, a lesser number of iterations is needed for certificate checking. Also, joining of any of those abstract states is not involved within the certificate checking process, thus checking is potentially faster for programs with complex branching structure. In some cases, the two values for *#Computed States* differ drastically, e.g. for s3_srvr_11_f-u-c_f-t.cil 72432 states are computed compared to 10221 states during checking which gives a reduction factor of 7. The running time was also more efficient in the checking process with 106699 ms compared to 29797 ms. For another entry – s3_srvr_6_f-u-c_f-t.cil – we computed 59646 abstract states compared to 9387 abstract states which is roughly a reduction factor of 6 and had more efficient runtimes with 83424 ms compared to 28363 ms. Indeed we always observe that if we compute in the generation process clearly more abstract states, checking is more efficient.

We conclude that the efficiency of certificate checking strongly depends on the program structure. For programs with loops and a lot of branching certificate checking is indeed considerably faster than a complete analysis. In case of loop-free programs certificate checking is less efficient due to the dominating overhead of parsing the certificate. Since realistic programs typically have complex structures including loops, we conjecture that certificate checking will pay off for larger real-world programs. However, more experiments are needed to confirm this conjecture.

Let us now consider **RQ2**. We expect that the size of the certificates depends mainly on two aspects. On the one hand on the total number of abstract states in general, i.e. the reach-set which is computed. For our data-flow analysis this is equal to the number of locations[4]. On the other hand on the total number of computed dependencies per abstract state. In our experiments the certificate size goes up to 4764343 bytes ($\approx$4, 5 MB). This corresponds to approximately 8.5 KB per location which is large. The certificates are larger than the actual original files, but in our opinion they are not so large that they become unusable. If the consumer has large memory storage like todays modern PCs usually have, the advantages of faster property validation of a program outweighs the extra certificate transfer payload. However, if we have limited end systems – like e.g. mobile devices – storage is a more critical issue. For future experiments we thus want to investigate the size of certificates of policy-dependent analyses and

---

[4] Still, the number of computed states might be much larger.

expect these to be drastically smaller than the policy-independent ones with which we experimented here.

5   Related Work

In the area of proof-carrying code [32], the concept of using abstract reachability graphs as certificates is not novel but is mainly used for safety trace-properties. In several works of *Albert et al.* [4], they call this approach *abstraction-carrying code* (ACC) and use a fixpoint computation of the abstract reachability graph as well. In following works they present several optimizations like reduced certificates [3] in the sense of a smallest subset of abstract states needed to restore the complete abstract reachability graph in a single analysis run or incremental difference [2] where the difference in the succeeding abstract states is computed.

Jakobs and Wehrheim [23] integrated configurable certification in CPACHECKER as an ACC-approach, where they integrated several optimizations as well like reduced certificates [22] and compact proof witnesses [24]. Our approach builds upon this approach, but focuses on the hyperproperty non-interference.

Other proof-carrying code technique resolve around checking generated theorem proving results. *Chaieb* [12] computes invariants for programs. The correctness of the invariants are transformed to *Isabelle/HOL*-proofs and delivered as checkable certificates to the consumer. *Loidl et al.* [28] also present a PCC-technique focused on heap consumption. They developed a certificate checking technique that is extended with a heap consumption logic. These are transformed to *Isabelle/HOL*-proofs as results that can be checked on consumer side as certificate. *Bidmeshki et al.* [11] consider a PCHIP framework where HDL code is analysed and checked for security-related properties like hardware-trojans. The theorem proofs they construct are *COQ*-proofs. *Jin et al.* [25] also consider HDL code and construct *COQ*-proofs as well. They consider information flow scenarios in circuits.

6   Conclusion

In this paper we presented a proof-carrying code technique for information flow analysis, based on an existing data-flow analysis and on the CPC-approach of Jakobs and Wehrheim. We proved soundness and relative completeness of our approach. Our experiments showed that the certificate checking time often gets smaller than the analysis time. However, it also showed that certificates only pay off when the analysis itself is complex, i.e., typically when the fixpoint computation involves a large number of iterations. The reason for this is that certificate checking involves certificate parsing, and certificate sizes are so far relatively large.

Future Work. In future works we will consequently try to reduce the certificate size. This can for instance be done by using the policy-dependent analysis instead of a policy-independent analysis, like we mentioned in the experimental section. Also by using policy-dependent analysis results as certificate we could modify the checking mechanism to be more efficient. For example one optimization could be integrating checking the policy refinement relations we described in [34] beforehand.

In this paper we tackled the problem of providing proof-carrying code mechanism for non-interference. Non-interference is a so called hyperproperty [7], which is a type of property that needs the consideration of several program paths for property verification. The theory of hyperproperties was recently introduced. Hyperproperties stand in contrast to trace properties which can argue about a property by consideration of single traces. So far validation techniques for hyperproperties –like ours as well – rely on over-approximating the hyperproperty to a trace property – e.g. a data-flow analysis or a model-checking approach. Monitoring and testing-techniques [1] based on HyperLTL are in development. HyperLTL extends LTL to quantify over paths. So far known techniques extend modelchecking techniques for LTL in such a way that they can be used for HyperLTL to work. Also tool implementation already exists like EAHyper [15] which checks the satisfiability of a decidable subclass of hyperproperties or MCHyper [16], a modelchecking approach for checking a decidable subclass of hyperproperties. In general we plan to investigate analysis techniques for several hyperproperties in more detail and plan to develop proof-carrying code techniques for such analyses.

References

1. Agrawal, S., Bonakdarpour, B.: Runtime verification of k-safety hyperproperties in HyperLTL. In: Proceedings of 29th IEEE Computer Security Foundations Symposium, CSF 2016, Lisbon, June/July 2016, pp. 239–252. IEEE CS Press, Washington, DC (2016). https://doi.org/10.1109/csf.2016.24
2. Albert, E., Arenas, P., Puebla, G.: An incremental approach to abstraction-carrying code. In: Hermann, M., Voronkov, A. (eds.) LPAR 2006. LNCS (LNAI), vol. 4246, pp. 377–391. Springer, Heidelberg (2006). https://doi.org/10.1007/11916277_26
3. Albert, E., Arenas-Sánchez, P., Puebla, G., Hermenegildo, M.V.: Reduced certificates for abstraction-carrying code. In: Etalle, S., Truszczynski, M. (eds.) ICLP 2006. LNCS, vol. 4079, pp. 163–178. Springer, Heidelberg (2006). https://doi.org/10.1007/11799573_14
4. Albert, E., Puebla, G., Hermenegildo, M.: Abstraction-carrying code. In: Baader, F., Voronkov, A. (eds.) LPAR 2005. LNCS (LNAI), vol. 3452, pp. 380–397. Springer, Heidelberg (2005). https://doi.org/10.1007/978-3-540-32275-7_25
5. Amtoft, T., Banerjee, A.: Information flow analysis in logical form. In: Giacobazzi, R. (ed.) SAS 2004. LNCS, vol. 3148, pp. 100–115. Springer, Heidelberg (2004). https://doi.org/10.1007/978-3-540-27864-1_10
6. Arzt, S., et al.: FlowDroid: precise context, flow, field, object-sensitive and lifecycle-aware taint analysis for Android apps. In: Proc. of 2014 ACM SIGPLAN Conference on Programming Language Design and Implementation, PLDI 2014, Edinburgh, June 2014, pp. 259–269. ACM Press, New York (2014). https://doi.org/10.1145/2594291.2594299

7. Assaf, M., Naumann, D.A., Signoles, J., Totel, E., Tronel, F.: Hypercollecting semantics and its application to static analysis of information flow. In: Proceedings of 44th ACM SIGPLAN Symposium on Principles of Programming Languages, POPL 2017, Paris, January 2017, pp. 874–887. ACM Press, New York (2017). https://doi.org/10.1145/3009837.3009889

8. Barthe, G., Crégut, P., Grégoire, B., Jensen, T., Pichardie, D.: The MOBIUS proof carrying code infrastructure. In: de Boer, F.S., Bonsangue, M.M., Graf, S., de Roever, W.-P. (eds.) FMCO 2007. LNCS, vol. 5382, pp. 1–24. Springer, Heidelberg (2008). https://doi.org/10.1007/978-3-540-92188-2_1

9. Beyer, D.: Software verification with validation of results. In: Legay, A., Margaria, T. (eds.) TACAS 2017. LNCS, vol. 10206, pp. 331–349. Springer, Heidelberg (2017). https://doi.org/10.1007/978-3-662-54580-5_20

10. Beyer, D., Henzinger, T.A., Théoduloz, G.: Configurable software verification: concretizing the convergence of model checking and program analysis. In: Damm, W., Hermanns, H. (eds.) CAV 2007. LNCS, vol. 4590, pp. 504–518. Springer, Heidelberg (2007). https://doi.org/10.1007/978-3-540-73368-3_51

11. Bidmeshki, M., Makris, Y.: Toward automatic proof generation for information flow policies in third-party hardware IP. In: Proceedings of 2015 IEEE International Symposium on Hardware-Oriented Security and Trust, HOST 2015, Washington, DC, May 2015, pp. 163–168. IEEE CS Press, Washington, DC (2015). https://doi.org/10.1109/hst.2015.7140256

12. Chaieb, A.: Proof-producing program analysis. In: Barkaoui, K., Cavalcanti, A., Cerone, A. (eds.) ICTAC 2006. LNCS, vol. 4281, pp. 287–301. Springer, Heidelberg (2006). https://doi.org/10.1007/11921240_20

13. Darvas, Á., Hähnle, R., Sands, D.: A theorem proving approach to analysis of secure information flow. In: Hutter, D., Ullmann, M. (eds.) SPC 2005. LNCS, vol. 3450, pp. 193–209. Springer, Heidelberg (2005). https://doi.org/10.1007/978-3-540-32004-3_20

14. Enck, W., et al.: TaintDroid: an information-flow tracking system for realtime privacy monitoring on smartphones. ACM Trans. Comput. Syst. 32(2), 5 (2014). https://doi.org/10.1145/2619091

15. Finkbeiner, B., Hahn, C., Stenger, M.: EAHyper: satisfiability, implication, and equivalence checking of hyperproperties. In: Majumdar, R., Kunčak, V. (eds.) CAV 2017. LNCS, vol. 10427, pp. 564–570. Springer, Cham (2017). https://doi.org/10.1007/978-3-319-63390-9_29

16. Finkbeiner, B., Rabe, M.N., Sánchez, C.: Algorithms for model checking Hyper-LTL and HyperCTL*. In: Kroening, D., Păsăreanu, C.S. (eds.) CAV 2015. LNCS, vol. 9206, pp. 30–48. Springer, Cham (2015). https://doi.org/10.1007/978-3-319-21690-4_3

17. Foley, S.N.: Aggregation and separation as noninterference properties. J. Comput. Sec. 1(2), 159–188 (1992). https://doi.org/10.3233/jcs-1992-1203

18. Le Guernic, G., Banerjee, A., Jensen, T., Schmidt, D.A.: Automata-based confidentiality monitoring. In: Okada, M., Satoh, I. (eds.) ASIAN 2006. LNCS, vol. 4435, pp. 75–89. Springer, Heidelberg (2007). https://doi.org/10.1007/978-3-540-77505-8_7

19. Hammer, C., Snelting, G.: Flow-sensitive, context-sensitive, and object-sensitive information flow control based on program dependence graphs. Int. J. Inf. Sec. 8(6), 399–422 (2009). https://doi.org/10.1007/s10207-009-0086-1

20. Horwitz, S., Reps, T.W.: The use of program dependence graphs in software engineering. In: Proceedings of 14th International Conference on Software Engineering, ICSE 1992, Melbourne, May 1992, pp. 392–411. ACM Press, New York (1992). https://doi.org/10.1145/143062.143156

21. Hunt, S., Sands, D.: On flow-sensitive security types. In: Proceedings of 33rd ACM SIGPLAN-SIGACT Symposium on Principles of Programming Languages, POPL 2006, Charleston, SC, January 2006, pp. 79–90. ACM Press, New York (2006). https://doi.org/10.1145/1111037.1111045

22. Jakobs, M.-C.: Speed up configurable certificate validation by certificate reduction and partitioning. In: Calinescu, R., Rumpe, B. (eds.) SEFM 2015. LNCS, vol. 9276, pp. 159–174. Springer, Cham (2015). https://doi.org/10.1007/978-3-319-22969-0_12

23. Jakobs, M., Wehrheim, H.: Certification for configurable program analysis. In: Proceedings of 2014 International Symposium on Model Cheking for Software, SPIN 2014, San Jose, CA, July 2014, pp. 30–39. ACM Press, New York (2014). https://doi.org/10.1145/2632362.2632372

24. Jakobs, M.-C., Wehrheim, H.: Compact proof witnesses. In: Barrett, C., Davies, M., Kahsai, T. (eds.) NFM 2017. LNCS, vol. 10227, pp. 389–403. Springer, Cham (2017). https://doi.org/10.1007/978-3-319-57288-8_28

25. Jin, Y., Yang, B., Makris, Y.: Cycle-accurate information assurance by proof-carrying based signal sensitivity tracing. In: Proceedings of 2013 International Symposium on Hardware-Oriented Security and Trust, HOST 2013, Austin, TX, June 2013, pp. 99–106. IEEE CS Press, Washington, DC (2013). https://doi.org/10.1109/hst.2013.6581573

26. Joshi, R., Leino, K.R.M.: A semantic approach to secure information flow. Sci. Comput. Program. 37(1–3), 113–138 (2000). https://doi.org/10.1016/s0167-6423(99)00024-6

27. Lengauer, T., Tarjan, R.E.: A fast algorithm for finding dominators in a flowgraph. ACM Trans. Program. Lang. Syst. 1(1), 121–141 (1979). https://doi.org/10.1145/357062.357071

28. Loidl, H., MacKenzie, K., Jost, S., Beringer, L.: A proof-carrying-code infrastructure for resources. In: Proceedings of 4th Latin-American Symposium on Dependable Computing, LADC 2009, João Pessoa, September 2009, pp. 127–134. IEEE CS Press, Washington, DC (2009). https://doi.org/10.1109/ladc.2009.13

29. Lortz, S., Mantel, H., Starostin, A., Bähr, T., Schneider, D., Weber, A.: Cassandra: towards a certifying app store for Android. In: Proceedings of 4th ACM Workshop on Security and Privacy in Smartphones and Mobile Devices, SPSM 2014, Scottsdale, AZ, November 2014, pp. 93–104. ACM Press, New York (2014). https://doi.org/10.1145/2666620.2666631

30. Magazinius, J., Russo, A., Sabelfeld, A.: On-the-fly inlining of dynamic security monitors. Comput. Sec. 31(7), 827–843 (2012). https://doi.org/10.1016/j.cose.2011.10.002

31. Mantel, H.: On the composition of secure systems. In: Proceedings of 2002 IEEE Symposium on Security and Privacy, S&P 2002, Berkeley, CA, May 2002, pp. 88–101. IEEE CS Press, Washington, DC (2002). https://doi.org/10.1109/secpri.2002.1004364

32. Necula, G.C.: Proof-carrying code. In: Conference on Record of 24th ACM SIGPLAN-SIGACT Symposium on Principles of Programming Languages, POPL 1997, Paris, January 1997, pp. 106–119. ACM Press, New York (1997). https://doi.org/10.1145/263699.263712

33. Töws, M., Wehrheim, H.: A CEGAR scheme for information flow analysis. In: Ogata, K., Lawford, M., Liu, S. (eds.) ICFEM 2016. LNCS, vol. 10009, pp. 466–483. Springer, Cham (2016). https://doi.org/10.1007/978-3-319-47846-3_29

34. Töws, M., Wehrheim, H.: Policy dependent and independent information flow analyses. In: Duan, Z., Ong, L. (eds.) ICFEM 2017. LNCS, vol. 10610, pp. 362–378. Springer, Cham (2017). https://doi.org/10.1007/978-3-319-68690-5_22

35. Vachharajani, N., et al.: RIFLE: an architectural framework for user-centric information-flow security. In: Proceedings of 37th Annual International Symposium on Microarchitecture, MICRO-37, Portland, OR, December 2004, pp. 243–254. IEEE CS Press, Washington, DC (2004). https://doi.org/10.1109/micro.2004.31

36. Volpano, D.M., Irvine, C.E., Smith, G.: A sound type system for secure flow analysis. J. Comput. Sec. 4(2–3), 167–188 (1996). https://doi.org/10.3233/jcs-1996-42-304

The Smallest FSSP Partial Solutions for One-Dimensional Ring Cellular Automata: Symmetric and Asymmetric Synchronizers

Hiroshi Umeo$^{(\boxtimes)}$, Naoki Kamikawa, and Gen Fujita

Osaka Electro-Communication University,
18-8 Hatsu-cho, Neyagawa-shi, Osaka 572-8530, Japan
umeo@cyt.osakac.ac.jp

Abstract. A synchronization problem in cellular automata has been known as the Firing Squad Synchronization Problem (FSSP) since its development, where the FSSP gives a finite-state protocol for synchronizing a large scale of cellular automata. A quest for smaller state FSSP solutions has been an interesting problem for a long time. Umeo, Kamikawa and Yunès (2009) answered partially by introducing a concept of partial FSSP solutions and proposed a full list of the smallest four-state *symmetric* powers-of-2 FSSP protocols that can synchronize any one-dimensional (1D) ring cellular automata of length $n = 2^k$ for any positive integer $k \geq 1$. Afterwards, Ng (2011) also added a list of *asymmetric* FSSP partial solutions, thus completing the four-state powers-of-2 FSSP partial solutions. The number four is the lower bound in the class of FSSP protocols. A question: are there any four-state partial solutions other than powers-of-2? has remained open. In this paper, we answer the question by proposing a new class of the smallest symmetric and asymmetric four-state FSSP protocols that can synchronize any 1D ring of length $n = 2^k - 1$ for any positive integer $k \geq 2$. We show that the class includes a rich variety of FSSP protocols that consists of 39 *symmetric* and 132 *asymmetric* solutions, ranging from minimum-time to linear-time in synchronization steps. In addition, we make an investigation into several interesting properties of these partial solutions, such as swapping general states, reversal protocols, and a duality property between them.

1 Introduction

We study a synchronization problem that gives a finite-state protocol for synchronizing a large scale of cellular automata. A synchronization problem in cellular automata has been known as the Firing Squad Synchronization Problem (FSSP) since its development, in which it was originally proposed by J. Myhill in Moore [6] to synchronize some/all parts of self-reproducing cellular automata. The FSSP has been studied extensively for more than fifty years in [1–12].

A minimum-time (i.e., $(2n - 2)$-step) FSSP algorithm was developed first by Goto [4] for synchronizing any one-dimensional (1D) array of length $n \geq 2$.

© Springer Nature Switzerland AG 2018
B. Fischer and T. Uustalu (Eds.): ICTAC 2018, LNCS 11187, pp. 455–471, 2018.
https://doi.org/10.1007/978-3-030-02508-3_24

The algorithm required many thousands of internal states for its finite-state realization. Afterwards, Waksman [11], Balzer [1], Gerken [3] and Mazoyer [5] also developed a minimum-time FSSP algorithm and reduced the number of states required, each with 16, 8, 7 and 6 states, respectively. On the other hand, Balzer [1], Sanders [8] and Berthiaume et al. [2] have shown that there exists no four-state synchronization algorithm. Thus, an existence or non-existence of five-state FSSP protocol has been an open problem for a long time. Umeo, Kamikawa and Yunès [9] answered partially by introducing a concept of *partial versus full* FSSP solutions and proposing a full list of the smallest four-state symmetric powers-of-2 FSSP partial protocols that can synchronize any 1D ring cellular automata of length $n = 2^k$ for any positive integer $k \geq 1$. Afterwards, Ng [7] also added a list of asymmetric FSSP partial solutions, thus completing the four-state powers-of-2 FSSP partial solutions. A question: are there any four-state partial solutions other than powers-of-2? has remained open.

In this paper, we answer the question by proposing a new class of the smallest four-state FSSP protocols that can synchronize any 1D ring of length $n = 2^k - 1$ for any positive integer $k \geq 2$. We show that the class includes a rich variety of FSSP protocols that consists of 39 symmetric and 132 asymmetric solutions, ranging from minimum-time to linear-time in synchronization steps. In addition, we make an investigation into several interesting properties of these partial solutions, such as swapping general states, a duality between them, inclusion of powers-of-2 solutions, reflected solutions and so on. In Sect. 2, we give a description of the 1D FSSP on rings and review some basic results on ring FSSP algorithms. Section 3 presents a new class the symmetric and asymmetric partial solutions for rings. Due to the space of available, we focus our attention to the symmetric solutions and only give an overview for the asymmetric ones. Section 4 gives a summary and discussions of the paper.

2   Firing Squad Synchronization Problem on Rings

2.1   Definition of the FSSP on Rings

The FSSP on rings is formalized in terms of the model of cellular automata. Figure 1 shows a 1D ring cellular automaton consisting of n cells, denoted by C_i, where $1 \leq i \leq n$. All cells are identical finite state automata. The ring cellular automaton operates in lock-step mode such that the next state of each cell is determined by both its own present state and the present states of its right and left neighbors. All cells (*soldiers*), except one cell, are initially in the *quiescent* state at time $t = 0$ and have the property whereby the next state of a quiescent cell having quiescent neighbors is the quiescent state. At time $t = 0$ the cell C_1 (*general*) is in the *fire-when-ready* state, which is an initiation signal to the ring.

The FSSP is stated as follows: given a ring of n identical cellular automata, including a *general* cell which is activated at time $t = 0$, we want to give the description (state set and next-state function) of the automata so that, *at some future time*, all of the cells will *simultaneously* and, *for the first time*, enter a special *firing* state. The set of states and the next-state function must be

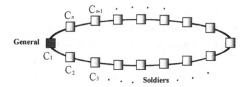

Fig. 1. One-dimensional (1D) ring cellular automaton

independent of n. Without loss of generality, we assume $n \geq 2$. The tricky part of the problem is that the same kind of soldier having a fixed number of states must be synchronized, regardless of the length n of the ring.

A formal definition of the FSSP on rings is as follows: a cellular automaton $\mathcal{M}$ is a pair $\mathcal{M} = (Q, \delta)$, where

1. Q is a finite set of states with three distinguished states G, Q, and F. G is an initial general state, Q is a quiescent state, and F is a firing state, respectively.
2. δ is a next-state function such that $\delta : Q^3 \to Q$.
3. The quiescent state Q must satisfy the following conditions: $\delta(Q, Q, Q) = Q$.

A ring cellular automaton $\mathcal{M}_n$ of length n, consisting of n copies of $\mathcal{M}$, is a 1D ring whose positions are numbered from 1 to n. Each $\mathcal{M}$ is referred to as a cell and denoted by C_i, where $1 \leq i \leq n$. We denote a state of C_i at time (step) t by S_i^t, where $t \geq 0, 1 \leq i \leq n$. A *configuration* of $\mathcal{M}_n$ at time t is a function $\mathcal{C}^t : [1, n] \to Q$ and denoted as $S_1^t S_2^t \dots S_n^t$. A *computation* of $\mathcal{M}_n$ is a sequence of configurations of $\mathcal{M}_n, \mathcal{C}^0, \mathcal{C}^1, \mathcal{C}^2, \dots, \mathcal{C}^t, \dots$, where $\mathcal{C}^0$ is a given initial configuration. The configuration at time $t+1$, $\mathcal{C}^{t+1}$, is computed by synchronous applications of the next-state function δ to each cell of $\mathcal{M}_n$ in $\mathcal{C}^t$ such that:

$$S_1^{t+1} = \delta(S_{n-1}^t, S_1^t, S_2^t), \ S_i^{t+1} = \delta(S_{i-1}^t, S_i^t, S_{i+1}^t), \text{ for any } i, 2 \leq i \leq n-1, \text{ and}$$
$$S_n^{t+1} = \delta(S_{n-1}^t, S_n^t, S_1^t).$$

A *synchronized configuration* of $\mathcal{M}_n$ at time t is a configuration $\mathcal{C}^t$, $S_i^t = F$, for any $1 \leq i \leq n$.

The FSSP is to obtain an $\mathcal{M}$ such that, for any $n \geq 2$,

1. A synchronized configuration at time $t = T(n)$, $\mathcal{C}^{T(n)} = \overbrace{F, \cdots, F}^{n}$ can be computed from an initial configuration $\mathcal{C}^0 = G \overbrace{Q, \cdots, Q}^{n-1}$.
2. For any t, i such that $1 \leq t \leq T(n) - 1, 1 \leq i \leq n, S_i^t \neq F$.

2.2 Full vs. Partial Solutions

One has to note that any solution in the original FSSP problem is to synchronize any array of length $n \geq 2$. We call it **full** solution. Berthiaume et al. [2] presented an eight-state full solution for the ring. On the other hand, Umeo, Kamikawa, and Yunès [9] and Ng [7] constructed a rich variety of 4-state protocols that can synchronize some infinite set of rings, but not all. We call such protocol **partial** solution. Here, we summarize recent developments on those small-state solutions in the ring FSSP. Berthiaume, Bittner, Perkovic, Settle, and Simon [2] gave time and state lower bounds for the ring FSSP, described in Theorems 1, 2 and 3, below.

Theorem 1. *The minimum time in which the ring FSSP could occur is no earlier than n steps for any ring of length n.*

Theorem 2. *There exists no 3-state **full** solution to the ring FSSP.*

Theorem 3. *There exists no 4-state, symmetric, minimal-time **full** solution to the ring FSSP.*

Umeo, Kamikawa, and Yunès [9] introduced a concept of **partial** solutions to the FSSP, gave a state lower bound, and showed that there exist 17 symmetric 4-state partial solutions to the ring FSSP.

Theorem 4. *There exists no 3-state **partial** solution to the ring FSSP.*

Theorem 5. *There exist **17 symmetric** 4-state **partial** solutions to the ring FSSP for the ring of length $n = 2^k$ for any positive integer $k \geq 1$.*

Ng [7] added a list of 80 asymmetric 4-state solutions, this completing the powers-of-two solutions.

Theorem 6. *There exist **80 asymmetric** 4-state **partial** solutions to the ring FSSP for the ring of length $n = 2^k$ for any positive integer $k \geq 1$.*

2.3   A New Quest for Four-State Partial Solutions for Rings

- **Four-state ring cellular automata**
  Let $\mathcal{M}$ be a four-state ring cellular automaton $\mathcal{M} = \{\mathcal{Q}, \delta\}$, where $\mathcal{Q}$ is an internal state set $\mathcal{Q} = \{\mathtt{A}, \mathtt{F}, \mathtt{G}, \mathtt{Q}\}$ and δ is a next-state function such that $\delta : \mathcal{Q}^3 \to \mathcal{Q}$. Without loss of generality, we assume that $\mathtt{Q}$ is a quiescent state with a property $\delta(\mathtt{Q}, \mathtt{Q}, \mathtt{Q}) = \mathtt{Q}$, $\mathtt{G}$ is a general state, $\mathtt{A}$ is an auxiliary state and F is the *firing* state, respectively. The initial configuration is $\mathtt{G} \overbrace{\mathtt{Q Q}, ..., \mathtt{Q}}^{n-1}$ for $n \geq 2$. We say that an FSSP solution is *symmetric* if its transition table has a property such that $\delta(x, y, z) = \delta(z, y, x)$, for any state x, y, z in $\mathcal{Q}$. Otherwise, the FSSP solution is called *asymmetric*.

- **A computer investigation into four-state FSSP solutions for rings**
  Figure 2 is a four-state transition table, where a symbol • shows a possible state in $\mathcal{Q} = \{\mathtt{A}, \mathtt{F}, \mathtt{G}, \mathtt{Q}\}$. Note that we have totally 4^{26} possible transition rules. We make a computer investigation into the transition rule set that might yield possible FSSP solutions. Our strategy is based on a backtracking searching. A similar technique was employed first successfully in Ng [7]. Due to the space available, we omit the details of the backtracking searching strategy. The outline of those solutions will be described in the next section.

Q	Right State				G	Right State				A	Right State		
	Q	G	A			Q	G	A			Q	G	A
Left State Q	Q	•	•		Left State Q	•	•	•		Left State Q	•	•	•
G	•	•	•		G	•	•	•		G	•	•	•
A	•	•	•		A	•	•	•		A	•	•	•

Fig. 2. Four-state transition table

Table 1. Time complexity and number of transition rules for 39 symmetric partial solutions

Symmetric partial solutions	Time complexity	# of transition rules
R_{S_1}	$T_G(n) = T_A(n) = n$	23
R_{S_2}	$T_G(n) = T_A(n) = n$	23
R_{S_3}	$T_G(n) = n$	23
R_{S_4}	$T_G(n) = n$	20
R_{S_5}	$T_G(n) = n$	27
R_{S_6}	$T_G(n) = n$	24
R_{S_7}	$T_G(n) = n$	23
R_{S_8}	$T_G(n) = T_A(n) = n$	24
R_{S_9}	$T_G(n) = T_A(n) = n$	25
R_{S_10}	$T_G(n) = T_A(n) = n$	27
R_{S_11}	$T_G(n) = T_A(n) = n$	24
R_{S_12}	$T_G(n) = n$	21
R_{S_13}	$T_G(n) = T_A(n) = n$	23
R_{S_14}	$T_G(n) = T_A(n) = n$	23
R_{S_15}	$T_G(n) = T_A(n) = n$	26
R_{S_16}	$T_G(n) = T_A(n) = n$	27
R_{S_17}	$T_G(n) = T_A(n) = n$	23
R_{S_18}	$T_G(n) = T_A(n) = n$	22
R_{S_19}	$T_G(n) = T_A(n) = n$	22
R_{S_20}	$T_G(n) = n$	26
R_{S_21}	$T_G(n) = T_A(n) = n$	25
R_{S_22}	$T_G(n) = T_A(n) = n$	26
R_{S_23}	$T_G(n) = T_A(n) = n$	26
R_{S_24}	$T_G(n) = n$	27
R_{S_25}	$T_G(n) = T_A(n) = n + 1$	27
R_{S_26}	$T_G(n) = T_A(n) = n + 1$	24
R_{S_27}	$T_G(n) = T_A(n) = n + 1$	24
R_{S_28}	$T_G(n) = n + 1$	22
R_{S_29}	$T_G(n) = n + 1, T_A(n) = n$	23
R_{S_30}	$T_G(n) = n + 1$	25
R_{S_31}	$T_G(n) = T_A(n) = n + 1$	24
R_{S_32}	$T_G(n) = T_A(n) = n + 1$	25
R_{S_33}	$T_G(n) = n + 1$	24
R_{S_34}	$T_G(n) = n + 1$	22
R_{S_35}	$T_G(n) = T_A(n) = n + 1$	24
R_{S_36}	$T_G(n) = T_A(n) = n + 1$	24
R_{S_37}	$T_G(n) = T_A(n) = n + 1$	24
R_{S_38}	$T_G(n) = n + 2, T_A(n) = n + 1$	24
R_{S_39}	$T_G(n) = (3n + 1)/2, T_A(n) = n + 1$	25

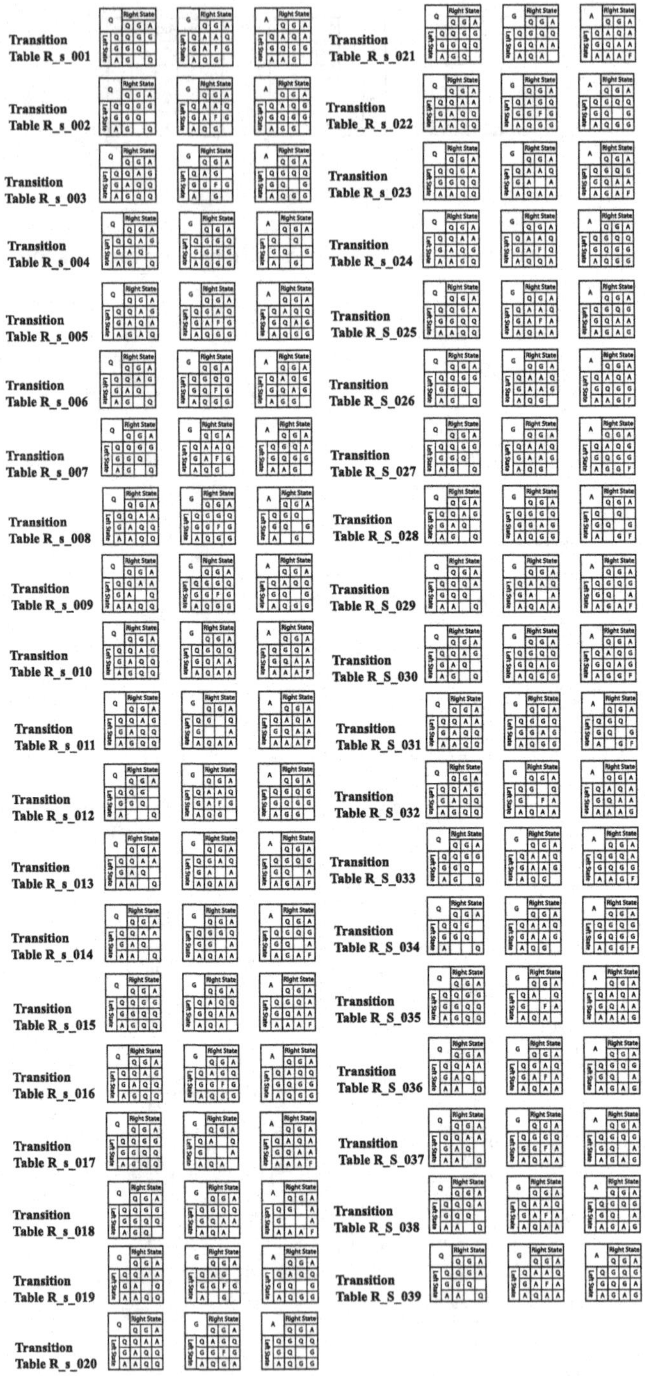

Fig. 3. Transition tables for 39 minimum-time, nearly minimum-time and non-minimum-time symmetric solutions

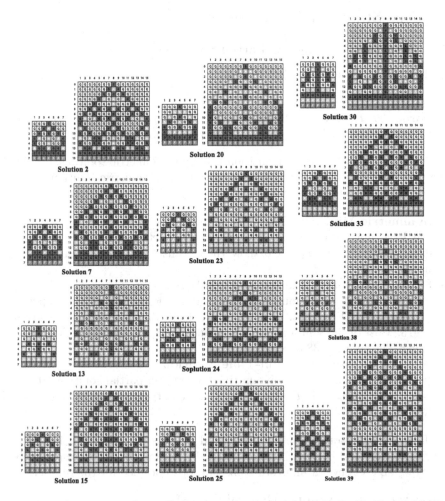

Fig. 4. Snapshots on 7 and 15 cells for symmetric solutions 2, 7, 13, 15, 20, 23, 24, 25, 30, 33, 38, and 39

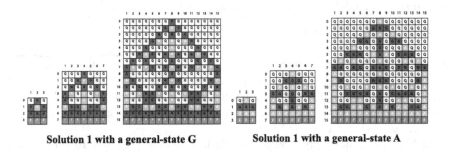

Solution 1 with a general-state G   **Solution 1 with a general-state A**

Fig. 5. Synchronized configurations on 3, 7, and 15 cells with a general-state G (left) and A (right), respectively, in the Solution 1

3   Four-State Partial Solutions

3.1   Four-State Symmetric Partial Solutions

In this section, we will establish the following theorem with a help of computer investigation.

Theorem 7. *There exist **39 symmetric** 4-state partial solutions to the ring FSSP for the ring of length $n = 2^k - 1$ for any positive integer $k \geq 2$.*

Let $R_{S\_i}, 1 \leq i \leq 39$ be a transition table for symmetric solutions obtained. We refer to the ith symmetric transition table as symmetric solution i, where $1 \leq i \leq 39$. The details are as follows:

- **Symmetric Minimum-Time Solutions:**
  We have got 24 minimum-time symmetric partial solutions operating in exactly $T(n) = n$ steps. We show their transition rules $R_{S\_i}, 1 \leq i \leq 24$ in Fig. 3.
- **Symmetric Nearly Minimum-Time Solutions:**
  We have got 14 nearly minimum-time symmetric partial solutions operating in $T(n) = n + O(1)$ steps. Their transition rules $R_{S\_i}, 25 \leq i \leq 38$ are given in Fig. 3. Most of the solutions, that is, solutions 25–37 operate in $T(n) = n + 1$ steps. The solution 38 operates in $T(n) = n + 2$ steps.
- **Symmetric Non-Minimum-Time Solution:**
  It is seen that one non-minimum-time symmetric partial solution 39 exists. Its time complexity is $T(n) = (3n + 1)/2$. The transition rule R_{S_39} is given in Fig. 3.

Here, we give some snapshots on 7 and 15 cells for minimum-time, nearly minimum-time and non-minimum-time FSSP solutions in Fig. 4, respectively.

Now, we give several interesting observations obtained for the rule set.

Observation 1 (Swapping General States)
It is noted that some solutions have a property that both of the states G and A can be an initial general state and yield successful synchronizations from each general state without introducing any additional transition rules.

For example, solution 1 can synchronize any ring of length $n = 2^k - 1, k \geq 2$ in $T(n) = n$ steps, starting from an initial configuration G $\overbrace{Q, \cdots, Q}^{n-1}$ and A $\overbrace{Q, \cdots, Q}^{n-1}$, respectively. Let $T_{G-R_{S\_i}}(n)$ (or simply $T_G(n)$, if the rule number is specified) and $T_{A-R_{S\_i}}(n)$ ($T_A(n)$) be synchronization steps starting the solution R_{S_i} from the initial general-state G and A, respectively, for rings of length n. Then, we have $T_{G-R_{S\_1}}(n) = T_{A-R_{S\_1}}(n) = n$.

In Fig. 5, we show synchronized configurations on 3, 7, and 15 cells with a general-state G (left) and A (right), respectively, for the solution 1. In Table 1, we give the time complexity and number of transition rules for each symmetric solution. The observation does not always hold for all symmetric rules. For example, the solution 3 can synchronize any ring of length $n = 2^k - 1, k \geq 2$ in $T(n) = n$ steps from the general state G, but not from the state A.

The Observation 1 yields the following *duality* relation among the four-state rule sets.

Observation 2 (Duality)

Let x and y be any four-state FSSP solution for rings and x is obtained from y by swapping the states G and A in y and vice versa. We say that the two solutions x and y are *dual* concerning the states G and A. The relation is denoted as $x \overset{Dual}{\leftrightarrows} y$. We have:

$$R_{S\_1} \overset{Dual}{\leftrightarrows} R_{S\_14}, \quad R_{S\_2} \overset{Dual}{\leftrightarrows} R_{S\_13},$$
$$R_{S\_8} \overset{Dual}{\leftrightarrows} R_{S\_17}, \quad R_{S\_9} \overset{Dual}{\leftrightarrows} R_{S\_21},$$
$$R_{S\_10} \overset{Dual}{\leftrightarrows} R_{S\_16}, \quad R_{S\_15} \overset{Dual}{\leftrightarrows} R_{S\_22},$$
$$R_{S\_18} \overset{Dual}{\leftrightarrows} R_{S\_19}, \quad R_{S\_26} \overset{Dual}{\leftrightarrows} R_{S\_37},$$
$$R_{S\_27} \overset{Dual}{\leftrightarrows} R_{S\_36}, \quad R_{S\_31} \overset{Dual}{\leftrightarrows} R_{S\_35}.$$

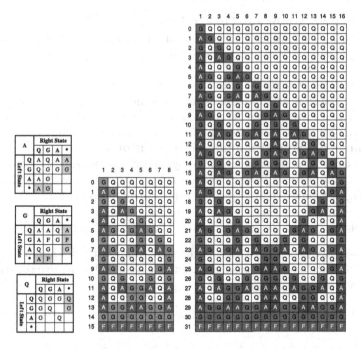

Fig. 6. An array solution (left) converted from ring solution R_{S_1} and synchronized configurations (right) on arrays consisting of 8 and 16 cells with a general-state G (Color figure online)

Observation 3 (Converting Ring Solutions to Array Ones)

It is noted that most of the symmetric solutions presented above can be converted into the solutions for arrays, that is, conventional 1D array with the general at one end, without introducing any additional state. For example, Fig. 6 shows the transition rules and snapshots on arrays consisting of 8 and 16 cells for a converted solution operating in non-optimum-steps. The solution can be obtained from the Solution 1 by adding 11 rules shown in Fig. 6 (leftmost one), illustrated with yellow small squares. All of the transition rules introduced newly are involved with the left and right end states, denoted by *. The converted 4-state array protocol can synchronize any 1D array of length $n = 2^k$ with the left-end general in $2n - 1$ steps, where k is any positive integer $k \geq 1$.

3.2   Four-State Asymmetric Partial Solutions

In this section we will establish the following theorem with a help of computer investigation.

Theorem 8. *There exist **132 asymmetric** 4-state partial solutions to the ring FSSP for the ring of length $n = 2^k - 1$ for any positive integer $k \geq 2$.*

Let $R_{AS\_i}, 1 \leq i \leq 132$ be ith transition table for asymmetric solutions obtained in this paper. We refer to the table as asymmetric solution i, where $1 \leq i \leq 132$. Their breakdown is as follows:

- **Asymmetric Minimum-Time Solutions:**
  We have got 60 minimum-time asymmetric partial solutions operating in exactly $T(n) = n$ steps. Their transition rule sets $R_{AS\_i}, 1 \leq i \leq 60$, are given in Figs. 7 and 8.
- **Asymmetric Nearly Minimum-Time Solutions:**
  We have got 56 nearly minimum-time asymmetric partial solutions operating in $T(n) = n + O(1)$ steps. Transition rule sets $R_{AS\_i}, 61 \leq i \leq 116$, shown in Figs. 8 and 9, are the nearly minimum-time solutions obtained.
- **Asymmetric Non-Minimum-Time Solutions:**
  We have got 16 non-minimum-time asymmetric partial solutions operating in non-minimum-steps. Their transition rules are denoted by $R_{AS\_i}, 117 \leq i \leq 132$. Figure 9 shows those transition rules. Each solution in $R_{S\_i}, 117 \leq i \leq 124$ operates in $T(n) = 3n/2 \pm O(1)$ steps, respectively. Each solution with the rule set R_{S_125} and R_{S_130} operates in $T(n) = 2n + O(1)$ steps, respectively.

In Table 2 we give an overview of the time complexity and number of transition rules for each asymmetric solution. In Figs. 7, 8, and 9, we give the transition rule for each asymmetric solution.

Table 2. Time complexity and number of transition rules for 132 asymmetric solutions

Asymmetric partial solutions	Time complexity	# of transition rules
$R_{AS\_i}, 1 \leq i \leq 60$	$T(n) = n$	22–26
$R_{AS\_i}, 61 \leq i \leq 116$	$T(n) = n + O(1)$	25–27
$R_{AS\_i}, 117 \leq i \leq 124$	$T(n) = 3n/2 \pm O(1)$	24–27
$R_{AS\_i}, 125 \leq i \leq 132$	$T(n) = 2n + O(1)$	24–27

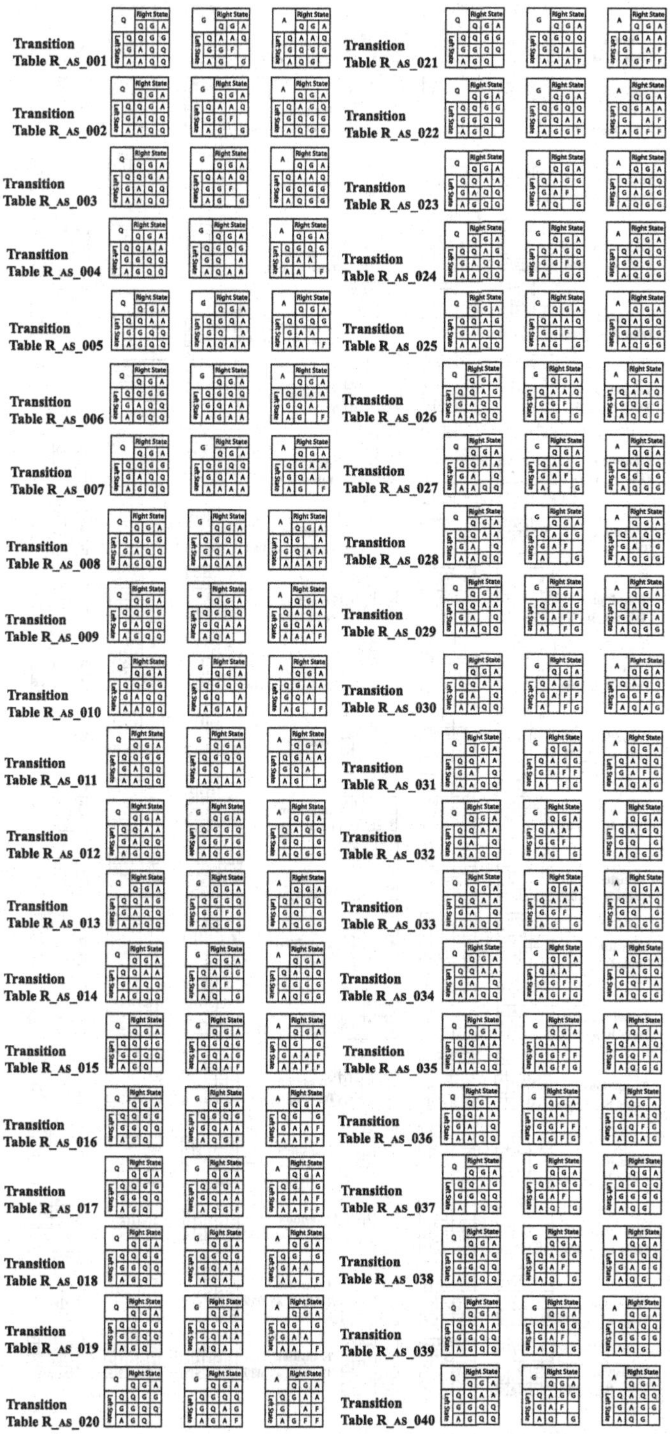

Fig. 7. Transition tables R_{AS_i}, $1 \leq i \leq 40$, for minimum-time asymmetric solutions

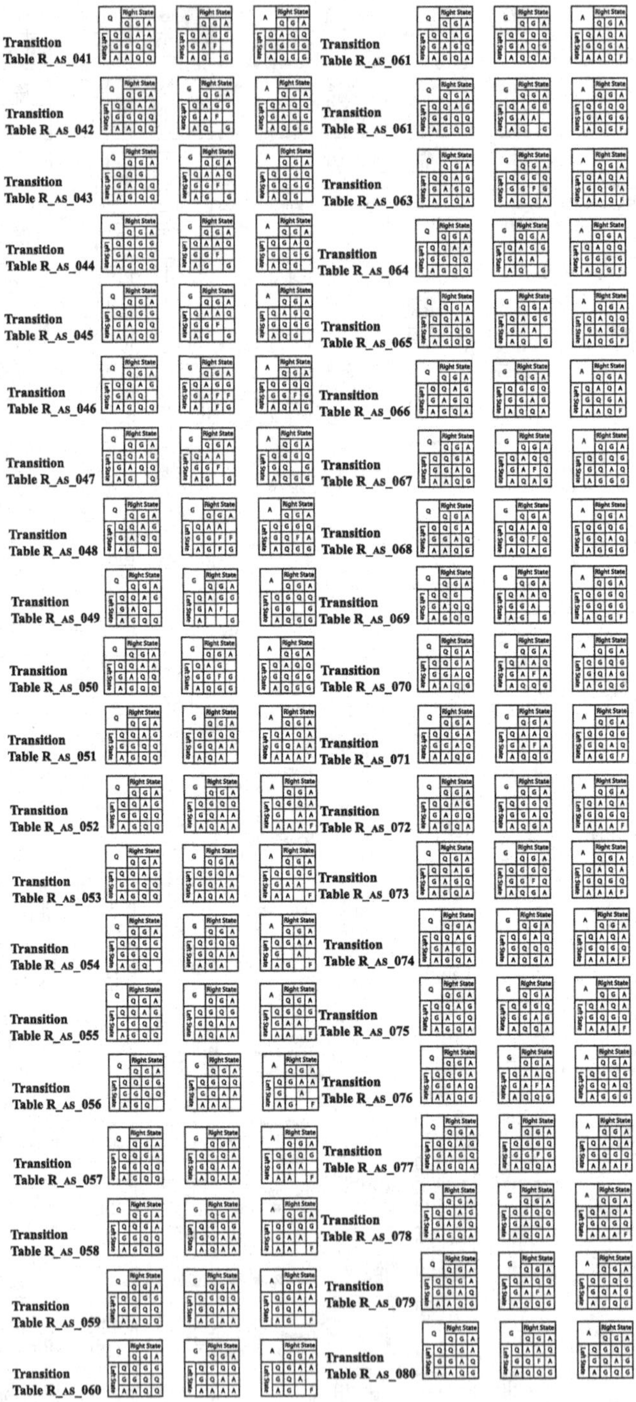

Fig. 8. Transition tables R_{AS_i}, $41 \leq i \leq 80$, for minimum-time and nearly-minimum-time asymmetric solutions

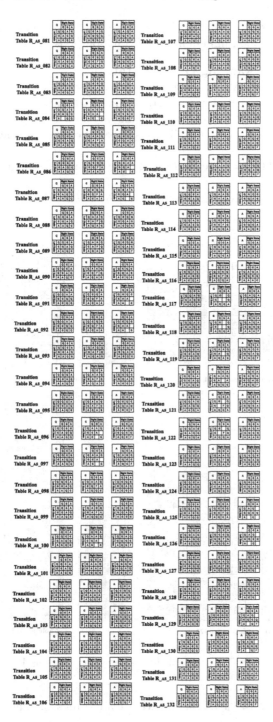

Fig. 9. Transition tables R_{AS_i}, $81 \leq i \leq 132$, for nearly-minimum-time and non-minimum-time asymmetric solutions

Here we give some snapshots on 7 and 15 cells for minimum-time, nearly minimum-time and non-minimum-time FSSP solutions, respectively, in Fig. 10.

Observation 4 (Swapping General States)

It is noted that some asymmetric solutions have a property that both of the states G and A can be an initial general state and yield successful synchronizations from each general state without introducing any additional transition rules. For example, asymmetric solution 1, R_{AS_1}, can synchronize any ring of length $n = 2^k - 1, k \geq 2$ in $T(n) = n$ steps, starting from an initial configuration $G \overbrace{Q, \cdots, Q}^{n-1}$ and $A \overbrace{Q, \cdots, Q}^{n-1}$, respectively and we have $T_G(n) = T_A(n) = n$.

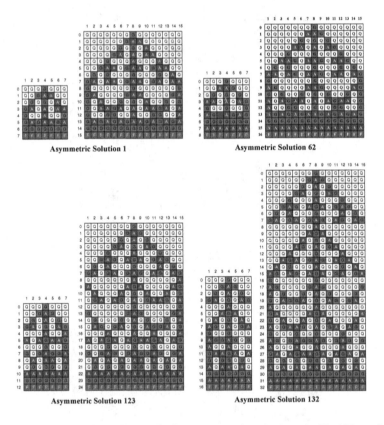

Fig. 10. Snapshots on 7 and 15 cells for asymmetric solutions 1, 62, 123, and 132

The Observation 4 yields the following *duality* relation among the four-state rule sets.

Observation 5 (Duality)
A duality relation exists among the asymmetric solutions. For example, we have:

$$R_{AS\_1} \overset{Dual}{\leftrightarrows} R_{AS\_4}, R_{AS\_2} \overset{Dual}{\leftrightarrows} R_{AS\_57}.$$

Observation 6 (Inclusion of Powers-of-2 Rule)
It is noted that some solutions can synchronize not only rings of length $2^k - 1, k \geq 2$ but also rings of length $2^k, k \geq 1$. For example, solution 130 can synchronize any ring of length $n = 2^k - 1, k \geq 2$ in $T(n) = 2n + 1$ steps and simultaneously the solution can synchronize any ring of length $n = 2^k, k \geq 1$ in $T(n) = 2n - 1$ steps. See the snapshots given in Fig. 11 on 7, 8, 15, and 16 cells for the solution 130. A relatively large number of solutions includes powers-of-2 solutions as a proper subset of rules.

Now we show a one to one correspondence between 4-state asymmetric solutions. First, we establish the following generic property for the asymmetric FSSP solution for rings. Let x be any k-state transition table defined on a k-state set $Q_x = \{s_1, s_2, ..., s_k\}$ and x^R be the k-state table defined on Q_x such that:

$$x_{s_\ell}^R(i,j) = x_{s_\ell}(j,i), \text{ for any } 1 \leq i, j, \ell \leq k.$$

Here $x_{s_\ell}(j,i)$ is a state on the ith row, jth column on the state transition matrix concerning the state s_ℓ in x. The transition table x^R is the reflected table concerning the principal diagonal of the table x, which is obtained by transposition. We describe the relation as $x \overset{Reflection}{\leftrightarrows} x^R$. Now we have:

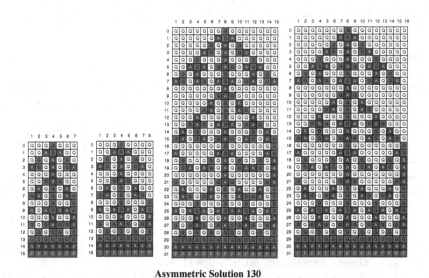

Asymmetric Solution 130

Fig. 11. Snapshots on 7, 8, 15, and 16 cells for asymmetric solutions 130.

Theorem 9. *Let x be any k-state FSSP ring solution with time complexity $T_x(n)$. Then, x^R is also an FSSP ring solution with time complexity $T_{x^R}(n) = T_x(n)$.*

Observation 7 (Reflection)
For every asymmetric rule in R_{AS_i}, $1 \leq i \leq 132$, the rule has one corresponding asymmetric rule in R_{AS_i}, $1 \leq i \leq 132$. For example, R_{AS_1} is the reflected rule of R_{AS_40} and vice versa:

$$R_{AS\_1} \overset{Reflection}{\leftrightarrows} R_{AS\_40}.$$

4   Summary and Discussions

A quest for the smaller state FSSP solutions has been an interesting problem for a long time. We have answered to the question by proposing a new class of the smallest four-state FSSP protocols that can synchronize any 1D ring of length $n = 2^k - 1$ for any positive integer $k \geq 2$. We show that the class includes a rich variety of FSSP protocols that consists of 39 symmetric and 132 asymmetric solutions, ranging from minimum-time to linear-time in synchronization steps. Some interesting properties in the structure of 4-state partial solutions have been discussed. We strongly believe that no smallest solutions exist other than the ones proposed for length 2^k rings in Umeo, Kamikawa and Yunès [9] and Ng [7] and for rings of length $2^k - 1$ in this paper. A question: how many 4-state partial solutions are there for arrays? remains open. We think that there would be a large number of the smallest 4-state partial solutions for arrays. Its number would be larger than several thousands. The structure of the 4-state array partial synchronizers is far more complex than the 4-state ring partial synchronizers.

References

1. Balzer, R.: An 8-state minimal time solution to the firing squad synchronization problem. Inf. Control **10**(1), 22–42 (1967). https://doi.org/10.1016/s0019-9958(67)90032-0
2. Berthiaume, A., Bittner, T., Perković, L., Settle, A., Simon, J.: Bounding the firing synchronization problem on a ring. Theor. Comput. Sci. **320**(2–3), 213–228 (2004). https://doi.org/10.1016/j.tcs.2004.01.036
3. Gerken, H.D.: Über Synchronisationsprobleme bei Zellularautomaten. Diplomarbeit, Institut für Theoretische Informatik, Technische Universität Braunschweig (1987)
4. Goto, E.: A minimal time solution of the firing squad problem. Dittoed Course Notes Appl. Math. **298**(with an illustration in color), 52–59 (1962)
5. Mazoyer, J.: A six-state minimal time solution to the firing squad synchronization problem. Theor. Comput. Sci. **50**, 183–238 (1987)
6. Moore, E.F.: The firing squad synchronization problem. In: Moore, E.F. (ed.) Sequential Machines, Selected Papers, pp. 213–214. Addison-Wesley, Reading (1964)

7. Ng, W.L.: Partial Solutions for the Firing Squad Synchronization Problem on Rings. ProQuest Publications, Ann Arbor (2011)
8. Sanders, P.: Massively parallel search for transition-tables of polyautomata. In: Jesshope, C., Jossifov, V., Wilhelmi, W. (eds.) Proc. of 6th Int, Workshop on Parallel Processing by Cellular Automata and Arrays, pp. 99–108. Akademie (1994)
9. Umeo, H., Kamikawa, N., Yunès, J.-B.: A family of smallest symmetrical four-state firing squad synchronization protocols for ring arrays. Parallel Process. Lett. **19**(2), 299–313 (2009). https://doi.org/10.1142/s0129626409000237
10. Umeo, H., Yanagihara, T.: A smallest five-state solution to the firing squad synchronization problem. In: Durand-Lose, J., Margenstern, M. (eds.) MCU 2007. LNCS, vol. 4664, pp. 291–302. Springer, Heidelberg (2007). https://doi.org/10.1007/978-3-540-74593-8_25
11. Waksman, A.: An optimum solution to the firing squad synchronization problem. Inf. Control **9**(1), 66–78 (1966). https://doi.org/10.1016/s0019-9958(66)90110-0
12. Yunès, J.-B.: A 4-states algebraic solution to linear cellular automata synchronization. Inf. Process. Lett. **107**(2), 71–75 (2008). https://doi.org/10.1016/j.ipl.2008.01.009

Convex Language Semantics for Nondeterministic Probabilistic Automata

Gerco van Heerdt[1], Justin Hsu[2(✉)], Joël Ouaknine[3,4], and Alexandra Silva[1]

[1] Department of Computer Science, University College London, London, UK
{g.vanheerdt,a.silva}@cs.ucl.ac.uk
[2] Department of Computer Sciences, University of Wisconsin-Madison,
Madison, WI, USA
justhsu@cs.wisc.edu
[3] Max Planck Institute for Software Systems, Saarbrücken, Germany
[4] Department of Computer Science, Oxford University, Oxford, UK
joel@mpi-sws.org

Abstract. We explore language semantics for automata combining probabilistic and nondeterministic behaviors. We first show that there are precisely two natural semantics for probabilistic automata with nondeterminism. For both choices, we show that these automata are strictly more expressive than deterministic probabilistic automata, and we prove that the problem of checking language equivalence is undecidable by reduction from the threshold problem. However, we provide a discounted metric that can be computed to arbitrarily high precision.

1 Introduction

Probabilistic automata are fundamental models of randomized computation. They have been used in the study of such topics as the semantics and correctness of probabilistic programming languages [18,20], randomized algorithms [24,25], and machine learning [3,26]. Removing randomness but adding nondeterminism, nondeterministic automata are established tools for describing concurrent and distributed systems [27].

Interest in systems that exhibit both random and nondeterministic behaviors goes back to Rabin's randomized techniques to increase the efficiency of distributed algorithms in the 1970s and 1980s [24,25]. This line of research yielded several automata models supporting both nondeterministic and probabilistic choices [4,16,28]. Many formal techniques and tools were developed for these models, and they have been successfully used in verification tasks [15,16,19,30], but there are many ways of combining nondeterminism and randomization, and there remains plenty of room for further investigation.

This work was partially supported by ERC starting grant ProFoundNet (679127), ERC consolidator grant AVS-ISS (648701), a Leverhulme Prize (PLP-2016-129), and an NSF grant (1637532).

B. Fischer and T. Uustalu (Eds.): ICTAC 2018, LNCS 11187, pp. 472–492, 2018.
https://doi.org/10.1007/978-3-030-02508-3_25

In this paper we study nondeterministic probabilistic automata (NPAs) and propose a novel probabilistic language semantics. NPAs are similar to Segala systems [28] in that transitions can make combined nondeterministic and probabilistic choices, but NPAs also have an output weight in $[0, 1]$ for each state, reminiscent of observations in Markov Decision Processes. This enables us to define the expected weight associated with a word in a similar way to what one would do for standard nondeterministic automata—the output of an NPA on an input word can be computed in a *deterministic* version of the automaton, using a careful choice of algebraic structure for the state space.

Equivalence in our semantics is language equivalence (also known as trace equivalence), which is coarser than probabilistic bisimulation [7,9,17,32], which distinguishes systems with different branching structure even if the total weight assigned to a word is the same. This generalizes the classical difference between branching and linear semantics [31] to the probabilistic setting, with different target applications calling for different semantics.

After reviewing mathematical preliminaries in Sect. 2, we introduce the NPA model and explore its semantics in Sect. 3. We show that there are precisely two natural ways to define the language semantics of such systems—by either taking the maximum or the minimum of the weights associated with the different paths labeled by an input word. The proof of this fact relies on an abstract view on these automata generating probabilistic languages with algebraic structure. Specifically, probabilistic languages have the structure of a *convex algebra*, analogous to the join-semilattice structure of standard languages. These features can abstractly be seen as so-called *Eilenberg-Moore algebras* for a monad—the distribution and the powerset monads, respectively—which can support new semantics and proof techniques (see, e.g., [6,7]).

In Sect. 4, we compare NPAs with standard, deterministic probabilistic automata (DPAs) as formulated by Rabin [23]. Our semantics ensures that NPAs recover DPAs in the special case when there is no nondeterministic choice. More interestingly, we show that there are weighted languages accepted by NPAs that are not accepted by any DPA. We use the theory of linear recurrence sequences to give a separation even for weighted languages over a unary alphabet.

In Sect. 5, we turn to equivalence. We prove that language equivalence of NPAs is undecidable by reduction from so-called *threshold problems*, which are undecidable [5,12,22]. The hard instances encoding the threshold problem are equivalences between probabilistic automata over a two-letter alphabet. Thus, the theorem immediately implies that equivalence of NPAs is undecidable when the alphabet size is at least two. The situation for automata over unary alphabets is more subtle; in particular, the threshold problem over a unary alphabet is not known to be undecidable. However, we give a reduction from the Positivity problem on linear recurrence sequences, a problem where a decision procedure would necessarily entail breakthroughs in open problems in number theory [21]. Finally, we show that despite the undecidability result we can provide a discounted metric that can be computed to arbitrarily high precision.

We survey related work and conclude in Sect. 6.

2   Preliminaries

Before we present our main technical results, we review some necessary mathematical background on convex algebras, monads, probabilistic automata, and language semantics.

2.1   Convex Algebra

A set A is a *convex algebra*, or a *convex set*, if for all $n \in \mathbb{N}$ and tuples $(p_i)_{i=1}^n$ of numbers in $[0,1]$ summing up to 1 there is an operation denoted $\sum_{i=1}^n p_i(-)_i \colon A^n \to A$ satisfying the following properties for $(a_1, \ldots, a_n) \in A^n$:

Projection. If $p_j = 1$ (and hence $p_i = 0$ for all $i \neq j$), we have $\sum_{i=1}^n p_i a_i = a_j$.

Barycenter. For any n tuples $(q_{i,j})_{j=1}^m$ in $[0,1]$ summing up to 1, we have

$$\sum_{i=1}^n p_i \left(\sum_{j=1}^m q_{i,j} a_j \right) = \sum_{j=1}^m \left(\sum_{i=1}^n p_i q_{i,j} \right) a_j.$$

Informally, a convex algebra structure gives a way to take finite convex combinations of elements in a set A. Given this structure, we can define convex subsets and generate them by elements of A.

Definition 1. *A subset $S \subseteq A$ is* convex *if it is closed under all convex combinations. (Such a set can also be seen as a convex subalgebra.) A convex set S is* generated *by a set $G \subseteq A$ if for all $s \in S$, there exist $n \in \mathbb{N}$, $(p_i)_{i=1}^n$, $(g_i)_{i=1}^n \in G^n$ such that $s = \sum_i p_i g_i$. When G is finite, we say that S is* finitely generated.

We can also define morphisms between convex sets.

Definition 2. *An* affine map *between two convex sets A and B is a function $h \colon A \to B$ commuting with convex combinations:*

$$h \left(\sum_{i=1}^n p_i a_i \right) = \sum_{i=1}^n p_i h(a_i).$$

2.2   Monads and Their Algebras

Our definition of language semantics will be based on the category theoretic framework of monads and their algebras. Monads can be used to model computational side-effects such as nondeterminism and probabilistic choice. An algebra allows us to interpret such side-effects within an object of the category.

Definition 3. *A* monad *(T, η, μ) consists of an endofunctor T and two natural transformations: a unit $\eta \colon Id \Rightarrow T$ and a multiplication $\mu \colon TT \Rightarrow T$, making the following diagrams commute.*

$$
\begin{array}{ccc}
T & \xrightarrow{\ \eta\ } & TT \\
{\scriptstyle T\eta} \downarrow & \diagdown & \downarrow {\scriptstyle \mu} \\
TT & \xrightarrow[\ \mu\ ]{} & T
\end{array}
\qquad\qquad
\begin{array}{ccc}
TTT & \xrightarrow{\ T\mu\ } & TT \\
{\scriptstyle \mu} \downarrow & & \downarrow {\scriptstyle \mu} \\
TT & \xrightarrow[\ \mu\ ]{} & T
\end{array}
$$

When there is no risk of confusion, we identify a monad with its endofunctor. An example of a monad in the category of sets is the triple $(\mathcal{P}, \{-\}, \bigcup)$, where $\mathcal{P}$ denotes the finite powerset functor sending each set to the set of its finite subsets, $\{-\}$ is the singleton operation, and $\bigcup$ is set union.

Definition 4. *An* algebra *for a monad* (T, η, μ) *is a pair* (X, h) *consisting of a carrier set* X *and a function* $h\colon TX \to X$ *making the following diagrams commute.*

$$
\begin{array}{ccc}
X & \xrightarrow{\eta} & TX \\
& \searrow & \downarrow h \\
& & X
\end{array}
\qquad\qquad
\begin{array}{ccc}
TTX & \xrightarrow{Th} & TX \\
\mu \downarrow & & \downarrow h \\
TX & \xrightarrow{h} & X
\end{array}
$$

Definition 5. *A* homomorphism *from an algebra* (X, h) *to an algebra* (Y, k) *for a monad* T *is a function* $f\colon X \to Y$ *making the diagram below commute.*

$$
\begin{array}{ccc}
TX & \xrightarrow{Tf} & TY \\
h \downarrow & & \downarrow k \\
X & \xrightarrow{f} & Y
\end{array}
$$

The algebras for the finite powerset monad are precisely the join-semilattices with bottom, and their homomorphisms are maps that preserve finite joins. The algebras for any monad together with their homomorphisms form a category.

2.3 Distribution and Convex Powerset Monads

We will work with two monads closely associated with convex sets. In the category of sets, the *distribution monad* $(\mathcal{D}, \delta, m)$ maps a set X to the set of distributions over X with finite support. The unit $\delta\colon X \to \mathcal{D}X$ maps $x \in X$ to the point distribution at x. For the multiplication $m\colon \mathcal{D}\mathcal{D}X \to \mathcal{D}X$, let $d \in \mathcal{D}\mathcal{D}X$ be a finite distribution with support $\{d_1, \ldots, d_n\} \subseteq \mathcal{D}X$ and define $m(d) = \sum_{i=1}^{n} p_i d_i$, where p_i is the probability of producing d_i under d. The category of algebras for the distribution monad is precisely the category of convex sets and affine maps—we will often convert between these two representations implicitly.

In the category of convex sets, the *finitely generated nonempty convex powerset monad* [7] $(\mathcal{P}_c, \{-\}, \bigcup)$ maps a convex set A to the set of finitely generated nonempty convex subsets of A.[1] The convex algebra structure on $\mathcal{P}_cA$ is given by $\sum_{i=1}^{n} p_i U_i = \{\sum_{i=1}^{n} p_i u_i \mid u_i \in U_i \text{ for all } 1 \le i \le n\}$ with every $U_i \in \mathcal{P}_cA$. The unit map $\{-\}\colon A \to \mathcal{P}_cA$ maps $a \in A$ to a singleton convex set $\{a\}$, and the multiplication $\bigcup\colon \mathcal{P}_c\mathcal{P}_cA \to \mathcal{P}_cA$ is again the union operation, which collapses nested convex sets.

As an example, we can consider this monad on the convex algebra $[0, 1]$. The result is a finitely generated convex set.

---

[1] In prior work [7], the monad was defined to take all convex subsets rather than just the finitely generated ones. However, since all the monad operations preserve finiteness of the generators, the restricted monad we consider is also well-defined.

Lemma 1. *The convex set $\mathcal{P}_c[0,1]$ is generated by its elements $\{0\}$, $\{1\}$, and $[0,1]$, i.e., $\mathsf{Conv}(\{\{0\},\{1\},[0,1]\}) = \mathcal{P}_c[0,1]$.*

Proof. The finitely generated nonempty convex subsets of $[0,1]$ are of the form $[p,q]$ for $p,q \in [0,1]$, and $[p,q] = p\{1\} + (q-p)[0,1] + (1-q)\{0\}$.   □

To describe automata with both nondeterministic and probabilistic transitions, we will work with convex powersets of distributions. The functor $\mathcal{P}_c\mathcal{D}$ taking sets X to the set of finitely generated nonempty convex sets of distributions over X can be given a monad structure.

Explicitly, writing $\omega_A \colon \mathcal{D}\mathcal{P}_cA \to \mathcal{P}_cA$ for the (affine) convex algebra structure on $\mathcal{P}_cA$ for any convex algebra A, the composite monad $(\mathcal{P}_c\mathcal{D}, \hat{\delta}, \hat{m})$ is given by

$$
\begin{array}{ccc}
X & \quad & \mathcal{P}_c\mathcal{D}\mathcal{P}_c\mathcal{D}X \\
{\scriptstyle \delta}\downarrow \quad \overset{\hat{\delta}}{\dashrightarrow} & & {\scriptstyle \mathcal{P}_c\omega}\downarrow \quad \overset{\hat{m}}{\dashrightarrow} \\
\mathcal{D}X \xrightarrow{\{-\}} \mathcal{P}_c\mathcal{D}X & & \mathcal{P}_c\mathcal{P}_c\mathcal{D}X \xrightarrow{\ \bigcup\ } \mathcal{P}_c\mathcal{D}X
\end{array}
\qquad (1)
$$

For all convex sets A and finite nonempty subsets $S \subseteq A$, we can define the *convex closure* of S (sometimes called the *convex hull*) $\mathsf{Conv}(S) \in \mathcal{P}_cA$ by

$$
\mathsf{Conv}(S) = \{\alpha(d) \mid d \in \mathcal{D}A, \mathsf{supp}(d) \subseteq S\},
$$

where $\alpha \colon \mathcal{D}A \to A$ is the convex algebra structure on A. Conv is in fact a natural transformation, a fact we will use later.

Lemma 2. *For all convex sets (A,α) and (B,β), affine maps $f \colon A \to B$, and finite nonempty subsets $S \subseteq A$, $(\mathcal{P}_cf \circ \mathsf{Conv})(S) = (\mathsf{Conv} \circ \mathcal{P}f)(S)$.*

Proof. We will first show that

$$
\{\mathcal{D}f(d) \mid d \in \mathcal{D}A, \mathsf{supp}(d) \subseteq S\} = \{d \in \mathcal{D}B \mid \mathsf{supp}(d) \subseteq \{f(a) \mid a \in S\}\} \quad (2)
$$

for all finite nonempty $S \subseteq A$. For the inclusion from left to right, note that for each $d \in \mathcal{D}A$ such that $\mathsf{supp}(d) \subseteq S$ we have $b \in \mathsf{supp}(\mathcal{D}f(d))$ only if there exists $a \in S$ such that $f(a) = b$. Thus, $\mathsf{supp}(\mathcal{D}f(d)) \subseteq \{f(a) \mid a \in S\}$. Conversely, consider $d \in \mathcal{D}B$ such that $\mathsf{supp}(d) \subseteq \{f(a) \mid a \in S\}$. We define $d' \in \mathcal{D}A$ by

$$
d'(a) = \frac{d(f(a))}{|\{a' \in S \mid f(a') = f(a)\}|}.
$$

Then

$$
\begin{aligned}
\mathcal{D}f(d')(b) &= \sum_{a \in A, f(a)=b} d'(a) && (\text{definition of } \mathcal{D}f) \\
&= \sum_{a \in A, f(a)=b} \frac{d(f(a))}{|\{a' \in S \mid f(a') = f(a)\}|} && (\text{definition of } d') \\
&= \sum_{a \in A, f(a)=b} \frac{d(b)}{|\{a' \in S \mid f(a') = b\}|} = d(b).
\end{aligned}
$$

Now we have

$$(\mathcal{P}_c f \circ \mathsf{Conv})(S)$$

$$= \mathcal{P}_c f(\{\alpha(d) \mid d \in \mathcal{D}A, \mathsf{supp}(d) \subseteq S\}) \qquad \text{(definition of Conv)}$$

$$= \{f(\alpha(d)) \mid d \in \mathcal{D}A, \mathsf{supp}(d) \subseteq S\} \qquad \text{(definition of } \mathcal{P}_c f)$$

$$= \{\beta(\mathcal{D}f(d)) \mid d \in \mathcal{D}A, \mathsf{supp}(d) \subseteq S\} \qquad (f \text{ is affine})$$

$$= \{\beta(d) \mid d \in \mathcal{D}B, \mathsf{supp}(d) \subseteq \{f(a) \mid a \in S\}\} \qquad (2)$$

$$= \mathsf{Conv}(\{f(a) \mid a \in S\}) \qquad \text{(definition of Conv)}$$

$$= (\mathsf{Conv} \circ \mathcal{P}f)(S) \qquad \text{(definition of } \mathcal{P}f). \qquad \square$$

2.4   Automata and Language Semantics

In this section we review the general language semantics for automata with side-effects provided by a monad (see, e.g., [2,14,29]). This categorical framework is the foundation of our language semantics for NPA.

Definition 6. *Given a monad (T, η, μ) in the category of sets, an output set O, and a (finite) alphabet A, a T-automaton is defined by a tuple $(S, s_0, \gamma, \{\tau_a\}_{a \in A})$, where S is the set of* states, $s_0 \in S$ *is the* initial state, $\gamma \colon S \to O$ *is the output function, and $\tau_a \colon S \to TS$ for $a \in A$ are the* transition functions.

This abstract formulation encompasses many standard notions of automata. For instance, we recover deterministic (Moore) automata by letting T be the identity monad; deterministic acceptors are a further specialization where the output set is the set $2 = \{0, 1\}$, with 0 modeling rejecting states and 1 modeling accepting states. If we use the powerset monad, we recover nondeterministic acceptors.

Any T-automaton can be determinized, using a categorical generalization of the powerset construction [29].

Definition 7. *Given a monad (T, η, μ) in the category of sets, an output set O with a T-algebra structure $o \colon TO \to O$, and a (finite) alphabet A, a T-automaton $(S, s_0, \gamma, \{\tau_a\}_{a \in A})$ can be determinized into the deterministic automaton $(TS, s_0', \gamma', \{\tau_a'\}_{a \in A})$ given by $s_0' = \eta(s_0) \in TS$ and*

$$\gamma' \colon TS \to O \qquad\qquad \tau_a' \colon TS \to TS$$
$$\gamma' = o \circ T\gamma \qquad\qquad \tau_a' = \mu \circ T\tau_a.$$

This construction allows us to define the language semantics of any T-automaton as the semantics of its determinization. More formally, we have the following definition.

Definition 8. *Given a monad (T, η, μ) in the category of sets, an output set O with a T-algebra structure $o \colon TO \to O$, and a (finite) alphabet A, the language accepted by a T-automaton $\mathcal{A} = (S, s_0, \gamma, \{\tau_a\}_{a \in A})$ is the function $\mathcal{L}_\mathcal{A} \colon A^* \to O$ given by $\mathcal{L}_\mathcal{A} = (l_\mathcal{A} \circ \eta)(s_0)$, where $l_\mathcal{A} \colon TS \to O^{A^*}$ is defined inductively by*

$$l_\mathcal{A}(s)(\varepsilon) = (o \circ T\gamma)(s) \qquad l_\mathcal{A}(s)(av) = l_\mathcal{A}((\mu \circ T\tau_a)(s))(v).$$

As an example, we recover deterministic probabilistic automata (DPAs) by taking T to be the distribution monad $\mathcal{D}$ and letting the output set be the interval $[0,1]$. That is, a DPA with finite[2] state space S has an output function of type $S \to [0,1]$, and each of its transition functions is of type $S \to \mathcal{D}S$. To give a semantics to such an automaton, we use the usual $\mathcal{D}$-algebra structure $\mathbb{E} \colon \mathcal{D}[0,1] \to [0,1]$ computing the expected weight.

More concretely, the semantics works as follows. Let $(S, s_0, \gamma, \{\tau_a\}_{a \in A})$ be a DPA. At any time while reading a word, we are in a convex combination of states $\sum_{i=1}^{n} p_i s_i$ (equivalently, a distribution over states). The current output is given by evaluating the sum $\sum_{i=1}^{n} p_i \gamma(s_i)$. On reading a symbol $a \in A$, we transition to the convex combination of convex combinations $\sum_{i=1}^{n} p_i \tau_a(s_i)$, say $\sum_{i=1}^{n} p_i \sum_{j=1}^{m_i} q_{i,j} s_{i,j}$, which is collapsed to the final convex combination $\sum_{i=1}^{n} \sum_{j=1}^{m_i} p_i q_{i,j} s_{i,j}$ (again, a distribution over states).

Remark 1. One may wonder if the automaton model would be more expressive if the initial state s_0 in an automaton $(S, s_0, \gamma, \{\tau_a\}_{a \in A})$ would be an element of TS rather than S. This is not the case, since we can always add a new element to S that simulates s_0 by setting its output to $(o \circ T\gamma)(s_0)$ and its transition on $a \in A$ to $(\mu \circ T\tau_a)(s_0)$.

For instance, DPAs allowing a distribution over states as the initial state can be represented by an initial state distribution μ, an output vector γ, and transitions τ_a. In typical presentations, μ and γ are represented as weight vectors over states, and the τ_a are encoded by stochastic matrices.

3   Nondeterministic Probabilistic Automata

We work with an automaton model supporting probabilistic and nondeterministic behaviors, inspired by Segala [28]. On each input letter, the automaton can choose from a finitely generated nonempty convex set of distributions over states. After selecting a distribution, the automaton then transitions to its next state probabilistically. Each state has an output weight in $[0,1]$. The following formalization is an instantiation of Definition 6 with the monad $\mathcal{P}_c\mathcal{D}$.

Definition 9. *A nondeterministic probabilistic automaton (NPA) over a (finite) alphabet A is defined by a tuple $(S, s_0, \gamma, \{\tau_a\}_{a \in A})$, where S is a finite set of states, $s_0 \in S$ is the initial state, $\gamma \colon S \to [0,1]$ is the output function, and $\tau_a \colon S \to \mathcal{P}_c\mathcal{D}S$ are the transition functions indexed by inputs $a \in A$.*

---

[2] All concrete automata considered in this paper will have a finite state space, but this is not required by Definition 6. The distribution monad, for example, does not preserve finite sets in general.

As an example, consider the NPA below.

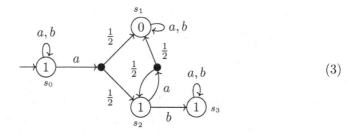

(3)

States are labeled by their direct output (i.e., their weight from γ) while out-going edges represent transitions. Additionally, we write the state name next to each state. We only indicate a set of generators of the convex subset that a state transitions into. If one of these generators is a distribution with nonsingleton support, then a transition into a black dot is depicted, from which the outgoing transitions represent the distribution. Those edges are labeled with probabilities.

Our NPAs recognize weighted languages. The rest of the section is concerned with formally defining this semantics, based on the general framework from Sect. 2.4.

3.1 From Convex Algebra to Language Semantics

To define language semantics for NPAs, we will use the monad structure of $\mathcal{P}_c\mathcal{D}$. To be able to use the semantics from Sect. 2.4, we need to specify a $\mathcal{P}_c\mathcal{D}$-algebra structure $o\colon \mathcal{P}_c\mathcal{D}[0,1] \to [0,1]$. Moreover, our model should naturally coincide with DPAs when transitions make no nondeterministic choices, i.e., when each transition function maps each state to a singleton distribution over states. Thus, we require the $\mathcal{P}_c\mathcal{D}$-algebra o to extend the expected weight function $\mathbb{E}$, making the diagram below commute.

$$
\begin{array}{c}
\mathcal{D}[0,1] \\
{\scriptstyle \{-\}}\downarrow \qquad \searrow^{\mathbb{E}} \\
\mathcal{P}_c\mathcal{D}[0,1] \xrightarrow{\ o\ } [0,1]
\end{array}
\qquad (4)
$$

3.2 Characterizing the Convex Algebra on $[0,1]$

While in principle there could be many different $\mathcal{P}_c\mathcal{D}$-algebras on $[0,1]$ leading to different language semantics for NPAs, we show that (i) each algebra extending the $\mathcal{D}$-algebra on $[0,1]$ is fully determined by a $\mathcal{P}_c$-algebra on $[0,1]$, and (ii) there are exactly two $\mathcal{P}_c$-algebras on $[0,1]$: the map computing the minimum and the map computing the maximum.

Proposition 1. *Any $\mathcal{P}_c\mathcal{D}$-algebra on $[0,1]$ extending $\mathbb{E}\colon \mathcal{D}[0,1] \to [0,1]$ is of the form $\mathcal{P}_c\mathcal{D}[0,1] \xrightarrow{\mathcal{P}_c\mathbb{E}} \mathcal{P}_c[0,1] \xrightarrow{\alpha} [0,1]$, where α is a $\mathcal{P}_c$-algebra.*

Proof. Let $o\colon \mathcal{P}_c\mathcal{D}[0,1] \to [0,1]$ be a $\mathcal{P}_c\mathcal{D}$-algebra extending $\mathbb{E}$. We define

$$\alpha = \mathcal{P}_c[0,1] \xrightarrow{\mathcal{P}_c\delta} \mathcal{P}_c\mathcal{D}[0,1] \xrightarrow{o} [0,1].$$

Indeed, the diagram

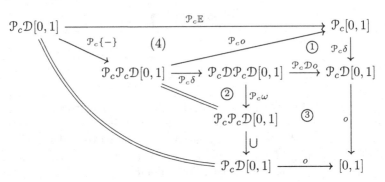

① naturality of δ ② ω is a convex algebra   ③ o is a $\mathcal{P}_c\mathcal{D}$-algebra

commutes, so it only remains to show that α is a $\mathcal{P}_c$-algebra. This can be seen from the commutative diagrams below.

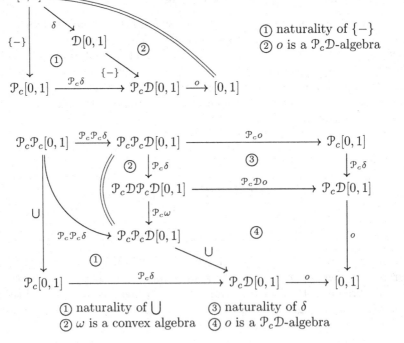

① naturality of $\bigcup$ ③ naturality of δ
② ω is a convex algebra   ④ o is a $\mathcal{P}_c\mathcal{D}$-algebra

□

Proposition 2. *The only $\mathcal{P}_c$-algebras on the convex set $[0,1]$ are* min *and* max.

Proof. Let $\alpha \colon \mathcal{P}_c[0,1] \to [0,1]$ be a $\mathcal{P}_c$-algebra. Then for any $r \in [0,1]$, $\alpha(\{r\}) = r$, and the diagram below must commute.

$$
\begin{array}{ccc}
\mathcal{P}_c\mathcal{P}_c[0,1] & \xrightarrow{\;\mathcal{P}_c\alpha\;} & \mathcal{P}_c[0,1] \\
{\scriptstyle \cup}\Big\downarrow & & \Big\downarrow{\scriptstyle \alpha} \\
\mathcal{P}_c[0,1] & \xrightarrow{\quad \alpha \quad} & [0,1]
\end{array}
\tag{5}
$$

Furthermore, α is an affine map. Since $\mathsf{Conv}(\{\{0\},\{1\},[0,1]\}) = \mathcal{P}_c[0,1]$ by Lemma 1, $\alpha(\{0\}) = 0$, and $\alpha(\{1\}) = 1$, α is completely determined by $\alpha([0,1])$. We now calculate that

$$
\begin{aligned}
\alpha([0,1]) &= \alpha\left(\bigcup\{[0,p] \mid p \in [0,1]\}\right) \\
&= (\alpha \circ \bigcup \circ \mathsf{Conv})(\{\{0\},[0,1]\}) \\
&= (\alpha \circ \mathcal{P}_c\alpha \circ \mathsf{Conv})(\{\{0\},[0,1]\}) && (5) \\
&= (\alpha \circ \mathsf{Conv} \circ \mathcal{P}\alpha)(\{\{0\},[0,1]\}) && (\text{Lemma 2}) \\
&= (\alpha \circ \mathsf{Conv})(\{\alpha(\{0\}),\alpha([0,1])\}) && (\text{definition of } \mathcal{P}\alpha) \\
&= (\alpha \circ \mathsf{Conv})(\{0,\alpha([0,1])\}) \\
&= \alpha([0,\alpha([0,1])]) \\
&= \alpha(\alpha([0,1])[0,1] + (1-\alpha([0,1]))\{0\}) \\
&= \alpha([0,1]) \cdot \alpha([0,1]) + (1-\alpha([0,1])) \cdot \alpha(\{0\}) && (\alpha \text{ is affine}) \\
&= \alpha([0,1])^2 + (1-\alpha([0,1])) \cdot 0 \\
&= \alpha([0,1])^2.
\end{aligned}
$$

Thus, we have either $\alpha([0,1]) = 0$ or $\alpha([0,1]) = 1$. Consider any finitely generated nonempty convex subset $[p,q] \subseteq [0,1]$. If $\alpha([0,1]) = 0$, then Lemma 1 gives

$$
\begin{aligned}
\alpha([p,q]) &= \alpha(p\{1\} + (q-p)[0,1] + (1-q)\{0\}) \\
&= p \cdot \alpha(\{1\}) + (q-p) \cdot \alpha([0,1]) + (1-q) \cdot \alpha(\{0\}) \\
&= p \cdot 1 + (q-p) \cdot 0 + (1-q) \cdot 0 = p = \min([p,q]);
\end{aligned}
$$

if $\alpha([0,1]) = 1$, then

$$
\begin{aligned}
\alpha([p,q]) &= \alpha(p\{1\} + (q-p)[0,1] + (1-q)\{0\}) \\
&= p \cdot \alpha(\{1\}) + (q-p) \cdot \alpha([0,1]) + (1-q) \cdot \alpha(\{0\}) \\
&= p \cdot 1 + (q-p) \cdot 1 + (1-q) \cdot 0 = q = \max([p,q]).
\end{aligned}
$$

We now show that min is an algebra; the case for max is analogous. We have

$$
\min\left(\sum_{i=1}^{n} r_i[p_i, q_i]\right) = \min\left(\left[\sum_{i=1}^{n} r_i \cdot p_i, \sum_{i=1}^{n} r_i \cdot q_i\right]\right)
$$

$$
= \sum_{i=1}^{n} r_i \cdot p_i
$$

$$
= \sum_{i=1}^{n} r_i \cdot \min([p_i, q_i]),
$$

so min is an affine map. Furthermore, clearly $\min(\{r\}) = r$ for all $r \in [0,1]$, and for all $S \in \mathcal{P}_c\mathcal{P}_c[0,1]$,

$$
\min\left(\bigcup S\right) = \min(\{\min(T) \mid T \in S\}) = (\min \circ \mathcal{P}_c\min)(S). \qquad \square
$$

Corollary 1. *The only $\mathcal{P}_c\mathcal{D}$-algebras on $[0,1]$ extending $\mathbb{E}$ are $\mathcal{P}_c\mathcal{D}[0,1] \xrightarrow{\mathcal{P}_c\mathbb{E}} \mathcal{P}_c[0,1] \xrightarrow{\min} [0,1]$ and $\mathcal{P}_c\mathcal{D}[0,1] \xrightarrow{\mathcal{P}_c\mathbb{E}} \mathcal{P}_c[0,1] \xrightarrow{\max} [0,1]$.*

Consider again the NPA (3). Since we can always choose to remain in the initial state, the max semantics assigns 1 to each word for this automaton. The min semantics is more interesting. Consider reading the word aa. On the first a, we transition from s_0 to $\mathsf{Conv}\{s_0, \frac{1}{2}s_1 + \frac{1}{2}s_2\} \in \mathcal{P}_c\mathcal{D}S$. Reading the second a gives

$$
\mathsf{Conv}\left\{\mathsf{Conv}\left\{s_0, \tfrac{1}{2}s_1 + \tfrac{1}{2}s_2\right\}, \tfrac{1}{2}\{s_1\} + \tfrac{1}{2}\left\{\tfrac{1}{2}s_1 + \tfrac{1}{2}s_2\right\}\right\} \in \mathcal{P}_c\mathcal{D}\mathcal{P}_c\mathcal{D}S.
$$

Now we first apply $\mathcal{P}_c\omega$ to eliminate the outer distribution, arriving at

$$
\mathsf{Conv}\left\{\mathsf{Conv}\left\{s_0, \tfrac{1}{2}s_1 + \tfrac{1}{2}s_2\right\}, \left\{\tfrac{3}{4}s_1 + \tfrac{1}{4}s_2\right\}\right\} \in \mathcal{P}_c\mathcal{P}_c\mathcal{D}S.
$$

Taking the union yields

$$
\mathsf{Conv}\left\{s_0, \tfrac{1}{2}s_1 + \tfrac{1}{2}s_2, \tfrac{3}{4}s_1 + \tfrac{1}{4}s_2\right\} \in \mathcal{P}_c\mathcal{D}S,
$$

which leads to the convex subset of distributions over outputs

$$
\mathsf{Conv}\left\{1, \tfrac{1}{2}\cdot 0 + \tfrac{1}{2}\cdot 1, \tfrac{3}{4}\cdot 0 + \tfrac{1}{4}\cdot 1\right\} \in \mathcal{P}_c\mathcal{D}[0,1].
$$

Calculating the expected weights gives $\mathsf{Conv}\{1, \frac{1}{2}, \frac{1}{4}\} \in \mathcal{P}_c[0,1]$, which has a minimum of $\frac{1}{4}$. One can show that on reading any word $u \in A^*$ the automaton outputs 2^{-n}, where n is the length of the longest sequence of a's occurring in u.

The semantics coming from max and min are highly symmetrical; in a sense, they are two representations of the same semantics.[3] Technically, we establish the following relation between the two semantics—this will be useful to avoid repeating proofs twice for each property.

---

[3] The max semantics is perhaps preferable since it recovers standard nondeterministic finite automata when there is no probabilistic choice and the output weights are in $\{0,1\}$, but this is a minor point.

Proposition 3. *Consider an NPA* $\mathcal{A} = (S, s_0, \gamma, \{\tau_a\}_{a \in A})$ *under the* min *semantics. Define* $\gamma' \colon S \to [0,1]$ *by* $\gamma'(s) = 1 - \gamma(s)$, *and consider the NPA* $\mathcal{A}' = (S, s_0, \gamma', \{\tau_a\}_{a \in A})$ *under the* max *semantics. Then* $\mathcal{L}_{\mathcal{A}'}(u) = 1 - \mathcal{L}_{\mathcal{A}}(u)$ *for all* $u \in A^*$.

Proof. We prove a stronger property by induction on u: for all $x \in \mathcal{P}_c \mathcal{D} S$ and $u \in A^*$, we have $l_{\mathcal{A}'}(x)(u) = 1 - l_{\mathcal{A}}(x)(u)$. This is sufficient because $\mathcal{A}$ and $\mathcal{A}'$ have the same initial state. We have

$$l_{\mathcal{A}'}(x)(\varepsilon)$$

$$= (\max \circ \mathcal{P}_c \mathbb{E} \circ \mathcal{P}_c \mathcal{D} \gamma')(x) \qquad \text{(Definition 8)}$$

$$= (\max \circ \mathcal{P}_c \mathbb{E})\left(\left\{\lambda p. \sum_{s \in S, \gamma'(s)=p} d(s) \,\middle|\, d \in x\right\}\right) \qquad \text{(definition of } \mathcal{P}_c \mathcal{D} \gamma')$$

$$= \max\left(\left\{\sum_{p \in [0,1]} p \sum_{s \in S, \gamma'(s)=p} d(s) \,\middle|\, d \in x\right\}\right) \qquad \text{(definition of } \mathcal{P}_c \mathbb{E})$$

$$= \max\left(\left\{\sum_{p \in [0,1]} p \sum_{s \in S, \gamma(s)=1-p} d(s) \,\middle|\, d \in x\right\}\right) \qquad \text{(definition of } \gamma')$$

$$= \max\left(\left\{\sum_{p \in [0,1]} (1-p) \sum_{s \in S, \gamma(s)=p} d(s) \,\middle|\, d \in x\right\}\right)$$

$$= \max\left(\left\{\sum_{p \in [0,1]} (1-p) \cdot \mathcal{D}\gamma(d)(p) \,\middle|\, d \in x\right\}\right)$$

$$= \max\left(\left\{1 - \sum_{p \in [0,1]} p \cdot \mathcal{D}\gamma(d)(p) \,\middle|\, d \in x\right\}\right)$$

$$= 1 - \min\left(\left\{\sum_{p \in [0,1]} p \cdot \mathcal{D}\gamma(d)(p) \,\middle|\, d \in x\right\}\right)$$

$$= 1 - (\min \circ \mathcal{P}_c \mathbb{E})(\{\mathcal{D}\gamma(d) \mid d \in x\}) \qquad \text{(definition of } \mathcal{P}_c \mathbb{E})$$

$$= 1 - (\min \circ \mathcal{P}_c \mathbb{E} \circ \mathcal{P}_c \mathcal{D}\gamma)(x) \qquad \text{(definition of } \mathcal{P}_c \mathcal{D}\gamma')$$

$$= 1 - l_{\mathcal{A}}(x)(\varepsilon) \qquad \text{(Definition 8)}.$$

Furthermore,

$$l_{\mathcal{A}'}(x)(av) = l_{\mathcal{A}'}\left(\left(\bigcup \circ \mathcal{P}_c \omega \circ \mathcal{P}_c \mathcal{D}\tau_a\right)(x)\right)(v) \qquad \text{(Definition 8)}$$

$$= 1 - l_{\mathcal{A}}\left(\left(\bigcup \circ \mathcal{P}_c \omega \circ \mathcal{P}_c \mathcal{D}\tau_a\right)(x)\right)(v) \qquad \text{(induction hypothesis)}$$

$$= 1 - l_{\mathcal{A}}(x)(av) \qquad \text{(Definition 8)}. \qquad \square$$

4   Expressive Power of NPAs

Our convex language semantics for NPAs coincides with the standard semantics for DPAs when all convex sets in the transition functions are singleton sets. In this section, we show that NPAs are in fact strictly more expressive than DPAs. We give two results. First, we exhibit a concrete language over a binary alphabet that is recognizable by a NPA, but not recognizable by any DPA. This argument uses elementary facts about the Hankel matrix, and actually shows that NPAs are strictly more expressive than weighted finite automata (WFAs).

Next, we separate NPAs and DPAs over a unary alphabet. This argument is substantially more technical, relying on deeper results from number theory about linear recurrence sequences.

4.1   Separating NPAs and DPAs: Binary Alphabet

Consider the language $\mathcal{L}_a\colon \{a,b\}^* \to [0,1]$ by $\mathcal{L}_a(u) = 2^{-n}$, where n is the length of the longest sequence of a's occurring in u. Recall that this language is accepted by the NPA (3) using the min algebra.

Theorem 1. *NPAs are more expressive than DPAs. Specifically, there is no DPA, or even WFA, accepting $\mathcal{L}_a$.*

Proof. Assume there exists a WFA accepting $\mathcal{L}_a$, and let $l(u)$ for $u \in \{a,b\}^*$ be the language of the linear combination of states reached after reading the word u. We will show that the languages $l(a^n b)$ for $n \in \mathbb{N}$ are linearly independent. Since the function that assigns to each linear combination of states its accepted language is a linear map, this implies that the set of linear combinations of states of the WFA is a vector space of infinite dimension, and hence the WFA cannot exist.

The proof is by induction on a natural number m. Assume that for all natural numbers $i \leq m$ the languages $l(a^i b)$ are linearly independent. For all $i \leq m$ we have $l(a^i b)(a^m) = 2^{-m}$ and $l(a^i b)(a^{m+1}) = 2^{-m-1}$; however, $l(a^{m+1} b)(a^m) = l(a^{m+1} b)(a^{m+1}) = 2^{-m-1}$. If $l(a^{m+1} b)$ is a linear combination of the languages $l(a^i b)$ for $i \leq m$, then there are constants $c_1, \dots, c_m \in \mathbb{R}$ such that in particular

$$(c_1 + \cdots + c_m)2^{-m} = 2^{-m-1} \qquad \text{and} \qquad (c_1 + \cdots + c_m)2^{-m-1} = 2^{-m-1}.$$

These equations cannot be satisfied. Therefore, for all natural numbers $i \leq m+1$ the languages $l(a^i b)$ are linearly independent. We conclude by induction that for all $m \in \mathbb{N}$ the languages $l(a^i b)$ for $i \leq m$ are linearly independent, which implies that all languages $l(a^n b)$ for $n \in \mathbb{N}$ are linearly independent. $\qquad \square$

A similar argument works for NPAs under the max algebra semantics—one can easily repeat the argument in the above theorem for the language accepted by the NPA resulting from applying Proposition 3 to the NPA (3).

4.2 Separating NPAs and DPAs: Unary Alphabet

We now turn to the unary case. A weighted language over a unary alphabet can be represented by a sequence $\langle u_i \rangle = u_0, u_1, \ldots$ of real numbers. We will give such a language that is recognizable by a NPA but not recognizable by any WFA (and in particular, any DPA) using results on *linear recurrence sequences*, an established tool for studying unary weighted languages.

We begin with some mathematical preliminaries. A sequence of real numbers $\langle u_i \rangle$ is a *linear recurrence sequence* (LRS) if for some integer $k \in \mathbb{N}$ (the *order*), constants $u_0, \ldots, u_{k-1} \in \mathbb{R}$ (the *initial conditions*), and coefficients $b_0, \ldots, b_{k-1} \in \mathbb{R}$, we have

$$u_{n+k} = b_{k-1} u_{n-1} + \cdots + b_0 u_n$$

for every $n \in \mathbb{N}$. A well-known example of an LRS is the *Fibonacci sequence*, an order-2 LRS satisfying the recurrence $f_{n+2} = f_{n+1} + f_n$. Another example of an LRS is any constant sequence, i.e., $\langle u_i \rangle$ with $u_i = c$ for all i.

Linear recurrence sequences are closed under linear combinations: for any two LRS $\langle u_i \rangle, \langle v_i \rangle$ and constants $\alpha, \beta \in \mathbb{R}$, the sequence $\langle \alpha u_i + \beta v_i \rangle$ is again an LRS (possibly of larger order). We will use one important theorem about LRSs. See the monograph by Everest et al. [11] for details.

Theorem 2 Skolem-Mahler-Lech). *If $\langle u_i \rangle$ is an LRS, then its zero set $\{i \in \mathbb{N} \mid u_i = 0\}$ is the union of a finite set along with finitely many arithmetic progressions (i.e., sets of the form $\{p + kn \mid n \in \mathbb{N}\}$ with $k \neq 0$).*

This is a celebrated result in number theory and not at all easy to prove. To make the connection to probabilistic and weighted automata, we will use two results. The first proposition follows from the Cayley-Hamilton Theorem.

Proposition 4 (see, e.g., [21]). *Let $\mathcal{L}$ be a weighted unary language recognizable by a weighted automaton W. Then the sequence of weights $\langle u_i \rangle$ with $u_i = \mathcal{L}(a^i)$ is an LRS, where the order is at most the number of states in W.*

While not every LRS can be recognized by a DPA, it is known that DPAs can recognize a weighted language encoding the sign of a given LRS.

Theorem 3 (Akshay et al. [1, Theorem 3, Corollary 4]). *Given any LRS $\langle u_i \rangle$, there exists a stochastic matrix M such that*

$$u_n \geq 0 \iff u^T M^n v \geq 1/4$$

for all n, where $u = (1, 0, \ldots, 0)$ and $v = (0, 1, 0, \ldots, 0)$. Equality holds on the left if and only if it holds on the right. The language $\mathcal{L}(a^n) = u^T M^n v$ is recognizable by a DPA with input vector u, output vector v, and transition matrix M (Remark 1). If the LRS is rational, M can be taken to be rational as well.

We are now ready to separate NPAs and WFAs over a unary alphabet.

Theorem 4. *There is a language over a unary alphabet that is recognizable by an NPA but not by any WFA (and in particular any DPA).*

Proof. We will work in the complex numbers $\mathbb{C}$, with i being the positive square root of -1 as usual. Let $a, b \in \mathbb{Q}$ be nonzero such that $z \triangleq a + bi$ is on the unit circle in $\mathbb{C}$, for instance $a = 3/5, b = 4/5$ so that $|a + bi| = a^2 + b^2 = 1$. Let $\bar{z} = a - bi$ denote the complex conjugate of z and let $\mathrm{Re}(z)$ denote the real part of a complex number. It is possible to show that z is not a root of unity, i.e., $z^k \neq 1$ for all $k \in \mathbb{N}$. Let $\langle x_n \rangle$ be the sequence $x_n \triangleq (z^n + \bar{z}^n)/2 = \mathrm{Re}(z^n)$. By direct calculation, this sequence has imaginary part zero and satisfies the recurrence·

$$x_{n+2} = 2ax_{n+1} - (a^2 + b^2)x_n$$

with $x_0 = 1$ and $x_1 = a$, so $\langle x_n \rangle$ is an order-2 rational LRS. By Theorem 3, there exists a stochastic matrix M and non-negative vectors u, v such that

$$x_n \geq 0 \iff u^T M^n v \geq 1/4$$

for all n, where equality holds on the left if and only if equality holds on the right. Note that $x_n = \mathrm{Re}(z^n) \neq 0$ since z is not a root of unity (so in particular $z^n \neq \pm i$), hence equality never holds on the right. Letting $\langle y_n \rangle$ be the sequence $y_n = u^T M^n v$, the (unary) language with weights $\langle y_n \rangle$ is recognized by the DPA with input u, output v and transition matrix M. Furthermore, the constant sequence $\langle 1/4 \rangle$ is recognizable by a DPA.

Now we define a sequence $\langle w_n \rangle$ with $w_n = \max(y_n, 1/4)$. Since $\langle y_n \rangle$ and $\langle 1/4 \rangle$ are recognizable by DPAs, $\langle w_n \rangle$ is recognizable by an NPA whose initial state nondeterministically chooses between the two DPAs (see Remark 1). Suppose for the sake of contradiction that it is also recognizable by a WFA. Then $\langle w_n \rangle$ is an LRS (by Proposition 4) and hence so is $\langle t_n \rangle$ with $t_n = w_n - y_n$. If we now consider the zero set

$$
\begin{aligned}
S &= \{n \in \mathbb{N} \mid t_n = 0\} \\
&= \{n \in \mathbb{N} \mid y_n > 1/4\} &&(y_n \neq 1/4) \\
&= \{n \in \mathbb{N} \mid x_n > 0\} &&(\text{Theorem 3}) \\
&= \{n \in \mathbb{N} \mid \mathrm{Re}(z^n) > 0\} &&(\text{by definition}),
\end{aligned}
$$

Theorem 2 implies that S is the union of a finite set of indices and along with a finite number of arithmetic progressions. Note that S cannot be finite—in the last line, z^n is dense in the unit circle since z is not a root of unity—so there must be at least one arithmetic progression $\{p + kn \mid n \in \mathbb{N}\}$. Letting $\langle r_n \rangle$ be

$$r_n = (z^p \cdot (z^k)^n + \bar{z}^p \cdot (\bar{z}^k)^n)/2 = \mathrm{Re}(z^p \cdot (z^k)^n) = x_{p+kn},$$

we have $p + kn \in S$, so $r_n > 0$ for all $n \in \mathbb{N}$, but this is impossible since it is dense in $[-1, 1]$ (because z^k is not a root of unity for $k \neq 0$, so $z^p \cdot (z^k)^n$ is dense in the unit circle).

Hence, the unary weighted language $\langle w_n \rangle$ can be recognized by an NPA but not by a WFA.   □

5   Checking Language Equivalence of NPAs

Now that we have a coalgebraic model for NPA, a natural question is whether there is a procedure to check language equivalence of NPAs. We will show that language equivalence of NPAs is undecidable by reduction from the *threshold problem* on DPAs. Nevertheless, we can define a metric on the set of languages recognized by NPAs to measure their similarity. While this metric cannot be computed exactly, it can be approximated to any given precision in finite time.

5.1   Undecidability and Hardness

Theorem 5. *Equivalence of NPAs is undecidable when $|A| \geq 2$ and the $\mathcal{P}_c\mathcal{D}$-algebra on $[0,1]$ extends the usual $\mathcal{D}$-algebra on $[0,1]$.*

Proof. Let X be a DPA and $\kappa \in [0,1]$. We define NPAs Y and Z as follows:

Here the node labeled X represents a copy of the automaton X—the transition into X goes into the initial state of X. Note that the edges are labeled by A to indicate a transition for every element of A. We see that $\mathcal{L}_Y(\varepsilon) = \kappa = \mathcal{L}_Z(\varepsilon)$ and (for α either min or max, as follows from Corollary 1)

$$\mathcal{L}_Y(av) = (\alpha \circ \mathsf{Conv})(\{\kappa, \mathcal{L}_X(v)\}) \qquad \mathcal{L}_Z(av) = \kappa.$$

Thus, if $\alpha = $ min, then $\mathcal{L}_Y = \mathcal{L}_Z$ if and only if $\mathcal{L}_X(v) \geq \kappa$ for all $v \in A^*$; if $\alpha = $ max, then $\mathcal{L}_Y = \mathcal{L}_Z$ if and only if $\mathcal{L}_X(v) \leq \kappa$ for all $v \in A^*$. Both of these threshold problems are undecidable for alphabets of size at least 2 [5,12,22]. □

The situation for automata over unary alphabets is more subtle; in particular, the threshold problem is not known to be undecidable in this case. However, there is a reduction to a long-standing open problem on LRSs.

Given an LRS $\langle u_i \rangle$, the *Positivity* problem is to decide whether u_i is nonnegative for all $i \in \mathbb{N}$ (see, e.g., [21]). While the decidability of this problem has remained open for more than 80 years, it is known that a decision procedure for Positivity would necessarily entail breakthroughs in open problems in number theory. That is, it would give an algorithm to compute the *homogeneous Diophantine approximation type* for a class of transcendental numbers [21]. Furthermore, the Positivity problem can be reduced to the threshold problem on unary probabilistic automata. Putting everything together, we have the following reduction.

Corollary 2. *The Positivity problem for linear recurrence sequences can be reduced to the equivalence problem of NPAs over a unary alphabet.*

Proof. The construction in Theorem 5 shows that the lesser-than threshold problem can be reduced to the equivalence problem for NPAs with max semantics, so we show that Positivity can be reduced to the lesser-than threshold problem on probabilistic automata with a unary alphabet. Given any rational LRS $\langle u_i \rangle$, clearly $\langle -u_i \rangle$ is an LRS as well, so by Theorem 3 there exists a rational stochastic matrix M such that

$$-u_n > 0 \iff u^T M^n v > 1/4$$

for all n, where $u = (1, 0, \ldots, 0)$ and $v = (0, 1, 0, \ldots, 0)$. Taking M to be the transition matrix, v to be the input vector, and u to be the output vector, the probabilistic automaton corresponding to the right-hand side is a nonsatisfying instance to the threshold problem with threshold $\leq 1/4$ if and only if the $\langle u_i \rangle$ is a satisfying instance of the Positivity problem.

Applying Proposition 3 yields an analogous reduction from Positivity to the equivalence problem of NPAs with min semantics.   □

5.2   Checking Approximate Equivalence

The previous negative results show that deciding exact equivalence of NPAs is computationally intractable (or at least very difficult, for a unary alphabet). A natural question is whether we might be able to check approximate equivalence. In this section, we show how to approximate a metric on weighted languages. Our metric will be *discounted*—differences in weights of longer words will contribute less to the metric than differences in weights of shorter words.

Given $c \in [0, 1)$ and two weighted languages $l_1, l_2 \colon A^* \to [0, 1]$, we define

$$d_c(l_1, l_2) = \sum_{u \in A^*} |l_1(u) - l_2(u)| \cdot \left(\frac{c}{|A|}\right)^{|u|}.$$

Suppose that l_1 and l_2 are recognized by given NPAs. Since $d_c(l_1, l_2) = 0$ if and only if the languages (and automata) are equivalent, we cannot hope to compute the metric exactly. We can, however, compute the weight of any finite word under l_1 and l_2. Combined with the discounting in the metric, we can approximate this metric d_c within any desired (nonzero) error.

Theorem 6. *There is a procedure that given $c \in [0, 1)$, $\kappa > 0$, and computable functions $l_1, l_2 \colon A^* \to [0, 1]$ outputs $x \in \mathbb{R}_+$ such that $|d_c(l_1, l_2) - x| \leq \kappa$.*

Proof. Let $n = \lceil \log_c((1 - c) \cdot \kappa) \rceil \in \mathbb{N}$ and define

$$x = \sum_{u \in A^*, |u| < n} |l_1(u) - l_2(u)| \cdot \left(\frac{c}{|A|}\right)^{|u|}.$$

This sum is over a finite set of finite strings and the weights of $l_1(u)$ and $l_2(u)$ can all be computed exactly, so x is computable as well. Now we can bound

$$|d_c(l_1, l_2) - x| = \sum_{u \in A^*, |u| \geq n} |l_1(u) - l_2(u)| \cdot \left(\frac{c}{|A|}\right)^{|u|} \leq \sum_{u \in A^*, |u| \geq n} \left(\frac{c}{|A|}\right)^{|u|}$$

$$= \sum_{i \in \mathbb{N}, i \geq n} |A|^i \cdot \left(\frac{c}{|A|}\right)^i = \sum_{i \in \mathbb{N}, i \geq n} c^i = \frac{c^n}{1 - c} \leq \kappa,$$

where the last step is because $n \geq \log_c((1 - c) \cdot \kappa)$, and thus $c^n \leq (1 - c) \cdot \kappa$, noting that $c \in [0, 1)$ and $\kappa > 0$. $\qquad \square$

We leave approximating other metrics on weighted languages—especially nondiscounted metrics—as an intriguing open question.

6 Conclusions

We have defined a novel probabilistic language semantics for nondeterministic probabilistic automata (NPAs). We proved that NPAs are strictly more expressive than deterministic probabilistic automata, and that exact equivalence is undecidable. We have shown how to approximate the equivalence question to arbitrary precision using a discounted metric. There are two directions for future work that we would like to explore. First, it would be interesting to see if different metrics can be defined on probabilistic languages and what approximate equivalence procedures they give rise to. Second, we would like to explore whether we can extend logical characterization results in the style of Panangaden et al. [10,13]. Finally, it would be interesting to investigate the class of languages recognizable by our NPAs.

Related Work. There are many papers studying probabilitic automata and variants thereof. The work in our paper is closest to the work of Segala [28] in that our automaton model has both nondeterminism and probabilistic choice. However, we enrich the states with an output weight that is used in the definition of the language semantics. Our language semantics is coarser than probabilistic (convex) bisimilarity [28] and bisimilarity on distributions [17]. In fact, in contrast to the hardness and undecidability results we proved for probabilistic language equivalence, bisimilarity on distributions can be shown to be decidable [17] with the help of convexity. The techniques we use in defining the semantics are closely related to the recent categorical understanding of bisimilarity on distributions [7].

Acknowledgements. We thank Nathanaël Fijalkow and the anonymous reviewers for their useful suggestions to improve the paper. The semantics studied in this paper has been brought to our attention in personal communication by Filippo Bonchi, Ana Sokolova, and Valeria Vignudelli. Their interest in this semantics is mostly motivated by its relationship with trace semantics previously proposed in the literature. This is the subject of a forthcoming publication [8].

References

1. Akshay, S., Antonopoulos, T., Ouaknine, J., Worrell, J.: Reachability problems for Markov chains. Inf. Process. Lett. **115**(2), 155–158 (2015). https://doi.org/10.1016/j.ipl.2014.08.013
2. Arbib, M.A., Manes, E.G.: Fuzzy machines in a category. Bull. Aust. Math. Soc. **13**(2), 169–210 (1975). https://doi.org/10.1017/s0004972700024412
3. Balle, B., Castro, J., Gavaldà, R.: Adaptively learning probabilistic deterministic automata from data streams. Mach. Learn. **96**(1–2), 99–127 (2014). https://doi.org/10.1007/s10994-013-5408-x
4. Bernardo, M., De Nicola, R., Loreti, M.: Revisiting trace and testing equivalences for nondeterministic and probabilistic processes. Log. Methods Comput. Sci. 10(1), Article no. 16 (2014). https://doi.org/10.2168/lmcs-10(1:16)2014
5. Blondel, V.D., Canterini, V.: Undecidable problems for probabilistic automata of fixed dimension. Theory Comput. Syst. **36**, 231–245 (2003). https://doi.org/10.1007/s00224-003-1061-2
6. Bonchi, F., Pous, D.: Hacking nondeterminism with induction and coinduction. Commun. ACM **58**(2), 87–95 (2015). https://doi.org/10.1145/2713167
7. Bonchi, F., Silva, A., Sokolova, A.: The power of convex algebras. In: Meyer, R., Nestmann, U. (eds.) Proceedings of 28th International Conference on Concurrency Theory, CONCUR 2017, Berlin, September 2017. Leibniz International Proceedings in Informatics, vol. 85, Article no. 23. Dagstuhl Publishing, Saarbrücken/Wadern (2017). https://doi.org/10.4230/lipics.concur.2017.23
8. Bonchi, F., Sokolova, A., Vignudelli, V.: Trace semantics for nondeterministic probabilistic automata via determinization. arXiv preprint 1808.00923 (2018). https://arxiv.org/abs/1808.00923
9. Deng, Y., van Glabbeek, R.J., Hennessy, M., Morgan, C.: Testing finitary probabilistic processes. In: Bravetti, M., Zavattaro, G. (eds.) CONCUR 2009. LNCS, vol. 5710, pp. 274–288. Springer, Heidelberg (2009). https://doi.org/10.1007/978-3-642-04081-8_19
10. Desharnais, J., Edalat, A., Panangaden, P.: A logical characterization of bisimulation for labeled Markov processes. In: Proceedings of 13th Annual IEEE Symposium on Logic in Computer Science. LICS 1998, Indianapolis, IN, June 1998, pp. 478–487. IEEE CS Press, Washington, D.C. (1998). https://doi.org/10.1109/lics.1998.705681
11. Everest, G., van der Poorten, A.J., Shparlinski, I.E., Ward, T.: Recurrence Sequences, Mathematical surveys and monographs, vol. 104. American Mathematical Society, Providence (2003)
12. Fijalkow, N.: Undecidability results for probabilistic automata. ACM SIGLOG News **4**(4), 10–17 (2017). https://doi.org/10.1145/3157831.3157833
13. Fijalkow, N., Klin, B., Panangaden, P.: Expressiveness of probabilistic modal logics, revisited. In: Chatzigiannakis, Y., Indyk, P., Kuhn, F., Muscholl, A. (eds.) Proc. of 44th Int. Coll. on Automata, Languages and Programming, ICALP 2017, Warsaw, July 2017. Leibniz International Proceedings in Informatics, vol. 80, Article no. 105. Dagstuhl Publishing, Saarbrücken/Wadern (2017). https://doi.org/10.4230/lipics.icalp.2017.105
14. Goncharov, S., Milius, S., Silva, A.: Towards a coalgebraic Chomsky hierarchy (extended abstract). In: Díaz, J., Lanese, I., Sangiorgi, D. (eds.) TCS 2014. LNCS, vol. 8705, pp. 265–280. Springer, Heidelberg (2014). https://doi.org/10.1007/978-3-662-44602-7_21

15. Henzinger, T.A.: Quantitative reactive modeling and verification. Comput. Sci. Res. Dev. **28**(4), 331–344 (2013). https://doi.org/10.1007/s00450-013-0251-7

16. Hermanns, H., Katoen, J.: The how and why of interactive Markov chains. In: de Boer, F.S., Bonsangue, M.M., Hallerstede, S., Leuschel, M. (eds.) FMCO 2009. LNCS, vol. 6286, pp. 311–337. Springer, Heidelberg (2010). https://doi.org/10. 1007/978-3-642-17071-3_16

17. Hermanns, H., Krcál, J., Kretínský, J.: Probabilistic bisimulation: naturally on distributions. In: Baldan, P., Gorla, D. (eds.) CONCUR 2014. LNCS, vol. 8704, pp. 249–265. Springer, Heidelberg (2014). https://doi.org/10.1007/978-3-662-44584-6_18

18. Kozen, D.: Semantics of probabilistic programs. In: Proceedings of 20th Annual Symposium on Foundations of Computer Science, FOCS 1979, San Juan, PR, October 1979, pp. 101–114. IEEE CS Press, Washington, D.C. (1979). https://doi.org/10.1109/sfcs.1979.38

19. Kwiatkowska, M., Norman, G., Parker, D.: PRISM 4.0: verification of probabilistic real-time systems. In: Gopalakrishnan, G., Qadeer, S. (eds.) CAV 2011. LNCS, vol. 6806, pp. 585–591. Springer, Heidelberg (2011). https://doi.org/10.1007/978-3-642-22110-1_47

20. Legay, A., Murawski, A.S., Ouaknine, J., Worrell, J.: On automated verification of probabilistic programs. In: Ramakrishnan, C.R., Rehof, J. (eds.) TACAS 2008. LNCS, vol. 4963, pp. 173–187. Springer, Heidelberg (2008). https://doi.org/10. 1007/978-3-540-78800-3_13

21. Ouaknine, J., Worrell, J.: Positivity problems for low-order linear recurrence sequences. In: Proceedings of 25th Annual ACM-SIAM Symposium on Discrete Algorithms, SODA 2014, Portland, OR, January 2014, pp. 366–379. SIAM (2014). https://doi.org/10.1137/1.9781611973402

22. Paz, A.: Introduction to Probabilistic Automata. Academic Press, New York/London (1971). https://doi.org/10.1016/c2013-0-11297-4

23. Rabin, M.O.: Probabilistic automata. Inf. Control **6**(3), 230–245 (1963). https://doi.org/10.1016/s0019-9958(63)90290-0

24. Rabin, M.O.: Probabilistic algorithms. In: Traub, J.F. (ed.) Algorithms and Complexity: New Directions and Recent Results, pp. 21–39. Academic Press, New York (1976)

25. Rabin, M.O.: N-process mutual exclusion with bounded waiting by $4 \log_2 N$-valued shared variable. J. Comput. Syst. Sci. **25**(1), 66–75 (1982). https://doi.org/10. 1016/0022-0000(82)90010-1

26. Ron, D., Singer, Y., Tishby, N.: The power of amnesia: learning probabilistic automata with variable memory length. Mach. Learn. **25**(2), 117–149 (1996). https://doi.org/10.1023/a:1026490906255

27. Sassone, V., Nielsen, M., Winskel, G.: Models for concurrency: towards a classification. Theor. Comput. Sci. **170**(1–2), 297–348 (1996). https://doi.org/10.1016/s0304-3975(96)80710-9

28. Segala, R.: Modeling and verification of randomized distributed real-time systems. Ph.D. thesis, Massachusetts Institute of Technology, Cambridge (1995)

29. Silva, A., Bonchi, F., Bonsangue, M.M., Rutten, J.J.M.M.: Generalizing determinization from automata to coalgebras. Log. Methods Comput. Sci. 9(1), Article no. 9 (2013). https://doi.org/10.2168/lmcs-9(1:9)2013

30. Swaminathan, M., Katoen, J.P., Olderog, E.R.: Layered reasoning for randomized distributed algorithms. Form. Asp. Comput. **24**(4), 477–496 (2012). https://doi.org/10.1007/s00165-012-0231-x
31. Vardi, M.Y.: Branching vs. linear time: final showdown. In: Margaria, T., Yi, W. (eds.) TACAS 2001. LNCS, vol. 2031, pp. 1–22. Springer, Heidelberg (2001)
32. Vignudelli, V.: Behavioral equivalences for higher-order languages with probabilities. Ph.D. thesis, Univ. di Bologna (2017)

Fast Computations on Ordered Nominal Sets

David Venhoek, Joshua Moerman, and Jurriaan Rot$^{(\boxtimes)}$

Institute for Computing and Information Sciences, Radboud Universiteit,
Postbus 9010, 6500 GL Nijmegen, The Netherlands
david@venhoek.nl, {joshua.moerman,jrot}@cs.ru.nl

Abstract. We show how to compute efficiently with nominal sets over the total order symmetry, by developing a direct representation of such nominal sets and basic constructions thereon. In contrast to previous approaches, we work directly at the level of orbits, which allows for an accurate complexity analysis. The approach is implemented as the library ONS (Ordered Nominal Sets).

Our main motivation is nominal automata, which are models for recognising languages over infinite alphabets. We evaluate ONS in two applications: minimisation of automata and active automata learning. In both cases, ONS is competitive compared to existing implementations and outperforms them for certain classes of inputs.

1 Introduction

Automata over infinite alphabets are natural models for programs with unbounded data domains. Such automata, often formalised as *register automata*, are applied in modelling and analysis of communication protocols, hardware, and software systems (see [4, 10, 15, 16, 22, 26] and references therein). Typical infinite alphabets include sequence numbers, timestamps, and identifiers. This means one can model data flow in such automata beside the basic control flow provided by ordinary automata. Recently, it has been shown in a series of papers that such models are amenable to learning [1, 6, 7, 11, 21, 29] with the verification of (closed source) TCP implementations as a prominent example [13].

A foundational approach to infinite alphabets is provided by the notion of *nominal set*, originally introduced in computer science as an elegant formalism for name binding [14, 25]. Nominal sets have been used in a variety of applications in semantics, computation, and concurrency theory (see [24] for an overview). Bojańczyk et al. introduce *nominal automata*, which allow one to model languages over infinite alphabets with different symmetries [4]. Their results are parametric in the structure of the data values. Important examples of data domains are ordered data values (e.g., timestamps) and data values that can only be compared for equality (e.g., identifiers). In both data domains, nominal automata and register automata are equally expressive [4].

Important for applications of nominal sets and automata are implementations. A couple of tools exist to compute with nominal sets. Notably, Nλ [17]

© Springer Nature Switzerland AG 2018
B. Fischer and T. Uustalu (Eds.): ICTAC 2018, LNCS 11187, pp. 493–512, 2018.
https://doi.org/10.1007/978-3-030-02508-3_26

and LOIS [18, 19] provide a general purpose programming language to manipulate infinite sets.[1] Both tools are based on SMT solvers and use logical formulas to represent the infinite sets. These implementations are very flexible, and the SMT solver does most of the heavy lifting, which makes the implementations themselves relatively straightforward. Unfortunately, this comes at a cost as SMT solving is in general PSPACE-hard. Since the formulas used to describe sets tend to grow as more calculations are done, running times can become unpredictable.

In the current paper, we use a direct representation, based on symmetries and orbits, to represent nominal sets. We focus on the *total order symmetry*, where data values are rational numbers and can be compared for their order. Nominal automata over the total order symmetry are more expressive than automata over the equality symmetry (i.e., traditional register automata [16]). A key insight is that the representation of nominal sets from [4] becomes rather simple in the total order symmetry; each orbit is presented solely by a natural number, intuitively representing the number of variables or registers.

Our main contributions include the following.

- We develop the *representation theory* of nominal sets over the total order symmetry. We give concrete representations of nominal sets, their products, and equivariant maps.
- We provide *time complexity bounds* for operations on nominal sets such as intersections and membership. Using those results we give the time complexity of Moore's minimisation algorithm (generalised to nominal automata) and prove that it is polynomial in the number of orbits.
- Using the representation theory, we are able to *implement nominal sets in a C++ library* ONS. The library includes all the results from the representation theory (sets, products, and maps).
- We *evaluate the performance* of ONS and compare it to Nλ and LOIS, using two algorithms on nominal automata: minimisation [5] and automata learning [21]. We use randomly generated automata as well as concrete, logically structured models such as FIFO queues. For random automata, our methods are drastically faster than the other tools. On the other hand, LOIS and Nλ are faster in minimising the structured automata as they exploit their logical structure. In automata learning, the logical structure is not available a-priori, and ONS is faster in most cases.

The structure of the paper is as follows. Section 2 contains background on nominal sets and their representation. Section 3 describes the concrete representation of nominal sets, equivariant maps and products in the total order symmetry. Section 4 describes the implementation ONS with complexity results, and Sect. 5 the evaluation of ONS on algorithms for nominal automata. Related work is discussed in Sect. 6, and future work in Sect. 7.

---

[1] Other implementations of nominal techniques that are less directly related to our setting (Mihda, Fresh OCaml, and Nominal Isabelle) are discussed in Sect. 6.

2   Nominal Sets

Nominal sets are infinite sets that carry certain symmetries, allowing a finite representation in many interesting cases. We recall their formalisation in terms of group actions, following [4,24], to which we refer for an extensive introduction.

Group Actions. Let G be a group and X be a set. A *(right) G-action* is a function $\cdot \colon X \times G \to X$ satisfying $x \cdot 1 = x$ and $(x \cdot g) \cdot h = x \cdot (gh)$ for all $x \in X$ and $g, h \in G$. A set X with a G-action is called a *G-set* and we often write xg instead of $x \cdot g$. The *orbit* of an element $x \in X$ is the set $\{xg \mid g \in G\}$. A G-set is always a disjoint union of its orbits (in other words, the orbits partition the set). We say that X is *orbit-finite* if it has finitely many orbits, and we denote the number of orbits by $N(X)$.

A map $f \colon X \to Y$ between G-sets is called *equivariant* if it preserves the group action, i.e., for all $x \in X$ and $g \in G$ we have $f(x)g = f(xg)$. If an equivariant map f is bijective, then f is an *isomorphism* and we write $X \cong Y$. A subset $Y \subseteq X$ is equivariant if the corresponding inclusion map is equivariant. The *product* of two G-sets X and Y is given by the Cartesian product $X \times Y$ with the pointwise group action on it, i.e., $(x, y)g = (xg, yg)$. Union and intersection of X and Y are well-defined if the two actions agree on their common elements.

Nominal Sets. A *data symmetry* is a pair $(\mathcal{D}, G)$ where $\mathcal{D}$ is a set and G is a subgroup of $\mathrm{Sym}(\mathcal{D})$, the group of bijections on $\mathcal{D}$. Note that the group G naturally acts on $\mathcal{D}$ by defining $xg = g(x)$. In the most studied instance, called the *equality symmetry*, $\mathcal{D}$ is a countably infinite set and $G = \mathrm{Sym}(\mathcal{D})$. In this paper, we will mostly focus on the *total order symmetry* given by $\mathcal{D} = \mathbb{Q}$ and $G = \{\pi \mid \pi \in \mathrm{Sym}(\mathbb{Q}), \pi \text{ is monotone}\}$.

Let $(\mathcal{D}, G)$ be a data symmetry and X be a G-set. A set of data values $S \subseteq \mathcal{D}$ is called a *support* of an element $x \in X$ if for all $g \in G$ with $\forall s \in S : sg = s$ we have $xg = x$. A G-set X is called *nominal* if every element $x \in X$ has a finite support.

Example 1. We list several examples for the total order symmetry. The set $\mathbb{Q}^2$ is nominal as each element $(q_1, q_2) \in \mathbb{Q}^2$ has the finite set $\{q_1, q_2\}$ as its support. The set has the following three orbits: $\{(q_1, q_2) \mid q_1 < q_2\}$, $\{(q_1, q_2) \mid q_1 > q_2\}$ and $\{(q_1, q_2) \mid q_1 = q_2\}$.

For a set X, the set of all subsets of size $n \in \mathbb{N}$ is denoted by $\mathcal{P}_n(X) = \{Y \subseteq X \mid \#Y = n\}$. The set $\mathcal{P}_n(\mathbb{Q})$ is a single-orbit nominal set for each n, with the action defined by direct image: $Yg = \{yg \mid y \in Y\}$. The group of monotone bijections also acts by direct image on the full power set $\mathcal{P}(\mathbb{Q})$, but this is *not* a nominal set. For instance, the set $\mathbb{Z} \in \mathcal{P}(\mathbb{Q})$ of integers has no finite support.

If $S \subseteq \mathcal{D}$ is a support of an element $x \in X$, then any set $S' \subseteq \mathcal{D}$ such that $S \subseteq S'$ is also a support of x. A set $S \subseteq \mathcal{D}$ is a *least support* of $x \in X$ if it is a support of x and $S \subseteq S'$ for any support S' of x. The existence of least supports is crucial for representing orbits. Unfortunately, even when elements have a finite support, in general they do not always have a least support. A data symmetry

$(\mathcal{D}, G)$ is said to *admit least supports* if every element of every nominal set has a least support. Both the equality and the total order symmetry admit least supports. (See [4] for other (counter)examples of data symmetries admitting least supports.) Having least supports is useful for a finite representation.

Given a nominal set X, the size of the least support of an element $x \in X$ is denoted by $\dim(x)$, the *dimension* of x. We note that all elements in the orbit of x have the same dimension. For an orbit-finite nominal set X, we define $\dim(X) = \max\{\dim(x) \mid x \in X\}$. For a single-orbit set O, observe that $\dim(O) = \dim(x)$ where x is any element $x \in O$.

2.1   Representing Nominal Orbits

We represent nominal sets as collections of single orbits. The finite representation of single orbits is based on the theory of [4], which uses the technical notions of *restriction* and *extension*. We only briefly report their definitions here. However, the reader can safely move to the concrete representation theory in Sect. 3 with only a superficial understanding of Theorem 2 below.

The *restriction* of an element $\pi \in G$ to a subset $C \subseteq \mathcal{D}$, written as $\pi|_C$, is the restriction of the function $\pi : \mathcal{D} \to \mathcal{D}$ to the domain C. The restriction of a group G to a subset $C \subseteq \mathcal{D}$ is defined as $G|_C = \{\pi|_C \mid \pi \in G, C\pi = C\}$. The *extension* of a subgroup $S \leq G|_C$ is defined as $\mathrm{ext}_G(S) = \{\pi \in G \mid \pi|_C \in S\}$. For $C \subseteq \mathcal{D}$ and $S \leq G|_C$, define $[C, S]^{ec} = \{\{sg \mid s \in \mathrm{ext}_G(S)\} \mid g \in G\}$, i.e., the set of right cosets of $\mathrm{ext}_G(S)$ in G. Then $[C, S]^{ec}$ is a single-orbit nominal set.

Using the above, we can formulate the representation theory from [4] that we will use in the current paper. This gives a finite description for all single-orbit nominal sets X, namely a finite set C together with some of its symmetries.

Theorem 2. *Let X be a single-orbit nominal set for a data symmetry $(\mathcal{D}, G)$ that admits least supports and let $C \subseteq \mathcal{D}$ be the least support of some element $x \in X$. Then there exists a subgroup $S \leq G|_C$ such that $X \cong [C, S]^{ec}$.*

The proof [4] uses a bit of category theory: it establishes an equivalence of categories between single-orbit sets and the pairs (C, S). We will not use the language of category theory much in order to keep the paper self-contained.

3   Representation in the Total Order Symmetry

This section develops a concrete representation of nominal sets over the total order symmetry, as well as their equivariant maps and products. It is based on the abstract representation theory from Sect. 2.1. From now on, by *nominal set* we always refer to a nominal set over the total order symmetry. Hence, our data domain is $\mathbb{Q}$ and we take G to be the group of monotone bijections.

3.1   Orbits and Nominal Sets

From the representation in Sect. 2.1, we find that any single-orbit set X can be represented as a tuple (C, S). Our first observation is that the finite group of 'local symmetries', S, in this representation is always trivial, i.e., $S = I$, where $I = \{1\}$ is the trivial group. This follows from the following lemma and $S \leq G|_C$.

Lemma 3. *For every finite subset $C \subset \mathbb{Q}$, we have $G|_C = I$.*

Immediately, we see that $(C, S) = (C, I)$, and hence that the orbit is fully represented by the set C. A further consequence of Lemma 3 is that each *element* of an orbit can be uniquely identified by its least support. This leads us to the following characterisation of $[C, I]^{ec}$.

Lemma 4. *Given a finite subset $C \subset \mathbb{Q}$, we have $[C, I]^{ec} \cong \mathcal{P}_{\#C}(\mathbb{Q})$.*

By Theorem 2 and the above lemmas, we can represent an orbit by a single integer n, the size of the least support of its elements. This naturally extends to (orbit-finite) nominal sets with multiple orbits by using a multiset of natural numbers, representing the size of the least support of each of the orbits. These multisets are formalised here as functions $f \colon \mathbb{N} \to \mathbb{N}$.

Definition 5. *Given a function $f \colon \mathbb{N} \to \mathbb{N}$, we define a nominal set $[f]^{o}$ by*

$$[f]^{o} = \bigcup_{\substack{n \in \mathbb{N} \\ 1 \leq i \leq f(n)}} \{i\} \times \mathcal{P}_n(\mathbb{Q}).$$

Proposition 6. *For every orbit-finite nominal set X, there is a function $f \colon \mathbb{N} \to \mathbb{N}$ such that $X \cong [f]^{o}$ and the set $\{n \mid f(n) \neq 0\}$ is finite. Furthermore, the mapping between X and f is one-to-one up to isomorphism of X when restricting to $f \colon \mathbb{N} \to \mathbb{N}$ for which the set $\{n \mid f(n) \neq 0\}$ is finite.*

The presentation in terms of a function $f \colon \mathbb{N} \to \mathbb{N}$ enforces that there are only finitely many orbits of any given dimension. The first part of the above proposition generalises to arbitrary nominal sets by replacing the codomain of f by the class of all sets and adapting Definition 5 accordingly. However, the resulting correspondence will no longer be one-to-one.

As a brief example, let us consider the set $\mathbb{Q} \times \mathbb{Q}$. The elements (a, b) split in three orbits, one for $a < b$, one for $a = b$ and one for $a > b$. These have dimension 2, 1 and 2 respectively, so the set $\mathbb{Q} \times \mathbb{Q}$ is represented by the multiset $\{1, 2, 2\}$.

3.2   Equivariant Maps

We show how to represent equivariant maps, using two basic properties. Let $f : X \to Y$ be an equivariant map. The first property is that the direct image of an orbit (in X) is again an orbit (in Y), that is to say, f is defined 'orbit-wise'. Second, equivariant maps cannot introduce new elements in the support (but they can drop them). More precisely:

Lemma 7. *Let* $f\colon X \to Y$ *be an equivariant map, and* $O \subseteq X$ *a single orbit. The direct image* $f(O) = \{f(x) \mid x \in O\}$ *is a single-orbit nominal set.*

Lemma 8. *Let* $f\colon X \to Y$ *be an equivariant map between two nominal sets* X *and* Y*. Let* $x \in X$ *and let* C *be a support of* x*. Then* C *supports* $f(x)$*.*

Hence, equivariant maps are fully determined by associating two pieces of information for each orbit in the domain: the orbit on which it is mapped and a string denoting which elements of the least support of the input are preserved. These ingredients are formalised in the first part of the following definition. The second part describes how these ingredients define an equivariant function. Proposition 10 then states that every equivariant function can be described in this way.

Definition 9. *Let* $H = \{(I_1, F_1, O_1), \dots, (I_n, F_n, O_n)\}$ *be a finite set of tuples where the* I_i*'s are disjoint single-orbit nominal sets, the* O_i*'s are single-orbit nominal sets with* $\dim(O_i) \leq \dim(I_i)$*, and the* F_i*'s are bit strings of length* $\dim(I_i)$ *with exactly* $\dim(O_i)$ *ones.*

Given a set H *as above, we define* $f_H\colon \bigcup I_i \to \bigcup O_i$ *as the unique equivariant function such that, given* $x \in I_i$ *with least support* C*,* $f_H(x)$ *is the unique element of* O_i *with support* $\{C(j) \mid F_i(j) = 1\}$*, where* $F_i(j)$ *is the j-th bit of* F_i *and* $C(j)$ *is the j-th smallest element of* C*.*

Proposition 10. *For every equivariant map* $f\colon X \to Y$ *between orbit-finite nominal sets* X *and* Y *there is a set* H *as in Definition 9 such that* $f = f_H$*.*

Consider the example function $\min\colon \mathcal{P}_3(\mathbb{Q}) \to \mathbb{Q}$ which returns the smallest element of a 3-element set. Note that both $\mathcal{P}_3(\mathbb{Q})$ and $\mathbb{Q}$ are single orbits. Since for the orbit $\mathcal{P}_3(\mathbb{Q})$ we only keep the smallest element of the support, we can thus represent the function $\min$ with $\{(\mathcal{P}_3(\mathbb{Q}), 100, \mathbb{Q})\}$.

3.3   Products

The product $X \times Y$ of two nominal sets is again a nominal set and hence, it can be represented itself in terms of the dimension of each of its orbits as shown in Sect. 3.1. However, this approach has some disadvantages.

Example 11. We start by showing that the orbit structure of products can be non-trivial. Consider the product of $X = \mathbb{Q}$ and the set $Y = \{(a, b) \in \mathbb{Q}^2 \mid a < b\}$. This product consists of five orbits, more than one might naively expect from the fact that both sets are single-orbit:

$$\{(a, (b, c)) \mid a, b, c \in \mathbb{Q}, a < b < c\}, \{(a, (a, b)) \mid a, b \in \mathbb{Q}, a < b\},$$
$$\{(b, (a, c)) \mid a, b, c \in \mathbb{Q}, a < b < c\}, \{(b, (a, b)) \mid a, b \in \mathbb{Q}, a < b\},$$
$$\{(c, (a, b)) \mid a, b, c \in \mathbb{Q}, a < b < c\}.$$

We find that this product is represented by the multiset $\{2, 2, 3, 3, 3\}$. Unfortunately, this is not sufficient to accurately describe the product as it abstracts away from the relation between its elements with those in X and Y. In particular, it is not possible to reconstruct the projection maps from such a representation.

The essence of our representation of products is that each orbit O in the product $X \times Y$ is described entirely by the dimension of O together with the two (equivariant) projections $\pi_1 : O \to X$ and $\pi_2 : O \to Y$. This combination of the orbit and the two projection maps can already be represented using Propositions 6 and 10. However, as we will see, a combined representation for this has several advantages. For discussing such a representation, let us first introduce what it means for tuples of a set and two functions to be isomorphic:

Definition 12. *Given nominal sets* X, Y, Z_1 *and* Z_2, *and equivariant functions* $l_1 \colon Z_1 \to X$, $r_1 \colon Z_1 \to Y$, $l_2 \colon Z_2 \to X$ *and* $r_2 \colon Z_2 \to Y$, *we define* $(Z_1, l_1, r_1) \cong (Z_2, l_2, r_2)$ *if there exists an isomorphism* $h : Z_1 \to Z_2$ *such that* $l_1 = l_2 \circ h$ *and* $r_1 = r_2 \circ h$.

Our goal is to have a representation that, for each orbit O, produces a tuple (A, f_1, f_2) isomorphic to the tuple (O, π_1, π_2). The next lemma gives a characterisation that can be used to simplify such a representation.

Lemma 13. *Let* X *and* Y *be nominal sets and* $(x, y) \in X \times Y$. *If* C, C_x, *and* C_y *are the least supports of* (x, y), x, *and* y *respectively, then* $C = C_x \cup C_y$.

With Proposition 10 we represent the maps π_1 and π_2 by tuples (O, F_1, O_1) and (O, F_2, O_2) respectively. Using Lemma 13 and the definitions of F_1 and F_2, we see that at least one of $F_1(i)$ and $F_2(i)$ equals 1 for each i.

We can thus combine the strings F_1 and F_2 into a single string $P \in \{L, R, B\}^*$ as follows. We set $P(i) = L$ when only $F_1(i)$ is 1, $P(i) = R$ when only $F_2(i)$ is 1, and $P(i) = B$ when both are 1. The string P fully describes the strings F_1 and F_2. This process for constructing the string P gives it two useful properties. The number of Ls and Bs in the string gives the size dimension of O_1. Similarly, the number of Rs and Bs in the string gives the dimension of O_2. We will call strings with that property *valid*. In conclusion, to describe a single orbit of the product $X \times Y$, a valid string P together with the images of π_1 and π_2 is sufficient.

Definition 14. *Let* $P \in \{L, R, B\}^*$, *and* $O_1 \subseteq X$, $O_2 \subseteq Y$ *be single-orbit sets. Given a tuple* (P, O_1, O_2), *where the string* P *is valid, define*

$$[(P, O_1, O_2)]^t = (\mathcal{P}_{|P|}(\mathbb{Q}), f_{H_1}, f_{H_2}),$$

where $H_i = \{(\mathcal{P}_{|P|}(\mathbb{Q}), F_i, O_i)\}$ *and the string* F_1 *is defined as the string* P *with* Ls *and* Bs *replaced by* 1s *and* Rs *by* 0s. *The string* F_2 *is similarly defined with the roles of* L *and* R *swapped.*

Proposition 15. *There exists a one-to-one correspondence between the orbits* $O \subseteq X \times Y$, *and tuples* (P, O_1, O_2) *satisfying* $O_1 \subseteq X$, $O_2 \subseteq Y$, *and where* P *is a valid string, such that* $[(P, O_1, O_2)]^t \cong (O, \pi_1|_O, \pi_2|_O)$.

From the above proposition it follows that we can generate the product $X \times Y$ simply by enumerating all valid strings P for all pairs of orbits (O_1, O_2) of X and Y. Given this, we can calculate the multiset representation of a product from the multiset representations of both factors.

Theorem 16. *For $X \cong [f]^{\circ}$ and $Y \cong [g]^{\circ}$ we have $X \times Y \cong [h]^{\circ}$, where*

$$h(n) = \sum_{\substack{0 \le i,j \le n \\ i+j \ge n}} f(i)g(j) \binom{n}{j}\binom{j}{n-i}.$$

Example 17. To illustrate some aspects of the above representation, let us use it to calculate the product of Example 11. First, we observe that both $\mathbb{Q}$ and $S = \{(a,b) \in \mathbb{Q}^2 \mid a < b\}$ consist of a single orbit. Hence any orbit of the product corresponds to a triple $(P, \mathbb{Q}, S)$, where the string P satisfies $|P|_L + |P|_B = \dim(\mathbb{Q}) = 1$ and $|P|_R + |P|_B = \dim(S) = 2$. We can now find the orbits of the product $\mathbb{Q} \times S$ by enumerating all strings satisfying these equations. This yields:

- LRR, corresponding to the orbit $\{(a, (b, c)) \mid a, b, c \in \mathbb{Q}, a < b < c\}$,
- RLR, corresponding to the orbit $\{(b, (a, c)) \mid a, b, c \in \mathbb{Q}, a < b < c\}$,
- RRL, corresponding to the orbit $\{(c, (a, b)) \mid a, b, c \in \mathbb{Q}, a < b < c\}$,
- RB, corresponding to the orbit $\{(b, (a, b)) \mid a, b \in \mathbb{Q}, a < b\}$, and
- BR, corresponding to the orbit $\{(a, (a, b)) \mid a, b \in \mathbb{Q}, a < b\}$.

Each product string fully describes the corresponding orbit. To illustrate, consider the string BR. The corresponding bit strings for the projection functions are $F_1 = 10$ and $F_2 = 11$. From the lengths of the string we conclude that the dimension of the orbit is 2. The string F_1 further tells us that the left element of the tuple consists only of the smallest element of the support. The string F_2 indicates that the right element of the tuple is constructed from both elements of the support. Combining this, we find that the orbit is $\{(a, (a, b)) \mid a, b \in \mathbb{Q}, a < b\}$.

3.4   Summary

We summarise our concrete representation in the following table. Propositions 6, 10 and 15 correspond to the three rows in the table.

Object	Representation
Single orbit O	Natural number $n = \dim(O)$
Nominal set $X = \bigcup_i O_i$	Multiset of these numbers
Map from single orbit $f \colon O \to Y$	The orbit $f(O)$ and a bit string F
Equivariant map $f \colon X \to Y$	Set of tuples $(O, F, f(O))$, one for each orbit
Orbit in a product $O \subseteq X \times Y$	The corresponding orbits of X and Y, and a string P relating their supports
Product $X \times Y$	Set of tuples (P, O_X, O_Y), one for each orbit

Notice that in the case of maps and products, the orbits are inductively represented using the concrete representation. As a base case we can represent single orbits by their dimension.

4   Implementation and Complexity of ONS

The ideas outlined above have been implemented in the C++ library ONS.[2] The library can represent orbit-finite nominal sets and their products, (disjoint) unions, and maps. A full description of the possibilities is given in the documentation included with ONS.

As an example, the following program computes the product from Example 11. Initially, the program creates the nominal set A, containing the entirety of $\mathbb{Q}$. Then it creates a nominal set B, such that it consists of the orbit containing the element $(1, 2) \in \mathbb{Q} \times \mathbb{Q}$. For this, the library determines to which orbit of the product $\mathbb{Q} \times \mathbb{Q}$ the element $(1, 2)$ belongs, and then stores a description of the orbit as described in Sect. 3. Note that this means that it internally never needs to store the element used to create the orbit. The function nomset_product then uses the enumeration of product strings mentioned in Sect. 3.3 to calculate the product of A and B. Finally, it prints a representative element for each of the orbits in the product. These elements are constructed based on the description of the orbits stored, filled in to make their support equal to sets of the form $\{1, 2, \ldots, n\}$.

```
nomset<rational> A = nomset_rationals();
nomset<pair<rational, rational>> B({rational(1),rational(2)});

auto AtimesB = nomset_product(A, B);    // compute the product
for (auto orbit : AtimesB)
    cout << orbit.getElement() << "␣";
```

Running this gives the following output ('/1' signifies the denominator):

```
(1/1,(2/1,3/1))  (1/1,(1/1,2/1))  (2/1,(1/1,3/1))
(2/1,(1/1,2/1))  (3/1,(1/1,2/1))
```

Internally, orbit is implemented following the theory presented in Sect. 3, storing the dimension of the orbit it represents. It also contains sufficient information to reconstruct elements given their least support, such as the product string for orbits resulting from a product. The class nomset then uses a standard set data structure to store the collection of orbits contained in the nominal set it represents.

In a similar way, eqimap stores equivariant maps by associating each orbit in the domain with the image orbit and the string representing which of the least support to keep. This is stored using a map data structure. For both nominal sets and equivariant maps, the underlying data structure is currently implemented using trees.

4.1   Complexity of Operations

Using the concrete representation of nominal sets, we can determine the complexity of common operations. To simplify such an analysis, we will make the following assumptions:

---

[2] ONS can be found at https://github.com/davidv1992/ONS.

- The comparison of two orbits takes $O(1)$.
- Constructing an orbit from an element takes $O(1)$.
- Checking whether an element is in an orbit takes $O(1)$.

These assumptions are justified as each of these operations takes time proportional to the size of the representation of an individual orbit, which in practice is small and approximately constant. For instance, the orbit $\mathcal{P}_n(\mathbb{Q})$ is represented by just the integer n and its type.

Theorem 18. *If nominal sets are implemented with a tree-based set structure (as in* ONS*), the complexity of the following set operations is as follows. Recall that* $N(X)$ *denotes the number of orbits of* X. *We use* p *and* f *to denote functions implemented in whatever way the user wants, which we assume to take* $O(1)$ *time. The software assumes these are equivariant, but this is not verified.*

Operation	Complexity
Test $x \in X$	$O(\log N(X))$
Test $X \subseteq Y$	$O(\min(N(X) + N(Y), N(X) \log N(Y)))$
Calculate $X \cup Y$	$O(N(X) + N(Y))$
Calculate $X \cap Y$	$O(N(X) + N(Y))$
Calculate $\{x \in X \mid p(x)\}$	$O(N(X))$
Calculate $\{f(x) \mid x \in X\}$	$O(N(X) \log N(X))$
Calculate $X \times Y$	$O(N(X \times Y)) \subseteq O(3^{\dim(X)+\dim(Y)} N(X) N(Y))$

Proof. Since most parts are proven similarly, we only include proofs for the first and last item.

Membership. To decide $x \in X$, we first construct the orbit containing x, which is done in constant time. Then we use a logarithmic lookup to decide whether this orbit is in our set data structure. Hence, membership checking is $O(\log(N(X)))$.

Products. Calculating the product of two nominal sets is the most complicated construction. For each pair of orbits in the original sets X and Y, all product orbits need to be generated. Each product orbit itself is constructed in constant time. By generating these orbits in-order, the resulting set takes $O(N(X \times Y))$ time to construct.

We can also give an explicit upper bound for the number of orbits in terms of the input. Recall that orbits in a product are represented by strings of length at most $\dim(X) + \dim(Y)$. (If the string is shorter, we pad it with one of the symbols.) Since there are three symbols (L, R and B), the product of X and Y will have at most $3^{\dim(X)+\dim(Y)} N(X) N(Y)$ orbits. It follows that taking products has time complexity of $O(3^{\dim(X)+\dim(Y)} N(X) N(Y))$. $\qquad\square$

5   Results and Evaluation in Automata Theory

In this section we consider applications of nominal sets to automata theory. As mentioned in the introduction, nominal sets are used to formalise languages over infinite alphabets. These languages naturally arise as the semantics of register automata. The definition of register automata is not as simple as that of ordinary finite automata. Consequently, transferring results from automata theory to this setting often requires non-trivial proofs. Nominal automata, instead, are defined as ordinary automata by replacing finite sets with orbit-finite nominal sets. The theory of nominal automata is developed in [4] and it is shown that many, but not all, algorithms from automata theory transfer to nominal automata.

As an example we consider the following language on rational numbers:

$$\mathcal{L}_{\text{int}} = \{a_1 b_1 \cdots a_n b_n \mid a_i, b_i \in \mathbb{Q}, a_i < a_{i+1} < b_{i+1} < b_i \text{ for all } i\}.$$

We call this language the *interval language* as a word $w \in \mathbb{Q}^*$ is in the language when it denotes a sequence of nested intervals. This language contains arbitrarily long words. For this language it is crucial to work with an infinite alphabet as for each finite set $C \subset \mathbb{Q}$, the restriction $\mathcal{L}_{\text{int}} \cap C^*$ is just a finite language. Note that the language is equivariant: $w \in \mathcal{L}_{\text{int}} \iff wg \in \mathcal{L}_{\text{int}}$ for any monotone bijection g, because nested intervals are preserved by monotone maps.[3] Indeed, $\mathcal{L}_{\text{int}}$ is a nominal set, although it is not orbit-finite.

Informally, the language $\mathcal{L}_{\text{int}}$ can be accepted by the automaton depicted in Fig. 1. Here we allow the automaton to store rational numbers and compare them to new symbols. For example, the transition from q_2 to q_3 is taken if any value c between a and b is read and then the currently stored value a is replaced by c. For any other value read at state q_2 the automaton transitions to the sink state q_4. Such a transition structure is made precise by the notion of nominal automata.

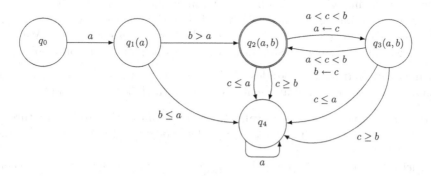

Fig. 1. Example automaton that accepts the language $\mathcal{L}_{\text{int}}$.

---

[3] The G-action on words is defined point-wise: $(w_1 \ldots w_n)g = (w_1 g) \ldots (w_n g)$.

Definition 19. *A nominal language is an equivariant subset $L \subseteq A^*$ where A is an orbit-finite nominal set.*

Definition 20. *A nominal deterministic finite automaton is a tuple (S, A, F, δ), where S is an orbit-finite nominal set of states, A is an orbit-finite nominal set of symbols, $F \subseteq S$ is an equivariant subset of final states, and $\delta: S \times A \to S$ is the equivariant transition function.*

Given a state $s \in S$, we define the usual acceptance condition: a word $w \in A^*$ is accepted if w denotes a path from s to a final state.

The automaton in Fig. 1 can be formalised as a nominal deterministic finite automaton as follows. Let $S = \{q_0, q_4\} \cup \{q_1(a) \mid a \in \mathbb{Q}\} \cup \{q_2(a, b) \mid a < b \in \mathbb{Q}\} \cup \{q_3(a, b) \mid a < b \in \mathbb{Q}\}$ be the set of states, where the group action is defined as one would expect. The transition we described earlier can now be formally defined as $\delta(q_2(a, b), c) = q_3(c, b)$ for all $a < c < b \in \mathbb{Q}$. By defining δ on all states accordingly and defining the final states as $F = \{q_2(a, b) \mid a < b \in \mathbb{Q}\}$, we obtain a nominal deterministic automaton $(S, \mathbb{Q}, F, \delta)$. The state q_0 accepts the language $\mathcal{L}_{\text{int}}$.

Testing. We implement two algorithms on nominal automata, minimisation and learning, to benchmark ONS. The performance of ONS is compared to two existing libraries for computing with nominal sets, Nλ and LOIS. The following automata will be used.

Random Automata. As a primary test suite, we generate random automata as follows. The input alphabet is always $\mathbb{Q}$ and the number of orbits and dimension k of the state space S are fixed. For each orbit in the set of states, its dimension is chosen uniformly at random between 0 and k, inclusive. Each orbit has a probability $\frac{1}{2}$ of consisting of accepting states.

To generate the transition function δ, we enumerate the orbits of $S \times \mathbb{Q}$ and choose a target state uniformly from the orbits S with small enough dimension. The bit string indicating which part of the support is preserved is then sampled uniformly from all valid strings. We will denote these automata as $\text{rand}_{N(S),k}$. The choices made here are arbitrary and only provide basic automata. We note that the automata are generated orbit-wise and this may favour our tool.

Structured Automata. Besides random automata we wish to test the algorithms on more structured automata. We define the following automata.

FIFO(n) Automata accepting valid traces of a finite FIFO data structure of size n. The alphabet is defined by two orbits: $\{\text{Put}(a) \mid a \in \mathbb{Q}\}$ and $\{\text{Get}(a) \mid a \in \mathbb{Q}\}$.

$ww(n)$ Automata accepting the language of words of the form ww, where $w \in \mathbb{Q}^n$.

$\mathcal{L}_{\max}$ The language $\mathcal{L}_{\max} = \{wa \in \mathbb{Q}^* \mid a = \max(w_1, \dots, w_n)\}$ where the last symbol is the maximum of previous symbols.

$\mathcal{L}_{\text{int}}$ The language accepting a series of nested intervals, as defined above.

In Table 1 we report the number of orbits for each automaton. The first two classes of automata were previously used as test cases in [21]. These two classes are also equivariant w.r.t. the equality symmetry. The extra bit of structure allows the automata to be encoded more efficiently, as we do not need to encode a transition for each orbit in $S \times A$. Instead, a more symbolic encoding is possible. Both LOIS and Nλ allow to use this more symbolic representation. Our tool, ONS, only works with nominal sets and the input data needs to be provided orbit-wise. Where applicable, the automata listed above were generated using the same code as used in [21], ported to the other libraries as needed.

5.1 Minimising Nominal Automata

For languages recognised by nominal DFAs, a Myhill-Nerode theorem holds which relates states to right congruence classes [4]. This guarantees the existence of unique minimal automata. We say an automaton is *minimal* if its set of states has the least number of orbits and each orbit has the smallest dimension possible.[4] We generalise Moore's minimisation algorithm to nominal DFAs (Algorithm 1) and analyse its time complexity using the bounds from Sect. 4.

Algorithm 1. Moore's minimisation algorithm for nominal DFAs

Require: Nominal automaton (S, A, F, δ).
1: $i \leftarrow 0$, $\equiv_{-1} \leftarrow S \times S$, $\equiv_0 \leftarrow F \times F \cup (S \backslash F) \times (S \backslash F)$
2: **while** $\equiv_i \neq \equiv_{i-1}$ **do**
3:    $\equiv_{i+1} = \{(q_1, q_2) \mid (q_1, q_2) \in \equiv_i \wedge \forall a \in A, (\delta(q_1, a), \delta(q_2, a)) \in \equiv_i\}$
4:    $i \leftarrow i + 1$
5: **end while**
6: $E \leftarrow S/_{\equiv_i}$
7: $F_E \leftarrow \{e \in E \mid \forall s \in e, s \in F\}$
8: Let δ_E be the map such that, if $s \in e$ and $\delta(s, a) \in e'$, then $\delta_E(e, a) = e'$.
9: **return** (E, A, F_E, δ_E).

Theorem 21. *The runtime complexity of Moore's algorithm on nominal deterministic automata is $O(3^{5k} k \operatorname{N}(S)^3 \operatorname{N}(A))$, where $k = \dim(S \cup A)$.*

Proof. This is shown by counting operations, using the complexity results of set operations stated in Theorem 18. We first focus on the while loop on lines 2 through 5. The runtime of an iteration of the loop is determined by line 3, as this is the most expensive step. Since the dimensions of S and A are at most k, computing $S \times S \times A$ takes $O(\operatorname{N}(S)^2 \operatorname{N}(A) 3^{5k})$. Filtering $S \times S$ using that then takes $O(\operatorname{N}(S)^2 3^{2k})$. The time to compute $S \times S \times A$ dominates, hence each iteration of the loop takes $O(\operatorname{N}(S)^2 \operatorname{N}(A) 3^{5k})$.

---

[4] Abstractly, an automaton is minimal if it has no proper quotients. Minimal deterministic automata are unique up to isomorphism.

Next, we need to count the number of iterations of the loop. Each iteration of the loop gives rise to a new partition, which is a refinement of the previous partition. Furthermore, every partition generated is equivariant. Note that this implies that each refinement of the partition does at least one of two things: distinguish between two orbits of S previously in the same element(s) of the partition, or distinguish between two members of the same orbit previously in the same element of the partition. The first can happen only $N(S) - 1$ times, as after that there are no more orbits lumped together. The second can only happen $\dim(S)$ times per orbit, because each such a distinction between elements is based on splitting on the value of one of the elements of the support. Hence, after $\dim(S)$ times on a single orbit, all elements of the support are used up. Combining this, the longest chain of partitions of S has length at most $O(k\,N(S))$.

Since each partition generated in the loop is unique, the loop cannot run for more iterations than the length of the longest chain of partitions on S. It follows that there are at most $O(k\,N(S))$ iterations of the loop, giving the loop a complexity of $O(k\,N(S)^3\,N(A)3^{5k})$.

The remaining operations outside the loop have a lower complexity than that of the loop, hence the complexity of Moore's minimisation algorithm for a nominal automaton is $O(k\,N(S)^3\,N(A)3^{5k})$.

The above theorem shows in particular that minimisation of nominal automata is fixed-parameter tractable (FPT) with the dimension as fixed parameter. The complexity of Algorithm 1 for nominal automata is very similar to the $O((\#S)^3\#A)$ bound given by a naive implementation of Moore's algorithm for ordinary DFAs. This suggest that it is possible to further optimise an implementation with similar techniques used for ordinary automata.

Implementations. We implemented the minimisation algorithm in ONS. For Nλ and LOIS we used their implementations of Moore's minimisation algorithm [17–19]. For each of the libraries, we wrote routines to read in an automaton from a file and, for the structured test cases, to generate the requested automaton. For ONS, all automata were read from file. The output of these programs was manually checked to see if the minimisation was performed correctly.

Results. The results (shown in Table 1) for random automata show a clear advantage for ONS, which is capable of running all supplied testcases in less than one second. This in contrast to both LOIS and Nλ, which take more than 2 h on the largest random automata.

The results for structured automata show a clear effect of the extra structure. Both Nλ and LOIS remain capable of minimising the automata in reasonable amounts of time for larger sizes. In contrast, ONS benefits little from the extra structure. Despite this, it remains viable: even for the larger cases it falls behind significantly only for the largest FIFO automaton and the two largest ww automata.

Table 1. Running times for Algorithm 1 implemented in the three libraries. $N(S)$ is the size of the input and $N(S^{\min})$ the size of the minimal automaton. For ONS, the time used to generate the automaton is reported separately (in grey).

Type	$N(S)$	$N(S^{\min})$	ONS	Gen.	Nλ	LOIS
$\text{rand}_{5,1}$ (x10)	5	n/a	0.02s	n/a	0.82s	3.14s
$\text{rand}_{10,1}$ (x10)	10	n/a	0.03s	n/a	17.03s	1m 32s
$\text{rand}_{10,2}$ (x10)	10	n/a	0.09s	n/a	35m 14s	> 60m
$\text{rand}_{15,1}$ (x10)	15	n/a	0.04s	n/a	1m 27s	10m 20s
$\text{rand}_{15,2}$ (x10)	15	n/a	0.11s	n/a	55m 46s	> 60m
$\text{rand}_{15,3}$ (x10)	15	n/a	0.46s	n/a	> 60m	> 60m
FIFO(2)	13	6	0.01s	0.01s	1.37s	0.24s
FIFO(3)	65	19	0.38s	0.09s	11.59s	2.4s
FIFO(4)	440	94	39.11s	1.60s	1m 16s	14.95s
FIFO(5)	3686	635	> 60m	39.78s	6m 42s	1m 11s
$ww(2)$	8	8	0.00s	0.00s	0.14s	0.03s
$ww(3)$	24	24	0.19s	0.02s	0.88s	0.16s
$ww(4)$	112	112	26.44s	0.25s	3.41s	0.61s
$ww(5)$	728	728	> 60m	6.37s	10.54s	1.80s
$\mathcal{L}_{\max}$	5	3	0.00s	0.00s	2.06s	0.03s
$\mathcal{L}_{\text{int}}$	5	5	0.00s	0.00s	1.55s	0.03s

5.2 Learning Nominal Automata

Another application that we implemented in ONS is *automata learning*. The aim of automata learning is to infer an unknown regular language $\mathcal{L}$. We use the framework of active learning as set up by Angluin [2] where a learning algorithm can query an oracle to gather information about $\mathcal{L}$. Formally, the oracle can answer two types of queries:

1. *membership queries*, where a query consists of a word $w \in A^*$ and the oracle replies whether $w \in \mathcal{L}$, and
2. *equivalence queries*, where a query consists of an automaton $\mathcal{H}$ and the oracle replies positively if $\mathcal{L}(\mathcal{H}) = \mathcal{L}$ or provides a counterexample if $\mathcal{L}(\mathcal{H}) \neq \mathcal{L}$.

With these queries, the L* algorithm can learn regular languages efficiently [2]. In particular, it learns the unique minimal automaton for $\mathcal{L}$ using only finitely many queries. The L* algorithm has been generalised to νL* in order to learn *nominal* regular languages [21]. In particular, it learns a nominal DFA (over an infinite alphabet) using only finitely many queries. We implement νL* in the presented library and compare it to its previous implementation in Nλ. The algorithm is not polynomial, unlike the minimisation algorithm described above. However, the authors conjecture that there is a polynomial algorithm.[5] For the correctness, termination, and comparison with other learning algorithms see [21].

---

[5] See   https://joshuamoerman.nl/papers/2017/17popl-learning-nominal-automata.html for a sketch of the polynomial algorithm.

Implementations. Both implementations in $N\lambda$ and ONs are direct implementations of the pseudocode for $\nu L^\star$ with no further optimisations. The authors of LOIS implemented $\nu L^\star$ in their library as well.[6] They reported similar performance as the implementation in $N\lambda$ (private communication). Hence we focus our comparison on $N\lambda$ and ONs. We use the variant of $\nu L^\star$ where counterexamples are added as columns instead of prefixes.

The implementation in $N\lambda$ has the benefit that it can work with different symmetries. Indeed, the structured examples, FIFO and ww, are equivariant w.r.t. the equality symmetry as well as the total order symmetry. For that reason, we run the $N\lambda$ implementation using both the equality symmetry and the total order symmetry on those languages. For the languages $\mathcal{L}_{max}$, $\mathcal{L}_{int}$ and the random automata, we can only use the total order symmetry.

To run the $\nu L^\star$ algorithm, we implement an external oracle for the membership queries. This is akin to the application of learning black box systems [29]. For equivalence queries, we constructed counterexamples by hand. All implementations receive the same counterexamples. We measure CPU time instead of real time, so that we do not account for the external oracle.

Results. The results (Table 2) for random automata show an advantage for ONs. Additionally, we report the number of membership queries, which can vary for each implementation as some steps in the algorithm depend on the internal ordering of set data structures.

In contrast to the case of minimisation, the results suggest that $N\lambda$ cannot exploit the logical structure of FIFO(n), $\mathcal{L}_{max}$ and $\mathcal{L}_{int}$ as it is not provided a priori. For $ww(2)$ we inspected the output on $N\lambda$ and saw that it learned some logical structure (e.g., it outputs $\{(a,b) \mid a \neq b\}$ as a single object instead of two orbits $\{(a,b) \mid a < b\}$ and $\{(a,b) \mid b < a\}$). This may explain why $N\lambda$ is still competitive. For languages which are equivariant for the equality symmetry, the $N\lambda$ implementation using the equality symmetry can learn with much fewer queries. This is expected as the automata themselves have fewer orbits. It is interesting to see that these languages can be learned more efficiently by choosing the right symmetry.

6   Related Work

As stated in the introduction, $N\lambda$ [17] and LOIS [18] use first-order formulas to represent nominal sets and use SMT solvers to manipulate them. This makes both libraries very flexible and they indeed implement the equality symmetry as well as the total order symmetry. As their representation is not unique, the efficiency depends on how the logical formulas are constructed. As such, they do not provide complexity results. In contrast, our direct representation allows for complexity results (Sect. 4) and leads to different performance characteristics (Sect. 5).

---

[6] Can be found on https://github.com/eryxcc/lois/blob/master/tests/learning.cpp.

Table 2. Running times and number of membership queries for the $\nu L^\star$ algorithm. For $N\lambda$ we used two version: $N\lambda^{ord}$ uses the total order symmetry $N\lambda^{eq}$ uses the equality symmetry.

Model	$N(S)$	$\dim(S)$	Ons		$N\lambda^{ord}$		$N\lambda^{eq}$	
			time	MQs	time	MQs	time	MQs
$\mathrm{rand}_{5,1}$	4	1	2 m 7 s	2321	39 m 51 s	1243		
$\mathrm{rand}_{5,1}$	5	1	0.12 s	404	40 m 34 s	435		
$\mathrm{rand}_{5,1}$	3	0	0.86 s	499	30 m 19 s	422		
$\mathrm{rand}_{5,1}$	5	1	>60 m	n/a	>60 m	n/a		
$\mathrm{rand}_{5,1}$	4	1	0.08 s	387	34 m 57 s	387		
FIFO(1)	3	1	0.04 s	119	3.17 s	119	1.76 s	51
FIFO(2)	6	2	1.73 s	2655	6 m 32 s	3818	40.00 s	434
FIFO(3)	19	3	46 m 34 s	298400	>60 m	n/a	34 m 7 s	8151
$ww(1)$	4	1	0.42 s	134	2.49 s	77	1.47 s	30
$ww(2)$	8	2	4 m 26 s	3671	3 m 48 s	2140	30.58 s	237
$ww(3)$	24	3	>60 m	n/a	>60 m	n/a	>60 m	n/a
$\mathcal{L}_{\max}$	3	1	0.01 s	54	3.58 s	54		
$\mathcal{L}_{\mathrm{int}}$	5	2	0.59 s	478	1 m 23 s	478		

A second big difference is that both $N\lambda$ and Lois implement a "programming paradigm" instead of just a library. This means that they overload natural programming constructs in their host languages (Haskell and C++ respectively). For programmers this means they can think of infinite sets without having to know about nominal sets.

It is worth mentioning that an older (unreleased) version of $N\lambda$ implemented nominal sets with orbits instead of SMT solvers [3]. However, instead of characterising orbits (e.g., by its dimension), they represent orbits by a representative element. The authors of $N\lambda$ have reported that the current version is faster [17].

The theoretical foundation of our work is the main representation theorem in [4]. We improve on that by instantiating it to the total order symmetry and distil a concrete representation of nominal sets. As far as we know, we provide the first implementation of the representation theory in [4].

Another tool using nominal sets is Mihda [12]. Here, only the equality symmetry is implemented. This tool implements a translation from π-calculus to history-dependent automata (HD-automata) with the aim of minimisation and checking bisimilarity. The implementation in OCaml is based on *named sets*, which are finite representations for nominal sets. The theory of named sets is well-studied and has been used to model various behavioural models with local names. For those results, the categorical equivalences between named sets, nominal sets and a certain (pre)sheaf category have been exploited [8,9]. The total order symmetry is not mentioned in their work. We do, however, believe that similar equivalences between categories can be stated. Interestingly, the product of named sets is similar to our representation of products of nominal sets: pairs of elements together with data which denotes the relation between data values.

Fresh OCaml [27] and Nominal Isabelle [28] are both specialised in name-binding and α-conversion used in proof systems. They only use the equality symmetry and do not provide a library for manipulating nominal sets. Hence they are not suited for our applications.

On the theoretical side, there are many complexity results for register automata [15,23]. In particular, we note that problems such as emptiness and equivalence are NP-hard depending on the type of register automaton. This does not easily compare to our complexity results for minimisation. One difference is that we use the total order symmetry, where the local symmetries are always trivial (Lemma 3). As a consequence, all the complexity required to deal with groups vanishes. Rather, the complexity is transferred to the input of our algorithms, because automata over the equality symmetry require more orbits when expressed over the total order symmetry. Another difference is that register automata allow for duplicate values in the registers. In nominal automata, such configurations will be encoded in different orbits. An interesting open problem is whether equivalence of unique-valued register automata is in PTIME [23].

Orthogonal to nominal automata, there is the notion of symbolic automata [10,20]. These automata are also defined over infinite alphabets but they use predicates on transitions, instead of relying on symmetries. Symbolic automata are finite state (as opposed to infinite state nominal automata) and do not allow for storing values. However, they do allow for general predicates over an infinite alphabet, including comparison to constants.

7   Conclusion and Future Work

We presented a concrete finite representation for nominal sets over the total order symmetry. This allowed us to implement a library, ONS, and provide complexity bounds for common operations. The experimental comparison of ONS against existing solutions for automata minimisation and learning show that our implementation is much faster in many instances. As such, we believe ONS is a promising implementation of nominal techniques.

A natural direction for future work is to consider other symmetries, such as the equality symmetry. Here, we may take inspiration from existing tools such as Mihda (see Sect. 6). Another interesting question is whether it is possible to translate a nominal automaton over the total order symmetry which accepts an equality language to an automaton over the equality symmetry. This would allow one to efficiently move between symmetries. Finally, our techniques can potentially be applied to timed automata by exploiting the intriguing connection between the nominal automata that we consider and timed automata [5].

Acknowledgement. We would like to thank Szymon Toruńczyk and Eryk Kopczyński for their prompt help when using the LOIS library. For general comments and suggestions we would like to thank Ugo Montanari and Niels van der Weide. At last, we want to thank the anonymous reviewers for their comments.

References

1. Aarts, F., Fiterau-Brostean, P., Kuppens, H., Vaandrager, F.: Learning register automata with fresh value generation. In: Leucker, M., Rueda, C., Valencia, F.D. (eds.) ICTAC 2015. LNCS, vol. 9399, pp. 165–183. Springer, Cham (2015). https://doi.org/10.1007/978-3-319-25150-9_11

2. Angluin, D.: Learning regular sets from queries and counterexamples. Inf. Comput. **75**(2), 87–106 (1987). https://doi.org/10.1016/0890-5401(87)90052-6

3. Bojańczyk, M., Braud, L., Klin, B., Lasota, S.: Towards nominal computation. In: Proceedings of 39th ACM SIGPLAN-SIGACT Symposium on Principles of Programming Languages, POPL 2012, Philadelphia, PA, USA, pp. 401–412. ACM Press, New York (2012). https://doi.org/10.1145/2103656.2103704

4. Bojańczyk, M., Klin, B., Lasota, S.: Automata theory in nominal sets. Log. Methods Comput. Sci. 10(3), Article no. 4 (2014). https://doi.org/10.2168/lmcs-10(3:4)2014

5. Bojańczyk, M., Lasota, S.: A machine-independent characterization of timed languages. In: Czumaj, A., Mehlhorn, K., Pitts, A., Wattenhofer, R. (eds.) ICALP 2012. LNCS, vol. 7392, pp. 92–103. Springer, Heidelberg (2012). https://doi.org/10.1007/978-3-642-31585-5_12

6. Bollig, B., Habermehl, P., Leucker, M., Monmege, B.: A fresh approach to learning register automata. In: Béal, M.-P., Carton, O. (eds.) DLT 2013. LNCS, vol. 7907, pp. 118–130. Springer, Heidelberg (2013). https://doi.org/10.1007/978-3-642-38771-5_12

7. Cassel, S., Howar, F., Jonsson, B., Steffen, B.: Active learning for extended finite state machines. Formal Asp. Comput. **28**(2), 233–263 (2016). https://doi.org/10.1007/s00165-016-0355-5

8. Ciancia, V., Kurz, A., Montanari, U.: Families of symmetries as efficient models of resource binding. Electron. Notes Theor. Comput. Sci. **264**(2), 63–81 (2010). https://doi.org/10.1016/j.entcs.2010.07.014

9. Ciancia, V., Montanari, U.: Symmetries, local names and dynamic (de)-allocation of names. Inf. Comput. **208**(12), 1349–1367 (2010). https://doi.org/10.1016/j.ic.2009.10.007

10. D'Antoni, L., Veanes, M.: The power of symbolic automata and transducers. In: Majumdar, R., Kunčak, V. (eds.) CAV 2017. LNCS, vol. 10426, pp. 47–67. Springer, Cham (2017). https://doi.org/10.1007/978-3-319-63387-9_3

11. Drews, S., D'Antoni, L.: Learning symbolic automata. In: Legay, A., Margaria, T. (eds.) TACAS 2017. LNCS, vol. 10205, pp. 173–189. Springer, Heidelberg (2017). https://doi.org/10.1007/978-3-662-54577-5_10

12. Ferrari, G.L., Montanari, U., Tuosto, E.: Coalgebraic minimization of HD-automata for the π-calculus using polymorphic types. Theor. Comput. Sci. **331**(2–3), 325–365 (2005). https://doi.org/10.1016/j.tcs.2004.09.021

13. Fiterău-Broştean, P., Janssen, R., Vaandrager, F.: Combining model learning and model checking to analyze TCP implementations. In: Chaudhuri, S., Farzan, A. (eds.) CAV 2016. LNCS, vol. 9780, pp. 454–471. Springer, Cham (2016). https://doi.org/10.1007/978-3-319-41540-6_25

14. Gabbay, M., Pitts, A.M.: A new approach to abstract syntax with variable binding. Formal Asp. Comput. **13**(3–5), 341–363 (2002). https://doi.org/10.1007/s001650200016

15. Grigore, R., Tzevelekos, N.: History-register automata. Log. Methods Comput. Sci. 12(1), Article no. 7 (2016). https://doi.org/10.2168/lmcs-12(1:7)2016

16. Kaminski, M., Francez, N.: Finite-memory automata. Theor. Comput. Sci. **134**(2), 329–363 (1994). https://doi.org/10.1016/0304-3975(94)90242-9

17. Klin, B., Szynwelski, M.: SMT solving for functional programming over infinite structures. In: Atkey, R., Krishnaswami, N.R. (eds.) Proc. of 6th Workshop on Mathematically Structured Functional Programming, MSFP 2016 (Eindhoven, Apr. 2016). Electronic Proceedings in Theoretical Computer Science, vol. 207, pp. 57–75. Open Publishing Association, Sydney (2016). https://doi.org/10.4204/eptcs.207.3

18. Kopczynski, E., Toruńczyk, S.: LOIS: an application of SMT solvers. In: King, T., Piskac, R. (eds.) Proceedings of 14th International Workshop on Satisfiability Modulo Theories, SMT 2016, Coimbra, July 2016. CEUR Workshop Proceedings, vol. 1617, pp. 51–60. CEUR-WS.org (2016). http://ceur-ws.org/Vol-1617/paper5.pdf

19. Kopczynski, E., Toruńczyk, S.: LOIS: syntax and semantics. In: Proceedings of 44th ACM SIGPLAN Symposium on Principles of Programming Languages, POPL 2017, Paris, January 2017, pp. 586–598. ACM Press, New York (2017). https://doi.org/10.1145/3009837.3009876

20. Maler, O., Mens, I.-E.: A generic algorithm for learning symbolic automata from membership queries. In: Aceto, L., Bacci, G., Bacci, G., Ingólfsdóttir, A., Legay, A., Mardare, R. (eds.) Models, Algorithms, Logics and Tools. LNCS, vol. 10460, pp. 146–169. Springer, Cham (2017). https://doi.org/10.1007/978-3-319-63121-9_8

21. Moerman, J., Sammartino, M., Silva, A., Klin, B., Szynwelski, M.: Learning nominal automata. In: Proceedings of 44th ACM SIGPLAN Symposium on Principles of Programming Languages, POPL 2017, Paris, January 2017, pp. 613–625. ACM Press, New York (2017). https://doi.org/10.1145/3009837.3009879

22. Montanari, U., Pistore, M.: An introduction to history dependent automata. Electron. Notes Theor. Comput. Sci. **10**, 170–188 (1998). https://doi.org/10.1016/s1571-0661(05)80696-6

23. Murawski, A.S., Ramsay, S.J., Tzevelekos, N.: Bisimilarity in fresh-register automata. In: Proceedings of 30th Annual ACM/IEEE Symposium on Logic in Computer Science, LICS 2015, Kyoto, July 2015, pp. 156–167. IEEE CS Press (2015). https://doi.org/10.1109/lics.2015.24

24. Pitts, A.M.: Nominal Sets: Names and Symmetry in Computer Science. Cambridge Tracts in Theoretical Computer Science, vol. 57. Cambridge University Press, Cambridge (2013). https://doi.org/10.1017/cbo9781139084673

25. Pitts, A.M.: Nominal techniques. SIGLOG News **3**(1), 57–72 (2016). http://doi.acm.org/10.1145/2893582.2893594

26. Segoufin, L.: Automata and logics for words and trees over an infinite alphabet. In: Ésik, Z. (ed.) CSL 2006. LNCS, vol. 4207, pp. 41–57. Springer, Heidelberg (2006). https://doi.org/10.1007/11874683_3

27. Shinwell, M.R., Pitts, A.M.: Fresh Objective Caml user manual. Technical report, Computer Laboratory, University of Cambridge (2005)

28. Urban, C., Tasson, C.: Nominal techniques in Isabelle/HOL. In: Nieuwenhuis, R. (ed.) CADE 2005. LNCS (LNAI), vol. 3632, pp. 38–53. Springer, Heidelberg (2005). https://doi.org/10.1007/11532231_4

29. Vaandrager, F.W.: Model learning. Commun. ACM **60**(2), 86–95 (2017). https://doi.org/10.1145/2967606

Non-preemptive Semantics
for Data-Race-Free Programs

Siyang Xiao[1]($^{(\boxtimes)}$), Hanru Jiang[1], Hongjin Liang[2], and Xinyu Feng[2]

[1] University of Science and Technology of China, Hefei 230027, China
{yutio888,hanru219}@mail.ustc.edu.cn
[2] State Key Laboratory for Novel Software Technology, Nanjing University,
Nanjing 210023, China
{hongjin,xyfeng}@nju.edu.cn

Abstract. It is challenging to reason about the behaviors of concurrent programs because of the non-deterministic interleaving execution of threads. To simplify the reasoning, we propose a non-preemptive semantics for data-race-free (DRF) concurrent programs, where a thread yields the control of the CPU only at certain carefully-chosen program points. We formally prove that DRF concurrent programs behave the same in the standard interleaving semantics and in our non-preemptive semantics. We also propose a novel formulation of data-race-freedom in our non-preemptive semantics, called NPDRF, which is proved equivalent to the standard DRF notion in the interleaving semantics.

Keywords: Data-race-freedom · Interleaving semantics
Non-preemptive semantics

1 Introduction

Interleaving semantics has been widely used as standard operational semantics for concurrent programs, where the execution of a thread can be preempted at any program point and the control is switched to a different thread. Reasoning about multi-threaded concurrent programs in this semantics is challenging because the number of possible interleaving executions can be exponential (with respect to the length of the program).

On the other hand, for a large class of programs, it is a waste of effort to enumerate and verify all the possible interleavings, because many of them actually lead to the same result. For instance, the simple program in Fig. 1(a) has six possible interleavings, but all of these interleavings result in the same final state ($x = r1 = 42, y = r2 = 24$). Thus, to analyze the final result of the program in Fig. 1(a), we can reason about only one interleaving instead of all the six, which dramatically reduces the verification effort. The question is, can we

This work is supported in part by grants from National Natural Science Foundation of China (NSFC) under Grant Nos. 61502442 and 61632005.

B. Fischer and T. Uustalu (Eds.): ICTAC 2018, LNCS 11187, pp. 513–531, 2018.
https://doi.org/10.1007/978-3-030-02508-3_27

x := 42; ‖ y := 24;	x := 42; ‖ y := 24;	x := 42; ‖ ⟨r1 := z⟩;

$$
\begin{array}{c|c}
\texttt{x := 42;} & \texttt{y := 24;} \\
\texttt{r1 := x;} & \texttt{r2 := y;}
\end{array}
\qquad
\begin{array}{c|c}
\texttt{x := 42;} & \texttt{y := 24;} \\
\texttt{r1 := x;} & \texttt{r2 := y;} \\
\langle\texttt{z := x}\rangle; & \langle\texttt{y := z}\rangle;
\end{array}
\qquad
\begin{array}{c|c}
\texttt{x := 42;} & \langle\texttt{r1 := z}\rangle; \\
\langle\texttt{z := 1}\rangle; & \texttt{if (r1=1)} \\
& \quad\texttt{r2 := x;}
\end{array}
$$

(a)   (b)   (c)

Fig. 1. Data-race-free programs

systematically reduce the number of interleavings without reducing the possible behaviors of a concurrent program?

Actually it is well-known that, for data-race-free (DRF) programs, we only need to consider interleavings at synchronization points. Informally a data race occurs when multiple threads access the same memory location concurrently and at least one of the accesses is a write. All the three programs in Fig. 1 are data-race-free. Here we use the atomic statement $\langle S \rangle$ to mean that the execution of S is atomic, i.e. it cannot be interrupted by other threads. Thus the two accesses of z in Fig. 1(b) are well synchronized, and the program is data-race-free. In Fig. 1(c), although both threads access the shared variable x outside of the atomic statement, they cannot be accessed *concurrently* (assuming the initial value of z is 0) because the read of x in the second thread can only be executed (if executed at all) after the write of z, which then happens after the write of x.

Although it is a folklore theorem that the behaviors of DRF programs under the standard interleaving semantics should be equivalent to those in some non-preemptive semantics where a thread yields the control of the CPU at will at certain program points, it is not obvious where these program points should be, especially if we want to minimize such program points to reduce as many possible interleavings as possible. And what if the language allows other effects other than memory accesses, such as I/O operations? Would non-termination of programs affect the choice of these program points?

For instance, a straightforward approach is to treat both the entry and the exit of atomic blocks $\langle S \rangle$ as program points to allow interleaving (i.e. switching between threads). But can we just use only one of them instead of both? If yes, are the entry and the exit points equally good? It is quite interesting to see that we can pick the exit of the block as the only switching point, and the behaviors under preemptive semantics are still preserved. However, the entry point does not work, which may lead to strictly less behaviors than preemptive semantics if the program following the atomic block does not terminate.

In this paper we formally study the non-preemptive semantics of DRF programs, and discuss the possible variations of the semantics and how they affect the equivalence with the preemptive semantics. The paper makes the following contributions:

- We define the notion of DRF operationally based on the preemptive operational semantics.
- We propose non-preemptive semantics for DRF programs. In addition to memory accesses, our language allows externally observable operations such

as I/O operations. Threads in the semantics can be preempted only at the end of each atomic block or after the I/O operations. We discuss how non-termination could affect the choice of switching points.

- We define the semantics equivalence based on the set of execution traces in each semantics. Then we formally prove that our non-preemptive semantics is equivalent to the preemptive one for DRF programs.
- We also give a new operational notion of DRF in the non-preemptive semantics, which is called NPDRF. We prove that NPDRF is equivalent to the original definition of DRF in the preemptive semantics. This allows one to study DRF programs fully within the non-preemptive semantics.

Related Work. Non-preemptive (or cooperative) semantics has been studied in various settings, for example in high scalability thread libraries [4,11,14], as alternative models for structuring or reasoning about concurrency [1,6,12,15], and in program analysis [16].

Beringer *et al.* [5] made a proposal of proving compilation correctness under a cooperative setting in order to reuse the compiler correctness proofs for sequential settings. Their proposal is based on the conjecture that when the source program is proved to be data-race-free, its behavior would be the same under cooperative semantics. We prove this conjecture in this paper.

Ferreira *et al.* [8] proposed a grainless semantics relating concurrent separation logic and relaxed memory models. Their grainless semantics execute non-atomic instructions in big steps, and cannot be interrupted by other threads, which is similar to cooperative semantics where program sections between atomic blocks are not interfered by other threads. They also proved DRF programs behave the same under interleaving semantics and grainless semantics in their setting. Our semantics and formulation of DRF are sufficiently different from theirs. Moreover, there is no in-depth discussion on how non-termination of programs affects the choice of the switching points to minimize the interleaving.

Collingbourne *et al.* [7] and Kojima *et al.* [10] studied the equivalence between interleaving semantics and the lock-step semantics usually used in graphics processing units (GPUs). They found that race-free programs executed in the standard interleaving semantics and the lock-step semantics should get the same result. However, the lock-step semantics require that each thread execute exactly the same set of operations in parallel. It is designed specially for GPU and is sufficiently different from the non-preemptive semantics we study here.

There has been much work formalizing DRF, e.g., DRF-0 [2] and DRF-1 [3]. Marino *et al.* [13] proposed a memory model called DRFx. They proposed a new concept called region conflict freedom, which requires no conflicting memory accesses between program sections instead of instructions, therefore enables efficient SC violation detecting. Their notion of region conflict freedom is similar to our NPDRF: regions are code snippets no larger than code snippets between critical sections, while in our NPDRF, we compare memory accesses of executions between atomic steps. They did not have a formal operational formulation as we do. Hower et al. [9] proposed the notion of heterogeneous-race-free (SC-HRF) for

$$\begin{array}{ll} \langle x := 1 \rangle; & \Big\| \quad \langle r := x \rangle; \\ \textbf{while(true) do skip;} & \quad \textbf{print}(r); \end{array}$$

$$\begin{array}{ll} \textbf{print}(1); & \Big\| \quad \textbf{print}(0); \\ \textbf{print}(2); & \end{array}$$

(a)   (b)

$$\begin{array}{ll} \textbf{print}(1); & \Big\| \quad \textbf{print}(0); \\ \textbf{while(true) do skip;} & \quad \textbf{while(true) do skip;} \end{array}$$

(c)

Fig. 2. More examples about non-preemptive executions

scoped synchronization in heterogeneous systems, which is for a different setting from ours.

Organizations. In the rest of this paper, we make some informal discussion about non-preemptive semantics in Sect. 2. Then we introduce the basic technical settings about the language and the preemptive semantics in Sect. 3. In Sect. 4, we give the definition of our non-preemptive semantics and discuss the equivalence of preemptive semantics and non-preemptive semantics. In Sect. 5, we discuss the notion of data-race-freedom in our non-preemptive semantics (called NPDRF) and the equivalence of NPDRF and DRF. Section 6 concludes this paper.

2   Informal Discussions of the Non-preemptive Semantics

In this section we informally compare the program behaviors in preemptive semantics and non-preemptive semantics with different choices of switching points, based on which we give a principle to ensure the semantics equivalence.

In Fig. 2(a), assuming the initial value of x is 0, the program may either print out 1 or print out 0 in the preemptive semantics, or generate no output at all if the scheduling is unfair. In non-preemptive semantics, if we allow switching at the exit of atomic blocks, we can get the same set of possible behaviors. However, if we choose the entry as the only switching point, it is impossible to print out 1. This is because the left thread does not terminate after the write of x, so there is no chance for the second thread to run.

Our language has the **print**(e) command as a representative I/O command. When we observe program behaviors, we observe the sequences of externally observable I/O events. To allow the non-preemptive semantics to generate the same set of event sequences as in the preemptive semantics, we must allow switching at each I/O command. In Fig. 2(b), it would be impossible to observe the sequence "102" if we disallow switching at each print command.

This is easy to understand if we view each print command as a write to a shared tape[1]. However, it would be interesting to see what would happen if we

---

[1] In this case, we don't view two concurrent print commands as a data race. Instead, we assume there is an implicit enclosing atomic block for each **print**(e).

project the whole output sequence to each thread and observe the resulting set of subsequences instead of the whole sequence. That is, we assume each thread has its own tape for outputs. For the program in Fig. 2(b), we can observe the subsequence "12" for the left thread and "0" for the right, no matter we allow switching at the print command or not.

However, the next example in Fig. 2(c) shows that, even if we only observe thread-local output sequences, we still need to treat the print command as an switching point, otherwise it would be impossible to see both outputs in non-preemptive semantics.

Figure 2(a) and (c) show that non-termination of the code segment between synchronization (or I/O) points plays an important role when we choose the switching points. Essentially this is because, in non-preemptive semantics, non-termination of these code segments prevents the switching from the current thread to another. Although such code segment never accesses shared resources in DRF programs, they should be viewed similarly as the accesses of shared resources—they all generate external effects affecting other threads.

Based on the above discussion, we follow the principle below when deciding switching points in our non-preemptive semantics to ensure its equivalence to the preemptive semantics:

There must be at least one switching point between any two consecutive externally observable effects generated at runtime in the same thread.

Here *externally observable effects* are those that either affect behaviors of other threads or generate externally observable events.

It is interesting to note that if a non-terminating code segment comes before an atomic block, there is no switching point in between if we do not treat the entry of the atomic block as an switching point. This actually does *not* violate the above principle because the atomic block never gets executed if it follows a non-terminating code segment. Therefore there are NO two consecutive externally observable effects generated at runtime.

In the following sections we formalize the ideas in our definition of non-preemptive semantics and prove that it preserves the behaviors of DRF programs in preemptive semantics.

3   The Language and Preemptive Semantics

The syntax of the language is shown in Fig. 3. In the language we distinguish variables from memory cells. The whole program P consists of n sequential threads, each with its own local variables (like thread-local registers). They communicate through a shared heap (i.e. memory).

The arithmetic expressions e and boolean expressions b are pure in that they do not access the heap. The commands $x := [e]$ and $[e] := e'$ reads and writes heap cells at the location e, respectively. The **print**(e) command generates externally observable output of the value of e.

The atomic statement $\langle S \rangle$ executes S sequentially, which cannot be interrupted by other threads. It can be viewed as a convenient abstraction for hardware supported atomic operations (such as the **cas** instruction). Here S cannot

$$(Expr) \quad e ::= x \mid \mathbf{n} \mid e_1 + e_2 \mid e_1 - e_2 \mid \ldots$$

$$(Bexp) \quad b ::= \mathbf{true} \mid \mathbf{false} \mid e_1 = e_2 \mid e_1 < e_2 \mid \neg b \mid b_1 \wedge b_2 \mid b_1 \vee b_2 \mid \ldots$$

$$(Prim) \quad c ::= x := e \mid x := [e] \mid [e] := e' \mid \mathbf{print}(e)$$

$$(Stmt) \quad S ::= c \mid \mathbf{skip} \mid S; S \mid \langle S \rangle \mid \mathbf{if}(b) \; S_1 \; \mathbf{else} \; S_2 \mid \mathbf{while}(b) \; \mathbf{do} \; S$$

$$(Prog) \quad P ::= S_1 \parallel \ldots \parallel S_n$$

Fig. 3. Syntax of the language

contain other atomic blocks or print commands. This is enforced in our operational semantics rules presented below.

The state model is defined in Fig. 4. The world W contains the program P, the id of the current thread $\mathbf{t}$ and the program state σ. The state σ contains a heap h, a mapping ls that maps each thread id to its local store s, and a binary flag $\mathbf{d}$ indicating whether the current thread is executing inside an atomic block.

$$
\begin{aligned}
(World) \quad & W && ::= (P, \mathbf{t}, \sigma) \\
(ThrdId) \quad & \mathbf{t} && \in \mathbb{N} \\
(Addr) \quad & a && \in \mathbb{N} \\
(Store) \quad & s && \in Var \rightarrow Int \\
(StoreList) \quad & ls && \in ThrdID \rightarrow Store \\
(Heap) \quad & h && \in Addr \rightharpoonup Int \\
(Bit) \quad & \mathbf{d} && ::= 0 \mid 1 \\
(State) \quad & \sigma && ::= (h, ls, \mathbf{d}) \\
(LocSet) \quad & rs, ws && \in \mathcal{P}(Addr) \\
(FootPrint) \quad & \delta && ::= (rs, ws) \qquad \mathbf{emp} \overset{\mathrm{def}}{=} (\emptyset, \emptyset) \\
(Label) \quad & \iota && ::= \gamma \mid \mathbf{out} \; n \\
(iLabel) \quad & \gamma && ::= \tau \mid \mathbf{sw} \mid \mathbf{atm}
\end{aligned}
$$

Fig. 4. Runtime constructs and footprints

Footprint-Based Semantics. Thread execution is defined as labeled transition in the form of $(S, (h, s)) \xrightarrow{\iota}_{\delta} (S', (h', s'))$. Figure 5 shows selected rules for thread-local transitions. Each step is associated with a label ι and a footprint δ. The label contains the information about this step. There are two class of labels, the internal labels γ and the externally observable output event ($\mathbf{out}$ n). An internal label γ can record a step inside an atomic block ($\mathbf{atm}$), a context switch ($\mathbf{sw}$, which is used only in the whole program transitions in Fig. 6), or a regular silent step (τ). Note the ATOM rule only allows τ-steps inside the atomic block,

$$\frac{[\![e]\!]_s = n \quad s' = s[x \rightsquigarrow n]}{(x := e, (h, s)) \xrightarrow[\text{emp}]{\tau} (\textbf{skip}, (h, s'))} \text{(ASSN)} \qquad \frac{[\![e]\!]_s = l \quad h[l] = n \quad s' = s[x \rightsquigarrow n]}{(x := [e], (h, s)) \xrightarrow[(\{l\}, \emptyset)]{\tau} (\textbf{skip}, (h, s'))} \text{(LD)}$$

$$\frac{[\![e]\!]_s = l \quad [\![e']\!]_s = n \quad l \in \text{dom}(h) \quad h' = h[l \rightsquigarrow n]}{([e] := e', (h, s)) \xrightarrow[(\emptyset, \{l\})]{\tau} (\textbf{skip}, (h', s))} \text{(ST)} \qquad \frac{[\![e]\!]_s = l \quad l \notin \text{dom}(h)}{([e] := e', (h, s)) \xrightarrow[\text{emp}]{\tau} \textbf{abort}} \text{(ST-ABT)}$$

$$\frac{[\![e]\!]_s = n}{(\textbf{print}(e), (h, s)) \xrightarrow[\text{emp}]{\text{out } n} (\textbf{skip}, (h, s))} \text{(PRT)} \qquad \frac{(S, (h, s)) \xrightarrow[\delta]{\tau} (S', (h', s'))}{(\langle S \rangle, (h, s)) \xrightarrow[\delta]{\text{atm}} (\langle S' \rangle, (h', s'))} \text{(ATOM)}$$

$$\frac{}{(\langle \textbf{skip} \rangle, (h, s)) \xrightarrow[\text{emp}]{\text{atm}} (\textbf{skip}, (h, s))} \text{(ATOM-END)}$$

Fig. 5. Selected rules for thread-local transitions

which are converted to **atm**-steps looking from outside of the block. Therefore the block $\langle S \rangle$ cannot contain other atomic blocks or print commands in S.

The footprint δ is defined as a pair (rs, ws), where rs and ws are the sets of memory locations read or written during the transition. The record of footprint allows us to define data-races below. When a step makes no memory accesses, the footprint is defined as **emp**, where rs and ws are both empty set.

Transitions of the global configuration W are defined in the form of $W \xRightarrow{\iota}_\delta W'$ in Fig. 6. The THRD rule shows a step of execution outside of atomic blocks. The flag **d** must be 0 in this case. It is set to 1 when executing inside the atomic block (the ATOMIC rule), and reset to 0 at the end (the ATOMIC-END rule). The SWITCH rule says the execution of the current thread can be switched to a different one at any time as long as the current thread is not executing an atomic block (i.e. the bit **d** must be 0). Here we use the label **sw** to indicate this is a switch step. Its use will be explained below.

W may also lead to **abort** if the execution of the current thread aborts (the ABT rule). It leads to a special configuration **done** if every individual thread terminates (the DONE rule).

Multi-step Transitions. We use $(S, (h, s)) \xrightarrow{\iota}_\delta {}^+ (S', (h', s'))$ to represent multi-step transitions that the label of each transition is ι. Here δ is the accumulation of the footprints generated. We may ommit the label or the footprint when they are irrelevant in the context. Similarly $\xrightarrow{\iota}_\delta {}^*$ represents transitions of zero or multiple steps. In the case of zero step, δ is **emp**. $W \xRightarrow{\iota}_\delta {}^+ W'$ and $W \xRightarrow{\iota}_\delta {}^* W'$ are similarly defined in the global semantics. In particular, $W \xRightarrow{\gamma}_\delta {}^* W'$ means only internal labels γ are generated during the transitions. The labels in these steps can be τ, **atm** or **sw**. Labels in different steps do not have to be the same in

$$\frac{P(t) = S \quad ls(t) = s \quad \iota \neq \mathbf{atm} \quad (S,(h,s)) \overset{\iota}{\underset{\delta}{\longmapsto}} (S',(h',s')) \quad ls' = ls[t \rightsquigarrow s']}{(P,t,(h,ls,0)) \overset{\iota}{\underset{\delta}{\Rightarrow}} (P[t \rightsquigarrow S'], t, (h', ls', 0))} \text{ (THRD)}$$

$$\frac{P(t) = S \quad S = \langle S_2 \rangle \vee S = \langle S_2 \rangle; S_3 \quad ls(t) = s}{S_2 \neq \mathbf{skip} \quad (S,(h,s)) \overset{\mathbf{atm}}{\underset{\delta}{\longmapsto}} (S',(h',s')) \quad ls' = ls[t \rightsquigarrow s']}{(P,t,(h,ls,d)) \overset{\mathbf{atm}}{\underset{\delta}{\Longrightarrow}} (P[t \rightsquigarrow S'], t, (h', ls', 1))} \text{ (ATOMIC)}$$

$$\frac{P(t) = S \quad S = \langle \mathbf{skip} \rangle \vee S = \langle \mathbf{skip} \rangle; S_2 \quad ls(t) = s \quad (S,(h,s)) \overset{\mathbf{atm}}{\underset{\mathrm{emp}}{\longmapsto}} (S',(h,s))}{(P,t,(h,ls,d)) \overset{\mathbf{atm}}{\underset{\mathrm{emp}}{\Longrightarrow}} (P[t \rightsquigarrow S'], t, (h, ls, 0))} \text{ (ATOMIC-END)}$$

$$\frac{P(t) = S \quad ls(t) = s \quad (S,(h,s)) \overset{\iota}{\underset{\delta}{\longmapsto}} \mathbf{abort}}{(P,t,(h,ls,d)) \overset{\iota}{\underset{\delta}{\Rightarrow}} \mathbf{abort}} \text{ (ABT)}$$

$$\frac{P(t') \neq \mathbf{skip}}{(P,t,(h,s,0)) \overset{\mathbf{sw}}{\underset{\mathrm{emp}}{\Longrightarrow}} (P,t',(h,s,0))} \text{ (SWITCH)} \qquad \frac{P = \mathbf{skip} \parallel \cdots \parallel \mathbf{skip}}{(P,t,\sigma) \overset{\tau}{\underset{\mathrm{emp}}{\Rightarrow}} \mathbf{done}} \text{ (DONE)}$$

Fig. 6. Selected rules for global transitions

this case. We also use a natural number k as the superscript to indicate a k-step transition.

Event Traces and Program Behaviors. The behavior of a concurrent program is defined as an externally observable event trace $\mathcal{B}$, which is a finite or infinite sequence of output values generated in the output event (**out** n), with possible ending events **done** or **abort**. An empty trace is represented as ϵ. Traces are co-inductively defined in Fig. 7.

The trace ends with **done** or **abort** if the execution terminates normally or aborts, respectively. When the program generates observable events (by the **print** command), the output value is put on the trace. Co-inductively defined, a trace can be infinite, which represents a diverging execution generating infinite number of outputs.

We allow a trace to be finite but not end with **done** or **abort**. In this case, after generating the last output recorded on the trace, the program runs forever but does not generate any more observable events (called silent divergence). Note our definition of silent divergence in the last rule in Fig. 7 requires there must always be non-switch steps (which can be τ steps or **atm** steps) executing. This prevents the execution that keeps switching between threads but does not execute any code.

Definition of Data Races. Below we first define conflict of footprints in Definition 1, which indicates conflicting accesses of shared memory. Two footprints

$$\frac{W \overset{\rightarrow}{\Rightarrow}{}^{+} \textbf{abort}}{Etr(W, \textbf{abort})} \qquad \frac{W \overset{\rightarrow}{\Rightarrow}{}^{*} W' \quad W' \xrightarrow{\ \text{out } n\ } W'' \quad Etr(W'', \mathcal{B})}{Etr(W, n :: \mathcal{B})}$$

$$\frac{W \overset{\rightarrow}{\Rightarrow}{}^{+} \textbf{done}}{Etr(W, \textbf{done})} \qquad \frac{W \overset{\rightarrow}{\Rightarrow}{}^{*} W' \quad W' \xrightarrow{\ \tau/\textbf{atm}\ } W'' \quad Etr(W'', \epsilon)}{Etr(W, \epsilon)}$$

$$ProgEtr((P, \sigma), \mathcal{B}) \quad \text{iff} \quad \exists \mathsf{t}. Etr((P, \mathsf{t}, \sigma), \mathcal{B})$$

Fig. 7. Definition of event trace in preemptive semantics

δ and δ' are conflicting, i.e. $\delta \frown \delta'$, if there exists a memory location in one of them also shows up in the *write* set of the other.

Definition 1 (Conflicting footprints). $\delta \frown \delta'$ iff $((\delta.rs \cap \delta'.ws \neq \emptyset) \vee (\delta.ws \cap \delta'.rs \neq \emptyset) \vee (\delta.ws \cap \delta'.ws \neq \emptyset))$.

In Fig. 8, we define data races operationally in the preemptive semantics. The key idea is that, during the program execution, we predict the footprints of any two threads and see if they are conflicting. Note that we only do the prediction at switching points. That is, footprints of threads are predicted only when the threads can indeed be switched to run. We cannot do the prediction when executing inside an atomic block, where switching is disallowed.

The first two rules inductively define the predicate $predict(W, \mathsf{t}, \delta, \mathsf{d})$. Suppose we execute thread t in W (which may or may not be the current thread t') zero or multiple steps. The accumulated footstep is δ. We let d be 1 if the predicted steps are in an atomic block, and 0 otherwise.

Then $W \Longmapsto \texttt{Race}$ if there exist two threads whose predicted footprints are conflicting, and at least one of them is not executing an atomic block. Since we assume that atomic blocks cannot be executed at the same time, atomic blocks that generate conflicting footprints are not considered as a data race.

We define $(P, \sigma) \Longmapsto \texttt{Race}$ if it predicts a data race after zero or multiple steps of execution starting from a certain thread. $\mathsf{DRF}(P, \sigma)$ holds if (P, σ) never reaches a race.

In both PREDICT-0 and PREDICRT-1 rules, the flag in W must be 0, indicating the current thread t' is not inside an atomic block (so the execution is at a switching point). Otherwise the predict rule is able to make use of the intermediate state during the execution of an atomic block that is invisible to other threads, and predict conflicting footprints that is not possible during execution. We can see this problem from the example program in Fig. 9. Assuming the heap cells are initialized with 0, it is easy to see the program is race-free since the second thread has no chance to write to the memory location 1. However, if we permit prediction inside an atomic block, we are able to make prediction at the program point right after the statement ([0] := 42;) in the first thread. Then in the predicted execution the second thread can reach the first branch of the conditional statement and write to location 1 since location 0 now contains 42.

$$\frac{W = (P, \mathsf{t}', (h, ls, 0)) \quad P(\mathsf{t}) = S \quad ls(\mathsf{t}) = s \quad (S, (h, s)) \xrightarrow[\delta]{\tau}{}^* (S', (h', s'))}{predict(W, \mathsf{t}, \delta, 0)} \text{ (PREDICT-0)}$$

$$\frac{W = (P, \mathsf{t}', (h, ls, 0)) \quad P(\mathsf{t}) = S \quad ls(\mathsf{t}) = s \quad (S, (h, s)) \xrightarrow[\delta]{\mathbf{atm}}{}^* (S', (h', s'))}{predict(W, \mathsf{t}, \delta, 1)} \text{ (PREDICT-1)}$$

$$\frac{\mathsf{t}_1 \neq \mathsf{t}_2 \quad predict(W, \mathsf{t}_1, \delta_1, \mathsf{d}_1) \quad predict(W, \mathsf{t}_2, \delta_2, \mathsf{d}_2)}{\delta_1 \frown \delta_2 \quad (\mathsf{d}_1 = 0 \lor \mathsf{d}_2 = 0)} \text{ (RACE)}$$
$$\frac{}{W \Longmapsto \mathbf{Race}}$$

$$\frac{(P, \mathsf{t}, \sigma) \Rightarrow^* W \quad W \Longmapsto \mathbf{Race}}{(P, \sigma) \Longmapsto \mathbf{Race}} \qquad \frac{\neg (P, \sigma) \Longmapsto \mathbf{Race}}{\mathsf{DRF}(P, \sigma)}$$

Fig. 8. Definition of races and data-race-freedom

```
⟨[0] := 42;     ⟨x := [0];                        [1] := 42;
 [0] := 0;⟩  ‖   if(x = 42) [1] := 42 else skip ⟩  ‖
```

Fig. 9. Example of an DRF program

We can also predict that the third thread writes to location 1 as well. This kind of conflicting footprints would never be generated during the actual execution of the program and should not be considered as data race.

4   Non-preemptive Semantics

Below we define our non-preemptive semantics, and prove its equivalence with preemptive semantics for DRF programs. As explained before, the key point of non-preemptive semantics is to reduce the potential interleaving in concurrency. It is done by limiting thread-switching to certain program points (called switching points). Thus the code fragment between switching points can be reasoned about as sequential code, and interleaving is only considered at those switching points.

4.1   Semantics

The non-preemptive semantics is defined in Fig. 10. We use three switching rules in our non-preemptive semantics, i.e. the NP-ATOM-SW rule, the OUT-SW rule and the END-SW rule, to show that switching can occur only at the end of atomic blocks, the **print** command, and the end of the current thread, respectively. The other rules are similar to their counterparts in the preemptive semantics.

$$\frac{P(t) = S \quad ls(t) = s \quad ls' = ls[t \rightsquigarrow s'] \quad (S,(h,s)) \xmapsto[\delta]{\tau} (S',(h',s'))}{(P,t,(h,ls,0)) :\xRightarrow[\delta]{\tau} (P[t \rightsquigarrow S'],t,(h',ls',0))} \text{ (NP-THRD)}$$

$$\frac{\begin{array}{c} P(t) = S \quad S = \langle S_a \rangle \vee S = \langle S_a \rangle; S_b \quad S_a \neq \textbf{skip} \\ ls(t) = s \quad ls' = ls[t \rightsquigarrow s'] \quad (S,(h,s)) \xmapsto[\delta]{\textbf{atm}} (S',(h',s')) \end{array}}{(P,t,(h,ls,d)) :\xRightarrow[\delta]{\textbf{atm}} (P[t \rightsquigarrow S'],t,(h',ls',1))} \text{ (NP-ATOM)}$$

$$\frac{\begin{array}{c} P(t) = S \quad S = \langle \textbf{skip} \rangle \vee S = \langle \textbf{skip} \rangle; S'' \quad ls(t) = s \\ (S,(h,s)) \xmapsto[\text{emp}]{\textbf{atm}} (S',(h,s)) \quad t' = t \vee P(t') \neq \textbf{skip} \end{array}}{(P,t,(h,ls,d)) :\xRightarrow[\text{emp}]{\textbf{sw}} (P[t \rightsquigarrow S'],t',(h,ls,0))} \text{ (NP-ATOM-SW)}$$

$$\frac{P(t) = S \quad (S,(h,ls)) \xmapsto[\text{emp}]{\textbf{out } n} (S',(h,ls)) \quad t' = t \vee P(t') \neq \textbf{skip}}{(P,t,(h,ls,0)) :\xRightarrow[\text{emp}]{\textbf{out } n} (P[t \rightsquigarrow S'],t',(h,ls,0))} \text{ (OUT-SW)}$$

$$\frac{P(t) = \textbf{skip} \quad \sigma.d = 0 \quad P(t') \neq \textbf{skip}}{(P,t,\sigma) :\xRightarrow[\text{emp}]{\textbf{sw}} (P,t',\sigma)} \text{ (END-SW)}$$

$$\frac{P = \textbf{skip} \parallel \cdots \parallel \textbf{skip}}{(P,t,\sigma) :\xRightarrow[\text{emp}]{\tau} \textbf{done}} \text{ (NP-DONE)}$$

$$\frac{P(t) = S \quad ls(t) = s \quad (S,(h,s)) \xmapsto[\text{emp}]{\tau} \textbf{abort}}{(P,t,(h,ls,d)) :\xRightarrow[\text{emp}]{\tau} \textbf{abort}} \text{ (NP-ABT)}$$

Fig. 10. Non-preemptive semantics

Event Traces in Non-preemptive Semantics. The definition of event traces in the non-preemptive semantics is almost the same as that in preemptive semantics (see Fig. 11). The last rule is simpler here because in the non-preemptive

$$\frac{W :\xRightarrow{} {}^+ \textbf{abort}}{NPEtr(W,\textbf{abort})} \qquad \frac{W :\xRightarrow{} {}^* W' \quad W' :\xRightarrow{\textbf{out } n} W'' \quad NPEtr(W'',\mathcal{B})}{NPEtr(W,n::\mathcal{B})}$$

$$\frac{W :\xRightarrow{} {}^+ \textbf{done}}{NPEtr(W,\textbf{done})} \qquad \frac{W :\xRightarrow{} {}^+ W' \quad NPEtr(W',\epsilon)}{NPEtr(W,\epsilon)}$$

$$ProgNPEtr((P,\sigma),\mathcal{B}) \text{ iff } \exists t.NPEtr((P,t,\sigma),\mathcal{B})$$

Fig. 11. Definition of $ProgNPEtr((P,\sigma),\mathcal{B})$.

semantics every context switch is tied with a non-switch step, as explained above. It is impossible for a program to keep switching without executing any code.

4.2 Equivalence with Preemptive Semantics

In this section we prove that, for any DRF program, it behaves the same in the preemptive semantics as in the non-preemptive semantics. Since we define the behavior of a program by the trace of observable events, essentially we require the program to have the same set of event traces in both semantics. The goal is formalized as Theorem 1. As an implicit assumption, the programs we consider must be safe.

Since every step in the non-preemptive semantics can be easily converted to preemptive steps, it is obvious that every event trace in the non-preemptive semantics can be produced in the preemptive semantics.

However, it is non-trivial to prove the other direction: the preemptive semantics cannot generate more event traces than the non-preemptive semantics.

The main idea of the proof is that under data-race-freedom, we can exchange the execution orders of any τ-steps of different threads in preemptive semantics. Note that the orders of atomic steps or print steps cannot be exchanged even when the program is data-race-free.

Then we can fix the order of atomic steps and the print step in the preemptive semantics and reorder all the other steps to form a non-preemptive-like execution. Recall that the non-preemptive semantics allows the threads to switch at the print steps and at the end of atomic blocks. Thus by reordering the steps, we can always let the program start executions in a thread until it reaches a print or the end of an atomic block, and then switch to another thread.

In the following lemmas we describe how to exchange the execution order of threads in preemptive semantics. For convenience, we write W^i to represent a world by setting the current thread id in W to i.

Lemma 1 says the orders of local transitions can be exchanged, as long as the footprints are not conflicting. The reorder would not change the final state, the labels and the generated footprints.

Lemma 1 (Reorder of thread-local transitions)

$$\text{If } (S_1, (h, s_1)) \xmapsto[\delta_1]{\iota_1} (S_1', (h', s_1')) \wedge (S_2, (h', s_2)) \xmapsto[\delta_2]{\iota_2} (S_2', (h'', s_2')) \wedge \neg(\delta_1 \frown \delta_2)$$

$$\text{then } \exists h'''. \ (S_2, (h, s_2)) \xmapsto[\delta_2]{\iota_2} (S_2', (h''', s_2')) \wedge (S_1, (h''', s_1)) \xmapsto[\delta_1]{\iota_1} (S_1', (h'', s_1'))$$

Lemma 2 says if there are two consecutive steps from two threads generating conflicting footprints, then the predicted execution of the two threads starting from the *same* state generating conflicting footprints too. That is, the prediction would not miss the race. We need this lemma because the prediction of different threads starts from the same state in the RACE rule in Fig. 8.

Lemma 2 (Lemma for conflicting thread-local transitions)

$$\text{If } (S_1, (h, s_1)) \xmapsto[\delta_1]{\iota_1} (S_1', (h', s_1')) \wedge (S_2, (h', s_2)) \xmapsto[\delta_2]{\iota_2} (S_2', (h'', s_2')) \wedge (\delta_1 \frown \delta_2)$$

$$\text{then } \exists \iota_2', \delta_2', S_2'', h''', s_2''. \ (S_2, (h, s_2)) \xmapsto[\delta_2']{\iota_2'} (S_2'', (h''', s_2'')) \wedge (\delta_1 \frown \delta_2')$$

Lemma 3 says we can reorder consecutive τ-steps from threads i and j if there is no data race. Lemma 4 shows the reorder of τ steps and atomic steps from different threads. Lemma 5 reorders the internal γ-steps and a print step from different threads. These lemmas are proved by applying Lemmas 1 and 2.

Lemma 3 (Reorder of silent steps)

For any $i, j, W, W_1, W_1', W_2, \delta_1, \delta_2$.
if $W.\sigma.d = 0 \wedge W^i \underset{\delta_1}{\overset{\tau}{\Rightarrow}}{}^* W_1 \wedge W_1^j \underset{\delta_2}{\overset{\tau}{\Rightarrow}}{}^* W_2 \wedge i \neq j$,
then either $W \Longmapsto Race$
or $\exists W_3. W^j \underset{\delta_2}{\overset{\tau}{\Rightarrow}}{}^* W_3 \wedge W_3^i \underset{\delta_1}{\overset{\tau}{\Rightarrow}}{}^* W_2^i$.

Lemma 4 (Reorder of silent steps and atomic steps)

For any $i, j, W, W_1, W_2, \delta_1, \delta_2$.
if $W.\sigma.d = 0 \wedge W_2.\sigma.d = 0 \wedge W^i \underset{\delta_1}{\overset{\tau}{\Rightarrow}}{}^* W_1 \wedge W_1^j \underset{\delta_2}{\overset{atm}{\Longrightarrow}}{}^* W_2 \wedge i \neq j$,
then either $W \Longmapsto Race$
or $\exists W_3. W^j \underset{\delta_2}{\overset{atm}{\Longrightarrow}}{}^* W_3 \wedge W_3^i \underset{\delta_1}{\overset{\tau}{\Rightarrow}}{}^* W_2^i$.

Lemma 5 (Reorder of internal steps and a print step)

For any $i, j, W, W_1, W_2, \delta_1, n$.
if $W.\sigma.d = 0 \wedge W^i \underset{\delta_1}{\overset{\gamma}{\Rightarrow}}{}^* W_1 \wedge W_1^j \underset{emp}{\overset{out\ n}{\Longrightarrow}} W_2 \wedge i \neq j$,
then $\exists W_3. W^j \underset{emp}{\overset{out\ n}{\Longrightarrow}} W_3 \wedge W_3^i \underset{\delta_1}{\overset{\tau}{\Rightarrow}}{}^* W_2^i$.

Then we can prove Theorem 1, saying that preemptive semantics and non-preemptive semantics behave the same.

Theorem 1 (Semantics equivalence)

For any P *and* σ, *if* $\mathsf{DRF}(P, \sigma)$,
then $\forall \mathcal{B}, ProgEtr(P, \sigma, \mathcal{B}) \iff ProgNPEtr(P, \sigma, \mathcal{B})$.

Proof "$\Longleftarrow$": As explained before, since every step in the non-preemptive semantics can be easily converted to preemptive steps, it is obvious that every event trace in the non-preemptive semantics can be produced in the preemptive semantics.

"$\Longrightarrow$": We consider the following cases of $\mathcal{B}$. We need to construct a non-preemptive execution for each case:

- case (1): $\mathcal{B} = \mathbf{done}$. We prove this case by induction on the number k of atomic blocks.
  0 : There is no atomic blocks. We prove this case by induction on the number of threads. If there is only one thread, we are immediately done. Otherwise, we choose any thread t to execute first and delay other threads by exchanging their steps with the thread t by Lemma 3. Then after the termination of the thread t, we can switch to another thread in the non-preemptive semantics. Then by induction hypothesis we are done.

$k + 1$: Let $\mathbf{t}$ be the first thread that is going to execute an atomic block. Then we exchange the τ-steps from other threads with the steps of thread $\mathbf{t}$ by Lemmas 3 and 4, so that we first execute thread $\mathbf{t}$ to the end of its atomic block, and then switch to execute the τ-steps from other threads. In this way we successfully reduce the number of atomic blocks by 1, and then by induction hypothesis, we are done.

- case (2): $\mathcal{B} = \mathbf{abort}$. This case is vacant by the assumption of safety.
- case (3): $\mathcal{B} = \epsilon$. If the number of atomic blocks is finite, there must be a point where the last atomic block ends. Then by induction on the number of atomic blocks we can construct a non-preemptive execution to that point by swapping other thread with the thread that is going to execute atomic block, similarly to case (1). Then we know that there is at least one thread $\mathbf{t}$ keep running forever, otherwise the program will terminate. We can let $\mathbf{t}$ execute all the time by exchanging other threads with it. Then we successfully construct a diverging execution for non-preemptive semantics.

Otherwise, there are infinite atomic blocks. The execution is a stream of small execution sections, each consisting of several silent steps in different threads and a single atomic block. We can exchange any silent step with the atomic block by Lemma 4 unless the silent step is in the same thread of the atomic block. Then we can merge the exchanged silent step part into the following section since it contains no atomic block. Therefore the first section consists steps of the same thread, then it can be converted to non-preemptive execution. Then by coinduction we can construct a diverging execution for non-preemptive semantics by converting every section to non-preemptive.

$$\frac{W = (P, \mathbf{t}', (h, ls, 0)) \quad P(\mathbf{t}) = S \quad ls(\mathbf{t}) = s \\ (S, (h, s)) \xrightarrow[\delta]{\tau}{}^* (S', (h', s'))}{nppredict(W, \mathbf{t}, \delta, 0)} \text{(NP-PREDICT-0)}$$

$$\frac{W = (P, \mathbf{t}', (h, ls, 0)) \quad P(\mathbf{t}) = S \quad ls(\mathbf{t}) = s \\ (S, (h, s)) \xrightarrow[\delta]{\tau}{}^* (S', (h', s')) \quad (S', (h', s')) \xrightarrow[\delta']{\mathbf{atm}}{}^* (S'', (h'', s''))}{nppredict(W, \mathbf{t}, \delta \cup \delta', 1)} \text{(NP-PREDICT-1)}$$

$$\frac{\mathbf{t}_1 \neq \mathbf{t}_2 \quad nppredict(W, \mathbf{t}_1, \delta_1, \mathbf{d}_1) \quad nppredict(W, \mathbf{t}_2, \delta_2, \mathbf{d}_2) \\ \delta_1 \frown \delta_2 \quad (\mathbf{d}_1 = 0 \vee \mathbf{d}_2 = 0)}{W :\Longmapsto \mathbf{Race}} \text{(NP-RACE)}$$

$$\frac{(P, \mathbf{t}, \sigma) :\Rightarrow^* W' \quad W' :\xrightarrow{\mathbf{sw}/(\mathbf{out}\ n)} W'' \quad W'' :\Longmapsto \mathbf{Race}}{(P, \sigma) :\Longmapsto \mathbf{Race}} \text{(SWITCH-RACE)}$$

$$\frac{(P, \mathbf{t}, \sigma) :\Longmapsto \mathbf{Race}}{(P, \sigma) :\Longmapsto \mathbf{Race}} \text{(INIT-RACE)} \qquad \frac{\neg (P, \sigma) :\Longmapsto \mathbf{Race}}{\mathsf{NPDRF}(P, \sigma)}$$

Fig. 12. Predicting race in non-preemptive semantics

- case (4): $\mathcal{B} = n :: \mathcal{B}'$. We prove this case by coinduction. Then we do induction on the number of atomic blocks and by applying Lemma 3 and Lemma 5, similarly to case (1) above.

5   Data-Race-Freedom in Non-preemptive Semantics

Theorem 1 shows that we can reason about a program in non-preemptive semantics instead of in preemptive semantics, as long as the program satisfies DRF in preemptive semantics. Below we present a notion of data-race-freedom in non-preemptive semantics (NPDRF) which is equivalent to DRF, making it possible to reason about the program solely under non-preemptive semantics.

We define NPDRF in Fig. 12. Similar to the DRF defined in Fig. 8, we predict the footprints of the execution (in the non-preemptive semantics now) of any two threads and see if they are conflicting (see the NP-RACE rule). The INIT-RACE rule and the SWITCH-RACE rule say the prediction can only be made either at the initial program configuration, or at a switch point. This is to ensure the prediction is made only at states from which the thread can indeed be switched to. Otherwise the prediction may not correspond to any actual execution.

The NP-PREDICT-0 rule is similar to the PREDICT-0 rule in Fig. 8. The tricky part is in the NP-PREDICT-1 rule. To predict the footprints of program steps inside atomic blocks, we need to execute the preceding silent steps as well (i.e. the τ-steps in the NP-PREDICT-1 rule). This is because the prediction starts only at a switching point, which must be outside of atomic blocks. Therefore we may never reach the atomic block directly without executing the preceding code outside of the atomic block first.

For example, in the program in Fig. 13, both the statements ($\langle [0] := 1 \rangle$) and ($[0] := 1$) writes to address 0. We can predict at the point before ($\langle [0] := 1 \rangle$) to get a data race in the preemptive semantics, following the DRF definition in Fig. 8. However, in our non-preemptive semantics, it is impossible to predict at the program point right before ($\langle [0] := 1 \rangle$), which is not a switch point. Instead, we have to do the prediction from the beginning of the left thread and execute the preceding **skip** as well.

Note that the prediction will never go across a switch point (e.g. the end of an atomic block). That's why we only consider τ-steps and **atm** steps in the NP-PREDICT-0 rule and the NP-PREDICT-1 rule.

Equivalence Between DRF and NPDRF. Below we prove that our novel notion NPDRF under the non-preemptive semantics is equivalent to DRF in the

$$
\begin{array}{c|c}
\textbf{skip;} & [0] := 1 \\
\langle [0] := 1 \rangle &
\end{array}
$$

Fig. 13. Example of data race

preemptive semantics. First we prove that the two different ways to predict data races in Figs. 8 and 12 are equivalent, as shown in Lemmas 6 and 7.

Lemma 6 (Lemma for prediction and np-prediction)
For any W, t, δ, d, if $predict(W, t, \delta, d)$, then $nppredict(W, t, \delta, d)$.

Proof. If $d = 0$ then it is immediate by the rules PREDICT-0 and NP-PREDICT-0.

Otherwise $d = 1$. In NP-PREDICT-1 rule, zero step is acceptable for the first part of silent steps, and the union of a footprint δ and emp is δ. Then by unfolding the definition of *predict* and by NP-PREDICT-1 rule we are done.

Lemma 7 (Lemma for data race prediction)
For any k, W and W', if $W \xrightarrow{\tau/sw}_k W' \wedge W' \Longmapsto Race$, then $W :\Longmapsto Race$.

Proof. By induction on k.

0 : By unfolding the definition, we know there exist t_1, t_2, δ_1, δ_2, d_1 and d_2 such that $t_1 \neq t_2$, $predict(W, t_1, \delta_1, d_1)$, $predict(W, t_2, \delta_2, d_2)$, $\delta_1 \frown \delta_2$ and $d_1 = 0 \vee d_2 = 0$.
Then by applying Lemma 6, we can transform *predict* to *nppredict*.
By NP-RACE rule it is done.

$k+1$: We know there exists W_0 and δ_0 such that $W \xrightarrow[\delta_0]{\tau/sw} W_0$ and $W_0 \xrightarrow{\tau/sw}_k W'$.
Then from the induction hypothesis, we know $W_0 :\Longmapsto Race$. By unfolding the definition, we know there exist t_1, t_2, δ_1, δ_2, d_1 and d_2 such that $t_1 \neq t_2$, $predict(W, t_1, \delta_1, d_1)$, $predict(W, t_2, \delta_2, d_2)$, $\delta_1 \frown \delta_2$ and $d_1 = 0 \vee d_2 = 0$. Suppose the step generating δ_0 is executed by the thread t_0.

- If $(t_0 = t_1 \wedge \neg(\delta_0 \frown \delta_2)) \vee (t_0 = t_2 \wedge \neg(\delta_0 \frown \delta_1))$, then we can merge it into the prediction by swapping the other thread with this step.
- If $(t_0 \neq t_1 \wedge t_0 \neq t_2 \wedge \neg(\delta_0 \frown \delta_1) \wedge \neg(\delta_0 \frown \delta_2))$, then we know the step is irrelevent and we can delay the thread t_0 by swapping the two threads with this step.
- Otherwise, $(t_0 = t_1 \wedge \delta_0 \frown \delta_2) \vee (t_0 = t_2 \wedge \delta_0 \frown \delta_1) \vee (t_0 \neq t_1 \wedge t_0 \neq t_2 \wedge (\delta_0 \frown \delta_1 \vee \delta_0 \frown \delta_2))$.
  Then we can predict a data race from W.
  In all cases, we can predict a data race from W.

It is very important that a data race should be predicted at switching point. Lemma 7 only concerns the equivalence of prediction. Thus we need to prove the equivalence of data races in preemptive semantics and non-preemptive semantics in Lemma 8.

Lemma 8 (Equivalence of data races in preemptive semantics and non-preemptive semantics)
For any P and σ, we have $((P, \sigma) \Longmapsto Race) \Longleftrightarrow ((P, \sigma) :\Longmapsto Race)$.

Proof. "⟸": According to the semantics, non-preemptive steps can be converted to preemptive steps directly. Then the problem is reduced to proving that the multi-step prediction of NP-PREDICT-1 in Fig. 12 can be simulated by the prediction in Fig. 8. Informally, we can rearrange the predicting executions defined in Fig. 12 by making the non-conflicting steps sequentially proceeding until the real conflicting steps, and predict in the way as in Fig. 8.

"⟹": After unfolding the definitions, we prove this case by induction on the number k of event steps.

0 : By induction on the number i of atomic blocks during the execution (except the predicted racing atomic steps).

   0 : By applying Lemma 7 and INIT-RACE rule.

   $i + 1$: Similar to the proof for Theorem 1. If there is no preemptive data race until the end of the first atomic block, then the thread of the first atomic block can execute without being interrupted by other threads, and then the number of atomic blocks can be reduced by 1. Afterwards we apply the induction hypothesis and predict a non-preemptive data race either at the end of the first atomic block (INIT-RACE rule) or a few steps later and right after a switching point (SWITCH-RACE rule). In both cases we are done by SWITCH-RACE rule.

   Otherwise, there is at least one preemptive data race before the end of first atomic block. Since data race cannot be predicted inside the atomic block, the prediction must be made before the first atomic block. Then by Lemma 7 we can predict a non-preemptive data race at the beginning of the execution. Thus we are done by INIT-RACE rule.

$k + 1$: We know the first thread to event step is thread m. By induction on the number i of atomic blocks before the first event step.

   0 : By applying Lemmas 3 and 5 we can let thread m execute first unless there is a data race before the first event step, which is reduced to case (k=0). Then the number of event steps is reduced by 1 and then by applying induction hypothesis we can predict a non-preemptive data race after the first event step (INIT-RACE rule) or a few steps later and right after a switching point (SWITCH-RACE rule). Then by SWITCH-RACE rule we are done.

   $i + 1$: If there is no preemptive data race until the end of the first atomic block, then the thread of the first atomic block can execute without being interrupted by other threads, and then the number of atomic blocks can be reduced by 1. Afterwards we apply the induction hypothesis and predict a non-preemptive data race either at the end of the first atomic block (INIT-RACE rule) or a few steps later and right after a switching point (SWITCH-RACE rule). In both cases we are done by SWITCH-RACE rule.

   Otherwise, there is at least one preemptive data race before the end of first atomic block, which is reduced to case (k = 0).

Theorem 2 (Equivalence between DRF and NPDRF)
For any P and σ, we have DRF(P, σ) ⟺ NPDRF(P, σ)

Proof. By applying Lemma 8.

6 Conclusion

In this paper, we propose a formal definition of the non-preemptive semantics, which restricts the interleavings of concurrent threads to certain carefully-chosen program points. We prove that data-race-free programs behave the same in our non-preemptive semantics as in the standard preemptive semantics. Here the behaviors include termination and I/O events. Our results can be used to reduce the complexity of reasoning about data-race-free programs.

We also define a notion of data-race-freedom in non-preemptive semantics (called NPDRF), which is proved to be equivalent to the standard data-race-freedom in preemptive semantics. This makes reasoning solely under our non-preemptive semantics possible.

References

1. Abadi, M., Plotkin, G.: A model of cooperative threads. In: Proceedings of 36th Annual ACM SIGPLAN-SIGACT Symposium on Principles of Programming Languages, POPL 2009, Savannah, GA, January 2009, pp. 29–40. ACM Press, New York (2009). https://doi.org/10.1145/1480881.1480887
2. Adve, S.V., Hill, M.D.: Weak ordering: a new definition. In: Proceedings of 17th Annual International Symposium on Computer Architecture, ISCA 1990, Seattle, WA, June 1990, pp. 2–14. ACM Press, New York (1990). https://doi.org/10.1145/325164.325100
3. Adve, S.V., Hill, M.D.: A unified formalization of four shared-memory models. IEEE Trans. Parallel Distrib. Syst. 4(6), 613–624 (1993). https://doi.org/10.1109/71.242161
4. von Behren, R., Condit, J., Zhou, F., Necula, G.C., Brewer, E.: Capriccio: scalable threads for internet services. In: Proceedings of 19th ACM Symposium on Operating Systems Principles, SOSP 2003, Bolton Landing, NY, October 2003, pp. 268–281. ACM Press, New York (2003). https://doi.org/10.1145/945445.945471
5. Beringer, L., Stewart, G., Dockins, R., Appel, A.W.: Verified compilation for shared-memory C. In: Shao, Z. (ed.) ESOP 2014. LNCS, vol. 8410, pp. 107–127. Springer, Heidelberg (2014). https://doi.org/10.1007/978-3-642-54833-8_7
6. Boudol, G.: Fair cooperative multithreading. In: Caires, L., Vasconcelos, V.T. (eds.) CONCUR 2007. LNCS, vol. 4703, pp. 272–286. Springer, Heidelberg (2007). https://doi.org/10.1007/978-3-540-74407-8_19
7. Collingbourne, P., Donaldson, A.F., Ketema, J., Qadeer, S.: Interleaving and lock-step semantics for analysis and verification of GPU kernels. In: Felleisen, M., Gardner, P. (eds.) ESOP 2013. LNCS, vol. 7792, pp. 270–289. Springer, Heidelberg (2013). https://doi.org/10.1007/978-3-642-37036-6_16
8. Ferreira, R., Feng, X., Shao, Z.: Parameterized memory models and concurrent separation logic. In: Gordon, A.D. (ed.) ESOP 2010. LNCS, vol. 6012, pp. 267–286. Springer, Heidelberg (2010). https://doi.org/10.1007/978-3-642-11957-6_15
9. Hower, D.R., et al.: Heterogeneous-race-free memory models. In: Architectural Support for Programming Languages and Operating Systems, ASPLOS 2014, Salt Lake City, UT, March 2014, pp. 427–440. ACM Press (2014). https://doi.org/10.1145/2541940.2541981

10. Kojima, K., Igarashi, A.: A Hoare logic for GPU kernels. ACM Trans. Comput. Log. **18**(1), Article No. 3 (2017). https://doi.org/10.1145/3001834
11. Li, P., Zdancewic, S.: Combining events and threads for scalable network services implementation and evaluation of monadic, application-level concurrency primitives. In: Proceedings of 28th ACM SIGPLAN Conference on Programming Language Design and Implementation, PLDI 2007, San Diego, CA, June 2007, pp. 189–199. ACM Press, New York (2007). https://doi.org/10.1145/1250734.1250756
12. Loring, M.C., Marron, M., Leijen, D.: Semantics of asynchronous JavaScript. In: Proceedings of 13th ACM SIGPLAN Int. Symposium on Dynamic Languages, DLS 2017, Vancouver, BC, October 2017, pp. 51–62. ACM Press, New York (2017). https://doi.org/10.1145/3133841.3133846
13. Marino, D., Singh, A., Millstein, T., Musuvathi, M., Narayanasamy, S.: DRFx: a simple and efficient memory model for concurrent programming languages. In: Proceedings of 31st ACM SIGPLAN Conference on Programming Language Design and Implementation, PLDI 2010, Toronto, ON, June 2010, pp. 351–362. ACM Press, New York (2010). https://doi.org/10.1145/1806596.1806636
14. Vouillon, J.: Lwt: a cooperative thread library. In: Proceedings of the of 2008 ACM SIGPLAN Workshop on ML, ML 2008, Victoria, BC, September 2008, pp. 3–12. ACM Press, New York (2008). https://doi.org/10.1145/1411304.1411307
15. Yi, J., Disney, T., Freund, S.N., Flanagan, C.: Cooperative types for controlling thread interference in Java. In: Proceedings of 2012 International Symposium on Software Testing and Analysis, ISSTA 2012, Minneapolis, MN, July 2012, pp. 232–242. ACM Press (2012). https://doi.org/10.1145/2338965.2336781
16. Yi, J., Sadowski, C., Flanagan, C.: Cooperative reasoning for preemptive execution. In: Proceedings of 16th ACM Symposium on Principles and Practice of Parallel Programming, PPoPP 2011, San Antonio, TX, February 2011, pp. 147–156. ACM Press, New York (2011). https://doi.org/10.1145/1941553.1941575

Author Index

Accattoli, Beniamino 37

Badouel, Éric 62
Barnat, Jiří 313
Berglund, Martin 80, 99
Bertot, Yves 3
Bester, Willem 99
Britz, Katarina 211

Chantawibul, Apiwat 116
Cheney, James 376

D'Argenio, Pedro R. 132
Dahlqvist, Fredrik 153
Djeumen Djatcha, Rodrigue Aimé 62

Felgenhauer, Bertram 173
Feng, Xinyu 513
Fujita, Gen 455

Gerber, Aurona 211
Goncharov, Sergey 191

Harmse, Henriette 211
Hsu, Justin 472

Janin, David 231
Jiang, Hanru 513
Johnsen, Einar Broch 252
Jonáš, Martin 273

Kamikawa, Naoki 455

Lanotte, Ruggero 292
Lauko, Henrich 313
Liang, Hongjin 513

Moerman, Joshua 493
Monti, Raúl E. 132

Nestra, Härmel 333
Nguena Timo, Omer 354

Ouaknine, Joël 472

Parlant, Louis 153
Petrenko, Alexandre 354

Ramesh, S. 354
Rapp, Franziska 173
Rauch, Christoph 191
Ricciotti, Wilmer 376
Ročkai, Petr 313
Rot, Jurriaan 493
Rybakov, Mikhail 396

Schaefer, Ina 80
Schröder, Lutz 191
Seki, Hiroyuki 415
Senda, Ryoma 415
Shkatov, Dmitry 396
Silva, Alexandra 153, 472
Sobociński, Paweł 116
Steffen, Martin 252
Strejček, Jan 273
Stumpf, Johanna Beate 252
Sulzmann, Martin 11

Takata, Yoshiaki 415
Thiemann, Peter 11
Tini, Simone 292
Töws, Manuel 435
Tveito, Lars 252

Umeo, Hiroshi 455

van der Merwe, Brink 99
van Heerdt, Gerco 472
Venhoek, David 493

Wehrheim, Heike 435

Xiao, Siyang 513

Printed in the United States
By Bookmasters